PRENTICE HALL

LITERATURE

COPPER

BRONZE

SILVER

GOLD

PLATINUM

THE AMERICAN EXPERIENCE

THE BRITISH TRADITION

WORLD MASTERPIECES

PRENTICE HALL

LITERATURE
PLATINUM

PARAMOUNT EDITION

LANDSCHAFT, CANNES, 1934
Max Beckmann
San Francisco Museum of Modern Art

PRENTICE HALL
Englewood Cliffs, New Jersey
Needham, Massachusetts

ISBN 0-13-722430-3

5 6 7 8 9 10   97 96 95

Art credits begin on page 1022.

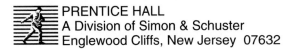

PRENTICE HALL
A Division of Simon & Schuster
Englewood Cliffs, New Jersey 07632

STAFF CREDITS FOR PRENTICE HALL LITERATURE

Publisher: Eileen Thompson

Editorial: Ellen Bowler, Douglas McCollum, Philip Fried, Kelly Ackley, Eric Hausmann, Lauren Weidenman

Multicultural/ESL: Marina Liapunov, Barbara T. Stone

Marketing: Mollie Ledwith, Belinda Loh

National Language Arts Consultants: Ellen Lees Backstrom, Ed.D., Craig A. McGhee, Karen Massey Riley, Vennisa Travers, Gail Witt

Permissions: Doris Robinson

Design: Susan Walrath, Carmela Pereira, Leslie Osher, AnnMarie Roselli

Visual Research: Libby Forsyth, Emily Rose, Martha Conway

Production: Suse Bell, Joan McCulley, Elizabeth Torjussen, Amy E. Fleming, Lynn Contrucci, Garret Schenck, Lorraine Moffa

Publishing Technology: Andrew Black, Deborah J. Jones, Monduane Harris, Cleasta Wilburn, Greg Myers

Pre-Press Production: Laura Sanderson, Natalia Bilash, Denise Herckenrath

Print and Bind: Rhett Conklin, Gertrude Szyferblatt

ACKNOWLEDGMENTS

Grateful acknowledgment is made to the following for permission to reprint copyrighted material:

Margaret Walker Alexander
Lines from "I Want to Write" by Margaret Walker, originally published in *Crisis* magazine (NAACP), May 1934. Reprinted in *October Journey,* 1973, by Margaret Walker (Broadside Press). Reprinted by permission of Margaret Walker Alexander.

Samuel Allen
"To Satch" by Samuel Allen is reprinted by permission of the author.

American Council for Nationalities Service
"Chee's Daughter" by Juanita Platero and Siyowin Miller. Originally published in *Common Ground,* 1948. Reprinted by permission.

(Continued on page 1018.)

CONTENTS

SHORT STORIES

READING ACTIVELY 2
MODEL
Anita Desai .... Games at Twilight 3

PLOT   **Jack Finney** .... Contents of the Dead Man's
                                      Pocket 17
W. W. Jacobs .... The Monkey's Paw 31
    Multicultural Connection: Fate in World Folklore 37
Carl Stephenson .... Leiningen Versus the Ants 43
R. K. Narayan .... Old Man of the Temple 61
    Multicultural Connection: Ghost Stories Around the World 62

CHARACTERIZATION   **William Melvin Kelley** .... A Visit to Grandmother 69
Juanita Platero and
    Siyowin Miller .... Chee's Daughter 77
Mark Twain .... Luck 89

POINT OF VIEW   **Darryl Babe Wilson** .... Diamond Island: Alcatraz 97
    One Writer's Process: Darryl Babe Wilson
    and "Diamond Island" 104
Julio Cortázar .... Axolotl 107
Italo Calvino .... Mushrooms in the City 115

SETTING   **Ray Bradbury** .... There Will Come Soft Rains 121
Josephina Niggli .... The Street of the Cañon 127
    Multicultural Connection: Marriage Customs 128
Stephen Vincent Benét ..... By the Waters of Babylon 135
Doris Lessing .... Through the Tunnel 147

SYMBOL, TONE,   **Toshio Mori** .... Abalone, Abalone, Abalone 157
AND IRONY   **Colette** .... The Portrait 161
Edgar Allan Poe .... The Masque of the
                                  Red Death 167

Multicultural Connection: Poe's Influence
  Around the World 174
Saki (H. H. Munro) .... The Open Window 177
Isaac Asimov .... The Machine That Won
                                  the War 183

THEME   **Bei Dao** .... The Homecoming Stranger 191
Multicultural Connection: Political Strife
  and Human Suffering 204
Alan Paton .... Sunlight in Trebizond Street 207
Chinua Achebe .... Civil Peace 215
Isak Dinesen .... The Ring 221

READING AND RESPONDING 228
MODEL
Anne Tyler .... With All Flags Flying 229

YOUR WRITING PROCESS: Exposition/Persuasion
  Writing a News Report 242

YOUR WRITING PROCESS: Narration
  Writing an Imaginary Narrative 244

DRAMA

READING ACTIVELY 248
Howard Koch .... Invasion From Mars 251

THE GREEK THEATER   **Sophocles** .... Antigone 275
Multicultural Connection: Burial Customs
  Across Cultures 287

THE SHAKESPEAREAN   **William Shakespeare** .... The Tragedy of
THEATER   Julius Caesar 309

YOUR WRITING PROCESS: Creative Writing
  Writing a New Version of a Scene 398

YOUR WRITING PROCESS: Description
  Writing a Descriptive Memo 400

NONFICTION

READING ACTIVELY 404
MODEL
James Thurber .... The Dog That Bit People 405

BIOGRAPHIES AND PERSONAL ACCOUNTS

Van Wyck Brooks .... Emily Dickinson 415
Langston Hughes .... Marian Anderson: Famous
Concert Singer 427
Dylan Thomas .... A Child's Christmas in Wales .. 433
   Multicultural Connection: Christmas in Different Places 435
Truman Capote .... A Christmas Memory 443

TYPES OF ESSAYS

Rudolfo A. Anaya .... *from* In Commemoration:
One Million Volumes 457
N. Scott Momaday .... *from* The Way to
Rainy Mountain 465
Annie Dillard .... Flood 473
Evan S. Connell .... *from* The White Lantern 481
Lorraine Hansberry .... On Summer 493
Mary Gordon .... Mary Cassatt 499
   One Writer's Process: Mary Gordon and "Mary Cassatt" 504

ESSAYS IN THE ARTS AND SCIENCES

Lewis Thomas .... Notes on Punctuation
(Language Arts) 507
Theodore H. White .... The American Idea (History) ... 511
Aaron Copland .... The Creative Process in Music
(Music) 515
Ann Beattie .... Alex Katz's *The Table* (Art) 523
Rachel Carson .... The Marginal World
(Science) 527

READING AND RESPONDING 534
MODEL
Thomas Boswell .... Glove's Labor Lost 535

YOUR WRITING PROCESS: Exposition
   Writing a Reflective Essay 540

YOUR WRITING PROCESS: Narration
   Writing a Reminiscence 542

POETRY

READING ACTIVELY 546
MODEL
Naomi Long Madgett .... Alabama Centennial 547

NARRATIVE POETRY   **John Keats** .... La Belle Dame sans Merci 553
Robert Frost .... Two Tramps in Mud Time 557
Henry Wadsworth Longfellow The Wreck of the Hesperus 563

DRAMATIC POETRY   **Rudyard Kipling** .... Danny Deever 569
W. H. Auden .... O What Is That Sound 573
Multicultural Connection: Poetry and the Oral Tradition 575
Edgar Allan Poe .... Eldorado 577

THE SPEAKER   **Gwendolyn Brooks** .... The Sonnet-Ballad 582
AND TONE   **Dorothy Parker** .... One Perfect Rose 584
Samuel Allen (Paul Vesey) .. To Satch 585
Multicultural Connection: Negro Baseball Leagues 586

LYRIC POETRY   **Paul Verlaine** .... Autumn Song 590
Gabriela Mistral .... I Am Not Lonely 591
Naomi Shihab Nye .... Making a Fist 592
Amy Lowell .... Generations 594
Yevgeny Yevtushenko ...... When Your Face
  Came Rising 595
James Wright .... A Blessing 598
Octavio Paz .... The Street 600
Mary Oliver .... A Letter from Home 601

FIGURATIVE   **Lucille Clifton** .... miss rosie 606
LANGUAGE   **Sharon Olds** .... Size and Sheer Will 607
Eve Merriam .... Metaphor 608
Philip Booth .... First Lesson 609
Amy Lowell .... Night Clouds 612
Mbuyiseni Oswald Mtshali .. Sunset 613
Colleen J. McElroy .... à pied 614
One Writer's Process: Colleen J. McElroy and "à pied" 616
Emily Dickinson .... The Wind—tapped like
  a tired Man 618

IMAGERY	**Theodore Roethke**	Big Wind	622
	A. R. Ammons	Loss	623
	Jorge Luis Borges	Afterglow	624
	Jean Toomer	Reapers	628
	Elizabeth Bishop	The Fish	629
	Robert Francis	Pitcher	632
	Nazim Hikmet	The Bees	633
MUSICAL DEVICES	**Robert Burns**	My Heart's in the Highlands	638
	Alfred, Lord Tennyson	The Splendor Falls	640
	Pawnee	Buffalo Dance Song	642
	Carl Sandburg	Jazz Fantasia	644
	John McCrae	In Flanders Fields	646
FORMS	**William Shakespeare**	Shall I Compare Thee to a Summer's Day?	650
	Elinor Wylie	Puritan Sonnet	652
	Hyakuchi, Chiyojo, Bashō, and Issa	Four Haiku	655
	John Updike	Letter Slot	660
	Lawrence Ferlinghetti	Constantly Risking Absurdity	661
THEMES	**Frank Horne**	To James	666
	Karl Shapiro	Auto Wreck	668
	Quincy Troupe	The Old People Speak of Death	670
	Wisława Szymborska	The Number Pi	673
	READING AND RESPONDING		676
	MODEL		
	John Updike	Ex-Basketball Player	677
	YOUR WRITING PROCESS: Creative Writing		
	Writing a Poem		680
	YOUR WRITING PROCESS: Exposition		
	Writing a Report of Information		682
THE HEROIC TRADITION	**READING ACTIVELY**		686
	T. H. White	Arthur Becomes King of Britain	690
	Sir Thomas Malory	The Marriage of King Arthur	701
	Alfred, Lord Tennyson	Morte d'Arthur	704

R. K. Narayan . . . . *from* the Ramayana:
Rama's Initiation 717
D. T. Niane . . . . *from* Sundiata: An Epic
of Old Mali 725
Lo Kuan-Chung . . . . K'ung-ming Borrows
Some Arrows 733
Miguel de Cervantes . . . . *from* Don Quixote 739

YOUR WRITING PROCESS: Exposition/Persuasion
Writing a Profile of a Hero 746

YOUR WRITING PROCESS: Exposition
Writing a Plan for a Mural Design 748

THE NOVEL

READING ACTIVELY 752
John Knowles . . . . A Separate Peace
Chapters 1–4 757
Chapters 5–10 791
Chapters 11–13 843
Buchi Emecheta . . . . The Wrestling Match
Chapters 1–7 879
Multicultural Connection: The Age-Group 886
Chapters 8–14 907
Multicultural Connection: The Universal Appeal of Wrestling . . 925

YOUR WRITING PROCESS: Exposition
Writing a Book Introduction 930

YOUR WRITING PROCESS: Persuasion
Writing a Persuasive Recommendation 932

ADDITIONAL FEATURES

Handbook of the Writing Process 934
Handbook of Grammar and Revising Strategies 942
Handbook of Literary Terms and Techniques 971
Glossary 993
Index of Fine Art 1004
Index of Skills 1007
Index of Titles by Themes 1011
Index of Authors and Titles 1015
Acknowledgments (continued) 1018

PRENTICE HALL

LITERATURE
PLATINUM

*To sit alone with a book spread out before you, and to hold
intimate conversations with . . . unseen generations—such
is a pleasure beyond compare.*

—The Pillow Book

MIDTOWN SUNSET, 1981
Romare Bearden
Courtesy of the Estate of Romare Bearden

SHORT STORIES

Originally *fiction* meant anything made up, created, or shaped. Today we have refined the definition to mean a prose story based on the imagination of the author. Fiction writers may imitate the forms of nonfiction or use true or historically accurate details in their stories. At the same time, they write not to re-create reality but to entertain and perhaps to comment on human existence.

One of the most popular forms of fiction, the short story was first defined by Edgar Allan Poe. He was sure that "worldly interests" prevented most readers from concentrating on reading. He felt that a short, concentrated tale that could be read in one sitting and that created a single, powerful impression was the best type of fiction. Today, innumerable writers have followed Poe's recommendations, creating stories on a vast array of subjects. For instance, this unit includes short stories ranging from a tale of three wishes to a story of an empty house after a nuclear war.

As opposed to other types of fiction, short stories are characterized by a limited number of characters, restricted settings, and a narrow range of action. Short stories, however, share common elements with other forms. Seven of those elements are examined in this unit—plot, characterization, point of view, setting, symbols, tone and irony, and theme. *Plot* refers to the series of events that make up the story. *Characterization* is the creation of reasonable facsimiles of human beings with all their warts and smiles. *Point of view* is the perspective of the story, the voice or speaker who is doing the narrating. *Setting* refers to the natural or artificial environment in which the story takes place. A *symbol* may be understood to mean something beyond itself. Every short story has a *tone,* or attitude, that the writer conveys toward the story itself and toward you, the reader. A special element sometimes used in creating tone is *irony,* in which writers use language or situations that are the opposite of what is expected. Finally, *theme* is what the short story reveals about life, the central idea presented throughout the work.

These, then, are the major tools short story writers have at their disposal. Understanding the elements of the story will help you discover the author's intentions and what is being said about life and the human experience. Although you, the reader, might be studying one of the elements, it is important to realize that a short story is unified, that all elements happen at once in the tale. As you read, consider the whole as well as the parts.

READING ACTIVELY

Short Stories

A short story is fiction—a work of literature in which the characters and events are created by the author. Fiction allows you to explore new worlds, share joys and sorrows of characters, and learn from their experiences.

Reading short stories is an active process. It is a process in which you envision what is happening in the story and derive meaning from the picture you are envisioning. You do this through the following active-reading strategies:

QUESTION What questions come to mind as you are reading? For example, why do the characters act as they do? What causes events to happen? Why does the writer include certain information? Look for answers to your questions as you read.

VISUALIZE Use details from the story to create a picture in your mind. As you read along, change your picture as the story unfolds and your understanding grows. If you find yourself confused, try to state your confusion. Use your visualization to clarify whatever hasn't been clear to you.

PREDICT What do you think will happen? Look for hints in the story that seem to suggest a certain outcome. As you read on, you will see if your predictions are correct.

On pages 3–13 you will see an example of active reading by Marlene Sanchez of Oñate High School in Las Cruces, New Mexico. The notes in the side column include Marlene's thoughts and comments as she read "Games at Twilight." Your own thoughts as you read the story may be different because each reader responds differently to a story.

CONNECT Bring your own experience and knowledge to the story. Make connections with what you know about similar situations or people in your life.

Also make connections between one event and another in the story. Try to summarize how all the pieces of the story fit together.

RESPOND Think about what the story means. What does it say to you? What feelings does it evoke in you? What has the story added to your understanding of people and of life in general?

Try to use these strategies as you read the stories in this unit. The strategies will help you increase your understanding and enjoyment of literature.

MODEL

Games at Twilight
Anita Desai

Question: *What are the "games at twilight"? Who plays them?*

It was still too hot to play outdoors. They had had their tea, they had been washed and had their hair brushed, and after the long day of confinement in the house that was not cool but at least a protection from the sun, the children strained to get out. Their faces were red and bloated with the effort, but their mother would not open the door, everything was still curtained and shuttered in a way that stifled the children, made them feel that their lungs were stuffed with cotton wool and their noses with dust and if they didn't burst out into the light and see the sun and feel the air, they would choke.

Predict: *This story must be set in a hot climate or in a hot season. Maybe it takes place during summer.*

"Please, Ma, please," they begged. "We'll play in the veranda and porch—we won't go a step out of the porch."

"You will, I know you will, and then—"

"No—we won't, we won't," they wailed so horrendously that she actually let down the bolt of the front door so that they burst out like seeds from a crackling, over-ripe pod into the veranda, with such wild, maniacal yells that she retreated to her bath and the shower of talcum powder and the fresh sari[1] that were to help her face the summer evening.

Connect: *The mother wears a sari; the story probably takes place in India, where people must protect themselves from the sun and the heat. That is why the children couldn't play outside.*

They faced the afternoon. It was too hot. Too bright. The white walls of the veranda glared stridently in the sun. The bougainvillea[2] hung about it, purple and magenta, in livid balloons. The garden outside was like a tray made of beaten brass, flattened out on the red gravel and the stony soil in all shades of metal—aluminum, tin, copper and brass. No life stirred at this arid time of day—the birds still drooped, like dead fruit, in the papery tents of the trees; some squirrels lay

Visualize: *These descriptions make the heat seem like oven heat.*

---

1. sari (sä′ rē) *n.*: A long piece of cloth wrapped around the body forming a skirt and draped over one shoulder; worn by Hindu women.
2. bougainvillea (boo gən vil′ ē ə) *n.*: Woody, tropical vines with flowers.

limp on the wet earth under the garden tap. The outdoor dog lay stretched as if dead on the veranda mat, his paws and ears and tail all reaching out like dying travelers in search of water. He rolled his eyes at the children—two white marbles rolling in the purple sockets, begging for sympathy—and attempted to lift his tail in a wag but could not. It only twitched and lay still.

Then, perhaps roused by the shrieks of the children, a band of parrots suddenly fell out of the eucalyptus tree, tumbled frantically in the still, sizzling air, then sorted themselves out into battle formation and streaked away across the white sky.

Question: *Why does the author call "play" children's "business"? Isn't play supposed to be fun, not serious?*

The children, too, felt released. They too began tumbling, shoving, pushing against each other, frantic to start. Start what? Start their business. The business of the children's day which is—play.

"Let's play hide-and-seek."

"Who'll be It?"

"You be It."

"Why should I? You be—"

"You're the eldest—"

"That doesn't mean—"

Connect: *The children seem to take their play very seriously, as if it were "business."*

The shoves became harder. Some kicked out. The motherly Mira intervened. She pulled the boys roughly apart. There was a tearing sound of cloth but it was lost in the heavy panting and angry grumbling and no one paid attention to the small sleeve hanging loosely off a shoulder.

"Make a circle, make a circle!" she shouted, firmly pulling and pushing till a kind of vague circle was formed. "Now clap!" she roared and, clapping, they all chanted in melancholy unison: "Dip, dip, dip—my blue ship—" and every now and then one or the other saw he was safe by the way his hands fell at the crucial moment—palm on palm, or back of hand on palm—and dropped out of the circle with a yell and a jump of relief and jubilation.

Visualize: *This description lets you see every little kid jumping and running to find a hiding space, while Raghu stands on the porch.*

Raghu was It. He started to protest, to cry "You cheated—Mira cheated—Anu cheated—" but it was too late, the others had all already streaked away. There was no one to hear when he called out, "Only in the veranda—the porch—Ma said—Ma *said* to stay in the porch!" No one had stopped to listen, all he saw were their brown legs flashing through the dusty shrubs, scrambling up brick walls, leaping over compost heaps and hedges, and then the porch stood empty in the purple shade of the bougainvillea and the garden was as empty as before; even the limp squirrels had whisked away, leaving everything gleaming, brassy and bare.

Only small Manu suddenly reappeared, as if he had dropped out of an invisible cloud or from a bird's claws, and stood for a moment in the center of the yellow lawn, chewing his finger and near to tears as he heard Raghu shouting, with his head pressed against the veranda wall, "Eighty-three, eighty-five, eighty-nine, ninety . . . " and then made off in a panic, half of him wanting to fly north, the other half counseling south. Raghu turned just in time to see the flash of his white shorts and the uncertain skittering of his red sandals, and charged after him with such a bloodcurdling yell that Manu stumbled over the hosepipe, fell into its rubber coils and lay there weeping, "I won't be It—you have to find them all—all—All!"

"I know I have to, idiot," Raghu said, superciliously kicking him with his toe. "You're dead," he said with satisfaction, licking the beads of perspiration off his upper lip, and then stalked off in search of worthier prey, whistling spiritedly so that the hiders should hear and tremble.

Ravi heard the whistling and picked his nose in a panic, trying to find comfort by burrowing the finger deep—deep into that soft tunnel. He felt himself too exposed, sitting on an upturned flower pot behind the garage. Where could he burrow? He could run around the garage if he heard Raghu come—around and around and around—but he hadn't much faith in his short legs when matched against Raghu's long, hefty, hairy footballer legs.[3] Ravi had a frightening glimpse of them as Raghu combed the hedge of crotons and hibiscus,[4] trampling delicate ferns underfoot as he did so. Ravi looked about him desperately, swallowing a small ball of snot in his fear.

The garage was locked with a great heavy lock to which the driver had the key in his room, hanging from a nail on the

Predict: *Raghu will catch Manu.*

Connect: *Manu was too easily caught, so Raghu wants his next victims to be more challenging.*

---

3. footballer legs: The powerful legs of a soccer player.
4. crotons (krōt′ 'nz) **and hibiscus** (hī bis′ kəs): Types of tropical shrubs.

wall under his work-shirt. Ravi had peeped in and seen him still sprawling on his string-cot in his vest and striped underpants, the hair on his chest and the hair in his nose shaking with the vibrations of his phlegm-obstructed snores. Ravi had wished he were tall enough, big enough to reach the key on the nail, but it was impossible, beyond his reach for years to come. He had sidled away and sat dejectedly on the flower pot. That at least was cut to his own size.

But next to the garage was another shed with a big green door. Also locked. No one even knew who had the key to the lock. That shed wasn't opened more than once a year when Ma turned out all the old broken bits of furniture and rolls of matting and leaking buckets, and the white ant hills were broken and swept away and Flit sprayed into the spider webs and rat holes so that the whole operation was like the looting of a poor, ruined and conquered city. The green leaves of the door sagged. They were nearly off their rusty hinges. The hinges were large and made a small gap between the door and the walls—only just large enough for rats, dogs, and, possibly, Ravi to slip through.

Ravi had never cared to enter such a dark and depressing mortuary[5] of defunct household goods seething with such unspeakable and alarming animal life but, as Raghu's whistling grew angrier and sharper and his crashing and storming in the hedge wilder, Ravi suddenly slipped off the flower pot and through the crack and was gone. He chuckled aloud with astonishment at his own temerity so that Raghu came out of the hedge, stood silent with his hands on his hips, listening, and finally shouted "I heard you! I'm coming! *Got* you—" and came charging round the garage only to find the upturned flower pot, the yellow dust, the crawling of white ants in a mud-hill against the closed shed door—nothing. Snarling, he bent to pick up a stick and went off, whacking it against the garage and shed walls as if to beat out his prey.

Ravi shook, then shivered with delight, with self-congratulation. Also with fear. It was dark, spooky in the shed. It had a muffled smell, as of graves. Ravi had once got

Visualize: *The shed seems like a hiding spot where no one would dare to look for Ravi.*

Predict: *Ravi wants to hide in the shed; maybe he will get stuck there.*

---

5. mortuary (môr′ chōō er ē) *n.*: A place where dead bodies are kept before being buried or cremated.

locked into the linen cupboard and sat there weeping for half an hour before he was rescued. But at least that had been a familiar place, and even smelled pleasantly of starch, laundry and, reassuringly, of his mother. But the shed smelled of rats, ant hills, dust and spider webs. Also of less definable, less recognizable horrors. And it was dark. Except for the white-hot cracks along the door, there was no light. The roof was very low. Although Ravi was small, he felt as if he could reach up and touch it with his finger tips. But he didn't stretch. He hunched himself into a ball so as not to bump into anything, touch or feel anything. What might there not be to touch him and feel him as he stood there, trying to see in the dark? Something cold, or slimy—like a snake. Snakes! He leapt up as Raghu whacked the wall with his stick—then, quickly realizing what it was, felt almost relieved to hear Raghu, hear his stick. It made him feel protected.

But Raghu soon moved away. There wasn't a sound once his footsteps had gone around the garage and disappeared. Ravi stood frozen inside the shed. Then he shivered all over. Something had tickled the back of his neck. It took him a while to pick up the courage to lift his hand and explore. It was an insect—perhaps a spider—exploring *him*. He squashed it and wondered how many more creatures were watching him, waiting to reach out and touch him, the stranger.

There was nothing now. After standing in that position—his hand still on his neck, feeling the wet splodge of the squashed spider gradually dry—for minutes, hours, his legs began to tremble with the effort, the inaction. By now he could see enough in the dark to make out the large solid shapes of old wardrobes, broken buckets and bedsteads piled on top of each other around him. He recognized an old bathtub—patches of enamel glimmered at him and at last he lowered himself onto its edge.

He contemplated slipping out of the shed and into the fray. He wondered if it would not be better to be captured by Raghu and be returned to the milling crowd as long as he could be in the sun, the light, the free spaces of the garden and the familiarity of his brothers, sisters and cousins. It would be evening soon. Their games would become legitimate. The parents would sit out on the lawn on cane basket chairs and watch them as they tore around the garden or gathered in knots to share a loot of mulberries or black, teeth-splitting *jamun*[6] from the garden trees. The gardener would fix the hosepipe to the water tap and water would fall lavishly through the air to the ground, soaking the dry yellow grass and the red gravel and arousing the sweet, the intoxicating scent of water on dry earth—that loveliest scent in the world. Ravi sniffed for a whiff of it. He half-rose from the bathtub, then heard the despairing scream of one of the girls as Raghu bore down upon her. There was the sound of a crash, and of rolling about in the bushes, the shrubs, then screams and accusing sobs of, ''I touched the den—'' ''You did not—'' ''I did—'' ''You liar, you did *not*'' and then a fading away and silence again.

Predict: *Ravi will get out of the shed soon.*

Ravi sat back on the harsh edge of the tub, deciding to hold out a bit longer. What fun if they were all found and caught—he alone left unconquered! He had never known that sensation. Nothing more wonderful had ever happened to him than being taken out by an uncle and bought a whole slab of chocolate all to himself, or being flung into the soda-man's pony cart and driven up to the gate by the friendly driver with the red beard and pointed ears. To defeat Raghu—that hirsute,[7] hoarse-voiced football champion—and to be the winner in a circle of older, bigger, luckier children—that would be thrilling beyond imagination. He hugged his knees together and smiled to himself almost shyly at the thought of so much victory, such laurels.[8]

Connect: *Ravi is driven by his ambition to win, especially if it means beating the older children.*

There he sat smiling, knocking his heels against the bathtub, now and then getting up and going to the door to put his ear to the broad crack and listening for sounds of the game, the pursuer and the pursued, and then returning to his seat with the dogged determination of the true winner, a breaker of records, a champion.

---

6. jamun (jä′ m$\overline{oo}$n′) *n.*: A tart fruit with reddish-purple pulp and juice.
7. hirsute (hʉr′ s$\overline{oo}$t′) *adj.*: Hairy.
8. laurels (lôr′ əlz) *n.*: Foliage from the laurel tree, worn in a crown as a symbol of victory in a contest.

Visualize: *As it's getting darker in the shed, you can see Ravi sitting there, getting lonelier.*

Predict: *Now that Ravi has been gone for so long and it's dark, people must be worried about him.*

Predict: *He won't win, after all.*

Connect: *The disappointment of not being recognized as the winner overwhelms Ravi.*

It grew darker in the shed as the light at the door grew softer, fuzzier, turned to a kind of crumbling yellow pollen that turned to yellow fur, blue fur, gray fur. Evening. Twilight. The sound of water gushing, falling. The scent of earth receiving water, slaking its thirst in great gulps and releasing that green scent of freshness, coolness. Through the crack Ravi saw the long purple shadows of the shed and the garage lying still across the yard. Beyond that, the white walls of the house. The bougainvillea had lost its lividity, hung in dark bundles that quaked and twittered and seethed with masses of homing sparrows. The lawn was shut off from his view. Could he hear the children's voices? It seemed to him that he could. It seemed to him that he could hear them chanting, singing, laughing. But what about the game? What had happened? Could it be over? How could it when he was still not found?

It then occurred to him that he could have slipped out long ago, dashed across the yard to the veranda and touched the "den." It was necessary to do that to win. He had forgotten. He had only remembered the part of hiding and trying to elude the seeker. He had done that so successfully, his success had occupied him so wholly that he had quite forgotten that success had to be clinched by that final dash to victory and the ringing cry of "Den!"

With a whimper he burst through the crack, fell on his knees, got up and stumbled on stiff, benumbed legs across the shadowy yard, crying heartily by the time he reached the veranda so that when he flung himself at the white pillar and bawled, "Den! Den! Den!" his voice broke with rage and pity at the disgrace of it all and he felt himself flooded with tears and misery.

Out on the lawn, the children stopped chanting. They all turned to stare at him in amazement. Their faces were pale and triangular in the dusk. The trees and bushes around them stood inky and sepulchral,[9] spilling long shadows across them. They stared, wondering at his reappearance, his passion, his wild animal howling. Their mother rose from her basket chair and came toward him, worried, annoyed, saying,

---

9. sepulchral (sə pul′ krəl) *adj.*: Dismal; gloomy.

HIDE AND SEEK
Tony Wong
Courtesy of the Artist

Games at Twilight   11

"Stop it, stop it, Ravi. Don't be a baby. Have you hurt yourself?" Seeing him attended to, the children went back to clasping their hands and chanting "The grass is green, the rose is red. . . . "

Visualize: *You can just see him carrying on hysterically.*

But Ravi would not let them. He tore himself out of his mother's grasp and pounded across the lawn into their midst, charging at them with his head lowered so that they scattered in surprise. "I won, I won, I won," he bawled, shaking his head so that the big tears flew. "Raghu didn't find me. I won, I won—"

It took them a minute to grasp what he was saying, even who he was. They had quite forgotten him. Raghu had found all the others long ago. There had been a fight about who was to be It next. It had been so fierce that their mother had emerged from her bath and made them change to another game. Then they had played another and another. Broken mulberries from the tree and eaten them. Helped the driver wash the car when their father returned from work. Helped the gardener water the beds till he roared at them and swore he would complain to their parents. The parents had come out, taken up their positions on the cane chairs. They had begun to play again, sing and chant. All this time no one had remembered Ravi. Having disappeared from the scene, he had disappeared from their minds. Clean.

"Don't be a fool," Raghu said roughly, pushing him aside, and even Mira said, "Stop howling, Ravi. If you want to play, you can stand at the end of the line," and she put him there very firmly.

The game proceeded. Two pairs of arms reached up and met in an arc. The children trooped under it again and again in a lugubrious[10] circle, ducking their heads and intoning

"The grass is green,
The rose is red;
Remember me
When I am dead, dead, dead, dead . . . "

---

10. lugubrious (lə gōō′ brē əs) *adj.*: Sad and mournful, especially in an exaggerated way.

And the arc of thin arms trembled in the twilight, and the heads were bowed so sadly, and their feet tramped to that melancholy refrain so mournfully, so helplessly, that Ravi could not bear it. He would not follow them, he would not be included in this funeral game. He had wanted victory and triumph—not a funeral. But he had been forgotten, left out and he would not join them now. The ignominy[11] of being forgotten—how could he face it? He felt his heart go heavy and ache inside him unbearably. He lay down full length on the damp grass, crushing his face into it, no longer crying, silenced by a terrible sense of his insignificance.

---

11. ignominy (ig' nə min' ē) *n.*: Shame; dishonor.

Respond: *Ravi's obsession with winning the game interfered with his enjoyment of it. Ironically, the children who were caught are now happily playing another game. Ravi was so carried away with the glory of winning that he forgot how to achieve his goal.*

Anita Desai (1937–   ), born of an Indian father and a German mother, has been called one of India's most gifted writers. She was educated in Delhi, and her work has won widespread critical acclaim. Of Desai's talent, the critic Victoria Glendinning said, "She has the gift of opening up a closed world and making it clearly visible and, by the end, familiar." Desai lives in Bombay with her husband and their four children.

RESPONDING TO THE SELECTION

Your Response

1. Put yourself in Ravi's place. What would you have done after Raghu left the shed area? Explain your answer.
2. If you could talk to Ravi, what would you tell him about games?

Recalling

3. Where does Ravi hide?
4. What causes Ravi to lose the game even though he wasn't caught?

Interpreting

5. How does Ravi feel about Raghu?
6. What do we know about Ravi's personality based on the choices he makes in the story?
7. What bitter lesson does Ravi learn at the end of the story?

Applying

8. Do you think that Ravi's "sense of insignificance" at the end of the story will remain strong? Explain.

ANALYZING LITERATURE

Understanding Motivation

Motivation is the cause of a character's actions. Motives can arise from events involving the character, from the character's emotional needs, or from a combination of both. For example, Ravi is afraid of the shed. Yet he is motivated to overcome his fear because he wants to win the game and because he is afraid of Raghu.

1. What motivates Ravi to refuse to join the children in their evening game?
2. What motivates the children to play other games while Ravi is still hiding?

CRITICAL THINKING AND READING

Recognizing Relevant Details

Relevant details give information that is central to the situation, plot, or characters. Paying at-

tention to relevant details can give you insight into a character's motives or a character's effect on others. For instance, when Raghu finds Manu, Raghu kicks him and whistles "so that the hiders should hear and tremble." Later, Desai describes Raghu as a football champion. These details imply that Raghu frightens the other children.

1. Which details of the shed contribute to your understanding of Ravi's determination to avoid Raghu?
2. Ravi feels protected when he hears Raghu pound on the shed with his stick. How does this detail relate to Ravi's decision to stay in the shed?
3. When Raghu catches one of the girls, she insists that she "touched the den." How does this detail relate to the outcome of the story?

THINKING AND WRITING

Writing About Motivation

Reading about characters in a story is in some ways like being with people in real life. Now that you have spent some time with Ravi, perhaps you can guess how the events of the story will motivate him in the future. Imagine the next few days, months, or years of his life, and think of how Ravi's behavior might be influenced by his experience in the shed. Then predict the effect of this experience on his behavior, supporting your prediction with evidence from the story.

LEARNING OPTION

Art. Take another look at the pictures on pages 6 and 11. They were not painted to illustrate "Games at Twilight," yet they depict scenes similar to the ones depicted in the story. How do these paintings relate to the story? Try to find other photographs or works of fine art that remind you of the story. You might look in a museum or in books of art in the library. If possible, bring to class the pictures you have found and show them to your classmates.

Plot

REGATTAS AT ARGENTEUIL, 1875
Claude Monet
Paris, Louvre/Giraudon/Art Resource

Contents of the Dead Man's Pocket

Plot

The **plot** of a story is a series of related events moving from a problem to a solution. A plot often begins with **exposition,** which presents the characters and the situation, including the conflict. The **conflict,** the source of tension in a story, is the struggle between opposing forces. Tension builds to a **climax,** or turning point, of this conflict. Following the climax, the **resolution** shows how the problems are worked out. The plot may also have **complications,** events that stand in the way of resolving the conflict. In "Contents of the Dead Man's Pocket," Tom faces a series of complications as he tries to complete one simple but dangerous task.

Focus

Ambition motivates people to work hard, achieve goals, and improve themselves. Although ambition can lead to success, it can also cloud judgment. Before you read "Contents of the Dead Man's Pocket," think about your own ambitions. How have they led to success? Have they clouded your judgment at times? In what ways have you rearranged your priorities because of your ambitions? Answer these questions in a journal entry. After you read the story, you might want to return to your journal and write about how the story affected you.

Vocabulary

Knowing the following words will help you as you read "Contents of the Dead Man's Pocket."

convoluted (kän və lōōt′ id) *adj.*: Intricate; twisted (p. 19)

grimace (gri məs′) *n.*: A twisted facial expression (p. 22)

deftness (deft′ nis) *n.*: Skillfulness (p. 22)

imperceptibly (im pər sep′ tə blē) *adv.*: In such a slight way as to be almost unnoticeable (p. 23)

reveling (rev′ 'l iŋ) *v.*: Taking great pleasure in (p. 25)

interminable (in tʉr′ mi nə b'l) *adj.*: Seemingly endless (p. 26)

Jack Finney

(1911–   ) was born in Milwaukee, Wisconsin. Finney has worked in advertising and in journalism in addition to writing fiction. In 1956 one of Finney's science-fiction stories was made into the movie *The Invasion of the Body Snatchers.* In most of his work, Finney creates suspense and makes his readers experience terror through his portrayal of the everyday world. This is the method he uses in "Contents of the Dead Man's Pocket."

Contents of the Dead Man's Pocket

Jack Finney

At the little living-room desk Tom Benecke rolled two sheets of flimsy[1] and a heavier top sheet, carbon paper sandwiched between them, into his portable. *Interoffice Memo,* the top sheet was headed, and he typed tomorrow's date just below this; then he glanced at a creased yellow sheet, covered with his own handwriting, beside the typewriter. "Hot in here," he muttered to himself. Then, from the short hallway at his back, he heard the muffled clang of wire coat hangers in the bedroom closet, and at this reminder of what his wife was doing he thought: Hot, no—guilty conscience.

He got up, shoving his hands into the back pockets of his gray wash slacks, stepped to the living-room window beside the desk and stood breathing on the glass, watching the expanding circlet of mist, staring down through the autumn night at Lexington Avenue,[2] eleven stories below. He was a tall, lean, dark-haired young man in a pullover sweater, who looked as though he had played not football, probably, but basketball in college. Now he placed the heels of his hands against the top edge of the lower window frame and shoved upward. But as usual the window didn't budge, and he had to lower his hands and then shoot them hard upward to jolt the window open a few inches. He dusted his hands, muttering.

But still he didn't begin his work. He crossed the room to the hallway entrance and, leaning against the doorjamb, hands shoved into his back pockets again, he

---

1. flimsy (flim′ zē) *n.*: Thin typing paper for making carbon copies.
2. Lexington Avenue: A major avenue on New York City's East Side.

called, "Clare?" When his wife answered, he said, "Sure you don't mind going alone?"

"No." Her voice was muffled, and he knew her head and shoulders were in the bedroom closet. Then the tap of her high heels sounded on the wood floor and she appeared at the end of the little hallway, wearing a slip, both hands raised to one ear, clipping on an earring. She smiled at him—a slender, very pretty girl with light brown, almost blonde, hair—her prettiness emphasized by the pleasant nature that showed in her face. "It's just that I hate you to miss this movie; you wanted to see it too."

"Yeah, I know." He ran his fingers through his hair. "Got to get this done though."

She nodded, accepting this. Then, glancing at the desk across the living room, she said, "You work too much, though, Tom —and too hard."

He smiled. "You won't mind though, will you, when the money comes rolling in and I'm known as the Boy Wizard of Wholesale Groceries?"

"I guess not." She smiled and turned back toward the bedroom.

Tom sat at his desk again; then a few moments later Clare appeared, dressed and ready to leave. "Just after seven," she said. "I can make the beginning of the first feature."

He walked to the front-door closet to help her on with her coat. He kissed her then and, for an instant, holding her close, smelling the perfume she had used, he was tempted to go with her; it was not actually true that he had to work tonight, though he very much wanted to. This was his own project, unannounced as yet in his office, and it could be postponed. But then they won't see it till Monday, he thought once again, and if I give it to the boss tomorrow he

might read it over the weekend . . . "Have a good time," he said aloud. He opened the door for her, feeling the air from the building hallway, smelling faintly of floor wax, stream gently past his face.

He watched her walk down the hall, flicked a hand in response as she waved, and then he started to close the door, but it resisted for a moment. As the door opening narrowed, the current of warm air from the hallway, channeled through this smaller opening now, suddenly rushed past him with accelerated force. Behind him he heard the slap of the window curtains against the wall and the sound of paper fluttering from his desk, and he had to push to close the door.

Turning, he saw a sheet of white paper drifting to the floor in a series of arcs, and another sheet, yellow, moving toward the window, caught in the dying current flowing through the narrow opening. As he watched, the paper struck the bottom edge of the window and hung there for an instant, plastered against the glass and wood. Then as the moving air stilled completely the curtains swinging back from the wall to hang free again, he saw the yellow sheet drop to the window ledge and slide over out of sight.

He ran across the room, grasped the bottom edge of the window and tugged, staring through the glass. He saw the yellow sheet, dimly now in the darkness outside, lying on the ornamental ledge a yard below the window. Even as he watched, it was moving, scraping slowly along the ledge, pushed by the breeze that pressed steadily against the building wall. He heaved on the window with all his strength and it shot open with a bang, the window weight rattling in the casing. But the paper was past his reach and, leaning out into the night, he watched it scud steadily along the ledge to the south, half plastered against the building wall. Above the muffled sound of the street traffic far below, he could hear the dry scrape of its movement, like a leaf on the pavement.

The living room of the next apartment to the south projected a yard or more farther out toward the street than this one; because of this the Beneckes paid seven and a half dollars less rent than their neighbors. And now the yellow sheet, sliding along the stone ledge, nearly invisible in the night, was stopped by the projecting blank wall of the next apartment. It lay motionless, then, in the corner formed by the two walls—a good five yards away, pressed firmly against the ornate corner ornament of the ledge, by the breeze that moved past Tom Benecke's face.

He knelt at the window and stared at the yellow paper for a full minute or more, waiting for it to move, to slide off the ledge and fall, hoping he could follow its course to the street, and then hurry down in the elevator and retrieve it. But it didn't move, and then he saw that the paper was caught firmly between a projection of the convoluted corner ornament and the ledge. He thought about the poker from the fireplace, then the broom, then the mop—discarding each thought as it occurred to him. There was nothing in the apartment long enough to reach that paper.

It was hard for him to understand that he actually had to abandon it—it was ridiculous—and he began to curse. Of all the papers on his desk, why did it have to be this one in particular! On four long Saturday afternoons he had stood in supermarkets counting the people who passed certain displays, and the results were scribbled on that yellow sheet. From stacks of trade publications, gone over page by page in snatched half hours at work and during evenings at home, he had copied facts, quotations, and

figures onto that sheet. And he had carried it with him to the Public Library on Fifth Avenue, where he'd spent a dozen lunch hours and early evenings adding more. All were needed to support and lend authority to his idea for a new grocery-store display method; without them his idea was a mere opinion. And there they all lay, in his own improvised shorthand—countless hours of work—out there on the ledge.

For many seconds he believed he was going to abandon the yellow sheet, that there was nothing else to do. The work could be duplicated. But it would take two months, and the time to present this idea was *now*, for use in the spring displays. He struck his fist on the window ledge. Then he shrugged. Even though his plan were adopted, he told himself, it wouldn't bring him a raise in pay—not immediately, anyway, or as a direct result. It won't bring me a promotion either, he argued—not of itself.

But just the same, and he couldn't escape the thought, this and other independent projects, some already done and others planned for the future, would gradually mark him out from the score of other young men in his company. They were the way to change from a name on the payroll to a name in the minds of the company officials. They were the beginning of the long, long climb to where he was determined to be, at the very top. And he knew he was going out there in the darkness, after the yellow sheet fifteen feet beyond his reach.

By a kind of instinct, he instantly began making his intention acceptable to himself by laughing at it. The mental picture of himself sidling along the ledge outside was absurd—it was actually comical—and he smiled. He imagined himself describing it; it would make a good story at the office and, it occurred to him, would add a special interest and importance to his memorandum, which would do it no harm at all.

To simply go out and get his paper was an easy task—he could be back here with it in less than two minutes—and he knew he wasn't deceiving himself. The ledge, he saw, measuring it with his eye, was about as wide as the length of his shoe, and perfectly flat. And every fifth row of brick in the face of the building, he remembered—leaning out, he verified this—was indented half an inch, enough for the tips of his fingers, enough to maintain balance easily. It occurred to him that if this ledge and wall were only a yard aboveground—as he knelt at the window staring out, this thought was the final confirmation of his intention—he could move along the ledge indefinitely.

On a sudden impulse, he got to his feet, walked to the front closet and took out an old tweed jacket; it would be cold outside. He put it on and buttoned it as he crossed the room rapidly toward the open window. In the back of his mind he knew he'd better hurry and get this over with before he thought too much, and at the window he didn't allow himself to hesitate.

He swung a leg over the sill, then felt for and found the ledge a yard below the window with his foot. Gripping the bottom of the window frame very tightly and carefully, he slowly ducked his head under it, feeling on his face the sudden change from the warm air of the room to the chill outside. With infinite care he brought out his other leg, his mind concentrating on what he was doing. Then he slowly stood erect. Most of the putty, dried out and brittle, had dropped off the bottom edging of the window frame, he found, and the flat wooden edging provided a good gripping surface, a half inch or more deep, for the tips of his fingers.

Now, balanced easily and firmly, he stood on the ledge outside in the slight, chill breeze, eleven stories above the street, staring into his own lighted apartment, odd and different-seeming now.

First his right hand, then his left, he carefully shifted his fingertip grip from the puttyless window edging to an indented row of bricks directly to his right. It was hard to take the first shuffling sideways step then —to make himself move—and the fear stirred in his stomach, but he did it, again by not allowing himself time to think. And now—with his chest, stomach, and the left side of his face pressed against the rough cold brick—his lighted apartment was suddenly gone, and it was much darker out here than he had thought.

Without pause he continued—right foot, left foot, right foot, left—his shoe soles shuffling and scraping along the rough stone, never lifting from it, fingers sliding along the exposed edging of brick. He moved on the balls of his feet, heels lifted slightly; the ledge was not quite as wide as he'd expected. But leaning slightly inward toward the face of the building and pressed against it, he could feel his balance firm and secure, and moving along the ledge was quite as easy as he had thought it would be. He could hear the buttons of his jacket scraping steadily along the rough bricks and feel them catch momentarily, tugging a little, at each mortared crack. He simply did not permit himself to look down, though the compulsion to do so never left him; nor did he allow himself actually to think. Mechanically—right foot, left foot, over and again—he shuffled along crabwise, watching the projecting wall ahead loom steadily closer . . .

Then he reached it, and, at the corner —he'd decided how he was going to pick up the paper—he lifted his right foot and placed it carefully on the ledge that ran along the projecting wall at a right angle to the ledge on which his other foot rested. And now, facing the building, he stood in the corner formed by the two walls, one foot on the ledging of each, a hand on the shoulder-high indentation of each wall. His forehead was pressed directly into the corner against the cold bricks, and now he carefully lowered first one hand, then the other, perhaps a foot farther down, to the next indentation in the rows of bricks.

Very slowly, sliding his forehead down the trough of the brick corner and bending his knees, he lowered his body toward the paper lying between his outstretched feet. Again he lowered his fingerholds another

foot and bent his knees still more, thigh muscles taut, his forehead sliding and bumping down the brick V. Half squatting now, he dropped his left hand to the next indentation and then slowly reached with his right hand toward the paper between his feet.

He couldn't quite touch it, and his knees now were pressed against the wall; he could bend them no farther. But by ducking his head another inch lower, the top of his head now pressed against the bricks, he lowered his right shoulder and his fingers had the paper by a corner, pulling it loose. At the same instant he saw, between his legs and

far below, Lexington Avenue stretched out for miles ahead.

He saw, in that instant, the Loew's theater sign, blocks ahead past Fiftieth Street: the miles of traffic signals, all green now; the lights of cars and street lamps; countless neon signs; and the moving black dots of people. And a violent instantaneous explosion of absolute terror roared through him. For a motionless instant he saw himself externally—bent practically double, balanced on this narrow ledge, nearly half his body projecting out above the street far below—and he began to tremble violently, panic flaring through his mind and muscles, and he felt the blood rush from the surface of his skin.

In the fractional moment before horror paralyzed him, as he stared between his legs at that terrible length of street far beneath him, a fragment of his mind raised his body in a spasmodic jerk to an upright position again, but so violently that his head scraped hard against the wall, bouncing off it, and his body swayed outward to the knife edge of balance, and he very nearly plunged backward and fell. Then he was leaning far into the corner again, squeezing and pushing into it, not only his face but his chest and stomach, his back arching; and his fingertips clung with all the pressure of his pulling arms to the shoulder-high half-inch indentation in the bricks.

He was more than trembling now; his whole body was racked with a violent shuddering beyond control, his eyes squeezed so tightly shut it was painful, though he was past awareness of that. His teeth were exposed in a frozen grimace, the strength draining like water from his knees and calves. It was extremely likely, he knew, that he would faint, to slump down along the wall, his face scraping, and then drop backward, a limp weight, out into nothing. And to save his life he concentrated on holding

onto consciousness, drawing deliberate deep breaths of cold air into his lungs, fighting to keep his senses aware.

Then he knew that he would not faint, but he could neither stop shaking nor open his eyes. He stood where he was, breathing deeply, trying to hold back the terror of the glimpse he had had of what lay below him; and he knew he had made a mistake in not making himself stare down at the street, getting used to it and accepting it, when he had first stepped out onto the ledge.

It was impossible to walk back. He simply could not do it. He couldn't bring himself to make the slightest movement. The strength was gone from his legs; his shivering hands—numb, cold and desperately rigid—had lost all deftness; his easy ability to move and balance was gone. Within a step or two, if he tried to move, he knew that he would stumble clumsily and fall.

Seconds passed, with the chill faint wind pressing the side of his face, and he could hear the toned-down volume of the street traffic far beneath him. Again and again it slowed and then stopped, almost to silence; then presently, even this high, he would hear the click of the traffic signals and the subdued roar of the cars starting up again. During a lull in the street sounds, he called out. Then he was shouting *"Help!"* so loudly it rasped his throat. But he felt the steady pressure of the wind, moving between his face and the blank wall, snatch up his cries as he uttered them, and he knew they must sound directionless and distant. And he remembered how habitually, here in New York, he himself heard and ignored shouts in the night. If anyone heard him, there was no sign of it, and presently Tom Benecke knew he had to try moving; there was nothing else he could do.

Eyes squeezed shut, he watched scenes in his mind like scraps of motion-picture film—he could not stop them. He saw himself stumbling suddenly sideways as he crept along the ledge and saw his upper body arc outward, arms flailing. He saw a dangling shoestring caught between the ledge and the sole of his other shoe, saw a foot start to move, to be stopped with a jerk, and felt his balance leaving him. He saw himself falling with a terrible speed as his body revolved in the air, knees clutched tight to his chest, eyes squeezed shut, moaning softly.

Out of utter necessity, knowing that any of these thoughts might be reality in the very next seconds, he was slowly able to shut his mind against every thought but what he now began to do. With fear-soaked slowness, he slid his left foot an inch or two toward his own impossibly distant window. Then he slid the fingers of his shivering left hand a corresponding distance. For a moment he could not bring himself to lift his right foot from one ledge to the other; then he did it, and became aware of the harsh exhalation of air from his throat and realized that he was panting. As his right hand, then, began to slide along the brick edging, he was astonished to feel the yellow paper pressed to the bricks underneath his stiff fingers, and he uttered a terrible, abrupt bark that might have been a laugh or a moan. He opened his mouth and took the paper in his teeth, pulling it out from under his fingers.

By a kind of trick—by concentrating his entire mind on first his left foot, then his left hand, then the other foot, then the other hand—he was able to move, almost imperceptibly, trembling steadily, very nearly without thought. But he could feel the terrible strength of the pent-up horror on just the other side of the flimsy barrier he had erected in his mind; and he knew that if it broke through he would lose this thin artificial control of his body.

During one slow step he tried keeping his eyes closed; it made him feel safer, shutting him off a little from the fearful reality of where he was. Then a sudden rush of giddiness swept over him and he had to open his eyes wide, staring sideways at the cold rough brick and angled lines of mortar, his cheek tight against the building. He kept his eyes open then, knowing that if he once let them flick outward, to stare for an instant at the lighted windows across the street, he would be past help.

He didn't know how many dozens of tiny sidling steps he had taken, his chest, belly, and face pressed to the wall; but he knew the slender hold he was keeping on his mind and body was going to break. He had a sudden mental picture of his apartment on just the other side of this wall—warm, cheerful, incredibly spacious. And he saw himself striding through it, lying down on the floor on his back, arms spread wide, reveling in its unbelievable security. The impossible remoteness of this utter safety, the contrast between it and where he now stood, was more than he could bear. And the barrier broke then, and the fear of the awful height he stood on coursed through his nerves and muscles.

A fraction of his mind knew he was going to fall, and he began taking rapid blind steps with no feeling of what he was doing, sidling with a clumsy desperate swiftness, fingers scrabbling along the brick, almost hopelessly resigned to the sudden backward pull and swift motion outward and down. Then his moving left hand slid onto not brick but sheer emptiness, an impossible gap in the face of the wall, and he stumbled.

His right foot smashed into his left anklebone; he staggered sideways, began falling, and the claw of his hand cracked against glass and wood, slid down it, and his fingertips were pressed hard on the puttyless edging of his window. His right hand smacked gropingly beside it as he fell to his knees; and, under the full weight and direct downward pull of his sagging body, the open window dropped shudderingly in its frame till it closed and his wrists struck the sill and were jarred off.

For a single moment he knelt, knee bones against stone on the very edge of the ledge, body swaying and touching nowhere else, fighting for balance. Then he lost it, his shoulders plunging backward, and he flung his arms forward, his hands smashing against the window casing on either side; and—his body moving backward—his fingers clutched the narrow wood stripping of the upper pane.

For an instant he hung suspended between balance and falling, his fingertips pressed onto the quarter-inch wood strips. Then, with utmost delicacy, with a focused concentration of all his senses, he increased even further the strain on his fingertips hooked to these slim edgings of wood. Elbows slowly bending, he began to draw the full weight of his upper body forward, knowing that the instant his fingers slipped off these quarter-inch strips he'd plunge backward and be falling. Elbows imperceptibly bending, body shaking with the strain, the sweat starting from his forehead in great sudden drops, he pulled, his entire being and thought concentrated in his fingertips. Then suddenly, the strain slackened and ended, his chest touching the window sill, and he was kneeling on the ledge, his forehead pressed to the glass of the closed window.

Dropping his palms to the sill, he stared into his living room—at the red-brown davenport across the room, and a magazine he had left there; at the pictures on the walls and the gray rug; the entrance to the hallway; and at his papers, typewriter and desk, not two feet from his nose. All was as he had left it—this was past all belief—only a few minutes before.

His head moved, and in faint reflection from the glass before him he saw the yellow paper clenched in his front teeth. Lifting a hand from the sill he took it from his mouth; the moistened corner parted from the paper, and he spat it out.

For a moment, in the light from the living room, he stared wonderingly at the yellow sheet in his hand and then crushed it into the side pocket of his jacket.

He couldn't open the window. It had been pulled not completely closed, but its lower edge was below the level of the outside sill; there was no room to get his fingers underneath it. Between the upper sash and the lower was a gap not wide enough —reaching up, he tried—to get his fingers into; he couldn't push it open. The upper window panel, he knew from long experience, was impossible to move, frozen tight with dried paint.

Very carefully observing his balance, the fingertips of his left hand again hooked to the narrow stripping of the window casing, he drew back his right hand, palm facing the glass, and then struck the glass with the heel of his hand.

His arm rebounded from the pane, his body tottering, and he knew he didn't dare strike a harder blow.

But in the security and relief of his new position, he simply smiled; with only a sheet of glass between him and the room just before him, it was not possible that there wasn't a way past it. Eyes narrowing, he thought for a few moments about what to do. Then his eyes widened, for nothing occurred to him. But still he felt calm: the trembling, he realized, had stopped. At the back of his mind there still lay the thought that once he was again in his home, he could give release to his feelings. He actually *would* lie on the

floor, rolling, clenching tufts of the rug in his hands. He would literally run across the room, free to move as he liked, jumping on the floor, testing and reveling in its absolute security, letting the relief flood through him, draining the fear from his mind and body. His yearning for this was astonishingly intense, and somehow he understood that he had better keep this feeling at bay.

He took a half dollar from his pocket and struck it against the pane, but without any hope that the glass would break and with very little disappointment when it did not. After a few moments of thought he drew his leg up onto the ledge and picked loose the knot of his shoelace. He slipped off the shoe and, holding it across the instep, drew back his arm as far as he dared and struck the leather heel against the glass. The pane rattled, but he knew he'd been a long way from breaking it. His foot was cold and he slipped the shoe back on. He shouted again, experimentally, and then once more, but there was no answer.

The realization suddenly struck him that he might have to wait here till Clare came home, and for a moment the thought was funny. He could see Clare opening the front door, withdrawing her key from the lock, closing the door behind her, and then glancing up to see him crouched on the other side of the window. He could see her rush across the room, face astounded and frightened, and hear himself shouting instructions: "Never mind how I got here! Just open the wind—" She couldn't open it, he remembered, she'd never been able to; she'd always had to call him. She'd have to get the building superintendent or a neighbor, and he pictured himself smiling and answering their questions as he climbed in. "I just wanted to get a breath of fresh air, so—"

He couldn't possibly wait here till Clare came home. It was the second feature she'd wanted to see, and she'd left in time to see the first. She'd be another three hours or—He glanced at his watch; Clare had been gone eight minutes. It wasn't possible, but only eight minutes ago he had kissed his wife goodbye. She wasn't even at the theater yet!

It would be four hours before she could possibly be home, and he tried to picture himself kneeling out here, fingertips hooked to these narrow strippings, while first one movie, preceded by a slow listing of credits, began, developed, reached its climax and then finally ended. There'd be a newsreel next, maybe, and then an animated cartoon, and then interminable scenes from coming pictures. And then, once more, the beginning of a full-length picture—while all the time he hung out here in the night.

He might possibly get to his feet, but he was afraid to try. Already his legs were cramped, his thigh muscles tired; his knees hurt, his feet felt numb and his hands were stiff. He couldn't possibly stay out here for four hours, or anywhere near it. Long before that his legs and arms would give out; he would be forced to try changing his position often—stiffly, clumsily, his coordination and strength gone—and he would fall. Quite realistically, he knew that he would fall; no one could stay out here on this ledge for four hours.

A dozen windows in the apartment building across the street were lighted. Looking over his shoulder, he could see the top of a man's head behind the newspaper he was reading; in another window he saw the blue-gray flicker of a television screen. No more than twenty-odd yards from his back were scores of people, and if just one of them would walk idly to his window and glance out. . . . For some moments he stared over his shoulder at the lighted rectangles, waiting. But no one appeared. The man reading his paper turned a page and then continued his reading. A figure passed another of the windows and was immediately gone.

In the inside pocket of his jacket he found a little sheaf of papers, and he pulled one out and looked at it in the light from the living room. It was an old letter, an advertisement of some sort; his name and address, in purple ink, were on a label pasted to the envelope. Gripping one end of the envelope in his teeth, he twisted it into a tight curl. From his shirt pocket he brought out a book of matches. He didn't dare let go the casing with both hands, but, with the twist of paper in his teeth, he opened the matchbook with his free hand; then he bent one of the matches in two without tearing it from the folder, its red-tipped end now touching the striking surface. With his thumb, he rubbed the red tip across the striking area.

He did it again, then again, and still again, pressing harder each time, and the match suddenly flared, burning his thumb. But he kept it alight, cupping the matchbook in his hand and shielding it with his body. He held the flame to the paper in his mouth till it caught. Then he snuffed out the match flame with his thumb and forefinger, careless of the burn, and replaced the book in his pocket. Taking the paper twist in his hand, he held it flame down, watching the flame crawl up the paper, till it flared bright. Then he held it behind him over the street, moving it from side to side, watching it over his shoulder, the flame flickering and guttering in the wind.

There were three letters in his pocket and he lighted each of them, holding each till the flame touched his hand and then dropping it to the street below. At one point, watching over his shoulder while the last of the letters burned, he saw the man across the street put down his paper and stand —even seeming, to Tom, to glance toward his window. But when he moved, it was only to walk across the room and disappear from sight.

There were a dozen coins in Tom Benecke's pocket and he dropped them, three or four at a time. But if they struck anyone, or if anyone noticed their falling, no one connected them with their source, and no one glanced upward.

His arms had begun to tremble from the steady strain of clinging to this narrow perch, and he did not know what to do now and was terribly frightened. Clinging to the window stripping with one hand, he again searched his pockets. But now—he had left his wallet on his dresser when he'd changed clothes—there was nothing left but the yellow sheet. It occurred to him irrelevantly that his death on the sidewalk below would be an eternal mystery; the window closed —why, how, and from where could he have fallen? No one would be able to identify his body for a time, either—the thought was somehow unbearable and increased his fear. All they'd find in his pockets would be the yellow sheet. *Contents of the dead man's pockets,* he thought, *one sheet of paper bearing penciled notations—incomprehensible.*

He understood fully that he might actually be going to die; his arms, maintaining his balance on the ledge, were trembling steadily now. And it occurred to him then with all the force of a revelation that, if he fell, all he was ever going to have out of life he would then, abruptly, have had. Nothing, then, could ever be changed; and nothing more—no least experience or pleasure —could ever be added to his life. He wished, then, that he had not allowed his wife to go off by herself tonight—and on similar nights. He thought of all the evenings he had spent away from her, working; and he regretted them. He thought wonderingly of his fierce ambition and of the direction his life had taken; he thought of the hours he'd spent by himself, filling the yellow sheet that had brought him out here. *Contents of the dead man's pockets,* he thought with sudden fierce anger, *a wasted life.*

He was simply not going to cling here till he slipped and fell; he told himself that now. There was one last thing he could try; he had been aware of it for some moments, refusing to think about it, but now he faced it. Kneeling here on the ledge, the fingertips of one hand pressed to the narrow strip of wood, he could, he knew, draw his other hand back a yard perhaps, fist clenched tight, doing it very slowly till he sensed the outer limit of balance, then, as hard as he was able from the distance, he could drive his fist forward against the glass. If it broke, his fist smashing through, he was safe; he might cut himself badly, and probably would, but with his arm inside the room, he would be secure. But if the glass did not break, the rebound, flinging his arm back, would topple him off the ledge. He was certain of that.

He tested his plan. The fingers of his left hand clawlike on the little stripping, he drew back his other fist until his body began teetering backward. But he had no leverage now—he could feel that there would be no force to his swing—and he moved his fist slowly forward till he rocked forward on his knees again and could sense that his swing would carry its greatest force. Glancing down, however, measuring the distance from his fist to the glass, he saw that it was less than two feet.

It occurred to him that he could raise his arm over his head, to bring it down against the glass. But, experimenting in slow motion, he knew it would be an awkward blow without the force of a driving punch, and not nearly enough to break the glass.

Facing the window, he had to drive a blow from the shoulder, he knew now, at a distance of less than two feet; and he did not know whether it would break through the heavy glass. It might; he could picture it happening, he could feel it in the nerves of his arm. And it might not; he could feel that too—feel his fist striking this glass and being instantaneously flung back by the unbreaking pane, feel the fingers of his other hand breaking loose, nails scraping along the casing as he fell.

He waited, arm drawn back, fist balled, but in no hurry to strike; this pause, he knew, might be an extension of his life. And to live even a few seconds longer, he felt, even out here on this ledge in the night, was infinitely better than to die a moment earlier than he had to. His arm grew tired, and he brought it down and rested it.

Then he knew that it was time to make the attempt. He could not kneel here hesitating indefinitely till he lost all courage to act, waiting till he slipped off the ledge. Again he drew back his arm, knowing this time that he would not bring it down till he struck. His elbow protruding over Lexington Avenue far below, the fingers of his other hand pressed down bloodlessly tight against the narrow stripping, he waited, feeling the sick tenseness and terrible excitement building. It grew and swelled toward the moment of action, his nerves tautening. He thought of Clare—just a wordless, yearning thought —and then drew his arm back just a bit more, fist so tight his fingers pained him, and knowing he was going to do it. Then with full power, with every last scrap of strength he could bring to bear, he shot his arm forward toward the glass, and he said, *"Clare!"*

He heard the sound, felt the blow, felt himself falling forward, and his hand closed on the living-room curtains, the shards and fragments of glass showering onto the floor. And then, kneeling there on the ledge, an arm thrust into the room up to the shoulder, he began picking away the protruding slivers and great wedges of glass from the window frame, tossing them in onto the rug. And, as he grasped the edges of the empty window frame and climbed into his home, he was grinning in triumph.

He did not lie down on the floor or run through the apartment, as he had promised himself; even in the first few moments it seemed to him natural and normal that he should be where he was. He simply turned to his desk, pulled the crumpled yellow sheet from his pocket and laid it down where it had been, smoothing it out; then he absently laid a pencil across it to weight it down. He shook his head wonderingly, and turned to walk toward the closet.

There he got out his topcoat and hat and, without waiting to put them on, opened the front door and stepped out, to go find his wife. He turned to pull the door closed and the warm air from the hall rushed through the narrow opening again. As he saw the yellow paper, the pencil flying, scooped off the desk and, unimpeded by the glassless window, sail out into the night and out of his life, Tom Benecke burst into laughter and then closed the door behind him.

RESPONDING TO THE SELECTION

Your Response

1. Do you identify with Tom? Why or why not?
2. How did you react to the story's ending?

Recalling

3. Why does Tom go out on the ledge?
4. How is Tom's journey back different from the one to the corner of the ledge?
5. Describe the progression of Tom's thoughts as he attempts to return to his apartment.
6. How does Tom succeed in getting back into his apartment?

Interpreting

7. Explain what the paper that flew out the window represents to Tom.
8. Explain how Tom's thoughts and feelings affect his physical ability to return to his apartment, thereby increasing the tension.
9. Contrast Tom's attitude at the beginning of the story with his attitude at the end.
10. At the end of this story, why does Tom laugh?
11. Why is this story called "Contents of the Dead Man's Pocket"?

Applying

12. Tom's perilous position causes him to examine his life. Do you think people can ever truly change after examining their lives? Explain your answer.

ANALYZING LITERATURE

Understanding Plot

The **plot** of a story is a series of events related to the solution of a problem or conflict. The plot includes **exposition,** which introduces the situation; **conflict,** or the struggle between opposing forces; a **climax,** or turning point; and the **resolution,** or outcome. It may also include complications that delay the resolution of the conflict. Without complications "Contents of the Dead Man's Pocket" would progress like this: Tom

edged his way along the ledge, picked up the paper, and returned home safely.

Study the plot diagram below.

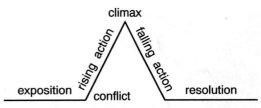

1. Describe the major conflict in the story.
2. What complicates the opening situation?
3. What is the moment of climax in the story?
4. Why does the story continue after Tom gets safely back into the apartment?

THINKING AND WRITING

Writing About Plot

A local book club is holding a contest to pick the best short story of the year. Write a statement to the nominating committee telling why you think "Contents of the Dead Man's Pocket" should (or should not) be a candidate for the award. Include an analysis of the plot, telling why it is special and why you were impressed (or not impressed) by it. When you revise your statement, make it as forceful and convincing as possible.

LEARNING OPTION

Performance. What do you think Tom said to his wife when he found her or when she returned to the apartment? With a partner write a dialogue between Tom and Clare. Explore the ways in which Tom would tell Clare what happened after she left the apartment. Capture Clare's reaction as you and your partner imagine it. Then act out your dialogue in class. You might want to use props in your enactment. For example, you could re-create the scene with a desk, a yellow slip of paper, a fan for wind, and other props.

GUIDE FOR READING

The Monkey's Paw

Suspense and Foreshadowing

Suspense is the quality of the story that keeps you reading to find out what will happen. Authors often use foreshadowing to help build suspense. **Foreshadowing** refers to the use of hints about what is going to happen. In "The Monkey's Paw," the hints are clear enough to let you know something frightening is in store but ambiguous enough to keep you guessing.

Focus

From childhood into adulthood, everyone has wishes. People are usually happy when their wishes come true. Some wishes, however, don't turn out as planned. Think of wishes you've had in the past. When a wish came true, was the result what you had hoped for? If a wish didn't come true, was it for the best in the long run? Copy the following chart in your journal; then list a few of your wishes and their positive and negative outcomes.

POSITIVE OUTCOME	WISH	NEGATIVE OUTCOME

Vocabulary

Knowing the following words will help you as you read "The Monkey's Paw."

doughty (dout' ē) *adj.*: Brave; valiant (p. 32)

talisman (tal' is mən) *n.*: Anything believed to have magical power (p. 34)

antimacassar (an' ti mə kas' ər) *n.*: A small cover on the arms or back of a chair or sofa to prevent soiling (p. 34)

credulity (krə dōo' lə tē) *n.*: A tendency to believe too readily (p. 34)

prosaic (prō zā' ik) *adj.*: Commonplace; ordinary (p. 35)

avaricious (av' ə rish' əs) *adj.*: Greedy for riches (p. 35)

bibulous (bib' yōo ləs) *adj.*: Given to drinking alcoholic beverages (p. 35)

fusillade (fyōo sə lād') *n.*: Something that is like the rapid firing of many firearms (p. 40)

W. W. Jacobs

(1863–1943) was born in London, England, and lived as a child in a house on a Thames River dock. There, he had a chance to hear strange tales of foreign lands told by the passing seafarers. As an adult, Jacobs made use of this experience by writing strange tales of his own. Many of his stories artfully combine everyday life with elements of the supernatural. "The Monkey's Paw" is one such tale. First published in 1902, it was made into a successful play a year later.

The Monkey's Paw

W. W. Jacobs

Without, the night was cold and wet, but in the small parlor of Laburnam Villa the blinds were drawn and the fire burned brightly. Father and son were at chess, the former, who possessed ideas about the game involving radical changes, putting his king into such sharp and unnecessary perils that it even provoked comment from the white-haired old lady knitting placidly by the fire.

"Hark at the wind," said Mr. White, who, having seen a fatal mistake after it was too late, was amiably desirous of preventing his son from seeing it.

"I'm listening," said the latter, grimly surveying the board as he stretched out his hand. "Check."[1]

"I should hardly think that he'd come tonight," said his father, with his hand poised over the board.

"Mate,"[2] replied the son.

"That's the worst of living so far out," bawled Mr. White, with sudden and un-looked-for violence; "of all the beastly, slushy, out-of-the-way places to live in, this is the worst. Pathway's a bog, and the road's a torrent. I don't know what people are thinking about. I suppose because only two houses on the road are let, they think it doesn't matter."

"Never mind, dear," said his wife, sooth-ingly; "perhaps you'll win the next one."

Mr. White looked up sharply, just in time to intercept a knowing glance between mother and son. The words died away on his lips, and he hid a guilty grin in his thin gray beard.

"There he is," said Herbert White, as the gate banged to loudly and heavy foot-steps came toward the door.

The old man rose with hospitable haste, and opening the door, was heard condoling with the new arrival. The new arrival also condoled with himself, so that Mrs. White said, "Tut, tut!" and coughed gently as her husband entered the room, followed by a tall, burly man, beady of eye and rubicund of visage.[3]

"Sergeant Major Morris," he said, intro-ducing him.

The sergeant major shook hands, and taking the proffered seat by the fire, watched contentedly while his host got out tumblers and stood a small copper kettle on the fire.

At the third glass his eyes got brighter, and he began to talk, the little family circle regarding with eager interest this visitor from distant parts, as he squared his broad shoulders in the chair and spoke of wild

---

1. check (chek) n.: A move in chess that threatens to capture the king.
2. mate (māt) n.: Checkmate, a chess move in which the king is captured and the game is over.

3. rubicund (roo′ bi kund′) **of visage** (viz′ ij): Having a red complexion.

scenes and doughty deeds; of wars and plagues and strange peoples.

"Twenty-one years of it," said Mr. White, nodding at his wife and son. "When he went away he was a slip of a youth in the warehouse. Now look at him."

"He don't look to have taken much harm," said Mrs. White, politely.

"I'd like to go to India myself," said the old man, "just to look round a bit, you know."

"Better where you are," said the sergeant major, shaking his head. He put down the empty glass, and sighing softly, shook it again.

"I should like to see those old temples and fakirs and jugglers," said the old man. "What was that you started telling me the other day about a monkey's paw or something, Morris?"

"Nothing," said the soldier, hastily. "Leastways nothing worth hearing."

"Monkey's paw?" said Mrs. White, curiously.

"Well, it's just a bit of what you might call magic, perhaps," said the sergeant major, offhandedly.

His three listeners leaned forward eagerly. The visitor absent-mindedly put his empty glass to his lips and then set it down again. His host filled it for him.

"To look at," said the sergeant major, fumbling in his pocket, "it's just an ordinary little paw, dried to a mummy."

He took something out of his pocket and proffered it. Mrs. White drew back with a grimace, but her son, taking it, examined it curiously.

"And what is there special about it?" inquired Mr. White as he took it from his son, and having examined it, placed it upon the table.

"It had a spell put on it by an old fakir," said the sergeant major, "a very holy man.

He wanted to show that fate ruled people's lives, and that those who interfered with it did so to their sorrow. He put a spell on it so that three separate men could each have three wishes from it."

His manner was so impressive that his hearers were conscious that their light laughter jarred somewhat.

"Well, why don't you have three, sir?" said Herbert White, cleverly.

The soldier regarded him in the way that middle age is wont to regard presumptuous youth. "I have," he said, quietly, and his blotchy face whitened.

"And did you really have the three wishes granted?" asked Mrs. White.

"I did," said the sergeant major, and his glass tapped against his strong teeth.

"And has anybody else wished?" persisted the old lady.

"The first man had his three wishes, yes," was the reply; "I don't know what the first two were, but the third was for death. That's how I got the paw."

His tones were so grave that a hush fell upon the group.

"If you've had your three wishes, it's no good to you now, then, Morris," said the old man at last. "What do you keep it for?"

The soldier shook his head. "Fancy, I suppose," he said, slowly. "I did have some idea of selling it, but I don't think I will. It has caused enough mischief already. Besides, people won't buy. They think it's a fairy tale, some of them, and those who do think anything of it want to try it first and pay me afterward."

"If you could have another three wishes," said the old man, eyeing him keenly, "would you have them?"

"I don't know, said the other. "I don't know."

He took the paw, and dangling it between his forefinger and thumb, suddenly

threw it upon the fire. White, with a slight cry, stooped down and snatched it off.

"Better let it burn," said the soldier, solemnly.

"If you don't want it, Morris," said the other, "give it to me."

"I won't," said his friend doggedly. "I threw it on the fire. If you keep it, don't blame me for what happens. Pitch it on the fire again, like a sensible man."

The other shook his head and examined

his new possession closely. "How do you do it?" he inquired.

"Hold it up in your right hand and wish aloud," said the sergeant major, "but I warn you of the consequences."

"Sounds like the *Arabian Nights,*"[4] said Mrs. White, as she rose and began to set the supper. "Don't you think you might wish for four pairs of hands for me?"

Her husband drew the talisman from pocket, and then all three burst into laughter as the sergeant major, with a look of alarm on his face, caught him by the arm. "If you must wish," he said, gruffly, "wish for something sensible."

Mr. White dropped it back in his pocket, and placing chairs, motioned his friend to the table. In the business of supper the talisman was partly forgotten, and afterward the three sat listening in an enthralled fashion to a second installment of the soldier's adventures in India.

"If the tale about the monkey's paw is not more truthful than those he has been telling us," said Herbert, as the door closed behind their guest, just in time for him to catch the last train, "we shan't make much out of it."

"Did you give him anything for it, Father?" inquired Mrs. White, regarding her husband closely.

"A trifle," said he, coloring slightly. "He didn't want it, but I made him take it. And he pressed me again to throw it away."

"Likely," said Herbert, with pretended horror. "Why, we're going to be rich, and famous and happy. Wish to be an emperor, Father, to begin with; then you can't be bossed around."

He darted round the table, pursued by the maligned Mrs. White armed with an antimacassar.

Mr. White took the paw from his pocket and eyed it dubiously. "I don't know what to wish for, and that's a fact," he said, slowly. "It seems to me I've got all I want."

"If you only cleared the house, you'd be quite happy, wouldn't you?" said Herbert, with his hand on his shoulder. "Well, wish for two hundred pounds,[5] then; that'll just do it."

His father, smiling shamefacedly at his own credulity, held up the talisman, as his son, with a solemn face somewhat marred by a wink at his mother, sat down at the piano and struck a few impressive chords.

"I wish for two hundred pounds," said the old man distinctly.

A fine crash from the piano greeted the words, interrupted by a shuddering cry from the old man. His wife and son ran toward him.

"It moved," he cried, with a glance of disgust at the object as it lay on the floor. "As I wished it twisted in my hand like a snake."

"Well, I don't see the money," said his son as he picked it up and placed it on the table, "and I bet I never shall."

"It must have been your fancy, Father," said his wife, regarding him anxiously.

He shook his head. "Never mind, though; there's no harm done, but it gave me a shock all the same."

They sat down by the fire again while the two men finished their pipes. Outside, the wind was higher than ever, and the old man started nervously at the sound of a door banging upstairs. A silence unusual and

---

4. Arabian Nights: A story collection from the ancient Near East.

5. pounds *n*.: English money.

depressing settled upon all three, which lasted until the old couple rose to retire for the night.

"I expect you'll find the cash tied up in a big bag in the middle of your bed," said Herbert, as he bade them good night, "and something horrible squatting up on top of the wardrobe watching you as you pocket your ill-gotten gains."

Herbert sat alone in the darkness, gazing at the dying fire, and seeing faces in it. The last face was so horrible and so simian[6] that he gazed at it in amazement. It got so vivid that, with a little uneasy laugh, he felt on the table for a glass containing a little water to throw over it. His hand grasped the monkey's paw, and with a little shiver he wiped his hand on his coat and went up to bed.

II

In the brightness of the wintry sun next morning as it streamed over the breakfast table Herbert laughed at his fears. There was an air of prosaic wholesomeness about the room which it had lacked on the previous night, and the dirty, shriveled little paw was pitched on the sideboard with a carelessness which betokened no great belief in its virtues.

"I suppose all old soldiers are the same," said Mrs. White. "The idea of our listening to such nonsense! How could wishes be granted in these days? And if they could, how could two hundred pounds hurt you, Father?"

"Might drop on his head from the sky," said the frivolous Herbert.

---

6. simian (sim′ ē ən) *adj.*: Monkeylike.

"Morris said the things happened so naturally," said his father, "that you might if you so wished attribute it to coincidence."

"Well, don't break into the money before I come back," said Herbert, as he rose from the table. "I'm afraid it'll turn you into a mean, avaricious man, and we shall have to disown you."

His mother laughed, and following him to the door, watched him down the road, and, returning to the breakfast table, was very happy at the expense of her husband's credulity. All of which did not prevent her from scurrying to the door at the postman's knock, nor prevent her from referring somewhat shortly to retired sergeant majors of bibulous habits when she found that the post brought a tailor's bill.

"Herbert will have some more of his funny remarks, I expect, when he comes home," she said, as they sat at dinner.

"I dare say," said Mr. White, "but for all that, the thing moved in my hand; that I'll swear to."

"You thought it did," said the old lady soothingly.

"I say it did," replied the other. "There was no thought about it; I had just—What's the matter?"

His wife made no reply. She was watching the mysterious movements of a man outside, who, peering in an undecided fashion at the house, appeared to be trying to make up his mind to enter. In mental connection with the two hundred pounds, she noticed that the stranger was well dressed, and wore a silk hat of glossy newness. Three times he paused at the gate, and then walked on again. The fourth time he stood with his hand upon it, and then with sudden resolution flung it open and walked up the path. Mrs. White at the same moment placed her hands behind her, and hurriedly unfastening the strings of her apron, put that useful article of apparel beneath the cushion of her chair.

She brought the stranger, who seemed ill at ease, into the room. He gazed at her furtively, and listened in a preoccupied fashion as the old lady apologized for the appearance of the room, and her husband's coat, a garment which he usually reserved for the garden. She then waited patiently for him to broach his business, but he was at first strangely silent.

"I—was asked to call," he said at last, and stooped and picked a piece of cotton from his trousers. "I come from 'Maw and Meggins.'"

The old lady started. "Is anything the matter?" she asked, breathlessly. "Has anything happened to Herbert? What is it? What is it?"

Her husband interposed. "There, there, mother," he said, hastily. "Sit down, and don't jump to conclusions. You've not brought bad news, I'm sure, sir," and he eyed the other wistfully.

"I'm sorry—" began the visitor.

"Is he hurt?" demanded the mother, wildly.

The visitor bowed in assent. "Badly hurt," he said quietly, "but he is not in any pain."

"Oh, thank God!" said the old woman, clasping her hands. "Thank God for that! Thank—"

She broke off suddenly as the sinister meaning of the assurance dawned upon her and she saw the awful confirmation of her fears in the other's averted face. She caught her breath, and turning to her husband, laid her trembling old hand upon his. There was a long silence.

"He was caught in the machinery," said the visitor at length, in a low voice.

"Caught in the machinery," repeated Mr. White, in a dazed fashion, "yes."

He sat staring blankly out at the window, and taking his wife's hand between his own, pressed it as he had been wont to do in their old courting days nearly forty years before.

"He was the only one left to us," he said, turning gently to the visitor. "It is hard."

The other coughed, and, rising, walked slowly to the window. "The firm wished me to convey their sincere sympathy with you in your great loss," he said, without looking round. "I beg that you will understand I am only their servant and merely obeying orders."

There was no reply; the old woman's face was white, her eyes staring, and her breath inaudible; on the husband's face was a look such as his friend the sergeant might have carried into his first action.

"I was to say that Maw and Meggins disclaim all responsibility," continued the other. "They admit no liability at all, but in consideration of your son's services they wish to present you with a certain sum as compensation."

Mr. White dropped his wife's hand, and rising to his feet, gazed with a look of horror at his visitor. His dry lips shaped the words, "How much?"

"Two hundred pounds," was the answer.

Unconscious of his wife's shriek, the old man smiled faintly, put out his hands like a sightless man, and dropped, a senseless heap, to the floor.

III

In the huge new cemetery, some two miles distant, the old people buried their dead, and came back to a house steeped in shadow and silence. It was all over so quickly that at first they could hardly realize it, and remained in a state of expectation as though of something else to happen —something else which was to lighten this load, too heavy for old hearts to bear.

But the days passed, and expectation gave place to resignation—the hopeless resignation of the old, sometimes miscalled

MULTICULTURAL CONNECTION

Fate in World Folklore

If there is a message in "The Monkey's Paw," it is that people should not meddle with fate. The concept of fate, a power that determines the outcome of events before they occur, is one that dates back to the earliest civilizations.

As seen by Ancient Greeks. The ancient Greeks went so far as to personify fate in three goddesses called the Fates. These daughters of Nyx, the god of night, were often represented as three old women. Clotho spun the thread of life; Lachesis measured it out; and Atropos cut the thread, ending life. The Fates' decisions were unalterable.

Dame Fortuna. The ancient Romans personified fate as one woman. Her name was Fortuna, and you can readily see the link between this name and our own word *fortune*. Romans consulted this goddess about the future, and in their art they showed her with a horn of plenty because she was the giver of abundance. They also showed her with a rudder, symbolizing her control of fate.

In the Middle Ages, this goddess was often shown controlling a wheel or globe of fortune. The turning of this sphere indicated that one's fortune was subject to many ups and downs.

Determining all events. The belief in fate as determining all events in heaven and on earth was adopted by later Western European societies. It can be seen most dramatically in Elizabethan England through the plays of William Shakespeare and his contemporaries. The three Fates make a notable appearance in Shakespeare's tragedy *Macbeth*. Here, however, they are depicted as three witches who accurately prophesy the rise and fall of the play's hero, the Scottish lord Macbeth.

The magical number three. It is no accident that the monkey's paw grants three wishes to three people. The very number three is considered magical and filled with fateful meaning in many cultures. In the fabled Eastern storybook *The Thousand and One Nights*, the magic genie in Aladdin's lamp also grants three wishes. Again, fate sees to it that the wishes of the unwise and evil lead only to their downfall.

Why do people believe in fate? As Americans, we like to think we are free to choose our own destinies. However, the idea of fate for many societies has helped people to accept life's good and bad. Many have found comfort in the face of disaster and death by believing that it was "meant to be."

Exploring and Sharing

Research examples of the use of the number three in fairy tales and stories from other countries. Share your findings with the class.

apathy. Sometimes they hardly exchanged a word, for now they had nothing to talk about, and their days were long to weariness.

It was about a week after that the old man, waking suddenly in the night, stretched out his hand and found himself alone. The room was in darkness, and the sound of subdued weeping came from the window. He raised himself in bed and listened.

"Come back," he said, tenderly. "You will be cold."

"It is colder for my son," said the old woman, and wept afresh.

The sound of her sobs died away on his ears. The bed was warm, and his eyes heavy with sleep. He dozed fitfully, and then slept until a sudden wild cry from his wife awoke him with a start.

The paw!" she cried wildly. "The monkey's paw!"

He started up in alarm. "Where? Where is it? What's the matter?"

She came stumbling across the room toward him. "I want it," she said quietly. "You've not destroyed it?"

"It's in the parlor, on the bracket," he replied, marveling. "Why?"

She cried and laughed together, and bending over, kissed his cheek.

"I only just thought of it," she said hysterically. "Why didn't I think of it before? Why didn't *you* think of it?"

"Think of what?" he questioned.

"The other two wishes," she replied rapidly. "We've only had one."

"Was not that enough?" he demanded, fiercely.

"No," she cried triumphantly; "we'll have one more. Go down and get it quickly, and wish our boy alive again."

The man sat up in bed and flung the bedclothes from his quaking limbs. "You are mad!" he cried, aghast.

"Get it," she panted; "get it quickly, and wish—Oh, my boy, my boy!"

Her husband struck a match and lit the candle. "Get back to bed," he said unsteadily. "You don't know what you are saying."

"We had the first wish granted," said the old woman feverishly; "why not the second?"

"A coincidence," stammered the old man.

"Go and get it and wish," cried his wife, quivering with excitement.

The old man turned and regarded her, and his voice shook. "He has been dead ten days, and besides he—I would not tell you else, but—I could only recognize him by his clothing. If he was too terrible for you to see then, how now?"

"Bring him back," cried the old woman, and dragged him toward the door. "Do you think I fear the child I have nursed?"

He went down in the darkness, and felt his way to the parlor, and then to the mantelpiece. The talisman was in its place, and a horrible fear that the unspoken wish might bring his mutilated son before him ere he could escape from the room seized upon him, and he caught his breath as he found that he had lost the direction of the door. His brow cold with sweat, he felt his way round the table, and groped along the wall until he found himself in the small passage with the unwholesome thing in his hand.

Even his wife's face seemed changed as he entered the room. It was white and expectant, and to his fears seemed to have an unnatural look upon it. He was afraid of her.

"*Wish!*" she cried, in a strong voice.

"It is foolish and wicked," he faltered.

"*Wish!*" repeated his wife.

He raised his hand. "I wish my son alive again."

The talisman fell to the floor, and he regarded it fearfully. Then he sank trem-

bling into a chair as the old woman, with burning eyes, walked to the window and raised the blind.

He sat until he was chilled with the cold, glancing occasionally at the figure of the old woman peering through the window. The candle-end, which had burned below the rim of the china candlestick, was throwing pulsating shadows on the ceiling and walls, until, with a flicker larger than the rest, it expired. The old man, with an unspeakable sense of relief at the failure of the talisman, crept back to his bed, and a minute or two afterward the old woman came silently and apathetically beside him.

Neither spoke, but lay silently listening to the ticking of the clock. A stair creaked, and a squeaky mouse scurried noisily through the wall. The darkness was oppressive, and after lying for some time screwing up his courage, he took the box of matches, and striking one, went downstairs for a candle.

At the foot of the stairs the match went out, and he paused to strike another; and at the same moment a knock, so quiet and stealthy as to be scarcely audible, sounded on the front door.

The matches fell from his hand and spilled in the passage. He stood motionless, his breath suspended until the knock was repeated. Then he turned and fled swiftly back to his room, and closed the door behind him. A third knock sounded through the house.

"What's that?" cried the old woman, starting up.

"A rat," said the old man in shaking tones—"a rat. It passed me on the stairs."

His wife sat up in bed listening. A loud knock resounded through the house.

"It's Herbert!" she screamed. "It's Herbert!"

She ran to the door, but her husband was before her, and catching her by the arm, held her tightly.

"What are you going to do?" he whispered hoarsely.

"It's my boy; it's Herbert!" she cried, struggling mechanically. "I forgot it was two miles away. What are you holding me for? Let go. I must open the door."

"Don't let it in," cried the old man, trembling.

"You're afraid of your own son," she cried, struggling. "Let me go. I'm coming, Herbert; I'm coming."

There was another knock, and another. The old woman with a sudden wrench broke free and ran from the room. Her husband followed to the landing, and called after her appealingly as she hurried downstairs. He heard the chain rattle back and the bottom bolt drawn slowly and stiffly from the socket. Then the old woman's voice, strained and panting.

"The bolt," she cried, loudly. "Come down. I can't reach it."

But her husband was on his hands and knees groping wildly on the floor in search of the paw. If he could only find it before the thing outside got in. A perfect fusillade of knocks reverberated through the house, and he heard the scraping of a chair as his wife put it down in the passage against the door. He heard the creaking of the bolt as it came slowly back, and at the same moment he found the monkey's paw, and frantically breathed his third and last wish.

The knocking ceased suddenly, although the echoes of it were still in the house. He heard the chair drawn back and the door opened. A cold wind rushed up the staircase, and a long loud wail of disappointment and misery from his wife gave him courage to run down to her side, and then to the gate beyond. The street lamp flickering opposite shone on a quiet and deserted road.

RESPONDING TO THE SELECTION

Your Response

1. Were you surprised at the end of the story? Explain.
2. How has this story affected you?

Recalling

3. According to the sergeant major, what power does the monkey's paw have?
4. In what way is Mr. White's first wish fulfilled?
5. What evidence from the story indicates that his other two wishes were fulfilled?

Interpreting

6. How does the opening setting of the cold, wet night and the warm, cozy fire set the mood?
7. The sergeant major states that the wishes were granted so naturally that they seemed like co-incidence. Explain the events of the story as coincidence.
8. Explain whether you think the events of the story prove the fakir's point that "fate ruled people's lives and those who interfered with it did so to their sorrow."

Applying

9. Suppose someone gave you a talisman that would grant three wishes. After reading this story, what would you do?

ANALYZING LITERATURE

Understanding Suspense

Suspense is the quality of a story that keeps you reading to find out what will happen. In "The Monkey's Paw," the suspense arouses a feeling of dread as you wonder what terrible results Mr. White's wishes will have. Jacobs uses foreshadowing to build suspense.

Decide if each of these quotations from "The Monkey's Paw" is an example of foreshadowing. If so, explain how it helps build suspense.

1. "'If you keep it, don't blame me for what happens.'" (page 33)

2. "'Come back. . . . You will be cold.'" (page 38)
3. "'If he was too terrible for you to see then, how now?'" (page 38)

CRITICAL THINKING AND READING

Predicting Outcomes

As you read, you make predictions about what will happen next. At what point in the story did you first predict the following events, and what was the basis for your prediction?

1. Herbert is killed in an accident.
2. Mrs. White asks her husband to wish her son alive again.

THINKING AND WRITING

Writing About Mood

Suppose that you were asked to make suggestions for a television show based on "The Monkey's Paw." Write a memo to the director suggesting ways to create the proper mood. Suggest a location, actors for each part, and music that will create the mood. Give reasons for your choices. Revise to be sure your ideas are clear.

LEARNING OPTIONS

1. **Cross-curricular Connection.** With two or three classmates, listen to pieces of music that might be used to introduce each part of the story. You might be familiar with music that could accompany the story, or you might want to look for some pieces at your library. In your group discuss which pieces best reflect the mood of each part of the story. Play your selections for the class, explaining why your group chose each piece.
2. **Writing.** How did you expect "The Monkey's Paw" to end? Write an alternative ending to the story. For example, suppose that Mr. or Mrs. White used their last wish differently. What would you have them wish for? Be sure to use descriptive details in your ending.

GUIDE FOR READING

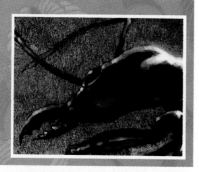

Leiningen Versus the Ants

Internal and External Conflict

A short story generally contains a **conflict,** which is a struggle between opposing forces. A conflict can be internal or external. An **internal conflict** takes place within a character, as he or she struggles with opposing feelings, beliefs, or needs. An **external conflict** is one that occurs between two or more characters or between a character and a natural force.

Focus

Nature can be formidable. Hurricanes, tornadoes, tidal waves, and volcanic eruptions are just a few natural occurrences that can devastate people and the environment in which they live. In "Leiningen Versus the Ants," a natural disaster takes the form of a swarm of ants. What natural disasters can you imagine? Draw a plot diagram of a story about a natural disaster. Be creative; use original ideas that would make an intriguing story, should you decide to write one later. The following diagram will help get you started. Use specific events in yours.

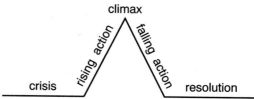

Vocabulary

Knowing the following words will help you as you read "Leiningen Versus the Ants."

saurians (sôr′ ē ənz) *n.*: Lizardlike animals (p. 43)

pampas (pam′ pəz) *n.*: Treeless plains in South America (p. 45)

peons (pē′ änz) *n.*: Laborers in Spanish America (p. 45)

flout (flout) *v.*: Show contempt for (p. 46)

weir (wir) *n.*: A low dam (p. 47)

provender (präv′ ən dər) *n.*: Food (p. 50)

alluvium (ə lōō′ vē əm) *n.*: Material such as sand or gravel deposited by moving water (p. 58)

fomentations (fō′ mən tā′ shənz) *n.*: Applications of warm, moist substances in the treatment of an injury (p. 58)

Carl Stephenson

(1893–   ) was born in Germany and has lived there all his life. "Leiningen Versus the Ants" was first published in 1938, and it has been widely read ever since, appearing in numerous collections of short stories. According to Stephenson's literary agent, "Leiningen Versus the Ants" may be the only story that Stephenson will allow to be published during his lifetime.

Leiningen Versus the Ants

Carl Stephenson

"Unless they alter their course, and there's no reason why they should, they'll reach your plantation in two days at the latest."

Leiningen sucked placidly at a cigar about the size of a corn cob and for a few seconds gazed without answering at the agitated District Commissioner. Then he took the cigar from his lips and leaned slightly forward. With his bristling gray hair, bulky nose, and lucid eyes, he had the look of an aging and shabby eagle.

"Decent of you," he murmured, "paddling all this way just to give me the tip. But you're pulling my leg, of course, when you say I must do a bunk. Why, even a herd of saurians couldn't drive me from this plantation of mine."

The Brazilian official threw up lean and lanky arms and clawed the air with wildly distended fingers. "Leiningen!" he shouted, "you're insane! They're not creatures you can fight—they're an elemental—an 'act of God!' Ten miles long, two miles wide— ants, nothing but ants! And every single one of them a fiend from hell; before you can spit three times they'll eat a full-grown buffalo to the bones. I tell you if you don't clear out at once there'll be nothing left of you but a skeleton picked as clean as your own plantation."

Leiningen grinned. "Act of God, my eye! Anyway, I'm not going to run for it just because an elemental's on the way. And don't think I'm the kind of fathead who tries to fend off lightning with his fists, either. I use my intelligence, old man. With me, the brain isn't a second blind gut;[1] I know what it's there for. When I began this model farm and plantation three years ago, I took into account all that could conceivably happen to it. And now I'm ready for anything and everything—including your ants."

The Brazilian rose heavily to his feet. "I've done my best," he gasped. "Your obstinacy endangers not only yourself, but the lives of your four hundred workers. You don't know these ants!"

Leiningen accompanied him down to the river, where the government launch was moored. The vessel cast off. As it moved downstream, the exclamation mark neared the rail and began waving arms frantically. Long after the launch had disappeared round the bend, Leiningen thought he could still hear that dimming, imploring voice. "You don't know them, I tell you! *You don't know them!*"

But the reported enemy was by no means unfamiliar to the planter. Before he started work on his settlement, he had lived long enough in the country to see for himself the fearful devastations sometimes wrought by these ravenous insects in their campaigns for food. But since then he had planned measures of defense accordingly, and these, he was convinced, were in every way adequate to withstand the approaching peril.

Moreover, during his three years as planter, Leiningen had met and defeated drought, flood, plague, and all other "acts of God" which had come against him—unlike his fellow settlers in the district, who had made little or no resistance. This unbroken success he attributed solely to the observance of his lifelong motto: *The human brain needs only to become fully aware of its powers to conquer even the elements.* Dullards reeled senselessly and aimlessly into the abyss; cranks, however brilliant, lost their heads when circumstances suddenly altered or accelerated and ran into stone walls; sluggards drifted with the current until they were caught in whirlpools and dragged under. But such disasters, Leiningen contended, merely strengthened his argument that intelligence, directed aright, invariably makes man the master of his fate.

Yes, Leiningen had always known how to grapple with life. Even here, in this Brazilian wilderness, his brain had triumphed over every difficulty and danger it had so far encountered. First he had vanquished primal forces by cunning and organization, then he had enlisted the resources of modern science to increase miraculously the yield of his plantation. And now he was sure he would prove more than a match for the "irresistible" ants.

That same evening, however, Leiningen assembled his workers. He had no intention of waiting till the news reached their ears from other sources. Most of them had been born in the district; the cry, "The ants are coming!" was to them an imperative signal for instant, panic-stricken flight, a spring for life itself. But so great was the Indians' trust in Leiningen, in Leiningen's word, and in Leiningen's wisdom, that they received his curt tidings, and his orders for the imminent struggle, with the calmness with which they were given. They waited, unafraid, alert, as if for the beginning of a new game or hunt which he had just described to them. The ants were indeed mighty, but not so mighty as the boss. Let them come!

---

1. blind gut: Reference to the appendix, which may have no function.

They came at noon the second day. Their approach was announced by the wild unrest of the horses, scarcely controllable now either in stall or under rider, scenting from afar a vapor instinct with horror.

It was announced by a stampede of animals, timid and savage, hurtling past each other; jaguars and pumas flashing by nimble stags of the pampas; bulky tapirs, no longer hunters, themselves hunted, outpacing fleet kinkajous; maddened herds of cattle, heads lowered, nostrils snorting, rushing through tribes of loping monkeys, chattering in a dementia[2] of terror; then followed the creeping and springing denizens of bush and steppe, big and little rodents, snakes, and lizards.

Pell-mell the rabble swarmed down the hill to the plantation, scattered right and left before the barrier of the water-filled ditch, then sped onwards to the river, where, again hindered, they fled along its banks out of sight.

This water-filled ditch was one of the defense measures which Leiningen had long since prepared against the advent of the ants. It encompassed three sides of the plantation like a huge horseshoe. Twelve feet across, but not very deep, when dry it could hardly be described as an obstacle to either man or beast. But the ends of the "horseshoe" ran into the river which formed the northern boundary, and fourth side, of the plantation. And at the end nearer the house and outbuildings in the middle of the plantation, Leiningen had constructed a dam by means of which water from the river could be diverted into the ditch.

So now, by opening the dam, he was able to fling an imposing girdle of water, a huge quadrilateral with the river as its base, completely around the plantation, like the moat encircling a medieval city. Unless the ants

were clever enough to build rafts, they had no hope of reaching the plantation, Leiningen concluded.

The twelve-foot water ditch seemed to afford in itself all the security needed. But while awaiting the arrival of the ants, Leiningen made a further improvement. The western section of the ditch ran along the edge of a tamarind wood,[3] and the branches of some great trees reached over the water. Leiningen now had them lopped so that ants could not descend from them within the "moat."

The women and children, then the herds of cattle, were escorted by peons on rafts over the river, to remain on the other side in absolute safety until the plunderers had departed. Leiningen gave this instruction, not because he believed the noncombatants were in any danger, but in order to avoid hampering the efficiency of the defenders.

Finally, he made a careful inspection of the "inner moat"—a smaller ditch lined with concrete, which extended around the hill on which stood the ranch house, barns, stables, and other buildings. Into this concrete ditch emptied the inflow pipes from three great petrol[4] tanks. If by some miracle the ants managed to cross the water and reach the plantation, this "rampart of petrol" would be an absolutely impassable protection for the besieged and their dwellings and stock. Such, at least, was Leiningen's opinion.

He stationed his men at irregular distances along the water ditch, the first line of defense. Then he lay down in his hammock and puffed drowsily away at his pipe until a peon came with the report that the ants had been observed far away in the south.

---

2. **dementia** (di men′ shə) n.: Insanity or madness.

3. **tamarind** (tam′ ə rind) **wood:** A grove of leafy trees found in the tropics.
4. **petrol** (pet′ rəl) adj.: Gasoline.

Leiningen mounted his horse, which at the feel of its master seemed to forget its uneasiness, and rode leisurely in the direction of the threatening offensive. The southern stretch of ditch—the upper side of the quadrilateral—was nearly three miles long; from its center one could survey the entire countryside. This was destined to be the scene of the outbreak of war between Leiningen's brain and twenty square miles of life-destroying ants.

It was a sight one could never forget. Over the range of hills, as far as eye could see, crept a darkening hem, ever longer and broader, until the shadow spread across the slope from east to west, then downward, downward, uncannily swift, and all the green herbage of that wide vista was being mown as by a giant sickle, leaving only the vast moving shadow, extending, deepening, and moving rapidly nearer.

When Leiningen's men, behind their barrier of water, perceived the approach of the long-expected foe, they gave vent to their suspense in screams and imprecations. But as the distance began to lessen between the "sons of hell" and the water ditch, they relapsed into silence. Before the advance of that awe-inspiring throng, their belief in the powers of the boss began to steadily dwindle.

Even Leiningen himself, who had ridden up just in time to restore their loss of heart by a display of unshakable calm, even he could not free himself from a qualm of malaise. Yonder were thousands of millions of voracious jaws bearing down upon him and only a suddenly insignificant, narrow ditch lay between him and his men and being gnawed to the bones "before you can spit three times."

Hadn't his brain for once taken on more than it could manage? If the blighters decided to rush the ditch, fill it to the brim with their corpses, there'd still be more than enough to destroy every trace of that cranium of his. The planter's chin jutted; they hadn't got him yet, and he'd see to it they never would. While he could think at all, he'd flout both death and the devil.

The hostile army was approaching in perfect formation; no human battalions, however well drilled, could ever hope to rival the precision of that advance. Along a front that moved forward as uniformly as a straight line, the ants drew nearer and nearer to the water ditch. Then, when they learned through their scouts the nature of the obstacle, the two outlying wings of the army detached themselves from the main body and marched down the western and eastern sides of the ditch.

This surrounding maneuver took rather more than an hour to accomplish; no doubt the ants expected that at some point they would find a crossing.

During this outflanking movement by the wings, the army on the center and southern front remained still. The besieged were therefore able to contemplate at their leisure the thumb-long, reddish-black, long-legged insects; some of the Indians believed they could see, too, intent on them, the brilliant, cold eyes, and the razor-edged mandibles,[5] of this host of infinity.

It is not easy for the average person to imagine that an animal, not to mention an insect, can *think*. But now both the brain of Leiningen and the brains of the Indians began to stir with the unpleasant foreboding that inside every single one of that deluge of insects dwelled a thought. And that thought was: Ditch or no ditch, we'll get to your flesh!

Not until four o'clock did the wings reach the "horseshoe" ends of the ditch, only to find these ran into the great river. Through some kind of secret telegraphy, the

_____

5. **mandibles** (man′ də b′lz) *n*.: Biting jaws.

report must then have flashed very swiftly indeed along the entire enemy line. And Leiningen, riding—no longer casually—along his side of the ditch, noticed by energetic and widespread movements of troops that for some unknown reason the news of the check had its greatest effect on the southern front, where the main army was massed. Perhaps the failure to find a way over the ditch was persuading the ants to withdraw from the plantation in search of spoils more easily attainable.

An immense flood of ants, about a hundred yards in width, was pouring in a glimmering black cataract down the far slope of the ditch. Many thousands were already drowning in the sluggish creeping flow, but they were followed by troop after troop, who clambered over their sinking comrades, and then themselves served as dying bridges to the reserves hurrying on in their rear.

Shoals of ants were being carried away by the current into the middle of the ditch, where gradually they broke asunder and then, exhausted by their struggles, vanished below the surface. Nevertheless, the wavering, floundering hundred-yard front was remorselessly if slowly advancing toward the besieged on the other bank. Leiningen had been wrong when he supposed the enemy would first have to fill the ditch with their bodies before they could cross; instead, they merely needed to act as steppingstones, as they swam and sank, to the hordes ever pressing onwards from behind.

Near Leiningen a few mounted herdsmen awaited his orders. He sent one to the weir—the river must be dammed more strongly to increase the speed and power of the water coursing through the ditch.

A second peon was dispatched to the outhouses to bring spades and petrol sprinklers. A third rode away to summon to the zone of the offensive all the men, except the observation posts, on the nearby sections of the ditch, which were not yet actively threatened.

The ants were getting across far more quickly than Leiningen would have deemed possible. Impelled by the mighty cascade behind them, they struggled nearer and nearer to the inner bank. The momentum of the attack was so great that neither the tardy flow of the stream nor its downward pull could exert its proper force; and into the gap left by every submerging insect, hastened forward a dozen more.

When reinforcements reached Leiningen, the invaders were halfway over. The planter had to admit to himself that it was only by a stroke of luck for him that the ants were attempting the crossing on a relatively short front: had they assaulted simultaneously along the entire length of the ditch, the outlook for the defenders would have been black indeed.

Even as it was, it could hardly be described as rosy, though the planter seemed quite unaware that death in a gruesome form was drawing closer and closer. As the war between his brain and the "act of God" reached its climax, the very shadow of annihilation began to pale to Leiningen, who now felt like a champion in a new Olympic game, a gigantic and thrilling contest, from which he was determined to emerge victor. Such, indeed, was his aura of confidence that the Indians forgot their fear of the peril only a yard or two away; under the planter's supervision, they began fervidly digging up to the edge of the bank and throwing clods of earth and spadefuls of sand into the midst of the hostile fleet.

The petrol sprinklers, hitherto used to destroy pests and blights on the plantation, were also brought into action. Streams of evil-reeking oil now soared and fell over an enemy already in disorder through the bombardment of earth and sand.

The ants responded to these vigorous and successful measures of defense by further developments of their offensive. Entire clumps of huddling insects began to roll down the opposite bank into the water. At the same time, Leiningen noticed that the ants were now attacking along an ever-widening front. As the numbers both of his men and his petrol sprinklers were severely limited, this rapid extension of the line of battle was becoming an overwhelming danger.

To add to his difficulties, the very clods of earth they flung into that black floating carpet often whirled fragments toward the defenders' side, and here and there dark ribbons were already mounting the inner bank. True, wherever a man saw these they could still be driven back into the water by spadefuls of earth or jets of petrol. But the file of defenders was too sparse and scattered to hold off at all points these landing parties, and though the peons toiled like mad men, their plight became momently more perilous.

One man struck with his spade at an enemy clump, did not draw it back quickly enough from the water; in a trice the wooden haft swarmed with upward scurrying insects. With a curse, he dropped the spade into the ditch; too late, they were already on his body. They lost no time; wherever they encountered bare flesh they bit deeply; a few, bigger than the rest, carried in their hindquarters a sting which injected a burning and paralyzing venom. Screaming, frantic with pain, the peon danced and twirled like a dervish.[6]

Realizing that another such casualty, yes, perhaps this alone, might plunge his men into confusion and destroy their morale, Leiningen roared in a bellow louder than the yells of the victim: "Into the petrol, idiot! Douse your paws in the petrol!" The dervish ceased his pirouette as if transfixed, then tore off his shirt and plunged his arm and the ants hanging to it up to the shoulder in one of the large open tins of petrol. But even then the fierce mandibles did not slacken; another peon had to help him squash and detach each separate insect.

Distracted by the episode, some defenders had turned away from the ditch. And now cries of fury, a thudding of spades, and a wild trampling to and fro, showed that the ants had made full use of the interval, though luckily only a few had managed to get across. The men set to work again desperately with the barrage of earth and sand. Meanwhile an old Indian, who acted as medicine man to the plantation workers, gave the bitten peon a drink he had prepared some hours before, which, he claimed, possessed the virtue of dissolving and weakening ants' venom.

Leiningen surveyed his position. A dispassionate observer would have estimated the odds against him at a thousand to one. But then such an onlooker would have reckoned only by what he saw—the advance of myriad battalions of ants against the futile efforts of a few defenders—and not by the unseen activity that can go on in a man's brain.

For Leiningen had not erred when he decided he would fight elemental with elemental. The water in the ditch was beginning to rise; the stronger damming of the river was making itself apparent.

Visibly the swiftness and power of the masses of water increased, swirling into quicker and quicker movement its living black surface, dispersing its pattern, carrying away more and more of it on the hastening current.

Victory had been snatched from the very jaws of defeat. With a hysterical shout of joy,

6. **dervish** (dər' vish) n.: One who performs a ritual Moslem whirling dance.

the peons feverishly intensified their bombardment of earth clods and sand.

And now the wide cataract down the opposite bank was thinning and ceasing, as if the ants were becoming aware that they could not attain their aim. They were scurrying back up the slope to safety.

All the troops so far hurled into the ditch had been sacrificed in vain. Drowned and floundering insects eddied in thousands along the flow, while Indians running on the bank destroyed every swimmer that reached the side.

Not until the ditch curved toward the east did the scattered ranks assemble again in a coherent mass. And now, exhausted and half-numbed, they were in no condition to ascend the bank. Fusillades of clods drove them round the bend toward the mouth of the ditch and then into the river, wherein they vanished without leaving a trace.

The news ran swiftly along the entire chain of outposts, and soon a long scattered line of laughing men could be seen hastening along the ditch toward the scene of victory.

For once they seemed to have lost all their native reserve, for it was in wild abandon now they celebrated the triumph—as if there were no longer thousands of millions of merciless, cold and hungry eyes watching them from the opposite bank, watching and waiting.

The sun sank behind the rim of the tamarind wood and twilight deepened into night. It was not only hoped but expected that the ants would remain quiet until dawn. But to defeat any forlorn attempt at a crossing, the flow of water through the ditch was powerfully increased by opening the dam still further.

In spite of this impregnable barrier, Leiningen was not yet altogether convinced that the ants would not venture another surprise attack. He ordered his men to camp along the bank overnight. He also detailed parties of them to patrol the ditch in two of his motor cars and ceaselessly to illuminate the surface of the water with headlights and electric torches.

After having taken all the precautions he deemed necessary, the farmer ate his supper with considerable appetite and went to bed. His slumbers were in no wise disturbed by the memory of the waiting, live, twenty square miles.

Dawn found a thoroughly refreshed and active Leiningen riding along the edge of the ditch. The planter saw before him a motionless and unaltered throng of besiegers. He studied the wide belt of water between them and the plantation, and for a moment almost regretted that the fight had ended so soon and so simply. In the comforting, matter-of-fact light of morning, it seemed to him now that the ants hadn't the ghost of a chance to cross the ditch. Even if they plunged headlong into it on all three fronts at once, the force of the now powerful current would inevitably sweep them away. He had got quite a thrill out of the fight—a pity it was already over.

He rode along the eastern and southern sections of the ditch and found everything in order. He reached the western section, opposite the tamarind wood, and here, contrary to the other battle fronts, he found the enemy very busy indeed. The trunks and branches of the trees and the creepers of the lianas,[7] on the far bank of the ditch, fairly swarmed with industrious insects. But instead of eating the leaves there and then, they were merely gnawing through the stalks, so that a thick green shower fell steadily to the ground.

No doubt they were victualing columns

_____

7. lianas (lē a′ nəz) *n.*: Climbing vines found in the tropics.

sent out to obtain provender for the rest of the army. The discovery did not surprise Leiningen. He did not need to be told that ants are intelligent, that certain species even use others as milch cows, watchdogs, and slaves. He was well aware of their power of adaptation, their sense of discipline, their marvelous talent for organization.

His belief that a foray to supply the army was in progress was strengthened when he saw the leaves that fell to the ground being dragged to the troops waiting outside the wood. Then all at once he realized the aim that rain of green was intended to serve.

Each single leaf, pulled or pushed by dozens of toiling insects, was borne straight to the edge of the ditch. Even as Macbeth watched the approach of Birnam Wood in the hands of his enemies,[8] Leiningen saw the tamarind wood move nearer and nearer in the mandibles of the ants. Unlike the fey Scot, however, he did not lose his nerve; no witches had prophesied his doom,[9] and if they had he would have slept just as soundly. All the same, he was forced to admit to himself that the situation was now far more ominous than that of the day before.

He had thought it impossible for the ants to build rafts for themselves—well, here they were, coming in thousands, more than enough to bridge the ditch. Leaves after leaves rustled down the slope to the water, where the current drew them away from the bank and carried them into midstream. And every single leaf carried several ants. This time the farmer did not trust to the alacrity of his messengers. He galloped away, leaning from his saddle and yelling orders as he rushed past outpost after outpost: "Bring petrol pumps to the southwest front! Issue spades to every man along the line facing the wood!" And arrived at the eastern and southern sections, he dispatched every man except the observation posts to the menaced west.

Then, as he rode past the stretch where the ants had failed to cross the day before, he witnessed a brief but impressive scene. Down the slope of the distant hill there came toward him a singular being, writhing rather than running, an animallike blackened statue with a shapeless head and four quivering feet that knuckled under almost ceaselessly. When the creature reached the far bank of the ditch and collapsed opposite Leiningen, he recognized it as a pampas stag, covered over and over with ants.

It had strayed near the zone of the army. As usual, they had attacked its eyes first.

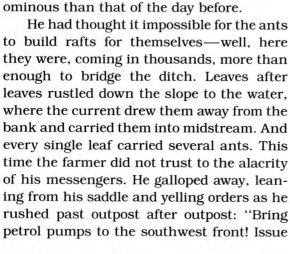

---

8. Macbeth . . . enemies: In William Shakespeare's play *Macbeth*, soldiers carried boughs from Birnam Wood to hide behind as they attacked a castle.
9. fey (fā) **Scot . . . doom:** "Fey Scot" refers to Macbeth, whose death was foretold by three witches.

Blinded, it had reeled in the madness of hideous torment straight into the ranks of its persecutors, and now the beast swayed to and fro in its death agony.

With a shot from his rifle Leiningen put it out of its misery. Then he pulled out his watch. He hadn't a second to lose, but for life itself he could not have denied his curiosity the satisfaction of knowing how long the ants would take—for personal reasons, so to speak. After six minutes the white polished bones alone remained. That's how he himself would look before you can —Leiningen spat once, and put spurs to his horse.

The sporting zest with which the excitement of the novel contest had inspired him the day before had now vanished; in its place was a cold and violent purpose. He would send these vermin back to the hell where they belonged, somehow, anyhow. Yes, but how was indeed the question; as things stood at present it looked as if the devils would raze him and his men from the earth instead. He had underestimated the might of the enemy; he really would have to bestir himself if he hoped to outwit them.

The biggest danger now, he decided, was the point where the western section of the ditch curved southward. And arrived there, he found his worst expectations justified. The very power of the current had huddled the leaves and their crews of ants so close together at the bend that the bridge was almost ready.

True, streams of petrol and clumps of earth still, prevented a landing. But the number of floating leaves was increasing

ever more swiftly. It could not be long now before a stretch of water a mile in length was decked by a green pontoon over which the ants could rush in millions.

Leiningen galloped to the weir. The damming of the river was controlled by a wheel on its bank. The planter ordered the man at the wheel first to lower the water in the ditch almost to vanishing point, next to wait a moment, then suddenly to let the river in again. This maneuver of lowering and raising the surface, of decreasing then increasing the flow of water through the ditch, was to be repeated over and over again until further notice.

This tactic was at first successful. The water in the ditch sank, and with it the film of leaves. The green fleet nearly reached the bed and the troops on the far bank swarmed down the slope to it. Then a violent flow of water at the original depth raced through the ditch, overwhelming leaves and ants, and sweeping them along.

This intermittent rapid flushing prevented just in time the almost completed fording of the ditch. But it also flung here and there squads of the enemy vanguard simultaneously up the inner bank. These seemed to know their duty only too well, and lost no time accomplishing it. The air rang with the curses of bitten Indians. They had removed their shirts and pants to detect the quicker the upward-hastening insects; when they saw one, they crushed it; and fortunately the onslaught as yet was only by skirmishers.

Again and again, the water sank and rose, carrying leaves and drowned ants away with it. It lowered once more nearly to its bed; but this time the exhausted defenders waited in vain for the flush of destruction. Leiningen sensed disaster; something must have gone wrong with the machinery of the dam. Then a sweating peon tore up to him:

"They're over!"

While the besieged were concentrating upon the defense of the stretch opposite the wood, the seemingly unaffected line beyond the wood had become the theater of decisive action. Here the defenders' front was sparse and scattered; everyone who could be spared had hurried away to the south.

Just as the man at the weir had lowered the water almost to the bed of the ditch, the ants on a wide front began another attempt at a direct crossing like that of the preceding day. Into the emptied bed poured an irresistible throng. Rushing across the ditch, they attained the inner bank before the Indians fully grasped the situation. Their frantic screams dumbfounded the man at the weir. Before he could direct the river anew into the safeguarding bed he saw himself surrounded by raging ants. He ran like the others, ran for his life.

When Leiningen heard this, he knew the plantation was doomed. He wasted no time bemoaning the inevitable. For as long as there was the slightest chance of success, he had stood his ground; and now any further resistance was both useless and dangerous. He fired three revolver shots into the air—the prearranged signal for his men to retreat instantly within the "inner moat." Then he rode toward the ranch house.

This was two miles from the point of invasion. There was therefore time enough to prepare the second line of defense against the advent of the ants. Of the three great petrol cisterns near the house, one had already been half emptied by the constant withdrawals needed for the pumps during the fight at the water ditch. The remaining petrol in it was now drawn off through underground pipes into the concrete trench which encircled the ranch house and its outbuildings.

And there, drifting in twos and threes, Leiningen's men reached him. Most of them were obviously trying to preserve an air of calm and indifference, belied, however, by their restless glances and knitted brows. One could see their belief in a favorable outcome of the struggle was already considerably shaken.

The planter called his peons around him.

"Well, lads," he began, "we've lost the first round. But we'll smash the beggars yet, don't you worry. Anyone who thinks otherwise can draw his pay here and now and push off. There are rafts enough and to spare on the river and plenty of time still to reach 'em."

Not a man stirred.

Leiningen acknowledged his silent vote of confidence with a laugh that was half a grunt. "That's the stuff, lads. Too bad if you'd missed the rest of the show, eh? Well, the fun won't start till morning. Once these blighters turn tail, there'll be plenty of work for everyone and higher wages all round. And now run along and get something to eat; you've earned it all right."

In the excitement of the fight the greater part of the day had passed without the men once pausing to snatch a bite. Now that the ants were for the time being out of sight, and the "wall of petrol" gave a stronger feeling of security, hungry stomachs began to assert their claims.

The bridges over the concrete ditch were removed. Here and there solitary ants had reached the ditch; they gazed at the petrol meditatively, then scurried back again. Apparently they had little interest at the moment for what lay beyond the evil-reeking barrier, the abundant spoils of the plantation were the main attraction. Soon the trees, shrubs and beds for miles around were hulled with ants zealously gobbling the yield of long weary months of strenuous toil.

As twilight began to fall, a cordon of ants marched around the petrol trench, but as yet made no move toward its brink. Leiningen posted sentries with headlights and electric torches, then withdrew to his office, and began to reckon up his losses. He estimated these as large, but, in comparison with his bank balance, by no means unbearable. He worked out in some detail a scheme of intensive cultivation which would enable him, before very long, to more than compensate himself for the damage now being wrought to his crops. It was with a contented mind that he finally betook himself to bed where he slept deeply until dawn, undisturbed by any thought that next day little more might be left of him than a glistening skeleton.

He rose with the sun and went out on the flat roof of his house. And a scene like one from Dante[10] lay around him; for miles in every direction there was nothing but a black, glittering multitude, a multitude of rested, sated, but nonetheless voracious ants; yes, look as far as one might, one could see nothing but that rustling black throng, except in the north, where the great river drew a boundary they could not hope to pass. But even the high stone breakwater, along the bank of the river, which Leiningen had built as a defense against inundations, was, like the paths, the shorn trees and shrubs, the ground itself, black with ants.

So their greed was not glutted in razing that vast plantation? Not by a long chalk; they were all the more eager now on a rich and certain booty—four hundred men, numerous horses, and bursting granaries.

At first it seemed that the petrol trench would serve its purpose. The besiegers sensed the peril of swimming it, and made no move to plunge blindly over its brink. Instead they devised a better maneuver;

---

10. Dante (dän' tā): Italian poet (1265–1321) who wrote *The Divine Comedy*, describing the horrors of hell.

they began to collect shreds of bark, twigs and dried leaves and dropped these into the petrol. Everything green, which could have been similarly used, had long since been eaten. After a time, though, a long procession could be seen bringing from the west the tamarind leaves used as rafts the day before.

Since the petrol, unlike the water in the outer ditch, was perfectly still, the refuse stayed where it was thrown. It was several hours before the ants succeeded in covering an appreciable part of the surface. At length, however, they were ready to proceed to a direct attack.

Their storm troops swarmed down the concrete side, scrambled over the supporting surface of twigs and leaves, and impelled these over the few remaining streaks of open petrol until they reached the other side. Then they began to climb up this to make straight for the helpless garrison.

During the entire offensive, the planter sat peacefully, watching them with interest, but not stirring a muscle. Moreover, he had ordered his men not to disturb in any way whatever the advancing horde. So they squatted listlessly along the bank of the ditch and waited for a sign from the boss.

The petrol was now covered with ants. A few had climbed the inner concrete wall and were scurrying toward the defenders.

"Everyone back from the ditch!" roared Leiningen. The men rushed away, without the slightest idea of his plan. He stooped forward and cautiously dropped into the ditch a stone which split the floating carpet and its living freight, to reveal a gleaming patch of petrol. A match spurted, sank down to the oily surface—Leiningen sprang back; in a flash a towering rampart of fire encompassed the garrison.

This spectacular and instant repulse threw the Indians into ecstasy. They ap-plauded, yelled and stamped. Had it not been for the awe in which they held their boss, they would infallibly have carried him shoulder high.

It was some time before the petrol burned down to the bed of the ditch, and the wall of smoke and flame began to lower. The ants had retreated in a wide circle from the devastation, and innumerable charred fragments along the outer bank showed that the flames had spread from the holocaust in the ditch well into the ranks beyond, where they had wrought havoc far and wide.

Yet the perseverance of the ants was by no means broken; indeed, each setback seemed only to whet it. The concrete cooled, the flicker of the dying flames wavered and vanished, petrol from the second tank poured into the trench—and the ants marched forward anew to the attack.

The foregoing scene repeated itself in every detail, except that on this occasion less time was needed to bridge the ditch, for the petrol was now already filmed by a layer of ash. Once again they withdrew; once again petrol flowed into the ditch. Would the creatures never learn that their self-sacrifice was utterly senseless? It really was senseless, wasn't it? Yes, of course it was senseless—provided the defenders had an *unlimited* supply of petrol.

When Leiningen reached this stage of reasoning, he felt for the first time since the arrival of the ants that his confidence was deserting him. His skin began to creep; he loosened his collar. Once the devils were over the trench there wasn't a chance for him and his men. What a prospect, to be eaten alive like that!

For the third time the flames immolated the attacking troops, and burned down to extinction. Yet the ants were coming on again as if nothing had happened. And meanwhile Leiningen had made a discovery that chilled him to the bone—petrol was no longer flowing into the ditch. Something must be blocking the outflow pipe of the third and last cistern—a snake or a dead rat? Whatever it was, the ants could be held off no longer, unless petrol could by some method be led from the cistern into the ditch.

Then Leiningen remembered that in an outhouse nearby were two old disused fire engines. The peons dragged them out of the shed, connected their pumps to the cistern, uncoiled and laid the hose. They were just in time to aim a stream of petrol at a column of ants that had already crossed and drive them back down the incline into the ditch. Once more an oily girdle surrounded the garrison, once more it was possible to hold the position—for the moment.

It was obvious, however, that this last resource meant only the postponement of defeat and death. A few of the peons fell on their knees and began to pray; others, shrieking insanely, fired their revolvers at the black, advancing masses, as if they felt their despair was pitiful enough to sway fate itself to mercy.

At length, two of the men's nerves broke: Leiningen saw a naked Indian leap over the north side of the petrol trench, quickly followed by a second. They sprinted with incredible speed toward the river. But their fleetness did not save them; long before they could attain the rafts, the enemy covered their bodies from head to foot.

In the agony of their torment, both sprang blindly into the wide river, where enemies no less sinister awaited them. Wild screams of mortal anguish informed the breathless onlookers that crocodiles and sword-toothed piranhas were no less ravenous than ants, and even nimbler in reaching their prey.

In spite of this bloody warning, more and more men showed they were making up their minds to run the blockade. Anything, even a fight midstream against alligators, seemed better than powerlessly waiting for death to come and slowly consume their living bodies.

Leiningen flogged his brain till it reeled. Was there nothing on earth could sweep this devils' spawn back into the hell from which it came?

Then out of the inferno of his bewilderment rose a terrifying inspiration. Yes, one hope remained, and one alone. It might be possible to dam the great river completely, so that its waters would fill not only the water ditch but overflow into the entire gigantic "saucer" of land in which lay the plantation.

The far bank of the river was too high for the waters to escape that way. The stone breakwater ran between the river and the plantation; its only gaps occurred where the "horseshoe" ends of the water ditch passed into the river. So its waters would not only be forced to inundate into the plantation, they would also be held there by the breakwater until they rose to its own high level. In half an hour, perhaps even earlier, the plantation and its hostile army of occupation would be flooded.

The ranch house and outbuildings stood upon rising ground. Their foundations were higher than the breakwater, so the flood would not reach them. And any remaining ants trying to ascend the slope could be repulsed by petrol.

It was possible—yes, if one could only get to the dam! A distance of nearly two miles lay between the ranch house and the weir—two miles of ants. Those two peons had managed only a fifth of that distance at the cost of their lives. Was there an Indian daring enough after that to run the gauntlet five times as far? Hardly likely; and if there were, his prospect of getting back was almost nil.

No, there was only one thing for it, he'd have to make the attempt himself; he might just as well be running as sitting still, anyway, when the ants finally got him. Besides, there *was* a bit of a chance. Perhaps the ants weren't so almighty, after all; perhaps he had allowed the mass suggestion of that evil black throng to hypnotize him, just as a snake fascinates and overpowers.

The ants were building their bridges. Leiningen got up on a chair. "Hey, lads, listen to me!" he cried. Slowly and listlessly, from all sides of the trench, the men began to shuffle toward him, the apathy of death already stamped on their faces.

"Listen, lads!" he shouted. "You're frightened of those beggars, but I'm proud of you. There's still a chance to save our lives —by flooding the plantation from the river. Now one of you might manage to get as far as the weir—but he'd never come back. Well, I'm not going to let you try it; if I did, I'd be worse than one of those ants. No, I called the tune, and now I'm going to pay the piper.

"The moment I'm over the ditch, set fire to the petrol. That'll allow time for the flood to do the trick. Then all you have to do is to wait here all snug and quiet till I'm back. Yes, I'm coming back, trust me"—he grinned—"when I've finished my slimming cure."

He pulled on high leather boots, drew heavy gauntlets over his hands, and stuffed the spaces between breeches and boots, gauntlets and arms, shirt and neck, with rags soaked in petrol. With close-fitting mosquito goggles he shielded his eyes, knowing too well the ants' dodge of first robbing their victim of sight. Finally, he plugged his nostrils and ears with cotton-wool, and let the peons drench his clothes with petrol.

He was about to set off when the old Indian medicine man came up to him; he had a wondrous salve, he said, prepared from a species of chafer[11] whose odor was intolerable to ants. Yes, this odor protected these chafers from the attacks of even the most murderous ants. The Indian smeared the boss's boots, his gauntlets, and his face over and over with the extract.

Leiningen then remembered the paralyzing effect of ants' venom, and the Indian gave him a gourd full of the medicine he had administered to the bitten peon at the water ditch. The planter drank it down without noticing its bitter taste; his mind was already at the weir.

He started off toward the northwest corner of the trench. With a bound he was over—and among the ants.

The beleaguered garrison had no opportunity to watch Leiningen's race against death. The ants were climbing the inner bank again—the lurid ring of petrol blazed aloft. For the fourth time that day the reflection from the fire shone on the sweating faces of the imprisoned men, and on the reddish-black cuirasses[12] of their oppressors. The red and blue, dark-edged flames leaped vividly now, celebrating what? The funeral pyre of the four hundred, or of the hosts of destruction?

Leiningen ran. He ran in long, equal strides, with only one thought, one sensation, in his being—he *must* get through. He dodged all trees and shrubs; except for the split seconds his soles touched the ground, the ants should have no opportunity to alight on him. That they would get to him soon, despite the salve on his boots, the petrol on his clothes, he realized only too well, but he knew even more surely that he

---

11. chafer (chāf′ ər) *n.*: Insect that feeds on plants.
12. cuirasses (kwi ras′ əz) *n.*: Body armor; here, the ants' outer bodies.

must, and that he would, get to the weir.

Apparently the salve was some use after all; not until he had reached halfway did he feel ants under his clothes, and a few on his face. Mechanically, in his stride, he struck at them, scarcely conscious of their bites. He saw he was drawing appreciably nearer the weir—the distance grew less and less—sank to five hundred—three—two—hundred yards.

Then he was at the weir and gripping the ant-hulled wheel. Hardly had he seized it when a horde of infuriated ants flowed over his hands, arms, and shoulders. He started the wheel—before it turned once on its axis the swarm covered his face. Leiningen strained like a madman, his lips pressed tight; if he opened them to draw breath . . .

He turned and turned; slowly the dam lowered until it reached the bed of the river. Already the water was overflowing the ditch. Another minute, and the river was pouring through the nearby gap in the breakwater. The flooding of the plantation had begun.

Leiningen let go the wheel. Now, for the first time, he realized he was coated from head to foot with a layer of ants. In spite of the petrol, his clothes were full of them, several had got to his body or were clinging to his face. Now that he had completed his task, he felt the smart raging over his flesh from the bites of sawing and piercing insects.

Frantic with pain, he almost plunged into the river. To be ripped and slashed to shreds by piranhas? Already he was running the return journey, knocking ants from his gloves and jacket, brushing them from his bloodied face, squashing them to death under his clothes.

One of the creatures bit him just below the rim of his goggles; he managed to tear it away, but the agony of the bite and its etching acid drilled into the eye nerves; he saw now through circles of fire into a milky mist, then he ran for a time almost blinded, knowing that if he once tripped and fell. . . . The old Indian's brew didn't seem much good; it weakened the poison a bit, but didn't get rid of it. His heart pounded as if it would burst; blood roared in his ears; a giant's fist battered his lungs.

Then he could see again, but the burning girdle of petrol appeared infinitely far away; he could not last half that distance. Swift-changing pictures flashed through his head, episodes in his life, while in another part of his brain a cool and impartial onlooker informed this ant-blurred, gasping, exhausted bundle named Leiningen that such a rushing panorama of scenes from one's past is seen only in the moment before death.

A stone in the path . . . too weak to avoid it . . . the planter stumbled and collapsed. He tried to rise . . . he must be pinned under a rock . . . it was impossible . . . the slightest movement was impossible. . . .

Then all at once he saw, starkly clear and huge, and, right before his eyes, furred with ants, towering and swaying in its death agony, the pampas stag. In six minutes —gnawed to the bones. He *couldn't* die like that! And something outside him seemed to drag him to his feet. He tottered. He began to stagger forward again.

Through the blazing ring hurtled an apparition which, as soon as it reached the ground on the inner side, fell full length and did not move. Leiningen, at the moment he made that leap through the flames, lost consciousness for the first time in his life. As he lay there, with glazing eyes and lacerated face, he appeared a man returned from the grave. The peons rushed to him, stripped off his clothes, tore away the ants from a body that seemed almost one open wound; in some places the bones were showing. They carried him into the ranch house.

As the curtain of flames lowered, one could see in place of the illimitable host of ants an extensive vista of water. The thwarted river had swept over the plantation, carrying with it the entire army. The water had collected and mounted in the great "saucer," while the ants had in vain attempted to reach the hill on which stood the ranch house. The girdle of flames held them back.

And so, imprisoned between water and fire, they had been delivered into the annihilation that was their god. And near the farther mouth of the water ditch, where the stone mole had its second gap, the ocean swept the lost battalions into the river, to vanish forever.

The ring of fire dwindled as the water mounted to the petrol trench and quenched the dimming flames. The inundation rose higher and higher: because its outflow was impeded by the timber and underbrush it had carried along with it, its surface required some time to reach the top of the high stone breakwater and discharge over it the rest of the shattered army.

It swelled over ant-stippled shrubs and bushes, until it washed against the foot of the knoll whereon the besieged had taken refuge. For a while an alluvium of ants tried again and again to attain the dry land, only to be repulsed by streams of petrol back into the merciless flood.

Leiningen lay on his bed, his body swathed from head to foot in bandages. With fomentations and salves, they had managed to stop the bleeding, and had dressed his many wounds. Now they thronged around him, one question in every face. Would he recover? "He won't die," said the old man who had bandaged him, "if he doesn't want to."

The planter opened his eyes. "Everything in order?" he asked.

"They're gone," said his nurse. He held out to his master a gourd full of a powerful sleeping-draft. Leiningen gulped it down.

"I told you I'd come back," he murmured, "even if I am a bit streamlined."

Your Response

1. Put yourself in Leiningen's place. What would you have done differently? Why?

Recalling

2. What threat do the ants pose to Leiningen?
3. At what point in the story does it first seem that Leiningen has snatched victory "from the very jaws of defeat"? How do the ants recover?
4. How does Leiningen finally defeat the ants?

Interpreting

5. Why do you think Leiningen was so determined to stay and fight the ants?
6. What qualities do you think make Leiningen well equipped to fight the ants? What qualities might make him dangerous to others?
7. What behavior of the ants makes them appear to be intelligent beings?
8. Early in the story, Leiningen's motto is stated: *The human brain needs only to become fully aware of its power to conquer even the elements.* Explain how the events of the story either support or invalidate his motto.

Applying

9. By staying to fight the ants, Leiningen risked others' lives as well as his own. Do you think he was justified? Why or why not?

ANALYZING LITERATURE

Examining Conflicts

An **internal conflict** is a struggle that takes place within a character who struggles with differing ideas and feelings. The peons have internal conflicts between their fear of the ants and their belief in Leiningen. An **external conflict** occurs between two or more characters or between a character and natural forces.

1. Give an example of an internal conflict that pits intellect against instinct.
2. Give an example of an external conflict that pits intellect against instinct.

CRITICAL THINKING AND READING

Recognizing Causes and Effects

Situations have both causes and effects. The **causes** are the reasons why something happens. The **effects** are the results or outcomes of the situation.

1. Describe each of Leiningen's lines of defense against the ants.
2. Explain the effect of each line of defense.

THINKING AND WRITING

Writing About Conflict

Imagine that you are a reporter covering Leiningen's war against the ants. To write your final summary story, decide what the conflict was really about and why it was important. Also list some high points of the fighting. Write a story that helps your readers understand what went on. When you revise your story, be sure that it answers these questions: who? what? where? when? why? and how?

LEARNING OPTIONS

1. **Art.** Based on Stephenson's description, draw a map of Leiningen's plantation. On your map use symbols to show the measures Leiningen took to defend the plantation. Draw lines indicating the distance the ants advanced at each stage. In addition create symbols to show the strategies the ants used against Leiningen. Finally, make a key to explain the symbols on your map.
2. **Community Connections.** How have people in your community banded together in response to a crisis? Think of a situation in which members of your community have tried to solve or alleviate a problem through a group effort. Commend this effort in a letter to the editor of your local newspaper.

Old Man of the Temple

R. K. Narayan

(1906–   ) grew up in Madras and attended Maharaja's College in Mysore, South India. His first novel was published in 1935. In 1958 he won the National Prize of the Indian Literary Academy, his country's highest literary honor. In addition to novels, Indian legends, and his autobiography, Narayan has also written short stories. The one you are about to read takes place, as do many of Narayan's works, in India—in this case on a road passing through a village.

Fantasy

A **fantasy** is a work of fiction that features characters, places, or events that could not actually happen. When writers write fantasy, they let their imaginations run freely in order to create the impossible. When readers read fantasy, they suspend disbelief in order to accept the impossible. Fantasy fascinates us. We enjoy reading about ghosts, magic spells, wizards, dragons, and other fantastic elements. Peter Pan's Never-Never Land beckons to most of us at one time or another. Our spines tingle as we stand with Ichabod Crane and face the Headless Horseman. But fantasy must also contain elements of real life. The fantasy "Old Man of the Temple" combines realistic elements and fantastic details to entertain the reader.

Focus

Before you read "Old Man of the Temple," brainstorm to compile a list of books you have read or movies you have seen that combine elements of reality and fantasy. It might be fun to brainstorm in a group of three or four people. In your group, discuss books or movies in which the characters and events take place in a context that is both real and fantastic. Keep your discussion in mind as you read "Old Man of the Temple."

Vocabulary

Knowing the following words will help you as you read "Old Man of the Temple."

sobriety (sə brī′ ə tē) *n.*: Moderation, especially in the use of alcoholic beverages (p. 61)

awry (ə rī′) *adj.*: Not straight; askew (p. 61)

literally (lit′ ər əl ē) *adv.*: Word for word; not imaginatively; actually; in fact (p. 63)

longevity (län jev′ ə tē) *n.*: The length or duration of a life (p. 64)

imperative (im per′ ə tiv) *adj.*: Absolutely necessary; urgent (p. 65)

venture (ven′ chər) *n.*: A chance (p. 65)

Old Man of the Temple

R. K. Narayan

The Talkative Man said:

It was some years ago that this happened. I don't know if you can make anything of it. If you do, I shall be glad to hear what you have to say; but personally I don't understand it at all. It has always mystified me. Perhaps the driver was drunk; perhaps he wasn't.

I had engaged a taxi for going to Kumbum, which, as you may already know, is fifty miles from Malgudi.[1] I went there one morning and it was past nine in the evening when I finished my business and started back for the town. Doss,[2] the driver, was a young fellow of about twenty-five. He had often brought his car for me and I liked him. He was a well-behaved, obedient fellow, with a capacity to sit and wait at the wheel, which is really a rare quality in a taxi driver. He drove the car smoothly, seldom swore at passers-by, and exhibited perfect judgment, good sense, and sobriety; and so I preferred him to any other driver whenever I had to go out on business.

It was about eleven when we passed the village Koopal,[3] which is on the way down. It was the dark half of the month and the surrounding country was swallowed up in the night. The village street was deserted.

Everyone had gone to sleep; hardly any light was to be seen. The stars overhead sparkled brightly. Sitting in the back seat and listening to the continuous noise of the running wheels, I was half lulled into a drowse.

All of a sudden Doss swerved the car and shouted: "You old fool! Do you want to kill yourself?"

I was shaken out of my drowse and asked: "What is the matter?"

Doss stopped the car and said, "You see that old fellow, sir. He is trying to kill himself. I can't understand what he is up to."

I looked in the direction he pointed and asked, "Which old man?"

"There, there. He is coming towards us again. As soon as I saw him open that temple door and come out I had a feeling, somehow, that I must keep an eye on him."

I took out my torch, got down, and walked about, but could see no one. There was an old temple on the roadside. It was utterly in ruins; most portions of it were mere mounds of old brick; the walls were awry; the doors were shut to the main doorway, and brambles and thickets grew over and covered them. It was difficult to guess with the aid of the torch alone what temple it was and to what period it belonged.

"The doors are shut and sealed and don't look as if they had been opened for centuries now," I cried.

"No, sir," Doss said coming nearer. "I saw the old man open the doors and come

---

1. Kumbum (kəm′ bəm) . . . **Malgudi** (mäl g$\overline{oo}$′ dē): Malgudi is a fictional city about which Narayan often writes.
2. Doss (däs)
3. Koopal (k$\overline{oo}$ päl′)

out. He is standing there; shall we ask him to open them again if you want to go in and see?''

I said to Doss, "Let us be going. We are wasting our time here."

We went back to the car. Doss sat in his seat, pressed the self-starter, and asked without turning his head, "Are you permitting this fellow to come with us, sir? He says he will get down at the next milestone."

"Which fellow?" I asked.

Doss indicated the space next to him.

"What is the matter with you, Doss? Have you had a drop of drink or something?"

"I have never tasted any drink in my life, sir," he said, and added, "Get down, old boy. Master says he can't take you."

"Are you talking to yourself?"

"After all, I think we needn't care for these unknown fellows on the road," he said.

"Doss," I pleaded. "Do you feel confident you can drive? If you feel dizzy don't drive."

"Thank you, sir," said Doss. "I would rather not start the car now. I am feeling a little out of sorts." I looked at him anxiously. He closed his eyes, his breathing became heavy and noisy, and gradually his head sank.

"Doss, Doss," I cried desperately. I got down, walked to the front seat, opened the door, and shook him vigorously. He opened his eyes, assumed a hunched-up position, and rubbed his eyes with his hands, which trembled like an old man's.

"Do you feel better?" I asked.

"Better! Better! Hi! Hi!" he said in a thin, piping voice.

MULTICULTURAL CONNECTION

Ghost Stories Around the World

Many of us love to hear a scary ghost story, especially on a cold, windy night. It is not surprising then that these gruesome tales are told all over the world.

Ghostly ancestors. In many cultures, ghosts are believed to be dead ancestors. Every August in Japan, the Bon Festival is observed to welcome relatives from the land of the dead. However, not all ghosts are welcome. The "gaki," or hungry ghosts, are the spirits of the homeless and are angry because they were not admitted to paradise.

In a story from Benin, West Africa, a young woman wanders into the market of the dead by mistake and meets the ghosts of her grandmother, mother, and brother. When she returns home, she breaks her promise not to tell where she has been and returns to the market with a friend.

Angry, the dead prevent them from leaving.

Spirits with a message. European ghost stories usually speak of spirits who return to complete unfinished tasks. In a story from Holland, the spirit of a rich miser returns to his house each night to count and recount the gold coins he had hidden while he was still alive.

A Halloween legend. In the United States, ghosts play a big part in Halloween. Even the jack-o'lantern derives from an old Irish ghost story. Upon his death a man named Jack, known for his mean behavior, was denied entrance to heaven and hell. With nowhere to go, Jack's ghost began to roam the Earth. To find his way in the dark, Jack put a piece of coal from hell's fire inside a turnip he was gnawing—his jack-o'lantern!

To Share in Class

Do you know any ghost stories from other countries? Share them with the class.

"What has happened to your voice? You sound like someone else," I said.

"Nothing. My voice is as good as it was. When a man is eighty he is bound to feel a few changes coming on."

"You aren't eighty, surely," I said.

"Not a day less," he said. "Is nobody going to move this vehicle? If not, there is no sense in sitting here all day. I will get down and go back to my temple."

"I don't know how to drive," I said. "And unless you do it, I don't see how it can move."

"Me!" exclaimed Doss. "These new chariots! God knows what they are drawn by, I never understand, though I could handle a pair of bullocks[4] in my time. May I ask a question?"

"Go on," I said.

"Where is everybody?"

"Who?"

"Lots of people I knew are not to be seen at all. All sorts of new fellows everywhere, and nobody seems to care. Not a soul comes near the temple. All sorts of people go about but not one who cares to stop and talk. Why doesn't the king ever come this way? He used to go this way at least once a year before."

"Which king?" I asked.

"Let me go, you idiot," said Doss, edging towards the door on which I was leaning. "You don't seem to know anything." He pushed me aside, and got down from the car. He stooped as if he had a big hump on his back, and hobbled along towards the temple. I followed him, hardly knowing what to do. He turned and snarled at me: "Go away, leave me alone. I have had enough of you."

"What has come over you, Doss?" I asked.

"Who is Doss, anyway? Doss, Doss, Doss. What an absurd name! Call me by my name or leave me alone. Don't follow me calling 'Doss, Doss.'"

"What is your name?" I asked.

"Krishna Battar,[5] and if you mention my name people will know for a hundred miles around. I built a temple where there was only a cactus field before. I dug the earth, burnt every brick, and put them one upon another, all single-handed. And on the day the temple held up its tower over the surrounding country, what a crowd gathered! The king sent his chief minister . . ."

"Who was the king?"

"Where do you come from?" he asked.

"I belong to these parts certainly, but as far as I know there has been only a collector at the head of the district. I have never heard of any king."

"Hi! Hi! Hi!" he cackled, and his voice rang through the gloomy silent village. "Fancy never knowing the king! He will behead you if he hears it."

"What is his name?" I asked.

This tickled him so much that he sat down on the ground, literally unable to stand the joke any more. He laughed and coughed uncontrollably.

"I am sorry to admit," I said, "that my parents have brought me up in such utter ignorance of worldly affairs that I don't know even my king. But won't you enlighten me? What is his name?"

"Vishnu Varma,[6] the emperor of emperors . . ."

I cast my mind up and down the range of my historical knowledge but there was no one by that name. Perhaps a local chief of pre-British days, I thought.

"What a king! He often visited my tem-

---

4. **bullocks** (bo͝ol′ əks) *n*.: Oxen; steers.

ple or sent his minister for the Annual Festival of the temple. But now nobody cares."

"People are becoming less godly nowadays," I said. There was silence for a moment. An idea occurred to me, I can't say why. "Listen to me," I said. "You ought not to be here any more."

"What do you mean?" he asked, drawing himself up, proudly.

"Don't feel hurt; I say you shouldn't be here any more because you are dead."

"Dead! Dead!" he said. "Don't talk nonsense. How can I be dead when you see me before you now? If I am dead how can I be saying this and that?"

"I don't know all that," I said. I argued and pointed out that according to his own story he was more than five hundred years old, and didn't he know that man's longevity was only a hundred? He constantly interrupted me, but considered deeply what I said.

He said: "It is like this . . . I was coming through the jungle one night after visiting my sister in the next village. I had on me some money and gold ornaments. A gang of robbers set upon me. I gave them as good a fight as any man could, but they were too many for me. They beat me down and knifed me; they took away all that I had on me and left thinking they had killed me. But soon I got up and tried to follow them. They were gone. And I returned to the temple and have been here since . . ."

I told him, "Krishna Battar, you are dead, absolutely dead. You must try and go away from here."

"What is to happen to the temple?" he asked.

"Others will look after it."

"Where am I to go? Where am I to go?"

"Have you no one who cares for you?" I asked.

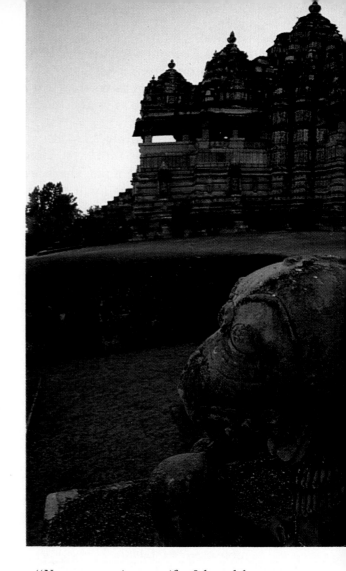

"None except my wife. I loved her very much."

"You can go to her."

"Oh, no. She died four years ago . . ."

Four years! It was very puzzling. "Do you say four years back from now?" I asked.

"Yes, four years ago from now." He was clearly without any sense of time.

So I asked, "Was she alive when you were attacked by thieves?"

"Certainly not. If she had been alive she would never have allowed me to go through the jungle after nightfall. She took very good

care of me.''

"See here," I said. "It is imperative you should go away from here. If she comes and calls you, will you go?"

"How can she when I tell you that she is dead?"

I thought for a moment. Presently I found myself saying, "Think of her, and only of her, for a while and see what happens. What was her name?"

"Seetha,[7] a wonderful girl . . ."

_____
7. Seetha (sē′ thə)

"Come on, think of her." He remained in deep thought for a while. He suddenly screamed, "Seetha is coming! Am I dreaming or what? I will go with her . . ." He stood up, very erect; he appeared to have lost all the humps and twists he had on his body. He drew himself up, made a dash forward, and fell down in a heap.

Doss lay on the rough ground. The only sign of life in him was his faint breathing. I shook him and called him. He would not open his eyes. I walked across and knocked on the door of the first cottage. I banged on the door violently.

Someone moaned inside, "Ah, it is come!"

Someone else whispered, "You just cover your ears and sleep. It will knock for a while and go away." I banged on the door and shouted who I was and where I came from.

I walked back to the car and sounded the horn. Then the door opened, and a whole family crowded out with lamps. "We thought it was the usual knocking and we wouldn't have opened if you hadn't spoken."

"When was this knocking first heard?" I asked.

"We can't say," said one. "The first time I heard it was when my grandfather was living; he used to say he had even seen it once or twice. It doesn't harm anyone, as far as I know. The only thing it does is bother the bullock carts passing the temple and knock on the doors at night . . ."

I said as a venture, "It is unlikely you will be troubled any more."

It proved correct. When I passed that way again months later I was told that the bullocks passing the temple after dusk never shied now and no knocking on the doors was heard at nights. So I felt that the old fellow had really gone away with his good wife.

RESPONDING TO THE SELECTION

Your Response

1. The Talkative Man says, "I don't know if you can make anything of it. If you do, I shall be glad to hear what you have to say . . ." If you had the opportunity to address the Talkative Man's comment, what would you say to him?

Recalling

2. The trip is interrupted when something unusual appears to have happened to Doss. Explain what seems to have happened.
3. How is peace and quiet finally restored?

Interpreting

4. How does the narrator become aware of the existence of an unexpected visitor?
5. Why did the narrator knock on the cottage door? What does the narrator's conversation with the occupants of the cottage add to the story?
6. What do you think happens to Doss at the end of the story? Support your answer.
7. How would you describe the mood or atmosphere of this story? How does the setting contribute to this mood?

Applying

8. *Requiescat in pace,* a Latin saying for "Rest in peace," is often used at funeral or memorial services. Why might this saying make a good title for this story?

ANALYZING LITERATURE

Investigating Fantasy

Fantasy contains elements that could not exist in real life. These may include events in the plot, strange characters with magical powers, and imaginary places.

1. List the elements of fantasy that occur in "Old Man of the Temple."
2. At what point does "Old Man of the Temple" become a fantasy rather than a realistic story?

3. Explain how the realistic feelings of the characters help the fantasy seem more believable.

CRITICAL THINKING AND READING

Making Inferences From Evidence

An **inference** is a conclusion based on given facts and past experience. Since authors tend to leave much unsaid, you often need to make inferences when you read. When you infer, you use the evidence the author provides.

What is the most likely inference you would draw from the evidence in each of the following scenes from the story?

1. Doss sees an old man who is not visible to the person telling the story.
2. All of a sudden, Doss begins to speak and move as though he were an old man.

THINKING AND WRITING

Writing Fantasy

Choose an ordinary event—one that occurs often in real life. You might choose a family eating dinner or two friends walking to school. Turn the event into a fantasy by including characters and details that could not possibly occur in real life. After you have planned your fantasy, write a first draft. As you revise, make sure that your ideas are presented clearly and that you have really exercised your imagination.

LEARNING OPTION

Performance. In a Readers Theater, you act out stories without scenery or costumes, using only your voice, face, and gestures. Actors read their lines from the story. Often someone is assigned to read those parts of the story that are not spoken directly by the characters themselves.

With several classmates prepare a Readers Theater presentation of "Old Man of the Temple." Be sure that the person playing Doss collapses gently to the floor so that no injury occurs.

Characterization

EVENING, MONHEGAN ISLAND
Samuel Reindorf

GUIDE FOR READING

William Melvin Kelley

(1937–   ) was born in New York City. He was educated at Harvard University and has taught at several colleges. Kelley's stories focus on the problems of individuals, some of them black. Kelley has said, "I am not a sociologist or a politician or a spokesman. Such people try to give answers. A writer, I think, should ask questions." In "A Visit to Grandmother," Kelley shows members of an African American family seeking answers to their own questions.

A Visit to Grandmother

Direct and Indirect Characterization

Characterization is the way a writer brings a character to life. Sometimes a writer uses **direct characterization**—directly telling you about the character's personality. More frequently a writer uses **indirect characterization,** revealing personality through a physical description of the character; through the character's thoughts, words, and actions; and through other characters' comments. Kelley uses indirect characterization in "A Visit to Grandmother," for example, when the grandmother tells a story that reveals a great deal about herself and one of her children.

Focus

"A Visit to Grandmother" explores family relationships. Whether a family has two members or ten, misunderstandings are common. Disagreements among siblings or between a parent and a son or daughter can result from misunderstandings. Tension can be healthy, however, when it leads people to communicate and work out their differences. Through a stressful confrontation, the characters in this story gain a better understanding of one another. Think about close friends or relatives. Write a journal entry about a confrontation you've had with someone close to you. In your journal explore how the confrontation clarified misunderstandings between you and that person. Think about your experience as you read "A Visit to Grandmother."

Vocabulary

Knowing the following words will help you as you read "A Visit to Grandmother."

indulgence (in dul′ jəns) *n.*: Leniency; forgiveness (p. 70)
grimacing (grim′ əs iŋ) *v.*: Making a twisted or distorted facial expression (p. 70)

lacquered (lak′ ərd) *adj.*: Coated with a varnish made from shellac or resin (p. 74)

A Visit to Grandmother

William Melvin Kelley

Chig knew something was wrong the instant his father kissed her. He had always known his father to be the warmest of men, a man so kind that when people ventured timidly into his office, it took only a few words from him to make them relax, and even laugh. Doctor Charles Dunford cared about people.

But when he had bent to kiss the old lady's black face, something new and almost ugly had come into his eyes: fear, uncertainty, sadness, and perhaps even hatred.

Ten days before in New York, Chig's father had decided suddenly he wanted to go to Nashville to attend his college class reunion, twenty years out. Both Chig's brother and sister, Peter and Connie, were packing for camp and besides were too young for such an affair. But Chig was seventeen, had nothing to do that summer, and his father asked if he would like to go along. His father had given him additional reasons: "All my running buddies got their diplomas and were snapped up by them crafty young gals, and had kids within a year—now all those kids, some of them gals, are your age."

The reunion had lasted a week. As they packed for home, his father, in a far too offhand way, had suggested they visit Chig's grandmother. "We this close. We might as well drop in on her and my brothers."

So, instead of going north, they had gone farther south, had just entered her house.

And Chig had a suspicion now that the reunion had been only an excuse to drive south, that his father had been heading to this house all the time.

His father had never talked much about his family, with the exception of his brother, GL, who seemed part con man, part

practical joker and part Don Juan;[1] he had spoken of GL with the kind of indulgence he would have shown a cute, but ill-behaved and potentially dangerous, five-year-old.

Chig's father had left home when he was fifteen. When asked why, he would answer: "I wanted to go to school. They didn't have a Negro high school at home, so I went up to Knoxville and lived with a cousin and went to school."

They had been met at the door by Aunt Rose, GL's wife, and ushered into the living room. The old lady had looked up from her seat by the window. Aunt Rose stood between the visitors.

The old lady eyed his father. "Rose, who that? Rose?" She squinted. She looked like a doll, made of black straw, the wrinkles in her face running in one direction like the head of a broom. Her hair was white and coarse and grew out straight from her head. Her eyes were brown—the whites, too, seemed light brown—and were hidden behind thick glasses, which remained somehow on a tiny nose. "That Hiram?" That was another of his father's brothers. "No, it ain't Hiram; too big for Hiram." She turned then to Chig. "Now that man, he look like Eleanor, Charles's wife, but Charles wouldn't never send my grandson to see me. I never even hear from Charles." She stopped again.

"It Charles, Mama. That who it is." Aunt Rose, between them, led them closer. "It Charles come all the way from New York to see you, and brung little Charles with him."

The old lady stared up at them. "Charles? Rose, that really Charles?" She turned away, and reached for a handkerchief in the pocket of her clean, ironed,

flowered housecoat, and wiped her eyes. "God have mercy. Charles." She spread her arms up to him, and he bent down and kissed her cheek. That was when Chig saw his face, grimacing. She hugged him; Chig watched the muscles in her arms as they tightened around his father's neck. She half rose out of her chair. "How are you, son?"

Chig could not hear his father's answer.

She let him go, and fell back into her chair, grabbing the arms. Her hands were as dark as the wood, and seemed to become part of it. "Now, who that standing there? Who that man?"

"That's one of your grandsons, Mama." His father's voice cracked. "Charles Dunford, junior. You saw him once, when he was a baby, in Chicago. He's grown now."

"I can see that, boy!" She looked at Chig squarely. "Come here, son, and kiss me once." He did. "What they call you? Charles too?"

"No, ma'am, they call me Chig."

She smiled. She had all her teeth, but they were too perfect to be her own. "That's good. Can't have two boys answering to Charles in the same house. Won't nobody at all come. So you that little boy. You don't remember me, do you. I used to take you to church in Chicago, and you'd get up and hop in time to the music. You studying to be a preacher?"

"No, ma'am. I don't think so. I might be a lawyer."

"You'll be an honest one, won't you?"

"I'll try."

"Trying ain't enough! You be honest, you hear? Promise me. You be honest like your daddy."

"All right. I promise."

"Good. Rose, where's GL at? Where's that thief? He gone again?"

"I don't know, Mama." Aunt Rose looked embarrassed. "He say he was going by the store. He'll be back."

---

1. Don Juan (dän' wän'): An idle, immoral nobleman who enjoyed a great appeal for women.

"Well, then where's Hiram? You call up those boys, and get them over here—now! You got enough to eat? Let me go see." She started to get up. Chig reached out his hand. She shook him off. "What they tell you about me, Chig? They tell you I'm all laid up? Don't believe it. They don't know nothing about old ladies. When I want help, I'll let you know. Only time I'll need help getting anywheres is when I dies and they lift me into the ground."

She was standing now, her back and shoulders straight. She came only to Chig's chest. She squinted up at him. "You eat much? Your daddy ate like two men."

"Yes, ma'am."

"That's good. That means you ain't nervous. Your mama, she ain't nervous. I remember that. In Chicago, she'd sit down by a window all afternoon and never say nothing, just knit." She smiled. "Let me see what we got to eat."

"I'll do that, Mama." Aunt Rose spoke softly. "You haven't seen Charles in a long time. You sit and talk."

The old lady squinted at her. "You can do the cooking if you promise it ain't because you think I can't."

Aunt Rose chuckled. "I know you can do it, Mama."

"All right. I'll just sit and talk a spell." She sat again and arranged her skirt around her short legs.

Chig did most of the talking, told all about himself before she asked. His father spoke only when he was spoken to, and then, only one word at a time, as if by coming back home, he had become a small boy again, sitting in the parlor while his mother spoke with her guests.

When Uncle Hiram and Mae, his wife, came they sat down to eat. Chig did not have to ask about Uncle GL's absence; Aunt Rose

volunteered an explanation: "Can't never tell where the man is at. One Thursday morning he left here and next thing we knew, he was calling from Chicago, saying he went up to see Joe Louis[2] fight. He'll be here though; he ain't as young and footloose as he used to be." Chig's father had mentioned driving down that GL was about five years older than he was, nearly fifty.

Uncle Hiram was somewhat smaller than Chig's father; his short-cropped kinky hair was half gray, half black. One spot, just off his forehead, was totally white. Later, Chig found out it had been that way since he was twenty. Mae (Chig could not bring himself to call her Aunt) was a good deal younger than Hiram, pretty enough so that Chig would have looked at her twice on the street. She was a honey-colored woman, with long eyelashes. She was wearing a white sheath.

At dinner, Chig and his father sat on one side, opposite Uncle Hiram and Mae; his grandmother and Aunt Rose sat at the ends. The food was good; there was a lot and Chig ate a lot. All through the meal, they talked about the family as it had been thirty years before, and particularly about the young GL. Mae and Chig asked questions; the old lady answered; Aunt Rose directed the discussion, steering the old lady onto the best stories; Chig's father laughed from time to time; Uncle Hiram ate.

"Why don't you tell them about the horse, Mama?" Aunt Rose, over Chig's weak protest, was spooning mashed potatoes onto his plate. "There now, Chig."

"I'm trying to think." The old lady was holding her fork halfway to her mouth, looking at them over her glasses. "Oh, you talking about that crazy horse GL brung home that time."

---

2. Joe Louis: U.S. boxer (1914—1981), and the world heavyweight champion from 1937 to 1949.

"That's right, Mama." Aunt Rose nodded and slid another slice of white meat on Chig's plate.

Mae started to giggle. "Oh, I've heard this. This is funny, Chig."

The old lady put down her fork and began: Well, GL went out of the house one day with an old, no-good chair I wanted him to take over to the church for a bazaar, and he met up with this man who'd just brung in some horses from out West. Now, I reckon you can expect one swindler to be in every town, but you don't rightly think there'll be two, and God forbid they should ever meet —but they did, GL and his chair, this man and his horses. Well, I wished I'd-a been there; there must-a been some mighty high-powered talking going on. That man with his horses, he told GL them horses was half-Arab, half-Indian, and GL told that man the chair was an antique he'd stole from some rich white folks. So they swapped. Well, I was a-looking out the window and seen GL dragging this animal to the house. It looked pretty gentle and its eyes was most closed and its feet was shuffling.

"GL, where'd you get that thing?" I says.

"I swapped him for that old chair, Mama," he says. "And made myself a bargain. This is even better than Papa's horse."

Well, I'm a-looking at this horse and noticing how he be looking more and more wide awake every minute, sort of warming up like a teakettle until, I swears to you, that horse is blowing steam out its nose.

"Come on, Mama," GL says, "come on and I'll take you for a ride." Now George, my husband, God rest his tired soul, he'd brung home this white folks' buggy which had a busted wheel and fixed it and was to take it back that day and GL says: "Come on, Mama, we'll use this fine buggy and take us a ride."

"GL," I says, "no, we ain't. Them white folks'll burn us alive if we use their buggy. You just take that horse right on back." You see, I was sure that boy'd come by that animal ungainly.

"Mama, I can't take him back," GL says.

"Why not?" I says.

"Because I don't rightly know where that man is at," GL says.

"Oh," I says. "Well, then I reckon we stuck with it." And I turned around to go back into the house because it was getting late, near dinner time, and I was cooking for ten.

"Mama," GL says to my back. "Mama, ain't you coming for a ride with me?"

"Go on, boy. You ain't getting me inside kicking range of that animal." I was eying that beast and it was boiling hotter all the time. I reckon maybe that man had drugged it. "That horse is wild, GL," I says.

"No, he ain't. He ain't. That man say he is buggy and saddle broke and as sweet as the inside of a apple."

My oldest girl, Essie, had-a come out on the porch and she says: "Go on, Mama. I'll cook. You ain't been out the house in weeks."

"Sure, come on, Mama," GL says. "There ain't nothing to be fidgety about. This horse is gentle as a rose petal." And just then that animal snorts so hard it sets up a little dust storm around its feet.

"Yes, Mama," Essie says, "you can see he gentle." Well, I looked at Essie and then at that horse because I didn't think we could be looking at the same animal. I should-a figured how Essie's eyes ain't never been so good.

"Come on, Mama," GL says.

"All right," I says. So I stood on the porch and watched GL hitching that horse up to the white folks' buggy. For a while there, the animal was pretty quiet, pawing a little, but not much. And I was feeling a little better about riding with GL behind that crazy-looking horse. I could see how GL was happy I was going with him. He was scurrying around that animal buckling buckles and strapping straps, all the time smiling, and that made me feel good.

Then he was finished, and I must say, that horse looked mighty fine hitched to that buggy and I knew anybody what climbed up there would look pretty good too. GL came around and stood at the bottom of the steps, and took off his hat and bowed and said: "Madam," and reached out his hand to me and I was feeling real elegant like a fine lady. He helped me up to the seat and then got up beside me and we moved out down our alley. And I remember how black folks come out on their porches and shook their heads, saying: "Lord now, will you look at Eva Dunford, the fine lady! Don't she look good sitting up there!" And I pretended not to hear and sat up straight and proud.

We rode on through the center of town, up Market Street, and all the way out where Hiram is living now, which in them days was all woods, there not being even a farm in sight and that's when that horse must-a first realized he weren't at all broke or tame or maybe thought he was back out West again, and started to gallop.

"GL," I says, "now you ain't joking with your mama, is you? Because if you is, I'll strap you purple if I live through this."

Well, GL was pulling on the reins with all his meager strength, and yelling, "Whoa, you. Say now, whoa!" He turned to me just long enough to say, "I ain't fooling with you, Mama. Honest!"

I reckon that animal weren't too satisfied with the road, because it made a sharp right turn just then, down into a gulley and struck out across a hilly meadow. "Mama," GL yells. "Mama, do something!"

I didn't know what to do, but I figured I had to do something so I stood up, hopped down onto the horse's back and pulled it to a stop. Don't ask me how I did that; I reckon it was that I was a mother and my baby asked me to do something, is all.

"Well, we walked that animal all the way home; sometimes I had to club it over the nose with my fist to make it come, but we made it, GL and me. You remember how tired we was, Charles?"

"I wasn't here at the time." Chig turned to his father and found his face completely blank, without even a trace of a smile or a laugh.

"Well, of course you was, son. That happened in . . . in . . . it was a hot summer that year and—"

"I left here in June of that year. You wrote me about it."

The old lady stared past Chig at him. They all turned to him; Uncle Hiram looked up from his plate.

"Then you don't remember how we all laughed?"

"No, I don't, Mama. And I probably wouldn't have laughed. I don't think it was funny." They were staring into each other's eyes.

"Why not, Charles?"

"Because in the first place, the horse was gained by fraud. And in the second place, both of you might have been seriously injured or even killed." He broke off their stare and spoke to himself more than to any of them: "And if I'd done it, you would've beaten me good for it."

"Pardon?" The old lady had not heard him; only Chig had heard.

Chig's father sat up straight as if preparing to debate. "I said that if I had done it, if I had done just exactly what GL did, you would have beaten me good for it, Mama." He was looking at her again.

"Why you say that, son?" She was leaning toward him.

"Don't you know? Tell the truth. It can't hurt me now." His voice cracked, but only once. "If GL and I did something wrong, you'd beat me first and then be too tired to beat him. At dinner, he'd always get seconds and I wouldn't. You'd do things with him, like ride in that buggy, but if I wanted you to do something with me, you were always too busy." He paused and considered whether to say what he finally did say: "I cried when I left here. Nobody loved me, Mama. I cried all the way up to Knoxville. That was the last time I ever cried in my life."

"Oh, Charles." She started to get up, to come around the table to him.

He stopped her. "It's too late."

"But you don't understand."

"What don't I understand? I understood then; I understand now."

Tears now traveled down the lines in her face, but when she spoke, her voice was clear. "I thought you knew. I had ten children. I had to give all of them what they needed most." She nodded. "I paid more mind to GL. I had to. GL could-a ended up swinging if I hadn't. But you was smarter. You was more growed up than GL when you was five and he was ten, and I tried to show you that by letting you do what you wanted to do."

"That's not true, Mama. You know it. GL was light-skinned and had good hair and looked almost white and you loved him for that."

"Charles, no. No, son. I didn't love any one of you more than any other."

"That can't be true." His father was standing now, his fists clenched tight. "Admit it, Mama . . . please!" Chig looked at him, shocked; the man was actually crying.

"It may not-a been right what I done, but I ain't no liar." Chig knew she did not really understand what had happened, what he wanted of her. "I'm not lying to you, Charles."

Chig's father had gone pale. He spoke very softly. "You're about thirty years too late, Mama." He bolted from the table. Silverware and dishes rang and jumped. Chig heard him hurrying up to their room.

They sat in silence for awhile and then heard a key in the front door. A man with a new, lacquered straw hat came in. He was wearing brown and white two-tone shoes with very pointed toes and a white summer suit. "Say now! Man! I heard my brother was in town. Where he at? Where that rascal?"

He stood in the doorway, smiling broadly, an engaging, open, friendly smile, the innocent smile of a five-year-old.

Your Response

1. Do you identify with any of the characters in the story? Explain.

Recalling

2. What is the reason Chig's father, Charles, gives for visiting Chig's grandmother?
3. What reasons does Charles give for leaving home when he was fifteen?
4. What is Charles's reaction to the story that Mama tells about the horse?
5. How does Mama explain the difference in the way she treated her children?

Interpreting

6. Why is there "fear, uncertainty, sadness, and perhaps even hatred" in Charles's eyes when he kisses his mother?
7. Describe Charles's attitude toward GL.
8. Why is GL the center of attention?
9. Why do you think Charles has not visited his mother before? What draws him back now?
10. What do you think Charles's relationship with his mother will be like in the future?

Applying

11. What are some possible effects of not clearing up misunderstandings?

ANALYZING LITERATURE

Understanding Characterization

With **direct characterization,** the author tells you directly what a character is like. With **indirect characterization,** the author allows you to discover what a character is like through the dialogue and action of the character or through other characters' comments. In "A Visit to Grandmother," Kelley uses indirect characterization to present GL. Even though GL doesn't appear until the end of the story, you know a great deal about him from what other characters say.

1. List three things you learn about GL indirectly.

2. Explain how the author reveals each of the details you listed.

CRITICAL THINKING AND READING

Making Inferences About Characters

When authors reveal characters indirectly, you make **inferences,** or reasonable conclusions based on evidence, to know what the characters are like. For example, when Aunt Rose offers to cook dinner, you might infer that she is a considerate person.

What inferences about the characters can you make from the following statements?

1. Mama: "'Only time I'll need help getting anywheres is when I dies and they lift me into the ground.'"
2. Charles: "'. . . spoke only when he was spoken to . . . as if by coming back home, he had become a small boy again . . .'"

THINKING AND WRITING

Writing a Character Sketch

Think of somebody you know who is an unusually interesting or memorable character. Write an article for a magazine in which you show the special qualities of the person. Include examples of things the person has done and said to illustrate your statements about what he or she is like. Try to get across the sense that the person is truly special. Revise your article, making sure your points are clear.

LEARNING OPTION

Writing. In the story Charles mentions that his mother wrote to him about the incident with the horse. If Charles had written back to his mother, what might his letter have said? Put yourself in Charles's place and write a letter to Mama in response to her letter about the horse. In your letter try to capture Charles's feelings based on what you learn about him in the story.

GUIDE FOR READING

Chee's Daughter

Round and Flat Characters

Round characters in stories appear to be fully developed people. They possess a wide and complex range of character traits, or personal qualities, and their actions can be as contradictory or as difficult to predict as those of your friends. **Flat characters** appear to have only one or two superficial character traits. Even though the story centers on Chee's daughter, she is a flat character—always an affectionate child.

Focus

"Chee's Daughter" explores the survival of traditional values and customs in a modern world. Think of a tradition in your culture. Make a cluster diagram of the tradition. Include advantages and disadvantages of the tradition in your cluster. The cluster diagram below may help get you started. As you read "Chee's Daughter," consider the role that tradition plays in the lives of the various characters.

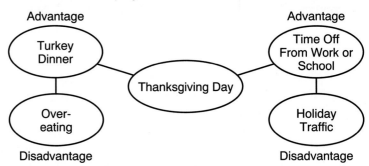

Vocabulary

Knowing the following words will help you as you read "Chee's Daughter."

flicker (flik′ ər) *adj.*: Of a species of woodpecker (p. 77)

mesas (mā′ səz) *n.*: Flattened hills with steep sides (p. 80)

queue (kyōō) *n.*: A braid or pigtail worn down one's back (p. 81)

indolence (in′ də ləns) *n.*: Idleness; a dislike for work (p. 81)

jerked (jʉrkt) *adj.*: Preserved by cutting into strips and drying in the sun (p. 81)

deference (def′ ər əns) *n.*: Respect and consideration (p. 85)

surmised (sər mīzd′) *v.*: Guessed; inferred (p. 85)

Juanita Platero

and

Siyowin Miller

met in 1929, when Platero was living on a Navajo reservation in New Mexico and Miller was living in California. The two women collaborated on the novel *The Winds Erase Your Footprints,* which took them several years to write. The theme of that novel, as well as of "Chee's Daughter," which first appeared in *Common Ground* magazine, is the Native Americans' struggle to preserve ancient ways amid modern culture.

Chee's Daughter

Juanita Platero and Siyowin Miller

THE CANYON
Jack Dudley
Courtesy of the Artist

The hat told the story, the big, black, drooping Stetson.[1] It was not at the proper angle, the proper rakish angle for so young a Navajo.[2] There was no song, and that was not in keeping either. There should have been at least a humming, a faint, all-to-himself "he he he heya," for it was a good horse he was riding, a slender-legged, high-stepping buckskin that would race the wind with light knee-urging. This was a day for singing, a warm winter day, when the touch of the sun upon the back belied the snow high on distant mountains.

Wind warmed by the sun touched his high-boned cheeks like flicker feathers, and still he rode on silently, deeper into Little Canyon, until the red rock walls rose straight upward from the stream bed and only a narrow piece of blue sky hung above. Abruptly the sky widened where the canyon walls were pushed back to make a wide place, as though in ancient times an angry stream had tried to go all ways at once.

This was home—this wide place in the

---

1. Stetson (stet′ s'n) *n*.: A man's hat, worn especially by Western cowboys.
2. Navajo (nav′ ə hō′) *n*.: Member of the largest Indian nation in the U.S., who live in Arizona, New Mexico, and Utah.

Chee's Daughter 77

canyon—levels of jagged rock and levels of rich red earth. This was home to Chee, the rider of the buckskin, as it had been to many generations before him.

He stopped his horse at the stream and sat looking across the narrow ribbon of water to the bare-branched peach trees. He was seeing them each springtime with their age-gnarled limbs transfigured beneath veils of blossom pink; he was seeing them in autumn laden with their yellow fruit, small and sweet. Then his eyes searched out the indistinct furrows of the fields beside the stream, where each year the corn and beans and squash drank thirstily of the overflow from summer rains. Chee was trying to outweigh today's bitter betrayal of hope by gathering to himself these reminders of the integrity of the land. Land did not cheat! His mind lingered deliberately on all the days spent here in the sun caring for the young plants, his songs to the earth and to the life springing from it—". . . In the middle of the wide field . . . Yellow Corn Boy . . . He has started both ways . . . ," then the harvest and repayment in full measure. Here was the old feeling of wholeness and of oneness with the sun and earth and growing things.

Chee urged the buckskin toward the family compound where, secure in a recess of overhanging rock, was his mother's dome-shaped hogan,[3] red rock and red adobe like the ground on which it nestled. Not far from the hogan was the half-circle of brush like a dark shadow against the canyon wall—corral for sheep and goats. Farther from the hogan, in full circle, stood the horse corral made of heavy cedar branches sternly interlocked. Chee's long thin lips curved into a smile as he passed his daughter's tiny hogan squatted like a round Pueblo

oven beside the corral. He remembered the summer day when together they sat back on their heels and plastered wet adobe all about the circling wall of rock and the woven dome of piñon twigs. How his family laughed when the Little One herded the bewildered chickens into her tiny hogan as the first snow fell.

Then the smile faded from Chee's lips and his eyes darkened as he tied his horse to a corral post and turned to the strangely empty compound. "Someone has told them," he thought, "and they are inside weeping." He passed his mother's deserted loom on the south side of the hogan and pulled the rude wooden door toward him, bowing his head, hunching his shoulders to get inside.

His mother sat sideways by the center fire, her feet drawn up under her full skirts. Her hands were busy kneading dough in the chipped white basin. With her head down, her voice was muffled when she said, "The meal will soon be ready, son."

Chee passed his father sitting against the wall, hat over his eyes as though asleep. He passed his older sister who sat turning mutton ribs on a crude wire grill over the coals, noticed tears dropping on her hands. "She cared more for my wife than I realized," he thought.

Then because something must be said sometime, he tossed the black Stetson upon a bulging sack of wool and said, "You have heard, then." He could not shut from his mind how confidently he had set the handsome new hat on his head that very morning, slanting the wide brim over one eye: he was going to see his wife and today he would ask the doctors about bringing her home; last week she had looked so much better.

His sister nodded but did not speak. His mother sniffled and passed her velveteen sleeve beneath her nose. Chee sat down, leaning against the wall. "I suppose I was a

---

3. hogan (hō' gōn) n.: Traditional Navajo dwelling, built of wood and adobe (ə dō' bē), unburnt, sun-dried brick.

CARMEN
James Asher
Courtesy of the artist

fool for hoping all the time. I should have expected this. Few of our people get well from the coughing sickness.[4] But *she* seemed to be getting better."

His mother was crying aloud now and blowing her nose noisily on her skirt. His father sat up, speaking gently to her.

Chee shifted his position and started a cigarette. His mind turned back to the Little One. At least she was too small to understand what had happened, the Little One who had been born three years before in the sanitarium where his wife was being treated for the coughing sickness, the Little One he had brought home to his mother's hogan to be nursed by his sister whose baby was a few months older. As she grew fat-cheeked and sturdy-legged, she followed him about like a shadow; somehow her baby mind had grasped that of all those at the hogan who cared for her and played with her, he—Chee—belonged most to her. She sat cross-legged at his elbow when he worked silver at the forge; she rode before him in the saddle when he drove the horses to water; often she lay wakeful on her sheep-pelts until he stretched out for the night in the darkened hogan and she could snuggle warm against him.

Chee blew smoke slowly and some of the sadness left his dark eyes as he said, "It is not as bad as it might be. It is not as though we are left with nothing."

Chee's sister arose, sobs catching in her throat, and rushed past him out the door-

---

4. coughing sickness: Tuberculosis.

way. Chee sat upright, a terrible fear possessing him. For a moment his mouth could make no sound. Then: "The Little One! Mother, where is she?"

His mother turned her stricken face to him. "Your wife's people came after her this morning. They heard yesterday of their daughter's death through the trader at Red Sands."

Chee started to protest but his mother shook her head slowly. "I didn't expect they would want the Little One either. But there is nothing you can do. She is a girl child and belongs to her mother's people; it is custom."

Frowning, Chee got to his feet, grinding his cigarette into the dirt floor. "Custom! When did my wife's parents begin thinking about custom? Why, the hogan where they live doesn't even face the East!"[5] He started toward the door. "Perhaps I can overtake them. Perhaps they don't realize how much we want her here with us. I'll ask them to give my daughter back to me. Surely, they won't refuse."

His mother stopped him gently with her outstretched hand. "You couldn't overtake them now. They were in the trader's car. Eat and rest, and think more about this."

"Have you forgotten how things have always been between you and your wife's people?" his father said.

That night, Chee's thoughts were troubled—half-forgotten incidents became disturbingly vivid—but early the next morning he saddled the buckskin and set out for the settlement of Red Sands. Even though his father-in-law, Old Man Fat, might laugh, Chee knew that he must talk to him. There were some things to which Old Man Fat might listen.

Chee rode the first part of the fifteen miles to Red Sands expectantly. The sight of sandstone buttes[6] near Cottonwood Spring reddening in the morning sun brought a song almost to his lips. He twirled his reins in salute to the small boy herding sheep toward many-colored Butterfly Mountain, watched with pleasure the feathers of smoke rising against tree-darkened western mesas from the hogans sheltered there. But as he approached the familiar settlement sprawled in mushroom growth along the highway, he began to feel as though a scene from a bad dream was becoming real.

Several cars were parked around the trading store which was built like two log hogans side by side, with red gas pumps in front and a sign across the tar-paper roofs: *Red Sands Trading Post—Groceries Gasoline Cold Drinks Sandwiches Indian Curios.* Back of the trading post an unpainted frame house and outbuildings squatted on the drab, treeless land. Chee and the Little One's mother had lived there when they stayed with his wife's people. That was according to custom—living with one's wife's people—but Chee had never been convinced that it was custom alone which prompted Old Man Fat and his wife to insist that their daughter bring her husband to live at the trading post.

Beside the post was a large hogan of logs, with brightly painted pseudo-Navajo[7] designs on the roof—a hogan with smoke-smudged windows and a garish blue door which faced north to the highway. Old Man Fat had offered Chee a hogan like this one. The trader would build it if he and his wife would live there and Chee would work at his forge making silver jewelry where tourists

---

5. East: By ancient custom, the hogan door is built facing east.

6. buttes (byo͞ots) *n.:* Flat-topped rock formations.
7. pseudo- (so͞o′ dō) **Navajo** *adj.:* False or imitation Navajo.

could watch him. But Chee had asked instead for a piece of land for a cornfield and help in building a hogan far back from the highway and a corral for the sheep he had brought to this marriage.

A cold wind blowing down from the mountains began to whistle about Chee's ears. It flapped· the gaudy Navajo rugs which were hung in one long bright line to attract tourists. It swayed the sign *Navajo Weaver at Work* beside the loom where Old Man Fat's wife sat hunched in her striped blanket, patting the colored thread of a design into place with a wooden comb. Tourists stood watching the weaver. More tourists stood in a knot before the hogan where the sign said: *See Inside a Real Navajo Home 25c.*

Then the knot seemed to unravel as a few people returned to their cars: some had cameras; and there against the blue door Chee saw the Little One standing uncertainly. The wind was plucking at her new purple blouse and wide green skirt; it freed truant strands of soft dark hair from the meager queue into which it had been tied with white yarn.

"Isn't she cunning!" one of the women tourists was saying as she turned away.

Chee's lips tightened as he began to look around for Old Man Fat. Finally he saw him passing among the tourists collecting coins.

Then the Little One saw Chee. The uncertainty left her face and she darted through the crowd as her father swung down from his horse. Chee lifted her in his arms, hugging her tight. While he listened to her breathless chatter, he watched Old Man Fat bearing down on them, scowling.

As his father-in-law walked heavily across the graveled lot, Chee was reminded of a statement his mother sometimes made: "When you see a fat Navajo, you see one who hasn't worked for what he has."

Old Man Fat was fattest in the middle. There was indolence in his walk even though he seemed to hurry, indolence in his cheeks so plump they made his eyes squint, eyes now smoldering with anger.

Some of the tourists were getting into their cars and driving away. The old man said belligerently to Chee, "Why do you come here? To spoil our business? To drive people away?"

"I came to talk with you," Chee answered, trying to keep his voice steady as he faced the old man.

"We have nothing to talk about," Old Man Fat blustered and did not offer to touch Chee's extended hand.

"It's about the Little One." Chee settled his daughter more comfortably against his hip as he weighed carefully all the words he had planned to say. "We are going to miss her very much. It wouldn't be so bad if we knew that *part* of each year she could be with us. That might help you too. You and your wife are no longer young people and you have no young ones here to depend upon." Chee chose his next words remembering the thriftlessness of his wife's parents, and their greed. "Perhaps we could share the care of this little one. Things are good with us. So much snow this year will make lots of grass for the sheep. We have good land for corn and melons."

Chee's words did not have the expected effect. Old Man Fat was enraged. "Farmers, all of you! Long-haired farmers! Do you think everyone must bend his back over the shorthandled hoe in order to have food to eat?" His tone changed as he began to brag a little. "We not only have all the things from cans at the trader's, but when the Pueblos come past here on their way to town we buy their salty jerked mutton, young corn for roasting, dried sweet peaches."

Chee's dark eyes surveyed the land

along the highway as the old man continued to brag about being "progressive." *He* no longer was tied to the land. He and his wife made money easily and could *buy* all the things they wanted. Chee realized too late that he had stumbled into the old argument between himself and his wife's parents. They had never understood his feelings about the land—that a man took care of his land and it in turn took care of him. Old Man Fat and his wife scoffed at him, called him a Pueblo farmer, all during that summer when he planted and weeded and harvested. Yet they ate the green corn in their mutton stews, and the chili paste from the fresh ripe chilis, and the tortillas from the cornmeal his wife ground. None of this working and sweating in the sun for Old Man Fat, who talked proudly of his easy way of living—collecting money from the trader who rented this strip of land beside the highway, collecting money from the tourists.

Yet Chee had once won that argument. His wife had shared his belief in the integrity of the earth, that jobs and people might fail one but the earth never would. After that first year she had turned from her own people and gone with Chee to Little Canyon.

Old Man Fat was reaching for the Little One. "Don't be coming here with plans for my daughter's daughter," he warned. "If you try to make trouble, I'll take the case to the government man in town."

The impulse was strong in Chee to turn and ride off while he still had the Little One in his arms. But he knew his time of victory would be short. His own family would uphold the old custom of children, especially girl children, belonging to the mother's people. He would have to give his daughter up if the case were brought before the Headman of Little Canyon, and certainly he would have no better chance before a strange white man in town.

He handed the bewildered Little One to her grandfather who stood watching every movement suspiciously. Chee asked, "If I brought you a few things for the Little One, would that be making trouble? Some velvet for a blouse, or some of the jerky she likes so well . . . this summer's melon?"

Old Man Fat backed away from him. "Well," he hesitated, as some of the anger disappeared from his face and beads of greed shone in his eyes. "Well," he repeated. Then as the Little One began to squirm in his arms and cry, he said, "No! No! Stay away from here, you and all your family."

The sense of his failure deepened as Chee rode back to Little Canyon. But it was not until he sat with his family that evening in the hogan, while the familiar bustle of meal preparing went on about him, that he began to doubt the wisdom of the things he'd always believed. He smelled the coffee boiling and the oily fragrance of chili powder dusted into the bubbling pot of stew; he watched his mother turning round crusty fried bread in the small black skillet. All around him was plenty—a half of mutton hanging near the door, bright strings of chili drying, corn hanging by the braided husks, cloth bags of dried peaches. Yet in his heart was nothing.

He heard the familiar sounds of the sheep outside the hogan, the splash of water as his father filled the long drinking trough from the water barrel. When his father came in, Chee could not bring himself to tell a second time of the day's happenings. He watched his wiry, soft-spoken father while his mother told the story, saw his father's queue of graying hair quiver as he nodded his head with sympathetic exclamations.

Chee's doubting, acrid thoughts kept forming: Was it wisdom his father had passed on to him or was his inheritance only the stubbornness of a long-haired Navajo resisting change? Take care of the land and it will take care of you. True, the land had always given him food, but now food was not enough. Perhaps if he had gone to school he would have learned a different kind of wisdom, something to help him now. A schoolboy might even be able to speak convincingly to this government man whom Old Man threatened to call, instead of sitting here like a clod of earth itself—Pueblo farmer indeed! What had the land to give that would restore his daughter?

In the days that followed, Chee herded sheep. He got up in the half-light, drank the hot coffee his mother had ready, then started the flock moving. It was necessary to drive the sheep a long way from the hogan to find good winter forage. Sometimes Chee met friends or relatives who were on their way to town or to the road camp where they hoped to get work; then there was friendly banter and an exchange of news. But most of the days seemed endless; he could not walk far enough or fast enough from his memories of the Little One or from his bitter thoughts. Sometimes it seemed his daughter trudged beside him, so real he could almost hear her footsteps—the muffled pad-pad of little feet clad in deerhide. In the glare of a snow bank he would see her vivid face, brown eyes sparkling. Mingling with the tinkle of sheep bells he heard her laughter.

When, weary of following the small sharp hoof marks that crossed and recrossed in the snow, he sat down in the shelter of a rock, it was only to be reminded that in his thoughts he had forsaken his brotherhood with the earth and sun and growing things. If he remembered times when he had flung himself against the earth to rest, to lie there in the sun until he could no longer feel where he left off and the earth began, it was to remember also that now he sat like an alien against the same

earth; the belonging-together was gone. The earth was one thing and he was another.

It was during the days when he herded sheep that Chee decided he must leave Little Canyon. Perhaps he would take a job silversmithing for one of the traders in town. Perhaps, even though he spoke little English, he could get a job at the road camp with his cousins; he would ask them about it.

Springtime transformed the mesas. The peach trees in the canyon were shedding fragrance and pink blossoms on the gentled wind. The sheep no longer foraged for the yellow seeds of chamiso[8] but ranged near the hogan with the long-legged new lambs, eating tender young grass.

Chee was near the hogan on the day his cousins rode up with the message for which he waited. He had been watching with mixed emotions while his father and his sister's husband cleared the fields beside the stream.

"The boss at the camp says he needs an extra hand, but he wants to know if you'll be willing to go with the camp when they move it to the other side of the town?" The tall cousin shifted his weight in the saddle.

The other cousin took up the explanation. "The work near here will last only until the new cut-off beyond Red Sands is finished. After that, the work will be too far away for you to get back here often."

That was what Chee had wanted—to get away from Little Canyon—yet he found himself not so interested in the job beyond town as in this new cut-off which was almost finished. He pulled a blade of grass, split it thoughtfully down the center as he

---

8. chamiso (c/hə mē′ sō) *n.*: Densely growing desert shrub.

asked questions of his cousins. Finally he said: "I need to think more about this. If I decide on this job I'll ride over."

Before his cousins were out of sight down the canyon Chee was walking toward the fields, a bold plan shaping in his mind. As the plan began to flourish, wild and hardy as young tumbleweed, Chee added his own voice softly to the song his father was singing: ". . . In the middle of the wide field . . . Yellow Corn Boy . . . I wish to put in."

Chee walked slowly around the field, the rich red earth yielding to his footsteps. His plan depended upon this land and upon the things he remembered most about his wife's people.

Through planting time Chee worked zealously and tirelessly. He spoke little of the large new field he was planting because he felt so strongly that just now this was something between himself and the land. The first days he was ever stooping, piercing the ground with the pointed stick, placing the corn kernels there, walking around the field and through it, singing, ". . . His track leads into the ground . . . Yellow Corn Boy . . . his track leads into the ground." After that, each day Chee walked through his field watching for the tips of green to break through; first a few spikes in the center and then more and more until the corn in all parts of the field was above ground. Surely, Chee thought, if he sang the proper songs, if he cared for this land faithfully, it would not forsake him now, even though through the lonely days of winter he had betrayed the goodness of the earth in his thoughts.

Through the summer Chee worked long days, the sun hot upon his back, pulling weeds from around young corn plants; he planted squash and pumpkin; he terraced a small piece of land near his mother's hogan and planted carrots and onions and the moisture-loving chili. He was increasingly restless. Finally he told his family what he hoped the harvest from this land would bring him. Then the whole family waited with him, watching the corn: the slender graceful plants that waved green arms and bent to embrace each other as young winds wandered through the field, the maturing plants flaunting their pollen-laden tassels in the sun, the tall and sturdy parent corn with new-formed ears and a froth of purple, red and yellow corn-beards against the dusty emerald of broad leaves.

Summer was almost over when Chee slung the bulging packs across two pack ponies. His mother helped him tie the heavy rolled pack behind the saddle of the buck-skin. Chee knotted the new yellow kerchief about his neck a little tighter, gave the broad black hat brim an extra tug, but these were only gestures of assurance and he knew it. The land had not failed him. That part was done. But this he was riding into? Who could tell?

When Chee arrived at Red Sands, it was as he had expected to find it—no cars on the highway. His cousins had told him that even the Pueblo farmers were using the new cut-off to town. The barren gravel around the Red Sands Trading Post was deserted. A sign banged against the dismantled gas pumps *Closed until further notice.*

Old Fat Man came from the crude summer shelter built beside the log hogan from a few branches of scrub cedar and the sides of wooden crates. He seemed almost friendly when he saw Chee.

"Get down, my son," he said, eyeing the bulging packs. There was no bluster in his voice today and his face sagged, looking somewhat saddened; perhaps because his cheeks were no longer quite full enough to push his eyes upward at the corners. "You are going on a journey?"

Chee shook his head. "Our fields gave us

so much this year, I thought to sell or trade this to the trader. I didn't know he was no longer here."

Old Man Fat sighed, his voice dropping to an injured tone. "He says he and his wife are going to rest this winter; then after that he'll build a place up on the new highway."

Chee moved as though to be traveling on, then jerked his head toward the pack ponies. "Anything you need?"

"I'll ask my wife," Old Man Fat said as he led the way to the shelter. "Maybe she has a little money. Things have not been too good with us since the trader closed. Only a few tourists come this way." He shrugged his shoulders. "And with the trader gone —no credit."

Chee was not deceived by his father-in-law's unexpected confidences. He recognized them as a hopeful bid for sympathy and, if possible, something for nothing. Chee made no answer. He was thinking that so far he had been right about his wife's parents: their thriftlessness had left them with no resources to last until Old Man Fat found another easy way of making a living.

Old Man Fat's Wife was in the shelter working at her loom. She turned rather wearily when her husband asked with noticeable deference if she would give him money to buy supplies. Chee surmised that the only income here was from his mother-in-law's weaving.

She peered around the corner of the shelter at the laden ponies, and then she looked at Chee. "What do you have there, my son?"

Chee smiled to himself as he turned to pull the pack from one of the ponies, dragged it to the shelter where he untied the ropes. Pumpkins and hardshelled squash tumbled out, and the ears of corn —pale yellow husks fitting firmly over plump ripe kernels, blue corn, red corn,

PRIVATE PERFORMANCE
Lois Johnson
Courtesy of the artist

yellow corn, many-colored corn, ears and ears of it—tumbled into every corner of the shelter.

"Yooooh," Old Man Fat's Wife exclaimed as she took some of the ears in her hands. Then she glanced up at her son-in-law. "But we have no money for all this. We have sold almost everything we own—even the brass bed that stood in the hogan."

Old Man Fat's brass bed. Chee concealed his amusement as he started back for another pack. That must have been a hard parting. Then he stopped, for, coming from the cool darkness of the hogan was the Little One, rubbing her eyes as though she had been asleep. She stood for a moment in the doorway and Chee saw that she was dirty, barefoot, her hair uncombed, her little blouse shorn of all its silver buttons. Then she ran toward Chee, her arms outstretched. Heedless of Old Man Fat and his wife, her father caught her in his arms, her hair falling in a dark cloud across his face, the sweetness of her laughter warm against his shoulder.

It was the haste within him to get this slow waiting game played through to the finish that made Chee speak unwisely. It was the desire to swing her before him in the saddle and ride fast to Little Canyon that prompted his words. "The money doesn't matter. You still have something. . . ."

Chee knew immediately that he had overspoken. The old woman looked from him to the corn spread before her. Unfriendliness began to harden in his father-in-law's face. All the old arguments between himself and his wife's people came pushing and crowding in between them now.

Old Man Fat began kicking the ears of corn back onto the canvas as he eyed Chee angrily. "And you rode all the way over here thinking that for a little food we would give up our daughter's daughter?"

Chee did not wait for the old man to reach for the Little One. He walked dazedly to the shelter, rubbing his cheek against her soft dark hair and put her gently into her grandmother's lap. Then he turned back to the horses. He had failed. By his own haste he had failed. He swung into the saddle, his hand touching the roll behind it. Should he ride on into town?

Then he dismounted, scarcely glancing at Old Man Fat, who stood uncertainly at the corner of the shelter, listening to his wife. "Give me a hand with this other pack of corn, Grandfather," Chee said, carefully keeping the small bit of hope from his voice.

Puzzled, but willing, Old Man Fat helped carry the other pack to the shelter, opening it to find more corn as well as carrots and round pale yellow onions. Chee went back for the roll behind the buckskin's saddle

and carried it to the entrance of the shelter where he cut the ropes and gave the canvas a nudge with his toe. Tins of coffee rolled out, small plump cloth bags; jerked meat from several butcherings spilled from a flour sack, and bright red chilis splashed like flames against the dust.

"I will leave all this anyhow," Chee told them. "I would not want my daughter or even you old people to go hungry."

Old Man Fat picked up a shiny tin of coffee, then put it down. With trembling hands he began to untie one of the cloth bags—dried sweet peaches.

The Little One had wriggled from her grandmother's lap, unheeded, and was on her knees, digging her hands into the jerked meat.

"There is almost enough food here to last all winter," Old Man Fat's Wife sought the eyes of her husband.

Chee said, "I meant it to be enough. But that was when I thought you might send the Little One back with me." He looked down at his daughter noisily sucking jerky. Her mouth, both fists were full of it. "I am sorry that you feel you cannot bear to part with her."

Old Man Fat's Wife brushed a straggly wisp of gray hair from her forehead as she turned to look at the Little One. Old Man Fat was looking too. And it was not a thing to see. For in that moment the Little One ceased to be their daughter's daughter and became just another mouth to feed.

"And why not?" the old woman asked wearily.

Chee was settled in the saddle, the barefooted Little One before him. He urged the buckskin faster, and his daughter clutched his shirtfront. The purpling mesas flung back the echo: ". . . My corn embrace each other. In the middle of the wide field . . . Yellow Corn Boy embrace each other."

RESPONDING TO THE SELECTION

Your Response

1. What was your reaction when Chee learned that his daughter had been taken from him?
2. In similar circumstances would you have acted as Chee did? Explain.

Recalling

3. Why does Chee's family allow Old Man Fat to take away Chee's daughter?
4. What is the "old argument" between Chee and Old Man Fat?
5. How does Chee get his daughter back?

Interpreting

6. Find three passages from the story that show Chee's belief in and relationship with the land.
7. How do Chee's beliefs and way of life differ from Old Man Fat's?
8. Why does losing his daughter make Chee doubt his beliefs and way of life?

Applying

9. Suppose you had to decide whether Chee or Old Man Fat should have custody of Chee's daughter. What factors would you consider?

ANALYZING LITERATURE

Identifying Flat and Round Characters

Flat characters have few traits. In "Chee's Daughter," for example, Chee's mother is characterized only by her belief in tradition and her grief over her daughter-in-law's death. **Round characters,** on the other hand, are complex. They are fully formed, like real people.

List all of the characters in "Chee's Daughter." Explain whether each is round or flat.

CRITICAL THINKING AND READING

Recognizing Stereotypes

A **stereotype** is an oversimplified idea about what a person or group is like. It is a view that does not allow for individual differences. In "Chee's Daughter," for example, the tourists who gather at the trading post likely see the Navajos there as stereotypes of the Navajo Indian, whereas the Navajos probably view the tourists as stereotypes of tourists. Generally, stereotypes are examples of flat characters.

Actual people, however, are not so easily defined, which is why the stereotypical character seems false. A stereotypical character in a book or movie rarely makes us feel that we know humans better.

Explain how each of these remarks is based on a stereotype.

1. "When you see a fat Navajo, you see one who hasn't worked for what he has."
2. "Farmers, all of you! Long-haired farmers! Do you think everyone must bend his back over the shorthandled hoe in order to have food to eat?"

THINKING AND WRITING

Comparing and Contrasting Characters

Suppose you worked at the trading store when Chee and his wife lived there, and you witnessed the growing conflict between Chee and Old Man Fat. Write an essay describing the two men and explaining why they will have trouble getting along. Before you begin, list the ways the two men are alike and the ways they are different. Use this information to organize your essay. Finally, revise your work.

LEARNING OPTION

Cross-curricular Connection. Setting figures prominently in "Chee's Daughter." The story gives you a strong sense of the Southwest and the Navajos' place in it. Study the art that accompanies the selection. Find additional paintings or photographs that evoke Southwest scenes. Library books, magazines, and a museum might be good sources of art. Paste down the images you find and write captions for each one. If possible, make imaginative connections to "Chee's Daughter."

GUIDE FOR READING

Mark Twain

(1835–1910) is the pen name of Samuel Langhorne Clemens, one of America's greatest writers. He was born in Florida, Missouri, and grew up in nearby Hannibal. Twain worked as a printer and a riverboat pilot, prospected for gold, and gave lectures around the world. His pen name is from the cry of Mississippi riverboatmen: "By the mark, twain!"—assessing the river as two fathoms deep. His two most widely read novels are *The Adventures of Tom Sawyer* (1876) and *The Adventures of Huckleberry Finn* (1885).

Luck

Static and Dynamic Characters

Characters can be classified as either static or dynamic. **Static characters** do not change during the course of the story. They remain the same no matter what happens to them. **Dynamic characters** change and sometimes learn as a result of the events of the story. The changes they undergo affect their personality traits, attitudes, and beliefs.

Focus

As the title indicates, luck figures prominently in the story you are about to read. Luck plays a big role in shaping the main character's reputation as a hero. Make word webs with the words *luck* and *hero*. (The word webs below may help get you started.) Write down characteristics of each word. Do any characteristics overlap? Keep your web diagrams in mind as you read "Luck."

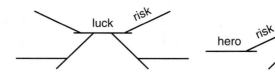

Vocabulary

Knowing the following words will help you as you read "Luck."

zenith (zē′ nith) *n.*: The highest point (p. 89)

countenance (koun′ tə nəns) *n.*: The expression on a person's face (p. 89)

veracity (və ras′ ə tē) *n.*: Truthfulness; honesty (p. 89)

guileless (gīl′ lis) *adj.*: Without slyness or cunning; frank (p. 90)

prodigious (prə dij′ əs) *adj.*: Enormous (p. 91)

sublimity (sə blim′ ə tē) *n.*: A noble or exalted state (p. 91)

Luck

Mark Twain

It was at a banquet in London in honor of one of the two or three conspicuously illustrious[1] English military names of this generation. For reasons which will presently appear, I will withhold his real name and titles, and call him Lieutenant-General Lord Arthur Scoresby, V.C., K.C.B., etc., etc., etc. What a fascination there is in a renowned name! There sat the man, in actual flesh, whom I had heard of so many thousands of times since that day, thirty years before, when his name shot suddenly to the zenith from a Crimean battlefield,[2] to remain forever celebrated. It was food and drink to me to look, and look, and look at that demigod; scanning, searching, noting: the quietness, the reserve, the noble gravity of his countenance; the simple honesty that expressed itself all over him; the sweet unconsciousness of his greatness—unconsciousness of the hundreds of admiring eyes fastened upon him, unconsciousness of the deep, loving, sincere worship welling out of the breasts of those people and flowing toward him.

The clergyman at my left was an old acquaintance of mine—clergyman now, but had spent the first half of his life in the camp and field, and as an instructor in the military school at Woolwich. Just at the moment I have been talking about, a veiled and singular light glimmered in his eyes, and he leaned down and muttered confidentially to me—indicating the hero of the banquet with a gesture:

"Privately—he's an absolute fool."

This verdict was a great surprise to me. If its subject had been Napoleon,[3] or Socrates,[4] or Solomon,[5] my astonishment could not have been greater. Two things I was well aware of: that the Reverend was a man of strict veracity, and that his judgment of men was good. Therefore I knew, beyond doubt or question, that the world was mistaken about this hero: he *was* a fool. So I meant to find out, at a convenient moment, how the Reverend, all solitary and alone, had discovered the secret.

Some days later the opportunity came, and this is what the Reverend told me:

About forty years ago I was an instructor in the military academy at Woolwich. I was

---

1. **conspicuously** (kən spik′ yŏŏ wəs lē) **illustrious** (il us′ trē əs): Outstandingly famous.
2. **Crimean** (krī mē′ ən) **battlefield:** A place of battle during the Crimean War (1854–1856), in which Russia was defeated in trying to dominate southeastern Europe.

3. **Napoleon** (nə pō′ lē ən): Napoleon Bonaparte (1769–1821), French military leader and emperor of France from 1804 to 1815.
4. **Socrates** (säk′ rə tēz′): Athenian philosopher and teacher (470?–399 B.C.).
5. **Solomon** (säl′ ə mən): In the Bible, the King of Israel who built the first temple and was noted for his wisdom.

"HINT TO MODERN SCULPTORS AS
AN ORNAMENT TO A FUTURE SQUARE"
*Hand-colored etching
by James Gillray*

present in one of the sections when young Scoresby underwent his preliminary examination. I was touched to the quick with pity; for the rest of the class answered up brightly and handsomely, while he—why, dear me, he didn't know *anything*, so to speak. He was evidently good, and sweet, and lovable, and guileless; and so it was exceedingly painful to see him stand there, as serene as a graven image, and deliver himself of answers which were veritably miraculous for stupidity and ignorance. All the compassion in me was aroused in his behalf. I said to myself, when he comes to be examined again, he will be flung over, of course; so it will be simply a harmless act of charity to ease his fall as much as I can. I took him aside, and found that he knew a little of Caesar's history;[6] and as he didn't know anything else, I went to work and drilled him like a galley slave on a certain line of stock questions concerning Caesar which I knew would be used. If you'll believe me, he went through with flying colors on examination day! He went through on that purely superficial "cram," and got compliments too, while others, who knew a thousand times more than he, got plucked. By some strangely lucky accident—an accident not likely to happen twice in a century—he was asked no question outside of the narrow limits of his drill.

It was stupefying. Well, all through his course I stood by him, with something of the sentiment which a mother feels for a crippled child; and he always saved himself —just by miracle, apparently.

Now of course the thing that would expose him and kill him at last was mathematics. I resolved to make his death as easy as I could; so I drilled him and crammed him, and crammed him and drilled him, just on the line of questions which the examiners would be most likely to use, and then launched him on his fate. Well, sir, try to conceive of the result: to my consternation he took the first prize! And with it he got a perfect ovation in the way of compliments.

Sleep? There was no more sleep for me for a week. My conscience tortured me day and night. What I had done I had done purely through charity, and only to ease the poor youth's fall—I never had dreamed of any such preposterous result as the thing that had happened. I felt as guilty and miserable as the creator of Frankenstein. Here

was a woodenhead whom I had put in the way of glittering promotions and prodigious responsibilities, and but one thing could happen: he and his responsibilities would all go to ruin together at the first opportunity.

The Crimean War had just broken out. Of course there had to be a war, I said to myself: we couldn't have peace and give this donkey a chance to die before he is found out. I waited for the earthquake. It came. And it made me reel when it did come. He was actually gazetted[7] to a captaincy in a marching regiment! Better men grow old and gray in the service before they climb to a sublimity like that. And who could ever have foreseen that they would go and put such a load of responsibility on such green and inadequate shoulders? I could just barely have stood it if they had made him a cornet;[8] but a captain—think of it! I thought my hair would turn white.

Consider what I did—I who so loved repose and inaction. I said to myself, I am responsible to the country for this, and I must go along with him and protect the country against him as far as I can. So I took my poor little capital that I had saved up through years of work and grinding economy, and went with a sigh and bought a cornetcy in his regiment, and away we went to the field.

And there—oh dear, it was awful. Blunders?—why, he never did anything *but* blunder. But, you see, nobody was in the fellow's secret—everybody had him focused wrong, and necessarily misinterpreted his performance every time—consequently they took his idiotic blunders for inspirations of genius; they did, honestly! His mildest blunders were enough to make a man in his right mind cry; and they did

---

6. Caesar's (sē′ zərz) **history:** The account of Julius Caesar (100?–44 B.C.), Roman emperor from 49 to 44 B.C.

7. gazetted (gə zet′ əd) *v.*: Officially promoted.
8. cornet (kôr net′) *n.*: A British cavalry officer who carried his troop's flag.

make me cry—and rage and rave too, privately. And the thing that kept me always in a sweat of apprehension was the fact that every fresh blunder he made increased the luster of his reputation! I kept saying to myself, he'll get so high, that when discovery does finally come, it will be like the sun falling out of the sky.

He went right along up, from grade to grade, over the dead bodies of his superiors, until at last, in the hottest moment of the battle of * * * * down went our colonel, and my heart jumped into my mouth, for Scores-by was next in rank! Now for it, said I; we'll all land in Sheol[9] in ten minutes, sure.

The battle was awfully hot; the allies were steadily giving way all over the field. Our regiment occupied a position that was vital; a blunder now must be destruction. At this crucial moment, what does this immortal fool do but detach the regiment from its place and order a charge over a neighboring hill where there wasn't a suggestion of an

---

9. Sheol (shē' ōl) *n.*: In the Bible, a place in the depths of the earth where the dead are thought to dwell.

SCOTLAND FOREVER
Elizabeth Butler
Leeds City Art Galleries

enemy. "There you go!" I said to myself; "this *is* the end at last."

And away we did go, and were over the shoulder of the hill before the insane movement could be discovered and stopped. And what did we find? An entire and unsuspected Russian army in reserve! And what happened? We were eaten up? That is necessarily what would have happened in ninety-nine cases out of a hundred. But no, those Russians argued that no single regiment would come browsing around there at such a time. It must be the entire English

army, and that the sly Russian game was detected and blocked; so they turned tail, and away they went, pell-mell, over the hill and down into the field, in wild confusion, and we after them; they themselves broke the solid Russian center in the field, and tore through, and in no time there was the most tremendous rout you ever saw, and the defeat of the allies was turned into a sweeping and splendid victory! Marshal Canrobert looked on, dizzy with astonishment, admiration, and delight; and sent right off for Scoresby, and hugged him, and decorated him on the field, in presence of all the armies!

And what was Scoresby's blunder that time? Merely the mistaking his right hand for his left—that was all. An order had come to him to fall back and support our right; and instead, he fell *forward* and went over the hill to the left. But the name he won that day as a marvelous military genius filled the world with his glory, and that glory will never fade while history books last.

He is just as good and sweet and lovable and unpretending as a man can be, but he doesn't know enough to come in when it rains. Now that is absolutely true. He is the supremest fool in the universe; and until half an hour ago nobody knew it but himself and me. He has been pursued, day by day and year by year, by a most phenomenal and astonishing luckiness. He has been a shining soldier in all our wars for a generation; he has littered his whole military life with blunders, and yet has never committed one that didn't make him a knight or a baronet or a lord or something. Look at his breast; why, he is just clothed in domestic and foreign decorations. Well, sir, every one of them is the record of some shouting stupidity or other; and taken together, they are proof that the very best thing in all this world that can befall a man is to be born lucky. I say again, as I said at the banquet, Scoresby's an absolute fool.

RESPONDING TO THE SELECTION

Your Response

1. In the story, we hear only the clergyman's evaluation of Scoresby. If you could ask Scoresby about his experiences, what would you ask him?

Recalling

2. How does the clergyman describe Scoresby?
3. How does the clergyman feel about Scoresby when he first meets him?
4. Describe two things the clergyman does in order to help Scoresby.
5. Trace the series of lucky events that put Scoresby in a position of leadership.
6. How does Scoresby achieve his "greatest victory"?

Interpreting

7. How does the narrator's first impression of Scoresby contrast with the view of him given by the clergyman?
8. Compare and contrast Scoresby and the clergyman.
9. Do you agree with the clergyman that Scoresby is a fool? Explain your answer. In what way is the clergyman also a fool?

Applying

10. The clergyman states that "the very best thing in the world is to be born lucky." In your opinion, to what extent does luck play a role in a person's success? Give examples to support your opinion.

ANALYZING LITERATURE

Recognizing Static Characters

Dynamic characters grow and change in response to the events of a story. They are different at the end of the story. **Static characters,** on the other hand, do not change in any fundamental way. Their personalities, opinions, and attitudes are fixed.

In "Luck," Scoresby is an example of a static character. According to the clergyman, not only is he a fool as a youth and as an older man, but his personality remains the same in other ways.

Find descriptions of Scoresby that indicate he remains the same at each of the following points in his life.

1. while a student in the military academy
2. while a young officer in the Crimean War
3. while an older military hero

CRITICAL THINKING AND READING

Recognizing Humor

Some character traits are more likely than others to produce humor. A character such as Scoresby, who is a foolish bungler, may be humorous in a number of ways. For example, his actions may bring unexpected or absurd results, or humorous misunderstandings may arise from his foolishness.

How does Scoresby's character lend humor to each of these situations?

1. the banquet at which hundreds of admirers come to honor Scoresby
2. the major victory Scoresby won in the Crimean War

THINKING AND WRITING

Writing About a Person

Think about someone whom you might nominate for a "Person of the Year" award. List this person's main character traits, and freewrite about them. Use this information to write a description of this person for the nominating committee. Include examples of things the person has said and done to illustrate the traits that you see but that might not be apparent to the committee. When you revise your description, add any anecdotes you can think of that would convince the committee to consider this person as "Person of the Year."

Point of View

STAIRWAY, c. 1925
Edward Hopper
Collection of Whitney Museum of American Art

GUIDE FOR READING

Diamond Island: Alcatraz

First Person Point of View

Point of view is the position or perspective from which the events of a story are seen. When the author uses *first-person* point of view, the narrator is also a character in the story. As a character, the narrator participates in the events and tells the story using the first-person pronoun "I." The "I" in "Diamond Island: Alcatraz" is sometimes the narrator and sometimes the narrator's grandfather, who tells a story within the story.

Focus

To Native Americans, Alcatraz island in San Francisco Bay has a significance that is much different from its identity as the site of a federal prison (1934–1963). In Wilson's words, "it is time to give the island of Alcatraz a proper identity and a *real* history." In a group of three or four people, discuss what you know about Alcatraz island. Keep your group discussion in mind as you read "Diamond Island: Alcatraz." Then, after reading the story, get together with your group to discuss how the story added to your knowledge of the island and your understanding of its importance.

Vocabulary

Knowing the following words will help you as you read "Diamond Island: Alcatraz."

expended (ek spend′ id) *v.*: To have spent or used by consuming (p. 98)

momentum (mō men′ təm) *n.*: The ongoing force of a moving object (p. 98)

redolence (red′ ′l əns) *n.*: The quality of being fragrant or sweet smelling (p. 99)

autonomous (ô tän′ ə məs) *adj.*: Independent (p. 102)

Darryl Babe Wilson

(1939–   ) lives in Tucson, Arizona, where he teaches Native American studies at the University of Arizona. As a Native American, Wilson has written about the struggles of his people. He has also interviewed Native Americans from Barrow, Alaska, to the Mayan Peninsula for his book *Voices from the Earth.* As the title suggests, the interviews deal with our ecological problems.

Educated at the University of California at Davis, Wilson is a widely recognized poet and short story writer. About his heritage he writes, "It is imperative that *we* [Native Americans] write our history and *we* remind American society that *we* do, in fact, own a history, a long and beautiful history, a history that is timeless in its preciousness and precious in its timelessness."

Diamond Island: Alcatraz

Allisti Ti-Tanin-Miji
(rock)   (rainbow)

Darryl Babe Wilson

**PHOTO OF A NATIVE
AMERICAN MALE**
(Wailaki tribe)
Edward S. Curtis
Southwest Museum,
Los Angeles

There was a single letter in the mailbox. Somehow it seemed urgent. The address, although it was labored over, could hardly be deciphered—square childlike print that did not complete the almost individual letters. Inside, five pages written on both sides. Blunt figures. Each word pressed heavily into the paper. I could not read it but I could feel the message. "Al traz" was in the first paragraph, broken and scattered, but there. At the very bottom of the final page—running out of space—he scrawled his name. It curved down just past the right-hand corner. The last letter of his name, *n*, did not fit: *Gibso.* It was winter, 1971. I hurried to his home.

Grandfather lived at Atwam, 100 miles east of Redding, California, in a little shack out on the flat land. His house was old and crooked just like in a fairy tale. His belongings were few and they, too, were old and worn. I always wanted to know his age and often asked some of the older of our people if they could recall when Grandfather was born. After silences that sometimes seemed more than a year, they always shook their silver-gray heads and answered: "I dunno. He was old and wrinkled with white hair for as long as I can remember. Since I was just a child." He must have been born between 1850 and 1870.

Thanksgiving weekend, 1989. It is this time of the year when I think about Grandfather and his ordeal. I keep promising myself that I will write his story down because it is time to give the island of Alcatraz a proper identity and a "real" history. It is easy for modern people to think that the history of Alcatraz began when a foreign ship sailed into the bay and a stranger named Don Juan Manuel de Ayala[1] observed the "rock" and recorded "Alcatraz" in a log book in 1775. That episode, that sailing and that recording was only moments ago.

Grandfather said that long ago the Sacramento Valley was a huge freshwater lake, that it was "as long as the land" (from the northern part of California to the southern), and that a great shaking of an angry spirit within the earth caused part of the coastal range to crumble into the outer-ocean. When the huge lake finally drained and the waves from the earthquake finally settled, there was the San Francisco Bay, and there, in isolation and containing a "truth," was Diamond Island (Alcatraz).

He told me the story one winter in his little one-room house in Atwam. It is bitter cold there during winters. I arrived late in the evening, tires of my truck spinning up his driveway. The driveway was a series of frozen, broken mudholes in a general direction across a field to his home. The headlights bounced out of control.

My old 1948 Chevy pickup was as cold inside as it was outside. The old truck kept going, but it was a fight to make it go in the winter. It was such a struggle that we called it "Mr. Miserable." Mr. Miserable and I came to a jolting halt against a snowbank that was the result of someone shoveling a walk in the front yard. We expended our momentum. The engine died with a sputtering cough. Lights flopped out.

It was black outside but the crusted snow lay like a ghost upon the earth and faded away in every direction. The night sky trembled with the fluttering of a million stars—all diamond blue. Wind whipped broken tumbleweeds across his neglected yard. The snow could not conceal the yard's chaos.

The light in the window promised warmth. Steam puffing from every breath, I hurried to his door. The snow crunched underfoot, sounding like a horse eating a crisp apple. The old door lurched open with a complaint. Grandfather's fatigued, centenarian[2] body a black silhouette against the brightness—bright although he had but a single shadeless lamp to light the entire house. I saw a skinned bear once. It looked just like Grandfather. Short, stout arms and bowed legs. Compact physique. Muscular—not fat. Thick chest. Powerful. Natural.

Old powder-blue eyes strained to see who was out there in the dark. "Hallo.

---

1. Don Juan Manuel de Ayala (dän hwän män wel' dä ä yä' lä): An eighteenth-century Spanish explorer who was the first European to enter San Francisco Bay.

2. centenarian (sen' tə ner' ē ən) *adj.*: At least one hundred years old.

You're just the man I'm lookin' for." Coffee aroma exploded from the open door. Coffee. Warmth!

Grandfather stood back and I entered the comfort of his jumbled little bungalow. It was cozy in there. He was burning juniper wood. Juniper, cured for a summer, has a clean, delicate aroma—a perfume. After a healthy handshake we huddled over steaming cups of coffee. Grandfather looked long at me. I think that he was not totally convinced that I was there. The hot coffee was good. It was not a fancy Colombian, aromatic blend, but it was so good!

We were surrounded by years of Grandfather's collections. It was like a museum. Everything was very old and worn. It seemed that every part of the clutter had a history—sometimes a history that remembered the origin of the earth, like the bent pail filled with obsidian[3] that he had collected from Glass Mountain many summers before, "just in case."

He also had a radio that he was talked into purchasing when he was a young working man in the 1920s. The radio cost $124. I think he got conned by that merchant and the episode magnified in mystery when he recalled that it was not until 1948 before he got the electric company to put a line to his home. By that time he forgot about the radio and he did not remember to turn it on until 1958. It worked. There was an odor of oldness—like a mouse that died then dried to a stiffness through the years—a redolence of old neglected newspapers.

The old person in the old house under the old moon began to tell the story of his escape from "the rock" long ago. He gathered himself together and reached back into a painful past. The silence was long and I

thought that he might be crying silently. Then, with a quiver in his voice, he started telling the story that he wanted me to know:

"Alcatraz island. Where the Pit River runs into the sea is where I was born, long ago. *Alcatraz,* that's the white man's name for it. To our people, in our legends, we always knew it as *Allisti Ti-tanin-miji* [Rock Rainbow], Diamond Island. In our legends, that's where the Mouse Brothers, the twins, were told to go when they searched for a healing treasure for our troubled people long, long ago. They were to go search at the end of *It A-juma* [Pit River]. They found it. They brought it back. But it is lost now. It is said, the 'diamond' was to bring goodness to all our people, everywhere.

"We always heard that there was a 'diamond' on an island near the great salt water. We were always told that the 'diamond' was a thought, or a truth. Something worth very much. It was not a jewelry. It sparkled and it shined, but it was not a jewelry. It was more. Colored lights came from inside it with every movement. That is why we always called it [Alcatraz] *Allisti Ti-tanin-miji.*" With a wave of an ancient hand and words filled with enduring knowledge, Grandfather spoke of a time long past.

In one of the many raids upon our people of the Pit River country, his pregnant mother was taken captive and forced, with other Indians, to make the long and painful march to Alcatraz in the winter. At that same time, the military was "sweeping" California. Some of our people were "removed" to the Round Valley Reservation at Covelo; others were taken east by train in open cattle cars during the winter to Quapa, Oklahoma. Still others were taken out into the ocean at Eureka and thrown overboard into icy waters.

Descendants of those that were taken in chains to Quapa are still there. Some of

---

3. obsidian (əb sid′ ē ən) *n.*: Hard, dark-colored or black volcanic glass.

those cast into the winter ocean at Eureka made it back to land and returned to Pit River country. A few of those defying confinement, the threat of being shot by "thunder sticks," and dark winter nights of a cold Alcatraz-made-deadly by churning, freezing currents, made it back to Pit River country, too.

Grandfather said, "I was very small, too small to remember, but my grandmother remembered it all. The guards allowed us to swim around the rock. Every day, my mother swam. Every day, the people swam. We were not just swimming. We were gaining strength. We were learning the currents. We had to get home.

"When it was time, we were ready. We left at darkness. Grandmother said that I was a baby and rode my mother's back, clinging as she swam from Alcatraz to solid ground in night. My Grandmother remembered that I pulled so hard holding on that I broke my mother's necklace. It is still there in the water . . . somewhere." With a pointing of a stout finger southward, Grandfather indicated where "there" was.

Quivering with emotion, he hesitated. He trembled. "I do not remember if I was scared," Grandfather said, crooked, thick fingers rubbing a creased and wrinkled chin covered with white stubble. "I must have been."

When those old, cloudy eyes dripped tears down a leathery, crevassed[4] face, and long silences were between his sentences, often I trembled too. He softly spoke of his memory.

Our cups were long empty; *maliss* (fire) needed attention. The moon was suspended in the frozen winter night—round, bright, scratched and scarred—when Grandfather finally paused in his thinking. The old cast-iron heater grumbled and screamed when I slid open the top to drop in a fresh log. Sparks flew up into the darkness then disappeared. I slammed the top closed. Silence, again.

Grandfather continued, "There was not real diamonds on the island. At least I don't think so. I always thought the diamonds were not diamonds but some kind of understanding, some kind of good thought—or something." He shook a white, shaggy head and looked off into the distance into a time that was so long ago that the mountains barely remembered. For long moments he reflected, he gathered his thoughts. He knew that I "wrote things down on paper."

The night was thick. To the north a coyote howled. Far to the west an old coyote rasped a call to the black wilderness, a supreme presence beneath starry skies with icy freedom all around.

"When first I heard about the 'diamond,' I thought it might be a story of how we escaped. But after I heard that story so many times, I don't think so. I think there was a truth there that the Mouse Brothers were instructed to get and bring back long ago to help our people. I don't think that I know where that truth is now. Where can it be? It must be deep inside *Axo-Yet* [Mount Shasta[5]] or *Sa Titt* [Medicine Lake]. It hides from our people. The truth hides from us. It must not like us. It denies us."

The One-as-Old-as-the-Mountains made me wonder about this story. It seems incredible that there was such an escape from Alcatraz. Through American propaganda I have been trained to believe that it was

---

4. crevassed (krə vast') *adj.*: Deeply cracked.

5. Mount Shasta (shas' tə): A volcanic mountain in northern California.

SAN FRANCISCO, 1849
Attributed to Joshua Peirce

impossible to escape from that isolated rock because of the currents and because of the freezing temperature as the powerful ocean and the surging rivers merged in chaos. I was convinced—until I heard Grandfather's story and until I realized that he dwelled within a different "time," a different "element." He dwelled within a spirituality of a natural source. In his world, I was only a foreign infant. It is true today that when I talk with the old people I feel like *nilladu-wi-* (a white man). I feel like some domesti-

cated creature addressing original royalty—knowing that the old ones were pure savage, born into the wild, free.

In his calm manner, Grandfather proceeded. "We wandered for many nights. We hid during the day. It is said that we had to go south for three nights before we could turn north. [My people landed at San Francisco and had to sneak to what is now San Jose, traveling at night with no food until they could turn northward.] They [the U.S. Army] were after us. They were after us all. We had to be careful. We had to be careful and not make mistakes. We headed north for two nights.

"We came to a huge river. We could not cross it. It was swift. My mother walked far upstream then jumped in. Everybody followed. The river washed us to the other shore [possibly the Benicia Straits]. We rested for two days eating dead fish that we found along the river. We could not build a fire because they would see the smoke and catch us so we must eat it [fish] raw. At night we traveled again. Again we traveled, this time for two nights also.

"There is a small island of mountains in the great valley [Sutter Buttes]. When we reached that place one of the young men climbed the highest peak. He was brave. We were all brave. It was during the sunlight. We waited for him to holler as was the plan. We waited a long, long time. Then we heard: 'Axo-Yet! Axo-Yet! To-ho-ja-toki! To-ho-ja-toki Tanjan' [Mount Shasta! Mount Shasta! North direction!]. Our hearts were happy. We were close to home. My mother squeezed me to her. We cried. I know we cried. I was there. So was my mother and grandmother."

Grandfather has been within the earth for many snows now. The volumes of knowledge that were buried with him are lost to my generation, a generation that needs original knowledge now more than ever, if we are to survive as a distinct and autonomous people. Perhaps a generation approaching will be more aware, more excited with tradition and custom and less satisfied to being off balance somewhere between the world of the "white man" and the world of the "Indian," and will seek this knowledge.

It is nearing winter, 1989. Snows upon *Axo-Yet* (Mount Shasta) are deep. The glaring white makes Grandfather's hair nearly yellow—now that I better recall the coarse strands that I often identified as "silver." That beautiful mountain. The landmark that caused the hunted warrior 140 years ago to forget the tragic episode that could have been the termination of our nation, and, standing with the sun shining full upon him, hollered to a frightened people waiting below: *"Axo-Yet! Axo-Yet! To-ho-ja-toki Tanjan!"*

Perhaps the approaching generation will seek and locate *Allisti Ti-tanin-miji* within the mountains. Possibly that generation will reveal many truths to this world society that is immense and confused in its immensity. An old chief of the Pit River country, "Charlie Buck," said often: "Truth. It is truth that will set us free." Along with Grandfather, I think that it was a "truth" that the Mouse Brothers brought to our land from Diamond Island long ago. A truth that needs to be understood, appreciated, and acknowledged. A truth that needs desperately to be found and known for its value.

Grandfather's letter is still in my files. I still can't read it, but if I could, I am sure that the message would be the same as this story that he gave to me as the moon listened and the winds whispered across a frozen Atwam, during a sparkling winter night long ago.

RESPONDING TO THE SELECTION

Your Response

1. If you could ask Grandfather a question about his story, what would you ask? Why?
2. If you could tell a future generation a story from your youth, what would it be? Explain.

Recalling

3. How did Grandfather learn the story of his family's escape from Alcatraz—an event that took place when he was a small boy?
4. According to the story, what does the "diamond" of Diamond Island represent?

Interpreting

5. Interpret the narrator's comment on page 98, "That episode, that sailing and that recording was only a moment ago." What does the comment suggest about the history of Alcatraz island?
6. Why did Grandfather ask the narrator to visit?
7. In your words, explain why the author's generation needs "original knowledge" in order to survive.

Applying

8. What do people in your culture do to preserve their heritage—their identity—as a culture?

ANALYZING LITERATURE

Analyzing First-Person Point of View

A first-person narrator tells mainly what he or she thinks, feels, and observes. As a result, the narrator's attitudes shape the story. In addition to communicating his own attitudes, the narrator of this story also conveys his grandfather's beliefs and observations. He does this by recording a story that his grandfather told him nearly twenty years before.

1. Discuss two ways in which first-person narration enables the author to use Grandfather's story most effectively.

2. What does the narrator reveal about his feelings toward Grandfather and Alcatraz island?

CRITICAL THINKING AND READING

Determining the Author's Purpose

An author who writes in the first person wants the reader to know the narrator's thoughts and feelings. Exploring these thoughts and feelings can provide insight into the author's motives for writing a story. In the case of "Diamond Island: Alcatraz," the author is the narrator. What do the emotions and ideas that Wilson expresses reveal about his purpose in writing "Diamond Island: Alcatraz"? Refer to passages from the story to support your answer.

THINKING AND WRITING

Writing in the First Person

What stories do you know that you think should be preserved for future generations? Choose one, and write about it in the first person. Like Wilson, you might choose to write about a story that was shared with you and affected you deeply. You could also write about a story from your life, your family, your school, or your community. Try to interview someone who can give you his or her first-hand observations of the events in your story. Finally, in your narration, include hints to the reader about your purpose for writing the story.

LEARNING OPTION

Art. Draw a map of Grandfather's return to Pit River country from Alcatraz. In order to begin, consult a map of the areas described by Grandfather. On your map, illustrate Grandfather's story at key locations. For example, you might want to draw a necklace at the point where Grandfather pulls at his mother's necklace as they struggle through the icy currents.

ONE WRITER'S PROCESS

Darryl Babe Wilson and "Diamond Island"

PREWRITING

A Writer's Inspiration Much of Darryl Babe Wilson's inspiration comes from his desire to preserve what he calls "the long and beautiful history" of Native Americans.

A "Lost" History Wilson insists that Native American writers "cannot wait for the Americans to 'find' us and to acknowledge our right to exist—a right that was a gift to us from the moment the stars were scattered in the vastness and songs were given us to sing that awesome power. We must take pen in hand, place the proper words in the exact sequence, and move this society to awaken."

The Storytelling Gift For many generations, Native American history was passed down by word of mouth. More recently, writers such as Darryl Babe Wilson have begun to "take pen in hand." "Diamond Island: Alcatraz" was the result of an impulse flitting through what Wilson calls his "thought processor." How does this work? Wilson explains it this way: "When it is time for the story or poem to appear, it does. If I am not prepared to record that thought at the moment of its appearance, then it vanishes. I must be on guard to 'capture' a thought that has made itself 'visible' enough so that I can put it down in words with enough velocity to insure its survival."

DRAFTING

The Story Approaches "The manuscript came in three parts," he recalls. The first portion to appear was the body of Grandfather's story. Then a period of waiting followed. "At this point I did not pursue completion of the manuscript—since I had no idea how or when it would be complete. And, like allowing a curious fawn to approach, I patiently waited for more 'instruction' from the element within me that places the words upon the page. The following morning the beginning three pages arrived."

Beginnings and Endings Once the various pieces of "Diamond Island: Alcatraz" had arrived, Wilson began to sense how to fit them together. He realized that the three pages describing Grandfather's letter and his house in Atwam formed the story's beginning. "And how much more appropriate it is that the beginning of the story began at the beginning!"

Of course, not all stories begin at the beginning. Wilson points this out by noting that "often a story beginning with the closing line is more effective."

Releasing Your Voice As you can see, the creation of the story took patience. Yet Wilson stresses that when inspiration arrives, the writer must seize upon it. "Do not doubt," he says. "Do not hesitate. When you write, splash your words upon the paper by the bucketful, and sprinkle ideas throughout your effort as you rewrite and earth's energy surges through you. . . . It is all a matter of listening to the voice that is within you whispering, singing, clamoring to be released. Release it!"

REVISING

Searching for the Better Word Wilson seldom tinkers with the broad outline of a narrative. He does revise the language, however. "There is always the search for a better word," he says, "or for the elimination of 'dead wood'—too many words that clutter the meaning and are an obstacle to clarity."

How does a writer find that better word? "Examine new words," Wilson insists. "Make them awaken, get up, sing and dance. If you were to play baseball, you would be required to spend hours and hours of practice and trial and error. Apply yourself and your talents to writing, to creating with words, with the same velocity that Babe Ruth needed to play baseball."

Advice Helps Wilson wrote "Diamond Island: Alcatraz" for a university-level creative writing class. Each student in the class received a copy of Wilson's draft and contributed suggestions and comments. Generally Wilson found the comments of his fellow students "very constructive and encouraging."

"Do not fear criticism," Wilson says. "Welcome it. When someone says, 'This is not good, this is not clear, this is incomplete,' don't cringe in fear. Rather, ask them why it is so. Then make the adjustments within your wisdom-bank to use in your future expressions."

Sharpening the Details The class instructor also gave Wilson advice about revisions. One particular part of the story they discussed was Grandfather's description of the escape from Alcatraz.

Look at the box. The darkened words are some of those Wilson added to this description as he revised it. According to the author, these revisions underlined the sense of danger.

PUBLISHING

Moving the Reader Much of Darryl Babe Wilson's writing is motivated by the author's wish to honor and preserve Native American culture. Sometimes this wish makes Wilson unsure about whether to publish a story. "One of the greatest problems I have," he explains, "is that I am not certain that I am authorized to 'present' the story once it has been 'captured' and recorded. I constantly have to wonder if the ancient ones of my nation would give approval."

Along with his cultural goals, Wilson also admits to a much simpler motivation—moving the reader. "Whenever I reread something and it moves me, then I know it moves other people, too," he says.

Grandfather said, "I was very small, **too small to remember,** but my grandmother remembered it **all. The guards allowed us to swim around the rock. Every day, my mother swam. Every day, the people swam. We were not just swimming. We were gaining strength. We were learning the currents. We had to get home."**

"When it was time, we were ready. We left at darkness. Grandmother** said that I was a baby and rode my mother's back, clinging as she swam from Alcatraz to solid ground in night. My Grandmother remembered that I pulled so hard holding on that I broke my mother's necklace. It is still **there** in the water . . . somewhere." **With a pointing of a stout finger southward, Grandfather indicated where "there" was.**

THINKING ABOUT THE PROCESS

1. Which aspect of his writing does Wilson change the most during the revision stage?
2. **Writing** Do you usually start your stories with the beginning, middle, or end? Try taking a story that you have already written and rearranging the pieces in a different order so that the end is now the beginning. Describe what effect this has on the story.

GUIDE FOR READING

Axolotl

Narrator's Perspective

The **narrator's perspective** is his or her outlook on what occurs. Be careful not to assume that the author is the narrator; good writers use different voices as they tell stories. Instead, imagine a live human voice telling the story as you read it. Try to hear the voice. What do you learn about the narrator? How does the narrator feel about the story? How does the story affect him or her? Is the information we get from the narrator reliable given his or her position in the story? Answering these questions as you read will give you insight into the narrator's perspective. In "Axolotl" the narrator begins as an observer in an aquarium. By the end of the story, his perspective has changed dramatically.

Focus

In this story a man becomes fascinated by a species of salamander called an axolotl (ak′ sə lät′ ′l). Have you or has someone you know ever become so fascinated by something that you gave up your normal routine? Freewrite about this experience. Then, as you read, note the similarities between the experience you describe and the one Cortázar describes.

Vocabulary

Knowing the following words will help you as you read "Axolotl."

obliquely (ə blēk′ lē) *adv.*: In a slanted, sloping way (p. 107)

banal (bā′ nəl) *adj.*: Commonplace; trite (p. 107)

disconcerted (dis′ kən surt′ id) *adj.*: Embarrassed; confused (p. 108)

diminutive (də min′ yoo tiv) *adj.*: Tiny (p. 109)

undulation (un′ dyoo lā′ shən) *n.*: Regular wavelike movement, alternating from side to side (p. 109)

unfathomable (un′ fath′ əm ə bəl) *adj.*: Incapable of being understood or measured (p. 110)

anthropomorphic (an′ thrə pō′ môr′ fik) *adj.*: Having or suggesting human characteristics (p. 110)

ignoble (ig nō′ bəl) *adj.*: Common (p. 110)

implacable (im plā′ kə bəl) *adj.*: Unable to be appeased or pacified (p. 110)

Julio Cortázar

(1914–1984) was born in Belgium to Argentine parents and held dual citizenship in Argentina and France. His sense of belonging to both Europe and Latin America was an important theme in his life.

Cortázar is best known for his experimental fiction. His writing often surprises readers with fantasy. In his words, "The fantastic is something that one must never say good-bye to lightly. The man of the future . . . will have to find the bases of a reality which is truly his and, at the same time, maintain the capacity of dreaming and playing . . . since it is through those doors that the Other, the fantastic dimension, and the unexpected will always slip, . . ." The narrator of "Axolotl" slips through "those doors."

Axolotl

Julio Cortázar

translated by Paul Blackburn

There was a time when I thought a great deal about the axolotls. I went to see them in the aquarium at the Jardin des Plantes[1] and stayed for hours watching them, observing their immobility, their faint movements. Now I am an axolotl.

I got to them by chance one spring morning when Paris was spreading its peacock tail after a wintry Lent.[2] I was heading down the boulevard Port-Royal, then I took Saint-Marcel and L'Hôpital and saw green among all that gray and remembered the lions. I was friend of the lions and panthers, but had never gone into the dark, humid building that was the aquarium. I left my bike against the gratings and went to look at the tulips. The lions were sad and ugly and my panther was asleep. I decided on the aquarium, looked obliquely at banal fish until, unexpectedly, I hit it off with the axolotls. I stayed watching them for an hour and left, unable to think of anything else.

In the library at Sainte-Geneviève, I consulted a dictionary and learned that axolotls are the larval stage[3] (provided with gills) of a species of salamander of the genus *Ambystoma*.[4] That they were Mexican I knew already by looking at them and their little pink Aztec[5] faces and the placard[6] at the top of the tank. I read that specimens of them had been found in Africa capable of living on dry land during the periods of drought, and continuing their life under water when the rainy season came. I found their Spanish name, *ajolote*,[7] and the mention that they were edible, and that their oil was used (no longer used, it said) like cod-liver oil.

I didn't care to look up any of the specialized works, but the next day I went back to the Jardin des Plantes. I began to go every morning, morning and afternoon some days. The aquarium guard smiled perplexedly, taking my ticket. I would lean up against the iron bar in front of the tanks and set to watching them. There's nothing strange in this, because after the first minute I knew that we were linked, that something infinitely lost and distant kept pulling us together. It had been enough to detain me that first morning in front of the sheet of glass where

---

1. Jardin des Plantes (zhår den′ dä plänt′): The Garden of Plants in Paris, France; it has botanical gardens, hothouses, a zoo, and various museums.
2. Lent: The forty weekdays from Ash Wednesday to Easter, observed by many Christians as a period of repentance.
3. larval stage: Period of time before an animal changes structurally and becomes an adult.

4. *Ambystoma* (am′ bi stō′ mə)
5. Aztec (az′ tek) *adj.*: Of the Aztecs, a Native American civilization that flourished before Cortés's conquest of Mexico.
6. placard (plak′ ärd) *n.*: Poster or card displayed for public notice.
7. *ajolote* (â hō lō′ te)

EL PEZ LUMINOSO (THE LUMINOUS FISH), 1956
Juan Soriano
Collection INBA—Museo de Arte Moderno, Mexico

some bubbles rose through the water. The axolotls huddled on the wretched narrow (only I can know how narrow and wretched) floor of moss and stone in the tank. There were nine specimens, and the majority pressed their heads against the glass, looking with their eyes of gold at whoever came near them. Disconcerted, almost ashamed, I felt it a lewdness to be peering at these silent and immobile figures heaped at the bottom of the tank. Mentally I isolated one, situated on the right and somewhat apart from the others, to study it better. I saw a rosy little body, translucent (I thought of those Chi-

fingers with minutely human nails. And then I discovered its eyes, its face. Inexpressive features, with no other trait save the eyes, two orifices, like brooches, wholly of transparent gold, lacking any life but looking, letting themselves be penetrated by my look, which seemed to travel past the golden level and lose itself in a diaphanous[8] interior mystery. A very slender black halo ringed the eye and etched it onto the pink flesh, onto the rosy stone of the head, vaguely triangular, but with curved and irregular sides which gave it a total likeness to a statuette corroded by time. The mouth was masked by the triangular plane of the face, its considerable size would be guessed only in profile; in front a delicate crevice barely slit the lifeless stone. On both sides of the head where the ears should have been, there grew three tiny sprigs red as coral, a vegetal outgrowth, the gills, I suppose. And they were the only thing quick about it; every ten or fifteen seconds the sprigs pricked up stiffly and again subsided. Once in a while a foot would barely move, I saw the diminutive toes poise mildly on the moss. It's that we don't enjoy moving a lot, and the tank is so cramped—we barely move in any direction and we're hitting one of the others with our tail or our head—difficulties arise, fights, tiredness. The time feels like it's less if we stay quietly.

It was their quietness that made me lean toward them fascinated the first time I saw the axolotls. Obscurely I seemed to understand their secret will, to abolish space and time with an indifferent immobility. I knew better later; the gill contraction, the tentative reckoning of the delicate feet on the stones, the abrupt swimming (some of them swim with a simple undulation of the body) proved to me that they were capable of

nese figurines of milky glass), looking like a small lizard about six inches long, ending in a fish's tail of extraordinary delicacy, the most sensitive part of our body. Along the back ran a transparent fin which joined with the tail, but what obsessed me was the feet, of the slenderest nicety, ending in tiny

---

8. diaphanous (dī af′ ə nəs) *adj.*: Fine or gauzy in texture; indistinct.

escaping that mineral lethargy in which they spent whole hours. Above all else, their eyes obsessed me. In the standing tanks on either side of them, different fishes showed me the simple stupidity of their handsome eyes so similar to our own. The eyes of the axolotls spoke to me of the presence of a different life, of another way of seeing. Gluing my face to the glass (the guard would cough fussily once in a while), I tried to see better those diminutive golden points, that entrance to the infinitely slow and remote world of these rosy creatures. It was useless to tap with one finger on the glass directly in front of their faces; they never gave the least reaction. The golden eyes continued burning with their soft, terrible light; they continued looking at me from an unfathomable depth which made me dizzy.

And nevertheless they were close. I knew it before this, before being an axolotl. I learned it the day I came near them for the first time. The anthropomorphic features of a monkey reveal the reverse of what most people believe, the distance that is traveled from them to us. The absolute lack of similarity between axolotls and human beings proved to me that my recognition was valid, that I was not propping myself up with easy analogies. Only the little hands . . . But an eft, the common newt, has such hands also, and we are not at all alike. I think it was the axolotls' heads, that triangular pink shape with the tiny eyes of gold. That looked and knew. That laid the claim. They were not *animals.*

It would seem easy, almost obvious, to fall into mythology. I began seeing in the axolotls a metamorphosis which did not succeed in revoking a mysterious humanity. I imagined them aware, slaves of their bodies, condemned infinitely to the silence of the abyss, to a hopeless meditation. Their blind gaze, the diminutive gold disk without expression and nonetheless terribly shining, went through me like a message: "Save us, save us." I caught myself mumbling words of advice, conveying childish hopes. They continued to look at me, immobile; from time to time the rosy branches of the gills stiffened. In that instant I felt a muted pain; perhaps they were seeing me, attracting my strength to penetrate into the impenetrable thing of their lives. They were not human beings, but I had found in no animal such a profound relation with myself. The axolotls were like witnesses of something, and at times like horrible judges. I felt ignoble in front of them; there was such a terrifying purity in those transparent eyes. They were larvas, but larva means disguise and also phantom. Behind those Aztec faces, without expression but of an implacable cruelty, what semblance was awaiting its hour?

I was afraid of them. I think that had it not been for feeling the proximity of other visitors and the guard, I would not have been bold enough to remain alone with them. "You eat them alive with your eyes, hey," the guard said, laughing; he likely thought I was a little cracked. What he didn't notice was that it was they devouring me slowly with their eyes, in a cannibalism of gold. At any distance from the aquarium, I had only to think of them, it was as though I were being affected from a distance. It got to the point that I was going every day, and at night I thought of them immobile in the darkness, slowly putting a hand out which immediately encountered another. Perhaps their eyes could see in the dead of night, and for them the day continued indefinitely. The eyes of axolotls have no lids.

I know now that there was nothing strange, that that had to occur. Leaning over in front of the tank each morning, the recognition was greater. They were suffering, every fiber of my body reached toward that

TODA LA SABIDURIA VIENE DEL CIELO
(ALL THE WISDOM COMES FROM THE SKY), 1991
Arnaldo Roche Rabell
Galeria Alejandro Gallo

stifled pain, that stiff torment at the bottom of the tank. They were lying in wait for something, a remote dominion destroyed, an age of liberty when the world had been that of the axolotls. Not possible that such a terrible expression which was attaining the overthrow of that forced blankness on their stone faces should carry any message other than one of pain, proof of that eternal sentence, of that liquid hell they were undergoing. Hopelessly, I wanted to prove to myself that my own sensibility was projecting a nonexistent consciousness upon the axolotls. They and I knew. So there was nothing strange in what happened. My face was pressed against the glass of the aquarium, my eyes were attempting once more to penetrate the mystery of those eyes of gold without iris, without pupil. I saw from very close up the face of an axolotl immobile next to the glass. No transition and no surprise, I saw my face against the glass, I saw it on the outside of the tank, I saw it on the other side of the glass. Then my face drew back and I understood.

Only one thing was strange: to go on thinking as usual, to know. To realize that was, for the first moment, like the horror of a man buried alive awakening to his fate. Outside, my face came close to the glass again, I saw my mouth, the lips compressed with the effort of understanding the axolotls. I was an axolotl and now I knew instantly that no understanding was possible. He was outside the aquarium, his thinking was a thinking outside the tank. Recognizing him, being him himself, I was an axolotl and in my world. The horror began—I learned in the same moment—of believing myself prisoner in the body of an axolotl, metamorphosed into him with my human mind intact, bur-

ied alive in an axolotl, condemned to move lucidly among unconscious creatures. But that stopped when a foot just grazed my face, when I moved just a little to one side and saw an axolotl next to me who was looking at me, and understood that he knew also, no communication possible, but very clearly. Or I was also in him, or all of us were thinking humanlike, incapable of expression, limited to the golden splendor of our eyes looking at the face of the man pressed against the aquarium.

He returned many times, but he comes less often now. Weeks pass without his showing up. I saw him yesterday, he looked at me for a long time and left briskly. It seemed to me that he was not so much interested in us any more, that he was coming out of habit. Since the only thing I do is think, I could think about him a lot. It occurs to me that at the beginning we continued to communicate, that he felt more than ever one with the mystery which was claiming him. But the bridges were broken between him and me, because what was his obsession is now an axolotl, alien to his human life. I think that at the beginning I was capable of returning to him in a certain way—ah, only in a certain way—and of keeping awake his desire to know us better. I am an axolotl for good now, and if I think like a man it's only because every axolotl thinks like a man inside his rosy stone semblance. I believe that all this succeeded in communicating something to him in those first days, when I was still he. And in this final solitude to which he no longer comes, I console myself by thinking that perhaps he is going to write a story about us, that, believing he's making up a story, he's going to write all this about axolotls.

RESPONDING TO THE SELECTION

Your Response

1. Do you think the narrator is crazy? Why or why not?

Recalling

2. Describe axolotls.
3. How does the narrator become more and more obsessed with the axolotls? What happens at the end of the story?

Interpreting

4. Which details of the story are realistic? Which are fantastic?
5. How are the human narrator and axolotls similar? How are they different?
6. What is especially fascinating about the axolotls' eyes?
7. In what way is the narrator being devoured by the axolotls?
8. What does the axolotl mean when he says that "the bridges were broken between him and me"?
9. Is the fantastic change that occurs at the end of the story similar to any changes that occur in the real world? Explain.

Applying

10. Do you think this story would make a good film? Why or why not?

ANALYZING LITERATURE

Understanding the Narrator's Perspective

The author of this story plays games with the narrator's perspective, or vantage point, in order to startle readers out of their ordinary ways of thinking. Throughout the story the first-person narrator refers to himself as "I." Yet the perspective of the "I" at the beginning of the story is much different from that at the end.

1. At what point in the story does the narrator's perspective change in an important way?

2. In your own words, describe this change in perspective. What causes this change?

CRITICAL THINKING AND READING

Identifying Shifts in Perspective

You can trace the changes in perspective in this story by keeping a close eye on the pronouns. At one point the first-person narrator seems to divide into an axolotl self and a human self. The narrator signals this shift by referring to the human self as *he.*

1. Locate the point at which the narrator first refers to his human self as *he.* How does this shift reveal a change in his perspective?
2. How do the axolotl self and the human self grow more distant at the end of the story?

THINKING AND WRITING

Writing From a Different Perspective

"Axolotl" is about a change in perspective that is also a dramatic change in physical form. Use your imagination to write a short story as if you were another creature entirely. It may help to choose an animal that you are very familiar with. Describe what it feels like to be this creature and write about a specific experience.

LEARNING OPTIONS

1. **Art.** The art accompanying this selection was not originally meant to illustrate "Axolotl." Nevertheless, qualities of each painting resemble qualities of the story. Write a brief note about each painting, describing how the art detracts from or enhances your enjoyment of "Axolotl."
2. **Writing.** The only person who speaks to the narrator in the story is the aquarium guard. Imagine that you are the guard and that you have been asked to report on the narrator's behavior. Write three or four paragraphs describing your observations and opinions of the narrator.

GUIDE FOR READING

Mushrooms in the City

Third-Person Limited Point of View

A story with a **third-person limited point of view** is told by an outside observer. The observer tells the events from the limited perspective, or vantage point, of just one character. The person telling the story refers to that character in the third person—by name, or as *he* or *she*—and presents only what that character knows, thinks, and feels. Any other characters in the story are seen through that one character's eyes only. Such a point of view may seem narrow, but what it lacks in breadth, it makes up for in depth and intensity. The third-person limited point of view makes it possible for the reader to really understand one character's experience and often to sympathize with that character's views and situation.

Focus

Marcovaldo, the main character of "Mushrooms in the City," observes nature even though he lives in a city. Using a chart like the one below, list unusual examples of natural life that you have observed. Then compare your observations with Marcovaldo's.

	Where Seen	When Seen
Birds		
Other Animals		
Insects		
Plants		

Vocabulary

Knowing the following words will help you as you read "Mushrooms in the City."

stipulated (stip′ yōō lāt′ əd) *adj.*: Agreed upon; guaranteed (p. 115)

assimilating (ə sim′ ə lāt iŋ) *v.*: Taking in; absorbing (p. 115)

ecstatically (ek stat′ ik lē) *adv.*: With great joy (p. 115)

incredulous (in krej′ oo ləs)

adj.: Unbelieving; doubtful (p. 116)

jurisdiction (joor′ is dik′ s·hən) *n.*: Area of responsibility (p. 116)

eradicated (ē rad′ i kāt′ əd) *v.*: Completely wiped out (p. 116)

Italo Calvino

(1923–1985) fought against the Germans as a member of the Italian Resistance during World War II. He studied at the University of Turin after the war. For the rest of his life, he collected and edited traditional Italian folk tales and, at the same time, wrote original short stories and novels. His original works, such as this one, have been called "modern fables" because they use elements of the fable form to comment on modern life. The writer and critic John Gardner called Calvino "one of the world's best" writers of fables.

Mushrooms in the City

Italo Calvino
translated by William Weaver

The wind, coming to the city from far away, brings it unusual gifts, noticed by only a few sensitive souls, such as hay-fever victims, who sneeze at the pollen from flowers of other lands.

One day, to the narrow strip of ground flanking a city avenue came a gust of spores from God knows where; and some mushrooms germinated. Nobody noticed them except Marcovaldo,[1] the worker who caught his tram[2] just there every morning.

This Marcovaldo possessed an eye ill-suited to city life: billboards, traffic lights, shop windows, neon signs, posters, no matter how carefully devised to catch the attention, never arrested his gaze, which might have been running over the desert sands. Instead, he would never miss a leaf yellowing on a branch, a feather trapped by a roof tile; there was no horsefly on a horse's back, no worm hole in a plank, or fig peel squashed on the sidewalk that Marcovaldo didn't remark and ponder over, discovering the changes of season, the yearnings of his heart, and the woes of his existence.

Thus, one morning, as he was waiting for the tram that would take him to Sbav and Co.,[3] where he was employed as an unskilled laborer, he noticed something unusual near the stop, in the sterile, encrusted strip of earth beneath the avenue's line of trees; at certain points, near the tree trunks, some bumps seemed to rise and, here and there, they had opened, allowing roundish subterranean bodies to peep out.

Bending to tie his shoes, he took a better look: they were mushrooms, real mushrooms, sprouting right in the heart of the city! To Marcovaldo the gray and wretched world surrounding him seemed suddenly generous with hidden riches; something could still be expected of life, beyond the hourly wage of his stipulated salary, with inflation index,[4] family grant, and cost-of-living allowance.

On the job he was more absent-minded than usual; he kept thinking that while he was there unloading cases and boxes, in the darkness of the earth the slow, silent mushrooms, known only to him, were ripening their porous[5] flesh, were assimilating underground humors,[6] breaking the crust of clods. "One night's rain would be enough," he said to himself, "then they would be ready to pick." And he couldn't wait to share his discovery with his wife and his six children.

"I'm telling you!" he announced during their scant supper. "In a week's time we'll be eating mushrooms! A great fry! That's a promise!"

And to the smaller children, who did not know what mushrooms were, he explained ecstatically the beauty of the numerous spe-

---

1. Marcovaldo (mär′ kō val′ dō)
2. tram (tram) *n.*: An open railway car; a streetcar.
3. Sbav (sbəv) **and Co.:** Sbav and Company.

4. inflation index (in flā′ shən in′ deks): Adjustment of wages to increase automatically as the cost of living increases.
5. porous (pôr′ əs) *adj.*: Full of pores through which air, light, or liquids might pass.
6. humors (hyōō′ mərz) *n.*: Juices.

Mushrooms in the City **115**

cies, the delicacy of their flavor, the way they should be cooked; and so he also drew into the discussion his wife, Domitilla,[7] who until then had appeared rather incredulous and abstracted.

"Where are these mushrooms?" the children asked. "Tell us where they grow!"

At this question Marcovaldo's enthusiasm was curbed by a suspicious thought: Now if I tell them the place, they'll go and hunt for them with the usual gang of kids, word will spread through the neighborhood, and the mushrooms will end up in somebody else's pan! And so that discovery, which had promptly filled his heart with universal love, now made him wildly possessive, surrounded him with jealous and distrusting fear.

"I know where the mushrooms are, and I'm the only one who knows," he said to his children, "and God help you if you breathe a word to anybody."

The next morning, as he approached the tram stop, Marcovaldo was filled with apprehension. He bent to look at the ground and, to his relief, saw that the mushrooms had grown a little, but not much, and were still almost completely hidden by the earth.

He was bent in this position when he realized there was someone behind him. He straightened up at once and tried to act indifferent. It was the street cleaner, leaning on his broom and looking at him.

This street cleaner, whose jurisdiction included the place where the mushrooms grew, was a lanky youth with eyeglasses. His name was Amadigi,[8] and Marcovaldo had long harbored a dislike of him, perhaps because of those eyeglasses that examined the pavement of the streets, seeking any trace of nature, to be eradicated by his broom.

7. **Domitilla** (dō mē tē′ la)
8. **Amadigi** (am′ ə dēj′ ē)

It was Saturday; and Marcovaldo spent his free half-day circling the bed of dirt with an absent air, keeping an eye on the street cleaner in the distance and on the mushrooms, and calculating how much time they needed to ripen.

That night it rained: like peasants who, after months of drought, wake up and leap with joy at the sound of the first drops, so Marcovaldo, alone in all the city, sat up in bed and called to his family: "It's raining! It's raining!" and breathed in the smell of moistened dust and fresh mold that came from outside.

At dawn—it was Sunday—with the children and a borrowed basket, he ran immediately to the patch. There were the mushrooms, erect on their stems, their caps high over the still-soaked earth. "Hurrah!" —and they fell to gathering them.

"Papà! Look how many that man over there has found," Michelino[9] said, and his father, raising his eyes, saw Amadigi standing beside them, also with a basket full of mushrooms under his arm.

"Ah, you're gathering them, too?" the street cleaner said. "Then they're edible? I picked a few, but I wasn't sure . . . Farther down the avenue some others have sprouted, even bigger ones . . . Well, now that I know, I'll tell my relatives; they're down there arguing whether it's a good idea to pick them or not . . ." And he walked off in a hurry.

Marcovaldo was speechless: even bigger mushrooms, which he hadn't noticed, an unhoped-for harvest, being taken from him like this, before his very eyes. For a moment he was almost frozen with anger, fury, then —as sometimes happens—the collapse of individual passion led to a generous impulse. At that hour, many people were wait-

9. **Michelino** (mik′ ə lē′ nō)

ing for the tram, umbrellas over their arms, because the weather was still damp and uncertain. "Hey, you! Do you want to eat fried mushrooms tonight?" Marcovaldo shouted to the crowd of people at the stop. "Mushrooms are growing here by the street! Come along! There's plenty for all!" And he walked off after Amadigi, with a string of people behind him.

They all found plenty of mushrooms, and lacking baskets, they used their open umbrellas. Somebody said: "It would be nice to have a big feast, all of us together!" But, instead, each took his own share and went home.

They saw one another again soon, however; that very evening, in fact, in the same ward of the hospital, after the stomach pump had saved them all from poisoning. It was not serious, because the number of mushrooms eaten by each person was quite small.

Marcovaldo and Amadigi had adjacent beds; they glared at each other.

MUSHROOMS, 1940
Sir William Nicholson
Tate Gallery, London

RESPONDING TO THE SELECTION

Your Response

1. If you were Marcovaldo, what would you have done differently after you discovered the mushrooms?
2. Were you surprised by the way the story ended? Explain.

Recalling

3. Describe how Marcovaldo feels about city life.
4. Why does Marcovaldo rejoice when it rains?

Interpreting

5. What do the mushrooms represent for Marcovaldo? Do the other characters value them in the same way he does? Explain.
6. What do you think was the author's purpose in writing the story? Which sentence comes closest to summing up the central idea?
7. How does the surprise ending reinforce the story's central idea or theme?

Applying

8. This story presents a particular attitude about nature and its gifts. Explain that attitude in your own words, and show how the same attitude relates to the use of natural resources today.

ANALYZING LITERATURE

Appreciating Point of View

This story is told from the **third-person limited point of view.** Everything is seen through the eyes of Marcovaldo, and nothing is revealed that Marcovaldo does not know or feel. For example, what we find out about other characters we learn from Marcovaldo's viewpoint.

1. How does Marcovaldo feel about Amadigi, the streetcleaner? Give quotations from the story that support your conclusion.
2. How does Marcovaldo view his wife and children? Does he see them as sympathetic?
3. Are you as a reader sympathetic to Marcovaldo?

THINKING AND WRITING

Changing the Point of View

Suppose this story were written from Amadigi's point of view. How would he feel about the mushrooms and about Marcovaldo's actions? To get insight into Amadigi's feelings, play the role of Amadigi with another classmate playing Marcovaldo. Then rewrite the story from Amadigi's point of view. Work with your partner to make sure that you have not included anything that Amadigi could not know. You may want to read your revised draft to your classmates and ask them if your version of the story makes them feel more sympathetic to Amadigi.

LEARNING OPTIONS

1. **Speaking and Listening.** With a partner role-play a conversation Marcovaldo and Amadigi might have had as they lay in their hospital beds. First, write a dialogue consistent with Calvino's story and its characters. Practice acting out the dialogue with your partner. Then perform your skit for the class.
2. **Cross-curricular Connection.** If Marcovaldo had done his homework about the mushrooms, he might have avoided going to the hospital. Imagine that you are a botanist and that Marcovaldo has come to you for advice about the mushrooms. Write a brief explanation of what you would tell Marcovaldo. Before you begin writing, consult resources in your life-science or biology classroom. Explore what to look for when identifying mushrooms as poisonous or harmless, and include what you find in your explanation to Marcovaldo.
3. **Writing.** Imagine that you are a journalist in the city where Marcovaldo lives. You have been assigned to cover the story of how the people waiting for the tram ended up in the hospital. Create a short, humorous piece that sums up how the events of the day "mushroomed."

Setting

ROAD WITH CYPRESS AND STAR
Vincent van Gogh
Collection: State Museum, Kröller-Müller Otterlo, The Netherlands

GUIDE FOR READING

There Will Come Soft Rains

Ray Bradbury

(1920–) is one of the world's most celebrated science-fiction writers. He was born in Waukegan, Illinois, and grew up along the western shores of Lake Michigan. He began reading the stories of Edgar Allan Poe as a child and also developed a fascination with horror movies and fantasy—especially futuristic fantasy. In many of his stories, including "There Will Come Soft Rains," Bradbury describes a future that reflects the possible outcomes of today's technology.

Setting

The **setting** of a story is the time and place of the story's action. In some stories the author may merely establish the setting as a background for the action. In others the setting is vitally important, as important as the characters and plot. A horror story, for example, often needs a setting such as a musty old house with creaking floors to be effective. Bradbury sets "There Will Come Soft Rains" in a house that is anything but musty and old. In fact, the setting is so important that it is actually the central character in the story.

Focus

The house in "There Will Come Soft Rains" is automated. Think about the machines and equipment that you rely on in daily life. How many of them are computerized? In a group of three, brainstorm about ways in which computers have affected everyday life. Keep your discussion in mind as you read "There Will Come Soft Rains."

Vocabulary

Knowing the following words will help you as you read "There Will Come Soft Rains."

warrens (wôr′ ənz) *n.*: Maze-like passages (p. 121)

titanic (tī tan′ ik) *adj.*: Having great power (p. 122)

paranoia (par′ ə nɔi′ ə) *n.*: A mental disorder characterized by delusions of persecution (p. 122)

cavorting (kə vôrt′ iŋ) *v.*: Leaping or prancing about (p. 122)

spoors (spoorz) *n.*: Droppings of wild animals (p. 123)

okapi (ō kä′ pē) *n.*: An African animal related to the giraffe but with a much shorter neck (p. 123)

tremulous (trem′ yoo ləs) *adj.*: Trembling; quivering (p. 123)

psychopathic (sī′ kə patĥ′ ik) *adj.*: With a mental disorder (p. 124)

There Will Come Soft Rains

Ray Bradbury

In the living room the voice-clock sang, *Tick-tock, seven o'clock, time to get up, time to get up, seven o'clock!* as if it were afraid that nobody would. The morning house lay empty. The clock ticked on, repeating and repeating its sounds into the emptiness. *Seven-nine, breakfast time, seven-nine!*

In the kitchen the breakfast stove gave a hissing sigh and ejected from its warm interior eight pieces of perfectly browned toast, eight eggs sunnyside up, sixteen slices of bacon, two coffees, and two cool glasses of milk.

"Today is August 4, 2026," said a second voice from the kitchen ceiling, "in the city of Allendale, California." It repeated the date three times for memory's sake. "Today is Mr. Featherstone's birthday. Today is the anniversary of Tilita's marriage. Insurance is payable, as are the water, gas, and light bills."

Somewhere in the walls, relays clicked, memory tapes glided under electric eyes.

Eight-one, tick-tock, eight-one o'clock, off to school, off to work, run, run, eight-one! But no doors slammed, no carpets took the soft tread of rubber heels. It was raining outside. The weather box on the front door sang quietly: "Rain, rain, go away; rubbers, raincoats for today . . ." And the rain tapped on the empty house, echoing.

Outside, the garage chimed and lifted its door to reveal the waiting car. After a long wait the door swung down again.

At eight-thirty the eggs were shriveled and the toast was like stone. An aluminum wedge scraped them into the sink, where hot water whirled them down a metal throat which digested and flushed them away to the distant sea. The dirty dishes were dropped into a hot washer and emerged twinkling dry.

Nine-fifteen, sang the clock, *time to clean.*

Out of warrens in the wall, tiny robot mice darted. The rooms were acrawl with the small cleaning animals, all rubber and metal. They thudded against chairs, whirling their mustached runners, kneading the rug nap, sucking gently at hidden dust. Then, like mysterious invaders, they popped into their burrows. Their pink electric eyes faded. The house was clean.

Ten o'clock. The sun came out from behind the rain. The house stood alone in a city of rubble and ashes. This was the one house left standing. At night the ruined city gave off a radioactive glow which could be seen for miles.

Ten-fifteen. The garden sprinklers whirled up in golden founts, filling the soft morning air with scatterings of brightness. The water pelted windowpanes, running down the charred west side where the house had been burned evenly free of its white paint. The entire west face of the house was black, save for five places. Here the silhouette in paint of a man mowing a lawn. Here, as in a photograph, a woman bent to pick flowers. Still farther over, their images burned on wood in one titanic instant, a small boy, hands flung into the air; higher up, the image of a thrown ball, and opposite him a girl, hands raised to catch a ball which never came down.

The five spots of paint—the man, the woman, the children, the ball—remained. The rest was a thin charcoaled layer.

The gentle-sprinkler rain filled the garden with falling light.

Until this day, how well the house had kept its peace. How carefully it had inquired, "Who goes there? What's the password?" and, getting no answer from lonely foxes and whining cats, it had shut up its windows and drawn shades in an old-maidenly preoccupation with self-protection which bordered on a mechanical paranoia.

It quivered at each sound, the house did. If a sparrow brushed a window, the shade snapped up. The bird, startled, flew off! No, not even a bird must touch the house!

The house was an altar with ten thousand attendants, big, small, servicing, attending, in choirs. But the gods had gone away, and the ritual of the religion continued senselessly, uselessly.

Twelve noon.

A dog whined, shivering, on the front porch.

The front door recognized the dog voice and opened. The dog, once huge and fleshy, but now gone to bone and covered with sores, moved in and through the house, tracking mud. Behind it whirred angry mice, angry at having to pick up mud, angry at inconvenience.

For not a leaf fragment blew under the door but what the wall panels flipped open and the copper scrap rats flashed swiftly out. The offending dust, hair, or paper, seized in miniature steel jaws, was raced back to the burrows. There, down tubes which fed into the cellar, it was dropped into the sighing vent of an incinerator which sat like evil Baal[1] in a dark corner.

The dog ran upstairs, hysterically yelping to each door, at last realizing, as the house realized, that only silence was here.

It sniffed the air and scratched the kitchen door. Behind the door, the stove was making pancakes which filled the house with a rich baked odor and the scent of maple syrup.

The dog frothed at the mouth, lying at the door, sniffing, its eyes turned to fire. It ran wildly in circles, biting at its tail, spun in a frenzy, and died. It lay in the parlor for an hour.

Two o'clock, sang a voice.

Delicately sensing decay at last, the regiments of mice hummed out as softly as blown gray leaves in an electrical wind.

Two-fifteen.

The dog was gone.

In the cellar, the incinerator glowed suddenly and a whirl of sparks leaped up the chimney.

Two thirty-five.

Bridge tables sprouted from patio walls. Playing cards fluttered onto pads in a shower of pips. Glasses manifested on an oaken bench with egg-salad sandwiches. Music played.

But the tables were silent and the cards untouched.

At four o'clock the tables folded like great butterflies back through the paneled walls.

Four-thirty.

The nursery walls glowed.

Animals took shape: yellow giraffes, blue lions, pink antelopes, lilac panthers cavorting in crystal substance. The walls were glass. They looked out upon color and fantasy. Hidden films clocked through well-oiled sprockets, and the walls lived. The nursery

---

1. Baal (bā′ əl): A false god or idol.

floor was woven to resemble a crisp, cereal meadow. Over this ran aluminum roaches and iron crickets, and in the hot still air butterflies of delicate red tissue wavered among the sharp aroma of animal spoors! There was the sound like a great matted yellow hive of bees within a dark bellows, the lazy bumble of a purring lion. And there was the patter of okapi feet and the murmur of a fresh jungle rain, like other hoofs, falling upon the summer-starched grass. Now the walls dissolved into distances of parched weed, mile on mile, and warm endless sky. The animals drew away into thorn brakes and water holes.

It was the children's hour.

Five o'clock. The bath filled with clear hot water.

Six, seven, eight o'clock. The dinner dishes manipulated like magic tricks, and in the study a *click.* In the hearth a fire now blazed up warmly.

Nine o'clock. The beds warmed their hidden circuits, for nights were cool here.

Nine-five. A voice spoke from the study ceiling:

"Mrs. McClellan, which poem would you like this evening?"

The house was silent.

The voice said at last, "Since you express no preference, I shall select a poem at random." Quiet music rose to back the voice. "Sara Teasdale. As I recall, your favorite. . . ."

*There will come soft rains and the
   smell of the ground,
And swallows circling with their
   shimmering sound;*

*And frogs in the pools singing at
   night,
And wild plum trees in tremulous
   white;*

*Robins will wear their feathery fire,
Whistling their whims on a low
   fence-wire;*

*And not one will know of the war,
   not one
Will care at last when it is done.*

*Not one would mind, neither bird
   nor tree,
If mankind perished utterly;*

*And Spring herself, when she woke
   at dawn
Would scarcely know that we were
   gone."*

The fire burned on the stone hearth. The empty chairs faced each other between the silent walls, and the music played.

At ten o'clock the house began to die.

The wind blew. A falling tree bough crashed through the kitchen window. Cleaning solvent, bottled, shattered over the stove. The room was ablaze in an instant!

"Fire!" screamed a voice. The house lights flashed, water pumps shot water from the ceilings. But the solvent spread on the linoleum, licking, eating, under the kitchen door, while the voices took it up in chorus: "Fire, fire, fire!"

The house tried to save itself. Doors sprang tightly shut, but the windows were broken by the heat and the wind blew and sucked upon the fire.

The house gave ground as the fire in ten billion angry sparks moved with flaming ease from room to room and then up the stairs. While scurrying water rats squeaked from the walls, pistoled their water, and ran for more. And the wall sprays let down showers of mechanical rain.

But too late. Somewhere, sighing, a pump shrugged to a stop. The quenching rain ceased. The reserve water supply which had filled baths and washed dishes for many quiet days was gone.

The fire crackled up the stairs. It fed upon Picassos and Matisses[2] in the upper halls, like delicacies, baking off the oily flesh, tenderly crisping the canvases into black shavings.

Now the fire lay in beds, stood in windows, changed the colors of drapes!

And then, reinforcements.

From attic trapdoors, blind robot faces peered down with faucet mouths gushing green chemical.

The fire backed off, as even an elephant must at the sight of a dead snake. Now there were twenty snakes whipping over the floor, killing the fire with a clear cold venom of green froth.

But the fire was clever. It had sent flame outside the house, up through the attic to the pumps there. An explosion! The attic brain which directed the pumps was shattered into bronze shrapnel on the beams.

The fire rushed back into every closet and felt of the clothes hung there.

The house shuddered, oak bone on bone, its bared skeleton cringing from the heat, its wire, its nerves revealed as if a surgeon had torn the skin off to let the red veins and capillaries quiver in the scalded air. Help, help! Fire! Run, run! Heat snapped mirrors like the first brittle winter ice. And the voices wailed Fire, fire, run, run, like a tragic nursery rhyme, a dozen voices, high, low, like children dying in a forest, alone, alone. And the voices fading as the wires popped their sheathings like hot chestnuts. One, two, three, four, five voices died.

In the nursery the jungle burned. Blue lions roared, purple giraffes bounded off. The panthers ran in circles, changing color, and ten million animals, running before the fire, vanished off toward a distant steaming river. . . .

Ten more voices died. In the last instant under the fire avalanche, other choruses, oblivious, could be heard announcing the time, playing music, cutting the lawn by remote-control mower, or setting an umbrella frantically out and in the slamming and opening front door, a thousand things happening, like a clock shop when each clock strikes the hour insanely before or after the other, a scene of maniac confusion, yet unity; singing, screaming, a few last cleaning mice darting bravely out to carry the horrid ashes away! And one voice, with sublime disregard for the situation, read poetry aloud in the fiery study, until all the film spools burned, until all the wires withered and the circuits cracked.

The fire burst the house and let it slam flat down, puffing out skirts of spark and smoke.

In the kitchen, an instant before the rain of fire and timber, the stove could be seen making breakfasts at a psychopathic rate, ten dozen eggs, six loaves of toast, twenty dozen bacon strips, which, eaten by fire, started the stove working again, hysterically hissing!

The crash. The attic smashing into kitchen and parlor. The parlor into cellar, cellar into subcellar. Deep freeze, armchair, film tapes, circuits, beds, and all like skeletons thrown in a cluttered mound deep under.

Smoke and silence. A great quantity of smoke.

Dawn showed faintly in the east. Among the ruins, one wall stood alone. Within the wall, a last voice said, over and over again and again, even as the sun rose to shine upon the heaped rubble and steam:

"Today is August 5, 2026, today is August 5, 2026, today is . . ."

---

2. Picassos (pi kä′sōz) **and Matisses** (mä tēs′əz): Works by the painters Pablo Picasso and Henri Matisse.

RESPONDING TO THE SELECTION

Your Response

1. What do you think Bradbury intended to convey about nuclear war in the story?
2. Did Teasdale's poem "There Will Come Soft Rains" add to your appreciation of Bradbury's story? Explain.

Recalling

3. List some activities the house performs.
4. Explain what has happened to the occupants of the house.
5. Explain what happens to the dog.
6. Describe the final hours of the house.

Interpreting

7. Why does the house keep going, even without human occupants?
8. What can you infer about the quality of the lives of the former inhabitants? Explain the evidence that supports your answer.
9. An allusion is a reference to another work. Why do you think Bradbury chose to have the house broadcast the Sara Teasdale poem?
10. Compare the house, both in its normal operation and in its final hours, to a human.
11. Why do you think the story ends with a voice within one wall repeating the date?

Applying

12. There have been many books, movies, and television shows about the end of the world. What qualities make this story different from others with which you are familiar?

ANALYZING LITERATURE

Understanding Setting

The **setting** is the time and place of a story's action. Some stories contain more information about setting than others. In "There Will Come Soft Rains," the setting is significant, and Bradbury gives you precise information about the time of the events and a detailed description of the place where they occur.

1. When does the story take place?
2. Give two details from the story that reinforce the time period.
3. In what kind of community does it occur?
4. Why does this setting make the story effective?

CRITICAL THINKING AND READING

Understanding the Effect of Setting

The events in some stories could happen almost anywhere. The events in others could happen only in a particular setting. You can recognize the importance of a setting when you examine whether the events are dependent on the setting or whether they could happen elsewhere.

1. List three events in the story that could happen only in the future.
2. List three events in the story that could happen in an ordinary house today.
3. Explain whether the events in this story depend on the given setting.

THINKING AND WRITING

Writing About a Place

Suppose that you work for the chamber of commerce of a town or city you know. Write a description of one attraction in the town. The description is for a brochure aimed at getting people to visit. Tell what the place looks like, how people use it, and what makes it special. As you revise, replace dull verbs with vivid ones.

LEARNING OPTION

Art. Imagine that you have been commissioned to illustrate "There Will Come Soft Rains." At key points in the story, sketch out illustrations of how you interpret Bradbury's descriptions. In your sketches try to capture the house as a character in the story. In addition try to convey the destruction of humanity integral to the story.

GUIDE FOR READING

The Street of the Cañon

Local Color

When the setting of a story emphasizes the characteristics of a particular locality, the story has local color. **Local color** refers to the use of details about the customs and way of life in a specific place. "The Street of the Cañon" is so filled with local color that after you read it, you may feel as if you have actually been to the Mexican village in which it is set.

Josephina Niggli

(1910–) was born in Monterey, Mexico, where her father, a Texan, was working on the railroad and her mother was a concert violinist. During the Mexican Revolution, the family fled to San Antonio, Texas, where Niggli grew up. Niggli began writing when she was quite young, and her first collection of poems and sketches, *Mexican Silhouettes,* appeared when she was only eighteen. "The Street of the Cañon" is excerpted from *Mexican Village,* which was published in 1945.

Focus

"The Street of the Cañon" takes you into a Mexican village. As you read the story, you will notice details that reveal the culture and traditions of the people in the village. Think about the culture from which you come. Consider the particular foods your family eats, special holidays you celebrate, or clothes you and your family members wear on special occasions. Copy the drawing of the street below. On the street make simple drawings symbolizing aspects of your culture. Think of a name for the street that would identify your culture.

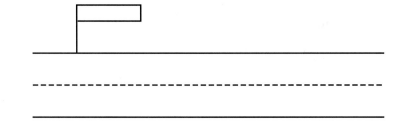

Vocabulary

Knowing the following words will help you as you read "The Street of the Cañon."

officious (ə fish′ əs) *adj.*: Overly ready to serve (p. 127)

mottled (mät′ ′ld) *adj.*: Marked with spots of different shades (p. 129)

nonchalantly (nän sʰə länt′ lē) *adv.*: Casually; indifferently (p. 129)

audaciously (ô dā′ sʰəs lē) *adv.*: In a bold manner (p. 129)

imperiously (im pir′ ē əs lē) *adv.*: Arrogantly (p. 129)

plausibility (plô′ zə bil′ it ē) *n.*: Believability (p. 130)

The Street of the Cañon

from *Mexican Village*

Josephina Niggli

It was May, the flowering thorn was sweet in the air, and the village of San Juan Iglesias in the Valley of the Three Marys was celebrating. The long dark streets were empty because all of the people, from the lowest-paid cowboy to the mayor, were helping Don Roméo Calderón celebrate his daughter's eighteenth birthday.

On the other side of the town, where the Cañon Road led across the mountains to the Sabinas Valley, a tall slender man, a package clutched tightly against his side, slipped from shadow to shadow. Once a dog barked, and the man's black suit merged into the blackness of a wall. But no voice called out, and after a moment he slid into the narrow, dirt-packed street again.

The moonlight touched his shoulder and spilled across his narrow hips. He was young, no more than twenty-five, and his black curly head was bare. He walked swiftly along, heading always for the distant sound of guitar and flute. If he met anyone now, who could say from which direction he had come? He might be a trader from Monterrey, or a buyer of cow's milk from farther north in the Valley of the Three Marys. Who would guess that an Hidalgo[1] man dared to walk alone in the moonlit streets of San Juan Iglesias?

Carefully adjusting his flat package so that it was not too prominent, he squared his shoulders and walked jauntily across the street to the laughter-filled house. Little boys packed in the doorway made way for him, smiling and nodding to him. The long, narrow room with the orchestra at one end was filled with whirling dancers. Rigid-backed chaperones were gossiping together, seated in their straight chairs against the plaster walls. Over the scene was the yellow glow of kerosene lanterns, and the air was hot with the too-sweet perfume of gardenias, tuberoses, and the pungent scent of close-packed humanity.

The man in the doorway, while trying to appear at ease, was carefully examining every smiling face. If just one person recognized him, the room would turn on him like a den of snarling mountain cats, but so far all the laughter-dancing eyes were friendly.

Suddenly a plump, officious little man, his round cheeks glistening with perspiration, pushed his way through the crowd. His voice, many times too large for his small body, boomed at the man in the doorway. "Welcome, stranger, welcome to our house." Thrusting his arm through the stranger's, and almost dislodging the package, he started to lead the way through the maze of dancers. "Come and drink a toast to my daughter—to my beautiful Sarita. She is eighteen this night."

---

1. Hidalgo (ē dal′go) *adj*.: A nearby village.

In the square patio the gentle breeze ruffled the pink and white oleander bushes. A long table set up on sawhorses held loaves of flaky crusted French bread, stacks of thin, delicate tortillas, plates of barbecued beef, and long red rolls of spicy sausages. But most of all there were cheeses, for the Three Marys was a cheese-eating valley. There were yellow cheese and white cheese and curded cheese from cow's milk. There was even a flat white cake of goat cheese from distant Linares, a delicacy too expensive for any but feast days.

To set off this feast were bottles of beer floating in ice-filled tin tubs, and another table was covered with bottles of mescal, of tequila, of maguey wine.

Don Roméo Calderón thrust a glass of tequila into the stranger's hand. ''Drink, friend, to the prettiest girl in San Juan. As pretty as my fine fighting cocks, she is. On her wedding day she takes to her man, and may she find him soon, the best fighter in my flock. Drink deep, friend. Even the rivers flow with wine.''

The Hidalgo man laughed and raised his glass high. ''May the earth be always fertile beneath her feet.''

Someone called to Don Roméo that more guests were arriving, and with a final delighted pat on the stranger's shoulder, the little man scurried away. As the young fellow smiled after his retreating host, his eyes caught and held another pair of eyes

MULTICULTURAL CONNECTION

Marriage Customs

Courtship and marriage customs play an important role in this story. In Western cultures, love and marriage usually go hand in hand: first love, then marriage. However, in many societies, especially in the East and the Middle East, the pattern is reversed.

Arranged marriages. In Eastern and Middle Eastern countries, the match between two people is carefully regulated, based on their suitability to each other and social status. It is hoped that once these factors are satisfied, love may follow. Even in the West, until modern times, romantic love was not a prerequisite for marriage.

Marriages that are arranged by families are more common in societies that still favor large or extended families. Dating is frowned upon; young people rely on their parents to find them a husband or wife. It is also common for a matchmaker, who may be a friend or relative or even a professional broker, to arrange a marriage that is acceptable to both people.

Mutual attraction and "love marriage." By contrast, in societies in which the small or nuclear family has replaced the large, extended family, families rarely become involved in matchmaking; children usually choose their own mates based not on socioeconomic considerations but on mutual attraction.

It is interesting to note that even in Western societies some sort of "arranged marriage" exists, especially among royalty and the extremely wealthy. As a final note, even in non-Western societies, marriage by one's own choice, or "love marriage" as it is sometimes called, is gaining popularity and acceptance because of Western influence.

Exploring on Your Own

How do you think dating and marriage will change in the twenty-first century? Get together with a group of classmates and brainstorm to answer this question. Then present your ideas to the class.

—laughing black eyes set in a young girl's face. The last time he had seen that face it had been white and tense with rage, and the lips clenched tight to prevent an outgushing stream of angry words. That had been in February, and she had worn a white lace shawl over her hair. Now it was May, and a gardenia was a splash of white in the glossy dark braids. The moonlight had mottled his face that February night, and he knew that she did not recognize him. He grinned impudently back at her, and her eyes widened, then slid sideways to one of the chaperones. The fan in her small hand snapped shut. She tapped its parchment tip against her mouth and slipped away to join the dancing couples in the front room. The gestures of a fan translate into a coded language on the frontier. The stranger raised one eyebrow as he interpreted the signal.

But he did not move toward her at once. Instead, he inched slowly back against the table. No one was behind him, and his hands quickly unfastened the package he had been guarding so long. Then he nonchalantly walked into the front room.

The girl was sitting close to a chaperone. As he came up to her he swerved slightly toward the bushy-browed old lady.

"Your servant, señora. I kiss your hands and feet."

The chaperone stared at him in astonishment. Such fine manners were not common to the town of San Juan Iglesias.

"Eh, you're a stranger," she said. "I thought so."

"But a stranger no longer, señora, now that I have met you." He bent over her, so close she could smell the faint fragrance of talcum on his freshly shaven cheek. "Will you dance the *parada* with me?"

This request startled her eyes into popping open beneath the heavy brows. "So, my young rooster, would you flirt with me, and I old enough to be your grandmother?"

"Can you show me a prettier woman to flirt with in the Valley of the Three Marys?" he asked audaciously.

She grinned at him and turned toward the girl at her side. "This young fool wants to meet you, my child."

The girl blushed to the roots of her hair and shyly lowered her white lids. The old woman laughed aloud.

"Go out and dance, the two of you. A man clever enough to pat the sheep has a right to play with the lamb."

The next moment they had joined the circle of dancers and Sarita was trying to control her laughter.

"She is the worst dragon in San Juan. And how easily you won her!"

"What is a dragon," he asked imperiously, "when I longed to dance with you?"

"Ay," she retorted, "you have a quick tongue. I think you are a dangerous man."

In answer he drew her closer to him, and turned her toward the orchestra. As he reached the chief violinist he called out, "Play the *Virgencita*, 'The Shy Young Maiden.'"

The violinist's mouth opened in soundless surprise. The girl in his arms said sharply, "You heard him, the *Borachita*, 'The Little Drunken Girl.'"

With a relieved grin, the violinist tapped his music stand with his bow, and the music swung into the sad farewell of a man to his sweetheart:

Farewell, my little drunken one,
I must go to the capital
To serve the master
Who makes me weep for my return.

The stranger frowned down at her. "Is this a joke, señorita?" he asked coldly.

"No," she whispered, looking about her quickly to see if the incident had been observed. "But the *Virgencita* is the favorite song of Hidalgo, a village on the other side of the mountains in the next valley. The people of Hidalgo and San Juan Iglesias do not speak.''

"That is a stupid thing," said the man from Hidalgo as he swung her around in a large turn. "Is not music free as air? Why should one town own the rights to a song?"

The girl shuddered slightly. "Those people from Hidalgo—they are wicked monsters. Can you guess what they did not six months since?"

The man started to point out that the space of time from February to May was three months, but he thought it better not to appear too wise. "Did these Hidalgo monsters frighten you, señorita? If they did, I personally will kill them all."

She moved closer against him and tilted her face until her mouth was close to his ear. "They attempted to steal the bones of Don Rómolo Balderas."

"Is it possible?" He made his eyes grow round and his lips purse up in disdain. "Surely not that! Why, all the world knows that Don Rómolo Balderas was the greatest historian in the entire Republic. Every school child reads his books. Wise men from Quintana Roo to the Río Bravo bow their heads in admiration to his name. What a wicked thing to do!" He hoped his virtuous tone was not too virtuous for plausibility, but she did not seem to notice.

"It is true! In the night they came. Three devils!"

"Young devils, I hope."

"Young or old, who cares? They were devils. The blacksmith surprised them even as they were opening the grave. He raised such a shout that all of San Juan rushed to his aid, for they were fighting, I can tell you. Especially one of them—their leader."

"And who was he?"

"You have heard of him doubtless. A proper wild one named Pepe Gonzalez."

"And what happened to them?"

"They had horses and got away, but one, I think, was hurt."

The Hidalgo man twisted his mouth remembering how Rubén the candymaker had ridden across the whitewashed line high on the cañon trail that marked the division between the Three Marys' and the Sabinas' sides of the mountains, and then had fallen in a faint from his saddle because his left arm was broken. There was no candy in Hidalgo for six weeks, and the entire Sabinas Valley resented that broken arm as fiercely as did Rubén.

The stranger tightened his arm in reflexed anger about Sarita's waist as she said, "All the world knows that the men of Hidalgo are sons of the mountain witches."

"But even devils are shy of disturbing the honored dead," he said gravely.

"'Don Rómolo was born in our village,' Hidalgo says. 'His bones belong to us.' Well, anyone in the valley can tell you he died in San Juan Iglesias, and here his bones will stay! Is that not proper? Is that not right?"

To keep from answering, he guided her through an intricate dance pattern that led them past the patio door. Over her head he could see two men and a woman staring with amazement at the open package on the table.

His eyes on the patio, he asked blandly, "You say the leader was one Pepe Gonzalez? The name seems to have a familiar sound."

"But naturally. He has a talent." She tossed her head and stepped away from him as the music stopped. It was a dance of two *paradas*. He slipped his hand through her arm and guided her into place in the large oval of parading couples. Twice around the room and the orchestra would play again.

"A talent?" he prompted.

"For doing the impossible. When all the world says a thing cannot be done, he does it to prove the world wrong. Why, he climbed to the top of the Prow, and not even the long vanished Joaquín Castillo had ever climbed that mountain before. And this same Pepe caught a mountain lion with nothing to aid him but a rope and his two bare hands."

"He doesn't sound such a bad friend," protested the stranger, slipping his arm around her waist as the music began to play the merry song of the soap bubbles:

Pretty bubbles of a thousand colors
That ride on the wind
And break as swiftly
As a lover's heart.

The events in the patio were claiming his attention. Little by little he edged her closer to the door. The group at the table had considerably enlarged. There was a low murmur of excitement from the crowd.

"What has happened?" asked Sarita, attracted by the noise.

"There seems to be something wrong at the table," he answered, while trying to peer over the heads of the people in front of him. Realizing that this might be the last moment of peace he would have that evening, he bent toward her.

"If I come back on Sunday, will you walk around the plaza with mé?"

She was startled into exclaiming, "Ay, no!"

"Please. Just once around."

"And you think I'd walk more than once with you, señor, even if you were no stranger? In San Juan Iglesias, to walk around the plaza with a girl means a wedding."

"Ha, and you think that is common to San Juan alone? Even the devils of Hidalgo respect that law." He added hastily at her puzzled upward glance. "And so they do in all the villages." To cover his lapse he said softly, "I don't even know your name."

A mischievous grin crinkled the corners of her eyes. "Nor do I know yours, señor.

SEÑORA SABASA GARCIA, 1806–1807
Francisco José de Goya
National Gallery of Art, Washington
Andrew W. Mellon Collection

Strangers do not often walk the streets of San Juan."

Before he could answer, the chattering in the patio swelled to louder proportions. Don Roméo's voice lay on top, like thick cream on milk. "I tell you it is a jewel of a cheese. Such flavor, such texture, such whiteness. It is a jewel of a cheese."

"What has happened?" Sarita asked of a woman at her elbow.

"A fine goat's cheese appeared as if by magic on the table. No one knows where it came from."

"Probably an extra one from Linares," snorted a fat bald man on the right.

"Linares never made such a cheese as this," said the woman decisively.

"Silence!" roared Don Roméo. "Old Tío[2] Daniel would speak a word to us."

A great hand of silence closed down over the mouths of the people. The girl was standing on tiptoe trying vainly to see what was happening. She was hardly aware of the stranger's whispering voice although she remembered the words that he said. "Sunday night—once around the plaza."

She did not realize that he had moved away, leaving a gap that was quickly filled by the blacksmith.

Old Tío Daniel's voice was a shrill squeak, and his thin, stringy neck jutted forth from his body like a turtle's from its shell. "This is no cheese from Linares," he said with authority, his mouth sucking in over his toothless gums between his sentences. "Years ago, when the great Don Rómolo Balderas was still alive, we had such cheese as this—ay, in those days we had it. But after he died and was buried in our own sainted ground, as was right and proper . . ."

"Yes, yes," muttered voices in the crowd. He glared at the interruption. As soon as there was silence again, he continued:

"After he died, we had it no more. Shall I tell you why?"

"Tell us, Tío Daniel," said the voices humbly.

"Because it is made in Hidalgo!"

The sound of a waterfall, the sound of a wind in a narrow cañon, and the sound of an angry crowd are much the same. There were no distinct words, but the sound was enough.

"Are you certain, Tío?" boomed Don Roméo.

"As certain as I am that a donkey has long ears. The people of Hidalgo have been famous for generations for making cheese like this—especially that wicked one, that owner of a cheese factory, Timotéo Gonzalez, father to Pepe, the wild one, whom we have good cause to remember."

"We do, we do," came the sigh of assurance.

"But on the whole northern frontier there are no vats like his to produce so fine a product. Ask the people of Chihuahua, of Sonora. Ask the man on the bridge at Laredo, or the man in his boat at Tampico, 'Hola,[3] friend, who makes the finest goat cheese?' And the answer will always be the same, 'Don Timotéo of Hidalgo.'"

It was the blacksmith who asked the great question. "Then where did that cheese come from, and we haters of Hidalgo these ten long years?"

No voice said, "The stranger," but with one fluid movement every head in the patio turned toward the girl in the doorway. She also turned, her eyes wide with something that she realized to her own amazement was more apprehension than anger.

But the stranger was not in the room. When the angry, muttering men pushed through to the street, the stranger was not on the plaza. He was not anywhere in sight. A few of the more religious crossed themselves for fear that the Devil had walked in their midst. "Who was he?" one voice asked another. But Sarita, who was meekly listening to a lecture from Don Roméo on the propriety of dancing with strangers, did not have to ask. She had a strong suspicion that she had danced that night within the circling arm of Pepe Gonzalez.

---

2. Tío (tē′ ō): Spanish for uncle.

3. Hola (ō′la): Spanish exclamation meaning "Hey there."

RESPONDING TO THE SELECTION

Your Response

1. Based on this excerpt, would you like to read more of *Mexican Village*? Why or why not?

Recalling

2. What kind of welcome does Pepe Gonzalez receive at the party?
3. What two things does Pepe set out to do at the party?
4. What outrageous deed had men from Hidalgo attempted in San Juan Iglesias three months previously?
5. What causes an uproar among the guests?

Interpreting

6. What does Pepe's caution in arriving in the village suggest about his motives?
7. Describe Pepe's personality.
8. Compare and contrast the villagers' treatment of the stranger with the way they probably would have knowingly treated Pepe.
9. Give three reasons Pepe Gonzalez might have had for leaving the cheese.
10. How does Sarita know who the stranger is?

Applying

11. What do you think will happen now between Pepe and Sarita and between the two villages? Give your reasons for making those predictions.

ANALYZING LITERATURE

Appreciating Local Color

Local color includes any descriptions that highlight the special qualities of a place or of a person. By using local color, authors help you feel what a community is like. Readers familiar with the setting can recognize the truth of the local color presented. Readers unfamiliar with the community can get a real feeling of what it is like.

1. From this story list five details that give the feeling of a small Mexican village.
2. What events in this story depend on the details of local color?
3. List five details of local color about a city, town, or neighborhood with which you are familiar.

CRITICAL THINKING AND READING

Making Inferences About Characters

The customs and traditions of the place where a story occurs can be an important aspect of the setting. The rules of the community affect the people who live there. When an author does not directly state how the setting affects a character, you can make inferences about the relationship based on the facts the author does include.

1. What effect do the customs of the village have on Sarita?
2. Why is walking around the plaza so significant to both Sarita and Pepe?

THINKING AND WRITING

Describing a Place

Think of a city, town, or neighborhood that you find interesting. Write a letter to a friend recommending that he or she visit the place. Include details of local color that will help your friend understand the special flavor of the location. When you revise, include two more details of local color.

LEARNING OPTION

Art. Niggli establishes a mood of mystery in the story. For example, her descriptions of the Hidalgo man (a stranger) dressed in black and the "moonlit streets of San Juan Iglesias" give the story an aura of romantic secrecy. Choose a scene in the story and illustrate it. In your illustration try to convey a sense of mystery.

GUIDE FOR READING

By the Waters of Babylon

Time as an Aspect of Setting

The **setting** of a story is both the time and the place of the action. In certain stories the time in which the story takes place is an important aspect, suggesting what has happened or will happen in history. In "By the Waters of Babylon," the time period may at first be unclear, but when you recognize it, you will understand the significance of the story.

Focus

The title "By the Waters of Babylon" is an allusion to Psalm 137 in the Bible. According to the Bible, the Israelites grieved over their separation from their homeland, "Zion," and their captivity by the Babylonians. In Psalm 137 the Israelites remember Zion and weep for it.

> By the rivers of Babylon, there we sat down,
>   yea, we wept, when we remembered Zion.
> We hanged our harps upon the willows in the midst
>   thereof.
> For there they that carried us away captive required of us
>   a song; and they that wasted us required of us mirth,
>   saying,
> "Sing us one of the songs of Zion."
> How shall we sing the Lord's song in a strange land?

As you read "By the Waters of Babylon," consider how these lines from the psalm relate to the story.

Vocabulary

Knowing the following words will help you as you read "By the Waters of Babylon."

purified (pyoor′ ə fīd) v.: Cleansed; rid of impurities (p. 135)

boasted (bōst′ əd) v.: Showed too much pride; bragged (p. 135)

bowels (bou′ əlz) n.: Intestines; guts (p. 138)

slain (slān) adj.: Killed (p. 138)

Stephen Vincent Benét

(1898–1943) was born in Bethlehem, Pennsylvania. He is perhaps best known for his epic poem *John Brown's Body,* for which he won a Pulitzer Prize in 1929. Although he was also the author of novels and short stories, Benét thought of himself primarily as a poet. The story you are about to read began as a poem, which Benét then transformed into a short story called "The Place of the Gods." He changed the title for its publication in the collection *Thirteen O'Clock* in 1937.

By the Waters of Babylon

Stephen Vincent Benét

The north and the west and the south are good hunting ground, but it is forbidden to go east. It is forbidden to go to any of the Dead Places except to search for metal, and then he who touches the metal must be a priest or the son of a priest. Afterwards, both the man and the metal must be purified! These are the rules and the laws; they are well made. It is forbidden to cross the great river and look upon the place that was the Place of the Gods—this is most strictly forbidden. We do not even say its name though we know its name. It is there that spirits live, and demons—it is there that there are the ashes of the Great Burning. These things are forbidden—they have been forbidden since the beginning of time.

My father is a priest; I am the son of a priest. I have been in the Dead Places near us, with my father—at first, I was afraid. When my father went into the house to search for the metal, I stood by the door and my heart felt small and weak. It was a dead man's house, a spirit house. It did not have the smell of man, though there were old bones in a corner. But it is not fitting that a priest's son should show fear. I looked at the bones in the shadow and kept my voice still.

Then my father came out with the metal —a good, strong piece. He looked at me with both eyes but I had not run away. He gave me the metal to hold—I took it and did not die. So he knew that I was truly his son and would be a priest in my time. That was when I was very young—nevertheless, my brothers would not have done it, though they are good hunters. After that, they gave me the good piece of meat and the warm corner by the fire. My father watched over me—he was glad that I should be a priest. But when I boasted or wept without a reason, he punished me more strictly than my brothers. That was right.

After a time, I myself was allowed to go into the dead houses and search for metal. So I learned the ways of those houses—and if I saw bones, I was no longer afraid. The bones are light and old—sometimes they will fall into dust if you touch them. But that is a great sin.

I was taught the chants and the spells —I was taught how to stop the running of blood from a wound and many secrets. A priest must know many secrets—that was what my father said. If the hunters think we do all things by chants and spells, they may believe so—it does not hurt them. I was taught how to read in the old books and how

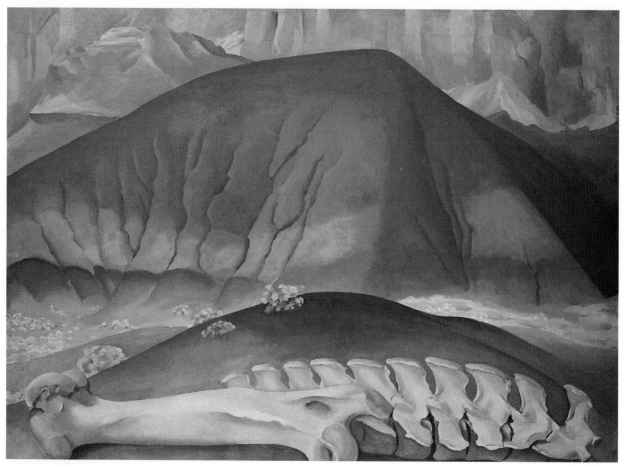

RED HILLS AND BONES, 1941
Georgia O'Keeffe
Philadelphia Museum of Art: The Alfred Stieglitz Collection

to make the old writings—that was hard and took a long time. My knowledge made me happy—it was like a fire in my heart. Most of all, I liked to hear of the Old Days and the stories of the gods. I asked myself many questions that I could not answer, but it was good to ask them. At night, I would lie awake and listen to the wind—it seemed to me that it was the voice of the gods as they flew through the air.

We are not ignorant like the Forest People—our women spin wool on the wheel, our priests wear a white robe. We do not eat grubs from the tree, we have not forgotten the old writings, although they are hard to understand. Nevertheless, my knowledge and my lack of knowledge burned in me—I wished to know more. When I was a man at last, I came to my father and said, "It is time for me to go on my journey. Give me your leave."

He looked at me for a long time, stroking his beard, then he said at last, "Yes. It is time." That night, in the house of the priesthood, I asked for and received purification. My body hurt but my spirit was a cool stone. It was my father himself who questioned me about my dreams.

He bade me look into the smoke of the fire and see—I saw and told what I saw. It was what I have always seen—a river, and, beyond it, a great Dead Place and in it the gods walking. I have always thought about that. His eyes were stern when I told him—he was no longer my father but a priest. He said, "This is a strong dream."

"It is mine," I said, while the smoke waved and my head felt light. They were singing the Star song in the outer chamber and it was like the buzzing of bees in my head.

He asked me how the gods were dressed and I told him how they were dressed. We know how they were dressed from the book, but I saw them as if they were before me. When I had finished, he threw the sticks three times and studied them as they fell.

"This is a very strong dream," he said. "It may eat you up."

"I am not afraid," I said and looked at him with both eyes. My voice sounded thin in my ears but that was because of the smoke.

He touched me on the breast and the forehead. He gave me the bow and the three arrows.

"Take them," he said. "It is forbidden to travel east. It is forbidden to cross the river. It is forbidden to go to the Place of the Gods. All these things are forbidden."

"All these things are forbidden," I said, but it was my voice that spoke and not my spirit. He looked at me again.

"My son," he said. "Once I had young dreams. If your dreams do not eat you up, you may be a great priest. If they eat you, you are still my son. Now go on your journey."

I went fasting, as is the law. My body hurt but not my heart. When the dawn came, I was out of sight of the village. I prayed and purified myself, waiting for a sign. The sign was an eagle. It flew east.

Sometimes signs are sent by bad spirits. I waited again on the flat rock, fasting, taking no food. I was very still—I could feel the sky above me and the earth beneath. I waited till the sun was beginning to sink. Then three deer passed in the valley, going east—they did not wind me or see me. There was a white fawn with them—a very great sign.

I followed them, at a distance, waiting for what would happen. My heart was troubled about going east, yet I knew that I must go. My head hummed with my fasting—I did not even see the panther spring upon the white fawn. But, before I knew it, the bow was in my hand. I shouted and the panther lifted his head from the fawn. It is not easy to kill a panther with one arrow but the arrow went through his eye and into his brain. He died as he tried to spring—he rolled over, tearing at the ground. Then I knew I was meant to go east—I knew that was my journey. When the night came, I made my fire and roasted meat.

It is eight suns' journey to the east and a man passes by many Dead Places. The Forest People are afraid of them but I am not. Once I made my fire on the edge of a Dead Place at night and, next morning, in the dead house, I found a good knife, little rusted. That was small to what came afterward, but it made my heart feel big. Always when I looked for game, it was in front of my arrow, and twice I passed hunting parties of the Forest People without their knowing. So I knew my magic was strong and my journey clean, in spite of the law.

Toward the setting of the eighth sun, I came to the banks of the great river. It was half-a-day's journey after I had left the god-road—we do not use the god-roads now for they are falling apart into great blocks of stone, and the forest is safer going. A long way off, I had seen the water through trees but the trees were thick. At last, I came out upon an open place at the top of a cliff. There was the great river below, like a giant in the sun. It is very long, very wide. It could eat all the streams we know and still be thirsty. Its name is Ou-dis-sun, the Sacred, the Long. No man of my tribe had seen it, not even my father, the priest. It was magic and I prayed.

Then I raised my eyes and looked south. It was there, the Place of the Gods.

How can I tell what it was like—you do not know. It was there, in the red light, and they were too big to be houses. It was there with the red light upon it, mighty and ruined. I knew that in another moment the gods would see me. I covered my eyes with my hands and crept back into the forest.

Surely, that was enough to do, and live. Surely it was enough to spend the night upon the cliff. The Forest People themselves do not come near. Yet, all through the night, I knew that I should have to cross the river and walk in the places of the gods, although the gods ate me up. My magic did not help me at all and yet there was a fire in my bowels, a fire in my mind. When the sun rose, I thought, "My journey has been clean. Now I will go home from my journey." But, even as I thought so, I knew I could not. If I went to the place of the gods, I would surely die, but, if I did not go, I could never be at peace with my spirit again. It is better to lose one's life than one's spirit, if one is a priest and the son of a priest.

Nevertheless, as I made the raft, the tears ran out of my eyes. The Forest People could have killed me without fight, if they had come upon me then, but they did not

come. When the raft was made, I said the sayings for the dead and painted myself for death. My heart was cold as a frog and my knees like water, but the burning in my mind would not let me have peace. As I pushed the raft from the shore, I began my death song—I had the right. It was a fine song.

> "I am John, son of John," I sang.
> "My people are the Hill People.
> They are the men.
> I go into the Dead Places but I am not
> slain.
> I take the metal from the Dead Places
> but I am not blasted.
> I travel upon the god-roads and am
> not afraid. E-yah! I have killed the
> panther, I have killed the fawn!
> E-yah! I have come to the great river.
> No man has come there before.
> It is forbidden to go east, but I have
> gone, forbidden to go on the great
> river, but I am there.
> Open your hearts, you spirits, and
> hear my song.
> Now I go to the Place of the Gods, I
> shall not return.
> My body is painted for death and my
> limbs weak, but my heart is big as
> I go to the Place of the Gods!"

All the same, when I came to the Place of the Gods, I was afraid, afraid. The current of the great river is very strong—it gripped my raft with its hands. That was magic, for the river itself is wide and calm. I could feel evil spirits about me, in the bright morning; I could feel their breath on my neck as I was swept down the stream. Never have I been so much alone—I tried to think of my knowledge, but it was a squirrel's heap of winter nuts. There was no strength in my knowledge any more, and I felt small and naked as a new-hatched bird—alone upon the great river, the servant of the gods.

Yet, after a while, my eyes were opened and I saw. I saw both banks of the river—I saw that once there had been god-roads across it, though now they were broken and fallen like broken vines. Very great they were, and wonderful and broken—broken in the time of the Great Burning when the fire fell out of the sky. And always the current took me nearer to the Place of the Gods, and the huge ruins rose before my eyes.

I do not know the customs of rivers—we are the People of the Hills. I tried to guide my raft with the pole but it spun around. I thought the river meant to take me past the Place of the Gods and out into the Bitter Water of the legends. I grew angry then—my heart felt strong. I said aloud, "I am a priest and the son of a priest!" The gods heard me—they showed me how to paddle with the pole on one side of the raft. The current changed itself—I drew near to the Place of the Gods.

When I was very near, my raft struck and turned over. I can swim in our lakes—I swam to the shore. There was a great spike of rusted metal sticking out into the river—I hauled myself up upon it and sat there, panting. I had saved my bow and two arrows and the knife I found in the Dead Place but that was all. My raft went whirling downstream toward the Bitter Water. I looked after it, and thought if it had trod me under, at least I would be safely dead. Nevertheless, when I had dried my bow-string and re-strung it, I walked forward to the Place of the Gods.

It felt like ground underfoot; it did not burn me. It is not true what some of the tales say, that the ground there burns forever, for I have been there. Here and there were the marks and stains of the Great Burning, on the ruins, that is true. But they were old marks and old stains. It is not true either, what some of our priests say, that it is an island covered with fogs and enchantments. It is not. It is a great Dead Place—greater than any Dead Place we know. Everywhere in it there are god-roads, though most are cracked and broken. Everywhere there are the ruins of the high towers of the gods.

How shall I tell what I saw? I went carefully, my strung bow in my hand, my skin ready for danger. There should have been the wailings of spirits and the shrieks of demons, but there were not. It was very silent and sunny where I had landed—the wind and the rain and the birds that drop seeds had done their work—the grass grew in the cracks of the broken stone. It is a fair island—no wonder the gods built there. If I had come there, a god, I also would have built.

How shall I tell what I saw? The towers are not all broken—here and there one still stands, like a great tree in a forest, and the birds nest high. But the towers themselves look blind, for the gods are gone. I saw a fish-hawk, catching fish in the river. I saw a little dance of white butterflies over a great heap of broken stones and columns. I went there and looked about me—there was a carved stone with cut-letters, broken in half. I can read letters but I could not understand these. They said UBTREAS. There was also the shattered image of a man or a god. It had been made of white stone and he wore his hair tied back like a woman's. His name was ASHING, as I read on the cracked half of a stone. I thought it wise to pray to ASHING, though I do not know that god.

How shall I tell what I saw? There was no smell of man left, on stone or metal. Nor were there many trees in that wilderness of stone. There are many pigeons, nesting and dropping in the towers—the gods must have loved them, or, perhaps, they used them for sacrifices. There are wild cats that roam the god-roads, green-eyed, unafraid of man. At night they wail like demons but they are not demons. The wild dogs are more dangerous, for they hunt in a pack, but them I did not meet till later. Everywhere there are the carved stones carved with magical numbers or words.

I went North—I did not try to hide myself. When a god or a demon saw me, then I would die, but meanwhile I was no longer afraid. My hunger for knowledge burned in me—there was so much that I could not understand. After awhile, I knew that my belly was hungry. I could have hunted for my meat, but I did not hunt. It is known that the gods did not hunt as we do—they got their food from enchanted boxes and jars. Sometimes these are still found in the Dead Places—once, when I was a child and foolish, I opened such a jar and tasted it and found the food sweet. But my father found out and punished me for it strictly, for, often, that food is death. Now, though, I had long gone past what was forbidden, and I entered the likeliest towers, looking for the food of the gods.

I found it at last in the ruins of a great temple in the mid-city. A mighty temple it must have been, for the roof was painted like the sky at night with its stars—that much I could see, though the colors were faint and dim. It went down into great caves and tunnels—perhaps they kept their slaves there. But when I started to climb down, I heard the squeaking of rats, so I did not go—rats are unclean, and there must have been many tribes of them, from the squeaking. But near there, I found food, in the heart of a ruin, behind a door that still opened. I ate only the fruits from the jars—they had a very sweet taste. There was drink, too, in bottles of glass—the drink of the gods was strong and made my head swim. After I had eaten and drunk, I slept on the top of a stone, my bow at my side.

When I woke, the sun was low. Looking down from where I lay, I saw a dog sitting on his haunches. His tongue was hanging out of his mouth; he looked as if he were laughing. He was a big dog, with a gray-brown coat, as big as a wolf. I sprang up and shouted at him but he did not move—he just sat there as if he were laughing. I did not like that. When I reached for a stone to throw, he moved swiftly out of the way of the stone. He was not afraid of me; he looked at me as if I were meat. No doubt I could have killed him with an arrow, but I did not know if there were others. Moreover, night was falling.

I looked about me—not far away there was a great, broken god-road, leading North. The towers were high enough, but not so high, and while many of the dead-houses were wrecked, there were some that stood. I went toward this god-road, keeping to the heights of the ruins, while the dog followed. When I had reached the god-road, I saw that there were others behind him. If I had slept later, they would have come upon me asleep and torn out my throat. As it was, they were sure enough of me; they did not hurry. When I went into the dead-house, they kept watch at the entrance—doubtless they thought they would have a fine hunt. But a dog cannot open a door and I knew, from the books, that the gods did not like to live on the ground but on high.

I had just found a door I could open when the dogs decided to rush. Ha! They were surprised when I shut the door in their faces—it was a good door, of strong metal. I could hear their foolish baying beyond it, but I did not stop to answer them. I was in darkness—I found stairs and climbed. There were many stairs, turning around till my head was dizzy. At the top was another door—I found the knob and opened it. I was in a long small chamber—on one side of it was a bronze door that could not be opened, for it had no handle. Perhaps there was a magic word to open it, but I did not have the word. I turned to the door in the opposite side of the wall. The lock of it was broken and I opened it and went in.

Within, there was a place of great riches. The god who lived there must have been a powerful god. The first room was a small anteroom—I waited there for some time, telling the spirits of the place that I came in peace and not as a robber. When it seemed to me that they had had time to hear me, I went on. Ah, what riches! Few, even, of the windows had been broken—it was all as it had been. The great windows that looked over the city had not been broken at all though they were dusty and streaked with many years. There were coverings on the floors, the colors not greatly faded, and the chairs were soft and deep. There were pictures upon the walls, very strange, very wonderful—I remember one of a bunch of flowers in a jar—if you came close to it, you could see nothing but bits of color, but if you stood away from it, the flowers might have been picked yesterday. It made my heart feel strange to look at this picture—and to look at the figure of a bird, in some hard clay, on a table and see it so like our birds. Everywhere there were books and writings, many in tongues that I could not read. The god who lived there must have been a wise god and full of knowledge. I felt I had right there, as I sought knowledge also.

Nevertheless, it was strange. There was a washing-place but no water—perhaps the gods washed in air. There was a cooking-place but no wood, and though there was a machine to cook food, there was no place to put fire in it. Nor were there candles or lamps—there were things that looked like lamps but they had neither oil nor wick. All these things were magic, but I touched them and lived—the magic had gone out of them. Let me tell one thing to show. In the washing-place, a thing said "Hot" but it was not hot to the touch—another thing said "Cold" but it was not cold. This must have been a strong magic but the magic was gone. I do not understand—they had ways—I wish that I knew.

It was close and dry and dusty in their house of the gods. I have said the magic was gone but that is not true—it had gone from the magic things but it had not gone from the place. I felt the spirits about me, weighing upon me. Nor had I ever slept in a Dead Place before—and yet, tonight, I must sleep there. When I thought of it, my tongue felt dry in my throat, in spite of my wish for knowledge. Almost I would have gone down again and faced the dogs, but I did not.

I had not gone through all the rooms when the darkness fell. When it fell, I went back to the big room looking over the city and made fire. There was a place to make fire and a box with wood in it, though I do not think they cooked there. I wrapped myself in a floor-covering and slept in front of the fire—I was very tired.

Now I tell what is very strong magic. I woke in the midst of the night. When I woke, the fire had gone out and I was cold. It seemed to me that all around me there were whisperings and voices. I closed my eyes to shut them out. Some will say that I slept again, but I do not think that I slept. I could feel the spirits drawing my spirit out of my body as a fish is drawn on a line.

Why should I lie about it? I am a priest and the son of a priest. If there are spirits, as they say, in the small Dead Places near us, what spirits must there not be in that great Place of the Gods? And would not they wish to speak? After such long years? I know that I felt myself drawn as a fish is drawn on a line. I had stepped out of my body—I could see my body asleep in front of the cold fire, but it was not I. I was drawn to look out upon the city of the gods.

It should have been dark, for it was night, but it was not dark. Everywhere there were lights—lines of light—circles and blurs of light—ten thousand torches would not have been the same. The sky itself was alight—you could barely see the stars for the glow in the sky. I thought to myself "This is strong magic" and trembled. There was a roaring in my ears like the rushing of rivers. Then my eyes grew used to the light and my ears to the sound. I knew that I was seeing the city as it had been when the gods were alive.

That was a sight indeed—yes, that was a sight: I could not have seen it in the body—my body would have died. Everywhere went the gods, on foot and in chariots—there were gods beyond number and counting and their chariots blocked the streets. They had turned night to day for their pleasure—they did not sleep with the sun. The noise of their coming and going was the noise of many waters. It was magic what they could do—it was magic what they did.

I looked out of another window—the great vines of their bridges were mended and the god-roads went East and West. Restless, restless, were the gods and always in motion! They burrowed tunnels under rivers—they flew in the air. With unbelievable tools they did giant works—no part of

the earth was safe from them, for, if they wished for a thing, they summoned it from the other side of the world. And always, as they labored and rested, as they feasted and made love, there was a drum in their ears—the pulse of the giant city, beating and beating like a man's heart.

Were they happy? What is happiness to the gods? They were great, they were mighty, they were wonderful and terrible. As I looked upon them and their magic, I felt like a child—but a little more, it seemed to me, and they would pull down the moon from the sky. I saw them with wisdom beyond wisdom and knowledge beyond knowledge. And yet not all they did was well done—even I could see that—and yet their wisdom could not but grow until all was peace.

Then I saw their fate come upon them and that was terrible past speech. It came upon them as they walked the streets of their city. I have been in the fights with the Forest People—I have seen men die. But this was not like that. When gods war with gods, they use weapons we do not know. It was fire falling out of the sky and a mist that poisoned. It was the time of the Great Burning and the Destruction. They ran about like ants in the streets of their city—poor gods, poor gods! Then the towers began to fall. A few escaped—yes, a few. The legends tell it. But, even after the city had become a Dead Place, for many years the poison was still in the ground. I saw it happen, I saw the last of them die. It was darkness over the broken city, and I wept.

All this, I saw. I saw it as I have told it, though not in the body. When I woke in the morning, I was hungry, but I did not think first of my hunger, for my heart was perplexed and confused. I knew the reason for the Dead Places but I did not see why it had

CITY NIGHT, 1926
Georgia O'Keeffe
The Minneapolis Institute of Arts

happened. It seemed to me it should not have happened, with all the magic they had. I went through the house looking for an answer. There was so much in the house I could not understand—and yet I am a priest and the son of a priest. It was like being on one side of the great river, at night, with no light to show the way.

Then I saw the dead god. He was sitting in his chair, by the window, in a room I had not entered before and, for the first moment, I thought that he was alive. Then I saw the skin on the back of his hand—it was like dry leather. The room was shut, hot and dry—no doubt that had kept him as he was. At first I was afraid to approach him—then the fear left me. He was sitting looking out over the city—he was dressed in the clothes of the gods. His age was neither young nor old—I could not tell his age. But there was wisdom in his face and great sadness. You could see that he would have not run away. He had sat at his window, watching his city die—then he himself had died. But it is better to lose one's life than one's spirit—and you could see from the face that his spirit had not been lost. I knew, that, if I touched him, he would fall into dust—and yet, there was something unconquered in the face.

That is all of my story, for then I knew he was a man—I knew then that they had been men, neither gods nor demons. It is a great knowledge, hard to tell and believe. They were men—they went a dark road, but they were men. I had no fear after that—I had no fear going home, though twice I fought off the dogs and once I was hunted for two days by the Forest People. When I saw my father again, I prayed and was purified. He touched my lips and my breast, he said, "You went away a boy. You come back a man and a priest." I said, "Father, they were men! I have been in the Place of the Gods and seen it! Now slay me, if it is the law—but still I know they were men."

He looked at me out of both eyes. He said, "The law is not always the same shape—you have done what you have done. I could not have done it my time, but you come after me. Tell!"

I told and he listened. After that, I wished to tell all the people but he showed me otherwise. He said, "Truth is a hard deer to hunt. If you eat too much truth at once, you may die of the truth. It was not idly that our fathers forbade the Dead Places." He was right—it is better the truth should come little by little. I have learned that, being a priest. Perhaps, in the old days, they ate knowledge too fast.

Nevertheless, we make a beginning. It is not for the metal alone we go to the Dead Places now—there are the books and the writings. They are hard to learn. And the magic tools are broken—but we can look at them and wonder. At least, we make a beginning. And, when I am chief priest we shall go beyond the great river. We shall go to the Place of the Gods—the place new-york—not one man but a company. We shall look for the images of the gods and find the god ASHING and the others—the gods Li-coln and Biltmore[1] and Moses.[2] But they were men who built the city, not gods or demons. They were men. I remember the dead man's face. They were men who were here before us. We must build again.

---

1. Biltmore: A hotel in New York City.
2. Moses: Robert Moses, former New York City municipal official.

Your Response

1. How do you respond to the line from the story that says, "But it is better to lose one's life than one's spirit . . ."?
2. Father says, "Perhaps, in the old days, they ate knowledge too fast." In your opinion does our society "eat knowledge too fast"? Explain your answer.

Recalling

3. In what way is John different from his brothers? What are his responsibilities?
4. Why does John set out on his journey? Why is John's journey particularly dangerous?
5. Describe three things John sees in the Place of the Gods.
6. What significant piece of information about the "gods" does John learn on his journey?

Interpreting

7. What is the significance of the journey to John and his people?
8. Explain why John's father wants to keep secret what John has learned about the Place of the Gods.
9. Explain the title of this story. Why is it appropriate that this story would appear in a collection called *Thirteen O'Clock*?

Applying

10. How do you think John's people can best avoid repeating the mistakes that led to the destruction of civilization in the past?

ANALYZING LITERATURE

Recognizing Time in Setting

Setting has two components: time and place. **Time** can be particularly important in some stories, so important that it can take on the concrete reality of a place. Thus, we often refer to the future or the past as *where,* rather than *when,* the story takes place.

1. When does this story take place?
2. Find at least three facts, incidents, or details that reveal the time period.
3. UBTREAS refers to the Subtreasury Building. To what do the following refer? a. ASHING; b. Ou-dis-sun.
4. What is meant by the Dead Places? Compare and contrast the world of John's people with the world of those who lived in the Place of the Gods.

THINKING AND WRITING

Writing to Contrast Settings

Imagine that you somehow survived the war that destroyed the Place of the Gods and that the place was where you live. Write a message to leave for future generations telling what the place was like immediately before and immediately after the war. Your purpose is to teach future people about the past and to help them avoid the same fate. When you revise your message, add at least two more visual details so that people who have never seen your city or anything like it will be able to picture it.

LEARNING OPTION

Writing. Imagine that John's son is now the head priest and is leading his people into New York City. Prepare a list of instructions for his people. List the things they should bring with them as well as what they should be prepared to see. Make sure that your list includes specific and direct instructions. You may wish to consult a travel book about New York City.

GUIDE FOR READING

Through the Tunnel

Atmosphere

Atmosphere is the mood or the overall feeling in a story. A writer may establish atmosphere by describing specific details of the setting in order to create a desired effect. For example, describing a dark night, the noise of the wind, and the appearance of light and shadows will create an atmosphere of suspense and prepare you to be frightened by the action. Dialogue and action may also contribute to the atmosphere.

Focus

This story is about a boy who works hard to achieve a goal. What goal would you like to attain? Using the format you see below, state your goal in a box. On the lines pointing to the box, list the ways in which you intend to reach your goal (use more than three lines if necessary). Then, as you read the story, evaluate what Jerry does to achieve his objective.

1. ———————————
2. ——————————— → GOAL
3. ———————————

Vocabulary

Knowing the following words will help you as you read "Through the Tunnel."

contrition (kən trish′ ən) *n.*: A feeling of remorse for having done something wrong (p. 147)
promontories (präm′ ən tôr′ ēz) *n.*: High places extending out over a body of water (p. 147)
luminous (lōō′ mə nəs) *adj.*: Giving off light (p. 147)
supplication (sup′ lə kā′ shən) *n.*: The act of asking humbly and earnestly (p. 148)
frond (fränd) *n.*: A leaflike shoot of seaweed (p. 150)
convulsive (kən vul′ siv) *adj.*: Marked by an involuntary muscular contraction (p. 152)
gout (gout) *n.*: A spurt, splash, a glob (p. 153)

Doris Lessing

(1919–   ) was born in Persia (now Iran) of British parents and raised in a remote area of southern Africa. She left school at fifteen and had a variety of jobs, including children's nurse, telephone operator, and typist. She moved to England in 1949 and published her first novel, *The Grass Is Singing,* the following year. Most of Lessing's work centers on social and political questions. "Through the Tunnel," however, focuses on the inner life of a single child.

Through the Tunnel

Doris Lessing

Going to the shore on the first morning of the vacation, the young English boy stopped at a turning of the path and looked down at a wild and rocky bay, and then over to the crowded beach he knew so well from other years. His mother walked on in front of him, carrying a bright striped bag in one hand. Her other arm, swinging loose, was very white in the sun. The boy watched that white, naked arm, and turned his eyes, which had a frown behind them, toward the bay and back again to his mother. When she felt he was not with her, she swung around. "Oh, there you are, Jerry!" she said. She looked impatient, then smiled. "Why, darling, would you rather not come with me? Would you rather—" She frowned, conscientiously worrying over what amusements he might secretly be longing for, which she had been too busy or too careless to imagine. He was very familiar with that anxious, apologetic smile. Contrition sent him running after her. And yet, as he ran, he looked back over his shoulder at the wild bay; and all morning, as he played on the safe beach, he was thinking of it.

Next morning, when it was time for the routine of swimming and sunbathing, his mother said, "Are you tired of the usual beach, Jerry? Would you like to go somewhere else?"

"Oh, no!" he said quickly, smiling at her out of that unfailing impulse of contrition —a sort of chivalry. Yet, walking down the path with her, he blurted out, "I'd like to go and have a look at those rocks down there."

She gave the idea her attention. It was a wild-looking place, and there was no one there; but she said, "Of course, Jerry. When you've had enough, come to the big beach. Or just go straight back to the villa, if you like." She walked away, that bare arm, now slightly reddened from yesterday's sun, swinging. And he almost ran after her again, feeling it unbearable that she should go by herself, but he did not.

She was thinking, Of course he's old enough to be safe without me. Have I been keeping him too close? He mustn't feel he ought to be with me. I must be careful.

He was an only child, eleven years old. She was a widow. She was determined to be neither possessive nor lacking in devotion. She went worrying off to her beach.

As for Jerry, once he saw that his mother had gained her beach, he began the steep descent to the bay. From where he was, high up among red-brown rocks, it was a scoop of moving bluish green fringed with white. As he went lower, he saw that it spread among small promontories and inlets of rough, sharp rock, and the crisping, lapping surface showed stains of purple and darker blue. Finally, as he ran sliding and scraping down the last few yards, he saw an edge of white surf and the shallow, luminous movement of water over white sand, and, beyond that, a solid, heavy blue.

THE BEACH TREAT (detail)
Suzanne Nagler Photograph © Stephen Tucker
Collection of Mr. and Mrs. X. Daniel Kafcas

He ran straight into the water and began swimming. He was a good swimmer. He went out fast over the gleaming sand, over a middle region where rocks lay like discolored monsters under the surface, and then he was in the real sea—a warm sea where irregular cold currents from the deep water shocked his limbs.

When he was so far out that he could look back not only on the little bay but past the promontory that was between it and the big beach, he floated on the buoyant surface and looked for his mother. There she was, a speck of yellow under an umbrella that looked like a slice of orange peel. He swam back to shore, relieved at being sure she was there, but all at once very lonely.

On the edge of a small cape that marked the side of the bay away from the promontory was a loose scatter of rocks. Above them, some boys were stripping off their clothes. They came running, naked, down to the rocks. The English boy swam toward them, but kept his distance at a stone's throw. They were of that coast; all of them were burned smooth dark brown and speaking a language he did not understand. To be with them, of them, was a craving that filled his whole body. He swam a little closer; they turned and watched him with narrowed, alert dark eyes. Then one smiled and waved. It was enough. In a minute, he had swum in and was on the rocks beside them, smiling with a desperate, nervous supplication. They shouted cheerful greetings at him; and then, as he preserved his nervous, uncomprehending smile, they understood that he was a foreigner strayed from his own beach, and they proceeded to forget him. But he was happy. He was with them.

They began diving again and again from a high point into a well of blue sea between rough, pointed rocks. After they had dived and come up, they swam around, hauled themselves up, and waited their turn to dive again. They were big boys—men, to Jerry.

He dived, and they watched him; and when he swam around to take his place, they made way for him. He felt he was accepted and he dived again, carefully, proud of himself.

Soon the biggest of the boys poised himself, shot down into the water, and did not come up. The others stood about, watching. Jerry, after waiting for the sleek brown head to appear, let out a yell of warning; they looked at him idly and turned their eyes back toward the water. After a long time, the boy came up on the other side of a big dark rock, letting the air out of his lungs in a sputtering gasp and a shout of triumph. Immediately the rest of them dived in. One moment, the morning seemed full of chattering boys; the next, the air and the surface of the water were empty. But through the heavy blue, dark shapes could be seen moving and groping.

Jerry dived, shot past the school of underwater swimmers, saw a black wall of rock looming at him, touched it, and bobbed up at once to the surface, where the wall was a low barrier he could see across. There was no one visible; under him, in the water, the dim shapes of the swimmers had disappeared. Then one, and then another of the boys came up on the far side of the barrier of rock, and he understood that they had swum through some gap or hole in it. He plunged down again. He could see nothing through the stinging salt water but the blank rock. When he came up the boys were all on the diving rock, preparing to attempt the feat again. And now, in a panic of failure, he yelled up, in English, "Look at me! Look!" and he began splashing and kicking in the water like a foolish dog.

They looked down gravely, frowning. He knew the frown. At moments of failure, when he clowned to claim his mother's attention, it was with just this grave, embarrassed inspection that she rewarded him.

Through his hot shame, feeling the pleading grin on his face like a scar that he could never remove, he looked up at the group of big brown boys on the rock and shouted, *"Bonjour! Merci! Au revoir! Monsieur, monsieur!"*[1] while he hooked his fingers round his ears and waggled them.

Water surged into his mouth; he choked, sank, came up. The rock, lately weighted with boys, seemed to rear up out of the water as their weight was removed. They were flying down past him, now, into the water; the air was full of falling bodies. Then the rock was empty in the hot sunlight. He counted one, two, three. . . .

At fifty, he was terrified. They must all be drowning beneath him, in the watery caves of the rock! At a hundred, he stared around him at the empty hillside, wondering if he should yell for help. He counted faster, faster, to hurry them up, to bring them to the surface quickly, to drown them quickly—anything rather than the terror of counting on and on into the blue emptiness of the morning. And then, at a hundred and sixty, the water beyond the rock was full of boys blowing like brown whales. They swam back to the shore without a look at him.

He climbed back to the diving rock and sat down, feeling the hot roughness of it under his thighs. The boys were gathering up their bits of clothing and running off along the shore to another promontory. They were leaving to get away from him. He cried openly, fists in his eyes. There was no one to see him, and he cried himself out.

It seemed to him that a long time had passed, and he swam out to where he could see his mother. Yes, she was still there, a yellow spot under an orange umbrella. He swam back to the big rock, climbed up, and

---

1. Bonjour! . . . monsieur (bōn zhōōr′ . . . mə syö′): Babbling of commonly known French words: "Hello! Thank you! Goodbye! Sir, sir!"

dived into the blue pool among the fanged and angry boulders. Down he went, until he touched the wall of rock again. But the salt was so painful in his eyes that he could not see.

He came to the surface, swam to shore and went back to the villa to wait for his mother. Soon she walked slowly up the path, swinging her striped bag, the flushed, naked arm dangling beside her. "I want some swimming goggles," he panted, defiant and beseeching.

She gave him a patient, inquisitive look as she said casually, "Well, of course, darling."

But now, now, now! He must have them this minute, and no other time. He nagged and pestered until she went with him to a shop. As soon as she had bought the goggles, he grabbed them from her hand as if she were going to claim them for herself, and was off, running down the steep path to the bay.

Jerry swam out to the big barrier rock, adjusted the goggles, and dived. The impact of the water broke the rubber-enclosed vacuum, and the goggles came loose. He understood that he must swim down to the base of the rock from the surface of the water. He fixed the goggles tight and firm, filled his lungs, and floated, face down, on the water. Now he could see. It was as if he had eyes of a different kind—fish eyes that showed everything clear and delicate and wavering in the bright water.

Under him, six or seven feet down, was a floor of perfectly clean, shining white sand, rippled firm and hard by the tides. Two grayish shapes steered there, like long, rounded pieces of wood or slate. They were fish. He saw them nose toward each other, poise motionless, make a dart forward, swerve off, and come around again. It was like a water dance. A few inches above them the water sparkled as if sequins were drop-ping through it. Fish again—myriads of minute fish, the length of his fingernail, were drifting through the water, and in a moment he could feel the innumerable tiny touches of them against his limbs. It was like swimming in flaked silver. The great rock the big boys had swum through rose sheer out of the white sand—black, tufted lightly with greenish weed. He could see no gap in it. He swam down to its base.

Again and again he rose, took a big chestful of air, and went down. Again and again he groped over the surface of the rock, feeling it, almost hugging it in the desperate need to find the entrance. And then, once, while he was clinging to the black wall, his knees came up and he shot his feet out forward and they met no obstacle. He had found the hole.

He gained the surface, clambered about the stones that littered the barrier rock until he found a big one, and, with this in his arms, let himself down over the side of the rock. He dropped, with the weight, straight to the sandy floor. Clinging tight to the anchor of stone, he lay on his side and looked in under the dark shelf at the place where his feet had gone. He could see the hole. It was an irregular, dark gap; but he could not see deep into it. He let go of his anchor, clung with his hands to the edges of the hole, and tried to push himself in.

He got his head in, found his shoulders jammed, moved them in sidewise, and was inside as far as his waist. He could see nothing ahead. Something soft and clammy touched his mouth; he saw a dark frond moving against the grayish rock, and panic filled him. He thought of octopuses, of clinging weed. He pushed himself out backward and caught a glimpse, as he retreated, of a harmless tentacle of seaweed drifting in the mouth of the tunnel. But it was enough. He reached the sunlight, swam to shore, and lay on the diving rock. He looked down into the blue well of water. He knew he must find his way through that cave, or hole, or tunnel, and out the other side.

First, he thought, he must learn to control his breathing. He let himself down into the water with another big stone in his arms, so that he could lie effortlessly on the bottom of the sea. He counted. One, two, three. He counted steadily. He could hear the movement of blood in his chest. Fifty-one, fifty-two. . . . His chest was hurting. He let go of the rock and went up into the air. He saw that the sun was low. He rushed to the villa and found his mother at her supper. She said only "Did you enjoy yourself?" and he said "Yes."

All night the boy dreamed of the water-filled cave in the rock, and as soon as breakfast was over he went to the bay.

That night, his nose bled badly. For hours he had been underwater, learning to hold his breath, and now he felt weak and dizzy. His mother said, "I shouldn't overdo things, darling, if I were you."

That day and the next, Jerry exercised his lungs as if everything, the whole of his life, all that he would become, depended upon it. Again his nose bled at night, and his mother insisted on his coming with her the next day. It was a torment to him to waste a day of his careful self-training, but he stayed with her on that other beach, which now seemed a place for small children, a place where his mother might lie safe in the sun. It was not his beach.

He did not ask for permission, on the following day, to go to his beach. He went, before his mother could consider the complicated rights and wrongs of the matter. A day's rest, he discovered, had improved his count by ten. The big boys had made the passage while he counted a hundred and sixty. He had been counting fast, in his fright. Probably now, if he tried, he could get through that long tunnel, but he was not

going to try yet. A curious, most unchildlike persistence, a controlled impatience, made him wait. In the meantime, he lay underwater on the white sand, littered now by stones he had brought down from the upper air, and studied the entrance to the tunnel. He knew every jut and corner of it, as far as it was possible to see. It was as if he already felt its sharpness about his shoulders.

He sat by the clock in the villa, when his mother was not near, and checked his time. He was incredulous and then proud to find he could hold his breath without strain for two minutes. The words "two minutes," authorized by the clock, brought close the adventure that was so necessary to him.

In another four days, his mother said casually one morning, they must go home. On the day before they left, he would do it. He would do it if it killed him, he said defiantly to himself. But two days before they were to leave—a day of triumph when he increased his count by fifteen—his nose bled so badly that he turned dizzy and had to lie limply over the big rock like a bit of seaweed, watching the thick red blood flow onto the rock and trickle slowly down to the sea. He was frightened. Supposing he turned dizzy in the tunnel? Supposing he died there, trapped? Supposing—his head went around, in the hot sun, and he almost gave up. He thought he would return to the house and lie down, and next summer, perhaps, when he had another year's growth in him—*then* he would go through the hole.

But even after he had made the decision, or thought he had, he found himself sitting up on the rock and looking down into the water; and he knew that now, this moment, when his nose had only just stopped bleeding, when his head was still sore and throbbing—this was the moment when he would try. If he did not do it now, he never would. He was trembling with fear that he would not go; and he was trembling with horror at that long, long tunnel under the rock, under the sea. Even in the open sunlight, the barrier rock seemed very wide and very heavy; tons of rock pressed down on where he would go. If he died there, he would lie until one day—perhaps not before next year—those big boys would swim into it and find it blocked.

He put on his goggles, fitted them tight, tested the vacuum. His hands were shaking. Then he chose the biggest stone he could carry and slipped over the edge of the rock until half of him was in the cool, enclosing water and half in the hot sun. He looked up once at the empty sky, filled his lungs once, twice, and then sank fast to the bottom with the stone. He let it go and began to count. He took the edges of the hole in his hands and drew himself into it, wriggling his shoulders in sidewise as he remembered he must, kicking himself along with his feet.

Soon he was clear inside. He was in a small rockbound hole filled with yellowish-gray water. The water was pushing him up against the roof. The roof was sharp and pained his back. He pulled himself along with his hands—fast, fast—and used his legs as levers. His head knocked against something; a sharp pain dizzied him. Fifty, fifty-one, fifty-two. . . . He was without light, and the water seemed to press upon him with the weight of rock. Seventy-one, seventy-two. . . . There was no strain on his lungs. He felt like an inflated balloon, his lungs were so light and easy, but his head was pulsing.

He was being continually pressed against the sharp roof, which felt slimy as well as sharp. Again he thought of octopuses, and wondered if the tunnel might be filled with weed that could tangle him. He gave himself a panicky, convulsive kick forward, ducked his head, and swam. His feet and hands moved freely, as if in open water. The hole must have widened out. He thought he

must be swimming fast, and he was frightened of banging his head if the tunnel narrowed.

A hundred, a hundred and one . . . The water paled. Victory filled him. His lungs were beginning to hurt. A few more strokes and he would be out. He was counting wildly; he said a hundred and fifteen, and then, a long time later, a hundred and fifteen again. The water was a clear jewel-green all around him. Then he saw, above his head, a crack running up through the rock. Sunlight was falling through it, showing the clean, dark rock of the tunnel, a single mussel shell, and darkness ahead.

He was at the end of what he could do. He looked up at the crack as if it were filled with air and not water, as if he could put his mouth to it to draw in air. A hundred and fifteen, he heard himself say inside his head—but he had said that long ago. He must go on into the blackness ahead, or he would drown. His head was swelling, his lungs cracking. A hundred and fifteen, a hundred and fifteen pounded through his head, and he feebly clutched at rocks in the dark, pulling himself forward, leaving the brief space of sunlit water behind. He felt he was dying. He was no longer quite conscious. He struggled on in the darkness between lapses into unconsciousness. An immense, swelling pain filled his head, and then the darkness cracked with an explosion of green light. His hands, groping forward, met nothing; and his feet, kicking back, propelled him out into the open sea.

He drifted to the surface, his face turned up to the air. He was gasping like a fish. He felt he would sink now and drown; he could not swim the few feet back to the rock. Then he was clutching it and pulling himself up on to it. He lay face down, gasping. He could see nothing but a red-veined, clotted dark. His eyes must have burst, he thought; they were full of blood. He tore off his goggles and

a gout of blood went into the sea. His nose was bleeding, and the blood had filled the goggles.

He scooped up handfuls of water from the cool, salty sea, to splash on his face, and did not know whether it was blood or salt water he tasted. After a time, his heart quieted, his eyes cleared, and he sat up. He could see the local boys diving and playing half a mile away. He did not want them. He wanted nothing but to get back home and lie down.

In a short while, Jerry swam to shore and climbed slowly up the path to the villa. He flung himself on his bed and slept, waking at the sound of feet on the path outside. His mother was coming back. He rushed to the bathroom, thinking she must not see his face with bloodstains, or tearstains, on it. He came out of the bathroom and met her as she walked into the villa, smiling, her eyes lighting up.

"Have a nice morning?" she asked, laying her hand on his warm brown shoulder a moment.

"Oh, yes, thank you," he said.

"You look a bit pale." And then, sharp and anxious, "How did you bang your head?"

"Oh, just banged it," he told her.

She looked at him closely. He was strained; his eyes were glazed-looking. She was worried. And then she said to herself, Oh, don't fuss! Nothing can happen. He can swim like a fish.

They sat down to lunch together.

"Mummy," he said, "I can stay under water for two minutes—three minutes, at least." It came bursting out of him.

"Can you, darling?" she said. "Well, I shouldn't overdo it. I don't think you ought to swim any more today."

She was ready for a battle of wills, but he gave in at once. It was no longer of the least importance to go to the bay.

Through the Tunnel   153

RESPONDING TO THE SELECTION

Your Response

1. What qualities do you admire in Jerry? Which don't you admire? Explain your answers.
2. Do you think Jerry's victory is worth the pain and risks entailed? Why or why not?

Recalling

3. Describe Jerry's encounter with the local boys. What effect does it have on him?
4. How does Jerry prepare for his task?

Interpreting

5. Describe Jerry's relationship with his mother at the beginning of the story. How does it change by the end of the story? Cite specific instances in the story that helped you form your opinions.
6. What must Jerry prove to himself by swimming through the tunnel?
7. Jerry experiences both external and internal conflicts as he swims through the tunnel. Explain both his conflicts.
8. There are both literal and figurative aspects to the title. Explain both.
9. How has Jerry changed in the course of this story? Why is going to the bay "no longer of the least importance"?

Applying

10. Why do many young people set up situations in which they challenge themselves? Give some examples.

ANALYZING LITERATURE

Identifying Atmosphere

Atmosphere is the prevalent feeling created by a story or a scene. Descriptions of a story's setting often help establish the atmosphere, but dialogue and action may also play a role in defining a story's mood. The atmosphere developed in a story sets up your expectations about the events and the outcome. In "Through the Tunnel,"

when Jerry abandons his mother's beach, he leaves behind the carefree atmosphere of a vacation resort, and you expect him to have some sort of adventure.

1. Compare the atmosphere of the two beaches.
2. Describe the atmosphere when Jerry is under water.
3. In what way does the atmosphere affect your expectations when Jerry starts swimming through the tunnel?

THINKING AND WRITING

Writing About Art

Look at the pieces of fine art used on pages 148 and 153 in this story. For each piece of art, list details that create the atmosphere of the work. Then write a few paragraphs in which you discuss whether you think these pieces appropriately capture the atmospheres of Jerry's world and his mother's world. If you think they do not, explain why. When you revise your work, add sensory details that appeal to more than one sense in your descriptions of the atmospheres in the paintings.

LEARNING OPTIONS

1. **Art.** Doris Lessing uses vivid word pictures to describe the setting of this story. Using her words as a guide, draw a picture to illustrate the story. You may wish to show the bay, the rocks, or the underwater tunnel. You may add any details that you wish, but be sure to include the elements described by the author.
2. **Cross-curricular Connection.** If you were to produce this story on television or in a movie, what music would you use? In a group of three or four people, exchange ideas about what type of music would best accompany the story. Your group might have specific suggestions in mind, or you might need to listen to several pieces of music before choosing one. When your group has made its selection, bring in the music and play it for the class.

Symbol, Tone, and Irony

STREET SCENE IN LOWER NEW YORK, c. 1926
Glenn O. Coleman
Collection of Whitney Museum of American Art

GUIDE FOR READING

Toshio Mori

(1910–1980) was born in Oakland and raised in San Leandro, California. During World War II, he was interned in the Topaz Relocation Center in Utah, where he was camp historian. He began to publish his stories in magazines during the 1940's while he was still in Topaz. After the war Mori returned to San Leandro. *Yokohama, California,* his first collection of short stories, was published in 1949. Mori worked most of his adult life in a small family nursery, as do both characters in "Abalone, Abalone, Abalone."

Abalone, Abalone, Abalone

Symbols

A **symbol** is an object, a person, or an event that represents something else. A writer may use a symbol to make a point, to create a mood, or to reinforce a theme. Many common symbols have obvious or universal meanings. Thus a single green leaf can represent springtime and hope, or a gray cloud can represent darkness and despair. Within a given work, a symbol takes its meaning from the work itself. While the object that is a symbol exists as an integral part of the story, it represents something larger or more significant beyond the story, such as an idea or a belief.

Focus

In "Abalone, Abalone, Abalone," a man who collects abalone shells intrigues the narrator. What can you learn about people by studying their hobbies or their collections? For example, many people collect coins, stamps, or baseball cards. What might these collections mean for their collectors? In a group of three or four, discuss collections of yours or of people you know. Explore the symbolic significance of these collections. Keep your discussion in mind as you read "Abalone, Abalone, Abalone."

Vocabulary

Knowing the following words will help you as you read "Abalone, Abalone, Abalone."

abalone (ab′ ə lō′ nē) *n.*: A shellfish with a flat shell that has a pearly lining (p. 157)
nursery (nʉr′ sə rē) *n.*: A place where young trees and plants are grown (p. 157)

luster (lus′ tər) *n.*: Soft, reflected light; brilliance (p. 158)
hues (hyo͞oz) *n.*: Colors; shades of a given color (p. 158)
akin (ə kin′) *adj.*: Having a similar quality or character (p. 158)

Abalone, Abalone, Abalone

Toshio Mori

Before Mr. Abe went away I used to see him quite often at his nursery. He was a carnation grower just as I am one today. At noontime I used to go to his front porch and look at his collection of abalone shells.

They were lined up side by side against the side of his house on the front porch. I was curious as to why he bothered to collect them. It was a lot of bother polishing them. I had often seen him sit for hours on Sundays and noon hours polishing each one of the shells with the greatest of care. Of course I knew these abalone shells were pretty. When the sun strikes the insides of these shells it is something beautiful to behold. But I could not understand why he continued collecting them when the front porch was practically full.

He used to watch for me every noon hour. When I approached he would look out of his room and bellow, "Hello, young man!"

"Hello, Abe-*san*,"[1] I said. "I came to see the abalone shells."

Then he came out of the house and we sat on the front porch. But he did not tell me why he collected these shells. I think I have asked him dozens of times but each time he closed his mouth and refused to answer.

"Are you going to pass this collection of abalone shells on to your children?" I said.

"No," he said. "I want my children to collect for themselves. I wouldn't give it to them."

"Why?" I said. "When you die?"

Mr. Abe shook his head. "No. Not even when I die," he said. "I couldn't give the children what I see in these shells. The children must go out for themselves and find their own shells."

"Why, I thought this collecting hobby of abalone shells was a simple affair," I said.

"It is simple. Very simple," he said. But he would not tell me further.

For several years I went steadily to his front porch and looked at the beautiful shells. His collection was getting larger and larger. Mr. Abe sat and talked to me and on each occasion his hands were busy polishing the shells.

"So you are still curious?" he said.

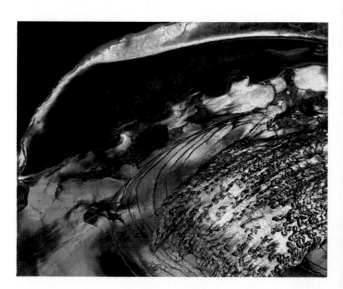

---

1. Abe-san: Mister Abe. *San* is a Japanese term of respect often added to a person's name.

"Yes," I said.

One day while I was hauling the old soil from the benches and replacing it with new soil I found an abalone shell half buried in the dust between the benches. So I stopped working. I dropped my wheelbarrow and went to the faucet and washed the abalone shell with soap and water. I had a hard time taking the grime off the surface.

After forty minutes of cleaning and polishing the old shell it became interesting. I began polishing both the outside and the inside of the shell. I found after many minutes of polishing that I could not do very much with the exterior side. It had scabs of the sea which would not come off by scrubbing and the surface itself was rough and hard. And in the crevices the grime stuck so that even with a needle it did not become clean.

But on the other side, the inside of the shell, the more I polished the more luster I found. It had me going.[2] There were colors which I had not seen in the abalone shells before or anywhere else. The different hues, running berserk in all directions, coming together in harmony. I guess I could say they were not unlike a rainbow which men once

---

2. It had me going: It had gripped my interest.

symbolized. As soon as I thought of this I thought of Mr. Abe.

I remember running to his place, looking for him. "Abe-*san!*" I said when I found him. "I know why you are collecting the abalone shells!"

He was watering the carnation plants in the greenhouse. He stopped watering and came over to where I stood. He looked me over closely for awhile and then his face beamed.

"All right," he said. "Do not say anything. Nothing, mind you. When you have found the reason why you must collect and preserve them, you do not have to say anything more."

"I want you to see it, Abe-*san,*" I said.

"All right. Tonight," he said. "Where did you find it?"

"In my old greenhouse, half buried in the dust," I said.

He chuckled. "That is pretty far from the ocean," he said, "but pretty close to you."

At each noon hour I carried my abalone shell and went over to Mr. Abe's front porch. While I waited for his appearance I kept myself busy polishing the inside of the shell with a rag.

One day I said, "Abe-*san,* now I have three shells."

"Good!" he said. "Keep it up!"

"I have to keep them all," I said. "They are very much alike and very much different."

"Well! Well!" he said and smiled.

That was the last I saw of Abe-*san.* Before the month was over he sold his nursery and went back to Japan. He brought his collection along and thereafter I had no one to talk to at the noon hour. This was before I discovered the fourth abalone shell, and I should like to see Abe-*san* someday and watch his eyes roll as he studies me whose face is now akin to the collectors of shells or otherwise.

RESPONDING TO THE SELECTION

Your Response

1. Are you a collector? Why or why not?
2. Do you identify with the narrator? With Mr. Abe? Explain.

Recalling

3. Why is the narrator drawn to Mr. Abe's nursery day after day?
4. Explain how Mr. Abe responds to the narrator's questions.
5. How does the narrator change after he finds an abalone shell?

Interpreting

6. What is it that Mr. Abe wants his children to discover for themselves?
7. Why does the narrator feel he must save every abalone shell he finds?
8. In what ways is an abalone shell like a rainbow?

Applying

9. Suppose that you were the narrator and Mr. Abe offered to give you his shell collection. Would you accept it? Why or why not?
10. What is the satisfaction of collecting something yourself rather than acquiring an already assembled collection?

ANALYZING LITERATURE

Interpreting Symbols

A **symbol** is anything that represents something outside itself, usually an idea, a belief, or a feeling. A writer may include a symbol to reinforce the point of the story. Sometimes one symbol can represent more than one idea. For example, a rainbow can represent the fulfillment of a dream or wish. It can also represent the return of peace.

1. Describe an abalone shell.
2. Why does Mr. Abe collect abalone shells?
3. What is it that Mr. Abe sees in them?
4. What might the abalone shells symbolize?

CRITICAL THINKING AND READING

Interpreting Connotative Meaning

In addition to their literal dictionary definitions, many words also have **connotative meanings,** or ideas and feelings that they suggest. For example, the word *greenhouse* suggests a sheltered environment, damp heat, and lush vegetation. What are some connotations of the following words and phrases?

1. front porch   3. shells
2. noon   4. soap and water

THINKING AND WRITING

Writing About a Symbol

Suppose that Mr. Abe had not told the narrator that he did "not have to say any more." How might the narrator have explained his discovery and his new-found need to collect abalone shells? Write a letter from the narrator to Mr. Abe explaining what the shells mean to him and expressing his new-found understanding of Mr. Abe and his collection. When you revise, be sure your explanation is logical and clear.

LEARNING OPTIONS

1. **Cross-curricular Connection.** Write a brief description of abalone shells and their characteristics. You might start with the details you read in the story; then expand on them. For example, explain why abalone shells are shiny on the inside and rough on the outside. An encyclopedia or a book on marine life might be a good information source.
2. **Art.** Suppose this story were being placed in a collection of stories about shells. You have been asked to supply cover art for the book. Locate pictures of abalone shells or of other shells that might interest you, and design a cover using the pictures you find. Magazines and postcards might be good sources of pictures.

GUIDE FOR READING

The Portrait

Symbols

A **symbol** in a literary work is a person, a place, or an object whose significance goes beyond its literal meaning. Writers use symbols to help them convey abstract or complicated ideas. For example, the appearance in a story of a mysterious figure wearing black may suggest the presence of danger or death. Symbols often trigger more than one association in a reader's mind and, therefore, open the meaning of a work to more than one interpretation.

Focus

A portrait has special meaning for the two main characters in "The Portrait." Find a picture or photograph that stores a special memory for you. What memory comes to life when you look at the picture? What feelings does the picture stir in you? In your journal make a word web with a label of the picture in the center. As an example, see the word-web diagram below. On the lines from the center, write the associations you make with the picture. Think of ways in which the memory has changed meaning for you over time. As you read "The Portrait," pay attention to what a memory means to the women in the story.

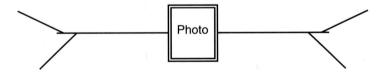

Vocabulary

Knowing the following words will help you as you read "The Portrait."

terse (turs) *adj.*: Brief; to the point (p. 162)

fickle (fik′ əl) *adj.*: Unfaithful; changeable (p. 162)

pathos (pā′ thäs) *n.*: Compassion; sympathy (p. 162)

ingrate (in′ grāt) *n.*: Unappreciative person (p. 162)

malevolence (mə lev′ ə ləns) *n.*: Ill will; malice (p. 164)

prosaic (prō zā′ ik) *adj.*: Ordinary; unimaginative (p. 164)

svelte (svelt) *adj.*: Slim; attractively slender (p. 164)

disdain (dis dān′) *n.*: Sense of superiority (p. 164)

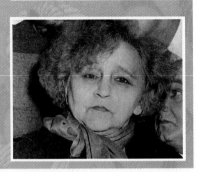

Colette

(1873–1954) was born Sidonie Gabrielle Colette in France. When she was eighteen, her family arranged for her to marry thirty-five-year-old Henry Gauthier-Villars. Her husband introduced Colette to the artistic life of Paris. There she wrote and published stories based on her youth. Later these stories were recognized as the early work of an exceptionally lyrical writer with a love of nature. Her novels and stories, such as "The Portrait," show an acute understanding of the female character.

The Portrait

Colette
translated by Matthew Ward

Both women opened the windows of their adjoining rooms at the same time, rattling the blinds, half closed against the sun, and smiled at one another as they leaned over the wooden balcony.

"What weather!"

"And the sea doesn't have a wrinkle!"

"Just one lucky streak. Did you see how much the wisteria's grown since last year?"

"And the honeysuckle! It's got its shoots caught in the blinds now."

"Are you going to rest, Lily?"

"I'm getting me a sweater and going down! I can't sit still the first day . . . What are you going to do, Alice?"

"Arrange things in my linen closet. It still has the scent of last year's lavender. Go on, I'll amuse myself like a madwoman. You go about your little affairs!"

Lily's short, bleached hair bounced goodbye like a puppet's, and a moment later Alice saw her, apple-green, going down into the sandy garden, poorly protected against the wind from the sea.

Alice laughed good-naturedly. "She's so plump!"

She looked down contentedly at her long white hands and crossed her thin forearms on the wooden rail, breathing in the salt and iodine that enriched the air. The breeze did not disturb a single strand of her hair, done in the "Spanish style," smoothed back,

THE SISTERS, 1940
Stanley Spencer
Leeds City Art Galleries

forehead and ears uncovered, quite flatter-ing to her fine, straight nose, but quite hard on everything else that was showing the decline in her: horizontal wrinkles above her eyebrows, hollow cheeks, the dark cir-cles of an insomniac[1] around her eyes. Her friend Lily blamed the severe hairstyle. "What can I say? I think that when fruit gets a little dry it needs some greenery!"

To which Alice replied, "Not everybody forty-five can wear her hair like a girl in the Folies!"[2]

They lived in perfect harmony, and this daily teasing was fuel for the fire of their friendship. Elegant and bony, Alice would voluntarily point out, "You might say my weight hasn't changed since the year my husband died. I've kept a blouse I had when I was a girl, out of curiosity: you'd think it was made for me yesterday!"

Lily did not mention any marriage, and for good reason. Her forties, after a dizzy youth, had endowed her with an irreducible plumpness.

"I'm plump, it's true," she would de-clare. "But you look at my face: not one wrinkle! And the same goes for the rest! Now, you must admit that's something."

And she would cast a malicious glance at Alice's hollow cheeks, at the scarf or fox[3] meant to hide the tendons in her neck, or her collarbones forming the cross bar of the letter T . . .

But it was love, more than rivalry, that bound the two friends together: the same handsome man, famous long before he grew old, had rejected them both. For Alice, a few letters from the great man were evidence that for a few weeks he had found her jealous

eyes, her irresistible elegance as a skinny, cleverly veiled brunette to his liking. All that Lily had from him was a telegram, one tele-gram, strangely terse and urgent. Shortly afterward he forgot both of them and the "What? You knew him too?" of the two friends was followed by nearly sincere con-fessions which they made tirelessly again and again.

"I never understood his sudden silence," admitted Alice. "But there was a moment in our life when I could have been, I'm sure of it, the friend, the spiritual guide to that fickle man, whom no one has been able to hold on to . . ."

"Well, my dear, I won't argue with you there," countered Lily. "The friend, the guide . . . I've never understood those big words. What I do know is that between him and me . . . Oh, heavens! What fire! We weren't thinking about pathos, take my word for it! I felt, right here, as clearly as I'm talking to you, that I could have ruled that man through the flesh. And then it fell apart . . . It always falls apart."

Content, in short, with their equal disap-pointments, having reached the age when women begin adorning little chapels, they had hung, in the drawing room of Lily's villa where they lived together, sharing expenses for two months, a portrait of the ingrate, the best portrait, the one used by all the daily papers and the illustrated magazines. A photographic enlargement, touched up, en-hanced with only highlights like an impas-sioned etching, softened with some pink on the mouth, some blue on the eyes, like a watercolor . . .

"It's not what you'd call a work of art," Alice would say, "but when you knew him as I did—as we did, Lily, it's alive!"

For two years now they had happily re-signed themselves to a kind of devout solitude, entertaining friends, inoffensive

---

1. insomniac (in săm′ nē ak′) *n.*: Someone who has a chronic inability to sleep.
2. Folies (fôl′ ēz): A famous French stage show.
3. fox: The skin of a whole fox used as a scarf.

IN THE STUDIO
William Merritt Chase
Collection of Arthur G. Altschul

The Portrait **163**

women and older well-bred men. Growing old? Well, heavens, yes, growing old, you have to get used to the idea . . . Growing old, under the eyes of that youthful portrait, in the glimmer of a beautiful memory . . . Growing old in good health, in the course of short, restful little trips, in the course of well-prepared little meals.

"Now, isn't this better than hanging around dance halls, masseuses,[4] and gambling parlors?" Lily would say.

Alice would nod in agreement and add: "Everything is so pale, next to a memory like that . . ."

When she finished straightening the closet, Alice changed her dress, buckled a white leather belt around her waist, and smiled. "The same hole as last year! It really is amusing!"

But she scolded herself for not having greeted, downstairs in the drawing room, "their" portrait . . .

"Alice! Alice! Are you coming down?" called Lily's voice from below. Alice leaned out over the balcony.

"In a minute! What is it?"

"Come down . . . Something strange . . . Come on!"

Vaguely excited, always ready for some romantic encounter, she ran downstairs and found Lily standing in front of "their" portrait, taken down from its hook and set on an armchair in the light. The exceptionally humid weather, some combination of salt and paint, had, in ten months in the darkness of the closed villa, worked an intelligent disaster, an act of destruction in which chance had armed itself with an almost miraculous malevolence. Mold growing on the great man's Roman chin had drawn the whitish beard of an unkempt old man, the paper had blistered, puffing the cheeks up into two lymphatic[5] pouches. A few grains of black charcoal, slipping down from the hair across the entire portrait, loaded the conqueror's face with wrinkles and years . . . Alice put her white hands over her eyes.

"It's . . . it's vandalism!"

Lily, ever prosaic, sighed out a long "Good God . . ." adding feverishly, "We're not going to leave it there, are we?"

"Lord, no! I'd be sick!"

They looked at each other. Lily found Alice's svelte figure young-looking, and Alice was unable to ward off a feeling of envy: "What a complexion Lily has! Like a peach!"

Their lunch rang with unusual chatter, during which there was talk of massages, diets, dresses, and the local casino. They spoke, as if incidentally, about the prolonged youth of certain artists and about their publicized love affairs. For no apparent reason, Lily exclaimed, "Hmph! Short and sweet? I prefer long and happy!" and Alice distractedly mentioned the same man's name four or five times, the name of one of their friends who would be spending—"or else I'm very much mistaken"—the summer in the neighborhood . . . A feverish desire to escape, a rush of wicked designs, made them eat, drink, smoke, and talk freely. But in the drawing room Alice turned her face away pityingly as she walked past the portrait, and it was the frivolous Lily, rubicund[6] and a little tipsy, who exhaled the smoke through her nostrils at the great man with disdain.

"Poor old thing!"

---

4. masseuses (ma stz əz) *n.*: Women whose work is giving massages.

5. lymphatic (lim fat′ ik) *adj.*: Containing or conveying lymph, a clear, yellowish fluid that resembles blood plasma.

6. rubicund (roo′ bə kund′) *adj.*: Reddish; ruddy.

RESPONDING TO THE SELECTION

Your Response

1. Suppose you were a niece or nephew of Alice or Lily. What advice would you give your aunt?

2. What insight into human life do you think Colette conveyed in "The Portrait"?

Recalling

3. How old are Alice and Lily, and what are we told about each one's past?

4. Who is the man in the portrait?

Interpreting

5. In what aspect of her appearance does each woman take pride? What does this suggest about what the women value?

6. How does each woman see her relationship with the man in the portrait? How might an outside observer view these relationships?

7. What do images like "adorning little chapels" and "devout solitude" suggest about the women and the portrait?

8. Why are the women so upset when they find the portrait destroyed?

9. How do the women adjust to the loss of the portrait? Has its loss changed them in any basic way?

Applying

10. The main characters in this story have a very definite attitude toward growing old. What is an alternative attitude toward this inescapable fact of life?

ANALYZING LITERATURE

Interpreting a Symbol

Writers make use of symbols to help them convey their insights into human life. A **symbol** is a person, a place, an object, or an event that has significance beyond its obvious meaning. For example, the central symbol of this story, the portrait, is destroyed by the natural forces of salt and humidity. This event is plausible on the literal level but is also meant to suggest that natural forces will in time change everything, including humans.

1. What meaning does the portrait have to the women beyond its obvious significance as a picture of an old boyfriend?

2. What is the symbolic significance of the portrait having been "touched up"?

CRITICAL THINKING AND READING

Comparing and Contrasting Characters

When you **compare** characters, you point out the similarities between them. When you **contrast** characters, you indicate the differences between them.

1. Compare and contrast Alice and Lily.

2. Decide whether you think they are more alike than different, or vice versa. Give reasons for your opinion.

THINKING AND WRITING

Writing a Sequel

At the end of the story, "a feverish desire to escape" drives the two women to talk briskly about the upcoming summer. Discuss with a partner what the two are trying to escape and what you think they are likely to do next. Then write a sequel to the story describing how Lily and Alice spend the summer. Include an appropriate symbol in your sequel.

LEARNING OPTION

Cross-curricular Connection. Give Alice and Lily a scientific explanation for the decay of the portrait. Use the life science resources in your school to find out how humidity can cause mold to grow and how, in turn, mold affects objects. Write your explanation in the form of a letter to the women. In your letter advise them about precautions they can take to avoid similar decay of other paintings they own.

GUIDE FOR READING

The Masque of the Red Death

Allegory

An **allegory** is a story intended to be read on a symbolic level. In an allegorical story, the characters, settings, and events are intended to have meanings independent of the action in the surface story. For example, the palace in "The Masque of the Red Death" may stand for the entire world. In fact, the entire story can be seen as a symbol representing a truth about a condition of life.

Focus

In "The Masque of the Red Death," Prince Prospero tries desperately to avoid his fate. What happens seems to bear out this statement: "Our hour is marked, and no one can claim a moment of life beyond what fate has predestined" (Napoleon Bonaparte). Before you read the story, write a journal entry in response to Napoleon's words. In your journal explore to what extent humans can and cannot control their fate.

Vocabulary

Knowing the following words will help you as you read "The Masque of the Red Death."

masque (mask) *n.*: A costume ball or masquerade theme (p. 167)

august (ô gust') *adj.*: Imposing and magnificent (p. 167)

candelabrum (kan' də lä' brəm) *n.*: A large branched candlestick (p. 168)

piquancy (pē' kan sē) *n.*: A pleasantly sharp quality (p. 170)

arabesque (ar' ə besk') *adj.*: Elaborately designed (p. 170)

disapprobation (dis ap' rə bā' shən) *n.*: Disapproval (p. 170)

phantasm (fan' taz'm) *n.*: Something apparently seen but having no physical reality (p. 170)

habiliments (hə bil' ə mənts) *n.*: Clothing (p. 171)

mummer (mum' ər) *n.*: A masked and costumed person who acts out pantomimes (p. 172)

Edgar Allan Poe

(1809–1849) was born in Boston, Massachusetts. When his parents died, Poe was adopted by Mr. and Mrs. John Allan and raised in Richmond, Virginia. In his short life, Poe wrote a large number of poems and short stories as well as some works of criticism. A masterful craftsman of the short story, his stories usually create a single, horrifying effect. "The Masque of the Red Death," which was first published in 1842, has the eerie and mysterious quality so many of Poe's tales possess.

The Masque of the Red Death

Edgar Allan Poe

The "Red Death" had long devastated the country. No pestilence had ever been so fatal, or so hideous. Blood was its Avatar[1] and its seal—the redness and the horror of blood. There were sharp pains, and sudden dizziness, and then profuse bleeding at the pores, with dissolution. The scarlet stains upon the body and especially upon the face of the victim, were the pest ban which shut him out from the aid and from the sympathy of his fellow men. And the whole seizure, progress and termination of the disease, were the incidents of half an hour.

But the Prince Prospero was happy and dauntless and sagacious. When his dominions were half depopulated, he summoned to his presence a thousand hale and light-hearted friends from among the knights and dames of his court, and with these retired to the deep seclusion of one of his castellated abbeys.[2] This was an extensive and magnificent structure, the creation of the prince's own eccentric yet august taste. A strong and lofty wall girdled it in. This wall had gates of iron. The courtiers, having entered, brought furnaces and massy[3] hammers and welded the bolts. They resolved to leave means neither of ingress or egress[4] to the sudden impulses of despair or of frenzy from within. The abbey was amply provisioned. With such precautions the courtiers might bid defiance to contagion. The external world could take care of itself. In the meantime it was folly to grieve, or to think. The prince had provided all the appliances of pleasure. There were buffoons, there were improvisatori,[5] there were ballet dancers, there were musicians, there was Beauty, there was wine. All these and security were within. Without was the "Red Death."

It was toward the close of the fifth or sixth month of his seclusion, and while the pestilence raged most furiously abroad, that the Prince Prospero entertained his thousand friends at a masked ball of the most unusual magnificence.

It was a voluptuous scene, that masquerade. But first let me tell of the rooms in which it was held. There were seven—an imperial suite. In many palaces, however, such suites form a long and straight vista, while the folding doors slide back nearly to the walls on either hand, so that the view of

---

1. Avatar (av′ ə tär′) *n.*: A symbol or manifestation of an unseen force.
2. castellated (kas′ tə lā′ tid) **abbeys** (ab′ ēz): Monasteries or convents with castle-like towers.
3. massy (mas′ ē) *adj.*: Massive or large.

4. ingress (in′ gres) **or egress** (ē′ gres): Entering or leaving.
5. improvisatori (im′ prə vē zə tôr′ ē) *n.*: Poets who improvise, or create verses without previous thought.

the whole extent is scarcely impeded. Here the case was very different; as might have been expected from the duke's love of the bizarre. The apartments were so irregularly disposed that the vision embraced but little more than one at a time. There was a sharp turn at every twenty or thirty yards, and at each turn a novel effect. To the right and left, in the middle of each wall, a tall and narrow Gothic window looked out upon a closed corridor which pursued the windings of the suite. These windows were of stained glass whose color varied in accordance with the prevailing hue of the decorations of the chamber into which it opened. That at the eastern extremity was hung, for example, in blue—and vividly blue were its windows. The second chamber was purple in its orna-

ments and tapestries, and here the panes were purple. The third was green through-out, and so were the casements. The fourth was furnished and lighted with orange—the fifth with white—the sixth with violet. The seventh apartment was closely shrouded in black velvet tapestries that hung all over the ceiling and down the walls, falling in heavy folds upon a carpet of the same material and hue. But in this chamber only, the color of the windows failed to correspond with the decorations. The panes here were scarlet—a deep blood color. Now in no one of the seven apartments was there any lamp or candelabrum amid the profusion of golden ornaments that lay scattered to and fro or depended from the roof. There was no light of any kind emanating from lamp or candle

within the suite of chambers. But in the corridors that followed the suite, there stood, opposite to each window, a heavy tripod, bearing a brazier[6] of fire that projected its rays through the tinted glass and so glaringly illumined the room. And thus were produced a multitude of gaudy and fantastic appearances. But in the western or black chamber the effect of the firelight that streamed upon the dark hangings through the blood-tinted panes, was ghastly in the extreme, and produced so wild a look upon the countenances of those who entered, that there were few of the company bold enough to set foot within its precincts at all.

---

6. brazier (brā′ zhər) *n.*: A metal pan or bowl to hold burning coals or charcoal.

It was in this apartment, also, that there stood against the western wall a gigantic clock of ebony. Its pendulum swung to and fro with a dull, heavy, monotonous clang; and when the minute-hand made the circuit of the face, and the hour was to be stricken, there came from the brazen lungs of the clock a sound which was clear and loud and deep and exceedingly musical, but of so peculiar a note and emphasis that, at each lapse of an hour, the musicians of the orchestra were constrained to pause, momentarily, in their performance, to hearken to the sound; and thus the waltzers perforce ceased their evolutions; and there was a brief disconcert of the whole gay company; and, while the chimes of the clock yet rang, it was observed that the giddiest grew pale, and the more aged and sedate passed their hands over their brows as if in confused reverie or meditation. But when the echoes had fully ceased, a light laughter at once pervaded the assembly; the musicians looked at each other and smiled as if at their own nervousness and folly, and made whispering vows, each to the other, that the next chiming of the clock should produce in them no similar emotion; and then, after the lapse of sixty minutes, (which embrace three thousand and six hundred seconds of the Time that flies), there came yet another chiming of the clock, and then were the same disconcert and tremulousness and meditation as before.

But, in spite of these things, it was a gay and magnificent revel. The tastes of the duke were peculiar. He had a fine eye for colors and effects. He disregarded the decora[7] of mere fashion. His plans were bold and fiery, and his conceptions glowed with barbaric luster. There are some who would have thought him mad. His followers felt that he

---

7. decora (dā kôr′ ə) *n.*: Requirements of good taste.

was not. It was necessary to hear and see and touch him to be *sure* that he was not.

He had directed, in great part, the movable embellishments of the seven chambers, upon occasion of this great fête; and it was his own guiding taste which had given character to the masqueraders. Be sure they were grotesque. There were much glare and glitter and piquancy and phantasm—much of what has been since seen in *Hernani*.[8] There were arabesque figures with unsuited limbs and appointments. There were delirious fancies such as the madman fashions. There was much of the beautiful, much of the wanton, much of the bizarre, something of the terrible, and not a little of that which might have excited disgust. To and fro in the seven chambers there stalked, in fact, a multitude of dreams. And these—the dreams—writhed in and about, taking hue from the rooms, and causing the wild music of the orchestra to seem as the echo of their steps. And, anon, there strikes the ebony clock which stands in the hall of the velvet. And then, for a moment, all is still, and all is silent save the voice of the clock. The dreams are stiff-frozen as they stand. But the echoes of the chime die away—they have endured but an instant—and a light, half-subdued laughter floats after them as they depart. And now again the music swells, and the dreams live, and writhe to and fro more merrily than ever, taking hue from the many-tinted windows through which stream the rays from the tripods. But to the chamber which lies most westwardly of the seven, there are now none of the maskers who venture; for the night is waning away; and there flows a ruddier light through the blood-colored panes; and the blackness of the sable drapery appalls; and

to him whose foot falls upon the sable carpet, there comes from the near clock of ebony a muffled peal more solemnly emphatic than any which reaches *their* ears who indulge in the more remote gaieties of the other apartments.

But these other apartments were densely crowded, and in them beat feverishly the heart of life. And the revel went whirlingly on, until at length there commenced the sounding of midnight upon the clock. And then the music ceased, as I have told; and the evolutions of the waltzers were quieted; and there was an uneasy cessation of all things as before. But now there were twelve strokes to be sounded by the bell of the clock; and thus it happened, perhaps, that more of thought crept, with more of time, into the meditations of the thoughtful among those who reveled. And thus, too, it happened, perhaps, that before the last echoes of the last chime had utterly sunk into silence, there were many individuals in the crowd who had found leisure to become aware of the presence of a masked figure which had arrested the attention of no single individual before. And the rumor of this new presence having spread itself whisperingly around, there arose at length from the whole company a buzz, or murmur, expressive of disapprobation and surprise—then, finally, of terror, of horror, and of disgust.

In an assembly of phantasms such as I have painted, it may well be supposed that no ordinary appearance could have excited such sensation. In truth the masquerade license of the night was nearly unlimited; but the figure in question had out-Heroded Herod,[9] and gone beyond the bounds of even the prince's indefinite decorum. There are

---

8. Hernani: An extravagant drama by the French author Victor Hugo.

9. out-Heroded Herod: Behaved excessively, just as King Herod did. In the Bible, Herod slaughtered innocent babies, hoping to kill Jesus.

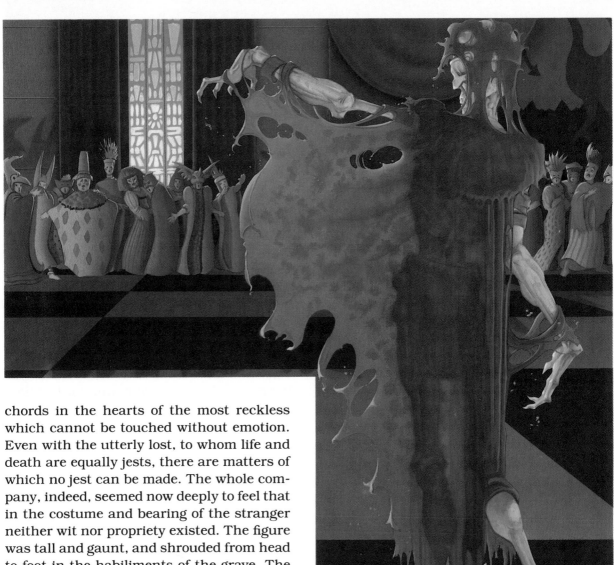

chords in the hearts of the most reckless which cannot be touched without emotion. Even with the utterly lost, to whom life and death are equally jests, there are matters of which no jest can be made. The whole company, indeed, seemed now deeply to feel that in the costume and bearing of the stranger neither wit nor propriety existed. The figure was tall and gaunt, and shrouded from head to foot in the habiliments of the grave. The mask which concealed the visage was made so nearly to resemble the countenance of a stiffened corpse that the closest scrutiny must have had difficulty in detecting the cheat. And yet all this might have been endured, if not approved, by the mad revelers around. But the mummer had gone so far as to assume the type of the Red Death. His vesture was dabbled in *blood*—and his broad brow, with all the features of the face, was besprinkled with the scarlet horror.

When the eyes of Prince Prospero fell upon this spectral image (which with a slow and solemn movement, as if more fully to sustain its role, stalked to and fro among the waltzers) he was seen to be convulsed, in the first moment with a strong shudder either of terror or distaste; but, in the next, his brow reddened with rage.

"Who dares?" he demanded hoarsely of the courtiers who stood near him—"who dares insult us with this blasphemous mockery? Seize him and unmask him —that we may know whom we have to hang at sunrise, from the battlements!"

It was in the eastern or blue chamber in which stood the Prince Prospero as he uttered these words. They rang throughout the seven rooms loudly and clearly—for the prince was a bold and robust man, and the music had become hushed at the waving of his hand.

It was in the blue room where stood the prince, with a group of pale courtiers by his side. At first, as he spoke, there was a slight rushing movement of this group in the direction of the intruder, who at the moment was also near at hand, and now, with deliberate and stately step, made closer approach to the speaker. But from a certain nameless awe with which the mad assumptions of the mummer had inspired the whole party, there were found none who put forth hand to seize him; so that, unimpeded, he passed within a yard of the prince's person; and, while the vast assembly, as if with one impulse, shrank from the centers of the rooms to the walls, he made his way uninterruptedly, but with the same solemn and measured step which had distinguished him from the first, through the blue chamber to the purple—through the purple to the green—through the green to the orange —through this again to the white—and even thence to the violet, ere a decided movement had been made to arrest him. It was then, however, that the Prince Prospero, maddening with rage and the shame of his own momentary cowardice, rushed hurriedly through the six chambers, while none followed him on account of a deadly terror that had seized upon all. He bore aloft a drawn dagger, and had approached, in rapid impetuosity, to within three or four feet of the retreating figure, when the latter, having attained the extremity of the velvet apartment, turned suddenly and confronted his pursuer. There was a sharp cry—and the dagger dropped gleaming upon the sable carpet, upon which, instantly afterwards, fell prostrate in death the Prince Prospero. Then, summoning the wild courage of despair, a throng of the revelers at once threw themselves into the black apartment, and, seizing the mummer, whose tall figure stood erect and motionless within the shadow of the ebony clock, gasped in unutterable horror at finding the grave cerements[10] and corpselike mask which they handled with so violent a rudeness, untenanted by any tangible form.

And now was acknowledged the presence of the Red Death. He had come like a thief in the night. And one by one dropped the revelers in the blood-bedewed halls of their revel, and died each in the despairing posture of his fall. And the life of the ebony clock went out with that of the last of the gay. And the flames of the tripods expired. And Darkness and Decay and the Red Death held illimitable dominion over all.

---

10. cerements (sĭr′ mənts) *n.*: Wrappings or shroud.

Your Response
1. What did you expect from the masked figure?
2. Would you have attended the ball? Explain.

Recalling
3. Why do Prince Prospero and his followers retreat to his palace?
4. Describe the series of rooms in which the entertainment takes place.
5. Explain how the party is disrupted.

Interpreting
6. Compare life outside the palace with the life of the people Prospero brought inside.
7. What do you learn about Prospero from his desire to keep his palace free of the plague?
8. What mood or effect is created by the colors and the lighting in the rooms of the ball?
9. Why does the clock have such a dramatic effect on the dancers?
10. Why does the visitor frighten the guests?
11. Explain how Poe builds terror in the story.

Applying
12. Ugo Betti has written, "Every tiny part of us cries out against the idea of dying, and hopes to live forever." Explain whether you think Poe would agree.

ANALYZING LITERATURE

Understanding Allegory
In an **allegory** the characters, settings, and events are an interconnected series of symbols. The deeper or symbolic meaning of the story may contain a lesson about life.

1. What might each symbol from "The Masque of the Red Death" represent?
   a. Prince Prospero   d. the number 7
   b. the masquerade   e. the clock
   c. the masked figure
2. What is the allegorical lesson in the story?

CRITICAL THINKING AND READING

Interpreting Connotative Meaning
The **connotative meaning** of a word is what the word suggests beyond its literal dictionary meaning. Authors can use the connotative meanings of words to help establish symbols. For example, the color red connotes blood and death. Poe uses that connotation in describing the appearance of the masked figure.

1. What are some connotations of the following colors from the story?
   a. green   c. white
   b. orange   d. black
2. Find three words or phrases that suggest the quality of a nightmare.

THINKING AND WRITING

Writing About Allegory
Write a key that future readers can use to unlock the meaning of "The Masque of the Red Death." Tell what you believe the various events, characters, and aspects of the setting stand for, giving reasons for your assumptions. Then relate these symbols to the larger lesson Poe is presenting. When you revise your work, be sure your interpretation is clear and makes sense.

LEARNING OPTIONS

1. **Writing.** Write an obituary for Prince Prospero. Include details about his character and the circumstances surrounding his death. You might also use your imagination to make up details.
2. **Art.** Imagine that you are the set engineer for a movie of "The Masque of the Red Death." Your supervisor has asked you to design the set. In your design plans, you must include a detailed map of the palace. Based on Poe's description, draw a map of Prospero's palace. Try to capture the macabre atmosphere.

MULTICULTURAL CONNECTION

Poe's Influence Around the World

A fruitful exchange. Edgar Allan Poe borrowed richly from the world he visited through the books and magazines he read. Then, through his own works, he gave back equally richly to the world beyond his study. It was a fruitful exchange.

The British, French, Greek, and Arabic influences on his writings are obvious. Just as obvious are his influences on modern world culture. He gave new twists to tales of horror, inspiring such modern practitioners of the form as Stephen King, Anne Rice, and film director Alfred Hitchcock. His poetry changed the face of French literature, leading to the nineteenth-century Symbolist movement. The writers in this movement, like Poe, sought to escape from humdrum, everyday reality.

Poe's writings also influenced the French artists Eugène Delacroix and Edouard Manet, and the Belgian painter James Ensor (see page 175).

Magical Realism. Poe has had nearly as great an influence on Latin American literature as on French literature. His fantasies and tales of horror have contributed to the development in Latin America of a school of fiction called "Magical Realism." In this type of fiction, the line between the magical and the realistic is worn away, replaced with a world that is both at the same time. It is too real to be fantasy and too fantastic to be real. In Gabriel García Márquez's *Autumn of the Patriarch*, for example, decades of time pass with virtually no sign of change or aging in the novel's protagonist, a dictator. He appears to be truly and literally immortal. Then he dies and the winds of change immediately blow through his world, bringing years of decay in the instant of their wake.

In addition to Colombia's García Márquez, other Latin American writers whose work features the qualities of Magical Realism include Argentina's Jorge Luis Borges, Mexico's Carlos Fuentes, Peru's Mario Vargas Llosa, Chile's Isabel Allende, and Brazil's Julio Cortázar. All of them, but particularly Borges and Cortázar, who has translated Poe, show Poe's influence. It is an influence that has come full circle. In the United States, writers like Maxine Hong Kingston and John Edgar Wideman have brought a touch of Magical Realism to their fiction.

Father of the detective story. There is one place above all others, however, where Edgar Allan Poe's contribution to the world is unmistakable. He invented a genre of writing, the detective story, that now has nearly universal popularity. Detective stories, and their close cousins, the thriller and the mystery novel, have taken root in the literary soil of nearly every culture in which they have found an audience. With each transplanting, something unique has resulted. Among Poe's literary children are such detectives as Arthur Conan Doyle's Sherlock Holmes; Agatha Christie's Miss Marple; Tony Hillerman's Lieutenant Joe Leaphorn of the Navajo Tribal Police; Chester Himes's Harlem detectives Coffin Ed Johnson and Grave

Digger Jones; and James Lee Burke's Cajun detective Dave Robicheaux.

Exploring on Your Own

1. Use crayons or pastel colors to draw your own illustration for "The Masque of the Red Death."
2. With classmates, work in a small group to write a detective story of your own. You may first want to read an anthology of detective stories to prepare for this assignment.

Further Reading

Himes, Chester. *The Collected Stories of Chester Himes* (New York: Thunder's Mouth Press, 1991). This book contains stories from one of America's neglected masters.

Poe, Edgar Allan. *The Fall of the House of Usher and Other Writings* (New York: Penguin, 1988).

LES MASQUES ET LA MORT, 1897
James Ensor
© *Estate of James Ensor/VAGA, New York, 1993*

GUIDE FOR READING

The Open Window

Tone in Dialogue

The **tone** of a story is the attitude implied toward the characters, situation, and readers. The characters within a story may also convey a tone toward a situation or toward other characters. A character's tone might be respectful or sympathetic or challenging, for example. Characters' attitudes are revealed primarily through their dialogue and actions. You can infer characters' tones from their choice of words and from their intent. Each of the three characters in "The Open Window" who speaks at length has an identifiable tone.

Focus

Before you read "The Open Window," explore how your tone of voice can affect the meaning of what you say. With a partner read the following sentences using different tones for the italicized words. Read each italicized word with a sincere tone, a sarcastic tone, and a tone of surprise.

1. Last night, I saw an *amusing* movie.
2. The plot was *interesting*.
3. The main character, a fifteen-year-old girl, was *extraordinary*.
4. Her imagination was her *specialty*.

As you read "The Open Window," pay attention to each character's tone of voice.

Vocabulary

Knowing the following words will help you as you read "The Open Window."

delusion (di lo͞o′ zhən) *n.*: A false belief held in spite of evidence to the contrary (p. 180)

imminent (im′ ə nənt) *adj.*: Likely to happen presently; threatening (p. 180)

mackintosh (mak′ in täsh′) *n.*: A waterproof raincoat (p. 180)

pariah (pə rī′ ə) *adj.*: Despised; outcast (p. 180)

Saki

(1870–1916) is the pen name of H. H. Munro. Saki was born in Burma, which was then a British colony, but when his mother died, Saki was sent to England to be raised by two aunts. His earliest works were political satires, which appeared in newspapers. He worked for several newspapers as a foreign correspondent. In 1914 Saki enlisted in the army and was killed in battle during World War I. Saki's stories, including "The Open Window," are noted for their wit and humor.

The Open Window

Saki

"My aunt will be down presently, Mr. Nuttel," said a very self-possessed young lady of fifteen; "in the meantime you must try and put up with me."

Framton Nuttel endeavored to say the correct something that should duly flatter the niece of the moment without unduly discounting the aunt that was to come. Privately he doubted more than ever whether these formal visits on a succession of total strangers would do much towards helping the nerve cure which he was supposed to be undergoing.

"I know how it will be," his sister had said when he was preparing to migrate to this rural retreat; "you will bury yourself down there and not speak to a living soul, and your nerves will be worse than ever from moping. I shall just give you letters of introduction to all the people I know there. Some of them, as far as I can remember, were quite nice."

Framton wondered whether Mrs. Sappleton, the lady to whom he was presenting one of the letters of introduction, came into the nice division.

"Do you know many of the people round here?" asked the niece, when she judged that they had had sufficient silent communion.

"Hardly a soul," said Framton. "My sister was staying here, at the rectory, you know, some four years ago, and she gave me letters of introduction to some of the people here."

DOROTHY
William Merritt Chase
Indianapolis Museum of Art

He made the last statement in a tone of distinct regret.

"Then you know practically nothing about my aunt?" pursued the self-possessed young lady.

"Only her name and address," admitted the caller. He was wondering whether Mrs. Sappleton was in the married or widowed state. An undefinable something about the room seemed to suggest masculine habitation.

"Her great tragedy happened just three years ago," said the child; "that would be since your sister's time."

"Her tragedy?" asked Framton; somehow in this restful country spot tragedies seemed out of place.

"You may wonder why we keep that window wide open on an October afternoon," said the niece, indicating a large French window that opened on to a lawn.

"It is quite warm for the time of the year," said Framton; "but has that window got anything to do with the tragedy?"

"Out through that window, three years ago to a day, her husband and her two young brothers went off for their day's shooting. They never came back. In crossing the moor to their favorite snipe-shooting ground[1] they were all three engulfed in a treacherous piece of bog. It had been that dreadful wet summer, you know, and places that were safe in other years gave way suddenly without warning. Their bodies were never recovered. That was the dreadful part of it." Here the child's voice lost its self-possessed note and became falteringly human. "Poor aunt always thinks that they will come back some day, they and the little brown spaniel that was lost with them, and walk in at that window just as they used to do. That is why the window is kept open every evening till it is quite dusk. Poor dear aunt, she has often told me how they went out, her husband with his white waterproof coat over his arm, and Ronnie, her youngest brother, singing, 'Bertie, why do you bound?' as he always did to tease her, because she said it got on her nerves. Do you know, sometimes on still, quiet evenings like this, I almost get a creepy feeling that they will walk in through that window—"

She broke off with a little shudder. It was a relief to Framton when the aunt bustled into the room with a whirl of apologies for being late in making her appearance.

"I hope Vera has been amusing you?" she said.

"She has been very interesting," said Framton.

"I hope you don't mind the open window," said Mrs. Sappleton briskly; "my husband and brothers will be home directly from shooting, and they always come in this way. They've been out for snipe in the marshes today, so they'll make a fine mess over my poor carpets. So like you menfolk, isn't it?"

She rattled on cheerfully about the shooting and the scarcity of birds, and the prospects for duck in the winter. To Framton, it was all purely horrible. He made a desperate but only partially successful effort to turn the talk on to a less ghastly topic; he was conscious that his hostess was giving him only a fragment of her attention, and her eyes were constantly straying past him to the open window and the lawn beyond. It was certainly an unfortunate coincidence that he should have paid his visit on this tragic anniversary.

"The doctors agree in ordering me complete rest, an absence of mental excitement, and avoidance of anything in the nature of violent physical exercise," announced

---

1. snipe-shooting ground: Area for hunting snipe, wading birds who live chiefly in marshy places and have long, flexible bills.

THE HUNTERS
Gari Melchers
Private Collection

Framton, who labored under the tolerably wide-spread delusion that total strangers and chance acquaintances are hungry for the least detail of one's ailments and infirmities, their cause and cure. "On the matter of diet they are not so much in agreement," he continued.

"No?" said Mrs. Sappleton, in a voice which only replaced a yawn at the last moment. Then she suddenly brightened into alert attention—but not to what Framton was saying.

"Here they are at last!" she cried. "Just in time for tea, and don't they look as if they were muddy up to the eyes!"

Framton shivered slightly and turned towards the niece with a look intended to convey sympathetic comprehension. The child was staring out through the open window with dazed horror in her eyes. In a chill shock of nameless fear Framton swung round in his seat and looked in the same direction.

In the deepening twilight three figures were walking across the lawn towards the window; they all carried guns under their arms, and one of them was additionally burdened with a white coat hung over his shoulders. A tired brown spaniel kept close at their heels. Noiselessly they neared the house, and then a hoarse young voice chanted out of the dusk: "I said, Bertie, why do you bound?"

Framton grabbed wildly at his stick and hat; the hall door, the gravel drive, and the front gate were dimly noted stages in his headlong retreat. A cyclist coming along the road had to run into the hedge to avoid imminent collision.

"Here we are, my dear," said the bearer of the white mackintosh, coming in through the window; "fairly muddy, but most of it's dry. Who was that who bolted out as we came up?"

"A most extraordinary man, a Mr. Nuttel," said Mrs. Sappleton; "could only talk about his illnesses, and dashed off without a word of goodbye or apology when you arrived. One would think he had seen a ghost."

"I expect it was the spaniel," said the niece calmly; "he told me he had a horror of dogs. He was once hunted into a cemetery somewhere on the banks of the Ganges[2] by a pack of pariah dogs, and had to spend the night in a newly dug grave with the creatures snarling and grinning and foaming just above him. Enough to make anyone lose their nerve."

Romance at short notice was her specialty.

---

2. **Ganges** (gan' jēz): A river in northern India and Bangladesh.

Your Response

1. If you were Mr. Nuttel, what would you have said to Vera as the men came through the window?

Recalling

2. For what reason is Framton Nuttel living in the country? Why is he visiting the Sappletons?
3. How does Vera explain the open window?
4. Explain what causes Framton to rush from the house so suddenly.
5. How does Vera explain Framton's departure?

Interpreting

6. Contrast the outstanding character traits of Framton and Vera. What qualities or traits of Framton make him susceptible to her story?
7. At what point do you realize that Vera is telling a story? Cite evidence from the story that shows her intent.
8. Saki concludes the story with the statement "Romance at short notice was her specialty." Explain the meaning of *romance*.
9. Explain how this story can be thought of as having a double ending.

Applying

10. Explain how a person's expectations can lead him or her to misunderstand or misinterpret obvious facts.

ANALYZING LITERATURE

Recognizing Tone in Dialogue

When you converse with someone, you can recognize that person's **tone** from his or her manner of speaking. The person's tone might be sarcastic or serious, for example. The dialogue in short stories reveals the characters' tone in the same way. In "The Open Window," Framton's tone remains polite throughout the story, showing a respectful attitude toward the Sappletons.

1. What is Vera's tone when speaking to Framton? What evidence indicates this tone?

2. What is Mrs. Sappleton's tone toward Framton before his sudden departure? What words or details reveal her tone?
3. Verbal irony occurs when someone means the opposite of what is said. Find two examples of verbal irony in this story.

CRITICAL THINKING AND READING

Making Inferences About Characters

From the characters' dialogue and actions, you can make inferences about the characters themselves. For example, Mrs. Sappleton's suppressed yawn shows her to be bored with Framton's conversation about his condition.

1. What is Framton's social status compared with that of the Sappletons?
2. What kind of person is Framton?
3. What kind of person is Vera? Look up the meaning of her name. What do you think was the author's purpose in choosing the name Vera for this character?

THINKING AND WRITING

Writing About Tone

Suppose that you went to tea at the Sappletons' when Framton was there. Write a journal entry describing the experience. Describe each family member and his or her tone of voice in conversing with you. Conclude with the opinion you formed of the family during the tea. Review your entry, adding at least two lines of dialogue that reveal characters' tones.

LEARNING OPTION

Writing. Write a letter to Mr. Nuttel's sister from his point of view. Tell her what happened at Mrs. Sappleton's and how the incident has affected your nervous condition. In your letter try to use a tone appropriate for Mr. Nuttel.

GUIDE FOR READING

Isaac Asimov

(1920–1992) was born in the Soviet Union. When he was three, his family emigrated to the United States, and Asimov grew up in Brooklyn, New York. He is the author of some three hundred books on a variety of subjects, including the sciences (astronomy, mathematics, and biochemistry), history, Shakespeare, and the Bible. Asimov remains best known, however, for his works of science fiction including novels like *Fantastic Voyage* and short stories like "The Machine That Won the War."

The Machine That Won the War

Verbal Irony and Irony of Situation

Irony is a contrast between what is and what seems to be. There are different kinds of irony. In **verbal irony** a writer or speaker says one thing but means another, usually the opposite. You use verbal irony when you describe someone you like as "really bad." **Irony of situation** refers to the difference between what is expected to happen and what actually happens. Having a machine turn out to be a war hero might seem ironic, but in "The Machine That Won the War," that is just the beginning.

Focus

Increasingly advanced technology forces people, at one time or another, to work with machines. Microwave ovens, VCRs, and computers are just a few examples of machines that some people work with daily. Machines can increase human efficiency and productivity a thousandfold; at the same time, machines can frustrate people who aren't used to working with them. Recall a time when you had difficulty operating a machine. In your journal tell about that experience and explore your reactions to it.

Keep your experiences with machines in mind as you read "The Machine That Won the War."

Vocabulary

Knowing the following words will help you as you read "The Machine That Won the War."

erratic (i rat′ ik) *adj.*: Irregular; random (p. 183)

grisly (griz′ lē) *adj.*: Horrifying; gruesome (p. 183)

imperturbable (im′ pər tʉr′ bə b'l) *adj.*: Unable to be excited or disturbed (p. 183)

oracle (ôr′ ə k'l) *n.*: A source of knowledge or wise counsel (p. 183)

surcease (sʉr sēs′) *n.*: An end (p. 184)

subsidiary (səb sid′ ē er′ ē) *adj.*: Secondary; supporting (p. 184)

circumvent (sʉr′ kəm vent′) *v.*: Prevent from happening (p. 185)

The Machine That Won the War

Isaac Asimov

The celebration had a long way to go and even in the silent depths of Multivac's underground chambers, it hung in the air.

If nothing else, there was the mere fact of isolation and silence. For the first time in a decade, technicians were not scurrying about the vitals of the giant computer, the soft lights did not wink out their erratic patterns, the flow of information in and out had halted.

It would not be halted long, of course, for the needs of peace would be pressing. Yet now, for a day, perhaps for a week, even Multivac might celebrate the great time, and rest.

Lamar Swift took off the military cap he was wearing and looked down the long and empty main corridor of the enormous computer. He sat down rather wearily in one of the technician's swing-stools, and his uniform, in which he had never been comfortable, took on a heavy and wrinkled appearance.

He said, "I'll miss it all after a grisly fashion. It's hard to remember when we weren't at war with Deneb, and it seems against nature now to be at peace and to look at the stars without anxiety."

The two men with the Executive Director of the Solar Federation were both younger than Swift. Neither was as gray. Neither looked quite as tired.

John Henderson, thin-lipped and finding it hard to control the relief he felt in the midst of triumph, said, "They're destroyed! They're destroyed! It's what I keep saying to myself over and over and I still can't believe it. We all talked so much, over so many years, about the menace hanging over Earth and all its worlds, over every human being, and all the time it was true, every word of it. And now we're alive and it's the Denebians who are shattered and destroyed. They'll be no menace now, ever again."

"Thanks to Multivac," said Swift, with a quiet glance at the imperturbable Jablonsky, who through all the war had been Chief Interpreter of science's oracle. "Right, Max?"

Jablonsky shrugged. He said, "Well, that's what *they* say." His broad thumb moved in the direction of his right shoulder, aiming upward.

"Jealous, Max?"

"Because they're shouting for Multivac? Because Multivac is the big hero of mankind in this war?" Jablonsky's craggy face took on an air of suitable contempt. "What's that to me? Let Multivac be the machine that won the war, if it pleases them."

Henderson looked at the other two out of the corners of his eyes. In this short interlude that the three had instinctively sought out in the one peaceful corner of a metropolis gone mad; in this entr'acte[1] between the dangers of war and the difficulties of peace; when, for one moment, they might all find surcease; he was conscious only of his weight of guilt.

Suddenly, it was as though that weight were too great to be borne longer. It had to be thrown off, along with the war; now!

Henderson said, "Multivac had nothing to do with victory. It's just a machine."

"A big one," said Swift.

"Then just a big machine. No better than the data fed it." For a moment, he stopped, suddenly unnerved at what he was saying.

Jablonsky looked at him. "You should know. You supplied the data. Or is it just that you're taking the credit?"

"*No*," said Henderson angrily. "There is no credit. What do you know of the data Multivac had to use; predigested from a hundred subsidiary computers here on Earth, on the Moon, on Mars, even on Titan. With Titan always delayed and always feeling that its figures would introduce an unexpected bias."

"It would drive anyone mad," said Swift, with gentle sympathy.

Henderson shook his head. "It wasn't just that. I admit that eight years ago when I replaced Lepont as Chief Programmer, I was nervous. But there was an exhilaration about things in those days. The war was still long range; an adventure without real danger. We hadn't reached the point where manned vessels had had to take over and where interstellar warps could swallow up a planet clean, if aimed correctly. But then, when the real difficulties began—"

Angrily—he could finally permit anger —he said, "You know nothing about it."

_____
1. entr'acte (än trakt') *n*.: Interval.

"Well," said Swift. "Tell us. The war is over. We've won."

"Yes." Henderson nodded his head. He had to remember that. Earth had won, so all had been for the best. "Well, the data became meaningless."

"Meaningless? You mean that literally?" said Jablonsky.

"Literally. What would you expect? The trouble with you two was that you weren't out in the thick of it. You never left Multivac, Max, and you, Mr. Director, never left the Mansion except on state visits where you saw exactly what they wanted you to see."

"I was not as unaware of that," said Swift, "as you may have thought."

"Do you know," said Henderson, "to what extent data concerning our production capacity, our resource potential, our trained manpower—everything of importance to the war effort, in fact—had become unreliable and untrustworthy during the last half of the war? Group leaders, both civilian and military, were intent on projecting their own improved image, so to speak, so they obscured the bad and magnified the good. Whatever the machines might do, the men who programmed them and interpreted the results had their own skins to think of and competitors to stab. There was no way of stopping that. I tried, and failed."

"Of course," said Swift, in quiet consolation. "I can see that you would."

"Yet I presume you provided Multivac with data in your programming?" Jablonsky said. "You said nothing to us about unreliability."

"How could I tell you? And if I did, how could you afford to believe me?" demanded Henderson, savagely. "Our entire war effort was geared to Multivac. It was the one great weapon on our side, for the Denebians had nothing like it. What else kept up morale in the face of doom but the assurance that Multivac would always predict and circumvent any Denebian move, and would always direct and prevent the circumvention of our moves? Great Space, after our Spy-warp was blasted out of hyperspace we lacked any reliable Denebian data to feed Multivac and we didn't dare make *that* public."

"True enough," said Swift.

"Well, then," said Henderson, "if I told you the data was unreliable, what could you have done but replace me and refuse to believe me? I couldn't allow that."

"What did you do?" said Jablonsky.

"Since the war is won, I'll tell you what I did. I corrected the data."

"How?" asked Swift.

"Intuition, I presume. I juggled them till they looked right. At first, I hardly dared. I changed a bit here and there to correct what were obvious impossibilities. When the sky didn't collapse about us, I got braver. Toward the end, I scarcely cared. I just wrote out the necessary data as it was needed. I even had the Multivac Annex prepare data for me according to a private programming pattern I had devised for the purpose."

"Random figures?" said Jablonsky.

"Not at all. I introduced a number of necessary biases."

Jablonsky smiled, quite unexpectedly, his dark eyes sparkling behind the crinkling of the lower lids. "Three times a report was brought to me about unauthorized uses of the Annex, and I let it go each time. If it had mattered, I would have followed it up and spotted you, John, and found out what you were doing. But, of course, nothing about Multivac mattered in those days, so you got away with it."

"What do you mean, nothing mattered?" asked Henderson, suspiciously.

"Nothing did. I suppose if I had told you this at the time, it would have spared you your agony, but then if you had told me what you were doing, it would have spared me mine. What made you think Multivac was in working order, whatever the data you supplied it?"

"Not in working order?" said Swift.

"Not really. Not reliably. After all, where were my technicians in the last years of the war? I'll tell you, they were feeding computers on a thousand different space devices. They were gone! I had to make do with kids I couldn't trust and veterans who were out-of-date. Besides, do you think I could trust the solid-state components coming out of Cryogenics[2] in the last years? Cryogenics wasn't any better placed as far as personnel was concerned than I was. To me, it didn't matter whether the data being supplied Multivac were reliable or not. The *results* weren't reliable. That much I knew."

"What did you do?" asked Henderson.

"I did what you did, John. I introduced the bugger factor. I adjusted matters in accordance with intuition—and that's how the machine won the war."

Swift leaned back in the chair and stretched his legs out before him. "Such revelations. It turns out then that the material handed me to guide me in my decision-making capacity was a man-made interpretation of man-made data. Isn't that right?"

"It looks so," said Jablonsky.

"Then I perceive I was correct in not placing too much reliance upon it," said Swift.

"You didn't?" Jablonsky, despite what he had just said, managed to look professionally insulted.

---

2. Cryogenics (krī′ ə jen′ iks): Here, a department concerned with the science of low-temperature phenomena.

"I'm afraid I didn't. Multivac might seem to say, Strike here, not there; do this, not that; wait, don't act. But I could never be certain that what Multivac seemed to say, it really did say; or what it really said, it really meant. I could never be certain."

"But the final report was always plain enough, sir," said Jablonsky.

"To those who did not have to make the decision, perhaps. Not to me. The horror of the responsibility of such decisions was unbearable and not even Multivac was sufficient to remove the weight. But the point is I was justified in doubting and there is tremendous relief in that."

Caught up in the conspiracy of mutual confession, Jablonsky put titles aside. "What was it you did then, Lamar? After all, you did make decisions. How?"

"Well, it's time to be getting back perhaps, but—I'll tell you first. Why not? I did make use of a computer, Max, but an older one than Multivac, much older."

He groped in his own pocket and brought out a scattering of small change; old-fashioned coins dating to the first years

before the metal
shortage had brought
into being a credit system
tied to a computer-complex.

Swift smiled rather sheepishly.
"I still need these to make money seem
substantial to me. An old man finds it hard
to abandon the habits of youth." He
dropped the coins, one by one, back into
his pocket.

He held the last coin between his fingers,
staring absently at it. "Multivac is not the
first computer, friends, nor the best-known,

nor the one that can most efficiently lift the load of decision from the shoulders of the executive. A machine *did* win the war, John; at least a very simple computing device did; one that I used every time I had a particularly hard decision to make.''

With a faint smile of reminiscence, he flipped the coin he held. It glinted in the air as it spun and came down in Swift's outstretched palm. His hand closed over it and brought it down on the back of his left hand. His right hand remained in place, hiding the coin.

"Heads or tails, gentlemen?" said Swift.

Responding to the Selection

Your Response

1. What was your opinion of Multivac as you read the story?

Recalling

2. What is the reason for the celebration at the opening of the story? Why is Multivac a hero?
3. What does each man reveal about his wartime activities?
4. What is the primitive computing device that Swift used?

Interpreting

5. Why do the three men decide to make their confessions?
6. Explain how each character's wartime activities may have affected the victory.
7. In what way was Multivac responsible for winning the war?

Applying

8. Do you think it is possible that a machine can determine the course of human events? Explain your answer.

Analyzing Literature

Recognizing Irony

In **verbal irony** what is said is different from, or opposite to, what is meant. Verbal irony often calls more attention to the intended meaning than a direct statement would. In **irony of situation,** there is a contrast between what appears to be true and what really is true. You or the characters are led to expect a certain outcome, but something quite different actually occurs. For example, in this story, it appears to everyone that the Multivac systems succeeded and were responsible for the victory. However, Henderson had to create data to make Multivac work as it should have. This entire story depends on a series of ironic revelations about how the war was won.

1. Explain why the title of this short story is ironic.
2. Explain how each man's confession is ironic.
3. Why is Swift's confession especially ironic?
4. Every day advances are being made in the field of artificial intelligence. What is artificial intelligence? Why is the term itself ironic?

Thinking and Writing

Writing About a Title

Imagine that you are working as an assistant to Isaac Asimov. He has just finished writing this story and he wants your advice about the title he is considering. Write Asimov a memorandum explaining why you think the title he chose is a good one for the story, or suggest another and explain why you think it is better. Include reasons that relate both to the plot of the story and to Asimov's method of developing it. When you revise the memo, include a quotation from the story to support your position.

Theme

GIRL LOOKING AT LANDSCAPE, 1957
Richard Diebenkorn
Collection of Whitney Museum of American Art

GUIDE FOR READING

Bei Dao

(1949–   ) was born in Beijing, where he was educated at one of the country's best schools. In 1966 his education was interrupted by the Cultural Revolution, a movement to "purify" China by persecuting leaders and intellectuals. Bei Dao, like many teenagers, participated in this movement. However, he soon became disillusioned with it and turned to writing poetry. Eventually he earned a reputation as China's foremost young poet. Nevertheless, his highly personal poetry and his support for human rights angered the Chinese regime.

Bei Dao was in Berlin when student protesters were massacred at Tiananmen Square (June 4, 1989). Since that time, he has lived in exile, apart from his wife and daughter.

The Homecoming Stranger

Theme

Theme is the central message or general insight into life that the author conveys in a story. Modern writers don't usually express theme directly. Rather, they suggest it through the elements of plot, character, and setting. For example, one aspect of this story's setting that relates to the theme is the Cultural Revolution, which is explained below.

Focus

In 1966 the Communist government under Mao Zedong undertook the Cultural Revolution. Teenagers, organized into paramilitary groups called Red Guards, arrested leaders viewed as corrupt or lacking in revolutionary zeal. In the chaotic aftermath of this movement, millions of Chinese were imprisoned or exiled, and the lives of an entire generation of Chinese were disrupted. Get together with several classmates and try to imagine what it was like to be a member of the Red Guard. How would it have felt to march through the streets and arrest party officials, government leaders, and teachers? Keep your discussion in mind as you read about a family that suffered under the Cultural Revolution.

Vocabulary

Knowing the following words will help you as you read "The Homecoming Stranger."

rehabilitation (rē′ hə bil′ ə tā′ shən) n.: Restoration of rank, privileges, and property (p. 191)
delineated (di lin′ ē āt′ id) v.: Depicted; described (p. 192)
resplendent (ri splen′ dənt) adj.: Splendid; dazzling (p. 192)
repudiated (ri pyoo′ dē āt′ id) v.: Denied (p. 194)
ubiquitous (yoo bik′ wə təs) adj.: Present everywhere, at the same time (p. 195)

compunction (kəm puŋk′ shən) n.: Sense of guilt or regret (p. 196)
conciliatory (kən sil′ e ə tôr′ ē) adj.: Soothing (p. 198)
imploring (im plôr′ iŋ) adj.: As if begging or asking (p. 200)
pensively (pen′ siv lē) adv.: Sadly; reflectively (p. 200)

The Homecoming Stranger

Bei Dao

translated by Bonnie S. McDougall and Chen Maiping

1

Papa was back.

After exactly twenty years of reform through labor, which took him from the Northeast to Shanxi,[1] and then from Shanxi to Gansu,[2] he was just like a sailor swept overboard by a wave, struggling blindly against the undertow until miraculously he is tossed by another wave back onto the same deck.

The verdict was: it was entirely a misjudgment, and he has been granted complete rehabilitation. That day, when the leaders of the Theater Association honored our humble home to announce the decision, I almost jumped up: when did you become so clever? Didn't the announcement that he was an offender against the people come out of your mouths too? It was Mama's eyes, those calm yet suffering eyes, that stopped me.

Next came the dress rehearsal for the celebration: we moved from a tiny pigeon loft into a three-bedroom apartment in a big building; sofas, bookcases, desks, and chrome folding chairs appeared as if by magic (I kept saying half-jokingly to Mama that these were the troupe's props); relatives and friends came running in and out all day, until the lacquer doorknob was rubbed shiny by their hands, and even those uncles and aunts who hadn't shown up all those years rushed to offer congratulations . . . all right, cheer, sing, but what does all this have to do with me? My Papa died a long time ago, he died twenty years ago, just when a little four- or five-year-old girl needed a father's love—that's what Mama, the school, kind-hearted souls, and the whole social upbringing that starts at birth told me. Not only this, you even wanted me to hate him, curse him, it's even possible you'd have given me a whip so I could lash him viciously! Now it's the other way round, you're wearing a different face. What do you want me to do? Cry or laugh?

Yesterday at dinner time, Mama was even more considerate than usual, endlessly filling my bowl with food. After the meal, she drew a telegram from the drawer and handed it to me, showing not the slightest sign of any emotion.

"Him?"

"He arrives tomorrow, at 4:50 in the afternoon."

I crumpled the telegram, staring numbly into Mama's eyes.

"Go and meet him, Lanlan." She avoided my gaze.

"I have a class tomorrow afternoon."

"Get someone to take it for you."

I turned toward my room. "I won't go."

"Lanlan." Mama raised her voice. "He is your father, after all!"

---

1. **Shanxi** (shän′ shē′): Province of northeast China.
2. **Gansu** (gän′ sü′): Province of northwest China.

"Father?" I muttered, turning away fiercely, as if overcome with fear at the meaning of this word. From an irregular spasm in my heart, I realized it was stitches from the old wound splitting open one by one.

I closed the composition book spread in front of me: Zhang Xiaoxia,[3] 2nd Class, 5th Year. A spirited girl, her head always slightly to one side in a challenging way, just like me as a child. Oh yes, childhood. For all of us life begins with those pale blue copybooks, with those words, sentences, and punctuation marks smudged by erasers; or, to put it more precisely, it begins with a certain degree of deception. The teachers delineated life with halos, but which of them does not turn into a smoke ring or an iron hoop?

Shadows flowed in from the long old-fashioned windows, dulling the bright light on the glass desktop. The entire staff-room was steeped in drowsy tranquillity. I sighed, tidied my things, locked the door and crossing the deserted school grounds walked toward home.

The apartment block with its glittering lights was like a huge television screen, the unlit windows composing an elusive image. After a little while some of the windows lit up, and some went dark again. But the three windows on the seventh floor remained as they were: one bright, two dark. I paced up and down for a long time in the vacant lot piled with white lime and fir poles. On a crooked, broken signboard were the words: "Safety First."

Strange, why is it that in all the world's languages, this particular meaning comes out as the same sound: Papa. Fathers of different colors, temperaments, and status all derive the same satisfaction from this sound. Yet I still can't say it. What do I know

about him? Except for a few surviving old photographs retaining a childhood dream (perhaps every little girl would have such dreams): him, sitting on an elephant like an Arab sheik, a white cloth wound round his head, a resplendent mat on the elephant's back, golden tassels dangling to the ground . . . there were only some plays that once created a sensation and a thick book on dramatic theory which I happened to see at the wastepaper salvage station. What else was there? Yes, add those unlucky letters, as punctual and drab as a clock; stuck in those brown paper envelopes with their red frames, they were just like death notices, suffocating me. I never wrote back, and afterward, I threw them into the fire without even looking at them. Once, a dear little duckling was printed on a snow-white envelope, but when I tore it open and looked, I was utterly crushed. I was so upset I cursed all ugly ducklings, counting up their vices one by one: greed, pettiness, slovenliness . . . because they hadn't brought me good luck. But what luck did I deserve?

The elevator had already closed for the day, and I had to climb all the way up. I stopped outside the door to our place and listened, holding my breath. From inside came the sounds of the television hum and the clichés of an old film. God, give me courage!

As soon as I opened the door, I heard my younger brother's gruff voice: "Sis's back." He rushed up as if making an assault on the enemy, helping me take off my coat. He was almost twenty, but still full of a childish attachment to me, probably because I had given him the maternal love which had seemed too heavy a burden for Mama in those years.

The corridor was very dark and the light from the kitchen split the darkness in two. He was standing in the doorway of the room

---

3. Zhang Xiaoxia (jöŋ shou′ shä′)

opposite, standing in the other half of darkness, and next to him was Mama. The reflection from the television screen flickered behind their shoulders.

A moment of dead silence.

Finally, he walked over, across the river of light. The light, the deathly white light, slipped swiftly over his wrinkled and mottled neck and face. I was struck dumb: was this shriveled little old man him? Father. I leaned weakly against the door.

He hesitated a moment and put out his hand. My small hand disappeared in his stiff, big-jointed hand. These hands didn't match his body at all.

"Lanlan." His voice was very low, and trembled a little.

Silence.

"Lanlan," he said again, his voice becoming a little more positive, as if he were waiting eagerly for something.

But what could I say?

"You're back very late. Have you had dinner?" said Mama.

"Mm." My voice was so weak.

"Why is everyone standing? Come inside," said Mama.

He took me by the hand. I followed obediently. Mama turned on the light and switched off the television with a click. We sat down on the sofa. He was still clutching my hand tightly, staring at me intently. I evaded his eyes and let my gaze fall on the blowup plastic doll on the windowsill.

An unbearable silence.

"Lanlan," he called once again.

I was really afraid the doll might explode, sending brightly colored fragments flying all over the room.

"Have you had your dinner?"

I nodded vigorously.

"Is it cold outside?"

"No." Everything was so normal, the doll wouldn't burst. Perhaps it would fly away suddenly like a hydrogen balloon, out the window, above the houses full of voices, light, and warmth, and go off to search for the stars and moon.

"Lanlan." His voice was full of compassion and pleading.

All of a sudden, my just-established confidence swiftly collapsed. I felt a spasm of alarm. Blood pounded at my temples. Fiercely I pulled back my hand, rushed out the door into my own room, and flung myself headfirst onto the bed. I really felt like bursting into tears.

The door opened softly; it was Mama. She came up to the bed, sat down in the darkness and stroked my head, neck, and shoulders. Involuntarily, my whole body began to tremble as if with cold.

"Don't cry, Lanlan."

Cry? Mama, if I could still cry the tears would surely be red, they'd be blood.

She patted me on the back. "Go to sleep, Lanlan, everything will pass."

Mama left.

Everything will pass. Huh, it's so easily said, but can twenty years be written off at one stroke? People are not reeds, or leeches, but oysters, and the sands of memory will flow with time to change into a part of the body itself, teardrops will never run dry.

. . . a basement. Mosquitoes thudded against the searing light bulb. An old man covered with cuts and bruises was tied up on the pommel horse, his head bowed, moaning hoarsely. I lay in the corner sobbing. My knees were cut to ribbons by the broken glass; blood and mud mixed together . . .

I was then only about twelve years old. One night, when Mama couldn't sleep, she suddenly hugged me and told me that Papa was a good man who had been wrongly accused. At these words hope flared up in the child's heart: for the first time she might be able to enjoy the same rights as other children. So I ran all around, to the school, the Theater Association, the neighborhood committee, and the Red Guard[4] headquar-

ters, to prove Papa's innocence to them. Disaster was upon us, and those louts took me home savagely for investigation. I didn't know what was wrong with Mama, but she repudiated all her words in front of her daughter. All the blame fell on my small shoulders. Mama repented, begged, wished herself dead, but what was the use? I was

---

4. Red Guard Groups of young students that, during the Cultural Revolution, formed a fanatical arm of the Communist party. They reported and arrested people believed to be ''suspect'' in their support of the Revolution.

UNTITLED (PEOPLE ARRESTED DURING THE CULTURAL REVOLUTION)
James McMullan

struggled against, given heavy labor, and punished by being made to kneel on broken glass.

. . . the old man raised his bloody face: "Give me some water, water, water!" Staring with frightened eyes, I forgot the pain, huddling tightly into the corner. When dawn came and the old man breathed his last, I fainted with fright too. The blood congealed on my knees . . .

Can I blame Mama for this?

2

The sky was so blue it dazzled the eyes, its intense reflections shining on the ground. My hair tied up in a ribbon, I was holding a small empty bamboo basket and standing amidst the dense waist-high grass. Suddenly, from the jungle opposite appeared an elephant, the tassels of the mat on its back dangling to the ground; Papa sat proudly on top, a white turban on his head. The elephant's trunk waved to and fro, and with a snort it curled round me and placed me up in front of Papa. We marched forward, across the coconut grove streaked with leaping sunlight, across the hills and gullies gurgling with springs. I suddenly turned my head and cried out in alarm. A little old man was sitting behind me, his face blurred with blood; he was wearing convict clothes and on his chest were printed the words "Reform Through Labor." He was moaning hoarsely, "Give me some water, water, water . . ."

I woke up in fright.

It was five o'clock, and outside it was still dark. I stretched out my hand and pulled out the drawer of the bedside cupboard, fumbled for cigarettes, and lit one. I drew back fiercely and felt more relaxed. The white cloud of smoke spread through the darkness and finally floated out through the small open-shuttered window. The glow from the ciga-

rette alternately brightened and dimmed as I strained to see clearly into the depths of my heart, but other than the ubiquitous silence, the relaxation induced by the cigarette, and the vague emptiness left by the nightmare, there was nothing.

I switched on the desk lamp, put on my clothes, and opened the door quietly. There was a light on in the kitchen and a rustling noise. Who was up so early? Who?

Under the light, wearing a black cotton-padded vest, he was crouching over the wastepaper basket with his back toward me, meticulously picking through everything; spread out beside him were such spoils as vegetable leaves, trimmings, and fish heads.

I coughed.

He jumped and looked round in alarm, his face deathly white, gazing in panic toward me.

The fluorescent light hummed.

He stood up slowly, one hand behind his back, making an effort to smile. "Lanlan, I woke you up."

"What are you doing?"

"Oh, nothing, nothing." He was flustered and kept wiping his trousers with his free hand.

I put out my hand. "Let me see."

After some hesitation he handed the thing over. It was just an ordinary cigarette pack, with nothing odd about it except that it was soiled in one corner.

I lifted my head, staring at him in bewilderment.

"Oh, Lanlan," beads of sweat started from his balding head, "yesterday I forgot to examine this cigarette pack when I threw it away, just in case I wrote something on it; it would be terrible if the team leader saw it."

"Team leader?" I was even more baffled. "Who's the team leader?"

"The people who oversee us prisoners are called team leaders." He fished out a handkerchief and wiped the sweat away. "Of course, I know, it's beyond their reach, but better to find it just in case . . ."

My head began to buzz. "All right, that's enough."

He closed his mouth tightly, as if he had even bitten out his tongue. I really hadn't expected our conversation would begin like this. For the first time I looked carefully at him. He seemed even older and paler than yesterday, with a short grayish stubble over his sunken cheeks, wrinkles that seemed to have been carved by a knife around his lackluster eyes, and an ugly sarcoma[5] on the tip of his right ear. I could not help feeling some compassion for him.

"Was it very hard there?"

"It was all right, you get used to it."

Get used to it! A cold shiver passed through me. Dignity. Wire netting. Guns. Hurried footsteps. Dejected ranks. Death. I crumpled up the cigarette pack and tossed it into the wastepaper basket. "Go back to sleep, it's still early."

"I've had enough sleep, reveille's[6] at 5:30." He turned to tidy up the scattered rubbish.

Back in my room, I pressed my face against the ice-cold wall. It was quite unbearable to begin like this, what should I do next? Wasn't he a man of great integrity before? Ah, Hand of Time, you're so cruel and indifferent, to knead a man like putty, you destroyed him before his daughter could remember her father's real face clearly . . . eventually I calmed down, packed my things into my bag, and put on my overcoat.

Passing through the kitchen, I came to a standstill. He was at the sink, scrubbing his

big hands with a small brush, the green soap froth dripping down like sap.

"I'm going to work."

"So early?" He was so absorbed he did not even raise his head.

"I'm used to it."

I did not turn on the light, going down along the darkness, along each flight of stairs.

3

For several days in a row I came home very late. When Mama asked why, I always offered the excuse that I was busy at school. As soon as I got home, I would dodge into the kitchen and hurriedly rake up a few left-overs, then bore straight into my own little nest. I seldom ran into him, and even when we did meet I would hardly say a word. Yet it seemed his silence contained enormous compunction, as if to apologize for that morning, for his unexpected arrival, for my unhappy childhood, these twenty years and my whole life.

My brother was always running in like a spy to report on the situation, saying things like: "He's planted a pot of peculiar dried-up herbs." "All afternoon he stared at the fish in the tank." "He's burned a note again" . . . I would listen without any reaction. As far as I was concerned, it was all just a continuation of that morning, not worth making a fuss about. What was strange was my brother, talking about such things so flatly, not tinged by any emotion at all, not feeling any heavy burden on his mind. It was no wonder; since the day he was born Papa had already flown far away, and besides, in those years he was brought up in his Grandma's home, and with Mama's wings and mine in turn hanging over Grandma's little window as well, he never saw the ominous sky.

---

5. sarcoma (sär kō′ mə) *n.*: Malignant tumor that develops in the skin.
6. reveille (rev′ ə lē) *n.*: Signal to waken soldiers.

One evening, as I was lying on the bed smoking, someone knocked at the door. I hurriedly stuffed the cigarette butt in a small tin box as Mama came in.

"Smoking again, Lanlan?"

As if nothing had happened I turned over the pages of a novel beside my pillow.

"The place smells of smoke, open a window."

Thank heavens, she hadn't come to nag. But then I realized that there was something strange in her manner. She sat down beside the small desk, absently picked up the ceramic camel pen-rack and examined it for a moment before returning it to its original place. How would one put it in diplomatic language? Talks, yes, formal talks . . .

"Lanlan, you're not a child anymore." Mama was weighing her words.

It had started; I listened with respectful attention.

"I know you've resented me since you were little, and you've also resented him and resented everyone else in the world, because you've had enough suffering . . . but Lanlan, it isn't only you who's suffered."

"Yes, Mama."

"When you marry Jianping,[7] and have children, you'll understand a mother's suffering . . ."

"We don't want children if we can't be responsible for their future."

"You're blaming us, Lanlan," Mama said painfully.

"No, not blaming. I'm grateful to you, Mama, it wasn't easy for you in those years . . ."

"Do you think it was easy for him?"

"Him?" I paused. "I don't know, and I don't want to know either. As a person, I respect his past . . ."

"Don't you respect his present? You should realize, Lanlan, his staying alive required great courage!"

"That's not the problem, Mama. You say this because you lived together for many years, but I, I can't make a false display of affection . . ."

"What are you saying!" Mama grew angry and raised her voice. "At least one should fulfill one's own duties and obligations!"

"Duties? Obligations?" I started to laugh, but it was more painful than crying. "I heard a lot about them during those years. I don't want to lose any more, Mama."

"But what have you gained?"

"The truth."

"It's a cold and unfeeling truth!"

"I can't help it," I spread out my hands, "that's how life is."

"You're too selfish!" Mama struck the desk with her hand and got up, the loose flesh on her face trembling. She stared furiously at me for a moment, then left, shutting the door heavily.

Selfish, I admit it. In those years selfishness was a kind of instinct, a means of self-defense. What could I rely on except this? Perhaps I shouldn't have provoked Mama's anger, perhaps I should really be a good girl and love Papa, Mama, my brother, life, and myself.

4

During the break between classes, I went into the reception office and rang Jianping.

"Hello, Jianping, come over this evening."

"What's up? Lanlan?" he was shouting, over the clatter of the machines his voice sounding hoarse and weary.

"He's back."

"Who? Your father?"

---

7. **Jianping** (jen′ pin′)

DAWEI, 1982 (detail)
Sun Jingbo

"Clever one, come over and help; it's an absolutely awful situation."

He started to laugh.

"Huh, if you laugh, just watch out!" I clenched my fists and banged down the receiver.

It's true, Jianping has the ability to head off disaster. The year when the production brigade chief withheld the grain ration from us educated youth,[8] it was he who led the whole bunch of us to snatch it all back. Although I normally appear to be quite sharp-witted, I always have to hide behind his broad shoulders whenever there's a crisis.

That afternoon I had no classes and

---

8. educated youth: During the Cultural Revolution, educated people (young and old) were distrusted and persecuted.

---

hurried home early. Mama had left a note on the table, saying that she and Papa had gone to call on some old friends and would eat when they returned. I kneaded some dough, minced the meat filling, and got everything ready to wrap the dumplings.

Jianping arrived. He brought with him a breath of freshness and cold, his cheeks flushed red, brimming with healthy vitality. I snuggled up against him at once, my cheek pressed against the cold buttons on his chest, like a child who feels wronged but has nowhere to pour out her woes. I didn't say anything, what could I say?

We kissed and hugged for a while, then sat down and wrapped dumplings, talking and joking as we worked. From gratitude, relaxation, and the vast sleepiness that follows affection, I was almost on the verge of tears.

When my brother returned, he threw off his work clothes, drank a mouthful of water, and flew off like a whirlwind.

It was nearly eight when they got home. As they came in, it gave them quite a shock to see us. Mama could not then conceal a conciliatory and motherly smile of victory; Papa's expression was much more complicated. Apart from the apologetic look of the last few days, he also seemed to feel an irrepressible pleasure at this surprise, as well as a precautionary fear.

"This is Jianping, this is . . ." My face was suffocated with red.

"This is Lanlan's father," Mama filled in.

Jianping held out his hand and boomed, "How do you do, Uncle!"

Papa grasped Jianping's hand, his lips trembling for a long time. "So you're, so you're Jianping, fine, fine . . ."

Delivering the appropriate courtesies, Jianping gave the old man such happiness he was at a loss what to do. It was quite clear to me that his happiness had nothing to do with these remarks, but was because he felt that at last he'd found a bridge between him and me, a strong and reliable bridge.

At dinner, everyone seemed to be on very friendly terms, or at least that's how it appeared on the surface. Several awkward silences were covered over by Jianping's jokes. His conversation was so witty and lively that it even took me by surprise.

After dinner, Papa took out his Zhong-hua[9] cigarettes from a tin cigarette case to offer to Jianping. This set them talking about the English method of drying tobacco and moving on to soil salinization,[10] insect pests among peanuts and vine-grafting. I sat bolt upright beside them, smiling like a mannequin in a shop window.

Suddenly, my smile began to vanish. Surely this was a scene from a play? Jian-ping was the protagonist—a clever son-in-law, while I, I was the meek and mild new bride. For reasons only the devil could tell, everyone was acting to the hilt, striving to forget something in this scene. Acting happiness, acting calmness, acting glossed-over suffering. I suddenly felt that Jianping was an outsider to the fragmented, shattered suffering of this family.

I began to consider Jianping in a different light. His tone, his gestures, even his appearance, all had an unfamiliar flavor. This wasn't real, this wasn't the old him. Could strangeness be contagious? How frightening.

Jianping hastily threw me an inquiring glance, as if expecting me to repay the role he was playing with a commending smile. This made me feel even more disgusted. I

was disgusted with him, and with myself, disgusted with everything the world is made of, happiness and sorrow, reality and sham, good and evil.

Guessing this, he wound up the conversation. He looked at his watch, said a few thoroughly polite bits of nonsense, and got to his feet.

As usual, I accompanied him to the bus stop. But along the way, I said not a single word, keeping a fair distance from him. He dejectedly thrust his hands in his pockets, kicking a stone.

An apartment block ahead hid the night. I felt alone. I longed to know how human beings survive behind these countless containers of suffering, broken families. Yet in these containers, memory is too frightening. It can only deepen the suffering and divide every family until everything turns to powder.

When we reached the bus stop, he stood with his back to me, gazing at the distant lights. "Lanlan, do I still need to explain?"

"There's no need."

He leaped onto the bus. Its red taillights flickering, it disappeared round the corner.

5

Today there was a sports meet at the school, but I didn't feel like it at all. Yesterday afternoon, Zhang Xiaoxia kept pestering me to come and watch her in the 100 meter race. I just smiled, without promising anything. She pursed her little mouth and, fanning her cheeks, which were streaming with sweat, with her handkerchief, stared out the window in a huff. I put my hands on her shoulders and turned her round. "I'll go then, all right?" Her face broadening into dimples, she struggled free of me in embarrassment and ran off. How easy it is to deceive a child.

---

9. Zhonghua (jơơŋ′ hwä′): A trademark of one of the best cigarettes in China.
10. soil salinization (sal′ ə nə zā′ shən) n.: Process of contaminating soil with salts.

I stretched, and started to get dressed. The winter sunlight seeped through the fogged-up window, making everything seem dim and quiet, like an extension of sleep and dreams. When I came out of my room, it was quiet and still; evidently everyone had gone out. I washed my hair and put my washing to soak, dashing busily to and fro. When everything was done, I sat down to eat breakfast. Suddenly I sensed that someone was standing behind me, and when I looked round it was Papa, standing stiffly in the kitchen doorway and staring at me blankly.

"Didn't you go out?" I asked.

"Oh, no, no, I was on the balcony. You're not going to school today?"

"No. What is it?"

"I thought," he hesitated, "we might go for a walk in the park, what do you think?" There was an imploring note in his voice.

"All right." Although I didn't turn round, I could feel that his eyes had brightened.

It was a warm day, but the morning mist had still not faded altogether, lingering around eaves and treetops. Along the way, we said almost nothing. But when we entered the park, he pointed at the tall white poplars[11] by the side of the road. "The last time I brought you here, they'd just been planted." But I didn't remember it at all.

After walking along the avenue for a while, we sat down on a bench beside the lake. On the cement platform in front of us, several old wooden boats, corroded by wind and rain, were lying upside down, dirt and dry leaves forming a layer over them. The ice on the surface of the water crackled from time to time.

He lit a cigarette.

"Those same boats," he said pensively.

"Oh?"

_____
11. poplars (päp′ lərz) _n._: Trees of the willow family.

"There're still the same boats. You used to like sitting in the stern, splashing with your bare feet and shouting, 'Motorboat! Motorboat!'" The shred of a smile of memory appeared on his face. "Everyone said you were like a boy . . ."

"Really?"

"You liked swords and guns; whenever you went into a toy shop you'd always want to come out with a whole array of weapons."

"Because I didn't know what they were used for."

All at once, a shadow covered his face and his eyes darkened. "You were still a child then . . ."

Silence, a long silence. The boats lying on the bank were turned upside down here. They were covering a little girl's silly cries, a father's carefree smile, soft-drink bottle-tops, a blue satin ribbon, children's books and toy guns, the taste of earth in the four seasons, the passage of twenty years . . .

"Lanlan," he said suddenly, his voice very low and trembling. "I, I beg your pardon."

My whole body began to quiver.

"When your mother spoke of your life in these years, it was as if my heart was cut with a knife. What is a child guilty of?" His hand clutched at the air and came to rest against his chest.

"Don't talk about these things," I said quietly.

"To tell you the truth, it was for you that I lived in those years. I thought if I paid for my crime myself, perhaps life would be a bit better for my child, but . . ." he choked with sobs, "you can blame me, Lanlan, I didn't have the ability to protect you, I'm not worthy to be your father . . ."

"No, don't don't . . ." I was trembling, my whole body went weak, all I could do was wave my hands. How selfish I was! I thought only of myself, immersed myself only in my

RISE WITH FORCE AND SPIRIT, 1988
James Bama
The Greenwich Workshop, Inc., Trumbull, CT

own sufferings, even making suffering a kind of pleasure and a wall of defense against others. But how did he live? For you, for your selfishness, for your heartlessness! Can the call of blood be so feeble? Can what is called human nature have completely died out in my heart?

"... twenty years ago, the day I left the house, it was a Sunday. I took an afternoon train, but I left at dawn; I didn't want you to remember this scene. Standing by your little bed, the tears streaming down, I thought to myself: 'Little Lanlan, shall we ever meet again?' You were sleeping so soundly and sweetly, with your little round dimples . . . the evening before as you were going to bed, you hugged my neck and said in a soft voice, 'Papa, will you take me out tomorrow?' 'Papa's busy tomorrow.' You went into a sulk and pouted unhappily. I had to promise. Then you asked again, 'Can we go rowing?' 'Yes, we'll go rowing.' And so you went to sleep quite satisfied. But I deceived you, Lanlan, when you woke up the next day, what could you think . . .''

"Papa!" I blurted out, flinging myself on his shoulder and crying bitterly.

With trembling hands he stroked my head. "Lanlan, my child."

"Forgive me, Papa," I said, choked with sobs. "I'm still your little Lanlan, always . . .''

"My little Lanlan, always.''

A bird whose name I don't know hovered over the lake, crying strangely, adding an even deeper layer of desolation to this bleak winter scene.

I lay crying against Papa's shoulder for a long time. My tears seeped drop by drop into the coarse wool of his overcoat. I seemed to smell the pungent scent of tobacco mingling with the smell of mud and sweat. I seemed to see him in the breaks between heavy labor, leaning wearily against the pile of dirt and rolling a cigarette staring into the distance through the fork between the guard's legs. He was pulling a cart, struggling forward on the miry road, the cartwheels screeching, churning up black mud sods. The guard's legs. He was digging the earth shovelful after shovelful, straining himself to fling it toward the pit side. The guard's legs. He was carrying his bowl, greedily draining the last mouthful of vegetable soup. The guard's legs . . . I dared not think anymore, I dared not. My powers of imagining suffering were limited after all. But he actually lived in a place beyond the powers of human imagination. Minute after minute, day after day, oh

God, a full twenty years . . . no, amidst suffering, people should be in communication with one another, suffering can link people's souls even more than happiness, even if the soul is already numb, already exhausted . . .

"Lanlan, look,'' he drew a beautiful necklace from his pocket, "I made this just before I left there from old toothbrush handles. I wanted to give you a kind of present, but then I was afraid you wouldn't want this crude toy . . .''

"No, I like it." I took the necklace, moving the beads lightly to and fro with my finger, each of these wounded hearts . . .

On the way back, Papa suddenly bent over and picked up a piece of paper, turning it over and over in his hand. Impulsively I pulled up his arm and laid my head on his shoulder. In my heart I understood that this was because of a new strangeness, and an attempt to resist this strangeness.

Here on this avenue, I seemed to see a scene from twenty years earlier. A little girl with a blue ribbon in her hair, both fists outstretched, totters along the edge of the concrete road. Beside her walks a middle-aged man relaxed and at ease. A row of little newly planted poplars separates them. And these little trees, as they swiftly swell and spread, change into a row of huge insurmountable bars. Symbolizing this are twenty years of irregular growth rings.

"Papa, let's go."

He tossed away the piece of paper and wiped his hand carefully on his handkerchief. We walked on again.

Suddenly I thought of Zhang Xiaoxia. At this moment, she'll actually be in the race. Behind rises a puff of white smoke from the starting gun, and amid countless faces and shrill cries falling away behind her, she dashes against the white finishing tape.

RESPONDING TO THE SELECTION

Your Response

1. Put yourself in Lanlan's place. How would you have felt seeing your father for the first time in twenty years?

Recalling

2. Where has Lanlan's father been for twenty years?

3. How do Lanlan's reactions to her father change during the story?

Interpreting

4. Why does Lanlan have difficulty saying the word *Papa*?

5. Lanlan's mother calls her selfish. Explain why you agree or disagree with this accusation.

6. Why is Lanlan grateful to Jianping at first and then resentful of him?

7. What accounts for the differences in Lanlan's attitude toward her father at the beginning and end of the story?

8. What has Lanlan learned by the end of the story?

9. What is the meaning of the story's final image?

Applying

10. What insight did this story give you about how the Cultural Revolution affected people's lives?

ANALYZING LITERATURE

Analyzing Theme

A story's **theme** is the insight into life that it offers. Theme is rarely stated directly in modern stories; rather, it is implied through plot, character, setting, and imagery. For example, in "The Homecoming Stranger," the emotions felt by Lanlan are suggestive of the theme.

1. How do Lanlan's changing feelings toward her father reveal the theme?

2. How do details like the necklace made "from old toothbrush handles" convey theme?

3. Express the theme of the story in your own words.

4. Is the insight into life that this story conveys relevant to you as well as to a Chinese reader? Explain.

CRITICAL THINKING AND READING

Recognizing Figurative Language

Sometimes authors use **figurative language**—words that are not meant to be interpreted literally. The purpose of such language is to evoke a strong response in readers by causing them to see things in new ways. Following are examples of figurative language. Explain how each contributes to the story's meaning by conveying an idea or a feeling in a fresh way.

1. "'Father?' I muttered, turning away fiercely, as if overcome with fear at the meaning of this word. From an irregular spasm in my heart, I realized it was stitches from the old wound splitting open one by one." (page 192)

2. ". . . in those years, he [her brother] was brought up in his Grandma's home, and with Mama's wings and mine in turn hanging over Grandma's little window as well, he never saw the ominous sky." (page 196)

THINKING AND WRITING

Exploring Theme

Imagine that you are a reporter from a Chinese newspaper. You are writing a feature about the effects of the Cultural Revolution, and you want to interview Lanlan. Plan your interview by preparing a list of questions for her. Then write the answers that she would probably give. Use your questions and answers to bring out what Lanlan has learned from her experience. As you revise your interview, make sure that you have portrayed Lanlan as she appears in the story.

MULTICULTURAL CONNECTION

Political Strife and Human Suffering

In Bei Dao's moving "The Homecoming Stranger," the human costs of political strife become clear. The disruption caused by a father's twenty-year imprisonment suddenly ends. However, the family members must learn to live with one another again.

Parallel suffering. Bei Dao, a poet as well as a short-story writer, is actually living through an experience similar to that of his own fictional character. Like the father in the story, Bei Dao has been separated from his daughter. Because he protested against the injustices of the Chinese government, he cannot return to China, where his wife and daughter are living.

The sadness of this situation is reflected in a poem he wrote for his daughter, whose nickname, Tiantian, includes two Chinese characters that resemble a pair of windows: 田田 The word *picture* in Chinese also includes this windowlike character.

A Picture
for Tiantian's fifth birthday

Morning arrives in a sleeveless
    dress
apples tumble all over the earth
my daughter is drawing a picture
how vast is a five-year-old sky
your name has two windows
one opens towards a sun with no
    clock-hands
the other opens towards your father
who has become a hedgehog in
    exile
taking with him a few unintelligible
    characters
and a bright red apple
he has left your painting
how vast is a five-year-old sky

Both the father in the poem and the father in the story suffer similarly. The poet-father worries as he studies a "sun with no clock-hands," which is a frighteningly timeless, perhaps eternal, clock. His exile has no scheduled end and, therefore, there are no means to measure its length. When will it end? *Will it end?* These questions can't be answered.

The father in "The Homecoming Stranger" could not measure his suffering until his exile ended. At first there is only *his* loss, *his* pain, *his* separation. However, the family also suffered without him.

Two political movements. The events that led to this suffering involved two political movements in China: the Cultural Revolution, which lasted from 1965 to 1976, and the Democracy Movement of the 1980's. Both were primarily youth movements. Both turned China upside down.

Stoking the fires of chaos. During the Cultural Revolution, young students joined the Red Guards, a fanatical arm of the Communist party. Their job was to stoke the fires of revolutionary change. Encouraged by Mao Zedong, China's dictator, and supported by the army, they were to report anyone who was "suspect" in his or her support of the Revolution.

Red Guards arrested neighbors. They turned in teachers, school officials, bus drivers, shopkeepers, farmers, and clerks. (The father in Bei Dao's story is a victim of the Red Guards.) They betrayed friends, parents, and siblings. No evidence was required, just an accusation. To defend someone was to risk being accused. Few took the risk. Prison, beatings, banishments from home, and executions were among the punishments. Schools were closed for several years, local governments were shut down, and business and trade were disrupted.

The Democracy Movement. Eventually, because chaos threatened to engulf China, the government put an end to the Cultural Revolution. Radicals were arrested and punished. Mao Zedong died. Reforms slowly allowed for debate, and the Democracy Movement began with poems, essays, songs, and stories printed and posted on a public wall in Beijing.

One of those making contributions to the Democracy Wall was a former Red Guard writing under the name Bei Dao, which means "northern island" in Chinese. Even as it waned, the excesses of the Cultural Revolution had disillusioned Bei Dao. Its human costs were too great, the suffering pointless. His poems and stories addressed this suffering. Bei Dao soon became one of the leading intellectuals of the Democracy Movement.

Blood in the square. For a time, particularly during the days of late 1988 and early 1989, progress seemed unstoppable. There was a massive rally in Tiananmen Square. A Statue of Liberty was displayed before thousands of students and workers gathered in the square. Less than a generation before, young people had led the forces of repression. Now they were leading the movement for reform, with no weapons other than their courage and their hope for a more democratic society.

As the world watched, the crackdown began. Television broadcast the startling sight of a young man blocking the advance of a line of tanks. For an inspiring moment, the forces of repression blinked rather than shot. The tanks halted. A few nights later, however, new troops entered Beijing, and the Tiananmen Square protesters were routed in a bloody massacre. Smoke and darkness covered their work, but the morning sun showed an empty, blood-stained square.

Exile: A worldwide theme. Thousands were arrested. Those who escaped arrest and the violence of the night went into hiding. Some went into exile. Bei Dao, who was traveling abroad, could not return home to his wife and daughter.

Bei Dao had written "The Homecoming Stranger" from the outside looking in. Now he writes from inside his own suffering, looking out at a world where there are still too many people like him. They are people in exile from Cuba, South Africa, China, Burma, Haiti, El Salvador, Nicaragua, and many other places. Like Bei Dao, they work to end repression.

Activities

1. **Cross-curricular Connection.** Draw a map of contemporary China. Label places such as Beijing, Shanxi, and Sansu that are mentioned in the story.
2. **Writing.** Pretend that Lanlan is the daughter in *A Picture* and write a poem that expresses her thoughts and feelings.
3. **Speaking and Listening.** Go to see the movie *A World Apart,* which tells the story of the difficulties between a mother and daughter caught in the struggle against apartheid in South Africa. With classmates, prepare a debate concerning the questions raised in the movie.
4. **Cross-curricular Connection.** Read the book *Think Chinese, Speak Chinese* (New York: Regents Publishing Company, Inc., 1978) to learn more about the written characters of the Chinese language. You can then prepare posters explaining how Chinese characters are written.

GUIDE FOR READING

Sunlight in Trebizond Street

Interior Monologue

An **interior monologue** is a method of telling a story in which the writer brings the reader inside the mind of the narrator, who is the main character. The readers feel that they are experiencing the character's thoughts, feelings, and memories as they are occurring. The effect is a very intense and intimate atmosphere in which emotions are heightened and involvement with the narrator is very strong.

Alan Paton

(1903–1988) was born in the Union of South Africa. In 1948 he published *Cry, the Beloved Country,* an internationally successful novel contrasting the beauty of the South African landscape with the horrors of racial oppression. One of the first white South Africans to publicly denounce the official apartheid policies, Paton in his later years turned to political action and nonfiction, until writing the novel *Ah, But Your Land Is Beautiful* in 1981. "Sunlight in Trebizond Street" appears in *Knocking on the Door,* a collection of short stories and nonfiction.

Focus

The narrator of "Sunlight in Trebizond Street" is in a military prison, where he spends most of the time alone. Imagine that you were unjustly imprisoned. Think about the people and things you would miss. Then write a letter to a friend or relative from captivity. In your letter record your thoughts and feelings about the experience, as well as your curiosities about the outside world.

Vocabulary

Knowing the following words will help you as you read "Sunlight in Trebizond Street."

certitude (sʉrt′ ə tōōd′) *n.*: Certainty; assurance (p. 207)

arrogant (ar′ ə gənt) *adj.*: Proud; haughty (p. 208)

incessantly (in ses′ ənt lē) *adv.*: Without stopping; ceaselessly (p. 210)

superfluous (sə pʉr′ flōō əs) *adj.*: Unnecessary; useless (p. 210)

desultory (des′ əl tôr′ ē) *adj.*: Purposeless (p. 210)

sardonically (sär dän′ ik lē) *adv.*: Sarcastically (p. 211)

subversion (səb vʉr′ zhən) *n.*: Attempts to overthrow the government (p. 212)

decadent (dek′ ə dənt) *adj.*: Decayed or declining, especially in morals (p. 212)

Sunlight in Trebizond Street

Alan Paton

Today the lieutenant said to me, *I'm going to do you a favor.* I don't answer him. I don't want his favors. *I'm not supposed to do it,* he said. *If I were caught I'd be in trouble.* He looks at me as though he wanted me to say something, and I could have said, *that'd break my heart,* but I don't say it. I don't speak unless I think it will pay me. That's my one fast rule.

Don't you want me to do you a favor? he asks. *I don't care,* I said, *if you do me a favor or you don't. But if you want to do it, that's your own affair.*

You're a stubborn devil, aren't you? I don't answer that, but I watch him. I have been watching Caspar for a long time, and I have come to the conclusion that he has a grudging respect for me. If the major knew his job, he'd take Caspar away, give me someone more exciting, more dangerous.

Don't you want to get out? I don't answer. There are two kinds of questions I don't answer, and he knows it. One is the kind he needs the answers to. The other is the kind to which he knows the answers already. Of course I want to get out, away from those hard staring eyes, whose look you can bear only if your own are hard and staring too. And I want to eat some tasty food, and drink some wine, in some place with soft music and hidden lights. And I want . . . but I do not think of that. I have made a rule.

How many days have you been here? I don't answer that, because I don't know any more. And I don't want Caspar to know that I don't. When they took away the first Bible, it was 81. By an effort of will that exhausted me, I counted up to 105. And I was right, up to 100 at any rate, for on that day they came to inform me, with almost a kind of ceremony, that duly empowered under Act so-and-so, Section so-and-so, they were going to keep me another 100, and would release me when I "answered satisfactorily." That shook me, though I tried to hide it from them. But I lost my head a little, and called out quite loudly, "Hooray for the rule of law." It was foolish. It achieved exactly nothing. After 105 I nearly went to pieces. The next morning I couldn't remember if it were 106 or 107. After that you can't remember any more. You lose your certitude. You're like a blind man who falls over a stool in the well-known house. There's no birthday, no trip to town, no letter from abroad, by which to remember. If you try going back, it's like going back to look for something you dropped yesterday in the desert, or in the forest, or in the water of the lake. Something is gone from you that you'll never find again.

It took me several days to convince myself that it didn't matter all that much. Only one thing mattered, and that was to give them no access to my private self. Our heroic model was B.B.B. He would not speak, or cry out, or stand up, or do anything they told him to do. He would not even look at them, if such a thing is possible. Solitude did not affect him, for he could withdraw into a solitude of his own, a kind of state of suspended being. He died in one such solitude. Some say he withdrew too far and could not come back. Others say he was tortured to death, that in the end the pain stabbed its way into the solitude. No one knows.

So far they haven't touched me. And if they touched me, what would I do? Pain might open the door to that private self. It's my fear of that that keeps me from being arrogant. I have a kind of superstition that pride gets punished sooner than anything else. It's a relic of my lost religion.

You're thinking deep, said Caspar, *I'll come tomorrow. I expect to bring you interesting news.*

Caspar said to me, *Rafael Swartz has been taken in.* It's all I can do to hide from him that for the first time I stand before him in my private and naked self. I dare not pull the clothes round me, for he would know what he had done. Why doesn't he bring instruments, to measure the sudden uncontrollable kick of the heart, and the sudden tensing of the muscles of the face, and the contraction of the pupils? Or does he think he can tell without them? He doesn't appear to be watching me closely. Perhaps he puts down the bait carelessly, confident that the prey will come. But does he not know that the prey is already a thousand times aware? I am still standing naked, but I try to look as though I am wearing clothes.

Rafael Swartz. Is he brave? Will he keep them waiting 1,000 days, till in anger they let him go? Or will he break as soon as one of them casually picks up the poker that has been left carelessly in the coals?

He's a rat, says Caspar. *He has already ratted on you.* I say foolishly, *How can he rat on me? I'm here already.*

You're here, Caspar agreed. He said complainingly, *But you don't tell us anything. Swartz is going to tell us things that you won't tell. Things you don't want us to know. Tell me, doctor, who's the boss?*

I don't answer him. I begin to feel my clothes stealing back on me. I could now look at Caspar confidently, but that I mustn't do. I must wait till I can do it casually.

I don't know when I'll see you again, he said, quite like conversation. *I'll be spending time with Swartz. I expect to have interesting talks with him. And if there's anything I think you ought to know, I'll be right back. Goodbye, doctor.*

He stops at the door. *There's one thing you might like to know. Swartz thinks you brought him in.*

He looks at me. *He thinks that,* he says, *because we told him so.*

John Forrester always said to me when parting, *Have courage.* Have I any courage? Have I any more courage than Rafael Swartz? And who am I to know the extent of his courage? Perhaps they are lying to me. Perhaps when they told him I had brought him in, he laughed at them and said, *It's an old trick but you can't catch an old dog with it.*

Don't believe them, Rafael. And I shan't believe them either. Have courage, Rafael, and I shall have courage too.

Caspar doesn't come. It's five days now.

PORTRAIT OF LUCIAN FREUD
Francis Bacon
Whitworth Art Gallery
University of Manchester

Sunlight in Trebizond Street **209**

At least I think it's five. I can't even be sure of that now. Have courage, Rafael.

It must be ten days now. I am not myself. My stomach is upset. I go to and fro the whole day, and it leaves me weak and drained. But though my body is listless, my imagination works incessantly. What is happening there, in some other room, like this, perhaps in this building too? I know it is useless imagining it, but I go on with it. I've stopped saying, *Have courage, Rafael*, on the grounds that if he has lost his courage, it's too late, and if he hasn't lost his courage, it's superfluous. But I'm afraid. It's coming too close.

Who's your boss? asks Caspar, and of course I don't reply. He talks about Rafael Swartz and Lofty Coombe and Helen Columbus, desultory talk, with now and then desultory questions. The talk and the questions are quite pointless. Is the lieutenant a fool or is he not?

He says to me, *You're a dark horse, aren't you, doctor? Leading a double life, and we didn't know.*

I am full of fear. It's coming too close. I can see John Forrester now, white-haired and benevolent, what they call a man of distinction, the most miraculous blend of tenderness and steel that any of us will ever know. He smiles at me as though to say, *Keep up your courage, we're thinking of you every minute of the day.*

What does Caspar mean, my double life? Of course I led a double life, that's why I'm here. Does he mean some other double life? And how would they know? Could Rafael have known?

Can't you get away, my love? I'm afraid of you, I'm afraid for us all. What did I tell you? I can't remember. I swore an oath to tell no one. But with you I can't remember. And I swore an oath that there would never be any woman at all. That was my crime.

When I first came here, I allowed myself to remember you once a day, for about one minute. But now I am thinking of you more and more. Not just love, fear too. Did I tell you who we were?

Love, why don't you go? Tell them you didn't know I was a revolutionary. Tell them anything, but go.

As for myself, my opinion of myself is unspeakable. I thought I was superior, that I could love a woman, and still be remote and unknowable. We take up this work like children. We plot and plan and are full of secrets. Everything is secret except our secrecy.

What is happening now? Today the major comes with the lieutenant, and the mere sight of him sets my heart pounding. The major's not like Caspar. He does not treat me as superior or inferior. He says *Sit down*, and I sit. He says to me, *So you still won't cooperate?* Such is my foolish state that I say to him, *Why should I cooperate? There's no law which says I must cooperate. In fact the law allows for my not cooperating, and gives you the power to detain me until I do.*

The major speaks to me quite evenly. He says, *Yes, I can detain you, but I can do more than that, I can break you. I can send you out of here an old broken man, going about with your head down, mumbling to yourself, like Samuelson.*

He talks to me as though I were an old man already. *You wouldn't like that, doctor. You like being looked up to by others. You like to pity others, it gives you a boost, but it would be hell to be pitied by them. In Fordsville they thought the sun shone out your eyes. Our name stinks down there because we took you away.*

We can break you, doctor, he said. *We don't need to give you shock treatment, or hang you up by the feet. There are many other ways. But it isn't convenient. We don't want you drooling round Fordsville.* He adds sardonically, *It would spoil our image.*

He looks at me judicially, but there's a hard note in his voice. *It's inconvenient, but there may be no other way. And if there's no other way, we'll break you. Now listen carefully. I'm going to ask you a question.*

He keeps quiet for a minute, perhaps longer. He wants me to think over his threat earnestly. He says, *Who's your boss?*

After five minutes he stands up. He turns to Caspar. *All right, lieutenant, you can go ahead.*

What can Caspar go ahead with? Torture? for me? or for Rafael Swartz? My mind shies away from the possibility that it might be for you. But what did he mean by the double life? Their cleverness, which might some other time have filled me with admiration, fills me now with despair. They drop a fear into your mind, and then they go away. They're busy with other things, intent on their job of breaking, but you sit alone for days and think about the last thing they said. Ah, I am filled with fear for you. There are 3,000 million people in the world, and I can't get one of them to go to you and say, *Get out, this day, this very minute.*

Barbara Trevelyan, says Caspar, *it's a smart name. You covered it up well, doctor, so we're angry at you. But there's someone angrier than us. Didn't you promise on oath to have no friendship outside the People's League, more especially with a woman? What is your boss going to say?*

Yes, I promised. But I couldn't go on living like that, cut off from all love, from all

persons, from all endearment. I wanted to mean something to somebody, a live person, not a cause. I am filled with shame, not so much that I broke my promise, but because I couldn't make an island where there was only our love, only you and me. But the world had to come in, and the great plan for the transformation of the world, and forbidden knowledge, dangerous knowledge, and . . . I don't like to say it, perhaps boasting came in too, dangerous boasting. My head aches with pain, and I try to remember what I told you.

You are having your last chance today, says Caspar. *If you don't talk today, you won't need to talk any more. Take your choice. Do you want her to tell us, or will you?*

I don't know. If I talk, then what was the use of these 100 days? Some will go to prison, some may die. If I don't tell, if I let her tell, then they will suffer just the same. And the shame will be just as terrible.

It doesn't matter, says Caspar, *if you tell or she tells. They'll kill you either way. Because we're going to let you go.*

He launches another bolt at me. *You see, doctor, she doesn't believe in the cause, she believes only in you. Tomorrow she won't even do that. Because we're going to tell her that you brought her in.*

Now he is watching me closely. Something is moving on my face. Is it an insect? or a drop of sweat? Don't tell them, my love. Listen my love, I am sending a message to you. Don't tell them, my love.

Do you remember what Rafael Swartz used to boast at those meetings in the good old days, that he'd follow you to hell? Well, he'd better start soon, hadn't he? Because that's where you are now.

He takes off his watch and puts it on the table. *I give you five minutes,* he said, *and they're the last you'll ever get. Who's your* boss? He puts his hands on the table too, and rests his forehead on them. Tired he is, tired with breaking men. He lifts his head and puts on his watch and stands up. There is a look on his face I haven't seen before, hating and vicious.

You're all the same, aren't you? Subversion most of the time, and women in between. Marriage, children, family, that's for the birds, that's for our decadent society. You want to be free, don't you? You paint FREEDOM *all over the town. Well you'll be free soon, and it'll be the end of you.*

Lofty and Helen and Le Grange. And now Rafael. Is there anyone they can't break? Does one grow stronger or weaker as the days go by? I say a prayer for you tonight, to whatever God may be . . .

Did I say Rafael's name? I'm sorry, Rafael, I'm not myself today. Have courage, Rafael. Don't believe what they say. And I shan't believe either.

Five days? Seven days? More? I can't remember. I hardly sleep now. I think of you and wonder what they are doing to you. I try to remember what I told you. Did I tell you I was deep in? Did I tell you how deep? Did I tell you any of their names? It's a useless question, because I don't know the answer to it. If the answer came suddenly into my mind, I wouldn't know it for what it was.

Ah, never believe that I brought you in. It's an old trick, the cruellest trick of the cruellest profession in the world. Have courage, my love. Look at them out of your gray honest eyes and tell them you don't know anything at all, that you were just a woman in love.

Caspar says to me, *You're free.* What am I supposed to do? Should my face light up with joy? It might have done, only a few days ago. *Do you know why we're letting you go?* Is there point in not answering? I shake my head.

Because we've found your boss, that's why. When he sees I am wary, not knowing whether to believe or disbelieve, he says, *John Forrester's the name. He doesn't know what to believe either, especially when we told him you had brought him in. Doctor, don't come back here any more. You're not made for this game. You've only lasted this long because of orders received. Don't ask me why. Come, I'll take you home.*

Outside in the crowded street the sun is shining. The sunlight falls on the sooty trees in Trebizond Street, and the black leaves dance in the breeze. The city is full of noise and life, and laughter too, as though no one cared what might go on behind those barricaded walls. There is an illusion of freedom in the air.

Your Response

1. What qualities do you admire in the narrator?
2. If you could ask the narrator a question about his experience, what would you ask?

Recalling

3. What do the lieutenant and the major want from the narrator? Do they get it from him?

Interpreting

4. What are you not told about the narrator and his situation?
5. Why does the narrator make rules for himself? What is he trying to maintain?
6. Who is Rafael Swartz and how are his fate and that of the narrator linked?
7. How does the narrator's love for Barbara affect his actions? Does it strengthen or weaken him?
8. What kind of man is the major? What is his method for "breaking" the narrator?
9. Do the authorities get what they want in the end? Why is the narrator's release merely "an illusion of freedom"?

Applying

10. The narrator is trapped in an extreme set of circumstances where maximum pressure is being brought to bear upon him. Do you think such circumstances are fair tests of a person's character or moral strength? Why or why not?

ANALYZING LITERATURE

Appreciating the Interior Monologue

An **interior monologue** brings the reader inside the mind of the main character, who shares his thoughts, feelings, and memories directly. In this story we enter the inner world of a prisoner who is being pressured for information by ruthless members of the military. The interior monologue creates a feeling of intense involvement between the reader and the main character.

1. What are some of the hopes, fears, and memories the narrator shares?
2. How does knowing the thoughts and feelings of the narrator make you feel about him?
3. Why was the interior monologue form an especially good choice for this story?

CRITICAL THINKING AND READING

Recognizing Ambiguity

Ambiguity in a literary work is a quality of uncertainty that exists because more than one interpretation of a character or an event is possible. A good story often suggests more than it tells, thereby involving the reader in the process of creating meaning.

"Sunlight in Trebizond Street" leaves the reader with a degree of uncertainty about several issues. Consider the following questions:

1. How do the authorities find out John Forrester's name?
2. Do we know for sure what will happen to the narrator after his release?

THINKING AND WRITING

Interpreting a Character

How would you evaluate the behavior of the main character in this story? Is he a brave man? A coward? A victim? A fool? Should he be judged by a special set of standards because of his extraordinary circumstances? Brainstorm with a group of classmates before writing your interpretation of the narrator's character. When you revise your paper, be sure you have included details from the story that support your opinion of the narrator.

LEARNING OPTION

Writing. Write a continuation of the story, starting with the narrator's release. Begin with an interior monologue of the narrator's response to the "illusion of freedom in the air."

GUIDE FOR READING

Civil Peace

Theme

The **theme** of a story is the central idea or insight into life that the story reveals. Often a writer will include in a story key statements that point to the theme. Key statements are those that go beyond the specific events of the story and indicate something that is true about life in general. Recognizing and understanding these key statements can help you to identify a story's theme.

Chinua Achebe

(1930–   ), educated in his homeland of Nigeria and in London, has directed a radio station and started a publishing company in Nigeria, taught in Nigerian and American universities, and involved himself in local Nigerian politics. His greatest achievement, however, has been as a novelist. His novels, including *Things Fall Apart* (1958) and *Anthills of the Savannah* (1988), convey the tragic history of tribal Africa's encounter with European power. Achebe is the editor of an anthology, *African Short Stories,* in which his "Civil Peace" appears.

Focus

Throughout "Civil Peace" the main character repeats the African proverb "Nothing puzzles God." Proverbs are important in many cultures. As part of an oral tradition, they are a means of teaching and preserving valuable ideas by passing them from generation to generation. What wisdom is imparted in the following Ibo proverb? "A man who answers every summons by the town crier will not plant yams in his field." What proverbs have you learned as you grew up? Write down several proverbs that were passed down in your family or culture. See how the proverbs you listed compare with those that your classmates wrote down.

Vocabulary

Knowing the following words will help you as you read "Civil Peace."

inestimable (in es′ tə mə bəl) *adj.*: Priceless; beyond reckoning (p. 215)

disreputable (dis rep′ yōō tə bəl) *adj.*: Not respectable (p. 215)

amenable (ə mē′ nə bəl) *adj.*: Responsive; open (p. 215)

edifice (ed′ i fis) *n.*: Building (p. 215)

destitute (des′ tə tōōt′) *adj.*: Poverty-stricken; in great need (p. 216)

imperious (im pir′ ē əs) *adj.*: Commanding; powerful (p. 217)

commiserate (kə miz′ ər āt′) *v.*: Sympathize; share sufferings (p. 218)

Civil Peace

Chinua Achebe

Jonathan Iwegbu[1] counted himself extraordinarily lucky. "Happy survival!" meant so much more to him than just a current fashion of greeting old friends in the first hazy days of peace. It went deep to his heart. He had come out of the war with five inestimable blessings—his head, his wife Maria's head and the heads of three out of their four children. As a bonus he also had his old bicycle—a miracle too but naturally not to be compared to the safety of five human heads.

The bicycle had a little history of its own. One day at the height of the war it was commandeered "for urgent military action." Hard as its loss would have been to him he would still have let it go without a thought had he not had some doubts about the genuineness of the officer. It wasn't his disreputable rags, nor the toes peeping out of one blue and one brown canvas shoe, nor yet the two stars of his rank done obviously in a hurry in biro,[2] that troubled Jonathan; many good and heroic soldiers looked the same or worse. It was rather a certain lack of grip and firmness in his manner. So Jonathan, suspecting he might be amenable to influence, rummaged in his raffia[3] bag and produced the two pounds with which he had been going to buy firewood which his wife,

Maria, retailed to camp officials for extra stock-fish and corn meal, and got his bicycle back. That night he buried it in the little clearing in the bush where the dead of the camp, including his own youngest son, were buried. When he dug it up again a year later after the surrender all it needed was a little palm-oil greasing. "Nothing puzzles God," he said in wonder.

He put it to immediate use as a taxi and accumulated a small pile of Biafran[4] money ferrying camp officials and their families across the four-mile stretch to the nearest tarred road. His standard charge per trip was six pounds and those who had the money were only glad to be rid of some of it in this way. At the end of a fortnight[5] he had made a small fortune of one hundred and fifteen pounds.

Then he made the journey to Enugu and found another miracle waiting for him. It was unbelievable. He rubbed his eyes and looked again and it was still standing there before him. But, needless to say, even that monumental blessing must be accounted also totally inferior to the five heads in the family. This newest miracle was his little house in Ogui Overside. Indeed nothing puzzles God! Only two houses away a huge concrete edifice some wealthy contractor had put up just before the war was a moun-

---

1. Iwegbu (i wem′ bōō).
2. biro (bir′ ō) *n.*: A ballpoint pen.
3. raffia (raf′ ē ə) *n.*: Fiber from palm leaves used to make baskets, hats, and so on.

---

4. Biafran (bē äf′ rən) *adj.*: From the east part of the Gulf of Guinea on the west coast of Africa.
5. fortnight (fôrt′ nīt) *n.*: Two weeks.

tain of rubble. And here was Jonathan's little zinc house of no regrets built with mud blocks quite intact! Of course the doors and windows were missing and five sheets off the roof. But what was that? And anyhow he had returned to Enugu early enough to pick up bits of old zinc and wood and soggy sheets of cardboard lying around the neighborhood before thousands more came out of their forest holes looking for the same things. He got a destitute carpenter with one old hammer, a blunt plane and a few bent and rusty nails in his tool bag to turn this assortment of wood, paper and metal into door and window shutters for five Nigerian shillings or fifty Biafran pounds. He paid the pounds, and moved in with his overjoyed family carrying five heads on their shoulders.

His children picked mangoes near the military cemetery and sold them to soldiers' wives for a few pennies—real pennies this time—and his wife started making breakfast akara balls[6] for neighbors in a hurry to start life again. With his family earnings he took his bicycle to the villages around and bought fresh palm-wine which he mixed generously in his rooms with the water which had recently started running again in the public tap down the road, and opened up a bar for soldiers and other lucky people with good money.

At first he went daily, then every other day and finally once a week, to the offices of the Coal Corporation where he used to be a miner, to find out what was what. The only thing he did find out in the end was that that little house of his was even a greater blessing than he had thought. Some of his fellow ex-miners who had nowhere to return at the end of the day's waiting just slept outside the doors of the offices and cooked what

meal they could scrounge together in Bournvita tins.[7] As the weeks lengthened and still nobody could say what was what Jonathan discontinued his weekly visits altogether and faced his palm-wine bar.

But nothing puzzles God. Came the day of the windfall when after five days of endless scuffles in queues[8] and counterqueues in the sun outside the Treasury he had twenty pounds counted into his palms as ex-gratia[9] award for the rebel money he had turned in. It was like Christmas for him and for many others like him when the payments began. They called it (since few could manage its proper official name) *egg-rasher.*

As soon as the pound notes were placed in his palm Jonathan simply closed it tight over them and buried fist and money inside

---

6. akara (ə kär′ ə) **balls:** Balls made of cooked yams.

7. Bournvita (bôrn vē′ tə) **tins:** A brand of canned goods. The cans were used as cooking pots when empty of their contents.

8. queues (kyo̅o̅z) *n.*: Lines.

9. ex gratia (eks grä′ s̸hē ə): As a favor.

his trouser pocket. He had to be extra careful because he had seen a man a couple of days earlier collapse into near-madness in an instant before that oceanic crowd because no sooner had he got his twenty pounds than some heartless ruffian picked it off him. Though it was not right that a man in such an extremity of agony should be blamed yet many in the queues that day were able to remark quietly at the victim's carelessness, especially after he pulled out the innards of his pocket and revealed a hole in it big enough to pass a thief's head. But of course he had insisted that the money had been in the other pocket, pulling it out too to show its comparative wholeness. So one had to be careful.

Jonathan soon transferred the money to his left hand and pocket so as to leave his right free for shaking hands should the need arise, though by fixing his gaze at such an elevation as to miss all approaching human faces he made sure that the need did not arise, until he got home.

He was normally a heavy sleeper but that night he heard all the neighborhood noises die down one after another. Even the night watchman who knocked the hour on some metal somewhere in the distance had fallen silent after knocking one o'clock. That must have been the last thought in Jonathan's mind before he was finally carried away himself. He couldn't have been gone for long, though, when he was violently awakened again.

"Who is knocking?" whispered his wife lying beside him on the floor.

"I don't know," he whispered back breathlessly.

The second time the knocking came it was so loud and imperious that the rickety old door could have fallen down.

"Who is knocking?" he asked them, his voice parched and trembling.

"Na tief-man and him people," came the cool reply. "Make you hopen de door."[10] This was followed by the heaviest knocking of all.

Maria was the first to raise the alarm, then he followed and all their children.

"Police-o! Thieves-o! Neighbors-o! Police-o! We are lost! We are dead! Neighbors, are you asleep? Wake up! Police-o!"

This went on for a long time and then stopped suddenly. Perhaps they had scared the thief away. There was total silence. But only for a short while.

"You done finish?" asked the voice outside. "Make we help you small. Oya, everybody!"

"Police-o! Tief-man-so! Neighbors-o! we done loss-o! Police-o! . . ."

There were at least five other voices besides the leader's.

Jonathan and his family were now completely paralyzed by terror. Maria and the children sobbed inaudibly like lost souls. Jonathan groaned continuously.

The silence that followed the thieves' alarm vibrated horribly. Jonathan all but begged their leader to speak again and be done with it.

"My frien," said he at long last, "we don try our best for call dem but I tink say dem all done sleep-o . . . So wetin we go do now? Sometaim you wan call soja? Or you wan make we call dem for you? Soja better pass police. No be so?"

"Na so!" replied his men. Jonathan thought he heard even more voices now than before and groaned heavily. His legs were sagging under him and his throat felt like sandpaper.

---

10. "Na tief-man . . . hopen de door": The man is speaking English with an accent and mixed with some of the word forms and grammar of his own language. He is saying, "I am not a thief with my accomplices. Open the door." As you read the rest of the story, read aloud when characters speak this way and try to figure out what they are saying.

"My frien, why you no de talk again. I de ask you say you wan make we call soja?"

"No."

"Awrighto. Now make we talk business. We no be bad tief. We no like for make trouble. Trouble done finish. War done finish and all the katakata wey de for inside. No Civil War again. This time na Civil Peace. No be so?"

"Na so!" answered the horrible chorus.

"What do you want from me? I am a poor man. Everything I had went with this war. Why do you come to me? You know people who have money. We . . ."

"Awright! We know say you no get plenty money. But we sef no get even anini. So derefore make you open dis window and give us one hundred pound and we go commot. Orderwise we de come for inside now to show you guitar-boy like dis . . ."

A volley of automatic fire rang through the sky. Maria and the children began to weep aloud again.

"Ah, missisi de cry again. No need for dat. We done talk say we na good tief. We just take our small money and go nwayorly. No molest. Abi we de molest?"

"At all!" sang the chorus.

"My friends," began Jonathan hoarsely. "I hear what you say and I thank you. If I had one hundred pounds . . ."

"Lookia my frien, no be play we come play for your house. If we make mistake and step for inside you no go like am-o. So derefore . . ."

"To God who made me; if you come inside and find one hundred pounds, take it and shoot me and shoot my wife and children. I swear to God. The only money I have in this life is this twenty-pounds *egg-rasher* they gave me today . . ."

"Ok. Time de go. Make you open dis window and bring the twenty pound. We go manage am like dat."

There were now loud murmurs of dissent among the chorus: "Na lie de man de lie; e get plenty money . . . Make we go inside and search properly well . . . Wetin be twenty pound? . . ."

"Shurrup!" rang the leader's voice like a lone shot in the sky and silenced the murmuring at once. "Are you dere? Bring the money quick!"

"I am coming," said Jonathan fumbling in the darkness with the key of the small wooden box he kept by his side on the mat.

At the first sign of light as neighbors and others assembled to commiserate with him he was already strapping his five-gallon demijohn[11] to his bicycle carrier and his wife, sweating in the open fire, was turning over akara balls in a wide clay bowl of boiling oil. In the corner his eldest son was rinsing out dregs of yesterday's palm-wine from old beer bottles.

"I count it as nothing," he told his sympathizers, his eyes on the rope he was tying. "What is *egg-rasher*? Did I depend on it last week? Or is it greater than other things that went with the war? I say, let *egg-rasher* perish in the flames! Let it go where everything else has gone. Nothing puzzles God."

---

11. demijohn (dem′ i jän′) *n*.: A large bottle.

RESPONDING TO THE SELECTION

Your Response

1. In what ways do you identify with Jonathan? Explain.

Recalling

2. What does Jonathan Iwegbu count as his greatest blessings? For what else is he grateful?
3. How do Jonathan and his family behave after their money is stolen?

Interpreting

4. What can you infer from details in the story about the war that has just ended? How did the war affect the lives of people like Jonathan?
5. Describe the character of the leader of the thieves. Do you think he and his followers are hardened criminals?
6. Although Jonathan and his family are terrified of the thieves, the encounter has its comic side. What is the source of the humor in the scene?
7. Why is "Civil Peace" an appropriate title for this story? Consider the meanings of the word *civil.*
8. How would you sum up Jonathan's attitude toward life?

Applying

9. Although a poor man by Western standards, Jonathan places a limited value on material wealth. Do you think it is easier for a poor person or a rich one to accept the loss of material possessions? Explain your answer.

ANALYZING LITERATURE

Understanding Key Statements

Key statements in a story often help reveal the central idea or theme. **Key statements** often go beyond the events of a particular story and point to a general truth about life. In "Civil Peace" Chinua Achebe makes use of a tribal proverb that has been important in African life. This proverb also acts as a key statement that throws light on the central meaning of his story.

1. What does the key saying "Happy Survival" reveal about Jonathan's values?
2. Why do you think the proverb "Nothing puzzles God" is repeated in the story? How does it help reveal the story's theme?

CRITICAL THINKING AND READING

Summarizing a Story

To **summarize** a story is to state the main events in your own words. A good summary can help you see the structure of a story and the overall point that the story is making.

Write a paragraph summarizing the main events of this story. Conclude with a sentence that suggests the meaning of the events.

THINKING AND WRITING

Rewriting Dialogue

Rewrite the spoken words of the thieves in standard English. Read your dialogue aloud, and compare it with other students' versions. Discuss differences and work together to prepare a final version. Then act out the robbery scene. First use the original dialogue and then the rewritten version.

LEARNING OPTION

Cross-curricular Connection. Imagine that the publisher of "Civil Peace" has asked you to provide an introductory note for the story. You decide to give background material on the Nigerian Civil War. Ask a social studies teacher in your school to suggest sources of information for your note. Write two or three paragraphs of background information that will help readers of "Civil Peace" understand the story better.

GUIDE FOR READING

Isak Dinesen

(1885–1962) was the pen name of Karen Blixen, a member of an aristocratic Danish family. In 1914 Karen and her husband established a coffee plantation in British East Africa. In 1931, ten years after they were divorced, she went bankrupt and lost her farm because coffee prices had fallen. She describes these years in her memoir, *Out of Africa*. After returning to Denmark, she wrote fiction in both English and Danish, including the collection *Anecdotes of Destiny* from which this story is taken.

The Ring

A Crystallized Moment

In some stories the theme or overall meaning is revealed in one **crystallized moment** in which time seems to stand still and the main character makes a tremendous discovery that changes him or her profoundly. Understanding the truth revealed in the crystallized moment is the key to understanding such a story's theme.

Focus

In "The Ring" a young woman has an experience that changes her life. As a result of the experience, the woman learns something about herself and the circumstances of her life that changes her outlook. You or someone you know well has probably had such an experience, a moment in which time stood still. Write about the experience in your journal. Create a verbal portrait of that moment and also discuss its subsequent effects. Keep your writing in mind as you read "The Ring."

Vocabulary

Knowing the following words will help you as you read "The Ring."

railleries (rāl′ ər ēz) *n.*: Good-natured teasing; jests (p. 221)

solicitously (sə lis′ ə təs lē) *adv.*: With great care (p. 221)

gamboling (gam′ bəl iŋ) *v.*: Leaping playfully (p. 223)

scrutinized (skroot′ 'n īzd′) *v.*: Inspected carefully (p. 223)

sylvan (sil′ vən) *adj.*: Wooded (p. 223)

covert (kuv′ ərt) *n.*: Hiding place (p. 224)

phosphorescent (fäs′ fə res′ ənt) *adj.*: Glowing from within (p. 225)

The Ring

Isak Dinesen

On a summer morning a hundred and fifty years ago a young Danish squire[1] and his wife went out for a walk on their land. They had been married a week. It had not been easy for them to get married, for the wife's family was higher in rank and wealthier than the husband's. But the two young people, now twenty-four and nineteen years old, had been set on their purpose for ten years; in the end her haughty parents had had to give in to them.

They were wonderfully happy. The stolen meetings and secret, tearful love letters were now things of the past. To God and man they were one; they could walk arm in arm in broad daylight and drive in the same carriage, and they would walk and drive so till the end of their days. Their distant paradise had descended to earth and had proved, surprisingly, to be filled with the things of everyday life: with jesting and railleries, with breakfasts and suppers, with dogs, haymaking and sheep. Sigismund,[2] the young husband, had promised himself that from now there should be no stone in his bride's path, nor should any shadow fall across it. Lovisa,[3] the wife, felt that now,

every day and for the first time in her young life, she moved and breathed in perfect freedom because she could never have any secret from her husband.

To Lovisa—whom her husband called Lise—the rustic atmosphere of her new life was a matter of wonder and delight. Her husband's fear that the existence he could offer her might not be good enough for her filled her heart with laughter. It was not a long time since she had played with dolls; as now she dressed her own hair, looked over her linen press and arranged her flowers she again lived through an enchanting and cherished experience: one was doing everything gravely and solicitously, and all the time one knew one was playing.

It was a lovely July morning. Little woolly clouds drifted high up in the sky, the air was full of sweet scents. Lise had on a white muslin frock and a large Italian straw hat. She and her husband took a path through the park; it wound on across the meadows, between small groves and groups of trees, to the sheep field. Sigismund was going to show his wife his sheep. For this reason she had not brought her small white dog, Bijou,[4] with her, for he would yap at the lambs and frighten them, or he would annoy the sheep dogs. Sigismund prided himself on his

---

1. **squire** (skwīr) *n*.: A country gentleman or landowner.
2. **Sigismund** (sig′ əs mənd)
3. **Lovisa** (lō vē′ sə)

4. **Bijou** (bē′ jo͞o)

sheep; he had studied sheep-breeding in Mecklenburg[5] and England, and had brought back with him Cotswold rams[6] by which to improve his Danish stock.[7] While they walked he explained to Lise the great possibilities and difficulties of the plan.

She thought: "How clever he is, what a lot of things he knows!" and at the same time: "What an absurd person he is, with his sheep! What a baby he is! I am a hundred years older than he."

But when they arrived at the sheepfold[8] the old sheepmaster Mathias[9] met them with the sad news that one of the English lambs was dead and two were sick. Lise saw that her husband was grieved by the tidings; while he questioned Mathias on the matter she kept silent and only gently pressed his arm. A couple of boys were sent off to fetch the sick lambs, while the master and servant went into the details of the case. It took some time.

Lise began to gaze about her and to think of other things. Twice her own thoughts made her blush deeply and happily, like a red rose, then slowly her blush died away, and the two men were still talking about sheep. A little while after their conversation caught her attention. It had turned to a sheep thief.

This thief during the last months had broken into the sheepfolds of the neighborhood like a wolf, had killed and dragged away his prey like a wolf and like a wolf had left no trace after him. Three nights ago the shepherd and his son on an estate ten miles away

had caught him in the act. The thief had killed the man and knocked the boy senseless, and had managed to escape. There were men sent out to all sides to catch him, but nobody had seen him.

Lise wanted to hear more about the horrible event, and for her benefit old Mathias went through it once more. There had been a long fight in the sheep house, in many places the earthen floor was soaked with blood. In the fight the thief's left arm was broken; all the same, he had climbed a tall fence with a lamb on his back. Mathias added that he would like to string up the murderer with these two hands of his, and Lise nodded her head at him gravely in approval. She remembered Red Riding-hood's wolf,[10] and felt a pleasant little thrill running down her spine.

Sigismund had his own lambs in his mind, but he was too happy in himself to wish anything in the universe ill. After a minute he said: "Poor devil."

Lise said: "How can you pity such a terrible man? Indeed Grandmamma was right when she said that you were a revolutionary and a danger to society!" The thought of Grandmamma, and of the tears of past days, again turned her mind away from the gruesome tale she had just heard.

The boys brought the sick lambs and the men began to examine them carefully, lifting them up and trying to set them on their legs; they squeezed them here and there and made the little creatures whimper. Lise shrank from the show and her husband noticed her distress.

"You go home, my darling," he said, "this will take some time. But just walk ahead slowly, and I shall catch up with you."

---

5. Mecklenburg (mek′ lən bŭrg′): A region in northeast Germany.

6. Cotswold (käts′ wôld) **rams:** Male sheep of a breed originally from southwest central England.

7. Danish stock: The rest of Sigismund's sheep were of a breed from Denmark.

8. sheepfold (shēp′ fōld′) *n*.: A pen or enclosure for sheep.

9. Mathias (mə thī′ əs)

---

10. Red Ridinghood's wolf: The wolf in the fairy tale who masqueraded as Red Ridinghood's grandmother in order to eat the child when she came to visit.

So she was turned away by an impatient husband to whom his sheep meant more than his wife. If any experience could be sweeter than to be dragged out by him to look at those same sheep, it would be this. She dropped her large summer hat with its blue ribbons on the grass and told him to carry it back for her, for she wanted to feel the summer air on her forehead and in her hair. She walked on very slowly, as he had told her to do, for she wished to obey him in everything. As she walked she felt a great new happiness in being altogether alone, even without Bijou. She could not remember that she had ever before in all her life been altogether alone. The landscape around her was still, as if full of promise, and it was hers. Even the swallows cruising in the air were hers, for they belonged to him, and he was hers.

She followed the curving edge of the grove and after a minute or two found that she was out of sight to the men by the sheep house. What could now, she wondered, be sweeter than to walk along the path in the long flowering meadow grass, slowly, slowly, and to let her husband overtake her there? It would be sweeter still, she reflected, to steal into the grove and to be gone, to have vanished from the surface of the earth from him when, tired of the sheep and longing for her company, he should turn the bend of the path to catch up with her.

An idea struck her; she stood still to think it over.

A few days ago her husband had gone for a ride and she had not wanted to go with him, but had strolled about with Bijou in order to explore her domain. Bijou then, gamboling, had led her straight into the grove. As she had followed him, gently forcing her way into the shrubbery, she had suddenly come upon a glade in the midst of it, a narrow space like a small alcove with hangings of thick green and golden bro-cade,[11] big enough to hold two or three people in it. She had felt at that moment that she had come into the very heart of her new home. If today she could find the spot again she would stand perfectly still there, hidden from all the world. Sigismund would look for her in all directions; he would be unable to understand what had become of her and for a minute, for a short minute—or, perhaps, if she was firm and cruel enough, for five—he would realize what a void, what an unendurably sad and horrible place the universe would be when she was no longer in it. She gravely scrutinized the grove to find the right entrance to her hiding-place, then went in.

She took great care to make no noise at all, therefore advanced exceedingly slowly. When a twig caught the flounces of her ample skirt she loosened it softly from the muslin, so as not to crack it. Once a branch took hold of one of her long golden curls; she stood still, with her arms lifted, to free it. A little way into the grove the soil became moist; her light steps no longer made any sound upon it. With one hand she held her small handkerchief to her lips, as if to emphasize the secretness of her course. She found the spot she sought and bent down to divide the foliage and make a door to her sylvan closet. At this the hem of her dress caught her foot and she stopped to loosen it. As she rose she looked into the face of a man who was already in the shelter.

He stood up erect, two steps off. He must have watched her as she made her way straight toward him.

She took him in in one single glance. His face was bruised and scratched, his hands and wrists stained with dark filth. He was dressed in rags, barefooted, with tatters wound round his naked ankles. His arms hung down to his sides, his right hand

---

11. brocade (brō kād′) n.: A rich cloth with a raised design woven into it.

ADAM AND EVE
Edvard Munch
Munch Museum, Oslo

clasped the hilt of a knife. He was about her own age. The man and the woman looked at each other.

This meeting in the wood from beginning to end passed without a word; what happened could only be rendered by pantomime. To the two actors in the pantomime it was timeless; according to a clock it lasted four minutes.

She had never in her life been exposed to danger. It did not occur to her to sum up her position, or to work out the length of time it would take to call her husband or Mathias, whom at this moment she could hear shouting to his dogs. She beheld the man before her as she would have beheld a forest ghost: the apparition itself, not the sequels[12] of

---

12. **sequels** (sē′ kwəlz) *n*.: Things that follow or come afterward; effects or consequences.

it, changes the world to the human who faces it.

Although she did not take her eyes off the face before her she sensed that the alcove had been turned into a covert. On the ground a couple of sacks formed a couch; there were some gnawed bones by it. A fire must have been made here in the night, for there were cinders strewn on the forest floor.

After a while she realized that he was observing her just as she was observing him. He was no longer just run to earth and crouching for a spring, but he was wondering, trying to know. At that she seemed to see herself with the eyes of the wild animal at bay in his dark hiding-place: her silently approaching white figure, which might mean death.

He moved his right arm till it hung down

straight before him between his legs. Without lifting the hand he bent the wrist and slowly raised the point of the knife till it pointed at her throat. The gesture was mad, unbelievable. He did not smile as he made it, but his nostrils distended, the corners of his mouth quivered a little. Then slowly he put the knife back in the sheath by his belt.

She had no object of value about her, only the wedding ring which her husband had set on her finger in church, a week ago. She drew if off, and in this movement dropped her handkerchief. She reached out her hand with the ring toward him. She did not bargain for her life. She was fearless by nature, and the horror with which he inspired her was not fear of what he might do to her. She commanded him, she besought him to vanish as he had come, to take a dreadful figure out of her life, so that it should never have been there. In the dumb movement her young form had the grave authoritativeness of a priestess conjuring down some monstrous being by a sacred sign.[13]

He slowly reached out his hand to hers, his finger touched hers, and her hand was steady at the touch. But he did not take the ring. As she let it go it dropped to the ground as her handkerchief had done.

For a second the eyes of both followed it. It rolled a few inches toward him and stopped before his bare foot. In a hardly perceivable movement he kicked it away and again looked into her face. They remained like that, she knew not how long, but she felt that during that time something happened, things were changed.

He bent down and picked up her handkerchief. All the time gazing at her, he again drew his knife and wrapped the tiny bit of cambric[14] round the blade. This was difficult for him to do because his left arm was broken. While he did it his face under the dirt and suntan slowly grew whiter till it was almost phosphorescent. Fumbling with both hands, he once more stuck the knife into the sheath. Either the sheath was too big and had never fitted the knife, or the blade was much worn—it went in. For two or three more seconds his gaze rested on her face; then he lifted his own face a little, the strange radiance still upon it, and closed his eyes.

The movement was definitive[15] and unconditional. In this one motion he did what she had begged him to do: he vanished and was gone. She was free.

She took a step backward, the immovable, blind face before her, then bent as she had done to enter the hiding-place, and glided away as noiselessly as she had come. Once outside the grove she stood still and looked round for the meadow path, found it and began to walk home.

Her husband had not yet rounded the edge of the grove. Now he saw her and helloed to her gaily; he came up quickly and joined her.

The path here was so narrow that he kept half behind her and did not touch her. He began to explain to her what had been the matter with the lambs. She walked a step before him and thought: All is over.

After a while he noticed her silence, came up beside her to look at her face and asked, "What is the matter?"

She searched her mind for something to say, and at last said: "I have lost my ring."

"What ring?" he asked her.

She answered, "My wedding ring."

As she heard her own voice pronounce

---

13. priestess . . . sign: A female priest of some pagan religion who could cause horrible creatures to disappear by performing some kind of magic spell.

14. cambric (kām′ brik) n.: Very fine, thin linen.
15. definitive (dē fin′ ə tiv) adj.: Final; conclusive.

the words she conceived[16] their meaning.

Her wedding ring. "With this ring"—dropped by one and kicked away by another—"with this ring I thee wed." With this lost ring she had wedded herself to something. To what? To poverty, persecution, total loneliness. To the sorrows and the sinfulness of this earth. "And what therefore God has joined together let man not put asunder."[17]

"I will find you another ring," her husband said. "You and I are the same as we were on our wedding day; it will do as well. We are husband and wife today too, as much as yesterday, I suppose."

Her face was so still that he did not know if she had heard what he said. It touched him that she should take the loss of his ring so to heart. He took her hand and kissed it. It was cold, not quite the same hand as he had last kissed. He stopped to make her stop with him.

"Do you remember where you had the ring on last?" he asked.

"No," she answered.

"Have you any idea," he asked, "where you may have lost it?"

"No," she answered. "I have no idea at all."

---

16. conceived (kən sēv′d′) v.: Understood.

17. "With this ring . . . not put asunder": These words are from the wedding vows Lovisa made during her wedding ceremony.

THE LONELY ONES, 1899
Edvard Munch
Munch Museum, Oslo

RESPONDING TO THE SELECTION

Your Response

1. If you were Lise, what would you have done in the grove?
2. Why do you think Lise lies to Sigismund?

Recalling

3. Describe Lise and Sigismund and their state of mind as the story opens.
4. What happens between Lise and the thief?

Interpreting

5. What kind of life has Lise had up until the time she encounters the thief?
6. What reasons does she have for entering the glade? What does she imagine will happen if she hides there?
7. What feelings does the sight of the thief arouse in her?
8. Why does Lise offer the thief her wedding ring after he has put away his knife? Why does he refuse it?
9. At the beginning Lise is confident that "she could never have any secret from her husband." How does the dialogue at the end indicate how much she has changed?

Applying

10. What do the events of this story suggest about people's knowledge of how they will behave in moments of unexpected danger?

ANALYZING LITERATURE

Understanding the Crystallized Moment

A **crystallized moment** in a literary work is an instant of concentrated experience in which the main character makes a discovery that radically changes him or her. The wordless encounter between Lise and the thief brings about an unmistakable change in her, but the nature of the encounter itself is mysterious.

1. Find evidence from the story that indicates the extraordinary importance of what happened in the glade.
2. If Lise was open, innocent, and immature before her encounter, what has she become afterward?

CRITICAL THINKING AND READING

Appreciating Details

Although "The Ring" is an original creation by Isak Dinesen, it has many characteristics of a fairy tale or medieval romance. For example, the story is set in a distant past, and the main characters are young, strong, and happy like the princes and princesses of fairy tales.

1. What specific fairy-tale character is mentioned in the story? Why might that character be compared to a character in "The Ring"?
2. What aspects of the physical setting add a romantic or fairy-tale atmosphere?
3. What kind of power is Lise described as exercising over the thief?

THINKING AND WRITING

Writing a Fairy Tale

As Isak Dinesen did in "The Ring," use elements of the fairy tale to write a story about a young character's first encounter with danger and death. Begin by outlining the characteristics of your hero and your villain. Then write the first draft of your story. When you revise, make sure that you have made clear how the confrontation has changed the main character.

LEARNING OPTION

Performance. Work with others to prepare a dramatic reading of "The Ring." Be sure you have someone to play the narrator and the four characters. Use your voice, body, and facial expressions to convey your character's emotions.

READING AND RESPONDING

The Short Story

As an active reader, you are involved with a story and take meaning from it. You apply your active reading strategies to the plot, the characters, the setting, and the theme—the elements that work together to create a complete, effective story. Your response is your reaction to the story and its elements. It is what you think, what you feel, and what the story means to you.

RESPONDING TO PLOT The plot is what happens in a short story. The sequence of events in the plot centers on a conflict, or struggle, between opposing forces. Your knowledge of the plot structure will help you make connections and predictions. Your involvement in the plot will affect your response to the resolution of the conflict and will determine whether or not you are satisfied with the story's ending.

RESPONDING TO CHARACTERS Characters are the people—and sometimes the animals—in a story. Like real people, characters have traits and personalities that determine the way they behave. They think and feel just as real people think and feel. When you read, let yourself identify with the characters: Share their feelings and emotions, compare your own ideas with theirs, and think about what you would do in their place.

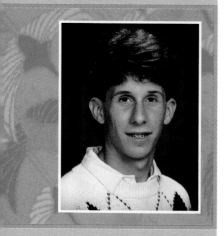

On pages 229–240, you will see how Josh Lee, a student at Sunnyslope High School, Phoenix, Arizona, actively read and responded to "With All Flags Flying." The notes in the side column include Josh's thoughts and comments as he read the story.

RESPONDING TO SETTING Setting is the time and the place in which the events in a story occur. The time might be in the past or in the future, and it might cover a minute or a span of years. The location might be a foreign country or someone's back yard. As you read actively, respond to the author's details about the setting. What kind of atmosphere, or mood, does the author create? How does the setting affect the plot and the characters? How does it affect you?

RESPONDING TO THEME Theme is the general idea about life presented in a story. It is what the story means to you. As you read, you will notice how the author has constructed the story to reveal the theme. Does the main character learn something about life? Is the theme stated or implied? What does this story say to you?

MODEL

With All Flags Flying

Anne Tyler

Weakness was what got him in the end. He had been expecting something more definite—chest pains, a stroke, arthritis—but it was only weakness that put a finish to his living alone. A numbness in his head, an airy feeling when he walked. A wateriness in his bones that made it an effort to pick up his coffee cup in the morning. He waited some days for it to go away, but it never did. And meanwhile the dust piled up in corners; the refrigerator wheezed and creaked for want of defrosting. Weeds grew around his rosebushes.

He was awake and dressed at six o'clock on a Saturday morning, with the patchwork quilt pulled up neatly over the mattress. From the kitchen cabinet he took a hunk of bread and two Fig Newtons, which he dropped into a paper bag. He was wearing a brown suit that he had bought on sale in 1944, a white T-shirt and copper-toed work boots. These and his other set of underwear, which he put in the paper bag along with a razor, were all the clothes he took with him. Then he rolled down the top of the bag and stuck it under his arm, and stood in the middle of the kitchen staring around him for a moment.

The house had only two rooms, but he owned it—the last scrap of the farm that he had sold off years ago. It stood in a hollow of dying trees beside a superhighway in Baltimore County. All it held was a few sticks of furniture, a change of clothes, a skillet and a set of dishes. Also odds and ends, which disturbed him. If his inventory were complete, he would have to include six clothespins, a salt and a pepper shaker, a broken-toothed comb, a cheap ballpoint pen—oh, on and on, past logical numbers. Why should he be so cluttered? He was eighty-two years old. He had grown from an

Character: *When people get old, they often get tired, and this man is obviously tired. His weakness frustrates him. He can no longer live alone.*

Setting: *The ugly weeds around the beautiful rose bushes won't go away, just like his weakness won't go away.*

Character: *Material things are not important to the man; he takes only the bare essentials.*

Plot: *It seems like he is leaving his solitude forever. He is leaving his house and his old ways of living.*

infant owning nothing to a family man with a wife, five children, everyday and Sunday china and a thousand appurtenances, down at last to solitary old age and the bare essentials again, but not bare enough to suit him. Only what he needed surrounded him. Was it possible he needed so much?

Now he had the brown paper bag; that was all. It was the one satisfaction in a day he had been dreading for years.

He left the house without another glance, heading up the steep bank toward the superhighway. The bank was covered with small, crawling weeds planted especially by young men with scientific training in how to prevent soil erosion. Twice his knees buckled. He had to sit and rest, bracing himself against the slope of the bank. The scientific weeds, seen from close up, looked straggly and gnarled. He sifted dry earth through his fingers without thinking, concentrating only on steadying his breath and calming the twitching muscles in his legs.

Once on the superhighway, which was fairly level, he could walk for longer stretches of time. He kept his head down and his fingers clenched tight upon the paper bag, which was growing limp and damp now. Sweat rolled down the back of his neck, fell in drops from his temples. When he had been walking maybe half an hour he had to sit down again for a rest. A black motorcycle buzzed up from behind and stopped a few feet away from him. The driver was young and shabby, with hair so long that it drizzled out beneath the back of his helmet.

"Give you a lift, if you like," he said. "You going somewhere?"

"Just into Baltimore."

"Hop on."

He shifted the paper bag to the space beneath his arm, put on the white helmet he was handed and climbed on behind the driver. For safety he took a clutch of the boy's shirt, tightly at first and then more loosely when he saw there was no danger. Except for the helmet, he was perfectly comfortable. He felt his face cooling and stiffening in the wind, his body learning to lean gracefully with the tilt of the motorcycle as it swooped from lane to lane. It was a fine way to spend his last free day.

Half an hour later they were on the outskirts of Baltimore, stopped at the first traffic light. The boy turned his head and shouted, "Whereabouts did you plan on going?"

"I'm visiting my daughter, on Belvedere near Charles Street."

"I'll drop you off, then," the boy said. "I'm passing right by there."

The light changed, the motor roared. Now that they were in traffic, he felt more conspicuous, but not in a bad way. People in their automobiles seemed sealed in, overprotected; men in large trucks must envy the way the motorcycle looped in and out, hornetlike, stripped to the bare essentials of a motor and two wheels. By tugs at the boy's shirt and single words shouted into the wind he directed him to his daughter's house, but he was sorry to have the ride over so quickly.

His daughter had married a salesman and lived in a plain, square stone house that the old man approved of. There were sneakers and a football in the front yard, signs of a large, happy family. A bicycle lay in the driveway. The motorcycle stopped just inches from it. "Here we are," the boy said.

"Well, I surely do thank you."

He climbed off, fearing for one second that his legs would give way beneath him and spoil everything that had gone before. But no, they held steady. He took off the helmet and handed it to the boy, who waved and roared off. It was a really magnificent roar, ear-dazzling. He turned toward the house, beaming in spite of himself, with his head feeling cool and light now that the helmet was gone. And there was his daughter on the front porch, laughing. "Daddy, what on *earth*?" she said. "Have you turned into a teeny-bopper?" Whatever that was. She came rushing down the steps to hug him—a plump, happy-looking woman in an apron. She was getting on toward fifty now. Her hands were like her mother's, swollen and veined. Gray had started dusting her hair.

"You never *told* us," she said. "Did you ride all this way on a motorcycle? Oh, why didn't you find a telephone and call? I would have come. How long can you stay for?"

"Now . . ." he said, starting toward the house. He was thinking of the best way to put it. "I came to a decision. I won't be living alone any more. I want to go to an old folks' home.

Theme: *The end of the ride is a painful reminder that his youth is gone. Life passes quickly. Like the motorcycle ride, youth doesn't last long. To me, this means don't wish your life away; enjoy youth.*

Setting: *The setting suggests a loving, happy family that enjoys its youth.*

Character: *He beams in spite of himself because he realizes that he can still have fun. He temporarily shed his "old skin" and felt free.*

That's what I *want*," he said, stopping on the grass so she would be sure to get it clear. "I don't want to live with you—I want an old folks' home." Then he was afraid he had worded it too strongly. "It's nice *visiting* you, of course," he said.

"Why, Daddy, you know we always asked you to come and live with us."

"I know that, but I decided on an old folks' home."

"We couldn't do that. We won't even talk about it."

"Clara, my mind is made up."

Then in the doorway a new thought hit her, and she suddenly turned around. "Are you sick?" she said. "You always said you would live alone as long as health allowed."

"I'm not up to that any more," he said.

"What is it? Are you having some kind of pain?"

"I just decided, that's all," he said. "What I *will* rely on you for is the arrangements with the home. I know it's a trouble."

"We'll talk about that later," Clara said. And she firmed the corners of her mouth exactly the way her mother used to do when she hadn't won an argument but wasn't planning to lose it yet either.

In the kitchen he had a glass of milk, good and cold, and the hunk of bread and the two Fig Newtons from his paper bag. Clara wanted to make him a big breakfast, but there was no sense wasting what he had brought. He munched on the dry bread and washed it down with milk, meanwhile staring at the Fig Newtons, which lay on the smoothed-out bag. They were the worse for their ride—squashed and pathetic-looking, the edges worn down and crumbling. They seemed to have come from somewhere long ago and far away. "Here, now, we've got cookies I baked only yesterday," Clara said; but he said, "No, no," and ate the Fig Newtons, whose warmth on his tongue filled him with a vague, sad feeling deeper than homesickness. "In my house," he said, "I left things a little messy. I hate to ask it of you, but I didn't manage to straighten up any."

"Don't even think about it," Clara said. "I'll take out a suitcase tomorrow and clean everything up. I'll bring it all back."

"I don't want it. Take it to the poor people."

"Don't want any of it? But, Daddy—"

He didn't try explaining it to her. He finished his lunch in silence and then let her lead him upstairs to the guest room.

Clara had five boys and a girl, the oldest twenty. During the morning as they passed one by one through the house on their way to other places, they heard of his arrival and trooped up to see him. They were fine children, all of them, but it was the girl he enjoyed the most. Francie. She was only thirteen, too young yet to know how to hide what she felt. And what she

Character: *The clutter has tired him. He doesn't want to be bothered with "things," objects that he has to think about and keep in order. He only wants the bare essentials.*

Character: *Francie and her innocent preoccupation with love bring joy to her grandfather.*

Character: *Francie is my favorite character. She has no hate inside her. The author reveals a lot about Francie in a short amount of time. We learn that she is unsure and inexperienced with love, but loving, kind, smart, and adventurous at the same time.*

Character: *The family loves him so much; they really want him to stay with them. Maybe he won't live with them because he wants to be around people his own age. People his age might understand him more than the family does.*

Character: *At least he realizes how lucky he is. It's emotionally healthy for him to feel so good about his children and their families. He also feels good about his life, except he hadn't looked forward to weakening.*

felt was always about love, it seemed: whom she just loved, who she hoped loved her back. Who was just a darling. Had thirteen-year-olds been so aware of love in the old days? He didn't know and didn't care; all he had to do with Francie was sit smiling in an armchair and listen. There was a new boy in the neighborhood who walked his English sheepdog past her yard every morning, looking toward her house. Was it because of her, or did the dog just like to go that way? When he telephoned her brother Donnie, was he hoping for her to answer? And when she did answer, did he want her to talk a minute or hand the receiver straight to Donnie? But what would she say to him, anyway? Oh, all her questions had to do with where she might find love, and everything she said made the old man wince and love her more. She left in the middle of a sentence, knocking against a doorknob as she flew from the room, an unlovable-looking tangle of blond hair and braces and scrapes and Band-Aids. After she was gone the room seemed too empty, as if she had accidentally torn part of it away in her flight.

Getting into an old folks' home was hard. Not only because of lack of good homes, high expenses, waiting lists; it was harder yet to talk his family into letting him go. His son-in-law argued with him every evening, his round, kind face anxious and questioning across the supper table. "Is it that you think you're not welcome here? You are, you know. You were one of the reasons we bought this big house." His grandchildren when they talked to him had a kind of urgency in their voices, as if they were trying to impress him with their acceptance of him. His other daughters called long distance from all across the country and begged him to come to them if he wouldn't stay with Clara. They had room, or they would make room; he had no idea what homes for the aged were like these days. To all of them he gave the same answer: "I've made my decision." He was proud of them for asking, though. All his children had turned out so well, every last one of them. They were good, strong women with happy families, and they had never given him a moment's worry. He was luckier than he had a right to be. He had felt lucky all his life, dangerously lucky, cursed by luck; it had seemed some disaster must be waiting to even things up. But the luck had held. When his wife died it was at a late age, sparing her the pain she would have had to face, and his life had continued in its steady, reasonable pattern with no more sorrow than any other man's. His final lot was to weaken, to crumble and to die—only a secret disaster, not the one he had been expecting.

He walked two blocks daily, fighting off the weakness. He shelled peas for Clara and mended little household articles, which gave him an excuse to sit. Nobody noticed how he arranged to climb the stairs only once a day, at bedtime. When he had empty time he chose a chair without rockers, one that would not be a symbol of age and weariness and lack of work. He rose every morning at six and stayed in his room a full hour, giving his legs enough warning to face the day ahead. Never once did he disgrace himself by falling down in front of people. He dropped nothing more important than a spoon or a fork.

Plot: *His actions suggest his determination to stay strong. He didn't want to act like an old man, falling down and dropping things. That would be disgraceful. Instead, he kept his dignity by keeping busy, exercising, and doing odd jobs around the house.*

Meanwhile the wheels were turning; his name was on a waiting list. Not that that meant anything, Clara said. "When it comes right down to driving you out there, I just won't let you go," she told him. "But I'm hoping you won't carry things that far. Daddy, won't you put a stop to this foolishness?"

He hardly listened. He had chosen long ago what kind of old age he would have; everyone does. Most, he thought, were weak, and chose to be loved at any cost. He had seen women turn soft and sad, anxious to please, and had watched with pity and impatience their losing battles. And he had once known a schoolteacher, no weakling at all, who said straight out that when she grew old she would finally eat all she wanted and grow fat without worry. He admired that—a simple plan, dependent upon no one. "I'll sit in an armchair," she had said, "with a lady's magazine in my lap and a box of homemade fudge on the lampstand. I'll get as fat as I like and nobody will give a hang." The schoolteacher was thin and pale, with a kind of stooped, sloping figure that was popular at the time. He had lost track of her long ago, but he liked to think that she had kept her word. He imagined her fifty years later, cozy and fat in a puffy chair, with one hand moving constantly between her mouth and the candy plate. If she had died young or changed her mind or put off her eating till another decade, he didn't want to hear about it.

Theme: *It's sad that he thinks needing love is a sign of weakness. On the contrary, giving love and allowing yourself to be loved are strong qualities in a person—at any age.*

He had chosen independence. Nothing else had even occurred to him. He had lived to himself, existed on less money than his family would ever guess, raised his own vegetables and refused all gifts but an occasional tin of coffee. And now he would sign himself into the old folks' home and enter on his own two feet, relying only on the impersonal care of nurses and cleaning women. He could have chosen to die alone of neglect, but for his daughters that would have been a burden too—a different kind of burden, much worse. He was sensible enough to see that.

Meanwhile, all he had to do was to look as busy as possible in a chair without rockers and hold fast against his family. Oh, they gave him no peace. Some of their attacks were obvious—the arguments with his son-in-law over the supper table—and some were subtle; you had to be on your guard every minute for those. Francie, for instance, asking him questions about what she called the "olden days." Inviting him to sink unnoticing into doddering reminiscence. "Did I see Granny ever? I don't remember her. Did she like me? What kind of person was she?" He stood his ground, gave monosyllabic answers. It was easier than he had expected. For him, middle age tempted up more memories. Nowadays events had telescoped. The separate agonies and worries—the long, hard births of each of his children, the youngest daughter's chronic childhood earaches, his wife's last illness—were smoothed now into a single, summing-up sentence: He was a widowed farmer with five daughters, all married, twenty grandchildren and three great-grandchildren. "Your grandmother was a fine woman," he told Francie; "just fine." Then he shut up.

Francie, not knowing that she had been spared, sulked and peeled a strip of sunburned skin from her nose.

Clara cried all the way to the home. She was the one who was driving; it made him nervous. One of her hands on the steering wheel held a balled-up tissue, which she had stopped using. She let tears run unchecked down her face and drove jerkily with a great deal of brake-slamming and gear-gnashing.

"Clara, I wish you wouldn't take on so," he told her. "There's no need to be sad over *me*."

"I'm not sad so much as mad," Clara said. "I feel like this

is something you're doing *to* me, just throwing away what I give. Oh, why do you have to be so stubborn? It's still not too late to change your mind.''

The old man kept silent. On his right sat Francie, chewing a thumbnail and scowling out the window, her usual self except for the unexplainable presence of her other hand in his, tight as wire. Periodically she muttered a number; she was counting red convertibles, and had been for days. When she reached a hundred, the next boy she saw would be her true love.

He figured that was probably the reason she had come on this trip—a greater exposure to red convertibles.

Whatever happened to DeSotos?[1] Didn't there use to be a car called a roadster?[2]

They parked in the U-shaped driveway in front of the home, under the shade of a poplar tree. If he had had his way, he would have arrived by motorcycle, but he made the best of it—picked up his underwear sack from between his feet, climbed the front steps ramrod-straight. They were met by a smiling woman in blue who had to check his name on a file and ask more questions. He made sure to give all the answers himself, overriding Clara when necessary. Meanwhile Francie spun on one squeaky sneaker heel and examined the hall, a cavernous, polished square with old-fashioned parlors on either side of it. A few old people were on the plush couches, and a nurse sat idle beside a lady in a wheelchair.

They went up a creaking elevator to the second floor and down a long, dark corridor deadened by carpeting. The lady in blue, still carrying a sheaf of files, knocked at number 213. Then she flung the door open on a narrow green room flooded with sunlight.

''Mr. Pond,'' she said, ''this is Mr. Carpenter. I hope you'll get on well together.''

Mr. Pond was one of those men who run to fat and baldness in old age. He sat in a rocking chair with a gilt-edged Bible on his knees.

''How-do,'' he said. ''Mighty nice to meet you.''

Character: He doesn't want to believe that Francie took the trip out of her fondness for him. He seems to avoid feeling loved because, to him, needing love is weak.

Character: He still wants the freedom and "sparseness" of the motorcycle. "Overriding" Clara's answers to the receptionist's questions also reflects his fierce independence.

Setting: The "creaking elevator" reminds me of the old man's creaking muscles. At the same time, the "lady in blue," the green room, and the sunlight have a relaxing effect. This will be good for the old man.

---

1. DeSotos: Car model of the 1950's.
2. roadster (rōd′ stər) *n.*: An early sportscar with an open cab and a ''rumble seat'' in the rear.

They shook hands cautiously, with the women ringing them like mothers asking their children to play nicely with each other. "Ordinarily I sleep in the bed by the window," said Mr. Pond, "but I don't hold it in much importance. You can take your pick."

"Anything will do," the old man said.

Clara was dry-eyed now. She looked frightened.

"You'd best be getting on back now," he told her. "Don't you worry about me. I'll let you know," he said, suddenly generous now that he had won, "if there is anything I need."

Clara nodded and kissed his cheek. Francie kept her face turned away, but she hugged him tightly, and then she looked up at him as she stepped back. Her eyebrows were tilted as if she were about to ask him one of her questions. Was it her the

boy with the sheepdog came for? Did he care when she answered the telephone?

They left, shutting the door with a gentle click. The old man made a great business out of settling his underwear and razor in a bureau drawer, smoothing out the paper bag and folding it, placing it in the next drawer down.

"Didn't bring much," said Mr. Pond, one thumb marking his page in the Bible.

"I don't need much."

"Go on—take the bed by the window. You'll feel better after awhile."

"I *wanted* to come," the old man said.

"That there window is a front one. If you look out, you can see your folks leave."

He slid between the bed and the window and looked out. No reason not to. Clara and Francie were just climbing into the car, the sun lacquering the tops of their heads. Clara was blowing her nose with a dot of tissue.

"*Now* they cry," said Mr. Pond, although he had not risen to look out himself. "Later they'll buy themselves a milkshake to celebrate."

"I wanted to come. I made them bring me."

"And so they did. *I* didn't want to come. My son wanted to put me here—his wife was expecting. And so he did. It all works out the same in the end."

"Well, I could have stayed with one of my daughters," the old man said. "But I'm not like some I have known. Hanging around making burdens of themselves, hoping to be loved. Not me."

"If you don't care about being loved," said Mr. Pond, "how come it would bother you to be a burden?"

Then he opened the Bible again, at the place where his thumb had been all the time and went back to reading.

The old man sat on the edge of the bed, watching the tail of Clara's car flash as sharp and hard as a jewel around the bend of the road. Then, with nobody to watch that mattered, he let his shoulders slump and eased himself out of his suit coat, which he folded over the foot of the bed. He slid his suspenders down and let them dangle at his waist. He took off his copper-toed work boots and set them on the floor neatly side

Plot: *It seems as though he now regrets his decision to live in the nursing home. The whole time he insisted on going, maybe he was hiding his true feelings.*

Character: *I totally disagree with Mr. Pond. Mr. Carpenter's family loves him; they will not "celebrate" Mr. Carpenter's decision. Mr. Pond is being insensitive to Mr. Carpenter.*

Character: *Mr. Carpenter is insecure about love, so he avoids it. For him, avoiding love also means avoiding the disappointments that accompany love. Not wanting to make a burden of himself suggests that he doesn't want to give up the control over his life.*

To me, this story sends a strong message to people of all ages, but especially to young people. Mr. Carpenter reminded me to enjoy the sweetness of life every day. Doing so is difficult for young people who have the pressures of school and parents. However, pressures and painful experiences will always exist. Even so, it's important not to let them interfere with being young. I would hate to end up in an old-age home looking back on the things I could have done in my youth.

by side. And although it was only noon, he lay down full-length on top of the bedspread. Whiskery lines ran across the plaster of the ceiling high above him. There was a cracking sound in the mattress when he moved; it must be covered with something waterproof.

The tiredness in his head was as vague and restless as anger; the weakness in his knees made him feel as if he had just finished some exhausting exercise. He lay watching the plaster cracks settle themselves into pictures, listening to the silent, neuter voice in his mind form the words he had grown accustomed to hearing now: Let me not give in at the end. Let me continue gracefully till the moment of my defeat. Let Lollie Simpson be alive somewhere even as I lie on my bed; let her be eating homemade fudge in an overstuffed armchair and growing fatter and fatter.

Anne Tyler (1941–   ) was born in Minneapolis, Minnesota. During her childhood her family moved frequently, and she lived in many communities in the South and the Midwest. At age sixteen she entered Duke University, where she majored in Russian. Since 1965 Tyler has been writing full time. In 1967 Tyler moved to Baltimore, Maryland, the setting of most of her work, including "With All Flags Flying." Many of her novels, including *Dinner at the Homesick Restaurant* and *The Accidental Tourist,* have been best sellers.

RESPONDING TO THE SELECTION

Your Response

1. Do you identify with any of the characters in the story? Explain.
2. What do you think will be important to you in your old age?

Recalling

3. Why does Mr. Carpenter decide not to live alone anymore?
4. How does he plan to live the rest of his life?
5. How does his family feel about his plan?
6. What obstacles does he encounter?
7. Explain whether Mr. Carpenter is able to carry out his plan.

Interpreting

8. What is Mr. Carpenter's attitude about possessions and unnecessary things? Support your answer with examples from the story.
9. Why is Mr. Carpenter so determined not to move in with his daughter and her family?
10. What does Mr. Pond mean when he says, "It all works out the same in the end"?

Applying

11. If you had been in Mr. Carpenter's shoes, what would you have done? Explain your answer.

ANALYZING LITERATURE

Recognizing Characters as Symbols

Characters can represent ideas, beliefs, and feelings; that is, they can be used as **symbols.** The symbolism of a character comes out of the character's strong traits or pattern of behavior. For example, Florence Nightingale, known for her nursing care, can stand for compassion.

What do you think each of the following characters represents?

1. Mr. Carpenter
2. Lollie Simpson (the teacher)
3. Francie

CRITICAL THINKING AND READING

Recognizing Generalizations

A **generalization** is a statement or principle, inferred from a number of specific examples, that has broad general application. "All his children had turned out well" is a generalization. Each of Mr. Carpenter's children has made a good life for herself, so the statement covers five specific instances. If one of his children had turned out badly, the generalization would not be valid.

1. Why is the following statement a generalization: "And what [Francie] felt was always about love."
2. What generalization does Mr. Carpenter make about old people?

THINKING AND WRITING

Writing With a Symbol

Brainstorm with your classmates to come up with possibilities for a character who may be used as a symbol. The character's personality, behavior, or appearance should reflect the idea or feeling the character stands for. Then write about an incident in which the character's behavior or appearance demonstrates the quality or idea for which the character is a symbol. When you revise your paper, try to replace general words with specific ones.

LEARNING OPTION

Community Connections. Volunteer in a local nursing home or retirement home for a day. By the end of the day, you will have a sense of how the residents feel about themselves and their lives just by helping to care for their needs. Compare what you learned about the people in the home with what your classmates observed in the people they met. Did you or any of your classmates meet a resident like Mr. Carpenter? Explain.

YOUR WRITING PROCESS

WRITING A NEWS REPORT

"I talk out the lines as I write."

Tennessee Williams

Suppose one of your favorite short story writers has accepted an invitation to give a reading at your school and everyone in the community is welcome to attend. Also, imagine that you are the reporter for cultural events on a local news program produced by students. How would you broadcast the news of the reading to generate interest?

Focus

Assignment: Write a TV news report that zeroes in on suspenseful events in one of this unit's short stories.
Purpose: To inform viewers and to draw them to the reading.
Audience: People in the community with a special interest in your school.

Prewriting

1. Review the short stories. Look back at the stories in this unit and choose one that you feel enthusiastic about. Imagine that the story's author will give a reading of it at your school.

2. Highlight the plot. Make a diagram tracing the development of the story's plot.

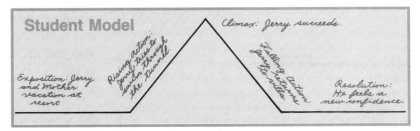

Student Model

Climax: Jerry succeeds.

Rising action: Jerry tries to swim through the tunnel.

Falling action: Jerry returns to villa.

Exposition: Jerry and Mother vacation at resort

Resolution: He feels a new confidence.

3. Discover an interesting slant. The story's events may be interesting, but the special "spin" you give them will hook your viewers' attention. To discover an interesting slant for your report, cluster answers around this question: What insight into life do the story's events convey?

Drafting

1. Hook your viewers with a snappy opening. Write an opening to grab your audience's attention by presenting your special slant. Try asking viewers a question, or fascinate them with a provocative idea.

2. Selectively follow your diagram of the plot. Use the diagram you sketched as a guide for writing the body of your report, but don't give away all of the story. Since one of your purposes for writing is to generate interest, you'll not want to spoil the ending for viewers. Instead, build their expectations. Lead them up to the climactic moment and then leave them suspended, waiting to hear more.

3. Focus on sound. Because viewers will be listening to your report, not reading it, your words should appeal to their ears. Try to include sound devices such as repetition and alliteration, but don't overdo it.

Student Model

His pulse pounding, his lungs about to burst like a balloon, Jerry struggles on into the darkness—struggles against pain, panic, and his fears of dying.

Revising and Editing

1. Have a classmate read your draft or tape-record it. Listen to your report critically as viewers will. Does it have a beginning, a middle, and an end and flow smoothly from one part to the next?

2. Consult with your classmates. Read your news report to a partner or to an editing group. You might ask them questions like these:

- Are there passages that seem to drag?
- Do I give away too much of the plot or not enough?
- Would this report make you want to attend the reading?

Writer's Hint

Whenever possible, use the active, not the passive voice to keep your report lively and easy to follow.

Options for Publishing

- Read your news report to the class and ask for comments.
- Prepare a videotape of your report as it would appear on a TV newscast. Before filming, work with a director to rehearse your posture, gestures, and delivery. Invite teachers and students to a screening.

Reviewing Your Writing Process

1. How did you decide on a way to hook your viewers' attention?

2. Did you refer to a diagram of the story's plot as you drafted your report? Why or why not?

3. What was the most challenging part of this assignment? Explain.

YOUR WRITING PROCESS

WRITING AN IMAGINARY NARRATIVE

"When you catch an adjective, kill it."

Mark Twain

Picture this: You are a staff writer at *Future Trends* magazine, and your editor assigns you a story on possible educational developments in the American high school fifty years in the future. She says that she wants a "fresh angle." As an ace reporter, you decide that your article will take the form of a diary entry written by a tenth-grade student in the mid-twenty-first century.

> **Focus**
>
> **Assignment:** Write a diary entry about your day at a school of the future.
> **Purpose:** To show how high schools will be different in fifty years.
> **Audience:** Readers of a magazine that predicts future developments in various fields.

Prewriting

1. Review some futuristic stories. To begin, review the Benét, Bradbury, and Asimov short stories in this unit. Consider the kinds of details these writers include in their narratives. Keep in mind that you are writing about a future time in which things will probably differ considerably from the way they are today.

2. Brainstorm to come up with ideas about school life. Use a cluster diagram to help you explore the different aspects of the high school of the future. What activities will students participate in? What subjects will they study? Also, don't forget to consider the "look" of the school building and the structure of a typical school day.

Student Model

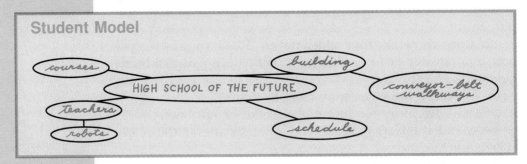

3. Freewrite about some of these aspects. Picture yourself wandering through the halls of the school and jot down what you see. Remember, this is freewriting. You don't have to worry about neat transitions or "making sense" of what comes to your mind.

Drafting

1. Review the diary format. A diary is a collection of entries of a personal nature, written in the first person. Sometimes a diary entry takes the form of a "letter" to the journal from the writer ("Dear Diary . . ."), but other diary techniques include straightforward descriptions, recorded dialogues, or purely emotional reactions. Any of these techniques can be used in combination with the others to make a chronological record of your day.

2. Consider the "accuracy" of your narrative. Use details that are plausible, given the time period and the location you are considering. Try to base your predictions on some current trends you notice in American society in general and high schools in particular.

Revising and Editing

1. Review your work for plausibility as well as interest. Check your work to make sure that the predictions you make are not only based on current trends but are also a bit surprising.

2. Test your diary entry on a peer editor. Exchange your entry with a classmate, and consider the following questions as you review each other's work:
- Is the correct diary format used?
- Are the predictions plausible?
- Are the details consistent throughout?
- Is the diary entry imaginative and informative?

3. Proofread your work. Check to see that your writing is error-free.

Grammar Tip

When you write a first-person narrative, you relate a personal experience. The experience is part of your memory, and you draw on emotional associations to give it meaning. Use the first-person pronouns *I* and *me,* and tell the story as you see it.

Options for Publishing

- Collect all the diary entries written in the class into a "magazine" and add imaginative illustrations. Make the magazine available to other classes.
- Submit your diary entry to your school newspaper as a feature article entitled "Students Predict the Future Classroom."

Reviewing Your Writing Process

1. What problems did you encounter when thinking and writing about a future time?

2. In what ways is it harder to write about future events than about past or present ones? In what ways is it easier?

RAISED STAGE WITH MASKS, NARRATOR, AND AUDITORIUM, 1981
David Hockney
© *David Hockney, 1981*

DRAMA

One of our earliest literary forms, drama evolved from man's tribal past. Ancient people would act out great triumphs, deep fears, or heartfelt wishes in early religious rites. Still a religious ritual, drama became an art form in fifth-century B.C. Greece, where ancient myths were retold in dramatic form at religious festivals. Ancient playwrights shaped drama into its modern form, with acts and scenes performed by a large cast. The Greek philosopher Aristotle divided all drama into tradegy, which tells of the downfall of a noble or heroic individual, and comedy, which describes the regeneration or reformation of a group or society. Even with the rise of Christianity, drama remained connected to religion through much of its history. During the medieval period, drama was reborn in the mystery and morality plays of the Catholic Church. Eventually old Greek and Roman manuscripts were discovered, translated, and produced on stage. By the end of the sixteenth century, English drama entered a golden age with William Shakespeare. Currently drama throughout the world has taken many and varied forms, from musicals to biting satires.

The word *drama* comes from the Greek word *dran,* meaning "to do" or "to act." It is this doing or acting quality that makes drama unique in literature. While plays share many elements with prose fiction and poetry—plot, character, point of view, setting, tone, symbolism, and theme—the greatest difference is that drama is designed to be presented by actors on a stage before an audience. Actors speak to one another or to the audience, bringing life to their characters through tone of voice, expressions, and movement. On the stage, sets and props help to create a specific place and underscore ideas the playwright is trying to convey. Costumes, lighting, music, and sound effects add to the total effect of the drama. Even the audience plays a part, for its reactions provide feedback to the actors.

In this unit you will read plays by the Greek playwright Sophocles, and by William Shakespeare as well as a play by a modern author.

READING ACTIVELY

Drama

Let us examine the elements of drama. First, as a story, a play shows a character in conflict—facing a problem that gets progressively worse until it reaches a crisis, the climax. At this point a decisive action solves the problem. This action speedily brings about the end of the story. Second, a play is told through dialogue and action. Because the audience cannot look directly into the minds of the characters to see what they are thinking and feeling, the audience must infer those thoughts or feelings by "reading" the actions. A character who pounds his fist on a table is angry. One who bites her nails is nervous.

Plays are meant to be performed. When you read a play, you are reading a script. The stage directions, printed in italics within brackets, are intended to show the actors when and how to move and speak. They suggest to the director what kinds of sound effects and lighting are needed and what the stage should look like. Stage directions use a particular vocabulary. *Right, left, up, down,* and *center* refer to areas of the stage as the actors see it. To help you visualize what is meant when a stage direction tells an actor to move up center, for example, picture the stage like this:

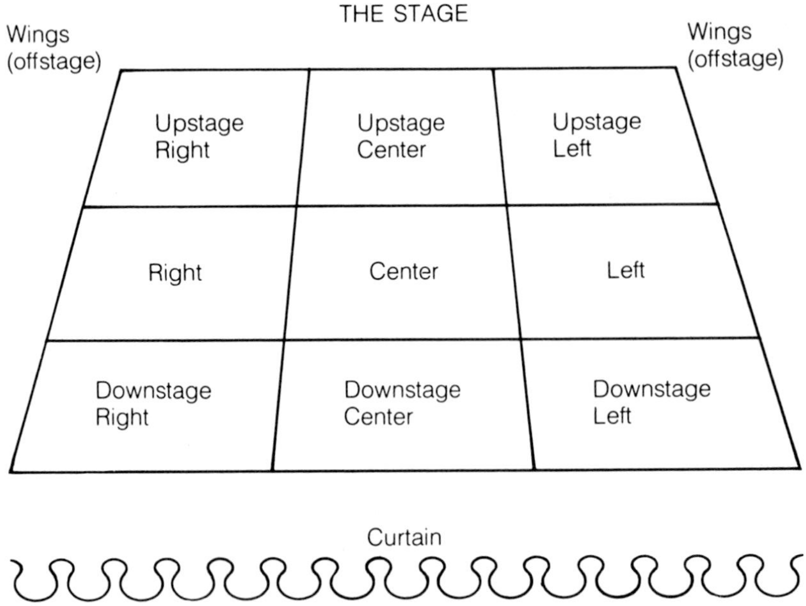

THE STAGE

Wings (offstage)

Wings (offstage)

Upstage Right	Upstage Center	Upstage Left
Right	Center	Left
Downstage Right	Downstage Center	Downstage Left

Curtain

Just as you read stories actively, you should also read drama actively. Reading actively involves seeing the play in your mind while you continually question the meaning of what the actors are saying and doing.

The following strategies will help you read drama actively so that you will enjoy and appreciate the plays in this unit.

VISUALIZE Picture the stage and the characters in action. Use the directions and information supplied by the playwright to create the scene in your mind. Hear the characters speak; listen to their tone of voice. Let them show you what is happening.

QUESTION What is each character like? What situation does each character face? How are the characters in conflict with one another? What motives and traits does each character reveal by his or her words and actions?

PREDICT Building on your knowledge of the play's central conflict and the characters' motives, predict what you think will happen. How will the conflict be resolved? What will become of each character?

CLARIFY Be sure that you can make sense of the characters' words or actions. If something is not clear to you, perhaps you need to review to find a clue in earlier words or actions. Look for answers to your questions, and check your predictions.

CONNECT Occasionally pause to review what has happened. What is the central conflict? How is it being resolved? Try to summarize how the characters' actions and words fit together. Use your own knowledge and experience to make connections between events and real life.

RESPOND Finally, think about all the elements of the play. What does the play mean? What has it revealed about life? What does it say to you?

You will be a more effective reader if you use these strategies when you read drama, and you will better understand the dramatist's purpose.

GUIDE FOR READING

Howard Koch

(1902–   ), born in New York, has lived much of his life there and in Hollywood. He has written for the stage, screen, and radio. Koch won an Oscar for his screenplay for the movie *Casablanca.* He said his goal was to "dramatize as honestly as I can any aspect of the human condition in its social framework, with an emphasis on life-supporting values." When his radio play *Invasion From Mars,* based on the novel *War of the Worlds* by H. G. Wells, was broadcast, many listeners believed it to be real.

Invasion From Mars

Radio Play

A **radio play** is read by actors for a radio broadcast rather than performed on a stage. Since the play is heard and not seen, you must rely on the dialogue, sound effects, and music to develop the characters and plot, and to indicate the passage of time. You also must imagine the characters' appearance and actions.

Focus

On Halloween night 1938, *Invasion From Mars* was broadcast. Many listeners panicked as they heard the radio announcers describe the Martian invasion of New Jersey. Create a brief news bulletin about a fictional event in your community. Make it seem realistic by answering the following questions:

> Who? Where? Why?
>
> What? When? How?

As you read *Invasion From Mars*, compare your bulletin with those in the play.

Vocabulary

Knowing the following words will help you as you read *Invasion From Mars.*

mortal (môr′ t'l) *adj.*: That which must die (p. 251)

scrutinized (skro͞ot′ 'n īzd′) *v.*: Examined closely (p. 251)

complacence (kəm plās′ 'ns) *n.*: Self-satisfaction (p. 251)

serene (sə rēn′) *adj.*: Undisturbed (p. 251)

conjecture (kən jek′ chər) *n.*: An inference based on incomplete or inconclusive evidence (p. 253)

silhouettes (sil′ o͞o wetz′) *n.*: Outlines of things that appear dark against a light background (p. 256)

Invasion From Mars

Howard Koch

CHARACTERS

Three Announcers

Orson Welles

Carl Phillips, radio commentator

Professor Richard Pierson, astronomer

A Policeman

Mr. Wilmuth, a farmer

Brigadier General Montgomery Smith

Harry McDonald

Captain Lansing

Secretary of the Interior

Soldiers of the 22nd Field Artillery:
An officer, a gunner, and an observer

Lieutenant Voght, commander of an
Army bomber plane

Five Radio Operators

A Stranger

COLUMBIA BROADCASTING SYSTEM

ORSON WELLES AND MERCURY THEATRE

ON THE AIR

SUNDAY, OCTOBER 30, 1938

8:00 TO 9:00 P.M.

ANNOUNCER. The Columbia Broadcasting System and its affiliated[1] stations present Orson Welles and the Mercury Theatre on the Air in a radio play by Howard Koch suggested by the H. G. Wells novel *The War of the Worlds.*

[*Mercury Theatre Musical Theme*]

ANNOUNCER. Ladies and gentlemen: the director of the Mercury Theatre and star of these broadcasts, Orson Welles . . .

ORSON WELLES. We know now that in the early years of the twentieth century this world was being watched closely by intelligences greater than man's and yet as mortal as his own. We know now that as human beings busied themselves about their various concerns they were scrutinized and studied, perhaps almost as narrowly as a man with a microscope might scrutinize the transient[2] creatures that swarm and multiply in a drop of water. With infinite complacence people went to and fro over the earth about their little affairs, serene in the assurance of their dominion[3] over this small spinning fragment of solar driftwood which by chance or design man has inherited out of the dark mystery of Time and Space. Yet across an immense ethereal[4] gulf, minds that are to our minds as ours are to the beasts in the jungle, intellects vast, cool and unsympathetic, regarded this earth with envious eyes and slowly and surely drew their plans

---

2. transient (tran′ shənt) *adj.*: Not permanent; passing quickly.

3. dominion (də min′ yən) *n.*: Power to rule.

4. ethereal (i thir′ ē əl) *adj.*: Of the upper regions of space.

---

1. affiliated (ə fil′ē āt əd) *adj.*: Associated.

against us. In the thirty-eighth year of the twentieth century came the great disillusionment.[5]

It was near the end of October. Business was better. The war was over. More men were back at work. Sales were picking up. On this particular evening, October 30, the Crossley service[6] estimated that thirty-two million people were listening in on radios.

ANNOUNCER. . . . for the next twenty-four hours not much change in temperature. A slight atmospheric disturbance of undetermined origin is reported over Nova Scotia,[7] causing a low pressure area to move down rather rapidly over the northeastern states, bringing a forecast of rain, accompanied by winds of light gale force. Maximum temperature 66; minimum 48. This weather report comes to you from the Government Weather Bureau.

. . . We now take you to the Meridian Room in the Hotel Park Plaza in downtown New York, where you will be entertained by the music of Ramón Raquello and his orchestra.

[*Spanish theme song . . . fades.*]

ANNOUNCER THREE. Good evening, ladies and gentlemen. From the Meridian Room in the Park Plaza in New York City, we bring you the music of Ramón Raquello and his orchestra. With a touch of the Spanish, Ramón Raquello leads off with "La Cumparsita."

[*Piece starts playing.*]

ANNOUNCER TWO. Ladies and gentlemen, we interrupt our program of dance music to bring you a special bulletin from the Intercontinental Radio News. At twenty minutes before eight, central time, Professor Farrell of the Mount Jennings Observatory, Chicago, Illinois, reports observing several explosions of incandescent gas, occurring at regular intervals on the planet Mars.

The spectroscope[8] indicates the gas to be hydrogen and moving toward the earth with enormous velocity. Professor Pierson of the observatory at Princeton[9] confirms Farrell's observation, and describes the phenomenon as (quote) like a jet of blue flame shot from a gun (unquote). We now return you to the music of Ramón Raquello, playing for you in the Meridian Room of the Park Plaza Hotel, situated in downtown New York.

[*Music plays for a few moments until piece ends . . . sound of applause*]

Now a tune that never loses favor, the ever-popular "Star Dust." Ramón Raquello and his orchestra . . .

[*Music*]

ANNOUNCER TWO. Ladies and gentlemen, following on the news given in our bulletin a moment ago, the Government Meteorological Bureau has requested the large observatories of the country to keep an astronomical watch on any further disturbances occurring on the planet Mars. Due to the unusual nature of this occurrence, we have arranged an interview with the noted astronomer, Professor Pierson, who will give us his views on this event. In a few moments we will take you to the Princeton Observatory at Princeton, New Jersey. We return you until then to the music of Ramón Raquello and his orchestra.

---

5. disillusionment (dis′ i lōō′ zhən mənt) *n.*: Disappointment.
6. Crossley service: A service that estimated the size of radio audiences as the Nielsen rating service estimates the size of television audiences today.
7. Nova Scotia (nō′və skō′ shə): A southeastern province of Canada.

8. spectroscope (spek′ trə skōp′) *n.*: A scientific instrument used to identify substances.
9. Princeton: A university in Princeton, New Jersey.

ANNOUNCER TWO. We are ready now to take you to the Princeton Observatory at Princeton where Carl Phillips, our commentator, will interview Professor Richard Pierson, famous astronomer. We take you now to Princeton, New Jersey.

[*Echo chamber*]

PHILLIPS. Good evening, ladies and gentlemen. This is Carl Phillips, speaking to you from the observatory at Princeton. I am standing in a large semi-circular room, pitch black except for an oblong split in the ceiling. Through this opening I can see a sprinkling of stars that cast a kind of frosty glow over the intricate mechanism of the huge telescope. The ticking sound you hear is the vibration of the clockwork. Professor Pierson stands directly above me on a small platform, peering through the giant lens. I ask you to be patient, ladies and gentlemen, during any delay that may arise during our interview. Beside his ceaseless watch of the heavens, Professor Pierson may be interrupted by telephone or other communications. During this period he is in constant touch with the astronomical centers of the world . . . Professor, may I begin our questions?

PIERSON. At any time, Mr. Phillips.

PHILLIPS. Professor, would you please tell our radio audience exactly what you see as you observe the planet Mars through your telescope?

PIERSON. Nothing unusual at the moment, Mr. Phillips. A red disk swimming in a blue sea. Transverse[10] stripes across the disk. Quite distinct now because Mars happens to

_____
10. transverse (trans vʉrs′) *adj.*: Crossing from side to side.

be at the point nearest the earth . . . in opposition, as we call it.

PHILLIPS. In your opinion, what do these transverse stripes signify, Professor Pierson?

PIERSON. Not canals, I can assure you, Mr. Phillips, although that's the popular conjecture of those who imagine Mars to be inhabited. From a scientific viewpoint the stripes are merely the result of atmospheric conditions peculiar to the planet.

PHILLIPS. Then you're quite convinced as a scientist that living intelligence as we know it does not exist on Mars?

PIERSON. I should say the chances against it are a thousand to one.

PHILLIPS. And yet how do you account for these gas eruptions occurring on the surface of the planet at regular intervals?

PIERSON. Mr. Phillips, I cannot account for it.

PHILLIPS. By the way, Professor, for the benefit of our listeners, how far is Mars from the earth?

PIERSON. Approximately forty million miles.

PHILLIPS. Well, that seems a safe enough distance.

PHILLIPS. Just a moment, ladies and gentlemen, someone has just handed Professor Pierson a message. While he reads it, let me remind you that we are speaking to you from the observatory in Princeton, New Jersey, where we are interviewing the world-famous astronomer, Professor Pierson . . . One moment, please. Professor Pierson has passed me a message which he has just received . . . Professor, may I read the message to the listening audience?

PIERSON. Certainly, Mr. Phillips.

PHILLIPS. Ladies and gentlemen, I shall read

you a wire addressed to Professor Pierson from Dr. Gray of the National History Museum, New York. "9:15 P.M. eastern standard time. Seismograph[11] registered shock of almost earthquake intensity occurring within a radius of twenty miles of Princeton. Please investigate. Signed, Lloyd Gray, Chief of Astronomical Division." . . . Professor Pierson, could this occurrence possibly have something to do with the disturbances observed on the planet Mars?

PIERSON. Hardly, Mr. Phillips. This is probably a meteorite[12] of unusual size and its arrival at this particular time is merely a coincidence. However, we shall conduct a search, as soon as daylight permits.

PHILLIPS. Thank you, Professor. Ladies and gentlemen, for the past ten minutes we've been speaking to you from the observatory at Princeton, bringing you a special interview with Professor Pierson, noted astronomer. This is Carl Phillips speaking. We now return you to our New York studio.

[*Fade in piano playing*]

ANNOUNCER TWO. Ladies and gentlemen, here is the latest bulletin from the Intercontinental Radio News. Montreal, Canada: Professor Morse of McGill University reports observing a total of three explosions on the planet Mars, between the hours of 7:45 P.M. and 9:20 P.M., eastern standard time. This confirms earlier reports received from American observatories. Now, nearer home, comes a special announcement from Trenton,[13] New Jersey. It is reported that at 8:50 P.M. a huge, flaming object, believed to be a meteorite, fell on a farm in the neighborhood of Grovers Mill, New Jersey, twenty-two miles from Trenton. The flash in the sky was visible within a radius of several hundred miles and the noise of the impact was heard as far north as Elizabeth.

We have dispatched a special mobile unit to the scene, and will have our commentator, Mr. Phillips, give you a word description as soon as he can reach there from Princeton. In the meantime, we take you to the Hotel Martinet in Brooklyn, where Bobby Millette and his orchestra are offering a program of dance music.

[*Swing band for twenty seconds . . . then cut*]

ANNOUNCER TWO. We take you now to Grovers Mill, New Jersey.

[*Crowd noises . . . police sirens*]

PHILLIPS. Ladies and gentlemen, this is Carl Phillips again, at the Wilmuth farm, Grovers Mill, New Jersey. Professor Pierson and myself made the eleven miles from Princeton in ten minutes. Well, I . . . I hardly know where to begin, to paint for you a word picture of the strange scene before my eyes, like something out of a modern *Arabian Nights*.[14] Well, I just got here. I haven't had a chance to look around yet. I guess that's it. Yes, I guess that's the . . . thing, directly in front of me, half buried in a vast pit. Must have struck with terrific force. The ground is covered with splinters of a tree it must have struck on its way down. What I can see of the . . . object itself doesn't look very much like a meteor, at least not the meteors I've seen. It looks more like a huge cylinder. It has a diameter of . . . what would you say, Professor Pierson?

PIERSON. [*Off*] About thirty yards.

---

11. seismograph (sīz′ mə graf′) *n.*: An instrument that records the intensity and duration of earthquakes.
12. meteorite (mēt′ ē ə rīt′) *n.*: Part of a heavenly body that passes through the atmosphere and falls to the earth's surface as a piece of matter.
13. Trenton (tren′ tən): The capital of New Jersey.

14. *Arabian Nights:* A collection of tales from Arabia, India, and Persia.

PHILLIPS. About thirty yards . . . The metal on the sheath[15] is . . . well, I've never seen anything like it. The color is sort of yellowish-white. Curious spectators now are pressing close to the object in spite of the efforts of the police to keep them back. They're getting in front of my line of vision. Would you mind standing on one side, please?

POLICEMAN. One side, there, one side.

PHILLIPS. While the policemen are pushing the crowd back, here's Mr. Wilmuth, owner of the farm here. He may have some interesting facts to add. . . . Mr. Wilmuth, would you please tell the radio audience as much as you remember of this rather unusual visitor that dropped in your backyard? Step closer, please. Ladies and gentlemen, this is Mr. Wilmuth.

WILMUTH. I was listenin' to the radio.

PHILLIPS. Closer and louder, please.

WILMUTH. Pardon me!

PHILLIPS. Louder, please, and closer.

WILMUTH. Yes, sir—while I was listening to the radio and kinda drowsin', that Professor fellow was talkin' about Mars, so I was half dozin' and half . . .

PHILLIPS. Yes, Mr. Wilmuth. Then what happened?

WILMUTH. As I was sayin', I was listenin' to the radio kinda halfways . . .

PHILLIPS. Yes, Mr. Wilmuth, and then you saw something?

WILMUTH. Not first off. I heard something.

PHILLIPS. And what did you hear?

WILMUTH. A hissing sound. Like this: sssssss . . . kinda like a fourt' of July rocket.

PHILLIPS. Then what?

WILMUTH. Turned my head out the window and would have swore I was to sleep and dreamin'.

PHILLIPS. Yes?

WILMUTH. I seen a kinda greenish streak and then zingo! Somethin' smacked the ground. Knocked me clear out of my chair!

PHILLIPS. Well, were you frightened, Mr. Wilmuth?

WILMUTH. Well, I—I ain't quite sure. I reckon I—I was kinda riled.[16]

PHILLIPS. Thank you, Mr. Wilmuth. Thank you.

WILMUTH. Want me to tell you some more?

PHILLIPS. No . . . That's quite all right, that's plenty.

PHILLIPS. Ladies and gentlemen, you've just heard Mr. Wilmuth, owner of the farm where this thing has fallen. I wish I could convey the atmosphere . . . the background of this . . . fantastic scene. Hundreds of cars are parked in a field in back of us. Police are trying to rope off the roadway leading into the farm. But it's no use. They're breaking right through. Their headlights throw an enormous spot on the pit where the object's half buried. Some of the more daring souls are venturing near the edge. Their silhouettes stand out against the metal sheen.

[*Faint humming sound*]

One man wants to touch the thing . . . he's having an argument with a policeman. The policeman wins. . . . Now, ladies and gentlemen, there's something I haven't mentioned in all this excitement, but it's becoming more distinct. Perhaps you've caught it already on your radio. Listen:

---

15. sheath (shēth) *n.*: A case or covering.

16. riled (rīl'd) *v.*: Irritated; angered.

[*Long pause*] . . . Do you hear it? It's a curious humming sound that seems to come from inside the object. I'll move the microphone nearer. Here. [*Pause*] Now we're not more than twenty-five feet away. Can you hear it now? Oh, Professor Pierson!

PIERSON. Yes, Mr. Phillips?

PHILLIPS. Can you tell us the meaning of that scraping noise inside the thing?

PIERSON. Possibly the unequal cooling of its surface.

PHILLIPS. Do you still think it's a meteor, Professor?

PIERSON. I don't know what to think. The metal casing is definitely extraterrestrial . . . not found on this earth. Friction[17] with the earth's atmosphere usually tears holes in a meteorite. This thing is smooth and, as you can see, of cylindrical shape.

PHILLIPS. Just a minute! Something's happening! Ladies and gentlemen, this is terrific! This end of the thing is beginning to flake off! The top is beginning to rotate like a screw! The thing must be hollow!

VOICES.
She's a movin'!
Look, the darn thing's unscrewing!
Keep back, there! Keep back, I tell you!
Maybe there's men in it trying to escape!
It's red hot, they'll burn to a cinder!
Keep back there. Keep those idiots back!

[*Suddenly the clanking sound of a huge piece of falling metal*]

VOICES.
She's off! The top's loose!
Look out there! Stand back!

PHILLIPS. Ladies and gentlemen, this is the most terrifying thing I have ever witnessed . . . Wait a minute! *Someone's crawling out*

of the hollow top. Someone or . . . something. I can see peering out of that black hole two luminous disks . . . are they eyes? It might be a face. It might be . . .

[*Shout of awe from the crowd*]

PHILLIPS. Good heavens, something's wriggling out of the shadow like a gray snake. Now it's another one, and another. They look like tentacles to me. There, I can see the thing's body. It's large as a bear and it glistens like wet leather. But that face. It . . . it's indescribable. I can hardly force myself to keep looking at it. The eyes are black and gleam like a serpent. The mouth is V-shaped with saliva dripping from its rimless lips that seem to quiver and pulsate. The monster or whatever it is can hardly move. It seems weighed down by . . . possibly gravity or something. The thing's raising up. The crowd falls back. They've seen enough. This is the most extraordinary experience. I can't find words . . . I'm pulling this microphone with me as I talk. I'll have to stop the description until I've taken a new position. Hold on, will you please, I'll be back in a minute.

[*Fade into piano*]

ANNOUNCER TWO. We are bringing you an eyewitness account of what's happening on the Wilmuth farm, Grovers Mill, New Jersey. [*More piano*] We now return you to Carl Phillips at Grovers Mill.

PHILLIPS. Ladies and gentlemen (Am I on?). Ladies and gentlemen, here I am, back of a stone wall that adjoins Mr. Wilmuth's garden. From here I get a sweep of the whole scene. I'll give you every detail as long as I can talk. As long as I can see. More state police have arrived. They're drawing up a cordon[18] in front of the pit, about thirty of

---

17. friction (frik′ shən) *n.*: Resistance.

18. cordon (kôr′ d'n) *n.*: A line or circle of police stationed around an area to guard it.

them. No need to push the crowd back now. They're willing to keep their distance. The captain is conferring with someone. We can't quite see who. Oh yes, I believe it's Professor Pierson. Yes, it is. Now they've parted. The professor moves around one side, studying the object, while the captain and two policemen advance with something in their hands. I can see it now. It's a white handkerchief tied to a pole . . . a flag of truce. If those creatures know what that means . . . what anything means! . . . *Wait!* Something's happening!

[*Hissing sound followed by a humming that increases in intensity*]

A humped shape is rising out of the pit. I can make out a small beam of light against a mirror. What's that? There's a jet of flame springing from that mirror, and it leaps right at the advancing men. It strikes them head on! Good Lord, they're turning into flame!

[*Screams and unearthly shrieks*]

Now the whole field's caught fire. [*Explosion*] The woods . . . the barns . . . the gas tanks of automobiles . . . it's spreading everywhere. It's coming this way. About twenty yards to my right . . .

[*Crash of microphone . . . then dead silence*]

ANNOUNCER TWO. Ladies and gentlemen, due to circumstances beyond our control, we are unable to continue the broadcast from Grovers Mill. Evidently there's some difficulty with our field transmission. However, we will return to that point at the earliest opportunity. In the meantime, we have a late bulletin from San Diego, California. Professor Indellkoffer, speaking at a dinner of the

California Astronomical Society, expressed the opinion that the explosions on Mars are undoubtedly nothing more than severe volcanic disturbances on the surface of the planet. We continue now with our piano interlude.

[*Piano . . . then cut*]

Ladies and gentlemen, I have just been handed a message that came in from Grovers Mill by telephone. Just a moment. At least forty people, including six state troopers lie dead in a field east of the village of Grovers Mill, their bodies burned and distorted beyond all possible recognition. The next voice you hear will be that of Brigadier General Montgomery Smith, commander of the state militia[19] at Trenton, New Jersey.

SMITH. I have been requested by the governor of New Jersey to place the counties of Mercer and Middlesex as far west as Princeton, and east to Jamesburg, under martial law.[20] No one will be permitted to enter this area except by special pass issued by state or military authorities. Four companies of state militia are proceeding from Trenton to Grovers Mill, and will aid in the evacuation of homes within the range of military operations. Thank you.

ANNOUNCER. You have just been listening to General Montgomery Smith, commanding the state militia at Trenton. In the meantime, further details of the catastrophe at Grovers Mill are coming in. The strange creatures after unleashing their deadly assault, crawled back in their pit and made no attempt to prevent the efforts of the firemen to recover the bodies and extinguish the fire. Combined fire departments of Mercer Coun-

ty are fighting the flames which menace the entire countryside.

We have been unable to establish any contact with our mobile unit at Grovers Mill, but we hope to be able to return you there at the earliest possible moment. In the meantime we take you—uh, just one moment please.

[*Long pause*]

[*Whisper*] Ladies and gentlemen, I have just been informed that we have finally established communication with an eyewitness of the tragedy. Professor Pierson has been located at a farmhouse near Grovers Mill where he has established an emergency observation post. As a scientist, he will give you his explanation of the calamity. The next voice you hear will be that of Professor Pierson, brought to you by direct wire. Professor Pierson.

PIERSON. Of the creatures in the rocket cylinder at Grovers Mill, I can give you no authoritative information—either as to their nature, their origin, or their purposes here on earth. Of their destructive instrument I might venture some conjectural explanation. For want of a better term, I shall refer to the mysterious weapon as a heat ray. It's all too evident that these creatures have scientific knowledge far in advance of our own. It is my guess that in some way they are able to generate an intense heat in a chamber of practically absolute nonconductivity.[21] This intense heat they project in a parallel beam against any object they choose, by means of a polished parabolic[22] mirror of unknown composition, much as the mirror of a lighthouse projects a beam of light. That is my conjecture of the origin of the heat ray . . .

---

19. militia (mə lish′ ə) *n.*: An army of citizens rather than professional soldiers, called out in time of emergency.
20. martial law (mär′ shəl lô′) *n.*: Temporary rule by the military authorities.

21. nonconductivity (nän′ kən duk tiv′ə tē) *n.*: The ability to contain and not transmit heat.
22. parabolic (par′ ə bäl′ ik) *adj.*: Bowl-shaped.

ANNOUNCER TWO. Thank you, Professor Pierson. Ladies and gentlemen, here is a bulletin from Trenton. It is a brief statement informing us that the charred body of Carl Phillips has been identified in a Trenton hospital. Now here's another bulletin from Washington, D.C.

Office of the director of the National Red Cross reports ten units of Red Cross emergency workers have been assigned to the headquarters of the state militia stationed outside of Grovers Mill, New Jersey. Here's a bulletin from state police, Princeton Junction: The fires at Grovers Mill and vicinity now under control. Scouts report all quiet in the pit, and no sign of life appearing from the mouth of the cylinder . . . And now, ladies and gentlemen, we have a special statement from Mr. Harry McDonald, vice-president in charge of operations.

McDONALD. We have received a request from the militia at Trenton to place at their disposal our entire broadcasting facilities. In view of the gravity of the situation, and believing that radio has a definite responsibility to serve in the public interest at all times, we are turning over our facilities to the state militia at Trenton.

ANNOUNCER. We take you now to the field headquarters of the state militia near Grovers Mill, New Jersey.

CAPTAIN. This is Captain Lansing of the signal corps,[23] attached to the state militia now engaged in military operations in the vicinity of Grovers Mill. Situation arising from the reported presence of certain individuals of unidentified nature is now under complete control.

The cylindrical object which lies in a pit directly below our position is surrounded on all sides by eight battalions of infantry, without heavy fieldpieces,[24] but adequately armed with rifles and machine guns. All cause for alarm, if such cause ever existed, is now entirely unjustified. The things, whatever they are, do not even venture to poke their heads above the pit. I can see their hiding place plainly in the glare of the searchlights here. With all their reported resources, these creatures can scarcely stand up against heavy machine-gun fire. Anyway, it's an interesting outing for the troops. I can make out their khaki uniforms, crossing back and forth in front of the lights. It looks almost like a real war. There appears to be some slight smoke in the woods bordering the Millstone River. Probably fire started by campers. Well, we ought to see some action soon. One of the companies is deploying[25] on the left flank.[26] A quick thrust and it will all be over. Now wait a minute! I see something on top of the cylinder. No, it's nothing but a shadow. Now the troops are on the edge of the Wilmuth farm. Seven thousand armed men closing in on an old metal tube. Wait, that wasn't a shadow! It's something moving . . . solid metal . . . kind of a shieldlike affair rising up out of the cylinder . . . It's going higher and higher. Why, it's standing on legs . . . actually rearing up on a sort of metal framework. Now it's reaching above the trees and the searchlights are on it! Hold on!

ANNOUNCER TWO. Ladies and gentlemen, I have a grave announcement to make. Incredible as it may seem, both the observations of science and the evidence of our eyes lead to the inescapable assumption[27] that those strange beings who landed in the Jer-

---

23. signal corps: The part of the army in charge of communications.

24. fieldpieces (fēld' pēs əz) n.: Mobile artillery.
25. deploying (dē ploi' iŋ) v.: Spreading out.
26. flank (flaŋk) n.: Side.
27. assumption (ə sump' shən) n.: Idea accepted as true without proof.

sey farmlands tonight are the vanguard[28] of an invading army from the planet Mars. The battle which took place tonight at Grovers Mill has ended in one of the most startling defeats ever suffered by an army in modern times; seven thousand men armed with rifles and machine guns pitted against a single fighting machine of the invaders from Mars. One hundred and twenty known survivors. The rest strewn over the battle area from Grovers Mill to Plainsboro crushed and trampled to death under the metal feet of the monster, or burned to cinders by its heat ray. The monster is now in control of the middle section of New Jersey and has effectively cut the state through its center. Communication lines are down from Pennsylvania to the Atlantic Ocean. Railroad tracks are torn and service from New York to Philadelphia discontinued except routing some of the trains through Allentown and Phoenixville.[29] Highways to the north, south, and west are clogged with frantic human traffic. Police and army reserves are unable to control the mad flight. By morning the fugitives will have swelled Philadelphia, Camden and Trenton, it is estimated, to twice their normal population.

At this time martial law prevails throughout New Jersey and eastern Pennsylvania. We take you now to Washington for a special broadcast on the National Emergency . . . the Secretary of the Interior . . .

SECRETARY. Citizens of the nation: I shall not try to conceal the gravity of the situation that confronts the country, nor the concern of your government in protecting the lives and property of its people. However, I wish to impress upon you—private citizens and public officials, all of you—the urgent need of calm and resourceful action. Fortunately, this formidable enemy is still confined to a comparatively small area, and we may place our faith in the military forces to keep them there. In the meantime placing our faith in God we must continue the performance of our duties each and every one of us, so that we may confront this destructive adversary with a nation united, courageous, and consecrated[30] to the preservation of human supremacy on this earth. I thank you.

ANNOUNCER. You have just heard the Secretary of the Interior speaking from Washington. Bulletins too numerous to read are piling up in the studio here. We are informed that the central portion of New Jersey is blacked out from radio communication due to the effect of the heat ray upon power lines and electrical equipment. Here is a special bulletin from New York. Cables received from English, French, German scientific bodies offering assistance. Astronomers report continued gas outbursts at regular intervals on planet Mars. Majority voice opinion that enemy will be reinforced by additional rocket machines. Attempts made to locate Professor Pierson of Princeton, who has observed Martians at close range. It is feared he was lost in recent battle. Langham Field, Virginia: Scouting planes report three Martian machines visible above treetops, moving north toward Somerville with population fleeing ahead of them. Heat ray not in use; although advancing at express-train speed, invaders pick their way carefully. They seem to be making conscious effort to avoid destruction of cities and countryside. However, they stop to uproot power lines, bridges, and railroad tracks. Their apparent objective is to crush resistance, paralyze

---

28. vanguard (van′ gärd) *n.*: The part of an army that goes ahead of the main body in an advance.
29. Allentown and Phoenixville: Cities in eastern Pennsylvania.

30. consecrated (kän′ sə krāt′ əd) *adj.*: Dedicated.

communication, and disorganize human society.

Here is a bulletin from Basking Ridge, New Jersey: Raccoon hunters have stumbled on a second cylinder similar to the first embedded in the great swamp twenty miles south of Morristown. U.S. army fieldpieces are proceeding from Newark to blow up second invading unit before cylinder can be opened and the fighting machine rigged. They are taking up position in the—foothills of Watchung Mountains.[31] Another bulletin from Langham Field, Virginia: Scouting planes report enemy machines, now three in number, increasing speed northward kicking over houses and trees in their evident haste to form a conjunction[32] with their allies south of Morristown. Machines also sighted by telephone operator east of Middlesex within ten miles of Plainfield. Here's a bulletin from Winston Field, Long Island. Fleet of army bombers carrying heavy explosives flying north in pursuit of enemy. Scouting planes act as guides. They keep speeding enemy in sight. Just a moment please. Ladies and gentlemen, we've run special wires to the artillery line in adjacent villages to give you direct reports in the zone of the advancing enemy. First we take you to the battery of the 22nd Field Artillery, located in the Watchung Mountains.

OFFICER. Range, thirty-two meters.

GUNNER. Thirty-two meters.

OFFICER. Projection, thirty-nine degrees.

GUNNER. Thirty-nine degrees.

OFFICER. Fire! [*Boom of heavy gun . . . pause*]

OBSERVER. One hundred and forty yards to the right, sir.

OFFICER. Shift range . . . thirty-one meters.

GUNNER. Thirty-one meters.

OFFICER. Projection . . . thirty-seven degrees.

GUNNER. Thirty-seven degrees.

OFFICER. Fire! [*Boom of heavy gun . . . pause*]

OBSERVER. A hit, sir! We got the tripod[33] of one of them. They've stopped. The others are trying to repair it.

OFFICER. Quick, get the range! Shift thirty meters.

GUNNER. Thirty meters.

OFFICER. Projection . . . twenty-seven degrees.

GUNNER. Twenty-seven degrees.

OFFICER. Fire! [*Boom of heavy gun . . . pause*]

OBSERVER. Can't see the shell land, sir. They're letting off a smoke.

OFFICER. What is it?

OBSERVER. A black smoke, sir. Moving this way. Lying close to the ground. It's moving fast.

OFFICER. Put on gas masks. [*Pause*] Get ready to fire. Shift to twenty-four meters.

GUNNER. Twenty-four meters.

OFFICER. Projection, twenty-four degrees.

GUNNER. Twenty-four degrees.

OFFICER. Fire! [*Boom*]

OBSERVER. Still can't see, sir. The smoke's coming nearer.

---

31. **Watchung** (wäch′ uŋ) **Mountains:** A range of low mountains in New Jersey.
32. **conjunction** (kən juŋk′ shən) n.: Union.

33. **tripod** (trī′ päd) n.: Three-legged support.

OFFICER. Get the range. [*Coughs*]

OBSERVER. Twenty-three meters. [*Coughs*]

OFFICER. Twenty-three meters. [*Coughs*]

GUNNER. Twenty-three meters. [*Coughs*]

OBSERVER. Projection, twenty-two degrees. [*Coughing*]

OFFICER. Twenty-two degrees. [*Fade in coughing*]

[*Fading in . . . sound of airplane motor*]

COMMANDER. Army bombing plane, V-8-43, off Bayonne, New Jersey, Lieutenant Voght, commanding eight bombers. Reporting to Commander Fairfax, Langham Field . . . This is Voght, reporting to Commander Fairfax, Langham Field . . . Enemy tripod machines now in sight. Reinforced by three machines from the Morristown cylinder . . . Six altogether. One machine partially crippled. Believed hit by shell from army gun in Watchung Mountains. Guns now appear silent. A heavy black fog hanging close to the earth . . . of extreme density,[34] nature unknown. No sign of heat ray. Enemy now turns east, crossing Passaic River into the Jersey marshes. Another straddles the Pulaski Skyway.[35] Evident objective is New York City. They're pushing down a high tension power station. The machines are close together now, and we're ready to attack. Planes circling, ready to strike. A thousand yards and we'll be over the first —eight hundred yards . . . six hundred . . . four hundred . . . two hundred . . . There they go! The giant arm raised . . . Green flash! They're spraying us with flame! Two thousand feet. Engines are giving out. No chance to release bombs. Only one thing

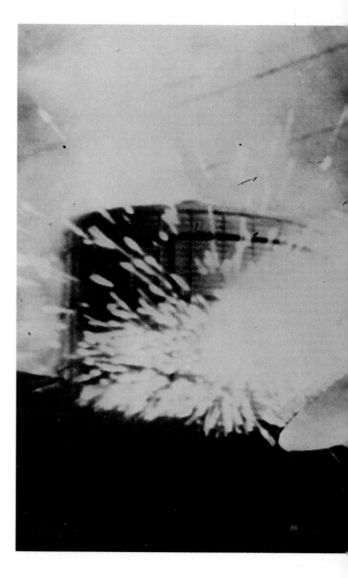

left . . . drop on them, plane and all. We're diving on the first one. Now the engine's gone! Eight . . .

OPERATOR ONE. This is Bayonne, New Jersey, calling Langham Field . . .

This is Bayonne, New Jersey, calling Langham Field . . .

Come in, please . . . Come in, please . . .

OPERATOR TWO. This is Langham Field . . . go ahead . . .

---

34. density (den′ sə tē) *n.*: Thickness.
35. Pulaski (poo las′ kē) **Skyway:** An elevated highway in eastern New Jersey.

OPERATOR ONE. Eight army bombers in engagement with enemy tripod machines over Jersey flats.[36] Engines incapacitated[37] by heat ray. All crashed. One enemy machine destroyed. Enemy now discharging heavy black smoke in direction of—

OPERATOR THREE. This is Newark, New Jersey . . .

---

36. flats *n.*: Low-lying marshlands.
37. incapacitated (in′ kə pas′ ə tāt əd) *adj.*: Disabled.

This is Newark, New Jersey . . .

Warning! Poisonous black smoke pouring in from Jersey marshes. Reaches South Street. Gas masks useless. Urge population to move into open spaces . . . automobiles use Routes 7, 23, 24 . . . Avoid congested areas. Smoke now spreading over Raymond Boulevard . . .

OPERATOR FOUR. 2X2L . . . calling CQ . . .
2X2L . . . calling CQ . . .
2X2L . . . calling 8X3R . . .
Come in, please . . .

OPERATOR FIVE. This is 8X3R . . . coming back at 2X2L.

OPERATOR FOUR. How's reception? How's reception? K, please. Where are you, 8X3R?
What's the matter? Where are you?

[Bells ringing over city gradually diminishing]

ANNOUNCER. I'm speaking from the roof of Broadcasting Building, New York City. The bells you hear are ringing to warn the people to evacuate the city as the Martians approach. Estimated in last two hours three million people have moved out along the roads to the north, Hutchison River Parkway still kept open for motor traffic. Avoid bridges to Long Island . . . hopelessly jammed. All communication with Jersey shore closed ten minutes ago. No more defenses. Our army wiped out . . . artillery, air force, everything wiped out. This may be the last broadcast. We'll stay here to the end . . . People are holding service below us . . . in the cathedral.

[Voices singing hymn]

Now I look down the harbor. All manner of boats, overloaded with fleeing population, pulling out from docks.

[Sound of boat whistles]

Streets are all jammed. Noise in crowds like New Year's Eve in city. Wait a minute . . . Enemy now in sight above the Palisades.[38] Five great machines. First one is crossing river. I can see it from here, wading the Hudson like a man wading through a brook . . . A bulletin's handed me . . . Martian cylinders are falling all over the country. One outside Buffalo, one in Chicago, St. Louis . . . seem to be 'timed and spaced. . . . Now the first machine reaches the shore. He stands watching, looking over the city. His steel, cowlish[39] head is even with the skyscrapers. He waits for the others. They rise like a line of new towers on the city's west side . . . Now they're lifting their metal hands. This is the end now. Smoke comes out . . . black smoke, drifting over the city. People in the streets see it now. They're running toward the East River . . . thousands of them, dropping in like rats. Now the smoke's spreading faster. It's reached Times Square. People trying to run away from it, but it's no use. They're falling like flies. Now the smoke's crossing Sixth Avenue . . . Fifth Avenue . . . one hundred yards away . . . it's fifty feet . . .

OPERATOR FOUR. 2X2L calling CQ . . .
2X2L calling CQ . . .
2X2L calling CQ . . . New York.
Isn't there anyone on the air?
Isn't there anyone . . .
2X2L—

ANNOUNCER. You are listening to a CBS presentation of Orson Welles and the Mercury Theatre on the Air in an original dramatization of *The War of the Worlds* by H. G. Wells. The performance will continue after a brief intermission.

---

38. Palisades (pal′ ə sādz′): The line of steep cliffs in northeastern New Jersey and southeastern New York on the west shore of the Hudson River.
39. cowlish (koul′ ish) *adj.*: Hood-shaped.

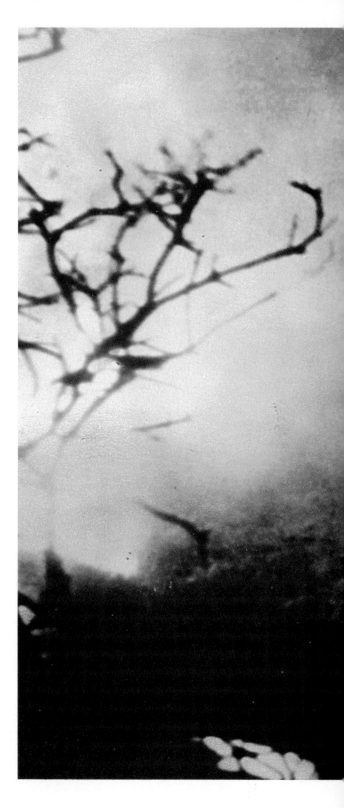

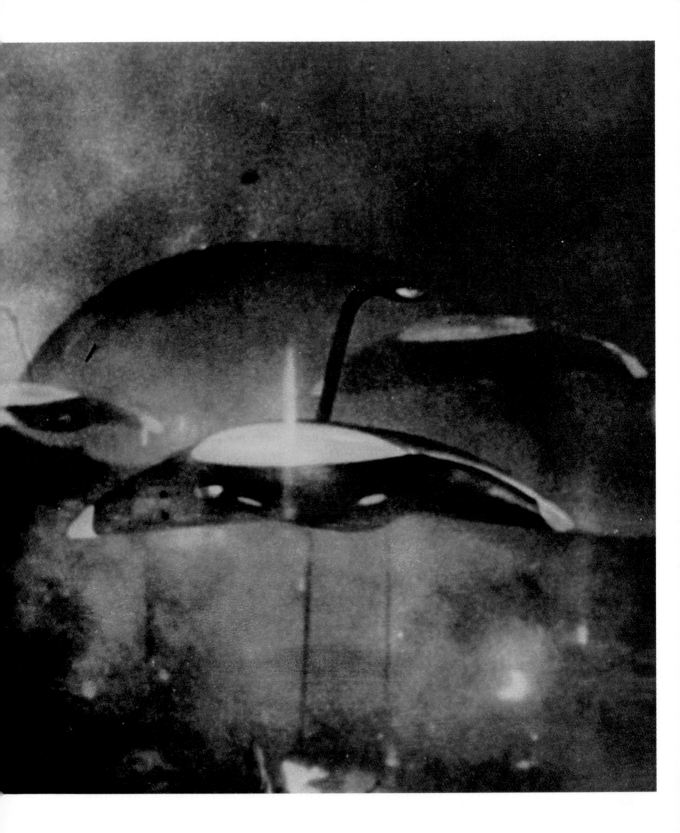

This is the Columbia . . . Broadcasting System.

[*Music*]

PIERSON. As I set down these notes on paper, I'm obsessed by the thought that I may be the last living man on earth. I have been hiding in this empty house near Grovers Mill—a small island of daylight cut off by the black smoke from the rest of the world. All that happened before the arrival of these monstrous creatures in the world now seems part of another life . . . a life that has no continuity with the present, furtive[40] existence of the lonely derelict who pencils these words on the back of some astronomical notes bearing the signature of Richard Pierson. I look down, at my blackened hands, my torn shoes, my tattered clothes, and I try to connect them with a professor who lives at Princeton, and who on the night of October 30, glimpsed through his telescope an orange splash of light on a distant planet. My wife, my colleagues, my students, my books, my observatory, my . . . my world . . . where are they? Did they ever exist? Am I Richard Pierson? What day is it? Do days exist without calendars? Does time pass when there are no human hands left to wind the clocks? . . . In writing down my daily life I tell myself I shall preserve human history between the dark covers of this little book that was meant to record the movements of the stars . . . But to write I must live, and to live I must eat . . . I find moldy bread in the kitchen, and an orange not too spoiled to swallow. I keep watch at the window. From time to time I catch sight of a Martian above the black smoke.

The smoke still holds the house in its black coil . . . But at length there is a hissing sound and suddenly I see a Martian mounted on his machine, spraying the air with a jet of steam, as if to dissipate[41] the smoke. I watch in a corner as his huge metal legs nearly brush against the house. Exhausted by terror, I fall asleep . . . It's morning. Sun streams in the window. The black cloud of gas has lifted, and the scorched meadows to the north look as though a black snowstorm has passed over them. I venture from the house. I make my way to a road. No traffic. Here and there a wrecked car, baggage overturned, a blackened skeleton. I push on north. For some reason I feel safer trailing these monsters than running away from them. And I keep a careful watch. I have seen the Martians feed. Should one of their machines appear over the top of trees, I am ready to fling myself flat on the earth. I come to a chestnut tree. October, chestnuts are ripe. I fill my pockets. I must keep alive. Two days I wander in a vague northerly direction through a desolate world. Finally I notice a living creature . . . a small red squirrel in a beech tree. I stare at him, and wonder. He stares back at me. I believe at that moment the animal and I shared the same emotion . . . the joy of finding another living being . . . I push on north. I find dead cows in a brackish[42] field. Beyond, the charred ruins of a dairy. The silo remains standing guard over the waste land like a lighthouse deserted by the sea. Astride the silo perches a weathercock. The arrow points north.

Next day I came to a city vaguely familiar in its contours, yet its buildings strangely dwarfed and leveled off, as if a giant had sliced off its highest towers with a capricious[43] sweep of his hand. I reached the

---

40. furtive (fur′ tiv) *adj.*: Sneaky; secretive.

41. dissipate (dis′ ə pāt′) *v.*: Scatter.
42. brackish (brak′ ish) *adj.*: Salty and marshy.
43. capricious (ka prish′əs) *adj.*: Without apparent reason.

outskirts. I found Newark, undemolished, but humbled by some whim of the advancing Martians. Presently, with an odd feeling of being watched, I caught sight of something crouching in a doorway. I made a step toward it, and it rose up and became a man—a man, armed with a large knife.

STRANGER. Stop . . . Where did you come from?

PIERSON. I come from . . . many places. A long time ago from Princeton.

STRANGER. Princeton, huh? That's near Grovers Mill!

PIERSON. Yes.

STRANGER. Grovers Mill . . . [*Laughs as at a great joke*] There's no food here. This is my country . . . all this end of town down to the river. There's only food for one . . . Which way are you going?

PIERSON. I don't know. I guess I'm looking for—for people.

STRANGER. [*Nervously*] What was that? Did you hear something just then?

PIERSON. Only a bird [*Marvels*] . . . A live bird!

STRANGER. You get to know that birds have shadows these days . . . Say, we're in the open here. Let's crawl into this doorway and talk.

PIERSON. Have you seen any Martians?

STRANGER. They've gone over to New York. At night the sky is alive with their lights. Just as if people were still living in it. By daylight you can't see them. Five days ago a couple of them carried something big across the flats from the airport. I believe they're learning how to fly.

PIERSON. Fly!

STRANGER. Yeah, fly.

PIERSON. Then it's all over with humanity. Stranger, there's still you and I. Two of us left.

STRANGER. They got themselves in solid; they wrecked the greatest country in the world. Those green stars, they're probably falling somewhere every night. They've only lost one machine. There isn't anything to do. We're done. We're licked.

PIERSON. Where were you? You're in a uniform.

STRANGER. What's left of it. I was in the militia—national guard . . . That's good! Wasn't any war any more than there's war between men and ants.

PIERSON. And we're edible ants. I found that out . . . What will they do to us?

STRANGER. I've thought it all out. Right now we're caught as we're wanted. The Martian only has to go a few miles to get a crowd on the run. But they won't keep doing that. They'll begin catching us systematic like —keeping the best and storing us in cages and things. They haven't begun on us yet!

PIERSON. Not begun!

STRANGER. Not begun. All that's happened so far is because we don't have sense enough to keep quiet . . . bothering them with guns and such stuff and losing our heads and rushing off in crowds. Now instead of our rushing around blind we've got to fix ourselves up according to the way things are now. Cities, nations, civilization, progress . . . done.

PIERSON. But if that's so, what is there to live for?

STRANGER. There won't be any more concerts for a million years or so, and no nice little dinners at restaurants. If it's amusement you're after, I guess the game's up.

PIERSON. And what is there left?

STRANGER. Life . . . that's what! I want to live. And so do you! We're not going to be exterminated. And I don't mean to be caught, either, and tamed, and fattened like an ox.

PIERSON. What are you going to do?

STRANGER. I'm going on . . . right under their feet. I gotta plan. We humans as humans are finished. We don't know enough. We gotta learn plenty before we've got a chance. And we've got to live and keep free while we learn. I've thought it all out, see.

PIERSON. Tell me the rest.

STRANGER. Well, it isn't all of us that are made for wild beasts, and that's what it's got to be. That's why I watched you. All these little office workers that used to live in these houses—they'd be no good. They haven't any stuff to 'em. They just used to run off to work. I've seen hundreds of 'em, running wild to catch their commuters' train in the morning for fear that they'd get canned if they didn't; running back at night afraid they won't be in time for dinner. Lives insured and a little invested in case of accidents. And on Sundays, worried about the hereafter. The Martians will be a godsend for those guys. Nice roomy cages, good food, no worries. After a week or so chasing about the fields on empty stomachs they'll come and be glad to be caught.

PIERSON. You've thought it all out, haven't you?

STRANGER. You bet I have! And that isn't all. These Martians will make pets of some of them, train 'em to do tricks. Who knows? Get sentimental over the pet boy who grew up and had to be killed. And some, maybe, they'll train to hunt us.

PIERSON. No, that's impossible. No human being . . .

STRANGER. Yes, they will. There's people who'll do it gladly. If one of them ever comes after me . . .

PIERSON. In the meantime, you and I and others like us . . . where are we to live when the Martians own the earth?

STRANGER. I've got it all figured out. We'll live underground. I've been thinking about the sewers. Under New York are miles and miles of 'em. The main ones are big enough for anybody. Then there's cellars, vaults, underground storerooms, railway tunnels, subways. You begin to see, eh? And we'll get a bunch of strong people together. No weak ones, that rubbish, out.

PIERSON. And you meant me to go?

STRANGER. Well, I gave you a chance, didn't I?

PIERSON. We won't quarrel about that. Go on.

STRANGER. And we've got to make safe places for us to stay in, see, and get all the books we can—science books. That's where people like you come in, see? We'll raid the museums, we'll even spy on the Martians. It may not be so much we have to learn before —just imagine this: four or five of their own fighting machines suddenly start off—heat rays right and left and not a Martian in 'em. Not a Martian in 'em! But humans —humans who have learned the way how. It may even be in our time. Gee! Imagine having one of them lovely things with its heat ray wide and free! We'd turn it on Martians, we'd turn it on people. We'd bring everybody down to their knees.

PIERSON. That's your plan?

STRANGER. You and me and a few more of us we'd own the world.

PIERSON. I see.

STRANGER. Say, what's the matter? Where are you going?

PIERSON. Not to your world . . . Good-bye, stranger . . .

PIERSON. After parting with the artilleryman, I came at last to the Holland Tunnel.[44] I entered that silent tube anxious to know the fate of the great city on the other side of the Hudson. Cautiously I came out of the tunnel and made my way up Canal Street.

I reached Fourteenth Street, and there again were black powder and several bodies, and an evil ominous[45] smell from the gratings of the cellars of some of the houses. I wandered up through the Thirties and Forties;[46] I stood alone on Times Square.[47] I caught sight of a lean dog running down Seventh Avenue with a piece of dark brown meat in his jaws, and a pack of starving mongrels at his heels. He made a wide circle around me, as though he feared I might prove a fresh competitor. I walked up Broadway in the direction of that strange powder —past silent shopwindows, displaying their mute wares to empty sidewalks—past the Capitol Theatre, silent, dark—past a shooting gallery, where a row of empty guns faced an arrested line of wooden ducks. Near Columbus Circle I noticed models of 1939 motorcars in the showrooms facing empty streets. From over the top of the General Motors Building, I watched a flock of black birds circling in the sky. I hurried on. Suddenly I caught sight of the hood of a Martian machine, standing somewhere in Central Park, gleaming in the late afternoon sun. An insane idea! I rushed recklessly across Columbus Circle and into the Park. I climbed a small hill above the pond at Sixtieth Street. From there I could see, standing in a silent row along the mall, nineteen of those great metal Titans,[48] their cowls empty, their steel arms hanging listlessly by their sides. I looked in vain for the monsters that inhabit those machines.

Suddenly, my eyes were attracted to the immense flock of black birds that hovered directly below me. They circled to the ground, and there before my eyes, stark and silent, lay the Martians, with the hungry birds pecking and tearing brown shreds of flesh from their dead bodies. Later when their bodies were examined in laboratories, it was found that they were killed by the putrefactive[49] and disease bacteria against which their systems were unprepared . . . slain, after all man's defenses had failed, by the humblest thing that God in His wisdom put upon this earth.

Before the cylinder fell there was a general persuasion that through all the deep of space no life existed beyond the petty surface of our minute sphere. Now we see further. Dim and wonderful is the vision I have conjured up in my mind of life spreading slowly from this little seedbed of the solar system throughout the inanimate vastness of sidereal[50] space. But that is a remote dream. It may be that the destruction of the Martians is only a reprieve.[51] To them, and not to us, is the future ordained perhaps.

---

44. Holland Tunnel: A tunnel under the Hudson River between New York and New Jersey.
45. ominous (äm′ ə nəs) *adj*.: Threatening; sinister.
46. Thirties and Forties: Numbered streets across Manhattan.
47. Times Square: The center of the theater district in New York City.

48. Titans (tī′ tənz) *n*.: Giants.
49. putrefactive (pyōō′ trə fak′ tiv) *adj*.: Rotting; decomposing.
50. sidereal (sī dir′ ē əl) *adj*.: Of the stars.
51. reprieve (ri prēv′) *n*.: Postponement.

Strange it now seems to sit in my peaceful study at Princeton writing down this last chapter of the record begun at a deserted farm in Grovers Mill. Strange to see from my window the university spires dim and blue through an April haze. Strange to watch children playing in the streets. Strange to see young people strolling on the green, where the new spring grass heals the last black scars of a bruised earth. Strange to watch the sightseers enter the museum where the disassembled parts of a Martian machine are kept on public view. Strange when I recall the time when I first saw it, bright and clean-cut, hard and silent, under the dawn of that last great day.

[*Music*]

This is Orson Welles, ladies and gentlemen, out of character to assure you that The War of the Worlds has no further significance than as the holiday offering it was intended to be. The Mercury Theatre's own radio version of dressing up in a sheet and jumping out of a bush and saying Boo! Starting now, we couldn't soap all your windows and steal all your garden gates, by tomorrow night . . . so we did the next best thing. We annihilated the world before your very ears, and utterly destroyed the Columbia Broadcasting System. You will be relieved, I hope, to learn that we didn't mean it, and that both institutions are still open for business. So good-bye everybody, and remember, please, for the next day or so, the terrible lesson you learned tonight. That grinning, glowing, globular invader of your living room is an inhabitant of the pumpkin patch, and if your doorbell rings and nobody's there, that was no Martian . . . it's Hallowe'en.

RESPONDING TO THE SELECTION

Your Response

1. How would you have felt if you were Richard Pierson?
2. When *Invasion From Mars* was aired, many listeners who did not know it was a radio play panicked. Did you think this selection seemed like an actual radio news broadcast? Why or why not?

Recalling

3. What are the first signs of an unusual occurrence?
4. Describe the sight at the landing as seen by the people of Grovers Mill.
5. What is the first reaction of the people at Grovers Mill to the "thing"? How does their reaction change?
6. What methods are used to try to thwart the invaders? What are the results of these attempts?
7. What finally destroys the invaders?

Interpreting

8. In what ways does the invaders' takeover seem to show intelligent planning?
9. Explain why Pierson rejects the Stranger's plan for resistance. How does his attitude contrast with that of the Stranger?

Applying

10. This radio play was broadcast on Halloween in 1938. How would an audience today react to such a broadcast? Explain your answer.

ANALYZING LITERATURE

Understanding the Radio Play

A **radio play,** which is read by actors for a radio broadcast rather than performed on a stage, relies on dialogue, sound effects, and music to create the scenes in your mind. There are no visual cues. The dialogue reveals characters and carries the plot along. The sound effects and music may indicate the passage of time or create mood.

1. Describe how you envision Grovers Mill when the aliens first land.
2. Give three examples of the use of music to indicate passage of time. Discuss the different lengths of time.
3. With what kind of expression do you think the last paragraph spoken by Pierson should be read? Why?
4. Explain whether or not you think a radio broadcast is an especially effective format for this play. Would the play be as successful produced as a television broadcast or as a movie? Explain your answer.

CRITICAL THINKING AND READING

Evaluating Technique

When *Invasion From Mars* was first broadcast, many people believed it was a report of an actual invasion. The playwright presents the play in a newscast format, which creates realism and suspense. Within this format he uses four techniques that make the play seem like an authentic broadcast. Give examples of each of the following techniques used in the play, and explain how each example contributes to the apparent authenticity of it.

1. news bulletin
2. interview
3. eyewitness account
4. official statement

THINKING AND WRITING

Writing a Drama Review

Imagine that you were in New York City when *Invasion From Mars* was first broadcast. You observed hundreds of people panicking in the streets as a result of the broadcast. Make notes describing this reaction. Then use your notes in writing a review of the radio play for a New York City newspaper. Explain the relationship between the play and the panic. Comment on the effectiveness of the play. Discuss the authentic sound of the play's broadcast and what elements of the play contribute to this authenticity. Revise your review by adding quotations from the play.

LEARNING OPTIONS

1. **Cross-curricular Connection.** In *Invasion From Mars,* astronomers observe the planet Mars. Find current information about Mars, using a science textbook, an encyclopedia, a nonfiction book, or magazine articles. Research the planet's size, color, visible features, satellites, average temperatures, relative distance from Earth, and other characteristics. Then create either a chart or a diagram to illustrate your findings about Mars.

2. **Speaking and Listening.** *Invasion From Mars* was written to be read aloud on the radio. With three to five classmates, take turns reading part of the play aloud. First decide as a group which portion of the play to read. Then choose specific roles, and determine what music and sound effects will enhance your reading. After you have rehearsed, perform your reading for the rest of the class. Your group might want to tape-record and later review the performance.

THE GREEK THEATER

Theater was a celebration in ancient Greece. The Athenians of the fifth century B.C. held festivals to honor Dionysos (dī′ ə nī′ səs), their god of wine. During these holidays citizens gathered to watch competitions between playwrights. Playwrights presented plays derived from well-known myths. These plays showed events that exposed arrogance and that emphasized reverence for the gods.

Thousands of Athenians saw the plays. In seats that rose away from a level, semicircular orchestral area, they would view performances with limited numbers of characters and scenes interspersed with songs. There were no curtains to allow for changes of scenery between acts. No violence or irreverence was depicted on stage, although such matters were central to the plots of many plays. Such events occurred and were reported offstage.

The Presentation of the Plays

Ancient Greek playwrights used a consistent format for most of the productions. Plays opened with a prologue (pro‾′ lôg), or exposition, which presented the background to situate the conflict. The entering chorus then sang a parados (par′ əd əs), or opening song. This was followed by the first scene. The chorus's song, called an ode, divided scenes, serving the same purpose as a curtain does in modern theater.

The Chorus. The role of the chorus is central to the production and important for interpreting the meaning of the plays. During the odes a leader called the choragos (kō rā′ gəs) might exchange thoughts with the group in a dialogue. During that recital the group rotates first from right to left, singing the strophe (strō′ fē). Then the choral members move in the opposite direction during the antistrophe (an tis′ trə fē). An epode (ep′ ōd) was included in some odes as a sort of final stanza. At the conclusion there was a paean (pē′ ən) of thanksgiving to Dionysos and an exodos (ek′ sə dəs), or final exiting scene. Clearly, the chorus played an essential part of any play's success.

The Oedipus Myth

Sophocles wrote three tragedies about the royal family of Thebes, a city in northeastern Greece. Called the Theban plays, these tragedies were *Oedipus the King, Oedipus at Colonus,* and *Antigone.* The story of these plays was as familiar to the audience as the story of Noah's Ark or of Jonah and the whale is to many people today.

Abandoned at Birth. Oedipus (ed′ ə pəs) was abandoned at birth by his parents, the Theban king Laios (lā′ yəs) and his wife, Iocaste (yō kas′ tə). A fortuneteller proclaimed in an oracle that the infant would kill his father and marry his mother. Wishing to avoid that fate, the couple had Oedipus taken off to be abandoned on a mountaintop by a servant who was to assure the baby's death. They assumed this mission was completed. In fact, the servant pitied the newborn and gave him to a childless couple in a distant city who raised the boy without ever mentioning his adoption.

A Famous Riddle. When Oedipus left that city to start his adult life, he still did not know that his real father was Laios and that his mother was Iocaste. His travels took him toward Thebes, where he killed a man without knowing it was Laios. Oedipus' fame grew after he confronted the Sphinx, a monster that killed those unable to answer its riddle. The riddle was this: What creature walks on four legs at dawn, two legs at noon, and three legs in the evening? Oedipus answered man, a being who crawls as an infant on all fours, walks erect in midlife, and uses a third leg in the form of a cane during old age. The Sphinx leaped into the sea after Oedipus gave the correct answer, and Oedipus was received as a hero in the city.

A Royal Marriage. Iocaste, now a widow, agreed to marry the unknown champion. The couple lived happily for years and raised four children of their own. Then a plague befell the city. Priests claimed it was sent as punishment for some unknown sin. During an investigation of his own background, Oedipus learned the truth of his childhood. In horror at this revelation, Iocaste committed suicide and Oedipus blinded himself. Iocaste's brother, Creon (krē′än), took control of the city and allowed one of Oedipus' children, Antigone (an tig′ ə nē′), to lead Oedipus into exile where he died.

A Daughter Mourns. After her return to Thebes, Antigone was deeply troubled by her experience. Her sister, Ismene (is mē′ nē), and brothers, Eteocles (ē tē′ ə klēz′) and Polyneices (päl′ i nī′ sēz′), were also burdened by their family background. They were haunted by the curse that caused their father to fulfill his own prophecy and to condemn his sons to kill each other for control of Thebes.

Order Restored. By the time *Antigone* opens, Creon has restored some order to Thebes. The civil war between the brothers has just ended. Eteocles and Polyneices have killed each other in combat. The former supported Creon's established order and was buried with honors. The latter rebelled with the forces of Argos against Thebes, and Creon ordered that his corpse be left to rot. Antigone's decision to disobey that command is central to the play.

GUIDE FOR READING

Antigone, Prologue through Scene 2

Plot Structure in Drama

Plot is the sequence of events that make up a story. In a well-told novel or play, one action leads to another in a natural way, and the action moves toward the resolution of a conflict. The protagonist is the central character whom viewers usually favor. The antagonists stand in conflict to the protagonist. This tension leads to a climax, the high point of conflict, after which the action turns.

Focus

At the beginning of the play, Antigone decides to break a law by burying her brother Polyneices. Although her decision has serious consequences, Antigone feels she must follow her conscience. Think of an example from history or current events in which someone broke the law for reasons of conscience. Then copy the diagram that follows and fill in the information about the example you have chosen.

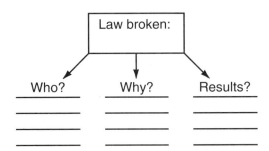

Vocabulary

Knowing the following words will help you as you read *Antigone,* Prologue through Scene 2.

carrion (kar′ ē ən) *adj.*: Flesh-eating (p. 276)

sated (sāt′ əd) *v.*: Satisfied or pleased (p. 278)

anarchists (an′ ər kists) *n.*: Those who disrespect laws or rules (p. 281)

sententiously (sen ten′ shəs lē) *adv.*: Pointed; expressing much in a few words (p. 281)

sultry (sul′ trē) *adj.*: Oppressively hot or moist; inflamed (p. 283)

transcends (tran sendz′) *v.*: Goes above or beyond limits; exceeds (p. 288)

Sophocles

(c. 496–406 B.C.), who was born in Athens, is regarded as one of the world's greatest playwrights, and his plays have had an enduring influence on many other writers. During his long life he wrote more than one hundred plays, but only seven have survived. Sophocles frequently won first place in the competitions that judged the plays performed in the Dionysian festivals. His ability to see current values in old myths thrilled his contemporaries, and audiences since have continued to appreciate the freshness and vitality of his world view.

Antigone

Sophocles

translated by Dudley Fitts and Robert Fitzgerald

PERSONS REPRESENTED

Antigone (an tig′ ə nē′), daughter of Oedipus, former King of Thebes

Ismene (is mē′ nē), another daughter of Oedipus

Eurydice (yoo rid′ ə sē′), wife of Creon

Creon (krē′ än), King of Thebes, uncle of Antigone and Ismene

Haimon (hī′ mən), Creon's son, engaged to Antigone

Teiresias (tī rē′ sē əs), a blind prophet

A Sentry

A Messenger

Chorus

Choragos (kō rā′ gəs), leader of the chorus

A Boy, who leads Teiresias

Guards

Servants

Scene. *Before the palace of* CREON, *King of Thebes. A central double door, and two lateral doors. A platform extends the length of the façade, and from this platform three steps lead down into the "orchestra," or chorus-ground.* **Time.** *Dawn of the day after the repulse of the Argive[1] army from the assault on Thebes.*

Prologue

[ANTIGONE *and* ISMENE *enter from the central door of the Palace.*]

---

1. Argive (är′ gīv): From Argos, the capital of a section of ancient Greece.

ANTIGONE. Ismene, dear sister,
You would think that we had already
    suffered enough
For the curse on Oedipus:[2]
I cannot imagine any grief
That you and I have not gone through. And
    now—
Have they told you of the new decree of our
    King Creon?

ISMENE. I have heard nothing: I know
That two sisters lost two brothers, a
    double death

---

2. curse on Oedipus: This curse refers to the fate of Oedipus, who was doomed by a decree of the gods to kill his father and marry his mother while ignorant of their true identities.

In a single hour; and I know that the
    Argive army
10 Fled in the night; but beyond this, nothing.

ANTIGONE. I thought so. And that is why I
    wanted you
To come out here with me. There is
    something we must do.

ISMENE. Why do you speak so strangely?

ANTIGONE. Listen, Ismene:

15 Creon buried our brother Eteocles
With military honors, gave him a soldier's
    funeral,
And it was right that he should; but
    Polyneices,
Who fought as bravely and died as
    miserably,—
They say that Creon has sworn
No one shall bury him, no one mourn for
20   him,
But his body must lie in the fields, a sweet
    treasure
For carrion birds to find as they search for
    food.
That is what they say, and our good Creon
    is coming here
To announce it publicly; and the
    penalty—
Stoning to death in the public square!
25   There it is,
And now you can prove what you are:
A true sister, or a traitor to your family.

ISMENE. Antigone, you are mad! What could
    I possibly do?

ANTIGONE. You must decide whether you
    will help me or not.

ISMENE. I do not understand you. Help you
30   in what?

ANTIGONE. Ismene, I am going to bury him.
    Will you come?

ISMENE. Bury him!. You have just said the
    new law forbids it.

ANTIGONE. He is my brother. And he is your
    brother, too.

ISMENE. But think of the danger! Think
    what Creon will do!

ANTIGONE. Creon is not strong enough to
35   stand in my way.

ISMENE. Ah sister!
Oedipus died, everyone hating him
For what his own search brought to light,
    his eyes
Ripped out by his own hand; and Iocaste
    died,
His mother and wife at once: she twisted
40   the cords
That strangled her life; and our two
    brothers died,
Each killed by the other's sword. And we
    are left:
But oh, Antigone,
Think how much more terrible than these
Our own death would be if we should go
45   against Creon
And do what he has forbidden! We are only
    women,
We cannot fight with men, Antigone!
The law is strong, we must give in to the
    law
In this thing, and in worse. I beg the Dead
To forgive me, but I am helpless: I must
50   yield
To those in authority. And I think it is
    dangerous business
To be always meddling.

ANTIGONE.   If that is what you think,
I should not want you, even if you asked to
    come.
You have made your choice and you can be
    what you want to be.
55 But I will bury him; and if I must die,

I say that this crime is holy: I shall lie
  down
With him in death, and I shall be as dear
To him as he to me.
                    It is the dead,
Not the living, who make the longest
  demands:
We die for ever . . .
60   You may do as you like,
Since apparently the laws of the gods
  mean nothing to you.

ISMENE. They mean a great deal to me; but I
  have no strength
To break laws that were made for the
  public good.

ANTIGONE. That must be your excuse, I
  suppose. But as for me,
I will bury the brother I love.

65 ISMENE.   Antigone,
I am so afraid for you!

ANTIGONE.   .   You need not be:
You have yourself to consider, after all.

ISMENE. But no one must hear of this, you
  must tell no one!
I will keep it a secret, I promise!

ANTIGONE.   Oh tell it! Tell everyone!
Think how they'll hate you when it all
70   comes out
If they learn that you knew about it all the
  time!

ISMENE. So fiery! You should be cold with
  fear.

ANTIGONE. Perhaps. But I am doing only
  what I must.

ISMENE. But can you do it? I say that you
  cannot.

ANTIGONE. Very well: when my strength
75   gives out, I shall do no more.

ISMENE. Impossible things should not be
  tried at all.

ANTIGONE. Go away, Ismene:
I shall be hating you soon, and the dead
  will too,
For your words are hateful. Leave me my
  foolish plan:
I am not afraid of the danger; if it means
80   death,
It will not be the worst of deaths—death
  without honor.

ISMENE. Go then, if you feel that you must.
You are unwise.
But a loyal friend indeed to those who love
  you.

[*Exit into the Palace.* ANTIGONE *goes off, left.
Enter the* CHORUS.]

Parodos

CHORUS.   [STROPHE 1]
Now the long blade of the sun, lying
Level east to west, touches with glory
Thebes of the Seven Gates.³ Open,
     unlidded
Eye of golden day! O marching light
Across the eddy and rush of Dirce's
5   stream,⁴
Striking the white shields of the enemy
Thrown headlong backward from the blaze
     of morning!

CHORAGOS. Polyneices their commander
Roused them with windy phrases,
10 He the wild eagle screaming
Insults above our land,
His wings their shields of snow,
His crest their marshalled helms.

CHORUS.   [ANTISTROPHE 1]
Against our seven gates in a yawning ring
The famished spears came onward in the
15   night;
But before his jaws were sated with our
     blood,
Or pinefire took the garland of our towers,
He was thrown back; and as he turned,
     great Thebes—
No tender victim for his noisy power—
Rose like a dragon behind him, shouting
20   war.

CHORAGOS. For God hates utterly
The bray of bragging tongues;
And when he beheld their smiling,
Their swagger of golden helms,
25 The frown of his thunder blasted
Their first man from our walls.

----

3. Seven Gates: The city of Thebes was defended by
walls containing seven entrances.
4. Dirce's (dʉr′sēz) **stream:** A small river near
Thebes into which the body of Dirce, one of the city's
early queens, was thrown after her murder.

CHORUS.   [STROPHE 2]
We heard his shout of triumph high in the
     air
Turn to a scream; far out in a flaming arc
He fell with his windy torch, and the earth
     struck him.
And others storming in fury no less than
30   his
Found shock of death in the dusty joy of
     battle.

CHORAGOS. Seven captains at seven gates
Yielded their clanging arms to the god
That bends the battle-line and breaks it.
35 These two only, brothers in blood,
Face to face in matchless rage,
Mirroring each the other's death,
Clashed in long combat.

CHORUS.   [ANTISTROPHE 2]
But now in the beautiful morning of
     victory
Let Thebes of the many chariots sing for
40   joy!
With hearts for dancing we'll take leave of
     war:
Our temples shall be sweet with hymns of
     praise,
And the long night shall echo with our
     chorus.

Scene 1

CHORAGOS. But now at last our new King is
     coming:
Creon of Thebes, Menoikeus'⁵ son.
In this auspicious dawn of his reign
What are the new complexities
5 That shifting Fate has woven for him?
What is his counsel? Why has he
     summoned
The old men to hear him?

[Enter CREON *from the Palace, center. He*

----

5. Menoikeus (me nŏi′ kē əs)

addresses the CHORUS *from the top step.*]

CREON. Gentlemen: I have the honor to inform you that our Ship of State, which
10 recent storms have threatened to destroy, has come safely to harbor at last, guided by the merciful wisdom of Heaven. I have summoned you here this morning because I know that I can depend upon you:
15 your devotion to King Laïos was absolute; you never hesitated in your duty to our late ruler Oedipus; and when Oedipus died, your loyalty was transferred to his children. Unfortunately, as you know, his two
20 sons, the princes Eteocles and Polyneices, have killed each other in battle; and I, as the next in blood, have succeeded to the full power of the throne.

I am aware, of course, that no Ruler can
25 expect complete loyalty from his subjects until he has been tested in office. Nevertheless, I say to you at the very outset that I have nothing but contempt for the kind of Governor who is afraid, for whatever
30 reason, to follow the course that he knows is best for the State; and as for the man who sets private friendship above the public welfare—I have no use for him, either. I call God to witness that if I saw
35 my country headed for ruin, I should not be afraid to speak out plainly; and I need hardly remind you that I would never have any dealings with an enemy of the people. No one values friendship more highly
40 than I; but we must remember that friends made at the risk of wrecking our Ship are not real friends at all.

These are my principles, at any rate, and that is why I have made the following
45 decision concerning the sons of Oedipus: Eteocles, who died as a man should die, fighting for his country, is to be buried
65 with full military honors, with all the ceremony that is usual when the greatest

50 heroes die; but his brother Polyneices, who broke his exile to come back with fire and sword against his native city and the shrines of his fathers' gods, whose one idea was to spill the blood of his blood
55 and sell his own people into slavery — Polyneices, I say, is to have no burial: no man is to touch him or say the least prayer for him; he shall lie on the plain, unburied; and the birds and the scaveng-
60 ing dogs can do with him whatever they like.

This is my command, and you can see the wisdom behind it. As long as I am King, no traitor is going to be honored with the loyal man. But whoever shows by word and deed that he is on the side of the State—he shall have my respect while he is living, and my reverence when he is dead.

CHORAGOS. If that is your will, Creon son of
70 Menoikeus,
You have the right to enforce it: we are
    yours.

CREON. That is my will. Take care that you
    do your part.

CHORAGOS. We are old men: let the younger
    ones carry it out.

CREON. I do not mean that: the sentries
    have been appointed.

CHORAGOS. Then what is it that you would
75 have us do?

CREON. You will give no support to whoever
    breaks this law.

CHORAGOS. Only a crazy man is in love with
    death!

CREON. And death it is; yet money talks,
    and the wisest
Have sometimes been known to count a
    few coins too many.

[*Enter* SENTRY *from left.*]

80 **SENTRY.** I'll not say that I'm out of breath
    from running, King, because every time I
    stopped to think about what I have to tell
    you, I felt like going back. And all the time
    a voice kept saying, "You fool, don't you
85 know you're walking straight into trou-
    ble?"; and then another voice: "Yes, but if
    you let somebody else get the news to
    Creon first, it will be even worse than that
    for you!" But good sense won out, at least
90 I hope it was good sense, and here I am
    with a story that makes no sense at all;
    but I'll tell it anyhow, because, as they
    say, what's going to happen's going to
    happen, and—

CREON. Come to the point. What have you to
95 say?

SENTRY. I did not do it. I did not see who did
    it. You must not punish me for what
    someone else has done.

CREON. A comprehensive defense! More
    effective, perhaps,
100 If I knew its purpose. Come: what is it?

SENTRY. A dreadful thing . . . I don't know
    how to put it—

CREON. Out with it!

SENTRY.   Well, then;
The dead man—
                      Polyneices—

[*Pause. The* SENTRY *is overcome, fumbles for
words.* CREON *waits impassively.*]

                                out there—
                                someone,—
New dust on the slimy flesh!

[*Pause. No sign from* CREON.]

Someone has given it burial that way, and
105 Gone . . .

[*Long pause.* CREON *finally speaks with
deadly control.*]

CREON. And the man who dared do this?

SENTRY.   I swear I

Do not know! You must believe me!
                                Listen:
The ground was dry, not a sign of digging,
    no,
Not a wheeltrack in the dust, no trace of
    anyone.
It was when they relieved us this morning:
110 and one of them,
The corporal, pointed to it.
                        There it was,
The strangest—
                    Look:
The body, just mounded over with light
    dust: you see?

Not buried really, but as if they'd covered it
Just enough for the ghost's peace. And no
115   sign
Of dogs or any wild animal that had been
   there.

And then what a scene there was! Every
   man of us
Accusing the other: we all proved the other
   man did it,
We all had proof that we could not have
   done it.
We were ready to take hot iron in our
120   hands,
Walk through fire, swear by all the gods,
It was not I!
I do not know who it was, but it was not
   I!

[CREON'S *rage has been mounting steadily,*
but the SENTRY *is too intent upon his story to*
notice it.]

And then, when this came to nothing,
   someone said
125 A thing that silenced us and made us stare
Down at the ground: you had to be told the
   news,
And one of us had to do it! We threw the
   dice,
And the bad luck fell to me. So here I am,
No happier to be here than you are to have
   me:
Nobody likes the man who brings bad
130   news.

CHORAGOS. I have been wondering, King:
   can it be that the gods have done this?

CREON. [*Furiously*] Stop!
Must you doddering wrecks
Go out of your heads entirely? "The gods!"
135 Intolerable!
The gods favor this corpse? Why? How had
   he served them?
Tried to loot their temples, burn their
   images,

Yes, and the whole State, and its laws with
   it!
Is it your senile opinion that the gods love
   to honor bad men?
A pious thought!—
140   No, from the very beginning
There have been those who have
   whispered together,
Stiff-necked anarchists, putting their
   heads together,
Scheming against me in alleys. These are
   the men,
And they have bribed my own guard to do
   this thing.
145 Money!   [*Sententiously*]
There's nothing in the world so
   demoralizing as money.
Down go your cities,
Homes gone, men gone, honest hearts
   corrupted,
Crookedness of all kinds, and all for
   money!

[*To* SENTRY]

                            But you—!
150 I swear by God and by the throne of God,
The man who has done this thing shall
   pay for it!
Find that man, bring him here to me, or
   your death
Will be the least of your problems: I'll
   string you up
Alive, and there will be certain ways to
   make you
155 Discover your employer before you die;
And the process may teach you a lesson
   you seem to have missed:
The dearest profit is sometimes all too
   dear:
That depends on the source. Do you
   understand me?
A fortune won is often misfortune.

SENTRY. King, may I speak?

160 **CREON.**   Your very voice distresses me.

SENTRY. Are you sure that it is my voice,
and not your conscience?

CREON. By God, he wants to analyze me
now!

SENTRY. It is not what I say, but what has
been done, that hurts you.

CREON. You talk too much.

SENTRY.   Maybe; but I've done nothing.

CREON. Sold your soul for some silver: that's
165   all you've done.

SENTRY. How dreadful it is when the right
judge judges wrong!

CREON. Your figures of speech
May entertain you now; but unless you
bring me the man,
You will get little profit from them in the
end.

[*Exit* CREON *into the Palace.*]

170 SENTRY. "Bring me the man"—!
I'd like nothing better than bringing him
the man!
But bring him or not, you have seen the
last of me here.
At any rate, I am safe!

[Exit SENTRY.]

Ode I

CHORUS.   [STROPHE 1]
Numberless are the world's wonders, but
    none
More wonderful than man; the stormgray
    sea
Yields to his prows, the huge crests bear
    him high;
Earth, holy and inexhaustible, is graven
With shining furrows where his plows
5   have gone
Year after year, the timeless labor of
    stallions.

             [ANTISTROPHE 1]
The lightboned birds and beasts that cling
    to cover,
The lithe fish lighting their reaches of dim
    water,
All are taken, tamed in the net of his
    mind;
The lion on the hill, the wild horse
10   windy-maned,
Resign to him; and his blunt yoke has
    broken
The sultry shoulders of the mountain bull.

             [STROPHE 2]
Words also, and thought as rapid as air,
He fashions to his good use; statecraft is
    his,
And his the skill that deflects the arrows
15   of snow,
The spears of winter rain: from every wind
He has made himself secure—from all but
    one:
In the late wind of death he cannot stand.

             [ANTISTROPHE 2]
O clear intelligence, force beyond all
    measure!
20 O fate of man, working both good and evil!
When the laws are kept, how proudly his
    city stands!
When the laws are broken, what of his city
    then?
Never may the anarchic man find rest at
    my hearth,
Never be it said that my thoughts are his
    thoughts.

Scene 2

[*Re-enter* SENTRY *leading* ANTIGONE.]

CHORAGOS. What does this mean? Surely
    this captive woman
Is the Princess, Antigone. Why should she
    be taken?

SENTRY. Here is the one who did it! We
    caught her
In the very act of burying him.—Where is
    Creon?

5 **CHORAGOS.** Just coming from the house.

[*Enter* CREON, *center.*]

CREON.   What has happened?
Why have you come back so soon?

SENTRY. [*Expansively*]   O King,
A man should never be too sure of
    anything:
I would have sworn
That you'd not see me here again: your
    anger
Frightened me so, and the things you
10   threatened me with;
But how could I tell then
That I'd be able to solve the case so soon?
No dice-throwing this time: I was only too
    glad to come!

Here is this woman. She is the guilty one:
15 We found her trying to bury him.
Take her, then; question her; judge her as
    you will.
I am through with the whole thing now,
    and glad of it.

CREON. But this is Antigone! Why have you brought her here?

SENTRY. She was burying him, I tell you!

20 **CREON.** [*Severely*]   Is this the truth?

SENTRY. I saw her with my own eyes. Can I say more?

CREON. The details: come, tell me quickly!

SENTRY.   It was like this:
After those terrible threats of yours, King,
We went back and brushed the dust away from the body.
25 The flesh was soft by now, and stinking,
So we sat on a hill to windward and kept guard.
No napping this time! We kept each other awake.
But nothing happened until the white round sun
Whirled in the center of the round sky over us:
30 Then, suddenly,

A storm of dust roared up from the earth, and the sky
Went out, the plain vanished with all its trees
In the stinging dark. We closed our eyes and endured it.
The whirlwind lasted a long time, but it passed;
And then we looked, and there was
35 Antigone!
I have seen
A mother bird come back to a stripped nest, heard
Her crying bitterly a broken note or two
For the young ones stolen. Just so, when this girl
Found the bare corpse, and all her love's
40 work wasted,
She wept, and cried on heaven to damn the hands
That had done this thing.
           And then she brought more dust
And sprinkled wine three times for her brother's ghost.

We ran and took her at once. She was not
    afraid,
Not even when we charged her with what
45   she had done.
She denied nothing.
                And this was a comfort to me,
And some uneasiness: for it is a good thing
To escape from death, but it is no great
    pleasure
To bring death to a friend.
                            Yet I always say
There is nothing so comfortable as your
50   own safe skin!

CREON. [*Slowly, dangerously*] And you,
    Antigone,
You with your head hanging,—do you
    confess this thing?

ANTIGONE. I do. I deny nothing.

CREON. [*To* SENTRY]   You may go.

[*Exit* SENTRY.]

[*To* ANTIGONE] Tell me, tell me briefly:
Had you heard my proclamation touching
55   this matter?

ANTIGONE. It was public. Could I help
    hearing it?

CREON. And yet you dared defy the law.

ANTIGONE.   I dared.
It was not God's proclamation. That final
    Justice
That rules the world below makes no such
    laws.
60 Your edict, King, was strong,
    But all your strength is weakness itself
        against
    The immortal unrecorded laws of God.
    They are not merely now: they were, and
        shall be,
    Operative forever, beyond man utterly.

    I knew I must die, even without your
65   decree:

I am only mortal. And if I must die
Now, before it is my time to die,
Surely this is no hardship: can anyone
Living, as I live, with evil all about me,
Think Death less than a friend? This death
70   of mine
Is of no importance; but if I had left my
    brother
Lying in death unburied, I should have
    suffered.
Now I do not.
                You smile at me. Ah Creon,
Think me a fool, if you like; but it may well
    be
75 That a fool convicts me of folly.

CHORAGOS. Like father, like daughter: both
    headstrong, deaf to reason!
She has never learned to yield.

CREON.   She has much to learn.
The inflexible heart breaks first, the
    toughest iron
Cracks first, and the wildest horses bend
    their necks
At the pull of the smallest curb.
80   Pride? In a slave?
This girl is guilty of a double insolence,
Breaking the given laws and boasting of it.
Who is the man here,
She or I, if this crime goes unpunished?
85 Sister's child, or more than sister's child,
Or closer yet in blood—she and her sister
Win bitter death for this!

[*To* SERVANTS]   Go, some of you,
Arrest Ismene. I accuse her equally.
Bring her: you will find her sniffling in the
    house there.

Her mind's a traitor: crimes kept in the
90   dark
Cry for light, and the guardian brain
    shudders;
But how much worse than this
Is brazen boasting of barefaced anarchy!

ANTIGONE. Creon, what more do you want
than my death?

CREON.   Nothing.
That gives me everything.

95 **ANTIGONE.**   Then I beg you: kill me.
This talking is a great weariness: your
     words
Are distasteful to me, and I am sure that
     mine
Seem so to you. And yet they should not
     seem so:
I should have praise and honor for what I
     have done.
100 All these men here would praise me
Were their lips not frozen shut with fear of
     you.

[*Bitterly*]

Ah the good fortune of kings,
Licensed to say and do whatever they
     please!

CREON. You are alone here in that opinion.

ANTIGONE. No, they are with me. But they
105   keep their tongues in leash.

CREON. Maybe. But you are guilty, and they
     are not.

ANTIGONE. There is no guilt in reverence for
     the dead.

CREON. But Eteocles—was he not your
     brother too?

ANTIGONE. My brother too.

CREON.   And you insult his memory?

ANTIGONE. [*Softly*] The dead man would not
110   say that I insult it.

CREON. He would: for you honor a traitor as
     much as him.

ANTIGONE. His own brother, traitor or not,
     and equal in blood.

CREON. He made war on his country.
     Eteocles defended it.

ANTIGONE. Nevertheless, there are honors
     due all the dead.

CREON. But not the same for the wicked as
115   for the just.

ANTIGONE. Ah Creon, Creon,
Which of us can say what the gods hold
     wicked?

CREON. An enemy is an enemy, even dead.

ANTIGONE. It is my nature to join in love, not
     hate.

CREON. [*Finally losing patience*] Go join
120   them, then; if you must have your love,
Find it in hell!

CHORAGOS. But see, Ismene comes:

[*Enter* ISMENE, *guarded.*]

Those tears are sisterly, the cloud
That shadows her eyes rains down gentle
     sorrow.

CREON. You too, Ismene,
Snake in my ordered house, sucking my
125   blood
Stealthily—and all the time I never knew
That these two sisters were aiming at my
     throne!
              Ismene,
Do you confess your share in this crime, or
     deny it?
Answer me.

ISMENE. Yes, if she will let me say so. I am
130   guilty.

ANTIGONE. [*Coldly*] No, Ismene. You have no
     right to say so.
You would not help me, and I will not have
     you help me.

ISMENE. But now I know what you meant;
     and I am here

To join you, to take my share of
   punishment.

ANTIGONE. The dead man and the gods who
135   rule the dead
Know whose act this was. Words are not
   friends.

ISMENE. Do you refuse me, Antigone? I want
   to die with you:
I too have a duty that I must discharge to
   the dead.

ANTIGONE. You shall not lessen my death by
   sharing it.

ISMENE. What do I care for life when you are
140   dead?

ANTIGONE. Ask Creon. You're always
   hanging on his opinions.

ISMENE. You are laughing at me. Why,
   Antigone?

ANTIGONE. It's a joyless laughter, Ismene.

ISMENE.   But can I do nothing?

ANTIGONE. Yes. Save yourself. I shall not
   envy you.
There are those who will praise you; I shall
145   have honor, too.

ISMENE. But we are equally guilty!

ANTIGONE.   No more, Ismene.
You are alive, but I belong to Death.

CREON. [*To the* CHORUS] Gentlemen, I beg you
   to observe these girls:
One has just now lost her mind; the other,
150 It seems, has never had a mind at all.

ISMENE. Grief teaches the steadiest minds to
   waver, King.

CREON. Yours certainly did, when you
   assumed guilt with the guilty!

ISMENE. But how could I go on living
   without her?

CREON.   You are.
She is already dead.

ISMENE.   But your own son's bride!

CREON. There are places enough for him to
155   push his plow.
I want no wicked women for my sons!

ISMENE. O dearest Haimon, how your father
   wrongs you!

CREON. I've had enough of your childish
   talk of marriage!

MULTICULTURAL CONNECTION

Burial Customs Across Cultures

The central conflict in this play relates
to the observance of burial customs. Though
death is of course universal, funeral rites
vary greatly around the globe.

Ancient traditions. The most universal
and oldest method of burial is under the
ground. Eskimos covered the corpse with a
pile of stones or a small igloo. Both the
Vikings and Egyptians buried their dead
along with their servants, pets, and prized
belongings so that they would have them in
the afterlife.

In Western cultures, water burial is rare.
Some inhabitants of the South Pacific, however, place the body in a canoe and launch
it into the water.

Cremation, the burning of a body, was
practiced extensively in the ancient world
and is still common in many Asian countries. In Laos cremation is a privilege extended to those who died "fortunately," having led a full and rewarding life.

Exploring on Your Own

Research the burial customs of a culture
other than your own. Then tell your class about
the history and meaning of these customs.

CHORAGOS. Do you really intend to steal this
   girl from your son?

160 CREON. No; Death will do that for me.

CHORAGOS.   Then she must die?

CREON. [*Ironically*] You dazzle me.
                    —But enough of this talk!

[*To* GUARDS] You, there, take them away and
   guard them well:
For they are but women, and even brave
   men run
When they see Death coming.

[*Exit* ISMENE, ANTIGONE, *and* GUARDS.]

Ode II

CHORUS.   [STROPHE 1]
Fortunate is the man who has never tasted
   God's vengeance!
Where once the anger of heaven has
   struck, that house is shaken
Forever: damnation rises behind each child
Like a wave cresting out of the black
   northeast,
5 When the long darkness undersea roars up
And bursts drumming death upon the
   windwhipped sand.

                    [ANTISTROPHE 1]
I have seen this gathering sorrow from
   time long past
Loom upon Oedipus' children: generation
   from generation
Takes the compulsive rage of the enemy
   god.

10 So lately this last flower of Oedipus' line
Drank the sunlight! but now a passionate
   word
And a handful of dust have closed up all
   its beauty.

                    [STROPHE 2]
   What mortal arrogance
   Transcends the wrath of Zeus?[6]
Sleep cannot lull him, nor the effortless
15   long months
Of the timeless gods: but he is young
   forever,
And his house is the shining day of high
   Olympos.[7]
   All that is and shall be,
   And all the past, is his.
No pride on earth is free of the curse of
20   heaven.

                    [ANTISTROPHE 2]
   The straying dreams of men
   May bring them ghosts of joy:
But as they drowse, the waking embers
   burn them;
Or they walk with fixed eyes, as blind men
   walk.
But the ancient wisdom speaks for our
25   own time:
   Fate works most for woe
   With Folly's fairest show.
Man's little pleasure is the spring of
   sorrow.

---

6. Zeus (zo͞os): The king of all Greek gods, who is
both timeless and all-powerful.

7. Olympos (ō lim′ pəs): A mountain in Greece,
where the gods were believed to live in ease and
splendor.

RESPONDING TO THE SELECTION

Your Response

1. Antigone and Ismene disagree over the burial of Polyneices. With whom do you agree?
2. In his speech on pages 279–280 King Creon indicates what kind of ruler he will be. Do you share his vision of leadership? Why or why not?

Recalling

3. Briefly summarize Creon's remarks to the chorus about the ship of state.

Interpreting

4. Explain what Ismene means when she says, "We are only women,/We cannot fight with men, Antigone!"
5. How might Ismene's advice to her sister seem cowardly to certain readers?
6. Because she insisted on burying her brother's body, Antigone has broken the law. What does such defiance indicate about her personality?
7. In his argument with Antigone, Creon declares, "An enemy is an enemy, even dead." What does he mean? Do you agree? Why or why not?

Applying

8. Strength of will and moral courage are usually thought of as virtues. Can they also seem foolish? Explain your answer.

ANALYZING LITERATURE

Understanding Plot Structure

Plot structure, the sequence and relationships of events that make up a play or story, includes exposition and conflict. This structure provides a coherent frame for the actions of the characters.

1. The exposition presents the information and characters central to understanding the play. What essential information do you learn through the exposition?
2. What is the major conflict in this play?
3. What other conflicts exist?
4. How do you think Sophocles wants you to feel about each of these conflicts? Explain.

CRITICAL THINKING AND READING

Investigating the Role of the Chorus

The ode at the end of Scene 1 is famous. Some readers think Sophocles gives so important a statement to the chorus because he regards its members as a collective conscience for the community. Others disagree. They claim the chorus is best understood as another character, who is no more or less complicated than the other players. There is no single way to interpret the chorus and its role, but most commentators stress its importance.

1. Tell whether you think Sophocles uses the comments of the chorus to give voice to his own opinions about human nature. Explain.
2. Mention two ways in which the chorus helped the Greek playwrights.
3. What devices do modern playwrights use in place of a chorus?

THINKING AND WRITING

Assuming a Character's Identity

Suppose that you are Ismene writing a letter to Antigone. How would you address the sister you loved if you thought she were dooming herself? You might suggest other ways of showing respect to your brother's memory, or you might write about the future of your relationship once this crisis is past. As you revise, check for the following: Did you remain consistent and faithful to the voice of Ismene? Is your sincerity apparent?

LEARNING OPTION

Art. The Greeks built stone amphitheaters in which a whisper from the stage could be heard in the last row of seats. Using the photographs on pages 272–273 and information from other books, build a model of an ancient Greek theater. You may use cardboard, papier-mâché, or any other suitable material. When you are finished, display your model in class.

GUIDE FOR READING

Antigone, Scenes 3 through 5

Tragedy

A tragedy is a work of literature that results in a catastrophe for the main character. In ancient Greek drama, the main character was always a significant person, a king or a hero, and the cause of the tragedy was a tragic flaw, or weakness, in his or her character. There is some debate about the tragic hero in *Antigone.* Some claim Creon fills the definition fully and that Antigone is not to be regarded as more important simply because her name is used in the title. The exchanges between them seem to lead to an irreversible point from which neither of them can retreat. They are doomed, some say, either by fate or by a certain flaw in character that forces them to act as they do. Others see the flaw in Antigone. To them, her headstrongness is a form of pride, which makes her unyielding and leads to her doom.

Focus

In Scenes 3 and 5 of *Antigone,* Haimon and Teiresias reason with Creon but fail to get him to change his mind about punishing Antigone and Ismene. How would you try to change Creon's mind? List as many reasons as you can to persuade Creon not to punish the two sisters. As you read the rest of *Antigone,* compare your reasons with those used by Haimon and Teiresias in their arguments.

Vocabulary

Knowing the following words will help you as you read *Antigone,* Scenes 3 through 5.

deference (def′ ər əns) *n.*: A yielding in thought (p. 291)

vile (vīl) *adj.*: Extremely disgusting (p. 293)

piety (pī′ ə tē) *n.*: Holiness; respect for the divine (p. 294)

blasphemy (blas′ fə mē) *n.*: Disrespectful speech or action concerning God (p. 295)

lamentation (lam′ ən tā′ shən) *n.*: An expression of grief; weeping (p. 296)

chorister (kôr′ is tər) *n.*: A member of a chorus (p. 301)

Scene 3

CHORAGOS. But here is Haimon, King, the last of all your sons.
Is it grief for Antigone that brings him here,
And bitterness at being robbed of his bride?

[*Enter* HAIMON.]

CREON. We shall soon see, and no need of diviners.[1]
       —Son,
You have heard my final judgment on that
5 girl:
Have you come here hating me, or have you come
With deference and with love, whatever I do?

HAIMON. I am your son, father. You are my guide.
You make things clear for me, and I obey you.
No marriage means more to me than your
10 continuing wisdom.

CREON. Good. That is the way to behave: subordinate
Everything else, my son, to your father's will.
This is what a man prays for, that he may get
Sons attentive and dutiful in his house,
15 Each one hating his father's enemies,
Honoring his father's friends. But if his sons
Fail him, if they turn out unprofitably,
What has he fathered but trouble for himself
And amusement for the malicious?
               So you are right
20 Not to lose your head over this woman.

Your pleasure with her would soon grow cold, Haimon,
And then you'd have a hellcat in bed and elsewhere.
Let her find her husband in Hell!
Of all the people in this city, only she
Has had contempt for my law and broken
25 it.

Do you want me to show myself weak before the people?
Or to break my sworn word? No, and I will not.
The woman dies.
I suppose she'll plead "family ties." Well, let her.
30 If I permit my own family to rebel,
How shall I earn the world's obedience?
Show me the man who keeps his house in hand,
He's fit for public authority.
               I'll have no dealings
With lawbreakers, critics of the government:
Whoever is chosen to govern should be
35 obeyed—

---

1. diviners (də vīn′ ərz): Those who forecast the future.

Must be obeyed, in all things, great and
     small,
Just and unjust! O Haimon,
The man who knows how to obey, and that
     man only,
Knows how to give commands when the
     time comes.
You can depend on him, no matter how
40   fast
The spears come: he's a good soldier, he'll
     stick it out.

Anarchy, anarchy! Show me a greater evil!
This is why cities tumble and the great
     houses rain down,
This is what scatters armies!

No, no: good lives are made so by
45   discipline.
We keep the laws then, and the lawmakers,
And no woman shall seduce us. If we must
     lose,
Let's lose to a man, at least! Is a woman
     stronger than we?

CHORAGOS. Unless time has rusted my wits,
What you say, King, is said with point and
50   dignity.

HAIMON. [*Boyishly earnest*] Father:
Reason is God's crowning gift to man, and
     you are right
55 To warn me against losing mine. I cannot
     say—
I hope that I shall never want to
     say!—that you
Have reasoned badly. Yet there are other
     men
Who can reason, too; and their opinions
     might be helpful.
You are not in a position to know
     everything
That people say or do, or what they feel:
Your temper terrifies them—everyone
60 Will tell you only what you like to hear.
But I, at any rate, can listen; and I have
     heard them

Muttering and whispering in the dark
     about this girl.
They say no woman has ever, so
     unreasonably,
Died so shameful a death for a generous
     act:
"She covered her brother's body. Is this
65   indecent?
She kept him from dogs and vultures. Is
     this a crime?
Death?—She should have all the honor
     that we can give her!"

This is the way they talk out there in the
     city.

You must believe me:
Nothing is closer to me than your
70   happiness.
What could be closer? Must not any son
Value his father's fortune as his father
     does his?
I beg you, do not be unchangeable:
Do not believe that you alone can be right.
75 The man who thinks that,
The man who maintains that only he has
     the power
To reason correctly, the gift to speak, the
     soul—
A man like that, when you know him,
     turns out empty.

It is not reason never to yield to reason!

In flood time you can see how some trees
80   bend,
And because they bend, even their twigs
     are safe,
While stubborn trees are torn up, roots
     and all.
And the same thing happens in sailing:
Make your sheet fast, never slacken—and
     over you go,
Head over heels and under: and there's
85   your voyage.
Forget you are angry! Let yourself be
     moved!

I know I am young; but please let me say this:
The ideal condition
Would be, I admit, that men should be right by instinct;
90 But since we are all too likely to go astray,
The reasonable thing is to learn from those who can teach.

CHORAGOS. You will do well to listen to him, King,
If what he says is sensible. And you, Haimon,
Must listen to your father.—Both speak well.

CREON. You consider it right for a man of
95 my years and experience
To go to school to a boy?

HAIMON.   It is not right
If I am wrong. But if I am young, and right,
What does my age matter?

CREON. You think it right to stand up for an anarchist?

HAIMON. Not at all. I pay no respect to
100 criminals.

CREON. Then she is not a criminal?

HAIMON. The City would deny it, to a man.

CREON. And the City proposes to teach me how to rule?

HAIMON. Ah. Who is it that's talking like a boy now?

CREON. My voice is the one voice giving
105 orders in this City!

HAIMON. It is no City if it takes orders from one voice.

CREON. The State is the King!

HAIMON.   Yes, if the State is a desert.

[Pause]

CREON. This boy, it seems, has sold out to a woman.

HAIMON. If you are a woman: my concern is only for you.

CREON. So? Your "concern"! In a public
110 brawl with your father!

HAIMON. How about you, in a public brawl with justice?

CREON. With justice, when all that I do is within my rights?

HAIMON. You have no right to trample on God's right.

CREON. [Completely out of control] Fool, adolescent fool! Taken in by a woman!

HAIMON. You'll never see me taken in by
115 anything vile.

CREON. Every word you say is for her!

HAIMON. [Quietly, darkly]   And for you.
And for me. And for the gods under the earth.

CREON. You'll never marry her while she lives.

HAIMON. Then she must die.—But her death will cause another.

120 CREON. Another?
Have you lost your senses? Is this an open threat?

HAIMON. There is no threat in speaking to emptiness.

CREON. I swear you'll regret this superior tone of yours!
You are the empty one!

HAIMON.   If you were not my father,
125 I'd say you were perverse.

CREON. You girlstruck fool, don't play at words with me!

HAIMON. I am sorry. You prefer silence.

CREON.   Now, by God—!
I swear, by all the gods in heaven above us,
You'll watch it, I swear you shall!

[*To the* SERVANTS]   Bring her out!
Bring the woman out! Let her die before
130   his eyes!
Here, this instant, with her bridegroom
      beside her!

HAIMON. Not here, no; she will not die here,
      King.
And you will never see my face again.
Go on raving as long as you've a friend to
      endure you.

[*Exit* HAIMON.]

135 **CHORAGOS.** Gone, gone.
Creon, a young man in a rage is
      dangerous!

CREON. Let him do, or dream to do, more
      than a man can.
He shall not save these girls from death.

CHORAGOS.   These girls?
You have sentenced them both?

CREON.   No, you are right.
I will not kill the one whose hands are
140   clean.

CHORAGOS. But Antigone?

CREON. [*Somberly*] I will carry her far away
Out there in the wilderness, and lock her
Living in a vault of stone. She shall have
      food,
As the custom is, to absolve the State of
      her death.
145 And there let her pray to the gods of hell:
They are her only gods:
Perhaps they will show her an escape from
      death,
Or she may learn,
                    though late,
That piety shown the dead is pity in vain.

[*Exit* CREON.]

Ode III

CHORUS.   [STROPHE]
Love, unconquerable
Waster of rich men, keeper
Of warm lights and all-night vigil
In the soft face of a girl:
5   Sea-wanderer, forest-visitor!
Even the pure Immortals cannot escape
      you,
And mortal man, in his one day's dusk,
Trembles before your glory.

                                    [ANTISTROPHE]
Surely you swerve upon ruin
10   The just man's consenting heart,
As here you have made bright anger
Strike between father and son—
And none has conquered but Love!
A girl's glance working the will of heaven:
15   Pleasure to her alone who mocks us,
Merciless Aphrodite.[2]

Scene 4

CHORAGOS. [*As* ANTIGONE *enters guarded*] But
      I can no longer stand in awe of this,
Nor, seeing what I see, keep back my tears.
Here is Antigone, passing to that chamber
Where all find sleep at last.

ANTIGONE.   [STROPHE 1]
5   Look upon me, friends, and pity me
Turning back at the night's edge to say
Good-by to the sun that shines for me no
      longer;
Now sleepy Death
Summons me down to Acheron,[3] that cold
      shore:
There is no bridesong there, nor any
10   music.

_____

2. Aphrodite (af′ rə dīt′ ē): Goddess of beauty and
love, who is sometimes vengeful in her retaliation for
offenses.
3. Acheron (ak′ ə răn): A river in the underworld
over which the dead are ferried.

CHORUS. Yet not unpraised, not without a kind of honor,
You walk at last into the underworld;
Untouched by sickness, broken by no sword.
What woman has ever found your way to death?

ANTIGONE. [ANTISTROPHE 1]

15 How often I have heard the story of Niobe,[4]
Tantalos'[5] wretched daughter, how the stone
Clung fast about her, ivy-close: and they say
The rain falls endlessly
And sifting soft snow; her tears are never done.
20 I feel the loneliness of her death in mine.

CHORUS. But she was born of heaven, and you
Are woman, woman-born. If her death is yours,
A mortal woman's, is this not for you
Glory in our world and in the world beyond?

ANTIGONE. [STROPHE 2]

25 You laugh at me. Ah, friends, friends,
Can you not wait until I am dead? O Thebes,
O men many-charioted, in love with Fortune,
Dear springs of Dirce, sacred Theban grove,

Be witnesses for me, denied all pity,
30 Unjustly judged! and think a word of love
For her whose path turns
Under dark earth, where there are no more tears.

CHORUS. You have passed beyond human daring and come at last
Into a place of stone where Justice sits.
35 I cannot tell
What shape of your father's guilt appears in this.

ANTIGONE. [ANTISTROPHE 2]

You have touched it at last: that bridal bed
Unspeakable, horror of son and mother mingling:
Their crime, infection of all our family!
40 O Oedipus, father and brother!
Your marriage strikes from the grave to murder mine.
I have been a stranger here in my own land:
All my life
The blasphemy of my birth has followed me.

---

4. Niobe (nī′ ə bē′): A queen of Thebes who was turned to stone while weeping for her slain children. Her seven sons and seven daughters were killed by Artemis and Apollo, the divine twins of Leto. These gods ruined Niobe after Leto complained that Niobe insulted her by bragging of maternal superiority. It was Zeus who turned the bereaved Niobe to stone, but her lament continued and her tears created a stream.

5. Tantalos (tan′ tə ləs): Niobe's father, who was condemned to eternal frustration in the underworld because he revealed the secrets of the gods. Tantalos was tormented by being kept just out of reach of the water and food that was near him but which he could never reach to enjoy.

CHORUS. Reverence is a virtue, but strength
45 Lives in established law: that must prevail.
You have made your choice,
Your death is the doing of your conscious
    hand.

ANTIGONE.   [EPODE]
Then let me go, since all your words are
    bitter,
50 And the very light of the sun is cold to me.
Lead me to my vigil, where I must have
Neither love nor lamentation; no song, but
    silence.

[CREON *interrupts impatiently.*]

CREON. If dirges and planned lamentations
    could put off death,
Men would be singing forever.

[*To the* SERVANTS]   Take her, go!
You know your orders: take her to the
55   vault
And leave her alone there. And if she lives
    or dies,
That's her affair, not ours: our hands are
    clean.

ANTIGONE. O tomb, vaulted bride-bed in
    eternal rock,
Soon I shall be with my own again
Where Persephone[6] welcomes the thin
60   ghosts underground:
And I shall see my father again, and you,
    mother,
And dearest Polyneices—
                          dearest indeed
To me, since it was my hand
That washed him clean and poured the
    ritual wine:
65 And my reward is death before my time!

And yet, as men's hearts know, I have
    done no wrong,
I have not sinned before God. Or if I have,

I shall know the truth in death. But if the
    guilt
Lies upon Creon who judged me, then, I
    pray,
May his punishment equal my own.

70 **CHORAGOS.**   O passionate heart,
Unyielding, tormented still by the same
    winds!

CREON. Her guards shall have good cause to
    regret their delaying.

ANTIGONE. Ah! That voice is like the voice of
    death!

CREON. I can give you no reason to think
    you are mistaken.

ANTIGONE. Thebes, and you my fathers'
75   gods,
And rulers of Thebes, you see me now, the
    last
Unhappy daughter of a line of kings,
Your kings, led away to death. You will
    remember
What things I suffer, and at what men's
    hands,
Because I would not transgress the laws of
80   heaven.

[*To the* GUARDS, *simply*]

Come: let us wait no longer.

[*Exit* ANTIGONE, *left, guarded.*]

Ode IV

CHORUS.   [STROPHE 1]
All Danae's beauty[7] was locked away

---

6. Persephone (pər sef′ ə nē): Queen of the
underworld.

7. Danae's (dan′ ā ēz′) **beauty:** Danae was
imprisoned in a brazen, dark tower when it was
foretold that she would mother a son who would kill
her father. Her beauty attracted Zeus, who visited her
in the form of a shower of gold. Perseus was born of
the union, and Danae was exiled with the child over
stormy seas from which Zeus saved them. Years later,
as prophesied, the boy did kill the man he failed to
recognize as his grandfather.

In a brazen cell where the sunlight could
    not come:
A small room, still as any grave, enclosed
    her.
Yet she was a princess too,
And Zeus in a rain of gold poured love
5   upon her.
O child, child,
No power in wealth or war
Or tough sea-blackened ships
Can prevail against untiring Destiny!

                   [ANTISTROPHE 1]

10 And Dryas' son[8] also, that furious king,
Bore the god's prisoning anger for his
    pride:
Sealed up by Dionysos[9] in deaf stone,
His madness died among echoes.
So at the last he learned what dreadful
    power
15 His tongue had mocked:
For he had profaned the revels,
And fired the wrath of the nine
Implacable Sisters[10] that love the sound of
    the flute.

                   [STROPHE 2]

And old men tell a half-remembered tale
Of horror done where a dark ledge splits
20   the sea
And a double surf beats on the gray
    shores:
How a king's new woman, sick

---

8. Dryas' (drī′ əs) **son:** Lycorgos (lī kʉr′ gəs), whose
opposition to the worship of Dionysos was severely
punished by the gods. He drove the followers of the
god from Thrace and was driven insane for having
done so. Lycorgos recovered from his madness while
imprisoned in a cave but was later blinded by Zeus as
additional punishment for his offense.
9. Dionysos (dī′ ə nī′ səs): The god of wine, in
whose honor the Greek plays were performed.
10. nine Implacable Sisters: The nine muses, or
goddesses, of science and literature. They are the
daughters of Zeus and Mnemosyne (nē mäs′ ə
nē′)—Memory—who inspired invention and
influenced the production of art. They are called
implacable (im plak′ ə b'l) because they were
unforgiving and denied inspiration to anyone who
offended them.

With hatred for the queen he had
    imprisoned,
Ripped out his two sons' eyes with her
    bloody hands
While grinning Ares[11] watched the shuttle
25   plunge
Four times: four blind wounds crying for
    revenge,

                 [ANTISTROPHE 2]

Crying, tears and blood mingled.
    —Piteously born,
Those sons whose mother was of heavenly
    birth!
Her father was the god of the North Wind
30 And she was cradled by gales,
She raced with young colts on the
    glittering hills
And walked untrammeled in the open
    light:
But in her marriage deathless Fate found
    means
To build a tomb like yours for all her joy.

Scene 5

[*Enter blind* TEIRESIAS, *led by a boy. The
opening speeches of* TEIRESIAS *should be in
singsong contrast to the realistic lines of*
CREON.]

TEIRESIAS. This is the way the blind man
    comes, Princes, Princes,
Lock-step, two heads lit by the eyes of one.

CREON. What new thing have you to tell us,
    old Teiresias?

TEIRESIAS. I have much to tell you: listen to
    the prophet, Creon.

CREON. I am not aware that I have ever
5   failed to listen.

TEIRESIAS. Then you have done wisely,
    King, and ruled well.

---

11. Ares (er′ ēz): The god of war.

CREON. I admit my debt to you.[12] But what have you to say?

TEIRESIAS. This, Creon: you stand once more on the edge of fate.

CREON. What do you mean? Your words are a kind of dread.

10 **TEIRESIAS.** Listen, Creon:

I was sitting in my chair of augury,[13] at the place
Where the birds gather about me. They were all a-chatter,
As is their habit, when suddenly I heard
A strange note in their jangling, a scream, a
15 Whirring fury; I knew that they were fighting,
Tearing each other, dying
In a whirlwind of wings clashing. And I was afraid.
I began the rites of burnt-offering at the altar,
But Hephaistos[14] failed me: instead of bright flame,
There was only the sputtering slime of the
20 fat thigh-flesh
Melting: the entrails dissolved in gray smoke,
The bare bone burst from the welter. And no blaze!

This was a sign from heaven. My boy described it,

Seeing for me as I see for others.
25 I tell you, Creon, you yourself have brought
This new calamity upon us. Our hearths and altars
Are stained with the corruption of dogs and carrion birds
That glut themselves on the corpse of Oedipus' son.
The gods are deaf when we pray to them, their fire
Recoils from our offering, their birds of
30 omen
Have no cry of comfort, for they are gorged
With the thick blood of the dead.

                     O my son,
These are no trifles! Think: all men make mistakes,
But a good man yields when he knows his course is wrong,
And repairs the evil. The only crime is
35 pride.

Give in to the dead man, then: do not fight with a corpse—
What glory is it to kill a man who is dead?
Think, I beg you:
It is for your own good that I speak as I do.
You should be able to yield for your own
40 good.

CREON. It seems that prophets have made me their especial province.
All my life long
I have been a kind of butt for the dull arrows
Of doddering fortunetellers!

                    No, Teiresias:
45 If your birds—if the great eagles of God himself
Should carry him stinking bit by bit to heaven,
I would not yield. I am not afraid of pollution:
No man can defile the gods.

                  Do what you will,
Go into business, make money, speculate

---

12. my debt to you: Creon is here admitting that he would not have acquired the throne if Teiresias had not moved the former king, Oedipus, to an investigation of his own background that led eventually to his downfall. The news of his personal history, uncovered with help from Teiresias, forced Oedipus into exile.

13. chair of augury: The seat near the temple from which Teiresias would deliver his predictions about the future. Augury was the skill of telling such fortunes from a consideration of omens like the flight of birds or the position of stars.

14. Hephaistos (he fes′ təs): The god of fire and the forge. He would be invoked, as he is here by Teiresias, for aid in the starting of ceremonial fires.

In India gold or that synthetic gold from
50 Sardis,[15]
Get rich otherwise than by my consent to
    bury him.
Teiresias, it is a sorry thing when a wise
    man
Sells his wisdom, lets out his words for
    hire!

TEIRESIAS. Ah Creon! Is there no man left
in the world—

CREON. To do what?—Come, let's have the
55 aphorism![16]

TEIRESIAS. No man who knows that wisdom
outweighs any wealth?

CREON. As surely as bribes are baser than
any baseness.

TEIRESIAS. You are sick, Creon! You are
deathly sick!

CREON. As you say: it is not my place to
challenge a prophet.

TEIRESIAS. Yet you have said my prophecy is
60 for sale.

CREON. The generation of prophets has
always loved gold.

TEIRESIAS. The generation of kings has
always loved brass.

CREON. You forget yourself! You are
speaking to your King.

TEIRESIAS. I know it. You are a king because
of me.

CREON. You have a certain skill; but you
65 have sold out.

TEIRESIAS. King, you will drive me to words
that—

CREON.   Say them, say them!
Only remember: I will not pay you for
them.

TEIRESIAS. No, you will find them too costly.

CREON.   No doubt. Speak:
Whatever you say, you will not change my
will.

TEIRESIAS. Then take this, and take it to
70 heart!
The time is not far off when you shall pay
back
Corpse for corpse, flesh of your own flesh.
You have thrust the child of this world into
living night,
You have kept from the gods below the
child that is theirs:
The one in a grave before her death, the
75 other,

---

15. Sardis (sär′ dis): Capital of ancient Lydia, which
produced the first coins made from an alloy of gold
and silver.
16. aphorism (af′ ə riz′m): A brief, insightful saying.
Creon is taunting the prophet and suggesting that the
old man is capable only of relying on trite,
meaningless expressions instead of any original
thinking.

Dead, denied the grave. This is your crime:
And the Furies[17] and the dark gods of Hell
Are swift with terrible punishment for you.

Do you want to buy me now, Creon?

                        Not many days,
And your house will be full of men and
80   women weeping,
And curses will be hurled at you from far
Cities grieving for sons unburied, left to rot
Before the walls of Thebes.

These are my arrows, Creon: they are all
    for you.

85 But come, child: lead me home.   [*To* BOY]
Let him waste his fine anger upon younger
    men.
Maybe he will learn at last
To control a wiser tongue in a better head.

[*Exit* TEIRESIAS.]

CHORAGOS. The old man has gone, King, but
    his words
90 Remain to plague us. I am old, too,
But I cannot remember that he was ever
    false.

CREON. That is true. . . . It troubles me.
Oh it is hard to give in! but it is worse
To risk everything for stubborn pride.

CHORAGOS. Creon: take my advice.

95 CREON.   What shall I do?

CHORAGOS. Go quickly: free Antigone from
    her vault
And build a tomb for the body of
    Polyneices.

CREON. You would have me do this?

CHORAGOS.   Creon, yes!

And it must be done at once: God moves
100 Swiftly to cancel the folly of stubborn men.

CREON. It is hard to deny the heart! But I
Will do it: I will not fight with destiny.

CHORAGOS. You must go yourself, you
    cannot leave it to others.

CREON. I will go.
                        —Bring axes, servants:
105 Come with me to the tomb. I buried her, I
Will set her free.
                        Oh quickly!
My mind misgives—
The laws of the gods are mighty, and a
    man must serve them
To the last day of his life!

[*Exit* CREON.]

Pæan

CHORAGOS.   [STROPHE 1]
God of many names

CHORUS.   O Iacchos[18]
                              son
of Kadmeian Semele[19]
                        O born of the Thunder!
Guardian of the West
                        Regent
of Eleusis' plain[20]
                        O Prince of maenad Thebes[21]

_____

17. Furies (fyŏor′ ēz): The goddesses of vengence,
who made insane those whose crimes were
unpunished, especially those who had sinned against
their own families.

_____

18. Iacchos (ē′ ə kəs): One of several alternate
names for Dionysos.
19. Kadmeian Semele (sem′ ə lē′): Semele was a
mortal and the mother of Dionysos. She was the
daughter of Thebes' founder, Kadmos.
20. Eleusis' (i lōo′ sis) **plain:** Located north of
Athens, this plain was a site of worship for Dionysos
and Demeter, gods who protected the harvests of
grapes and corn.
21. maenad (mē′ nad) **Thebes:** The city is here
compared to a maenad, one of Dionysos' female
worshipers. Such a follower would be thought of as
uncontrolled or disturbed, much as Thebes was while
being upset by the civil war.

and the Dragon Field by rippling
5   Ismenos:[22]

CHORAGOS.   [ANTISTROPHE 1]
God of many names

CHORUS.   the flame of torches
flares on our hills
                    the nymphs of Iacchos
dance at the spring of Castalia:[23]

from the vine-close mountain
                    come ah come in ivy:
Evohe evohe![24] sings through the streets of
10   Thebes

CHORAGOS.   [STROPHE 2]
God of many names

CHORUS.   Iacchos of Thebes
heavenly Child
            of Semele bride of the Thunderer!
The shadow of plague is upon us:
                            come
with clement feet[25]
            oh come from Parnasos[26]
down the long slopes
15   across the lamenting water

CHORAGOS.   [ANTISTROPHE 2]
Io[27] Fire! Chorister of the throbbing stars!

---

22. Dragon Field . . . Ismenos (is mē′ nas): The Dragon Field was located by the banks of Ismenos, a river sacred to Apollo that flows near Thebes. The Dragon Field was where Kadmos miraculously created warriors by sowing the teeth of the dragon he killed there. Those men helped him establish the city.
23. Castalia (kas tā′ lē ə): Location of a site sacred to Apollo where his followers would worship.
24. Evohe (ē vō′ ē): A triumphant shout of affirmation (like "Amen") used at ceremonies dedicated to Dionysos.
25. clement feet: Clement means kind or favorable. The chorus is here asking Dionysos to step gently into the troubled path and to intervene in a healing manner.
26. Parnasos (pär nas′ əs): A mountain that was sacred to both Dionysos and Apollo. It is located in central Greece.
27. Io (ē′ ō): Greek word for "Behold" or "Hail."

O purest among the voices of the night!
Thou son of God, blaze for us!

CHORUS. Come with choric rapture of
    circling Maenads
Who cry *Io Iacche!*[28]
20   *God of many names!*

Exodos

[*Enter* MESSENGER, *left.*]

MESSENGER. Men of the line of Kadmos,[29]
    you who live
Near Amphion's citadel:[30]
                    I cannot say
Of any condition of human life "This is fixed,
This is clearly good, or bad." Fate raises up,
And Fate casts down the happy and
5   unhappy alike:
No man can foretell his Fate.
                    Take the case of Creon:
Creon was happy once, as I count happiness:
Victorious in battle, sole governor of the land,
Fortunate father of children nobly born.
And now it has all gone from him! Who
10   can say
That a man is still alive when his life's joy fails?
He is a walking dead man. Grant him rich,
Let him live like a king in his great house:
If his pleasure is gone, I would not give

---

28. Io Iacche (ē ō ē′ ə kē): A cry of celebration used by Dionysian worshipers.
29. Kadmos (kad′ məs): Founder of the city of Thebes whose daughter, Semele, gave birth to Dionysos.
30. Amphion's (am fī′ ən) **citadel:** Amphion was a king of Thebes who is credited with erecting the walls of the fortress, or citadel, by using his lyre so magically that its music caused the stones to move themselves into proper place.

So much as the shadow of smoke for all he
15   owns.

CHORAGOS. Your words hint at sorrow: what
   is your news for us?

MESSENGER. They are dead. The living are
   guilty of their death.

CHORAGOS. Who is guilty? Who is dead?
   Speak!

MESSENGER. Haimon.
Haimon is dead; and the hand that killed
   him
Is his own hand.

20 **CHORAGOS.**   His father's? or his own?

MESSENGER. His own, driven mad by the
   murder his father had done.

CHORAGOS. Teiresias, Teiresias, how clearly
   you saw it all!

MESSENGER. This is my news: you must
   draw what conclusions you can from it.

CHORAGOS. But look: Eurydice, our Queen:
25 Has she overheard us?

[*Enter* EURYDICE *from the Palace, center.*]

EURYDICE. I have heard something, friends:
As I was unlocking the gate of Pallas'[31]
   shrine,

For I needed her help today, I heard a voice
Telling of some new sorrow. And I fainted
There at the temple with all my maidens
30   about me.
But speak again: whatever it is, I can bear
   it:
Grief and I are no strangers.

MESSENGER.   Dearest Lady,
I will tell you plainly all that I have seen.
I shall not try to comfort you: what is the
   use,
Since comfort could lie only in what is not
35   true?
The truth is always best.
                  I went with Creon
To the outer plain where Polyneices was
   lying,
No friend to pity him, his body shredded by
   dogs.
We made our prayers in that place to
   Hecate[32]
And Pluto,[33] that they would be merciful.
40   And we bathed
The corpse with holy water, and we
   brought
Fresh-broken branches to burn what was
   left of it,
And upon the urn we heaped up a towering
   barrow
Of the earth of his own land.
              When we were done, we ran
To the vault where Antigone lay on her
45   couch of stone.
One of the servants had gone ahead,
And while he was yet far off he heard a
   voice
Grieving within the chamber, and he came
   back
And told Creon. And as the King went
   closer,

---

31. Pallas (pal' əs): Pallas Athena, the goddess of
wisdom.

32. Hecate (hek' ə tē): A goddess of the underworld.
33. Pluto (plo͞ot' ō): God of the underworld who
managed the souls of the departed.

50 The air was full of wailing, the words lost,
   And he begged us to make all haste. "Am I
      a prophet?"
   He said, weeping, "And must I walk this
      road,
   The saddest of all that I have gone before?
   My son's voice calls me on. Oh quickly,
      quickly!
   Look through the crevice there, and tell me
55 If it is Haimon, or some deception of the
      gods!"

   We obeyed; and in the cavern's farthest
      corner
   We saw her lying:
   She had made a noose of her fine linen veil
   And hanged herself. Haimon lay beside
60   her,
   His arms about her waist, lamenting her,
   His love lost underground, crying out
   That his father had stolen her away from
      him.

   When Creon saw him the tears rushed to
      his eyes
   And he called to him: "What have you
65   done, child? Speak to me.
   What are you thinking that makes your
      eyes so strange?
   O my son, my son, I come to you on my
      knees!"
   But Haimon spat in his face. He said not a
      word,
   Staring—
               And suddenly drew his sword
   And lunged. Creon shrank back, the blade
70   missed; and the boy,
   Desperate against himself, drove it half its
      length
   Into his own side, and fell. And as he died
   He gathered Antigone close in his arms
      again,
   Choking, his blood bright red on her white
      cheek.
   And now he lies dead with the dead, and
75   she is his

At last, his bride in the houses of the dead.

[*Exit* EURYDICE *into the Palace.*]

CHORAGOS. She has left us without a word.
   What can this mean?

MESSENGER. It troubles me, too; yet she
   knows what is best,
Her grief is too great for public
   lamentation,
And doubtless she has gone to her
80   chamber to weep
For her dead son, leading her maidens in
   his dirge.
CHORAGOS. It may be so: but I fear this deep
   silence.

[*Pause*]

MESSENGER. I will see what she is doing. I
   will go in.

[*Exit* MESSENGER *into the Palace.*]

[*Enter* CREON *with attendants, bearing* HAI-
MON's *body.*]

CHORAGOS. But here is the King himself: oh
   look at him,
85 Bearing his own damnation in his arms.
CREON. Nothing you say can touch me any
   more.
My own blind heart has brought me
From darkness to final darkness. Here you
   see
The father murdering, the murdered son—
90 And all my civic wisdom!

Haimon my son, so young, so young to die,
I was the fool, not you; and you died for
   me.

CHORAGOS. That is the truth; but you were
   late in learning it.

CREON. This truth is hard to bear. Surely a
   god
Has crushed me beneath the hugest weight
95   of heaven,
And driven me headlong a barbaric way

To trample out the thing I held most dear.

The pains that men will take to come to pain!

[*Enter* MESSENGER *from the Palace.*]

MESSENGER. The burden you carry in your hands is heavy,
But it is not all: you will find more in your
100 house.

CREON. What burden worse than this shall I find there?

MESSENGER. The Queen is dead.

CREON. O port of death, deaf world,
Is there no pity for me? And you, Angel of evil,
I was dead, and your words are death
105 again.
Is it true, boy? Can it be true?
Is my wife dead? Has death bred death?

MESSENGER. You can see for yourself.

[*The doors are opened, and the body of* EURYDICE *is disclosed within.*]

CREON. Oh pity!
All true, all true, and more than I can
110 bear!
O my wife, my son!

MESSENGER. She stood before the altar, and her heart
Welcomed the knife her own hand guided,
And a great cry burst from her lips for Megareus[34] dead,
And for Haimon dead, her sons; and her
115 last breath
Was a curse for their father, the murderer of her sons.
And she fell, and the dark flowed in through her closing eyes.

CREON. O God, I am sick with fear.

———————

34. Megareus (mə ga′ rē əs): Oldest son of Creon and Eurydice, who was killed in the civil war by Argive forces invading Thebes.

Are there no swords here? Has no one a blow for me?

MESSENGER. Her curse is upon you for the
120 deaths of both.

CREON. It is right that it should be. I alone am guilty.
I know it, and I say it. Lead me in,
Quickly, friends.
I have neither life nor substance. Lead me in.

CHORAGOS. You are right, if there can be
125 right in so much wrong.
The briefest way is best in a world of sorrow.

CREON. Let it come,
Let death come quickly, and be kind to me.
I would not ever see the sun again.

CHORAGOS. All that will come when it will;
130 but we, meanwhile,
Have much to do. Leave the future to itself.

CREON. All my heart was in that prayer!

CHORAGOS. Then do not pray any more: the sky is deaf.

CREON. Lead me away. I have been rash and foolish.
135 I have killed my son and my wife.
I look for comfort; my comfort lies here dead.
Whatever my hands have touched has come to nothing.
Fate has brought all my pride to a thought of dust.

[*As* CREON *is being led into the house, the* CHORAGOS *advances and speaks directly to the audience.*]

CHORAGOS. There is no happiness where there is no wisdom;
140 No wisdom but in submission to the gods.
Big words are always punished,
And proud men in old age learn to be wise.

RESPONDING TO THE SELECTION

Your Response

1. In Scene 3 Creon and Haimon express very different points of view. Which character's feelings do you most share? Explain.
2. Would you change the ending of this play in any way? Explain.

Recalling

3. According to Teiresias, what terrible punishment awaits Creon? What action does Creon take after Teiresias' prophecy?
4. What does the messenger tell Eurydice before she leaves the stage during the Exodos?

Interpreting

5. Explain the conflicts that drive Haimon to such extremes. Does he seem more concerned with the divine law to which Antigone turns for justification of her defiance or with the human law created by his father's power? Find support for your answer.
6. Toward the end of the Exodos, Creon says, "I have neither life nor substance." Why does he say that? In what ways has he been changed by the fate that altered his life?
7. Fate is said to dictate certain actions in the play. How great a role do you think Sophocles intended fate to have in determining the outcome of his story? Explain your answer.
8. The issue of individual conscience versus delegated authority, or human versus divine law, is at the center of this play. Explain the tensions that exist, and tell why you think one side has greater appeal than the other.

Applying

9. Antigone and Creon may be said to share at least one quality: an unwillingness to seem weak. Do you know anyone who is like that? How does that trait seem to influence the person's outlook on life?
10. On page 304 Creon says, "The pains that men will take to come to pain!" How do his words apply to contemporary society?

ANALYZING LITERATURE

Examining a Tragic Character

A tragic character is one who suffers a downfall. This character is marked with a tragic flaw that brings about his or her doom. The person may or may not be morally, physically, or intellectually superior. However, the character should be a significant presence in the play.

1. In your opinion, who is brought down most completely at the conclusion of the action? Find evidence to support your answer.
2. What is this character's tragic flaw? How does this flaw lead to the character's downfall?
3. What role, if any, does fate play in leading to the downfall?

CRITICAL THINKING AND READING

Predicting Outcomes

Some readers find the end of *Antigone* predictable. Others are shocked by a conclusion that seems more violent than what was expected.

1. (a) Did you guess how the play would end? (b) How accurate was your estimate?
2. Do you think that Sophocles was bound to have his characters ruined in so bloody a way? Why?

THINKING AND WRITING

Writing a Different Ending

Create a brief final speech (10–20 lines) in which the messenger will have a last chance to comment on the action. List three or four things that he will mention in the speech. You might begin with the line: "I shall go now over the world's paths to tell a sad story of . . ."

Before you revise, ask yourself the following: Has the messenger kept his remarks consistent with the vocabulary and voice of his early statements? Have the comments expressed some of the sentiments that viewers would expect? Has he clearly made a final comment on the outcome of the tragedy? Then proofread your paper and prepare a final draft.

Julius Caesar

The Tragedy of Julius Caesar is based on historical facts of the first century B.C. Julius Caesar (100?–44 B.C.), a brilliant military and political strategist, won a number of high offices. He was popular with the people but unpopular with his former political allies, who were jealous of him. William Shakespeare took the facts, which he found in a translation of *Plutarch's Lives of the Noble Greeks and Romans,* and developed them into a play. At the beginning of the play, the Roman Republic is at peace. In the course of the play, one man is assassinated and many others die. In *Julius Caesar,* Shakespeare was less concerned with the interplay of these events than he was with the motives of the protagonists. The play, therefore, is not so much about the life and death of the dictator Caesar but about the minds and motives of Caesar's murderers.

The Theater in Shakespeare's Day

Julius Caesar, like most of Shakespeare's plays, was produced in a public theater. Public theaters were built around roofless courtyards without artificial light. Performances, therefore, were given only during daylight hours. Surrounding the courtyard were three levels of galleries with benches where wealthier playgoers sat. Poorer spectators, called groundlings, stood and watched a play from the courtyard, which was called the pit.

Most of Shakespeare's plays were performed in the Globe Theatre. No one is certain exactly what the Globe looked like, though Shakespeare tells us it was round or octagonal. We know that it was open to the sky and held between 2,500 and 3,000 people. The discovery of its foundation in 1990 was exciting because the eventual excavation will reveal clues about the plays, the actors, and the audience. The tiny part of the foundation initially uncovered yielded a great number of hazelnut shells. Hazelnuts were Elizabethan popcorn; people munched on them all during a performance.

The stage was a platform that extended into the pit. Actors entered and left the stage from doors located behind the platform. The portion of the galleries behind and above the stage was used primarily as dressing and storage rooms. The second-level gallery right above the stage, however, was used as an upper stage. There was no scenery in the theaters of Shakespeare's day. Settings were indicated by references in the dialogue. As a result, one scene could follow another in rapid succession. The actors wore elaborate clothing—typical Elizabethan clothing, not costuming. Thus, the plays

SWAN THEATRE, LONDON, c. 1596
Drawing by Johannes DeWitt
The Granger Collection

produced in Shakespeare's day were fast-paced, colorful productions. Usually a play lasted two hours.

An important difference between Shakespeare's theater and today's is that acting companies of the sixteenth century were made up only of men and boys. Women did not perform on the stage, as it was not considered proper. Boys of eleven, twelve, or thirteen— before their voices changed—performed the female roles.

Some Common Elizabethan Words

The English language was somewhat different during Shakespeare's time. As you read *Julius Caesar,* most of the unfamiliar words and phrases you will encounter are explained in footnotes. The following, however, appear so frequently that learning them now will make your reading of the play easier.

anon: Soon	hither: Here
aye: Yes	marry: Indeed
betimes: Right now	prithee: Pray thee
e'en: Even	sooth: Truly
e'er: Ever	withal: In addition
hence: Away, from here	wont: Accustomed
hie: Hurry	

GUIDE FOR READING

William Shakespeare

(1564–1616) was born in Stratford-on-Avon, England. Little is known about his personal life, except that he married Anne Hathaway, became the father of three, and went to London to work as an actor, a playwright, and a poet. Despite the majesty of his poetry, Shakespeare was above all a playwright. His knowledge of acting and audiences gave him a great insight into what was dramatically workable. Shakespeare based *The Tragedy of Julius Caesar* on actual events that occurred in Rome in 44 B.C.

The Tragedy of Julius Caesar, Act I

Blank Verse

Blank verse is a poetic form written in the metrical pattern of iambic pentameter. *Iambic* means that an unaccented or unstressed syllable is followed by an accented or stressed one. *Pentameter* means that there are five iambs per line. In the following lines, / labels a stressed syllable and ∪ an unstressed one.

What tributaries follow him to Rome

To grace in captive bonds his chariot-wheels?
(Act I, Scene i, lines 34–35)

Focus

Shakespeare's work is the source of many well-known sayings. The following famous quotation, for instance, occurs in Act I, Scene ii: "The fault, dear Brutus, is not in our stars, / But in ourselves, that we are underlings." With a group of students, speculate on the meaning of this quotation. Then read Act I to see whether you were correct.

Vocabulary

Knowing the following words will help you as you read Act I of *The Tragedy of Julius Caesar*.

replication (rep' lə kā' shən) *n.*: Echo or reverberation (p. 311)

mettle (met' 'l) *n.*: Basic character (p. 311)

spare (sper) *adj.*: Lean or thin (p. 318)

infirmity (in fʉr' mə tē) *n.*: Bodily weakness (p. 320)

tempests (tem' pists) *n.*: Violent windstorms often with rain, snow, or hail (p. 322)

surly (sʉr' lē) *adv.*: In a proud, commanding way (p. 322)

portentous (pôr ten' təs) *adj.*: Foreboding; full of unspecified meaning (p. 322)

prodigious (prə dij' əs) *adj.*: Impressively forceful (p. 324)

The Tragedy of Julius Caesar

William Shakespeare

CHARACTERS

Julius Caesar
Octavius Caesar ⎱ triumvirs* after
Marcus Antonius ⎰ the death of
M. Aemilius Lepidus ⎰ Julius Caesar

Cicero
Publius ⎰ senators
Popilius Lena ⎰

Marcus Brutus
Cassius
Casca
Trebonius ⎰ conspirators against
Ligarius ⎰ Julius Caesar
Decius Brutus
Metellus Cimber

Cinna
Flavius ⎰ tribunes
Marullus ⎰

Artemidorus of Cnidos,
    a teacher of rhetoric

A Soothsayer
Cinna, a poet
Another Poet

Lucilius
Titinius ⎰ friends
Messala ⎰ to Brutus
Young Cato ⎰ and Cassius
Volumnius

Varro
Clitus
Claudius ⎰ servants
Strato ⎰ to Brutus
Lucius
Dardanius

Pindarus, servant to Cassius
Calpurnia, wife to Caesar
Portia, wife to Brutus
Senators, Citizens, Guards,
    Attendants, and so on

Scene: During most of the play, at Rome;
afterward near Sardis, and near Philippi.

---

*triumvirs (trī um′ vərz) *n.*: In ancient Rome, a group
of three rulers who share authority equally.

Act I

Scene i. *Rome. A street.*

[Enter Flavius, Marullus, and certain Commoners[1] over the stage.]

FLAVIUS. Hence! Home, you idle creatures, get you home!
    Is this a holiday? What, know you not,
    Being mechanical,[2] you ought not walk
    Upon a laboring day without the sign
5   Of your profession?[3] Speak, what trade art thou?

CARPENTER. Why, sir, a carpenter.

MARULLUS. Where is thy leather apron and thy rule?
    What dost thou with thy best apparel on?
    You, sir, what trade are you?

10 COBBLER. Truly, sir, in respect of a fine workman,[4] I am
    but, as you would say, a cobbler.[5]

MARULLUS. But what trade art thou? Answer me directly.

COBBLER. A trade, sir, that, I hope, I may use with a safe
    conscience, which is indeed, sir, a mender of bad
15   soles.

FLAVIUS. What trade, thou knave?[6] Thou naughty knave,
    what trade?

COBBLER. Nay, I beseech you, sir, be not out with me: yet,
    if you be out,[7] sir, I can mend you.[8]

MARULLUS. What mean'st thou by that? Mend me, thou
    saucy fellow?

20 COBBLER. Why, sir, cobble you.

FLAVIUS. Thou art a cobbler, art thou?

COBBLER. Truly, sir, all that I live by is with the awl:[9] I
    meddle with no tradesman's matters, nor women's
    matters; but withal, I am indeed, sir, a surgeon to old
25   shoes: when they are in great danger, I recover them.
    As proper men as ever trod upon neat's leather[10]
    have gone upon my handiwork.

FLAVIUS. But wherefore art not in thy shop today?
    Why dost thou lead these men about the streets?

1. commoners (käm′ ən ərz) *n.:* People not of the nobility or upper classes.

2. mechanical: Of the working class.

3. sign/Of your profession: Work clothes and tools.

4. in respect of a fine workman: In relation to a skilled worker.
5. cobbler: Mender of shoes or a clumsy, bungling worker.

6. knave (nāv) *n.:* A tricky rascal; a rogue.
7. be not out . . . if you be out: Be not angry . . . if you have worn-out shoes.
8. mend you: Mend your shoes or improve your disposition.

9. awl (ôl) *n.:* A small, pointed tool for making holes in leather.

10. neat's leather: Leather made from the hides of cattle.

COBBLER. Truly, sir, to wear out their shoes, to get
30   myself into more work. But indeed, sir, we make
holiday to see Caesar and to rejoice in his triumph.[11]

MARULLUS. Wherefore rejoice? What conquest brings he
home?

What tributaries[12] follow him to Rome,
35   To grace in captive bonds his chariot wheels?
You blocks, you stones, you worse than senseless
    things!
O you hard hearts, you cruel men of Rome,
Knew you not Pompey?[13] Many a time and oft
Have you climbed up to walls and battlements,
40   To tow'rs and windows, yea, to chimney tops,
Your infants in your arms, and there have sat
The livelong day, with patient expectation,
To see great Pompey pass the streets of Rome.
And when you saw his chariot but appear,
45   Have you not made an universal shout,
That Tiber[14] trembled underneath her banks
To hear the replication of your sounds
Made in her concave shores?[15]
And do you now put on your best attire?
50   And do you now cull out[16] a holiday?
And do you now strew flowers in his way
That comes in triumph over Pompey's blood?[17]
Be gone!
Run to your houses, fall upon your knees,
55   Pray to the gods to intermit the plague[18]
That needs must light on this ingratitude.

FLAVIUS. Go, go, good countrymen, and, for this fault,
Assemble all the poor men of your sort;
Draw them to Tiber banks and weep your tears
60   Into the channel, till the lowest stream
Do kiss the most exalted shores of all.[19]

                         [*All the Commoners exit.*]
See, whe'r their basest mettle[20] be not moved,
They vanish tongue-tied in their guiltiness.
Go you down that way toward the Capitol;
65   This way will I. Disrobe the images,
If you do find them decked with ceremonies.[21]

MARULLUS. May we do so?
You know it is the feast of Lupercal.[22]

11. triumph (trī′ əmf) *n.*:
In ancient Rome, a
procession celebrating the
return of a victorious
general and his army.

12. tributaries trib′ yoo
ter′ ēz) *n.*: Captives.

13. Pompey (päm′ pē): A
Roman general and
triumvir defeated by Caesar
in 48 B.C. and later
murdered.

14. Tiber (tī′ bər): River
that flows through Rome.
15. concave shores:
hollowed-out banks;
overhanging banks.
16. cull out: Pick out;
select.

17. Pompey's blood:
Pompey's sons, whom
Caesar has just defeated.
18. intermit the plague
(plāg): Stop the calamity or
trouble.

**19. the most exalted
shores of all:** The highest
banks.
**20. whe'r their basest
mettle:** Whether the most
inferior material of which
they are made.
**21. Disrobe the
images . . . decked with
ceremonies:** Strip the
statues . . . covered with
decorations.
22. feast of Lupercal
(loo′ pər kal): An ancient
Roman festival celebrated
on February 15.

FLAVIUS. It is no matter; let no images

70 Be hung with Caesar's trophies. I'll about

And drive away the vulgar[23] from the streets;

So do you too, where you perceive them thick.

These growing feathers plucked from Caesar's wing

Will make him fly an ordinary pitch,[24]

75 Who else would soar above the view of men

And keep us all in servile fearfulness. [*Exit.*]

Scene ii. *A public place.*

[*Enter Caesar, Antony (for the course),[1] Calpurnia, Portia, Decius, Cicero, Brutus, Cassius, Casca, a Soothsayer; after them, Marullus and Flavius.*]

CAESAR. Calpurnia!

CASCA. Peace, ho! Caesar speaks.

CAESAR. Calpurnia!

CALPURNIA. Here, my lord.

CAESAR. Stand you directly in Antonius' way

When he doth run his course. Antonius!

5 **ANTONY.** Caesar, my lord?

CAESAR. Forget not in your speed, Antonius,

To touch Calpurnia; for our elders say

The barren, touchèd in this holy chase,

Shake off their sterile curse.[2]

ANTONY. I shall remember:

10 When Caesar says "Do this," it is performed.

CAESAR. Set on, and leave no ceremony out.

SOOTHSAYER. Caesar!

CAESAR. Ha! Who calls?

CASCA. Bid every noise be still; peace yet again!

15 **CAESAR.** Who is it in the press[3] that calls on me?

I hear a tongue, shriller than all the music,

Cry "Caesar." Speak; Caesar is turned to hear.

SOOTHSAYER. Beware the ides of March.[4]

CAESAR. What man is that?

BRUTUS. A soothsayer bids you beware the ides of March.

23. vulgar (vul′ gər) *n.*: The common people.

24. pitch: The upward flight of a hawk.

1. for the course: Ready for the footrace that was part of the Lupercal festivities.

2. barren . . . sterile curse: It was believed that women who were unable to bear children (such as Calpurnia), if touched by a runner during this race, would then be able to bear children.

3. press *n.*: Crowd.

4. ides (īdz) **of March:** March 15.

20   **CAESAR.** Set him before me; let me see his face.

CASSIUS. Fellow, come from the throng; look upon
      Caesar.

CAESAR. What say'st thou to me now? Speak once again.

SOOTHSAYER. Beware the ides of March.

CAESAR. He is a dreamer, let us leave him. Pass.
    [*A trumpet sounds. Exit all but Brutus and Cassius.*]

25   **CASSIUS.** Will you go see the order of the course?[5]

    5. order of the course: The race.

BRUTUS. Not I.

CASSIUS. I pray you do.

BRUTUS. I am not gamesome:[6] I do lack some part
    Of that quick spirit[7] that is in Antony.
30   Let me not hinder, Cassius, your desires;
    I'll leave you.

    6. gamesome (gām' səm) *adj.*: Having a liking for sports.
    7. quick spirit: Lively disposition.

The Tragedy of Julius Caesar, Act I, Scene ii   313

CASSIUS. Brutus, I do observe you now of late;
  I have not from your eyes that gentleness
  And show of love as I was wont[8] to have;
35 You bear too stubborn and too strange a hand[9]
  Over your friend that loves you.

BRUTUS.   Cassius,
  Be not deceived: if I have veiled my look,
  I turn the trouble of my countenance
  Merely upon myself.[10] Vexèd I am
40 Of late with passions[11] of some difference,[12]
  Conceptions only proper to myself,[13]
  Which give some soil,[14] perhaps, to my behaviors;
  But let not therefore my good friends be grieved
  (Among which number, Cassius, be you one)
45 Nor construe any further my neglect
  Than that poor Brutus, with himself at war,
  Forgets the shows of love to other men.

CASSIUS. Then, Brutus, I have much mistook your pas-
    sion;
  By means whereof this breast of mine hath buried[15]
50 Thoughts of great value, worthy cogitations.[16]
  Tell me, good Brutus, can you see your face?

BRUTUS. No, Cassius; for the eye sees not itself
  But by reflection, by some other things.

CASSIUS. 'Tis just.[17]
55 And it is very much lamented,[18] Brutus,
  That you have no such mirrors as will turn
  Your hidden worthiness into your eye,
  That you might see your shadow.[19] I have heard
  Where many of the best respect[20] in Rome
60 (Except immortal Caesar), speaking of Brutus,
  And groaning underneath this age's yoke,[21]
  Have wished that noble Brutus had his eyes.

BRUTUS. Into what dangers would you lead me, Cassius,
  That you would have me seek into myself
65 For that which is not in me?

CASSIUS. Therefore, good Brutus, be prepared to hear;
  And since you know you cannot see yourself
  So well as by reflection, I, your glass
  Will modestly discover to yourself
70 That of yourself which you yet know not of.[22]
  And be not jealous on[23] me, gentle Brutus:

8. wont (wōnt): Accustomed.

9. bear . . . hand: Treat too harshly and too like a stranger.

10. If I . . . upon myself: If I have been less open, my troubled face is due entirely to personal matters.

11. passions: Feelings; emotions.

12. of some difference: In conflict.

13. Conceptions . . . myself: Thoughts that concern only me.

14. soil: Blemish.

15. By means . . . buried: Because of which I have kept to myself.

16. cogitations (kăj′ ə tā′ shənz) *n.:* Thoughts.

17. 'Tis just: It is true.

18. lamented (lə men′ t'd) *v.:* Regretted.

19. turn . . . shadow: Reflect your hidden noble qualities so you could see their image.

20. the best respect: Most respected people.

21. this age's yoke: The tyranny of Caesar.

22. Will modestly . . . know not of: Will without exaggeration make known to you the qualities you have that you are unaware of.

23. be not jealous on: Do not be suspicious of.

Were I a common laughter,[24] or did use
To stale with ordinary oaths my love
To every new protester;[25] if you know
That I do fawn on men and hug them hard,
75 And after scandal[26] them; or if you know
That I profess myself in banqueting
To all the rout,[27] then hold me dangerous.

[*Flourish of trumpets and shout.*]

BRUTUS. What means this shouting? I do fear the people
Choose Caesar for their king.

80 **CASSIUS.**   Ay, do you fear it?
Then must I think you would not have it so.

BRUTUS. I would not, Cassius, yet I love him well.
But wherefore do you hold me here so long?
What is it that you would impart to me?
85 If it be aught toward the general good,[28]
Set honor in one eye and death i' th' other,
And I will look on both indifferently;[29]
For let the gods so speed me,[30] as I love
The name of honor more than I fear death.

90 **CASSIUS.** I know that virtue to be in you, Brutus,
As well as I do know your outward favor.[31]
Well, honor is the subject of my story.
I cannot tell what you and other men
Think of this life, but for my single self,
95 I had as lief not be,[32] as live to be
In awe of such a thing as I myself.[33]
I was born free as Caesar; so were you:
We both have fed as well, and we can both
Endure the winter's cold as well as he:
100 For once, upon a raw and gusty day,
The troubled Tiber chafing with[34] her shores,
Caesar said to me "Darest thou, Cassius, now
Leap in with me into this angry flood,
And swim to yonder point?" Upon the word,
105 Accout'red[35] as I was, I plungèd in
And bade him follow: so indeed he did.
The torrent roared, and we did buffet[36] it
With lusty sinews,[37] throwing it aside
And stemming it with hearts of controversy.[38]
110 But ere we could arrive the point proposed,
Caesar cried "Help me, Cassius, or I sink!"
I, as Aeneas,[39] our great ancestor,

24. common laughter:
Object of ridicule.
**25. To stale . . . new
protester:** To make cheap
my friendship to anyone
who promises to be my
friend.
26. scandal: Slander;
gossip about.
**27. profess myself . . .
rout:** Declare my
friendship to the common
crowd.

28. aught . . . good:
Anything to do with the
public welfare.
29. indifferently: Without
preference or concern.
30. speed: Give good
fortune to.

31. favor: Face;
appearance.

32. as lief not be: Just as
soon not exist.
**33. such a thing as
myself:** Another human
being (Caesar).
34. chafing with: Raging
against.
35. Accout'red: Dressed
in armor.
36. buffet (buf' it) *v.*:
Struggle against.
37. lusty sinews (sin'
yo͞oz): Strong muscles.
**38. stemming
it . . . controversy:** Making
progress against it with our
intense rivalry.
39. Aeneas (ē nē' əs):
Trojan hero of the poet
Virgil's epic poem *Aeneid*,
who carried his old father,
Anchises, from the burning
city of Troy and later
founded Rome.

Did from the flames of Troy upon his shoulder
The old Anchises bear, so from the waves of Tiber
115 Did I the tired Caesar. And this man
Is now become a god, and Cassius is
A wretched creature, and must bend his body
If Caesar carelessly but nod on him.
He had a fever when he was in Spain,
120 And when the fit was on him, I did mark
How he did shake: 'tis true, this god did shake.
His coward lips did from their color fly,[40]
And that same eye whose bend[41] doth awe the world
Did lose his[42] luster: I did hear him groan;
125 Ay, and that tongue of his, that bade the Romans
Mark him and write his speeches in their books,
Alas, it cried, "Give me some drink, Titinius,"
As a sick girl. Ye gods! It doth amaze me,
A man of such a feeble temper[43] should
130 So get the start of[44] the majestic world,
And bear the palm[45] alone.

[Shout. Flourish of trumpets.]

BRUTUS. Another general shout?
I do believe that these applauses are
For some new honors that are heaped on Caesar.

135 CASSIUS. Why, man, he doth bestride the narrow world
Like a Colossus,[46] and we petty men
Walk under his huge legs and peep about
To find ourselves dishonorable[47] graves.
Men at some time are masters of their fates:
140 The fault, dear Brutus, is not in our stars,[48]
But in ourselves, that we are underlings.[49]
Brutus and Caesar: what should be in that "Cae-
sar"?
Why should that name be sounded[50] more than
yours?
Write them together, yours is as fair a name;
145 Sound them, it doth become the mouth as well;
Weigh them, it is as heavy; conjure[51] with 'em,
"Brutus" will start[52] a spirit as soon as "Caesar."
Now, in the names of all the gods at once,
Upon what meat doth this our Caesar feed,
150 That he is grown so great? Age, thou art shamed!
Rome, thou hast lost the breed of noble bloods!
When went there by an age, since the great flood,[53]
But it was famed with[54] more than with one man?

40. His coward lips . . . fly: The color fled from his lips, which were like cowardly soldiers fleeing from a battle.
41. bend n.: Glance.
42. his: Its.
43. feeble temper: Weak physical constitution.
44. get the start of: Become the leader of.
45. palm: Symbol of victory; victor's prize.

46. Colossus (kə läs′ əs) n.: A gigantic statue of Apollo, a god of Greek and Roman mythology, which was set at the entrance to the harbor of Rhodes about 280 B.C. and included among the seven wonders of the ancient world.
47. dishonorable (dis än′ ər ə b′l) adj.: Shameful (because they will not be of free men).
48. stars: Destinies. The stars were thought to control people's lives.
49. underlings: Inferior people.
50. sounded: Spoken or announced by trumpets.
51. conjure (kän jər) v.: Summon a spirit by a magic spell.
52. start: Raise.
53. great flood: In Greek mythology a flood that drowned everyone except Deucalion and his wife Pyrrha, saved by the god Zeus because of their virtue.
54. But it was famed with: Without the age being made famous by.

When could they say (till now) that talked of Rome,
155 That her wide walks encompassed but one man?
Now is it Rome indeed, and room enough,
When there is in it but one only man.
O, you and I have heard our fathers say,
There was a Brutus[55] once that would have brooked[56]
160 Th' eternal devil to keep his state in Rome
As easily as a king.

BRUTUS. That you do love me, I am nothing jealous;[57]
What you would work me to,[58] I have some aim;[59]
How I have thought of this, and of these times,
165 I shall recount hereafter. For this present,
I would not so (with love I might entreat you)
Be any further moved. What you have said
I will consider; what you have to say
I will with patience hear, and find a time
170 Both meet to hear and answer such high things.
Till then, my noble friend, chew[60] upon this:
Brutus had rather be a villager
Than to repute himself a son of Rome
Under these hard conditions as this time
Is like to lay upon us.

175 CASSIUS.   I am glad
That my weak words have struck but thus much show
Of fire from Brutus.

[*Enter Caesar and his Train.*]

BRUTUS. The games are done, and Caesar is returning.

CASSIUS. As they pass by, pluck Casca by the sleeve,
180 And he will (after his sour fashion) tell you
What hath proceeded worthy note today.

BRUTUS. I will do so. But look you, Cassius,
The angry spot doth glow on Caesar's brow,
And all the rest look like a chidden train:[61]
185 Calpurnia's cheek is pale, and Cicero
Looks with such ferret[62] and such fiery eyes
As we have seen him in the Capitol,
Being crossed in conference[63] by some senators.

CASSIUS. Casca will tell us what the matter is.

190 CAESAR. Antonius.

ANTONY. Caesar?

55. Brutus: Lucius Junius Brutus had helped expel the last King of Rome and had helped found the Republic in 509 B.C.
56. brooked: Put up with.
57. nothing jealous: Not at all doubting.
58. work me to: Persuade me of.
59. aim: Idea.

60. chew upon: Think about.

61. chidden train: Scolded attendants.
62. ferret (fer′ it) *n.*: A small animal like a weasel with reddish eyes.
63. crossed in conference: Opposed in debate.

CAESAR. Let me have men about me that are fat,
Sleek-headed men, and such as sleep a-nights.
Yond Cassius has a lean and hungry look;
195   He thinks too much: such men are dangerous.

ANTONY. Fear him not, Caesar, he's not dangerous;
He is a noble Roman, and well given.[64]

64. well given: Well disposed.

CAESAR. Would he were fatter! But I fear him not.
Yet if my name were liable to fear,
200   I do not know the man I should avoid
So soon as that spare Cassius. He reads much,
He is a great observer, and he looks
Quite through the deeds[65] of men. He loves no plays,
As thou dost, Antony; he hears no music;
205   Seldom he smiles, and smiles in such a sort[66]
As if he mocked himself, and scorned his spirit
That could be moved to smile at anything.

65. looks . . . deeds of men: Sees through people's actions to their motives.
66. sort: Way.

Such men as he be never at heart's ease
Whiles they behold a greater than themselves,
210 And therefore are they very dangerous.
I rather tell thee what is to be feared
Than what I fear; for always I am Caesar.
Come on my right hand, for this ear is deaf,
And tell me truly what thou think'st of him.
[*A trumpet sounds. Caesar and his Train exit.*]

CASCA. You pulled me by the cloak; would you speak
215 with me?

BRUTUS. Ay, Casca; tell us what hath chanced[67] today,
That Caesar looks so sad.

CASCA. Why, you were with him, were you not?

BRUTUS. I should not then ask Casca what had chanced.

220 **CASCA.** Why, there was a crown offered him; and being
offered him, he put it by[68] with the back of his hand,
thus; and then the people fell a-shouting.

BRUTUS. What was the second noise for?

CASCA. Why, for that too.

225 **CASSIUS.** They shouted thrice; what was the last cry for?

CASCA. Why, for that too.

BRUTUS. Was the crown offered him thrice?

CASCA. Ay, marry, was't, and he put it by thrice, every
time gentler than other; and at every putting-by
230 mine honest neighbors shouted.

CASSIUS. Who offered him the crown?

CASCA. Why, Antony.

BRUTUS. Tell us the manner of it, gentle Casca.

CASCA. I can as well be hanged as tell the manner of it: it
235 was mere foolery; I did not mark it. I saw Mark
Antony offer him a crown—yet 'twas not a crown
neither, 'twas one of these coronets[69]—and, as I told
you, he put it by once; but for all that, to my thinking,
he would fain[70] have had it. Then he offered it to him
240 again; then he put it by again; but to my thinking, he
was very loath to lay his fingers off it. And then he
offered it the third time. He put it the third time by;

and still as he refused it, the rabblement[71] hooted,
and clapped their chopt[72] hands, and threw up their
sweaty nightcaps,[73] and uttered such a deal of stinking breath because Caesar refused the crown, that it
had, almost, choked Caesar; for he swounded[74] and
fell down at it. And for mine own part, I durst not
laugh, for fear of opening my lips and receiving the
bad air.

CASSIUS. But, soft,[75] I pray you; what, did Caesar
swound?

CASCA. He fell down in the market place, and foamed at
mouth, and was speechless.

BRUTUS. 'Tis very like he hath the falling-sickness.[76]

CASSIUS. No, Caesar hath it not; but you, and I,
And honest Casca, we have the falling-sickness.[77]

CASCA. I know not what you mean by that, but I am sure
Caesar fell down. If the tag-rag people[78] did not clap
him and hiss him, according as he pleased and
displeased them, as they use[79] to do the players in the
theater, I am no true man.

BRUTUS. What said he when he came unto himself?

CASCA. Marry, before he fell down, when he perceived
the common herd was glad he refused the crown, he
plucked me ope his doublet[80] and offered them his
throat to cut. An I had been a man of any occupation,[81] if I would not have taken him at a word, I
would I might go to hell among the rogues. And so he
fell. When he came to himself again, he said,
if he had done or said anything amiss, he desired their
worships to think it was his infirmity.[82] Three or four
wenches,[83] where I stood, cried "Alas, good soul!"
and forgave him with all their hearts; but there's no
heed to be taken of them; if Caesar had stabbed their
mothers, they would have done no less.

BRUTUS. And after that, he came thus sad away?

CASCA. Ay.

CASSIUS. Did Cicero say anything?

CASCA. Ay, he spoke Greek.

CASSIUS. To what effect?

71. **rabblement** (rab' 'l mənt) n.: Mob.
72. **chopt** (chäpt) adj.: Chapped.
73. **nightcaps:** Workers' caps.
74. **swounded:** Swooned; fainted.

75. **soft:** Slowly.

76. **falling-sickness:** Epilepsy.
77. **We have the falling sickness:** We are becoming helpless under Caesar's rule.

78. **tag-rag people:** The rabble.
79. **use:** Are accustomed.

80. **doublet** (dub' lit) n.: Closefitting jacket.
81. **An I . . . occupation:** If I had been a workingman (or a man of action).

82. **infirmity** (in fur' mə tē) n.: Weakness; ailment.
83. **wenches** (wench əz) n.: Young women.

CASCA. Nay, an I tell you that, I'll ne'er look you i' th' face again. But those that understood him smiled at one another and shook their heads; but for mine own part, it was Greek to me. I could tell you more news
285 too: Marullus and Flavius, for pulling scarfs off Caesar's images, are put to silence.[84] Fare you well. There was more foolery yet, if I could remember it.

CASSIUS. Will you sup with me tonight, Casca?

CASCA. No, I am promised forth.[85]

290 **CASSIUS.** Will you dine with me tomorrow?

CASCA. Ay, if I be alive, and your mind hold,[86] and your dinner worth the eating.

CASSIUS. Good; I will expect you.

CASCA. Do so. Farewell, both.   [*Exit.*]

295 **BRUTUS.** What a blunt[87] fellow is this grown to be!
He was quick mettle[88] when he went to school.

CASSIUS. So is he now in execution[89]
Of any bold or noble enterprise,
However he puts on this tardy form.[90]
300 This rudeness is a sauce to his good wit,[91]
Which gives men stomach to disgest[92] his words
With better appetite.

BRUTUS. And so it is. For this time I will leave you.
Tomorrow, if you please to speak with me,
305 I will come home to you; or if you will,
Come home to me, and I will wait for you.

CASSIUS. I will do so. Till then, think of the world.[93]
                    [*Exit Brutus.*]

Well, Brutus, thou art noble; yet I see
Thy honorable mettle may be wrought
310 From that it is disposed;[94] therefore it is meet
That noble minds keep ever with their likes;
For who so firm that cannot be seduced?
Caesar doth bear me hard,[95] but he loves Brutus.
If I were Brutus now, and he were Cassius,
315 He should not humor[96] me. I will this night,
In several hands,[97] in at his windows throw,
As if they came from several citizens,
Writings, all tending to the great opinion[98]

84. for pulling . . . silence: For taking decorations off statues of Caesar, have been silenced (by being forbidden to take part in public affairs, exiled, or perhaps even executed).
85. am promised forth: Have a previous engagement.
86. hold: Does not change.

87. blunt: Dull; not sharp.
88. quick mettle: Of a lively disposition.
89. execution (ek′ sə kyo͞o′ shən) *n*.: A carrying out; doing.
90. tardy form: Sluggish appearance.
91. wit: Intelligence.
92. disgest: Digest.

93. the world: The present state of affairs.

94. wrought . . . is disposed: Shaped (like iron) in a way different from its usual form.
95. bear me hard: Dislikes me.
96. humor me: Win me over.
97. several hands: Different handwritings.
98. tending to the great opinion: Pointing out the great respect.

That Rome holds of his name; wherein obscurely
320   Caesar's ambition shall be glancèd at.[99]
And after this, let Caesar seat him sure;[100]
For we will shake him, or worse days endure. [*Exit.*]

99. glancèd at: Hinted at.
100. seat him sure: Establish himself securely.

Scene iii. *A street.*

[*Thunder and lightning. Enter from opposite sides, Casca and Cicero.*]

CICERO. Good even, Casca; brought you Caesar home?
Why are you breathless? And why stare you so?

CASCA. Are not you moved, when all the sway of earth[1]
Shakes like a thing unfirm? O Cicero,
5   I have seen tempests, when the scolding winds
Have rived[2] the knotty oaks, and I have seen
Th' ambitious ocean swell and rage and foam,
To be exalted with[3] the threat'ning clouds;
But never till tonight, never till now,
10   Did I go through a tempest dropping fire.
Either there is a civil strife in heaven,
Or else the world, too saucy[4] with the gods,
Incenses[5] them to send destruction.

1. all the sway of earth: The stable order of earth.

2. have rived: Have split.

3. exalted with: Lifted up to.

4. saucy: Rude; impudent.
5. Incenses: Enrages.

CICERO. Why, saw you anything more wonderful?

15   CASCA. A common slave—you know him well by sight—
Held up his left hand, which did flame and burn
Like twenty torches joined, and yet his hand,
Not sensible of[6] fire, remained unscorched.
Besides—I ha' not since put up my sword—
20   Against[7] the Capitol I met a lion,
Who glazed[8] upon me and went surly by
Without annoying me. And there were drawn
Upon a heap[9] a hundred ghastly[10] women,
Transformèd with their fear, who swore they saw
25   Men, all in fire, walk up and down the streets.
And yesterday the bird of night[11] did sit
Even at noonday upon the market place,
Hooting and shrieking. When these prodigies[12]
Do so conjointly meet,[13] let not men say,
30   "These are their reasons, they are natural,"
For I believe they are portentous things
Unto the climate that they point upon.[14]

6. sensible of: Sensitive to.
7. Against: Opposite or near.
8. glazed: Stared.
9. were drawn . . . heap: Huddled together.
10. ghastly (gast' lē) *adj.*: Ghostlike; pale.
11. bird of night: Owl.
12. prodigies (prăd'ə jēz) *n.*: Extraordinary happenings.
13. conjointly meet: Occur at the same time and place.
14. portentous (pôr ten' təs) *. . .* **upon:** Bad omens for the country they point to.

CICERO. Indeed, it is a strange-disposèd[15] time:
But men may construe things after their fashion,[16]
35 Clean from the purpose[17] of the things themselves.
Comes Caesar to the Capitol tomorrow?

CASCA. He doth; for he did bid Antonius
Send word to you he would be there tomorrow.

CICERO. Good night then, Casca; this disturbèd sky
Is not to walk in.

40 CASCA.   Farewell, Cicero.   [*Exit Cicero.*]

[*Enter Cassius.*]

CASSIUS. Who's there?

CASCA.   A Roman.

CASSIUS.   Casca, by your voice.

CASCA. Your ear is good. Cassius, what night is this?

CASSIUS. A very pleasing night to honest men.

CASCA. Who ever knew the heavens menace so?

CASSIUS. Those that have known the earth so full of
45   faults.
For my part, I have walked about the streets,
Submitting me unto the perilous night,
And thus unbracèd,[18] Casca, as you see,
Have bared my bosom to the thunder-stone;[19]
50 And when the cross[20] blue lightning seemed to open
The breast of heaven, I did present myself
Even in the aim and very flash of it.

CASCA. But wherefore did you so much tempt the
heavens?
It is the part[21] of men to fear and tremble
55 When the most mighty gods by tokens send
Such dreadful heralds to astonish[22] us.

CASSIUS. You are dull, Casca, and those sparks of life
That should be in a Roman you do want,[23]
Or else you use not. You look pale, and gaze,
60 And put on fear, and cast yourself in wonder,[24]
To see the strange impatience of the heavens;
But if you would consider the true cause
Why all these fires, why all these gliding ghosts,
Why birds and beasts from quality and kind,[25]

15. strange-disposèd:
Abnormal.
16. construe . . . fashion:
Explain in their own way.
**17. Clean from the
purpose:** Different from
the real meaning.

18. unbracèd: With jacket
open.
19. thunder-stone:
Thunderbolt.
20. cross: Zigzag.

21. part: Role.

**22. by tokens . . . to
astonish:** By portentous
signs send such awful
announcements to frighten
and stun.
23. want: Lack.
24. put on . . . in wonder:
Show fear and are amazed.

**25. from quality and
kind:** Acting contrary to
their nature.

65 Why old men, fools, and children calculate,[26]
    Why all these things change from their ordinance,[27]
    Their natures and preformèd faculties,
    To monstrous quality,[28] why, you shall find
    That heaven hath infused them with these spirits[29]
70 To make them instruments of fear and warning
    Unto some monstrous state.[30]
    Now could I, Casca, name to thee a man
    Most like this dreadful night,
    That thunders, lightens, opens graves, and roars
75 As doth the lion in the Capitol;
    A man no mightier than thyself, or me,
    In personal action, yet prodigious grown
    And fearful,[31] as these strange eruptions are.

CASCA. 'Tis Caesar that you mean, is it not, Cassius?

80 CASSIUS. Let it be who it is; for Romans now
    Have thews[32] and limbs like to their ancestors;
    But, woe the while![33] Our fathers' minds are dead,
    And we are governed with our mothers' spirits;
    Our yoke and sufferance[34] show us womanish.

85 CASCA. Indeed, they say the senators tomorrow
    Mean to establish Caesar as a king;
    And he shall wear his crown by sea and land,
    In every place save here in Italy.

    CASSIUS. I know where I will wear this dagger then;
90 Cassius from bondage will deliver[35] Cassius.
    Therein,[36] ye gods, you make the weak most strong;
    Therein, ye gods, you tyrants do defeat.
    Nor stony tower, nor walls of beaten brass,
    Nor airless dungeon, nor strong links of iron,
95 Can be retentive to[37] the strength of spirit;
    But life, being weary of these worldly bars,
    Never lacks power to dismiss itself.
    If I know this, know all the world besides,
    That part of tyranny that I do bear
    I can shake off at pleasure.   [Thunder still.]

100 CASCA.   So can I;
    So every bondman in his own hand bears
    The power to cancel his captivity.

    CASSIUS. And why should Caesar be a tyrant then?
    Poor man, I know he would not be a wolf
105 But that he sees the Romans are but sheep;

26. calculate: Make predictions.
27. ordinance: Regular behavior.
28. preformèd . . . quality: Established function to unnatural behavior.
29. infused . . . spirits: Filled them with supernatural powers.
30. monstrous state: Abnormal condition of government.

31. fearful: Causing fear.

32. thews (t͞hyo͞oz) *n.:* Muscles or sinews; strength.
33. woe the while!: Alas for the times.
34. yoke and sufferance: Slavery and meek acceptance of it.

35. will deliver: Will set free.
36. Therein: In that way (by using his dagger on himself).

37. be retentive to: Confine.

He were no lion, were not Romans hinds.[38]
Those that with haste will make a mighty fire
Begin it with weak straws. What trash is Rome,
What rubbish and what offal,[39] when it serves
110   For the base matter[40] to illuminate
So vile a thing as Caesar! But, O grief,
Where hast thou led me? I, perhaps, speak this
Before a willing bondman; then I know
My answer must be made.[41] But I am armed,
115   And dangers are to me indifferent.

CASCA. You speak to Casca, and to such a man
That is no fleering tell-tale.[42] Hold, my hand.
Be factious[43] for redress of all these griefs,[44]
And I will set this foot of mine as far
As who goes farthest.   [*They clasp hands.*]

120   **CASSIUS.**   There's a bargain made.
Now know you, Casca, I have moved already
Some certain of the noblest-minded Romans
To undergo[45] with me an enterprise
Of honorable dangerous consequence;[46]
125   And I do know, by this[47] they stay for me
In Pompey's porch;[48] for now, this fearful night,
There is no stir or walking in the streets,
And the complexion of the element[49]
In favor's like[50] the work we have in hand,
130   Most bloody, fiery, and most terrible.

[*Enter Cinna.*]

CASCA. Stand close[51] awhile, for here comes one in haste.

CASSIUS. 'Tis Cinna; I do know him by his gait;[52]
He is a friend. Cinna, where haste you so?

CINNA. To find out you. Who's that? Metellus Cimber?

135   **CASSIUS.** No, it is Casca, one incorporate[53]
To our attempts. Am I not stayed[54] for, Cinna?

CINNA. I am glad on't.[55] What a fearful night is this!
There's two or three of us have seen strange sights.

CASSIUS. Am I not stayed for? Tell me.

CINNA.   Yes, you are.
140   O Cassius, if you could
But win the noble Brutus to our party—

---

38. hinds (hīndz) *n.*: Female deer; peasants; servants.

39. offal (ôf' 'l) *n.*: Garbage.

40. base matter: Inferior or low material; foundation materials.

41. speak this . . . answer must be made: Say this before a willing servant of Caesar's; then I know I will have to answer for my words.

42. fleering tell-tale: Sneering tattletale.

43. factious (fak' shəs) *adj.*: Active in forming a faction or a political party.

44. redress (rē' dres) **of all these griefs:** Setting right all these grievances.

45. undergo: Undertake.

46. consequence (kän' sə kwens') *n.*: Importance.

47. by this: By this time.

48. Pompey's porch: Portico of Pompey's Theater.

49. complexion of the element: Condition of the sky; weather.

50. In favor's like: In appearance is like.

51. close: Hidden.

52. gait (gāt) *n.*: Way of moving.

53. incorporate (in kôr' pər it) *adj.*: United.

54. stayed: Waited.

55. on't: Of it.

CASSIUS. Be you content. Good Cinna, take this paper,
And look you lay it in the praetor's chair,[56]
Where Brutus may but find it;[57] and throw this
145 In at his window; set this up with wax
Upon old Brutus'[58] statue. All this done,
Repair to Pompey's porch, where you shall find us.
Is Decius Brutus and Trebonius there?

CINNA. All but Metellus Cimber, and he's gone
150 To seek you at your house. Well, I will hie,
And so bestow these papers as you bade me.

CASSIUS. That done, repair to Pompey's Theater.

                              [Exit Cinna.]

Come, Casca, you and I will yet ere day
See Brutus at his house; three parts of him
155 Is ours already, and the man entire
Upon the next encounter yields him ours.

CASCA. O, he sits high in all the people's hearts;
And that which would appear offense[59] in us,
His countenance,[60] like richest alchemy,[61]
160 Will change to virtue and to worthiness.

CASSIUS. Him, and his worth, and our great need of him,
You have right well conceited.[62] Let us go,
For it is after midnight, and ere day
We will awake him and be sure of him.   *[Exit.]*

56. praetor's (prē′ tərz)
chair: Roman magistrate's
(or judge's) chair.
57. Where . . . find it:
Where only Brutus (as the
chief magistrate) will find it.
58. old Brutus: Lucius
Junius Brutus, the founder
of Rome.

59. offense (ə fens′) *n.*:
Crime.
60. countenance (koun′
tə nəns) *n.*: Support.
61. alchemy (al′ kə mē)
n.: An early form of
chemistry in which the
goal was to change baser
metals into gold.
62. conceited (kən sēt′
id): Understood.

RESPONDING TO THE **S**ELECTION

Your Response

1. What is your reaction to the sight that Cassius, Casca, and Cinna observe during a stormy night?

Recalling

2. Explain why the tribunes have nothing but contempt for the common people of Rome.
3. What warning does the soothsayer give? What is Caesar's reaction to this warning?
4. Summarize Casca's report of what happened at the games.

5. Whom does Cassius say the night of unnatural events is like?

Interpreting

6. How does Cassius feel about Caesar? Why does Caesar fear Cassius?
7. Why is Brutus' participation essential to Cassius? In what essential way is he different from Cassius?
8. How does Cassius try to win Brutus over? What is it in Brutus that allows this technique to be effective?
9. Why do you think Caesar refused the crown?
10. Compare and contrast the reactions of Cicero

and Casca to the violent storm. What do their reactions tell you about each man? How does the storm itself help advance the plot?

Applying

11. The philosopher Jeremy Bentham has written, "Tyranny and anarchy are never far asunder." First discuss the meaning of this quotation. Then explain how it relates to this play.

ANALYZING LITERATURE

Understanding Blank Verse

The metrical pattern of blank verse is *iambic pentameter*—five sets of an accented syllable following an unaccented one. It is the natural rhythm of English speech. This line, for instance, could occur in dialogue of any kind:

"Set him before me; let me see his face." (Act I, Scene ii, line 20)

Within this pattern, however, some variation allows for natural speech rhythms. This line, for example, ends with an extra unaccented syllable and is said to have a feminine ending:

"I know that virtue to be in you, Brutus." (Act I, Scene ii, line 90)

The following line contains examples of two other variations: (1) an accented syllable followed by an unaccented one at the beginning of the line and (2) *elision,* a sliding over of one syllable to fit the meter:

"Caesar cried, 'Help me, Cassius, or I sink!'" (Act I, Scene ii, line 111).

1. Analyze Marullus' speech in Act I, Scene i, lines 34–43. Mark stressed syllables with ′. Mark unstressed syllables with ˘.
2. Which characters in Act I speak in blank verse? Which speak in prose? What do you think is the reason for this difference?

CRITICAL THINKING AND READING

Interpreting the Effect of Imagery

In this act the impression the audience forms of Caesar comes mainly from the way in which other characters describe him, often with imagery rather than in direct terms. For example, look at Flavius' speech in Act I, Scene i, lines 73–76. Flavius compares Caesar to a menacing bird of prey circling above the Romans to keep them in their place. The image portrays Caesar as a tyrant and threat to Roman liberty.

Analyze the imagery in the following speeches of Cassius and discuss what they contribute to the audience's idea of Caesar.

1. Act I, Scene ii, lines 135–138
2. Act I, Scene iii, lines 103–111

THINKING AND WRITING

Writing Blank Verse

Using Shakespeare's blank verse as a model, write at least eight lines of blank verse. Describe the character traits of a real or an imagined historical figure. When you have revised, mark the metrical patterns of your blank verse with ′ and ˘. Read your verse aloud.

LEARNING OPTION

Cross-curricular Connection. Find out more about Julius Caesar—his life, his family, his military career, his rise to power, and the reforms he carried out when he was in power. Use your social studies textbook or resources from your library to find information. Write a short biography of Caesar or a feature article about him for a newspaper or magazine.

GUIDE FOR READING

The Tragedy of Julius Caesar, Act II

Dramatic Irony

The term *irony* comes from the Greek word *eironeia,* which means dissembling or feigning ignorance. Irony always involves a contrast, a discrepancy between what is expected and what actually occurs, between the apparent and the real. Such contrast may appear in many forms. Verbal irony, for example, involves what is said being different from, or opposite to, what is meant. Irony of situation presents a contrast between what appears to be true and what really is true. **Dramatic irony** occurs when a character fails to recognize realities that are clear to the audience. For example, in Act I, Scene ii, when the soothsayer warns Caesar to beware the ides of March, the audience realizes that Caesar should heed the warning, but Caesar dismisses him as only a dreamer. In Act I, Scene ii, the audience hears Cassius' plan to throw letters written in several different handwritings into Brutus' window. Brutus will think the letters came from Roman citizens, but the audience knows they were written by Cassius.

Focus

There are many references in this play to foretelling the future. Get together with a group of classmates and debate the following question: Is it possible to predict future events? Then have someone from your group report to your class on the results of this informal debate.

Vocabulary

Knowing the following words will help you as you read Act II of *The Tragedy of Julius Caesar.*

augmented (ôg ment' id) *v.:* Made greater (p. 329)

entreated (in trēt' id) *v.:* Begged; pleaded with (p. 330)

conspiracy (kən spir' ə sē) *n.:* (1) A group plotting a harmful act (2) Such a plot (p. 331)

resolution (rez' ə lōo' shən) *n.:* Strong determination (p. 332)

exploit (eks' ploit) *n.:* Act or deed, especially a heroic achievement (p. 338)

imminent (im' ə nənt) *adj.:* About to happen (p. 341)

emulation (em' yə lā' shən) *n.:* Old word for envy or jealousy (p. 343)

Act II

Scene i. *Rome.*

[*Enter Brutus in his orchard.*]

BRUTUS. What, Lucius, ho!
    I cannot, by the progress of the stars,
    Give guess how near to day. Lucius, I say!
    I would it were my fault to sleep so soundly.
5   When, Lucius, when? Awake, I say! What, Lucius!

[*Enter Lucius.*]

LUCIUS. Called you, my lord?

BRUTUS. Get me a taper in my study, Lucius.
    When it is lighted, come and call me here.

LUCIUS. I will, my lord.   [*Exit.*]

10 **BRUTUS.** It must be by his death; and for my part,
    I know no personal cause to spurn at[1] him,
    But for the general.[2] He would be crowned.
    How that might change his nature, there's the question.
    It is the bright day that brings forth the adder,[3]
15   And that craves[4] wary walking. Crown him that,
    And then I grant we put a sting in him
    That at his will he may do danger with.
    Th' abuse of greatness is when it disjoins
    Remorse from power;[5] and, to speak truth of Caesar,
20   I have not known when his affections swayed[6]
    More than his reason. But 'tis a common proof[7]
    That lowliness[8] is young ambition's ladder,
    Whereto the climber upward turns his face;
    But when he once attains the upmost round,
25   He then unto the ladder turns his back,
    Looks in the clouds, scorning the base degrees[9]
    By which he did ascend. So Caesar may;
    Then lest he may, prevent.[10] And, since the quarrel
    Will bear no color for the thing he is,[11]
30   Fashion it[12] thus: that what he is, augmented
    Would run to these and these extremities;[13]
    And therefore think him as a serpent's egg
    Which hatched, would as his kind grow mischievous,
    And kill him in the shell.

1. spurn at: Kick against; rebel.
2. the general: The public good.

3. adder (ad' ər) *n.:* A poisonous snake.
4. craves: Requires.

5. disjoins . . . power: Separates mercy from power.
6. affections swayed: Emotions ruled.
7. proof: Experience.
8. lowliness: Humility.
9. base degrees: Low steps or people in lower positions.
10. lest . . . prevent: In case he may, we must stop him.
11. the quarrel . . . no color: Our complaint cannot be justified in view of what he now is.
12. Fashion it: State the case.
13. extremities (ek strem' ə tēz) *n.:* Extremes (of tyranny).

[*Enter Lucius.*]

35 **LUCIUS.** The taper burneth in your closet,[14] sir.
    Searching the window for a flint,[15] I found
    This paper thus sealed up, and I am sure
    It did not lie there when I went to bed.
    [*Gives him the letter.*]

BRUTUS. Get you to bed again; it is not day.
40 Is not tomorrow, boy, the ides of March?

LUCIUS. I know not, sir.

BRUTUS. Look in the calendar and bring me word.

LUCIUS. I will, sir.   [*Exit.*]

BRUTUS. The exhalations[16] whizzing in the air
45 Give so much light that I may read by them.
    [*Opens the letter and reads.*]

    ''Brutus, thou sleep'st; awake, and see thyself.
    Shall Rome, &c.[17] Speak, strike, redress.
    Brutus, thou sleep'st; awake.''

    Such instigations[18] have been often dropped
50 Where I have took them up.
    ''Shall Rome, &c.'' Thus must I piece it out:[19]
    Shall Rome stand under one man's awe?[20] What,
        Rome?
    My ancestors did from the streets of Rome
    The Tarquin[21] drive, when he was called a king.
55 ''Speak, strike, redress.'' Am I entreated
    To speak and strike? O Rome, I make thee promise,
    If the redress will follow, thou receivest
    Thy full petition at the hand of[22] Brutus!

[*Enter Lucius.*]

LUCIUS. Sir, March is wasted fifteen days. [*Knock within.*]

60 **BRUTUS.** 'Tis good. Go to the gate; somebody knocks.
    [*Exit Lucius.*]

    Since Cassius first did whet[23] me against Caesar,
    I have not slept.
    Between the acting of a dreadful thing
    And the first motion,[24] all the interim is
65 Like a phantasma,[25] or a hideous dream.
    The genius and the mortal instruments[26]
    Are then in council, and the state of a man,

14. closet: Study.
15. flint: Stone used to start a fire.

16. exhalations (eks' hə lā' shənz) *n.*: Meteors.

17. & c.: et cetera (Latin for *and so forth.*)

18. instigations (in' stə gā' shənz) *n.*: Urgings, incitements, or spurs to act.
19. piece it out: Figure out the meaning.
20. under one man's awe: In fearful reverence of one man.
21. Tarquin (tär' kwin) King of Rome driven out by Lucius Junius Brutus, Brutus' ancestor.

22. Thy full . . . hand of: All you ask from.

23. whet (hwet) *v.*: Sharpen; incite.
24. motion: Idea; suggestion.
25. all the . . . a phantasma: All the time between seems like a nightmare.
26. mortal instruments: Bodily powers.

Like to a little kingdom, suffers then
The nature of an insurrection.[27]

[Enter Lucius.]

70 LUCIUS. Sir, 'tis your brother[28] Cassius at the door,
Who doth desire to see you.

BRUTUS.   Is he alone?

LUCIUS. No, sir, there are moe[29] with him.

BRUTUS.   Do you know them?

LUCIUS. No, sir; their hats are plucked about their ears,
And half their faces buried in their cloaks,
75 That by no means I may discover them
By any mark of favor.[30]

BRUTUS.   Let 'em enter. [Exit Lucius.]
They are the faction. O conspiracy,
Sham'st thou to show thy dang'rous brow by night,
When evils are most free? O, then by day
80 Where wilt thou find a cavern dark enough
To mask thy monstrous visage? Seek none, con-
spiracy;
Hide it in smiles and affability:
For if thou path, thy native semblance on,[31]
Not Erebus[32] itself were dim enough
85 To hide thee from prevention.[33]

[Enter the conspirators, Cassius, Casca, Decius, Cinna, Metellus Cimber, and Trebonius.]

CASSIUS. I think we are too bold upon[34] your rest.
Good morrow, Brutus; do we trouble you?

BRUTUS. I have been up this hour, awake all night.
Know I these men that come along with you?

90 CASSIUS. Yes, every man of them; and no man here
But honors you; and every one doth wish
You had but that opinion of yourself
Which every noble Roman bears of you.
This is Trebonius.

BRUTUS.   He is welcome hither.

CASSIUS. This, Decius Brutus.

95 BRUTUS.   He is welcome too.

27. insurrection (in′ sə
rek′ sɦən) *n.*: Revolt.

28. brother:
Brother-in-law (Cassius
was married to Brutus'
sister).

29. moe: More.

30. discover . . . favor:
Identify them by their
appearance.

**31. path . . . semblance
on:** Walk looking as you
normally do.
32. Erebus (er′ ə bəs):
The dark place between
earth and Hades.
33. prevention: Being
discovered and stopped.
34. upon: In interfering
with.

CASSIUS. This, Casca; this, Cinna; and this, Metellus Cimber.

BRUTUS. They are all welcome.
What watchful cares do interpose themselves
Betwixt your eyes and night?[35]

100 **CASSIUS.** Shall I entreat[36] a word?   *[They whisper.]*

DECIUS. Here lies the east; doth not the day break here?

CASCA. No.

CINNA. O, pardon, sir, it doth; and yon gray lines
That fret[37] the clouds are messengers of day.

105 **CASCA.** You shall confess that you are both deceived.
Here, as I point my sword, the sun arises,
Which is a great way growing on[38] the south,
Weighing[39] the youthful season of the year.
Some two months hence, up higher toward the north
110 He first presents his fire; and the high[40] east
Stands as the Capitol, directly here.

BRUTUS. Give me your hands all over, one by one.

CASSIUS. And let us swear our resolution.

BRUTUS. No, not an oath. If not the face of men,
115 The sufferance of our souls, the time's abuse[41]—
If these be motives weak, break off betimes,[42]
And every man hence to his idle bed.
So let high-sighted[43] tyranny range on
Till each man drop by lottery.[44] But if these
120 (As I am sure they do) bear fire enough
To kindle cowards and to steel with valor
The melting spirits of women, then, countrymen,
What need we any spur but our own cause
To prick us to redress?[45] What other bond
125 Than secret Romans, that have spoke the word,
And will not palter?[46] And what other oath
Than honesty to honesty engaged[47]
That this shall be, or we will fall for it?
Swear priests and cowards and men cautelous,[48]
130 Old feeble carrions[49] and such suffering souls
That welcome wrongs; unto bad causes swear
Such creatures as men doubt; but do not stain
The even[50] virtue of our enterprise,
Nor th' insuppressive mettle[51] of our spirits,
135 To think that or our cause or[52] our performance

35. watchful . . . night:
Worries that keep you from
sleep.
36. entreat (in trēt′) *v.*:
Speak.

37. fret (fret) *v.*: Decorate
with a pattern.

38. growing on: Tending
toward.
39. Weighing:
Considering.
40. high: Due.

**41. the face . . . time's
abuse:** The sadness on
men's faces, the suffering
of our souls, the present
abuses.
42. betimes: Quickly.
43. high-sighted:
Arrogant (as a hawk about
to swoop down on its prey).
44. by lottery: By chance
or in his turn.

45. prick us to redress:
Goad or spur us on to
correct these evils.
46. palter (pôl′ tər) *v.*: Talk
insincerely.
47. honesty engaged:
Personal honor pledged.
48. cautelous: Cautious.
49. carrions (kar′ ē ənz)
n.: Decaying flesh.

50. even: Constant.
51. insuppressive mettle:
Uncrushable courage.
52. or . . . or: Either our
cause or.

Did need an oath; when every drop of blood
That every Roman bears, and nobly bears,
Is guilty of a several bastardy[53]
If he do break the smallest particle
140   Of any promise that hath passed from him.

CASSIUS. But what of Cicero? Shall we sound[54] him?
I think he will stand very strong with us.

CASCA. Let us not leave him out.

CINNA.   No, by no means.

METELLUS. O, let us have him, for his silver hairs
145   Will purchase us a good opinion,
And buy men's voices to commend our deeds.
It shall be said his judgment ruled our hands;
Our youths and wildness shall no whit[55] appear,
But all be buried in his gravity.

150   **BRUTUS.** O, name him not! Let us not break with him;[56]
For he will never follow anything
That other men begin.

CASSIUS.   Then leave him out.

CASCA. Indeed, he is not fit.

DECIUS. Shall no man else be touched but only Caesar?

53. guilty . . . bastardy:
Is no true Roman.

54. sound him: Find out
his opinion.

55. no whit (hwit) *n.*: Not
the least bit.

56. break with him:
Confide in him.

155   **CASSIUS.** Decius, well urged. I think it is not meet
       Mark Antony, so well beloved of Caesar,
       Should outlive Caesar; we shall find of[57] him
       A shrewd contriver;[58] and you know, his means;
       If he improve[59] them, may well stretch so far
160   As to annoy[60] us all; which to prevent,
       Let Antony and Caesar fall together.
      BRUTUS. Our course will seem too bloody, Caius Cassius,
       To cut the head off and then hack the limbs,
       Like wrath in death and envy afterwards;[61]
165   For Antony is but a limb of Caesar.
       Let's be sacrificers, but not butchers, Caius.
       We all stand up against the spirit of Caesar,
       And in the spirit of men there is no blood.
       O, that we then could come by Caesar's spirit,[62]
170   And not dismember Caesar! But, alas,
       Caesar must bleed for it. And, gentle[63] friends,
       Let's kill him boldly, but not wrathfully;
       Let's carve him as a dish fit for the gods,
       Not hew him as a carcass fit for hounds.
175   And let our hearts, as subtle masters do,
       Stir up their servants[64] to an act of rage,
       And after seem to chide 'em.[65] This shall make
       Our purpose necessary, and not envious;
       Which so appearing to the common eyes,
180   We shall be called purgers,[66] not murderers.
       And for Mark Antony, think not of him;
       For he can do no more than Caesar's arm
       When Caesar's head is off.

      CASSIUS.   Yet I fear him;
       For in the ingrafted[67] love he bears to Caesar—

185   **BRUTUS.** Alas, good Cassius, do not think of him.
       If he love Caesar, all that he can do
       Is to himself—take thought[68] and die for Caesar.
       And that were much he should,[69] for he is given
       To sports, to wildness, and much company.

190   **TREBONIUS.** There is no fear in him; let him not die,
       For he will live and laugh at this hereafter.
                            [*Clock strikes.*]

      BRUTUS. Peace! Count the clock.

      CASSIUS.   The clock hath stricken three.

      TREBONIUS. 'Tis time to part.

57. of: In.
58. contriver (kən trīv′ ər) *n.*: Schemer.
59. improve: Increase.
60. annoy: Harm.

61. Like . . . envy: As if we were killing in anger with hatred afterwards.

62. come by Caesar's spirit: Get hold of the principles of tyranny for which Caesar stands.
63. gentle: Honorable; noble.

64. servants: Their hands.
65. chide 'em: Scold them.

66. purgers: Healers.

67. ingrafted: Deeply rooted.

68. take thought: Become melancholy.
69. that were much he should: It is unlikely he would do that.

CASSIUS. But it is doubtful yet
Whether Caesar will come forth today or no;
195 For he is superstitious grown of late,
Quite from the main[70] opinion he held once
Of fantasy, of dreams, and ceremonies.[71]
It may be these apparent prodigies,
The unaccustomed terror of this night,
200 And the persuasion of his augurers[72]
May hold him from the Capitol today.

DECIUS. Never fear that. If he be so resolved,
I can o'ersway him;[73] for he loves to hear
That unicorns may be betrayed with trees,[74]
205 And bears with glasses,[75] elephants with holes,[76]
Lions with toils,[77] and men with flatterers;
But when I tell him he hates flatterers
He says he does, being then most flatterèd.
Let me work;
210 For I can give his humor the true bent,[78]
And I will bring him to the Capitol.

CASSIUS. Nay, we will all of us be there to fetch him.

BRUTUS. By the eighth hour; is that the uttermost?[79]

CINNA. Be that the uttermost, and fail not then.

215 **METELLUS.** Caius Ligarius doth bear Caesar hard,[80]
Who rated[81] him for speaking well of Pompey.
I wonder none of you have thought of him.

BRUTUS. Now, good Metellus, go along by him.
He loves me well, and I have given him reasons;
220 Send him but hither, and I'll fashion[82] him.

CASSIUS. The morning comes upon 's; we'll leave you,
Brutus.
And, friends, disperse yourselves; but all remember
What you have said, and show yourselves true
Romans.

BRUTUS. Good gentlemen, look fresh and merrily.
225 Let not our looks put on[83] our purposes,
But bear it[84] as our Roman actors do,
With untired spirits and formal constancy.[85]
And so good morrow to you every one.
[*Exit all but Brutus.*]
Boy! Lucius! Fast asleep? It is no matter;
230 Enjoy the honey-heavy dew of slumber.
Thou hast no figures nor no fantasies

70. Quite from the main: Quite changed from the strong.
71. ceremonies: Omens.
72. augurers (ô′ gər ərz) *n.*: Officials who interpreted omens to decide if they were favorable or unfavorable for an undertaking.
73. I can o'ersway him: I can change his mind.
74. unicorns . . . trees: The story that tells how standing in front of a tree and stepping aside at the last moment causes a charging unicorn to bury his horn in the tree and be caught.
75. glasses: Mirrors.
76. holes: Pitfalls.
77. toils: Nets; snares.
78. give his humor the true bent: Bend his feelings in the right direction.
79. uttermost: Latest.

80. doth bear Caesar hard: Has a grudge against Caesar.
81. rated: Berated.

82. fashion: Mold.

83. put on: Show.
84. bear it: Carry it off.
85. formal constancy: Consistent dignity.

Which busy care draws in the brains of men;
Therefore thou sleep'st so sound.

[*Enter Portia.*]

PORTIA.   Brutus, my lord.

BRUTUS. Portia, what mean you? Wherefore rise you now
235   It is not for your health thus to commit
        Your weak condition to the raw cold morning.

PORTIA. Nor for yours neither. Y'have ungently, Brutus,
        Stole from my bed; and yesternight at supper
        You suddenly arose and walked about,
240   Musing and sighing, with your arms across;
        And when I asked you what the matter was,
        You stared upon me with ungentle looks.
        I urged you further; then you scratched your head,
        And too impatiently stamped with your foot.
245   Yet I insisted, yet you answered not,
        But with an angry wafter[86] of your hand   **86. wafter:** Waving.
        Gave sign for me to leave you. So I did,
        Fearing to strengthen that impatience
        Which seemed too much enkindled, and withal
250   Hoping it was but an effect of humor,
        Which sometime hath his[87] hour with every man.   **87. his:** Its.
        It will not let you eat, nor talk, nor sleep,
        And could it work so much upon your shape
        As it hath much prevailed on your condition,[88]   **88. condition:** Disposition.
255   I should not know you[89] Brutus. Dear my lord,   **89. I should not know you:** I would not recognize you as.
        Make me acquainted with your cause of grief.

BRUTUS. I am not well in health, and that is all.

PORTIA. Brutus is wise and, were he not in health,
        He would embrace the means to come by it.

260 BRUTUS. Why, so I do. Good Portia, go to bed.

PORTIA. Is Brutus sick, and is it physical[90]   **90. physical:** Healthy.
        To walk unbracèd and suck up the humors[91]   **91. humors:** Dampness.
        Of the dank morning? What, is Brutus sick,
        And will he steal out of his wholesome bed,
265   To dare the vile contagion of the night,
        And tempt the rheumy and unpurgèd air[92]   **92. Tempt . . . air:** Risk the air that is likely to cause rheumatism and air that has not been purified by the sun.
        To add unto his sickness? No, my Brutus;
        You have some sick offense[93] within your mind,   **93. sick offense:** Harmful sickness.
        Which by the right and virtue of my place
270   I ought to know of; and upon my knees   **94. charm:** Beg.
        I charm[94] you, by my once commended[95] beauty,   **95. commended:** Praised.

By all your vows of love, and that great vow[96]
Which did incorporate and make us one,
That you unfold to me, your self, your half,
275 Why you are heavy,[97] and what men tonight
Have had resort to you; for here have been
Some six or seven, who did hide their faces
Even from darkness.

BRUTUS.   Kneel not, gentle Portia.

PORTIA. I should not need, if you were gentle Brutus.
280 Within the bond of marriage, tell me, Brutus,
Is it excepted[98] I should know no secrets
That appertain[99] to you? Am I your self
But, as it were, in sort or limitation,[100]
To keep with you at meals, comfort your bed,
And talk to you sometimes? Dwell I but in the
285   suburbs[101]
Of your good pleasure? If it be no more,
Portia is Brutus' harlot, not his wife.

BRUTUS. You are my true and honorable wife,
As dear to me as are the ruddy drops[102]
290 That visit my sad heart.

PORTIA. If this were true, then should I know this secret.
I grant I am a woman; but withal
A woman that Lord Brutus took to wife.
I grant I am a woman; but withal
295 A woman well reputed, Cato's daughter.[103]
Think you I am no stronger than my sex,
Being so fathered and so husbanded?
Tell me your counsels,[104] I will not disclose 'em.
I have made strong proof of my constancy,
300 Giving myself a voluntary wound
Here in the thigh; can I bear that with patience,
And not my husband's secrets?

BRUTUS.   O ye gods,
Render[105] me worthy of this noble wife!   [*Knock.*]
Hark, hark! One knocks. Portia, go in a while,
305 And by and by thy bosom shall partake
The secrets of my heart.
All my engagements[106] I will construe to thee,
All the charactery of my sad brows.[107]
Leave me with haste.   [*Exit Portia.*]

[*Enter Lucius and Caius Ligarius.*]

                    Lucius, who's that knocks?

96. great vow: Marriage vow.

97. heavy: Sorrowful.

98. excepted: Made an exception.
99. appertain (ap' ər tān') *v.*: Belong.
100. in sort or limitation: Within a limited way.
101. suburbs: Outskirts.

102. ruddy drops: Blood.

103. Cato's daughter: Marcus Porcius Cato had been an ally of Pompey and enemy of Caesar. He killed himself rather than be captured by Caesar.
104. counsels: Secrets.

105. Render (ren' dər) *v.*: Make.

106. engagements: Commitments.
107. All the charactery of my sad brows: All that is written on my face.

310 **LUCIUS.** Here is a sick man that would speak with you.

BRUTUS. Caius Ligarius, that Metellus spake of.
Boy, stand aside. Caius Ligarius! How?

CAIUS. Vouchsafe good morrow from a feeble tongue.

BRUTUS. O, what a time have you chose out,[108] brave
Caius,
315 To wear a kerchief![109] Would you were not sick!

CAIUS. I am not sick, if Brutus have in hand
Any exploit worthy the name of honor.

BRUTUS. Such an exploit have I in hand, Ligarius,
Had you a healthful ear to hear of it.

320 **CAIUS.** By all the gods that Romans bow before,
I here discard my sickness! Soul of Rome,
Brave son, derived from honorable loins,[110]
Thou, like an exorcist,[111] hast conjured up
My mortifièd spirit.[112] Now bid me run,
325 And I will strive with things impossible.
Yea, get the better of them. What's to do?

BRUTUS. A piece of work that will make sick men whole.

CAIUS. But are not some whole that we must make sick?

BRUTUS. That must we also. What it is, my Caius,
330 I shall unfold[113] to thee, as we are going
To whom it must be done.

CAIUS.   Set on[114] your foot,
And with a heart new-fired I follow you,
To do I know not what; but it sufficeth[115]
That Brutus leads me on.   [*Thunder.*]

BRUTUS.   Follow me, then.   [*Exit.*]

Scene ii. *Caesar's house.*

[*Thunder and lightning. Enter Julius Caesar in his nightgown.*]

CAESAR. Nor heaven nor earth have been at peace to-
night:
Thrice hath Calpurnia in her sleep cried out,
"Help, ho! They murder Caesar!" Who's within?

[*Enter a Servant.*]

SERVANT. My lord?

---

108. chose out: Picked out.

109. To wear a kerchief: Caius wears a scarf to protect him from drafts because he is sick.

110. derived from honorable loins: Descended from Lucius Junius Brutus, founder of Rome.

111. exorcist (ek' sôr sist) *n.*: One who calls up spirits.

112. mortifièd spirit: Paralyzed, as if dead, spirit.

113. unfold: Disclose.

114. Set on: Advance.

115. sufficeth (sə fis' eth) *v.*: Is enough.

5   **CAESAR.** Go bid the priests do present[1] sacrifice,
    And bring me their opinions of success.

    SERVANT. I will, my lord.   [*Exit.*]

[*Enter Calpurnia.*]

    CALPURNIA. What mean you, Caesar? Think you to walk
        forth?
    You shall not stir out of your house today.

    CAESAR. Caesar shall forth. The things that threatened
10   me
    Ne'er looked but on my back; when they shall see
    The face of Caesar, they are vanishèd.

    CALPURNIA. Caesar, I never stood on ceremonies,[2]
    Yet now they fright me. There is one within,
15   Besides the things that we have heard and seen,
    Recounts most horrid sights seen by the watch.[3]
    A lioness hath whelpèd[4] in the streets,
    And graves have yawned, and yielded up their dead;
    Fierce fiery warriors fought upon the clouds
20   In ranks and squadrons and right form of war,[5]
    Which drizzled blood upon the Capitol;
    The noise of battle hurtled[6] in the air,
    Horses did neigh and dying men did groan,
    And ghosts did shriek and squeal about the streets.
25   O Caesar, these things are beyond all use,[7]
    And I do fear them.

    CAESAR.   What can be avoided
    Whose end is purposed[8] by the mighty gods?
    Yet Caesar shall go forth; for these predictions
    Are to the world in general as to Caesar.[9]

30   **CALPURNIA.** When beggars die, there are no comets seen;
    The heavens themselves blaze forth[10] the death of
        princes.

    CAESAR. Cowards die many times before their deaths;
    The valiant never taste of death but once.
    Of all the wonders that I yet have heard,
35   It seems to me most strange that men should fear,
    Seeing that death, a necessary end,
    Will come when it will come.

[*Enter a Servant.*]

                What say the augurers?

1. present: Immediate.

2. stood on ceremonies: Paid attention to omens.

3. Recounts . . . watch: Tells about the awful sights seen by the watchman.
4. whelpèd: Given birth.

5. right form of war: Proper military formation of war.
6. hurtled (hŭrt′ 'ld) *v.*: Clashed together.

7. beyond all use: Contrary to all experience.

8. is purposed: Is intended.

9. For these . . . as to Caesar: Because these predictions apply to the rest of the world as much as they apply to Caesar.
10. blaze forth: Proclaim with meteors and comets.

SERVANT. They would not have you to stir forth today.
Plucking the entrails of an offering forth,[11]
40 They could not find a heart within the beast.

CAESAR. The gods do this in shame of[12] cowardice:
Caesar should be a beast without a heart
If he should stay at home today for fear.
No, Caesar shall not; Danger knows full well
45 That Caesar is more dangerous than he.
We are two lions littered[13] in one day,
And I the elder and more terrible,
And Caesar shall go forth.

CALPURNIA.   Alas, my lord,
Your wisdom is consumed in confidence.[14]
50 Do not go forth today. Call it my fear
That keeps you in the house and not your own.
We'll send Mark Antony to the Senate House,
And he shall say you are not well today.
Let me, upon my knee, prevail in this.

55 **CAESAR.** Mark Antony shall say I am not well,
And for thy humor,[15] I will stay at home.

[*Enter Decius.*]

Here's Decius Brutus, he shall tell them so.

DECIUS. Caesar, all hail! Good morrow, worthy Caesar;
I come to fetch you to the Senate House.

60 **CAESAR.** And you are come in very happy time[16]
To bear my greeting to the senators,
And tell them that I will not come today.
Cannot, is false; and that I dare not, falser:
I will not come today. Tell them so, Decius.

CALPURNIA. Say he is sick.

65 **CAESAR.**   Shall Caesar send a lie?
Have I in conquest stretched mine arm so far
To be afeard to tell graybeards[17] the truth?
Decius, go tell them Caesar will not come.

DECIUS. Most mighty Caesar, let me know some cause,
70 Lest I be laughed at when I tell them so.

CAESAR. The cause is in my will: I will not come.
That is enough to satisfy the Senate.
But for your private satisfaction,
Because I love you, I will let you know.

11. Plucking . . . forth:
Pulling out the insides of a
sacrificed animal.

12. in shame of: In order
to shame.

13. littered: Born.

14. confidence:
Overconfidence.

15. humor: Whim.

16. in very happy time:
At just the right moment.

**17. afeard to tell
graybeards:** Afraid to tell
old men (the senators).

75   Calpurnia here, my wife, stays me at home.
        She dreamt tonight she saw my statue,
        Which, like a fountain with an hundred spouts,
        Did run pure blood, and many lusty Romans
        Came smiling and did bathe their hands in it.
80   And these does she apply for[18] warnings and
            portents
        And evils imminent, and on her knee
        Hath begged that I will stay at home today.

    DECIUS. This dream is all amiss interpreted;
        It was a vision fair and fortunate:
85   Your statue spouting blood in many pipes,
        In which so many smiling Romans bathed,
        Signifies that from you great Rome shall suck
        Reviving blood, and that great men shall press
        For tinctures, stains, relics, and cognizance.[19]
90   This by Calpurnia's dream is signified.

    CAESAR. And this way have you well expounded[20] it.

    DECIUS. I have, when you have heard what I can say;
        And know it now, the Senate have concluded
        To give this day a crown to mighty Caesar.
95   If you shall send them word you will not come,
        Their minds may change. Besides, it were a mock
        Apt to be rendered,[21] for someone to say
        "Break up the Senate till another time,
        When Caesar's wife shall meet with better dreams."
100   If Caesar hide himself, shall they not whisper
        "Lo, Caesar is afraid"?
        Pardon me, Caesar, for my dear dear love
        To your proceeding[22] bids me tell you this,
        And reason to my love is liable.[23]

105 CAESAR. How foolish do your fears seem now, Calpurnia!
        I am ashamèd I did yield to them.
        Give me my robe,[24] for I will go.

[Enter Brutus, Ligarius, Metellus Cimber, Casca, Trebonius, Cinna, and Publius.]

        And look where Publius is come to fetch me.

    PUBLIUS. Good morrow, Caesar.

    CAESAR.   Welcome, Publius.
110   What, Brutus, are you stirred so early too?
        Good morrow, Casca. Caius Ligarius,

18. apply for: Consider to be.

19. shall press . . . cognizance: Decius interprets Calpurnia's dream with a double meaning. To Caesar he suggests that people will beg for badges to show they are Caesar's servants. To the audience, that people will seek remembrances of his death.

20. expounded (ik spoŭnd' əd) v.: Interpreted; explained.

21. mock . . . rendered: Jeering comment likely to be made.

22. proceeding: Advancing in your career.

23. reason . . . liable: My judgment is not as strong as my affection for you is.

24. robe: Toga.

Caesar was ne'er so much your enemy[25]
As that same ague[26] which hath made you lean.
What is't o'clock?

BRUTUS.   Caesar, 'tis strucken eight.

115   **CAESAR.** I thank you for your pains and courtesy.

[*Enter Antony.*]

See! Antony, that revels[27] long a-nights,
Is notwithstanding up. Good morrow, Antony.

ANTONY. So to most noble Caesar.

CAESAR.   Bid them prepare[28] within.
120   I am to blame to be thus waited for.
Now, Cinna; now, Metellus; what Trebonius,
I have an hour's talk in store for you;
Remember that you call on me today;

Be near me, that I may remember you.

125   **TREBONIUS.** Caesar, I will [*aside*] and so near will I be,
That your best friends shall wish I had been further.
CAESAR. Good friends, go in and taste some wine with
    me,
And we (like friends) will straightway go together.

**25. Caius Ligarius . . .
your enemy:** Caesar had
recently pardoned Ligarius
for supporting Pompey
during the civil war.
26. ague (ā′ gyōo) *n.:*
Fever.

27. revels (rev′ əlz) *v.:*
Makes merry.

28. prepare: Set out
refreshments.

BRUTUS. [*Aside*] That every like is not the same,[29] O Caesar,
The heart of Brutus earns[30] to think upon.   [*Exit.*]

Scene iii. *A street near the Capitol, close to Brutus' house.*

[*Enter Artemidorus, reading a paper.*]

ARTEMIDORUS. "Caesar, beware of Brutus; take heed of Cassius; come not near Casca; have an eye to Cinna; trust not Trebonius; mark well Metellus Cimber; Decius Brutus loves thee not; thou hast wronged
5   Caius Ligarius. There is but one mind in all these men, and it is bent against Caesar. If thou beest not immortal, look about you: security gives way to conspiracy.[1] The mighty gods defend thee!
                             Thy lover,[2] ARTEMIDORUS."

10   Here will I stand till Caesar pass along,
And as a suitor[3] will I give him this.
My heart laments that virtue cannot live
Out of the teeth of emulation.
If thou read this, O Caesar, thou mayest live;
15   If not, the Fates with traitors do contrive.[4]   [*Exit.*]

Scene iv. *Another part of the street.*

[*Enter Portia and Lucius.*]

PORTIA. I prithee, boy, run to the Senate House;
Stay not to answer me, but get thee gone.
Why dost thou stay?

LUCIUS.   To know my errand, madam.

PORTIA. I would have had thee there and here again
5   Ere I can tell thee what thou shouldst do there.
O constancy,[1] be strong upon my side;
Set a huge mountain 'tween my heart and tongue!
I have a man's mind, but a woman's might.[2]
How hard it is for women to keep counsel![3]
Art thou here yet?

10   **LUCIUS.**   Madam, what should I do?
Run to the Capitol, and nothing else?
And so return to you, and nothing else?

PORTIA. Yes, bring me word, boy, if thy lord look well,
For he went sickly forth; and take good note

15   What Caesar doth, what suitors press to him.
      Hark, boy, what noise is that?

      LUCIUS. I hear none, madam.

      PORTIA.   Prithee, listen well.
      I heard a bustling rumor like a fray,[4]   **4. fray** (frā) *n.*: Fight or
      And the wind brings it from the Capitol.   brawl.

20   **LUCIUS.** Sooth, madam, I hear nothing.

[*Enter the Soothsayer.*]

      PORTIA. Come hither, fellow. Which way hast thou been?

      SOOTHSAYER. At mine own house, good lady.

      PORTIA. What is't o'clock?

      SOOTHSAYER.   About the ninth hour, lady.

      PORTIA. Is Caesar yet gone to the Capitol?

25   **SOOTHSAYER.** Madam, not yet; I go to take my stand,
      To see him pass on to the Capitol.

      PORTIA. Thou hast some suit[5] to Caesar, hast thou not?   **5. suit** (sōōt) *n.*: Petition.

      SOOTHSAYER. That I have, lady; if it will please Caesar
      To be so good to Caesar as to hear me,
30   I shall beseech him to befriend himself.

      PORTIA. Why, know'st thou any harm's intended to-
      wards him?

      SOOTHSAYER. None that I know will be, much that I fear
      may chance.
      Good morrow to you. Here the street is narrow;
      The throng that follows Caesar at the heels,
35   Of senators, of praetors, common suitors,
      Will crowd a feeble man almost to death.
      I'll get me to a place more void,[6] and there   **6. void:** Empty.
      Speak to great Caesar as he comes along.   [*Exit.*]

      PORTIA. I must go in. Ay me, how weak a thing
40   The heart of woman is! O Brutus,
      The heavens speed[7] thee in thine enterprise![8]   **7. speed:** Prosper.
      Sure, the boy heard me—Brutus hath a suit   **8. enterprise** (en' tər
      That Caesar will not grant—O, I grow faint.   prīz') *n.*: Undertaking;
      Run, Lucius, and commend me[9] to my lord;   project.
45   Say I am merry; come to me again,   **9. commend** (kə mend')
      And bring me word what he doth say to thee.   *v.*: Give the kind regards
                                                       of.
                                    [*Exit separately.*]

RESPONDING TO THE SELECTION

Your Response

1. If you had been a Roman citizen, would you have joined the conspirators? Why or why not?
2. What is your opinion of Brutus' decision not to tell Portia about the plot against Caesar?

Recalling

3. In his soliloquy what reasons does Brutus give for killing Caesar?
4. Why is a meeting held at Brutus' house, and who attends the meeting?
5. Explain the two changes Brutus recommends in the assassination plan.
6. What reasons does Calpurnia, Caesar's wife, give for wanting him to stay home?
7. How is Caesar convinced to go to the Capitol and by whom?

Interpreting

8. Why do you think the writer left gaps in the letter that Lucius finds? What inferences do you draw from the way Brutus fills in these gaps?
9. Brutus justifies his actions by comparing Caesar to a serpent's egg in Act II, Scene i, lines 32–34. Explain how this is an example of a false analogy, or a comparison that is not logical.
10. Why does Brutus decide to go along with the conspirators? Explain whether or not you think his decision proves him honorable.

Applying

11. How might unwillingness to seem weak lead people to take unnecessary risks?

ANALYZING LITERATURE

Recognizing Irony

In addition to dramatic **irony,** in which the audience knows something a character does not, this act also contains ironic situations in which one character intentionally says something with a meaning that another character is not aware of. For example, Trebonius speaks ironically in Act II, Scene ii, lines 124–125. Caesar is unaware of the meaning, but the audience and Trebonius know the meaning.

1. First find and explain an example of dramatic irony in Act I or II.
2. Then find and explain an example of irony spoken by Decius in Act II, Scene ii.
3. Find and explain an example of irony spoken by Portia in Act II, Scene iv.

CRITICAL THINKING AND READING

Predicting Outcomes

An **outcome** is the natural result of what has gone before. To predict an outcome, you must consider both the action that has taken place and what has been said by and about the characters. For example, given what we have learned about Caesar in this act—his pride and his unwillingness to appear weak and fearful—it is reasonable to predict that he will go to the Capitol even if he is warned.

Predict outcomes to these questions and support them with evidence from Acts I and II.

1. Who will assume power after Caesar's death?
2. How will the people react to Caesar's death?

THINKING AND WRITING

Writing With Dramatic Irony

Write a short scene in which Calpurnia explains her dream and her fears to Portia. Portia must respond in a way that is truthful but that does not reveal what she knows about Brutus' intentions. The scene should follow Act II, Scene iv. You may write it in prose, rather than blank verse, if you prefer.

GUIDE FOR READING

The Tragedy of Julius Caesar, Act III

Aside, Soliloquy, and Monologue

In drama characters often make special kinds of speeches. One of these is the aside. An **aside** is a brief comment a character makes that is not heard by anyone else onstage and that reveals the character's thoughts or feelings. An example is Brutus' last two lines in Act II, Scene ii, lines 129–130.

Another special kind of speech is the soliloquy. A **soliloquy** is a speech made by a character alone onstage. Cassius' speech in Act I, Scene ii, lines 308–322 is an example of a soliloquy.

A type of speech similar to the soliloquy is the monologue. A **monologue** is a very long speech by one person without interruption from others onstage. Cassius' speech in Act I, Scene ii, lines 90–131 is an example of a monologue.

Focus

In Act III, scene ii, Mark Antony delivers a famous speech. Like effective speakers throughout history, Antony repeats key phrases to influence his audience. Get together with a group of classmates and make a chart in which you identify famous speeches and the key words that make them memorable.

Vocabulary

Knowing the following words will help you as you read Act III of *The Tragedy of Julius Caesar.*

suit (so͞ot) *n.*: Old word for "petition" (p. 347)

spurn (spʉrn) *v.*: Old word for "to kick disdainfully" (p. 348)

repealing (ri pēl′ iŋ) *n.*: Old word for "recalling," especially from exile (p. 348)

confounded (kən found′ id) *adj.*: Confused (p. 349)

mutiny (myo͞ot′ 'n ē) *n.*: Open rebellion against authority (p. 349)

malice (mal′ is) *n.*: A desire to harm or see harm done to others (p. 353)

oration (ô rā′ shən) *n.*: A formal speech, especially one given at a state occasion, ceremony, or funeral (p. 356)

discourse (dis kôrs′) *v.*: To speak formally and at length (p. 356)

vile (vīl) *adj.*: Depraved; ignoble (p. 357)

Act III

Scene i. *Rome. Before the Capitol.*

[*Flourish of trumpets. Enter Caesar, Brutus, Cassius, Casca, Decius, Metellus Cimber, Trebonius, Cinna, Antony, Lepidus, Artemidorus, Publius, Popilius, and the Soothsayer.*]

    CAESAR. The ides of March are come.

    SOOTHSAYER. Ay, Caesar, but not gone.

    ARTEMIDORUS. Hail, Caesar! Read this schedule.[1]

    DECIUS. Trebonius doth desire you to o'er-read,
5   At your best leisure, this his humble suit.

    ARTEMIDORUS. O Caesar, read mine first; for mine's a suit
        That touches Caesar nearer. Read it, great Caesar.

    CAESAR. What touches us ourself shall be last served.

    ARTEMIDORUS. Delay not, Caesar; read it instantly.

    CAESAR. What, is the fellow mad?

10   **PUBLIUS.**   Sirrah, give place.[2]

    CASSIUS. What, urge you your petitions in the street?
        Come to the Capitol.

[*Caesar goes to the Capitol, the rest following.*]

    POPILIUS. I wish your enterprise today may thrive.

    CASSIUS. What enterprise, Popilius?

    POPILIUS.   Fare you well.
        [*Advances to Caesar.*]

15   **BRUTUS.** What said Popilius Lena?

    CASSIUS. He wished today our enterprise might thrive.
        I fear our purpose is discoverèd.

    BRUTUS. Look how he makes to[3] Caesar; mark him.

    CASSIUS. Casca, be sudden,[4] for we fear prevention.
20   Brutus, what shall be done? If this be known,
        Cassius or Caesar never shall turn back,[5]
        For I will slay myself.

1. schedule (skej′ ōōl) *n.*: Paper.

2. give place: Get out of the way.

3. makes to: Approaches.

4. be sudden: Be quick.

5. Cassius . . . back: Either Cassius or Caesar will not return alive.

BRUTUS. Cassius, be constant.[6]
Popilius Lena speaks not of our purposes;
For look, he smiles, and Caesar doth not change.[7]

25 **CASSIUS.** Trebonius knows his time; for look you,
Brutus,
He draws Mark Antony out of the way.

[*Exit Antony and Trebonius.*]

DECIUS. Where is Metellus Cimber? Let him go
And presently prefer his suit[8] to Caesar.

BRUTUS. He is addressed.[9] Press near and second[10] him.

30 **CINNA.** Casca, you are the first that rears your hand.

CAESAR. Are we all ready? What is now amiss
That Caesar and his Senate must redress?[11]

METELLUS. Most high, most mighty, and most puissant[12]
Caesar,
Metellus Cimber throws before thy seat
An humble heart. [*Kneeling.*]

35 **CAESAR.** I must prevent thee, Cimber.
These couchings and these lowly courtesies[13]
Might fire the blood of ordinary men,
And turn preordinance and first decree
Into the law of children.[14] Be not fond[15]

40 To think that Caesar bears such rebel blood
That will be thawed from the true quality[16]
With that which melteth fools—I mean sweet words,
Low-crookèd curtsies, and base spaniel fawning.[17]
Thy brother by decree is banishèd.

45 If thou dost bend and pray and fawn for him,
I spurn thee like a cur out of my way.
Know, Caesar doth not wrong, nor without cause
Will he be satisfied.

METELLUS. Is there no voice more worthy than my own,

50 To sound more sweetly in great Caesar's ear
For the repealing of my banished brother?

BRUTUS. I kiss thy hand, but not in flattery, Caesar,
Desiring thee that Publius Cimber may
Have an immediate freedom of repeal.

CAESAR. What, Brutus?

55 **CASSIUS.** Pardon, Caesar; Caesar, pardon!

6. constant: Firm; calm.

7. change: Change the expression on his face.

8. presently prefer his suit: Immediately present his petition.
9. addressed: Ready.
10. second: Support.

11. amiss . . . redress: Wrong that Caesar and his Senate must correct.
12. puissant (pyo͞o′ i sənt) *adj.*: Powerful.

13. couchings . . . courtesies: Low bowings and humble gestures of reverence.

14. And turn . . . law of children: And change what has already been decided as children might change their minds.
15. fond *adj.*: Foolish.
16. rebel . . . quality: Unstable disposition that will be changed from firmness.
17. base spaniel fawning: Low doglike cringing.

As low as to thy foot doth Cassius fall
To beg enfranchisement[18] for Publius Cimber.

CAESAR. I could be well moved, if I were as you;
If I could pray to move,[19] prayers would move me;
60 But I am constant as the Northern Star,
Of whose true-fixed and resting[20] quality
There is no fellow[21] in the firmament.[22]
The skies are painted with unnumb'red sparks,
They are all fire and every one doth shine;
65 But there's but one in all doth hold his[23] place.
So in the world; 'tis furnished well with men,
And men are flesh and blood, and apprehensive;[24]
Yet in the number I do know but one
That unassailable holds on his rank,[25]
70 Unshaked of motion;[26] and that I am he,
Let me a little show it, even in this—
That I was constant. Cimber should be banished,
And constant do remain to keep him so.

CINNA. O Caesar—

CAESAR.   Hence! Wilt thou lift up Olympus?[27]

DECIUS. Great Caesar—

75 **CAESAR.**   Doth not Brutus bootless[28] kneel?

CASCA. Speak hands for me!   [*They stab Caesar.*]

CAESAR. *Et tu, Brutè?*[29] Then fall Caesar.   [*Dies.*]

CINNA. Liberty! Freedom! Tyranny is dead!
Run hence, proclaim, cry it about the streets.

80 **CASSIUS.** Some to the common pulpits,[30] and cry out
"Liberty, freedom, and enfranchisement!"

BRUTUS. People, and senators, be not affrighted.
Fly not; stand still; ambition's debt is paid.[31]

CASCA. Go to the pulpit, Brutus.

DECIUS.   And Cassius too.

85 **BRUTUS.** Where's Publius?

CINNA. Here, quite confounded with this mutiny.

METELLUS. Stand fast together, lest some friend of
     Caesar's
     Should chance—

18. **enfranchisement** (en fran′ chīz mənt) *n.*: Freedom.
19. **pray to move:** Beg others to change their minds.
20. **resting:** Immovable.
21. **fellow:** Equal.
22. **firmament** (fʉr′ mə mənt) *n.*: Sky.

23. **his:** Its.

24. **apprehensive** (ap′ rə hen′ siv) *adj.*: Able to understand.
25. **unassailable . . . rank:** Unattackable maintains his position.
26. **Unshaked of motion:** Unmoved by his own or others' impulses.

27. **Olympus** (ō lim′ pəs): Mountain in northern Greece that was, in Greek mythology, the home of the gods.
28. **bootless:** Uselessly.

29. *Et tu, Brutè?*: In Latin, *And you, Brutus?*

30. **pulpits** (pʊl′ pits) *n.*: Speakers' platforms.

31. **ambition's . . . paid:** Ambition received what it deserved.

The Tragedy of Julius Caesar, Act III, Scene i   349

BRUTUS. Talk not of standing. Publius, good cheer;
90   There is no harm intended to your person,
      Nor to no Roman else. So tell them, Publius.

CASSIUS. And leave us, Publius, lest that the people
      Rushing on us should do your age some mischief.

BRUTUS. Do so; and let no man abide[32] this deed
95   But we the doers.

[Enter Trebonius.]

32. let no man abide: Let no man take responsibility for.

CASSIUS. Where is Antony?

TREBONIUS.   Fled to his house amazed.[33]
Men, wives, and children stare, cry out and run,
As[34] it were doomsday.

BRUTUS.   Fates, we will know your pleasures.
That we shall die, we know; 'tis but the time,
100   And drawing days out, that men stand upon.[35]

CASCA. Why, he that cuts off twenty years of life
Cuts off so many years of fearing death.

BRUTUS. Grant that, and then is death a benefit.
So are we Caesar's friends, that have abridged
105   His time of fearing death. Stoop, Romans, stoop,
And let us bathe our hands in Caesar's blood
Up to the elbows, and besmear our swords.
Then walk we forth, even to the market place,
And waving our red weapons o'er our heads,
110   Let's all cry "Peace, freedom, and liberty!"

CASSIUS. Stoop then, and wash. How many ages hence
Shall this our lofty scene be acted over
In states unborn and accents yet unknown!

BRUTUS. How many times shall Caesar bleed in sport,[36]
115   That now on Pompey's basis lies along[37]
No worthier than the dust!

CASSIUS.   So oft as that shall be,
So often shall the knot[38] of us be called
The men that gave their country liberty.

DECIUS. What, shall we forth?

CASSIUS.   Ay, every man away.
120   Brutus shall lead, and we will grace his heels[39]
With the most boldest and best hearts of Rome.

[Enter a Servant.]

BRUTUS. Soft, who comes here? A friend of Antony's.
SERVANT. Thus, Brutus, did my master bid me kneel;
Thus did Mark Antony bid me fall down;
125   And, being prostrate, thus he bade me say:
Brutus is noble, wise, valiant, and honest;
Caesar was mighty, bold, royal, and loving.
Say I love Brutus and I honor him;
Say I feared Caesar, honored him, and loved him.

33. amazed: Astounded.

34. As: As if.

35. drawing . . . upon:
Prolonging life that people
care about.

36. in sport: In plays.
**37. on Pompey's basis
lies along:** By the pedestal
of Pompey's statue lies
stretched out.

38. Knot: Group.

39. grace his heels:
Honor him by following
him.

130	If Brutus will vouchsafe that Antony
	May safely come to him and be resolved[40]
	How Caesar hath deserved to lie in death,
	Mark Antony shall not love Caesar dead
	So well as Brutus living; but will follow
135	The fortunes and affairs of noble Brutus
	Thorough the hazards of this untrod state[41]
	With all true faith. So says my master Antony.

40. be resolved: Have it explained.

BRUTUS. Thy master is a wise and valiant Roman;
I never thought him worse.

41. Thorough . . . state: Through the dangers of this new state of affairs.

140   Tell him, so[42] please him come unto this place,
He shall be satisfied and, by my honor,
Depart untouched.

42. so: If it should.

SERVANT.   I'll fetch him presently.

[Exit Servant.]

BRUTUS. I know that we shall have him well to friend.[43]

43. to friend: As a friend.

CASSIUS. I wish we may. But yet have I a mind
145   That fears him much; and my misgiving still
Falls shrewdly to the purpose.[44]

[Enter Antony.]

44. my misgiving . . . to the purpose: My doubts always turn out to be justified.

BRUTUS. But here comes Antony. Welcome, Mark Antony.

ANTONY. O mighty Caesar! Dost thou lie so low?
Are all thy conquests, glories, triumphs, spoils,
150   Shrunk to this little measure? Fare thee well.
I know not, gentlemen, what you intend,
Who else must be let blood,[45] who else is rank.[46]
If I myself, there is no hour so fit
As Caesar's death's hour, nor no instrument
155   Of half that worth as those your swords, made rich
With the most noble blood of all this world.
I do beseech ye, if you bear me hard,[47]
Now, whilst your purpled hands[48] do reek and smoke,
Fulfill your pleasure. Live[49] a thousand years,
160   I shall not find myself so apt[50] to die;
No place will please me so, no mean of death,[51]
As here by Caesar, and by you cut off,
The choice and master spirits of this age.

45. be let blood: Be killed.
46. rank: Too powerful; in need of bloodletting.

47. bear me hard: Have a grudge against me.
48. purpled hands: Bloody hands.
49. Live: If I live.
50. apt: Ready.
51. mean of death: Way of dying.

BRUTUS. O Antony, beg not your death of us!
165   Though now we must appear bloody and cruel,
As by our hands and this our present act

You see we do, yet see you but our hands
And this the bleeding business they have done.

170 Our hearts you see not; they are pitiful;[52]
And pity to the general wrong of Rome—
As fire drives out fire, so pity pity[53]—
Hath done this deed on Caesar. For your part,
To you our swords have leaden[54] points, Mark
    Antony:
Our arms in strength of malice, and our hearts

175 Of brothers' temper,[55] do receive you in
With all kind love, good thoughts, and reverence.

CASSIUS. Your voice[56] shall be as strong as any man's
In the disposing of new dignities.[57]

BRUTUS. Only be patient till we have appeased

180 The multitude, beside themselves with fear,
And then we will deliver[58] you the cause
Why I, that did love Caesar when I struck him,
Have thus proceeded.

ANTONY.   I doubt not of your wisdom.
Let each man render me his bloody hand.

185 First, Marcus Brutus, will I shake with you;
Next, Caius Cassius, do I take your hand;
Now, Decius Brutus, yours; now yours, Metellus;
Yours, Cinna; and, my valiant Casca, yours;
Though last, not least in love, yours, good Trebonius.

190 Gentlemen all—alas, what shall I say?
My credit[59] now stands on such slippery ground
That one of two bad ways you must conceit[60] me,
Either a coward or a flatterer.
That I did love thee, Caesar, O, 'tis true!

195 If then thy spirit look upon us now,
Shall it not grieve thee dearer[61] than thy death
To see thy Antony making his peace,
Shaking the bloody fingers of thy foes,
Most noble, in the presence of thy corse?[62]

200 Had I as many eyes as thou hast wounds,
Weeping as fast as they stream forth thy blood,
It would become me better than to close[63]
In terms of friendship with thine enemies.
Pardon me, Julius! Here wast thou bayed,[64] brave
    hart;[65]

205 Here didst thou fall, and here thy hunters stand,
Signed in thy spoil[66] and crimsoned in thy lethe.[67]

52. pitiful: Full of pity.

53. pity pity: Pity for Rome drove out pity for Caesar.

54. leaden: Dull; blunt.

55. of brothers' temper: Filled with brotherly feelings.

56. voice: Vote.

57. dignities: Offices.

58. deliver: Tell to.

59. credit: Reputation.

60. conceit (kən sēt') v.: Think of.

61. dearer: More deeply.

62. corse: Corpse.

63. close (clōz) v.: To reach an agreement.

64. bayed: Cornered.

65. hart (härt) n.: Deer.

66. Signed in thy spoil: Marked by signs of your decaying parts.

67. lethe: A river in Hades, but in this case a river of blood.

O world, thou wast the forest to this hart;
And this indeed, O world, the heart of thee.
How like a deer, stroken[68] by many princes,
210   Dost thou here lie!

68. stroken: Struck down.

CASSIUS. Mark Antony—

ANTONY.   Pardon me, Caius Cassius.
The enemies of Caesar shall say this;
Then, in a friend, it is cold modesty.[69]

69. cold modesty: Calm, moderate speech.

CASSIUS. I blame you not for praising Caesar so;
215   But what compact[70] mean you to have with us?
Will you be pricked[71] in number of our friends,
Or shall we on,[72] and not depend on you?

70. compact (käm′ pakt) *n.:* Agreement.
71. pricked: Marked.
72. on: Proceed.

ANTONY. Therefore I took your hands, but was indeed
Swayed from the point by looking down on Caesar.
220   Friends am I with you all, and love you all,
Upon this hope, that you shall give me reasons
Why, and wherein, Caesar was dangerous.

BRUTUS. Or else were this a savage spectacle.
Our reasons are so full of good regard[73]
225   That were you, Antony, the son of Caesar,
You should be satisfied.

73. so full of good regard: So carefully considered.

ANTONY.   That's all I seek;
And am moreover suitor that I may
Produce[74] his body to the market place,
And in the pulpit, as becomes a friend,
230   Speak in the order[75] of his funeral.

74. Produce: Bring forth.

75. order: Course of the ceremonies.

BRUTUS. You shall, Mark Antony.

CASSIUS.   Brutus, a word with you.
[*Aside to Brutus*] You know not what you do; do not
    consent
That Antony speak in his funeral.
Know you how much the people may be moved
By that which he will utter?

235   BRUTUS.   By your pardon:
I will myself into the pulpit first,
And show the reason of our Caesar's death.
What Antony shall speak, I will protest[76]
He speaks by leave and by permission,
240   And that we are contented Caesar shall
Have all true rites and lawful ceremonies.
It shall advantage more than do us wrong.[77]

76. protest: Declare.

77. advantage . . . wrong: Benefit us more than hurt us.

CASSIUS. I know not what may fall;[78] I like it not.

BRUTUS. Mark Antony, here, take you Caesar's body.
245   You shall not in your funeral speech blame us,
       But speak all good you can devise of Caesar,
       And say you do't by our permission;
       Else shall you not have any hand at all
       About his funeral. And you shall speak
250   In the same pulpit whereto I am going,
       After my speech is ended.

ANTONY.   Be it so;
       I do desire no more.

BRUTUS. Prepare the body then, and follow us.

                    [*Exit all but Antony.*]

ANTONY. O pardon me, thou bleeding piece of earth,
255   That I am meek and gentle with these butchers!
       Thou art the ruins of the noblest man
       That ever livèd in the tide of times.[79]
       Woe to the hand that shed this costly blood!
       Over thy wounds now do I prophesy
260   (Which like dumb mouths do ope their ruby lips
       To beg the voice and utterance of my tongue),
       A curse shall light upon the limbs of men;
       Domestic fury and fierce civil strife
       Shall cumber[80] all the parts of Italy;
265   Blood and destruction shall be so in use,[81]
       And dreadful objects so familiar,
       That mothers shall but smile when they behold
       Their infants quartered with the hands of war,
       All pity choked with custom of fell deeds;[82]
270   And Caesar's spirit, ranging[83] for revenge,
       With Ate[84] by his side come hot from hell,
       Shall in these confines[85] with a monarch's voice
       Cry "Havoc,"[86] and let slip[87] the dogs of war,
       That this foul deed shall smell above the earth
275   With carrion[88] men, groaning for burial.

[*Enter Octavius' Servant.*]

       You serve Octavius Caesar, do you not?

SERVANT. I do, Mark Antony.

ANTONY. Caesar did write for him to come to Rome.

SERVANT. He did receive his letters and is coming,
280   And bid me say to you by word of mouth—
       O Caesar!   [*Seeing the body.*]

---

78. what may fall: What may happen.

79. tide of times: Course of all history.

80. cumber (kum' bər) *v.*: Distress; burden.
81. in use: Customary.

82. fell deeds: Cruel acts.
83. ranging: Roaming like a wild beast in search of prey.
84. Ate (ā' tē): Greek goddess personifying reckless ambition in man.
85. confines (kän' finz) *n.*: Boundaries.
86. Havoc: Latin for *no quarter*, a signal for general slaughter.
87. slip: Loose.
88. carrion (kar' ē ən) *adj.*: Dead and rotting.

ANTONY. Thy heart is big;[89] get thee apart and weep.
    Passion, I see, is catching, for mine eyes,
    Seeing those beads of sorrow stand in thine,
285   Began to water. Is thy master coming?

SERVANT. He lies tonight within seven leagues[90] of Rome.

ANTONY. Post[91] back with speed, and tell him what hath
    chanced.[92]
    Here is a mourning Rome, a dangerous Rome,
    No Rome of safety for Octavius yet.
290   Hie hence and tell him so. Yet stay awhile;
    Thou shalt not back till I have borne this corse
    Into the market place; there shall I try[93]
    In my oration how the people take
    The cruel issue[94] of these bloody men;
295   According to the which, thou shalt discourse
    To young Octavius of the state of things.
    Lend me your hand.   *[Exit.]*

89. big: Swollen with grief.

90. lies . . . seven leagues: Is camped tonight within twenty-one miles.
91. Post: Hasten.
92. hath chanced: Has happened.

93. try: Test.

94. cruel issue: Outcome of the cruelty.

Scene ii. *The Forum*

[Enter Brutus and goes into the pulpit, and Cassius, with the Plebeians.[1]]

PLEBEIANS. We will be satisfied![2] Let us be satisfied!

BRUTUS. Then follow me, and give me audience, friends.
    Cassius, go you into the other street
    And part the numbers.[3]
5   Those that will hear me speak, let 'em stay here;
    Those that will follow Cassius, go with him;
    And public reasons shall be renderèd
    Of Caesar's death.

FIRST PLEBEIAN.   I will hear Brutus speak.

SECOND PLEBEIAN. I will hear Cassius, and compare their
    reasons,
10   When severally[4] we hear them renderèd.
            [Exit Cassius, with some of the Plebeians.]
THIRD PLEBEIAN. The noble Brutus is ascended. Silence!

BRUTUS. Be patient till the last.
    Romans, countrymen, and lovers,[5] hear me for my
    cause, and be silent, that you may hear. Believe me
15   for mine honor, and have respect to mine honor, that
    you may believe. Censure[6] me in your wisdom, and

1. Plebeians (ple bē′ ənz) *n*.: Commoners; members of the lower class.
2. be satisfied: Get an explanation.

3. part the numbers: Divide the crowd.

4. severally (sev′ ər əl ē) *adv*.: Separately.

5. lovers: Dear friends.

6. Censure (sen′ sʰər) *v*.: Condemn as wrong; criticize.

awake your senses,[7] that you may the better judge. If there be any in this assembly, any dear friend of Caesar's, to him I say that Brutus' love to Caesar was no less than his. If then that friend demand why Brutus rose against Caesar, this is my answer: Not that I loved Caesar less, but that I loved Rome more. Had you rather Caesar were living, and die all slaves, than that Caesar were dead, to live all free men? As Caesar loved me, I weep for him; as he was fortunate, I rejoice at it; as he was valiant, I honor him; but, as he was ambitious, I slew him. There is tears, for his love; joy, for his fortune; honor, for his valor; and death, for his ambition. Who is here so base,[8] that would be a bondman?[9] If any, speak; for him have I offended. Who is here so rude,[10] that would not be a Roman? If any, speak; for him have I offended. Who is here so vile, that will not love his country? If any, speak; for him have I offended. I pause for a reply.

35   **ALL.** None, Brutus, none!

BRUTUS. Then none have I offended. I have done no more to Caesar than you shall do to Brutus. The question of his death is enrolled in the Capitol;[11] his glory not extenuated,[12] wherein he was worthy, nor his offenses enforced,[13] for which he suffered death.

40

[*Enter Mark Antony, with Caesar's body.*]

Here comes his body, mourned by Mark Antony, who, though he had no hand in his death, shall receive the benefit of his dying, a place in the commonwealth, as which of you shall not? With this I depart, that, as I slew my best lover for the good of Rome, I have the same dagger for myself, when it shall please my country to need my death.

45

ALL. Live, Brutus! Live, live!

FIRST PLEBEIAN. Bring him with triumph home unto his house.

50   **SECOND PLEBEIAN.** Give him a statue with his ancestors.

THIRD PLEBEIAN. Let him be Caesar.

FOURTH PLEBEIAN.   Caesar's better parts[14]
Shall be crowned in Brutus.

---

7. senses: Powers of reason.

8. base: Low.
9. bondman: Slave.
10. rude: Ignorant.

11. The question . . . in the Capitol: The whole matter of his death is on record in the Capitol.
12. extenuated (ik sten′ yōō wāt id) *v.*: Underrated.
13. enforced (in fôrs'd′) *v.*: Given force to.

14. parts: Qualities.

FIRST PLEBEIAN. We'll bring him to his house
     With shouts and clamors.

BRUTUS.   My countrymen—

SECOND PLEBEIAN. Peace! Silence! Brutus speaks.

55 **FIRST PLEBEIAN.**   Peace, ho!

BRUTUS. Good countrymen, let me depart alone,
     And, for my sake, stay here with Antony.
     Do grace to Caesar's corpse, and grace his speech
     Tending to Caesar's glories,[15] which Mark Antony
60   By our permission, is allowed to make.
     I do entreat you, not a man depart,
     Save I alone, till Antony have spoke.   [*Exit.*]

FIRST PLEBEIAN. Stay, ho! And let us hear Mark Antony.

THIRD PLEBEIAN. Let him go up into the public chair;
65   We'll hear him. Noble Antony, go up.

ANTONY. For Brutus' sake, I am beholding[16] to you.

FOURTH PLEBEIAN. What does he say of Brutus?

THIRD PLEBEIAN.   He says, for Brutus' sake,
     He finds himself beholding to us all.

FOURTH PLEBEIAN. 'Twere best he speak no harm of Bru-
     tus here!

FIRST PLEBEIAN. This Caesar was a tyrant.

70 **THIRD PLEBEIAN.**   Nay, that's certain.
     We are blest that Rome is rid of him.

SECOND PLEBEIAN. Peace! Let us hear what Antony can
     say.

ANTONY. You gentle Romans—

ALL.   Peace, ho! Let us hear him.

ANTONY. Friends, Romans, countrymen, lend me your
          ears;
75   I come to bury Caesar, not to praise him.
     The evil that men do lives after them,
     The good is oft interrèd with their bones;
     So let it be with Caesar. The noble Brutus
     Hath told you Caesar was ambitious.
80   If it were so, it was a grievous fault,
     And grievously hath Caesar answered[17] it.

**15. Do grace . . .
glories:** Honor Caesar's
body and the speech telling
of Caesar's achievements.

16. beholding: Indebted.

17. answered: Paid the
penalty for.

Here, under leave of Brutus and the rest
(For Brutus is an honorable man,
So are they all, all honorable men),
85   Come I to speak in Caesar's funeral.
He was my friend, faithful and just to me;
But Brutus says he was ambitious,
And Brutus is an honorable man.
He hath brought many captives home to Rome,
90   Whose ransoms did the general coffers fill;
Did this in Caesar seem ambitious?
When that the poor have cried, Caesar hath wept;
Ambition should be made of sterner stuff.
Yet Brutus says he was ambitious;
95   And Brutus is an honorable man.

You all did see that on the Lupercal
I thrice presented him a kingly crown,
Which he did thrice refuse. Was this ambition?
Yet Brutus says he was ambitious;

100 And sure he is an honorable man.
I speak not to disprove what Brutus spoke,
But here I am to speak what I do know.
You all did love him once, not without cause;
What cause withholds you then to mourn for him?

105 O judgment, thou art fled to brutish beasts,
And men have lost their reason! Bear with me;
My heart is in the coffin there with Caesar,
And I must pause till it come back to me.

FIRST PLEBEIAN. Methinks there is much reason in his
    sayings.

110 **SECOND PLEBEIAN.** If thou consider rightly of the matter,
    Caesar has had great wrong.

THIRD PLEBEIAN. Has he, masters?
    I fear there will a worse come in his place.

FOURTH PLEBEIAN. Marked ye his words? He would not
    take the crown,
    Therefore 'tis certain he was not ambitious.

115 **FIRST PLEBEIAN.** If it be found so, some will dear abide
    it.[18]

SECOND PLEBEIAN. Poor soul, his eyes are red as fire with
    weeping.

THIRD PLEBEIAN. There's not a nobler man in Rome than
    Antony.

FOURTH PLEBEIAN. Now mark him, he begins again to
    speak.

ANTONY. But yesterday the word of Caesar might
120 Have stood against the world; now lies he there,
    And none so poor to[19] do him reverence.
    O masters! If I were disposed to stir
    Your hearts and minds to mutiny and rage,
    I should do Brutus wrong and Cassius wrong,
125 Who, you all know, are honorable men.
    I will not do them wrong; I rather choose
    To wrong the dead, to wrong myself and you,
    Than I will wrong such honorable men.

18. dear abide it: Pay
dearly for it.

19. to: As to.

But here's a parchment with the seal of Caesar;
130   I found it in his closet; 'tis his will.
Let but the commons[20] hear this testament,
Which, pardon me, I do not mean to read,
And they would go and kiss dead Caesar's wounds,
And dip their napkins[21] in his sacred blood;
135   Yea, beg a hair of him for memory,
And dying, mention it within their wills,
Bequeathing it as a rich legacy
Unto their issue.[22]

FOURTH PLEBEIAN. We'll hear the will; read it, Mark Antony.

140   **ALL.** The will, the will! We will hear Caesar's will!

ANTONY. Have patience, gentle friends, I must not read it.
It is not meet you know how Caesar loved you.
You are not wood, you are not stones, but men;
And being men, hearing the will of Caesar,
145   It will inflame you, it will make you mad.
'Tis good you know not that you are his heirs;
For if you should, O, what would come of it?

FOURTH PLEBEIAN. Read the will! We'll hear it, Antony!
You shall read us the will, Caesar's will!

150   **ANTONY.** Will you be patient? Will you stay awhile?
I have o'ershot myself[23] to tell you of it.
I fear I wrong the honorable men
Whose daggers have stabbed Caesar; I do fear it.

FOURTH PLEBEIAN. They were traitors. Honorable men!

155   **ALL.** The will! The testament!

SECOND PLEBEIAN. They were villains, murderers! The will! Read the will!

ANTONY. You will compel me then to read the will?
Then make a ring about the corpse of Caesar,
160   And let me show you him that made the will.
Shall I descend? And will you give me leave?

ALL. Come down.

SECOND PLEBEIAN. Descend.   [*Antony comes down.*]

THIRD PLEBEIAN. You shall have leave.

165   **FOURTH PLEBEIAN.** A ring! Stand round.

FIRST PLEBEIAN. Stand from the hearse,[24] stand from the body!

SECOND PLEBEIAN. Room for Antony, most noble Antony!

ANTONY. Nay, press not so upon me; stand far off.

ALL. Stand back! Room! Bear back.

170   **ANTONY.** If you have tears, prepare to shed them now.
     You all do know this mantle;[25] I remember
     The first time ever Caesar put it on:
     'Twas on a summer's evening, in his tent,
     That day he overcame the Nervii.
175   Look, in this place ran Cassius' dagger through;
     See what a rent[26] the envious[27] Casca made;
     Through this the well-belovèd Brutus stabbed,
     And as he plucked his cursèd steel away,

24. hearse (hʉrs) *n.*: Coffin.

25. mantle (man' t'l) *n.*: Cloak; toga.

26. rent (rent) *n.*: Torn place.
27. envious (en' vē əs) *adj.*: Spiteful.

Mark how the blood of Caesar followed it,
180 As[28] rushing out of doors, to be resolved[29]
If Brutus so unkindly knocked, or no;
For Brutus, as you know, was Caesar's angel.
Judge, O you gods, how dearly Caesar loved him!
This was the most unkindest cut of all;
185 For when the noble Caesar saw him stab,
Ingratitude, more strong than traitors' arms,
Quite vanquished him. Then burst his mighty heart;
And, in his mantle muffling up his face,
Even at the base of Pompey's statue
190 (Which all the while ran blood) great Caesar fell.
O, what a fall was there, my countrymen!
Then I, and you, and all of us fell down,
Whilst bloody treason flourished[30] over us.
O, now you weep, and I perceive you feel
195 The dint[31] of pity; these are gracious drops.
Kind souls, what[32] weep you when you but behold
Our Caesar's vesture[33] wounded? Look you here,
Here is himself, marred as you see with[34] traitors.

FIRST PLEBEIAN. O piteous spectacle!

200 **SECOND PLEBEIAN.** O noble Caesar!

THIRD PLEBEIAN. O woeful day!

FOURTH PLEBEIAN. O traitors, villains!

FIRST PLEBEIAN. O most bloody sight!

SECOND PLEBEIAN. We will be revenged.

205 **ALL.** Revenge! About![35] Seek! Burn! Fire! Kill! Slay!
Let not a traitor live!

ANTONY. Stay, countrymen.

FIRST PLEBEIAN. Peace there! Hear the noble Antony.

SECOND PLEBEIAN. We'll hear him, we'll follow him, we'll
210 die with him!

ANTONY. Good friends, sweet friends, let me not stir you
up
To such a sudden flood of mutiny.
They that have done this deed are honorable.
What private griefs[36] they have, alas, I know not,
215 That made them do it. They are wise and honorable,
And will, no doubt, with reasons answer you.

28. As: As if.
29. to be resolved: To learn for certain.

30. flourished (flŭr′ ish'd) v.: Grew; triumphed.

31. dint (dint) n.: Force.
32. what: Why.
33. vesture (ves′ chər) n.: Clothing.
34. with: By.

35. About: Let's go.

36. griefs (grēfs) n.: Grievances.

I come not, friends, to steal away your hearts;
I am no orator, as Brutus is;
But (as you know me all) a plain blunt man
220 That love my friend, and that they know full well
That gave me public leave[37] to speak of him.
For I have neither writ, nor words, nor worth,
Action, nor utterance,[38] nor the power of speech
To stir men's blood; I only speak right on.[39]
225 I tell you that which you yourselves do know,
Show you sweet Caesar's wounds, poor poor dumb
   mouths,
And bid them speak for me. But were I Brutus,
And Brutus Antony, there were an Antony
Would ruffle up your spirits, and put a tongue
230 In every wound of Caesar's that should move
The stones of Rome to rise and mutiny.

ALL. We'll mutiny.

FIRST PLEBEIAN. We'll burn the house of Brutus.

THIRD PLEBEIAN. Away, then! Come, seek the conspirators.

ANTONY. Yet hear me, countrymen. Yet hear me speak.

235 **ALL.** Peace, ho! Hear Antony, most noble Antony!

ANTONY. Why, friends, you go to do you know not what:
Wherein hath Caesar thus deserved your loves?
Alas, you know not; I must tell you then:
You have forgot the will I told you of.

240 **ALL.** Most true, the will! Let's stay and hear the will.

ANTONY. Here is the will, and under Caesar's seal.
To every Roman citizen he gives,
To every several man, seventy-five drachmas.

SECOND PLEBEIAN. Most noble Caesar! We'll revenge his
death!

245 **THIRD PLEBEIAN.** O royal Caesar!

ANTONY. Hear me with patience.

ALL. Peace, ho!

ANTONY. Moreover, he hath left you all his walks,
His private arbors, and new-planted orchards,[40]
250 On this side Tiber; he hath left them you,

37. leave: Permission.

**38. neither writ . . .
utterance** (ut′ ər əns):
Neither written speech, nor
fluency, nor reputation, nor
gestures, nor style of
speaking.
39. right on: Directly.

40. walks . . . orchards:
Parks, his private trees,
and newly planted gardens.

And to your heirs forever: common pleasures,[41]
To walk abroad and recreate yourselves.
Here was a Caesar! When comes such another?

FIRST PLEBEIAN. Never, never! Come, away, away!
255   We'll burn his body in the holy place,
And with the brands[42] fire the traitors' houses.
Take up the body.

SECOND PLEBEIAN. Go fetch fire.

THIRD PLEBEIAN. Pluck down benches.

260   FOURTH PLEBEIAN. Pluck down forms, windows, anything!

            [*Exit Plebeians with the body.*]

ANTONY. Now let it work: Mischief, thou art afoot,
Take thou what course thou wilt.

[*Enter Servant.*]

                       How now, fellow?

SERVANT. Sir, Octavius is already come to Rome.

ANTONY. Where is he?

265   SERVANT. He and Lepidus are at Caesar's house.

ANTONY. And thither[43] will I straight to visit him;
He comes upon a wish. Fortune is merry,
And in this mood will give us anything.

SERVANT. I heard him say, Brutus and Cassius
270   Are rid[44] like madmen through the gates of Rome.

ANTONY. Belike[45] they had some notice of the people,[46]
How I had moved them. Bring me to Octavius.[*Exit.*]

Scene iii. *A street.*

[*Enter Cinna the Poet, and after him the Plebeians.*]

CINNA. I dreamt tonight that I did feast with Caesar,
And things unluckily charge my fantasy.[1]
I have no will to wander forth of doors,[2]
Yet something leads me forth.

5   FIRST PLEBEIAN. What is your name?

SECOND PLEBEIAN. Whither are you going?

41. common pleasures:
Public places of recreation.

42. brands: Torches.

43. thither: There.

44. are rid: Have ridden.
45. Belike: Probably.
46. notice of the people:
Word about the mood of
the people.

1. things . . . fantasy:
The events that have
happened weigh heavily on
my imagination.
2. of doors: Outdoors.

THIRD PLEBEIAN. Where do you dwell?

FOURTH PLEBEIAN. Are you a married man or a bachelor?

SECOND PLEBEIAN. Answer every man directly.

10 **FIRST PLEBEIAN.** Ay, and briefly.

FOURTH PLEBEIAN. Ay, and wisely.

THIRD PLEBEIAN. Ay, and truly, you were best.

CINNA. What is my name? Whither am I going? Where do I dwell? Am I a married man or a bachelor? Then, to
15 answer every man directly and briefly, wisely and truly: wisely I say, I am a bachelor.

SECOND PLEBEIAN. That's as much as to say, they are fools that marry; you'll bear me a bang³ for that, I fear. Proceed directly.

3. **bear me a bang:** Get a blow from me.

20 **CINNA.** Directly, I am going to Caesar's funeral.

FIRST PLEBEIAN. As a friend or an enemy?

CINNA. As a friend.

SECOND PLEBEIAN. That matter is answered directly.

FOURTH PLEBEIAN. For your dwelling, briefly.

25 **CINNA.** Briefly, I dwell by the Capitol.

THIRD PLEBEIAN. Your name, sir, truly.

CINNA. Truly, my name is Cinna.

FIRST PLEBEIAN. Tear him to pieces! He's a conspirator.

CINNA. I am Cinna the poet! I am Cinna the poet!

30 **FOURTH PLEBEIAN.** Tear him for his bad verses! Tear him for his bad verses!

CINNA. I am not Cinna the conspirator.

FOURTH PLEBEIAN. It is no matter, his name's Cinna; pluck but his name out of his heart, and turn him
35 going.⁴

4. **turn him going:** Send him on his way.

THIRD PLEBEIAN. Tear him, tear him! [*They attack him.*] Come, brands, ho! Firebrands!⁵ To Brutus', to Cassius'! Burn all! Some to Decius' house, and some to Casca's; some to Ligarius'! Away, go!
[*Exit all the Plebeians with Cinna.*]

5. **Firebrands:** People who stir up others to revolt.

RESPONDING TO THE SELECTION

Your Response

1. If you had been in the audience, how would you have responded to Antony's speech in Scene ii?

Recalling

2. What petition is presented to Caesar, and how does he respond to it?
3. What reason does Brutus give the people for the assassination?
4. How does Antony repeatedly refer to Brutus during the funeral oration?
5. What effect does Antony's speech have on the plebeians?

Interpreting

6. Why does Antony befriend the conspirators immediately after the assassination?
7. Why does Brutus allow Antony to speak at Caesar's funeral?
8. How does Caesar's will affect the people?

Applying

9. Antony convinces the crowd to accept his opinion of Caesar and the conspirators. Think of a modern leader who tries to influence public opinion. What techniques does he or she use?

ANALYZING LITERATURE

Examining Types of Speeches by Actors

Usually an **aside** is spoken by a character as if speaking to himself or herself. In this act, however, two characters speak asides not overheard by the others, and they reveal their true feelings. In a **soliloquy** a character alone onstage reveals and examines his or her thoughts and feelings. A **monologue** is a long speech spoken without interruption by one character in the presence of others. It may or may not reveal what the speaker really thinks or feels.

1. Compare what Cassius says to Antony in Act III, Scene i, line 177 with what he says to Bru-

tus in the aside beginning in line 232.
2. Compare what Antony says in Act III, Scene i, lines 218–222 with his soliloquy from line 254 on.
3. Examine Brutus' speech (Act III, Scene ii, line 12 on). To what extent is Brutus speaking his true feelings?

CRITICAL THINKING AND READING

Understanding Tone

Tone shows the speaker's attitude toward the subject and the audience. The tone of Antony's soliloquy over Caesar's body (Act III, Scene i, line 254 on) is that of sincere grief and rage, as you can infer from the language and sentence structure. Brutus' speech early in Scene ii begins with a reasonable tone and shifts to one urging the crowd's acceptance of the assassination.

1. Examine Antony's funeral oration.
2. Identify the tone and shifts in tone.
3. Give an example from the text to support each of your inferences about the tone.

THINKING AND WRITING

Writing About Background Music

Select a piece of music that would be an appropriate background for the assassination scene. Write a brief explanation of why the selection is appropriate. When you revise, make sure you have supported your choice.

LEARNING OPTION

Writing. Write either a newspaper obituary to announce Caesar's death or an epitaph for his grave or tomb. An obituary contains facts about someone's achievements and death. An epitaph is brief, gives the dates of birth and death, and often includes an inspiring or comforting verse. Use what you know about Caesar from reading Acts I–III to write the obituary or epitaph. If necessary, research additional facts about his life.

GUIDE FOR READING

The Tragedy of Julius Caesar, Act IV

Conflict

Conflict is a struggle between opposing forces. Some kind of conflict is essential for any piece of fiction or drama. The conflict may be external, involving a person and nature, two people, or two groups of people. Sometimes the conflict is internal, involving a person struggling to decide between two opposing ideas or values within himself or herself. The action in fiction or drama depends upon the conflict, which provides the tension as the action builds to the climax. In *The Tragedy of Julius Caesar,* several different types of conflict have been introduced. In earlier acts, we have seen conflict between Caesar and the conspirators, within Brutus over what the course of action should be, and between Cassius and Brutus over how to deal with Antony. Cassius and Brutus disagreed over whether Antony should be killed along with Caesar and whether he should be allowed to speak at Caesar's funeral. These conflicts have arisen because the two characters have differing attitudes toward people and situations.

Focus

Fill in a diagram like the one that follows to predict how the conflicts in the play will be resolved.

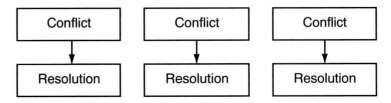

Vocabulary

Knowing the following words will help you as you read Act IV.

legacies (leg' ə sēz) *n.*: Money, property, or position left in a will to someone (p. 369)

slanderous (slan' dər əs) *adj.*: Damaging to a person's reputation (p. 369)

covert (kuv' ərt) *adj.*: Hidden; secret (p. 370)

chastisement (chas tīz' mənt) *n.*: Punishment; severe criticism (p. 373)

philosophy (fil äs' ə fē) *n.*: System of values (p. 377)

Act IV

Scene i. *A house in Rome.*

[*Enter Antony, Octavius, and Lepidus.*]

ANTONY. These many then shall die; their names are
  pricked.

OCTAVIUS. Your brother too must die; consent you, Lepidus?

LEPIDUS. I do consent—

OCTAVIUS.   Prick him down, Antony.

LEPIDUS. Upon condition Publius shall not live,
5   Who is your sister's son, Mark Antony.

ANTONY. He shall not live; look, with a spot I damn him.[1]
  But, Lepidus, go you to Caesar's house;
  Fetch the will hither, and we shall determine
  How to cut off some charge in legacies.

10 **LEPIDUS.** What, shall I find you here?

OCTAVIUS. Or[2] here or at the Capitol.   [*Exit Lepidus.*]

ANTONY. This is a slight unmeritable[3] man,
  Meet to be sent on errands; is it fit,
  The threefold world[4] divided, he should stand
  One of the three to share it?

15 **OCTAVIUS.**   So you thought him,
  And took his voice[5] who should be pricked to die
  In our black sentence and proscription.[6]

ANTONY. Octavius, I have seen more days[7] than you;
  And though we lay these honors on this man.
20 To ease ourselves of divers sland'rous loads,[8]
  He shall but bear them as the ass bears gold,
  To groan and sweat under the business,
  Either led or driven, as we point the way;
  And having brought our treasure where we will,
25 Then take we down his load, and turn him off,
  (Like to the empty ass) to shake his ears
  And graze in commons.[9]

OCTAVIUS.   You may do your will;
  But he's a tried and valiant soldier.

1. with a spot . . . him: With a mark on the tablet, I condemn him.

2. Or: Either.

3. slight unmeritable: Insignificant and without merit.

4. threefold world: Three areas of the Roman Empire—Europe, Asia, and Africa.

5. voice: Vote; opinion.

6. proscription: List of those sentenced to death or exile.

7. have seen more days: I am older.

8. divers sland'rous loads: Various burdens of blame.

9. in commons: On public pasture.

ANTONY. So is my horse, Octavius, and for that

30   I do appoint him store of provender.[10]

It is a creature that I teach to fight,

To wind,[11] to stop, to run directly on,

His corporal motion governed by my spirit.[12]

And, in some taste,[13] is Lepidus but so.

35   He must be taught, and trained, and bid go forth.

A barren-spirited[14] fellow; one that feeds

On objects, arts, and imitations,[15]

Which, out of use and staled[16] by other men,

Begin his fashion.[17] Do not talk of him

40   But as a property. And now, Octavius,

Listen great things. Brutus and Cassius

Are levying powers;[18] we must straight make head.[19]

Therefore let our alliance be combined,

Our best friends made, our means stretched;[20]

45   And let us presently go sit in council

How covert matters may be best disclosed,

And open perils surest answerèd.[21]

    OCTAVIUS. Let us do so; for we are at the stake,[22]

And bayed about with many enemies;

50   And some that smile have in their hearts, I fear,

Millions of mischiefs.[23]   [*Exit.*]

10. appoint . . . provender: Allot him a supply of food.

11. wind (wīnd) *v*.: Turn.

12. His . . . spirit: His body movements governed by my mind.

13. taste: Degree.

14. barren-spirited: Without ideas of his own.

15. feeds on objects, arts, and imitations: Enjoys curiosities, arts, and styles.

16. staled: Cheapened.

17. Begin his fashion: He begins to use. (He is hopelessly behind the times.)

18. levying powers: Enlisting troops.

19. straight make head: Quickly gather soldiers.

20. stretched: Used to the fullest advantage.

21. How . . . answerèd: How secrets may be discovered and dangers met.

22. at the stake: Like a bear tied to a stake and set upon by many dogs.

23. mischiefs: Plans to injure us.

Scene ii. *Camp near Sardis.*

[Drum. Enter Brutus, Lucilius, Lucius, and the Army. Titinius and Pindarus meet them.]

BRUTUS. Stand ho!

LUCILIUS. Give the word, ho! and stand.

BRUTUS. What now, Lucilius, is Cassius near?

LUCILIUS. He is at hand, and Pindarus is come
5   To do you salutation[1] from his master.

BRUTUS. He greets me well. Your master, Pindarus,
In his own change, or by ill officers,
Hath given me some worthy cause to wish
Things done undone;[2] but if he be at hand,
I shall be satisfied.

10   **PINDARUS.**   I do not doubt
But that my noble master will appear
Such as he is, full of regard and honor.

BRUTUS. He is not doubted. A word, Lucilius,
How he received you; let me be resolved.[3]

15   **LUCILIUS.** With courtesy and with respect enough,
But not with such familiar instances,[4]
Nor with such free and friendly conference[5]
As he hath used of old.

BRUTUS.   Thou hast described
A hot friend cooling. Ever note, Lucilius,
20   When love begins to sicken and decay
It useth an enforcèd ceremony.[6]
There are no tricks in plain and simple faith;
But hollow[7] men, like horses hot at hand,[8]
Make gallant show and promise of their mettle;
                         [Low march within.]
25   But when they should endure the bloody spur,
They fall their crests, and like deceitful jades
Sink in the trial.[9] Comes his army on?

LUCILIUS. They mean this night in Sardis to be quartered;
The greater part, the horse in general,[10]
Are come with Cassius.

[Enter Cassius and his Powers.]

30   **BRUTUS.**   Hark! He is arrived.
March gently[11] on to meet him.

---

1. To do you salutation: To bring you greetings.

2. In his own . . . done undone: Has changed in his feelings toward me or has received bad advice from subordinates and has made me wish we had not done what we did.

3. resolved: Fully informed.

4. familiar instances: Marks of friendship.
5. conference: Conversation.

6. enforcèd ceremony: Forced formality.
7. hollow: Insincere.
8. hot at hand: Full of spirit when reined in.

9. They fall . . . the trial: They drop their necks, and like worn-out worthless horses fail the test.
10. horse in general: Cavalry.

11. gently: Slowly.

CASSIUS. Stand, ho!

BRUTUS. Stand, ho! Speak the word along.

FIRST SOLDIER. Stand!

35 **SECOND SOLDIER.** Stand!

THIRD SOLDIER. Stand!

CASSIUS. Most noble brother, you have done me wrong.

BRUTUS. Judge me, you gods! Wrong I mine enemies?
    And if not so, how should I wrong a brother?

40 **CASSIUS.** Brutus, this sober form¹² of yours hides
        wrongs;
    And when you do them—

BRUTUS.   Cassius, be content.¹³
    Speak your griefs softly; I do know you well.
    Before the eyes of both our armies here
    (Which should perceive nothing but love from us)
45   Let us not wrangle. Bid them move away;
    Then in my tent, Cassius, enlarge¹⁴ your griefs,
    And I will give you audience.

CASSIUS.   Pindarus,
    Bid our commanders lead their charges¹⁵ off
    A little from this ground.

50 **BRUTUS.** Lucilius, do you the like, and let no man
    Come to our tent till we have done our conference.
    Let Lucius and Titinius guard our door.
               [Exit all but Brutus and Cassius.]

Scene iii. *Brutus' tent.*

CASSIUS. That you have wronged me doth appear in this:
    You have condemned and noted¹ Lucius Pella
    For taking bribes here of the Sardians;
    Wherein my letters, praying on his side,²
5   Because I knew the man, was slighted off.³

BRUTUS. You wronged yourself to write in such a case.

CASSIUS. In such a time as this it is not meet
    That every nice offense should bear his comment.⁴

BRUTUS. Let me tell you, Cassius, you yourself
10   Are much condemned to have an itching palm,⁵
    To sell and mart⁶ your offices for gold
    To undeservers.

12. sober form: Serious manner.

13. be content: Be patient.

14. enlarge: Freely express.

15. charges: Troops.

1. noted: Publicly denounced.
2. praying on his side: Pleading on his behalf.
3. slighted off: Disregarded.

4. every . . . comment: Every petty fault should receive its criticism.

5. condemned . . . palm: Accused of having a hand eager to accept bribes.
6. mart: trade.

CASSIUS.   I an itching palm?
    You know that you are Brutus that speaks this,
    Or, by the gods, this speech were else your last.

15   **BRUTUS.** The name of Cassius honors[7] this corruption,
    And chastisement doth therefore hide his head.

CASSIUS. Chastisement!

BRUTUS. Remember March, the ides of March remember.
    Did not great Julius bleed for justice' sake?
20   What villain touched his body, that did stab,
    And not[8] for justice? What, shall one of us,
    That struck the foremost man of all this world
    But for supporting robbers,[9] shall we now
    Contaminate our fingers with base bribes,
25   And sell the mighty space of our large honors[10]
    For so much trash[11] as may be graspèd thus?
    I had rather be a dog, and bay[12] the moon,
    Than such a Roman.

CASSIUS.   Brutus, bait[13] not me;
    I'll not endure it. You forget yourself
30   To hedge me in.[14] I am a soldier, I,
    Older in practice, abler than yourself
    To make conditions.[15]

BRUTUS.   Go to! You are not, Cassius.

CASSIUS. I am.

BRUTUS. I say you are not.

35   **CASSIUS.** Urge[16] me no more, I shall forget myself;
    Have mind upon your health;[17] tempt me no farther.

BRUTUS. Away, slight[18] man!

CASSIUS. Is't possible?

BRUTUS.   Hear me, for I will speak.
    Must I give way and room to your rash choler?[19]
40   Shall I be frighted when a madman stares?

CASSIUS. O ye gods, ye gods! Must I endure all this?

BRUTUS. All this? Ay, more: fret till your proud heart
    break.
    Go show your slaves how choleric[20] you are,
    And make your bondmen tremble. Must I budge?[21]
45   Must I observe you?[22] Must I stand and crouch
    Under your testy humor?[23] By the gods,
    You shall digest the venom of your spleen,[24]

7. honors: Gives respectability to.

8. And not: Except.
9. But . . . robbers: Here Brutus says, for the first time, that Caesar's officials were also involved in taking bribes and that this was a motive in his assassination.
10. honors: Offices.
11. trash: Dirty money.
12. bay: Howl at.

13. bait: Harass (as a bear tied to a stake is harassed by dogs).
14. hedge me in: Restrict my actions.

15. conditions: Decisions.

16. Urge: Drive.
17. health: Safety.

18. slight: Insignificant.

19. choler (käl′ ər) *n.*: Anger.
20. choleric (käl′ ər ik) *adj.*: Quick-tempered.
21. budge: Flinch away from you.
22. observe you: Show reverence toward you.
23. testy humor: Irritability.
24. digest . . . spleen: Eat the poison of your spleen. (The spleen was thought to be the source of anger.)

Though it do split you; for, from this day forth,
I'll use you for my mirth,[25] yea, for my laughter,
When you are waspish.[26]

50   CASSIUS.   Is it come to this?

BRUTUS. You say you are a better soldier:
  Let it appear so; make your vaunting[27] true,
  And it shall please me well. For mine own part,
  I shall be glad to learn of[28] noble men.

CASSIUS. You wrong me every way; you wrong me,
55   Brutus;
  I said, an elder soldier, not a better.
  Did I say, better?

BRUTUS.   If you did, I care not.

CASSIUS. When Caesar lived, he durst not thus have
  moved[29] me.

BRUTUS. Peace, peace, you durst not so have tempted
  him.

60   CASSIUS. I durst not?

BRUTUS. No.

CASSIUS. What? Durst not tempt him?

BRUTUS.   For your life you durst not.

CASSIUS. Do not presume too much upon my love;
  I may do that I shall be sorry for.

65   BRUTUS. You have done that you should be sorry for.
  There is no terror, Cassius, in your threats;
  For I am armed so strong in honesty
  That they pass by me as the idle wind,
  Which I respect not. I did send to you
70   For certain sums of gold, which you denied me;
  For I can raise no money by vile means.
  By heaven, I had rather coin my heart
  And drop my blood for drachmas than to wring
  From the hard hands of peasants their vile trash
75   By any indirection.[30] I did send
  To you for gold to pay my legions,
  Which you denied me. Was that done like Cassius?
  Should I have answered Caius Cassius so?
  When Marcus Brutus grows so covetous[31]

80   To lock such rascal counters[32] from his friends,
      Be ready, gods, with all your thunderbolts,
      Dash him to pieces!

CASSIUS.   I denied you not.

BRUTUS. You did.

CASSIUS.   I did not. He was but a fool
      That brought my answer back. Brutus hath rived[33]
         my heart.
85   A friend should bear his friend's infirmities;
      But Brutus makes mine greater than they are.

BRUTUS. I do not, till you practice them on me.

CASSIUS. You love me not.

BRUTUS.   I do not like your faults.

CASSIUS. A friendly eye could never see such faults.

90   **BRUTUS.** A flatterer's would not, though they do appear
      As huge as high Olympus.

CASSIUS. Come, Antony, and young Octavius, come,
      Revenge yourselves alone[34] on Cassius,
      For Cassius is aweary of the world:
95   Hated by one he loves; braved[35] by his brother;
      Checked like a bondman;[36] all his faults observed,
      Set in a notebook, learned and conned by rote[37]
      To cast into my teeth. O, I could weep
      My spirit from mine eyes! There is my dagger,
100   And here my naked breast; within, a heart
      Dearer than Pluto's mine,[38] richer than gold;
      If that thou be'st a Roman, take it forth.
      I, that denied thee gold, will give my heart.
      Strike as thou didst at Caesar; for I know,
      When thou didst hate him worst, thou lovedst him
105   better
      Than ever thou lovedst Cassius.

BRUTUS.   Sheathe your dagger.
      Be angry when you will, it shall have scope.[39]
      Do what you will, dishonor shall be humor.[40]
      O Cassius, you are yokèd[41] with a lamb
110   That carries anger as the flint bears fire,
      Who, much enforcèd,[42] shows a hasty spark,
      And straight is cold again.

32. rascal counters:
Worthless coins.

33. rived (rīv'd) *v.*:
Broken.

34. alone: Only.
35. braved: Bullied.
36. Checked like a bondman: Scolded like a slave.
37. conned by rote: Memorized.

38. Pluto's mine: The mythological Roman god of the underworld and of riches symbolized by his mine.

39. scope: Free play.
40. dishonor . . . humor: Any dishonorable acts will be considered just your irritable disposition.
41. yokèd: In partnership.
42. enforcèd: Provoked.

CASSIUS.   Hath Cassius lived
    To be but mirth and laughter to his Brutus
    When grief and blood ill-tempered vexeth him?

115 BRUTUS. When I spoke that, I was ill-tempered too.

CASSIUS. Do you confess so much? Give me your hand.

BRUTUS. And my heart too.

CASSIUS.   O Brutus!

BRUTUS.   What's the matter?

CASSIUS. Have not you love enough to bear with me
    When that rash humor which my mother gave me
    Makes me forgetful?

120 BRUTUS.   Yes, Cassius, and from henceforth,
    When you are over-earnest with your Brutus,
    He'll think your mother chides, and leave you so.[43]

[*Enter a Poet, followed by Lucilius, Titinius, and Lucius.*]

POET. Let me go in to see the generals;

43. your mother . . . so:
It is just your inherited
disposition and let it go at
that.

There is some grudge between 'em; 'tis not meet
125 They be alone.

LUCILIUS. You shall not come to them.

POET. Nothing but death shall stay me.

CASSIUS. How now? What's the matter?

POET. For shame, you generals! What do you mean?
130 Love, and be friends, as two such men should be;
For I have seen more years, I'm sure, than ye.

CASSIUS. Ha, ha! How vilely doth this cynic[44] rhyme!

44. cynic: Rude fellow.

BRUTUS. Get you hence, sirrah! Saucy fellow, hence!

CASSIUS. Bear with him, Brutus, 'tis his fashion.

135 **BRUTUS.** I'll know his humor when he knows his time.[45]
What should the wars do with these jigging[46] fools?
Companion,[47] hence!

45. I'll know . . . time: I'll
accept his eccentricity
when he chooses a proper
time to exhibit it.
46. jigging: Rhyming.
47. Companion: Fellow
(used to show contempt).

CASSIUS.   Away, away, be gone! [*Exit Poet.*]

BRUTUS. Lucilius and Titinius, bid the commanders
Prepare to lodge their companies tonight.

CASSIUS. And come yourselves, and bring Messala with
140   you
Immediately to us.   [*Exit Lucilius and Titinius.*]

BRUTUS.   Lucius, a bowl of wine. [*Exit Lucius.*]

CASSIUS. I did not think you could have been so angry.

BRUTUS. O Cassius, I am sick of many griefs.

CASSIUS. Of your philosophy you make no use,
145   If you give place to accidental evils.[48]

**48. Of your philosophy
. . . accidental evils:**
Brutus's philosophy was
Stoicism. As a Stoic he
believed that nothing evil
would happen to a good
man.

BRUTUS. No man bears sorrow better. Portia is dead.

CASSIUS. Ha? Portia?

BRUTUS. She is dead.

CASSIUS. How scaped I killing when I crossed you so?[49]
150   O insupportable and touching loss!
Upon[50] what sickness?

**49. How scaped . . . you
so?:** How did I escape
being killed when I
opposed you so?
50. Upon: As a result of.

BRUTUS.   Impatient of my absence,
And grief that young Octavius with Mark Antony
Have made themselves so strong—for with her death
That tidings came[51]—with this she fell distract,[52]
155 And (her attendants absent) swallowed fire.

51. tidings: News.
52. fell distract: Became
distraught.

CASSIUS. And died so?

BRUTUS.   Even so.

CASSIUS.   O ye immortal gods!

[*Enter Lucius, with wine and tapers.*]

BRUTUS. Speak no more of her. Give me a bowl of wine.
  In this I bury all unkindness, Cassius.   [*Drinks.*]

CASSIUS. My heart is thirsty for that noble pledge.
160   Fill, Lucius, till the wine o'erswell the cup;
    I cannot drink too much of Brutus' love.
                                    [*Drinks. Exit Lucius.*]

[*Enter Titinius and Messala.*]

BRUTUS. Come in, Titinius! Welcome, good Messala.
    Now sit we close about this taper here,
    And call in question[53] our necessities.

53. call in question:
Examine.

CASSIUS. Portia, art thou gone?

165 **BRUTUS.**   No more, I pray you.
    Messala, I have here receivèd letters
    That young Octavius and Mark Antony
    Come down upon us with a mighty power,[54]
    Bending their expedition toward Philippi.[55]

170 **MESSALA.** Myself have letters of the selfsame tenure.[56]

BRUTUS. With what addition?

54. power: Army.
55. Bending . . . Philippi
(fi lip′ ī): Directing their
rapid march toward
Philippi.
56. selfsame tenure:
Same message.

MESSALA. That by proscription and bills of outlawry
    Octavius, Antony, and Lepidus
    Have put to death an hundred senators.

175 **BRUTUS.** Therein our letters do not well agree.
    Mine speak of seventy senators that died
    By their proscriptions, Cicero being one.

CASSIUS. Cicero one?

MESSALA.   Cicero is dead,
    And by that order of proscription.
180   Had you your letters from your wife, my lord?

BRUTUS. No, Messala.

MESSALA. Nor nothing in your letters writ of her?

BRUTUS. Nothing, Messala.

MESSALA.   That methinks is strange.

BRUTUS. Why ask you? Hear you aught[57] of her in yours?

185   **MESSALA.** No, my lord.

BRUTUS. Now as you are a Roman, tell me true.

MESSALA. Then like a Roman bear the truth I tell,
For certain she is dead, and by strange manner.

BRUTUS. Why, farewell, Portia. We must die, Messala.
190   With meditating that she must die once,
I have the patience to endure it now.

MESSALA. Even so great men great losses should endure.

CASSIUS. I have as much of this in art[58] as you,
But yet my nature could not bear it so.

195   **BRUTUS.** Well, to our work alive.[59] What do you think
Of marching to Philippi presently?

CASSIUS. I do not think it good.

BRUTUS.   Your reason?

CASSIUS.   This it is:
'Tis better that the enemy seek us;
So shall he waste his means, weary his soldiers,
200   Doing himself offense,[60] whilst we, lying still,
Are full of rest, defense, and nimbleness.

BRUTUS. Good reasons must of force[61] give place to
      better.
The people 'twixt Philippi and this ground
Do stand but in a forced affection;[62]
205   For they have grudged us contribution.[63]
The enemy, marching along by them,
By them shall make a fuller number up,[64]
Come on refreshed, new-added[65] and encouraged;
From which advantage shall we cut him off
210   If at Philippi we do face him there,
These people at our back.

CASSIUS.   Hear me, good brother.

BRUTUS. Under your pardon.[66] You must note beside
That we have tried the utmost of our friends,
Our legions are brimful, our cause is ripe.
215   The enemy increaseth every day;
We, at the height, are ready to decline.
There is a tide in the affairs of men
Which, taken at the flood, leads on to fortune;
Omitted,[67] all the voyage of their life

57. aught (ôt) *n.:* Anything at all.

58. have . . . art: Have as much Stoicism in theory.
59. to our work alive: Let us go about the work we have to do as living men.

60. offense: Harm.

61. of force: Of necessity.

62. Do stand . . . affection: Support us only by fear of force.
63. grudged us contribution: Given us aid and supplies grudgingly.
64. shall make . . . up: Will add more to their numbers.
65. new-added: Reinforced.

66. Under your pardon: Excuse me.

67. Omitted: Neglected.

220   Is bound[68] in shallows and in miseries.
        On such a full sea are we now afloat,
        And we must take the current when it serves,
        Or lose our ventures.

        CASSIUS.   Then, with your will,[69] go on;
        We'll along ourselves and meet them at Philippi.

225   BRUTUS. The deep of night is crept upon our talk,
        And nature must obey necessity,
        Which we will niggard with a little rest.[70]
        There is no more to say?

        CASSIUS.   No more. Good night.
        Early tomorrow will we rise and hence.[71]

[*Enter Lucius.*]

        BRUTUS. Lucius, my gown.[72]   [*Exit Lucius.*]
230   Farewell, good Messala.
        Good night, Titinius. Noble, noble Cassius,
        Good night, and good repose.

        CASSIUS.   O my dear brother,
        This was an ill beginning of the night.
        Never come[73] such division 'tween our souls!
        Let it not, Brutus.

[*Enter Lucius, with the gown.*]

235   BRUTUS.   Everything is well.

        CASSIUS. Good night, my lord.

        BRUTUS.   Good night, good brother.

        TITINIUS, MESSALA. Good night, Lord Brutus.

        BRUTUS.   Farewell, every one.
                                            [*Exit.*]
        Give me the gown. Where is thy instrument?[74]

        LUCIUS. Here in the tent.

        BRUTUS.   What, thou speak'st drowsily?
        Poor knave,[75] I blame thee not; thou art
240   o'erwatched.[76]
        Call Claudius and some other of my men;
        I'll have them sleep on cushions in my tent.

        LUCIUS. Varro and Claudius!

[*Enter Varro and Claudius.*]

        VARRO. Calls my lord?

68. bound: Confined.

69. with your will: As you wish.

70. niggard . . . rest: Satisfy stingily with a short sleep.

71. hence: Leave.

72. gown: Nightgown.

73. Never come: May there never come.

74. instrument: Lute (probably).

75. knave (nāv) *n.*: Servant.
76. o'erwatched: Weary with too much watchfulness.

245   **BRUTUS.** I pray you, sirs, lie in my tent and sleep.
        It may be I shall raise[77] you by and by
        On business to my brother Cassius.

     VARRO. So please you, we will stand and watch your
          pleasure.

   BRUTUS. I will not have it so; lie down, good sirs;
250   It may be I shall otherwise bethink me.[78]
                  [*Varro and Claudius lie down.*]
       Look. Lucius, here's the book I sought for so;
       I put it in the pocket of my gown.

   LUCIUS. I was sure your lordship did not give it me.

   BRUTUS. Bear with me, good boy, I am much forgetful.
255   Canst thou hold up thy heavy eyes awhile,
       And touch[79] thy instrument a strain or two?

   LUCIUS. Ay, my lord, an't[80] please you.

   BRUTUS.   It does, my boy.
       I trouble thee too much, but thou art willing.

   LUCIUS. It is my duty, sir.

260   **BRUTUS.** I should not urge thy duty past thy might;
       I know young bloods[81] look for a time of rest.

   LUCIUS. I have slept, my lord, already.

   BRUTUS. It was well done, and thou shalt sleep again;
       I will not hold thee long. If I do live,
265   I will be good to thee.

[*Music, and a song.*]

       This is a sleepy tune. O murd'rous[82] slumber!
       Layest thou thy leaden mace[83] upon my boy,
       That plays thee music? Gentle knave, good night;
       I will not do thee so much wrong to wake thee.
270   If thou dost nod, thou break'st thy instrument;
       I'll take it from thee; and, good boy, good night.
       Let me see, let me see; is not the leaf[84] turned down
       Where I left reading? Here it is, I think.

[*Enter the Ghost of Caesar.*]

       How ill this taper burns. Ha! Who comes here?
275   I think it is the weakness of mine eyes
       That shapes this monstrous apparition.[85]
       It comes upon[86] me. Art thou anything?
       Art thou some god, some angel, or some devil,

77. raise: Wake.

78. otherwise bethink me: Change my mind.

79. touch: Play.

80. an't: If it.

81. bloods: Constitutions.

82. murd'rous: Deathlike.
83. mace (mās) *n.*: Staff of office (an allusion to the practice of tapping a person on the shoulder with a mace when arresting him).

84. leaf: Page.

85. monstrous apparition: Ominous ghost.
86. upon: Toward.

That mak'st my blood cold, and my hair to stare?[87]
280   Speak to me what thou art.

87. stare: Stand on end.

GHOST. Thy evil spirit, Brutus.

BRUTUS.   Why com'st thou?

GHOST. To tell thee thou shalt see me at Philippi.

BRUTUS. Well; then I shall see thee again?

GHOST. Ay, at Philippi.

285   **BRUTUS.** Why, I will see thee at Philippi then.

                                 [*Exit Ghost.*]
    Now I have taken heart thou vanishest.
    Ill spirit, I would hold more talk with thee.
    Boy! Lucius! Varro! Claudius! Sirs, awake!
    Claudius!

290   **LUCIUS.** The strings, my lord, are false.[88]

88. false: Out of tune.

BRUTUS. He thinks he still is at his instrument.
    Lucius, awake!

LUCIUS. My lord?

BRUTUS. Didst thou dream, Lucius, that thou so criedst
    out?

295   **LUCIUS.** My lord, I do not know that I did cry.

BRUTUS. Yes, that thou didst. Didst thou see anything?

LUCIUS. Nothing, my lord.

BRUTUS. Sleep again, Lucius. Sirrah Claudius!
    [*To Varro*] Fellow thou, awake!

300   **VARRO.** My lord?

CLAUDIUS. My lord?

BRUTUS. Why did you so cry out, sirs, in your sleep?

BOTH. Did we, my lord?

BRUTUS.   Ay. Saw you anything?

VARRO. No, my lord, I saw nothing.

CLAUDIUS.   Nor I, my lord.

305   **BRUTUS.** Go and commend me[89] to my brother Cassius;
    Bid him set on his pow'rs betimes before,[90]
    And we will follow.

89. commend: Carry my greetings.
90. set on . . . before: Advance his troops.

BOTH.   It shall be done, my lord.   [*Exit.*]

RESPONDING TO THE SELECTION

Your Response

1. With whom do you sympathize in Act IV—Brutus or Cassius?
2. What is your response to the episode in which Caesar's ghost visits Brutus?

Recalling

3. What three men rule Rome after Caesar's death? Describe each of them.
4. What is the immediate cause of the quarrel between Brutus and Cassius? How does Cassius defend himself?
5. How does Portia die? Describe Brutus' reaction and Cassius' reaction to the death.
6. What supernatural event occurs at the end of the act? Describe Brutus' reaction to the event.

Interpreting

7. How is the argument between Brutus and Cassius different from the one between Octavius and Antony in Scene i?
8. What does the ghost mean when he says to Brutus, "Thou shalt see me at Philippi"?

Applying

9. Charles Dickens once wrote, "An idea, like a ghost, according to the common notion of ghosts, must be spoken to a little before it will explain itself." First discuss the meaning of this quotation. Then provide an explanation for Caesar's ghost.

ANALYZING LITERATURE

Understanding Conflict

This act contains the bitter quarrel between the two old friends Brutus and Cassius, a conflict that does much to reveal the characters' natures.

1. Discuss the argument. How does it begin? How does it build? How is it resolved?
2. What does the argument show us about the characters' natures? Use examples from the play to support your inferences.

CRITICAL THINKING AND READING

Analyzing Arguments

An **argument** is a course of reasoning intended to prove a point. For example, Brutus' speech to the Roman crowd in Act III was an argument suggesting that Caesar's assassination was necessary to preserve the freedom of Roman citizens.

Contrast Cassius' and Brutus' arguments about going to Philippi in Act IV, Scene iii, lines 196–230. Whose arguments are stronger and more reasonable? Explain why.

THINKING AND WRITING

Rewriting in Contemporary Language

Rewrite in contemporary language the discussion between Brutus and Cassius in Act IV, Scene iii, lines 196–230. As you work, try to make the dialogue consistent with each man's character. When you have finished revising and proofreading your work, team up with a classmate to perform with one and then the other's version.

LEARNING OPTIONS

1. **Art.** Illustrate the scene in which Caesar's ghost visits Brutus. First draw Brutus as he sees the ghost but doesn't believe his eyes. Capture Brutus' disbelief in your drawing. Next draw Caesar's ghost as you interpret it.
2. **Cross-curricular Connection.** Find music that would be appropriate for Lucius to play at the end of Act IV. Your school or local library might have music tapes or compact disks that you could borrow and play for the rest of the class. Select music that captures the mood of the scene. If possible, try to find music played on a lute.

GUIDE FOR READING

The Tragedy of Julius Caesar, Act V

Tragedy

Tragedy is a dramatic form that was first defined about 330 B.C. by the Greek philosopher Aristotle. The main character in a tragedy is involved in a struggle of great significance that ends in disaster. This main character is a noble person of high rank whose ruin is caused by a **tragic flaw** or weakness. The tragic flaw may be excessive ambition, pride, jealousy, or some other common human frailty. The flaw inevitably leads to the character's downfall. Seeing that the actions are leading to disaster arouses emotions of pity and fear in the audience. By the time the tragedy ends, the audience has been cleansed of these emotions because they have exhausted them. This process is called a **catharsis.** A tragedy leaves not only the audience, but the main character as well, with greater insight and understanding of life.

Focus

If you were writing a tragedy for our own times, what kind of person would you choose as a tragic hero, what flaw would he or she have, and how would this flaw become evident? Answer these questions by filling in a chart like the one that follows.

Person	Character flaw	Situation

Make a similar chart for Brutus after you finish reading the play.

Vocabulary

Knowing the following words will help you as you read Act V of *The Tragedy of Julius Caesar.*

Epicurus (ep′ ə kyo͞or′ əs): A Greek philosopher who tried to find freedom from physical pain and emotional disturbance (p. 387)

ensign (en′ s'n) *n.:* Old word for a standard bearer; one who carries a flag (p. 387)

envy (en′ vē) *n.:* Feeling of desire for another's possessions or qualities and jealousy at not having them (p. 396)

Act V

Scene i. *The plains of Philippi.*

[*Enter Octavius, Antony, and their Army.*]

OCTAVIUS. Now, Antony, our hopes are answerèd;
    You said the enemy would not come down,
    But keep the hills and upper regions.
    It proves not so; their battles[1] are at hand;
5   They mean to warn[2] us at Philippi here,
    Answering before we do demand of them.[3]

ANTONY. Tut, I am in their bosoms,[4] and I know
    Wherefore[5] they do it. They could be content
    To visit other places, and come down
10   With fearful bravery,[6] thinking by this face[7]
    To fasten in our thoughts[8] that they have courage;
    But 'tis not so.

[*Enter a Messenger.*]

MESSENGER.   Prepare you, generals,
    The enemy comes on in gallant show;
    Their bloody sign[9] of battle is hung out,
15   And something to be done immediately.

ANTONY. Octavius, lead your battle softly[10] on
    Upon the left hand of the even[11] field.

OCTAVIUS. Upon the right hand I; keep thou the left.

ANTONY. Why do you cross me in this exigent?[12]

20 **OCTAVIUS.** I do not cross you; but I will do so.   [*March.*]

[*Drum. Enter Brutus, Cassius, and their Army; Lucilius, Titinius, Messala, and others.*]

BRUTUS. They stand, and would have parley.[13]

CASSIUS. Stand fast, Titinius, we must out and talk.

OCTAVIUS. Mark Antony, shall we give sign of battle?

ANTONY. No, Caesar, we will answer on their charge.[14]
    Make forth;[15] the generals would have some words.

OCTAVIUS. Stir not until the signal.

BRUTUS. Words before blows; is it so, countrymen?

---

1. **battles:** Armies.
2. **warn:** Challenge.
3. **Answering . . . of them:** Appearing in opposition to us before we challenge them.
4. **am in their bosoms:** Know what they are thinking.
5. **Wherefore:** Why.
6. **fearful bravery:** Awesome show of bravery covering up their fear.
7. **face:** Appearance.
8. **fasten in our thoughts:** Convince us.

9. **bloody sign:** Red flag.

10. **softly:** Slowly.
11. **even:** Level.

12. **exigent:** Critical situation.

13. **parley:** Conference between enemies.

14. **answer their charge:** Meet their advance.
15. **Make forth:** Go forward.

OCTAVIUS. Not that we love words better, as you do.

BRUTUS. Good words are better than bad strokes, Octavius.

ANTONY. In your bad strokes, Brutus, you give good
30   words;
        Witness the hole you made in Caesar's heart,
        Crying "Long live! Hail, Caesar!"

CASSIUS.   Antony,
        The posture[16] of your blows are yet unknown;
        But for your words, they rob the Hybla bees,[17]
        And leave them honeyless.

35 **ANTONY.**   Not stingless too.

BRUTUS. O, yes, and soundless too;
        For you have stol'n their buzzing, Antony,
        And very wisely threat before you sting.

ANTONY. Villains! You did not so, when your vile daggers
40   Hacked one another in the sides of Caesar.
        You showed your teeth[18] like apes, and fawned like
          hounds,
        And bowed like bondmen, kissing Caesar's feet;
        Whilst damnèd Casca, like a cur, behind
        Struck Caesar on the neck. O you flatterers!

45 **CASSIUS.** Flatterers! Now, Brutus, thank yourself;
        This tongue had not offended so today,
        If Cassius might have ruled.[19]

OCTAVIUS. Come, come, the cause.[20] If arguing make us
        sweat,
        The proof[21] of it will turn to redder drops.
50   Look,
        I draw a sword against conspirators.
        When think you that the sword goes up[22] again?
        Never, till Caesar's three and thirty wounds
        Be well avenged; or till another Caesar
55   Have added slaughter to the sword of traitors.[23]

BRUTUS. Caesar, thou canst not die by traitors' hands,
        Unless thou bring'st them with thee.

OCTAVIUS.   So I hope.
        I was not born to die on Brutus' sword.

16. posture: Quality.
17. Hybla bees: Bees, from the town of Hybla in Sicily, noted for their sweet honey.

18. showed your teeth: Grinned.

19. If Cassius might have ruled: If Cassius had had his way when he urged that Antony be killed.
20. cause: Business at hand.
21. proof: Test.

22. goes up: Goes into its scabbard.

23. till another Caesar . . . traitors: Until I, another Caesar, have also been killed by you.

BRUTUS. O, if thou wert the noblest of thy strain,[24]

60   Young man, thou couldst not die more honorable.

CASSIUS. A peevish[25] schoolboy, worthless of such honor,

    Joined with a masker and a reveler.[26]

ANTONY. Old Cassius still!

OCTAVIUS.   Come, Antony; away!

    Defiance, traitors, hurl we in your teeth.

65   If you dare fight today, come to the field;

    If not, when you have stomachs.[27]

                [Exit Octavius, Antony, and Army.]

CASSIUS. Why, now blow wind, swell billow, and swim bark![28]

    The storm is up, and all is on the hazard.[29]

BRUTUS. Ho, Lucilius, hark, a word with you.

           [Lucilius and Messala stand forth.]

LUCILIUS.   My lord?

       [Brutus and Lucilius converse apart.]

CASSIUS. Messala.

MESSALA.   What says my general?

70 **CASSIUS.**   Messala,

    This is my birthday; as this very day

    Was Cassius born. Give me thy hand, Messala:

    Be thou my witness that against my will

    (As Pompey was)[30] am I compelled to set[31]

75   Upon one battle all our liberties.

    You know that I held Epicurus strong,[32]

    And his opinion; now I change my mind.

    And partly credit things that do presage.[33]

    Coming from Sardis, on our former[34] ensign

80   Two mighty eagles fell,[35] and there they perched,

    Gorging and feeding from our soldiers' hands,

    Who to Philippi here consorted[36] us.

    This morning are they fled away and gone,

    And in their steads do ravens, crows, and kites[37]

85   Fly o'er our heads and downward look on us

    As we were sickly prey; their shadows seem

    A canopy most fatal,[38] under which

    Our army lies, ready to give up the ghost.

MESSALA. Believe not so.

---

24. noblest of thy strain: Best of your family.

25. peevish: Silly.

26. a masker and a reveler: One who takes part in masquerades and festivities.

27. stomachs: Appetites for battle.

28. bark: Ship.

29. on the hazard: At stake.

30. As Pompey was: Against his own judgment, Pompey was urged to do battle against Caesar. The battle resulted in Pompey's defeat and murder.

31. set: Stake.

32. held Epicurus strong: Believed in Epicurus's philosophy that the gods do not interest themselves in human affairs and that omens are merely superstitions.

33. presage: Foretell.

34. former: Foremost.

35. fell: Swooped down.

36. consorted: Accompanied.

37. ravens . . . kites: Birds that are bad omens.

38. a canopy most fatal: A rooflike covering foretelling death.

CASSIUS.   I but believe it partly,
90   For I am fresh of spirit and resolved
        To meet all perils very constantly.[39]

BRUTUS. Even so, Lucilius.

CASSIUS.   Now, most noble Brutus,
        The gods today stand friendly, that we may,
        Lovers in peace, lead on our days to age!
95   But since the affairs of men rests still incertain,[40]
        Let's reason with the worst that may befall.[41]
        If we do lose this battle, then is this
        The very last time we shall speak together.
        What are you then determinèd to do?

100   **BRUTUS.** Even by the rule of that philosophy
        By which I did blame Cato for the death
        Which he did give himself; I know not how,
        But I do find it cowardly and vile,
        For fear of what might fall, so to prevent
105   The time of life,[42] arming myself with patience
        To stay the providence[43] of some high powers
        That govern us below.

CASSIUS.   Then, if we lose this battle,
        You are contented to be led in triumph[44]
        Thorough the streets of Rome?

110   **BRUTUS.** No, Cassius, no; think not, thou noble Roman,
        That ever Brutus will go bound to Rome;
        He bears too great a mind. But this same day
        Must end that work the ides of March begun;
        And whether we shall meet again I know not.
115   Therefore our everlasting farewell take.
        Forever, and forever, farewell, Cassius!
        If we do meet again, why, we shall smile;
        If not, why then this parting was well made.

CASSIUS. Forever, and forever, farewell, Brutus!
120   If we do meet again, we'll smile indeed;
        If not, 'tis true this parting was well made.

BRUTUS. Why then, lead on. O, that a man might know
        The end of this day's business ere it come!
        But it sufficeth that the day will end,
125   And then the end is known. Come, ho! Away! [*Exit.*]

39. very constantly: Most resolutely.

40. rests still incertain: Always remain uncertain.
41. befall: Happen.

42. so to prevent . . . life: Thus to anticipate the natural end of life.
43. stay the providence: Await the ordained fate.

44. in triumph: As a captive in the victor's procession.

Scene ii. *The field of battle.*

[Call to arms sounds. Enter Brutus and Messala.]

    BRUTUS. Ride, ride, Messala, ride, and give these bills[1]
    Unto the legions on the other side.[2]
                       [Loud call to arms.]
    Let them set on at once; for I perceive
    But cold demeanor[3] in Octavius' wing,
5   And sudden push gives them the overthrow,[4]
    Ride, ride, Messala! Let them all come down.[5] *[Exit.]*

1. **bills:** Written orders.
2. **other side:** The wing of the army commanded by Cassius.
3. **cold demeanor** (di mēn′ ər): Lack of spirit in their conduct.
4. **sudden push . . . overthrow:** Sudden attack will defeat them.
5. **Let . . . down:** Attack all at once.

Scene iii. *The field of battle.*

[Calls to arms sound. Enter Cassius and Titinius.]

    CASSIUS. O, look, Titinius, look, the villains[1] fly!
    Myself have to mine own turned enemy.[2]
    This ensign here of mine was turning back;
    I slew the coward, and did take it[3] from him.

5   **TITINIUS.** O Cassius, Brutus gave the word too early,
    Who, having some advantage on Octavius,
    Took it too eagerly; his soldiers fell to spoil,[4]
    Whilst we by Antony are all enclosed.

1. **villains:** His own men.
2. **Myself . . . enemy:** I have become an enemy to my own soldiers.
3. **it:** The banner or standard.

4. **fell to spoil:** Began to loot.

[Enter Pindarus.]

    PINDARUS. Fly further off, my lord, fly further off!
10   Mark Antony is in your tents, my lord.
    Fly, therefore, noble Cassius, fly far off!

    CASSIUS. This hill is far enough. Look, look, Titinius!
    Are those my tents where I perceive the fire?

    TITINIUS. They are, my lord.

    CASSIUS.   Titinius, if thou lovest me,
15   Mount thou my horse and hide[5] thy spurs in him
    Till he have brought thee up to yonder troops
    And here again, that I may rest assured
    Whether yond troops are friend or enemy.

5. **hide:** Sink.

    TITINIUS. I will be here again even with a thought.[6] *[Exit.]*

6. **even with a thought:** As quick as a thought.

20   **CASSIUS.** Go, Pindarus, get higher on that hill;
    My sight was ever thick.[7] Regard[8] Titinius,
    And tell me what thou not'st about the field.

                         [Exit Pindarus.]

7. **thick:** Dim.
8. **Regard:** Observe.

This day I breathèd first. Time is come round,
And where I did begin, there shall I end.
25 My life is run his compass.[9] Sirrah, what news?

PINDARUS. [*Above*] O my lord!

CASSIUS. What news?

PINDARUS. [*Above*] Titinius is enclosèd round about
With horsemen that make to him on the spur;[10]
30 Yet he spurs on. Now they are almost on him.
Now, Titinius! Now some light.[11] O, he lights too!
He's ta'en![12] [*Shout.*] And, hark! They shout for joy.

CASSIUS. Come down; behold no more.
O, coward that I am, to live so long,
35 To see my best friend ta'en before my face!

[*Enter Pindarus.*]

Come hither, sirrah.
In Parthia did I take thee prisoner;
And then I swore thee, saving of thy life,
That whatsoever I did bid thee do,
40 Thou shouldst attempt it. Come now, keep thine
    oath.
Now be a freeman, and with this good sword,
That ran through Caesar's bowels, search[13] this
    bosom.
Stand not[14] to answer. Here, take thou the hilts,
And when my face is covered, as 'tis now,
45 Guide thou the sword—Caesar, thou art revenged,
Even with the sword that killed thee.   [*Dies.*]

PINDARUS. So, I am free; yet would not so have been,
Durst I have done my will. O Cassius!
Far from this country Pindarus shall run,
50 Where never Roman shall take note of him.   [*Exit.*]

[*Enter Titinius and Messala.*]

MESSALA. It is but change,[15] Titinius; for Octavius
Is overthrown by noble Brutus' power,
As Cassius' legions are by Antony.

TITINIUS. These tidings will well comfort Cassius.

MESSALA. Where did you leave him?

55 **TITINIUS.**   All disconsolate,
With Pindarus his bondman, on this hill.

---

9. his compass: Its full course.

10. make . . . spur: Ride toward him at top speed.

11. light: Dismount from their horses.
12. ta'en: Taken; captured.

13. search: Penetrate.

14. Stand not: Do not wait.

15. change: An exchange.

MESSALA. Is not that he that lies upon the ground?

TITINIUS. He lies not like the living. O my heart!

MESSALA. Is not that he?

TITINIUS.   No, this was he, Messala,
60   But Cassius is no more. O setting sun,
        As in thy red rays thou dost sink to night,
        So in his red blood Cassius' day is set.
        The sun of Rome is set. Our day is gone;
        Clouds, dews, and dangers come; our deeds are done!
65   Mistrust of my success[16] hath done this deed.

16. Mistrust . . . success:
Fear that I would not
succeed.

MESSALA. Mistrust of good success hath done this deed.
O hateful Error, Melancholy's child,[17]
Why dost thou show to the apt thoughts of men
The things that are not?[18] O Error, soon conceived,[19]
70 Thou never com'st unto a happy birth,
But kill'st the mother that engend'red thee![20]

TITINIUS. What, Pindarus! Where art thou, Pindarus?

MESSALA. Seek him, Titinius, whilst I go to meet
The noble Brutus, thrusting this report
75 Into his ears. I may say "thrusting" it;
For piercing steel and darts envenomèd[21]
Shall be as welcome to the ears of Brutus
As tidings of this sight.

TITINIUS. Hie you, Messala,
And I will seek for Pindarus the while. [*Exit Messala.*]

80 Why didst thou send me forth, brave[22] Cassius?
Did I not meet thy friends, and did not they
Put on my brows this wreath of victory,
And bid me give it thee? Didst thou not hear their
      shouts?
Alas, thou hast misconstrued everything!
85 But hold thee,[23] take this garland on thy brow;
Thy Brutus bid me give it thee, and I
Will do his bidding. Brutus, come apace,[24]
And see how I regarded[25] Caius Cassius.
By your leave,[26] gods. This is a Roman's part:[27]
90 Come, Cassius' sword, and find Titinius' heart. [*Dies.*]

[*Call to arms sounds. Enter Brutus, Messala, young Cato,
Strato, Volumnius, and Lucilius.*]

BRUTUS. Where, where, Messala, doth his body lie?

MESSALA. Lo, yonder, and Titinius mourning it.

BRUTUS. Titinius' face is upward.

CATO. He is slain.

BRUTUS. O Julius Caesar, thou art mighty yet!
95 Thy spirit walks abroad, and turns our swords
In our own proper entrails.[28]   [*Low calls to arms.*]

CATO. Brave Titinius!
Look, whe'r[29] he have not crowned dead Cassius.

---

17. Melancholy's child: One of despondent temperament.

18. Why dost . . . are not?: Why do you (despondent temperament) fill easily impressed men's thoughts with imagined fears?

19. conceived: Created.

20. mother . . . thee: Cassius (in this case) that conceived the error.

21. envenomèd: Poisoned.

22. brave: Noble.

23. hold thee: Wait a moment.

24. apace: Quickly.

25. regarded: Honored.

26. By your leave: With your permission.

27. part: Role; duty.

28. own proper entrails: Very own inner organs.

29. whe'r: Whether.

BRUTUS. Are yet two Romans living such as these?
The last of all the Romans, fare thee well!
100   It is impossible that ever Rome
Should breed thy fellow.[30] Friends, I owe moe tears
To this dead man than you shall see me pay.
I shall find time, Cassius; I shall find time.
Come, therefore, and to Thasos[31] send his body;
105   His funerals shall not be in our camp,
Lest it discomfort us.[32] Lucilius, come,
And come, young Cato; let us to the field.
Labeo and Flavius set our battles[33] on.
'Tis three o'clock; and, Romans, yet ere night
110   We shall try fortune in a second fight.   [*Exit.*]

30. fellow: Equal.

31. Thasos: An island not far from Philippi.

32. discomfort us: Discourage our soldiers.

33. battles: Armies.

Scene iv. *The field of battle.*

[*Call to arms sounds. Enter Brutus, Messala, young Cato, Lucilius, and Flavius.*]

BRUTUS. Yet, countrymen, O, yet hold up your heads!
         [*Exit, with followers.*]

CATO. What bastard[1] doth not? Who will go with me?
I will proclaim my name about the field.
I am the son of Marcus Cato,[2] ho!
5   A foe to tyrants, and my country's friend.
I am the son of Marcus Cato, ho!

[*Enter Soldiers and fight.*]

LUCILIUS. And I am Brutus, Marcus Brutus, I;
Brutus, my country's friend; know me for Brutus![3]
         [*Young Cato falls.*]
O young and noble Cato, art thou down?
10   Why, now thou diest as bravely as Titinius,
And mayst be honored, being Cato's son.

FIRST SOLDIER. Yield, or thou diest.

LUCILIUS.   Only I yield to die.[4]
There is so much that thou wilt kill me straight;[5]
Kill Brutus, and be honored in his death.

15   **FIRST SOLDIER.** We must not. A noble prisoner!

[*Enter Antony.*]

SECOND SOLDIER. Room, ho! Tell Antony, Brutus is ta'en.

1. bastard: Person who is not a true Roman.

2. Marcus Cato: Brutus's wife's father.

3. And I am . . . Brutus: Lucilius impersonates Brutus in order to protect him and confuse the enemy.

4. Only . . . die: I will surrender only to die.
5. much . . . straight: Much honor in it that you will kill me immediately.

FIRST SOLDIER. I'll tell thee news. Here comes the
    general.
    Brutus is ta'en, Brutus is ta'en, my lord.

ANTONY. Where is he?

20 **LUCILIUS.** Safe, Antony; Brutus is safe enough.
    I dare assure thee that no enemy
    Shall ever take alive the noble Brutus.
    The gods defend him from so great a shame!
    When you do find him, or alive or dead,
25   He will be found like Brutus, like himself.[6]

ANTONY. This is not Brutus, friend, but, I assure you,
    A prize no less in worth. Keep this man safe;
    Give him all kindness. I had rather have
    Such men my friends than enemies. Go on,
30   And see whe'r Brutus be alive or dead,
    And bring us word unto[7] Octavius' tent
    How everything is chanced.[8]   *[Exit.]*

6. like himself: Behaving in a noble way.

7. unto: In.

8. is chanced: Has happened.

Scene v. *The field of battle.*

[Enter Brutus, Dardanius, Clitus, Strato, and Volumnius.]

BRUTUS. Come, poor remains[1] of friends, rest on this
    rock.

CLITUS. Statilius showed the torchlight,[2] but, my lord,
    He came not back; he is or ta'en or slain.

BRUTUS. Sit thee down, Clitus. Slaying is the word;
5   It is a deed in fashion. Hark thee, Clitus.*[Whispers.]*

CLITUS. What, I, my lord? No, not for all the world!

BRUTUS. Peace then, no words.

CLITUS.   I'll rather kill myself.

BRUTUS. Hark thee, Dardanius.   *[Whispers.]*

DARDANIUS.   Shall I do such a deed?

CLITUS. O Dardanius!

10 **DARDANIUS.** O Clitus!

CLITUS. What ill request did Brutus make to thee?

DARDANIUS. To kill him, Clitus. Look, he meditates.

CLITUS. Now is that noble vessel[3] full of grief,
    That it runs over even at his eyes.

1. poor remains: Pitiful survivors.

2. showed the torchlight: Signaled with a torch.

3. vessel: Human being.

15 **BRUTUS.** Come hither, good Volumnius; list[4] a word.

VOLUMNIUS. What says my lord?

BRUTUS.   Why, this, Volumnius:
   The ghost of Caesar hath appeared to me
   Two several[5] times by night; at Sardis once,
   And this last night here in Philippi fields.
   I know my hour is come.

20 **VOLUMNIUS.**   Not so, my lord.

BRUTUS. Nay, I am sure it is, Volumnius.
   Thou seest the world, Volumnius, how it goes;
   Our enemies have beat us to the pit.[6]
                [Low calls to arms.]
It is more worthy to leap in ourselves
25   Than tarry till they push us.[7] Good Volumnius,
   Thou know'st that we two went to school together;
   Even for that our love of old, I prithee
   Hold thou my sword-hilts whilst I run on it.

VOLUMNIUS. That's not an office[8] for a friend, my lord.
                 [Call to arms still.]

30 **CLITUS.** Fly, fly, my lord, there is no tarrying here.

BRUTUS. Farewell to you; and you; and you, Volumnius.
   Strato, thou hast been all this while asleep;
   Farewell to thee too, Strato. Countrymen,
   My heart doth joy that yet in all my life
35   I found no man but he was true to me.
   I shall have glory by this losing day
   More than Octavius and Mark Antony
   By this vile conquest shall attain unto.[9]
   So fare you well at once, for Brutus' tongue
40   Hath almost ended his life's history.
   Night hangs upon mine eyes; my bones would rest,
   That have but labored to attain this hour.[10]
       [Call to arms sounds. Cry within, "Fly, fly, fly!"]

CLITUS. Fly, my lord, fly!

BRUTUS.   Hence! I will follow.
      [Exit Clitus, Dardanius, and Volumnius.]
   I prithee, Strato, stay thou by thy lord,
45   Thou art a fellow of a good respect.[11]
   Thy life hath had some smatch[12] of honor in it;
   Hold then my sword, and turn away thy face,
   While I do run upon it. Wilt thou, Strato?

4. list: Hear.

5. several: Separate.

6. pit: Trap or grave.

7. tarry . . . us: Wait until they kill us.

8. office: Task.

9. By this . . . unto: By this evil victory shall gain. (Brutus sees the victory of Octavius and Antony as causing the downfall of Roman freedom.)
10. this hour: Time of death.

11. respect: Reputation.
12. smatch: Smack or taste.

STRATO. Give me your hand first. Fare you well, my lord.

50 **BRUTUS.** Farewell, good Strato—Caesar, now be still;
    I killed not thee with half so good a will.   [*Dies.*]

[*Call to arms sounds. Retreat sounds. Enter Antony,
Octavius, Messala, Lucilius, and the Army.*]

OCTAVIUS. What man is that?

MESSALA. My master's man.[13] Strato, where is thy mas-
    ter?

STRATO. Free from the bondage you are in, Messala;
55   The conquerors can but make a fire of him.
    For Brutus only overcame himself,
    And no man else hath honor[14] by his death.

LUCILIUS. So Brutus should be found. I thank thee, Bru-
    tus,
    That thou hast proved Lucilius' saying[15] true.

60 **OCTAVIUS.** All that served Brutus, I will entertain them.[16]
    Fellow, wilt thou bestow[17] thy time with me?

STRATO. Ay, if Messala will prefer[18] me to you.

OCTAVIUS. Do so, good Messala.

MESSALA. How died my master, Strato?

65 **STRATO.** I held the sword, and he did run on it.

MESSALA. Octavius, then take him to follow thee,
    That did the latest service to my master.

ANTONY. This was the noblest Roman of them all.
    All the conspirators save[19] only he
70   Did that[20] they did in envy of great Caesar;
    He, only in a general honest thought
    And common good to all, made one of them.[21]
    His life was gentle,[22] and the elements
    So mixed[23] in him that Nature might stand up
75   And say to all the world, "This was a man!"

OCTAVIUS. According to his virtue,[24] let us use[25] him
    With all respect and rites of burial.
    Within my tent his bones tonight shall lie,
    Most like a soldier ordered honorably.[26]
80   So call the field[27] to rest, and let's away
    To part[28] the glories of this happy day.   [*Exit all.*]

---

13. man: Servant.

**14. no man else hath
honor:** No other man gains
honor.

15. Lucilius' saying: See
Act V, Scene iv, line 25.
16. entertain them: Take
them into my service.
17. bestow: Spend.
18. prefer: Recommend.

19. save: Except.
20. that: What.

21. made one of them:
Became one of the
conspirators.
22. gentle: Noble.
23. so mixed:
Well-balanced.
24. Virtue: Excellence.
25. use: Treat.

26. ordered honorably:
Treated with honor.
27. field: Army.
28. part: Share.

Your Response

1. What insights about life did you gain from the play?
2. How did you react to the extreme actions taken by Cassius, Brutus, and Titinius?

Recalling

3. On whose birthday does the battle take place, and how does he feel about the battle?
4. Explain the misunderstanding that led to Cassius' death.
5. Why does Brutus think it is time to die?

Interpreting

6. What does Cassius mean in Act V, Scene i, lines 45–47?
7. What does Brutus mean by his final words: "Caesar, now be still; / I killed not thee with half so good a will"?
8. How and why does Antony's attitude toward Brutus change from the beginning of the act to the end?

Applying

9. Who was the tragic hero of this play—Julius Caesar or Brutus? Form a team of three classmates to argue each side of a debate. Use evidence from the play to support your side's argument.

ANALYZING LITERATURE

Understanding Tragedy

The Greek philosopher Aristotle defined tragedy: "Tragedy, then, is an imitation of an action that is serious, complete, and of a certain magnitude." He explained that although the main character is noble, a tragedy must focus on action rather than on character development. The action should arouse feelings of pity and fear in the audience. The theme of a tragedy is the meaning of the central action and the main char-

acter's recognition of that meaning and its consequences.

1. What is the central action of this play?
2. What does Brutus see as the meaning of the central action and its consequences?
3. Explain the theme of this tragedy.

CRITICAL THINKING AND READING

Understanding Metaphorical Language

Metaphorical language describes one thing in terms of another. In Act V, Scene i, line 87, for example, Cassius says that the shadow of the birds of prey is a canopy, suggesting how dark and dense the shadow is.

Explain the metaphors that can be found where indicated.

1. Act V, Scene iii, line 15
2. Act V, Scene v, line 13
3. Act V, Scene v, line 23
4. Act V, Scene v, line 41

THINKING AND WRITING

Preparing an Argument

In Act V, Scene i, lines 39–44, Antony launches a bitter verbal attack against Brutus and Cassius. Brutus, however, makes no attempt to respond. Write a short speech in which Brutus *does* respond to Antony's criticism. Keep your tone consistent both with the situation and with what you know of Brutus' character.

LEARNING OPTION

Art. Work with a small group of classmates to plan and create scenery and sound effects for a performance of the final act of the play. If possible, make a recording of sound effects. Do rough sketches to show what the set would look like, or make a backdrop by painting scenes on an old sheet.

YOUR WRITING PROCESS

WRITING A NEW VERSION OF A SCENE

"The structure of a play is always the story of how the birds came home to roost."

Arthur Miller

Imagine that a producer has asked you to create a new version of a well-known play. Before she begins to invest her money, however, she wants to see a sample scene. Any of the plays in this unit could easily be adapted for another setting. *Julius Caesar,* for example, could be recast as a power struggle in contemporary Washington, D.C. The plot and theme would remain the same, but the setting, the characters' names, and their way of speaking would all change.

> **Focus**
>
> **Assignment:** Write a new version of a scene from a play.
> **Purpose:** To show the feasibility of creating a new version of a play.
> **Audience:** A producer.

Prewriting

1. Review plays. With a partner, look over the plays in this unit and choose one you feel would make a good candidate for a new version. Then select a particular scene or small section from that play to update. Discuss the following questions about your choice:

• What elements of the scene should stay the same?
• What elements of the scene should change, and why?
• How should the language in the new version differ from the language in the original?

2. Highlight changes. Make a diagram tracing the new elements of the scene. First review the original scene carefully, and then discuss changes with your partner.

Student Model

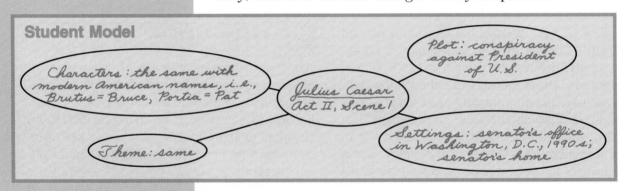

Characters: the same with modern American names, i.e., Brutus = Bruce, Portia = Pat

Plot: conspiracy against President of U.S.

Julius Caesar Act II, Scene 1

Settings: senator's office in Washington, D.C., 1990s; senator's home

Theme: same

3. Role-play to discover voices. After you and your partner have discussed and diagrammed the changes in your scene, think about how each character would talk in the new setting. With your partner, practice speaking as each character in your version.

Drafting

1. Use stage notes to explain the changes in your version. Write a brief introductory paragraph that explains how your version differs from the original. Check over your diagram to make sure you have included all the key changes. This introduction should summarize important information from characters' speeches as well as stimulate your audience's interest.

2. Focus on language. Make sure the characters' language is in tune with the new setting. Use contemporary vocabulary wherever applicable; also experiment with vivid language if it is appropriate for a character.

Student Model

Act II, Scene 1, lines 218–220

Original: (Brutus)
Now, good Metellus, go along by him.
He loves me well, and I have given him reasons;
Send him but hither, and I'll fashion him.

Updated Version: (Bruce)
Well, Michael, high-tail it over to the President's office.
His respect for me will bring him here.
When he gets here, we can proceed with our plan.

Revising and Editing

1. Get the form right. For instance, stage instructions appear in parentheses, and the name of the character speaking appears before his or her actual words. Use the plays in this book as models.

2. Do the characters' words match the characters? Keep the dialogue for each character consistent with his or her personality traits and the circumstances under which he or she is speaking.

3. Try for zero errors. Proofread the scene for errors in spelling, capitalization, and punctuation.

YOUR WRITING PROCESS

WRITING A DESCRIPTIVE MEMO

"I put a piece of paper under my pillow, and when I could not sleep I wrote in the dark."

Henry David Thoreau

Imagine that you have been chosen to supervise the creation of costumes and props for one of the plays in this unit. How would you most effectively share your ideas with others involved in the production? You could write a memo. Your descriptions of costumes and props would help the director and production assistants make important decisions about the best way to perform the play.

> ### Focus
> **Assignment:** Write a memo describing costumes and props for one of the plays in this unit.
> **Purpose:** To prepare for a production.
> **Audience:** The director and people in charge of gathering props and costumes.

Prewriting

1. Review memos. Business memos often contain information about work in progress. You might contact local businesses or your school administration to see an example of a memo. In a small group, discuss how you think the memo form would help you communicate ideas about costumes or props for a play.

2. Scan a play to list scenes, settings, and characters. Review one of the plays in this unit and choose one you would like to see produced on stage. How many acts or scenes does it contain and what are the settings? What props are needed? Who are the characters, and how do they dress?

3. Develop a costume/prop chart. A chart can help you organize your ideas.

> ### Student Model
>
> | Settings | Props | Characters/Costumes |
> | --- | --- | --- |
> | Radio station | Desk, phone | Announcers, Orson Welles/1930's men's suits |
> | Observatory | Telescope | Pierson & Phillips/ 1930's men's suits |

Drafting

1. Summarize your main ideas in an introductory paragraph. Let your fellow workers know what your memo will be about. Keep the introductory paragraph to the point.

Student Model

Memo From: Coordinator of Costumes and Props
Memo To: Director, Production Assistants
Re: Costumes and Props for *Invasion From Mars*

What follows is a description of specific props and costumes needed to produce *Invasion From Mars*. Since the play takes place in 1938, props and costumes should be appropriate to that time. As listed below, features of the Martian costumes are somber and ominous looking. Please respond to the following details and share your ideas at the next production meeting: Tuesday, 3:30 P.M., backstage.

---

2. Use descriptive language. As you describe the specific props and costumes needed for the play, use words and phrases that will help create clear mental pictures in the readers' minds. Include sensory details and vivid comparisons.

Revising and Editing

1. Share your draft with a small group of peer editors. Exchange memo drafts with members of a small group. Compare and contrast how the memos are organized. Help each other with ideas to make the memos as short and to the point as possible. You can be creative about the form of the memo; however, make sure that the heading indicates the sender, the receiver, and the subject of the memo.

2. Use a tone appropriate for your audience. Remember whom the memo is written for and use language appropriate for that audience. You can be somewhat informal when addressing fellow workers, but do not use slang or improper grammar.

3. Check for errors. Proofread your memo carefully for errors in spelling, punctuation, and usage. Remember that a well-written memo, with zero mistakes, will help readers receive your message without distractions.

Writer's Hint

Exact words will help you communicate ideas precisely. A thesaurus can help you find the specific words, including nouns, adjectives, and adverbs, necessary for effective descriptive writing.

Options for Publishing

• Read your memo to classmates, followed by a question-and-answer session about your ideas for costumes and props.
• Develop sketches to accompany your memo and display them as a bulletin board project.
• Refer to your memo as you prepare to produce the play you have selected.

Reviewing Your Writing Process

1. Did you find an actual memo to use as a model? If so, explain how you used it.

2. Did you use a chart to help you organize the material from the play? Why or why not?

3. Did you work with a partner or a small group? What was most helpful about using this writing strategy?

VIEW FROM A CAR
Emily A. Martin, Student, Erie, Pennsylvania
Courtesy of the Artist

NONFICTION

Nonfiction is simply literature that is true, that is based on facts—real people, actual places, and true incidents. Writers of nonfiction concern themselves with reality, not with the world of the imagination. This area of literature includes biographies, autobiographies, and essays.

Autobiographies and biographies try to create a portrait of an individual with words instead of paint. While some autobiographies and biographies are written about famous people, many are stories of individuals who have lived interesting lives or have lived ordinary lives in an interesting way. An autobiography tells of the events, experiences, and impressions in the life of the writer. It reveals the qualities and character of its subject. Since an autobiography is written by the individual, it will be a subjective work. A biography also reveals the character of the subject, but it is written by another person. Some biographers try to present the facts objectively and let the reader interpret the character and life of their subject, but most make subjective interpretations for the reader. These two forms of nonfiction can be considered types of history with a point of view and information about a way of life.

The word *essay* comes from the French *essais,* meaning "attempts" or "tries." One of the most flexible forms of literature, essays literally try out ideas about a subject on the reader. This literary form can be formal or informal; entertaining, persuasive, explanatory, or instructive; and can be written in any of the four major forms of discourse—description, exposition, narration, or persuasion. The subject matter can range from serious to silly.

Although nonfiction by definition must be based on fact, it shares many elements with fiction. Character can be developed, settings established, suspense built, and theme or purpose presented. Nonfiction can entertain just as fiction can present serious concerns and ideas about life.

As you read the selections in this unit, be aware of the elements that nonfiction shares with fiction. Notice the great variety within the nonfiction form—its ability to instruct, inform, amuse, and entertain. Note how the writers blend creative details with factual information.

READING ACTIVELY

Nonfiction

Nonfiction is a type of literature that deals with real people, events, and ideas. Nonfiction may instruct you, entertain you, keep you informed about the world, or satisfy your curiosity about real people and things.

Reading nonfiction actively means interacting with and responding to the information the author presents. You do this through the following strategies:

QUESTION Preview the material before you read it. For example, what questions come to mind? What is the author's purpose for writing? How does the author support the points presented? Why does the author include certain information? Look for answers to your questions as you read on.

PREDICT Predict what the author will say about the topic. How will the author support her or his points? Make new predictions as you read.

CONNECT Think of what you already know about the topic and make connections to what the author is saying. Take in new facts and ideas as you read and connect these to what you know. Doing so will help you to understand the information presented.

EVALUATE What do you think of the author's conclusions? What have you learned?

RESPOND Think about what the author has said. Allow yourself to respond personally. How do you feel about the topic? What will you do with this information?

Try to use these strategies as you read the selections in this unit. They will help you increase your enjoyment and understanding of nonfiction.

On pages 405–411 you will see an example of active reading by Beth Hasbrouck of Saint Dominic High School in Oyster Bay, New York. The notes in the side column include Beth's thoughts and comments as she read the selection. Your own thoughts will reflect what you bring to the reading and how you respond to it.

MODEL

The Dog That Bit People

James Thurber

Question: *Is the dog trained or wild? How many people does it bite?*

Probaby no one man should have as many dogs in his life as I have had, but there was more pleasure than distress in them for me except in the case of an Airedale named Muggs. He gave me more trouble than all the other fifty-four or -five put together, although my moment of keenest embarrassment was the time a Scotch terrier named Jeannie, who had just had six puppies in the clothes closet of a fourth floor apartment in New York, had the unexpected seventh and last at the corner of Eleventh Street and Fifth Avenue during a walk she had insisted on taking. Then, too, there was the prize winning French poodle, a great big black poodle—none of your little, untroublesome white miniatures—who got sick riding in the rumble seat[1] of a car with me on her way to the Greenwich Dog Show. She had a red rubber bib tucked around her throat and, since a rain storm came up when we were halfway through the Bronx, I had to hold over her a small green umbrella, really more of a parasol. The rain beat down fearfully and suddenly the driver of the car drove into a big garage, filled with mechanics. It happened so quickly that I forgot to put the umbrella down and I will always remember, with sickening distress, the look of incredulity mixed with hatred that came over the face of the particular hardened garage man that came over to see what we wanted, when he took a look at me and the poodle. All garage men, and people of that intolerant stripe, hate poodles with their curious hair cut, especially the pom-poms that you got to leave on their hips if you expect the dogs to win a prize.

Predict: *If Muggs caused so much trouble, the owner probably didn't keep him.*

Question: *Why does the author describe these other dogs? What is the purpose?*

Visualize: *This reference to pom-poms helps me picture the dog. It also adds humor to the essay.*

---

1. rumble seat: In some earlier automobiles, an open seat in the rear, behind the roofed seat, which could be folded shut when not in use.

But the Airedale, as I have said, was the worst of all my dogs. He really wasn't my dog, as a matter of fact: I came home from a vacation one summer to find that my brother Roy had bought him while I was away. A big, burly, choleric[2] dog, he always acted as if he thought I wasn't one of the family. There was a slight advantage in being one of the family, for he didn't bite the family as often as he bit strangers. Still, in the years that we had him he bit everybody but mother, and he made a pass at her once but missed. That was during the month when we suddenly had mice, and Muggs refused to do anything about them. Nobody ever had mice exactly like the mice we had that month. They acted like pet mice, almost like mice somebody had trained. They were so friendly that one night when mother entertained at dinner the Friraliras, a club she and my father had belonged to for twenty years, she put down a lot of little dishes with food in them on the pantry floor so that the mice would be satisfied with that and wouldn't come into the dining room. Muggs stayed out in the pantry with the mice, lying on the floor, growling to himself—not at the mice, but about all the people in the next room that he would have liked to get at. Mother slipped out into the pantry once to see how everything was going. Everything was going fine. It made her so mad to see Muggs lying there, oblivious of the mice—they came running up to her—that she slapped him and he slashed at her, but didn't make it. He was sorry immediately, mother said. He was always sorry, she said, after he bit someone, but we could not understand how she figured this out. He didn't act sorry.

Mother used to send a box of candy every Christmas to the people the Airedale bit. The list finally contained forty or more names. Nobody could understand why we didn't get rid of the dog. I didn't understand it very well myself, but we didn't get rid of him. I think that one or two people tried to poison Muggs—he acted poisoned once in a while—and old Major Moberly fired at him once with his service revolver near the Seneca Hotel in East Broad Street—but Muggs lived to be almost eleven years old and even when he could hardly get around he bit a Congressman who had called to see my father on business. My mother had never liked the Congressman

---

2. choleric (käl′ ər ik) *adj.*: Quick-tempered.

Nobody Knew Exactly What Was the Matter with Him

—she said the signs of his horoscope[3] showed he couldn't be trusted (he was Saturn with the moon in Virgo)—but she sent him a box of candy that Christmas. He sent it right back, probably because he suspected it was trick candy. Mother persuaded herself it was all for the best that the dog had bitten him, even though father lost an important business association because of it. "I wouldn't be associated with such a man," mother said, "Muggs could read him like a book."

We used to take turns feeding Muggs to be on his good side, but that didn't always work. He was never in a very good humor, even after a meal. Nobody knew exactly what was the matter with him, but whatever it was it made him irascible, especially in the mornings. Roy never felt very well in the morning, either, especially before breakfast, and once when he came downstairs and found that Muggs had moodily chewed up the morning paper he hit him in the face with a

Visualize: *The tone of the mother's comments helps me picture her defending Muggs. Her defense of him is amusing. A dog can't see through a person.*

Predict: *I predict that the family will take Muggs to be trained by a professional.*

---

3. horoscope (hôr′ ə skōp′) *n.:* The position of the planets and stars with relation to one another at a given time, especially at the time of a person's birth.

Predict: *I still think they will take him to a veterinarian or a specialist.*

Question: *Why didn't he bite anyone more than once? What is significant about this pattern?*

Clarify: *The mother treated Muggs as if he were human, defending him and making excuses for him.*

grapefruit and then jumped up on the dining room table, scattering dishes and silverware and spilling the coffee. Muggs' first free leap carried him all the way across the table and into a brass fire screen in front of the gas grate but he was back on his feet in a moment and in the end he got Roy and gave him a pretty vicious bite in the leg. Then he was all over it; he never bit anyone more than once at a time. Mother always mentioned that as an argument in his favor; she said he had a quick temper but that he didn't hold a grudge. She was forever defending him. I think she liked him because he wasn't well. "He's not strong," she would say, pityingly, but that was inaccurate; he may not have been well but he was terribly strong.

One time my mother went to the Chittenden Hotel to call on a woman mental healer who was lecturing in Columbus on the subject of "Harmonious Vibrations." She wanted to find out if it was possible to get harmonious vibrations into a dog. "He's a large tan-colored Airedale," mother explained. The woman said that she had never treated a dog but she advised my mother to hold the thought that he did not bite and would not bite. Mother was holding the thought the very next morning when Muggs got the iceman but she blamed that slip-up on the iceman. "If you didn't think he would bite you, he wouldn't," mother told him. He stomped out of the house in a terrible jangle of vibrations.

One morning when Muggs bit me slightly, more or less in passing, I reached down and grabbed his short stumpy tail and hoisted him into the air. It was a foolhardy thing to do and the last time I saw my mother, about six months ago, she said she didn't know what possessed me. I don't either, except that I was pretty mad. As long as I held the dog off the floor by his tail he couldn't get at me, but he twisted and jerked so, snarling all the time, that I realized I couldn't hold him that way very long. I carried him to the kitchen and flung him onto the floor and shut the door on him just as he crashed against it. But I forgot about the backstairs. Muggs went up the backstairs and down the frontstairs and had me cornered in the living room. I managed to get up onto the mantelpiece above the fireplace, but it gave way and came down with a tremendous crash throwing a large marble clock, several vases, and myself heavily to the floor. Muggs was so alarmed by the racket that when I picked myself up he had disappeared. We couldn't find him anywhere, although we whistled and shouted, until old Mrs. Detweiler called after dinner that night. Muggs had bitten her once, in the leg, and she came into the living room only after we assured her that Muggs had run away. She had just seated herself when, with a great growling and scratching of claws, Muggs emerged from under a davenport[4] where he had been quietly hiding all the time, and bit her again. Mother examined the bite and put arnica[5] on it and told Mrs. Detweiler that it was only a bruise. "He just bumped you," she said. But Mrs. Detweiler left the house in a nasty state of mind.

Lots of people reported our Airedale to the police but my father held a municipal office at the time and was on friendly terms with the police. Even so, the cops had been out a couple of times—once when Muggs bit Mrs. Rufus Sturtevant and again when he bit Lieutenant-Governor Malloy—but mother told them that it hadn't been Muggs' fault but the fault of the people who were bitten. "When he starts for them, they scream," she explained, "and that excites him." The cops

Question: *Why do people always try to belittle the harm or inconvenience that their pets cause other people? How could the mother call a bite a bruise or a bump?*

Predict: *The cops probably wanted them to keep Muggs tied up so that he couldn't bite people.*

---

4. davenport (dav′ ən pôrt′) *n*.: A large couch or sofa.
5. arnica (är′ ni kə) *n*.: A preparation made from certain plants, once used for treating sprains, bruises, and so forth.

Lots of People Reported Our Dog to the Police

suggested that it might be a good idea to tie the dog up, but mother said that it mortified him to be tied up and that he wouldn't eat when he was tied up.

Muggs at his meals was an unusual sight. Because of the fact that if you reached toward the floor he would bite you, we usually put his food plate on top of an old kitchen table with a bench alongside the table. Muggs would stand on the bench and eat. I remember that my mother's Uncle Horatio, who boasted that he was the third man up Missionary Ridge,[6] was splutteringly indignant when he found out that we fed the dog on a table because we were afraid to put his plate on the floor. He said he wasn't afraid of any dog that ever lived and that he would put the dog's plate on the floor if we would give it to him. Roy said that if Uncle Horatio had fed Muggs on the ground just before the battle he would have been the first man up Missionary Ridge. Uncle Horatio was furious. "Bring him in! Bring him in now!" he shouted. "I'll feed the—on the floor!" Roy was all for giving him a chance, but my father wouldn't hear of it. He said that Muggs had already been fed. "I'll feed him again!" bawled Uncle Horatio. We had quite a time quieting him.

In his last year Muggs used to spend practically all of his time outdoors. He didn't like to stay in the house for some reason or other—perhaps it held too many unpleasant memories for him. Anyway, it was hard to get him to come in and as a result the garbage man, the iceman, and the laundryman wouldn't come near the house. We had to haul the garbage down to the corner, take the laundry out and bring it back, and meet the iceman a block from home. After this had gone on for some time we hit on an ingenious arrangement for getting the dog in the house so that we could lock him up while the gas meter was read, and so on. Muggs was afraid of only one thing, an electrical storm. Thunder and lightning frightened him out of his senses (I think he thought a storm had broken the day the mantelpiece fell). He would rush into the house and hide under a bed or in a clothes closet. So we fixed up a thunder machine out of a long narrow piece of sheet iron with a wooden handle on one end. Mother would shake this vigorously when she wanted to get Muggs into the

---

6. Missionary Ridge: A height south of Chattanooga, Tennessee, that was the site of a Civil War battle.

house. It made an excellent imitation of thunder, but I suppose it was the most roundabout system for running a household that was ever devised. It took a lot out of mother.

A few months before Muggs died, he got to "seeing things." He would rise slowly from the floor, growling low, and stalk stiff-legged and menacing toward nothing at all. Sometimes the Thing would be just a little to the right or left of a visitor. Once a Fuller Brush salesman got hysterics. Muggs came wandering into the room like Hamlet[7] following his father's ghost. His eyes were fixed on a spot just to the left of the Fuller Brush man, who stood it until Muggs was about three slow, creeping paces from him. Then he shouted. Muggs wavered on past him into the hallway grumbling to himself but the Fuller man went on shouting. I think mother had to throw a pan of cold water on him before he stopped. That was the way she used to stop us boys when we got into fights.

Muggs died quite suddenly one night. Mother wanted to bury him in the family lot under a marble stone with some such inscription as "Flights of angels sing thee to thy rest" but we persuaded her it was against the law. In the end we just put up a smooth board above his grave along a lonely road. On the board I wrote with an indelible pencil "Cave Canem."[8] Mother was quite pleased with the simple classic dignity of the old Latin epitaph.

Clarify: *If Muggs had been disciplined properly, he wouldn't have been in the habit of growling and menacing.*

Respond: *This was an amusing essay. Even people who don't have dogs would find it funny because everyone has been exposed to dogs and dog-owners, like the mother in the essay.*

---

7. Hamlet: The tragic hero of the play *Hamlet* by William Shakespeare. Hamlet follows his father's ghost and learns that his father, a Danish king, had been murdered by Hamlet's uncle Claudius.
8. Cave canem (käʹ vā käʹ nəm): Latin for *Beware the dog.*

James Thurber (1894–1961) was a celebrated American humorist. Born in Columbus, Ohio, Thurber worked as a code clerk in the U.S. State Department and as a journalist. Much of his work first appeared in *The New Yorker* magazine. Thurber's works often humorously describe the anxieties of the average individual in modern society. Many of his works include cartoons of frightened men, menacing women, wicked children, and sad dogs. "The Dog That Bit People" is an example of Thurber's hilarious style.

Your Response

1. Thurber tells several amusing stories about Muggs. Which did you enjoy the most? Why?

Recalling

2. What is Muggs's most troublesome quality?
3. In dealing with Muggs, what is the advantage in being one of the family?
4. Describe Thurber's "foolhardy" experience with Muggs.
5. How does Mother explain that Muggs's reaction is the fault of other people?
6. How does Muggs eat his meals? Why does he eat this way?
7. How does Mother get Muggs into the house? Why does this method work?

Interpreting

8. How does Thurber feel about Muggs? Find evidence in the selection to support your answer.
9. Describe Mother. Find evidence in the selection to support your answer.

Applying

10. Thurber describes an aspect of his home life in a humorous way. What other aspects of daily life could be the subject of a humorous essay?

ANALYZING LITERATURE

Understanding the Humorous Essay

A **humorous essay** is a nonfiction composition that presents the author's thoughts on a subject in an amusing way. This lighthearted approach is intended to make the reader laugh.

A writer may create humor in an essay by describing a ridiculous situation in a serious way or by using exaggeration. Thurber uses anecdotes to enhance the humor of his essay in his description of Muggs as he tries to bite Roy.

1. Give an example of a ridiculous situation that Thurber describes in a serious way.

2. Give two examples of anecdotes that Thurber uses to enhance the humor of the essay.

CRITICAL THINKING AND READING

Supporting the Main Idea

A writer uses details to support the main idea of a literary work. Such details may include descriptions, phrases, examples, or anecdotes that provide evidence for the main idea. In "The Dog That Bit People," the main idea is that Muggs gave Thurber more distress than pleasure.

Give two examples of details from the essay that support this main idea.

THINKING AND WRITING

Describing a Pet

Pets sometimes seem more human than humans, with personalities that make their relationship with their owners seem outrageously funny to outsiders. Select an irascible, or irritable, pet that you have owned, have read about, or have seen in a television show or movie. (If you like, you may make up a pet.) List all the traits that make up this pet's peculiar personality. Using this list as your starting point, write an essay describing the animal. You may want to use exaggeration to make the pet's personality seem even more outrageous. When you revise, make sure you have included enough details to create a vivid picture of the pet. Proofread your essay and share it with your classmates.

LEARNING OPTION

Writing. Imagine that you are a news reporter. Your editor has assigned you to cover police reports. Develop a news story about Muggs's attack on a complaining party, such as Lieutenant-Governor Malloy or Mrs. Rufus Sturdevant. Plan out your story before you write it. Remember to answer the five standard "W" questions (who? what? where? when? why?) in your news story. When you have finished, you may wish to deliver your story as a radio announcement to the class.

Biographies and Personal Accounts

DIEGO MARTELLI
Edgar Degas
National Gallery of Scotland, Edinburgh

GUIDE FOR READING

Emily Dickinson

Characterization in Biography

The facts about a person's life can be obtained in an encyclopedia or other reference book. A biography attempts to go beyond the facts and portray the subject as a real person. By knowing the subject's joys, sorrows, problems, and influences, you gain a better understanding of the character of the subject. In this essay Brooks presents the character of Emily Dickinson in great detail.

Focus

Brooks's biography of Dickinson will give you a better understanding of her character and poetry. Suppose that a classmate were writing a biographical sketch of you for the school yearbook. What would you want the writer to emphasize about your personality, achievement, and background? Write an outline that your classmate could use to interview you. You need not disclose private information; share only what you're comfortable sharing. Then, as you read this account of Dickinson's life, think about the ways in which your life resembles and differs from hers.

Vocabulary

Knowing the following words will help you as you read "Emily Dickinson."

propriety (prə prī′ ə tē) *n.*: The quality of being proper, fitting, or suitable (p. 415)

punctilious (puŋk til′ ē əs) *adj.*: Very careful about every detail of behavior (p. 415)

abated (ə bāt′ id) *v.*: Lessened; ended (p. 415)

malign (mə līn′) *adj.*: Evil; harmful (p. 416)

cryptic (krip′ tik) *adj.*: Having a hidden meaning (p. 416)

transcendental (tran sen dent′ ′l) *adj.*: Supernatural; not concrete (p. 417)

Van Wyck Brooks

(1886–1963) was born in Plainfield, New Jersey. After graduating from Harvard University, he lived in Europe for several years and then taught at Stanford University. Shortly after his first book was published in 1909, he became well known as a writer of biography, criticism, and the history of American literature. *The Flowering of New England,* which was the first volume of that history, was a bestseller and won Brooks a Pulitzer Prize in 1937. In this essay he explores Emily Dickinson's life.

Emily Dickinson

Van Wyck Brooks

The Dickinsons lived in the principal house in Amherst. A large, square, red-brick mansion that stood behind a hemlock hedge, with three gates accurately closed, it was a symbol of rural propriety and all the substantialities of western New England. Edward Dickinson, the lawyer, had always had his office in the village and four times a day, in his broadcloth coat and beaver hat, with a gold-headed cane in his hand, he had passed through one of the gates, going or coming. A thin, severe punctilious man who had once been a member of Congress, a friend of Daniel Webster[1] in his youth, a Calvinist[2] of the strictest persuasion, he was a pillar of Amherst College until his death in 1874. The college had been founded, largely by his father, to check the sort of errors that were spreading from Harvard, and he never abated his rigor in the interests of pleasure. He was said to have laughed on one occasion, but usually he was as cold and still as the white marble mantel in his parlor. The story was told in Amherst, however, that once he had rung the church bell, as if to summon the people to a fire. The whole town came running, for he rang the bell excitedly. He wished to call attention to the sunset.

Tintype of Emily Dickinson

---

1. Daniel Webster (1782–1852): U. S. statesman and orator.
2. Calvinist (kal′ vin ist) *n*.: Follower of the theology of John Calvin (1509–1564), which emphasized the doctrine of predestination, salvation solely by God's grace, and a strict moral code.

Next door, behind the hemlock hedge, another ample dwelling stood, suggesting in its style an Italian villa. Here lived the Squire's son Austin, once his partner, who kept open house for the college. While the Dickinson mansion was somewhat forbidding, with the stamp of the Squire's grim ways and his invalid wife, the villa was a center of Hampshire hospitality that shared its rolling lawns and charming garden. Olmsted[3] had visited there, when he was planning Central Park, to examine the shrubs and trees, the plants and flowers; and distinguished guests at the college commencements and lecturers during the winter season were received and welcomed there as nowhere else. Emerson, Phillips, Beecher and Curtis[4] had stayed in this house next door, and Samuel Bowles of the *Springfield Republican* was an intimate friend of all the Dickinsons. The *Republican* was a school for journalists, known far and wide, and travelers,—Dickens and Kingsley[5] among them,—constantly stopped at Springfield in order to have a chat with Samuel Bowles. His paper was a sovereign authority in Amherst, and he often drove over for a call at the villa or the mansion, sometimes bringing manuscripts by well-known authors to show the Dickinson daughters before they were published. His favorite was Emily, who was older than Lavinia, but Emily usually "elfed it" when visitors came. She was always in the act of disappearing. Through the blinds of her western windows, overlooking the garden, she observed the hospitalities of the villa, and snatches of whatever was current in the books and talk of a college town, in the politics and thought of the moment, reached her when the guests had gone away. But even her oldest friends seldom saw her. While sometimes, in the evening, she flitted across the garden, she never left the place by day or night. To have

caught a fleeting glimpse of her was something to boast of, and a young girl across the way who watched at night for a light at her window was thrilled if Miss Emily's shadow appeared for a moment. There were nursemaids who thought she was a witch. They frightened the children by uttering her name, as if there were something malign in Miss Dickinson's queerness.

While her friends seldom saw her, and almost never face to face,—for she spoke from the shadows of the hallway, as they sat in the parlor, or sometimes down the stairs, —they were used to receiving little letters from her. These letters were also peculiar. Miss Dickinson rarely addressed the envelopes. Some other hand, perhaps her sister's, performed this office for her. More often the names of the person and town had been clipped from a printed paper and pasted together, as if it were a sort of violation to expose the strokes of her pen to the touch of the postman. The letters themselves were brief and cryptic, usually only a line or two: "Do you look out tonight?" for example. "The moon rides like a girl through a topaz town." Or "The frogs sing sweet today —they have such pretty, lazy times—how nice to be a frog." Or "Tonight the crimson children are playing in the West." Or "The lawn is full of south and the odors tangle, and I hear today for the first the river in the tree." Now and again, some fine phrase emerged from the silvery spray of words, —"Not what the stars have done, but what they are to do, is what detains the sky." Sometimes her notes had a humorous touch: "Father steps like Cromwell[6] when he gets the kindlings," or "Mrs. S. gets bigger, and rolls down the lane to church like a reverend marble." But her messages

---

3. Olmsted: Frederick Law Olmsted (1822–1903), the landscape architect who designed New York City's Central Park.

4. Emerson . . . Curtis: Men active in the intellectual life of the United States.

5. Dickens and Kingsley: Charles Dickens (1812–1870) and Charles Kingsley (1819–1875), English novelists.

---

6. Cromwell: Oliver Cromwell (1599–1658), English revolutionary leader.

often contained no words at all. She would lower baskets of goodies out of the window to children waiting below. At times, instead of a letter, she sent a poem, an odd little fragment of three or four lines, with a box of chocolate caramels or frosted cakes and a flower or a sprig of pine on top, heliotrope, perhaps, or an oleander blossom or a dandelion tied with a scarlet ribbon. Her letters were rhythmical, they scanned like the poems, and they were congested with images,—every phrase was an image; and the poems themselves suggested nursery rhymes or Dr. Watts's hymns, broken up and filled with a strange new content. They might have struck unsympathetic readers as a sort of transcendental baby talk. It was evident that Miss Dickinson had lost the art of communication, as the circle of her school friends understood it. She vibrated towards them, she put forth shy, impalpable[7] tentacles, she instantly signalized with a verse or a note every event in their lives. But she did not speak the language of the world outside her, and one gathered that she did not wish to touch it. She was rapt in a private world of sensations and thoughts. It was even observed that her handwriting went through three distinct phases and that towards the end the letters never touched. Each character, separately formed, stood quite alone.

She had been a recluse since the early sixties, and her family surmised the reason. She had fallen in love with a married man, a Philadelphia clergyman, and had buried herself at home by way of refuge. When her supposed lover supposedly pursued her there, her sister dashed across to the house next door and exclaimed to their brother Austin's wife, "Sue, come! That man is here. Father and mother are away, and I am afraid Emily will go away with him." Such was the family legend, which may have been apocryphal.[8] Undoubtedly, the clergyman came to see her, but probably only to call. Was he in love with Emily? Probably not. In any case, she did not go away. She withdrew from all activities outside the household, and her mind turned in upon itself. She had hitherto been eminently social, or as much so as her little world permitted. Born in 1830, in the red-brick mansion, she had grown up a lively girl who was always a center of attention. She was a capital[9] mimic. She travestied[10] the young-lady pieces, the "Battle of Prague" and others, which she played on the mahogany piano, and her old and funny stories enthralled her friends. Later they remembered that she placed bouquets of flowers in the pews of those she liked best, at church. Helen Hunt Jackson, now a well-known writer, had been her favorite playmate in early childhood. Dancing and card playing were not allowed in Amherst, but Noah Webster's granddaughter, who lived there, evaded the prohibition on behalf of her circle. She held "P.O.M." meetings for the Poetry of Motion, and Emily Dickinson excelled in this branch of learning. She joined in picnics and walks over the Amherst hills with groups of boys and girls from the town and the college. They had "sugaring-off" parties and valentine parties, and they often climbed Mount Norwottuck where they found ferns and lady-slippers; and sometimes they met at a brookside in the woods, where the boys went fishing and the girls made chowder. Emily was an ardent botanist. She knew the haunts of all the wild flowers in the region,

---

7. impalpable (im pal′ pə b'l) *adj.*: That which cannot be felt by touching.

8. apocryphal (ə pä′ krə f'l) *adj.*: Fictitious; false.
9. capital (kap′ ə t'l) *adj.*: Excellent.
10. travestied (trav′ is tēd) *v.*: Ridiculed; represented in a crude, distorted, or ridiculous way.

and sometimes she scrambled alone through the forest, perhaps with her big dog Carlo. She was an expert cook. At home she baked the bread and boiled her father's puddings, but her father was difficult to please. He read "lonely and rigorous books," she said, on Sunday afternoons, fearing that anything else might "joggle the mind;" and Shakespeare, the Bible, and Dr. Watts's hymns were the reading that he chose for his daughter. He did not like her to work in the garden, or to make visits without him, and when she was too witty he left the table. At fifteen she could not tell the time: her father supposed he had taught her, but she had not understood him, and she did

not dare to ask him again or ask anyone else who might have told him. Now and again, she rebelled. She smashed a plate or a teacup, and her friends and her brother found ways to provide her with books, hiding them in the box-bush that stood beside the front door or on the parlor piano, under the cover. In one way or another, she contrived to read most of the current authors, especially the Brontës and the Brownings, with Hawthorne, Coleridge, Irving, Keats and Ruskin. One of her special favorites was Sir Thomas Browne, and she loved the drollery[11] of Dickens. For the rest, she read Heine in German

---

11. drollery (drŏl' ər ē) *n.*: Wry humor.

Emily Dickinson's bedroom with a tintype of her on the table

and Emerson's poems, and Frank B. Sanborn's letters in the *Springfield Republican* kept her in the literary current. She was by no means passive in this house of duty. Once, at a funeral in Hadley, whither she had gone with her father in the family barouche,[12] she ran away for several hours with a young cousin from Worcester and drove back to Amherst in his buggy. At school, she declared her independence. She had been sent as a boarding pupil to Mary Lyon's seminary, where she had written her themes on the nature of sin. She had listened to lectures on total depravity[13] as if, like most of the other girls, she had meant to be a missionary's wife; but when, one day, Miss Lyon asked all the girls to rise, all who wished to be Christians, Emily alone refused to do so. She had found that she could not share the orthodox[14] faith. Otherwise her life went on, with a few journeys here and there, like that of any country lawyer's daughter. As a young girl, she had visited Boston. She remembered the concerts and Bunker Hill, the Chinese Museum and Mount Auburn; and later, on two occasions, she stayed in Cambridge, to receive some treatment for her eyes. When her father was serving his term in Congress, in 1854, she spent seven weeks in Washington with him. Her father's friends were struck by her charm and her wit. It was on her way home that she stopped at Philadelphia and received the sudden shock that had changed her life.

This was the whole of Miss Dickinson's story, so far as outward events were concerned, when Thomas Wentworth Higginson entered the picture. Higginson had written an appeal in *The Atlantic,* addressed to the rising generation. Remembering the days of *The Dial,* when the hazel wand, waved over New England, had indicated hidden springs of talent in many a country town, he said that to find a "new genius" was an editor's greatest privilege. If any such existed who read *The Atlantic,* let him court the editor,—"draw near him with soft approaches and mild persuasions." Higginson added a number of admonitions: "Charge your style with life . . . Tolerate no superfluities[15] . . . There may be years of crowded passion in a word, and half a life in a sentence." This appeal was anonymous, but many of the Amherst people knew who wrote the articles in *The Atlantic,* for Sanborn's literary gossip kept them posted; and presently Colonel Higginson, who was living in Worcester, received an odd little letter. The letter was unsigned, but the writer sent four poems, and she placed in a separate envelope the signature "Emily Dickinson." She begged this distant friend to be her "master." The poems puzzled Higginson. While he felt a curious power in them, he was not prepared for a "new genius" who broke so many rules as this lady in Amherst, who punctuated with dashes only and seemed to have small use for rhyme and merely wished to know if she was "clear." She did not ask him to publish the poems, and he did not pass them on to the editor, but he wrote her a sympathetic letter that was followed by a long correspondence. She continued to send him poems at intervals, signing her notes "your gnome" and "your scholar," but, although she asked him again if he would be her "preceptor,"[16] and he offered her a number of suggestions, she never changed a line or a word to please

---

12. barouche (bə rōōsh') *n.*: A horse-drawn carriage.
13. depravity (di prav' ə tē) *n.*: Wickedness.
14. orthodox (ôr' thə däks') *adj.*: Conforming to the usual beliefs.

15. superfluities (sōō' pər flōō' ə tēs) *n.*: Excesses.
16. preceptor (pri sep' tər) *n.*: Teacher.

him. In one note she said, "If I read a book and it makes my whole body so cold no fire can ever warm me, I know that is poetry. If I feel physically as if the top of my head were taken off, I know that is poetry. These are the only ways I know it. Is there any other way?" And once she replied, when he asked her for a photograph, "I had no portrait now, but am small, like the wren; and my hair is bold, like the chestnut burr; and my eyes like the sherry in the glass that the guest leaves." This feminine mystification piqued[17] the colonel. He wrote, "You enshroud yourself in this fiery mist and I cannot reach you, but only rejoice in the rare sparkles of light." When she told him that her companions were the hills and the sundown, he replied that she ought to come to Boston: she would find herself at home at Mrs. Sargent's. At last, in 1870, he went to Amherst. After a brief delay, while he waited in the parlor, he heard a faint footstep in the hallway and a shy, little childlike creature glided in. She carried two day-lilies, which she placed in his hand, saying, in a soft, breathless voice, "These are my introduction," adding in a whisper, "Forgive me if I am frightened. I never see strangers and hardly know what to say." She spoke of her household occupations and said that "people must have puddings," and she added a few detached, enigmatic[18] remarks. She seemed to the amiable Higginson as unique and remote as Undine or Mignon or Thekla.[19] But he was disturbed by the tension in the air and was glad he did not live too near this lady. There was something abnormal about her, he felt. He had never met anyone before who drained his nerve power so much.

At that time, Miss Dickinson was forty years old and had long since withdrawn from the world; and the friends who came to see her sister were used to the "hurrying whiteness" that was always just going through a door. She sometimes swept into the parlor, bowed and touched a hand or two, poised over the flowered Brussels carpet, and vanished like a ghost or an exhalation; but even these appearances had grown rarer and rarer. Only the neighbors' children really saw her. She had given up wearing colors and was always dressed in diaphanous[20] white, with a cameo pin that held the ruching[21] together. She was decisive in manner, anything but frail. Her complexion was velvety white, her lips were red. Her hair was bound with a chestnut-colored snood,[22] and when it was chilly she wore a little shoulder cape crocheted of soft white worsted run through with a ribbon. She often had a flower in her hand. She moved about in a sort of revery, flitting "as quick as a trout" when she was disturbed. This was one of her sister Lavinia's phrases. The children knew her "high, surprised voice." They knew her dramatic way of throwing up her hands as she ended one of the stories she liked to tell them. She made them her fellow conspirators. They followed her upstairs and heard her comments on the guests she had left in the parlor. She would say, with finger on lip, as feminine callers left, "Listen! Hear them kiss, the traitors!" Or, peeping down the stairs, she would say of some man, "Look, dear, his face is as

---

17. piqued (pēk'd) v.: Provoked.
18. enigmatic (en' ig mat' ik) adj.: Baffling.
19. Undine or Mignon or Thekla: Mysterious women.

20. diaphanous (dī af' ə nəs) adj.: Fine; gauzy.
21. ruching (roo' s̸hiŋ) n.: Pleats of lace at the neck of a dress.
22. snood (snood) n.: A baglike net worn at the back of the head to hold the hair.

pretty as a cloth pink," or "His face is as handsome and meaningless as the full moon." She remarked, apropos[23] of some scholarly person, "He has the facts, but not the phosphorescence[24] of learning." She said that her own ideal caller was always just going out of sight, and that it made her shiver to hear people talk as if they were "taking all the clothes off their souls." She called herself the "cow lily," because of the orange lights in her hair and her eyes, and she observed that the housemaid moved about "in a calico sarcophagus."[25] Once she said to her little niece, who was puzzled by her shy ways, "No one could ever punish a Dickinson by shutting her up alone." Meanwhile, her life went on with her flowers and her sister. She had a small conservatory, opening out of the dining room, a diminutive glass chamber with shelves around it; and there she grouped the ferns and the jasmine, the lilies and the heliotrope and the oxalis plants in their hanging baskets. She had a little watering pot, with a long, slender spout that was like the antenna of an insect, and she sat up all night at times in winter to keep her flowers from freezing. The garden was her special care, and occasionally one saw her at dusk through the gate fluttering about the porch like a moth in the moonlight. When it was damp, she knelt on an old red army blanket that she had thrown on the ground, to reach the flowers. Usually, on summer evenings, she sat for a while with Lavinia on the side piazza, overlooking the flagged path that led to the villa. There stood the giant daphne odora, moved out from the conservatory, and the two small oleanders in their tubs.

Meanwhile, since 1862, Miss Dickinson had been writing poems, although there were very few of her friends who knew it. They all knew the little rhymes she sent them with arbutus buds, but they did not know how seriously she pursued her writing, at night, beside the Franklin stove, in the upstairs corner bedroom, in the light that often glimmered over the snow. From her window she had caught suggestions that gave her a picture, a fancy, an image. Perhaps a boy passed whistling, or a neighbor on her way to church, or a dog with feet "like intermittent plush;" or perhaps she knew that a traveling circus was going to pass in the early morning, and she sat up to watch the "Algerian procession." A dead fly on the windowpane stirred her imagination, and once in the glare of a fire at night she saw a caterpillar measuring a leaf far down in the orchard. She saw the bluebirds darting round "with little dodging feet,"

The motions of the dipping birds,
The lightning's jointed road;

and all these observations went into her verses. She wrote on sheets of notepaper, which she sewed together, rolling and tying the bundles with a thread or a ribbon and tucking them away in the drawers of her bureau; although sometimes the back of an envelope served her as well, or a scrap of the *Springfield Republican*. But, casual in this, she was anything but casual,—she was a cunning workman,—in her composition. Poetry was her solitaire[26] and, so to speak, her journal, for, like Thoreau[27] in Concord, she watched the motions of her mind, re-

---

23. apropos (ap′ rə pō′) *adv.*: Aptly; fittingly for the occasion.
24. phosphorescence (fäs′ fə res′ 'ns) *n.*: Light.
25. sarcophagus (sär kãf′ ə gəs) *n.*: A stone coffin.

26. solitaire (säl′ ə tar′) *n.*: A card game played by one person.
27. Thoreau: Henry David Thoreau (1817–1862), U.S. naturalist and writer.

cording its ebbs and flows and the gleams that shot through it; and she labored over her phrases to make them right. Were they all her own? Were there echoes in them, or anything of the conventional, the rhetorical,[28] the fat? Were they clear, were they exact, were they compact? She liked the common hymn meters, and the meters of nursery jingles, which had been deeply ingrained in her mind as a child, and she seemed to take a rebellious joy in violating all their rules, fulfilling the traditional patterns while she also broke them. She was always experimenting with her rhymes and her rhythms, sometimes adding extra syllables to break up their monotony, sometimes deliberately twisting a rhyme, as Emerson did, for the sake of harshness, to escape the mellifluous[29] effect of conventional poems. Many of her pieces were like parodies of hymns, whose gentle glow in her mind had become heat lightning. For Emily Dickinson's light was quick. It was sudden, sharp and evanescent;[30] and this light was the dry light that is closest to the fire.

The visible setting of these poems was the New England countryside, the village, the garden, the household that she knew so well, a scene, the only scene she knew, that she invested with magic, so that the familiar objects became portents and symbols. Here were the hills, the changing seasons, the winter light, the light of spring, the bee, the mouse, the hummingbird, the cricket, the lonely houses off the road, the village inn, the lamppost that became, in the play of her fancy, sublime[31] or droll; and with what gifts of observation she caught the traits of her birds and insects, of everything that crept or ran or flew,—the snake "unbraiding in the sun," the robin's eyes, "like frightened beads," the umbrella of the bat that was "quaintly halved." She often seemed a little girl, amusing herself with childish whimsies, and, in fact, as the ward of her father, she remained in some ways adolescent; and, as she dressed to the end in the fashion of her early youth, so she retained the imagery of the child in the household. But her whimsies sometimes turned into bold ideas that expressed an all but fathomless[32] insight or wisdom. She saw the mountain, like her father, sitting "in his eternal chair;" her ocean had a "basement," like the house in Amherst, and her wind and snow swept the road like the brooms that she had been taught to use,—the brooms of the breeze swept vale and tree and hill. A journey to the Day of Judgment struck her as a "buggy ride," and she saw a "schoolroom" in the sky. She domesticated the universe and read her own experience into the motions of nature and the world she observed. The sun rose in the East for her "a ribbon at a time," and the "housewife in the evening West" came back to "dust the pond." Clouds for her were "millinery,"[33] mountains wore bonnets, shawls and sandals, eternity "rambled" with her, like her dog Carlo; the wind had fingers and combed the sky, and March walked boldly up and knocked like a neighbor. Volcanoes purred for her like cats, and she saw the planets "frisking about," and her Providence[34] kept a store on the village street, and she thought of death as

---

28. rhetorical (ri tôr′ i k′l) *adj.*: Elaborate in style.
29. mellifluous (mə lif′ loo wəs) *adj.*: Sweet and smooth.
30. evanescent (ev′ ə nes′ ′nt) *adj.*: Tending to fade from sight.
31. sublime (sə blīm′) *adj.*: Noble; exalted; majestic.

32. fathomless (fath′ əm lis) *adj.*: Too deep to be measured.
33. millinery (mil′ ə ner′ ē) *n.*: Women's hats.
34. Providence: God.

Emily Dickinson's house in Amherst, Massachusetts

coming with a broom and a dustpan. The moon slid down the stairs for her "to see who's there," and the grave for her was a little cottage where she could "lay the marble tea." One could not "fold a flood," she said, and "put it in a drawer," but she rolled up the months in mothballs and laid them away, as she had swept up the heart and put away love; and she saw hope, fear, time, future and past as persons to rally, tease, flee, welcome, mock or play with.

The turns of fancy that marked these poems were sharp and unpredictable, and yet they were singularly natural,—nothing was forced. Miss Dickinson lived in a world of paradox, for, while her eye was micro-

scopic, her imagination dwelt with mysteries and grandeurs. Ribbons and immortality were mingled in her mind, which passed from one to the other with the speed of lightning, though she sometimes took a mischievous pleasure in extravagant combinations of thought, uniting the droll and the sublime, the trivial and the grand. There was in this an element of the characteristic American humor that liked to play with incongruities,[35] and Miss Dickinson maintained in the poems of her later years the fun-loving spirit she had shown as a school-

---

35. incongruities (in′ kən grō͞o′ ə tēs) *n.*: Things lacking harmony or agreement; inconsistencies.

girl. To juxtapose[36] the great and the small, in unexpected ways, had been one of her prime amusements as the wit of her circle, and this, like the laconic[37] speech that also marked the Yankee, had remained an essential note of her style as a poet. "Shorter than a snake's delay," her poems were packed with meaning; and, swiftly as her images changed, they were scarcely able to keep the pace with which her mind veered from mood to mood, from faith to mockery, from mysticism to rationalism, through ecstasy, disillusion, anguish, joy. These poems were fairylike in their shimmer and lightness, they moved like bees upon a raft of air; and yet one felt behind them an energy of mind and spirit that only the rarest poets ever possessed. Was not Emily Dickinson's idiom[38] the final proof that she possessed it? Her style, her stamp, her form were completely her own.

Such were the games of solitaire that Miss Dickinson played in the silent room, as lonely as Jane Eyre,[39] in her red-curtained alcove, dreaming over the book with its pictures of the arctic wastes and the rock that stood up in the sea of billow and spray. Miss Dickinson had only this "acre of a rock," and yet what a harvest it yielded of grape and maize. Having but a crumb, she was sovereign of them all, as she said quite truly; for her constant theme was deprivation, the "banquet of abstemiousness,"[40] and this sharpened as nothing else her perception of values. When the well's dry, we know the worth of water, and she felt that she knew victory because she knew defeat, she felt that she knew love because she had lost it; and certainly for all she missed she made up in intensity. Where others merely glowed, she was incandescent.

---

36. juxtapose (juk′ stə pōz′) v.: Put side by side to show contrast.
37. laconic (lə kän′ ik) adj.: Using few words; terse.
38. idiom (id′ ē əm) n.: Language different from the literal; the style of artistic expression characteristic of an individual.

---

39. Jane Eyre (air): Heroine of the novel *Jane Eyre* by Charlotte Brontë.
40. abstemiousness (əb stē′ mē əs nes) n.: Moderation.

▮ RESPONDING TO THE SELECTION

Your Response

1. What insight into Dickinson's character did you find the most interesting? Why?
2. Brooks comments that Dickinson "had lost the art of communication, as the circle of her school friends understood it." How do you think that "the art of communication" among students today differs from what it was in Dickinson's time?

Recalling

3. Explain the event that caused Dickinson to withdraw socially.
4. What was Colonel Higginson's reaction to the first poems that Dickinson sent to him?

Interpreting

5. What in Dickinson's childhood and adolescence influenced the development of her character?
6. What is the author's attitude toward Emily Dickinson's unique style of poetry?
7. ". . . while her eye was microscopic, her imagination dwelt with mysteries and grandeurs." How does this statement relate to Dickinson's poetry?

Applying

8. How do you think that someone with a personality like Emily Dickinson's would be treated today?

ANALYZING LITERATURE

Understanding Characterization

One of the purposes of a biography is to present the subject as a person. To accomplish this, the **character** is revealed to help in understanding the motives behind the events of the subject's life. By understanding Dickinson's character, you are better able to understand her poetry.

> The Soul selects her own Society—
> Then—shuts the Door—
> To her divine Majority—
> Present no more—

1. To what aspect of Dickinson's character could this stanza of her poetry be referring?
2. Is your understanding of this stanza enhanced by the information in the essay? Support your answer.

CRITICAL THINKING AND READING

Drawing Conclusions About Characters

The author of a biography presents facts about a person's character and the events in his or her life. From this information you can **draw conclusions** that help you understand the character. For example, Dickinson had turned inward and become a recluse in her adult life. From these facts you could conclude that she was eccentric.

1. What inference can you make based on her character and her refusal to change any of her poetry based on Higginson's suggestions?
2. Give evidence to support this inference by Brooks: ". . . she did not speak the language of the world outside her, and one gathered that she did not wish to touch it."
3. Brooks says that Dickinson's "father was difficult to please." How could this have influenced Dickinson to withdraw from society?

THINKING AND WRITING

Writing About Emily Dickinson's Poetry

Choose two poems by Emily Dickinson and write a paragraph on each one. Include what the poem means to you and how Dickinson's character and life might have influenced its content.

Be sure to support your judgment with evidence from the poems and from this biographical sketch. When you revise, make sure you have included adequate support from your judgment. Proofread your paper and prepare a final draft.

LEARNING OPTIONS

1. **Writing.** Read the following quotations from Brooks's essay.
   (a) The visible setting of these poems was the New England countryside, the village, the garden, the household that she knew so well. . . ." (page 422)
   (b) ". . . she sometimes took a mischievous pleasure in . . . uniting . . . the trivial and the grand." (page 423)
   (c) "Miss Dickinson maintained in the poems of her later years the fun-loving spirit she had shown as a school girl." (pages 423–424)
   Now find a collection of Emily Dickinson's poetry in a library. Skim the collection, looking for poems that illustrate Brooks's comments. For each poem you choose, write a brief paragraph in which you explain how the poem supports Brooks's claim.
2. **Art.** As he explores Dickinson's character, Brooks refers to the imagery in her poems. For example, he says, "Volcanoes purred for her like cats." Choose three of the images Brooks refers to in his essay. Then find pictures (from magazines, postcards, or even your own photographs) that remind you of these images. If necessary, combine two or more pictures to suggest a Dickinson image. Tape down the pictures you find, and use the images Brooks includes in his essay as captions for the pictures.

GUIDE FOR READING

Langston Hughes

(1902–1967) was a poet, novelist, dramatist, and songwriter who first came to prominence as a leading artist of the Harlem Renaissance, an important literary movement of the 1920's. His life was similar in some ways to that of Marian Anderson. They were born in 1902 and became nationally and internationally recognized during their lifetimes. This essay first appeared in Langston Hughes's 1954 collection of biographies of famous black Americans.

Marian Anderson: Famous Concert Singer

Biography

A **biography** is an account of a person's life written by another individual. In many biographies the major events and accomplishments in the subject's life are covered from birth to death in chronological order. The biographer gathers these facts from firsthand documents such as letters and diaries, from interviews with people who knew the subject, or from other research done on the subject. These facts are then interwoven with the biographer's impressions or interpretation.

Focus

In "Marian Anderson: Famous Concert Singer," Langston Hughes discusses how Anderson, despite racial stereotypes and prejudice, made a successful career as a singer. Hughes emphasizes her strength of character by discussing the obstacles she overcame throughout her career. Get together with two or three classmates. Using your knowledge of American history, brainstorm to list the various types of obstacles African Americans faced in Anderson's time. (Remember that she became famous before the Civil Rights Movement of the 1960's.) Consider how such obstacles might have affected African American artists like Marian Anderson. Keep your discussion in mind as you read Hughes's impressions of her life and character.

Vocabulary

Knowing the following words will help you as you read "Marian Anderson: Famous Concert Singer."

arias (är′ ē əz) *n.*: Melodies in an opera, especially for solo voice with instrumental accompaniment (p. 427)

staunch (stônch) *adj.*: Steadfast; loyal (p. 427)

repertoire (rep′ ər twär) *n.*: The stock of songs that a singer is familiar with and is ready to perform (p. 430)

Marian Anderson: Famous Concert Singer

Langston Hughes

When Marian Anderson was born in a little red brick house in Philadelphia, a famous group of Negro singers, the Fisk Jubilee Singers, had already carried the spirituals all over Europe. And a colored woman billed as "Black Patti" had become famous on variety programs as a singer of both folk songs and the classics. Both Negro and white minstrels had popularized American songs. The all-Negro musical comedies of Bert Williams and George Walker had been successful on Broadway. But no well-trained colored singers performing the great songs of Schubert, Handel, and the other masters, or the arias from famous operas, had become successful on the concert stage. And most people thought of Negro vocalists only in connection with spirituals. Roland Hayes[1] and Marian Anderson were the first to become famous enough to break this stereotype.

Marian Anderson's mother was a staunch church worker who loved to croon the hymns of her faith about the house, as did the aunt who came to live with them when Marian's father died. Both parents were from Virginia. Marian's mother had been a schoolteacher there, and her father a farm boy. Shortly after they moved to Philadelphia where three daughters were born, the father died, and the mother went to work at Wanamaker's department store. But she saw to it that her children attended school and church regularly. The father had been an usher in the Union Baptist Church, so the congregation took an interest in his three little girls. Marian was the oldest and, before she was eight, singing in the Sunday school choir, she had already learned a great many hymns and spirituals by heart.

One day Marian saw an old violin in a pawnshop window marked $3.45. She set her mind on that violin, and began to save the nickels and dimes neighbors would give her for scrubbing their white front steps —the kind of stone steps so characteristic of Philadelphia and Baltimore houses —until she had $3.00. The pawnshop man let her take the violin at a reduced price. Marian never became very good on the violin. A few years later her mother bought a piano, so the child forgot all about it in favor of their newer instrument. By that time, too, her unusual singing voice had attracted the attention of her choir master, and at the age of fourteen she was promoted to a place in the main church choir. There she learned all four parts of all the hymns and anthems and could easily fill in anywhere from bass to soprano.

---

1. **Roland Hayes** (1887–1977): Famous African American tenor in the United States.

Marian Anderson with her accompanist Franz Rupp, 1949

Sensing that she had exceptional musical talent, some of the church members began to raise money so that she might have singing lessons. But her first teacher, a colored woman, refused to accept any pay for instructing so talented a child. So the church folks put their money into a trust fund called "Marian Anderson's Future," banking it until the time came for her to have advanced training. Meanwhile, Marian attended South Philadelphia High School for Girls and took part in various group concerts, usually doing the solo parts. When she was fifteen she sang a group of songs alone at a Sunday School Convention in Harrisburg and word of her talent began to spread about the state. When she was graduated from high school, the Philadelphia Choral Society, a Negro group, sponsored her further study and secured for her one of the best local teachers. Then in 1925 she journeyed to New York to take part, with three hundred other young singers, in the New York Philharmonic Competitions, where she won first place, and appeared with the orchestra at Lewisohn Stadium.

This appearance was given wide publicity, but very few lucrative engagements came in, so Marian continued to study. A Town Hall concert was arranged for her in New

York, but it was unsuccessful. Meanwhile, she kept on singing with various choral groups, and herself gave concerts in churches and at some of the Negro colleges until, in 1930, a Rosenald Fellowship made European study possible. During her first year abroad she made her debut in Berlin. A prominent Scandinavian concert manager read of this concert, but was attracted more by the name, *Anderson*, than by what the critics said about her voice. "Ah," he said, "a Negro singer with a Swedish name! She is bound to be a success in Scandinavia." He sent two of his friends to Germany to hear her, one of them being Kosti Vehanen who shortly became her accompanist and remained with her for many years.

Sure enough, Marian Anderson did become a great success in the Scandinavian countries, where she learned to sing in both Finnish and Swedish, and her first concert tour of Europe became a critical triumph. When she came back home to America, she gave several programs and appeared as soloist with the famous Hall Johnson Choir, but without financial success. However, the Scandinavian people, who had fallen in love with her, kept asking her to come back there. So, in 1933, she went again to Europe for 142 concerts in Norway, Sweden, Denmark, and Finland. She was decorated by the King of Denmark and the King of Sweden. Sibelius[2] dedicated a song to her. And the following spring she made her debut in Paris where she was so well received that she had to give three concerts that season at the Salle Gaveau.[3] Great successes followed in all the European capitals. In 1935 the famous conductor, Arturo Toscanini, listened to her sing at Salzburg.[4] He said,

"What I heard today one is privileged to hear only once in a hundred years." It was in Europe that Marian Anderson began to be acclaimed by critics as "the greatest singer in the world."

When Marian Anderson again returned to America, she was a seasoned artist. News of her tremendous European successes had preceded her, so a big New York concert was planned. But a few days before she arrived at New York, in a storm on the liner crossing the Atlantic, Marian fell and broke her ankle. She refused to allow this to interfere with her concert, however, nor did she even want people to know about it. She wore a very long evening gown that night so that no one could see the plaster cast on her leg. She propped herself in a curve of the piano before the curtains parted, and gave her New York concert standing on one foot! The next day Howard Taubman wrote enthusiastically in *The New York Times*:

> Marian Anderson has returned to her native land one of the great singers of our time. . . . There is no doubt of it, she was mistress of all she surveyed. . . . It was music making that proved too deep for words.

A coast-to-coast American tour followed. And, from that season on, Marian Anderson has been one of our country's favorite singers, rated, according to *Variety*,[5] among the top ten of the concert stage who earn over $100,000 a year. Miss Anderson has sung with the great symphony orchestras, and appeared on all the major radio and television networks many times, being a particular favorite with the millions of listeners to the Ford Hour. During the years she has returned often to Europe for concerts, and among the numerous honors accorded her

---

2. Sibelius: (si bā' lē oos) Jean Sibelius (1865–1957), a Finnish composer.
3. Salle Gaveau: (sal' ga vō') A concert hall in Paris, France.
4. Salzburg: A city in Austria, noted for its music festivals.

5. *Variety*: A show business newspaper.

abroad was a request for a command performance before the King and Queen of England, and a decoration from the government of Finland. Her concerts in South America and Asia have been as successful as those elsewhere. Since 1935 she has averaged over one hundred programs a year in cities as far apart as Vienna, Buenos Aires, Moscow, and Tokyo. Her recordings have sold millions of copies around the world. She has been invited more than once to sing at the White House. She has appeared in concert at the Paris Opera and at the Metropolitan Opera House in New York. Several colleges have granted her honorary degrees, and in 1944 Smith College made her a Doctor of Music.

In spite of all this, as a Negro, Marian Anderson has not been immune from those aspects of racial segregation which affect most traveling artists of color in the United States. In his book, *Marian Anderson,* her longtime accompanist, Vehanen, tells of hotel accommodations being denied her, and service in dining rooms often refused. Once after a concert in a Southern city, Vehanen writes that some white friends drove Marian to the railroad station and took her into the main waiting room. But a policeman ran them out, since Negroes were not allowed in that part of the station. Then they went into the smaller waiting room marked, COLORED. But again they were ejected, because *white* people were not permitted in the cubby hole allotted to Negroes. So they all had to stand on the platform until the train arrived.

The most dramatic incident of prejudice in all Marian Anderson's career occurred in 1939 when the Daughters of the American Revolution, who own Constitution Hall in Washington, refused to allow her to sing there. The newspapers headlined this and many Americans were outraged. In protest a committee of prominent people, including a number of great artists and distinguished figures in the government, was formed. Through the efforts of this committee, Marian Anderson sang in Washington, anyway —before the statue of Abraham Lincoln —to one of the largest crowds ever to hear a singer at one time in the history of the world. Seventy-five thousand people stood in the open air on a cold clear Easter Sunday afternoon to hear her. And millions more listened to Marian Anderson that day over the radio or heard her in the newsreels that recorded the event. Harold Ickes, then Secretary of the Interior, presented Miss Anderson to that enormous audience standing in the plaza to pay honor, as he said, not only to a great singer, but to the basic ideals of democracy and equality.

In 1943 Marian Anderson married Orpheus H. Fisher, an architect, and settled down—between tours—in a beautiful country house in Connecticut where she rehearses new songs to add to her already vast repertoire. Sometimes her neighbors across the fields can hear the rich warm voice that covers three octaves singing in English, French, Finnish, or German. And sometimes they hear in the New England air that old Negro spiritual, "Honor, honor unto the dying Lamb. . . ."

Friends say that Marian Anderson has invested her money in real estate and in government bonds. Certainly, throughout her career, she has lived very simply, traveled without a maid or secretary, and carried her own sewing machine along by train, ship, or plane to mend her gowns. When in 1941 in Philadelphia she was awarded the coveted Bok Award for outstanding public service, the $10,000 that came with the medallion she used to establish a trust fund for "talented American artists without regard to race or creed." Now, each year from this fund promising young musicians receive scholarships.

RESPONDING TO THE SELECTION

Your Response

1. After reading Hughes's essay, what are your impressions of Marian Anderson?

Recalling

2. How did Anderson's congregation help her?
3. Where did she first become a success?
4. What difficulties did Anderson face traveling in the United States?

Interpreting

5. Why was it so difficult for Anderson to gain success in the United States?
6. What does the incident involving her broken ankle reveal about Anderson's personality?
7. What was the significance of Anderson's concert in front of the Lincoln Memorial?

Applying

8. What young artists would you recommend for the award established by Marian Anderson?

ANALYZING LITERATURE

Understanding Biography

The account of a person's life written by another individual is a **biography.** Like most biographers, Hughes provides factual information about Marian Anderson's life, while emphasizing certain aspects of her character. In this way you get to know not only the events in Anderson's life, but also the strengths of her personality.

1. What incidents in the essay reveal Anderson's personality?
2. What aspects of Anderson's life has the author emphasized?

CRITICAL THINKING AND READING

Understanding a Biographer's Purpose

The **biographer's purpose** is the point he or she wants to make. A biographer will emphasize certain qualities or aspects of the subject in order to achieve that purpose. Two biographers who have the same subject may interpret factual information differently. For example, one might present certain facts about the difficulties Anderson faced as an African American concert singer. Another might present different information about her musical skill.

1. What is Hughes's purpose in this biography?
2. How might the purpose change if the essay were in a book about people from Philadelphia?

THINKING AND WRITING

Writing a Biography

Write a short biography of a friend or a family member. Your purpose is to present those characteristics of your subject that you admire. First, make a list of your subject's attributes and accomplishments. Then choose one incident in your subject's life that best presents your purpose. As you revise, be sure you have presented only the facts that fit your purpose.

LEARNING OPTIONS

1. **Cross-curricular Connection.** Find one or more of Anderson's recordings in a library and listen to it. As you listen, remember what you learned about Anderson from Hughes's essay. Beyond her exceptional musical talent, what do you hear in her singing? What qualities of her music do you think made her successful? Answer these questions as you introduce a song to play for the class.

2. **Multicultural Activity.** Think of other artists and athletes with different cultural backgrounds. What obstacles did they overcome to achieve success? How did they enrich their art or their sport? Choose an individual from a different culture. Then write a brief note explaining how he or she overcame obstacles to achieve greatness.

GUIDE FOR READING

A Child's Christmas in Wales

Autobiography

An **autobiography** is the story of a person's life written by that person. The writer of an autobiography can share personal thoughts and feelings and may comment on the effect of certain events on his or her life. As a result, you share in the life of the subject more intimately than in a biography. However, you must also be aware that all autobiographers present their lives subjectively; they do not reveal everything about themselves.

Focus

In "A Child's Christmas in Wales," Dylan Thomas writes affectionately about the impressions, emotions, and events he associates with his Christmas holidays. The way that we celebrate different holidays often includes events, foods, and other traditions that are particular to our ethnic or cultural heritage. Choose a joyful holiday that is part of your heritage. Tell your classmates how you celebrate it, and compare your traditions with the ones that they observe. Then, as you read this essay, notice what Christmas meant to one Welsh boy.

Vocabulary

Knowing the following words will help you as you read "A Child's Christmas in Wales."

bundling (bun′ dliŋ) v.: Moving quickly; bustling (p. 433)

sidle (sī′ d'l) v.: To move sideways in a sneaky manner (p. 433)

prey (prā) n.: An animal hunted or killed for food (p. 433)

wallowed (wäl′ ōd) v.: Enjoyed completely; took great pleasure (p. 434)

crocheted (krō shād′) v.: Made with thread or yarn woven together with hooked needles (p. 436)

brittle (brit′ 'l) adj.: Stiff and unbending; easily broken or shattered (p. 437)

trod (träd) v.: Walked (p. 437)

forlorn (fər lôrn′) adj.: Abandoned; deserted (p. 437)

Dylan Thomas

(1914–1953) grew up in a seaport in Wales, a country on the western coast of Great Britain. Although his education lasted only through grammar school, Thomas's brilliance as a poet was recognized with the publication of his first book, when he was only twenty. He also wrote the radio play *Under Milk Wood,* which has been adapted for stage, movie, and television productions. "A Child's Christmas in Wales" presents memories of several Christmas seasons of his youth, poetically blended together.

A Child's Christmas in Wales

Dylan Thomas

One Christmas was so much like another, in those years around the sea-town corner now and out of all sound except the distant speaking of the voices I sometimes hear a moment before sleep, that I can never remember whether it snowed for six days and six nights when I was twelve or whether it snowed for twelve days and twelve nights when I was six. All the Christmases roll down toward the two-tongued sea, like a cold and headlong moon bundling down the sky that was our street; and they stop at the rim of the ice-edged, fish-freezing waves, and I plunge my hands in the snow and bring out whatever I can find. In goes my hand into that wool-white bell-tongued ball of holidays resting at the rim of the carol-singing seas, and out come Mrs. Prothero and the firemen.

It was on the afternoon of the day of Christmas Eve, and I was in Mrs. Prothero's garden, waiting for cats, with her son Jim. It was snowing. It was always snowing at Christmas. December, in my memory, is white as Lapland, though there were no reindeers. But there were cats. Patient, cold and callous, our hands wrapped in socks, we waited to snowball the cats. Sleek and long as jaguars and horrible-whiskered, spitting and snarling, they would slink and sidle over the white back-garden walls, and the lynx-eyed hunters, Jim and I, fur-capped and moccasined trappers from Hudson Bay,[1] off Mumbles Road, would hurl our deadly snowballs at the green of their eyes. The wise cats never appeared. We were so still, Eskimo-footed arctic marksmen in the muffling silence of the eternal snows —eternal, ever since Wednesday—that we never heard Mrs. Prothero's first cry from her igloo at the bottom of the garden. Or, if we heard it at all, it was, to us, like the far-off challenge of our enemy and prey, the neighbor's polar cat. But soon the voice grew louder. "Fire!" cried Mrs. Prothero, and she beat the dinner-gong.

And we ran down the garden, with the snowballs in our arms, toward the house; and smoke, indeed, was pouring out of the dining room, and the gong was bombilating,[2] and Mrs. Prothero was annoucing ruin like a town crier in Pompeii.[3] This was

---

1. Hudson Bay: Inland sea in northeastern Canada.
2. bombilating (bäm′ bə lāt iŋ) v.: Making a buzzing, droning sound as though a bomb was approaching.
3. Pompeii (päm pā′ ē): City in Italy that was destroyed by the eruption of Mount Vesuvius in 79 A.D.

better than all the cats in Wales standing on the wall in a row. We bounded into the house, laden with snowballs, and stopped at the open door of the smoke-filled room.

Something was burning all right; perhaps it was Mr. Prothero, who always slept there after midday dinner with a newspaper over his face. But he was standing in the middle of the room, saying "A fine Christmas!" and smacking at the smoke with a slipper.

"Call the fire brigade," cried Mrs. Prothero as she beat the gong.

"They won't be there," said Mr. Prothero, "it's Christmas."

There was no fire to be seen, only clouds of smoke and Mr. Prothero standing in the middle of them, waving his slipper as though he were conducting.

"Do something," he said.

And we threw all our snowballs into the smoke—I think we missed Mr. Prothero —and ran out of the house to the telephone box.

"Let's call the police as well," Jim said.

"And the ambulance."

"And Ernie Jenkins, he likes fires."

But we only called the fire brigade, and soon the fire engine came and three tall men in helmets brought a hose into the house and Mr. Prothero got out just in time before they turned it on. Nobody could have had a noisier Christmas Eve. And when the firemen turned off the hose and were standing in the wet, smoky room, Jim's aunt, Miss Prothero, came downstairs and peered in at them. Jim and I waited, very quietly, to hear what she would say to them. She said the right thing, always. She looked at the three tall firemen in their shining helmets, standing among the smoke and cinders and dissolving snowballs, and she said: "Would you like anything to read?"

Years and years and years ago, when I was a boy, when there were wolves in Wales, and birds the color of red-flannel petticoats whisked past the harp-shaped hills, when we sang and wallowed all night and day in caves that smelt like Sunday afternoons in damp front farmhouse parlors, and we chased, with the jawbones of deacons, the English and the bears, before the motor car, before the wheel, before the duchess-faced horse, when we rode the daft[4] and happy hills bareback, it snowed and it snowed. But here a small boy says: "It snowed last year, too. I made a snowman and my brother knocked it down and I knocked my brother down and then we had tea."

"But that was not the same snow," I say. "Our snow was not only shaken from whitewash buckets down the sky, it came shawling[5] out of the ground and swam and drifted out of the arms and hands and bodies of the trees; snow grew overnight on the roofs of the houses like a pure and grandfather moss, minutely white-ivied the walls and settled on the postman, opening the gate, like a dumb, numb thunderstorm of white, torn Christmas cards."

"Were there postmen then, too?"

"With sprinkling eyes and wind-cherried noses, on spread, frozen feet they crunched up to the doors and mittened on them manfully. But all that the children could hear was a ringing of bells."

"You mean that the postman went rat-a-tat-tat and the doors rang?"

"I mean that the bells that the children could hear were inside them."

"I only hear thunder sometimes, never bells."

---

4. **daft:** Silly; foolish.
5. **shawling:** Draping like a shawl.

"There were church bells, too."

"Inside them?"

"No, no, no, in the bat-black, snow-white belfries, tugged by bishops and storks. And they rang their tidings over the bandaged town, over the frozen foam of the powder and ice-cream hills, over the crackling sea. It seemed that all the churches boomed for joy under my window; and the weathercocks crew for Christmas, on our fence."

"Get back to the postmen."

"They were just ordinary postmen, fond of walking and dogs and Christmas and the snow. They knocked on the doors with blue knuckles. . . ."

"Ours has got a black knocker. . . ."

"And then they stood on the white Welcome mat in the little, drifted porches and huffed and puffed, making ghosts with their breath, and jogged from foot to foot like small boys wanting to go out."

"And then the presents?"

MULTICULTURAL CONNECTION

Christmas in Different Places

Dylan Thomas's essay "A Child's Christmas in Wales" describes the Welsh Christmas customs he remembers so vividly from his childhood. It also suggests the similarities and differences in the celebration of Christmas around the world. Though different cultures have their own versions of Christmas, several customs, from the burning of the yule log to waiting for Saint Nicholas, are common in many countries.

Gift giving. One of the pleasant customs of Christmas is gift giving, a tradition that dates back to the story of the three Wise Men, who brought gifts to the Infant Jesus in Bethlehem. Today the gift-giver in many countries is Saint Nicholas, who comes at Christmastime on a sleigh and is referred to in some cultures as Santa Claus. In other places, he is simply a jolly old man who represents winter. In Russia, he is called Grandfather Frost and in France, he is *Père Noël*, which means Father Christmas.

Other traditions. Special sharing customs are often part of Christmas traditions. The Irish place a candle in the window, inviting travelers to share the warmth within. In Russia, an additional place is set at the Christmas table for the unexpected guest who might stop by. Austrians decorate a tree with bread crumbs to feed the birds.

Throughout the world, Christmas is celebrated on December 25, but other days are important to the festivities. In England, the day after Christmas is called Boxing Day, dating back to the time when on that day working people opened their boxed collections of tips and other special Christmas treats.

In Latin America, December 16 is the first night of *Las Posadas*, a reenactment of the search for lodging by Jesus' parents, Mary and Joseph. A celebration or fiesta commemorates their finding a place to stay.

Sharing

Interview friends or neighbors about winter holidays they celebrate, such as Hanuka, New Year's Day, or the African American holiday Kwanzaa. Tell the class about winter holidays you particularly enjoy.

"And then the Presents, after the Christmas box. And the cold postman, with a rose on his button-nose, tingled down the tea-tray-slithered run of the chilly glinting hill. He went in his ice-bound boots like a man on fish-monger's slabs.[6] He wagged his bag like a frozen camel's hump, dizzily turned the corner on one foot, and was gone."

"Get back to the Presents."

"There were the Useful Presents: engulfing mufflers of the old coach days, and mittens made for giant sloths;[7] zebra scarfs of a substance like silky gum that could be tug-o'-warred down to the galoshes;[8] blinding tam-o'-shanters[9] like patchwork tea cozies[10] and bunny-suited busbies[11] and balaclavas[12] for victims of head-shrinking tribes; from aunts who always wore wool next to the skin there were mustached and rasping vests that made you wonder why the aunts had any skin left at all; and once I had a little crocheted nose bag from an aunt now, alas, no longer whinnying with us. And pictureless books in which small boys, though warned with quotations not to, *would* skate on Farmer Giles' pond and did and drowned; and books that told me everything about the wasp, except why."

"Go on to the Useless Presents."

"Bags of moist and many-colored jelly babies[13] and a folded flag and a false nose and a tram-conductor's cap[14] and a machine that punched tickets and rang a bell; never a catapult;[15] once, by mistake that no one could explain, a little hatchet; and a celluloid duck that made, when you pressed it, a most unducklike sound, a mewing moo that an ambitious cat might make who wished to be a cow; and a painting book in which I could make the grass, the trees, the sea and the animals any color I pleased, and still the dazzling sky-blue sheep are grazing in the red field under the rainbow-billed and pea-green birds. Hard-boileds, toffee, fudge and allsorts, crunches, cracknels, humbugs, glaciers, marzipan, and butterwelsh[16] for the Welsh. And troops of bright tin soldiers who, if they could not fight, could always run. And Snakes-and-Families and Happy Ladders.[17] And Easy Hobbi-Games for Little Engineers, complete with instructions. Oh, easy for Leonardo![18] And a whistle to make the dogs bark to wake up the old man next door to make him beat on the wall with his stick to shake our picture off the wall. And a packet of cigarettes: you put one in your mouth and you stood at the corner of the street and you waited for hours, in vain, for an old lady to scold you for smoking a cigarette, and then with a smirk you ate it. And then it was breakfast under the balloons."

"Were there Uncles, like in our house?"

---

6. fishmonger's slabs: Flat, slimy surface on which fish are displayed for sale.

7. sloths: (slôths) Two-toed mammals that hang from trees.

8. galoshes: (gə läsh′ əz) Rubber overshoes or boots.

9. tam-o'-shanters: Scottish caps.

10. tea cozies: Knitted or padded covers placed over a teapot to keep the contents warm.

11. busbies (buz′ bēz): Tall fur hats worn as part of the full-dress uniforms of guardsmen in the British army.

12. balaclavas (bäl′ ə klä′ vəz): Knitted helmets with an opening for the nose and eyes.

13. jelly babies: Candies in the shape of babies.

14. tram conductor's cap: Streetcar or trolley car operator's cap.

15. catapult (kat′ ə pult′): An ancient military machine for throwing or shooting stones or spears; a slingshot.

16. hard-boileds, . . . butterwelsh: Various kinds of candy.

17. Snakes-and-Families and Happy Ladders: Games, the names of which Dylan Thomas mixes up on purpose. The games are actually Snakes-and-Ladders and Happy Families.

18. Leonardo: Leonardo da Vinci (1452–1519), an Italian painter, sculptor, architect, engineer, and scientist.

"There are always Uncles at Christmas. The same Uncles. And on Christmas mornings, with dog-disturbing whistle and sugar fags,[19] I would scour the swatched town for the news of the little world, and find always a dead bird by the white Post Office or by the deserted swings; perhaps a robin, all but one of his fires out. Men and women wading or scooping back from chapel, with taproom noses and wind-bussed cheeks, all albinos,[20] huddled their stiff black jarring feathers against the irreligious snow. Mistletoe hung from the gas brackets[21] in all the front parlors; there was sherry and walnuts and bottled beer and crackers by the dessert-spoons; and cats in their fur-abouts watched the fires; and the high-heaped fire spat, all ready for the chestnuts and the mulling pokers. Some few large men sat in the front parlors, without their collars, Uncles almost certainly, trying their new cigars, holding them out judiciously at arms' length, returning them to their mouths, coughing, then holding them out again as though waiting for the explosion; and some few small aunts, not wanted in the kitchen, nor anywhere else for that matter, sat on the very edges of their chairs, poised and brittle, afraid to break, like faded cups and saucers."

Not many those mornings trod the piling streets: an old man always, fawn-bowlered,[22] yellow-gloved and, at this time of year, with spats[23] of snow, would take his constitutional[24] to the white bowling green and back, as he would take it wet or fine on Christmas Day or Doomsday; sometimes two hale young men, with big pipes blazing, no overcoats and wind-blown scarfs, would trudge, unspeaking, down to the forlorn sea, to work up an appetite, to blow away the fumes, who knows, to walk into the waves until nothing of them was left but the two curling smoke clouds of their inextinguishable briars.[25] Then I would be slap-dashing home, the gravy smell of the dinners of others, the bird smell, the brandy, the pudding and mince, coiling up to my nostrils, when out of a snow-clogged side lane would come a boy the spit of myself, with a pink-tipped cigarette and the violet past of a black eye, cocky as a bullfinch, leering all to himself. I hated him on sight and sound, and would be about to put my dog whistle to my lips and blow him off the face of Christmas when suddenly he, with a violet wink, put *his* whistle to *his* lips and blew so stridently, so high, so exquisitely loud, that gobbling faces, their cheeks bulged with goose, would press against their tinseled windows, the whole length of the white echoing street. For dinner we had turkey and blazing pudding, and after dinner the Uncles sat in front of the fire, loosened all buttons, put their large moist hands over their watch chains, groaned a little and slept. Mothers, aunts and sisters scuttled to and fro, bearing tureens.[26] Auntie Bessie, who had already been frightened, twice, by a clock-work mouse, whimpered at the sideboard and had some elderberry wine. The dog was sick. Auntie Dosie had to have three aspirins, but Auntie Hannah, who liked port, stood in the

---

19. sugar fags: Candy cigarettes.
20. albinos (al bī′ nōz): People who because of a genetic factor have unusually pale skin and white hair.
21. gas brackets: Wall fixtures for gas lights.
22. fawn-bowlered: Tan-hatted.
23. spats: Coverings for the instep and ankle.
24. constitutional: A walk taken for one's health.

---

25. briars: Pipes.
26. tureens (too rēnz′): Deep dishes with covers.

Fritz Eichenberg etching

middle of the snowbound back yard, singing like a big-bosomed thrush. I would blow up balloons to see how big they would blow up to; and, when they burst, which they all did, the Uncles jumped and rumbled. In the rich and heavy afternoon, the Uncles breathing like dolphins and the snow descending, I would sit among festoons[27] and Chinese lanterns and nibble dates and try to make a model man-o'-war,[28] following the Instructions for Little Engineers, and produce what might be mistaken for a sea-going tramcar.

Or I would go out, my bright new boots squeaking, into the white world, on to the seaward hill, to call on Jim and Dan and Jack and to pad through the still streets, leaving huge deep footprints on the hidden pavements.

27. festoons: Wreaths and garlands.

28. man-o'-war: A warship.

"I bet people will think there's been hippos."

"What would you do if you saw a hippo coming down our street?"

"I'd go like this, bang! I'd throw him over the railings and roll him down the hill and then I'd tickle him under the ear and he'd wag his tail."

"What would you do if you saw *two* hippos?"

Iron-flanked and bellowing he-hippos clanked and battered through the scudding snow toward us as we passed Mr. Daniel's house.

"Let's post Mr. Daniel a snowball through his letter box."

"Let's write things in the snow."

"Let's write, 'Mr. Daniel looks like a spaniel' all over his lawn."

Or we walked on the white shore. "Can the fishes see it's snowing?"

The silent one-clouded heavens drifted on to the sea. Now we were snow-blind travelers lost on the north hills, and vast dewlapped[29] dogs, with flasks round their necks, ambled and shambled up to us, baying "Excelsior."[30] We returned home through the poor streets where only a few children fumbled with bare red fingers in the wheel-rutted snow and cat-called after us, their voices fading away, as we trudged uphill, into the cries of the dock birds and the hooting of ships out in the whirling bay. And then, at tea the recovered Uncles would be jolly; and the ice cake loomed in the center of the table like a marble grave. Auntie Hannah laced her tea with rum, because it was only once a year.

---

29. dewlapped: Having loose folds of skin hanging from the throat.
30. Excelsior (ek sel′ sē ôr′): Latin phrase meaning *onward and upward.*

Bring out the tall tales now that we told by the fire as the gaslight bubbled like a diver. Ghosts whooed like owls in the long nights when I dared not look over my shoulder; animals lurked in the cubbyhole under the stairs where the gas meter ticked. And I remember that we went singing carols once, when there wasn't the shaving of a moon to light the flying streets. At the end of a long road was a drive that led to a large house, and we stumbled up the darkness of the drive that night, each one of us afraid, each one holding a stone in his hand in case, and all of us too brave to say a word. The wind through the trees made noises as of old and unpleasant and maybe webfooted men wheezing in caves. We reached the black bulk of the house.

"What shall we give them? Hark the Herald?"

"No," Jack said, "Good King Wenceslas. I'll count three."

One, two, three, and we began to sing, our voices high and seemingly distant in the snow-felted darkness round the house that was occupied by nobody we knew. We stood close together, near the dark door.

Good King Wenceslas looked out
On the Feast of Stephen . . .

And then a small, dry voice, like the voice of someone who has not spoken for a long time, joined our singing: a small, dry, eggshell voice from the other side of the door: a small dry voice through the keyhole. And when we stopped running we were outside *our* house; the front room was lovely; balloons floated under the hot-water-bottle-gulping gas; everything was good again and shone over the town.

"Perhaps it was a ghost," Jim said.

Fritz Eichenberg etching

"Perhaps it was trolls,"[31] Dan said, who was always reading.

"Let's go in and see if there's any jelly left," Jack said. And we did that.

Always on Christmas night there was music. An uncle played the fiddle, a cousin sang "Cherry Ripe," and another uncle sang "Drake's Drum." It was very warm in the little house. Auntie Hannah, who had got on to the parsnip wine, sang a song about Bleeding Hearts and Death, and then another in which she said her heart was like a Bird's Nest; and then everybody laughed again; and then I went to bed. Looking through my bedroom window, out into the moonlight and the unending smoke-colored snow, I could see the lights in the windows of all the other houses on our hill and hear the music rising from them up the long, steadily falling night. I turned the gas down, I got into bed. I said some words to the close and holy darkness, and then I slept.

---

31. trolls: Mythical Scandinavian beings.

Your Response

1. Do you find something familiar in Thomas's memories? Explain.

Recalling

2. What does the opening passage indicate about the effects of time on Thomas's Christmas memory?
3. Describe the events concerning the fire in the Protheros' kitchen.
4. Describe at least four of the "Useful Presents."
5. How are the Uncles and Aunts described?
6. Explain what happened when the boys went caroling.

Interpreting

7. How does answering questions from a young boy affect the telling of the story?
8. In what ways was Christmas for the children different from Christmas for the adults?
9. What does the final sentence add to Thomas's memory of childhood?

Analyzing

10. Why do people's memories tend to blend together and exaggerate the past?

ANALYZING LITERATURE

Understanding Autobiography

A person writing an autobiography can reveal details and thoughts about certain events that would never be known through research.

1. Why do you think Dylan Thomas tells this memory of his childhood?
2. What details in the essay support your opinion?

CRITICAL THINKING AND READING

Recognizing Subjective Details

Objective details are impersonal. Details that are based on personal opinions and feelings are **subjective.** Dylan Thomas is not interested in providing an objective picture of his childhood. Instead, he wants to re-create the feelings, thoughts, and impressions of a young person at Christmas. His essay is therefore filled with subjective details. "It was snowing. It was always snowing at Christmas. December, in my memory, is white as Lapland, though there were no reindeers. But there were cats."

1. Find three examples of subjective information.
2. How does Dylan Thomas's use of subjective information reinforce the childlike quality of the essay?

THINKING AND WRITING

Writing an Autobiographical Sketch

Write a short, autobiographical sketch about a time in your life that has left an impression on your memory. Freewrite about your impressions and memories from another time. Try to re-create, as closely as possible, your feelings and thoughts as you are writing. As you revise, make sure you have included subjective as well as objective information.

LEARNING OPTIONS

1. **Writing.** Memories tend to fade over time, and people remember the same event in different ways. Choose a memory from your childhood. Write down what you recall; then interview family members or friends who are part of the memory. Finally, write a brief account of the event you are remembering, noting the ways in which others' recollections differ from yours.
2. **Multicultural Activity.** Design a greeting card or postcard for an important holiday in your culture. On the card illustrate the customs and traditions common to that holiday. If you design a postcard, write a brief note explaining the holiday and your illustrations as if you were sending the card to a friend. If you choose to create a greeting card, write a message inside that captures the spirit of the holiday. Share your card with your class.

GUIDE FOR READING

A Christmas Memory

Reminiscence

A **reminiscence** is an autobiographical account of an experience from the past. Unlike a full-length autobiography, which usually recounts most, if not all, of the writer's life, a reminiscence focuses on an experience of particular significance. It presents the events and the characters, as well as the special quality or meaning that keeps the memory alive and fresh in the writer's mind.

Focus

Think about a favorite relative or family friend who evokes happy childhood memories and feelings of affection. It may be a grandparent, aunt or uncle, or a close family friend. Make a sensory impressions chart with the following categories: sight, sound, touch, smell, taste. Under each sense, list the images that remind you of that person: a welcome expression in his or her eyes; a hearty laugh; an affectionate hug; a pleasant, comforting scent; special homemade food. As you read "A Christmas Memory," compare your impressions with Capote's.

Vocabulary

Knowing the following words will help you as you read "A Christmas Memory."

calico (kal′ ə kō) *adj.:* Made of cotton cloth, usually printed (p. 443)

inaugurating (in ô′ gyə rāt′ iŋ) *v.:* Making a formal beginning; celebrating the opening of (p. 444)

exhilarates (ig zil′ ə rāts) *v.:* Makes cheerful, lively; stimulates (p. 444)

dilapidated (di lap′ ə dāt′ id) *adj.:* Broken down; shabby and neglected (p. 444)

paraphernalia (par′ ə fər nāl′ yə) *n.:* Collection of articles; gear necessary for some activity (p. 444)

prosaic (prō zā′ ik) *adj.:* Commonplace; dull; ordinary (p. 446)

chastising (chas tīz′ iŋ) *adj.:* Punishing; scolding (p. 448)

Truman Capote

(1924–1984) was born in New Orleans, Louisiana, and spent most of his childhood in the care of relatives in the South. One of these relatives, an elderly cousin named Sook Faulk, was the inspiration for "A Christmas Memory." Capote also wrote short stories, novels, plays, screenplays, and travel sketches. His most successful work, *In Cold Blood,* is a "nonfiction novel," which combines factual reporting with imagination. He adapted a number of his works, including "A Christmas Memory," for television.

A Christmas Memory

Truman Capote

Imagine a morning in late November. A coming of winter morning more than twenty years ago. Consider the kitchen of a spreading old house in a country town. A great black stove is its main feature; but there is also a big round table and a fireplace with two rocking chairs placed in front of it. Just today the fireplace commenced its seasonal roar.

A woman with shorn white hair is standing at the kitchen window. She is wearing tennis shoes and a shapeless gray sweater over a summery calico dress. She is small and sprightly, like a bantam hen; but, due to a long youthful illness, her shoulders are pitifully hunched. Her face is remarkable—not unlike Lincoln's, craggy like that, and tinted by sun and wind; but it is delicate too, finely boned, and her eyes are sherry-colored and timid. "Oh my," she exclaims, her breath smoking the window-pane, "it's fruitcake weather!"

The person to whom she is speaking is myself. I am seven; she is sixty-something. We are cousins, very distant ones, and we have lived together—well, as long as I can remember. Other people inhabit the house, relatives; and though they have power over us, and frequently make us cry, we are not, on the whole, too much aware of them. We are each other's best friend. She calls me Buddy, in memory of a boy who was formerly her best friend. The other Buddy died in the 1880's, when she was still a child. She is still a child.

"I knew it before I got out of bed," she

Truman Capote and Miss Sook Faulk, "his friend" (Used with permission of the Estate of Truman Capote, Alan U. Schwartz, Executor)

says, turning away from the window with a purposeful excitement in her eyes. "The courthouse bell sounded so cold and clear. And there were no birds singing; they've gone to warmer country, yes indeed. Oh, Buddy, stop stuffing biscuit and fetch our buggy. Help me find my hat. We've thirty cakes to bake."

It's always the same: a morning arrives in November, and my friend, as though officially inaugurating the Christmas time of year that exhilarates her imagination and fuels the blaze of her heart, announces: "It's fruitcake weather! Fetch our buggy. Help me find my hat."

The hat is found, a straw cartwheel corsaged with velvet roses out-of-doors has faded: it once belonged to a more fashionable relative. Together, we guide our buggy, a dilapidated baby carriage, out to the garden and into a grove of pecan trees. The buggy is mine; that is, it was bought for me when I was born. It is made of wicker, rather unraveled, and the wheels wobble like a drunkard's legs. But it is a faithful object; springtimes, we take it to the woods and fill it with flowers, herbs, wild fern for our porch pots; in the summer, we pile it with picnic paraphernalia and sugar-cane fishing poles and roll it down to the edge of a creek; it has its winter uses, too: as a truck for hauling firewood from the yard to the kitchen, as a warm bed for Queenie, our tough little orange and white rat terrier who has survived distemper[1] and two rattlesnake bites. Queenie is trotting beside it now.

Three hours later we are back in the kitchen hulling[2] a heaping buggyload of windfall pecans. Our backs hurt from gathering them: how hard they were to find (the main crop having been shaken off the trees and sold by the orchard's owners, who are not us) among the concealing leaves, the frosted, deceiving grass. Caarackle! A cheery crunch, scraps of miniature thunder sound as the shells collapse and the golden mound of sweet oily ivory meat mounts in the milk-glass bowl. Queenie begs to taste, and now and again my friend sneaks her a

mite, though insisting we deprive ourselves. "We mustn't, Buddy. If we start, we won't stop. And there's scarcely enough as there is. For thirty cakes." The kitchen is growing dark. Dusk turns the window into a mirror: our reflections mingle with the rising moon as we work by the fireside in the firelight. At last, when the moon is quite high, we toss the final hull into the fire and, with joined sighs, watch it catch flame. The buggy is empty, the bowl is brimful.

We eat our supper (cold biscuits, bacon, blackberry jam) and discuss tomorrow. Tomorrow the kind of work I like best begins: buying. Cherries and citron,[3] ginger and vanilla and canned Hawaiian pineapple, rinds[4] and raisins and walnuts and whiskey and oh, so much flour, butter, so many eggs, spices, flavorings: why, we'll need a pony to pull the buggy home.

But before these purchases can be made, there is the question of money. Neither of us has any. Except for skinflint[5] sums persons in the house occasionally provide (a dime is considered very big money); or what we earn ourselves from various activities: holding rummage sales, selling buckets of hand-picked blackberries, jars of homemade jam and apple jelly and peach preserves, rounding up flowers for funerals and weddings. Once we won seventy-ninth prize, five dollars, in a national football contest. Not that we know a fool thing about football. It's just that we enter any contest we hear about: at the moment our hopes are centered on the fifty-thousand-dollar Grand Prize being offered to name a new brand of coffee (we suggested "A.M."; and, after some hesitation, for my friend thought it perhaps

---

1. distemper (dis tem′ pər) n.: An infectious virus disease of young dogs.
2. hulling: (hul′ iŋ) v.: Taking the shells off nuts.

3. citron (si′ trən) n.: A yellow, thick-skinned, lemonlike fruit.
4. rinds (rīnds) n.: The skins of oranges and lemons.
5. skinflint (skin′ flint′) adj.: Miserly.

sacrilegious,[6] the slogan "A.M.! Amen!"). To tell the truth, our only *really* profitable enterprise was the Fun and Freak Museum we conducted in a back-yard woodshed two summers ago. The Fun was a stereopticon[7] with slide views of Washington and New York lent us by a relative who had been to those places (she was furious when she discovered why we'd borrowed it); the Freak was a three-legged biddy chicken hatched by one of our own hens. Everybody hereabouts wanted to see that biddy: we charged grownups a nickel, kids two cents. And took in a good twenty dollars before the museum shut down due to the decease of the main attraction.

But one way and another we do each year accumulate Christmas savings, a Fruitcake Fund. These moneys we keep hidden in an ancient bead purse under a loose board under the floor under a chamber pot under my friend's bed. The purse is seldom removed from this safe location except to make a deposit, or, as happens every Saturday, a withdrawal; for on Saturdays I am allowed ten cents to go to the picture show. My friend has never been to a picture show, nor does she intend to: "I'd rather hear you tell the story, Buddy. That way I can imagine it more. Besides, a person my age shouldn't squander their eyes. When the Lord comes, let me see Him clear." In addition to never having seen a movie, she has never: eaten in a restaurant, traveled more than five miles from home, received or sent a telegram, read anything except funny papers and the Bible, worn cosmetics, cursed, wished someone harm, told a lie on purpose, let a hungry dog go hungry. Here are a few things she has done, does do: killed with a hoe the biggest rattlesnake ever seen in this county (sixteen rattles), dip snuff (secretly), tame hummingbirds (just try it) till they balance on her finger, tell ghost stories (we both believe in ghosts) so tingling they chill you in July, talk to herself, take walks in the rain, grow the prettiest japonicas[8] in town, know the recipe for every sort of old-time Indian cure, including a magical wart-remover.

Now, with supper finished, we retire to the room in a faraway part of the house where my friend sleeps in a scrap-quilt-covered iron bed painted rose pink, her favorite color. Silently, wallowing in the pleasures of conspiracy, we take the bead purse from its secret place and spill its contents on the scrap quilt. Dollar bills, tightly rolled and green as May buds. Somber fifty-cent pieces, heavy enough to weight a dead man's eyes. Lovely dimes, the liveliest coin, the one that really jingles. Nickels and quarters, worn smooth as creek pebbles. But mostly a hateful heap of bitter-odored pennies. Last summer others in the house contracted to pay us a penny for every twenty-five flies we killed. Oh, the carnage[9] of August: the flies that flew to heaven! Yet it was not work in which we took pride. And, as we sit counting pennies, it is as though we were back tabulating dead flies. Neither of us has a head for figures; we count slowly, lose track, start again. According to her calculations, we have $12.73. According to mine, exactly $13. "I do hope you're wrong, Buddy. We can't mess around with thirteen. The cakes will fall. Or put somebody in the cemetery. Why, I wouldn't dream of getting

---

6. sacrilegious (sak′ rə lij′ əs) *adj.*: Disrespectful or irreverent toward anything regarded as sacred.

7. stereopticon (ster′ ē äp′ ti kən) *n.*: An instrument with two eyepieces through which a pair of photographs of the same scene taken at slightly different angles are viewed to give a three-dimensional effect.

8. japonicas (jə pän′ i kəs) *n.*: Flowers such as camellias or Japanese quince.

9. carnage (kär′ nij) *n.*: Slaughter; massacre.

out of bed on the thirteenth." This is true: she always spends thirteenths in bed. So, to be on the safe side, we subtract a penny and toss it out the window.

Of the ingredients that go into our fruit-cakes, whiskey is the most expensive, as well as the hardest to obtain: State laws forbid its sale. But everybody knows you can buy a bottle from Mr. Haha Jones. And the next day, having completed our more prosaic shopping, we set out for Mr. Haha's business address, a "sinful " (to quote public opinion) fish-fry and dancing café down by the river. We've been there before, and on the same errand; but in previous years our dealings have been with Haha's wife, an iodine-dark Indian woman with brassy per-oxided hair and a dead-tired disposition. Actually, we've never laid eyes on her husband, though we've heard that he's an Indian too. A giant with razor scars across his cheeks. They call him Haha because he's so gloomy, a man who never laughs. As we approach his café (a large log cabin fes-tooned inside and out with chains of garish-gay naked light bulbs and standing by the river's muddy edge under the shade of river trees where moss drifts through the branch-es like gray mist) our steps slow down. Even Queenie stops prancing and sticks close by. People have been murdered in Haha's café. Cut to pieces. Hit on the head. There's a case coming up in court next month. Natu-rally these goings-on happen at night when the colored lights cast crazy patterns and the victrola[10] wails. In the daytime Haha's is shabby and deserted. I knock at the door, Queenie barks, my friend calls: "Mrs. Haha, ma'am? Anyone to home?"

Footsteps. The door opens. Our hearts overturn. It's Mr. Haha Jones himself! And he *is* a giant; he *does* have scars; he *doesn't*

---

10. **victrola** (vic trōl' ə) *n.*: A record player.

smile. No, he glowers at us through Satan-tilted eyes and demands to know: "What you want with Haha?"

For a moment we are too paralyzed to tell. Presently my friend half-finds her voice, a whispery voice at best: "If you please, Mr. Haha, we'd like a quart of your finest whis-key."

His eyes tilt more. Would you believe it? Haha is smiling! Laughing, too. "Which one of you is a drinkin' man?"

"It's for making fruitcakes, Mr. Haha. Cooking."

This sobers him. He frowns. "That's no way to waste good whiskey." Nevertheless, he retreats into the shadowed café and sec-onds later appears carrying a bottle of daisy-yellow unlabeled liquor. He demonstrates its sparkle in the sunlight and says: "Two dol-lars."

We pay him with nickels and dimes and pennies. Suddenly, as he jangles the coins in his hand like a fistful of dice, his face softens. "Tell you what," he proposes, pour-ing the money back into our bead purse, "just send me one of them fruitcakes in-stead."

"Well," my friend remarks on our way home, "there's a lovely man. We'll put an extra cup of raisins in *his* cake."

The black stove, stoked with coal and firewood, glows like a lighted pumpkin. Egg-beaters whirl, spoons spin round in bowls of butter and sugar, vanilla sweetens the air, ginger spices it; melting, nose-tingling odors saturate the kitchen, suffuse the house, drift out to the world on puffs of chimney smoke. In four days our work is done. Thirty-one cakes, dampened with whiskey, bask on window sills and shelves.

Who are they for?

Friends. Not necessarily neighbor friends: indeed, the larger share is intended for persons we've met maybe once, perhaps

yes. Also, the scrapbooks we keep of thank-you's on White House stationery, time-to-time communications from California and Borneo, the knife grinder's penny post cards, make us feel connected to eventful worlds beyond the kitchen with its view of a sky that stops.

Now a nude December fig branch grates against the window. The kitchen is empty, the cakes are gone; yesterday we carted the last of them to the post office, where the cost of stamps turned our purse inside out. We're broke. That rather depresses me, but my friend insists on celebrating—with two inches of whiskey left in Haha's bottle. Queenie has a spoonful in a bowl of coffee (she likes her coffee chicory-flavored and strong). The rest we divide between a pair of jelly glasses. We're both quite awed at the prospect of drinking straight whiskey; the taste of it brings screwed-up expressions and sour shudders. But by and by we begin to sing, the two of us singing different songs simultaneously. I don't know the words to mine, just: *Come on along, come on along, to the dark-town strutters' ball.* But I can dance: that's what I mean to be, a tap dancer in the movies. My dancing shadow rollicks on the walls; our voices rock the chinaware; we giggle: as if unseen hands were tickling us. Queenie rolls on her back, her paws plow the air, something like a grin stretches her black lips. Inside myself, I feel warm and sparky as those crumbling logs, carefree as the wind in the chimney. My friend waltzes round the stove, the hem of her poor calico skirt pinched between her fingers as though it were a party dress: *Show me the way to go home*

Enter: two relatives. Very angry. Potent[13] with eyes that scold, tongues that

not at all. People who've struck our fancy. Like President Roosevelt.[11] Like the Reverend and Mrs. J. C. Lucey, Baptist missionaries to Borneo who lectured here last winter. Or the little knife grinder who comes through town twice a year. Or Abner Packer, the driver of the six o'clock bus from Mobile,[12] who exchanges waves with us every day as he passes in a dust-cloud whoosh. Or the young Wistons, a California couple whose car one afternoon broke down outside the house and who spent a pleasant hour chatting with us on the porch (young Mr. Wiston snapped our picture, the only one we've ever had taken). Is it because my friend is shy with everyone *except* strangers that these strangers, and merest acquaintances, seem to us our truest friends? I think

---

11. President Roosevelt: Franklin Delano Roosevelt (1882–1945), thirty-second President of the United States (1933–1945).

12. Mobile (mō bēl′): City in Alabama.

---

13. potent (pōt′ 'nt) *adj.*: Powerful.

scald. Listen to what they have to say, the words tumbling together into a wrathful tune: "A child of seven! whiskey on his breath! are you out of your mind? feeding a child of seven! must be loony! road to ruination! remember Cousin Kate? Uncle Charlie? Uncle Charlie's brother-in-law? shame! scandal! humiliation! kneel, pray beg the Lord!"

Queenie sneaks under the stove. My friend gazes at her shoes, her chin quivers, she lifts her skirt and blows her nose and runs to her room. Long after the town has gone to sleep and the house is silent except for the chimings of clocks and sputter of fading fires, she is weeping into a pillow already as wet as a widow's handkerchief.

"Don't cry," I say, sitting at the bottom of her bed and shivering despite my flannel nightgown that smells of last winter's cough syrup, "don't cry," I beg, teasing her toes, tickling her feet, "you're too old for that."

"It's because," she hiccups, "I *am* too old. Old and funny."

"Not funny. Fun. More fun than anybody. Listen. If you don't stop crying you'll be so tired tomorrow we can't go cut a tree."

She straightens up. Queenie jumps on the bed (where Queenie is not allowed) to lick her cheeks. "I know where we'll find real pretty trees, Buddy. And holly, too. With berries big as your eyes. It's way off in the woods. Farther than we've ever been. Papa used to bring us Christmas trees from there: carry them on his shoulder. That's fifty years ago. Well, now: I can't wait for morning."

Morning. Frozen rime[14] lusters the grass; the sun, round as an orange and orange as hot-weather moons, balances on the horizon, burnishes the silvered winter woods. A wild turkey calls. A renegade hog grunts in the undergrowth. Soon, by the edge of knee-deep, rapid-running water, we have to abandon the buggy. Queenie wades the stream first, paddles across barking complaints at the swiftness of the current, the pneumonia-making coldness of it. We follow, holding our shoes and equipment (a hatchet, a burlap sack) above our heads. A mile more: of chastising thorns, burs and briers that catch at our clothes; of rusty pine needles brilliant with gaudy fungus and molted feathers. Here, there, a flash, a flutter, an ecstasy of shrillings remind us that not all the birds have flown south. Always, the path unwinds through lemony sun pools and pitch-black vine tunnels. Another creek to cross: a disturbed armada[15] of speckled trout froths the water round us, and frogs the size of plates practice belly flops; beaver workmen are building a dam. On the farther shore, Queenie shakes herself and trembles. My friend shivers, too: not with cold but enthusiasm. One of her hat's ragged roses sheds a petal as she lifts her head and inhales the pine-heavy air. "We're almost there; can you smell it, Buddy?" she says, as though we were approaching an ocean.

And, indeed, it is a kind of ocean. Scented acres of holiday trees, prickly-leafed holly. Red berries shiny as Chinese bells: black crows swoop upon them screaming. Having stuffed our burlap sacks with enough greenery and crimson to garland a dozen windows, we set about choosing a tree. "It should be," muses my friend, "twice as tall as a boy. So a boy can't steal the star." The one we pick is twice as tall as me. A brave handsome brute that survives thirty hatchet strokes before it keels with a creaking rending cry. Lugging it like a kill, we commence the long trek out. Every few yards we abandon the struggle, sit down

---

14. rime (rīm) *n.*: Frost.

15. armada (är mä′ də) *n.*: A fleet of warships.

and pant. But we have the strength of triumphant huntsmen; that and the tree's virile, icy perfume revive us, goad us on. Many compliments accompany our sunset return along the red clay road to town; but my friend is sly and noncommittal when passers-by praise the treasure perched in our buggy: what a fine tree and where did it come from? "Yonderways," she murmurs vaguely. Once a car stops and the rich mill owner's lazy wife leans out and whines: "Giveya two-bits cash for that ol tree." Ordinarily my friend is afraid of saying no; but on this occasion she promptly shakes her head: "We wouldn't take a dollar." The mill owner's wife persists. "A dollar, my foot! Fifty cents. That's my last offer. Goodness, woman, you can get another one." In answer, my friend gently reflects: "I doubt it. There's never two of anything."

Home: Queenie slumps by the fire and sleeps till tomorrow, snoring loud as a human.

A trunk in the attic contains: a shoebox of ermine[16] tails (off the opera cape of a curious lady who once rented a room in the house), coils of frazzled tinsel gone gold with age, one silver star, a brief rope of dilapidated, undoubtedly dangerous candy-like light bulbs. Excellent decorations, as far as they go, which isn't far enough: my friend wants our tree to blaze "like a Baptist window," droop with weighty snows of ornament. But we can't afford the made-in-Japan splendors at the five-and-dime. So we do what we've always done: sit for days at the kitchen table with scissors and crayons and stacks of colored paper. I make sketches and my friend cuts them out: lots of cats, fish too (because they're easy to draw), some apples, some watermelons, a few winged angels devised from saved-up sheets of candy-bar tin foil. We use safety pins to attach these creations to the tree; as a final touch, we sprinkle the branches with shredded cotton (picked in August for this purpose). My friend, surveying the effect, clasps her hands together. "Now honest, Buddy. Doesn't it look good enough to eat?" Queenie tries to eat an angel.

After weaving and ribboning holly wreaths for all the front windows, our next project is the fashioning of family gifts. Tie-dye scarves for the ladies, for the men a home-brewed lemon and licorice and aspirin syrup to be taken "at the first Symptoms of a Cold and after Hunting." But when it comes time for making each other's gift, my friend and I separate to work secretly. I would like to buy her a pearl-handled knife, a radio, a whole pound of chocolate-covered cherries (we tasted some once, and she always swears: "I could live on them, Buddy, Lord yes I could—and that's not taking His name in vain"). Instead, I am building her a kite. She would like to give me a bicycle (she's said so on several million occasions: "If only I could, Buddy. It's bad enough in life to do without something *you* want; but confound it, what gets my goat is not being able to give somebody something you want *them* to have. Only one of these days I will, Buddy. Locate you a bike. Don't ask how. Steal it, maybe"). Instead, I'm fairly certain that she is building me a kite—the same as last year, and the year before: the year before that we exchanged slingshots. All of which is fine by me. For we are champion kite-fliers who study the wind like sailors; my friend, more accomplished than I, can get a kite aloft when there isn't enough breeze to carry clouds.

Christmas Eve afternoon we scrape together a nickel and go to the butcher's to buy Queenie's traditional gift, a good gnawa-

---

16. ermine (ʉr′ mən) *adj.*: Of the soft white fur with black tips of a weasel.

ble beef bone. The bone, wrapped in funny paper, is placed high in the tree near the silver star. Queenie knows it's there. She squats at the foot of the tree staring up in a trance of greed: when bedtime arrives she refuses to budge. Her excitement is equaled by my own. I kick the covers and turn my pillow as though it were a scorching summer's night. Somewhere a rooster crows: falsely, for the sun is still on the other side of the world.

"Buddy, are you awake?" It is my friend, calling from her room, which is next to mine; and an instant later she is sitting on my bed holding a candle. "Well, I can't sleep a hoot," she declares. "My mind's jumping like a jack rabbit. Buddy, do you think Mrs. Roosevelt will serve our cake at dinner?" We huddle in the bed, and she squeezes my hand I-love-you. "Seems like your hand used to be so much smaller. I guess I hate to see you grow up. When you're grown up, will we still be friends?" I say always. "But I feel so bad, Buddy. I wanted so bad to give you a bike. I tried to sell my cameo[17] Papa gave me. Buddy"—she hesitates, as though embarrassed—"I made you another kite." Then I confess that I made her one, too; and we laugh. The candle burns too short to

---

17. cameo (kam′ ē ō′) *n.*: A shell or stone carved with a head in profile and used as jewelry.

hold. Out it goes, exposing the starlight, the stars spinning at the window like a visible caroling that slowly, slowly daybreak silences. Possibly we doze; but the beginnings of dawn splash us like cold water: we're up, wide-eyed and wandering while we wait for others to waken. Quite deliberately my friend drops a kettle on the kitchen floor. I tap-dance in front of closed doors. One by one the household emerges, looking as though they'd like to kill us both; but it's Christmas, so they can't. First, a gorgeous breakfast: just everything you can imagine —from flapjacks and fried squirrel to hominy grits and honey-in-the-comb. Which puts everyone in a good humor except my friend and me. Frankly, we're so impatient to get at the presents we can't eat a mouthful.

Well, I'm disappointed. Who wouldn't be? With socks, a Sunday school shirt, some handkerchiefs, a hand-me-down sweater and a year's subscription to a religious magazine for children. *The Little Shepherd.* It makes me boil. It really does.

My friend has a better haul. A sack of Satsumas,[18] that's her best present. She is proudest, however, of a white wool shawl knitted by her married sister. But she *says* her favorite gift is the kite I built her. And it *is* very beautiful; though not as beautiful as the one she made me, which is blue and scattered with gold and green Good Conduct stars; moreover, my name is painted on it, "Buddy."

"Buddy, the wind is blowing."

The wind is blowing, and nothing will do till we've run to a pasture below the house where Queenie has scooted to bury her bone (and where, a winter hence, Queenie will be buried, too). There, plunging through the healthy waist-high grass, we unreel our kites, feel them twitching at the string like sky fish as they swim into the wind. Satisfied, sun-warmed, we sprawl in the grass and peel Satsumas and watch our kites cavort. Soon I forget the socks and hand-me-down sweater. I'm as happy as if we'd already won the fifty-thousand-dollar Grand Prize in that coffee-naming contest.

"My, how foolish I am!" my friend cries, suddenly alert, like a woman remembering too late she has biscuits in the oven. "You know what I've always thought?" she asks in a tone of discovery, and not smiling at me but a point beyond. "I've always thought a body would have to be sick and dying before they saw the Lord. And I imagined that when He came it would be like looking at the Baptist window: pretty as colored glass with the sun pouring through, such a shine you don't know it's getting dark. And it's been a comfort: to think of that shine taking away all the spooky feeling. But I'll wager it never happens. I'll wager at the very end a body realizes the Lord has already shown Himself. That things as they are"—her hand circles in a gesture that gathers clouds and kites and grass and Queenie pawing earth over her bone—"just what they've always seen, was seeing Him. As for me, I could leave the world with today in my eyes."

This is our last Christmas together.

Life separates us. Those who Know Best decide that I belong in a military school. And so follows a miserable succession of bugle-blowing prisons, grim reveille-ridden summer camps. I have a new home too. But it doesn't count. Home is where my friend is, and there I never go.

And there she remains, puttering around the kitchen. Alone with Queenie. Then alone. ("Buddy dear," she writes in her wild hard-to-read script, "yesterday Jim Macy's horse kicked Queenie bad. Be thank-

---

18. **Satsumas** (sat′ soo məs) *n*.: Small, loose-skinned oranges.

ful she didn't feel much. I wrapped her in a Fine Linen sheet and rode her in the buggy down to Simpson's pasture where she can be with all her Bones . . .".) For a few Novembers she continues to bake her fruitcakes single-handed; not as many, but some: and, of course, she always sends me "the best of the batch." Also, in every letter she encloses a dime wadded in toilet paper: "See a picture show and write me the story." But gradually in her letters she tends to confuse me with her other friend, the Buddy who died in the 1880's; more and more thirteenths are not the only days she

stays in bed: a morning arrives in November, a leafless birdless coming of winter morning, when she cannot rouse herself to exclaim: "Oh my, it's fruitcake weather!"

And when that happens, I know it. A message saying so merely confirms a piece of news some secret vein had already received, severing from me an irreplaceable part of myself, letting it loose like a kite on a broken string. That is why, walking across a school campus on this particular December morning, I keep searching the sky. As if I expected to see, rather like hearts, a lost pair of kites hurrying toward heaven.

RESPONDING TO THE SELECTION

Your Response

1. What does the following quotation from the story mean to you? "It's bad enough in life to do without something *you* want; but confound it, what gets my goat is not being able to give somebody something you want *them* to have."

Recalling

2. Briefly describe Capote's cousin.
3. What are some of the ways that the two earn money?
4. What three tasks, in preparation for Christmas, do Capote and his cousin accomplish?
5. What gifts do Capote and his cousin exchange?

Interpreting

6. How does Capote feel about the other members of the household?
7. Why do Capote and his cousin send the fruitcakes to people they hardly know?
8. What are Capote's feelings about leaving and being apart from his cousin?
9. Reread the final paragraph. What does Capote mean by "a lost pair of kites hurrying toward heaven"?

Applying

10. What is the true meaning of gift giving?

ANALYZING LITERATURE

Understanding Reminiscence

A **reminiscence** is an autobiographical account of an experience in the writer's life. The most important aspect of a reminiscence is the special quality of memory that can impart a hazy, dreamlike character to remembered events.

1. Why does Capote use the present tense to describe events twenty years old?
2. Explain how "A Christmas Memory" is a reminiscence.

CRITICAL THINKING AND READING

Recognizing Emotive Language

Emotive language consists of words and phrases that trigger a specific emotional response in the reader. Writers often spend a great deal of time searching for the word or phrase that conveys a meaning or feeling exactly. This was especially true of Truman Capote, who claimed that he sometimes worked for days on a single sentence. Think of the feelings Capote evokes at the beginning of the story. The following are some of the words and phrases he uses: *sprightly; purposeful excitement; exhilarates her imagination; fuels the blaze of her heart.* This language evokes warm, happy feelings.

1. What emotion do you feel as the two approach the house of Haha Jones (page 446)? What words and phrases evoke this emotion?
2. What emotion do you feel at the end of the story? What words evoke this emotion?

THINKING AND WRITING

Comparing and Contrasting Memories

Write an essay comparing and contrasting "A Child's Christmas in Wales" and "A Christmas Memory." Consider the subject, setting, tone, and special meaning that each author conveys. As you write a draft, include specific examples from each story. Finally, revise your essay.

LEARNING OPTION

Art. Create a collage about a memory important to you. You might include photographs of your own or pictures you find in magazines that suggest the scene in your memory. Use as many different forms of expression as you can. For example, use words as well as pictures. In your collage try to communicate the special quality or meaning of the memory.

Types of Essays

A YOUNG GIRL READING, 1776
Jean-Honoré Fragonard
National Gallery of Art, Washington

GUIDE FOR READING

Rudolfo A. Anaya

(1937–   ) was born in Pastura, New Mexico. His poems, short stories, novels, and articles reflect his Mexican American heritage. He grew up hearing *cuentos* (stories) that were passed down by storytellers for generations. He explains, "The oral tradition of telling stories was part of my culture. . . . For those of us who listen to the Earth, and to the old legends and the myths of the people, the whispers of the blood draw us to our past."

His first novel, *Bless Me Ultima* (1972), won national acclaim for its moving depiction of the culture and history of New Mexico. Anaya lives in New Mexico and teaches creative writing and literature at the University of New Mexico in Albuquerque.

from In Commemoration: *One Million Volumes*

Expository Essay

An expository essay explains, defines, or interprets an idea, an event, or a process. The event that sparked Anaya's essay was the University of New Mexico's acquisition of the millionth volume for its library. Anaya's essay, originally delivered as a speech, explores the meaning of this event. It is a "commemoration," or celebration, that honors not just the University of New Mexico library, but libraries, books, and reading in general.

Focus

Imagine that your local library acquired its millionth volume. How would you promote the event to make people in your community appreciate its importance? What would a library with a million volumes have to offer to your community? Brainstorm with two or three classmates to list the benefits that a million-volume library would bring. Then sketch out plans for fliers, posters, and commercials to publicize your library's new status. Keep your discussion in mind as you read the essay.

Vocabulary

Knowing the following words will help you as you read this excerpt from "In Commemoration: *One Million Volumes.*"

induced (in dōōst′) *v.*: Caused (p. 457)

inherent (in hir′ ənt) *adj.*: Existing naturally and inseparably (p. 457)

litany (lit′ 'n ē) *n.*: Series of responsive religious readings (p. 458)

dilapidated (di lap′ ə dāt′ id) *adj.*: Broken down (p. 459)

satiated (sā′ s·hē āt′ id) *adj.*: Having had enough (p. 459)

enthralls (en t·hrôlz′) *v.*: Captivates; fascinates (p. 462)

labyrinth (lab′ ə rint·h) *n.*: Maze (p. 462)

poignant (poin′ yənt) *adj.*: Emotionally moving (p. 462)

fomentation (fō men tā′ s·hən) *n.*: Incitement; a stirring up (p. 462)

from In Commemoration: *One Million Volumes*

Rudolfo A. Anaya

A million volumes.

A magic number.

A million books to read, to look at, to hold in one's hand, to learn, to dream. . . .

I have always known there were at least a million stars. In the summer evenings when I was a child, we, all the children of the neighborhood, sat outside under the stars and listened to the stories of the old ones, los viejitos.[1] The stories of the old people taught us to wonder and imagine. Their adivinanzas[2] induced the stirring of our first questioning, our early learning.

I remember my grandfather raising his hand and pointing to the swirl of the Milky Way which swept over us. Then he would whisper his favorite riddle:

Hay un hombre con tanto dinero
Que no lo puede contar
Una mujer con una sábana tan
   grande
Que no la puede doblar.

There is a man with so much
   money
He cannot count it
A woman with a bedspread so
   large
She cannot fold it

We knew the million stars were the coins of the Lord, and the heavens were the bedspread of his mother, and in our minds the sky was a million miles wide. A hundred million. Infinite. Stuff for the imagination. And what was more important, the teachings of the old ones made us see that we were bound to the infinity of that cosmic dance of life which swept around us. Their teachings created in us a thirst for knowledge. Can this library with its million volumes bestow that same inspiration?

I was fortunate to have had those old and wise viejitos as guides into the world of nature and knowledge. They taught me with their stories; they taught me the magic of words. Now the words lie captured in ink, but the magic is still there, the power inherent in each volume. Now with book in hand we can participate in the wisdom of mankind.

---

1. **los viejitos** (lōs′ byä hē′ tōs)
2. **adivinanzas** (ä *the* vē nän′ säs) *n.*: Riddles.

ORION, 1984
Martin Wong
Exit Art Gallery, New York

Each person moves from innocence through rites of passage into the knowledge of the world, and so I entered the world of school in search of the magic in the words. The sounds were no longer the soft sounds of Spanish which my grandfather spoke; the words were in English, and with each new awareness came my first steps toward a million volumes. I, who was used to reading my oraciones en español[3] while I sat in the kitchen and answered the litany to the slap of my mother's tortillas,[4] I now stumbled from sound to word to groups of words, head throbbing, painfully aware that each new sound took me deeper into the maze of the new language. Oh, how I clutched the hands of my new guides then!

Learn, my mother encouraged me, learn. Be as wise as your grandfather. He could speak many languages. He could speak to the birds and the animals of the field.

Yes, I remember the cuentos[5] of my grandfather, the stories of the people. Words are a way, he said, they hold joy, and they

---

3. oraciones en español (ō̄ rä syō̄n′ es en es pa nyól): Prayers in Spanish.
4. tortillas (tō̄r tē′ yəs) *n.*: Thin, flat, round cakes of unleavened cornmeal.

5. cuentos (kwen′ tō̄s) *n.*: Stories.

are a deadly power if misused. I clung to each syllable which lisped from his tobacco-stained lips. That was the winter the snow came, he would say, it piled high and we lost many sheep and cattle, and the trees groaned and broke with its weight. I looked across the llano[6] and saw the raging blizzard, the awful destruction of that winter which was imbedded in our people's mind.

And the following summer, he would say, the grass of the llano grew so high we couldn't see the top of the sheep. And I would look and see what was once clean and pure and green. I could see a million sheep and the pastores[7] caring for them, as I now care for the million words that pasture in my mind.

But a million books? How can we see a million books? I don't mean just the books lining the shelves here at the University of New Mexico Library, not just the fine worn covers, the intriguing titles; how can we see the worlds that lie waiting in each book? A million worlds. A million million worlds. And the beauty of it is that each world is related to the next, as was taught to us by the old ones. Perhaps it is easier for a child to see. Perhaps it is easier for a child to ask: How many stars are there in the sky? How many leaves in the trees of the river? How many blades of grass in the llano? How many dreams in a night of dreams?

So I worked my way into the world of books, but here is the paradox, a book at once quenches the thirst of the imagination and ignites new fires. I learned that as I visited the library of my childhood, the Santa Rosa Library. It was only a dusty room in those days, a room sitting atop the town's fire department, which was comprised of one dilapidated fire truck used by the town's volunteers only in the direst emergencies. But in that small room I found my shelter and retreat. If there were a hundred books there we were fortunate, but to me there were a million volumes. I trembled in awe when I first entered that library, because I realized that if the books held as much magic as the words of the old ones, then indeed this was a room full of power.

Miss Pansy, the librarian, became my new guide. She fed me books as any mother would nurture her child. She brought me book after book, and I consumed them all. Saturday afternoons disappeared as the time of day dissolved into the time of distant worlds. In a world that occupied most of my other schoolmates with games, I took the time to read. I was a librarian's dream. My tattered library card was my ticket into the same worlds my grandfather had known, worlds of magic that fed the imagination.

Late in the afternoon, when I was satiated with reading, when I could no longer hold in my soul the characters that crowded there, I heard the call of the llano, the real world of my father's ranchito, the solid, warm world of my mother's kitchen. Then to the surprise and bewilderment of Miss Pansy, I would rush out and race down the streets of our town, books tucked under my shirt, in my pockets, clutched tightly to my breast. Mad with the insanity of books, I would cross the river to get home, shouting my crazy challenge even at la Llorona,[8] and that poor spirit of so many frightening cuentos would wither and withdraw. She was no match for me.

Those of you who have felt the same exhilaration from reading—or from love—

---

6. **llano** (yä′ nō̄) n.: Plain.
7. **pastores** (päs tō̄′ res) n.: Shepherds.

8. **la Llorona** (lä yō̄ rō̄′ nä): Spirit of many stories, famous for shouting and crying for her lost love.

will know about what I'm speaking. Alas, the people of the town could only shake their heads and pity my mother. At least one of her sons was a bit touched. Perhaps they were right, for few will trade a snug reality to float on words to other worlds.

And now there are a million volumes for us to read here at the University of New Mexico Library. Books on every imaginable subject, in every field, a history of the thought of the world which we must keep free of censorship, because we treasure our freedoms. It is the word *freedom* which eventually must reflect what this collection, or the collection of any library, is all about. We know that as we preserve and use the literature of all cultures, we preserve and regenerate our own. The old ones knew and taught me this. They eagerly read the few newspapers that were available. They kept their diaries, they wrote décimas[9] and cuentos, and they survived on their oral stories and traditions.

Another time, another library. I entered Albuquerque[10] High School Library prepared to study, because that's where we spent our study time. For better or for worse, I received my first contracts as a writer there. It was a place where budding lovers spent most of their time writing notes to each other, and when my friends who didn't have the gift of words found out I could turn a phrase I quickly had all the business I could do. I wrote poetic love notes for a dime apiece and thus worked my way through high school. And there were fringe benefits, because the young women knew very well who was writing the sweet words, and many a heart I was supposed to capture fell in love

---

9. décimas (dā′ sē mäs) *n.*: Ten-line stanzas.
10. Albuquerque (al′ bə kur′ kē): Capital of New Mexico.

LA BIBLIOTHÈQUE, (THE LIBRARY) 1949
Maria Elena Vieira da Silva
Musée National d'Art Moderne, Centre National d'Art et de Culture Georges Pompidou

from *In Commemoration:* One Million Volumes   461

with me. And so, a library is also a place where love begins.

A library should be the heart of a city. With its storehouse of knowledge, it liberates, informs, teaches, and enthralls. A library indeed should be the cultural center of any city. Amidst the bustle of work and commerce, the great libraries of the world have provided a sanctuary where scholars and common man alike come to enlarge and clarify knowledge, to read and reflect in quiet solitude.

I knew a place like this, I spent many hours in the old library on Central Avenue and Edith Street. But my world was growing, and quite by accident I wandered up the hill to enroll in the University of New Mexico. And what a surprise lay in store for me. The libraries of my childhood paled in comparison to this new wealth of books housed in Zimmerman Library. Here there were stack after stack of books, and ample space and time to wander aimlessly in this labyrinth of new frontiers.

I had known the communal memory of my people through the newspapers and few books my grandfather read to me and through the rich oral tradition handed down by the old ones; now I discovered the collective memory of all mankind at my fingertips. I had only to reach for the books that laid all history bare. Here I could converse with the writers from every culture on earth, old and new, and at the same time I began my personal odyssey, which would add a few books to the collection which in 1981 would come to house a million volumes.

Those were exciting times. Around me swirled the busy world of the university, in many respects an alien world. Like many fellow undergraduates, I sought refuge in the library. My haven during those student university years was the reading room of the west wing of the old library. There I found peace. The carved vigas[11] decorating the ceiling, the solid wooden tables and chairs and the warm adobe color of the stucco were things with which I was familiar. There I felt comfortable. With books scattered around me, I could read and doze and dream. I took my breaks in the warm sun of the portal, where I ate my tortilla sandwiches, which I carried in my brown paper bag. There, with friends, I sipped coffee as we talked of changing the world and exchanged idealistic dreams.

That is a rich and pleasant time in my memory. No matter how far across the world I find myself in the future, how deep in the creation of worlds with words, I shall keep the simple and poignant memories of those days. The sun set golden on the ocher walls, and the green pine trees and the blue spruce, sacred trees to our people, whispered in the breeze. I remembered my grandfather meeting with the old men of the village in the resolana[12] of one of the men's homes, or against the wall of the church on Sundays, and I remembered the things they said. Later, alone, dreaming against the sun-warmed wall of the library, I continued that discourse in my mind.

Yes, the library is a place where people should gather. It is a place for research, reading, and for the quiet fomentation of ideas, but because it houses the collective memory of our race, it should also be a place where present issues are discussed and debated and researched in order for us to gain the knowledge and insight to create a better future. The library should be a warm place that reflects the needs and aspirations of the people.

---

11. vigas (bē gäs) *n.*: Roof beams.
12. resolana (rä sō lä′ nä) *n.*: A place for enjoying the sun.

RESPONDING TO THE SELECTION

Your Response

1. Anaya appeals to people who have "felt the same exhilaration from reading" as he has felt. What reading has exhilarated you? Why?
2. Describe the place in which you most like to read. Explain why you find this place the most comfortable for reading.

Recalling

3. Name three things that Anaya compares to "a million volumes."
4. How and when did Anaya come to love words and reading?

Interreting

5. Interpret Anaya's comment, "that a book at once quenches the thirst of the imagination and ignites new fires" (p. 459).
6. Anaya repeatedly refers to the "magic" held in words and in books. How does he convey the magic of reading throughout his essay?
7. Why does Anaya associate libraries with freedom?
8. In what ways do books and reading help preserve a culture?

Applying

9. Anaya says that a library should "reflect the needs and aspirations of the people." What specific needs and aspirations do you think your library should reflect?

ANALYZING LITERATURE

Analyzing an Expository Essay

An **expository essay** can explain a process, or an event, analyze information, or compare and contrast ideas. Anaya pays tribute to Zimmerman Library in his expository essay by explaining the importance of books and reading. He also explains the different ways in which libraries can function. Throughout the essay, he draws from his personal experiences with libraries.

1. Anaya claims that reading engages people in a rite of passage from innocence to knowledge. How does he explain this process?
2. List three personal facts that Anaya shares in his essay. How does each fact you listed illustrate his beliefs about the importance of books, reading, and libraries?

CRITICAL THINKING AND READING

Appreciating Purpose

An expository essay is written for a purpose. Anaya wrote "In Commemoration: *One Million Volumes*" in response to a specific event—Zimmerman Library's one-millionth volume. In his essay Anaya celebrates this event. At the same time, he places the event in a larger context. Ultimately, he honors much more than the library's millionth volume. How does Anaya broaden his purpose to celebrate a universal idea?

THINKING AND WRITING

Writing a Tribute

Think of a local institution or building in your community that you would like to commemorate. Consider something that has personal significance, such as a park where you played as a child, a school building, or a library. Write an essay in which you explain why the place you chose deserves special recognition.

LEARNING OPTION

Community Connections. In what ways does your local library function as a cultural center? Is there a bulletin board for posting community events? Are there meeting rooms for presentations, classes, or club meetings? Are there typewriters or computers for public use? Present your findings in a brief article for your local newspaper. If your library doesn't offer many community resources, propose some for the library to consider. Draw from Anaya's essay for ideas.

Navarre Scott Momaday

(1934–   ), a Kiowa Indian, spent his youth on several Indian reservations where his parents taught. This contributed to his interest in Native American culture and history. Momaday earned a doctoral degree from Stanford University, where he now teaches English. His first novel, *House Made of Dawn,* was awarded a Pulitzer Prize. *The Way to Rainy Mountain* includes his impressions of contemporary Kiowa culture and world view, as well as their history and legends.

from The Way to Rainy Mountain

Imagery in a Narrative Essay

Imagery is the use of words and phrases to create pictures or images in the reader's mind. The most common image is visual, but writers also use images appealing to the senses of sound, taste, touch, and smell. The subject in a narrative essay is often an experience from the author's memory. Because memories include a great deal of information recorded through the senses, writers often rely on the use of imagery to convey their experiences graphically and accurately.

Focus

Myths are stories that were once widely accepted as truth and which serve to explain natural occurrences. In *The Way to Rainy Mountain*, Momaday writes about the myths his grandmother taught him concerning the creation of the world and the evolution of his Native American culture. Rainy Mountain is a landmark to him and his people. Think of a landmark in your area or in a place that is important to you. Draw an annotated map of this place. In your annotations show how the place is important to you or your culture. Highlight interesting areas of the place by using appropriate symbols. For example, if specific wildlife populate the area, you might want to include figures of the birds or animals. Share your map with classmates before reading from Momaday's essay.

Vocabulary

Knowing the following words will help you as you read this excerpt from *The Way to Rainy Mountain*.

writhe (rīth) *v.*: To twist in pain and agony (p. 465)

infirm (in furm') *adj.*: Weak; feeble (p. 465)

disposition (dis pə zish' ən) *n.*: Inclination; tendency; choice (p. 465)

pillage (pil' ij) *n.*: The act of robbing and destroying, especially during wartime (p. 465)

engender (in jen' dər) *v.*: To bring about; cause; produce (p. 467)

tenuous (ten' yoo wəs) *adj.*: Slight; flimsy; not substantial or strong (p. 468)

wariness (wer' ē nis) *n.*: Caution (p. 468)

opaque (ō pāk') *adj.*: Not letting light pass through (p. 469)

from The Way to Rainy Mountain

N. Scott Momaday

A single knoll rises out of the plain in Oklahoma, north and west of the Wichita Range.[1] For my people, the Kiowas, it is an old landmark, and they gave it the name Rainy Mountain. The hardest weather in the world is there. Winter brings blizzards, hot tornadic winds arise in the spring, and in summer the prairie is an anvil's edge.[2] The grass turns brittle and brown, and it cracks beneath your feet. There are green belts along the rivers and creeks, linear groves of hickory and pecan, willow and witch hazel. At a distance in July or August the steaming foliage seems almost to writhe in fire. Great green and yellow grasshoppers are everywhere in the tall grass, popping up like corn to sting the flesh, and tortoises crawl about on the red earth, going nowhere in the plenty of time. Loneliness is an aspect of the land. All things in the plain are isolate; there is no confusion of objects in the eye, but *one* hill or *one* tree or *one* man. To look upon that landscape in the early morning, with the sun at your back, is to lose the sense of proportion. Your imagination comes to life, and this, you think, is where Creation was begun.

I returned to Rainy Mountain in July. My grandmother had died in the spring, and I wanted to be at her grave. She had lived to be very old and at last infirm. Her only living daughter was with her when she died, and I was told that in death her face was that of a child.

I like to think of her as a child. When she was born, the Kiowas were living the last great moment of their history. For more than a hundred years they had controlled the open range from the Smoky Hill River to the Red, from the headwaters of the Canadian to the fork of the Arkansas and Cimarron. In alliance with the Comanches, they had ruled the whole of the southern Plains. War was their sacred business, and they were among the finest horsemen the world has ever known. But warfare for the Kiowas was preeminently a matter of disposition rather than of survival, and they never understood the grim, unrelenting advance of the U.S. Cavalry. When at last, divided and ill-provisioned, they were driven onto the Staked Plains in the cold rains of autumn, they fell into panic. In Palo Duro Canyon they abandoned their crucial stores to pillage and had nothing then but their lives. In order to save themselves, they surrendered to the soldiers at Fort Sill and were imprisoned in the old stone corral that now stands as a military museum. My grandmother was spared the humiliation of those high gray walls by eight or ten years, but she must have known from birth the affliction of defeat, the dark brooding of old warriors.

Her name was Aho, and she belonged to the last culture to evolve in North America.

---

1. Wichita (wich ə tô′) **Range:** A mountain range in southwestern Oklahoma.
2. anvil's edge: The edge of the iron or steel block on which metal objects are hammered into shape.

Her forebears came down from the high country in western Montana nearly three centuries ago. They were a mountain people, a mysterious tribe of hunters whose language has never been positively classified in any major group. In the late seventeenth century they began a long migration to the south and east. It was a journey toward the dawn, and it led to a golden age. Along the way the Kiowas were befriended by the Crows, who gave them the culture and religion of the Plains. They acquired horses, and their ancient nomadic spirit was suddenly free of the ground. They acquired Tai-me, the sacred Sun Dance doll, from that moment the object and symbol of their worship, and so shared in the divinity of the sun. Not least, they acquired the sense of destiny, therefore courage and pride. When they entered upon the southern Plains they had been transformed. No longer were they slaves to the simple necessity of survival; they were a lordly and dangerous society of fighters and thieves, hunters and priests of the sun. According to their origin myth, they entered the world through a hollow log. From one point of view, their migration was the fruit of an old prophecy, for indeed they emerged from a sunless world.

Although my grandmother lived out her long life in the shadow of Rainy Mountain, the immense landscape of the continental interior lay like memory in her blood. She could tell of the Crows, whom she had never seen, and of the Black Hills, where she had never been. I wanted to see in reality what she had seen more perfectly in the mind's eye, and traveled fifteen hundred miles to begin my pilgrimage.

Yellowstone,[3] it seemed to me, was the top of the world, a region of deep lakes and dark timber, canyons and waterfalls. But, beautiful as it is, one might have the sense of confinement there. The skyline in all directions is close at hand, the high wall of the woods and deep cleavages of shade. There is a perfect freedom in the mountains, but it belongs to the eagle and the elk, the badger and the bear. The Kiowas reckoned their stature by the distance they could see, and they were bent and blind in the wilderness.

Descending eastward, the highland meadows are a stairway to the plain. In July the inland slope of the Rockies is luxuriant with flax and buckwheat, stonecrop and larkspur. The earth unfolds and the limit of the land recedes. Clusters of trees, and animals grazing far in the distance, cause the vision to reach away and wonder to build upon the mind. The sun follows a longer course in the day, and the sky is immense beyond all comparison. The great billowing clouds that sail upon it are shadows that move upon the brain like water, dividing light. Farther down, in the land of the Crows and Blackfeet, the plain is yellow. Sweet clover takes hold of the hills and bends upon itself to cover and seal the soil. There the Kiowas paused on their way; they had come to the place where they must change their lives. The sun is at home on the plains. Precisely there does it have the certain character of a god. When the Kiowas came to the land of the Crows, they could see the dark lees of the hills at dawn across the Bighorn River, the profusion of light on the grain shelves, the oldest deity ranging after the solstices. Not yet would they veer southward to the caldron[4] of the land that lay below; they must wean their blood from the northern winter and hold the mountains a while longer in their view. They bore Tai-me in procession to the east.

---

3. Yellowstone: Yellowstone National Park, mostly in northwestern Wyoming but including narrow strips in southern Montana and eastern Idaho.

4. caldron (kôl′ drən) *n*.: Heat like that of a boiling kettle.

This map shows the area through which Momaday traveled as he retraced the route followed by the Kiowas nearly three centuries ago. The route stretched from the high country of what is today western Montana to the southern plains of what is now Kansas and Oklahoma.

A dark mist lay over the Black Hills, and the land was like iron. At the top of a ridge I caught sight of Devil's Tower upthrust against the gray sky as if in the birth of time the core of the earth had broken through its crust and the motion of the world was begun. There are things in nature that engender an awful quiet in the heart of man; Devil's Tower is one of them. Two centuries ago, because they could not do otherwise, the Kiowas made a legend at the base of the rock. My grandmother said:

Eight children were there at play, seven sisters and their brother.
Suddenly the boy was struck dumb; he trembled and began to run
upon his hands and feet. His fingers became claws, and his body
was covered with fur. Directly there was a bear where the boy had
been. The sisters were terrified; they ran, and the bear after them.
They came to the stump of a great tree, and the tree spoke to
them. It bade them climb upon it, and as they did so it began to
rise into the air. The bear came to kill them, but they were just
beyond its reach. It reared against the tree and scored the bark

all around with its claws. The seven sisters were borne into the
sky, and they became the stars of the Big Dipper.

ANNIE OLD CROW
James Bama
Courtesy of the artist

From that moment, and so long as the legend lives, the Kiowas have kinsmen in the night sky. Whatever they were in the mountains, they could be no more. However tenuous their well-being, however much they had suffered and would suffer again, they had found a way out of the wilderness.

My grandmother had a reverence for the sun, a holy regard that now is all but gone out of mankind. There was a wariness in her, and an ancient awe. She was a Christian in her later years, but she had come a long way about, and she never forgot her birthright. As a child she had been to the Sun Dances; she had taken part in those annual rites, and by them she had learned the restoration of her people in the presence of Tai-me. She was about seven when the last Kiowa Sun Dance was held in 1887 on the Washita River above Rainy Mountain Creek. The buffalo were gone. In order to consummate the ancient sacrifice—to impale the head of a buffalo bull upon the medicine tree—a delegation of old men journeyed into Texas, there to beg and barter for an animal from the Goodnight herd. She was ten when the Kiowas came together for the last time as a living Sun Dance culture. They could find no buffalo; they had to hang an old hide from the sacred tree. Before the dance could begin, a company of soldiers rode out from Fort Sill under orders to disperse the tribe. Forbidden without cause the essential act of their faith, having seen the wild herds slaughtered and left to rot upon the ground, the Kiowas backed away forever

from the medicine tree. That was July 20, 1890, at the great bend of the Washita. My grandmother was there. Without bitterness, and for as long as she lived, she bore a vision of deicide.[5]

Now that I can have her only in memory, I see my grandmother in the several postures that were peculiar to her: standing at the wood stove on a winter morning and turning meat in a great iron skillet; sitting at the south window, bent above her beadwork, and afterwards, when her vision failed, looking down for a long time into the fold of her hands; going out upon a cane, very slowly as she did when the weight of age came upon her; praying. I remember her most often at prayer. She made long, ram-

---

5. deicide (dē′ ə sīd′) *n.*: The killing of a god.

bling prayers out of suffering and hope, having seen many things. I was never sure that I had the right to hear, so exclusive were they of all mere custom and company. The last time I saw her she prayed standing by the side of her bed at night, naked to the waist, the light of a kerosene lamp moving upon her dark skin. Her long, black hair, always drawn and braided in the day, lay upon her shoulders and against her breasts like a shawl. I do not speak Kiowa, and I never understood her prayers, but there was something inherently sad in the sound, some merest hesitation upon the syllables of sorrow. She began in a high and descending pitch, exhausting her breath to silence; then again and again—and always the same intensity of effort, of something that is, and is not, like urgency in the human voice. Transported so in the dancing light among the shadows of her room, she seemed beyond the reach of time. But that was illusion; I think I knew then that I should not see her again.

Houses are like sentinels in the plain, old keepers of the weather watch. There, in a very little while, wood takes on the appearance of great age. All colors wear soon away in the wind and rain, and then the wood is burned gray and the grain appears and the nails turn red with rust. The windowpanes are black and opaque; you imagine there is nothing within, and indeed there are many ghosts, bones given up to the land. They stand here and there against the sky, and you approach them for a longer time than you expect. They belong in the distance; it is their domain.

Once there was a lot of sound in my grandmother's house, a lot of coming and going, feasting and talk. The summers there were full of excitement and reunion. The Kiowas are a summer people; they abide the cold and keep to themselves, but when the season turns and the land becomes warm and vital they cannot hold still; an old love of going returns upon them. The aged visitors who came to my grandmother's house when I was a child were made of lean and leather, and they bore themselves upright. They wore great black hats and bright ample shirts that shook in the wind. They rubbed fat upon their hair and wound their braids with strips of colored cloth. Some of them painted their faces and carried the scars of old and cherished enmities. They were an old council of warlords, come to remind and be reminded of who they were. Their wives and daughters served them well. The women might indulge themselves; gossip was at once the mark and compensation of their servitude. They made loud and elaborate talk among themselves, full of jest and gesture, fright and false alarm. They went abroad in fringed and flowered shawls, bright beadwork and German silver. They were at home in the kitchen, and they prepared meals that were banquets.

There were frequent prayer meetings, and great nocturnal feasts. When I was a child I played with my cousins outside, where the lamplight fell upon the ground and the singing of the old people rose up around us and carried away into the darkness. There were a lot of good things to eat, a lot of laughter and surprise. And afterwards, when the quiet returned, I lay down with my grandmother and could hear the frogs away by the river and feel the motion of the air.

Now there is a funeral silence in the rooms, the endless wake of some final word. The walls have closed in upon my grandmother's house. When I returned to it in mourning, I saw for the first time in my life how small it was. It was late at night, and there was a white moon, nearly full. I sat for a long time on the stone steps by the kitchen

OLD ONES TALKING
R. Brownell McGrew
Courtesy of the artist

door. From there I could see out across the land; I could see the long row of trees by the creek, the low light upon the rolling plains, and the stars of the Big Dipper. Once I looked at the moon and caught sight of a strange thing. A cricket had perched upon the handrail, only a few inches away from me. My line of vision was such that the creature filled the moon like a fossil. It had gone there, I thought, to live and die, for there, of all places, was its small definition made whole and eternal. A warm wind rose up and purled[6] like the longing within me.

The next morning I awoke at dawn and went out on the dirt road to Rainy Mountain. It was already hot, and the grasshoppers began to fill the air. Still, it was early in the morning, and the birds sang out of the shadows. The long yellow grass on the mountain shone in the bright light, and a scissortail[7] hied above the land. There, where it ought to be, at the end of a long and legendary way, was my grandmother's grave. Here and there on the dark stones were ancestral names. Looking back once, I saw the mountain and came away.

6. purled (purl'd) *v.*: Moved in ripples or with a murmuring sound; swirled.

7. scissortail (siz′ ər tāl′) *n.*: A pale gray and pink variety of flycatcher.

RESPONDING TO THE SELECTION

Your Response

1. Momaday's quest for the roots of his culture led to his new awareness and appreciation of it. Would such a quest interest you? Explain.
2. Referring to his grandmother's house, Momaday writes, "When I returned to it in mourning, I saw for the first time how small it was." Have you ever returned to a place and found it "smaller"? Explain.

Recalling

3. What did the Kiowas acquire that transformed their culture on their journey south?
4. What legend was inspired by Devil's Tower?
5. What happened when the Kiowas last came together as a living Sun Dance culture?
6. Describe the summer activities that Momaday remembers at his grandmother's house.

Interpreting

7. To what two people or things is Momaday paying respect on his visit to Rainy Mountain?
8. What aspects of her culture does Momaday believe his grandmother never lost?
9. What does seeing the Big Dipper and the image of the cricket at the end suggest about Momaday and the spirit of his people?

Applying

10. Frederick Douglass has written, "We have to do with the past only as we can make it useful to the present and the future." First discuss the meaning of this quotation. Do you agree with it? Do you think Momaday would agree with it? Explain your answers.

ANALYZING LITERATURE

Understanding Imagery in Essays

Imagery is the use of words and phrases to create pictures in the mind of the reader. Create a chart with a column for each of the five senses.

List details from the selection under each column. For example, under *Hearing,* you might list "cracks beneath your feet."

CRITICAL THINKING AND READING

Reading a Map

The Kiowa Indians traveled a great distance when they migrated from western Montana to the southern plains. Look at the map on page 467 and answer the following questions.

1. What direction did the Kiowas travel in their journey from the Yellowstone Park area to the Black Hills?
2. What was the distance of the journey from the Black Hills to the Wichita Mountain range?
3. Approximately how many square miles was the Kiowas' territory (page 465)?

THINKING AND WRITING

Writing About a Memorable Place

Imagine that you are writing an advertisement for a travel agent to convince people to visit a memorable place. Freewrite about impressions and thoughts you had when you visited this place; then write an essay about it. As you write, focus as much as possible on using images that will enable the reader to create a picture in his or her mind. Make sure that all of your descriptions are vivid and appeal to as many of the five senses as possible.

LEARNING OPTION

Art. In his essay Momaday makes a pilgrimage. He "wanted to see in reality what [his grandmother] had seen more perfectly in the mind's eye. . . ." As a result of his pilgrimage, he gained a greater sense of pride in his heritage. Discuss with your family what you know of your background, and draw a family tree to illustrate it. Then display your work for your class.

GUIDE FOR READING

Annie Dillard

(1945–   ) grew up in Tinker Creek, Virginia. "Flood" is set in Tinker Creek and presents, as much of her writing does, the natural world as its subject. The essay is an excerpt from Annie Dillard's Pulitzer Prize-winning first book, *Pilgrim at Tinker Creek,* and recalls the effects of Hurricane Agnes. This storm struck the eastern United States in 1972 and transformed the creek into a destructive force.

Flood

Descriptive Essay

A **descriptive essay,** through the use of imagery and other sensory language, creates a picture in the reader's mind. Dillard's essay is filled with sights, sounds, and smells intended to help you experience the flood as vividly as she did.

Focus

Throughout the seasons people must cope with harsh weather conditions. Whether you face extremely hot temperatures, drought, heavy snow or rain, or disastrous storms, the weather affects your way of life. Make a chart of weather conditions that you experience where you live. In the chart, list the effects each condition has on your region. Also list how the condition affects you individually. For example, if you live near a mountain, you might ski after a heavy snowfall. Keep your chart in mind as you read about how a flood affects people near Tinker Creek in Annie Dillard's essay "Flood."

Vocabulary

Knowing the following words will help you as you read "Flood."

obliterates (ə blit′ ə rāts) *v.:* Destroys; erases without a trace (p. 475)

opacity (ō pas′ ə tē) *n.:* The quality of not letting light pass through (p. 475)

usurped (yo͞o sʉrpt′) *v.:* Taken power over; held by force (p. 475)

mauled (môld) *adj.:* Roughly or clumsily handled (p. 476)

predator (pred′ ə tər) *n.:* An animal that eats other animals (p. 477)

malevolent (mə lev′ ə lənt) *adj.:* Intended as evil or harmful (p. 477)

repressed (ri prest′) *v.:* Held back; restrained (p. 477)

Flood

Annie Dillard

It's summer. We had some deep spring sunshine about a month ago, in a drought; the nights were cold. It's been gray sporadically, but not oppressively, and rainy for a week, and I would think: When is the real hot stuff coming, the mind-melting weeding weather? It was rainy again this morning, the same spring rain, and then this afternoon a different rain came: a pounding, three-minute shower. And when it was over, the cloud dissolved to haze. I can't see Tinker Mountain.[1] It's summer now: the heat is on. It's summer now all summer long.

The season changed two hours ago. Will my life change as well? This is a time for resolutions, revolutions. The animals are going wild. I must have seen ten rabbits in as many minutes. Baltimore orioles are here; brown thrashers seem to be nesting down by Tinker Creek across the road. The coot[2] is still around, big as a Thanksgiving turkey, and as careless; it doesn't even glance at a barking dog.

The creek's up. When the rain stopped today I walked across the road to the downed log by the steer crossing. The steers were across the creek, a black clot on a distant hill. High water had touched my log, the log I sit on, and dumped a smooth slope of muck in its lee. The water itself was an opaque pale green, like pulverized jade,[3] still high and very fast, lightless, like no earthly water. A dog I've never seen before, thin as death, was flushing rabbits.

A knot of yellow, fleshy somethings had grown up by the log. They didn't seem to have either proper stems or proper flowers, but instead only blind, featureless growth, like etiolated[4] potato sprouts in a root cellar. I tried to dig one up from the crumbly soil, but they all apparently grew from a single, well-rooted corm,[5] so I let them go.

Still, the day had an air of menace. A broken whiskey bottle by the log, the brown tip of a snake's tail disappearing between two rocks on the hill at my back, the rabbit the dog nearly caught, the rabies I knew was in the county, the bees who kept unaccountably fumbling at my forehead with their furred feet . . .

I headed over to the new woods by the creek, the motorbike woods. They were strangely empty. The air was so steamy I could barely see. The ravine separating the woods from the field had filled during high water, and a dead tan mud clogged it now. The horny orange roots of one tree on the ravine's jagged bank had been stripped of

1. **Tinker Mountain**: Mountain in Virginia.
2. **coot** (ko͞ot) *n.*: A ducklike, freshwater bird.

3. **pulverized jade** (pul′ və rīzd′ jād′): Crushed green stone.
4. **etiolated** (ēt′ ē ə lāt′ əd) *adj.*: Pale and stunted.
5. **corm** (kôrm) *n.*: An underground stem similar to a bulb.

soil; now the roots hung, an empty net in the air, clutching an incongruous light bulb stranded by receding waters. For the entire time that I walked in the woods, four jays flew around me very slowly, acting generally odd, and screaming on two held notes. There wasn't a breath of wind.

Coming out of the woods, I heard loud shots; they reverberated ominously in the damp air. But when I walked up the road, I saw what it was, and the dread quality of the whole afternoon vanished at once. It was a couple of garbage trucks, huge trash compacters humped like armadillos, and they were making their engines backfire to impress my neighbors' pretty daughters, high school girls who had just been let off the school bus. The long-haired girls strayed into giggling clumps at the corner of the road; the garbage trucks sped away glorious-

ly, as if they had been the Tarleton twins on thoroughbreds cantering away from the gates of Tara.[6] In the distance a white vapor was rising from the waters of Carvin's Cove and catching in trailing tufts in the mountains' sides. I stood on my own porch, exhilarated, unwilling to go indoors.

It was just this time last year that we had the flood. It was Hurricane Agnes, really, but by the time it got here, the weather bureau had demoted it to a tropical storm. I see by a clipping I saved that the date was June twenty-first, the solstice, midsummer's night, the longest daylight of the year; but I didn't notice it at the time. Everything was so exciting, and so very dark.

---

6. **Tarleton twins . . . of Tara:** Characters in the novel *Gone with the Wind.*

All it did was rain. It rained, and the creek started to rise. The creek, naturally, rises every time it rains; this didn't seem any different. But it kept raining, and, that morning of the twenty-first, the creek kept rising.

That morning I'm standing at my kitchen window. Tinker Creek is out of its four-foot banks, way out, and it's still coming. The high creek doesn't look like our creek. Our creek splashes transparently over a jumble of rocks; the high creek obliterates everything in flat opacity. It looks like somebody else's creek that has usurped or eaten our creek and is roving frantically to escape, big and ugly, like a blacksnake caught in a kitchen drawer. The color is foul, a rusty cream. Water that has picked up clay soils looks worse than other muddy waters, because the particles of clay are so fine; they spread out and cloud the water so that you can't see light through even an inch of it in a drinking glass.

Everything looks different. Where my eye is used to depth, I see the flat water, near, too near. I see trees I never noticed before, the black verticals of their rain-soaked trunks standing out of the pale water like pilings for a rotted dock. The stillness of grassy banks and stony ledges is gone; I see rushing, a wild sweep and hurry in one direction, as swift and compelling as a waterfall. The Atkins kids are out in their tiny rain gear, staring at the monster creek. It's risen up to their gates; the neighbors are gathering; I go out.

I hear a roar, a high windy sound more like air than like water, like the run-together whaps of a helicopter's propeller after the engine is off, a high million rushings. The air smells damp and acrid, like fuel oil, or insecticide. It's raining.

I'm in no danger; my house is high. I hurry down the road to the bridge. Neighbors who have barely seen each other all winter are there, shaking their heads. Few have ever seen it before: the water is *over* the bridge. Even when I see the bridge now, which I do every day, I still can't believe it: the water was *over* the bridge, a foot or two over the bridge, which at normal times is eleven feet above the surface of the creek.

Now the water is receding slightly; someone has produced empty metal drums, which we roll to the bridge and set up in a square to keep cars from trying to cross. It takes a bit of nerve even to stand on the bridge; the flood has ripped away a wedge of concrete that buttressed the bridge on the bank. Now one corner of the bridge hangs apparently unsupported while water hurls in an arch just inches below.

It's hard to take it all in, it's all so new. I look at the creek at my feet. It smashes under the bridge like a fist, but there is no end to its force; it hurtles down as far as I can see till it lurches round the bend, filling the valley, flattening, mashing, pushed, wider and faster, till it fills my brain.

It's like a dragon. Maybe it's because the bridge we are on is chancy, but I notice that no one can help imagining himself washed overboard, and gauging his chances for survival. You couldn't live. Mark Spitz[7] couldn't live. The water arches where the bridge's supports at the banks prevent its enormous volume from going wide, forcing it to go high; that arch drives down like a diving whale, and would butt you on the bottom. "You'd never know what hit you," one of the men says. But if you survived that part and managed to surface . . .? How fast can you live? You'd need a windshield. You couldn't keep your head up; the water under the surface is

---

7. **Mark Spitz:** Winner of seven gold medals in swimming in the 1972 Olympic Games.

fastest. You'd spin around like a sock in a clothes dryer. You couldn't grab onto a tree trunk without leaving that arm behind. No, you couldn't live. And if they ever found you, your gut would be solid red clay.

It's all I can do to stand. I feel dizzy, drawn, mauled. Below me the floodwater roils to a violent froth that looks like dirty lace, a lace that continuously explodes before my eyes. If I look away, the earth moves backwards, rises and swells, from the fixing of my eyes at one spot against the motion of the flood. All the familiar land looks as though it were not solid and real at all, but painted on a scroll like a backdrop, and that unrolled scroll has been shaken, so the earth sways and the air roars.

Everything imaginable is zipping by, almost too fast to see. If I stand on the bridge and look downstream, I get dizzy; but if I look upstream, I feel as though I am looking up the business end of an avalanche. There are dolls, split wood and kindling, dead fledgling songbirds, bottles, whole bushes and trees, rakes and garden gloves. Wooden, rough-hewn railroad ties charge by faster than any express. Lattice fencing bobs along, and a wooden picket gate. There are so many white plastic gallon milk jugs that when the flood ultimately recedes, they are left on the grassy banks looking from a distance like a flock of white geese.

I expect to see anything at all. In this one way, the creek is more like itself when it floods than at any other time: mediating, bringing things down. I wouldn't be at all surprised to see John Paul Jones coming round the bend, standing on the deck of the *Bon Homme Richard,*[8] or Amelia Earhart[9] waving gaily from the cockpit of her floating Lockheed. Why not a cello, a basket of breadfruit, a casket of antique coins? Here comes the Franklin expedition on snowshoes, and the three magi,[10] plus camels, afloat on a canopied barge!

The whole world is in flood, the land as well as the water. Water streams down the trunks of trees, drips from hat-brims, courses across roads. The whole earth seems to slide like sand down a chute; water pouring over the least slope leaves the grass flattened, silver side up, pointing downstream. Everywhere windfall and flotsam twigs and leafy boughs, wood from woodpiles, bottles, and saturated straw spatter the ground or streak it in curving windrows.[11] Tomatoes in flat gardens are literally floating in mud; they look as though they have been dropped whole into a boiling, brown-gravy stew. The level of the water table is at the top of the toe of my shoes. Pale muddy water lies on the flat so that it all but drowns the grass; it looks like a hideous parody[12] of a light snow on the field, with only the dark tips of the grass blades visible.

When I look across the street, I can't believe my eyes. Right behind the road's shoulder are waves, waves whipped in rhythmically peaking scallops, racing downstream. The hill where I watched the praying mantis lay her eggs is a waterfall that splashes into a brown ocean. I can't even remember where the creek usually runs—it is everywhere now. My log is gone for sure, I think—but in fact, I discover later, it holds, rammed between growing trees. Only the cable suspending the steers' fence is visible, and not the fence itself; the steers' pasture

---

8. John Paul Jones . . . the *Bon Homme Richard:* American naval officer and his ship. Both were involved in the Revolutionary War.
9. Amelia Earhart (1898–1937): U.S. pioneer aviator lost at sea.

10. three magi (mă′ jī): Three wise men from the East who brought gifts to the infant Jesus.
11. windrows (wĭnd′ rōs′) *n.*: Rows as of raked hay or windblown leaves.
12. parody (păr′ ə dē) *n.*: Poor imitation.

is entirely in flood, a brown river. The river leaps its banks and smashes into the woods where the motorbikes go, devastating all but the sturdiest trees. The water is so deep and wide it seems as though you could navigate the *Queen Mary*[13] in it, clear to Tinker Mountain.

What do animals do in these floods? I see a drowned muskrat go by like he's flying, but they all couldn't die; the water rises after every hard rain, and the creek is still full of muskrats. This flood is higher than their raised sleeping platforms in the banks; they must just race for high ground and hold on. Where do the fish go, and what do they do? Presumably their gills can filter oxygen out of this muck, but I don't know how. They must hide from the current behind any barriers they can find, and fast for a few days. They must: otherwise we'd have no fish; they'd all be in the Atlantic Ocean. What about herons and kingfishers,[14] say? They can't see to eat. It usually seems to me that when I see any animal, its business is urgent enough that it couldn't easily be suspended for forty-eight hours. Crayfish, frogs, snails, rotifers?[15] Most things must simply die. They couldn't live. Then I suppose that when the water goes down and clears, the survivors have a field day with no competition. But you'd think the bottom would be knocked out of the food chain— the whole pyramid would have no base plankton,[16] and it would crumble, or crash with a thud. Maybe enough spores[17] and larvae and eggs are constantly being borne down from slower upstream waters to repopulate . . . I don't know.

Some little children have discovered a snapping turtle as big as a tray. It's hard to believe that this creek could support a predator that size: its shell is a foot and a half across, and its head extends a good seven inches beyond the shell. When the children —in the company of a shrunken terrier —approach it on the bank, the snapper rears up on its thick front legs and hisses very impressively. I had read earlier that since turtles' shells are rigid, they don't have bellows lungs; they have to gulp for air. And, also since their shells are rigid, there's only room for so much inside, so when they are frightened and planning a retreat, they have to expel air from their lungs to make room for head and feet—hence the malevolent hiss.

The next time I look, I see that the children have somehow maneuvered the snapper into a washtub. They're waving a broom handle at it in hopes that it will snap the wood like a matchstick, but the creature will not deign[18] to oblige. The kids are crushed; all their lives they've heard that this is the one thing you do with a snapping turtle—you shove a broom handle near it, and it "snaps it like a matchstick." It's nature's way; it's sure-fire. But the turtle is having none of it. It avoids the broom handle with an air of patiently repressed rage. They let it go, and it beelines down the bank, dives unhesitatingly into the swirling floodwater, and that's the last we see of it.

A cheer comes up from the crowd on the bridge. The truck is here with a pump for the Bowerys' basement, hooray! We roll away the metal drums, the truck makes it

---

13. Queen Mary: A large ocean-going liner.
14. herons and kingfishers: Birds that catch fish to eat.
15. rotifers (rōt′ ə fers) *n.*: Microscopic invertebrates.
16. base plankton: Microscopic animal and plant life that is the first stage of the food chain.
17. spores: Small, usually one-celled reproductive bodies produced by bacteria, algae, mosses, ferns, and so forth.

18. deign (dān) *v.*: Do something regarded as beneath one's dignity.

over the bridge, to my amazement—the crowd cheers again. State police cruise by; everything's fine here; downstream people are in trouble. The bridge over by the Bings' on Tinker Creek looks like it's about to go. There's a tree trunk wedged against its railing, and a section of concrete is out. The Bings are away, and a young couple is living there, "taking care of the house." What can they do? The husband drove to work that morning as usual; a few hours later, his wife was evacuated from the front door in a *motorboat.*

I walk to the Bings'. Most of the people who are on our bridge eventually end up over there; it's just down the road. We straggle along in the rain, gathering a crowd. The men who work away from home are here, too; their wives have telephoned them at work this morning to say that the creek is rising fast, and they'd better get home while the gettin's good.

There's a big crowd already there; everybody knows that the Bings' is low. The creek is coming in the recreation-room windows; it's halfway up the garage door. Later that day people will haul out everything salvageable and try to dry it: books, rugs, furniture —the lower level was filled from floor to ceiling. Now on this bridge a road crew is trying to chop away the wedged tree trunk with a long-handled ax. The handle isn't so long that they don't have to stand on the bridge, in Tinker Creek. I walk along a low brick wall that was built to retain the creek away from the house at high water. The wall holds just fine, but now that the creek's receding, it's retaining water around the house. On the wall I can walk right out into the flood and stand in the middle of it. Now on the return trip I meet a young man who's going in the opposite direction. The wall is one brick wide; we can't pass. So we clasp hands and lean out backwards over the turbulent water; our feet interlace like teeth on a zipper, we pull together, stand, and continue on our ways. The kids have spotted a rattlesnake draping itself out of harm's way in a bush; now they all want to walk over the brick wall to the bush, to get bitten by the snake.

The little Atkins kids are here, and they are hopping up and down. I wonder if I hopped up and down, would the bridge go? I could stand at the railing as at the railing of a steamboat, shouting deliriously, "Mark three! Quarter-less-three! Half twain! Quarter twain![19] . . ." as the current bore the broken bridge out of sight around the bend before she sank. . . .

Everyone else is standing around. Some of the women are carrying curious plastic umbrellas that look like diving bells —umbrellas they don't put up, but on; they don't get under, but in. They can see out dimly, like goldfish in bowls. Their voices from within sound distant, but with an underlying cheerfulness that plainly acknowledges, "Isn't this ridiculous?" Some of the men are wearing their fishing hats. Others duck their heads under folded newspapers held not very high in an effort to compromise between keeping their heads dry and letting rain run up their sleeves. Following some form of courtesy, I guess, they lower these newspapers when they speak with you, and squint politely into the rain.

Women are bringing coffee in mugs to the road crew. They've barely made a dent in the tree trunk, and they're giving up. It's a job for power tools; the water's going down anyway, and the danger is past. Some kid starts doing tricks on a skateboard; I head home.

---

19. **"Mark three! . . . Quarter twain!":** Announcements of the depth in fathoms of the water as measured by marks on a lead line.

RESPONDING TO THE SELECTION

Your Response

1. Which of Dillard's descriptions did you find the most effective? Explain.

Recalling

2. How was the creek's appearance changed?
3. What was fascinating about the bridge near Dillard's home?
4. What are some of the things that rush by in the water?
5. Why does Dillard eventually head home?

Interpreting

6. How does the flood bring the neighbors together?
7. What is the effect on your imagination of the paragraph on page 476 describing the whole world as being in flood?
8. Why are the people attracted to the Bings' house?
9. How does the use of flashback and present tense affect your impression of the events?

Applying

10. Why do many people find extreme weather such as floods, blizzards, hurricanes, and even lightning storms so fascinating?

ANALYZING LITERATURE

Understanding Descriptive Essay

A **descriptive essay** contains words and phrases that appeal to the senses. Sensory language appeals most often to the sense of sight; however, most writers use language appealing to the other senses as well. This language is used to create pictures of people, places, or scenes in your imagination. For example, ". . . four jays flew around me very slowly, acting generally odd, and screaming on two held notes. There wasn't a breath of wind." These two sentences from the essay appeal to three senses: sight, sound, and touch.

1. Find three examples of language appealing to each of the five senses.
2. What is Dillard's purpose in describing her impression of the flood?

CRITICAL THINKING AND READING

Separating Fact From Opinion

A **fact** is information that can be proven true or false. An **opinion** is information that cannot be proven true or false because it is based on someone's judgment or feelings. A fact concerning this essay is that it is a description of a flooded creek. An opinion is that the essay beautifully re-creates the sights, sounds, and feelings of Dillard's experience.

Identify each of the following quotations from "Flood" as a statement of fact or opinion.

1. "I see by a clipping I saved that the date was June twenty-first . . . the longest daylight of the year."
2. "[The fish] must hide from the current behind any barriers they can find, and fast for a few days."
3. "I had read earlier that since turtles' shells are rigid, they don't have bellows lungs; they have to gulp for air."

THINKING AND WRITING

Writing About a Descriptive Essay

The following comment is from a review of *Pilgrim at Tinker Creek*.

"While readers and reviewers . . . appreciate Dillard's poetic descriptions of her natural world, they generally question how she is able to celebrate an existence which is often senseless and chaotic to her."

Do you agree or disagree with any or all of this statement? Write a short essay, supporting your opinion with examples from "Flood." Revise your essay, making sure you have included adequate support for your ideas.

GUIDE FOR READING

Evan S. Connell

(1924–   ) is an American novelist and essayist. Born in Kansas City, Missouri, Connell attended Dartmouth College and the University of Kansas and did graduate work at Stanford and Columbia. He served as a Navy pilot during World War II. His collection of essays entitled *The White Lantern* recounts the "irrational, marvelous passion of history's adventurers."

from The White Lantern

Narrative Essay

An essay is a brief composition in which the author offers an opinion or a point of view on a subject. A **narrative essay** tells a factual story from the author's point of view. Arranged in chronological order, the events have a definite beginning, middle, and end. They also take place over a limited period of time. In this essay the author writes about two arctic explorers and their expeditions to the South Pole.

Focus

How would you prepare for a journey to the Arctic? With three other students, list the types of equipment you would need. Then, if a map is available, plan out a route for your expedition. As you read from *The White Lantern,* compare your group's plans with those of Amundsen and Scott.

Vocabulary

Knowing the following words will help you as you read this excerpt from *The White Lantern.*

subsequently (sub′ si kwənt lē) *adv.*: Following (p. 481)

terse (tʉrs) *adj.*: Concise; polished (p. 481)

obligatory (ə blig′ ə tôr′ ē) *adj.*: Required; necessary (p. 481)

rigorously (rig′ ər əs lē) *adv.*: Strictly; harshly (p. 482)

logistics (lō jis′ tiks) *n.*: The providing and transporting of people and equipment (p. 483)

idyllic (ī dil′ ik) *adj.*: Pleasing and simple (p. 485)

disdain (dis dān′) *n.*: Scorn; lofty contempt (p. 486)

lethargic (li thär′ jik) *adj.*: Abnormally drowsy or dull; sluggish (p. 486)

predilection (pred ′l ek′ shən) *n.*: An inclination to like something; a special fondness (p. 487)

scrupulously (skroo′ pyə ləs lē) *adv.*: Conscientiously; painstakingly (p. 488)

from **The White Lantern**

Evan S. Connell

Amundsen and Scott are the illustrious names. They got to the Pole[1] within five weeks of each other, which suggests nothing more than good luck and bad luck; but there was such a difference in what happened subsequently that luck cannot explain it. The explanation must be found in the characters of the two men.

Roald Amundsen's opinion of luck is terse and revealing:

"Victory awaits those who have everything in order. People call this luck. Defeat awaits those who fail to take the necessary precautions. This is known as bad luck."

There we have it. To be lucky you must know what you are doing.

At the age of fifteen, after reading about Sir John Franklin's disastrous attempt to find a northwest passage, Amundsen began to get ready. He trained his body to endure hardship. He detested football, but forced himself to play it. He went skiing in the mountains whenever possible. He slept with his bedroom windows open all winter. He looked forward to the obligatory term of military service "both because I wanted to be a good citizen and because I felt that military training would be of great benefit to me as further preparation for my life."

When he was twenty-two he persuaded a friend to go with him on a miniature polar passage. West of Oslo[2] is a mile-high plateau extending nearly to the coast. In summer it is used by Lapp[3] herdsmen pasturing reindeer, but when winter arrives the Lapps descend to the valley and the plateau is deserted. There is no record of anyone ever having crossed it during winter. Amundsen resolved to cross it.

In the middle of their third night on the plateau he woke up because of a temperature change. Instead of sleeping on top of the snow he had burrowed into it, hoping to escape the wind, and while he lay snugly in the hole he had been pleased with himself for such a clever idea. He woke up lying on his back, feeling cramped. Without opening his eyes he tried to roll over but was unable to move. The damp snow of early evening had filled the entrance to his burrow, sifted over his sleeping bag, and then had frozen into a solid block of ice. He began struggling and shouting, but he was helpless—absolutely unable to move—and his voice probably was inaudible at the surface. He very soon quit shouting, he says, because it was hard to breathe, and he realized that if he did not keep quiet he would suffocate. Presumably his friend also had burrowed into the snow, which meant he must be trapped in the same way. Unless there

---

1. **Pole:** the South Pole.

2. **Oslo** (äs′ lō): Capital of Norway.
3. **Lapp** (lap) *adj.*: Of Lapland, an area in northern Norway, Sweden, and Finland.

Captain Amundsen

should be a quick thaw they both would die in these ice coffins.

Amundsen does not know whether he fell asleep or fainted, but the next time he became conscious he heard the sound of digging. His friend had slept on the surface, too exhausted to do anything else, and was astonished when he woke up to find himself alone. The only trace of Amundsen was a tuft of hair at one corner of his sleeping bag. Another snow flurry would have hidden him until the Lapps returned.

They got back in such poor shape that people who had seen them eight days earlier did not recognize them.

Commenting on this experience years later, Amundsen remarks that an "adventure" is merely an interruption of an explorer's serious work and indicates bad planning.

This trip across the Norwegian plateau seems to have been rigorously educational. What he learned from it, beyond the danger of burrowing, cannot even be estimated; but it is obvious that, like most extraordinary people, he knew how to distinguish the shape of the world from a grain of sand. Again and again he talks about preparation. Planning. Attention to detail.

He chose the site of his South Polar base only after studying every existing description of the Ross Ice Shelf[4] from the day it was discovered in 1841. Each member of his expedition was judiciously selected. Every bit of equipment, right down to the tent pegs and buttons, was inspected for weakness or inadequacy. He ordered the boots ripped apart and rebuilt according to his own ideas of comfort and safety. He insisted that a new dog whip be designed.

Aboard the *Fram*,[5] in addition to nineteen men, were almost 100 huskies. Amundsen was convinced that dogs were

---

4. Ross Ice Shelf: Frozen section of the Ross Sea along the coast of Antarctica.
5. Fram: The ship Amundsen's expedition used to get to Antarctica.

essential to success and he had a false deck constructed on the ship to protect them from the tropic sun. He watched their health as closely as he watched the health of his men. He had calculated the day-by-day weight of the sledges that must be hauled to the Pole, and he knew how much weight each animal could pull. As the journey progressed the sledges would become lighter, which meant that fewer dogs would be required. Logistics demanded, therefore, that at a certain point a certain number of dogs be slaughtered. Yet even in death they must contribute. He had calculated that the average dog carried fifty pounds of edible meat. He worked out the precise day on which he intended to kill each dog, and he adhered to this schedule almost exactly.

Amundsen says nothing about the liver, but Arctic Eskimos had known for a long time that you should not eat a husky's liver and he probably was aware of this. He would not have known just why the liver was dangerous, but it would be characteristic of him to credit the Eskimos with some valid reason for their belief.

On the central plateau twenty-four huskies were killed.

"We had agreed to shrink from nothing," he wrote. "The pemmican[6] was cooked remarkably quickly that evening and I was unusually industrious in stirring it. I am not a nervous man, but at the sound of the first shot I found myself trembling. Shot now followed shot in quick succession, echoing uncannily over the great white plain. Each time a trusty servant lost his life."

The Norwegians afterward referred to this campground as the Butcher's Shop.

At first they were reluctant to devour their trusty servants, but the cook Wisting knew his trade. He selected a young animal named Rex.

"I could not take my eyes off his work," says Amundsen.

The delicate little cutlets had an absolutely hypnotizing effect as they were spread out one by one over the snow. They recalled memories of old days, when no doubt a dog cutlet would have been less tempting than now—memories of dishes on which the cutlets were elegantly arranged side by side, with paper frills on the bones, and a neat pile of petits pois[7] in the middle. Ah, my thoughts wandered still farther afield—but that does not concern us now, nor has it anything to do with the South Pole. . . . The meat was excellent, quite excellent, and one cutlet after another disappeared with lightninglike rapidity. I must admit that they would have lost nothing by being a little more tender, but one must not expect too much of a dog. At this first meal I finished five cutlets myself, and looked in vain in the pot for more. Wisting appeared not to have reckoned on such a brisk demand.

About three o'clock on the afternoon of December 14, 1911, Amundsen's men calculated that they had reached the end of the trail.

There were no cheers, no orations. All together the five men grasped a Norwegian flag and thrust it into the snow: Amundsen, Sverre Hassel, Oskar Wisting, Helmer Hansen, Olav Bjaaland.

---

6. pemmican (pem′ i kən) *n*.: Dried meat.

7. petits pois (pə tē pwa′): French for "small green peas."

"Thus we plant thee, beloved flag, at the South Pole, and give to the plain on which it lies the name of King Haakon VII's plateau.[8]"

That brief speech was the only concession to ritual. One gets out of the way of protracted ceremonies in these regions, says Amundsen. The shorter they are, the better.

The Norwegians were in no hurry to leave. The trip had not been difficult, the weather was mild, and they had more than enough food. They stayed several days, taking measurements, circling the area on skis to be sure they truly had encompassed the Pole, and otherwise enjoyed themselves.

They were camped in the middle of a continent almost as large as Australia and Europe combined. The Ross Ice Shelf, over which they had traveled at the beginning, appears to be only a deep indentation on the map of Antarctica, although it is about the size of France. Ice has buried the entire continent—all of its mountains, plains, and valleys, with very few exceptions—in some places to a depth of two miles. Astronauts say that it is the earth's most noticeable feature and that it radiates light from the bottom of the world like a great white lantern.

Once upon a time Antarctica was different. There were pine forests, swamps, and fern jungles. Shackleton's party[9] found a seam of coal eight feet thick near the top of Beardmore Glacier. Scott, following the same route, came across fossilized twigs and leaves:

"The best leaf impressions and the most obvious were in the rotten clumps of weathered coal which split up easily to sheath-

knife and hammer. Every layer of these gave abundant vegetable remains. Most of the bigger leaves were like beech leaves in shape and venation, in size a little smaller than British beech."

On the Palmer Peninsula are traces of fig leaves, sequoia, and an evergreen called araucaria that reached a height of 150 feet and still grows in South America. At Mount Weaver, close to the Pole, is a petrified log eighteen inches in diameter; it dates from the Jurassic period, the age of dinosaurs. What reptiles, animals, and birds lived in prehistoric Antarctica is not known— except for some ancestral families of the penguin, one of which grew as tall as a man.

Nor does anybody know what changed the climate. There are theories, but not much agreement.

At present more than a million people live within a radius of 2,000 miles of the North Pole, yet within that radius of the South Pole—excluding the men at weather stations—there is no human life. There are no land animals or birds, only the indestructible aquatic penguin. There is not a single living tree. There are lichens clinging to exposed rocks, a little moss, some coarse grass, a few spiders and flies. The spiders do not spin webs because of the wind and the flies have no wings. These tiny creatures, as obstinate as Sir Douglas Mawson,[10] spend most of their lives frozen stiff, but thaw out several days a year and hurriedly go about their business in order to maintain the species. Such is life today in Antarctica, which may explain why King Haakon's real estate has never been developed.

Before starting the return journey Amundsen lashed a small Norwegian flag to a tent pole. Inside the tent he left a bag containing a letter to the king, just in case

---

8. King Haakon's (hô kōōnz′) **plateau:** They named the high, level area after King Haakon VII (1872–1957), king of Norway from 1905 to 1957.
9. Shackleton's party: A group of Antarctic explorers from Great Britain.

10. Sir Douglas Mawson: An Antarctic explorer.

The Five at the Pole

they should not make it back to their ship. He discarded some items: reindeerskin foot bags, mitts, a sextant, a hypsometer case—which is an instrument for measuring heights above sea level. And he addressed a letter to Scott.

"He will be here sooner or later," Amundsen told a member of the party. "I hope for his sake it will be sooner."

What Amundsen meant was that the weather could only get worse.

Their trip home sounds idyllic. They had marked the route, and the wind and sun were at their backs. They planned to travel eighteen miles a day, which they did without effort in less than five hours. There was so

much food that sometimes they threw away biscuits and pemmican, and fed chocolate to the dogs. The dogs had such an easy time pulling the sledges that they began to get fat.

"We were in high spirits and bowled along at a cracking pace. . . ."

They reached their base on January 25, the date Amundsen had selected two years earlier in Norway. A week later the *Fram* sailed with all aboard in perfect health.

Scott at this time was hundreds of miles away, writing in his diary: "February 2. Three out of five of us injured. We shall be lucky if we get through. . . ."

On March 18 he wrote: "Ill fortune presses. . . ."

March 19: "The weather doesn't give us a chance. . . ."

Earlier he had told a Melbourne journalist:[11] "We may get through, we may not. We may lose our lives. We may be wiped out. It is all a matter of providence and luck."

Shortly after that while en route to the Antarctic: ". . . fortune has determined to put every difficulty in our path."

Again, the following week: "I begin to wonder if fortune will ever turn her wheel."

At the start of the final journey: "The future is in the lap of the gods. . . ."

While struggling up Beardmore Glacier, unaware that Amundsen had just reached the Pole: "Our luck is very bad."

Eight days later: "I trust this may prove the turning point in our fortunes. . . ."

Near the end of March as he lay dying he wrote to the mother of one of his dead companions: "The ways of Providence are inscrutable. . . ."

And in his *Message to the Public,* found beside his body, he begins: "The causes of the disaster are not due to faulty organization, but to misfortune. . . ."

Perhaps. Perhaps he was right. Maybe all things rest in the lap of the gods. Maybe "faulty organization" was not the cause, though it is hard to forget something he had said ten years before:

"To my mind no journey ever made with dogs can approach the height of the fine conception which is realized when a party of men go forth to face hardships, dangers, and difficulties with their own unaided efforts, and by days and weeks of hard physical labor succeed in solving some problem of the great unknown. Surely in this case the conquest is more nobly and splendidly won."

It's arguable, of course, whether one should extract particular phrases from a man's life to offer as proof of anything. On the subject of luck, for example, Amundsen himself occasionally referred to it without disdain, in a rather idle fashion, as something to be hoped for.

Still, there's a difference. And the difference becomes more significant when you learn what others thought about Scott. As a child he was so lethargic and preoccupied that he was called "Old Moony." He seems to have been the storybook sissy: emotional, horrified at the sight of blood, physically weak, pampered by his mother and an older sister. A doctor who examined him before he joined the navy advised him to choose a different career.

Scott himself recognized his languid[12] disposition and tried to do something about it; and considering how rapidly he was promoted in the navy he must have changed. Yet in every photograph he looks bemused, tentative, almost doubtful. His stance, his expression—he lives far away from the frigid brutal world of Roald Amundsen. Biographer Peter Brent speaks of a brooding, melancholy air. "His mouth, with its full rounded lips, suggests a leaning toward sensuality and pleasure. . . ."

Scott's resemblance to his romantic kinsman, Sir Walter Scott, is startling; they look like brothers. And his written "impressions" of the Antarctic are what you might expect from a mystic poet, not an explorer:

The small green tent and the great white road.
The drift snow like finest flour penetrating every hole and corner—flickering up beneath one's head cov-

11. Melbourne (mel′ bərn) **journalist:** A news writer from a city in Australia.

12. languid (laŋ′ gwid) *adj.*: Weak; listless.

ering, pricking sharply as a sand blast.

The sun with blurred image peeping shyly through the wreathing drift giving pale shadowless light.

The eternal silence of the great white desert. Cloudy columns of snow drift advancing from the south, pale yellow wraiths, heralding the coming storm, blotting out one by one the sharp-cut lines of the land.

Given such a temperament, why was he chosen to lead an expedition? The answer seems to be that as a midshipman he won a whaleboat race. This sounds like a petty triumph, but among the excited spectators was Sir Clements Markham, president of the Royal Geographical Society. He invited Scott to supper and later commented: "I was much struck with his intelligence, information, and the charm of his manner."

Because of Markham's patronage, when a British exploratory party sailed for the Antarctic in 1901 its commander was Scott. Even then he admits he is out of place: "I may as well confess that I have no predilection for polar exploration. . . ."

Subsequently he married an actress, Kathleen Bruce, and began to associate with actors, authors, painters, and musicians— a doubtful lot. How much these people unsettled him can only be imagined. Once he wrote to Kathleen: "I seem to hold in reserve something that makes for success and yet to see no worthy field for it and so there is this consciousness of a truly deep unrest."

Now listen to Roald Amundsen on the same subject: "Success is a woman who has to be won, not courted. You've got to seize her and carry her off, not stand under her window with a mandolin."

In 1910 when the South Polar expedition departed Scott once more was put in charge. And it is a little strange—or perhaps not—that the London *Evening Standard* should remark: "We may never see them again."

Scott's wife also had premonitions, confiding to her diary:

"I had rather a horrid day today. I woke up having a bad dream about you, and then Peter came very close to me and said emphatically, 'Daddy won't come back,' as though in answer to my silly thoughts."

"I was very taken up with you all evening. I wonder if anything special is happening to you. Something odd happened to the clocks and watches between nine and ten P.M."

"I was still rather taken up by you and a wee bit depressed. As you ought about now to be returning to ship I see no reason for depression. I wonder."

Ernest Shackleton wrote to a New Zealand friend: "I suppose that we shall soon hear of Scott. I am inclined to think that we will hear from Amundsen first."

Today, from this distance, as one reads about the expedition, a feeling of doom soars overhead like an albatross.[13] Aboard ship —even before they reach Antarctica —things do not go well. Icebergs appear farther north than expected. Then a storm threatens the *Terra Nova*[14] and ten precious bags of coal which had not been lashed down must be jettisoned. At four in the morning the pumps become choked, water rises in the engine room, the men start bailing with buckets. A dog drowns. Two ponies die.

Upon reaching Antarctica they were unable to establish winter quarters on Cape

---

13. albatross (al′ bə trôs′) *n.*: A large sea bird often used as a symbol of a burden or source of distress.
14. Terra Nova: The ship Scott's expedition used to get to Antarctica.

Crozier as they had planned. Three motor sledges were brought along for heavy work but one sledge broke through the ice and sank, so that in order to get the ponies' fodder ashore the men harnessed themselves to bales of hay. And the expedition's photographer, standing quite literally on thin ice, was almost knocked into the water by a scheming killer whale.

About this time they got news of Amundsen, who had set up camp on an indentation sixty miles nearer the Pole. Scott wrote in his diary: "I never thought he could have got so many dogs safely to the ice. His plan for running them seems excellent. . . ."

Three more ponies died while the first depot was being stocked. Two more drowned when the ice disintegrated beneath them. And Scott writes: "I could not rid myself of the fear that misfortune was in the air. . . ."

Despite every problem he scrupulously kept his journal.

January 15: "We left our depot today with nine days' provisions, so that it ought to be a certain thing now, and the only appalling possibility the sight of the Norwegian flag forestalling ours."

January 16: "The worst has happened. . . . Bowers's sharp eyes detected what he thought was a cairn;[15] he was uneasy about it, but argued that it might be sastrugus.[16] Half an hour later he detected a black speck ahead. Soon we knew that this could not be a natural snow feature. We marched on, found that it was a black flag tied to a sledge bearer; nearby the remains of a camp; sledge tracks and ski tracks coming and going and the clear trace of dogs' paws —many dogs."

---

15. cairn (kern) *n.*: A cone-shaped heap of stones used as a marker or monument.
16. sastrugus (sas′ trσo gəs) *n.*: A wavelike ridge of hard snow formed by the wind and common in polar regions.

Next day Scott reached the Pole: "Great God! this is an awful place. . . ."

Inside the tent was Amundsen's message.

> Poleheim
> 15 December 1911
>
> Dear Captain Scott:
> As you are probably the first to reach this area after us, I will ask you kindly to forward this letter to King Haakon VII. If you can use any of the articles left in this tent, please do not hesitate to do so. The sledge left outside may be of use to you. With best regards, I wish you a safe return.
>
> Roald Amundsen

The British party stayed just long enough to verify the location. By their measurements, Amundsen's tent was only a few hundred yards from the geographical center.

It is hard to understand why they loitered on the way back. They did not have much food, the weather was savage, and they had 900 miles to go. But here is Scott's journal entry on February 8: "I decided to camp and spend the rest of the day geologizing. It has been extremely interesting. We found ourselves under perpendicular cliffs of Beacon sandstone, weathering rapidly and carrying veritable coal seams. From the last Wilson, with his sharp eyes, has picked several plant impressions, the last a piece of coal with beautifully traced leaves in layers, also some excellently preserved impressions of thick stems, showing cellular structure. In one place we saw the cast of small waves in the sand."

Why did they do this? Two explanations have been proposed. If they could bring back some scientific information that the Norwe-

Amundsen Taking a Sight

gians had overlooked their defeat would not be total. Certainly they knew that. The other explanation, which seeps through Scott's journal like a stain, is that they sensed they could never make it. By now they were crippled and suffering from the cold. Wilson had pulled a tendon in his leg. Evans's hands were so badly frozen that his fingernails had begun to drop off. Oates's feet were turning black. Scott had injured his shoulder. Bowers seems to be the only one in good shape.

Yet the next day they again stopped to collect geological specimens. Scott remarks on "the delight of setting foot on rock after 14 weeks of snow and ice."

A few days later Evans died.

Temperatures dropped so low that in the mornings it took them an hour to put on their footgear. The cooking oil was almost gone. Food rations were cut. Scott meditates: "I wonder what is in store for us. . . ."

On the fifteenth of March while they waited in the tent for a blizzard to let up

Oates said, "I am just going outside and may be some time." His feet had become so painful that he could hardly walk, and he did not want to delay the other men.

The bodies of Scott, Bowers, and Wilson were discovered eleven miles from a food depot. Their tent was almost buried by snow. The men lay in their sleeping bags, Wilson with his hands folded on his chest. Bowers also appeared to have died without anguish. Between them lay Scott, the flaps of his sleeping bag open. His diaries were in a green wallet underneath the bag, the last letters on a groundsheet beside him. His left arm was extended, his hand resting on Wilson's shoulder. The interior of the tent had been kept neat. There was an improvised lamp, a bag of tea, a bag of tobacco, and their scientific notes.

Outside stood the sledge. Along with the necessities, it carried thirty-five pounds of rock.

Scott's wife was aboard ship en route to New Zealand to meet him when she learned of his death—five days after the captain got the news by radio. The captain had been so distressed that he could not approach her. She reports in her diary that his hands trembled when he finally showed her the message. After reading it she said to him: "Oh, well, never mind! I expected that. Thanks very much. I will go and think about it."

Then, as she usually did each morning on the ship, she took a Spanish lesson. Then she ate lunch and discussed American politics and in the afternoon spent a while reading about the *Titanic*,[17] determined to avoid thinking of her husband's death until she was sure she could control herself.

Just as curious—perhaps more so—is the fact that Amundsen, the victor, is not as renowned as the loser. Quite a few people think Scott was the first man to reach the South Pole. There is no logical explanation for this belief, though his dramatic death may account for it, together with the fact that he and his companions are still there—frozen like insects or splinters on the side of the great white lantern. However, they won't stay there indefinitely. Calculations by scientists at McMurdo Sound indicate that the bodies now lie fifty feet beneath the surface and fifteen miles closer to the edge of the ice shelf. What this means is that sometime in the future Scott and his companions will be carried out to sea on an iceberg.

As for Roald Amundsen, who knows what became of him? Almost no one. He died on a gallant but useless errand, searching for General Umberto Nobile whose dirigible crash-landed in the Arctic. Amundsen's plane may have developed engine trouble; pieces of it were found off the Norwegian coast. The plane had been lent by the French government, which had at that time two modern seaplanes: one with a water-cooled engine, the other with an air-cooled engine. The French, exhibiting that singular wisdom we have come to associate with all federal government, provided Amundsen with the water-cooled engine for his long flight through subzero temperatures.

A Swedish pilot later rescued the Italian general.

Scott is now remembered and honored throughout the English-speaking world while Amundsen is not. One might say this is folly, because Amundsen has more to teach us. But in the end, of course, they are equally instructive.

---

17. *Titanic* (tī tan′ ik) *n.*: A ship considered unsinkable that hit an iceberg and sank in 1912 on its first voyage.

RESPONDING TO THE SELECTION

Your Response

1. Whom do you admire more, Amundsen or Scott? Give reasons for your answer.
2. What action would you take if you found yourself running short of supplies on a trip such as the one described in the essay?

Recalling

3. In what ways did Amundsen prepare for arctic exploration during his youth?
4. Why does Connell refer to Antarctica as a "white lantern"?
5. Which group reached the South Pole first?
6. What were some of the difficulties that Scott's party encountered?

Interpreting

7. What do Scott's and Amundsen's differing views of fortune or luck indicate about the differences in their personalities?
8. In what ways was Amundsen better prepared for the journey?
9. Whom does Connell admire more, Amundsen or Scott? Support your answer.

Applying

10. Reread the final paragraph of the essay. How are both explorers "equally instructive"?

ANALYZING LITERATURE

Understanding a Narrative Essay

Think of a **narrative essay** as a story that happens to be true. The events are related and take place over a distinct period of time. Using a definite sequence of events, Connell describes each explorer's journey to the South Pole. In addition, a narrative essay includes facts as well as the author's opinion about its subject.

1. How does Connell give the reader a sense of the time in which the events occurred?
2. What does Connell suggest as a possible explanation for the results of Scott's expedition?

CRITICAL THINKING AND READING

Using Comparison and Contrast

Comparison points out similarities between people or things; **contrast** points out differences. For example, on page 481 Connell describes Amundsen's attempts as a youngster to toughen himself. In contrast, he concludes that, as a child, Scott "seems to have been the storybook sissy: emotional, . . . physically weak, pampered by his mother . . ."

Contrast the attitudes of Amundsen and Scott toward each of the following: luck, success, adventure. Support your answers.

THINKING AND WRITING

Writing About a Narrative Essay

Write a brief essay, summarizing the characteristics of each explorer as Connell has presented them. Then evaluate the writer's attitudes toward Amundsen and Scott and decide whether his conclusions are fair or unfair.

LEARNING OPTIONS

1. **Performance.** Suppose that you were a reporter assigned to cover Amundsen's return from the South Pole. Prepare questions to ask him. Have a partner prepare answers from Amundsen's point of view. Although you may refer to the essay for factual information, you might also want to consult other sources in your library. Then, together with your partner, role-play the interview for your class.
2. **Cross-curricular Connection.** To find out more about why Antarctica is unsuitable for normal living, read about it in an encyclopedia or other reference books. Using what you learned from Connell's essay and your additional reading, write a short magazine article explaining why Antarctica is unsuitable for human life.

GUIDE FOR READING

On Summer

Persuasive Essay

A **persuasive essay** attempts to persuade the reader to accept an opinion. Although the opinion is usually subjective, the writer defends it by presenting facts and reasons in a logical and compelling manner. Persuasive essays are written to shed new light on the subject, to create interest in the subject, or to persuade the reader to act. In this essay, Lorraine Hansberry attempts to convince the reader of the virtues of summer.

Lorraine Hansberry

(1930–1965) was born and brought up in Chicago, Illinois. After high school, Hansberry studied art for two years before moving to New York City. While working at several jobs, she wrote *A Raisin in the Sun.* In 1959 this play became the first by a black woman to be produced on Broadway. This essay is from *To Be Young, Gifted, and Black,* a collection of writings that was published after her death.

Focus

People associate certain feelings and emotions with the seasons. The associations they make often depend on where they live. For example, winter in the northernmost parts of the United States is much colder than winter in the Deep South. What feelings, emotions, and activities do you associate with each of the seasons? Specifically, which do you associate with summer? In a group of three or four people, share your opinions of summer. As you read "On Summer," consider how your views and those of your peers compare with the author's opinions.

Vocabulary

Knowing the following words will help you as you read "On Summer."

aloofness (ə lo͞of′ nəs) *n.*: The state of being distant, removed, or uninvolved (p. 493)

melancholy (mel′ ən käl′ ē) *adj.*: Sadness; gloominess; depression (p. 493)

relief (ri lēf′) *n.*: The projection of shapes from a flat surface, so that they stand out (p. 493)

negotiate (ni gō′ shē āt) *v.*: To master or successfully move through a situation (p. 495)

palpable (pal′ pə b'l) *adj.*: Able to be perceived by the senses (p. 495)

ribald (rib′əld) *adj.*: Characterized by coarse or vulgar joking (p. 495)

On Summer

Lorraine Hansberry

It has taken me a good number of years to come to any measure of respect for summer. I was, being May-born, literally an "infant of the spring" and, during the later childhood years, tended, for some reason or other, to rather worship the cold aloofness of winter. The adolescence, admittedly lingering still, brought the traditional passionate commitment to melancholy autumn —and all that. For the longest kind of time I simply thought that *summer* was a mistake.

In fact, my earliest memory of anything at all is of waking up in a darkened room where I had been put to bed for a nap on a summer's afternoon, and feeling very, very hot. I acutely disliked the feeling then and retained the bias for years. It had originally been a matter of the heat but, over the years, I came actively to associate displeasure with most of the usually celebrated natural features and social by-products of the season: the too-grainy texture of sand; the too-cold coldness of the various waters we constantly try to escape into, and the icky-perspiry feeling of bathing caps.

It also seemed to me, esthetically[1] speaking, that nature had got inexcusably carried away on the summer question and let the whole thing get to be rather much. By duration alone, for instance, a summer's day seemed maddeningly excessive; an utter overstatement. Except for those few hours at either end of it, objects always appeared in too sharp a relief against backgrounds; shadows too pronounced and light too blinding. It always gave me the feeling of walking around in a motion picture which had been too artsily-craftsily exposed. Sound also had a way of coming to the ear without that muting influence, marvelously common to winter, across patios or beaches or through the woods. I suppose I found it too stark and yet too intimate a season.

My childhood Southside[2] summers were the ordinary city kind, full of the street games which the other rememberers have turned into fine ballets these days and rhymes that anticipated what some people insist on calling modern poetry:

Oh, Mary Mack, Mack, Mack
With the silver buttons, buttons, buttons
All down her back, back, back
She asked her mother, mother, mother
For fifteen cents, cents, cents
To see the elephant, elephant, elephant
Jump the fence, fence, fence
Well, he jumped so high, high, high
'Til he touched the sky, sky, sky
And he didn't come back, back, back
'Til the Fourth of Ju-ly, ly, ly!

---

1. esthetically (es thet' ik lē) *adv.*: Artistically.

2. Southside: A section of Chicago, Illinois.

Evenings were spent mainly on the back porches where screen doors slammed in the darkness with those really very special summertime sounds. And, sometimes, when Chicago nights got too steamy, the whole family got into the car and went to the park and slept out in the open on blankets. Those were, of course, the best times of all because the grownups were invariably reminded of having been children in rural parts of the country and told the best stories then. And it was also cool and sweet to be on the grass and there was usually the scent of freshly cut lemons or melons in the air. And Daddy would lie on his back, as fathers must, and explain about how men thought the stars above us came to be and how far away they were. I never did learn to believe that anything could be as far away as *that*. Especially the stars.

My mother first took us south to visit her Tennessee birthplace one summer when I was seven or eight, I think. I woke up on the back seat of the car while we were still driving through some place called Kentucky and my mother was pointing out to the beautiful hills on both sides of the highway and telling my brothers and my sister about how her father had run away and hidden

from his master in those very hills when he was a little boy. She said that his mother had wandered among the wooded slopes in the moonlight and left food for him in secret places. They were very beautiful hills and I looked out at them for miles and miles after that wondering who and what a *master* might be.

I remember being startled when I first saw my grandmother rocking away on her porch. All my life I had heard that she was a great beauty and no one had ever remarked that they meant a half century before. The woman that I met was as wrinkled as a prune and could hardly hear and barely see and always seemed to be thinking of other times. But she could still rock and talk and even make wonderful cupcakes which were like cornbread, only sweet. She was captivated by automobiles and, even though it was well into the Thirties,[3] I don't think she had ever been in one before we came down and took her driving. She was a little afraid of them and could not seem to negotiate the windows, but she loved driving. She died the next summer and that is all that I remember about her, except that she was born in slavery and had memories of it and they didn't sound anything like *Gone with the Wind.*[4]

Like everyone else, I have spent whole or bits of summers in many different kinds of places since then: camps and resorts in the Middle West and New York State; on an island; in a tiny Mexican village; Cape Cod, perched atop the Truro bluffs at Longnook Beach that Millay[5] wrote about; or simply strolling the streets of Provincetown[6] before the hours when the parties begin.

And, lastly, I do not think that I will forget days spent, a few summers ago, at a beautiful lodge built right into the rocky cliffs of a bay on the Maine coast. We met a woman there who had lived a purposeful and courageous life and who was then dying of cancer. She had, characteristically, just written a book and taken up painting. She had also been of radical viewpoint all her life; one of those people who energetically believe that the world *can* be changed for the better and spend their lives trying to do just that. And that was the way she thought of cancer; she absolutely refused to award it the stature of tragedy, a devastating instance of the brooding doom and inexplicability[7] of the absurdity of human destiny, etc., etc. The kind of characterization given, lately, as we all know, to far less formidable foes in life than cancer.

But for this remarkable woman it was a matter of nature in imperfection, implying, as always, work for man to do. It was an *enemy,* but a palpable one with shape and effect and source; and if it existed, it could be destroyed. She saluted it accordingly, without despondency, but with a lively, beautiful and delightfully ribald anger. There was one thing, she felt, which would prove equal to its relentless ravages and that was the genius of man. Not his mysticism, but man with tubes and slides and the stubborn human notion that the stars are very much within our reach.

The last time I saw her she was sitting

---

3. Thirties: The 1930's.
4. Gone with the Wind: A novel set in the South during the Civil War period.
5. Millay: Edna St. Vincent Millay (1892–1950), U.S. poet.

6. Provincetown: Resort town at the northern tip of Cape Cod, Massachusetts.
7. inexplicability (in eks′ pli kə bil′ ə tē) *n.*: A condition that cannot be explained.

surrounded by her paintings with her manuscript laid out for me to read, because, she
said, she wanted to know what a *young
person* would think of her thinking; one
must always keep up with what *young people* thought about things because, after all,
they were *change.*

Every now and then her jaw set in anger
as we spoke of things people should be
angry about. And then, for relief, she would
look out at the lovely bay at a mellow sunset
settling on the water. Her face softened with
love of all that beauty and, watching her, I
wished with all my power what I knew that
she was wishing: that she might live to see

at least one more *summer.* Through her eyes
I finally gained the sense of what it might
mean; more than the coming autumn with
its pretentious melancholy; more than an
austere and silent winter which must shut
dying people in for precious months; more
even than the frivolous spring, too full of too
many false promises, would be the gift of
another summer with its stark and intimate
assertion of neither birth nor death but life
at the apex; with the gentlest nights and,
above all, the longest days.

I heard later that she did live to see
another summer. And I have retained my
respect for the noblest of the seasons.

RESPONDING TO THE SELECTION

Your Response

1. Has this essay changed your feelings about summer? Why or why not?
2. Do you favor one season over the others? Explain your answer.

Recalling

3. What were Hansberry's feelings about summer before she met the woman in Maine?
4. What was the "radical viewpoint" on life of the woman in Maine?

Interpreting

5. What is Hansberry implying about adolescence when she refers to "the traditional passionate commitment to melancholy autumn"?
6. How do her childhood memories contrast with her statement that "For the longest kind of time I simply thought that *summer* was a mistake?"
7. Why did meeting the woman in Maine change Hansberry's mind about summer?

Applying

8. In his journal, André Gide wrote, "I should like to enjoy this summer flower by flower, as if it were to be the last one for me." How can you enjoy summer "flower by flower"?

ANALYZING LITERATURE

Understanding a Persuasive Essay

The goal of a **persuasive essay** is to convince the reader that an opinion is valid. Facts and reasons that support the writer's viewpoint are presented in a forceful, convincing way.

1. What are some of the facts and reasons that the author presents to persuade you?
2. Was Lorraine Hansberry successful in convincing you that summer is the "noblest of the seasons"? Explain your answer.

CRITICAL THINKING AND READING

Identifying Persuasive Techniques

Writers of persuasive essays use several techniques to present their opinions as convincingly as possible. One of these techniques, an appeal to your emotions, is used in "On Summer." By retelling memories of her childhood and her experience with the woman who had cancer, Hansberry is attempting to convince you that summer is the best season.

1. What specific emotions does Hansberry's essay appeal to?
2. Select two sentences that are especially effective. Explain their appeal.

THINKING AND WRITING

Summarizing an Essay

In a short essay, summarize the main points the author makes in "On Summer" that support her premise. Start by writing a brief outline of the essay to be sure you include all the important points. Then prepare a first draft. As you write, link each of the main points to the conclusion.

LEARNING OPTIONS

1. **Cross-curricular Connection.** In "On Summer," Hansberry describes characteristics of summer, such as "maddeningly excessive" days. What causes such effects? Find three qualities of summer noted in the essay and illustrate what causes them in words, drawings, or another form of your choice. You might want to use earth science resources in your school.
2. **Multicultural Activity.** If you were to spend the summer in another part of the world, it might not be summer as you know it. Choose a place and find out what summer is like there—either by reading or by talking to people familiar with the area. Then write a letter persuading a friend to join you in spending the summer there.

GUIDE FOR READING

Mary Cassatt

Essay of Appreciation

"Mary Cassatt" is an **essay of appreciation:** a discussion of the fine qualities that make its subject unique and significant. An encyclopedia article, a biography, or an art history book will offer facts about Mary Cassatt. In this essay, however, Gordon goes beyond facts to celebrate the artistic talents and accomplishments that make Mary Cassatt so admirable. Gordon also discusses what she appreciates most about Cassatt as a person.

Focus

Mary Cassatt spent most of her life painting in Europe. During her lifetime it was most unusual for an American woman to devote her life to art, to travel independently, and to remain single. Gordon considers such facts as she explores how people of Cassatt's time responded to her work. Look at two of Cassatt's paintings on pages 501 and 502. What do these scenes suggest to you? What do you think they reveal about Cassatt? Discuss each painting with a classmate and compare your impressions. Then keep your discussion in mind as you read the essay.

Vocabulary

Knowing the following words will help you as you read "Mary Cassatt."

paradoxes (par′ ə däks′ əz) *n.*: Seemingly contradictory statements (p. 499)

astringency (ə strin′ jən sē′) *n.*: A harsh, severe quality (p. 499)

exuberance (eg zōō′ bər əns) *n.*: A feeling of high spirits (p. 499)

credence (krēd′ ′ns) *n.*: An appearance of truth; belief (p. 500)

ambivalence (am biv′ ə ləns) *n.*: Conflicting feelings occurring simultaneously, such as love and hate (p. 500)

irascible (i ras′ ə bəl) *adj.*: Easily angered; quick-tempered (p. 502)

ardent (ärd′ ′nt) *adj.*: Intensely enthusiastic; devoted (p. 502)

Mary Gordon

(1949–   ) says that "there was never a time when [she] didn't want to be a writer." Gordon grew up in Queens, New York. When she was in high school, she wrote poetry almost exclusively; during that time writing was her "joy" and her "safe place."

As a novelist, Gordon has been described as passionate and perceptive. Her best-selling novels are *Final Payments, The Company of Women, Men and Angels,* and *The Other Side.* In addition, she has written *Temporary Shelter,* a highly acclaimed collection of short stories.

Gordon is also an eloquent essayist. Her discussion of Mary Cassatt comes from a collection of twenty-eight essays called *Good Boys and Dead Girls.*

Mary Cassatt

Mary Gordon

When Mary Cassatt's father was told of her decision to become a painter, he said: "I would rather see you dead." When Edgar Degas saw a show of Cassatt's etchings, his response was: "I am not willing to admit that a woman can draw that well." When she returned to Philadelphia after twenty-eight years abroad, having achieved renown as an Impressionist painter and the esteem of Degas, Huysmans, Pissarro, and Berthe Morisot, the *Philadelphia Ledger* reported: "Mary Cassatt, sister of Mr. Cassatt, president of the Pennsylvania Railroad, returned from Europe yesterday. She has been studying painting in France and owns the smallest Pekingese dog in the world."

Mary Cassatt exemplified the paradoxes of the woman artist. Cut off from the experiences that are considered the entitlement of her male counterpart, she has access to a private world a man can only guess at. She has, therefore, a kind of information he is necessarily deprived of. If she has almost impossible good fortune—means, self-confidence, heroic energy and dedication, the instinct to avoid the seductions of ordinary domestic life, which so easily become a substitute for creative work—she may pull off a miracle: she will combine the skill and surety that she has stolen from the world of men with the vision she brings from the world of women.

Mary Cassatt pulled off such a miracle. But if her story is particularly female, it is also American. She typifies one kind of independent American spinster who keeps reappearing in our history in forms as various as Margaret Fuller and Katharine Hepburn. There is an astringency in such women, a fierce discipline, a fearlessness, a love of work. But they are not inhuman. At home in the world, they embrace it with a kind of aristocratic greed that knows nothing of excess. Balance, proportion, an instinct for the distant and the formal, an exuberance, a vividness, a clarity of line: the genius of Mary Cassatt includes all these elements. The details of the combination are best put down to grace; the outlines may have been her birthright.

She was one of those wealthy Americans whose parents took the children abroad for their education and medical care. The James family comes to mind and, given her father's attitude toward her career, it is remarkable that Cassatt didn't share the fate of Alice James. But she had a remarkable mother, intelligent, encouraging of her children. When her daughter wanted to study in Paris, and her husband disapproved, Mrs. Cassatt arranged to accompany Mary as her chaperone.

From her beginnings as an art student, Cassatt was determined to follow the highest standards of craftsmanship. She went first to Paris, then to Italy, where she studied in Parma with Raimondi and spent many hours climbing up scaffolding (to the surprise of the natives) to study the work of Correggio and Parmigianino. Next, she was curious to visit Spain to look at the Spanish masters and to make use of the picturesque landscape and models. Finally, she returned to Paris, where she was to make her home, and worked with Degas, her sometime friend and difficult mentor. There has always been speculation as to whether or not they were lovers; her burning their correspondence gave the rumor credence. But I believe that they were not; she was, I think, too protective of her talent to make herself so vulnerable to Degas as a lover would have to be. But I suppose I don't believe it because I cherish, instead, the notion that a man and a woman can be colleagues and friends without causing an excuse for raised eyebrows. Most important, I want to believe they were not lovers because if they were, the trustworthiness of his extreme praise grows dilute.

She lived her life until late middle age among her family. Her beloved sister, Lydia, one of her most cherished models, had always lived as a semi-invalid and died early, in Mary's flat, of Bright's disease.[1] Mary was closely involved with her brothers and their children. Her bond with her mother was profound: when Mrs. Cassatt died, in 1895, Mary's work began to decline. At the severing of her last close familial tie, when her surviving brother died as a result of an illness he contracted when traveling with her to Egypt, she broke down entirely. "How we try for happiness, poor things, and how we don't find it. The best cure is hard work —if only one has the health for it," she said, and lived that way.

Not surprisingly, perhaps, Cassatt's reputation has suffered because of the prejudice against her subject matter. Mothers and children: what could be of lower prestige, more vulnerable to the charge of sentimentality? Yet if one looks at the work of Mary Cassatt, one sees how triumphantly she avoids the pitfalls of sentimentality because of the astringent rigor of her eye and craft. The Cassatt iconography[2] dashes in an instant the notion of the comfortable, easily natural fit of the maternal embrace. Again and again in her work, the child's posture embodies the ambivalence of his or her dependence. In *The Family*, the mother and child exist in positions of unease; the strong diagonals created by their postures of opposition give the pictures their tense strength, a strength that renders sentimental sweetness impossible. In *Ellen Mary Cassatt in a White Coat*, and *Girl in the Blue Arm Chair*, the children seem imprisoned and dwarfed by the trappings of respectable life. The lines of Ellen's coat, which create such a powerful framing device, entrap the round and living child. The sulky little girl in the armchair seems about to be swallowed up by the massive cylinders of drawing room furniture and the strong curves of emptiness that are the floor. In *The Bath*, the little girl has all the unformed charming awkwardness of a young child: the straight limbs, the loose stomach. But these are not the stuff of Gerber babies—even of the children of Millais. In this picture, the center of interest is not the relationship between the mother and the child but the strong vertical and diagonal stripes of the mother's dress, whose opposition shapes the picture with an insistence that is almost abstract.

Cassatt changed the iconography of the depiction of mothers and children. Hers do not look out into and meet the viewer's eye; neither supplicating nor seductive, they are absorbed in their own inner thoughts. Minds are at work here, a concentration unbroken by an awareness of themselves as objects to be gazed at by the world.

------

1. Bright's disease: A kidney ailment. Also known as nephritis (nē frīt′ əs).

2. iconography (ī kə näg′ rə fē) *n*.: The images that appear regularly in an artist's work or in all the works of a particular era.

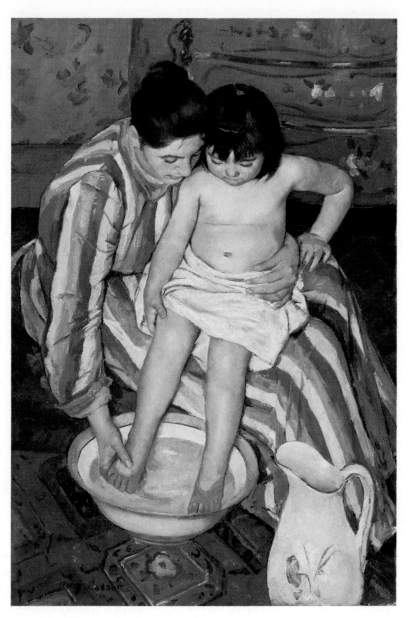

THE BATH, c. 1891
Mary Cassatt
The Art Institute of Chicago

The brilliance of Cassatt's colors, the clarity and solidity of her forms, are the result of her love and knowledge of the masters of European painting. She had a second career as adviser to great collectors: she believed passionately that America must, for the sake of its artists, possess masterpieces, and she paid no attention to the outrage of her European friends, who felt their treasures were being sacked by barbarians. A young man visiting her in her old age noted her closed mind regarding the movement of the moderns. She thought American painters should stay home and not become "café loafers in Paris. Why should they come to Europe?" she demanded. "When I was young it was different. . . . Our Museums had not great paintings for

THE FAMILY, c. 1892
Mary Cassatt
The Chrysler Museum, Norfolk, Virginia

the students to study. Now that has been corrected and something must be done to save our young over here.''

One can hear the voice of the old, irascible, still splendid aunt in that comment and see the gesture of her stick toward the Left Bank.[3] Cassatt was blinded by cataracts; the last years of her life were spent in a fog. She became ardent on the subjects of suffragism, socialism, and spiritualism; the horror of the First World War made her passionate in her conviction that mankind itself must change. She died at her country estate near Grasse, honored by the French, recipient of the Légion d'honneur,[4] but unappreciated in America, rescued only recently from misunderstanding, really, by feminist art critics. They allowed us to begin to see her for what she is: a master of line and color whose great achievement was to take the ''feminine'' themes of mothers, children, women with their thoughts alone, to endow them with grandeur without withholding from them the tenderness that fits so easily alongside the rigor of her art.

---

3. Left Bank: A district in Paris on the left bank of the Seine (sen) river, associated with artists.

4. Légion d'honneur (lā zhən' də nĕr'): Award given by the French Legion of Honor, founded in 1802 by Napoleon to recognize distinguished military or civil service.

RESPONDING TO THE SELECTION

Your Response

1. From what Gordon has told you, what do you admire most about Mary Cassatt?
2. How do you respond to Cassatt's comment "How we try for happiness, poor things, and how we don't find it. The best cure is hard work . . ."?

Recalling

3. Briefly summarize Cassatt's career.
4. According to Gordon what was Cassatt's great achievement?

Interpreting

5. Explain what Gordon means by "the paradoxes of the woman artist."
6. What do Degas's first responses to Cassatt's work and the newspaper report of her return from Europe suggest about attitudes toward women artists?
7. Why does Gordon deny that Cassatt's pictures are sentimental?
8. What do Mary Cassatt's paintings and career reveal about her personality?

Applying

9. How have attitudes toward women artists changed since Mary Cassatt's time?

ANALYZING LITERATURE

Analyzing an Essay of Appreciation

An **essay of appreciation** focuses on the fine qualities of a subject. Unlike narrative essays, in which there is a definite sequence of events, an essay of appreciation isn't necessarily chronological. For example, after briefly surveying Cassatt's career, Gordon discusses aspects of Cassatt's art and qualities of her personality.

1. How does Gordon show that Cassatt's success was remarkable for a nineteenth-century woman?
2. What does Gordon emphasize about Cassatt's treatment of her subject matter?

3. What does Gordon seem to appreciate most about Cassatt?

CRITICAL THINKING AND READING

Evaluating Conclusions About Art

After studying an artist's work, you draw conclusions about his or her skill. In her essay, Gordon draws conclusions about Mary Cassatt's art. For example, as she interprets Cassatt's paintings, Gordon concludes that Cassatt avoids sentimentality, or an obvious display of tender feelings. Gordon supports her conclusions by referring specifically to how Cassatt's painting *The Family* ". . . renders sentimental sweetness impossible."

1. After looking at Cassatt's paintings, do you agree that they are not sentimental? Explain.
2. After studying *The Bath,* do you share Gordon's conclusion that the relationship between the mother and child is not the focal point of the painting? Explain your answer.

THINKING AND WRITING

Writing an Essay of Appreciation

Write an essay of appreciation about an artist or performer, celebrating the qualities that make him or her unique. Explain what you appreciate most about your subject by drawing conclusions and supporting them with specific examples that illustrate your points. Finally, proofread your essay, and prepare a final draft.

LEARNING OPTION

Cross-curricular Connection. Study some of Cassatt's paintings. You might want to start with the ones Gordon mentions, but look at others as well. As you study the paintings, respond to them in your journal. Look for the qualities that Gordon values about Cassatt's work. What do you see in the paintings that reinforces Gordon's conclusions? What else do you see in Cassatt's art? Try to record as much as you can; you may want to return to your responses for future writing.

ONE WRITER'S PROCESS

Mary Gordon and "Mary Cassatt"

PREWRITING

Nonfiction Versus Fiction Although she is best known as a novelist, Mary Gordon is also a fine essayist. She makes the following distinction between these two types of writing: "Nonfiction is different from fiction primarily because in fiction you are always essentially standing in mid-air. Everything is your own invention."

Creating a Graceful Shape About her essay on Mary Cassatt, she says, "Before I could begin I did extensive research on the work and biography of Mary Cassatt, and a large part of the planning and revision was concerned with creating a graceful shape for the research I had done."

DRAFTING

Rituals and Habits Gordon has certain working conditions that she insists upon. She is very particular about notebooks and pens, and will write only "with one special fountain pen in a particular kind of notebook I get in England."

REVISING

Help From a Friend Gordon revises her work extensively. She has three friends—two writers and an editor—to whom she always shows her writing. She adds, "One instance when someone's advice was helpful was a friend's suggestion that I change the narrative voice of my first novel, *Final Payments*, from third person to first."

Adding More Detail To see the kinds of changes Gordon makes when revising, look at the following draft of a recent piece of writing and the revisions she made. Can you tell why she made the changes she did?

> **Draft**
> Memory: the cataract, the overwhelming annihilating flood. And what of the freezing power, of horror of shock, the immobilization of memory, the grey cold immobility, the other choice only other choice than death by drowning.
>
> **Revision**
> Memory: the cataract, the overwhelming flood. And what of the freezing power, of horror of shock, the paralysis, the grey cold stillness when memory stops dead and nothing moves in the grey windless plain, the place of stone, blind stone and you inhabit it because you must, it is the only place, you must choose it or death by drowning.

PUBLISHING

Commissioned Work Like many of her nonfiction pieces, Gordon's essay on Mary Cassatt was commissioned, or requested, by editors familiar with her work. She explains, "The editors of *Art and Antiques* contacted me about writing an article on Mary Cassatt, probably because in my novel *Men and Angels* I created a fictional character based in part on her." Here is a case, therefore, where a real person inspired a fictional character, who in turn inspired an essay on the real person!

THINKING ABOUT THE PROCESS

1. What are the benefits or drawbacks of revising extensively?
2. **Writing** Write a short narrative piece in the third person. Then change the narrative voice from third person to first. Share your revision with the class, and discuss your changes.

Essays in the Arts and Sciences

SONG, 1950
Ben Shahn
Hirshhorn Museum and Sculpture Garden
Smithsonian Institution

GUIDE FOR READING

Lewis Thomas

(1913–1993) was an American physician, scientist, and teacher who is remembered also as a gifted writer. In his brief essays, often published in the *New England Journal of Medicine,* Thomas offered his insights and opinions on a variety of topics. In his essay "Notes on Punctuation" from *The Medusa and the Snail: More Notes of a Biology Watcher* (1979), Thomas expressed his opinions about the useful but sometimes annoying marks that help writers convey structure and meaning.

Notes on Punctuation

Classification

Classification is an arrangement according to a systematic division into classes or groups. For example, a short-story writer can be grouped with his or her counterparts and then classified according to categories such as style, subject, and popularity. A classification essay divides the subject into major categories, arranges the categories in a sequence, and defines the categories. In "Notes on Punctuation" the writer classifies different types of punctuation as useful or not, and as those he likes and those he doesn't.

Focus

Devise a code for punctuation marks that uses words to translate the meaning and function of each mark. For example, STOP can be the code word for a period. For each punctuation mark you know, choose a meaningful code word. Then write a coded message on the chalkboard in your classroom and have classmates try to break the code by inserting the correct punctuation marks. Decode their messages as well. As you read "Notes on Punctuation," compare your ideas about punctuation with those in Thomas's essay.

Vocabulary

Knowing the following words will help you as you read "Notes on Punctuation."

deploying (dē ploi′ iŋ) *v.*: Using (p. 507)

ambiguity (am′ bə gyōō′ ə tē) *n.*: Uncertainty (p. 507)

implication (im′ plə kā′ shən) *n.*: Suggestion (p. 507)

banal (bā′ n'l) *adj.*: Without originality or freshness (p. 508)

unethical (un eth′ i k'l) *adj.*: Not moral; not conforming to certain rules (p. 508)

disown (dis ōn′) *v.*: To deny ownership of or responsibility for (p. 508)

clichés (klē shāz′) *n.*: Overused phrases or expressions (p. 508)

parsimonious (pär′ sə mō′ nē əs) *adj.*: Stingy (p. 508)

Notes on Punctuation

Lewis Thomas

There are no precise rules about punctuation (Fowler[1] lays out some general advice (as best he can under the complex circumstances of English prose (he points out, for example, that we possess only four stops (the comma, the semicolon, the colon and the period (the question mark and exclamation point are not, strictly speaking, stops; they are indicators of tone (oddly enough, the Greeks employed the semicolon for their question mark (it produces a strange sensation to read a Greek sentence which is a straightforward question: Why weepest thou; (instead of Why weepest thou? (and, of course, there are parentheses (which are surely a kind of punctuation making this whole matter much more complicated by having to count up the left-handed parentheses in order to be sure of closing with the right number (but if the parentheses were left out, with nothing to work with but the stops, we would have considerably more flexibility in the deploying of layers of meaning than if we tried to separate all the clauses by physical barriers (and in the latter case, while we might have more precision and exactitude for our meaning, we would lose the essential flavor of language, which is its wonderful ambiguity)))))))))))).

The commas are the most useful and usable of all the stops. It is highly important to put them in place as you go along. If you try to come back after doing a paragraph

and stick them in the various spots that tempt you you will discover that they tend to swarm like minnows into all sorts of crevices whose existence you hadn't realized and before you know it the whole long sentence becomes immobilized and lashed up squirming in commas. Better to use them sparingly, and with affection, precisely when the need for each one arises, nicely, by itself.

I have grown fond of semicolons in recent years. The semicolon tells you that there is still some question about the preceding full sentence; something needs to be added; it reminds you sometimes of the Greek usage. It is almost always a greater pleasure to come across a semicolon than a period. The period tells you that that is that; if you didn't get all the meaning you wanted or expected, anyway you got all the writer intended to parcel out and now you have to move along. But with a semicolon there you get a pleasant little feeling of expectancy; there is more to come; read on; it will get clearer.

Colons are a lot less attractive, for several reasons: firstly, they give you the feeling of being rather ordered around, or at least having your nose pointed in a direction you might not be inclined to take if left to yourself, and, secondly, you suspect you're in for one of those sentences that will be labeling the points to be made: firstly, secondly and so forth, with the implication that you haven't sense enough to keep track of a sequence of notions without having them numbered. Also, many writers use this system loosely and incompletely, starting out

1. Fowler: Henry Watson Fowler (1858–1933), an expert on the English language and author of *A Dictionary of Modern English Usage.*

with number one and number two as though counting off on their fingers and then going on and on without the succession of labels you've been led to expect, leaving you floundering about searching for the ninethly or seventeenthly that ought to be there but isn't.

Exclamation points are the most irritating of all. Look! they say, look at what I just said! How amazing is my thought! It is like being forced to watch someone else's small child jumping up and down crazily in the center of the living room shouting to attract attention. If a sentence really has something of importance to say, something quite remarkable, it doesn't need a mark to point it out. And if it is really, after all, a banal sentence needing more zing, the exclamation point simply emphasizes its banality!

Quotation marks should be used honestly and sparingly, when there is a genuine quotation at hand, and it is necessary to be very rigorous about the words enclosed by the marks. If something is to be quoted, the *exact* words must be used. If part of it must be left out because of space limitations, it is good manners to insert three dots to indicate the omission, but it is unethical to do this if it means connecting two thoughts which the original author did not intend to have tied together. Above all, quotation marks should not be used for ideas that you'd like to disown, things in the air so to speak. Nor should they be put in place around clichés; if you want to use a cliché you must take full responsibility for it yourself and not try to job it off on anon.,[2] or on society. The most objectionable misuse of quotation marks, but one which illustrates the dangers of misuse in ordinary prose, is seen in advertising, especially in advertisements for small restaurants, for example "just around the corner," or "a good place to eat." No single, identifiable, citable[3] person ever really said, for the record, "just around the corner," much less "a good place to eat," least likely of all for restaurants of the type that use this type of prose.

The dash is a handy device, informal and essentially playful, telling you that you're about to take off on a different tack but still in some way connected with the present course—only you have to remember that the dash is there, and either put a second dash at the end of the notion to let the reader know that he's back on course, or else end the sentence, as here, with a period.

The greatest danger in punctuation is for poetry. Here it is necessary to be as economical and parsimonious with commas and periods as with the words themselves, and any marks that seem to carry their own subtle meanings, like dashes and little rows of periods, even semicolons and question marks, should be left out altogether rather than inserted to clog up the thing with ambiguity. A single exclamation point in a poem, no matter what else the poem has to say, is enough to destroy the whole work.

The things I like best in T. S. Eliot's poetry, especially in the *Four Quartets,* are the semicolons. You cannot hear them, but they are there, laying out the connections between the images and the ideas. Sometimes you get a glimpse of a semicolon coming, a few lines farther on, and it is like climbing a steep path through woods and seeing a wooden bench just at a bend in the road ahead, a place where you can expect to sit for a moment, catching your breath.

Commas can't do this sort of thing; they can only tell you how the different parts of a complicated thought are to be fitted together, but you can't sit, not even take a breath, just because of a comma,

---

2. anon.: Abbreviation of *anonymous.*

3. citable (sīt′ ə b'l) *adj.*: Able to be named.

Your Response

1. What is your favorite comment in the essay? Why?
2. Agree or disagree with the following quotes from the essay:
   a. "The commas are the most useful and usable of all stops" (p. 507).
   b. "Exclamation points are the most irritating of all" (p. 508).

Recalling

3. What four stops and two indicators of tone does the English language include?
4. According to Thomas, what are the three most useful stops?
5. In the writer's opinion, which three punctuation marks present problems for writers? Give his reasons.
6. What is the writer's suggestion for punctuating poetry?

Interpreting

7. Do you think the purpose of this essay is to explain, entertain, or persuade?
8. What does the writer assume about the knowledge and needs of the audience?

Applying

9. Suppose that you used no punctuation marks in your writing. How would that affect your ability to write and your readers' ability to understand what you have written?

READING IN THE ARTS AND SCIENCES

Understanding Classification

Classification is an arrangement according to some systematic division into classes or groups. In "Notes on Punctuation," the classification of different types of punctuation as useful or not and as those the writer likes and those he doesn't depends largely on the writer's point of view.

For example, the writer says that exclamation points are irritating and unnecessary. However, the playwright of an emotional drama might feel that they are helpful in showing the actors where to infuse more emotion into their speech; an effusive person might feel that exclamation points are helpful in expressing his or her feelings.

1. The writer feels that dashes are "informal and essentially playful." How might a poet known for her quick wit feel about dashes?
2. The writer feels that quotation marks should be used "honestly and sparingly, when there is a genuine quotation at hand." How might a novelist known for his use of convincing dialogue feel about the use of quotation marks?

CRITICAL THINKING AND READING

Finding the Main Idea

The **main idea** is the most important idea expressed. Sometimes the main idea of a paragraph is stated directly in one sentence called the topic sentence. When the main idea is not stated directly but is implied, you must infer it.

1. Reread the first paragraph in column 1 on page 508. What is the main idea?
2. Reread the second paragraph in column 2 on page 508. What is the main idea?

THINKING AND WRITING

Writing About Language Arts

Select a punctuation mark that either helps you or irritates you when you read or write. Write a brief persuasive essay in which you try to convince other students to agree with your opinion. If you wish, use humor to make your point.

First, state the main idea you want your essay to convey. Then list the reasons or supporting details and examples for your main idea. List the best argument last in order to leave your readers with the strongest point. End your essay with a statement that summarizes or clinches your argument. Revise your essay to make sure it is persuasive, and proofread.

GUIDE FOR READING

Theodore H. White

(1915–1986), born in Boston, Massachusetts, spent most of his life as a foreign correspondent and political writer. He is best known for his Pulitzer Prize-winning book, *The Making of the President: 1960,* a report on the 1960 presidential campaign. White's adaptation of this book as a television documentary won an Emmy award in 1964. In "The American Idea," published in *The New York Times Magazine* (July 6, 1986), White celebrates the anniversary of American independence.

The American Idea

Definition

A **definition** describes the special qualities that identify a person, a place, an object, a process, or a concept and distinguishes it from others that may be similar. Writers may use definitions to explain, to entertain, to persuade, or to instruct.

Focus

At the foot of the Statue of Liberty is Emma Lazarus's poem that ends, "Give me your tired, your poor, your huddled masses yearning to breathe free. . . ." These words have welcomed refugees and other immigrants to America for more than a century. What draws people from all over the world to America's shores? Draw an American flag in your notebook. On the stripes list reasons that people come to live in the United States. (The drawing that follows may help get you started.) Compare your list to White's ideas as you read "The American Idea."

Vocabulary

Knowing the following words will help you as you read "The American Idea."

feisty (fīst' ē) *adj.*: Spunky; touchy and quarrelsome (p. 512)

pragmatic (prag mat' ik) *adj.*: Practical (p. 512)

subversion (səb vʉr' zhən) *n.*: A systematic attempt to overthrow a government from within (p. 512)

ministration (min' is trā' shən) *n.*: The act of serving as a minister or clergyman (p. 513)

The American Idea

Theodore H. White

The idea was there at the very beginning, well before Thomas Jefferson put it into words—and the idea rang the call.

Jefferson himself could not have imagined the reach of his call across the world in time to come when he wrote:

"We hold these truths to be self-evident, that all men are created equal, that they are endowed by their Creator with certain unalienable rights,[1] that among these are life, liberty, and the pursuit of happiness."

But over the next two centuries the call would reach the potato patches of Ireland, the ghettoes of Europe, the paddyfields of China, stirring farmers to leave their lands and townsmen their trades and thus unsettling all traditional civilizations.

It is the call from Thomas Jefferson, embodied in the great statue that looks down the Narrows of New York Harbor,[2] and in the immigrants who answered the call, that we now celebrate.

Some of the first European Americans had come to the new continent to worship God in their own way, others to seek their fortunes. But, over a century-and-a-half, the new world changed those Europeans, above all the Englishmen who had come to North America. Neither King nor Court nor Church could stretch over the ocean to the wild continent. To survive, the first emigrants had to learn to govern themselves. But the freedom of the wilderness whetted their appetites for more freedoms. By the time Jefferson drafted his call, men were in the field fighting for those new-learned freedoms, killing and being killed by English soldiers, the best-trained troops in the world, supplied by the world's greatest navy. Only something worth dying for could unite American volunteers and keep them in the field—a stated cause, a flag, a nation they could call their own.

When, on the Fourth of July, 1776, the colonial leaders who had been meeting as a Continental Congress in Philadelphia voted to approve Jefferson's Declaration of Independence, it was not puffed-up rhetoric for them to pledge to each other "our lives, our fortunes and our sacred honor." Unless

---

1. unalienable (un āl' yən ə b'l) **rights**: Rights that cannot be taken away. This quote is from the beginning of the Declaration of Independence, written by Thomas Jefferson and adopted July 4, 1776, by the Second Continental Congress.
2. Narrows of New York Harbor: The strait, or narrow channel of water, that connects Upper New York Bay with Lower New York Bay.

their new "United States of America" won the war, the Congressmen would be judged traitors as relentlessly as would the irregulars-under-arms[3] in the field.

The new Americans were tough men fighting for a very tough idea. How they won their battles is a story for the schoolbooks, studied by scholars, wrapped in myths by historians and poets. But what is most important is the story of the idea that made them into a nation, the idea that had an explosive power undreamed of in 1776.

All other nations had come into being among people whose families had lived for time out of mind on the same land where they were born. Englishmen are English, Frenchmen are French, Chinese are Chinese, while their governments come and go; their national states can be torn apart and remade without losing their nationhood. But Americans are a nation born of an idea; not the place, but the idea, created the United States Government.

The story we celebrate is the story of how this idea worked itself out, how it stretched and changed and how the call for "life, liberty and the pursuit of happiness" does still, as it did in the beginning, mean different things to different people.

The debate began with the drafting of the Declaration of Independence. That task was left to Jefferson of Virginia, who spent two weeks in an upstairs room in a Philadelphia boarding house penning a draft, while John Adams and Benjamin Franklin questioned, edited, hardened its phrases. By the end of that hot and muggy June, the three had reached agreement: the Declaration contained the ringing universal theme Jefferson strove for and, at the same time, voiced American grievances toughly enough

to please the feisty Adams and the pragmatic Franklin. After brief debate, Congress passed it.

As the years wore on, the great debate expanded between Jefferson and Adams. The young nation flourished and Jefferson chose to think of America's promise as a call to all the world, its promises universal. A few weeks before he died, he wrote, "May it be to the world, what I believe it will be (to some parts sooner, to others later, but finally to all), the signal of arousing men to burst their chains." To Adams, the call meant something else—it was the call for *American* independence, the cornerstone of an *American* state.

Their argument ran through their successive Administrations. Adams, the second President, suspected the French Revolutionaries;[4] Alien and Sedition Acts[5] were passed during his term of office to protect the American state and its liberties against French subversion. But Jefferson, the third President, welcomed the French. The two men, once close friends, became archrivals. Still, as they grew old, their rivalry faded; there was glory enough to share in what they had made; in 1812, they began a correspondence that has since become classic, remembering and taking comfort in the triumphs of their youth.

Adams and Jefferson lived long lives and died on the same day—the Fourth of July, 1826, 50 years to the day from the Continental Congress's approval of the Declaration. Legend has it that Adams breathed on his death bed, "Thomas Jefferson still survives." As couriers set out from Braintree[6] carrying the news of Adams's death, couri-

---

3. irregulars-under-arms: Fighters who do not belong to a regularly established army.

4. French Revolutionaries: People who revolted against the French king from 1789 to 1799.
5. Alien and Sedition Acts: A series of laws passed by the U.S. Congress in 1798 that restricted immigration and criticism of the government.
6. Braintree: The town in Massachusetts (now called Quincy) where John Adams lived and died.

ers were riding north from Virginia with the news of Jefferson's death. The couriers met in Philadelphia. Horace Greeley,[7] then a youth in Vermont, later remembered: ". . . When we learned . . . that Thomas Jefferson and John Adams, the author and the great champion, respectively, of the Declaration, had both died on that day, and that the messengers bearing South and North, respectively, the tidings of their decease, had met in Philadelphia, under the shadow of that Hall in which our independence was declared, it seemed that a Divine attestation[8] had solemnly hallowed and sanctified the great anniversary by the impressive ministration of Death."

---

7. Horace Greeley: A famous American newspaper publisher (1811–1872).

8. attestation (a′ tes tā′ shən) n.: Testimony or evidence.

RESPONDING TO THE SELECTION

Your Response

1. What does being an American mean to you?
2. Would you like to live in another country, either temporarily or permanently? Explain your answer.

Recalling

3. What is "the American idea"?
4. Why were the people in America ready to make the idea a reality?
5. What distinction does the writer make between the American nation and other nations?
6. Why did archrivals Jefferson and Adams finally become friends again?

Interpreting

7. According to legend, John Adams said these words on his deathbed: "Thomas Jefferson still survives." What do you think John Adams meant by that?

Applying

8. Do you agree with Jefferson or with Adams about how broadly the American idea should be interpreted? Explain your answer.

READING IN THE ARTS AND SCIENCES

Understanding Definition

A **definition** describes the qualities that identify and distinguish one element from others that may be similar. Definitions may explain, entertain, persuade, or instruct. Defining an idea in an essay helps the writer clarify his or her purpose for writing. One technique for defining is using examples, such as the examples White uses in his essay.

1. What definition does Jefferson give for the American idea?
2. What definition does Adams give for the American idea?
3. Do you think the writer uses definition to explain, to entertain, to persuade, or to instruct?
4. What examples of people who responded to the American idea does the writer include?

THINKING AND WRITING

Writing a Journal Entry About History

Imagine that you are living in America on July 4, 1776, when American independence is declared. Write a journal entry describing your thoughts and feelings about this new freedom and your inalienable rights to "life, liberty, and the pursuit of happiness." How will this event affect your way of life—as a farmer, blacksmith, or statesman? Describe, too, how you celebrated this good news. Draw on what you know of American life at that time. Revise your journal entry to be as historically accurate as possible. Proofread for errors in spelling, grammar, and punctuation.

GUIDE FOR READING

Aaron Copland

(1900–1990), born in Brooklyn, New York, was one of the greatest composers of music for the symphony orchestra, ballet, stage, films, and voice. His best-known works were based on American themes. Also a teacher and a writer, Copland said, "The more I live the life of music the more I am convinced that it is the freely imaginative mind that is at the core of all vital music making and music listening." In "The Creative Process in Music," he discusses how good music is created.

The Creative Process in Music

Process Analysis

Process analysis is the examination of the steps involved in a particular operation performed to bring about a desired result. The purposes of a process analysis essay may be to give directions and to provide information. In "The Creative Process in Music" the writer examines the elements involved in composing music.

Focus

Music is an art with universal appeal. Make a diagram like the following one, which is patterned on a musical staff. On each line write a different type of music that you enjoy and why you like it. Then, as you read this essay, see whether you gain a greater appreciation for classical music.

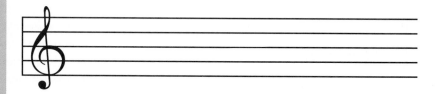

Vocabulary

Knowing the following words will help you as you read "The Creative Process in Music."

shrouded (shroud′ id) v.: Clothed or wrapped to conceal (p. 515)

perspective (pər spek′ tiv) n.: Point of view (p. 515)

dilettante (dil′ ə tänt′) n.: An amateur or dabbler in the arts (p. 515)

poignancy (poin′ yən sē) n.: The quality of being deeply affecting (p. 517)

metamorphoses (met′ ə môr′ fə sēz) n.: Changes in form, structure, or substance (p. 517)

criterion (krī tir′ ē ən) n.: A standard or rule for making a judgment (p. 517)

coherent (kō hir′ ənt) adj.: Logically connected or ordered (p. 520)

The Creative Process in Music

Aaron Copland

Most people want to know how things are made. They frankly admit, however, that they feel completely at sea when it comes to understanding how a piece of music is made. Where a composer begins, how he manages to keep going—in fact, how and where he learns his trade—all are shrouded in impenetrable darkness. The composer, in short, is a man of mystery to most people, and the composer's workshop an unapproachable ivory tower.[1]

One of the first things most people want to hear discussed in relation to composing is the question of inspiration. They find it difficult to believe that composers are not as preoccupied with that question as they had supposed. The layman[2] always finds it hard to realize how natural it is for the composer to compose. He has a tendency to put himself into the position of the composer and to visualize the problems involved, including that of inspiration, from the perspective of the layman. He forgets that composing to a composer is like fulfilling a natural function. It is like eating or sleeping. It is something that the composer happens to have been born to do; and, because of that, it loses the character of a special virtue in the composer's eyes.

The composer, therefore, confronted with the question of inspiration, does not say to himself: "Do I feel inspired?" He says to himself: "Do I feel like composing today?" And if he feels like composing, he does. It is more or less like saying to yourself: "Do I feel sleepy?" If you feel sleepy, you go to sleep. If you don't feel sleepy, you stay up. If the composer doesn't feel like composing, he doesn't compose. It's as simple as that.

Of course, after you have finished composing, you hope that everyone, including yourself, will recognize the thing you have written as having been inspired. But that is really an idea tacked on at the end.

Someone once asked me, in a public forum, whether I waited for inspiration. My answer was: "Every day!" But that does not, by any means, imply a passive waiting around for the divine afflatus.[3] That is exactly what separates the professional from the dilettante. The professional composer can sit down day after day and turn out some kind of music. On some days it will undoubt-

---

1. ivory (iʹ vər ē) **tower:** A place to which someone withdraws from daily life in order to think and create.
2. layman (lāʹ mən) *n.*: A person not belonging to or skilled in a given profession.

---

3. divine afflatus (ə flātʹ əs): Inspiration from heaven.

edly be better than on others; but the primary fact is the ability to compose. Inspiration is often only a by-product.

The second question that most people find intriguing is generally worded thus: "Do you or don't you write your music at the piano?" A current idea exists that there is something shameful about writing a piece of music at the piano. Along with that goes a mental picture of Beethoven[4] composing out in the fields. Think about it a moment and you will realize that writing away from the piano nowadays is not nearly so simple a matter as it was in Mozart[5] or Beethoven's day. For one thing, harmony[6] is so much more complex than it was then. Few composers are capable of writing down entire compositions without at least a passing reference to the piano. In fact, Stravinsky[7] in his *Autobiography* has even gone so far as to say that it is a bad thing to write music away from the piano because the composer should always be in contact with sound. That's a violent taking of the opposite side. But, in the end, the way in which a composer writes is a personal matter. The method is unimportant. It is the result that counts.

The really important question is: "What does the composer start with; where does he begin?" The answer to that is, Every composer begins with a musical idea—a *musical* idea, you understand, not a mental, literary, or extramusical idea.[8] Suddenly a theme comes to him. (Theme is used as synonymous with musical idea.) The composer starts with his theme; and the theme is a gift from Heaven. He doesn't know where it comes from—has no control over it. It comes almost like automatic writing.[9] That's why he keeps a book very often and writes themes down whenever they come. He collects musical ideas. You can't do anything about that element of composing.

The idea itself may come in various forms. It may come as a melody—just a one-line simple melody which you might hum to yourself. Or it may come to the composer as a melody with an accompaniment.[10] At times he may not even hear a melody; he may simply conceive an accompanimental figure to which a melody will probably be added later. Or, on the other hand, the theme may take the form of a purely rhythmic idea. He hears a particular kind of drumbeat, and that will be enough to start him off. Over it he will soon begin hearing an accompaniment and melody. The original conception, however, was a mere rhythm. Or, a different type of composer may possibly begin with a contrapuntal[11] web of two or three melodies which are heard at the same instant. That, however, is a less usual species of thematic inspiration.

All these are different ways in which the musical idea may present itself to the composer.

Now, the composer has the idea. He has a number of them in his book, and he examines them in more or less the way that you,

---

4. **Beethoven** (bā′ tō vən): Ludwig van (lōōt′ vig vän) Beethoven (1770–1827), a German composer whose work is known throughout the world.
5. **Mozart** (mō′ tsärt): Wolfgang Amadeus (Vôlf′ gäŋk′ ä′mä dā′ oos) Mozart (1756–1791), a famous Austrian composer.
6. **harmony** (här′ mə nē) *n.*: The study of chords in music; chords are combinations of tones sounded together.
7. **Stravinsky** (strə vin′ skē): Igor (ē′ gôr) Stravinsky (1882–1971), a United States composer and conductor who was born in Russia.
8. **extramusical idea:** An idea that is not from the field of music.

---

9. **automatic writing:** Writing a person does so quickly that he or she does not seem to know where the ideas come from.
10. **accompaniment** (ə kum′ pə ni mənt) *n.*: A part, usually instrumental, performed together with the main part for richer effect.
11. **contrapuntal** (kän′ trə pun′t ′l) *adj.*: Using one melody in contrast to or interaction with another.

the listener, would examine them if you looked at them. He wants to know what he has. He examines the musical line for its purely formal beauty. He likes to see the way it rises and falls, as if it were a drawn line instead of a musical one. He may even try to retouch it, just as you might in drawing a line, so that the rise and fall of the melodic contour might be improved.

But he also wants to know the emotional significance of his theme. If all music has expressive value, then the composer must become conscious of the expressive values of his theme. He may be unable to put it into so many words, but he feels it! He instinctively knows whether he has a gay or a sad theme, a noble or diabolic one. Sometimes he may be mystified himself as to its exact quality. But sooner or later he will probably instinctively decide what the emotional nature of his theme is, because that's the thing he is about to work with.

Always remember that a theme is, after all, only a succession of notes. Merely by changing the dynamics, that is, by playing it loudly and bravely or softly and timidly, one can transform the emotional feeling of the very same succession of notes. By a change of harmony a new poignancy may be given the theme; or by a different rhythmic treatment the same notes may result in a war dance instead of a lullaby. Every composer keeps in mind the possible metamorphoses of his succession of notes. First he tries to find its essential nature, and then he tries to find what might be done with it—how that essential nature may momentarily be changed.

As a matter of fact, the experience of most composers has been that the more complete a theme is the less possibility there is of seeing it in various aspects. If the theme itself, in its original form, is long enough and complete enough, the composer

may have difficulty in seeing it in any other way. It already exists in its definitive form. That is why great music can be written on themes that in themselves are insignificant. One might very well say that the less complete, the less important, the theme the more likely it is to be open to new connotations. Some of Bach's[12] greatest organ fugues[13] are constructed on themes that are comparatively uninteresting in themselves.

The current notion that all music is beautiful according to whether the theme is beautiful or not doesn't hold true in many cases. Certainly the composer does not judge his theme by that criterion alone.

Having looked at his thematic material, the composer must now decide what sound medium will best fit it. Is it a theme that belongs in a symphony, or does it seem more intimate in character and therefore better fitted for a string quartet? Is it a lyrical theme that would be used to best advantage in a song; or had it better be saved, because of its dramatic quality, for operatic treatment? A composer sometimes has a work half finished before he understands the medium for which it is best fitted.

Thus far I have been presupposing[14] an abstract[15] composer before an abstract theme. But actually I can see three different types of composers in musical history, each of whom conceives music in a somewhat different fashion.

The type that has fired public imagina-

---

12. Bach (bäkⱨ): Johann Sebastian (yō′hän si bas′ cⱨən) Bach (1685–1750), a famous German composer.
13. fugues (fyo͞ogs) *n.*: Musical compositions designed for a definite number of instruments or voices in which a theme is presented in one voice and then developed contrapuntally by each of the other voices.
14. presupposing (prē′ sə pōz′ iŋ) *v.*: Assuming beforehand.
15. abstract (ab strakt′) *adj.*: Apart from any particular example; theoretical.

tion most is that of the spontaneously inspired composer—the Franz Schubert[16] type, in other words. All composers are inspired of course, but this type is more spontaneously inspired. Music simply wells out of him. He can't get it down on paper fast enough. You can almost always tell this type of composer by his prolific output. In certain months, Schubert wrote a song a day. Hugo Wolf[17] did the same.

In a sense, men of this kind begin not so much with a musical theme as with a completed composition. They invariably work best in the shorter forms. It is much easier to improvise a song than it is to improvise a symphony. It isn't easy to be inspired in that spontaneous way for long periods at a stretch. Even Schubert was more successful in handling the shorter forms of music. The spontaneously inspired man is only one type of composer, with his own limitations.

Beethoven symbolizes the second type —the constructive type, one might call it. This type exemplifies my theory of the creative process in music better than any other, because in this case the composer really does begin with a musical theme. In Beethoven's case there is no doubt about it, for we have the notebooks in which he put the themes down. We can see from his notebooks how he worked over his themes —how he would not let them be until they were as perfect as he could make them. Beethoven was not a spontaneously inspired composer in the Schubert sense at all. He was the type that begins with a theme; makes it a germinal[18] idea; and upon that constructs a musical work, day after day, in painstaking fashion. Most compos-

ers since Beethoven's day belong to this second type.

The third type of creator I can only call, for lack of a better name, the traditionalist type. Men like Palestrina[19] and Bach belong in this category. They both exemplify the kind of composer who is born in a particular period of musical history, when a certain musical style is about to reach its fullest development. It is a question at such a time of creating music in a well-known and accepted style and doing it in a way that is better than anyone has done it before you.

Beethoven and Schubert started from a different premise. They both had serious pretensions[20] to originality! After all, Schubert practically created the song form singlehanded; and the whole face of music changed after Beethoven lived. But Bach and Palestrina simply improved on what had gone before them.

The traditionalist type of composer begins with a pattern rather than with a theme. The creative act with Palestrina is not the thematic conception so much as the personal treatment of a well-established pattern. And even Bach, who conceived forty-eight of the most varied and inspired themes in his *Well Tempered Clavichord*, knew in advance the general formal mold that they were to fill. It goes without saying that we are not living in a traditionalist period nowadays.

One might add, for the sake of completeness, a fourth type of composer—the pioneer type: men like Gesualdo[21] in the seventeenth century, Moussorgsky[22] and Berlioz[23]

---

16. Franz Schubert (sh͞oo′ bərt): A famous Austrian composer (1797–1828).
17. Hugo Wolf: A famous Austrian composer (1860–1903).
18. germinal (jʉr′ mə n'l) *adj.*: Serving as a basis for further development.

19. Palestrina (pä′ les trē′ nä): Giovanni (jô vän′ ē) Palestrina (1525?–1594), a famous Italian composer.
20. pretensions (pri ten′ shəns) *n.*: Claims.
21. Gesualdo (jā swal′ dō): Carlo Gesualdo (1560–1613), an Italian composer.
22. Moussorgsky (mus org′ skē): Modeste (mō des′ tə) Moussorgsky (1839–1881), a Russian composer.
23. Berlioz (ber lyōz′): Louis Hector Berlioz (1803–1869), a famous French composer.

BEETHOVEN'S STERBEZIMMER IM SCHWARZPANIERHAUS, 1827
Johann Nepomuk Hoechle
Historisches Museum der Stadt Wien

in the nineteenth, Debussy[24] and Edgar Varèse[25] in the twentieth. It is difficult to summarize the composing methods of so variegated a group. One can safely say that their approach to composition is the opposite of the traditionalist type. They clearly oppose conventional solutions of musical problems. In many ways, their attitude is experimental—they seek to add new harmonies, new sonorities,[26] new formal principles. The pioneer type was the characteristic one at the turn of the seventeenth century and also at the beginning of the twentieth century, but it is much less evident today.

But let's return to our theoretical composer. We have him with his idea—his musical idea—with some conception of its expressive nature, with a sense of what can be done with it, and with a preconceived notion of what medium is best fitted for it. Still he hasn't a piece. A musical idea is not the same as a piece of music. It only induces a piece of music. The composer knows very well that something else is needed in order to create the finished composition.

He tries, first of all, to find other ideas

---

24. Debussy (də bū sē'): Claude Debussy (1862–1918), a famous French composer.
25. Edgar Varèse (va rez'): A French composer (1883–1965).
26. sonorities (sə nôr' ə tēz) *n.*: Qualities of sound.

that seem to go with the original one. They may be ideas of a similar character, or they may be contrasting ones. These additional ideas will probably not be so important as the one that came first—usually they play a subsidiary role. Yet they definitely seem necessary in order to complete the first one. Still that's not enough! Some way must be found for getting from one idea to the next, and it is generally achieved through use of so-called bridge material.

There are also two other important ways in which the composer can add to his original material. One is the elongation process.[27] Often the composer finds that a particular theme needs elongating so that its character may be more clearly defined. Wagner[28] was a master at elongation. I referred to the other way when I visualized the composer's examining the possible metamorphoses of his theme. That is the much written-about development of his material, which is a very important part of his job.

All these things are necessary for the creation of a full-sized piece—the germinal idea, the addition of other lesser ideas, the elongation of the ideas, the bridge material for the connection of the ideas, and their full development.

Now comes the most difficult task of all—the welding together of all that material so that it makes a coherent whole. In the finished product, everything must be in its place. The listener must be able to find his way around in the piece. There should be no possible chance of his confusing the principal theme with the bridge material, or vice versa. The composition must have a beginning, a middle, and an end; and it is up to the composer to see to it that the listener always has some sense of where he is in relation to beginning, middle, and end. Moreover, the whole thing should be managed artfully so that none can say where the soldering[29] began—where the composer's spontaneous invention left off and the hard work began.

Of course, I do not mean to suggest that in putting his materials together the composer necessarily begins from scratch. On the contrary, every well-trained composer, has, as his stock in trade, certain formal structural molds on which to lean for the basic framework of his compositions. These formal molds I speak of have all been gradually evolved over hundreds of years as the combined efforts of numberless composers seeking a way to ensure the coherence of their compositions.

But whatever the form the composer chooses to adopt, there is always one great desideratum:[30] The form must have what in my student days we used to call "the long line." It is difficult adequately to explain the meaning of that phrase to the layman. To be properly understood in relation to a piece of music, it must be felt. In mere words, it simply means that every good piece of music must give us a sense of flow—a sense of continuity from first note to last. Every elementary music student knows the principle, but to put it into practice has challenged the greatest minds in music! A great symphony is a man-made Mississippi down which we irresistibly flow from the instant of our leave-taking to a long foreseen destination. Music must always flow, for that is part of its very essence, but the creation of that continuity and flow—that long line—constitutes the be-all and end-all of every composer's existence.

---

27. elongation (i lôŋ′ gā′ sʰən) **process**: The method by which the material is extended or lengthened.
28. Wagner (väg′ nər): Richard Wagner (1813—1883), a German composer.

29. soldering (säd′ ər iŋ) *n.*: Piecing together; uniting.
30. desideratum (di sid′ ə rät′ əm) *n.*: Something needed or wanted.

RESPONDING TO THE SELECTION

Your Response

1. Early in his essay, Copland says that most people "feel completely at sea when it comes to understanding how a piece of music is made." Are you a person who feels that way? Explain.

Recalling

2. How does the writer respond to the question people ask about inspiration?
3. How does the writer respond to the question people ask about composing at the piano?
4. Which four types of composers does the writer describe? Give an example of each one.

Interpreting

5. Why do you think the writer gives such a detailed account of the creative process of composing?
6. What does the writer's care in explaining the creative process tell you about him?

Applying

7. How does the creative process of composing music compare with or contrast to your own process of writing a composition? Name at least two similarities and two differences.

READING IN THE ARTS AND SCIENCES

Understanding Process Analysis

Process analysis, the examination of the steps involved in a particular operation performed to bring about a desired result, is used in "The Creative Process in Music" to examine the elements involved in composing music.

1. In what form do ideas enter the composer's mind?
2. What three things does a composer think about before developing a musical idea?
3. What are four ways in which a composer may develop a musical idea into a full composition?
4. Which is the most difficult part of the process?

5. What advice does the writer give for assessing the results of the process?

CRITICAL THINKING AND READING

Finding Supporting Details

The **main idea** of each paragraph is its most important point. The main idea may be stated directly or it may be implied. A writer includes **supporting details** that back up the main idea.

In "The Creative Process in Music," for example, the main idea could be stated as follows: *A composer creates a piece of fully developed music by using a particular creative process.* The writer develops this main point through the use of specific details, such as descriptions of the distinct parts of the music-making process.

Which of the following details support the main idea of the essay? Give reasons for your choices.

1. "Of course, after you have finished composing, you hope that everyone, including yourself, will recognize the thing you have written as having been inspired."
2. "Every composer begins with a musical idea."
3. "Having looked at his thematic material, the composer must now decide what sound medium will best fit it."

THINKING AND WRITING

Writing an Essay About Music

Choose a musical experience—whether that of a listener, a performer, or a musical composer—and write an essay explaining this process to students your age. First, list the steps involved, in the order in which they occur in the process. Then use this information to write your essay, describing each step. Revise your essay to include an example, such as an anecdote or a comparison. Proofread for errors in spelling, grammar, and punctuation.

GUIDE FOR READING

Ann Beattie

(1947–) writes novels and short stories concerned with young people who came of age in the 1960's and who became disillusioned in the following years. Her writing—particularly her description of people and objects—is characterized by attention to detail. This aspect of Beattie's writing suggests a reason for her interest in the painter Alex Katz, whose work invites you to look at a commonplace object "in its own right, instead of the way we usually look at it."

Alex Katz's *The Table*

Critical Writing

Critical writing is that concerned with judgments and evaluations of books, plays, movies, paintings, and other works of art. Critical writing usually describes a particular work of art and gives an opinion about it and reasons to support that opinion. An example of critical writing is a review of a ballet or a concert. In "Alex Katz's *The Table*," the writer evaluates a painting by Alex Katz.

Focus

Look ahead at the reproduction of Alex Katz's painting *The Table,* on page 524. Write a journal entry in response to the painting. In your journal describe the thoughts and feelings you have as you study the painting. Also include any questions you have about it and any possible answers to these questions. Keep your writing in mind as you read Beattie's essay.

Vocabulary

Knowing the meaning of the following words will help you as you read "Alex Katz's *The Table*."

perplexing (pər pleks′ iŋ) *adj.*: Puzzling; difficult to understand (p. 523)

conventional (kən ven′ shən 'l) *adj.*: Of the usual kind; customary (p. 523)

particularization (pər tik′ yə lər iz ā′ shən) *n.*: Presentation in minute detail (p. 523)

utilitarian (yo͞o til′ ə ter′ ē ən) *adj.*: Meant to be useful (p. 523)

provocativeness (prə väk′ ə tiv nis) *n.*: Stimulation; incitement (p. 523)

repository (ri päz′ ə tôr′ ē) *n.*: A place where things are stored and saved (p. 523)

inherently (in hir′ ənt lē) *adv.*: Basically; by its very nature (p. 523)

Alex Katz's *The Table*

Ann Beattie

Although Alex Katz is most often associated with painting people, he has painted everything from the branch of a tree to a picnic table. While it is difficult to say that the picnic table seen here is remarkable in and of itself, it is nevertheless a perplexing painting. If the painter can make us stare at it—if the table seems large and obvious and conventional but we are still drawn to it—we may have been given a clue about Katz's vision as well as a lesson in how to look and why.

As such, a picnic table is not very detailed. Detail is usually included so that something becomes more believable or unique in a way we may not have expected. Yet we would be foolish to look for particularization of a humble picnic table; we do not have the interest in detail the way we do when, say, we look at a bowl of fruit painted by Bonnard.[1] This is just a picnic table—yet what associations we all have with it: it is a symbol of summer and all that the season connotes; it is a timeless thing, something that will not likely be refined, improved and recycled into something *au courant*.[2] Its

form is a composite of horizontals, an assemblage that is a little more complex when seen at this angle than straight on, an object that is revealed to us as potentially less simple than we probably first thought. It is a nice painting. Easy to look at. The table is composed of dark and light, a representation of what a picnic table *essentially* looks like, rather than a very defined, scarred, splintery table affected by the elements. We associate this table with its utilitarian function, but since we do not see it functioning that way, it becomes mysterious, the way an empty movie house seems strange. What about this *thing,* this thing in its own right, instead of the way we usually think of it, defined by function? It forces us to admit that we rely on context—that context is linked in our minds with function—and that there is a provocativeness akin to nakedness when we must look at something in isolation. The table becomes a repository for our imaginings, a thing inherently useful, simple, and neutral. It is recognizable, though we may not have taken the time to stop and study it before. It also functions symbolically, and since we know what it represents, nothing needs to be done to interpret it. But we cannot be fooled into thinking that because it is inconspicuous, it is not important. At the very least, we are

---

1. Bonnard (bô när´): Pierre Bonnard (1864–1947), a French impressionist painter.
2. *au courant* (ō kōō rän´): French for "up-to-date."

THE TABLE
Alex Katz
Courtesy of Marlborough Gallery

told something about the artist's sensibility. This painting tells us what he finds worth presenting; that simple things have inherent beauty, even if it is a taken-for-granted beauty; and it suggests that things have an inherent quality. Though the table does not confound us or awaken us to some complexity we would never have imagined, having it presented this way still puzzles and attracts us. The picnic table is, if not of our dreams, of the painter's dreams, because his world is a dream, told to him and to us through symbols. This painting is a dream of color, of form, of the way light falls on the world. It also has enough openness, enough emptiness that is merely tinged with specificity that we at once believe in it, yet don't see it as so particular that we can only relate to it in some predetermined way. Given a symbol and a context, we may project a life upon it.

RESPONDING TO THE SELECTION

Your Response

1. Respond to the author's comment that "simple things have inherent beauty, even if it is a taken-for-granted beauty. . . ."

Recalling

2. What kind of table is depicted in the painting?
3. What kind of subject is Alex Katz best known for—landscapes, people, or objects?
4. How, according to the writer, does the painter make the table become mysterious and interesting in its own right?

Interpreting

5. What does the writer mean by saying the table is "a symbol of summer and all that the season connotes"?

Applying

6. Familiar objects or places may seem strange when viewed apart from their usual function. Think of an object or place that has seemed strange or mysterious to you because you suddenly saw it in a new way.

READING IN THE ARTS AND SCIENCES

Understanding Critical Writing

Critical writing makes a direct or an implied judgment of a work of art. Good critical writing helps you to perceive features of the work that you might fail to notice, and to form insights about the meaning of the work.

1. What is the writer's judgment about the painting *The Table*?
2. How does the essay enhance your first impression and appreciation of the painting?

CRITICAL THINKING AND READING

Making a Judgment About a Work of Art

Critical writing makes a judgment about a work of art. It also helps you to make your own judgment about it. In *The Table* the writer comments on details of the work and the artist's craft that support her view of the artist's achievement. For instance, she says that *The Table* does not invite the viewer to take an interest in minute detail, as does a still-life painting by Pierre Bonnard, whose attention to detail was remarkable. If you agree with the writer's comments, you are likely to share her overall estimate of the work. If you disagree with one or more of her observations, you may disagree with her overall judgment.

Reread the essay and answer the following questions.

1. Find two specific statements about the painting or the artist's craft that support the writer's view of the work, and summarize each statement.
2. Write a short statement expressing your own judgment of *The Table*.

THINKING AND WRITING

Writing About Art

Think of a painting or a photograph that you particularly like. First, jot down some features of the work that you consider noteworthy. Then use this information to write a critical paragraph about the picture that will help other students who are unfamiliar with it to share your appreciation. Revise the paragraph to be persuasive. Proofread for errors in spelling, grammar, and punctuation.

LEARNING OPTION

Art. Think of other objects that could be described "as potentially less simple than we probably first thought," as Beattie describes what is represented in *The Table*. Draw one of the objects that come to mind. Ask several classmates what associations they make with your drawing. What does the drawing symbolize to them? What do they think it symbolizes for you? Then respond to their drawings as well.

GUIDE FOR READING

The Marginal World

Observation and Inference

Observation is the act of carefully noting facts and events. Observation focuses on what you see, rather than on what you think or feel. More precise and systematic than the way you usually look at people and events, observation is often used by scientists in research.

Inference is a reasonable conclusion that you can draw based on evidence. Often you can make inferences based on factual information you have observed. In "The Marginal World," the writer's descriptions of sea life show her skill as an observer and allow her to make some inferences.

Focus

In this essay the author writes about the edge of the sea, a "marginal world." Think about areas you know that are on the edge or margin—for example, a traffic island or road divider. Write a brief description of this marginal, possibly ignored, place that will make people see it in a new way. Then see how Carson describes her marginal world.

Vocabulary

Knowing the following words will help you as you read "The Marginal World."

marginal (mär′ jən 'l) *adj*.: Occupying the borderland of a stable area (p. 527)

mutable (myo͞ot′ ə b'l) *adj*.: Capable of change (p. 527)

ephemeral (i fem′ ə rəl) *adj*.: Passing quickly (p. 529)

primeval (prī mē′ vəl) *adj*.: Ancient or primitive (p. 530)

essence (es′ 'ns) *n*.: Real nature of something (p. 530)

subjectively (səb jek′ tiv lē) *adv*.: Personally (p. 532)

manifestations (man′ ə fes tā′ shənz) *n*.: Appearances or evidence (p. 532)

cosmic (käz′ mik) *adj*.: Relating to the universe (p. 532)

Rachel Carson

(1907–1964), born in Springfield, Pennsylvania, was a naturalist who specialized in marine biology—the study of sea life. Carson spent several summers during college at the Marine Biological Laboratory in Woods Hole, Massachusetts. She later observed, "I am sure that the genesis of *The Sea Around Us* belongs to that first year at Woods Hole, when I began storing away facts about the sea—facts discovered in scientific literature or by personal observation and experience . . ."

The Marginal World

Rachel Carson

The edge of the sea is a strange and beautiful place. All through the long history of Earth it has been an area of unrest where waves have broken heavily against the land, where the tides have pressed forward over the continents, receded, and then returned. For no two successive days is the shoreline precisely the same. Not only do the tides advance and retreat in their eternal rhythms, but the level of the sea itself is never at rest. It rises or falls as the glaciers melt or grow, as the floor of the deep ocean basins shifts under its increasing load of sediments, or as the earth's crust along the continental margins warps up or down in adjustment to strain and tension. Today a little more land may belong to the sea, tomorrow a little less. Always the edge of the sea remains an elusive and indefinable boundary.

The shore has a dual nature, changing with the swing of the tides, belonging now to the land, now to the sea. On the ebb tide it knows the harsh extremes of the land world, being exposed to heat and cold, to wind, to rain and drying sun. On the flood tide it is a water world, returning briefly to the relative stability of the open sea.

Only the most hardy and adaptable can survive in a region so mutable, yet the area between the tide lines is crowded with plants and animals. In this difficult world of the shore, life displays its enormous toughness and vitality by occupying almost every conceivable niche. Visibly, it carpets the intertidal rocks; or half hidden, it descends into fissures and crevices, or hides under boulders, or lurks in the wet gloom of sea caves. Invisibly, where the casual observer would say there is no life, it lies deep in the sand, in burrows and tubes and passageways. It tunnels into solid rock and bores into peat and clay. It encrusts weeds or drifting spars[1] or the hard, chitinous[2] shell

---

1. spars (spärs) *n.*: Masts, booms, or other supports for sails.
2. chitinous (ki′ tən əs) *adj.*: Of a material which forms the tough outer covering of insects, crustaceans, and so on.

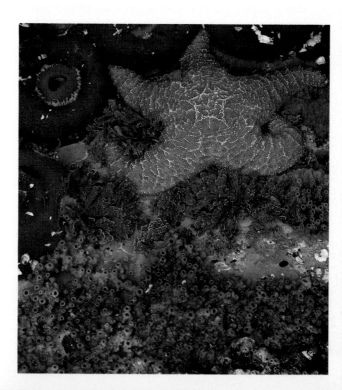

of a lobster. It exists minutely, as the film of bacteria that spreads over a rock surface or a wharf piling; as spheres of protozoa, small as pinpricks, sparkling at the surface of the sea; and as Lilliputian[3] beings swimming through dark pools that lie between the grains of sand.

The shore is an ancient world, for as long as there has been an earth and sea there has been this place of the meeting of land and water. Yet it is a world that keeps alive the sense of continuing creation and of the relentless drive of life. Each time that I enter it, I gain some new awareness of its beauty and its deeper meanings, sensing that intricate fabric of life by which one creature is linked with another, and each with its surroundings.

In my thoughts of the shore, one place stands apart for its revelation of exquisite beauty. It is a pool hidden within a cave that one can visit only rarely and briefly when the lowest of the year's low tides fall below it, and perhaps from that very fact it acquires some of its special beauty. Choosing such a tide, I hoped for a glimpse of the pool. The ebb was to fall early in the morning. I knew that if the wind held from the northwest and no interfering swell ran in from a distant storm the level of the sea should drop below the entrance to the pool. There had been sudden ominous showers in the night, with rain like handfuls of gravel flung on the roof. When I looked out into the early morning the sky was full of a gray dawn light but the sun had not yet risen. Water and air were pallid. Across the bay the moon was a luminous disc in the western sky, suspended above the dim line of distant shore—the full August moon, drawing the tide to the low, low levels of the threshold of the alien sea world. As I watched, a gull flew by, above the spruces. Its breast was rosy with the light of the unrisen sun. The day was, after all, to be fair.

Later, as I stood above the tide near the entrance to the pool, the promise of that rosy light was sustained. From the base of the steep wall of rock on which I stood, a moss-covered ledge jutted seaward into deep water. In the surge at the rim of the ledge the dark fronds[4] of oarweeds swayed, smooth and gleaming as leather. The projecting ledge was the path to the small hidden cave and its pool. Occasionally a swell, stronger than the rest, rolled smoothly over the rim and broke in foam against the cliff. But the intervals between such swells were long enough to admit me to the ledge and long enough for a glimpse of that fairy pool, so seldom and so briefly exposed.

And so I knelt on the wet carpet of sea moss and looked back into the dark cavern that held the pool in a shallow basin. The floor of the cave was only a few inches below the roof, and a mirror had been created in which all that grew on the ceiling was reflected in the still water below.

Under water that was clear as glass the pool was carpeted with green sponge. Gray patches of sea squirts[5] glistened on the ceiling and colonies of soft coral[6] were a pale apricot color. In the moment when I looked into the cave a little elfin starfish hung down, suspended by the merest thread, perhaps by only a single tube foot. It reached down to touch its own reflection, so perfectly delineated that there might have been, not

---

3. Lilliputian (lil′ə pyoo′ shən) *adj.:* Tiny and thus like the tiny people about six inches tall who inhabit Lilliput in the book *Gulliver's Travels* by Jonathan Swift.

4. fronds (frändz) *n.:* Leaves.
5. sea squirts: Sac-shaped water animals with tough outer coverings.
6. coral (kôr′əl) *n.:* Animals with tentacles at the top of tubelike bodies.

one starfish, but two. The beauty of the reflected images and of the limpid[7] pool itself was the poignant[8] beauty of things that are ephemeral, existing only until the sea should return to fill the little cave.

Whenever I go down into this magical zone of the low water of the spring tides, I look for the most delicately beautiful of all the shore's inhabitants—flowers that are not plant but animal, blooming on the threshold of the deeper sea. In that fairy cave I was not disappointed. Hanging from its roof were the pendent[9] flowers of the hydroid Tubularia, pale pink, fringed and delicate as the wind flower. Here were creatures so exquisitely fashioned that they seemed unreal, their beauty too fragile to exist in a world of crushing force. Yet every detail was functionally useful, every stalk and hydranth[10] and petallike tentacle fashioned for dealing with the realities of existence. I knew that they were merely waiting, in that moment of the tide's ebbing, for the return of the sea. Then in the rush of water, in the surge of surf and the pressure of the incoming tide, the delicate flower heads would stir with life. They would sway on their slender stalks, and their long tentacles would sweep the returning water, finding in it all that they needed for life.

And so in that enchanted place on the threshold of the sea the realities that possessed my mind were far from those of the land world I had left an hour before. In a different way the same sense of remoteness and of a world apart came to me in a twilight hour on a great beach on the coast of Georgia. I had come down after sunset and walked far out over sands that lay wet and gleaming, to the very edge of the retreating sea. Looking back across that immense flat, crossed by winding, waterfilled gullies and here and there holding shallow pools left by the tide, I was filled with awareness that this intertidal area, although abandoned briefly and rhythmically by the sea, is always reclaimed by the rising tide. There at the edge of low water the beach with its reminders of the land seemed far away. The only sounds were those of the wind and the sea and the birds. There was one sound of wind moving over water, and another of water sliding over the sand and tumbling down the faces of its own wave forms. The flats were astir with birds, and the voice of the willet[11] rang insistently. One of them stood at the edge of the water and gave its loud, urgent cry; an answer came from far up the beach and the two birds flew to join each other.

The flats took on a mysterious quality as dusk approached and the last evening light was reflected from the scattered pools and creeks. Then birds became only dark shadows, with no color discernible. Sanderlings[12] scurried across the beach like little ghosts, and here and there the darker forms of the willets stood out. Often I could come very close to them before they would start up in alarm—the sanderlings running, the willets flying up, crying. Black skimmers[13] flew along the ocean's edge silhouetted against the dull, metallic gleam, or they went flitting above the sand like large, dimly seen moths. Sometimes they "skimmed" the winding creeks of tidal water, where little spreading surface ripples marked the presence of small fish.

The shore at night is a different world, in

---

7. limpid (lim′ pid) *adj.*: Clear.
8. poignant (poin′ yənt) *adj.*: Emotionally moving.
9. pendent (pen′ dənt) *adj.*: Hanging.
10. hydranth (hī′ dranth) *n.*: Feeding individual.

11. willet (wil′ it) *n.*: Large, gray and white, long-legged wading bird.
12. sanderlings: Small, gray and white birds found on sandy beaches.
13. skimmers: Long-winged sea birds.

which the very darkness that hides the distractions of daylight brings into sharper focus the elemental realities. Once, exploring the night beach, I surprised a small ghost crab in the searching beam of my torch. He was lying in a pit he had dug just above the surf, as though watching the sea and waiting. The blackness of the night possessed water, air, and beach. It was the darkness of an older world, before Man. There was no sound but the all-enveloping, primeval sounds of wind blowing over water and sand, and of waves crashing on the beach. There was no other visible life—just one small crab near the sea. I have seen hundreds of ghost crabs in other settings, but suddenly I was filled with the odd sensation that for the first time I knew the creature in its own world—that I understood, as never before, the essence of its being. In that moment time was suspended; the world to which I belonged did not exist and I might have been an onlooker from outer space. The little crab alone with the sea became a symbol that stood for life itself—for the delicate, destructible, yet incredibly vital force that somehow holds its place amid the harsh realities of the inorganic world.

The sense of creation comes with memories of a southern coast, where the sea and the mangroves,[14] working together, are building a wilderness of thousands of small islands off the southwestern coast of Florida, separated from each other by a tortuous[15] pattern of bays, lagoons, and narrow waterways, I remember a winter day when the sky was blue and drenched with sunlight; though there was no wind one was conscious of flowing air like cold clear crystal. I had landed on the surf-washed tip of one of those islands, and then worked my way around to the sheltered bay side. There I found the tide far out, exposing the broad mud flat of a cove bordered by the mangroves with their twisted branches, their glossy leaves, and their long prop roots reaching down, grasping and holding the mud, building the land out a little more, then again a little more.

The mud flats were strewn with the shells of that small, exquisitely colored mollusk,[16] the rose tellin, looking like scattered

16. mollusk (mäl′ əsk) *n.*: One of a large group of soft-bodied animals with shells that include clams, oysters, mussels, snails, and so on.

---

14. mangroves (maŋ′ grōvs) *n.*: Tropical trees that grow in swampy ground with spreading branches that send down roots and thus form more trunks.
15. tortuous (tôr′ choo wəs) *adj.*: Full of twists and turns.

petals of pink roses. There must have been a colony nearby, living buried just under the surface of the mud. At first the only creature visible was a small heron[17] in gray and rusty plumage—a reddish egret that waded across the flat with the stealthy, hesitant movements of its kind. But other land creatures had been there, for a line of fresh tracks wound in and out among the mangrove roots, marking the path of a raccoon feeding on the oysters that gripped the supporting roots with projections from their shells. Soon I found the tracks of a shore bird, probably a sanderling, and followed

---

17. heron (her′ ən) *n.*: A wading bird with long legs and a long, tapered bill.

them a little; then they turned toward the water and were lost, for the tide had erased them and made them as though they had never been.

Looking out over the cove I felt a strong sense of the interchangeability of land and sea in this marginal world of the shore, and of the links between the life of the two. There was also an awareness of the past and of the continuing flow of time, obliterating much that had gone before, as the sea had that morning washed away the tracks of the bird.

The sequence and meaning of the drift of time were quietly summarized in the existence of hundreds of small snails—the mangrove periwinkles—browsing on the branches and roots of the trees. Once their ancestors had been sea dwellers, bound to the salt waters by every tie of their life processes. Little by little over the thousands and millions of years the ties had been broken, the snails had adjusted themselves to life out of water, and now today they were living many feet above the tide to which they only occasionally returned. And perhaps, who could say how many ages hence, there would be in their descendants not even this gesture of remembrance for the sea.

The spiral shells of other snails—these quite minute[18]—left winding tracks on the mud as they moved about in search of food. They were horn shells, and when I saw them I had a nostalgic moment when I wished I might see what Audubon[19] saw, a century and more ago. For such little horn shells were the food of the flamingo, once so numerous on this coast, and when I half closed my eyes I could almost imagine a flock of

---

18. minute (mī nōōt′) *adj.*: Tiny.
19. Audubon (ôd′ə bän′): John James Audubon (1785–1851), a famous ornithologist, naturalist, and painter, famed for his paintings of North American birds.

these magnificent flame birds feeding in that cove, filling it with their color. It was a mere yesterday in the life of the earth that they were there; in nature, time and space are relative matters, perhaps most truly perceived subjectively in occasional flashes of insight, sparked by such a magical hour and place.

There is a common thread that links these scenes and memories—the spectacle of life in all its varied manifestations as it has appeared, evolved, and sometimes died out. Underlying the beauty of the spectacle there is meaning and significance. It is the elusiveness of that meaning that haunts us, that sends us again and again into the natural world where the key to the riddle is hidden. It sends us back to the edge of the sea, where the drama of life played its first scene on earth and perhaps even its prelude;[20] where the forces of evolution are at work today, as they have been since the appearance of what we know as life; and where the spectacle of living creatures faced by the cosmic realities of their world is crystal clear.

_____

20. prelude (prel′ yo͞od) *n.*: Introduction.

RESPONDING TO THE SELECTION

Your Response

1. Carson describes how the "elusiveness of meaning" in nature haunts us. What natural objects or aspects of nature intrigue you? What sends you into the natural world in pursuit of the "elusive meaning"?

Recalling

2. In "The Marginal World," what time and special place does the writer describe first?
3. Why is this place rare and remote?
4. What special beauty does the writer find in this first place?
5. What second time, place, and experience does the writer describe?
6. What is the third time, place, and discovery the writer describes?

Interpreting

7. What broader meaning about life does this marginal world help you see?
8. Think of another title for this essay—one that states the meaning of the essay for you.

Applying

9. What other places could help you experience the interconnectedness of life?

READING IN THE ARTS AND SCIENCES

Observing and Making Inferences

Observation, the act of carefully reporting facts and events, focuses on what you see, rather than on what you think or feel. **Inference,** a reasonable conclusion that you can draw based on evidence, often can be made based on factual information you have observed. For example, a journalist may report on the events he or she observes in a foreign country's government, while a political analyst can make inferences based on these observations.

1. The writer makes observations about the sky when she visits the pool hidden within a cave at low tide. What inference does she make about the day?

2. The writer makes observations about the hundreds of snails browsing in trees. What inferences does she make about the snails?

CRITICAL THINKING AND READING

Recognizing Cause and Effect

Cause-and-effect relationships describe the connection between a cause, or reason, and its effects, or results. A cause makes something occur; an effect is the outcome of the cause.

1. What causes the following events?
   a. The shore is littered with mollusks and other shells.
   b. The level of the sea itself changes.
2. What are the effects of the following events?
   a. The snails move about in search of food.
   b. A flood tide comes in.

THINKING AND WRITING

Writing About Science

Choose one element of the marginal world of the seashore, such as the ebb tide, an animal, or a plant that lives in the intertidal world. First, list any scientific observation about this element that you can think of. Then use this information to write a vivid description of your subject that is both scientifically accurate and personally expressive. Revise your description to be a first-person observation of your subject in its natural world.

LEARNING OPTION

Art. In her essay Carson describes "that enchanted place on the threshold of the sea . . ." Find pictures in magazines or on postcards that capture the exquisite beauty that Carson describes. You might also have photographs of your own that capture the magical or mysterious quality of the shore. Tape down the pictures you find to create a montage. Use a quotation from "The Marginal World" as a caption for each picture. Display your montage for your class.

READING AND RESPONDING

Nonfiction

Nonfiction deals with actual people, places, things, and events. The nonfiction writer usually keeps several things in mind while writing: an idea to present (the topic), a purpose for presenting the idea, and an audience. To appreciate nonfiction fully, you should respond to the elements of nonfiction and the writer's techniques.

RESPONDING TO PURPOSE The purpose is the reason for writing. A writer usually has both a general purpose and a specific purpose. The general purpose may be to explain or inform, to describe, to persuade, or to entertain. The specific purpose may be to change the reader's thinking about the topic in some way. It may be to explain the effect of an incident on the writer's life, or it may be to make the reader understand and marvel at an event in nature. Your response to the writer's purpose will affect your understanding of the work.

RESPONDING TO IDEAS AND SUPPORT The main ideas are the most important points the writer wants to make. Main ideas can be facts or opinions. Support is the information the writer uses to develop, back up, or illustrate ideas. What do you think of the writer's ideas? Are they fully developed or illustrated? How do they relate to your own experience?

RESPONDING TO ORGANIZATION The writer organizes ideas and supporting details to accomplish his or her purpose and move the reader's thinking in the intended direction. The information may be arranged in chronological order, spatial order, order of importance, or any other order that best makes the ideas clear to the reader. How does the order help you grasp the writer's ideas?

RESPONDING TO TECHNIQUES Writers may use a variety of techniques to accomplish their purpose. They may use description, argumentation, comparison and contrast, or emotional language. They may also include anecdotes or quotations, or they may use an unexpected sentence structure to create an effect. How do the author's techniques affect your response?

On pages 535–538, you will see how Kristen Sweeney of Carmel High School in Carmel, Indiana, actively read and responded to "Glove's Labor Lost." The notes in the side column include Kristen's thoughts and comments while she read. Your thoughts and comments may be different.

MODEL

Glove's Labor Lost

Thomas Boswell

Each spring, when the ground loses its threadbare look, I wonder if I should buy a baseball glove. It is a quick, fleeting thought, "And what would you do with it?" I ask myself, and that is that.

For so many years the five-finger, Warren Spahn 300[1] with the trapper's web came up out of the wintry basement with a string tied around it and an old ball clamped inside the pocket. Pulling that string was a truer sign of spring than any robin.

My first glove, a parental gift at age eight, is now only a blurry memory, less vivid than the cowboy guns and garbage cans that I cherished at an earlier period. It was a very dark infielder model and it lived a hard life.

It was once soaked in linseed oil, because in the first stages of my growing addiction I confused linseed with neat's-foot oil, the proper glove preservative.

My rather academic parents thought linseed sounded foolish enough to be correct, so into the oil bath went the new glove. The linseeded glove quickly dried up, cracked like a stoned windshield, and literally flaked away.

During its years of disintegration, I laid plans for a real glove, one that would last a millennium, or at least until high school.

While the first glove was just another toy to be misused, the second, bought with money I saved for over a year, fell somewhere between the last toy and the first personal possession.

Once the money was saved, the shopping began. It took almost as long as the saving. For weeks I was late coming

---

1. Warren Spahn 300: A baseball mitt named for Warren Spahn, who won 363 games in his twenty-one years as a pitcher.

Purpose: *What does the title mean? Is the essay about a glove? What does "labor lost" mean?*

Purpose: *Specific seasons can bring back many childhood memories. Maybe this essay is about a childhood memory of spring.*

Ideas and Support: *The narrator remembers specific details about his old glove. He must have cherished it.*

Ideas and Support: *By "growing addiction," the narrator must mean that he became very attached to his glove.*

Technique: *The writer's use of this detail helps me relate to the essay. He and I have something in common— I saved thirteen paychecks to buy a CD player.*

home from school since, after getting off my bus downtown, I would be buffeted by the price tags, models, and signatures available at Irvings, Atlas, and Woodie's. My mother accused me of knowing every glove in the city personally. My father predicted, dourly, that I would grow up and marry a ball.

With a mixture of elation and sadness I settled on the Spahn 300. Before I handed over my thirty dollars to Atlas, I had owned every glove in town, and none of them. Now I had just one. I felt the same paradoxical emotion next when I picked a college.

The new, properly neat's-footed glove slept on my bed at night like a summer puppy and traveled back and forth to school every day, wrist strap looped through belt.

In the alley, beside my house, I saved many a home run from going over a hypothetical outfield fence, and before breakfast and after dinner fielded many a lazy bouncer off the garage wall.

The glove, a ball, and the brick wall of my house, covered with ivy, were my stadium and my major league. When the ball would stick in the ivy, I would dislodge it by throwing sticks and rocks, but only once, my glove. The Spahnie stuck thirty feet up in the ivy, barely peeking out, and my heart hung there, too.

In a still vivid instant, I saw it in my mind's eye lodged there for years, rotting, a testimony to my split-second insanity.

Once retrieved, the glove was never endangered again. I knew, because everyone told me, that it was much too good a glove for a young boy, and I kept it from the careless and uncaring hands of what seemed like hundreds of would-be borrowers. It taught me lessons in saying, "No."

In fact, when my junior high principal, Dick Babyak, sees me now, he still asks, sometimes, "Hey, Tom, can I borrow your glove?"

He still remembers that twenty years ago, when he was my principal, math teacher, and summer camp director rolled into one, I would not let him use it. He wasn't going to get me out in those Sunday camp softball games with my own glove.

The Spahnie stayed with me nearly ten years. I used it in practice in both high school and college, though I used the schools' big first baseman's mitts in games.

Purpose: *In college new priorities displaced the glove. The title must refer to the lost glove and the narrator's lost childhood.*

Ideas and Support: *The narrator remembers how simple life was in summer camp, as compared to how complicated adult life becomes.*

Response: *The narrator lost more than just his glove. He lost his childhood, which everyone does. However, the glove seems to anchor his memories and trigger important associations. Even though his glove and his childhood are gone, he can still relive his memories by borrowing a camper's glove and caring for it as he cared for his own.*

Eventually, I lent the glove to Babyak in the summer (to his endless amusement), and by high school I was playing on the same camp counselors' team with him. By my college days he had stepped out of most of the games, unable to hit the ball to the Mattaponi River[2] every time up, as he had once. I inherited his old position.

When I left college, I apparently left the Spahnie behind somewhere. Its role had dwindled considerably. Perhaps I left it on the Theta Delta[3] lawn the week of graduation.

Though service in Vietnam, graduate school, or a job were the uncertain possibilities in my near future, I spent one last summer working in the humid, but still idyllic world of scrapping children and hot macaroni in July.

When the first Sunday softball game came, I had no glove. From the pitcher's mound I watched the twelve-, thirteen-, and fourteen-year-olds running up to bat, tossing down their gloves. I looked for a mitt that seemed familiar, too big for its owner, and almost too well loved.

"Excuse me," I called to a new camper. "May I borrow your glove?"

He looked down, hesitated, then said, "Okay, sir. But take care of it."

"I'm not going to hurt it," I said.

---

2. Mattaponi River: A river in eastern Virginia.
3. Theta Delta: A college fraternity.

Thomas Boswell (1948–   ) is a sports reporter for the *Washington Post* and a contributing editor of *Inside Sports*. Boswell won the American Society of Newspaper Editors' prize for the best sports journalism in 1981 and is a three-time winner in the *Best Sports Stories* competition. Primarily, he writes about baseball. One critic has called him "the thinking person's writer about the thinking person's sport, baseball," adding the comment that "like the game itself, he is graceful, subtle, elegant, inexhaustibly interesting, and fun." "Glove's Labor Lost" appears in his book *How Life Imitates the World Series*.

RESPONDING TO THE SELECTION

Your Response

1. What did you appreciate most about Boswell's essay? Why?

Recalling

2. What was a truer sign of spring to the author than any robin?
3. Describe when and how the author acquired his first baseball glove.
4. Describe the steps involved in acquiring the second glove.
5. Name three ways the author kept his glove safe from harm.
6. What finally became of the glove?

Interpreting

7. In writing about a beloved baseball glove, the author tells us about himself. What do you learn from the essay about the kind of person the author is?
8. Why do you think the author included the last incident in the essay? What other incident does the last one resemble?

Applying

9. A personal narrative essay often appeals to a wide audience because it discusses an experience that is recognized by people in many different circumstances. Why might someone uninterested in baseball still enjoy this essay? If that person were to write an essay about his or her youth, what might that person write about in the essay instead of a baseball glove?

ANALYZING LITERATURE

Understanding a Personal Narrative

In a personal narrative essay like "Glove's Labor Lost," the author's purpose is to write about an aspect of his life that readers can relate to their own experiences.

1. Find three vivid adjectives in the essay. Explain why each is effective.

2. Give examples from the essay of two types of support—facts, opinions, reasons, details, examples, or incidents.
3. How is the essay arranged?
4. Do you think Boswell accomplished his purpose? Explain your answer.

CRITICAL THINKING AND READING

Making Inferences About an Author

In a personal narrative essay, you can make **inferences,** or judgments, based on evidence presented, about the author. What inferences can you draw from the following pieces of evidence?

1. "Each spring, . . . I wonder if I should buy a baseball glove."
2. ". . . the second, bought with money I saved for over a year, fell somewhere between the last toy and the first personal possession."

THINKING AND WRITING

Writing a Personal Narrative

Think of an object that you or someone you know might remember fondly. Write a narrative essay explaining how this object first became important to its owner and how it gathered meaning over time. When you have finished, make sure that you have used transitional words and phrases—such as *meanwhile, later,* and *eventually*—to indicate time relationships in your narrative. Finally, proofread your work, making sure that your usage, spelling, and punctuation are correct.

LEARNING OPTION

Writing. Imagine losing something very important to you. Design an advertisement describing the object. In your ad state why it is important that the item be returned. You might even consider offering a reward for the object's return. Remember that advertisements must grab people's attention, keep them interested, and leave them with a clear impression.

YOUR WRITING PROCESS

WRITING A REFLECTIVE ESSAY

> "The ideal view for daily writing, hour on hour, is the blank brick wall of a cold-storage warehouse. Failing this, a stretch of sky will do, cloudless if possible."
>
> **Edna Ferber**

Reflecting on an idea means thinking about it carefully in order to arrive at a personal conclusion. In this unit you have read reflective essays by writers such as Mary Gordon and Theodore White. Imagine that your school literary magazine is sponsoring an essay contest on the subject of humor. Get ready to explore what makes you laugh . . . and what doesn't.

Focus

Assignment: Write a reflective essay on your taste in humor.
Purpose: To form conclusions about what you think is funny.
Audience: Readers of your school's literary magazine.

Prewriting

1. Visualize humorous situations. Fold a sheet of paper in half vertically. Close your eyes and try to remember funny scenes, stories, and jokes from TV shows, movies, and your own life. In the left column, jot down a phrase that describes the funny situation or joke. In the right column, describe situations that may have seemed funny to others but not to you.

2. Look for contrasts. Study your two lists. Do you see any pairs of situations that contrast? You might wish to draw connecting lines between entries that seem to have a directly opposing relationship to each other.

Student Model

Funny	Not Funny
parodies of well-known politicians	slapstick humor
mistaken identities	ethnic or racial jokes
accurate impersonations	comic impressions that don't really resemble the subjects
puns and word plays	jokes about people I don't know
jokes that make you think	"put-down" stories

3. Draw conclusions. Look at the contrasting items on your lists and try to generalize some personal "humor rules." For example, a person might conclude that "character impersonations need to be accurate to be funny."

Drafting

1. Follow a structure. How will you organize your essay? Will you classify the different kinds of humor that appeal to you and then classify the kinds that don't? Or will you describe each "funny–not funny" pair? However you decide to present your material, make sure that you provide smooth transitions between points.

2. Use examples to illustrate your ideas. As in any good piece of writing, a reflective essay should contain concrete examples to help clarify points. Consult your prewriting lists and, if necessary, add additional examples to illustrate your "humor rules."

3. State your personal thoughts and feelings. Along with your principles of humor and examples, describe why you feel the way you do. Remember that a reflective essay expresses the personal thoughts, opinions, and feelings of the writer.

Revising and Editing

1. Is the essay reflective? As you review your writing, imagine you are a reader looking at the essay for the first time. Ask yourself whether it clearly communicates the writer's taste in humor. Decide whether the writer's personal thoughts and feelings about the subject come through.

2. Test your essay on peer editors. Exchange drafts with one or more classmates. Use a checklist of questions as you review one another's work.
- Are the main ideas clear?
- Are sufficient examples provided?
- Are the ideas organized effectively?
- Do all the ideas stick to the topic?
- Does the writing flow smoothly from point to point?
- Is the language vivid?

3. Vary your language. Use a variety of sentence structures and lengths in your writing. If necessary, add phrases and clauses to expand ideas. Replace vague verbs and nouns with concrete words. Avoid repetitious language, such as beginning each sentence with "I."

Grammar Tip
Transitions between ideas can be in the form of a word, a phrase, or a whole sentence. Words and phrases such as *similarly, in addition, moreover,* and *besides* can show that two ideas are alike or complementary in some way. Words and phrases such as *but, on the other hand, nevertheless,* and *despite* can show a contrast between ideas.

Options for Publishing
- Submit your essay to the school literary magazine or a statewide writing contest.
- Compile a class anthology of essays on humor and distribute it to other classes.
- Read your essay to friends and see whether they agree with your ideas about humor.

Reviewing Your Writing Process
1. Did the technique of visualization help you come up with ideas for writing? If not, what prewriting method worked best for you?
2. Do you think your writing style would have been different if you had written a reflective essay on a serious topic, such as illness? Explain.

YOUR WRITING PROCESS

WRITING A REMINISCENCE

Writing is a good way to recapture events and people from the past. A reminiscence like Truman Capote's "A Christmas Memory" paints a loving portrait of a very special woman whom the writer once knew. Suppose you wanted to describe an important event or person from your past to share with a new friend. What experience stands out most?

> **Focus**
>
> **Assignment:** Write a reminiscence.
> **Purpose:** To describe an important event or person from your past.
> **Audience:** A new friend who would like to know you better.

Prewriting

1. Create a cluster diagram to find a topic. Explore your thoughts by creating a cluster diagram around the central idea of "Memorable Events and People."

2. Draw a timeline. Once you have selected a subject for a reminiscence, think of it as a story with a beginning, middle, and end. Draw a timeline to help you form a shape for your recollection.

3. Brainstorm to recall details. Think of sensory details that will vividly convey a mood.

> **Student Model**
>
> Most frightening event: House destroyed by hurricane
>
> Sight: —Grandmother's china smashed to bits
> —shattered fish tank
> —sparks from downed electric lines
> Sound: —wind howling like a nightmare monster
> —crash of wall torn away
> —yelling of people in distance
> Smell: —earth-smelling wind
> —electrical wiring
> Touch: —Father's arms around me
> —splinters from flying glass
> Taste: —salty tears when I kissed Father's cheek
> —eating cold spaghetti, soggy bread

Drafting

1. Set the scene. Make sure your reminiscence gives a clear picture of where and when events occurred. Use your timeline to make sure you include all your important points.

2. Create a main impression. Use only details that develop the main impression or mood that you want to convey. Consult your brainstorming list to flesh out your writing.

3. Use dialogue. Dialogue helps to bring characters to life by allowing your audience to hear what they sound like. Try using dialogue to reveal characters' personalities, to advance the story, or to heighten the drama of a suspenseful moment.

Student Model

The wind was now roaring like a dragon that had poked its neck through the shattered picture window of the living room. Instinctively, we huddled more closely in the corner of the dark closet. Father hugged me tighter to him, shielding my head and face with his forearm.

"Oh, no. Oh, no," he whispered, sensing some worse tragedy to come. "The roof's about to go."

Then, for the first time, I was truly afraid.

Revising and Editing

1. Add figurative language. Using figurative language can help you add vivid imagery to your writing and appeal to your audience's imagination. Metaphors, similes, and personification can all be used to express colorful comparisons.

2. Use forceful, vivid verbs. Weed out bland verbs from your draft and replace them with strong verbs that add color.

Student Model

Suddenly true fear began to ~~move in~~ *tear at* my stomach *like a nest of fire ants*. In every room the wind-driven rain had *invaded* ~~entered~~ even locked drawers.

Grammar Tip

In descriptive writing, try playing with parts of speech. For example, add imagery to your writing by using nouns as verbs, the way the poet Dylan Thomas did:

"we waited to *snowball* the cats"

"snow . . . *white-ivied* the walls"

Options for Publishing

- Present your reminiscence as part of a reading at the local public library.
- Tape-record your writing along with that of other members of the class
- Include your reminiscence in a letter to a friend.

Reviewing Your Writing Process

1. How easy or difficult was it to capture the particular mood you wanted to express in your reminiscence?

2. Did you use a timeline to help you develop your story and organize your recollections? If not, what helped you accomplish these?

RED POPPIES
Georgia O'Keeffe
Private Collection

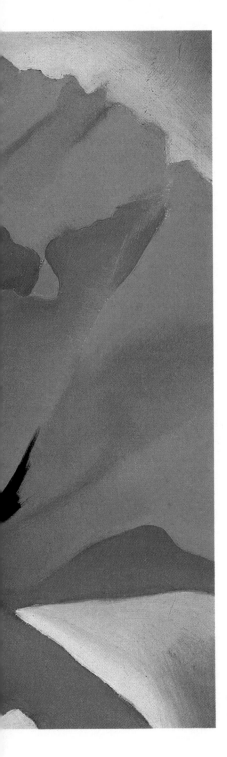

POETRY

Voltaire called poetry "the music of the soul," while Carl Sandburg defined it as "the synthesis of hyacinths and biscuits." Although there are almost as many definitions of poetry as there are poets, there is no neat, simple way to define poetry. Poems can be written in too many different forms and styles, on too many different subjects and emotions, and with too many different motives to describe in a single definition. Likewise, poetry cannot be defined by the way it looks. We think that poetry is a work with short lines, rhythm, perhaps some rhyme, and a lot of white space, yet some of the poems in this section do not have short lines, rhyme, or neat little stanzas. Poetry can look like prose or can actually form a picture with the placement of words. Poetry escapes definition by word or appearance.

If poetry defies definition, then how can it be studied? Poetry can tell a story, express an idea, define a character, convey an emotion, describe a setting, examine a situation—singly or all at once. A poem may even contain a wish, as in one poem in this section in which a narrator would like her admirer to send her a limousine every once in a while. Ideally, good poetry evokes an intellectual and emotional response from you, the reader.

Although on the surface poetry seems very different from fiction, it actually shares a great deal. Elements such as speaker or narrator, point of view, tone, style, and theme are common to all genres. However, there are significant ways in which poetry differs from prose. Poems often have economy, meaning that they are more condensed and compressed than prose so that each word contributes to a poem's total impact and meaning. Poems depend more on imagery, references to sensory impressions that create immediacy and vividness, often through comparison, allusion, or suggestion. Also, in poetry rhythm can be as important as the words, images, and ideas. Finally, the sound of a poem as it is read aloud or as it is heard in the mind is also important.

READING ACTIVELY

Poetry

Poetry is different from other forms of writing in its appearance, its use of language, and its musical qualities. The poet Walt Whitman wrote, "To have great poetry, there must be great audiences, too." How do you participate as an audience? You approach each poem actively. The following strategies will help you become an active reader of poetry:

QUESTION What is the poem saying? What questions come to mind as you are reading? Why does the writer include certain words and details? Look for answers to your questions as you read.

USE YOUR SENSES What images is the poet creating? How are these images developed? Let your imagination see the pictures in your mind, and let your senses respond to the poet's language.

LISTEN Much poetry is musical. Read the poem aloud so that you can hear the sound of it and feel its rhythm. Often the words and rhythm suggest a mood or feeling. Let the sound of the poem pull you into it. How does the sound affect you?

CONNECT Bring your own experience and knowledge to the poem. What images are familiar? Which are new to you?

PARAPHRASE Put the poem in your own words. When you can express a poem in your own words, you will better understand its meaning.

RESPOND How does the poem make you feel as you read? Respond to the poem as a whole, and decide what it says to *you*.

Try to use these strategies as you read the poems in this unit. By reading actively you will increase your enjoyment and understanding of poetry.

On pages 547–549 you will see how Reginald Carnegie from Northwestern High School in Detroit, Michigan, actively read the poem "Alabama Centennial." The notes in the side column include Reginald's thoughts and comments as he read the poem. Your own thoughts and comments as you read may be different.

Alabama Centennial

Naomi Long Madgett

Question: *Why is Alabama mentioned in the title?*

They said, "Wait." Well, I waited.
For a hundred years I waited
In cotton fields, kitchens, balconies,
In bread lines, at back doors, on chain gangs,
5   In stinking "colored" toilets
And crowded ghettos,
Outside of schools and voting booths.
And some said, "Later."
And some said, "Never!"

Senses: *These images appear to the senses of sight, smell, and touch.*

Connect: *There are still crowded ghettos in many inner cities today.*

10   Then a new wind blew, and a new voice
Rode its wings with quiet urgency,
Strong, determined, sure.
"No," it said. "Not 'never,' not 'later,'
Not even 'soon.'
15   Now.
Walk!"

Listen: *The sound of the voice in this stanza gives the poem an inspirational mood.*

And other voices echoed the freedom words,
"Walk together, children, don't get weary,"
Whispered them, sang them, prayed them, shouted them.
20   "Walk!"
And I walked the streets of Montgomery[1]
Until a link in the chain of patient acquiescence broke.

Then again: Sit down!
And I sat down at the counters of Greensboro.[2]

Paraphrase: *African Americans have had to endure many wrongs, but strong leaders and determined people faced their oppressors. The struggle for freedom is a hard-fought battle, one that African Americans must never stop fighting.*

---

1. Montgomery: Capital of Alabama; in 1955 Martin Luther King, Jr., led a boycott there that ended racial segregation on buses.
2. Greensboro: The largest city in North Carolina; in 1960 four African American students sat at a restricted lunch counter in Greensboro to protest racial segregation. This action prompted a wave of sit-in demonstrations throughout the South.

A 1965 Selma, Alabama, march in support of African American voting rights

25 Ride! And I rode the bus for freedom.
Kneel! And I went down on my knees in prayer and faith.
March! And I'll march until the last chain falls
Singing, "We shall overcome."

Not all the dogs and hoses in Birmingham[3]

---

3. Birmingham: In 1963 racial tensions in
Birmingham, Alabama, escalated until a bomb
exploded in an African American church, killing four
girls. As a result, interracial groups organized and
began working to prevent future incidents.

30 Nor all the clubs and guns in Selma[4]
    Can turn this tide.
    Not all the jails can hold these young black faces
    From their destiny of manhood,
    Of equality, of dignity,
35 Of the American Dream
    A hundred years past due.
    Now!

----

4. Selma: In 1965 King led a five-day march from
Selma, Alabama, to Montgomery to protest
discrimination in voter registration. Later that year
Congress passed the Voting Rights Act, which gave
100,000 African Americans the right to vote.

Respond: *This poem makes me feel that there is hope for African Americans. Although we have progressed since our arrival in this country, we have a ways to go, and at the rate we're going, not even my generation will see the outcome. However, nothing is going to stop African Americans from reaching their goal of true freedom.*

Naomi Long Madgett (1923–   ) was born in Norfolk, Virginia, to a clergyman and a teacher. When she was a child, she recalls discovering on the floor of her father's study the poetry of Langston Hughes and Alfred, Lord Tennyson; her poetry is influenced by their divergent styles. Madgett spent much of her career as a writing teacher and has written textbooks about writing and literature. She admits, "I would rather be a good poet than anything else I can imagine."

RESPONDING TO THE SELECTION

Your Response

1. What line or image made the strongest impression on you? Explain.
2. What does the "destiny . . . /Of the American Dream" mean to you?

Recalling

3. How long has the speaker been "waiting"?
4. Name some of the steps the speaker took to gain equality and dignity.

Interpreting

5. In the first line, who is "I"? Who are "they"?
6. Whose voice is the speaker referring to in line 10?
7. What does the image of the chain represent in line 22? In line 27?
8. Interpret the title "Alabama Centennial."

Applying

9. What other forms of discrimination against African Americans would you add to those mentioned in the poem?

ANALYZING LITERATURE

Appreciating Theme

Authors convey general insights into life through **theme,** the universal truth or message of a poem or work of prose. Poets can state a theme directly or convey it through images and dialogue

as well. In "Alabama Centennial" Madgett uses both of these techniques.

1. The last stanza is a direct statement of the theme. Express this theme in your own words.
2. How does the dialogue in the poem help you understand its theme?
3. How do the images of the "new wind" (line 10) and "tide" (line 31) contribute to theme?

CRITICAL THINKING AND READING

Understanding Allusions

An allusion is a brief reference to a person, a place, an event, or another literary work. Allusions convey a great deal of information. Referring to the poem's footnotes as a guide, explain how Madgett uses the names of cities to create a brief history of the civil rights movement. Then explain how these allusions contribute to the theme.

THINKING AND WRITING

Responding to Theme

As you read a poem, you bring your own experiences and attitudes to it and respond from your unique perspective. How do you respond to "Alabama Centennial"? What does the theme mean to you? Write about the theme in your journal. As you explore the theme, refer to specific lines and images that were especially powerful.

Narrative Poetry

CENTRAL PARK, 1901
Maurice Prendergast
Collection of Whitney Museum of American Art

GUIDE FOR READING

La Belle Dame sans Merci

Narrative Poetry

A **narrative poem** tells a story and is usually longer than other types of poems. Narrative poems may be the oldest form of poetry. Because few people could read many years ago, storytellers traveled from place to place telling about real and imagined events and people. These wanderers told stories to entertain listeners, but they were also the newscasters and historians of their time. The storytellers used rhymes and rhythms to help them remember the stories.

Like any story, a narrative poem has one or more characters, a setting, a conflict, and a series of events that come to a conclusion. Most narrative poems are divided into stanzas, or groups of lines that have the same rhyme pattern. In "La Belle Dame sans Merci," the second and fourth lines of each stanza rhyme.

Focus

The artist T. W. Waterhouse was inspired by Keats's poem to create the painting on page 553. Study the painting carefully, and try to imagine the two figures speaking to each other. Then write a short dialogue between the two people in the painting. Use these questions to help you get started:

- Who are these people and what is their relationship?
- Who seems to be in control? Why?
- What might they be saying to each other?

Keep your dialogue in mind as you read the poem.

Vocabulary

Knowing the following words will help you as you read "La Belle Dame sans Merci."

sedge (sej) *n.*: A grassy plant that grows in wet areas (l. 3)
thrall (thrôl) *n.*: Complete control; slavery (l. 40)
sojourn (sō′ jurn) *v.*: Stay temporarily (l. 45)

John Keats

(1795–1821) was born in England. Both of his parents died while he was still a boy, and his guardian sent Keats to school in London. Later, Keats studied surgery. He decided, however, to devote his life to writing poetry. He emphasized feeling and imagination over reason and logic in his poetry. Because he died young, Keats left only a small body of work. His poems, including the narrative poem "La Belle Dame sans Merci," communicate an appreciation of beauty and a sadness at its impermanence.

La Belle Dame sans Merci[1]

John Keats

LA BELLE DAME SANS MERCI
John W. Waterhouse
Hessiches Landes Museum, Darmstadt

O what can ail thee, knight-at-arms,
    Alone and palely loitering?
The sedge has withered from the lake,
    And no birds sing.

5   O what can ail thee, knight-at-arms,
    So haggard and so woe-begone?
The squirrel's granary is full,
    And the harvest's done.

---

1. La Belle Dame sans Merci: French for "The Beautiful Lady Without Pity."

I see a lily on thy brow,
10   With anguish moist and fever dew,
And on thy cheeks a fading rose
        Fast withereth too.

I met a lady in the meads,[2]
        Full beautiful—a faery's child,
15 Her hair was long, her foot was light,
        And her eyes were wild.

I made a garland for her head,
        And bracelets too, and fragrant zone;[3]
She looked at me as she did love,
20   And made sweet moan.

I set her on my pacing steed,
        And nothing else saw all day long,
For sidelong would she bend, and sing
        A faery's song.

25 She found me roots of relish sweet,
        And honey wild, and manna dew,[4]
And sure in language strange she said—
        'I love thee true.'

She took me to her elfin grot,[5]
30   And there she wept, and sighed full sore,
And there I shut her wild wild eyes
        With kisses four.

And there she lullèd me asleep,
        And there I dreamed—Ah! woe betide!
35 The latest dream I ever dreamed
        On the cold hill's side.

I saw pale kings and princes too,
        Pale warriors, death-pale were they all;
They cried—'La Belle Dame sans Merci
40   Hath thee in thrall!'

---

2. meads (mēdz) *n.*: Old-fashioned form of *meadow*.
3. fragrant (frā′ grənt) **zone** (zōn): A sweet-smelling plant.
4. manna (man′ ə) **dew** (do͞o): A sweet substance obtained from the bark of certain ash trees.
5. elfin (el′ fən) **grot**: A cave belonging to a fairy.

I saw their starved lips in the gloam,
   With horrid warning gapèd wide,
And I awoke and found me here,
   On the cold hill's side.

45 And this is why I sojourn here,
   Alone and palely loitering,
Though the sedge has withered from the lake,
   And no birds sing.

RESPONDING TO THE SELECTION

Your Response

1. In line 16, the speaker describes the lady's eyes as "wild." What do you think the speaker means by this description?

Recalling

2. What is the setting of the poem?
3. Describe the lady the knight meets.
4. Describe the knight's dream.

Interpreting

5. Explain how the people in the knight's dream relate to his present condition.
6. Why is the knight "alone and palely loitering"?

Applying

7. In ancient myths, the fertility of the land is tied to the health of a heroic figure such as a king or a knight. The land can be bountiful again only when a spell put on the heroic figure is broken. Explain how "La Belle Dame sans Merci" is similar to such a myth. Then explain why the fertility of the land would be of such vital importance to ancient peoples.

ANALYZING LITERATURE

Understanding Narrative Poetry

Because a narrative poem tells a story, some of its elements are the same as those in a short story. These elements include setting, characters, plot, conflict, and theme.

1. Which stanzas describe the setting and introduce the main character?
2. The subject of the sentences in stanzas 4–6 is different from the subject in stanzas 7–9. How does this shift help communicate what is happening in the story?
3. How does the last stanza tie everything together?

THINKING AND WRITING

Writing a Narrative Poem

Write a short narrative poem with or without rhyming lines. First, think of an interesting real or imagined event. Then list three or four pieces of information needed for the event to make sense to a reader. Plan a stanza of as many lines as you need for each piece of information. Use the first stanza to ask the question and the other stanzas to answer it. The last stanza should bring it to a close. When you revise your poem, make sure you have related the events in a logical order. Proofread your poem for errors in spelling.

GUIDE FOR READING

Two Tramps in Mud Time

The Speaker in Narrative Poetry

The **speaker** in a poem may actually be the voice of the poet, or the speaker may be the voice of a character in the poem invented by the poet. Even when a poet uses the pronoun *I* in a poem, the speaker may be fictional and not the poet himself or herself. Like other fictional characters, the speaker in a narrative poem may reveal information about himself or herself directly, through forthright statements, or indirectly, through hints and implications.

Focus

For the speaker in "Two Tramps in Mud Time," splitting wood is both work and play. What other kinds of work do people perform that can also be recreational? Answer this question by making a cluster diagram with "splitting wood" in the center; see the diagram that follows to get you started. In the circles branching from the center, name activities that can be performed both as work and as recreation. For example, some people perform yard work to keep their lawns healthy; at the same time, they enjoy fresh air, sunshine, and quiet time to themselves.

Keep your diagram in mind as you read the poem.

Vocabulary

Knowing the following words and expressions will help you as you read "Two Tramps in Mud Time."

put me off my aim: Made me miss what I was aiming at (l. 3)

playing possum: Pretending to be asleep or dead (l. 30)

hulking (hul' kiŋ) *adj.*: Large; heavy; clumsy (l. 49)

in twain (in twān): Together; side-by-side; as a pair (l. 63)

Robert Frost

(1874–1963) was one of the most popular American poets of the twentieth century. He was born in San Francisco, but his family moved to Massachusetts when he was eleven years old. As a young man, he worked as a farmer, a teacher, and an editor. Frost's first book of poetry was published in 1913. He later won four Pulitzer Prizes for poetry and a Congressional gold medal. In much of his poetry, Frost uses his experiences as a New England farmer to present his feelings about life.

Two Tramps in Mud Time

Robert Frost

Out of the mud two strangers came
And caught me splitting wood in the yard.
And one of them put me off my aim
By hailing cheerily "Hit them hard!"
5   I knew pretty well why he dropped behind
And let the other go on a way.
I knew pretty well what he had in mind:
He wanted to take my job for pay.

Good blocks of oak it was I split,
10 As large around as the chopping block;
And every piece I squarely hit
Fell splinterless as a cloven[1] rock.
The blows that a life of self-control
Spares to strike[2] for the common good,
15 That day, giving a loose to my soul,
I spent on the unimportant wood.

The sun was warm but the wind was chill.
You know how it is with an April day
When the sun is out and the wind is still,
20 You're one month on in the middle of May.
But if you so much as dare to speak,
A cloud comes over the sunlit arch,
A wind comes off a frozen peak,
And you're two months back in the middle of March.

25 A bluebird comes tenderly up to alight
And turns to the wind to unruffle a plume,
His song so pitched as not to excite
A single flower as yet to bloom.

---

1. cloven (klō′ vən) *adj.*: Split.
2. Spares to strike: Refrains from striking.

It is snowing a flake: and he half knew
30   Winter was only playing possum.
Except in color he isn't blue,
But he wouldn't advise a thing to blossom.

The water for which we may have to look
In summertime with a witching wand,[3]
35   In every wheelrut's now a brook,
In every print of a hoof a pond.
Be glad of water, but don't forget
The lurking frost in the earth beneath
That will steal forth after the sun is set
40   And show on the water its crystal teeth.

The time when most I loved my task
These two must make me love it more
By coming with what they came to ask.
You'd think I never had felt before
45   The weight of an ax-head poised aloft,
The grip on earth of outspread feet,
The life of muscles rocking soft
And smooth and moist in vernal[4] heat.

Out of the woods two hulking tramps
50   (From sleeping God knows where last night,
But not long since in the lumber camps).
They thought all chopping was theirs of right.
Men of the woods and lumberjacks,
They judged me by their appropriate tool.
55   Except as a fellow handled an ax
They had no way of knowing a fool.

Nothing on either side was said.
They knew they had but to stay their stay
And all their logic would fill my head:
60   As that I had no right to play
With what was another man's work for gain.
My right might be love but theirs was need.
And where the two exist in twain
Theirs was the better right—agreed.

---

3. witching wand: A twig that some people believe will
lead the holder to underground water.
4. vernal (vʉr′ nəl) *adj.*: Spring.

65 But yield who will to their separation,
My object in living is to unite
My avocation[5] and my vocation[6]
As my two eyes make one in sight.
Only where love and need are one,
70 And the work is play for mortal stakes,
Is the deed ever really done
For Heaven and the future's sakes.

---

5. avocation (a və kā′ s/hən) *n.*: Hobby.
6. vocation (vō kā′ s/hən) *n.*: Occupation.

RESPONDING TO THE SELECTION

Your Response

1. If, like the speaker, your goal in life was to unite your avocation and your vocation, what would you do? Explain.

Recalling

2. How, according to the speaker, does chopping wood give "a loose to [his] soul"?
3. How do the tramps probably earn a living?
4. How might the two tramps judge other men?
5. What does the speaker think the tramps want?
6. Does the speaker give them what they want? Explain your answer.

Interpreting

7. Explain lines 13–16. How does the speaker give "a loose to [his] soul"? What is the "unimportant wood"?
8. Why do the two tramps make the speaker love his work more?
9. How do you know that the speaker does or does not enjoy the outdoors? Find evidence in the poem to support your answer.

Applying

10. Do you agree with the speaker that the tramp's right was "the better right"? Explain your answer.

ANALYZING LITERATURE

Understanding the Speaker

The **speaker** in a narrative poem is the voice in the poem. Even if the speaker uses the pronoun *I*, you cannot assume the speaker is the voice of the poet. He or she may still be a fictional character. "Two Tramps in Mud Time" reveals several traits of an interesting speaker.

1. Of the nine stanzas, only the first two and the last three actually narrate the event. What are stanzas 3–5 about, and what does that topic reveal about the speaker?
2. The speaker is ambivalent—that is, he has conflicting feelings—about the two tramps. What are these conflicting feelings?

CRITICAL THINKING AND READING

Making Inferences About Characters

You make inferences about a character's personality as you do with people you meet. You look for clues in their words and actions.

1. Write the number of the line or lines that support each of the following inferences.

    a. The speaker is suspicious of strangers.

    b. He does not normally express his emotions.

    c. Chopping wood is a pleasure for him.

    d. He is sensitive to seasonal changes.

    e. He is aware of nature in its tiniest details.

    f. He is proud of his wood-chopping ability.

    g. He feels he should hire the two tramps.

    h. He has a clear understanding of what he wants his life to be like.

2. Based on your answers to the above questions, describe the speaker.

THINKING AND WRITING

Writing About the Speaker

The following comment about Frost's poems was written by Reginald L. Cook in *Robert Frost, A Living Voice.*

"To a mid-twentieth-century [reader], Frost's . . . poems . . . strike the legendary note of 'once upon a time.' . . . What was once common in Frost's experience has now become memory to an older generation."

Suppose you are writing a short review of Cook's book for your school paper. Write an explanation of how the speaker in "Two Tramps in Mud Time" is an example of what Cook meant. When you revise, make sure you have supported your explanation. Proofread for errors in spelling, grammar, and punctuation.

LEARNING OPTIONS

1. **Writing.** "Two Tramps in Mud Time" is narrated from the point of view of the person who is splitting wood. Rewrite the narrative—in either poetry or prose—from the point of view of one of the tramps. Describe the setting as *you* see it.

2. **Cross-curricular Connection.** Do some research about the role of wood as fuel, using these questions to guide you:

   • How many Americans use wood stoves today? For what purpose?

   • What is the difference between softwood and hardwood? How do they burn differently?

   • Is burning wood environmentally safer than burning oil or gas? Why or why not?

   • How is wood prepared for use as fuel?

   Present your findings in an informal report.

3. **Community Connections.** Cities and towns often employ people to perform jobs that others do as recreation. For example, many parks-and-recreation departments hire people to give swimming or tennis lessons to young people during the summer. Explore such opportunities in your community. You might start by phoning or writing to local government officials who can provide you with information. Then compile a master "Help Wanted" list, describing the various ways in which people can channel their recreational interests into part-time jobs in your community.

GUIDE FOR READING

The Wreck of the Hesperus

Suspense and Foreshadowing in Narrative Poetry

Suspense is as important in a narrative poem as in any other form of storytelling. **Suspense** is the building of curiosity so that readers want to find out what will happen next. One technique for maintaining suspense is **foreshadowing,** or giving hints of what is to come. A good writer plants hints in such a way that they do not interfere with the story. A good reader picks up the hints and watches for the events that have been foreshadowed. The title of the poem you are about to read foreshadows an event in the poem. What do you think that event will be?

Focus

Shipwrecks have been the subject of paintings, songs, poems, stories, and films for as long as there have been ships. What is the most memorable account of a shipwreck that you have read about, heard, or seen? Write a short description of one such account, including as many vivid images as possible. Then get together with two or three classmates and share your descriptions. In your group, discuss the reasons why storytellers and readers of stories enjoy tales of shipwrecks. What qualities of these stories intrigue people? What elements of the tales you shared in your group did each of you find the most interesting? Keep your discussion in mind as you read "The Wreck of the Hesperus."

Vocabulary

Knowing the following words will help you as you read "The Wreck of the Hesperus."

schooner (skōo′nər) *n.:* A ship with two or more masts, or supports for sails (l. 1)

spar (spär) *n.:* A pole that supports a sail (l. 35)

shrouds (shroudz) *n.:* A set of ropes used to tie a mast to the side of a ship (l. 73)

Henry Wadsworth Longfellow

(1807–1882) was born and lived in what is now Portland, Maine. During the nineteenth century, he became one of America's most popular poets. Some of his best-known poems are "Evangeline," "The Song of Hiawatha," "Paul Revere's Ride," and "The Village Blacksmith." Besides poetry, Longfellow wrote travel books and textbooks on foreign languages. He is best remembered, however, for his narrative poems such as "The Wreck of the Hesperus."

**THE WRECK OF
A TRANSPORT SHIP,
1810**
J.M.W. Turner
*Calouste Gulbenkian
Foundation Museum*

The Wreck of the Hesperus

Henry Wadsworth Longfellow

It was the schooner Hesperus,
    That sailed the wintry sea;
And the skipper had taken his little daughtèr,
    To bear him company.

5 Blue were her eyes as the fairy-flax,[1]
    Her cheeks like the dawn of day,
And her bosom white as the hawthorn buds,
    That ope[2] in the month of May.

The skipper he stood beside the helm,
10   His pipe was in his mouth,
And he watched how the veering flaw[3] did blow
    The smoke now West, now South.

---

1. fairy-flax (fer′ ē flaks) *n.*: The blue flowers of the
flax plant of fairies, or supernatural beings with magic powers.
2. ope (ōp) *v.*: Old-fashioned form of *open*.
3. veering (vir′ iŋ) **flaw:** Gust of wind that changes direction.

Then up and spake[4] an old sailòr,
    Had sailed to the Spanish Main,
15 "I pray thee, put into yonder port,
    For I fear a hurricane.

"Last night, the moon had a golden ring,
    And tonight no moon we see!"
The skipper, he blew a whiff from his pipe,
20   And a scornful laugh laughed he.

Colder and louder blew the wind,
    A gale from the Northeast,
The snow fell hissing in the brine,
    And the billows frothed like yeast.

25 Down came the storm, and smote amain,[5]
    The vessel in its strength;
She shuddered and paused, like a frighted[6] steed,
    Then leaped her cable's length.

"Come hither! come hither! my little daughtèr,
30   And do not tremble so;
For I can weather the roughest gale,
    That ever wind did blow."

He wrapped her warm in his seaman's coat
    Against the stinging blast;
35 He cut a rope from a broken spar,
    And bound her to the mast.

"O father! I hear the church-bells ring,
    O say, what may it be?"
"'Tis a fog-bell on a rock-bound coast!"—
40   And he steered for the open sea.

"O father! I hear the sound of guns,
    O say, what may it be?"
"Some ship in distress, that cannot live
    In such an angry sea!"

---

4. spake (spāk) *v.*: Old-fashioned form of *spoke*.
5. smote (smōt) **amain** (ə mān'): Struck violently.
6. frighted (frī' tid) *adj.*: Terrified.

45   "O father! I see a gleaming light,
         O say, what may it be?"
     But the father answered never a word,
         A frozen corpse was he.

     Lashed to the helm, all stiff and stark,
50   With his face turned to the skies,
     The lantern gleamed through the gleaming snow
         On his fixed and glassy eyes.

     Then the maiden clasped her hands and prayed
         That savèd she might be;
55   And she thought of Christ, who stilled the wave,
         On the Lake of Galilee.

     And fast through the midnight dark and drear
         Through the whistling sleet and snow,
     Like a sheeted ghost, the vessel swept
60   Towards the reef of Norman's Woe.

     And ever the fitful gusts between
         A sound came from the land;
     It was the sound of the trampling surf,
         On the rocks and the hard sea-sand.

65   The breakers were right beneath her bows,
         She drifted a dreary wreck,
     And a whooping billow swept the crew
         Like icicles from her deck.

     She struck where the white and fleecy waves
70   Looked soft as carded wool,
     But the cruel rocks, they gored her side
         Like the horns of an angry bull.

     Her rattling shrouds, all sheathed in ice,
         With the masts went by the board;
75   Like a vessel of glass, she stove and sank,
         Ho! ho! the breakers roared!

     At daybreak, on the bleak sea-beach,
         A fisherman stood aghast,
     To see the form of a maiden fair,
80   Lashed close to a drifting mast.

The salt sea was frozen on her breast,
  The salt tears in her eyes;
And he saw her hair, like the brown sea-weed,
  On the billows fall and rise.

85 Such was the wreck of the Hesperus,
  In the midnight and the snow!
Christ save us all from a death like this,
  On the reef of Norman's Woe!

▮R ESPONDING TO THE SELECTION

Your Response

1. Think of a time when you or someone you know discounted some advice. Did you or your friend make the right decision? Explain.

Recalling

2. Describe the setting of the poem.
3. Describe the two main characters.
4. Explain how the skipper is warned of an approaching hurricane. How does the skipper react to the warning?
5. What does he do to protect his daughter from the storm?
6. Explain what happens to the ship and its people.

Interpreting

7. Why does the skipper ignore the old sailor's warning?
8. Explain how the skipper's attitude toward the old sailor is consistent with his reaction to the storm.
9. Longfellow often wrote poems that contained moral lessons. What lesson do you think this poem presents? Find evidence in the poem to support your answer.

Applying

10. Taking pride in one's abilities can be considered a positive quality. Explain how it can also be a negative quality. Use examples from life to support your answer.

▮A NALYZING LITERATURE

Understanding Foreshadowing

Foreshadowing is hinting at what is to come. Foreshadowing serves a double purpose: It allows an author to prepare the reader for what is about to happen, and it gives the reader a chance to take part in the story by predicting what will happen without actually having been told about it. "The Wreck of the Hesperus" includes several examples of foreshadowing of later events.

1. How is the sea described in the first stanza?
2. What detail in the third stanza hints at what is to come?
3. How do lines 29–32 foreshadow the skipper's actions during the storm?
4. What detail in lines 57–60 suggests that there will be no survivors of the wreck?

▮T HINKING AND WRITING

Writing About Foreshadowing

Write a review of "The Wreck of the Hesperus." First, jot down notes explaining the poet's use of foreshadowing to heighten the suspense in the story. When you write your first draft, include specific details to illustrate the use of foreshadowing. When you revise, make sure you have explained the use of foreshadowing clearly. Proofread for errors in spelling, grammar, and punctuation.

Dramatic Poetry

PORTRAIT OF KITTY JAGGER, THE ARTIST'S WIFE
David Jagger

GUIDE FOR READING

Danny Deever

Dramatic Poetry

Dramatic Poetry is poetry in which one or more characters speak. By using the words of one or more speakers to tell directly what is happening, dramatic poetry creates the illusion that the reader is actually witnessing a dramatic event. The words of each speaker are often, but not always, enclosed in quotation marks.

Focus

"Danny Deever" takes place in a military setting. Explore your own associations with the military by writing down the first word you think of after reading each of the following words. Compare your responses to those of your classmates.

regiment	tank	bomber
sergeant	taps	stripes
veteran	recruit	draft
infantry	navy	general
bayonet	artillery	treason
court martial	purple heart	platoon
medal	lieutenant	saluted

Keep your associations in mind as you read "Danny Deever."

Vocabulary

Knowing the following words will help you as you read "Danny Deever."

whimpers (hwim′ pərz) *v.*: Makes a low, whining sound, as in crying or in fear (l. 27)
quickstep (kwik′ step′) *n.*: The pace used in normal military marching, as contrasted with the slower pace of the dead march (l. 29)

Rudyard Kipling

(1865–1936) in 1907 was the first English author to win the Nobel Prize for Literature. He produced a vast body of work including poems, stories, and novels. Born in Bombay, India, Kipling was sent at an early age to England for a formal education. Returning to India at about eighteen, Kipling worked as a journalist. Many of his early poems and stories first appeared in newspapers. "Danny Deever" was included in a collection of Kipling's poems called *Barracks Room Ballads.*

Danny Deever

Rudyard Kipling

"What are the bugles blowin' for?" said Files-on-Parade.[1]
"To turn you out, to turn you out," the Color-Sergeant[2] said.
"What makes you look so white, so white?" said Files-on-Parade.
"I'm dreadin' what I've got to watch," the Color-Sergeant said.

5   For they're hangin' Danny Deever, you can hear the Dead March play,
      The regiment's in 'ollow square[3]—they're hangin' him today;

---

1. Files-on-Parade: The soldier who directs marching formation.
2. Color-Sergeant: The flag-bearer.
3. 'ollow square: For a hanging, soldiers' ranks form three sides of a square; the fourth side is the gallows.

THE BATTLE OF BUNKER HILL
Howard Pyle
Delaware Art Museum

They've taken of his buttons off an' cut his stripes away,
An' they're hangin' Danny Deever in the mornin'.

"What makes the rear-rank breathe so 'ard?" said Files-on-Parade.
10 "It's bitter cold, it's bitter cold," the Color-Sergeant said.
"What makes that front-rank man fall down?" says Files-on-Parade.
"A touch o' sun, a touch o' sun," the Color-Sergeant said.
    They are hangin' Danny Deever, they are marchin' of 'im round,
    They 'ave 'alted Danny Deever by 'is coffin on the ground;
15   An' 'e'll swing in 'arf a minute for a sneakin' shootin' hound—
    O they're hangin' Danny Deever in the mornin'!

"'Is cot was right-'and cot to mine," said Files-on-Parade.
"'E's sleepin' out an' far tonight," the Color-Sergeant said.
"I've drunk 'is beer a score o' times," said Files-on-Parade.
20 "'E's drinkin' bitter beer alone," the Color-Sergeant said.
    They are hangin' Danny Deever, you must mark 'im to 'is place,
    For 'e shot a comrade sleepin'—you must look 'im in the face;
    Nine 'undred of 'is county an' the regiment's disgrace,
    While they're hangin' Danny Deever in the mornin'.

25 "What's that so black agin the sun?" said Files-on-Parade.
"It's Danny fightin' 'ard for life," the Color-Sergeant said.
"What's that that whimpers over'ead?" said Files-on-Parade.
"It's Danny's soul that's passin' now," the Color-Sergeant said.
    For they're done with Danny Deever, you can 'ear the quickstep play,
30   The regiment's in column, an' they're marchin' us away;
    Ho! the young recruits are shakin', an' they'll want their beer to-day,
    After hangin' Danny Deever in the mornin'.

RESPONDING TO THE SELECTION

Your Response

1. If you were in the regiment, how would you feel about having to watch the hanging? Explain.

Recalling

2. Describe the setting of "Danny Deever."
3. Of the two speakers in the poem, which has some prior experience with military executions?
4. For what crime is Danny Deever being executed?

Interpreting

5. In the second stanza, the Color-Sergeant explains one soldier's hard breathing by saying it is "bitter cold." He explains another soldier's fainting as the result of "a touch of sun." Are these conflicting explanations believable? What really accounts for the physical problems of the men?
6. What does Files-on-Parade mean when he says, "I've drunk 'is beer a score o'times"?
7. Compare and contrast Files-on-Parade and the Color-Sergeant.

Applying

8. The poem gives few facts about Danny Deever or his crime. Explain whether this lack of information makes you more or less sympathetic to him.

ANALYZING LITERATURE

Understanding Dramatic Poetry

The actual words of speakers play an important part in **dramatic poetry**—poetry that makes you feel that you are present witnessing dramatic events. In dramatic poetry, as in a play, the main action is conveyed through the words of speakers.

1. What effect is created by having Files-on-Parade and the Color-Sergeant speak in dialect?
2. The last half of each stanza of "Danny Deever" employs the same distinctive speech patterns used by Files-on-Parade and the Color-Sergeant. These lines, however, are not enclosed in quotation marks. Who do you think is speaking these words—another soldier, the poet, or some other observer?
3. Tell whether you think the poem would have been more effective if all the action had been revealed through the words of Files-on-Parade and the Color-Sergeant. Explain your answer.

LEARNING OPTION

Speaking and Listening. Dramatic poetry cries out to be read aloud. Actually hearing a poem will make you more aware of its rhyme scheme and its rhythms. To get still more out of reading dramatic poetry aloud, try making each speaker's voice sound a little different by capturing the flavor of the particular character. In addition, give questions and statements the proper inflection.

Practice reading "Danny Deever" aloud, experimenting with ways of making each speaker sound natural but different from the other. Decide whether you want the last four lines of each stanza to sound like the voices of the two soldiers or to contrast with them. When you are ready, give a reading of "Danny Deever" for your class.

GUIDE FOR READING

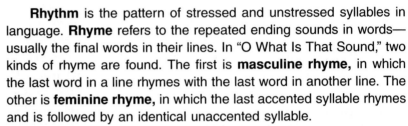

O What Is That Sound

Rhythm and Rhyme

Rhythm is the pattern of stressed and unstressed syllables in language. **Rhyme** refers to the repeated ending sounds in words—usually the final words in their lines. In "O What Is That Sound," two kinds of rhyme are found. The first is **masculine rhyme,** in which the last word in a line rhymes with the last word in another line. The other is **feminine rhyme,** in which the last accented syllable rhymes and is followed by an identical unaccented syllable.

In the following stanza from "O What Is That Sound," the stressed syllables are marked ′ and the unstressed syllables are marked ˇ. Notice the masculine (ear/dear) and feminine (drumming/coming) rhymes.

> Ŏ whát ǐs thàt sound whǐch sǒ thrílls thĕ ear
>
> Dówn ǐn thĕ válley drúmmǐng, drúmmǐng?
>
> Ónlly thĕ scárlĕt sóldiĕrs, dear,
>
> Thĕ sóldǐĕrs cómǐng.

Focus

In Auden's poem, two civilians are menaced by soldiers. Get together with a small group of students and think of situations in which soldiers threatened or oppressed a civilian population. Choose examples from history or current events. One example from American history would be Britain's use of soldiers to intimidate Americans just before the outbreak of the Revolutionary War. Keep your example in mind as you read Auden's poem.

Vocabulary

Knowing the following word will help you as you read the poem.
wheeling (hwēl′ iŋ) *v.*: Changing direction suddenly (l. 14)

Wystan Hugh Auden

(1907–1973) was born in England. He first attracted attention as a poet while a student at Oxford University in England and was recognized as a leading poet of his time while he was still a young man. In 1935 Auden married Erika Mann, daughter of the novelist Thomas Mann, to provide the British passport she needed to escape from Hitler's Germany. The poem "O What Is That Sound" suggests the predicament of someone less fortunate than Erika Mann.

O What
Is That Sound

W. H. Auden

O what is that sound which so thrills the ear
    Down in the valley drumming, drumming?
Only the scarlet soldiers, dear,
    The soldiers coming.

5 O what is that light I see flashing so clear
    Over the distance brightly, brightly?
Only the sun on their weapons, dear,
    As they step lightly.

O what are they doing with all that gear,
10   What are they doing this morning, this morning?
Only their usual maneuvers, dear,
    Or perhaps a warning.

O why have they left the road down there,
    Why are they suddenly wheeling, wheeling?
15 Perhaps a change in their orders, dear.
    Why are you kneeling?

O haven't they stopped for the doctor's care,
    Haven't they reined their horses, their horses?
Why, they are none of them wounded, dear,
20   None of these forces.

O is it the parson they want, with white hair,
    Is it the parson, is it, is it?
No, they are passing his gateway, dear,
    Without a visit.

25 O it must be the farmer who lives so near.
    It must be the farmer so cunning, so cunning?
They have passed the farmyard already, dear,
    And now they are running.

O where are you going? Stay with me here!
Were the vows you swore deceiving, deceiving?
No, I promised to love you, dear,
But I must be leaving.

O it's broken the lock and splintered the door,
O it's the gate where they're turning, turning;
Their boots are heavy on the floor
And their eyes are burning.

Responding to the Selection

Your Response

1. The woman in the poem appeals to the "vows" her companion made. Do you think he is being disloyal to her by leaving? Explain.

Recalling

2. What sound signals the soldiers' approach?
3. How can you tell if the soldiers are armed?
4. What inferences does one speaker make about the soldiers' reasons for approaching?
5. For what reason have the soldiers arrived?
6. What dishonorable act occurs?

Interpreting

7. How many speakers are there in the poem?
8. What is the probable relation between the speakers—relatives, business associates, sweethearts, friends, or other? Find evidence in the poem to support your answer.
9. Who do you think speaks the final two lines of the poem? Quote lines in the poem to support your answer.

Applying

10. How do the speakers' attitudes toward their neighbors and toward each other help explain their fear?
11. Newspapers teem with stories of civilians in other countries who are taken prisoner by soldiers for political crimes—real or imagined—against the state. Discuss a current political situation that might be an appropriate backdrop for this poem.

Analyzing Literature

Understanding Rhythm and Rhyme

Meter is the rhythmical pattern of a poem—the systematic way in which accented and unaccented syllables are arranged. Meter is usually described as consisting of units called feet. A **metrical foot** consists of one accented syllable and one or more unaccented ones. The common kinds of feet in English poetry follow.

iamb an unaccented syllable followed by an accented one

(bĕfóre)

anapest two unaccented syllables followed by an accented one

('Tw̆as th̆e níght . . .)

trochee one accented syllable followed by one unaccented syllable

(drúmmin̆g)

dactyl one accented syllable followed by two unaccented syllables

(ténd̆erl̆y).

Note that accented and unaccented syllables are marked by the symbols ′ and ˘.

Rhyme, or the matching of sounds at the ends of lines, may be masculine or feminine. In masculine rhyme, the last syllables of the final words in two or more lines rhyme (ear/dear, away/today).

In **feminine rhyme,** the accented syllables are followed by identical unaccented syllables (bríghtlў/líghtlў).

1. Each of the following words makes up a metrical foot in "O What Is That Sound." Use the symbols ′ and ˘ to indicate the accented and unaccented syllables. Then label each according to the kind of metrical foot it is.
   a. drumming   c. flashing
   b. indicate   d. suddenly
2. Analyze the metrical pattern of the first stanza of this poem.

3. Auden makes consistent use of feminine rhymes in this poem. Which lines in which stanzas rhyme in this way?

THINKING AND WRITING

Patterning the Style of the Poem

In "O What Is That Sound," the soldiers pass by the houses of a doctor, a parson, and a farmer. Imagine some other character whose house the soldiers might pass by. Then write a stanza about your character. Pattern your stanza after the rhythm and rhyme scheme of a stanza in "O What Is That Sound." When you revise, make sure the first two lines have been spoken by one speaker and the last two lines by the other.

MULTICULTURAL CONNECTION

Poetry and the Oral Tradition

W. H. Auden's "O What Is That Sound" is written as spoken dialogue, but the poem may be read as well as recited. Poetry in other cultures and times was not meant to be read but listened to, as it was spoken or sung by the poet or person reciting it.

The oral tradition of poetry goes back to the dawn of civilization, before written language existed. In ancient Greece, for example, poets called bards would sing about the deeds of great heroes and gods. The most famous bard was a legendary blind man named Homer, whose two greatest epic poems, the *Iliad* and the *Odyssey,* tell about the Trojan War fought between the Greeks and the Trojans and the return of a hero from that war. It is believed that these oral poems were finally written down at the end of Homer's life or even after his death.

This oral tradition lived on in twentieth-century Yugoslavia, where, in the 1930's, an American scholar studied native bards who could recite long poems although they couldn't read or write. The scholar believed that the bards did not memorize the poems but recited them spontaneously, improvising and changing them a little each time. Certain phrases, lines, and even whole scenes of their epic poems—like Homer's—were repeated, giving these long unrhymed poems a rhythm and form uniquely their own.

Exploring On Your Own

Find out more about the oral tradition in your own or another culture. This tradition might include sayings, folk tales, and poems. Then tell your class about what you have learned.

GUIDE FOR READING

Edgar Allan Poe

(1809–1849) was born in Boston, Massachusetts. Orphaned at an early age, Poe went to live with his godfather, John Allan, a wealthy Richmond, Virginia, merchant. Poe attended the University of Virginia for a year. After an unsuccessful try at a military career, Poe turned to journalism, a career to which he was far better suited. Although he achieved fame in his short lifetime, happiness and financial security eluded him. In "Eldorado" Poe writes of a search for a legendary city of gold.

Eldorado

Dialogue

Dialogue is talking between characters, or conversation. It is the direct representation of a character's words in a play, story, or poem. In dramatic poetry, dialogue is the main way in which the story of the poem is told. Dialogue in a poem may be set off by enclosing the speaker's words in quotation marks, or the beginning and end of a speaker's words may be suggested in some other way.

Focus

In the poem, "Eldorado" refers to the legendary country of riches and gold that was said to exist somewhere in South America. Poe wrote the poem after gold had been discovered in California in 1849. As a result of the discovery, thousands of people rushed to California to seek their fortunes. In "Eldorado," Poe describes a knight engaged in a similar quest.

The quest for wealth, power, or eternal fame is a common theme in literature. Like the knight in "Eldorado," characters can spend many years of their lives in quest of an elusive goal. Make a chart like the one that follows. Then list goals that you think are worth pursuing and others that you think are not. Keep your chart in mind as you read "Eldorado."

GOALS WORTH PURSUING	GOALS NOT WORTH PURSUING

THE BATTLE OF LIFE (THE GOLDEN KNIGHT)
Gustav Klimt
Courtesy Galerie St. Etienne, New York

Eldorado[1]

Edgar Allan Poe

Gaily bedight,[2]
A gallant knight,
In sunshine and in shadow,
Had journeyed long,
5   Singing a song,
In search of Eldorado.

But he grew old—
This knight so bold—

And o'er his heart a shadow
10   Fell as he found
No spot of ground
That looked like Eldorado.

And, as his strength
Failed him at length,
15 He met a pilgrim[3] shadow—
"Shadow," said he,
"Where can it be—
This land of Eldorado?"

"Over the Mountains
20   Of the Moon,
Down the Valley of the Shadow,
Ride, boldly ride,"
The shade[4] replied,—
"If you seek for Eldorado!"

---

1. Eldorado (el də rä′ dō): A legendary kingdom in South America, supposed to be rich in gold and precious stones and sought by sixteenth-century explorers.
2. bedight (bi dīt′) *adj.*: Adorned.

3. pilgrim *adj.*: Wanderer.
4. shade *n.*: Ghost.

1. Who are the speakers in this dramatic poem?
2. Why do they speak to one another at this particular time?
3. Explain how the conversation provides a dramatic climax to the poem.

RESPONDING TO THE SELECTION

Your Response

1. Poe describes the knight as "gallant" and "bold." After reading the poem, how would you describe the knight?
2. The shadow gives the knight advice about Eldorado. If you could give the knight advice, what would you tell him?

Recalling

3. Explain what the knight has been doing for a long time.
4. Does he feel he has been successful? Find evidence to support your answer.
5. What pair of rhyming words is repeated in each stanza of "Eldorado"?

Interpreting

6. Explain what is about to happen to the knight at the end of the poem. Find evidence in the poem to support your answer.

Applying

7. Eldorado is a symbol for an unattainable ideal. In this poem, does Poe seem to suggest that striving for unreachable goals is good or bad? Do you agree or disagree with him? Give reasons to support your opinion.

ANALYZING LITERATURE

Understanding Dialogue

   Dialogue represents the exact words of characters in a play, story, or poem. Dialogue is an important feature of dramatic poetry. When characters speak directly to one another about what is going on, the reader feels present at the scene. In "Eldorado" the dialogue provides a dramatic climax to the poem. Remember that a speaker's exact words in a poem are usually, but not always, enclosed in quotation marks.

LEARNING OPTIONS

1. **Art.** Draw the "pilgrim shadow" and the "Valley of the Shadow" from the poem. Make your drawing reflect your interpretation of each. You might consider the following questions before you begin to sketch: Does the shadow have a face? If so, what does the face look like? What is its expression? How is the shadow dressed? What is the shadow's posture? What does the name "Valley of the Shadow" suggest about how it would look? Once you have completed your drawings, share them with your class.

2. **Cross-curricular Connection.** During the Age of Discovery, many Spanish explorers sought the legendary country of Eldorado in South America. Among them were Jiménez de Quesada, a brother of Francisco Pizarro, and Francisco Orellana. These explorers, as well as others, journeyed over the Andes and down the mighty Amazon River, but none found the famed kingdom of gold. Read more about the quest for Eldorado in an encyclopedia or in other reference books in the library. Then write a short magazine article in which you discuss the fate of the explorers who sought Eldorado.

3. **Writing.** Write a short story about a character named L. Dorado, set in the present in your city or town. Use elements of Poe's poem to activate your imagination. For example, how would your Mr. or Ms. Dorado be "gaily bedight"? What might happen to a modern character who spent her or his life in search of a modern "Eldorado"?

The Speaker and Tone

COUPLE
Kees Van Dongen
Galleria d'Arte Moderna-Parigi/Servizio

GUIDE FOR READING

The Sonnet-Ballad

Gwendolyn Brooks (1917–   ) was born in Topeka, Kansas, but lived most of her life in Chicago, Illinois. She wrote her first poems at age seven and was regularly submitting her poetry to a Chicago newspaper by age sixteen. In 1950 she won the Pulitzer Prize for Poetry. "The Sonnet-Ballad" exemplifies Brooks's attempt in her writing to "feature people and their concerns—their troubles as well as their joys."

One Perfect Rose

Dorothy Parker (1893–1967) grew up in New York City. Beginning as a fashion writer and drama critic, she later wrote short stories, verse, and book reviews for *The New Yorker* and other magazines. Parker published several volumes of short stories and poetry, including *Enough Rope* (1926) and *Death and Taxes* (1931). She was famous for her wit and sarcasm. For example, when told that President Calvin Coolidge, known for his poker face and rigid manner, had died, she replied, "How can they tell?" "One Perfect Rose" exemplifies her sarcastic wit.

To Satch

Samuel Allen (1917–   ), who also writes under the name Paul Vesey, was born in Columbus, Ohio. After receiving a law degree from Harvard University, he practiced law for many years and wrote poetry and essays for publication. Eventually he chose to concentrate on his writing and a second career as a college professor of African and Afro-American literature. Among his many published works are *Ivory Tusks and Other Poems* (1968) and *Poems From Africa* (1973). "To Satch" glorifies the black baseball pitcher Satchel Paige.

Speaker and Tone

The **speaker** of a poem is the voice of the poem. The speaker and the poet are not necessarily the same, although the speaker can be the poet. The speaker can also be a character that the poet creates, as in "The Sonnet-Ballad." To identify the speaker, ask yourself whose point of view the poem expresses and whom the poem addresses.

Each speaker also uses a certain **tone**—the attitude the speaker takes toward the poem's subject. A speaker may use a serious tone, as in "The Sonnet-Ballad," or the speaker may take a humorous attitude, as in "One Perfect Rose." Speaker and tone cannot be separated. Understanding the speaker's tone can help you understand the poem's meaning.

In ordinary conversation, a speaker conveys a certain attitude, mainly through tone of voice. The word *yes,* for example, takes on a different meaning when said eagerly or angrily or laughingly. Poets must impart the same attitude using only the written word, by choosing precise words and arranging the lines with care.

Focus

To appreciate how a story or description can differ depending on the speaker, try this activity in a group of four people. Imagine that a sports car has just rear-ended a school bus in front of your school. Describe the accident from the points of view of different witnesses. Possible witnesses are as follows: the driver of the sports car, the driver of the school bus, a student riding the bus, a young child walking by, and a police officer making a report. Members of your group can also assume roles different from the ones listed. Keep in mind, however, that each different speaker is describing the same accident. Then, as you read each of the following poems, be aware of who is speaking.

Vocabulary

Knowing the following words will help you as you read these poems.

lamenting (lə men′ tiŋ) *v.*: Feeling or expressing great sorrow (p. 582)

coquettish (kō ket′ ish) *adj.*: Flirtatious (p. 583)

impudent (im′ pyo͞o dənt) *adj.*: Shamelessly bold or disrespectful (p. 583)

floweret (flou′ ər it) *n.*: A small flower (p. 584)

amulet (am′ yə lit) *n.*: A charm worn to protect against evil (p. 584)

The Sonnet-Ballad

Gwendolyn Brooks

Oh mother, mother, where is happiness?
They took my lover's tallness off to war,
Left me lamenting. Now I cannot guess
What I can use an empty heart-cup for.
5   He won't be coming back here any more.
Some day the war will end, but, oh, I knew
When he went walking grandly out that door
That my sweet love would have to be untrue.

Would have to be untrue. Would have to court
10 Coquettish death, whose impudent and strange
Possessive arms and beauty (of a sort)
Can make a hard man hesitate—and change.
And he will be the one to stammer, ''Yes.''
Oh mother, mother, where is happiness?

RESPONDING TO THE SELECTION

Your Response
1. The speaker of the poem says that she "cannot guess what [she] can use an empty heart-cup for." What suggestions do you have for her?

Recalling
2. What situation is the subject of this poem?
3. What does the speaker expect to happen to her lover?
4. What four adjectives describe death's characteristics?

Interpreting
5. To what do you think "my lover's tallness" refers in line 2? Explain your answer.
6. The speaker personifies death—talks about death as a person. Describe the kind of person death is in this poem.
7. How is death a rival? What is death's beauty?

Applying
8. What other situations might cause one to ask "Where is happiness?"

ANALYZING LITERATURE

Understanding Speaker and Tone

The **speaker** is the poem's voice. It may be the voice of the poet, of a character, or even of an object. The speaker in "The Sonnet-Ballad" is a young woman speaking to her mother.

The speaker's words communicate to the reader the **tone**—the speaker's attitude toward the poem's subject. The speaker's tone helps convey a poem's meaning and create its effect on its audience. For example, the speaker in "The Sonnet-Ballad" uses a serious, sad, somewhat bitter tone about the subject of a lover going off to war. But suppose the speaker laughed at this subject and made light of it. Changing the tone would change not only the poem's meaning but also would alter the audience's view and response.

1. What key verb used in line 3 helps set the poem's tone? Explain how it does so.
2. Describe the speaker of this poem. Why is she bitter?
3. Where does the speaker first state the poem's subject?
4. How does the speaker convey her attitude toward the poem's subject?
5. How might the tone of this poem be different if the speaker's true love were returning home from war instead of leaving?

One Perfect Rose

Dorothy Parker

A single flow'r he sent me, since we met.
    All tenderly his messenger he chose;
Deep-hearted, pure, with scented dew still wet—
    One perfect rose.

5   I knew the language of the floweret;
    "My fragile leaves," it said, "his heart enclose."
Love long has taken for his amulet
    One perfect rose.

Why is it no one ever sent me yet
10   One perfect limousine, do you suppose?
Ah no, it's always just my luck to get
    One perfect rose.

RESPONDING TO THE SELECTION

Your Response

1. If you were the speaker of the poem, how would you respond to receiving "one perfect rose"? If "one perfect rose" didn't suit you, what would you want instead?

Recalling

2. What event is described in the first line of this poem?
3. What would the speaker prefer to "one perfect rose"?

Interpreting

4. Describe the speaker of the poem.

Applying

5. Imagine that a similar poem about receiving "one perfect rose" was written by a teenage girl who had never before received flowers as a token of affection. How might this change in speaker affect the tone of the poem?

ANALYZING LITERATURE

Understanding Irony and Sarcasm

In verbal **irony,** the apparent meaning of the words is the opposite of the intended meaning. For example, when you say to a friend after everything has gone wrong, "Great day, isn't it?" you are using verbal irony.

1. What attitude does the speaker take toward the perfect rose in the first two stanzas?
2. What attitude is apparent in the last stanza?
3. How does the tone of this poem border on sarcasm, which is a biting form of irony?

To Satch[1]

Samuel Allen (Paul Vesey)

Sometimes I feel like I will *never* stop
Just go forever
Till one fine mornin'
I'm gonna reach up and grab me a handfulla stars
Swing out my long lean leg
And whip three hot strikes burnin' down the heavens
And look over at God and say
How about that!

---

1. Satch: Nickname (Satchel) for LeRoy Robert Paige
(1905–1982), legendary black baseball pitcher who,
after more than 20 years in the Negro leagues, entered
the major leagues in 1948.

Your Response

1. The speaker of "To Satch" describes grabbing "a handfulla stars" and then pitching three strikes. If you were to grab "a handfulla stars," what would you then do?

Recalling

2. How does the speaker say he feels?
3. What does the speaker say he will do?

Interpreting

4. What is the speaker's feeling about himself? What shows this feeling about himself?
5. The poem presents a picture in words to help convey the tone. What are the three parts of the image the speaker uses? What tone do the three parts of the image express?
6. Do you think this poem is a fitting tribute to the indomitable spirit of this legendary ball player? Explain your answer.
7. In the poem, the poet exaggerates the char- acter of Satchel Paige. What does this exag- geration add to the poem and its impact?

Applying

8. The baseball star Roy Campanella said, "You gotta be a man to play baseball for a living, but you gotta have a lot of little boy in you, too." Discuss the meaning of this quotation.

■ THINKING AND WRITING

Comparing and Contrasting Tones

Choose two of the poems in the poetry unit and compare and contrast their tone. First, reread the poems and list how they are alike and differ- ent in tone. Include specific details that contribute to the tone. Then use this information to write a paragraph of comparison and one of contrast. Be- gin with a general statement of the paragraph's topic. Revise each paragraph to make it persua- sive. Proofread for errors in spelling, grammar, and punctuation.

MULTICULTURAL CONNECTION

Negro Baseball Leagues

As early as 1867, African Americans were banned from baseball's first professional league. African Americans who loved the game formed their own professional teams. By 1900, there were five professional African American teams playing each other and twenty years later, after many failed at- tempts, eight teams organized to form the Negro National League. The Eastern Colored League soon followed, paving the way for the first Negro World Series in 1924.

Although they often played in the stadi- ums used by the white teams, the black teams were virtually ignored by the media. Racial discrimination often kept them out of hotels and forced them to sleep in their buses or in the ballparks where they had played earlier that day.

The first black major league star. In 1945, a promising African American rookie joined the black Kansas City Monarchs. His name was Jackie Robinson. Two years later, Robinson became the first African American player in modern major league baseball when he joined the Brooklyn Dodgers. He helped the Dodgers win six National League pennants and beat the New York Yankees in the 1955 World Series. Within a short time after Robinson's breakthrough, other tal- ented African Americans were signed on by major league teams.

Exploring

Research and discuss the contributions of African Americans to athletics.

Lyric Poetry

VIOLINIST AT THE WINDOW, 1917/18
Henri Matisse
Paris, Musée Nationale d'Art Moderne

GUIDE FOR READING

Autumn Song

Paul Verlaine (1844–1896) was a French poet who is now regarded as one of the most important writers of the nineteenth century. During his two-year imprisonment in Belgium for the attempted murder of a fellow poet, Verlaine wrote religious verse. Despite an irregular and unsettled life, he published several books of poetry that were recognized for their originality and lyricism. Much of his poetry, like "Autumn Song," focuses on feelings of isolation and anxiety.

I Am Not Lonely

Gabriela Mistral (1889–1957) is the pen name of Lucila Godoy Alcayaga, the first female poet, as well as the first Latin American, to win the Nobel Prize for Literature. Born in Chile, she was a prominent Latin American poet, educator, and diplomat. Her work often revolves around the theme of intimate relationships. Although she bore no children of her own, Mistral often celebrates birth and motherhood in her poems. "I Am Not Lonely" is from *Ternura* (Tenderness), her collection of children's songs, poems, and lullabies.

Making a Fist

Naomi Shihab Nye (1952–   ) was born in St. Louis, Missouri. A poet, songwriter, and story writer, she lives in San Antonio, Texas. She has twice traveled abroad as a participant in the Arts America program. Her poetry has been published internationally and has won several literary prizes. Among her works are collections of her poems, *Hugging the Jukebox* (1982) and *Yellow Glove* (1986). Her perception, imaginative sense of language, and ability to keep you close to experience is evident in "Making a Fist."

Generations

Amy Lowell (1874–1925) was born in Brookline, Massachusetts. She spent years reading, studying, and writing poetry before joining a group of radical poets called "Imagists," led by Ezra Pound. She became an energetic leader of the movement, which used precise, concrete images, free verse, and suggestion. She published several volumes of poetry and was posthumously awarded the 1926 Pulitzer Prize for *What's O'Clock.* The Imagist poets' vivid style that Lowell adopted and later refined is evident in "Generations."

When Your Face Came Rising

Yevgeny Yevtushenko (1933–   ), who was born in the Soviet Union, published his first book of poems as an adolescent in 1952. His criticism of his country's political rigidity brought official censure, but he has been allowed to travel and lecture throughout the world. In "When Your Face Came Rising," he writes openly about his fear, the fragility of joy, and the need for love in a world that seems barren.

Lyric Poetry

Lyric poetry is poetry that expresses a speaker's personal thoughts and feelings. In ancient Greece, such poems were sung to the music of a harplike instrument called a *lyre.* Lyric poems take their name and songlike quality from that stringed instrument.

Lyric poems express thoughts and feelings. For example, Verlaine writes about loss, Mistral about companionship, Nye and Yevtushenko about fear, and Lowell about the old and the young.

Focus

To understand how lyric poets evoke feelings through vivid words and images, draw a cluster diagram for a particular emotion. Then write down words and images you associate with the emotion you chose. See the diagram below.

Vocabulary

Knowing the following words will help you as you read these poems.

drone (drōn) *v.*: To make a continuous, dull humming sound (p. 590)

languorous (laŋ′ gər əs) *adj.*: Lacking vigor or vitality (p. 590)

monotone (män′ ə tōn′) *n.*: Uninterrupted repetition of the same tone (p. 590)

stripling (strip′ liŋ) *adj.*: Young or youthful (p. 594)

initiating (i nish′ ē āt iŋ) *v.*: Introducing or teaching about (p. 595)

Guide for Reading 589

Autumn Song

Paul Verlaine

translated by Bergen Applegate

Long sobbing winds,
The violins
   Of autumn drone,
Wounding my heart
5 With languorous¹ smart
   In monotone.

Choking and pale,
When on the gale
   The hour sounds deep,
10 I call to mind
Dead years behind,
   And I weep.

And I, going,
Borne by blowing
15   Winds and grief,
Flutter, here—there,
As on the air
   The dying leaf.

---

1. languorous (laŋ′ gər əs) *adj.*: Lacking vigor or vitality.

Responding to the Selection

Your Response

1. Do you share the speaker's impressions of autumn? Explain.

Recalling

2. What does the speaker recall that makes him weep?

Interpreting

3. What feeling is created by the opening stanza?

4. Search the poem for a reason that might explain the sorrow that the speaker seems to feel. Tell what might explain why he feels the way he does.

5. Explain the appropriateness of the speaker's comparison of himself to a fallen leaf.

Applying

6. Think of the other seasons of the year. What feeling do you associate with each?

I Am Not Lonely

Gabriela Mistral

translated by Langston Hughes

The night is left lonely
from the hills to the sea.
But I, who cradle you,
I am not lonely!

5   The sky is left lonely
should the moon fall in the sea.
But I, who cling to you,
I am not lonely!

The world is left lonely
10 and all know misery.
But I, who hug you close,
I am not lonely!

RESPONDING TO THE SELECTION

Your Response

1. Describe ways to dispel loneliness.

Recalling

2. What three things are lonely in the poem?
3. What is repeated in each stanza?

Interpreting

4. What is the relationship between the speaker and the person addressed as "you"? What verbs from the poem suggest this relationship?
5. What would make the night "lonely," as the speaker suggests in the first stanza?
6. How might the relationship between the people in the poem be similar to that between the sky and the moon?

Applying

7. What verbs besides the ones in this poem suggest the opposite of loneliness?

ANALYZING LITERATURE

Appreciating the Lyric Poem

Lyric poetry expresses intense personal feelings through vivid words and images that help you picture the experience and share it. By appealing to your emotions, the poet helps you identify with the feelings he or she conveys in the lyric. For example, one emotion that Mistral evokes is the feeling of loneliness.

1. What is another emotion that the poem evokes? Which words or images suggest this emotion?
2. Does the repetition in the poem help convey the poet's feelings? Explain.
3. Do you think that this poem would make a good song? Why or why not?

Making a Fist

Naomi Shihab Nye

For the first time, on the road north of Tampico,[1]
I felt the life sliding out of me,
a drum in the desert, harder and harder to hear.
I was seven, I lay in the car
5   watching palm trees swirl a sickening pattern
      past the glass.
My stomach was a melon split wide inside my skin.

"How do you know if you are going to die?"
I begged my mother.
We had been traveling for days.

---

1. Tampico (tam pē′ kō): Seaport in eastern Mexico.

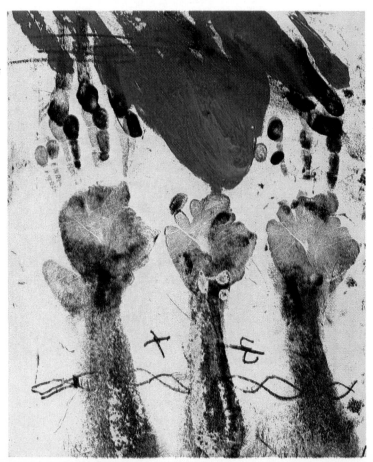

IMPRESSIONS OF HANDS, 1969
Antoni Tapies
The Museum of Modern Art, New York

10   With strange confidence she answered,
     "When you can no longer make a fist."

     Years later I smile to think of that journey,
     the borders we must cross separately,
     stamped with our unanswerable woes.
15   I who did not die, who am still living,
     still lying in the backseat behind all my questions,
     clenching and opening one small hand.

RESPONDING TO THE SELECTION

Your Response

1. Think back to when you were seven. What question or questions were you curious about?
2. Have you ever smiled to yourself when thinking about something you did as a child? Explain.

Recalling

3. What fear does the speaker express in line 2?
4. Which line first tells you what the speaker is feeling?
5. According to the speaker's mother, what happens "when you can no longer make a fist"?

Interpreting

6. In line 3, the speaker uses this powerful image: "a drum in the desert, harder and harder to hear." What is she describing with these words? Why is this description appropriate?
7. The images in the first two stanzas are clear, concrete pictures from the speaker's childhood. How does the last stanza contrast with the first two?
8. State in your own words the mother's response.
9. What is the significance of the title?

Applying

10. Explain one common method people use to deal with fear. Share this method with your classmates.

CRITICAL THINKING AND READING

Inferring Theme in Lyric Poetry

An **inference** is a reasonable conclusion that you draw from given facts or clues. You can infer the theme of a poem, when it is not evident, from specific details and images. The **theme** of a poem is its central meaning—the comment the poet is making about human life and values. In "Making a Fist," the poet comments on human life as a continuing journey and a test of survival. Her image of "life sliding out" of her early in the poem suggests that she has something to say about living and dying.

1. Dialogue in this poem is a clue to the theme. How does the dialogue between the child and her mother help you understand the poet's theme of survival?
2. The poet uses a fist as a symbol of life, yet it is not a fist that remains closed but one that is continually "clenching and opening." How does this detail in the poem relate to the poet's theme?

Generations

Amy Lowell

You are like the stem
Of a young beech-tree,
Straight and swaying,
Breaking out in golden leaves.
5 Your walk is like the blowing of a beech-tree
On a hill.
Your voice is like leaves
Softly struck upon by a South wind.
Your shadow is no shadow, but a scattered sunshine;
10 And at night you pull the sky down to you
And hood yourself in stars.

But I am like a great oak under a cloudy sky,
Watching a stripling beech grow up at my feet.

▐ RESPONDING TO THE SELECTION

Your Response

1. Does this poem show the main differences between youth and age? Explain.

Interpreting

2. When the poet speaks of the "young beech-tree," whom do you think the poet might be describing?
3. Using the poet's comparison to the beech-tree, how would you describe this person's physical appearance and movements?
4. Why is this poem called "Generations"?

Applying

5. This poem is written from the point of view of an older person speaking to a younger one. Explain how the feelings in the poem might change if the younger person were speaking.

▐ THINKING AND WRITING

Writing About Lyric Poetry

Choose one of the lyric poems you have read in this book. Then, using the definition of lyric poetry you have learned, write a brief essay explaining why the poem you selected is a lyric. First, list specific words and images from the poem that exemplify lyric poetry. Then use this information to write your essay for someone who is being introduced to lyric poetry for the first time.

When you have finished a rough draft, give it to a writing partner. Ask your partner to suggest two or three places where you might be more specific. Include those suggestions while revising your essay, making sure you have presented your information in a logical order. Proofread for errors in spelling, grammar, and punctuation.

When Your Face Came Rising

Yevgeny Yevtushenko

BIRTHDAY, 1915
Marc Chagall
Museum of Modern Art, New York

When your face came rising
above my crumpled life,
the only thing I understood at first
was how meager were all my possessions.
But your face cast a peculiar glow
on forests, seas, and rivers,
initiating into the colors of the world
uninitiated me.
I'm so afraid, I'm so afraid,
the unexpected dawn might end,

ending the discoveries, tears, and raptures,
but I refuse to fight this fear.
This fear—I understand—
is love itself. I cherish this fear,
not knowing how to cherish,
I, careless guardian of my love.
This fear has ringed me tightly.
These moments are so brief, I know,
and, for me, the colors will disappear
when once your face has set . . .

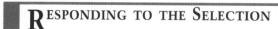

RESPONDING TO THE SELECTION

Your Response

1. Who in your life has dramatically influenced the way you see the world? Explain.

Recalling

2. What is it that the speaker fears?

Interpreting

3. How does the speaker's life differ after his friend's arrival?
4. Why is the speaker so afraid that "the unexpected dawn might end"?
5. What does the speaker mean when he admits that colors will disappear when he is no longer able to see his friend's face?

Applying

6. Are the feelings expressed in this poem similar to ones that all people experience from time to time? If so, are these feelings pleasant or painful? Explain.

THINKING AND WRITING

Responding to Lyric Poetry

Read "When Your Face Came Rising" again. Write a letter to the author in which you share your response to the poem. Begin by listing images or lines that seem particularly strong to you. Explain your response to sections that you favor. Trade first drafts of the letter with a partner in class and read each other's rough copies. See if you can find something worth commenting on in each other's letters. If your partner's remark prompts you to revise part of your letter, then change the original wording. Have your friend proofread your copy for errors in punctuation, spelling, and grammar before you begin writing the final draft of the letter.

A Blessing

James Wright (1927–1980) was born in Martins Ferry, Ohio, and graduated from Kenyon College and the University of Washington. A poet and a college English instructor, he has translated the works of Chilean writer Pablo Neruda and German writer Hermann Hesse. Among Wright's published works are *The Branch Will Not Break* (1963) and *Two Citizens* (1973). He received the Pulitzer Prize for Poetry in 1972. In "A Blessing," from *Collected Poems* (1971), he uses an image to generate, as a critic has described, "powerful emotions beyond the reach of logic or analysis."

The Street

Octavio Paz (1914–   ) was born in Mexico City, Mexico, and attended the National University there. He began his literary career at the age of seventeen and has since achieved international acclaim as a poet, critic, and social philosopher—in 1990 he was awarded the Nobel Prize for Literature. *The Green Wave* (1948) and *Sun Stone* (1963) have been translated into English and published in the United States. According to one critic, Octavio Paz sees his poems, such as "The Street," as "journeys" or "bridges of words" across which the poet travels from one side to another.

A Letter from Home

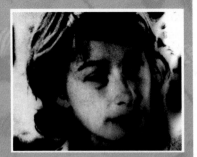

Mary Oliver (1935–   ) was born in Cleveland, Ohio, and attended Ohio State University and Vassar College. She traveled to England to live and work at Steepletop, the estate of deceased poet Edna St. Vincent Millay. Oliver now lives in Massachusetts and contributes poetry to periodicals in England and the United States. Her published works include *No Voyage and Other Poems* (1965) and *The River Styx, Ohio, and Other Poems* (1972). "A Letter from Home" expresses feelings Oliver may have felt while living in England.

Free Verse

Free verse is more open than poetry that uses conventional patterns of rhythm and rhyme. A poem written in free verse has no regular rhythm or line length and rarely has rhyme. Instead, poets who write in free verse usually try to imitate the rhythms of natural speech and invent new, individual arrangements of words and sounds that fit what they are saying and sound natural.

Focus

To understand the decisions faced by a poet writing in free verse, get together with several classmates and compare the following arrangements of the same words. How does each version change the way you read the lines? As you read the poems in this section, notice how the poets have arranged their lines.

Grandfather carried
his voice in the seamed palm of his right hand.

> Grandfather
> carried his voice in the seamed
> palm of his right hand.

Grandfather
carried
　　　　his voice
in
　　the seamed palm of his right hand.

> Grandfather carried his voice in the seamed
> palm of his right hand.

Vocabulary

Knowing the following words will help you as you read these poems.

caress (kə res′) *v.*: To touch or stroke lightly or lovingly (p. 599)

stricken (strik′ ′n) *adj.*: Hit or wounded, as if by a missile (p. 601)

A Blessing

James Wright

Just off the highway to Rochester, Minnesota,
Twilight bounds softly forth on the grass.
And the eyes of those two Indian ponies
Darken with kindness.
5   They have come gladly out of the willows
To welcome my friend and me.
We step over the barbed wire into the pasture
Where they have been grazing all day, alone.
They ripple tensely, they can hardly contain their
    happiness

10 That we have come.
   They bow shyly as wet swans. They love each other.
   There is no loneliness like theirs.
   At home once more,
   They begin munching the young tufts of spring in the
     darkness.
15 I would like to hold the slenderer one in my arms,
   For she has walked over to me
   And nuzzled my left hand.
   She is black and white,
   Her mane falls wild on her forehead,
20 And the light breeze moves me to caress her long ear
   That is delicate as the skin over a girl's wrist.
   Suddenly I realize
   That if I stepped out of my body I would break
   Into blossom.

RESPONDING TO THE SELECTION

Your Response

1. Describe a blessing that you or someone you know has experienced.
2. Have you ever felt as though you could "break / Into blossom"? Explain.

Recalling

3. What incident is the poet describing?
4. Describe what happens between the speaker and the slender, black-and-white pony.

Interpreting

5. A blessing may be defined as "anything that gives happiness." With that definition in mind, what significance does the poem's title have?
6. How does the speaker feel about his experience with the ponies?
7. What is the poet saying in the last three lines?

Applying

8. In a free-verse poem, pauses at the ends of lines are important to the poem's rhythm and meaning. Read the poem twice more, once *without* pauses at the end of each line and once *with* pauses. How did the different read-ings of the poem change your response to and understanding of it?

ANALYZING LITERATURE

Understanding Free Verse

Free verse is poetry that has no regular patterns of rhythm and rhyme. Free verse may sound more like prose than poetry because the verse lines are closely related to sentences. Yet the free-verse poet's use of line breaks indicates that the composition is, indeed, poetry.

1. Reread lines 5 and 6 of "A Blessing." What are the two parts of this complete thought? Explain why you think the poet divided these lines as he did.
2. Suppose the poet wrote the last three lines of his poem in one long line: "Suddenly I realize that if I stepped out of my body I would break into blossom." What would be lost as a result?
3. The rhythm of the poem is conversational un-til the last three lines. How does the poet em-phasize the significance of the last three lines?
4. Read the poem aloud. Do you find the poem musical? Explain your answer.

The Street

Octavio Paz
translated by Muriel Rukeyser

A long and silent street.
I walk in blackness and I stumble and fall
and rise, and I walk blind, my feet
stepping on silent stones and dry leaves.
5   Someone behind me also stepping on stones, leaves:
if I slow down, he slows;
if I run, he runs. I turn: nobody.
Everything dark and doorless.
Turning and turning among these corners
10   which lead forever to the street
where nobody waits for, nobody follows me,
where I pursue a man who stumbles
and rises and says when he sees me: nobody.

RESPONDING TO THE SELECTION

Your Response

1. Describe a time when you felt like the speaker in the poem.

Recalling

2. Describe the speaker's actions.

Interpreting

3. Reread the poem thinking of what it is like to be followed or to follow someone. The poet tries to suggest this idea in the pattern of the poem. Explain what this pattern suggests—for example, a bad dream or circumstances from which one can't escape.

Applying

4. Why is the mood of anxiety created by this poem especially appropriate for the modern world?

5. Julius Caesar once wrote, "As a rule, what is out of sight disturbs men's minds more seriously than what they see." Do you agree? Explain your answer.

CRITICAL THINKING AND READING

Recognizing Details That Create Mood

Most literary works have a **mood,** or dominant emotional atmosphere, that the writer seeks to establish. The mood sometimes can be described in a single word, such as *hopeful* or *sad;* other cases may require more involved descriptions. The details a poet uses can help you recognize the mood of a poem.

In free verse, poets may reinforce mood by using patterns of sound and rhythm. In "The Street," Octavio Paz supports a mood of anxiety through repeated words and rhythms. For example, the phrase "where nobody waits for, nobody follows me" enhances the anxious mood of flight.

1. Find another example of words, phrases, or details that add to the poem's mood. Explain your choice.

2. Which words in the poem are repeated? Give at least two reasons why the poet may have repeated these particular words.

A Letter from Home

Mary Oliver

She sends me news of bluejays, frost,
Of stars, and now the harvest moon
That rides above the stricken hills.
Lightly, she speaks of cold, of pain,
5   And lists what is already lost.
Here where my life seems hard and slow,
I read of glowing melons piled
Beside the door, and baskets filled
With fennel, rosemary and dill,[1]
10 While all she could not gather in
Or hide in leaves, grows black and falls.
Here where my life seems hard and strange,
I read her wild excitements when
Stars climb, frost comes, and bluejays sing.
15 The broken year will make no change
Upon her wise and whirling heart;—
She knows how people always plan
To live their lives, and never do.
She will not tell me if she cries.

20 I touch the crosses[2] by her name;
I fold the pages as I rise,
And tip the envelope, from which
Drift scraps of borage, woodbine, rue.[3]

---

1. fennel (fen′ əl), **rosemary** (rōz′ mer′ ē), **and dill**
(dil): Herbs used in cooking. Rosemary symbolizes
fidelity and remembrance.
2. crosses: Xs, symbols for kisses.
3. borage (bôr′ ij), **woodbine, rue** (rü): Herbs used
in cooking. Borage symbolizes courage and is thought
to drive away sadness. Rue symbolizes bitterness,
grief, and forgiveness.

Your Response

1. If you were away from home, what would you hope to read about in a letter from a close friend or relative?

Recalling

2. What are some of the topics the letter writer writes about?
3. Unlike many free-verse poems, this poem contains some scattered rhyming words, such as *frost* and *lost*. What other rhymes are used?

Interpreting

4. At what time of year does the action of the poem take place? Identify at least two clues from which you inferred the season.
5. How does the speaker react to the letter?
6. What comparison is implied between the letter writer's life and the speaker's life?
7. What do you know about the letter writer?
8. With a few exceptions, each line in the poem begins with an unaccented syllable followed by an accented one: "She sends," "Of stars," "That rides." How does this rhythm contribute to the mood of the poem?

Applying

9. Describe another situation in which you might have similar feelings to those of the speaker in this poem.

THINKING AND WRITING

Writing About Meaning in Free Verse

Choose one of the three free-verse poems in this book or another free-verse poem you like. Study the poem and list vivid words, phrases, sounds, and rhythms through which the poet expresses his or her ideas and feelings. Then use this information to write a paragraph explaining *what* the poem means and *how,* through the use of language and poetic devices, the poet communicates the meaning to you. Revise your paragraph to include examples that support your statements. Proofread for errors in spelling, grammar, and punctuation.

LEARNING OPTIONS

1. **Writing.** Write a letter to someone you don't see or speak to often. Before you begin writing, consider the following questions: What news do you have to share? What questions do you have for your reader? If you have pictures that might interest the person to whom you are writing, include them, and mention them in your letter.

2. **Cross-curricular Connection.** The letter-writer's world is represented in part by the herbs she mentions. Some herbs are used in perfumes; many are used in cooking; some are also known for their medicinal value. Certain herbs have symbolic significance, such as the ones explained in footnotes 1 and 3 on page 601. In your library find a book on herbs and read more about those mentioned in the poem—rosemary, fennel, dill, borage, woodbine, and rue. Present what you learn to your class.

3. **Language.** Notice how Oliver uses pronouns without antecedents in her poem. For example, "she" is never named; the reader must imagine who "she" is. Similarly, the word "what" in line 5 has no antecedent. As you read this line, you must infer "what" might have been lost. What inferences did you make as you read the poem? List some of your own ideas about the "she," "what," and "I" in the poem, and compare your answers to those of your classmates.

Figurative Language

MEDITERRANEAN LANDSCAPE
Pablo Picasso
Giraudon/Private Collection

GUIDE FOR READING

miss rosie

Lucille Clifton (1936–   ), born in Depew, New York, has written books for children as well as poetry for adults. The author of *The Black ABC's* and *Good News About the Earth,* Clifton won a National Endowment for the Arts award in 1970 and 1972. She lives in Baltimore, Maryland, where she is poet-in-residence at Coppin State College. Her book of poetry *An Ordinary Woman* and the poem "miss rosie" reflect Clifton's compassionate concern for the people and events of everyday life.

Size and Sheer Will

Sharon Olds (1942–   ) won two prestigious national awards for *The Dead and the Living* (1984), the collection from which "Size and Sheer Will" comes. A renowned teacher and poet, she earned her doctorate from Columbia University in New York City, where she now lives.

Olds often writes about intense emotions and explores her various roles as mother, daughter, and woman. In "Size and Sheer Will," she writes from a mother's perspective.

Metaphor

Eve Merriam (1916–1992) was a poet, biographer, radio writer, fashion-magazine editor, and teacher. Merriam found poetry "the most immediate and richest form of communication." She lived in New York City, where she joked that she would be the "last living inhabitant . . . when everyone else has quit for sub- or exurbia." Merriam lived in optimistic anticipation of what each new day has to offer. This optimism is reflected in "Metaphor."

First Lesson

Philip Booth (1925–   ), born in Hanover, New Hampshire, is a poet, a critic, and an English professor at Syracuse University in New York. Among the many awards Booth has won is the Bess Hokin prize, awarded by *Poetry* magazine, for his long poem "Letter from a Distant Land." Booth, a water-sports enthusiast, often writes about topics such as swimming in tidal streams and in the ocean, as is evident in "First Lesson."

Simile and Metaphor

Figurative language is language that is not literal but represents one thing in terms of another. Two common figures of speech are simile and metaphor.

A **simile** is a direct comparison between items that are unlike in most ways but similar in one respect. The comparison in a simile is usually made through the use of the words *like* and *as.*

A **metaphor** is an implied comparison that, like a simile, compares two items that are alike in one respect but unlike in others. However, instead of saying A is like B, a metaphor states that A *is* B—it equates the two items.

The following stanza from "The Day Is Done" by Henry Wadsworth Longfellow contains both simile and metaphor.

> The day is done, and the darkness
>   Falls from the wings of night,
> As a feather is wafted downward
>   From an eagle in his flight.

In this stanza, Longfellow uses the simile "*as* a feather is wafted downward" to describe the gentle approach of darkness. He uses the metaphor "wings of night" to depict the evening.

Focus

With a partner or in groups of three, choose one item from group A and one from group B. Then write a sentence about what the two items have in common: "Both _____ and _____ are . . ." Do this four or five times with different pairs of items. You might also want to try this activity with the similes and metaphors you find in "miss rosie," "Size and Sheer Will," "Metaphor," and "First Lesson."

Group A: a bicycle, a pair of glasses, scissors, an alarm clock, a clump of dirt, an elevator, garbage, a brown bag, a blank sheet of paper, a fish, a star

Group B: a baby, growing up, playing tennis, losing your temper, a football game, a shopping mall, a best friend, winning, laughter, an elephant, myself

Vocabulary

Knowing the following words will help you as you read these poems.

iridescent (ir′ i des′ ənt) *adj.*: Showing changes in color (p. 607)

elongated (ē lôŋ′ gāt′ id) *adj.*: Lengthened; stretched (p. 607)

miss rosie

Lucille Clifton

When I watch you
wrapped up like garbage
sitting, surrounded by the smell
of too old potato peels
5   or
when I watch you
in your old man's shoes
with the little toe cut out
sitting, waiting for your mind
10   like next week's grocery
I say
when I watch you
you wet brown bag of a woman
who used to be the best looking gal in Georgia
15   used to be called the Georgia Rose
I stand up
through your destruction
I stand up

RESPONDING TO THE SELECTION

Your Response

1. The speaker's tone suggests respect for miss rosie. Why is respect important?
2. How can people like miss rosie empower the people around them?

Recalling

3. Describe miss rosie.
4. What was miss rosie known as when she was young and beautiful?
5. What reaction does the speaker say she has when she views miss rosie's destruction?

Interpreting

6. Reread the simile in lines 9 and 10. What comparison is being made? What effect does this simile have? Explain your answer.
7. What has happened to miss rosie over the years?
8. What does the speaker mean in the last three lines?

Applying

9. The speaker in the poem gains determination to "stand up" from seeing the "destruction" of miss rosie. Can you think of instances in which a person gained strength or determination from witnessing the defeat of another?

Size and Sheer Will

Sharon Olds

The fine, green pajama cotton,
washed so often it is paper-thin and
iridescent, has split like a sheath
and the glossy white naked bulbs of
5   my son's toes thrust forth like crocus
this early Spring. The boy is growing
as fast as he can, elongated
wrists dangling, lean meat
showing between the shirt and the belt.
10 If there were a rack to stretch himself, he would
strap his slight body to it.
If there were a machine to enter,
skip the next ten years and be
sixteen immediately, this boy would
15 do it. All day long he cranes his
neck, like a plant in the dark with a single
light above it, or a sailor under
tons of green water, longing
for the surface, for his rightful life.

BOY WITH FLOAT
C. S. Mazarin
Courtesy of the Artist

■ RESPONDING TO THE SELECTION

Your Response

1. Why are children often eager to mature physically?
2. What advice would you give the narrator's son—or anyone who is eager to grow up quickly?

Recalling

3. Why have the boy's pajamas split?
4. How old is the narrator's son?

Interpreting

5. What do you think the title means?
6. Other than the ways described in the poem, how is the boy "growing as fast as he can"? What is the speaker implying about her son's emotional growth?
7. How do you think the speaker feels about her son's rapid growth?

Applying

8. The playwright George Bernard Shaw said that youth is "wasted on the young." Comment on this quotation. How does it relate to the poem? Do you think this remark is true? Why or why not?

■ THINKING AND WRITING

Writing About Simile

Explore a simile from "Size and Sheer Will." Begin by writing down the two items being compared (that is, the boy's toes and crocuses) and then list specific ways in which they are alike. Push your thinking beyond the obvious. Discuss your list with a partner and add even more ideas. Using your list, write a paragraph about why the simile is effective in the poem.

Metaphor

Eve Merriam

Morning is
a new sheet of paper
for you to write on.

Whatever you want to say,
5   all day,
until night
folds it up
and files it away.

The bright words and the dark words
10   are gone
until dawn
and a new day
to write on.

▉ RESPONDING TO THE SELECTION

Your Response

1. To what would you compare the morning? Why?
2. List three examples of "bright words" and three of "dark words."

Recalling

3. To what is morning compared?
4. What does night do at the end of the day?
5. What happens to words at night?

Interpreting

6. What does "files it away" in line 8 suggest?
7. What do you think the poet means by "bright words and the dark words" in line 9?

Applying

8. The poet says that morning is a new sheet of paper that you write on all day. Would the metaphor be more or less effective, in your opinion, if it said, "Each *day* is a new sheet of paper"? Give reasons for your opinion.

▉ ANALYZING LITERATURE

Understanding Metaphor

A **metaphor** compares two different items, usually by equating them. As with a simile, a good metaphor is more than mere description. Its purpose is, through only a few words, to present something familiar in a new light, giving you a new insight into its nature. In "Metaphor," morning is presented in terms of "a new sheet of paper."

1. What qualities do morning and a new sheet of paper share?
2. Why is this metaphor effective?

First Lesson

Philip Booth

Lie back, daughter, let your head
be tipped back in the cup of my hand.
Gently, and I will hold you. Spread
your arms wide, lie out on the stream
5   and look high at the gulls. A dead-
man's-float is face down. You will dive
and swim soon enough where this tidewater
ebbs to the sea. Daughter, believe
me, when you tire on the long thrash
10 to your island, lie up, and survive.
As you float now, where I held you
and let go, remember when fear
cramps your heart what I told you:
lie gently and wide to the light-year
15 stars, lie back, and the sea will hold you.

MELANIE AND ME SWIMMING
Michael Andrews
The Tate Gallery, London

RESPONDING TO THE SELECTION

Your Response

1. Name one of the most difficult things you ever did. Why was it difficult?

Recalling

2. What is the speaker teaching his daughter?
3. What specific instructions does he give her?

Interpreting

4. What does the poet mean by "you will dive and swim soon enough" (lines 6 and 7)?
5. What experience in life is being compared to floating face up in the water?
6. How does the father feel toward his daughter? Find evidence in the poem to support your answer.

Applying

7. Mark Van Doren has written, "The art of teaching is the art of assisting discovery." First discuss the meaning of this quotation. Then explain how it relates to "First Lesson."

THINKING AND WRITING

Writing About Metaphors

Create a metaphor for life that appeals to you—such as a journey, a game, or a race. Then write a brief essay for students being introduced to metaphors, explaining or showing how you can express what life is like by using only the metaphor you have chosen. Revise your essay to include examples to support your statements. Proofread for errors in spelling, grammar, and punctuation.

GUIDE FOR READING

Night Clouds

Amy Lowell (1874–1925) was famous for her readings and lectures, as well as for her poetry. She was awarded a Pulitzer Prize after her death for her volume entitled *What's O'Clock?* Lowell was a pioneer of the Imagist movement. Influenced by Japanese haiku poets, the Imagists focused on a single, precisely presented image. "Night Clouds" typifies Imagist poetry, with its strong central image and its rhythmic but irregular lines.

Sunset

Mbuyiseni Oswald Mtshali (1940–   ) was born in South Africa. His first book of poems, *Sounds of a Cowhide Drum,* sold more than 10,000 copies in its first year (1971). His writing often deals with is- sues related to racial tensions, but he also considers other problems. "I draw my themes," he says, "from my life as I live and experience it." In "Sunset" the poet wonders if even the vastness of the sun's rise and fall cannot be compared to the simple toss of a coin.

à pied

Colleen J. McElroy (1935–   ) was born and raised in St. Louis, Missouri, but she attended school in many different parts of the coun- try. She still retains a love of new places, and from her home in Seat- tle, Washington, she has traveled throughout this country and abroad. She has been just as adventurous in her mental journeys. In addition to writing poetry and fiction, she paints watercolors and writes film scripts. The poem "à pied" was inspired by something she saw . . . while traveling, of course!

The Wind—tapped like a tired Man

Emily Dickinson (1830–1886) spent most of her life in the small New England town of Amherst, Massachusetts. Lively and sociable as a young girl, she gradually became withdrawn and avoided all contact with strangers. Only seven of her poems were published during her lifetime. Dickinson is now recognized as a major writer of striking originality. The poem that follows displays one feature of her poetry—highly individualistic punctuation.

Figurative Language

Figurative language includes extended metaphor, symbol, and personification. An extended metaphor is a comparison made by equating two different items throughout the entire work. An example is "Night Clouds," in which clouds are equated with mares.

A symbol is an object, idea, or action that represents something other than itself. While common symbols have fixed meanings, like a dove as a symbol of peace, poetry often has its own symbols.

Personification is a figure of speech in which an object, animal, or idea is given the characteristics of a human. For example, in the line by A. E. Housman "And then the clock collected in the tower/ Its strength, and struck," the clock is given human characteristics.

Focus

Figurative language enables poets to convey meaning in original ways. Write one of the following pairs of words or phrases at the top of a sheet of paper. Below the pair, list ways in which the two things are alike. Push your imagination to go beyond the obvious.

a tree	a person
a pair of scissors	two good friends
making a pizza	writing a poem
clouds in the sky	horses in a field
the sun	a gold coin

Compare your list to your classmates' comparisons.

Vocabulary

Knowing the following words will help you as you read these four poems.

vermilion (vər mil′ yən) *adj.*: Bright red or reddish orange in color (p. 612)

azure (azh′ ər) *adj.*: Clear blue (p. 613)

forlorn (fôr lôrn′) *adj.*: Abandoned; deserted (p. 614)

incongruous (in kän′ groō əs) *adj.*: Lacking harmony of parts (p. 614)

commonplace (käm′ ən plas′)

adj.: Ordinary (p. 614)

careening (kə rēn′ iŋ) *v.*: Leaning from side to side while moving rapidly (p. 614)

countenance (koun′ tə nəns) *n.*: The face; facial features (p. 616)

tremulous (trem′ yōō ləs) *adj.*: Trembling; quivering (p. 616)

flurriedly (flur′ əd lē) *adv.*: In a flustered, agitated way (p. 616)

Night Clouds

Amy Lowell

The white mares of the moon rush along the sky
Beating their golden hoofs upon the glass Heavens;
The white mares of the moon are all standing on their hind legs
Pawing at the green porcelain doors of the remote Heavens.
Fly, Mares!
Strain your utmost.
Scatter the milky dust of stars,
Or the tiger sun will leap upon you and destroy you
With one lick of his vermilion tongue.

RESPONDING TO THE SELECTION

Your Response

1. How would you describe the clouds that are sometimes visible at night?
2. Why do you think that the speaker calls the clouds *mares* rather than *stallions?*

Recalling

3. Describe the appearance of the clouds.

Interpreting

4. Lowell uses an extended metaphor. List all the details that compare clouds to mares.
5. Why are the horses' hoofs "golden"?
6. To what does the "milky dust of stars" refer?
7. What is the effect of the phrase "tiger sun"?

Applying

8. The speaker in the poem urges the white mares of the moon to exert themselves to the utmost. What do you think is the implied message for the reader?

Sunset

Mbuyiseni Oswald Mtshali

The sun spun like
a tossed coin.
It whirled on the azure sky,
it clattered into the horizon,
it clicked in the slot,
and neon-lights popped
and blinked "Time expired,"
as on a parking meter.

THREE SUNS
Finnur Jonsson
National Gallery of Iceland, Listasafn Islands

RESPONDING TO THE SELECTION

Your Response

1. Mtshali compares the sun to "a tossed coin." What other object could you compare the sun to?

Recalling

2. What three sounds are you asked to hear in lines 4–6?

Interpreting

3. What is the significance of hearing such sounds?
4. Which lines or words do you think allow the speaker to share his perception of the sun most clearly? Provide reasons to back up your answer.
5. In what way does the setting sun's message remind the speaker of a parking meter? Do you think this comparison is appropriate? Explain.

Applying

6. Recall some sunsets you have watched. List three or four things that the setting sun brought to mind.

ANALYZING LITERATURE

Examining an Extended Metaphor

A metaphor speaks about a subject as if it were something else. An **extended metaphor** continues the comparisons for some time and may include several comparisons. The sustained comparison of the sun to a coin for the entire length of "Sunset" is an extended metaphor. Mtshali asks you to see and hear and imagine the coinlike impressions that the sun can make.

1. In what ways is the sun like a coin?
2. What advantage is gained by prolonging the comparison for the entire poem?
3. An extended metaphor should allow the reader to see the speaker's point of view more clearly as it continues. List words or lines from the text that allow you to do that.
4. As you analyze the actions assigned by the speaker to the sun (*spinning, whirling, clattering,* or *clicking*), other comparisons might suggest themselves. Name another action word that could describe the sun. Explain your answer.

à pied

Colleen J. McElroy

one shoe on the roadway presents
its own riddle of so much left
unsaid regardless of the condition:
scoured, unpolished and crumpled
5 like a drunk forever missing the next step
the tongue bent inward like some church
gossip who has said finally too much
and snapped that last accusation in
    public
the absence of laces or any restraints
10 and how everyone passing lurches away
from any entanglement

all roads at some time or other
have held a single shoe—the forlorn
reminder of someone careless enough
    to be trapped
15 like a teenager in the wash of fast travel
the incongruous one shoe out of step
without foot or wheels or movement
yet so commonplace as to almost
be forgotten by what is missing:
20 the left leg dangling bare
the child crying to be forgiven or the
    family
car careening on its mission of terror

one shoe on the road leaves it all
unsaid—the something that lies
25 without comment or recognition
in the heaviest of traffic or mid-lane
and turned sideways near the center
strip as if waiting for someone
to answer its description
30 if, as my father would say, the shoe fits
but this thing, so ordinary, cannot be
explained so easily like those strips
of rubber from burst tires

35 we'd soon as not remember how anyone
like a shoe may be lost in a crowd
or how part of what we know to be our
    lives
can become a stray digit or decimal
    point
an unrelated member of a set
yet any child from a divorce can tell
40 you how it feels to be abandoned
    midstream
while the family makes a fast break
for the nearest off-ramp—and we've all
heard of the countless armies

scattered like shoes in the traffic of war
45 along roads where city families once
took their Sunday country outings
but one shoe without ballroom or
    battleground
can never question the hurry of passing
it bends finally into its own loneliness
50 and unanswered questions of what
    might have happened
to its owner or what horror has befallen
    the other shoe

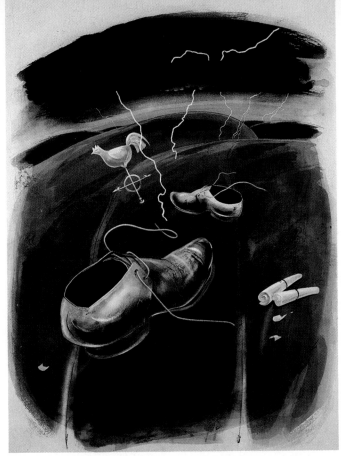

RESPONDING TO THE SELECTION

Your Response

1. Were you able to visualize the scenes and images described by the poet? Why or why not?

Recalling

2. Describe the sight that sparks the poet's associations in this poem.

Interpreting

3. The title of this poem, "à pied" (ä pyā′), is French for "on foot," as in "traveling on foot." Why is this title appropriate?

4. Why is the "one shoe on the roadway" a "riddle"?

5. Describe two situations or images that the poet associates with the shoe. What do these situations or images have in common with the shoe and with each other?

6. In what way is the poem about more than just an abandoned shoe?

7. Has the poet solved the riddle of the shoe, or has she deepened its mystery? Explain.

Applying

8. Write several additional lines for the poem expressing your own thoughts about a stray shoe.

LEARNING OPTION

Writing. Get together with several classmates and choose a common, everyday object that you can hold in your hand. Have each group member hold the object, describe an image or situation that the object suggests, and pass it on to the next person. When you have finished, combine your descriptions to make a poem, and choose a group member to read the poem aloud to your class.

ONE WRITER'S PROCESS

Colleen J. McElroy and "à pied"

PREWRITING

A Special Kind of Vision What most of us see when we pass an old shoe lying by the side of the road is just that—an old shoe. We may wonder briefly how it got there, but the moment passes.

Poets, however, cultivate a special kind of vision. As Colleen McElroy puts it, "Poems can turn the ordinary into the extraordinary."

Thus it should come as no surprise to learn that the idea for McElroy's "à pied" originated when she noticed a shoe in the middle of the road as she drove along the highway. Her mind started racing. "What myths could this shoe hold?" she wondered. "I began to think of the shoe not just as an item that caught my attention but as a symbol, one that linked my imagination to my curiosity about such questions as Who are we? and Where are we going?"

DRAFTING

The Ferment of Ideas It wasn't until traffic crawled to a stop a half mile later that McElroy had a chance to do anything about the ferment of ideas in her head. "I searched for my journal," she says, "a scrap of paper, anything to write on. I settled for the back of my travel itinerary."

Free Association Sitting at the wheel of her car, surrounded by bumper-to-bumper traffic, she started writing. "I wrote quickly, freely associating ideas without attention to punctuation or sentences. My notes became a scrawl of thoughts that even I had trouble deciphering later." First drafts are often frag-mented and messy because the goal is to write freely, without censoring oneself. McElroy's draft was barely legible, as you can see. At one point she even started a section upside down, but was too engrossed in getting her ideas on paper to turn the page around.

A Springboard Into the Unexpected "The appearance of the shoe became my springboard into what, at first glance, seemed easy," McElroy says. "But as I wrote, frantically in case the traffic cleared and left me, like the shoe, stranded mid-road, I looked for why the appearance of a lost shoe was both startling and expected. I thought of half a dozen possibilities. They arrived randomly. I would worry about shaping the poem in the next draft."

REVISING

An Army of Shoes It took McElroy several more drafts before she was satisfied with the poem. "The second draft," she says, "was basically the act of transferring my notes to a typewritten sheet. Along the way, I asked myself even more questions. . . . My imagination brought on a hoard of shoes, an army of shoes." Which shoes belonged in this particular poem, though? That was the question.

Tackling the third draft, McElroy still wasn't sure ". . . where the poem began." So she didn't try to begin at the beginning. "I started by looking for threads of ideas that could be grouped together—hopefully into stanzas. I also needed to listen for the music of the language, removing words that would interfere with my sense of music and tightening phrases that would strengthen the music."

Refining Language The chart below illustrates the process of refining the poem's language that McElroy talks about. At first glance, the changes may seem insignificant. "A lot" becomes "it all"; "it is something" becomes "the something"; "seen" becomes "passes" and then "lies"; "without comment" becomes "without comment or recognition." Yet all these changes together make the finished language much more specific and thus more effective. The finished lines have a pace and unstoppable motion that were missing initially.

Using Labels to Organize In her third draft, McElroy wrote numbers in the margin next to each section. This enabled her to shift sections around, creating stanzas. As she grouped and rearranged lines, she was letting the poem find its identity and rhythm.

"Most of all," she says, "I let the energy of my handwritten notes determine the pacing of the poem. . . ." She adds, "As I moved to the final draft, I had to confront the issue of the title." McElroy had been trying to force the word "shoe" into the title, but it simply didn't work. "Shoe seemed such a firm word," she says. "The lost shoe was more vulnerable, naked almost." McElroy felt sorry for the shoe. "Poor shoe," she recalls thinking, and out of that emotion came the title, "à pied," which is French for "on foot."

"After all," she points out, "it was not the highway or the cars or even the shoe, but the foot that had been left bare, and unprotected, without its shoe."

THINKING ABOUT THE PROCESS

1. At every stage of writing "à pied," McElroy asked herself questions. How can questioning oneself aid the writing process?
2. McElroy started writing down her thoughts immediately, even though she was in her car. What impact did this have on the final poem?
3. **Writing** Choose a spot to write and get comfortable. Give yourself two or three seconds, no more, to look around and pick an object. Then let your thoughts roam freely around that object for the next five minutes. Jot down everything that occurs to you, without censoring yourself. When you are finished, use your notes to create a short poem.

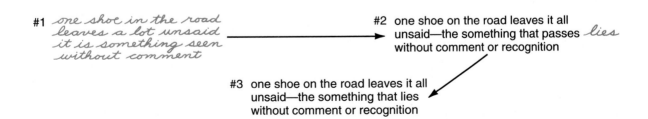

#1 one shoe in the road leaves a lot unsaid it is something seen without comment

#2 one shoe on the road leaves it all unsaid—the something that passes *lies* without comment or recognition

#3 one shoe on the road leaves it all unsaid—the something that lies without comment or recognition

The Wind—tapped like a tired Man

Emily Dickinson

The Wind—tapped like a tired Man—
And like a Host—"Come in"
I boldly answered—entered then
My Residence within

A Rapid—footless Guest—
To offer whom a Chair
Were as impossible as hand
A Sofa to the Air—

No Bone had He to bind Him—
His Speech was like the Push
Of numerous Humming Birds at once
From a superior Bush—

His Countenance—a Billow—
His Fingers, as He passed
Let go a music—as of tunes
Blown tremulous in Glass—

He visited—still flitting—
Then like a timid Man
Again, He tapped—'twas flurriedly—
And I became alone—

Responding to the Selection

Your Response

1. How does the personification in the poem help you see or think of the wind in new ways?

Recalling

2. Who or what is the "Guest" who enters the speaker's residence? Who is the "Host"?
3. What does the poet say the "Guest's" speech is like?

Interpreting

4. Why can't the "Host" offer the "Guest" a chair?
5. Look up the meanings of *flurry* in a dictionary. What related meaning of *flurry* makes *flurriedly* a good adverb for the "Guest" in this poem?

Applying

6. Emily Dickinson makes the dash stand for many things—a comma, a period, a semicolon, and even missing words that must be understood. However, not understanding her intent, the early publishers of her poems replaced the dashes with conventional punctuation. How do you think you would respond to this poem if it were punctuated in the regular way? Explain your answer.

Analyzing Literature

Understanding Personification

Personification is a figure of speech in which an object or idea is represented as a person. In "The Wind—tapped like a tired Man," the wind is personified as a weary man.

1. The wind is described as tapping like a tired man. How might a tired man tap on a window or a door?
2. The wind is described as a rapid, footless guest. What sounds might such a guest make when moving?
3. What offer might one make to a guest that is impossible to offer to the wind?
4. What impression of the wind does Emily Dickinson present through this poem?

Imagery

MEMORY, 1870
Elihu Vedder
Los Angeles County Museum of Art

Big Wind

Theodore H. Roethke (1908–1963), who was born in Michigan, is the author of more than a dozen books of poetry, as well as the author of children's books and essays. He has been recognized with numerous awards and degrees, including the Pulitzer Prize for Poetry and two National Book Awards. In "Big Wind" Roethke draws on the scenes of his childhood as the son of a greenhouse owner.

Loss

A. R. Ammons (1926–   ) began writing when he was a boy growing up in North Carolina. He published his first poems in 1955 while he was executive vice-president of a firm in Atlantic City, New Jersey. Since 1964 he has taught creative writing at Cornell University in Ithaca, New York, and has published many books of poems. In 1973 Ammons won the National Book Award for a collection of his poetry. "Loss" is typical of his work in the way that it transforms a small, ordinary moment into a vivid, memorable event.

Afterglow

Jorge Luis Borges (1899–1986) was born in Argentina, educated in Switzerland, and lived in Spain before returning to his native land. In addition to publishing many books of poetry, he helped to found three new, experimental journals. He served as director of the National Library and as Professor of English at the University of Buenos Aires. His work includes poetry and fiction that represent what he once called "spiritual adventures." "Afterglow" gives a glimpse into the lively mind of this talented writer as he tries to picture something that cannot be seen.

Imagery

Imagery is the use of vivid descriptions or figures of speech to create a mental image. In the poem "Night Clouds," the phrase "the milky dust of stars" paints a picture of a night sky.

Imagery also includes nonliteral uses of language, such as similes, metaphors, personification, and other figures of speech. No one believes, for example, that flowers really *dance* in the sunlight or that autumn leaves *scamper* in the wind. Such expressions are figures of speech used to create a mental image.

Often a vivid image can be achieved by joining ideas or words in unexpected combinations. In a poem about spring, E. E. Cummings used the words *mud-luscious* and *puddle-wonderful.* Such combinations bring the image into sharper focus.

Focus

Think of a natural event you have witnessed lately: the ripening of a tomato, a storm, or an animal amusing itself. Recall the event, as if you could replay it in slow motion. Then construct a chart of the five senses, and fill in as many details about the event as you can.

EVENT: _____

SIGHT	SOUND	SMELL	TASTE	TOUCH

The details you captured in words are images, the building blocks of poetry.

Vocabulary

Knowing the following words will help you as you read these poems.

pith (pith) *n.*: Force or strength (p. 622)

flailing (flāl^iŋ) *adj.*: Beating or striking with a thrashing movement (p. 622)

sumac (shoo^mak) *n.*: A type of small tree or shrub, often having a bitter sap; some varieties cause an itching rash (p. 623)

diffuse (di fyoos´) *adj.*: Widely spread or scattered (p. 623)

rigorous (rig^ər əs) *adj.*: Precisely accurate; strict (p. 623)

muted (myoot^ed) *adj.*: Silent; unspectacular (p. 624)

tautly (tôt^ lē) *adv.*: Showing strain; tense (p. 624)

Big Wind

Theodore Roethke

Where were the greenhouses going,
Lunging into the lashing
Wind driving water
So far down the river
5   All the faucets stopped?—
So we drained the manure-machine
For the steam plant,
Pumping the stale mixture
Into the rusty boilers,
10 Watching the pressure gauge
Waver over to red,
As the seams hissed
And the live steam
Drove to the far
15 End of the rose-house,
Where the worst wind was,
Creaking the cypress window-frames,
Cracking so much thin glass
We stayed all night,
20 Stuffing the holes with burlap;
But she rode it out,
That old rose-house,
She hove into the teeth of it,
The core and pith of that ugly storm,
25 Ploughing with her stiff prow,
Bucking into the wind-waves
That broke over the whole of her,
Flailing her sides with spray,
Flinging long strings of wet across the
    roof-top,
30 Finally veering, wearing themselves out,
    merely
Whistling thinly under the wind-vents;
She sailed until the calm morning,
Carrying her full cargo of roses.

Loss

A. R. Ammons

When the sun
falls behind the sumac
thicket the
wild
5   yellow daisies
in diffuse evening shade
lose their
rigorous attention
and
10 half-wild with loss
turn
any way the wind does
and lift their
petals up
15 to float
off their stems
and go

RESPONDING TO THE SELECTION

Your Response

1. How can feelings and behavior change as a result of the weather?

Recalling

2. What two forces of nature are at work in the poem?
3. How do the daisies react to each of the natural forces?

Interpreting

4. What change occurs at lines 5–17?
5. What kinds of words (parts of speech) create the contrast in imagery between the two parts of the poem?
6. What is the effect of having no punctuation, not even at the end?
7. Explain how the title relates to the poem. What do you think the loss is and why?

Applying

8. Describe another image from nature that would go with the title of this poem.

Afterglow

Jorge Luis Borges
translated by Norman Thomas di Giovanni

Sunset is always disturbing
whether theatrical or muted,
but still more disturbing
is that last desperate glow
5   that turns the plain to rust
when on the horizon nothing is left
of the pomp and clamor of the setting sun.
How hard holding on to that light, so tautly drawn and
        different,
that hallucination which the human fear of the dark
10 imposes on space
and which ceases at once
the moment we realize its falsity,
the way a dream is broken
the moment the sleeper knows he is dreaming.

■ RESPONDING TO THE SELECTION

Your Response

1. What feelings does a sunset inspire in you? Explain.

Recalling

2. When the sun does set, what is left on the horizon?

Interpreting

3. Why is sunset "always disturbing"?
4. What do you think the speaker means when he says it is "hard holding on to that light"?
5. Why is the "last desperate glow" especially disturbing?
6. In what way is the knowlege of a dreamer similar to that of a person who can no longer hold on to the sight he has described?

Applying

7. Think about an enjoyable experience you had while seeing some wonder of nature (perhaps a waterfall or fog). Briefly explain what thoughts you had afterward while recalling this experience.

■ ANALYZING LITERATURE

Examining an Image

By using descriptions that appeal to sight or touch or sound, poets help readers experience a topic. Examine this poem carefully for physical descriptions of the afterglow.

1. What two features of the setting sun are not left on the horizon?
2. How does the image in line 5 depict the influence of the afterglow on the plain?

NEWBURY HAYFIELDS AT SUNSET, 1862
Martin Johnson Heade
Memorial Art Gallery of the University of Rochester

CRITICAL THINKING AND READING

Analyzing the Overtones of an Image

A single word may be the center for an interpretation of the speaker's meaning in some poems. *Hallucination,* in line 9 of "Afterglow," may be such a word. Its dictionary definition is "the apparent perception of sights or sounds that are not actually present." But the speaker in "Afterglow" gives additional overtones to the word when he tells of the origin and termination of the hallucination.

1. Where does the speaker say the hallucination begins and ends?
2. What implications are associated with the word *hallucination*?
3. How do those associations influence your response to the poem?

THINKING AND WRITING

Writing About Imagery

Choose one of the poems you have read in this section. Reread the poem and search its lines for the details that enabled you to sense the physical dimensions the poet created with images. List those details in one column. In another, tell what sense the detail appeals to. Then write a brief explanation and evaluation of those images. After your first draft, swap with a partner and check over each other's work. Locate two places where changes might be made in these drafts. Suggest how variations in the writing might make these statements more coherent or more colorful. Also, be sure to review for errors in spelling, capitalization, and grammar. Then prepare a final copy of your own work.

GUIDE FOR READING

Reapers

Jean Toomer (1894–1967) was born in Washington, D.C., of French, Dutch, Welsh, German, Jewish, black, and Indian descent. He once said, "Because of these, my position in America has been a curious one. I have lived equally amid the two race groups." Toomer became famous at a young age with the publication of his book *Cane* (1923), which contained short stories, poems, and a short novel. In "Reapers" Toomer writes of a crew of farm workers mowing a field.

The Fish

Elizabeth Bishop (1911–1979) was born and raised in Massachusetts, but she loved to travel and spent many years living in Brazil. In 1945 Bishop entered a poetry contest along with 800 other contestants, and she won. As a result, her first book, *North and South* (1946), was published. "The Fish" was included in that book. Bishop was always a close observer of nature. She said in an interview, "I think geography goes first in my work, and then animals. But I like people, too."

Pitcher

Robert Francis (1901–   ) was born in Pennsylvania but now lives by himself in rural Massachusetts. He has written many books, including fiction such as *We Fly Away* (1948) and poetry such as *Come Out Into the Sun: Poems New and Selected* (1965). Francis has said, "By reducing my needs and doing all my own work, I am able to live on a very small income and have most of my time free for writing, reading, music, and gardening." "Pitcher" is one of many poems Francis has written about sports.

The Bees

Nazim Hikmet (1902–1963), a Turkish poet, is recognized as one of the great writers of the twentieth century. Because he opposed the policies of the Turkish government, he was sentenced to prison. Remarkably, he was able to write much of his best poetry in his prison cell. Within a year of his release, he was drafted, and he fled Turkey. He traveled to Moscow, Rome, Paris, Havana, Peking, and Tanganyika, and, in 1959, he became a citizen of Poland. His poems have been translated into fifty languages.

Mood

Mood is the atmosphere or dominant feeling or emotion conveyed in a poem. Poets use specific words, phrases, and images to express mood. In "The Fish" Bishop conveys a mood of sympathy. "I looked into his/eyes which were far larger than mine/but shallower, and yellowed,/the irises backed and packed/with tarnished tinfoil." These lines reflect a sympathetic mood as the speaker longs to understand the fish by looking into its eyes.

Focus

People experience a wide range of moods, from total despair to great joy. Design a mood thermometer like the one that follows to illustrate all the moods between these two extremes. Write a brief description of a mood on each of the temperature lines, and keep in mind that the moods should change gradually from despair (coldest) to joy (hottest).

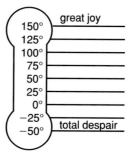

Keep your diagram in mind as you respond to the moods of the following poems.

Vocabulary

Knowing the following words will help you as you read these poems.

scythes (si*th*z) *n.:* Tools with long curving blades, used for mowing grass or grain (p. 628)

hones (hōnz) *n.:* Stones used for sharpening cutting tools (p. 628)

venerable (ven′ ər ə b′l) *adj.:* Worthy of respect because of age and character (p. 629)

errant (er′ ənt) *adj.:* Straying outside the proper path or bounds (p. 632)

arrant (ar′ ənt) *adj.:* Extreme (p. 632)

aberration (ab′ ər ā′ s h ən) *n.:* Something that goes astray (p. 632)

Reapers

Jean Toomer

Black reapers with the sound of steel on stones
Are sharpening scythes. I see them place the hones
In their hip-pockets as a thing that's done,
And start their silent swinging, one by one.
Black horses drive a mower through the weeds,
And there, a field rat, startled, squealing bleeds,
His belly close to ground. I see the blade,
Blood-stained, continue cutting weeds and shade.

RESPONDING TO THE SELECTION

Your Response

1. What other animals or even people are sometimes as helpless as the field rat in the poem?

Recalling

2. What are the reapers doing?
3. What happens to the field rat?

Interpreting

4. What does Toomer mean when he says, "I see the blade, / Blood-stained, continue cutting weeds and shade"?
5. What effect is created by the repetition of the sound *s* in the first two lines?
6. What do you think is the theme of this poem?

Applying

7. If the mower were to stop after the rat was hit, how would the mood of the poem change?

ANALYZING LITERATURE

Understanding Mood

Mood is the atmosphere or tone conveyed by a poem. Mood makes us feel a certain way after we have read a poem. A poet uses specific words, phrases, and images to create the mood of a poem. In "Reapers," Toomer uses sharp sounds—"the sound of steel on stones" and the squealing rat—to convey a feeling of harshness.

1. How does the color red (the bleeding rat, the blood-stained mower blade) contribute to the mood of the poem?
2. How does the reapers' "silent swinging" contribute to the mood of the poem?
3. What is the atmosphere at the end of the poem, when the mower keeps going after hitting the rat?

The Fish

Elizabeth Bishop

I caught a tremendous fish
and held him beside the boat
half out of water, with my hook
fast in a corner of his mouth.
5 He didn't fight.
He hadn't fought at all.
He hung a grunting weight,
battered and venerable
and homely. Here and there
10 his brown skin hung in strips
like ancient wallpaper,
and its pattern of darker brown
was like wallpaper:

shapes like full-blown roses
15 stained and lost through age.
He was speckled with barnacles,
fine rosettes[1] of lime,
and infested
with tiny white sea-lice,
20 and underneath two or three
rags of green weed hung down.
While his gills were breathing in
the terrible oxygen
—the frightening gills,

---

1. rosettes (rō zets′) *n.*: Patterns suggesting a rose.

25 fresh and crisp with blood,
that can cut so badly—
I thought of the coarse white flesh
packed in like feathers,
the big bones and the little bones,
30 the dramatic reds and blacks
of his shiny entrails,[2]
and the pink swim-bladder[3]
like a big peony.[4]
I looked into his eyes
35 which were far larger than mine
but shallower, and yellowed,
the irises[5] backed and packed
with tarnished tinfoil
seen through the lenses
40 of old scratched isinglass.[6]
They shifted a little, but not
to return my stare.
—It was more like the tipping
of an object toward the light.
45 I admired his sullen face,
the mechanism of his jaw,
and then I saw
that from his lower lip
—if you could call it a lip—

50 grim, wet, and weaponlike,
hung five old pieces of fish-line,
or four and a wire leader
with the swivel still attached,
with all their five big hooks
55 grown firmly in his mouth.
A green line, frayed at the end
where he broke it, two heavier lines,
and a fine black thread
still crimped from the strain and snap
60 when it broke and he got away.
Like medals with their ribbons
frayed and wavering,
a five-haired beard of wisdom
trailing from his aching jaw.
65 I stared and stared
and victory filled up
the little rented boat,
from the pool of bilge[7]
where oil had spread a rainbow
70 around the rusted engine
to the bailer[8] rusted orange,
the sun-cracked thwarts,[9]
the oarlocks on their strings,
the gunnels[10]—until everything
75 was rainbow, rainbow, rainbow!
And I let the fish go.

2. entrails (en′ trālz) *n.*: Intestines, guts.
3. swim-bladder: The gas-filled sac that gives buoyancy to a fish.
4. peony (pē′ ə nē) *n.*: A plant with large, showy flowers often red or pink in color.
5. irises (ī′ ris əz) *n.*: The iris is the round, colored part of an eye.
6. isinglass (ī′ z′n glas′) *n.*: A semitransparent substance obtained from fish bladders and sometimes used for windows.

7. bilge (bilj) *n.*: Dirty water in the bottom of a boat.
8. bailer (bā′ lər) *n.*: A scoop for removing water from a boat.
9. thwarts (thwôrts) *n.*: Rowers' seats lying across a boat.
10. gunnels (gun′ ′lz) *n.*: The upper edges of the sides of a boat.

RESPONDING TO THE SELECTION

Your Response

1. If you were the speaker, would you have let the fish go? Explain your answer.

Recalling

2. Describe the fish the speaker has caught.
3. What does the speaker find in the lower lip of the fish?
4. Explain what the speaker does with the fish.

Interpreting

5. Interpret lines 74–75: "—until everything/was rainbow, rainbow, rainbow!"
6. Why does the speaker let the fish go?

Applying

7. In this poem the speaker looks into the eyes of the fish and becomes a respecter of life—she throws the fish back. In what other small ways do people show that they are respecters of life?

THINKING AND WRITING

Writing About Mood

A critic has said about "The Fish" that it is one "of the most calmly beautiful, deeply sympathetic poems of our time." Expand on this statement by writing a review of the poem for a newspaper. Include the specific words, phrases, and images Bishop uses to create a mood that is "calmly beautiful" and "deeply sympathetic" in her poem. When you revise your review, include two more specific examples from the poem. Proofread for errors in spelling, grammar, and punctuation.

LEARNING OPTIONS

1. **Writing.** Elizabeth Bishop portrays one specific fish in astounding detail. Choose another animal with which you are familiar and write a description of it—either in prose or poetry. Let your reader see your subject in as much detail as Bishop uses. Try, as Bishop does, to create sympathy for the animal you describe. Let a friend or a classmate read your description and ask you questions about the animal you have chosen. Based on those questions, add even more detail.

2. **Cross-curricular Connection.** Bishop makes numerous references to anatomical and physiological details of the fish. Get together with two or three classmates and try to find answers to the following questions about fish. You might divide the questions among you and go to biology books or other reference books in your library. Then, as a group, discuss the ways in which the answers enhanced your appreciation of "The Fish."

   How do a fish's scales function?
   How do a fish's gills work?
   How many bones are in a fish's body? Are their skeletons like ours? Explain.
   How does a swim bladder function?
   Do fish see the way we see?

3. **Art.** Based on the speaker's description of the tremendous fish, create a drawing or painting that captures it in all of its rich detail. Perhaps you could even add real three-dimensional details to your artwork: strips of wallpaper, fish hooks, pictures of roses. Display your work of art on a bulletin board with a copy of the poem.

4. **Writing.** Marianne Moore, a contemporary of Elizabeth Bishop, has also written an often-anthologized poem called "The Fish." Find a copy of Moore's "The Fish," and compare and contrast it with Bishop's poem. As you study both poems, consider the following questions:

   Do the two fish look alike?
   How are the settings similar?
   Are the styles of writing similar?
   How are the speakers similar?
   Do the speakers feel the same way toward the fish?
   Are the themes of the poems at all similar? Why or why not?

   Then write a response to the poem you prefer, explaining your preference.

PITCHER
Mitchell Heinze

Pitcher

Robert Francis

His art is eccentricity, his aim
How not to hit the mark he seems to aim at,

His passion how to avoid the obvious,
His technique how to vary the avoidance.

The others throw to be comprehended. He
Throws to be a moment misunderstood.

Yet not too much. Not errant, arrant, wild,
But every seeming aberration willed.

Not to, yet still, still to communicate
Making the batter understand too late.

SUNRISE IN CRETE, 1981
Theo Hios
Courtesy of the Artist

The Bees

Nazim Hikmet

translated by Randy Blasing and Mutlu Konuk

The bees, like big drops of honey
carrying grapevines to the sun,
came flying out of my youth;
the apples, these heavy apples,
5   are also from my youth;
the gold-dust road,
these white pebbles in the stream,
my faith in songs,
my freedom from envy,
10 the cloudless day, this blue day,
the sea flat on its back, naked and warm,
my longing, these bright teeth and full lips—
they all came to this Caucasian village[1]
like big drops of honey on the legs of bees
15 out of my youth, the youth I left somewhere
                 before I was through.

---

1. Caucasian (kô kā′ zhən) **village** *adj.*: A village in
the Caucasus, a region in southeastern Europe
between the Black and Caspian seas.

RESPONDING TO THE SELECTION

Your Response

1. Do you have a memory of an earlier time in your life that is as warm and comforting as the speaker's memory in this poem? Explain.
2. The speaker refers to "[his] longing" in line 12. What do many young people long for?

Recalling

3. To what does the speaker compare the bees?
4. At the end of the poem, what does the speaker say happened to his youth?

Interpreting

5. What do the images of apples and honey suggest about the speaker's impressions of his youth?
6. What do the images of the sun (line 2), "the gold-dust road" (line 6), and "white pebbles in the stream" (line 7) have in common? Why might the speaker associate these images with his youth?
7. In lines 8–9, the speaker refers to faith and freedom. What do these references imply about the speaker's life after his youth?
8. How do lines 10–11 reflect the outlook or attitude that the speaker might have had as a youth?
9. Interpret the speaker's claim that he left his youth "somewhere / before [he] was through."

Applying

10. In *Song of My Youth,* Japanese author Ishikawa Takuboku wrote, "Like a kite / Cut from the string, / Lightly the soul of my youth /

CRITICAL THINKING AND READING

Understanding How Images Create Mood

The feelings and associations that emerge from an image contribute to the mood of a poem. Consider, for example, the qualities associated with bees. On the one hand, bees make honey, which is sweet. On the other hand, bees sting. Hikmet, however, emphasizes the sweetness associated with bees and honey. At the same time, he appeals to our sense of taste, which sparks an emotional response in the reader. The emotions we feel and the associations we make when we read an image help us determine the mood of a poem.

1. In your own words, what is the mood of the poem?
2. Find and list images in the poem that appeal to your sense of sight and touch. How do these images help create the mood?

LEARNING OPTION

Art. Choose an especially powerful image from the poem. Then draw or paint a picture of the image as you see it. In your work try to emphasize what you found especially moving about the image. In addition, try to capture how the image reflects the mood of the poem. Display your artwork for your class alongside a copy of the poem.

Musical Devices

SWING LANDSCAPE (detail), 1938
Stuart Davis
Indiana University Art Museum

GUIDE FOR READING

My Heart's in the Highlands

Robert Burns (1759–1796) was thought by many to be the greatest of Scottish poets. Known as the "Ayrshire ploughman," he was born in a small cottage in rural Alloway. Though the family was poor, Burns's father often bought books for the children with his scanty earnings. Burns learned to love the traditional songs and ballads of Scotland, and he began to write his own songs, including "My Heart's in the Highlands." Burns, however, could not sing the songs himself because he was tone deaf.

The Splendor Falls

Alfred, Lord Tennyson (1809–1892), was born in England. He wrote a great deal as a teenager and published his first book with his brother in 1827, called *Poems by Two Brothers.* His greatest poem, "In Memoriam," was published in 1850, the same year in which he was named Poet Laureate of England. He continued to write throughout his life, including collections of poetry such as *Charge of the Light Brigade and Other Poems* (1855). "The Splendor Falls" is set in the country Tennyson loved.

Buffalo Dance Song

The **Pawnee** are a Native American group that live mainly in the Pawnee, Oklahoma, area. They once lived in villages in what is now Nebraska. Once or twice a year, they left their villages to hunt buffalo on the plains. During the hunt the Pawnee lived in tepees made of buffalo skins. In addition to shelter, the buffalo was a source of meat and clothing. "Buffalo Dance Song" reflects how the Pawnee honored the buffalo.

Jazz Fantasia

Carl Sandburg (1878–1967) was born in Galesburg, Illinois. After first working for several Milwaukee newspapers, Sandburg went to the *Chicago Daily News.* While there, from 1917 to 1932, he worked as a reporter, an editorial writer, a motion picture editor, and a columnist. Sandburg won the Pulitzer Prize for History in 1939 for his book *Abraham Lincoln: The War Years.* He won the Pulitzer Prize for Poetry in 1951. The poem "Jazz Fantasia" is set in the city, about which Sandburg wrote many of his poems.

In Flanders Fields

John McCrae (1872–1918) was born in Guelph, Ontario, Canada. He became a physician, and in World War I he served as a medical officer in France. McCrae wrote poems during and about the war and is best remembered for his poem "In Flanders Fields," which was published by the British magazine *Punch* in 1915. The poem was reprinted in the United States to boost the morale of soldiers and encourage others to join the service. McCrae died of pneumonia in 1918.

Musical Devices

Sound devices are the tools of language that a poet uses to make a poem sound a certain way. Different devices achieve different effects. For example, **repetition** gives a poem the sound of a song. **Alliteration** is the repetition of the first sound of several words in a line. **Meter** is the formal organization of rhythms in a poem. Each line in the poem has a specific number of stresses if the poem is said aloud. **Assonance,** the repetition of vowel sounds, is still another sound device. **Onomatopoeia** is the use of words to imitate actual sounds.

Focus

Poets often try to use words that imitate or evoke specific sounds. Try your own hand at this device by finding or making up words to imitate the sounds described below.

two cats fighting
water draining out of a sink
the bird section of a pet store
roller skating on a rough sidewalk
the last seconds of a tied basketball game
a typing or keyboarding class
eating hot soup

Then compare your sound-words with those used by the poets.

Vocabulary

Knowing the following words will help you as you read these poems.

summits (sum' its) *n.:* The highest points of mountains (p. 640)

glens (glenz) *n.:* Secluded, narrow valleys between mountains (p. 640)

My Heart's in the Highlands

Robert Burns

My heart's in the Highlands,[1] my heart is not here,
My heart's in the Highlands a-chasing the deer,
A-chasing the wild deer and following the roe—[2]
My heart's in the Highlands, wherever I go!

5 Farewell to the Highlands, farewell to the North,
The birthplace of valor, the country of worth!
Wherever I wander, wherever I rove,
The hills of the Highlands forever I love.

Farewell to the mountains high cover'd with snow,
10 Farewell to the straths[3] and green valleys below,
Farewell to the forests and wild-hanging woods,
Farewell to the torrents and loud-pouring floods!

My heart's in the Highlands, my heart is not here,
My heart's in the Highlands a-chasing the deer,
15 A-chasing the wild deer and following the roe—
My heart's in the Highlands, wherever I go!

---

1. Highlands: Hilly areas in Scotland.
2. roe (rō) *n.*: A small, graceful European or Asiatic deer.
3. straths (strat͟hz) *n.*: Wide river valleys.

Your Response

1. Where is *your* heart? Why?
2. Does Burns's poem pique your interest in Scotland? Explain.

Recalling

3. Which two stanzas are repeated entirely?
4. To what does Burns say farewell in the second stanza? What two words in the second stanza characterize this place?
5. In the third stanza, what specific aspects of the place Burns loves does he mention?

Interpreting

6. What does Burns mean when he says, "My heart's in the Highlands, wherever I go"?
7. How does Burns feel about the Highlands?

Applying

8. Burns says, "my heart is not here." What kind of place do you imagine "here" to be?
9. William Shakespeare once wrote, "Praising what is lost/Makes the remembrance dear." Discuss the meaning of this quotation. Then explain how its meaning relates to "My Heart's in the Highlands."

ANALYZING LITERATURE

Understanding Repetition

Repetition is the repeating of words and phrases. It is a device that a poet uses to make a poem sound a certain way. By using repetition, Burns makes "My Heart's in the Highlands" sound like a song; he also emphasizes his idea. Burns not only repeats one entire stanza, he also repeats certain words, phrases, and rhymes throughout the poem. For instance, he uses the word *Highlands* eight times in the poem.

Parallelism refers to the repetition of the same grammatical form or structure. For example, notice that lines 1 and 2 both begin with the same grammatical structure—a possessive pronoun followed by a possessive noun followed by a preposition, an article, and a noun.

1. Which words and phrases are repeated in this poem? What effect is created by this repetition?
2. Which phrase is repeated most often in the poem? Why do you think the poet chose to repeat this phrase so often?
3. Which lines begin with a parallel structure? How does the use of parallel structure give the poem a musical quality?

LEARNING OPTIONS

1. **Cross-curricular Connection.** Knowing more about Scotland may help you identify with the speaker of "My Heart's in the Highlands." Read more about Scotland, with the following questions in mind:

   How large is Scotland? How many people live there today?

   What mountain ranges are in the Highlands?

   What are firths?

   What is Scotland's coastline like?

   What are its major rivers?

   What is a loch?

   Based on what you learned, write a letter to a tourist information center in Scotland, explaining why you would like to visit and requesting specific information that will help you plan your trip.

2. **Art.** Find recordings of Scottish bagpipe music in your library and listen to this national instrument of Scotland. After listening to several recordings, choose one that you think complements the poem, and play it for your class.

3. **Writing.** Imagine leaving your home to live elsewhere. Write a stanza or two of "farewells" in the style of "My Heart's in the Highlands." In your stanza(s) bid goodbye to anything that is special for you. Use repetition and parallelism. Try to make your images as specific and dramatic as those of Burns.

The Splendor Falls

Alfred, Lord Tennyson

The splendor falls on castle walls
    And snowy summits old in story:
    The long light shakes across the lakes,
    And the wild cataract[1] leaps in glory.
5 Blow, bugle, blow, set the wild echoes flying,
Blow, bugle; answer, echoes, dying, dying, dying.

    O hark, O hear! how thin and clear,
    And thinner, clearer, farther going!
    O sweet and far from cliff and scar[2]
10   The horns of Elfland[3] faintly blowing!
Blow, let us hear the purple glens replying:
Blow, bugle; answer, echoes, dying, dying, dying.

    O love, they die in yon rich sky,
    They faint on hill or field or river:
15   Our echoes roll from soul to soul,
    And grow for ever and for ever.
Blow, bugle, blow, set the wild echoes flying,
And answer, echoes, answer, dying, dying, dying.

---

1. cataract (kat′ ə rakt) *n.*: Waterfall.
2. scar (skär) *n.*: Steep, rocky place.
3. Elfland (elf′ land′): Fairyland.

Your Response

1. Did you visualize a particular landscape as you read the poem? Explain.

Recalling

2. Describe the setting for this poem.
3. To whom is the speaker in this poem speaking and to what are the people listening?
4. Explain what happens to what they hear.

Interpreting

5. What effect is created by the images in this poem?
6. Who are "they" in lines 13 and 14?
7. A refrain is a group of words repeated throughout the poem, usually at the end of stanzas. What is the refrain in this poem? What effect is created by the refrain?
8. What does the word *splendor* mean in the title of this poem? How can splendor fall? Interpret the meaning of the title.
9. This poem is sometimes called "The Bugle Song." Which title do you consider more effective? Why?

Applying

10. Explain why you do or do not think this is a love poem.

ANALYZING LITERATURE

Understanding Alliteration and Rhyme

Alliteration is the repetition of the first sound of several words in a line. In line 3 of "The Splendor Falls," Tennyson says, "The *l*ong *l*ight shakes across the *l*akes." He repeats the *l* in *long, light,* and *lakes.* He also uses internal rhyme to enhance the sound. **Internal rhyme** is created when two words with the same sound are used in one line of verse. In line 3 the words are *shakes* and *lakes.* By using these sounds, the poet creates an image of light rippling on the water of the lakes.

1. Name two lines and the words in them that illustrate Tennyson's use of alliteration. How does alliteration help create the images?
2. Give two examples of internal rhyme (other than *shakes* and *lakes*) from the poem.
3. Read the poem aloud. How does the use of alliteration contribute to its musical quality? How does the use of internal rhyme contribute to this quality?

LEARNING OPTIONS

1. **Writing.** Brainstorm to list other sounds, sights, sensations, or experiences that, like a bugle, repeat, roll, echo, and dwindle over time and distance. Examples are the ripples in a pond after a stone is tossed in, or perhaps experiences of love. Then try to write a poem about one of the images on your list. Use repetition, alliteration, and onomatopoeia to re-create the experience. Share your poem with your class by reading it aloud.
2. **Art.** Draw a landscape like the one Tennyson describes in this poem. You may want to include some of the features he mentions, for instance, "snowy summits," a "wild cataract," or "purple glens." In your use of line and color, try to re-create the mood that Tennyson evokes. Then you may want to exchange drawings with a classmate and see how someone else has visually interpreted the poem.

Buffalo Dance Song

from **the Pawnee**

Listen
the song of the aged father

The song
of the aged beloved

5 Our father
the buffalo heavy with age

Heavy with age
endlessly walking

Too heavy
10 to rise again if he should fall

Walking forever
walking forever

Humped high with age
head bent with age

15 Heavy with age
heavy with age

Aged buffalo
my aged father

UNTITLED (buffalo hunt)
New Bear (Gros Ventre Tribe)
Courtesy of Eastern Montana College Library

RESPONDING TO THE SELECTION

Your Response

1. The first word in the poem is "Listen." As you read the poem, describe what you heard as you "listened."

Recalling

2. Describe the buffalo honored in the poem.

Interpreting

3. Why does the speaker emphasize that the buffalo is "heavy"?
4. Why are the buffalo "endlessly walking"?
5. Interpret the metaphor of the buffalo as the "aged father."

Applying

6. Native Americans have tremendous respect for natural resources. What can people today do to show respect for the environment and preserve natural resources?

ANALYZING LITERATURE

Analyzing Repetition and Rhythm

The title of the poem indicates that "Buffalo Dance Song" is a musical poem. In addition the **repetition** and **rhythm** in the poem make it sound like a song. Poets employ these devices by establishing a pattern using the same sounds, words, and even lines. Repetition and rhythm are particularly effective because in some ways they mirror the music of the human body as the heart beats and as the person breathes in a rhythmic pattern. Repetition also helps the poet emphasize important words. As you read the poem again, concentrate on the repetition and rhythm.

1. What words are repeated most often? What does the repetition of these words indicate about how the Pawnee viewed the buffalo?
2. What phrases are repeated most often? How does the repetition of these phrases create rhythm?

CRITICAL THINKING AND READING

Understanding Purpose

The Pawnee held religious ceremonies to celebrate their sacred gifts, such as the buffalo. In these ceremonies great doctors and magicians performed their new feats, accompanied by singing, dancing, and music. Songs like "Buffalo Dance Song" were part of the ceremony. What purpose might "Buffalo Dance Song" or songs like it have served in a Pawnee festival?

THINKING AND WRITING

Writing a Musical Poem

What natural resources does our society depend on as the Pawnee depended on the buffalo? Write a poem that honors a natural resource. In your poem use repetition to emphasize important words. In your use of repetition, establish rhythm that has a musical quality. When you and your classmates have completed your poems, compile them in a volume and, as a group, decide on an appropriate title.

LEARNING OPTION

Community Connections. Many Native Americans were careful not to exploit the animals they hunted. By contrast many Europeans who settled in North America did not exercise such care. Recent environmental concerns, however, have heightened people's awareness of the need to conserve resources and reduce waste. What do you see in your community that reflects concern for the environment? For a week carry a small notebook, and make a note each time you engage in or observe environmental preservation. For example, if you separate your trash and recycle glass and aluminum, write it down. At the end of the week, compare your list to classmates' lists. Then, in a group of three or four students, discuss how people demonstrate concern for the environment.

Jazz Fantasia

Carl Sandburg

Drum on your drums, batter on your banjoes,
sob on the long cool winding saxophones.
Go to it, O jazzmen.

Sling your knuckles on the bottoms of the happy
tin pans, let your trombones ooze, and go husha-
husha-hush with the slippery sand-paper.

Moan like an autumn wind high in the lonesome treetops,
moan soft like you wanted somebody terrible, cry like a
racing car slipping away from a motorcycle cop,
bang-bang! you jazzmen, bang altogether drums, traps,
banjoes, horns, tin cans—make two people fight on the
top of a stairway and scratch each other's eyes in a
clinch[1] tumbling down the stairs.

Can[2] the rough stuff . . . now a Mississippi steamboat
pushes up the night river with a hoo-hoo-hoo-oo . . . and
the green lanterns calling to the high soft stars . . . a red
moon rides on the humps of the low river hills . . .go to it,
O jazzmen.

---

1. clinch (klinch) *n.*: Slang for *embrace.*
2. can: Slang for *stop.*

RESPONDING TO THE SELECTION

Your Response

1. Which kind of jazz would you rather hear—the kind described in stanzas 2 and 3 or the kind described in stanza 4? Why?

Recalling

2. What six instruments does Sandburg name in stanzas 1 and 2?
3. In stanza 3, what does the speaker say the music should make happen?
4. The mood of the poem changes in the last stanza. Name two images that indicate that the sound of the music has also changed.

Interpreting

5. In stanza 4, Sandburg writes, "Can the rough stuff." To what may he be referring?

Applying

6. Jazz is referred to as the only music that is purely "American." Why?

ANALYZING LITERATURE

Understanding Onomatopoeia

Onomatopoeia occurs when words imitate actual sounds. In "Jazz Fantasia" Sandburg says that the musicians go "husha-husha-hush with the slippery sandpaper." "Husha-husha-hush" imitates the sound of the sandpaper.

A poet can also use real words to suggest a sound. In "Jazz Fantasia" Sandburg says "batter on your banjoes." "Batter" suggests the sound the musicians make on their banjoes.

1. Name three examples of onomatopoeia in "Jazz Fantasia" other than those listed above.
2. In addition to the sounds made by the musicians with their instruments, what other sounds do you hear in "Jazz Fantasia"?

In Flanders Fields

John McCrae

In Flanders fields the poppies blow
Between the crosses, row on row,
    That mark our place; and in the sky
    The larks, still bravely singing, fly
5 Scarce heard amid the guns below.

We are the Dead. Short days ago
We lived, felt dawn, saw sunset glow,
    Loved and were loved, and now we lie
    In Flanders fields.

10 Take up our quarrel with the foe:
To you from failing hands we throw
    The torch; be yours to hold it high.
    If ye break faith with us who die
We shall not sleep, though poppies grow
    In Flanders fields.

Forms

PALENQUERA, 1988
Ana Mercedes Hoyos
Courtesy of the Artist

GUIDE FOR READING

Shall I Compare Thee to a Summer's Day?

William Shakespeare (1564–1616) was an actor, a theater owner, and a renowned playwright and poet. Among the best known of his thirty-eight plays, written over about twenty years, are *Hamlet, Macbeth, King Lear, Romeo and Juliet, A Midsummer Night's Dream,* and *The Merchant of Venice.* As early as 1591, Shakespeare began writing sonnets, the most popular poetic form in the England of his day. So well did he master this form, shown in "Shall I Compare Thee to a Summer's Day?" that the terms *Shakespearean sonnet* and *English sonnet* are interchangeable today.

Puritan Sonnet

Elinor Wylie (1885–1928) grew up in Washington, D.C., where her father served in the McKinley and Theodore Roosevelt administrations. She studied painting at the Corcoran Museum and wrote poetry, first as a hobby, then as a vocation. After one unhappy marriage, Wylie eloped with her second husband to England, where she spent several years writing. She returned in 1916 to the United States. "Puritan Sonnet" reveals her intense, vivid poetic style.

Sonnet

A **sonnet** is a fourteen-line lyric poem written in iambic pentameter (ten syllables, with each unaccented syllable followed by an accented one), with a particular rhyme scheme. An example is the first-line of Shakespeare's poem:

"Shall I compare thee to a summer's day?"

Robert Frost has said of the sonnet, "A true sonnet goes eight lines and then takes a turn for better or worse and goes six . . . lines more."

Focus

To write sonnets poets must be fascinated with rhymes and with syllables. Do some rhyme-playing of your own before you read the following sonnets. For example, how many words can you think of that rhyme with a simple word such as *cake*? At first you might think of the words *bake, fake, lake, flake, make, snake, rake, brake, take, steak, wake,* and *quake.* Then there are the two-syllabled rhymes such as *headache, clambake, opaque, daybreak, keepsake,* and *earthquake.* Some three-syllable words also rhyme with *cake: rattlesnake, undertake,* and *overtake.*

Now it's your turn. Work alone or with a partner and see how many words you can think of that rhyme with *tide.* (One rhyming dictionary lists no fewer than 250, including *bride, pink-eyed, outside, pacified,* and *identified.*) This experience will give you a sense of what sonnet writers go through to find just the right word, with just the right rhyme.

Vocabulary

Knowing the following words will help you as you read these sonnets.

temperate (tem′ pər it) *adj.*: Moderate in degree or quality (p. 650)

sheaves (shēvz) *n.*: Bunches of cut stalks of grain bound up in a bundle (p. 652)

Shall I Compare Thee to a Summer's Day?

William Shakespeare

Shall I compare thee to a summer's day?
Thou art more lovely and more temperate:
Rough winds do shake the darling buds of May,
And summer's lease hath all too short a date:
5 Sometime too hot the eye of heaven shines,
And often is his gold complexion dimmed;
And every fair from fair sometime declines,

By chance or nature's changing course untrimmed;[1]
But thy eternal summer shall not fade,
10   Nor lose possession of that fair thou owest;[2]
Nor shall Death brag thou wander'st in his shade,
When in eternal lines to time thou grow'st:
        So long as men can breathe, or eyes can see,
        So long lives this, and this gives life to thee.

———————

1. untrimmed (un trimd') *v*.: Not made or kept neat; disordered.
2. owest (ō' ist) *v*.: Own.

RESPONDING TO THE SELECTION

Your Response

1. To what would you compare a summer's day? Why?

Recalling

2. To what is the speaker comparing the subject of the poem?
3. What does the speaker say shall not fade?
4. What does the speaker say Death shall not do?

Interpreting

5. To whom is the poet speaking?
6. To what does "the eye of heaven" refer?
7. To what does the word *this* in the last line refer?
8. In the comparison does the beloved fare better or worse than a summer's day? Give details to support your opinion.
9. What makes the beloved immortal?

Applying

10. Do you agree with the statement made in the last two lines? What are some examples of this sentiment today?

ANALYZING LITERATURE

Understanding Shakespearean Sonnets

All sonnets have fourteen lines of iambic pentameter—a line of five unaccented syllables each followed by an accented syllable. An example is the following line from the poem.

Rough winds do shake the darling buds of May

A **Shakespearean sonnet,** also known as an English sonnet, consists of three quatrains (four-line groups) and a couplet (a two-line group). Each quatrain has alternating rhymes at the end of its lines *(ababcdcdefef)*. The two lines of the couplet rhyme at the end *(gg)*. Usually each quatrain explores a different aspect of the poem's central idea. The couplet sums up the poem or comments on what was said in the quatrains.

Discuss how the sonnet you just read fits the typical structure of an English, or Shakespearean, sonnet. How is it different from Frost's description on page 649?

Puritan Sonnet

Elinor Wylie

Down to the Puritan marrow of my bones
There's something in this richness that I hate.
I love the look, austere, immaculate,
Of landscapes drawn in pearly monotones.
5 There's something in my very blood that owns
Bare hills, cold silver on a sky of slate,
A thread of water, churned to milky spate[1]
Streaming through slanted pastures fenced with stones.

I love those skies, thin blue or snowy gray,
10 Those fields sparse-planted, rendering meager sheaves;
That spring, briefer than apple-blossom's breath,
Summer, so much too beautiful to stay,
Swift autumn, like a bonfire of leaves,
And sleepy winter, like the sleep of death.

---

1. spate: A flash flood.

RESPONDING TO THE SELECTION

Your Response

1. The speaker of the sonnet describes how she responds to the landscape from the "marrow of [her] bones" and her "blood." How do you respond to the landscape in which you live?

Recalling

2. What does the speaker of "Puritan Sonnet" say she loves in the first stanza?
3. What does the speaker of the poem hate?
4. What does the speaker say her very blood owns?
5. How does the speaker describe spring, summer, autumn, and winter?

Interpreting

6. Look up the word *Puritan* in a dictionary. How would you characterize someone who is a Pu-

ritan? Why is it appropriate that this word has the same root as the word *pure*?

7. How do the colors mentioned in the poem reflect a Puritan view? In what way is winter appropriate to a Puritan soul?

Applying

8. What kind of landscape, in your opinion, would be the opposite of a Puritan landscape?

ANALYZING LITERATURE

Understanding the Petrarchan Sonnet

The **Petrarchan sonnet,** also called the Italian sonnet, is a form of lyric poetry that was developed in thirteenth-century Italy. It is named after the famous Italian poet Francesco Petrarch (1304–1374).

The Petrarchan sonnet is usually divided into two stanzas. The first stanza, called the octave, is eight lines long; its rhyme scheme is *abbaabba*. The second stanza, called the sestet, is six lines long; its rhyme scheme is usually *cdecde*. The octave often presents a situation, and the sestet usually resolves or comments on it.

The Petrarchan sonnet usually is fourteen lines of iambic pentameter—a line of five unaccented syllables each followed by an accented syllable. An example is the following line:

"There's something in this richness that I hate."

In "Puritan Sonnet," iambic pentameter is not followed exactly.

1. Find an example in "Puritan Sonnet" in which iambic pentameter is not followed exactly. Why has the poet varied the rhythm?
2. Explain what situation is presented in the octave in "Puritan Sonnet" and what, if any, solution is provided in the sestet.

THINKING AND WRITING

Comparing and Contrasting Sonnets

Write a brief essay for a literary magazine in which you compare and contrast the two sonnets in this section. First, list the similarities and differences in structure (rhyme and meter), subject, and images. Then use this information to write your essay. Revise your essay to include examples to support your statements. Proofread for errors in spelling, grammar, and punctuation.

LEARNING OPTIONS

1. **Writing.** Brainstorm about the place in which you live. What do you love about it? What do you dislike about it? From your brainstorming choose the images that best convey your emotional response to your landscape. Using the images you chose, write a sonnet about your region. Model the title of your poem on Wylie's title, or invent one of your own.

2. **Cross-curricular Connection.** Who were the Puritans? When and where was Puritanism a strong influence? What did Puritans believe? Finding the answers to these questions might enhance your appreciation of the sonnet. Read more about the Puritans; then summarize what you have learned in a paragraph that could be used to introduce "Puritan Sonnet" to someone who has never read the poem.

3. **Language.** The language that Wylie uses in her sonnet reflects Puritan values. Study the adjectives she uses. What are the connotations of these words? For example, the word *austere* suggests sternness, strict self-discipline and self-denial, and plainness—qualities associated with Puritanism. Find more adjectives in the sonnet, and describe how each conveys qualities associated with Puritanism.

4. **Art.** As you read "Puritan Sonnet," what pictures came to your mind? Read the poem again, focusing on the images and colors. Draw or paint the pictures you see as you reread the poem. Try to capture the mood of the poem in your pictures. Finally, display your art for your class.

GUIDE FOR READING

Haiku

Hyakuchi was a Japanese haiku poet about whose life little is known. His haiku on page 655 reveals a spirit of quiet reflection.

Chiyojo (1703–1775) was another Japanese haiku poet about whom little is known. When her husband, a servant of a samurai, died, she became a nun and studied poetry with a well-known teacher of haiku.

Matsuo Bashō (1644–1694) was a master of a type of long, linked poem called a *regna* and traveled around the country teaching people how to write regna. A regna could consist of one hundred stanzas or more and was usually the work of two, three, or more poets in collaboration. The haiku evolved from the "starting verse" of a regna.

Kobayashi Issa (1762–1826) led a life of hardship and loss. Banished from his rural home as a teenager, Issa lived most of his life in urban poverty. All of his children died in infancy, and the young wives who bore them died before Issa. Through all his adversity, Issa seemed to draw strength from small creatures whose lives are fleeting and who appear overwhelmed by the elements.

Haiku

Haiku (hī′ kōō) is a lyric form of poetry from Japan consisting of seventeen syllables arranged in unrhymed lines of five, seven, and five syllables. Traditionally, haiku have as their subjects images from the natural world. Through the haiku's simple images, the poet tries to elicit a sudden, intense response in the reader.

Focus

Before you read the following haiku, look for photographs of natural objects or experiences that could be captured in a haiku. Then share the picture or pictures you found with two or three classmates. As a group, choose a picture and brainstorm for ways to describe the image in it, using lines of five or seven syllables. Then write a haiku about the image in the picture.

Vocabulary

Knowing the following word will help you as you read these haiku.
muses (myōōz′ əz) *v.*: Thinks deeply; meditates (p. 655)

Haiku

translated by Daniel C. Buchanan

思
う
ほ
ど
物
言
わ
ぬ
人
と
涼
み
け
り

Hyakuchi

With one who muses
But says not a single word
I enjoy the cool.

Chiyojo

月
を
見
て
我
は
こ
の
世
を
か
し
く
か
な

Having viewed the moon
I say farewell to this world
With heartfelt blessing.

落
ち
ざ
ま
に
水
こ
ぼ
し
け
り
花
椿

Bashō

Falling upon earth,
Pure water spills from the cup
Of the camellia.

SNOW-LADEN CAMELLIA AND SPARROW
Ando Hiroshige
Metropolitan Museum of Art

A SUDDEN SHOWER AT OHASHI
Ando Hiroshige
Metropolitan Museum of Art

春雨や
鼠のなめる
隅田川

Issa

A gentle spring rain.
Look, a rat is lapping
Sumida River.

Your Response

1. Which haiku was the most powerful for you? Explain.

Recalling

2. What does Bashō describe in his haiku?
3. What small creature does Issa write about in his haiku?
4. What natural object is central to the haiku by Chiyojo?
5. Who is with the speaker in the Hyakuchi haiku?

Interpreting

6. A haiku can make us see two things at the same time. What two things do we see in Issa's haiku?
7. Is the silence in the Hyakuchi haiku a comfortable or an uncomfortable one? Explain your answer.
8. How does Hyakuchi appeal to our senses of hearing and touch?
9. Which adjective best describes the attitude of the speaker in the Chiyojo haiku—bitter, kind, or remorseful? Give reasons for your answer.

Applying

10. The haiku by Hyakuchi deals with a moment of experience, not with a natural object. What other moments of experience can you think of that might be good subjects for haiku? Give reasons for your answer.

ANALYZING LITERATURE

Understanding Haiku

A **haiku** is a poem that consists of three unrhymed lines of five syllables, seven syllables, and five syllables. The subject is usually an image from nature or an intense moment of personal experience, which the haiku poet tries to put into words for the reader to share. Haiku have influenced many modern poets, including Ezra Pound and Amy Lowell.

In many haiku, the poet brings together seemingly unrelated images in startling and delightful ways. The poet also tries to appeal to more than one sense at the same time. The poet furthermore tries to condense in concentrated form a sequence of events.

1. To which of our senses does Bashō appeal?
2. To which of our senses does Issa appeal?
3. What emotions does Hyakuchi express?
4. What sequence of events occurs in Chiyojo's haiku?
5. Why do you suppose prepositions (such as *on, in,* and *over*) and articles (*a, an,* and *the*) are used so sparingly in English haiku and translations of haiku?

THINKING AND WRITING

Writing Haiku

Try your hand at writing a haiku. Choose as your subject one of your ideas from the Guide for Reading page. First, freewrite about it, describing the subject and your thoughts about it. Then use this information to write your haiku. Your haiku does not have to form a complete sentence but can present an image or suggest a feeling. Revise your haiku to make sure it has five syllables in the first line, seven syllables in the second, and five in the last. Proofread for spelling errors.

GUIDE FOR READING

Letter Slot

John Updike (1932–   ) is an American novelist, short-story writer, and poet. He was born in Shillington, Pennsylvania, where many of his early stories and novels are set. He attended Harvard College and was a staff member of *The New Yorker* magazine. Updike's work shows a deep concern for the pain and striving that are a part of human relationships. His novel *Rabbit Is Rich* won the 1982 Pulitzer Prize for Fiction. "Letter Slot" is his comment on a daily occurrence.

Constantly Risking Absurdity

Lawrence Ferlinghetti (1919–   ) was a leader in the American poetry revival in San Francisco in the 1950's. A founder of the first all-paperback bookstore, he later became a publisher of new poetry. Much of Ferlinghetti's poetry is political in focus, and its main theme is the opposition to violence, both in life and in art. Ferlinghetti has said that the function of the poet is "to uncover the secret meaning of things."

Concrete Poetry

Concrete poetry is poetry in which the lines form pictures. Concrete poetry uses the arrangement of words or lines of poetry on the page to convey meaning by forming a picture or an image of the poem's subject. Sometimes even the letters of words are used to create a picture. For example, a poem about sorrow might be written in the form of a teardrop. Although this visual approach to poetry became popular in the middle decades of this century, its history is much older. Poems whose shape matched their sense were written in the seventeenth century by English poets such as George Herbert.

Focus

Some concrete poems are written in the shape of their subjects— a swan, a pine tree, a tulip, a butterfly. The two poems that follow, however, are not written in the shape of things, but rather in the shape of actions: the first, the action of paper falling through a mail slot; the second, the action of an acrobat on a tightrope.

Think of the actions in the list that follows and how a poem might represent each by its shape. Then jot some notes or map out a way to capture the action on the page. Compare your ideas with those of your classmates. Finally, brainstorm for several more actions that might make good subjects for concrete poems.

playing hopscotch
jogging around a track
getting your teeth cleaned by a dentist
a leopard pacing back and forth in its cage
making popcorn
riding a bicycle
climbing a ladder

Vocabulary

Knowing the following words will help you as you read these poems.

spews (spyo͞oz) *v.*: Throws up from, or as from, the stomach (p. 660)

rime (rīm) *n.*: Another spelling for rhyme; poetry or verse in general (p. 661)

Letter Slot

John Updike

Once each day this broad mouth spews

Apologies,

bills,

rags,[1]

and news.

---

1. rags: Slang for newspapers.

RESPONDING TO THE SELECTION

Your Response

1. Did the concrete format of "Letter Slot" help you appreciate its subject? Explain.

Recalling

2. How often does the event occur?
3. What comes out of the "broad mouth"?

Interpreting

4. What is the "broad mouth"? Is the image of a "broad mouth" spewing a pleasant or an unpleasant one? Explain your answer.
5. What does this spewing suggest that the poet feels about this typical occurrence?

Applying

6. What kind of shape might you create for a concrete poem about a present?

ANALYZING LITERATURE

Understanding Concrete Poetry

An example of a concrete poem would be a poem about sorrow written in the shape of a teardrop. Although this visual approach to poetry became popular in the middle decades of this century, its history is much older. Poems whose shape matched their sense were written in the seventeenth century by English poets such as George Herbert.

1. What is the central idea of "Letter Slot"?
2. Explain how the arrangement of words in "Letter Slot" helps convey the central idea.

THINKING AND WRITING

Writing Concrete Poetry

Concrete poetry is poetry whose shape shows its meaning. The arrangement of its lines and words gives the poem a shape that matches or enhances its meaning.

Choose one of the subjects from the list you brainstormed. Choose a shape for the subject that matches the meaning of your subject. Freewrite about the subject, describing it and your thoughts. Then use this material to write a concrete poem to fit the shape. A concrete poem may consist of one or more complete sentences, several phrases, or even individual words or letters. Revise your poem to make sure it fits the shape you chose. Proofread for spelling errors.

Constantly Risking Absurdity

Lawrence Ferlinghetti

Constantly risking absurdity
     and death
   whenever he performs
     above the heads
5   of his audience
  the poet like an acrobat
   climbs on rime
    to a high wire of his own making
 and balancing on eyebeams
10   above a sea of faces
   paces his way
    to the other side of day
  performing entrechats[1]
    and sleight-of-foot tricks
15 and other high theatrics
    and all without mistaking
   any thing
    for what it may not be

  For he's the super realist
20   who must perforce[2] perceive
   taut truth
    before the taking of each stance or step
 in his supposed advance
    toward that still higher perch
25 where Beauty stands and waits
    with gravity
     to start her death-defying leap

---

1. entrechats (on' trə cha') *n.*: Leaps in which a
ballet dancer's legs crisscross several times.
2. perforce (pər fôrs') *adv.*: Necessarily.

And he
       a little charley chaplin[3] man

30   who may or may not catch
      her fair eternal form
           spreadeagled in the empty air
    of existence

---

3. Charley Chaplin: Charles Chaplin (1889–1977). British actor and producer, who worked in the U.S. from 1910 to 1952.

RESPONDING TO THE SELECTION

Your Response

1. Besides tightrope-walking, what other activities resemble writing?

Recalling

2. About whom is the poem written?
3. To what is the subject of the poem compared?
4. What must the "super realist" perceive?
5. Who stands on "that still higher perch" and "waits with gravity"?
6. What might or might not the "little charley chaplin man" do?

Interpreting

7. What common expression is "sleight-of-foot" in line 14 a play on?
8. What effect does this variation of the expression achieve?
9. The phrase "with gravity" in line 26 has at least two meanings. State and explain these meanings.
10. What does the description "a little charley chaplin man" suggest about the poet/acrobat?
11. What is the significance of the title?

Applying

12. A circus acrobat takes obvious risks. In what ways does a poet (or other artist) take risks? Explain your answer.

THINKING AND WRITING

Writing a Paraphrase of a Poem

To **paraphrase** is to restate the meaning of a written work in your own words. Paraphrasing can help you understand the theme of a written work. First, list the most important points in the order in which the poet uses them in "Constantly Risking Absurdity." Then use this information to write a paraphrase of the poem. Discuss how the poet develops the comparison of the poet to the acrobat. Revise your paraphrase, making sure you include a statement of the poem's theme. Proofread for errors in spelling, grammar, and punctuation.

Themes

GIRL WITH CAT
Franz Marc

GUIDE FOR READING

To James

Frank Horne (1899–1974) had a varied career as a college president, an optometrist, a race relations administrator, and a poet. As a student at the College of the City of New York, Horne distinguished himself as a track star. In "To James," Horne uses a race as a metaphor for life.

Auto Wreck

Karl Shapiro (1913–   ) has been a college professor, a critic, and an editor of *Poetry* and *Prairie Schooner,* as well as a distinguished American poet. He won a Pulitzer Prize in 1945 for *V-Letter and Other Poems,* which draws on his experience as a Jewish soldier in the United States Army during World War II. Shapiro has said that he would like to see the elimination "of the line between poetry and prose." The harsh realism of "Auto Wreck" reflects Shapiro's preferred poetic style.

The Old People Speak of Death

Quincy Troupe (1943–   ) is the son of Quincy Troupe, Sr., who was a famous baseball player in the segregated Negro Leagues. After graduating from college, Troupe played professional basketball in France. At first, basketball was more appealing than poetry; Troupe said, "Being a young man I wanted to shoot jump shots." However, he has since published four volumes of poetry and has written and edited several books.

The Number Pi

Wisława Szymborska (1923–   ) is a distinguished member of the post–World War II generation of writers in Poland. Her translators Magnus Krynski and Robert Maguire have called her "that rarest of phenomena: a serious poet who commands a large audience in her native land." For example, her book *A Great Number* met with astonishing success—10,000 copies were sold in only one week! Today Szymborska is internationally acclaimed as one of Poland's foremost contemporary poets.

Theme

Theme is the central idea of a story or poem, or the general idea or insight about life that the work reveals. Sometimes the writer states the theme directly, but more often only implies, or suggests, it. You can identify the theme through careful reading, analysis, and thought.

Focus

You might identify with one or more of the following general statements about life. Choose one and freewrite about it, relating it to your personal experience, thoughts, or observations.

- The world's a bubble, and the life of [a person]
  Less than a span. (Francis Bacon)
- And Life [is] a Fury slinging flame. (Alfred, Lord Tennyson)
- The life of a [person] is a circle from childhood to childhood and so it is in everything where power moves. (Black Elk)
- Life is a copycat and can be bullied into following the master artist who bids it come to heel. (Heywood Broun)
- Life is painting a picture, not doing a sum. (Oliver Wendell Holmes, Jr.)
- Life is but a day;
  A fragile dewdrop on its perilous way
  From a tree's summit. (John Keats)

After reviewing your freewriting, write your own sentence beginning "Life is . . ." Then, as you read the following poems, consider how your statement compares with the themes explored by these poets.

Vocabulary

Knowing the following words will help you as you read these poems.

sinews (sin′ yo͞oz) *n.*: Tendons—the fibrous cords attaching muscle to bone (p. 666)

deranged (di rānjd′) *adj.*: Disturbed out of the normal way of acting (p. 668)

douches (do͞osh′ əz) *v.*: Washes or flushes away (p. 668)

banal (bā′ n'l) *adj.*: Stale from overuse; commonplace (p. 668)

occult (ə kult′) *adj.*: Having to do with so-called mystic arts such as alchemy and astrology (p. 669)

expedient (ik spē′dē ənt) *adj.*: Useful; convenient (p. 669)

abyss (ə bis′) *n.*: An area too deep for measurement (p. 673)

To James

Frank Horne

Do you remember
how you won
that last race . . .?
how you flung your body
5   at the start . . .
how your spikes
ripped the cinders
in the stretch . . .
how you catapulted
10 through the tape . . .
do you remember . . .?
Don't you think
I lurched with you
out of those starting holes . . .?
15 Don't you think
my sinews tightened
at those first
few strides . . .
and when you flew into the stretch
20 was not all my thrill
of a thousand races
in your blood . . .?
At your final drive
through the finish line
25 did not my shout
tell of the
triumphant ecstasy
of victory . . .?

Live
30 as I have taught you
to run, Boy—
it's a short dash.
Dig your starting holes
deep and firm
35 lurch out of them

into the straightaway[1]
with all the power
that is in you
look straight ahead
40 to the finish line
think only of the goal
run straight
run high
run hard
45 save nothing
and finish
with an ecstatic burst
that carries you
hurtling
50 through the tape
to victory . . .

_____

1. straightaway (strāt′ ə wā′)
_n._: A straight course.

▎R ESPONDING TO THE SELECTION

Your Response

1. What game or sport would you consider a metaphor for your life? Explain.

Recalling

2. What is the outcome for James in the race described in the first part of the poem?
3. What does the speaker do at the end of James's final drive through the finish line?
4. What does the speaker tell James to do?

Interpreting

5. Does the speaker seem to be older, younger, or about the same age as James? Give reasons for your answer.
6. How does the speaker feel about James?
7. Find examples in the poem in which living one's life is compared to running a race. Explain the comparison.
8. What feeling about life does the speaker want James to have?

Applying

9. What other games, sports, or events could be used as a metaphor for life? Explain your choices.

▎A NALYZING LITERATURE

Understanding Theme

Theme, or the general idea or insight about life that the work reveals, often is only implied, or suggested. You can identify the theme of a poem through careful reading, analysis, and thought.

In "To James," the poet uses a race as a metaphor for life: "Live / as I have taught you / to run, Boy— / it's a short dash." Throughout the poem the speaker uses descriptions of a race to advise James about how to live.

State in your own words the theme of the poem.

Auto Wreck

Karl Shapiro

Its quick soft silver bell beating, beating,
And down the dark one ruby flare
Pulsing out red light like an artery,
The ambulance at top speed floating down
5 Past beacons and illuminated clocks
Wings in a heavy curve, dips down,
And brakes speed, entering the crowd.
The doors leap open, emptying light;
Stretchers are laid out, the mangled lifted
10 And stowed into the little hospital.
Then the bell, breaking the hush, tolls once,
And the ambulance with its terrible cargo
Rocking, slightly rocking, moves away,
As the doors, an afterthought, are closed.

15 We are deranged, walking among the cops
Who sweep glass and are large and composed.
One is still making notes under the light.
One with a bucket douches ponds of blood
Into the street and gutter.
20 One hangs lanterns on the wrecks that cling,
Empty husks of locusts, to iron poles.

Our throats were tight as tourniquets,[1]
Our feet were bound with splints, but now,
Like convalescents intimate and gauche,[2]
25 We speak through sickly smiles and warn
With the stubborn saw of common sense,
The grim joke and the banal resolution.
The traffic moves around with care,
But we remain, touching a wound
30 That opens to our richest horror.
Already old, the question Who shall die?
Becomes unspoken Who is innocent?

---

1. tourniquets (tŭr′ nə ketz) *n.*: Bandages to stop
bleeding by compressing a blood vessel.
2. gauche (gōsh) *adj.*: Awkward.

For death in war is done by hands;
Suicide has cause and stillbirth, logic;
35   And cancer, simple as a flower, blooms.
But this invites the occult mind,
Cancels our physics with a sneer,
And spatters all we knew of denouement[3]
Across the expedient and wicked stones.

---

3. denouement (dā' nū män') *n.:* Outcome or the end.

RESPONDING TO THE SELECTION

Your Response

1. The poet chose the title "Auto Wreck." What else could the poem's title be? Explain your answer.

Recalling

2. What do the first fourteen lines of the poem describe?
3. To what does the speaker compare himself and other onlookers?
4. What question does the speaker ask?
5. How does the speaker describe other forms of death?

Interpreting

6. What is it that pulses "out red light like an artery"? Explain your answer.
7. What does the tolling of the bell in line 11 suggest?
8. What is the "wound" in line 29? Give reasons for your answer.
9. To whom does "we" in the poem refer? Give reasons for your answer.
10. What does the image "empty husks of locusts" in line 21 suggest?

Applying

11. "Auto Wreck" describes a sudden death, beyond human understanding, which shocks observers out of their usual way of responding. Think of another human experience that could have such an effect.

LEARNING OPTIONS

1. **Community Connections.** Find out more about a local emergency medical service. Your library might be a good source of information, or you might want to interview someone who is trained as an emergency medical technician (EMT). Use the following questions to guide you:

   How does someone become an EMT?
   For whom do EMTs work?
   What skills are involved in EMT work?
   What's a typical work shift like?
   What are the most difficult aspects of the job?
   What are some of the rewarding aspects of the job?

   After you have the answers to these questions, report what you learned about your local emergency medical service to your class. You might want to invite an EMT to your presentation to answer additional questions your classmates might have. Discuss the ways in which EMT work does or does not appeal to you.

2. **Art.** Illustrate the poem as you interpret it. You might want to do one big illustration or several smaller drawings. Before you begin, decide whether you want to illustrate a close-up detail or a broad representation of the scene. Try to convey a sense of the poem's setting and mood.

The Old People Speak of Death

Quincy Troupe

the old people speak of death
frequently now
my grandmother speaks of those now
gone to spirit
5   now less than bone

they speak of shadows
that graced their days made lovelier
by their wings of light speak of years
& corpses of years of darkness
10   & of relationships buried
deeper even than residue of bone
gone now beyond hardness
gone now beyond form

they smile now from ingrown roots
15   of beginnings of those who have left us
& climbed back through the holes the old folks
left in their eyes
for them to enter through

eye walk back now with this poem
20   through the holes the old folks left in their eyes
for me to enter through walk back to where
eye see them there
the ones that have gone beyond hardness
the ones that have gone beyond form
25   see them there
darker than where roots began
& lighter than where they go
with their spirits
heavier than stone their memories
30   sometimes brighter than the flash
of sudden lightning

THE PROPHET #1, 1975–1976
Charles White
Heritage Gallery, Los Angeles

but green branches will grow
from these roots darker than time
& blacker than even the ashes of nations
35 sweet flowers will sprout
& wave their love-stroked language
in sun-tongued morning's shadow
the spirit in all our eyes

they have gone now back
40 to shadow as eye climb back out
from the holes of these old folks eyes
those spirits who sing through this poem
gone now back with their spirits
to fuse with greenness

45 enter stones & glue their invisible
faces upon the transmigration of earth
nailing winds singing guitar blues
voices through the ribcages
of these days
50 gone now to where the years run
darker than where roots begin
greener than what they bring

the old people speak of death
frequently now
55 my grandmother speaks of those now
gone to spirit
now less than bone

Your Response

1. What feeling does this poem communicate to you?

Recalling

2. Who "sings through [the] poem"?

Interpreting

3. What is the "eye" in the poem?
4. Who might the speaker's grandmother be talking about in lines 3–5?
5. Interpret the figure of speech in lines 19–21.
6. What is symbolized by the "green branches" (line 32) and the "roots" (line 33)?
7. What happens when the spirits "fuse with greenness" (line 44)?

Applying

8. Why do you think that it comforts some old people to talk about death or to remember those who have died?

ANALYZING LITERATURE

Understanding Theme Through Images

Theme, the universal truth or general insight into life that a work of literature conveys, can be stated directly or implied. In "The Old People Speak of Death," Troupe implies the theme through **images,** vivid descriptions or figures of speech that give the reader a mental picture. For example, Troupe uses several images of cycles in the poem. One of the most vivid images of a cycle is that of "sweet flowers [that] will sprout" in line 35. This image suggests a cycle of regeneration; some flowers sprout, bloom, and die, but eventually, new flowers grow.

1. How does the image of flowers sprouting suggest the theme to you?
2. Locate another image of a cycle and explain its relationship to theme in the poem.
3. In your own words, state the theme of the poem.

CRITICAL THINKING AND READING

Analyzing Repetition and Theme

Poets often use repetition as a tool to help them convey theme. Repeating certain images, lines, and even entire stanzas can reinforce important messages in the poem. Stressing ideas by repeating key words and phrases also makes these ideas more vivid and, therefore, more memorable in the reader's mind.

1. What message does Troupe emphasize by repeating the lines "gone now beyond hardness" and "gone now beyond form"?
2. In the last stanza, Troupe returns to the first stanza and repeats it exactly. How does this technique contribute to the theme?

THINKING AND WRITING

Responding to Theme

Write a journal entry in response to the poem. As you write, consider the following questions: How is the subject of the poem familiar to you? What images hold the most meaning for you? In what ways do you relate to the poem? Try to respond to the poem in detail; your response might make a good topic for a longer writing assignment in the future.

LEARNING OPTION

Cross-curricular Connection. The imagery in "The Old People Speak of Death" suggests the cyclical nature of life and death. For example, the image of "ashes" (line 34) implies the species of trees that replace themselves after fires. In fact, seeds of some trees won't germinate until they have been exposed to fire. In addition, certain plants, such as ivies, begonias, and geraniums, will grow new roots when their stems are cut and placed in water. Read more about this process in a gardening or horticulture book. Then experiment with a plant to see how new life can emerge from its seeds, stem, or leaves.

The Number Pi

Wisława Szymborska

**translated from the Polish by Grażyna Drabik,
Austin Flint, and Sharon Olds**

It's worth admiring, this number Pi
three point one four one.
Even the figures that follow are only the beginning
five nine two because Pi never ends.
5 It does not permit one to grasp it *six five three five* with a
    glance,
eight nine by calculation,
seven nine by imagination,
and even *three two three eight* by a joke, or a comparison
four six to anything
10 *two six four three* in the world.
The longest snake in the world ends after several meters.
In the same way, though somewhat later, fairy tale snakes
    end.
A pageant of figures making up the number Pi
does not stop at the edge of the page;
15 it can continue across the table, through the air,
through a wall, a leaf, a bird's nest, clouds, straight into
    the sky,
across the whole bulge and abyss of the sky.
The comet's tail is short as a mouse's!
The ray of a star so weak that it curves in space!
20 And here *two three fifteen three hundred nineteen*
my phone number your shirt size
the year one thousand nine hundred seventy-three sixth
    floor
the number of inhabitants sixty-five cents
the measurements around the hips two fingers a charade
    and a code
25 in which is said *my nightingale go fly, sing,*
and please *keep calm,*
and *the earth and the sky will pass,*

but not the number Pi, no, not it,
it has another perfectly good *five*,
30   a no mean *eight*,
a *seven* that is not its final,
urging, ah, urging sluggish eternity
to go on.

MATH MAN #4, 1967
Clarence Holbrook Carter
Courtesy of the Artist

RESPONDING TO THE SELECTION

Your Response

1. In the first line of the poem, the poet says that the number Pi is worth admiring. What do you find admirable about it?

Recalling

2. What is the relationship between the number Pi and the sky in the poem?
3. What general statement of fact does the poem illustrate about the number Pi?

Interpreting

4. What is conveyed by the juxtaposition of the approximate value of Pi and the words in the poem?
5. Interpret the image of a "pageant of figures" in line 13.
6. What distinguishes the images in the poem— a "comet's tail," the "ray of a star," a "phone number," a "shirt size"—from the number Pi? Why is the distinction important?
7. How does Pi urge "sluggish eternity/to go on" (lines 32–33)?

Applying

8. A phenomenon like the number Pi, which goes on to infinity, is hard to grasp. What are other examples of phenomena that reflect eternity or infinity?

CRITICAL THINKING AND READING

Appreciating Form

The form of a poem is its physical shape on the page. Often, the form a poet chooses suits the subject of a poem. In "The Number Pi," for example, Szymborska uses free verse, a form that has no regular rhyme or rhythm pattern and no exact meter. Similarly, Pi has no exact value. You might know Pi as 3.141, or the fraction 22/7, but these are only approximate values of the number Pi. As you read the poem again, notice how its form mirrors the subject.

1. Numbers such as "six five three five" (line 5)

are scattered throughout the poem. What is significant about these numbers?

2. How does the poet's use of imagery illustrate the fact that Pi is an irrational number and has no exact value?

THINKING AND WRITING

Responding to Theme

Write a journal entry in response to "The Number Pi." As you write, explore the answers to the following questions: What general insight into life did the poem suggest to you? In what ways did you relate to the message in the poem? How did you visualize the images as you read them? How did the pictures you formed help you understand the poem's theme? Try to capture the associations you made as you read the poem.

LEARNING OPTIONS

1. **Cross-curricular Connection.** Two mathematical formulas that include Pi are the formulas for finding the circumference of a circle ($C = \pi d$) and the area of a circle ($A = \pi r^2$). Test the truth of Pi. Find circular objects and apply these formulas. Measure the circumference, the area, and the diameter. Then, applying those values to the formulas, calculate the value of Pi. Is it 3.14159 or close? Report your procedures and your findings to your classmates.

2. **Cross-curricular Connection.** The mathematicians Tamura and Kanada recently calculated the first 16 million decimal places of Pi. Read about their accomplishment in an algebra book or in other resources in the library. Find out what method they used. Then write a short expository report explaining their method.

3. **Cross-curricular Connection.** Investigate another mathematical curiosity, the Fibonacci series of numbers. In a brief report—either oral or written—explain the sequence of numbers in this series, how it was discovered, and how it can be applied.

Poetry

Carl Sandburg wrote, "Poetry is the opening and closing of a door, leaving those who look through to guess about what was seen during a moment." Perhaps some "doors" were opened for you as you read and responded to the poems in this unit.

There is no precise definition of poetry, but it has special qualities that set it apart from other forms of literature. The language is imaginative, musical, and compact. The form may be unusual. Images and sound devices give you special insights into a poem.

Use your active reading strategies to respond fully to poetry.

RESPONDING TO LANGUAGE Poets use language to create new ways of seeing things. In doing so they often use figurative language, language that is not meant to be interpreted literally. These figures of speech enable you to see or think about something in a new and imaginative way. How does this language make you feel?

RESPONDING TO APPEARANCE Poetry can take a variety of forms. What does it look like on the page? Is its appearance related to the type of poetry it is, such as narrative or lyric? How does its appearance affect your expectations as you read it?

RESPONDING TO IMAGERY Poets appeal to your senses in developing images. Use your imagination and your senses to take in the images the poet might be creating. What senses are you using to respond to the images?

RESPONDING TO SOUND The music of poetry is created by sound devices. Read poems aloud, and let the rhythm and the rhyme flow naturally. Listen to alliteration, onomatopoeia, and other musical devices. What is the effect of these sound devices? How do they contribute to the meaning of the poem?

RESPONDING TO THEME Many poems convey an important idea or insight about life. What do you think is the message of the poem? What special meaning does the poem have for you? How can you connect it to your life?

On pages 677–678 you will see how Sarah Hong from Kalamazoo High School in Kalamazoo, Michigan, actively read and responded to "Ex-Basketball Player." The notes in the side column include Sarah's thoughts and comments as she read the poem. Your thoughts and comments may be different.

MODEL

Ex-Basketball Player

John Updike

Pearl Avenue runs past the high-school lot,
Bends with the trolley tracks, and stops, cut off
Before it has a chance to go two blocks,
At Colonel McComsky Plaza. Berth's Garage
5 Is on the corner facing west, and there,
Most days, you'll find Flick Webb, who helps Berth out.

Language: *The language in this stanza—"runs," "Bends," "stops"—helps me visualize the setting.*

Flick stands tall among the idiot pumps—
Five on a side, the old bubble-head style,
Their rubber elbows hanging loose and low.
10 One's nostrils are two S's, and his eyes
An E and O. And one is squat, without
A head at all—more of a football type.

Once Flick played for the high-school team, the Wizards.
He was good: in fact, the best. In '46
15 He bucketed[1] three hundred ninety points,
A county record still. The ball loved Flick.
I saw him rack up[2] thirty-eight or forty
In one home game. His hands were like wild birds.

He never learned a trade, he just sells gas,
20 Checks oil, and changes flats. Once in a while,
As a gag, he dribbles an inner tube,
But most of us remember anyway.
His hands are fine and nervous on the lug wrench.
It makes no difference to the lug wrench, though.

25 Off work, he hangs around Mae's luncheonette.
Grease-gray and kind of coiled, he plays pinball,
Smokes those thin cigars, nurses lemon phosphates.[3]
Flick seldom says a word to Mae, just nods
Beyond her face toward bright applauding tiers
30 Of Necco Wafers, Nibs, and Juju Beads.[4]

---

1. bucketed (buk′ it əd), *v.*: Scored.
2. rack up: Accumulate.
3. lemon phosphates (fos′ fātz): Carbonated water flavored with lemon syrup.
4. Necco . . . Beads: Packaged candy.

John Updike (1932–   ) is one of the foremost contemporary writers in the United States. Born in the small town of Shillington, Pennsylvania, Updike often uses this location as the setting of his writing. Updike brings to his short stories, novels, essays, and poems the eyes and ears of a keen observer. A recurring character in much of his work is the former high-school athlete who missed his chance for success.

RESPONDING TO THE SELECTION

Your Response

1. Why do you think it was difficult for Flick to live up to his early successes?

Recalling

2. How does Flick Webb earn his living?
3. What had Flick done in the past? Why did the speaker consider him "the best"?

Interpreting

4. How do you think Flick got his nickname? Support your answer with details from the poem.
5. Explain the speaker's changing attitude toward Flick.
6. How do you think the speaker would prefer for Flick to behave today? Support your answer with details from the poem.
7. High-school athletes are often the heroes of our youth. F. Scott Fitzgerald has written, "Show me a hero and I will write you a tragedy." In what way is Flick's life a tragedy?

Applying

8. The poet Dylan Thomas wrote, "A good poem helps to change the shape and significance of the universe, helps to extend everyone's knowledge of himself and the world around him." How does "Ex-Basketball Player" do this?

ANALYZING LITERATURE

Understanding Free Verse

Free verse is poetry that does not follow any regular pattern of rhythm. Instead, it gains its musical quality from the sounds of the language and the use of punctuation to indicate pauses and stops. Poets sometimes use free verse to give their poems a natural feeling.

Explain why the use of free verse is especially appropriate to the topic of "Ex-Basketball Player."

CRITICAL THINKING AND READING

Classifying

Classifying means grouping items according to a common element. For example, if you took an inventory of the clothes in your closet, you might group them into two categories: casual clothes and formal clothes.

1. Find all the verbs in this poem that could be classified as basketball terms.
2. Find the nouns that could be classified as gas-station terms.

THINKING AND WRITING

Writing Free Verse

Choose a sport you like to play or watch. Brainstorm to list all the details of the sport that seem especially vivid. Then, using free verse and colloquial language, write a brief poem describing an athlete playing this sport. When you revise, make sure your description is vivid. Proofread your poem and share it with your classmates.

LEARNING OPTION

Language. Colloquial language sounds like everyday conversation. It contains phrases and idioms commonly used in informal speech. For example, the speaker says that Flick "hangs around Mae's luncheonette." "Hangs around" is an informal way of saying "loiters about."

What is the meaning of each of the following colloquial phrases based on the verb *hang*?

1. hanging loose
2. hang back
3. hang together
4. get the hang of

YOUR WRITING PROCESS

WRITING A POEM

Poems are often celebrations of people, places, or events. Imagine that you have been asked by a record company to write a poem as a tribute to your favorite musician. What words and images would you use? The poems in this unit provide several forms and styles of celebration. Choose one . . . or create your own.

> ### Focus
>
> **Assignment:** Write a poem to be used for an audiocassette or CD insert.
> **Purpose:** To express your admiration for a musician or music group.
> **Audience:** Buyers of the audiocassette or CD.

Prewriting

1. Review the poems. Reread the poems you have read, especially "To Satch" by Samuel Allen, to see how the poets use images and figures of speech to express thoughts and feelings. How do the poets use formal features, such as stanzas and line lengths?

2. Ask yourself questions. Choose a musician or music group as a subject for your tribute. Then list questions to explore your thoughts and feelings about the subject.

Student Model

> The Beatles
> - Why are Lennon and McCartney considered such great songwriters?
> - Which are their most memorable songs?
> - How did they influence other musical groups?
> - What messages and attitudes do their songs express?

3. Focus your topic. Decide on the main quality of your subject that you would like to capture in your poem. What is the most important idea in your question list? Describe that idea in a phrase or image.

4. List details. Keeping your focus in mind, list words, phrases, or lines you might use in your poem. Note figures of speech that could add vivid images to the poem. Think of sound devices that could help make your poem sing.

Drafting

1. Develop your poem. Use your questions and list of details to create the lines of your poem. Help give your poem musical qualities by using rhyming words and patterns of accented syllables that create rhythm.

2. Give your poem a shape. Structure the lines of your poem. How short or long should they be? Where will each line break? Will your poem have stanzas? How will you arrange the words on the page?

Revising and Editing

1. Ask yourself questions. As you review your work, think about your purpose, your audience, and the effectiveness of the language in your poem. Make a list of questions to use as a checklist for revising.

Student Model

1. Did I clearly express why I admire this musician? Will my audience understand my reasons?
2. Does my poem express a central idea or feeling?
3. Is the form of the poem effective?
4. Did I use rhyme and rhythm to full benefit?
5. Are my words precise and my images concrete?

---

2. Share your poem with a partner. Read your poem aloud to a partner and discuss his or her responses. For example, ask your partner to identify the central idea or feeling the poem conveys and to explain which words, phrases, or images are most memorable. Discuss how people buying music by this artist might respond to your poem.

3. Proofread for consistency. In poetry it is not always necessary to follow the rules of grammar, capitalization, and punctuation. However, be consistent when handling mechanics. For example, if you decide not to use capital letters or periods, make sure you follow this style throughout your poem.

Writer's Hint

Similes make comparisons using the word *like* or *as.* **Metaphors** make direct comparisons. When using figurative language, make sure your words and images are precise. For instance, when comparing music to the sound of a bird, be specific by referring to the song of a particular kind of bird, such as a mourning dove.

Options for Publishing

• Join with other students to have a poetry reading in your school auditorium or local library. Invite other students, parents, and teachers. Play recordings by the musicians you are celebrating.

• Send your poem to the company that records music by the artist you chose. Share with the class any response you receive from the musician or company.

• Set your poem to music in the style of the musician you selected. Perform your song for the class.

Reviewing Your Writing Process

1. How did you decide which words, phrases, images, and form would best express the subject of your poem?

2. Did reading your poem aloud help you to identify its strengths and weaknesses? Explain.

YOUR WRITING PROCESS

WRITING A REPORT OF INFORMATION

Imagine that you are a police officer sent to the scene of a crime, accident, or other incident that occurs in one of the poems in this unit. How would you piece together the details of the event to write a clear police report for your supervisor? You rush to the scene, approach a witness, and demand, "Just the facts, m'am."

> **Focus**
>
> **Assignment:** Write a police report based on the events described in a poem.
> **Purpose:** To explain what happened and why police intervention was required.
> **Audience:** The commanding officer.

Prewriting

1. Review the poems. Narrative poems often tell stories that involve dramatic incidents. With a partner, look back at the poems in this unit and choose one that describes an accident, crime, or other moment of crisis that could be the subject for a police report.

2. Role-play the incident. After you have chosen a poem, review with your partner the events it describes. Dramatize the situation by taking on the roles of police officer and witness. The police officer should ask questions that encourage the witness to describe the incident.

> **Student Model**
>
> "Auto Wreck" by Karl Shapiro
> OFFICER: Where were you when you witnessed the accident?
> WITNESS: I was stopped at the traffic light.
> OFFICER: What did you see?
> WITNESS: A blue car pulled up to the light directly across from me. The light was red, so he stopped. But then he made a right on red. Just as he was turning, the silver car came streaking through the intersection, and hit him broadside . . . .

3. Take notes. Police officers always have a pen and pad ready. As the witness answers the questions, the officer should jot down important information that can be used to write a report of the incident.

4. Make a timeline. Assemble your notes and make a plan for your report. A timeline of events can help you organize the details for your writing. Remember that precision is crucial in a police report. Work with your partner to establish a clear and accurate sequence of events.

Student Model

Blue car stops at light	Blue car makes a right on red	Silver car streaks into intersection	Silver car hits blue car

---

Drafting

1. Stick to the facts. Remember that the commanding officer is interested only in the facts. As you develop the draft of your report, consult your notes and timeline to make sure you give a clear chronological account of the events.

2. Remember your purpose. Besides giving an accurate description of the incident, make sure you explain why police intervention was necessary. Will your supervisor be convinced by the reasons you give?

Revising and Editing

1. Check for accuracy. With your partner, read over the report to make sure it includes all the important facts about the incident. Is the sequence of events correct? Are there any significant questions that the report doesn't answer?

2. Form editing groups. Get together with one or two other writing teams and exchange the drafts of your reports. Respond to one another's work by using questions like the ones you used with your partner.

3. Eliminate errors. Reports such as police accounts need to be free of errors, including those in the mechanics of writing.

Writer's Hint

When you write a report of information, take the five W's test. Make sure you provide answers to the following questions about your subject: Who? What? When? Where? Why? Answers to these questions will help give your audience a clear picture of your topic.

Options for Publishing

• In class read aloud your police report along with the poem on which it is based. Ask the audience whether they think your report is an accurate reflection of the poem.

• Post students' police reports on a bulletin board. Give the display an appropriate title, such as "From the Police Blotter."

• Tape-record your report using background sound effects that re-create the setting of a police station. Play the recording for the class or your friends.

Reviewing Your Writing Process

1. Did role-playing the parts of police officer and witness help you gather information for your report? Why or why not?

2. What was most helpful in sharing your draft with other writing teams?

ENTRY OF KING ETZEL (ATTILA) INTO VIENNA
Albin Egger-Lienz

THE HEROIC TRADITION

Great legends develop in every culture, reflecting the history and beliefs of the people who create them. These stories serve the dual function of explaining important events in the history of a people and shaping these events into a heroic and memorable form. The various tales of different cultures have become part of the identifying marks of those cultures; other people can read these stories and get an immediate sense of how the culture was shaped and what figures and issues are central to its history.

In Great Britain, the tales surrounding the sixth-century leader King Arthur have become the greatest single expression of chivalrous behavior and courtly love. These legends have appealed to readers over the years because they present an appealing portrait of an ideal society. The best-known English compilation of the legends is *Le Morte d'Arthur* (1485), written by Sir Thomas Malory, himself a knight. Another of the enduring versions of the Arthur legend is *Idylls of the King* by Alfred, Lord Tennyson, which retells in poetry several of the most popular Arthurian adventures and stresses Arthur's great moral leadership. In *The Once and Future King* (1958), the writer T. H. White has modernized and combined the Arthur stories into a four-volume novel that suggests hope in our tumultuous times.

There is an equally strong tradition of heroic legends in Eastern and African cultures. The *Ramayana* is a great Indian epic, possibly originating as far back as the fourth century B.C. This heroic tale relates symbolic stories about the mythological characters Rama and Sita. In the African country of Mali, the story of *Sundiata* was told to D. T. Niane. *Sundiata* has been passed down in Mali from generation to generation for many centuries, told by storytellers who help preserve the history and culture of their people. In this story, the hero overcomes obstacles during a difficult childhood. In China, Lo Kuan-chung lived and wrote in the fourteenth century, during the Ming dynasty. His epic narrative, *Three Kingdoms,* based on two records of the fall of the Han dynasty, teaches values of loyalty and moral behavior. The last of the selections in this section is an excerpt from *Don Quixote,* written by the Spanish writer Miguel de Cervantes in the early seventeenth century. This story ridicules the literature of chivalry, such as the Arthurian legends. The hero is a self-declared knight who has misadventures rather than adventures; although his intentions are honorable, his attempts at heroism almost always fail.

Within each of these heroic stories, the customs, folklore, and history of a particular culture are entertainingly revealed.

READING ACTIVELY

The Heroic Tradition

Every culture has heroes who embody the values, strengths, and traditions of that culture. Legends develop around these characters and their heroic exploits. The legends may differ from culture to culture, but they all have certain features in common. For example, the hero often must overcome a difficult childhood to achieve success and heroic stature as an adult.

ARTHURIAN LEGENDS The King Arthur legend has been told in poetry and prose for more than a thousand years. A sixth-century account of the invasion of Britain by Saxon warriors tells of a heroic British general named Arturius. He led the Britons to a decisive victory over the Saxons and is believed to have been killed in battle. His remains were excavated six centuries later, in 1190, and his coffin bore an inscription that read, "Here lies buried the renowned King Arthur in the Isle of Avalon."

From these scant beginnings, the legend of King Arthur, the gloriously heroic king of the Britons, emerged. The legend was greatly enhanced by French writers who contributed the idea of the Round Table as well as several love stories involving Arthur, Guenevere, and Launcelot. But it was not until the late fifteenth century that the first unified English version of the Arthurian legend was produced in *Le Morte d'Arthur,* or *The Death of Arthur,* by Sir Thomas Malory. Malory's version is the basis for most subsequent versions of the legend of King Arthur.

THE RAMAYANA The *Ramayana* is a great Indian epic, possibly originating as far back as the fourth century B.C. This heroic tale is about the mythological characters Rama and Sita and their brave exploits against the forces of evil. The story has been the largest source of inspiration for Indian poets throughout the centuries, as each poet wishes to retell the story in his or her own words.

SUNDIATA In Mali, Africa, the *Sundiata* has been passed down through the generations for many centuries. Storytellers called *griots* preserve the history and culture of their country by telling these ancient legends. The griots of Mali are respected for their knowledge of the past; they go from village to village accumulating important anecdotes and information. In this epic, Sundiata is the disabled son of a disfigured princess and a handsome king. Although people scorn Sundiata for his disability, fortune-tellers predict that he will grow up to unite the many kingdoms of Mali into one great empire.

THREE KINGDOMS The great Chinese epic narrative *Three Kingdoms* takes place in the last years of the four-hundred-year Han dynasty. The epic depicts the disintegration of the dynasty, which many felt was due to corruption in the emperor's inner ruling circle. The main conflict is between those who remain loyal to the emperor and those who feel that the emperor must be overthrown.

DON QUIXOTE In the early seventeenth century, the Spanish writer Miguel de Cervantes wrote about Don Quixote, a character who decided to become a knight, and traveled around the country-side engaging in foolhardy acts of chivalry. The story parodies the chivalrous tradition that the Arthurian legends so imaginatively embody. Cervantes was able to write such an entertaining and complex version of Spanish life because he himself had experienced the good and bad aspects of that society. His critical eye, combined with a humorous and compassionate nature, makes him a writer for all ages: His work seems as relevant to today's society as it was to Spain in the seventeenth century.

Reading Strategies

You may have some difficulty understanding the language of the characters in these legends. Each tale reflects the culture and historic period during which the actions occurred. In the Arthurian legends, for example, the language is meant to convey a sense of courtly love; the knights and ladies speak a form of English used in medieval Britain, which sounds stiff and formal to us. Usually, you can use context clues to understand what each character is saying.

Finally, interact with the literature by using the active reading strategies: question, predict, visualize, connect, and respond. Stop to clarify dialogue that you do not immediately understand. By going back and reading the dialogue slowly and by putting it in its proper context, you can unravel its meaning.

Themes

You will encounter the following themes in the legends of King Arthur, the *Ramayana,* the *Sundiata, Three Kingdoms,* and *Don Quixote:*

- showing courage
- values and beliefs
- conflicts and challenges
- illusion and reality
- rites of passage

Arthur Becomes King of Britain

T(erence) H(anbury) White (1906–1964) was born in Bombay, India. At the age of thirty, he resigned a teaching position to research flying, filmmaking, falconry, and the Arthurian legends. His most famous work is the four-part novel *The Once and Future King* (1958), which took nearly twenty years to complete and became the basis for Lerner and Loewe's musical *Camelot* (1960). This excerpt shows the parodylike style of this retelling of Sir Thomas Malory's fifteenth-century romance *Le Morte d'Arthur*.

The Marriage of King Arthur

Sir Thomas Malory (c. 1400–1471) is believed to have been born in Warwickshire, England, where he was charged with various crimes that he may not have committed. It is possible he spent as many as twenty-one years in prison, where he wrote *Le Morte d'Arthur* (French for "The Death of Arthur"), based on the legend of King Arthur. Malory lived during a troubled time; he may have written this work—from which "The Marriage of King Arthur" is taken—to recapture the chivalric ideals that his age had lost.

Morte d'Arthur

Alfred, Lord Tennyson (1809–1892) was born in Somersby, Lincolnshire, England. Tennyson prepared for college at home. He attended Cambridge but never received a degree. He strove to perfect his craft as a poet, experimenting with different poetic forms. He wrote exquisite short lyrics as well as powerful longer works. This excerpt from the epic *Idylls of the King,* twelve narrative poems based on the Arthurian legends, describes the aftermath of Arthur's last great battle and his death.

Arthurian Legend

The Arthurian legend has been recorded over centuries. **Legends** are imaginative stories believed to have a historical basis. The real Arthur most probably was a primitive Welsh battle leader of the sixth century. He and his Round Table of knights became the very symbol of medieval chivalry. **Chivalry** was a code of brave and courteous conduct for knights in the Middle Ages. According to this system of morals and manners, a knight vowed to remain faithful to God, loyal to his king, and true to his lady-love.

One of the forms well-suited to the Arthurian legend is epic poetry. An epic is a long narrative poem that celebrates the life of a hero who embodies the values of a particular society. Epics were developed and performed by poet-musicians and passed down through generations. *Morte d'Arthur,* which was written down rather than improvised, is from Tennyson's epic poem *Idylls of the King.*

Focus

These three selections each deal with the Arthurian legend. What contemporary event could you base a legend on? Name an event, and list some of the details of that event that seem appropriate for a legend. Then, as you read, evaluate the aspects of the Arthurian legend that have made it appealing to such a wide audience.

Vocabulary

Knowing the following words will help you as you read the Arthurian legends.

stickler (stik′ lər) *n.*: A person who insists uncompromisingly on the observance of something specified (p. 691)

sumptuous (sump′ choo əs) *adj.*: Magnificent (p. 694)

palfrey (pôl′ frē) *n.*: A saddle horse, especially one for a woman (p. 695)

prowess (prou′ is) *n.*: Skill; bravery (p. 701)

homage (häm′ ij) *n.*: Public show of allegiance (p. 702)

forfeiture (fôr′ fə chər) *n.*: The act of giving up something as punishment (p. 702)

lamentation (lam′ ən tā′ shən) *n.*: Mourning (p. 712)

swarthy (swôr′ *th*ē) *adj.*: Having a dark complexion (p. 714)

Arthur Becomes King of Britain

T. H. White

King Pellinore arrived for the important weekend in a high state of flurry.

"I say," he exclaimed, "do you know? Have you heard? Is it a secret, what?"

"Is what a secret, what?" they asked him.

"Why, the King," cried his majesty. "You know, about the King?"

"What's the matter with the King?" inquired Sir Ector. "You don't say he's comin' down to hunt with those darned hounds of his or anythin' like that?"

CROWNING OF ARTHUR
The British Library Royal MS

"He's dead," cried King Pellinore tragically. "He's dead, poor fellah, and can't hunt any more."

Sir Grummore stood up respectfully and took off his cap.

"The King is dead," he said. "Long live the King."

Everybody else felt they ought to stand up too, and the boys' nurse burst into tears.

"There, there," she sobbed. "His loyal highness dead and gone, and him such a respectful gentleman. Many's the illuminated picture I've cut out of him, from the Illustrated Missals, aye, and stuck up over the mantel. From the time when he was in swaddling bands,[1] right through them world towers till he was a-visiting the dispersed areas as the world's Prince Charming, there wasn't a picture of 'im but I had it out, aye, and give 'im a last thought o' nights."

"Compose yourself, Nannie," said Sir Ector.

"It is solemn, isn't it?" said King Pellinore, "what? Uther the Conqueror, 1066 to 1216."

"A solemn moment," said Sir Grummore. "The King is dead. Long live the King."

"We ought to pull down the curtains," said Kay, who was always a stickler for good form, "or half-mast[2] the banners."

"That's right," said Sir Ector. "Somebody go and tell the sergeant-at-arms."

It was obviously the Wart's duty to execute this command, for he was now the junior nobleman present, so he ran out cheerfully to find the sergeant. Soon those who were left in the solar[3] could hear a voice crying out, "Nah then, one-two, special mourning fer 'is lite majesty, lower awai on the command Two!" and then the flapping of all the standards, banners, pennons, pennoncells, banderolls, guidons, streamers and cognizances[4] which made gay the snowy turrets of the Forest Sauvage.

"How did you hear?" asked Sir Ector.

"I was pricking through the purlieus[5] of the forest after that Beast, you know, when I met with a solemn friar of orders gray, and he told me. It's the very latest news."

"Poor old Pendragon," said Sir Ector.

"The King is dead," said Sir Grummore solemnly. "Long live the King."

"It is all very well for you to keep on mentioning that, my dear Grummore," exclaimed King Pellinore petulantly, "but who is this King, what, that is to live so long, what, accordin' to you?"

"Well, his heir," said Sir Grummore, rather taken aback.

"Our blessed monarch," said the Nurse tearfully, "never had no hair. Anybody that studied the loyal family knowed that."

"Good gracious!" exclaimed Sir Ector. "But he must have had a next-of-kin?"

"That's just it," cried King Pellinore in high excitement. "That's the excitin' part of it, what? No hair and no next of skin, and who's to succeed to the throne? That's what my friar was so excited about, what, and why he was asking who could succeed to what, what? What?"

"Do you mean to tell me," exclaimed Sir Grummore indignantly, "that there ain't no King of Gramarye?"

"Not a scrap of one," cried King Pellinore, feeling important. "And there have been signs and wonders of no mean might."

"I think it's a scandal," said Sir Grummore. "God knows what the dear old country is comin' to."

---

1. swaddling bands: Long, narrows bands of cloths wrapped around a newborn baby in former times.

2. half-mast (haf mast') v.: Hang a flag at half-mast.

3. solar (sō′ lər) n.: Here, sun room. *Solar* is often used as an adjective.

---

4. standards . . . cognizances (käg′ nə zən′ səz) n.: Banners or flags.

5. purlieus (pur′ lo͞oz) n.: An outlying part of a forest, exempted from forest laws.

"What sort of signs and wonders?" asked Sir Ector.

"Well, there has appeared a sort of sword in a stone, what, in a sort of a church. Not in the church, if you see what I mean, and not in the stone, but that sort of thing, what, like you might say."

"I don't know what the Church is coming to," said Sir Grummore.

"It's in an anvil,"[6] explained the King.

"The Church?"

"No, the sword."

"But I thought you said the sword was in the stone?"

"No," said King Pellinore. "The stone is outside the Church."

"Look here, Pellinore," said Sir Ector. "You have a bit of a rest, old boy, and start again. Here, drink up this horn of mead[7] and take it easy."

"The sword," said King Pellinore, "is stuck through an anvil which stands on a stone. It goes right through the anvil and into the stone. The anvil is stuck to the stone. The stone stands outside a church. Give me some more mead."

"I don't think that's much of a wonder," remarked Sir Grummore. "What I wonder at is that they should allow such things to happen. But you can't tell nowadays, what with all these Saxon agitators."[8]

"My dear fellah," cried Pellinore, getting excited again, "it's not where the stone is, what, that I'm trying to tell you, but what is written on it, what, where it is."

"What?"

"Why, on its pommel."[9]

"Come on, Pellinore," said Sir Ector. "You just sit quite still with your face to the

wall for a minute, and then tell us what you are talkin' about. Take it easy, old boy. No need for hurryin'. You sit still and look at the wall, there's a good chap, and talk as slow as you can."

"There are words written on this sword in this stone outside this church," cried King Pellinore piteously, "and these words are as follows. Oh, do try to listen to me, you two, instead of interruptin' all the time about nothin', for it makes a man's head go ever so."

"What are these words?" asked Kay.

"These words say this," said King Pellinore, "so far as I can understand from that old friar of orders gray."

"Go on, do," said Kay, for the King had come to a halt.

"Go on," said Sir Ector, "what do these words on this sword in this anvil in this stone outside this church, say?"

King Pellinore closed his eyes tight, extended his arms in both directions, and announced in capital letters, "Whoso Pulleth Out This Sword of this Stone and Anvil, is Rightwise King Born of All England."

"Who said that?" asked Sir Grummore.

"But the sword said it, like I tell you."

"Talkative weapon," remarked Sir Grummore skeptically.

"It was written on it," cried the King angrily. "Written on it in letters of gold."

"Why didn't you pull it out then?" asked Sir Grummore.

"But I tell you that I wasn't there. All this that I am telling you was told to me by that friar I was telling you of, like I tell you."

"Has this sword with this inscription been pulled out?" inquired Sir Ector.

"No," whispered King Pellinore dramatically. "That's where the whole excitement comes in. They can't pull this sword out at all, although they have all been tryin' like fun, and so they have had to proclaim a tournament all over England, for New Year's

---

6. anvil (an′vəl) *n*.: An iron or steel block.

7. mead (mēd) *n*.: A drink made of fermented honey and water, often with spices or fruit added.

8. Saxon (sak′ s'n) **agitators:** ancient Germanic people who conquered parts of England.

9. pommel (pum′ əl) *n*.: The round knob on the end of the hilt of some swords.

Day, so that the man who comes to the tournament and pulls out the sword can be King of all England forever, what, I say."

"Oh, father," cried Kay. "The man who pulls the sword out of the stone will be the King of England. Can't we go to the tournament, father, and have a shot?"

"Couldn't think of it," said Sir Ector.

"Long way to London," said Sir Grummore, shaking his head.

"My father went there once," said King Pellinore.

Kay said, "Oh, surely we could go? When I am knighted I shall have to go to a tournament somewhere, and this one happens at just the right date. All the best people will be there, and we should see the famous knights and great kings. It does not matter about the sword, of course, but think of the tournament, probably the greatest there has ever been in Gramarye, and all the things we should see and do. Dear father, let me go to this tourney, if you love me, so that I may bear away the prize of all, in my maiden fight."

"But, Kay," said Sir Ector, "I have never been to London."

"All the more reason to go. I believe that anybody who does not go for a tournament like this will be proving that he has no noble blood in his veins. Think what people will say about us, if we do not go and have a shot at that sword. They will say that Sir Ector's family was too vulgar and knew it had no chance."

"We all know the family has no chance," said Sir Ector, "that is, for the sword."

"Lot of people in London," remarked Sir Grummore, with a wild surmise. "So they say."

He took a deep breath and goggled at his host with eyes like marbles.

"And shops," added King Pellinore suddenly, also beginning to breathe heavily.

"Dang it!" cried Sir Ector, bumping his horn mug on the table so that it spilled. "Let's all go to London, then, and see the new King!"

They rose up as one man.

"Why shouldn't I be as good a man as my father?" exclaimed King Pellinore.

"Dash it all," cried Sir Grummore. "After all, it is the capital!"

"Hurray!" shouted Kay.

"Lord have mercy," said the nurse.

At this moment the Wart came in with Merlyn, and everybody was too excited to notice that, if he had not been grown up now, he would have been on the verge of tears.

"Oh, Wart," cried Kay, forgetting for the moment that he was only addressing his squire, and slipping back into the familiarity of their boyhood. "What do you think? We are all going to London for a great tournament on New Year's Day!"

"Are we?"

"Yes, and you will carry my shield and spears for the jousts, and I shall win the palm[10] of everybody and be a great knight!"

"Well, I am glad we are going," said the Wart, "for Merlyn is leaving us too."

"Oh, we shan't need Merlyn."

"He is leaving us," repeated the Wart.

"Leavin' us?" asked Sir Ector. "I thought it was we that were leavin'?"

"He is going away from the Forest Sauvage."

Sir Ector said, "Come now, Merlyn, what's all this about? I don't understand all this a bit."

"I have come to say Goodbye, Sir Ector," said the old magician. "Tomorrow my pupil Kay will be knighted, and the next week my other pupil will go away as his squire. I have outlived my usefulness here, and it is time to go."

---

10. win the palm: Be the winner. A palm leaf is a symbol of victory.

"Now, now, don't say that," said Sir Ector. "I think you're a jolly useful chap whatever happens. You just stay and teach me, or be the librarian or something. Don't you leave an old man alone, after the children have flown."

"We shall all meet again," said Merlyn. "There is no cause to be sad."

"Don't go," said Kay.

"I must go," replied their tutor. "We have had a good time while we were young, but it is in the nature of Time to fly. There are many things in other parts of the kingdom which I ought to be attending to just now, and it is a specially busy time for me. Come, Archimedes, say Goodbye to the company."

"Goodbye," said Archimedes tenderly to the Wart.

"Goodbye," said the Wart without looking up at all.

"But you can't go," cried Sir Ector, "not without a month's notice."

"Can't I?" replied Merlyn, taking up the position always used by philosophers who propose to dematerialize. He stood on his toes, while Archimedes held tight to his shoulder—began to spin on them slowly like a top—spun faster and faster till he was only a blur of grayish light—and in a few seconds there was no one there at all.

"Goodbye, Wart," cried two faint voices outside the solar window.

"Goodbye," said the Wart for the last time—and the poor fellow went quickly out of the room.

The knighting took place in a whirl of preparations. Kay's sumptuous bath had to be set up in the box room, between two towel-horses and an old box of selected games which contained a worn-out straw dart-board—it was called fléchette in those days—because all the other rooms were full of packing. The nurse spent the whole time constructing new warm pants for everybody, on the principle that the climate of any place outside the Forest Sauvage must be treacherous to the extreme, and, as for the sergeant, he polished all the armor till it was quite brittle and sharpened the swords till they were almost worn away.

At last it was time to set out.

Perhaps, if you happen not to have lived in the Old England of the twelfth century, or whenever it was, and in a remote castle on the borders of the Marshes at that, you will find it difficult to imagine the wonders of their journey.

The road, or track, ran most of the time along the high ridges of the hills or downs, and they could look down on either side of them upon the desolate marshes where the snowy reeds sighed, and the ice crackled, and the duck in the red sunsets quacked loud on the winter air. The whole country was like that. Perhaps there would be a moory marsh on one side of the ridge, and a forest of a hundred thousand acres on the other, with all the great branches weighted in white. They could sometimes see a wisp of smoke among the trees, or a huddle of buildings far out among the impassable reeds, and twice they came to quite respectable towns which had several inns to boast of, but on the whole it was an England without civilization. The better roads were cleared of cover for a bow-shot on either side of them, lest the traveler should be slain by hidden thieves.

They slept where they could, sometimes in the hut of some cottager who was prepared to welcome them, sometimes in the castle of a brother knight who invited them to refresh themselves, sometimes in the firelight and fleas of a dirty little hovel with a bush tied to a pole outside it—this was the signboard used at that time by inns—and once or twice on the open ground, all huddled together for warmth between their grazing chargers. Wherever they went and wherever they slept, the east wind whistled in the reeds, and the geese went over high in the starlight, honking at the stars.

London was full to the brim. If Sir Ector had not been lucky enough to own a little land in Pie Street, on which there stood a respectable inn, they would have been hard put to it to find a lodging. But he did own it, and as a matter of fact drew most of his dividends from that source, so they were able to get three beds between the five of them. They thought themselves fortunate.

On the first day of the tournament, Sir Kay managed to get them on the way to the lists at least an hour before the jousts could possibly begin. He had lain awake all night, imagining how he was going to beat the best barons in England, and he had not been able to eat his breakfast. Now he rode at the front of the cavalcade, with pale cheeks, and Wart wished there was something he could do to calm him down.

For country people, who only knew the dismantled tilting ground[11] of Sir Ector's castle, the scene which met their eyes was ravishing. It was a huge green pit in the earth, about as big as the arena of a football match. It lay ten feet lower than the surrounding country, with sloping banks, and the snow had been swept off it. It had been kept warm with straw, which had been cleared off that morning, and now the closeworn grass sparkled green in the white landscape. Round the arena there was a world of color so dazzling and moving and twinkling as to make one blink one's eyes. The wooden grandstands were painted in scarlet and white. The silk pavilions of famous people, pitched on every side, were azure and green and saffron and checkered.

The pennons and pennoncells which floated everywhere in the sharp wind were flapping with every color of the rainbow, as they strained and slapped at their flagpoles, and the barrier down the middle of the arena itself was done in chessboard squares of black and white. Most of the combatants and their friends had not yet arrived, but one could see from those few who had come how the very people would turn the scene into a bank of flowers, and how the armor would flash, and the scalloped sleeves of the heralds jig in the wind, as they raised their brazen trumpets to their lips to shake the fleecy clouds of winter with joyances[12] and fanfares.

"Good heavens!" cried Sir Kay. "I have left my sword at home."

"Can't joust without a sword," said Sir Grummore. "Quite irregular."

"Better go and fetch it," said Sir Ector. "You have time."

"My squire will do," said Sir Kay. "What an awful mistake to make! Here, squire, ride hard back to the inn and fetch my sword. You shall have a shilling[13] if you fetch it in time."

The Wart went as pale as Sir Kay was, and looked as if he were going to strike him. Then he said, "It shall be done, master," and turned his ambling palfrey against the stream of newcomers. He began to push his way toward their hostelry[14] as best he might.

"To offer me money!" cried the Wart to himself. "To look down at this beastly little donkey-affair off his great charger and to call me Squire! Oh, Merlyn, give me patience with the brute, and stop me from throwing his filthy shilling in his face."

When he got to the inn it was closed. Everybody had thronged to see the famous

---

11. tilting ground: Ground on which a joust takes place.

12. joyances (joi′ əns iz) *n.*: Old word for *rejoicing*.

13. shilling (s*h*il′ iŋ) *n.*: British silver coin.

14. hostelry (häs′ təl rē) *n.*: Inn.

tournament, and the entire household had followed after the mob. Those were lawless days and it was not safe to leave your house—or even to go to sleep in it—unless you were certain that it was impregnable.[15] The wooden shutters bolted over the downstairs windows were two inches thick, and the doors were double-barred.

"Now what do I do," asked the Wart, "to earn my shilling?"

He looked ruefully at the blind little inn, and began to laugh.

"Poor Kay," he said. "All that shilling stuff was only because he was scared and miserable, and now he has good cause to be. Well, he shall have a sword of some sort if I have to break into the Tower of London.

"How does one get hold of a sword?" he continued. "Where can I steal one? Could I waylay some knight even if I am mounted on an ambling pad, and take his weapons by force? There must be some swordsmith or armorer in a great town like this, whose shop would be still open."

He turned his mount and cantered off along the street. There was a quiet churchyard at the end of it, with a kind of square in front of the church door. In the middle of the square there was a heavy stone with an anvil on it, and a fine new sword was stuck through the anvil.

"Well," said the Wart, "I suppose it is some sort of war memorial, but it will have to do. I am sure nobody would grudge Kay a war memorial, if they knew his desperate straits."

He tied his reins round a post of the lych gate,[16] strode up the gravel path, and took hold of the sword.

"Come, sword," he said. "I must cry your mercy and take you for a better cause.

"This is extraordinary," said the Wart. "I feel strange when I have told of this sword, and I notice everything much more clearly. Look at the beautiful gargoyles[17] of the church, and of the monastery which it belongs to. See how splendidly all the famous banners in the aisle are waving. How nobly that yew[18] holds up the red flakes of its timbers to worship God. How clean the snow is. I can smell something like sweet briar— and is it music that I hear?"

It was music, whether of pan-pipes or of recorders, and the light in the churchyard was so clear, without being dazzling, that one could have picked a pin out twenty yards away.

"There is something in this place," said the Wart. "There are people. Oh, people, what do you want?"

Nobody answered him, but the music was loud and the light beautiful.

"People," cried the Wart, "I must take this sword. It is not for me, but for Kay. I will bring it back."

There was still no answer, and Wart turned back to the anvil. He saw the golden letters, which he did not read, and the jewels on the pommel, flashing in the lovely light.

"Come, sword," said the Wart.

He took hold of the handles with both hands, and strained against the stone. There was a melodious consort[19] on the recorders, but nothing moved.

The Wart let go of the handles, when they were beginning to bite into the palms of his hands, and stepped back, seeing stars.

"It is well fixed," he said.

He took hold of it again and pulled with all his might. The music played more strongly, and the light all about the churchyard

---

15. impregnable (im preg′ nə bəl) *adj.*: Not capable of being entered by force.
16. lych (lich) **gate:** A roofed gate at the entrace to a churchyard.

17. gargoyles (gär′ goilz) *n.*: Projecting ornaments, usually grotesquely carved animals or fantastic creatures, on a building.
18. yew (yo͞o) *n.*: Evergreen shrubs and trees of the yew family.
19. consort (kän′ sôrt) *n.*: Harmony of sounds.

glowed like amethysts; but the sword still stuck.

"Oh, Merlyn," cried the Wart, "help me to get this weapon."

These was a kind of rushing noise, and a long chord played along with it. All round the churchyard there were hundreds of old friends. They rose over the church wall all together, like the Punch-and-Judy[20] ghosts of remembered days, and there were badgers and nightingales and vulgar crows and hares and wild geese and falcons and fishes and dogs and dainty unicorns and solitary wasps and hedgehogs and griffins and the thousand other animals he had met. They loomed round the church wall, the lovers and helpers of the Wart, and they all spoke solemnly in turn. Some of them had come from the banners in the church, where they were painted in heraldry, some from the waters and the sky and the fields about— but all, down to the smallest shrew mouse, had come to help on account of love. Wart felt his power grow.

"Put you back into it," said a luce (or pike) off one of the heraldic banners, "as you once did when I was going to snap you up. Remember that power springs from the nape of the neck."

"What about those forearms," asked a badger gravely, "that are held together by a chest? Come along, my dear embryo,[21] and find your tool."

A merlin sitting at the top of the yew tree cried out, "Now then, Captain Wart, what is the first law of the foot? I thought I once heard something about never letting go."

"Don't work like a stalling woodpecker," urged a tawny owl affectionately. "Keep up a steady effort, my duck, and you will have it yet."

A white-front said. "Now, Wart, if you were once able to fly the great North Sea, surely you can coordinate a few little wing-muscles here and there? Fold your powers together, with the spirit of your mind, and it will come out like butter. Come along, Homo sapiens,[22] for all we humble friends of yours are waiting here to cheer."

The Wart walked up to the great sword for the third time. He put out his right hand softly and drew it out as gently as from a scabbard.

There was a lot of cheering, a noise like a hurdy-gurdy[23] which went on and on. In the middle of this noise, after a long time, he saw Kay and gave him the sword. The people at the tournament were making a frightful row.

"But this is not my sword," said Sir Kay.

"It was the only one I could get," said the Wart. "The inn was locked."

"It is a nice-looking sword. Where did you get it?"

"I found it stuck in a stone, outside a church."

Sir Kay had been watching the tilting nervously, waiting for his turn. He had not paid much attention to his squire.

"That is a funny place to find one," he said.

"Yes, it was stuck through an anvil."

"What?" cried Sir Kay, suddenly rounding upon him. "Did you just say this sword was stuck in a stone?"

"It was," said the Wart. "It was a sort of war memorial."

---

20. Punch-and-Judy: Puppets of the quarrelsome Punch and his wife, Judy, who constantly fight in a comical way.

21. embryo: (em′ brē ō) *n.*: Anything in an early stage of development.

22. Homo sapiens (hō′ mō sā′ pē ənz′): Human being.

23. hurdy-gurdy (hur′ dē gur′ dē) *n.*: A musical instrument, like a barrel organ, played by turning a crank.

Sir Kay stared at him for several seconds in amazement, opened his mouth, shut it again, licked his lips, then turned his back and plunged through the crowd. He was looking for Sir Ector, and the Wart followed after him.

"Father," cried Sir Kay, "come here a moment."

"Yes, my boy," said Sir Ector. "Splendid falls these professional chaps do manage. Why, what's the matter, Kay? You look as white as a sheet."

"Do you remember that sword which the King of England would pull out?"

"Yes."

"Well, here it is. I have it. It is in my hand. I pulled it out."

Sir Ector did not say anything silly. He looked at Kay and he looked at the Wart. Then he stared at Kay again, long and lovingly, and said, "We will go back to the church."

"Now then, Kay," he said, when they were at the church door. He looked at his firstborn kindly, but straight between the eyes. "Here is the stone, and you have the sword. It will make you the King of England. You are my son that I am proud of, and always will be, whatever you do. Will you promise me that you took it out by your own might?''

Kay looked at his father. He also looked at the Wart and at the sword.

Then he handed the sword to the Wart quite quietly.

He said, ''I am a liar. Wart pulled it out.''

As far as the Wart was concerned, there was a time after this in which Sir Ector kept telling him to put the sword back into the stone—which he did—and in which Sir Ector and Kay then vainly tried to take it out. The Wart took it out for them, and stuck it back again once or twice. After this, there was another time which was more painful.

He saw that his dear guardian was looking quite old and powerless, and that he was kneeling down with difficulty on a gouty[24] knee.

''Sir,'' said Sir Ector, without looking up, although he was speaking to his own boy.

''Please do not do this, father,'' said the Wart, kneeling down also. ''Let me help you up, Sir Ector, because you are making me unhappy.''

''Nay, nay, my lord,'' said Sir Ector, with some very feeble old tears. ''I was never your father nor of your blood, but I wote[25] well ye are of an higher blood than I wend[26] ye were.''

''Plenty of people have told me you are not my father,'' said the Wart, ''but it does not matter a bit.''

''Sir,'' said Sir Ector humbly, ''will ye be my good and gracious lord when ye are King?''

''Don't!'' said the Wart.

''Sir,'' said Sir Ector, ''I will ask no more of you but that you will make my son, your foster-brother, Sir Kay, seneschal[27] of all your lands.''

Kay was kneeling down too, and it was more than the Wart could bear.

''Oh, do stop,'' he cried. ''Of course he can be seneschal, if I have got to be this King, and, oh, father, don't kneel down like that, because it breaks my heart. Please get up, Sir Ector, and don't make everything so horrible. Oh, dear, oh, dear, I wish I had never seen that filthy sword at all.''

And the Wart also burst into tears.

---

24. gouty (gout′ ē) *adj.*: Having gout, a disease causing swelling and severe pain in the joints.

25. wote (wōt) *v.*: Old word meaning *know.*

26. wend (wend) *v.*: Here, old word meaning *thought.*

27. seneschal (sen′ ə shəl) *n.*: A steward in the house of a medieval noble.

RESPONDING TO THE SELECTION

Your Response

1. Put yourself in Wart's place. How would you have felt after finding a sword for Sir Kay?
2. Which character—Wart, Sir Kay, Merlyn, or another—was your favorite? Why?

Recalling

3. What news does King Pellinore bring? What is significant about this news?
4. Explain how the new King of England is to be chosen.

Interpreting

5. In what ways is the Wart's drawing the sword from the stone a moment of magic and mystery?
6. What do Sir Kay's explanations to Sir Ector about pulling the sword reveal about Sir Kay's character?
7. How does the Wart feel about becoming King?

Applying

8. Reread the words of encouragement given by the luce, the badger, the merlin, the tawny owl, and the white-front. How might their advice be pertinent to life in general?

ANALYZING LITERATURE

Understanding the Legend

A **legend** is an imaginative story handed down for generations and believed, but not proved, to have a historical basis. A legend provides information about the culture that created it. For instance, the idea of chivalry in King Arthur legends tells you that brave and courteous behavior in knights was valued by people of that time.

1. On the basis of this legend, what conclusions do you draw about loyalty to the king?
2. Do you think warfare was a common occurrence during this period? What evidence leads you to this opinion?

CRITICAL THINKING AND READING

Recognizing Tone

Tone is the attitude a writer takes toward his or her subject. You can recognize the tone of a literary work based on the attitude the writer shows through certain words and phrases. The tone of "Arthur Becomes King of Britain" is light and humorous.

1. Find three examples in this selection that provide evidence from which you can infer a light and humorous tone.
2. Find at least two examples in which the author seems to parody, or poke gentle fun at, the King Arthur legend.

LEARNING OPTIONS

1. **Art.** Create a cartoon or a comic strip to illustrate an important event in "Arthur Becomes King of Britain." You may wish to show King Pellinore announcing King Uther's death, Merlyn leaving, Sir Ector and the others going to London, or Wart pulling the sword out of the stone. Newspaper cartoons and comic strips can provide good models.
2. **Writing.** Imagine you are an eyewitness to the knights' tournament held in London. Write an account of this thrilling event for a newspaper called *Feudal Times.* In your account, answer the following questions: *Who? What? When? Where? Why? How?* Use vivid descriptive words to make your account come alive.
3. **Multicultural Activity.** The kings and knights in this selection belong to a political system called feudalism. Although "Arthur Becomes King of Britain" is set in medieval England, feudalism was also practiced in Japan as well as in other European countries. Use a social studies textbook, encyclopedia, or nonfiction book to find out more about feudalism. Then make a chart to compare and contrast the practice of feudalism in different countries.

The Marriage of King Arthur

Sir Thomas Malory

How King Arthur took a wife, and wedded Guenevere, daughter to Leodegrance, King of the Land of Cameliard, who had the Round Table

In the beginning of Arthur, after he was chosen king by adventure and by grace, most of the barons knew not that he was Uther Pendragon's son, unless Merlin told them. But yet many kings and lords made war against him for that cause, but well Arthur overcame them all. For most of the days of his life Arthur was ruled much by the counsel of Merlin. So it fell on a time King Arthur said unto Merlin, "My barons will let me have no rest, unless I take a wife, and I will none take but by thy counsel and by thine advice."

"It is well done," said Merlin, "that ye take a wife, for a man of your bounty[1] and noblesse[2] should not be without a wife. Now is there any that ye love more than another?"

"Yea," said King Arthur, "I love Guenevere, the daughter of King Leodegrance of the land of Cameliard, who holdeth in his house the Table Round that ye told me had been given to him by my father Uther. And this damsel is the most valiant and fairest lady that I know living, or yet that ever I could find."

"Sir," said Merlin, "as of her beauty and fairness she is one of the fairest alive, but if ye loved her not so well as ye do, I should find you a damsel of beauty and of goodness that should like you and please you, if your heart were not set; but as a man's heart is set, he will be loath to return."[3]

"That is truth," said King Arthur.

Then Merlin asked the king for men to go with him to enquire of Guenevere, and so the king granted him, and Merlin went forth unto King Leodegrance of Cameliard, and told him of the desire of the king that he would have for his wife Guenevere, his daughter.

"That is to me," said King Leodegrance, "the best tidings that ever I heard, that so worthy a king of prowess and noblesse will wed my daughter. And I would give him lands if I thought it would please him, but he has lands enough; instead I shall send him a gift that shall please him much more, for I shall give him the Table Round, which Uther Pendragon gave me, and when it is full complete, there is a hundred knights and fifty. A hundred good knights I have

---

1. **bounty** (bσun′ tē) *n.*: Generosity.
2. **noblesse** (nō bles′) *n.*: Nobility.
3. **loath** (lōṫh) **to return:** Reluctant to change his mind.

myself, but I faute[4] fifty, for so many have been slain in my days."

And so Leodegrance delivered his daughter Guenevere unto Merlin, and the Table Round with the hundred knights, and so they rode freshly, with great royalty, part of the way by water and part of the way by land, till they came nigh unto London.

How the Knights of the Round Table were ordained[5] and their sieges[6] blessed by the Bishop of Canterbury

When King Arthur heard of the coming of Guenevere and the hundred knights with the Table Round, then King Arthur made great joy for her coming and for that rich present and said openly, "This fair lady is welcome, for I have loved her long, and therefore there is nothing so lief to me. And these knights with the Round Table please me more than right great riches." And in all haste the king arranged for the marriage and the coronation in the most honorable way that could be devised.

"Now, Merlin," said King Arthur, "go thou and espy me in all this land fifty knights which be of most prowess and worship."

Within a short time Merlin had found twenty and eight knights, but no more could he find. Then the Bishop of Canterbury was fetched, and he blessed the sieges with great royalty and devotion, and there set the eight and twenty knights in their sieges. And when this was done Merlin said, "Fair sirs, ye must all arise and come to King Arthur to do him homage; then he will have the better will to maintain you."[7]

And so they arose and did their homage, and when they were gone Merlin found in every siege letters of gold that told the knight's name that had been sitting therein. But two sieges were void.[8]

And so anon came young Gawain and asked the king a gift. "Ask," said the king, "and I shall grant it you."

"Sir, I ask that ye will make me knight on the same day ye shall wed fair Guenevere."

"I will do it with a good will," said King Arthur, "and do unto you all the worship that I may, for I must because ye are my nephew, my sister's son.". . .

Then was the high feast made ready, and the king was wedded at Camelot unto Dame Guenevere, in the church of Saint Stephen's, with great solemnity. And as every man was set according to his degree,[9] Merlin went to all the knights of the Round Table, and bade them sit still, that none of them remove. . . .

Then the king established all his knights, and he gave lands to those that had no lands, and charged them never to do anything outrageous nor to commit murder, and always to flee treason; also, by no means to be cruel, but to give mercy unto him that asketh mercy, upon pain of forfeiture of their worship and lordship of King Arthur forevermore; and always to do ladies, damsels, and gentlewomen succor,[10] upon pain of death. Also, that no man do battle in a wrongful quarrel against the law or for world's goods. Unto this were all the knights sworn of the Table Round, both old and young. And every year were they sworn at the high feast of Pentecost.[11]

---

4. faute (fōt) *v.*: Lack.
5. ordained (ôr dānd') *v.*: Established.
6. sieges (sēj' əs) *n.*: Seats.
7. better will to maintain you: A stronger desire to provide for and to protect you.

8. void (void) *adj.*: Containing no matter; empty.
9. degree: Rank.
10. succor (suk' ər) *n.*: Aid; help.
11. Pentecost (pen' tə kôst') *n.*: A Christian religious celebration.

RESPONDING TO THE SELECTION

Your Response

1. Were you surprised by the way Guenevere became King Arthur's wife? Explain.
2. If you were a Round Table knight, which code of conduct would be most difficult for you to uphold? Why?

Recalling

3. What is King Leodegrance's response to Arthur's request to marry his daughter?
4. What else occurs on the day Arthur weds Guenevere?

Interpreting

5. Explain the significance of Leodegrance's gift to Arthur.
6. The King Arthur legends tell of a time in the early history of England when a belief in magic was supplanted by Christianity. What elements do you find of both magic and religion in this legend?

Applying

7. King Leodegrance gave Arthur the Round Table upon agreeing that Arthur would marry his daughter. How does this compare with customs today when two people marry?

ANALYZING LITERATURE

Understanding Chivalry

Chivalry, a knightly code of morals and manners in the Middle Ages, was more an ideal than a reality. Many of our modern ideas about heroism come in part from this vision of knighthood. The stirring idea of a brave and honorable knight who lives according to a high personal moral code has endured through the ages.

1. In your own words, summarize the code of conduct that Arthur establishes for his knights.
2. How does Merlin's response to King Arthur about marrying Guenevere fit in with the idea of chivalry?

3. Is chivalry alive in the modern world? Use examples from life to support your answer.

CRITICAL THINKING AND READING

Understanding Inversion

Inversion is a reversal of standard word order. An example of standard word order is "I went into the town to see the zebras in the zoo." An example of inverted word order is "Into the town to see the zebras in the zoo I went."

Inverted word order sounds somewhat artificial today but was commonly used in literature long ago. For example, King Arthur in "The Marriage of King Arthur" says that Guenevere is the "fairest lady . . . that ever I could find."

Find two other examples of inverted word order in this selection, and rewrite the sentence or phrase in standard word order.

THINKING AND WRITING

Writing About a Code of Conduct

Write an essay for a self-help magazine explaining a code of conduct appropriate for today. Use the list you developed earlier as the basis for your essay. First freewrite about why you think a code of conduct is valuable in life. Then use this information in writing your essay. Revise your essay to make sure you have included examples that support your opinion. Proofread for errors in spelling, grammar, and punctuation.

LEARNING OPTION

Writing. King Arthur asks Merlin to find fifty worthy knights for the Round Table. Write a speech to nominate a real historical figure, a fictional character, or a person you know who deserves a place at the Round Table. Explain why this person is a good candidate, and describe the talents or abilities he or she would contribute to the Round Table. Deliver your speech to the rest of the class.

Morte d'Arthur

Alfred, Lord Tennyson

The Epic

At Francis Allen's on the Christmas eve—
The game of forfeits[1] done—the girls all kissed
Beneath the sacred bush[2] and passed away—
The parson Holmes, the poet Everard Hall,
5   The host, and I sat round the wassail bowl,[3]
Then halfway ebbed; and there we held a talk,
How all the old honor had from Christmas gone,
Or gone or dwindled down to some odd games
In some odd nooks like this; till I, tired out
10   With cutting eights[4] that day upon the pond,
Where, three times slipping from the outer edge,
I bumped the ice into three several stars,
Fell in a doze; and half-awake I heard
The parson taking wide and wider sweeps,
15   Now harping on the church commissioners,
Now hawking at geology and schism;[5]
Until I woke, and found him settled down
Upon the general decay of faith
Right through the world: "at home was little left,
20   And none abroad; there was no anchor, none,
To hold by." Francis, laughing, clapped his hand
On Everard's shoulder, with "I hold by him."
"And I," quoth Everard, "by the wassail-bowl."
"Why yes," I said, "we knew your gift that way
25   At college; but another which you had—
I mean of verse (for so we held it then),

---

1. forfeits (fôr′ fits) *n.*: A game in which something is taken away as a penalty for making a mistake.
2. sacred bush: Mistletoe.
3. wassail bowl (wäs′əl bōl′) *n.*: Punch bowl.
4. cutting eights: Ice-skating so that skates cut figure eights in the ice.
5. schism (siz′ əm) *n.*: A division within an organization, especially a church, because of a difference of opinion.

What came of that?" "You know," said Frank, "he burnt
His epic, his King Arthur, some twelve books"—
And then to me demanding why: "O, sir,
30 He thought that nothing new was said, or else
Something so said 'twas nothing—that a truth
Looks freshest in the fashion of the day;
God knows; he has a mint of reasons; ask.
It pleased *me* well enough." "Nay, nay," said Hall,
35 "Why take the style of those heroic times?
For nature brings not back the mastodon,[6]
Nor we those times; and why should any man
Remodel models? these twelve books of mine
Were faint Homeric echoes,[7] nothing-worth,
40 Mere chaff and draff,[8] much better burnt." "But I,"
Said Francis, "picked the eleventh from this hearth,
And have it; keep a thing, its use will come.
I hoard it as a sugarplum for Holmes."
He laughed, and I, though sleepy, like a horse
45 That hears the corn-bin open, pricked my ears;
For I remembered Everard's college fame
When we were Freshmen. Then at my request
He brought it; and the poet, little urged,
But with some prelude of disparagement,
50 Read, mouthing out his hollow o's and a's,
Deep-chested music, and to this result.

Morte d'Arthur

So all day long the noise of battle rolled
Among the mountains by the winter sea,
Until King Arthur's table, man by man,
Had fallen in Lyonnesse[9] about their lord,
55 King Arthur; then, because his wound was deep,
The bold Sir Bedivere uplifted him,
Sir Bedivere, the last of all his knights,
And bore him to a chapel nigh the field,
60 A broken chancel[10] with a broken cross,
That stood on a dark strait of barren land.

---

6. mastodon (mas′ tə dän′) *n*.: An extinct animal resembling the
elephant but larger.

7. Homeric echoes (hō mer′ ik ek′ ōs): Imitations of the poems of the
Greek poet Homer (of about the eighth century B.C.).

8. chaff and draff: Anything worthless; dregs.

9. Lyonnesse (lī′ ə nes′): A legendary country off the southwestern
coast of England, supposed to have sunk beneath the sea.

10. chancel (chan′ səl) *n*.: The part of a church around the altar.

On one side lay the ocean, and on one
Lay a great water, and the moon was full.
    Then spake King Arthur to Sir Bedivere:
65   "The sequel of today unsolders[11] all
The goodliest fellowship of famous knights
Whereof this world holds record. Such a sleep
They sleep—the men I loved. I think that we
Shall never more, at any future time,
70   Delight our souls with talk of knightly deeds,
Walking about the gardens and the halls
Of Camelot, as in the days that were.
I perish by this people which I made—
Though Merlin sware that I should come again

---

11. unsolders (un säd′ ərs) *v.*: Separates.

75   To rule once more—but let what will be be,
I am so deeply smitten through the helm[12]
That without help I cannot last till morn.
Thou therefore take my brand[13] Excalibur,
Which was my pride; for thou rememberest how
80   In those old days, one summer noon, an arm
Rose up from out the bosom of the lake,
Clothed in white samite,[14] mystic, wonderful,
Holding the sword—and how I rowed across
And took it, and have worn it, like a king;
85   And, wheresoever I am sung or told
In aftertime, this also shall be known.
But now delay not; take Excalibur,
And fling him far into the middle mere;[15]
Watch what thou seest, and lightly[16] bring me word."
90   To him replied the bold Sir Bedivere:
"It is not meet,[17] Sir King, to leave thee thus,
Aidless, alone, and smitten through the helm.
A little thing may harm a wounded man.
Yet I thy hest will all perform at full,[18]
95   Watch what I see, and lightly bring thee word."
        So saying, from the ruined shrine he stepped
And in the moon athwart the place of tombs,
Where lay the mighty bones of ancient men,
Old knights, and over them the sea wind sang
100   Shrill, chill, with flakes of foam. He, stepping down
By zigzag paths and juts of pointed rock,
Came on the shining levels of the lake.
        There drew he forth the brand Excalibur,
And o'er him, drawing it, the winter moon,
105   Brightening the skirts of a long cloud, ran forth
And sparkled keen with frost against the hilt;
For all the haft[19] twinkled with diamond sparks,
Myriads[20] of topaz lights, and jacinth work[21]
Of subtlest jewelry. He gazed so long

---

12. helm: Helmet.
13. brand: Sword.
14. samite (sam' ĭt) *n.*: A heavy silk fabric.
15. mere (mir) *n.*: Lake.
16. lightly *adv.*: Quickly.
17. meet *adj.*: proper.
18. I thy hest will all perform at full: I will carry out your order completely.
19. haft *n.*: Handle or hilt of a sword.
20. myriads (mir' ē ədz) *n.*: Large numbers.
21. topaz (tō' paz) **. . . jacinth** (jā' sinth): Yellow and reddish-orange jewels.

110 That both his eyes were dazzled, as he stood,
This way and that dividing the swift mind,
In act to throw; but at the last it seemed
Better to leave Excalibur concealed
There in the many-knotted water flags,[22]
115 That whistled still and dry about the marge.[23]
So strode he back slow to the wounded king.
    Then spake King Arthur to Sir Bedivere:
"Hast thou performed my mission which I gave?
What is it thou hast seen, or what hast heard?"
120   And answer made the bold Sir Bedivere:
"I heard the ripple washing in the reeds,
And the wild water lapping on the crag."
    To whom replied King Arthur, faint and pale:
"Thou hast betrayed thy nature and thy name,
125 Not rendering[24] true answer, as beseemed[25]
Thy fealty, nor like a noble knight;
For surer sign had followed, either hand,
Or voice, or else a motion of the mere.
This is a shameful thing for men to lie.
130 Yet now, I charge thee, quickly go again
As thou art lief and dear, and do the thing
I bade thee, watch, and lightly bring me word."
    Then went Sir Bedivere the second time
Across the ridge, and paced beside the mere,
135 Counting the dewy pebbles, fixed in thought;
But when he saw the wonder of the hilt,
How curiously and strangely chased,[26] he smote
His palms together, and he cried aloud:
    "And if indeed I cast the brand away;
140 Surely a precious thing, one worthy note,
Should thus be lost forever from the earth,
Which might have pleased the eyes of many men.
What good should follow this, if this were done?
What harm, undone? deep harm to disobey,
145 Seeing obedience is the bond of rule.
Were it well to obey then, if a king demand
An act unprofitable, against himself?
The king is sick, and knows not what he does.
What record, or what relic of my lord

---

22. water flags: Marsh plants.
23. marge (märj) *n.*: Edge.
24. rendering (ren' dər iŋ) *v.*: Giving.
25. beseemed (bi sēm'd') *v.*: Was suitable to.
26. chased *v.*: Decorated by engraving or embossing.

150 Should be to aftertime, but empty breath
And rumors of a doubt? but were this kept,
Stored in some treasure-house of mighty kings,
Some one might show it at a joust of arms,
Saying, 'King Arthur's sword, Excalibur,
155 Wrought by the lonely maiden of the lake;
Nine years she wrought it, sitting in the deeps
Upon the hidden bases of the hills.'
So might some old man speak in the aftertime
To all the people, winning reverence;
160 But now much honor and much fame were lost."

    So spake he, clouded with his own conceit,
And hid Excalibur the second time,
And so strode back slow to the wounded king.
    Then spoke King Arthur, breathing heavily:
165 "What is it thou hast seen, or what hast heard?"
    And answer made the bold Sir Bedivere:
"I heard the water lapping on the crag,
And the long ripple washing in the reeds."
    To whom replied King Arthur, much in wrath:
170 "Ah, miserable and unkind, untrue,
Unknightly, traitor-hearted! Woe is me!
Authority forgets a dying king,
Laid widowed of the power in his eye
That bowed the will. I see thee what thou art,
175 For thou, the latest-left of all my knights,
In whom should meet the offices[27] of all,
Thou wouldst betray me for the precious hilt;
Either from lust of gold, or like a girl
Valuing the giddy pleasure of the eyes.
180 Yet, for a man may fail in duty twice,
And the third time may prosper, get thee hence;
But, if thou spare to fling Excalibur,
I will arise and slay thee with my hands."
    Then quickly rose Sir Bedivere, and ran,
185 And, leaping down the ridges lightly, plunged
Among the bulrush beds,[28] and clutched the sword,
And strongly wheeled and threw it. The great brand
Made lightnings in the splendor of the moon,
And flashing round and round, and whirled in an arch,
190 Shot like a streamer of the northern morn,[29]

---

27. offices *n.*: Duties.
28. bulrush (bool' rush) **beds:** Growth of marsh plants.
29. a streamer of the northern morn: The northern lights; the aurora borealis.

Seen where the moving isles of winter shock[30]
By night, with noises of the northern sea.
So flashed and fell the brand Excalibur;
But ere he dipped the surface, rose an arm
195 Clothed in white samite, mystic, wonderful,
And caught him by the hilt, and brandished him
Three times, and drew him under in the mere.
And lightly went the other to the king.
     Then spoke King Arthur, drawing thicker breath:
200 "Now see I by thine eyes that this is done.
Speak out; what is it thou hast heard, or seen?"
     And answer made the bold Sir Bedivere:
"Sir King, I closed mine eyelids, lest the gems
Should blind my purpose, for I never saw,
205 Nor shall see, here or elsewhere, till I die,
Not though I live three lives of mortal men,
So great a miracle as yonder hilt.
Then with both hands I flung him, wheeling him;
But when I looked again, behold an arm,
210 Clothed in white samite, mystic, wonderful,
That caught him by the hilt, and brandished him
Three times, and drew him under in the mere."
     And answer made King Arthur, breathing hard:
"My end draws nigh; 'tis time that I were gone.
215 Make broad thy shoulders to receive my weight,
And bear me to the margin,[31] yet I fear
My wound hath taken cold, and I shall die."
     So saying, from the pavement he half rose,
Slowly, with pain, reclining on his arm,
220 And looking wistfully with wide blue eyes
As in a picture. Him Sir Bedivere
Remorsefully regarded through his tears,
And would have spoken, but he found not words,
Then took with care, and kneeling on one knee,
225 O'er both his shoulders drew the languid hands,
And rising bore him through the place of tombs.
     But, as he walked, King Arthur panted hard,
Like one that feels a nightmare on his bed
When all the house is mute. So sighed the king,
230 Muttering and murmuring at his ear, "Quick, quick!
I fear it is too late, and I shall die."

---

30. the moving isles of winter shock: The icebergs crash.
31. margin (mär' jən) *n*.: Edge.

HOW SIR BEDIVERE CAST THE SWORD EXCALIBER INTO THE WATER
Aubrey Beardsley
Houghton Library, Harvard University

But the other swiftly strode from ridge to ridge,
Clothed with his breath, and looking, as he walked,
Larger than human on the frozen hills.
235 He heard the deep behind him, and a cry
Before. His own thought drove him like a goad.[32]
Dry clashed his harness[33] in the icy caves
And barren chasms, and all to left and right
The bare black cliff clanged round him, as he based
240 His feet on juts of slippery crag that rang
Sharp-smitten with the dint of armèd heels—
And on a sudden, lo! the level lake,
And the long glories of the winter moon.

      Then saw they how there hove a dusky barge,
245 Dark as a funeral scarf from stem to stern,
Beneath them; and descending they were ware
That all the decks were dense with stately forms
Black-stoled,[34] black-hooded, like a dream—by these
Three queens with crowns of gold—and from them rose
250 A cry that shivered to the tingling stars,
And, as it were one voice, an agony
Of lamentation, like a wind that shrills
All night in a waste land, where no one comes,
Or hath come, since the making of the world.

255   Then murmured Arthur, "Place me in the barge,"
And to the barge they came. There those three queens
Put forth their hands, and took the king, and wept.
But she that rose the tallest of them all
And fairest laid his head upon her lap,
260 And loosed the shattered casque,[35] and chafed his hands,
And called him by his name, complaining loud,
And dropping bitter tears against his brow
Striped with dark blood; for all his face was white
And colorless, and like the withered moon
265 Smote by the fresh beam of the springing east;
And all his greaves and cuisses dashed with drops
Of onset;[36] and the light and lustrous curls—

---

32. goad (gōd) *n.*: A sharp-pointed stick used to drive oxen.
33. harness (här' nis) *n.*: Armor.
34. black-stoled: Wearing long black scarves around their shoulders.
35. casque (kask) *n.*: Helmet.
36. greaves (grēvz) **and cuisses** (kwis' əs) **. . . onset:** Armor for the legs below the knee and for the thigh spattered with blood from the battle.

That made his forehead like a rising sun
High from the dais-throne—were parched with dust;
270 Or, clotted into points and hanging loose,
Mixed with the knightly growth that fringed his lips.
So like a shattered column lay the king;
Not like that Arthur who, with lance in rest,
From spur to plume a star of tournament,
275 Shot through the lists at Camelot, and charged
Before the eyes of ladies and of kings.

Then loudly cried the bold Sir Bedivere:
"Ah! my Lord Arthur, whither shall I go?
Where shall I hide my forehead and my eyes?
280 For now I see the true old times are dead,
When every morning brought a noble chance,
And every chance brought out a noble knight.
Such times have been not since the light that led
The holy Elders with the gift of myrrh.[37]
285 But now the whole ROUND TABLE is dissolved
Which was an image of the mighty world;
And I, the last, go forth companionless,
And the days darken round me, and the years,
Among new men, strange faces, other minds."

290 And slowly answered Arthur from the barge:
"The old order changeth, yielding place to new,
And God fulfills himself in many ways,
Lest one good custom should corrupt the world.
Comfort thyself: what comfort is in me?
295 I have lived my life, and that which I have done
May He within himself make pure! but thou,
If thou shouldst never see my face again,
Pray for my soul. More things are wrought by prayer
Than this world dreams of. Wherefore, let thy voice
300 Rise like a fountain for me night and day.
For what are men better than sheep or goats
That nourish a blind life within the brain,
If, knowing God, they lift not hands of prayer
Both for themselves and those who call them friend?
305 For so the whole round earth is every way
Bound by gold chains about the feet of God.
But now farewell. I am going a long way

---

37. the light . . . of myrrh (mur): The star that guided the three
Kings (the holy Elders) with their gift of incense (myrrh) to
Bethlehem at the time of the birth of Jesus.

With these thou seest—if indeed I go—
For all my mind is clouded with a doubt—
310   To the island-valley of Avilion;[38]
Where falls not hail, or rain, or any snow,
Nor ever wind blows loudly, but it lies
Deep-meadowed, happy, fair with orchard lawns
And bowery[39] hollows crowned with summer sea,
315   Where I will heal me of my grievous wound."
        So said he, and the barge with oar and sail
Moved from the brink, like some full-breasted swan
that, fluting a wild carol ere her death,
Ruffles her pure cold plume, takes the flood
320   With swarthy webs. Long stood Sir Bedivere
Revolving many memories, till the hull
Looked one black dot against the verge of dawn,
And on the mere the wailing died away.

        Here ended Hall, and our last light, that long
325   Had winked and threatened darkness, flared and fell;
At which the parson, sent to sleep with sound,
And waked with silence, grunted "Good!" but we
Sat rapt:[40] it was the tone with which he read—
Perhaps some modern touches here and there
330   Redeemed[41] it from the charge of nothingness—
Or else we loved the man, and prized his work;
I know not; but we sitting, as I said,
The cock crew loud, as at that time of year
The lusty bird takes every hour for dawn.
335   Then Francis, muttering, like a man ill-used,
"There now—that's nothing!" drew a little back,
And drove his heel into the smoldered log,
That sent a blast of sparkles up the flue.
And so to bed, where yet in sleep I seemed
340   To sail with Arthur under looming shores,
Point after point; till on to dawn, when dreams
Begin to feel the truth and stir of day,
To me, methought, who waited with the crowd,
There came a bark that, blowing forward, bore

---

38. island-valley of Avilion: The island paradise of
Avalon where heros were taken after death, according
to Celtic mythology and medieval romances.
39. bowery (bou′ər ē) *adj.*: Enclosed by overhanging
boughs of trees or by vines.
40. rapt *adj.*: Completely absorbed; engrossed.
41. Redeemed (ri dēmd′) *v.*: Rescued or saved.

345   King Arthur; like a modern gentleman
        Of stateliest port;[42] and all the people cried,
        "Arthur is come again: he cannot die."
        Then those that stood upon the hills behind
        Repeated—"Come again, and thrice as fair";
350   And, further inland, voices echoed—"Come
        With all good things, and war shall be no more."
        At this a hundred bells began to peal,
        That with the sound I woke, and heard indeed
        The clear church bells ring in the Christmas morn.

---

42. of stateliest port: Who carried himself in a most majestic or dignified manner.

▌R ESPONDING TO THE SELECTION

Your Response

1. King Arthur asks Sir Bedivere to throw Excalibur into a lake. What is your opinion of Sir Bedivere's actions? Explain.

Recalling

2. What occasion is being celebrated at the start of the poem?
3. In the poem within the poem, what has happened to King Arthur?
4. Describe Arthur's departure.

Interpreting

5. What does Arthur say will soon be lost forever? How, in lines 277–289, does Sir Bedivere echo Arthur's feelings?
6. What are Sir Bedivere's arguments for not throwing Excalibur into the lake?
7. Interpret Arthur's final words to Sir Bedivere.

Applying

8. The modern novelist F. Scott Fitzgerald has written, "Show me a hero and I will write you a tragedy." Do you think that the Arthurian legend is a tragedy? Explain your answer.

▌A NALYZING LITERATURE

Understanding Epic Poetry

Epic poetry is long narrative poetry that centers on the deeds of a single heroic individual who stands for the values of a society. Arthur's creation of Camelot represents an ideal of community and brotherhood founded on courage, faith, honor, love, and loyalty. Human weakness, however, and the world's evil eventually bring about the downfall of Camelot.

1. How is Arthur's decision to return Excalibur to the lake a final act of generosity and honor?
2. How do Sir Bedivere's actions relate to the theme of chivalry?

▌T HINKING AND WRITING

Writing About Epic Poetry

Write an essay for a literary magazine analyzing what qualities of *Morte d'Arthur* make it an epic. First list the values and attitudes that are embodied and expressed in this selection, the qualities that make Arthur a hero, and the ways in which the events and actions are larger than life. Develop this information in a draft of your essay. Revise your essay, making sure that your points are clear and that you have supported them with examples. Proofread for errors in spelling, grammar, and punctuation.

GUIDE FOR READING

Ramayana

The *Ramayana* is a great Indian epic, possibly dating as far back as the fourth century B.C. Relating stories about the life of the hero and others, the *Ramayana* has influenced nearly every aspect of Indian culture, from children's bedtime stories to religious studies. First written by the poet Valmiki in Sanskrit, the old Indian language used mostly for literature, this heroic tale has been translated into each of India's many languages, as well as languages around the world.

from the Ramayana
"Rama's Initiation"

The Epic Hero

The **epic hero** possesses certain qualities—bravery, great strength, and a desire to achieve immortality through his heroic deeds. The hero is based on a legendary or historic person who travels on a long and challenging journey. On the journey, the epic hero proves his wisdom, strength, and power in many different ways: He fights evil, falls in love, protects his honor, and rescues people in distress. Through the experiences of the hero, an epic reveals and preserves the folklore, values, and history of a culture.

Focus

This episode from the *Ramayana* shows how Rama proves his strength and his skills. All over the world, young people prove their mental, spiritual, and physical strength to themselves, to their peers, and to adults. On a sheet of paper make two lists. In the first, jot down the different ways that young people in your community prove their skills and strengths. In the second list, jot down the feelings that young people may experience when they are proving these powers.

Vocabulary

Knowing the following words will help you as you read the excerpt from the *Ramayana*.

austerities (ô ster′ ə tēz) *n.:* Self-denials (p. 717)

decrepitude (dē krep′ ə tōōd) *n.:* State of being worn out by old age or illness (p. 717)

sublime (sə blīm′) *adj.:* Noble; admirable (p. 717)

august (ô′ gust′) *adj.:* Worthy of respect because of age and dignity (p. 717)

stripling (strip′ liŋ) *n.:* A young boy passing into manhood (p. 718)

secular (sek′ yə lər) *adj.:* Not sacred or religious (p. 718)

obeisance (ō bā′ səns) *n.:* Gesture of respect (p. 718)

exuberance (eg zōō′ bər əns) *n.:* State of high spirits and good health (p. 721)

diminutive (də min′ yōō tiv) *adj.:* Smaller than average (p. 721)

esoteric (es′ ə ter′ ik) *adj.:* Beyond the understanding of most people (p. 722)

from the Ramayana
Rama's Initiation
R. K. Narayan

The new assembly hall, Dasaratha's[1] latest pride, was crowded all day with visiting dignitaries, royal emissaries, and citizens coming in with representations or appeals for justice. The King was always accessible, and fulfilled his duties as the ruler of Kosala without grudging the hours spent in public service.

On a certain afternoon, messengers at the gate came running in to announce, "Sage Viswamithra."[2] When the message was relayed to the King, he got up and hurried forward to receive the visitor. Viswamithra, once a king, a conqueror, and a dreaded name until he renounced his kingly role and chose to become a sage (which he accomplished through severe austerities), combined in himself the sage's eminence and the king's authority and was quick tempered and positive. Dasaratha led him to a proper seat and said, "This is a day of glory for us; your gracious presence is most welcome. You must have come from afar. Would you first rest?"

"No need," the sage replied simply. He had complete mastery over his bodily needs through inner discipline and austerities, and was above the effects of heat, cold, hunger, fatigue, and even decrepitude. The King later asked politely, "Is there anything I can do?" Viswamithra looked steadily at the King and answered, "Yes. I am here to ask of you a favor. I wish to perform, before the next full moon, a yagna[3] at Sidhasrama.[4] Doubtless you know where it is?"

"I have passed that sacred ground beyond the Ganges[5] many times."

The sage interrupted. "But there are creatures hovering about waiting to disturb every holy undertaking there, who must be overcome in the same manner as one has to conquer the five-fold evils[6] within before one can realize holiness. Those evil creatures are endowed with immeasurable powers of destruction. But it is our duty to pursue our aims undeterred. The yagna I propose to perform will strengthen the beneficial forces of this world, and please the gods above."

"It is my duty to protect your sublime effort. Tell me when, and I will be there."

The sage said, "No need to disturb your august self. Send your son Rama with me, and he will help me. He can."

"Rama!" cried the King, surprised, "When I am here to serve you."

---

1. Dasaratha's (dä sä rä′ täz)
2. Viswamithra (vish wä′ mē trä): Teacher of Rama, the main character of the *Ramayana*.

3. yagna (yäg nä′) *n*.: Sacrifice.
4. Sidhasrama (sēd häs rä′ mä)
5. Ganges (gan′ jēz): A river in northern India.
6. five-fold evils: Lust, anger, miserliness, egoism, and envy.

Viswamithra's temper was already stirring. "I know your greatness," he said, cutting the King short. "But I want Rama to go with me. If you are not willing, you may say so."

The air became suddenly tense. The assembly, the ministers and officials, watched in solemn silence. The King looked miserable. "Rama is still a child, still learning the arts and practicing the use of arms." His sentences never seemed to conclude, but trailed away as he tried to explain. "He is a boy, a child, he is too young and tender to contend with demons."

"But I know Rama," was all that Viswamithra said in reply.

"I can send you an army, or myself lead an army to guard your performance. What can a stripling like Rama do against those terrible forces . . . ? I will help you just as I helped Indra[7] once when he was harassed and deprived of his kingdom."

Viswamithra ignored his speech and rose to leave. "If you cannot send Rama, I need none else." He started to move down the passage.

The King was too stricken to move. When Viswamithra had gone half way, he realized that the visitor was leaving unceremoniously and was not even shown the courtesy of being escorted to the door. Vasishtha,[8] the King's priest and guide, whispered to Dasaratha, "Follow him and call him back," and hurried forward even before the King could grasp what he was saying. He almost ran as Viswamithra had reached the end of the hall and, blocking his way, said, "The King is coming; please don't go. He did not mean . . ."

A wry smile played on Viswamithra's face as he said without any trace of bitterness, "Why are you or anyone agitated? I came here for a purpose; it has failed; no reason to prolong my stay."

"Oh, eminent one, you were yourself a king once."

"What has that to do with us now?" asked Viswamithra, rather irked, since he hated all reference to his secular past and wanted always to be known as a Brahma Rishi.[9]

Vasishtha answered mildly, "Only to remind you of an ordinary man's feelings, especially a man like Dasaratha who had been childless and had to pray hard for an issue. . . ."

"Well, it may be so, great one; I still say that I came on a mission and wish to leave, since it has failed."

"It has not failed," said Vasishtha, and just then the King came up to join them in the passage; the assembly was on its feet.

Dasaratha made a deep obeisance and said, "Come back to your seat, Your Holiness."

"For what purpose, Your Majesty?" Viswamithra asked.

"Easier to talk seated . . ."

"I don't believe in any talk," said Viswamithra; but Vasishtha pleaded with him until he returned to his seat.

When they were all seated again, Vasishtha addressed the King: "There must be a divine purpose working through this seer, who may know but will not explain. It is a privilege that Rama's help should be sought. Do not bar his way. Let him go with the sage."

"When, oh when?" the King asked anxiously.

---

7. Indra (in' drə): A Hindu god associated with rain and thunderclouds.

8. Vasishtha (vä se' sh tä)

9. Brahma Rishi (brä' mä ri' she): Enlightened sage.

THE ADVENTURES OF RAMA—CEREMONY (detail)
School of Akbar
Freer Gallery of Art, Smithsonian Institution, Washington, D.C.

"Now," said Viswamithra. The King looked woebegone and desperate, and the sage relented enough to utter a word of comfort. "You cannot count on the physical proximity of someone you love, all the time. A seed that sprouts at the foot of its parent tree remains stunted until it is transplanted. Rama will be in my care, and he will be quite well. But ultimately, he will leave me too. Every human being, when the time comes, has to depart and seek his fulfillment in his own way."

"Sidhasrama is far away . . . ?" began the King.

"I'll ease his path for him, no need for a chariot to take us there," said Viswamithra reading his mind.

"Rama has never been separated from his brother Lakshmana.[10] May he also go with him?" pleaded the King, and he looked relieved when he heard Viswamithra say, "Yes, I will look after both, though their

---

10. Lakshmana (lăks mă′ nä)

mission will be to look after me. Let them get ready to follow me; let them select their favorite weapons and prepare to leave.''

Dasaratha, with the look of one delivering hostages into the hand of an enemy, turned to his minister and said, ''Fetch my sons.''

Following the footsteps of their master like his shadows, Rama and Lakshmana went past the limits of the city and reached the Sarayu River, which bounded the capital on the north. When night fell, they rested at a wooded grove and at dawn crossed the river. When the sun came over the mountain peak, they reached a pleasant grove over which hung, like a canopy, fragrant smoke from numerous sacrificial fires. Viswamithra explained to Rama, ''This is where God Shiva[11] meditated once upon a time and reduced to ashes the god of love when he attempted to spoil his meditation. From time immemorial saints praying to Shiva come here to perform their sacrifices, and the pall of smoke you notice is from their sacrificial fires.''

A group of hermits emerged from their seclusion, received Viswamithra, and invited him and his two disciples to stay with them for the night. Viswamithra resumed his journey at dawn and reached a desert region at midday. The mere expression ''desert'' hardly conveys the absolute aridity of this land. Under a relentless sun, all vegetation had dried and turned to dust, stone and rock crumbled into powdery sand, which lay in vast dunes, stretching away to the horizon. Here every inch was scorched and dry and hot beyond imagination. The ground was cracked and split, exposing enormous fissures everywhere. The distinction between dawn, noon, and evening did not exist here, as the sun seemed to stay overhead and burn the earth without moving. Bleached bones lay where animals had perished, including those of monstrous serpents with jaws open in deadly thirst; into these enormous jaws had rushed (says the poet) elephants desperately seeking shade, all dead and fossilized, the serpent and the elephant alike. Heat haze rose and singed the very heavens. While traversing this ground, Viswamithra noticed the bewilderment and distress on the faces of the young men, and transmitted to them mentally two *mantras*[12] (called ''Bala'' and ''Adi-Bala''). When they meditated on and recited these incantations, the arid atmosphere was transformed for the rest of their passage and they felt as if they were wading through a cool stream with a southern summer breeze blowing in their faces. Rama, ever curious to know the country he was passing through, asked, ''Why is this land so terrible? Why does it seem accursed?''

''You will learn the answer if you listen to this story—of a woman fierce, ruthless, eating and digesting all living creatures, possessing the strength of a thousand mad elephants.''

Thataka's Story

The woman I speak of was the daughter of Suketha,[13] a *yaksha*, a demigod of great valor, might, and purity. She was beautiful and full of wild energy. When she grew up she was married to a chieftain named Sunda. Two sons were born to them—Mareecha and Subahu[14]—who were endowed with

---

11. God Shiva (shē′ və): The Hindu god of destruction.

12. *mantras* (män′ träz): Sacred syllables.
13. Suketha (soō kā′ tä)
14. Mareecha (mä′ rē c̈hä) **and Subahu** (sä bä′ hoō)

enormous supernatural powers in addition to physical strength; and in their conceit and exuberance they laid waste their surroundings. Their father, delighted at their pranks and infected by their mood, joined in their activities. He pulled out ancient trees by their roots and flung them about, and he slaughtered all creatures that came his way. This depredation came to the notice of the great savant Agasthya[15] (the diminutive saint who once, when certain demoniac beings hid themselves at the bottom of the sea and Indra appealed for his help to track them, had sipped off the waters of the ocean). Agasthya had his hermitage in this forest, and when he noticed the destruction around, he cursed the perpetrator of this deed and Sunda fell dead. When his wife learned of his death, she and her sons stormed in, roaring revenge on the saint. He met their challenge by cursing them. "Since you are destroyers of life, may you become *asuras*[16] and dwell in the nether worlds." (Till now they had been demigods. Now they were degraded to demonhood.) The three at once underwent a transformation; their features and stature became forbidding, and their natures changed to match. The sons left to seek the company of superdemons. The mother was left alone and lives on here, breathing fire and wishing everything ill. Nothing flourishes here; only heat and sand remain. She is a scorcher. She carries a trident with spikes; a cobra entwined on her arm is her armlet. The name of this fearsome creature is Thataka.[17] Just as the presence of a little *loba* (meanness) dries up and disfigures a whole human personality, so does the presence of this monster turn

into desert a region which was once fertile. In her restlessness she constantly harasses the hermits at their prayers; she gobbles up anything that moves and sends it down her entrails.

THE ADVENTURES OF RAMA—
RAMA AND LAKSHMAN BATTLE THE DEMON RAKSHASAS
School of Akbar
Freer Gallery of Art, Smithsonian Institution, Washington, D.C.

---

15. savant (sə vänt′) **Agasthya** (ä gus tē yä′): A learned man named Agasthya.
16. *asuras* (ä sōō′ räz)
17. Thataka (tä tä′ kä)

Touching the bow slung on his shoulder, Rama asked, "Where is she to be found?"

Before Viswamithra could answer, she arrived, the ground rocking under her feet and a storm preceding her. She loomed over them with her eyes spitting fire, her fangs bared, her lips parted revealing a cavernous mouth; and her brows twitching in rage. She raised her trident and roared, "In this my kingdom, I have crushed out the minutest womb of life and you have been sent down so that I may not remain hungry."

Rama hesitated; for all her evil, she was still a woman. How could he kill her? Reading his thoughts, Viswamithra said, "You shall not consider her a woman at all. Such a monster must receive no consideration. Her strength, ruthlessness, appearance, rule her out of that category. Formerly God Vishnu himself killed Kyathi, the wife of Brigu,[18] who harbored the asuras fleeing his wrath, when she refused to yield them. Mandorai,[19] a woman bent upon destroying all the worlds, was vanquished by Indra and he earned the gratitude of humanity. These are but two instances. A woman of demoniac tendencies loses all consideration to be treated as a woman. This Thataka is more

dreadful than Yama, the god of death, who takes a life only when the time is ripe. But this monster, at the very scent of a living creature, craves to kill and eat. Do not picture her as a woman at all. You must rid this world of her. It is your duty."

Rama said, "I will carry out your wish."

Thataka threw her three-pronged spear at Rama. As it came flaming, Rama strung his bow and sent an arrow which broke it into fragments. Next she raised a hail of stones under which to crush her adversaries. Rama sent up his arrows, which shielded them from the attack. Finally Rama's arrow pierced her throat and ended her career; thereby also inaugurating Rama's life's mission of destroying evil and demonry in this world. The gods assembled in the sky and expressed their joy and relief and enjoined Viswamithra, "Oh, adept and master of weapons, impart without any reserve all your knowledge and powers to this lad. He is a savior." Viswamithra obeyed this injunction and taught Rama all the esoteric techniques in weaponry. Thereafter the presiding deities of various weapons, *asthras*,[20] appeared before Rama submissively and declared, "Now we are yours; command us night or day."

---

18. **Vishnu** (vēsh′ no͞o) . . . **Kyathi** (kyä′ tē) . . . **Brigu** (brē′ go͞o)
19. **Mandorai** (mänd rä′ ē)

20. *asthras* (äs′ träz)

RESPONDING TO THE SELECTION

Your Response

1. What scene do you find most exciting?
2. Toward which character in the story do you feel most sympathetic? Explain your choice.

Recalling

3. What does the sage Viswamithra request from King Dasaratha?
4. Why do Thataka and her sons want revenge against Agasthya?

Interpreting

5. Why is King Dasaratha surprised by Viswamithra's request and afraid to give him what he wants?
6. Why do you think Viswamithra dislikes all reference to his secular, or nonreligious, past?
7. Why do Thataka and her two sons undergo a physical transformation when they are cursed by Agasthya?
8. The gods declare Rama a savior. What qualities do you think they are referring to with this term?

Applying

9. Rama hesitates before killing Thataka because she is a woman. What does this imply about Indian society?

ANALYZING LITERATURE

Understanding the Epic Hero

The **epic hero** is the central character of an epic. Tales of the hero's experiences, like this excerpt, convey the qualities that a culture values when an individual passes from childhood to adulthood. For example, the gods in the *Ramayana* value a person's courage and skill. Rama must overcome his youthful doubts and hesitation to win their praise.

1. How does Rama begin the passage from childhood to adulthood?
2. How does Rama show his heroic powers?

3. How does the story of Thataka show that the Indian people value respect and order?

CRITICAL THINKING AND READING

Comparing and Contrasting Heroes

When you **compare** heroes, you look at the ways in which they are alike. When you **contrast** heroes, you see how they differ from each other. Because heroes reflect the cultures that create them, they can have many differences and similarities.

1. In the Arthurian legend, the young Arthur pulls a sword from a stone, thereby becoming king. Compare Arthur and Rama.
2. Rama shows great respect for his elders. Contrast his behavior with that of other fictional heroes.

THINKING AND WRITING

Writing About Initiation Rites

An initiation, or rite of passage, is a ceremony held to admit someone into a group. For example, people are initiated into adulthood in many ways. A girl might prove herself by composing and reciting a poem in order to join the Honor Society, or a father might give a son a family ring on his thirteenth birthday. Have you been initiated into adulthood? Write a journal entry describing at least one way that you have experienced the initiation process.

LEARNING OPTION

Cross-curricular Connection. Classical Indian music has always played a large part in Indian storytelling. Instruments such as the sitar, a stringed wooden instrument, create a haunting melodic background for descriptions of the heroic deeds of characters like Rama. In your library, research Indian music. Look for recordings that are associated in some way with the *Ramayana*. Bring in examples to share with your classmates.

GUIDE FOR READING

from Sundiata: An Epic of Old Mali

Epic Conflict

An **epic conflict** is the obstacle or series of problems a hero must overcome to achieve greatness and heroic stature. One recurring epic conflict is a difficult situation in childhood. In the traditional epic, the hero surmounts difficulties, conquers enemies, and finally emerges triumphant. Through these struggles, the hero passes from childhood to adulthood, proving his wisdom, bravery, and power. The character's struggle in the heroic story illuminates the history, customs, and folklore of the storyteller's culture.

Focus

In the story *Sundiata,* the central character, Mari Djata, has a difficult childhood. With a partner, brainstorm to create a list of fictional heroes who each had a difficult childhood. Describe the events that caused the difficulty in each case. Then, as you read *Sundiata,* consider how the situations you have talked about compare with Mari Djata's circumstances.

Vocabulary

Knowing the following words will help you as you read the excerpt from *Sundiata.*

fathom (fa*th*' əm) *v.*: Understand thoroughly (p. 725)

taciturn (tas' ə tʉrn) *adj.*: Uncommunicative (p. 726)

malicious (mə lish' əs) *adj.*: Intentionally harmful (p. 726)

infirmity (in fʉr' mə tē) *n.*: Physical weakness (p. 726)

innuendo (in' yo͞o en' dō) *n.*: Insinuation (p. 726)

diabolical (dī ə bäl' ik əl) *adj.*: Wicked; cruel (p. 726)

estranged (e strānjd') *adv.*: Removed from; at a distance (p. 726)

bequeathed (bē kwē*th*d') *v.*: Passed (p. 728)

affront (ə frunt') *n.*: Intentional insult (p. 729)

Sundiata

Mamadou Kouyate is the griot (grē' ō), or storyteller, who told the tale of Sundiata to D. T. Niane, the author of this selection. Though the original author is not known, the story of Sundiata has been told by the griots of Mali for many centuries. The griots call themselves the memory of their people, and they travel from village to village, teaching the history and legends of their ancestors to the new generations. Thus, the griots preserve their history and culture orally. After listening to the stories told by Griot Mamadou Kouyate, D. T. Niane wrote them down so that he could share the griot's wisdom with people from other parts of the world.

from Sundiata:
An Epic of Old Mali

D. T. Niane

CHARACTERS IN *SUNDIATA*

Balla Fasséké (bä′ lä fä sä′ kä): Griot, or counselor, of Sundiata.

Boukari (bo͞o kä′ rē): Son of the king and Namandjé, one of his wives; also called Manding (män′ diŋ) Boukari.

Dankaran Touman (dän′ kä rän to͞o′ män): Son of the king and his first wife, Sassouma, who is also called Sassouma Bérété.

Djamarou (jä mä′ ro͞o): Daughter of Sogolon and the king; sister of Sundiata and Kolonkan.

Farakourou (fä rä ko͞o′ ro͞o): Master of the forges.

Gnankouman Doua (nän ko͞o′ män do͞o′ə): The king's griot; also called simply, Doua.

Kolonkan (kō lõn′ kən): Sundiata's eldest sister.

Namandjé (nä män′ jē): One of the king's wives.

Naré Maghan (nä′ rä mäg′ hän): Sundiata's father.

Nounfaïri (no͞on′ fä ē′ rē): Soothsayer and smith; father of Farakourou.

Sassouma Bérété (sä so͞o′ mä be′ re te): The king's first wife.

Sogolon (sõ gõ lōn′): Sundiata's mother; also called Sogolon Kedjou (kä′ jo͞o).

Sundiata (so͞on dyä′ tä): Legendary king of Mali; referred to as Djata (dyä′ tä) and Sogolon Djata, which means "son of Sogolon." Sundiata is also called Mari (mä′ rē) Djata.

CHILDHOOD

God has his mysteries which none can fathom. You, perhaps, will be a king. You can do nothing about it. You, on the other hand, will be unlucky, but you can do nothing about that either. Each man finds his way already marked out for him and he can change nothing of it.

Sogolon's son had a slow and difficult childhood. At the age of three he still crawled along on all-fours while children of the same age were already walking. He had nothing of the great beauty of his father Naré Maghan. He had a head so big that he seemed unable to support it; he also had large eyes which would open wide whenever anyone entered his mother's house. He was taciturn and used to spend the whole day just sitting in the middle of the house. Whenever his mother went out he would crawl on all-fours to rummage about in the calabashes[1] in search of food, for he was very greedy.

Malicious tongues began to blab. What three-year-old has not yet taken his first steps? What three-year-old is not the despair of his parents through his whims and shifts of mood? What three-year-old is not the joy of his circle through his backwardness in talking? Sogolon Djata (for it was thus that they called him, prefixing his mother's name to his), Sogolon Djata, then, was very different from others of his own age. He spoke little and his severe face never relaxed into a smile. You would have thought that he was already thinking, and what amused children of his age bored him. Often Sogolon would make some of them come to him to keep him company. These children were already walking and she hoped that Djata, seeing his companions walking, would be tempted to do likewise. But nothing came of it. Besides, Sogolon Djata would brain the poor little things with his already strong arms and none of them would come near him any more.

The king's first wife was the first to rejoice at Sogolon Djata's infirmity. Her own son, Dankaran Touman, was already eleven. He was a fine and lively boy, who spent the day running about the village with those of his own age. He had even begun his initiation in the bush.[2] The king had had a bow made for him and he used to go behind the town to practice archery with his companions. Sassouma was quite happy and snapped her fingers at Sogolon, whose child was still crawling on the ground. Whenever the latter happened to pass by her house, she would say, "Come, my son, walk, jump, leap about. The jinn[3] didn't promise you anything out of the ordinary, but I prefer a son who walks on his two legs to a lion that crawls on the ground." She spoke thus whenever Sogolon went by her door. The innuendo would go straight home and then she would burst into laughter, that diabolical laughter which a jealous woman knows how to use so well.

Her son's infirmity weighed heavily upon Sogolon Kedjou; she had resorted to all her talent as a sorceress to give strength to her son's legs, but the rarest herbs had been useless. The king himself lost hope.

How impatient man is! Naré Maghan became imperceptibly estranged but Gnankouman Doua never ceased reminding him of the hunter's words. Sogolon became pregnant again. The king hoped for a son, but it was a daughter called Kolonkan. She resembled her mother and had nothing of her father's beauty. The disheartened king debarred Sogolon from his house and she lived in semi-disgrace for a while. Naré Maghan married the daughter of one of his allies, the king of the Kamaras. She was called Namandjé and her beauty was legendary. A year later she brought a boy into the world. When the king consulted soothsayers[4] on the destiny of this son, he received the reply that Namandjé's child would be the right hand of some mighty king. The king gave the newly-born the name of Boukari. He was to be called Manding Boukari or Manding Bory later on.

Naré Maghan was very perplexed. Could it be that the stiff-jointed son of Sogolon was the one the hunter soothsayer had foretold?

---

1. calabashes (kal′ ə bash′ iz) n.: The dried, hollow shells of gourds, used as bowls.
2. initiation in the bush: An education in tribal lore given to twelve-year-old West African boys so they can become full members of the tribe.

3. jinn (jin) n.: Supernatural beings that influence human affairs.
4. soothsayers (sooth′ sā′ ərz) n.: People who can foretell the future.

COVER OF *SUNDIATA*
Senegalese Glass Painting
From the Collection of Professor Donal Cruise-O'Brien

"The Almighty has his mysteries," Gnankouman Doua would say and, taking up the hunter's words, added, "The silk-cotton tree emerges from a tiny seed."

One day Naré Maghan came along to the house of Nounfaïri, the blacksmith seer of Niani. He was an old, blind man. He received the king in the anteroom which served as his workshop. To the king's question he replied, "When the seed germinates growth is not always easy; great trees grow slowly but they plunge their roots deep into the ground."

"But has the seed really germinated?" said the king.

"Of course," replied the blind seer. "Only the growth is not as quick as you would like it; how impatient man is."

This interview and Doua's confidence gave the king some assurance. To the great displeasure of Sassouma Bérété the king restored Sogolon to favor and soon another daughter was born to her. She was given the name of Djamarou.

However, all Niani talked of nothing else but the stiff-legged son of Sogolon. He was now seven and he still crawled to get about. In spite of all the king's affection, Sogolon was in despair. Naré Maghan aged and he felt his time coming to an end. Dankaran Touman, the son of Sassouma Bérété, was now a fine youth.

One day Naré Maghan made Mari Djata come to him and he spoke to the child as one speaks to an adult. "Mari Djata, I am growing old and soon I shall be no more among you, but before death takes me off I am going to give you the present each king gives his successor. In Mali every prince has his own griot. Doua's father was my father's griot, Doua is mine and the son of Doua, Balla Fasséké here, will be your griot. Be inseparable friends from this day forward. From his mouth you will hear the history of your ancestors, you will learn the art of governing Mali according to the principles which our ancestors have bequeathed to us. I have served my term and done my duty too. I have done everything which a king of Mali ought to do. I am handing an enlarged kingdom over to you and I leave you sure allies. May your destiny be accomplished, but never forget that Niani is your capital and Mali the cradle of your ancestors.''

The child, as if he had understood the whole meaning of the king's words, beckoned Balla Fasséké to approach. He made room for him on the hide he was sitting on and then said, "Balla, you will be my griot."

"Yes, son of Sogolon, if it pleases God," replied Balla Fasséké.

The king and Doua exchanged glances that radiated confidence.

The Lion's Awakening

A short while after this interview between Naré Maghan and his son the king died. Sogolon's son was no more than seven years old. The council of elders met in the king's palace. It was no use Doua's defending the king's will which reserved the throne for Mari Djata, for the council took no account of Naré Maghan's wish. With the help of Sassouma Bérété's intrigues, Dankaran Touman was proclaimed king and a regency council was formed in which the queen mother was all-powerful. A short time after, Doua died.

As men have short memories, Sogolon's son was spoken of with nothing but irony and scorn. People had seen one-eyed kings, one-armed kings, and lame kings, but a stiff-legged king had never been heard tell of. No matter how great the destiny promised for Mari Djata might be, the throne could not be given to someone who had no power in his legs; if the jinn loved him, let them begin by giving him the use of his legs. Such were the remarks that Sogolon heard every day. The queen mother, Sassouma Bérété, was the source of all this gossip.

Having become all-powerful, Sassouma Bérété persecuted Sogolon because the late Naré Maghan had preferred her. She banished Sogolon and her son to a back yard of the palace. Mari Djata's mother now occupied an old hut which had served as a lumber-room of Sassouma's.

The wicked queen mother allowed free passage to all those inquisitive people who wanted to see the child that still crawled at the age of seven. Nearly all the inhabitants of Niani filed into the palace and the poor Sogolon wept to see herself thus given over to public ridicule. Mari Djata took on a ferocious look in front of the crowd of sightseers. Sogolon found a little consolation only in the love of her eldest daughter, Kolonkan. She was four and she could walk. She seemed to understand all her mother's miseries and already she helped her with the housework. Sometimes, when Sogolon was attending to the chores, it was she who stayed beside her sister Djamarou, quite small as yet.

Sogolon Kedjou and her children lived on the queen mother's leftovers, but she kept a little garden in the open ground behind the village. It was there that she passed her brightest moments looking after her onions and gnougous.[5] One day she happened to be short of condiments and went to the queen mother to beg a little baobab leaf.[6]

---

5. gnougous (noo' gooz') *n.*: Root vegetables.
6. baobab (bā' ō bab') **leaf** *n.*: The baobab is a thick-trunked tree; its leaves are used to flavor foods.

"Look you," said the malicious Sassouma, "I have a calabash full. Help yourself, you poor woman. As for me, my son knew how to walk at seven and it was he who went and picked these baobab leaves. Take them then, since your son is unequal to mine." Then she laughed derisively with that fierce laughter which cuts through your flesh and penetrates right to the bone.

Sogolon Kedjou was dumbfounded. She had never imagined that hate could be so strong in a human being. With a lump in her throat she left Sassouma's. Outside her hut Mari Djata, sitting on his useless legs, was blandly eating out of a calabash. Unable to contain herself any longer, Sogolon burst into sobs and seizing a piece of wood, hit her son.

"Oh son of misfortune, will you never walk? Through your fault I have just suffered the greatest affront of my life! What have I done, God, for you to punish me in this way?"

Mari Djata seized the piece of wood and, looking at his mother, said, "Mother, what's the matter?"

"Shut up, nothing can ever wash me clean of this insult."

"But what then?"

"Sassouma has just humiliated me over a matter of a baobab leaf. At your age her own son could walk and used to bring his mother baobab leaves."

"Cheer up, Mother, cheer up."

"No. It's too much. I can't."

"Very well then, I am going to walk today," said Mari Djata. "Go and tell my father's smiths to make me the heaviest possible iron rod. Mother, do you want just the leaves of the baobab or would you rather I brought you the whole tree?"

"Ah, my son, to wipe out this insult I want the tree and its roots at my feet outside my hut."

Balla Fasséké, who was present, ran to the master smith, Farakourou, to order an iron rod.

Sogolon had sat down in front of her hut. She was weeping softly and holding her head between her two hands. Mari Djata went calmly back to his calabash of rice and began eating again as if nothing had happened. From time to time he looked up discreetly at his mother, who was murmuring in a low voice, "I want the whole tree, in front of my hut, the whole tree."

All of a sudden a voice burst into laughter behind the hut. It was the wicked Sassouma telling one of her serving women about the scene of humiliation and she was laughing loudly so that Sogolon could hear. Sogolon fled into the hut and hid her face under the blankets so as not to have before her eyes this heedless boy, who was more preoccupied with eating than with anything else. With her head buried in the bedclothes Sogolon wept and her body shook violently. Her daughter, Sogolon Djamarou, had come and sat down beside her and she said, "Mother, Mother, don't cry. Why are you crying?"

Mari Djata had finished eating and, dragging himself along on his legs, he came and sat under the wall of the hut for the sun was scorching. What was he thinking about? He alone knew.

The royal forges were situated outside the walls and over a hundred smiths worked there. The bows, spears, arrows and shields of Niani's warriors came from there. When Balla Fasséké came to order the iron rod, Farakourou said to him, "The great day has arrived then?"

"Yes. Today is a day like any other, but it will see what no other day has seen."

The master of the forges, Farakourou, was the son of the old Nounfaïri, and he was a soothsayer like his father. In his workshops there was an enormous iron bar wrought by his father, Nounfaïri. Everybody wondered what this bar was destined to be used for. Farakourou called six of his apprentices and told them to carry the iron bar to Sogolon's house.

When the smiths put the gigantic iron bar down in front of the hut the noise was so frightening that Sogolon, who was lying down, jumped up with a start. Then Balla Fasséké, son of Gnankouman Doua, spoke.

"Here is the great day, Mari Djata. I am speaking to you, Maghan, son of Sogolon. The waters of the Niger can efface the stain from the body, but they cannot wipe out an insult. Arise, young lion, roar, and may the bush know that from henceforth it has a master."

The apprentice smiths were still there, Sogolon had come out, and everyone was watching Mari Djata. He crept on all-fours and came to the iron bar. Supporting himself on his knees and one hand, with the other hand he picked up the iron bar without any effort and stood it up vertically. Now he was resting on nothing but his knees and held the bar with both his hands. A deathly silence had gripped all those present. Sogolon Djata closed his eyes, held tight, the muscles in his arms tensed. With a violent jerk he threw his weight on to it and his knees left the ground. Sogolon Kedjou was all eyes and watched her son's legs, which were trembling as though from an electric shock. Djata was sweating and the sweat ran from his brow. In a great effort he straightened up and was on his feet at one go—but the great bar of iron was twisted and had taken the form of a bow!

Then Balla Fasséké sang out the "Hymn to the Bow," striking up with his powerful voice:

"Take your bow, Simbon,
  Take your bow and let us go.
  Take your bow, Sogolon Djata."

When Sogolon saw her son standing she stood dumb for a moment, then suddenly she sang these words of thanks to God, who had given her son the use of his legs:

"Oh day, what a beautiful day,
Oh day, day of joy;
Allah[7] Almighty, you never created a
  finer day.
So my son is going to walk!"

Standing in the position of a soldier at ease, Sogolon Djata, supported by his enormous rod, was sweating great beads of sweat. Balla Fasséké's song had alerted the whole palace and people came running from all over to see what had happened, and each stood bewildered before Sogolon's son. The queen mother had rushed there and when she saw Mari Djata standing up she trembled from head to foot. After recovering his breath Sogolon's son dropped the bar and the crowd stood to one side. His first steps were those of a giant. Balla Fasséké fell into step and pointing his finger at Djata, he cried:

"Room, room, make room!
The lion has walked;
Hide antelopes,
Get out of his way."

Behind Niani there was a young baobab tree and it was there that the children of the town came to pick leaves for their mothers. With all his might the son of Sogolon tore up the tree and put it on his shoulders and went back to his mother. He threw the tree in front of the hut and said, "Mother, here are some baobab leaves for you. From henceforth it will be outside your hut that the women of Niani will come to stock up."

---

7. Allah (al' ə): The Muslim name for God.

RESPONDING TO THE SELECTION

Your Response

1. What did you think of the wicked queen mother's behavior toward Sogolon? Was her jealousy understandable? Explain.
2. How did you feel when the council of elders ignored Naré Maghan's wishes?

Recalling

3. Why did Sogolon's son, Mari Djata, have a difficult childhood?
4. What surprising announcement did Mari Djata make after Sassouma Bérété insulted his mother?

Interpreting

5. What did the soothsayer mean when he told the king, "great trees grow slowly"?
6. Why do you think Mari Djata did not respond to the crowds who tormented and teased him over the years?
7. Why had the master of the forges kept the iron bar made by his father in his workshop?
8. Why do you think Mari Djata is compared to a lion?

Applying

9. Why is patience a virtue when watching a child grow up?

ANALYZING LITERATURE

Understanding Epic Conflict

Through **epic conflict,** the hero of an epic confronts the obstacles that prevent him from achieving greatness and heroic stature. In *Sundiata,* Mari Djata overcomes a physical obstacle to take his rightful place as ruler.

1. How does Mari Djata's physical disability contribute to his effectiveness as a leader? How might his character have developed differently if he had not had to overcome this obstacle?
2. How do people react to Mari Djata as a result of his disability? How did Mari Djata respond to their behavior?

CRITICAL THINKING AND READING

Making Inferences About Culture

When you make inferences about a culture, you try to understand the culture through varied sources of information, such as stories, myths, or folk tales. The experiences of a hero reveal the customs and values of the hero's culture. For instance, the experiences of Mari Djata show you the importance of the king in Mali culture. They also show you that rumors and gossip were as evident and dangerous in Mali culture as they are in our own.

1. How does *Sundiata* show that the soothsayer is valued in Mali culture?
2. What does *Sundiata* reveal about the marriage customs in Mali?
3. What does *Sundiata* tell about the relationship between kings and griots in Mali?

THINKING AND WRITING

Writing in the Heroic Tradition

Write a brief episode in the life of Mari Djata showing how he fulfills the heroic tradition. Include cultural information you have learned from reading *Sundiata,* such as the attitudes and relationships between people.

LEARNING OPTIONS

1. **Speaking and Listening.** Families keep their histories alive in the same way that villages, towns, and countries keep them alive. Share a family story with the class. Your story might describe a grandparent's journey to the United States or a favorite story in your family about a holiday meal, a car trip, or the birth or death of a relative.
2. **Cross-curricular Connection.** Find information about the country of Mali. Focus on the aspects of life there that interest you; for example, the economy, or agriculture. When you complete your research, present your findings to the class in the form of a mini-documentary, using illustrations when possible.

GUIDE FOR READING

K'ung-ming Borrows Some Arrows

Historical Context

The **historical context** of a work of literature explains the important events of the period during which the work is set or was written. *Three Kingdoms* begins near the collapse of the Han dynasty in China (206 B.C.–A.D. 220). The Han era was one of political and cultural expansion. The collapse of the dynasty occurred when small factions began to fight for power and control.

Three Kingdoms tells of the attempt to reunify these factions after the fall of the dynasty. As the epic begins, Chancellor Ts'ao Ts'ao is plotting to overthrow the emperor. K'ung-ming, a hero of the epic, is an advisor who has sworn his loyalty to the emperor's cause.

Focus

"K'ung-ming Borrows Some Arrows" is about a man who advises and assists a military leader. Often the traits of a good leader may seem to conflict with each other; for example, a president might need to be compassionate when dealing with victims of poverty, but he might also need to be aggressive in the face of a serious threat to the nation's security. This idea of opposites working together to create a balanced whole is central to much of Eastern philosophy.

List several pairs of opposing traits you think an effective leader should possess. After you have read the selection, see if you can think of other traits to add.

Vocabulary

Knowing the following words will help you as you read "K'ung-ming Borrows Some Arrows."

subterfuge (sub′ tər fyo͞oj′) *n.*: A plan or action used to hide a true purpose (p. 733)

felicitations (fə lis′ i tā′ shənz) *n.*: Congratulations (p. 733)

levity (lev′ i tē) *n.*: Lack of seriousness; gaiety (p. 734)

trifle (trī′ fəl) *v.*: Deal lightly or in a joking way (p. 734)

mediocrity (mē′ dē äk′ rə tē) *n.*: Person of inferior abilities (p. 736)

flagrant (flā′ grənt) *adj.*: Outrageous (p. 736)

machinations (mak′ ə nā′ shənz) *n.*: Secret schemes (p. 736)

epitome (ē pit′ ə mē′) *n.*: A typical example (p. 736)

Lo Kuan-chung

(c. 1330–c. 1400) lived and wrote in China during the Ming dynasty, or period of family rule. His epic narrative *Three Kingdoms,* from which this selection is taken, is based largely on two records of the fall of the Han dynasty. Rather than simply retelling the historical facts of that period, Lo Kuan-chung dramatized them in a partly fictional work.

Written more than one thousand years after the collapse of this great dynasty, *Three Kingdoms* is considered a masterpiece of Chinese literature. Its characters and legends are known throughout China. For centuries they have served to teach values of loyalty, power, and social obligation.

K'ung-ming Borrows Some Arrows

from **Three Kingdoms**

Lo Kuan-Chung

translated by Moss Roberts

Chou Yü sent Lu Su to K'ung-ming to see if he had detected the subterfuge by which Ts'ai Mao was eliminated.

Lu Su: "Day after day I am taken up with military concerns and miss your good advice."

K'ung-ming: "Rather, I am the tardy one, having yet to convey my felicitations to the chief commandant Chou Yü!"

Lu Su: "What felicitations?"

"Why, for that very thing he sent you to ask whether I knew." The color left Lu Su's face. "But where did you learn of it, master?"

K'ung-ming: "The subterfuge was good enough to fool the messenger. As for Ts'ao Ts'ao, though he was hoodwinked this time, he will realize it quickly enough—except that he won't admit the mistake, that's all. But with the naval advisor dead the Southland has no major worry, so congratulations are certainly in order! But I hope you won't mention to Chou Yü that I knew about this beforehand, lest he become jealous and seek to do me harm."

Lu Su agreed, but could not help telling the whole truth to Chou Yü, who said in alarm: "We absolutely cannot let this man stay. I am determined to kill him."

Lu Su: "If you do, you will be the mockery of Ts'ao Ts'ao."

Chou Yü: "No, I can do it openly and legitimately. Wait and see."

The next day in the assembly of generals, Chou Yü asked K'ung-ming: "When we engage Ts'ao Ts'ao in battle, crossing arms on the river routes, what weapon should be our first choice?"

K'ung-ming: "On the Yangtze,[1] the bow and arrow."

Chou Yü: "Precisely. But we happen to be short of arrows. Dare I trouble you, master, to take responsibility for the production of one-hundred thousand shafts? This is a public service which you would favor me by not declining."

K'ung-ming: "Whatever you assign I will strive to achieve. Dare I ask by what time you will require them?"

Chou Yü: "Can you finish in ten days?"

K'ung-ming: "Ts'ao's army will arrive any moment. If we wait ten days, it will spoil everything."

Chou Yü: "How many days do you estimate you need, master?"

---

1. Yangtze (yaŋk′ sē) *n.*: Now the Chang River, the largest river and chief commercial highway of China.

K'ung-ming: "It will take only three before I can respectfully deliver the arrows."

Chou Yü: "There is no room for levity in the army."

K'ung-ming: "Dare I trifle with the chief commander? I beg to submit my oath in writing. Then if I fail to finish in three days, I deserve the maximum punishment."

This elated Chou Yü, who accepted the document.

K'ung-ming: "On the third day from tomorrow, send five hundred small craft to the river to transport the arrows."

After K'ung-ming left, Chou Yü said to Lu Su: "I will have the artisans delay things intentionally, just to be sure that he misses the appointed time. But go to him and bring me back information."

Lu Su went to K'ung-ming, who said: "I *did* tell you not to speak of this to Chou Yü. He is determined to kill me. I never dreamed you would refuse to cover for me. And now today he actually pulled this thing on me! How am I supposed to produce one-hundred thousand arrows in three days? You're the only one who can save me."

Lu Su: "You brought this on yourself. How could I save you?"

K'ung-ming: "I need you to lend me twenty vessels, with a crew of thirty for each. On the boats I want curtains of black cloth to conceal at least a thousand bales of straw that should be lined up on both sides. But you must not let Chou Yü know about it this time, or my plan will fail." And Lu Su obliged him, and even held his tongue.

The boats were ready, but neither on the first day nor on the second did K'ung-ming make any move. On the third day he secretly sent for Lu Su: "I called you especially to go with me to get the arrows." And linking the vessels with long ropes, they set out for the north shore and Ts'ao Ts'ao's fleet.

That night tremendous fogs rolled over the heavens, and the river mists were impenetrable. People could not see their companions who were directly in front of them. K'ung-ming urged his boats on.

From the ode "Great Mists Overhanging the Yangtze":

> Everywhere the fog, stock still:
> Not even a cartload can be spotted.
> All-obscuring grey vastness,
> Massive, without horizon.
> Whales hurtle over waves, and
> Dragons plunge and spew up mist.
> East they lose the shore at Chai
>   Sang,
> South the mountains of Hsia K'ou.
> Are we returning to the state without
>   form—
> To undivided Heaven and Earth?

At the fifth watch the boats were already nearing Ts'ao Ts'ao's river stations. K'ung-ming had the vessels lined up in single file, their prows pointed west. Then the crews began to volley with their drums and roar with their voices.

Lu Su was alarmed: "What do you propose if Ts'ao's men make a coordinated sally?"

K'ung-ming smiled: "I would be very surprised if Ts'ao Ts'ao dared plunge into this heavy a fog. Let us attend to the wine and take our pleasure. When the fog breaks we will return."

In his encampment, Ts'ao Ts'ao listened to the drumming and shouting. His new naval advisers rushed back and forth with bulletins. Ts'ao sent down an order: "The fog is so heavy it obscures the river. Enemy forces have arrived from nowhere. There must be an ambush. Our men must make absolutely no reckless movements. But let the archers fire upon the enemy at random." The naval advisers, fearing that the forces of the Southland were about to breach the camp, ordered the firing to commence. Soon

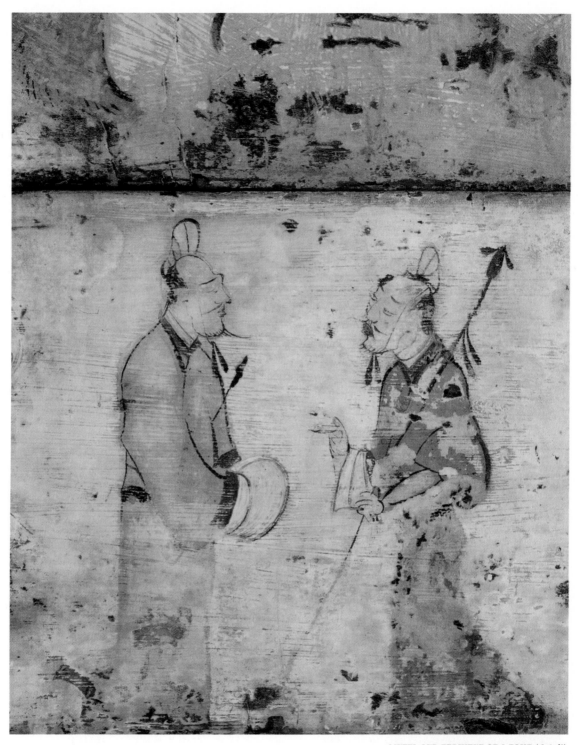

LINTEL AND PEDIMENT OF A TOMB (detail)
Anonymous Chinese Artist
Museum of Fine Arts, Boston

over ten-thousand men were concentrating their fire toward the center of the river, and the arrows came down like rain. K'ung-ming ordered the boats to reverse direction and press closer to the shore to take the arrows, while the crews continued their drumming and shouting.

When the sun rose high, dispersing the fog, K'ung-ming ordered the boats to rush homeward. The grass bales in gunnysacks bristled with arrow shafts. And K'ung-ming had each crew shout its thanks to the Chancellor for the arrows as it passed. By the time the reports reached Ts'ao Ts'ao, the light craft borne on swift currents were beyond overtaking, and Ts'ao Ts'ao was left with the agony of having played the fool.

K'ung-ming said to Lu Su: "Each boat has some five or six thousand arrows. So without costing the Southland the slightest effort, we have gained over one-hundred thousand arrows, which tomorrow we can return to Ts'ao's troops—to their decided discomfort."

Lu Su: "You are supernatural! How did you know there would be such a fog today?"

K'ung-ming: "A military commander must be versed in the patterns of the Heavens, must recognize the advantages of the terrain, must appreciate the odd chance, must understand the changes of the weather, must examine the maps of the formations, must be clear about the disposition of the troops—otherwise he is a mediocrity! Three days ago I calculated today's fog. That's why I took a chance on the three-day

limit. Chou Yü gave me ten days, but neither materials nor workmen, and plainly meant for my flagrant offense to kill me. But my fate is linked to Heaven. How could Chou Yü succeed?" When Chou Yü received Lu Su's report, he was amazed and resigned. "I cannot begin to approach his uncanny machinations and subtle calculations!"

When K'ung-ming came to Chou Yü, he was received with cordial admiration. "Master, we must defer to your superhuman powers of calculation."

K'ung-ming: "A petty subterfuge of common cunning, not worth your compliments."

Chou Yü: "Yesterday my sovereign urged us to advance. But I still lack the unexpected stratagem[2] that wins the battle. I appeal for your instruction."

K'ung-ming: "I am a run-of-the-mill mediocrity. What kind of surprise are you looking for?"

Chou Yü: "Yesterday I surveyed Ts'ao's naval stations. They are the epitome of strict order, all according to the book, invulnerable to any routine attack. I have one idea, but—"

K'ung-ming: "Refrain from speaking for a moment. We'll each write on our palms to see whether we agree or not." Each wrote, masking his word. They opened their hands together and laughed: the word was *fire*.

---

2. stratagem (strat′ ə jəm) *n.*: Trick or scheme for deceiving an enemy in war.

RESPONDING TO THE SELECTION

Your Response

1. What character do you think displays heroic qualities? Explain.
2. If you could talk to K'ung-ming, what would you tell him about Chou Yü?

Recalling

3. Why does Chou Yü trick K'ung-ming into agreeing to a plan he thinks K'ung-ming cannot achieve?
4. Why does K'ung-ming insist on delivering the arrows in three days' time rather than in ten days, as Chou Yü has asked?

Interpreting

5. Why does Lu Su agree to help K'ung-ming produce the arrows?
6. Why do K'ung-ming's crews make noises on the boats instead of waiting silently in the fog?
7. Explain why Chou Yü's attitude toward K'ung-ming changes.
8. What does K'ung-ming mean when he says "my fate is linked to Heaven"?

Applying

9. K'ung-ming uses fog to help him play a military trick. How might other elements of the weather or of nature be used as part of modern-day military tactics?

ANALYZING LITERATURE

Understanding Historical Context

By understanding the historical context of the epic *Three Kingdoms,* you will better appreciate this selection. At the time of this story, following the Han dynasty, there was a struggle for power in China between those who ruled by right of birth and those who sought to take control from the ruling clan. The conflicts in the epic reflect this struggle.

1. According to this selection, what qualities did a Chinese military leader require?

2. If you retold this story in a different historical context, which period in American history might be an appropriate setting? Explain.

CRITICAL THINKING AND READING

Appreciating Cultural Values

Literary works often reflect the cultural values, beliefs, and customs of the society in which the works were created. For example, Chinese parents tell their children to be like K'ung-ming rather than like the emperor.

1. What qualities of K'ung-ming might be most valued in Chinese society?
2. What features of other characters in this selection do you think have been valued or criticized in the course of Chinese history?

THINKING AND WRITING

Writing About Cultural Values

"K'ung-ming Borrows Some Arrows" contains many details that help form a picture of what was considered an ideal political leader in Chinese history. How does this portrait compare and contrast with the image that Americans have of an effective leader? Write a brief essay about the values you think are most important to people in both countries when they choose a leader. Before you write your draft, list the similarities and differences between the two cultures. When you revise, make sure each point of comparison and contrast is clear.

LEARNING OPTION

Multicultural Activity. With a small group of classmates, dramatize an episode in the life of a figure from Chinese history, such as the philosopher Confucius or the political leader Mao Zedong. Prepare a news story involving this figure and present it to the class.

GUIDE FOR READING

Miguel de Cervantes

(1547–1616) is one of the greatest writers in Spanish history. A poet and playwright as well as a novelist, Cervantes was born in a small town twenty miles outside of Madrid. At the age of twenty, he joined the Spanish army, later fought in a number of battles, and eventually became an accomplished soldier. While sailing home from the wars, he was captured and held prisoner by Algerian pirates for five years. Finally, at the age of thirty-three, Cervantes resettled in Madrid and began writing. Twenty-five years later, he completed the first part of his masterpiece *Don Quixote de la Mancha.*

from Don Quixote

Parody

A **parody** is a comical piece of writing that mocks the characteristics of a specific literary form. By exaggerating or humorously imitating the ideas, language, tone, or action in a work of literature, a parody calls attention to the ridiculous qualities of its subject. For example, *Don Quixote* is a parody that ridicules knights and the literature of chivalry. By exaggerating Don Quixote's behavior, Cervantes entertains his audience while making fun of the traditional knight in shining armor.

Focus

Don Quixote is about a man who uses his imagination to invent a new life for himself as a wandering medieval knight. Use your imagination and write down what you would like to be in your own fantasy world. Then make a list of ways your life would change. For instance, how would you dress? Where would you go? How would you get there? What name would you choose for yourself? What goals would you accomplish in your new life?

Vocabulary

Knowing the following words will help you as you read the excerpt from *Don Quixote.*

lucidity (lo͞o sid′ ə tē) *n.*: Clarity; ability to be understood (p. 739)

adulation (a′ jo͞o lā′ shən) *n.*: Excessive praise or admiration (p. 739)

interminable (in tʉr′ mi nə bəl) *adj.*: Lasting or seeming to last forever (p. 740)

affable (af′ ə bəl) *adj.*: Pleasant; friendly (p. 740)

sallying (sal′ ē iŋ) *v.*: Rushing forth suddenly (p. 740)

requisite (rek′ wə zit) *adj.*: Required by circumstances (p. 740)

sonorous (sə nôr′ əs) *adj.*: Having a powerful, impressive sound (p. 742)

veracious (və rā′ shəs) *adj.*: Truthful; accurate (p. 742)

vanquish (vaŋ′ kwish) *v.*: Conquer; force into submission (p. 742)

extolled (eks tōld′) *adj.*: Praised (p. 742)

The First Part of The Ingenious Gentleman Don Quixote of La Mancha[1]

Miguel de Cervantes
translated by John Ormsby

CHAPTER I

Which Treats of the Character and Pursuits of the Famous Gentleman Don Quixote of La Mancha

In a village of La Mancha, which I prefer to leave unnamed, there lived not long ago one of those gentlemen that keep a lance in the lance-rack, an old shield, a lean hack, and a greyhound for hunting. A stew of rather more beef than mutton, hash on most nights, bacon and eggs on Saturdays, lentils on Fridays, and a pigeon or so extra on Sundays consumed three quarters of his income. The rest went for a coat of fine cloth and velvet breeches and shoes to match for holidays, while on weekdays he cut a fine figure in his best homespun. He had in his house a housekeeper past forty, a niece under twenty, and a lad for the field and marketplace, who saddled the hack as well as handled the pruning knife. The age of this gentleman of ours was bordering on fifty. He was of a hardy constitution, spare, gaunt-featured, a very early riser, and fond of hunting. Some say that his surname was Quixada or Quesada (for there is no unanimity among those who write on the subject), although reasonable conjectures tend to show that he was called Quexana. But this scarcely affects our story; it will be enough not to stray a hair's breadth from the truth in telling it.

You must know that the above-named gentleman devoted his leisure (which was mostly all the year round) to reading books of chivalry—and with such ardor and avidity that he almost entirely abandoned the chase and even the management of his property. To such a pitch did his eagerness and infatuation go that he sold many an acre of tillage land to buy books of chivalry to read, bringing home all he could find.

But there were none he liked so well as those written by the famous Feliciano de Silva, for their lucidity of style and complicated conceits[2] were as pearls in his sight, particularly when in his reading he came upon outpourings of adulation and courtly challenges. There he often found passages like *"the reason of the unreason with which my reason is afflicted so weakens my reason that with reason I complain of your beauty"*; or again, *"the high heavens, that of your divinity divinely fortify you with the*

---

1. La Mancha: A province in south central Spain.
2. conceits (kən sēts′) *n*.: Elaborate comparisons or metaphors.

stars, render you deserving of the desert your greatness deserves."

Over this sort of folderol[3] the poor gentleman lost his wits, and he used to lie awake striving to understand it and worm out its meaning; though Aristotle[4] himself could have made out or extracted nothing, had he come back to life for that special purpose. He was rather uneasy about the wounds which Don Belianís gave and received, because it seemed to him that, however skilled the surgeons who had cured him, he must have had his face and body covered all over with seams and scars. He commended, however, the author's way of ending his book, with a promise to go on with that interminable adventure, and many a time he felt the urge to take up his pen and finish it just as its author had promised. He would no doubt have done so, and succeeded with it too, had he not been occupied with greater and more absorbing thoughts.

Many an argument did he have with the priest of his village (a learned man, and a graduate of Sigüenza[5]) as to which had been the better knight, Palmerín of England or Amadís of Gaul. Master Nicolás, the village barber, however, used to say that neither of them came up to the Knight of Phœbus, and that if there was any that could compare with *him* it was Don Galaor, the brother of Amadís of Gaul, because he had a spirit equal to every occasion, and was no wishy-washy knight or a crybaby like his brother, while in valor he was not a whit behind him.

In short, he became so absorbed in his books that he spent his nights from sunset to sunrise, and his days from dawn to dark, poring over them; and what with little sleep and much reading his brain shriveled up and he lost his wits. His imagination was stuffed with all he read in his books about enchantments, quarrels, battles, challenges, wounds, wooings, loves, agonies, and all sorts of impossible nonsense. It became so firmly planted in his mind that the whole fabric of invention and fancy he read about was true, that to him no history in the world was better substantiated. He used to say the Cid Ruy Díaz[6] was a very good knight but that he was not to be compared with the Knight of the Burning Sword who with one backstroke cut in half two fierce and monstrous giants. He thought more of Bernardo del Carpio because at Roncesvalles he slew Roland in spite of enchantments, availing himself of Hercules' trick when he strangled Antæus the son of Terra in his arms. He approved highly of the giant Morgante, because, although of the giant breed which is always arrogant and ill-mannered, he alone was affable and well-bred. But above all he admired Reinaldos of Montalbán, especially when he saw him sallying forth from his castle and robbing everyone he met, and when beyond the seas he stole that image of Mohammed which, as his history says, was entirely of gold. To have a bout of kicking at that traitor of a Ganelon he would have given his housekeeper, and his niece into the bargain.

In a word, his wits being quite gone, he hit upon the strangest notion that ever madman in this world hit upon. He fancied it was right and requisite, no less for his own greater renown than in the service of his country, that he should make a knight-errant of himself, roaming the world over in full armor and on horseback in quest of adventures. He would put into practice all that he had read

---

3. folderol (fäl′ də räl′) *n.*: Mere nonsense.
4. Aristotle (ar′ is tät′'l): Ancient Greek philosopher, renowned for his knowledge of many fields.
5. Sigüenza (sē gwän′ sä): One of a group of "minor universities" granting degrees that were often laughed at by Spanish humorists.

6. Cid Ruy Dí′az (sēd r$\overline{oo}$′ē dē′ äs): Famous Spanish soldier, Ruy Díaz de Vivar; called the Cid, a derivation of the Arabic word for lord.

DON QUIXOTE
Honoré Daumier
Neue Pinakothek, Munich

had no closed helmet, nothing but a simple morion.[8] This deficiency, however, his ingenuity made good, for he contrived a kind of half-helmet of pasteboard which, fitted on to the morion, looked like a whole one. It is true that, in order to see if it was strong and fit to withstand a cut, he drew his sword and gave it a couple of slashes, the first of which undid in an instant what had taken him a week to do. The ease with which he had knocked it to pieces disconcerted him somewhat, and to guard against the danger he set to work again, fixing bars of iron on the inside until he was satisfied with its strength. Then, not caring to try any more experiments with it, he accepted and commissioned it as a helmet of the most perfect construction.

He next proceeded to inspect his nag, which, with its cracked hoofs and more blemishes than the steed of Gonela, that *"tantum pellis et ossa fruit,"*[9] surpassed in his eyes the Bucephalus of Alexander or the Babieca of the Cid.[10] Four days were spent in thinking what name to give him, because (as he said to himself) it was not right that a horse belonging to a knight so famous, and one with such merits of its own, should be without some distinctive name. He strove to find something that would indicate what it had been before belonging to a knight-errant, and what it had now become. It was only reasonable that it should be given a new name to match the new career adopted by its master, and that the name should be a distinguished and full-sounding one, befitting the new order and calling it was about

of as being the usual practices of knights-errant: righting every kind of wrong, and exposing himself to peril and danger from which he would emerge to reap eternal fame and glory. Already the poor man saw himself crowned by the might of his arm Emperor of Trebizond[7] at least. And so, carried away by the intense enjoyment he found in these pleasant fancies, he began at once to put his scheme into execution.

The first thing he did was to clean up some armor that had belonged to his ancestors and had for ages been lying forgotten in a corner, covered with rust and mildew. He scoured and polished it as best he could, but the one great defect he saw in it was that it

---

7. Trebizond (treb′ i zänd′): In medieval times, a Greek empire off the southeast coast of the Black Sea.

8. morion (mōr′ ē än′) *n*.: Old-fashioned soldier's helmet with a brim, covering the top part of the head.

9. "tantum pellis et ossa fruit" (tän′ tum pel′ is et äs′ ə frōō′ it): A Latin phrase meaning "It was nothing but skin and bones."

10. Bucephalus (byōō sef′ ə ləs) **of Alexander or the Babieca** (bäb ē ā′ kä) **of the Cid:** Bucephalus was Alexander the Great's war horse; Babieca was the Cid's war horse.

to follow. And so, after having composed, struck out, rejected, added to, unmade, and remade a multitude of names out of his memory and fancy, he decided upon calling it Rocinante. To his thinking this was a lofty, sonorous name that nevertheless indicated what the hack's[11] status had been before it became what now it was, the first and foremost of all the hacks in the world.

Having got a name for his horse so much to his taste, he was anxious to get one for himself, and he spent eight days more pondering over this point. At last he made up his mind to call himself Don Quixote—which, as stated above, led the authors of this veracious history to infer that his name quite assuredly must have been Quixada, and not Quesada as others would have it. It occurred to him, however, that the valiant Amadis was not content to call himself Amadis and nothing more but added the name of his kingdom and country to make it famous and called himself Amadis of Gaul. So he, like a good knight, resolved to add on the name of his own region and style himself Don Quixote of La Mancha. He believed that this accurately described his origin and country, and that he did it honor by taking its name for his own.

So then, his armor being furbished, his morion turned into a helmet, his hack christened, and he himself confirmed, he came to the conclusion that nothing more was needed now but to look for a lady to be in love with, for a knight-errant without love was like a tree without leaves or fruit, or a body without a soul.

"If, for my sins, or by my good fortune," he said to himself, "I come across some giant hereabouts, a common occurrence with knights-errant, and knock him to the ground in one onslaught, or cleave him

asunder at the waist, or, in short, vanquish and subdue him, will it not be well to have someone I may send him to as a present, that he may come in and fall on his knees before my sweet lady, and in a humble, submissive voice say, 'I am the giant Caraculiambro, lord of the island of Malindrania, vanquished in single combat by the never sufficiently extolled knight Don Quixote of La Mancha, who has commanded me to present myself before your grace, that your highness may dispose of me at your pleasure'?"

Oh, how our good gentleman enjoyed the delivery of this speech, especially when he had thought of someone to call his lady! There was, so the story goes, in a village near his own a very good-looking farm-girl with whom he had been at one time in love, though, so far as is known, she never knew it nor gave a thought to the matter. Her name was Aldonza Lorenzo, and upon her he thought fit to confer the title of Lady of his Thoughts. Searching for a name not too remote from her own, yet which would aim at and bring to mind that of a princess and great lady, he decided upon calling her Dulcinea del Toboso, since she was a native of El Toboso. To his way of thinking, the name was musical, uncommon, and significant, like all those he had bestowed upon himself and his belongings.

CHAPTER VIII

Of the Good Fortune Which the Valiant Don Quixote Had in the Terrible and Undreamed-of Adventure of the Windmills, With Other Occurrences Worthy to Be Fitly Recorded

At this point they came in sight of thirty or forty windmills that are on that plain.

"Fortune," said Don Quixote to his squire, as soon as he had seen them, "is arranging matters for us better than we

---

11. **hack's:** Horse's.

**DON QUIXOTE
AND THE WINDMILL, c. 1900**
Francisco J. Torrome

could have hoped. Look there, friend Sancho Panza, where thirty or more monstrous giants rise up, all of whom I mean to engage in battle and slay, and with whose spoils we shall begin to make our fortunes. For this is righteous warfare, and it is God's good service to sweep so evil a breed from off the face of the earth."

"What giants?" said Sancho Panza.

"Those you see there," answered his master, "with the long arms, and some have them nearly two leagues[12] long."

"Look, your worship," said Sancho. "What we see there are not giants but windmills, and what seem to be their arms are the vanes that turned by the wind make the millstone go."

"It is easy to see," replied Don Quixote, "that you are not used to this business of adventures. Those are giants, and if you are afraid, away with you out of here and betake yourself to prayer, while I engage them in fierce and unequal combat."

So saying, he gave the spur to his steed Rocinante, heedless of the cries his squire Sancho sent after him, warning him that most certainly they were windmills and not giants he was going to attack. He, however, was so positive they were giants that he neither heard the cries of Sancho, nor perceived, near as he was, what they were.

"Fly not, cowards and vile beings," he shouted, "for a single knight attacks you."

A slight breeze at this moment sprang up, and the great vanes began to move.

"Though ye flourish more arms than the giant Briareus, ye have to reckon with me!" exclaimed Don Quixote, when he saw this.

So saying, he commended himself with all his heart to his lady Dulcinea, imploring her to support him in such a peril. With lance braced and covered by his shield, he charged at Rocinante's fullest gallop and attacked the first mill that stood in front of him. But as he drove his lance-point into the sail, the wind whirled it around with such force that it shivered the lance to pieces. It swept away with it horse and rider, and they

---

12. leagues: A league is about three miles.

were sent rolling over the plain, in sad condition indeed.

Sancho hastened to his assistance as fast as the animal could go. When he came up he found Don Quixote unable to move, with such an impact had Rocinante fallen with him.

"God bless me!" said Sancho. "Did I not tell your worship to watch what you were doing, because they were only windmills? No one could have made any mistake about it unless he had something of the same kind in his head."

"Silence, friend Sancho," replied Don Quixote. "The fortunes of war more than any other are liable to frequent fluctuations. Moreover I think, and it is the truth, that that same sage Frestón who carried off my study and books, has turned these giants into mills in order to rob me of the glory of vanquishing them, such is the enmity he bears me. But in the end his wicked arts will avail but little against my good sword."

"God's will be done," said Sancho Panza, and helping him to rise got him up again on Rocinante, whose shoulder was half dislocated. Then, discussing the adventure, they followed the road to Puerto Lápice, for there, said Don Quixote, they could not fail to find adventures in abundance and variety, as it was a well-traveled thoroughfare. For all that, he was much grieved at the loss of his lance, and said so to his squire.

"I remember having read," he added, "how a Spanish knight, Diego Pérez de Vargas by name, having broken his sword in battle, tore from an oak a ponderous bough or branch. With it he did such things that day, and pounded so many Moors, that he got the surname of Machuca, and he and his descendants from that day forth were called Vargas y Machuca. I mention this because from the first oak I see I mean to tear such a branch, large and stout. I am determined and resolved to do such deeds with it that

you may deem yourself very fortunate in being found worthy to see them and be an eyewitness of things that will scarcely be believed."

"Be that as God wills," said Sancho, "I believe it all as your worship says it. But straighten yourself a little, for you seem to be leaning to one side, maybe from the shaking you got when you fell."

"That is the truth," said Don Quixote, "and if I make no complaint of the pain it is because knights-errant are not permitted to complain of any wound, even though their bowels be coming out through it."

"If so," said Sancho, "I have nothing to say. But God knows I would rather your worship complained when anything ailed you. For my part, I confess I must complain however small the ache may be, unless this rule about not complaining applies to the squires of knights-errant also."

Don Quixote could not help laughing at his squire's simplicity, and assured him he might complain whenever and however he chose, just as he liked. So far he had never read of anything to the contrary in the order of knighthood.

Sancho reminded him it was dinner time, to which his master answered that he wanted nothing himself just then, but that Sancho might eat when he had a mind. With this permission Sancho settled himself as comfortably as he could on his beast, and taking out of the saddlebags what he had stowed away in them, he jogged along behind his master munching slowly. From time to time he took a pull at the wineskin with all the enjoyment that the thirstiest tavern-keeper in Málaga might have envied. And while he went on in this way, between gulps, he never gave a thought to any of the promises his master had made him, nor did he rate it as hardship but rather as recreation going in quest of adventures, however dangerous they might be.

RESPONDING TO THE SELECTION

Your Response

1. Which character in the story do you like best? Explain.
2. Sancho Panza waits patiently as Don Quixote gallops off to conquer imaginary enemies. How would you feel and act if you were Don Quixote's squire?

Recalling

3. How does Don Quixote spend his time before he becomes a knight-errant?
4. What sweeps Don Quixote and his horse over the plain?

Interpreting

5. What makes Don Quixote see the windmills as giants?
6. Why does Don Quixote want to use special names for people and things?
7. Why is Sancho Panza a particularly helpful squire to Don Quixote?

Applying

8. Don Quixote uses his imagination to live in the midst of his own fantasy. He sees what he wants to see and understands the world in the way that he chooses. What are the advantages and dangers of such an approach to life?

ANALYZING LITERATURE

Understanding Parody

A **parody** is a story, poem, or play that imitates or exaggerates a literary form. When writers exaggerate characteristics of literature or society, they encourage readers to look at values, cultures, and literary traditions in a new way. In making knightly bravery seem silly, Cervantes encourages you to think about what bravery means to you. When Don Quixote renames himself and his horse, Cervantes is poking fun at the medieval codes of knighthood. By making you laugh at knightly values, Cervantes encourages you to examine the values of the Middle Ages.

1. How does Cervantes poke fun at the way knights dressed?
2. How is the incident with the windmills an example of parody?
3. What other examples of parody can you find in the selection?

CRITICAL THINKING AND READING

Analyzing Tone in Parody

In **parody,** writers give a special importance to tone, or the attitude they take toward their subject. Exaggeration helps to create a comic tone and to make readers laugh at the silliness of the subject.

To identify the comic tone in *Don Quixote,* ask yourself, "Does Cervantes want me to view this action or character seriously or does he want me to laugh at the situation?" The following events help to create the comic tone in *Don Quixote.* Explain why each is funny.

1. Don Quixote devotes himself to reading books of chivalry.
2. Don Quixote asks Dulcinea for her support as he attacks the giants.
3. Don Quixote avoids complaining when in pain.

THINKING AND WRITING

Writing a Parody of a Fictional Hero

Choose a fictional hero as the subject for a parody. She or he might be a heroic character in a novel, movie, play, or television program. Jot down your hero's special characteristics. Then describe a day in your hero's life, exaggerating his or her characteristics in a funny way. When you finish writing, share your parody with classmates, and ask them if they can identify the hero you are parodying.

YOUR WRITING PROCESS

WRITING A PROFILE OF A HERO

Who are your heroes? Professional athletes? Famous musicians or writers? World leaders? What are the qualities of a hero? In some legends and epic tales, ordinary people prove their heroism through extraordinary acts of bravery or insight. What heroic character in this unit would you choose as the subject for a magazine profile?

Focus

Assignment: Write a profile of a hero.
Purpose: To describe a heroic figure's achievements and character traits.
Audience: Readers of a magazine about notable people.

Prewriting

1. What events shape a hero? Most heroic characters must overcome great difficulties to achieve their goals. Look over the legends and tales in this unit and choose your favorite hero. Then jot down notes about the kinds of conflicts or ordeals that the hero must face.

2. Create a character chart. Make a chart that summarizes the key qualities and abilities of your hero.

Student Model

Rama			
Brave	*Compassionate*	*Respectful*	*Strong*
goes with Viswamithra even though he is young and probably scared	hesitates before killing Thataka because she is a woman and might need protection	"I will carry out your wish."	manages to defeat Thataka, an evil demon

3. Focus your profile. List two or three of these character traits and briefly tell why they are important.

Strength—Important because Rama will confront dangerous situations requiring physical endurance.

Respect—Rama's respect for his father suggests the culture's high regard for elders.

Courage—Most important quality for a hero; without it Rama could not face the demons he must defeat.

4. Write a thesis statement. A good way to test whether you have narrowed down your topic adequately is to try stating it in a single sentence.

Rama demonstrates heroic qualities in his physical strength, respect for his elders, and courage in the face of danger.

Drafting

1. Grab the reader's attention. Begin your profile with a catchy introduction. You might use a quotation, a question, or a brief anecdote that illustrates a key quality of your hero.

2. Develop your profile. In the body of the profile, use separate paragraphs to discuss the key ideas you summarized in your thesis statement. Use specific details from the story to illustrate your points.

3. Write a conclusion. A good conclusion should not only summarize your ideas but also leave your readers with a stimulating or provocative point to consider.

Revising and Editing

1. Work with a peer editor. Ask your partner whether your profile conveys a clear sense of the heroic qualities of your subject.

2. Can I liven up my language? Ask yourself where you might replace vague verbs and nouns with more concrete words.

When you write a profile of someone, consider using **quotations** from your subject. By including significant comments spoken by your subject, you give the reader helpful insights into the personality of your hero and add liveliness to your writing.

• Assemble a classroom *Personalities* magazine that contains profiles of heroes from all walks of life.

• With your classmates, arrange a series of talks on "Heroes Through the Ages" and present your profile orally before another class.

• Create a piece of artwork that illustrates your profile and display both in a classroom exhibit.

1. Did creating a character chart help you generate ideas about the subject of your profile? Explain.

2. Did you discover certain grammar, spelling, or punctuation errors that recur in your writing? What can you do to avoid these kinds of errors in the future?

WRITING A PLAN FOR A MURAL DESIGN

Just as the imaginative stories in this unit use words to record the achievements of heroes, artists can visually depict heroic adventures in paintings and sculptures. Imagine that you have been asked by your school principal to plan the design for a mural depicting the achievements of a modern hero. How can you best communicate your plan to the artist who will create the mural?

> *"A work of art is not a matter of thinking beautiful thoughts or experiencing tender emotions (though those are its raw materials) but of intelligence, skill, taste, proportion, knowledge, discipline and industry; especially discipline."*
>
> **Evelyn Waugh**

Focus

Assignment: Write a plan for a mural design.
Purpose: To describe how the mural will look.
Audience: The artist who will create the mural for your school.

Prewriting

1. Share stories of modern heroes. Form a small group of classmates and discuss your definitions of a hero. Identify outstanding individuals who have made significant contributions to your community, the nation, or the world. Then choose a hero whose achievements could be effectively illustrated in a visual design.

2. Create a fact file. Write your hero's name at the top of a sheet of paper. Then add words and phrases under headings that summarize your hero's outstanding qualities and achievements. What makes your hero unique?

Student Model

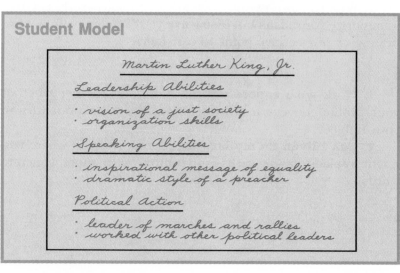

> Martin Luther King, Jr.
>
> *Leadership Abilities*
> · vision of a just society
> · organization skills
>
> *Speaking Abilities*
> · inspirational message of equality
> · dramatic style of a preacher
>
> *Political Action*
> · leader of marches and rallies
> · worked with other political leaders

3. Make a sketch. Make a rough sketch of the mural based on the qualities you noted in your fact file. Decide how these features could best be depicted in visual terms. Should the mural show lots of action, or focus on a quiet scene? What central mood do you want to express?

Drafting

1. Give an overview. Begin your plan with a summary of the key qualities you want the mural to convey about your hero. Describe the main impression the artist should capture.

Student Model

The mural should emphasize the qualities that make Martin Luther King, Jr., a role model for young people today: his outstanding leadership qualities, his universal message of freedom and equality, and his inspirational spirit of hope and victory. These features should be illustrated in a sequence of portraits and group scenes that express a mood of determination and victory.

---

2. Describe details. In the body of your plan, provide specific details and guidelines that will give the artist a clear picture of your design. Include information about images, scenes, colors, arrangements of figures, and general style. Use your sketch to help you develop your plan.

Revising and Editing

1. Take a break. Take time off from your writing by putting it aside for a while. Then take a fresh look at your plan. Be your own critic. Ask yourself if your plan will be clear and useful to the artist who will use it. Is any important information missing? Have you presented your ideas in a logical order?

2. Consult an art teacher. Ask an art teacher or artistic classmate to read over the draft of your plan. Can he or she suggest any improvements for your design?

3. Work with a peer editing group. Read your plan aloud to a small group of classmates. Have them try to sketch out the design as they listen. Does your plan clearly communicate your design for the mural?

Writer's Tip

In writing a plan for a mural, consider arranging the details of your description in a specific **spatial organization.** For example, you might describe elements of the design from left to right, top to bottom, or center to edges.

Options for Publishing

• Submit your design plan to a local artist who might be interested in creating a mural.
• As a class, choose one of the designs to develop into a mural. Then work together to create a life-size mural for the class or school.
• Exchange plans with other classmates and create miniature versions of each design. Display your work in class.

Reviewing Your Writing Process

1. How did you decide which method to use in arranging the details of your design plan?

2. Was taking time off from your writing useful? Explain.

3. What was the most challenging aspect of this writing project? Explain.

EARLY MORNING IN RO . . . , 1925
Paul Klee
The Museum of Modern Art, New York

THE NOVEL

Our word *novel,* meaning a long work of prose fiction, comes from the French word for "new." The first true works of fiction as we know it were the lengthy romances written in France and Spain during the sixteenth and seventeenth centuries. In fact, the French word for *novel* is still *roman.* The English used the Old French word *novel* to describe these stories and to differentiate them from medieval and classical romances, thus indicating they were something that was new. A distinct literary form was born.

Because of the increased levels of general education and literacy in the eighteenth century, growth of fiction in general and of the novel especially developed rapidly. Reading a novel even became a social event: In an age without television, people read to one another as a means of entertainment. A writer could write a novel and have it printed by a publisher. The publisher, in turn, could sell the story to this expanded audience and pay the author a percentage of the sales. With this wider audience and greater demand, novelists could earn a living with their words. The novel had arrived as a major genre of literature.

The novel has a plot as short stories do, but it is usually longer and more complex in its development and resolution. The creation of characters is important in a novel, for the writer has time to allow the reader to examine the innermost thoughts of the characters. Like most literature, novels have themes or ideas about life that the story reveals. A novelist writes from a point of view that could be first person or third person, limited or omniscient, like a writer of short stories or a poet. Certainly tone and style are elements of a novel as well.

Gothic romances, exciting espionage adventures, science-fiction thrillers, and biting social commentaries are but a few of the forms novels can take. In this unit you will read novels that present perceptive commentaries on life.

READING ACTIVELY

The Novel

BACKGROUND John Knowles was only thirty-three when *A Separate Peace* was first published in England in 1959. (It was published in the United States a year later.) The novel was an immediate success, winning the William Faulkner Foundation Award and the Rosenthal Award of the National Institute of Arts and Letters.

Devon School, the setting of *A Separate Peace,* is patterned after Phillips Exeter Academy, the boarding school Knowles attended in New Hampshire as a teenager during World War II. Knowles's experiences provided him with the background he needed to create the realistic atmosphere and characters of the book.

World War II affected most people in the United States in some way every day from December 7, 1941, when the Japanese bombed Pearl Harbor, until August 14, 1945, when the Japanese surrendered. The United States first entered the war in December 1941, declaring war on Germany and Italy as well as on Japan. Those three countries were the main members of the alliance called the Axis.

The countries opposing the Axis were called the Allies. Among the major powers of the Allies were the United States, Great Britain, and the Soviet Union. In 1942, the year in which the events of *A Separate Peace* begin, the Allies were taking a beating on all fronts. War materials were still in short supply. On the Pacific front, the Philippine Islands were being conquered; China was staggering before its Japanese enemy. On the European front, England was bombed nightly by the German Luftwaffe. Great Britain and the United States faced stiff opposition when they invaded Axis positions in North Africa.

On the home front, meanwhile, everyone pitched in to help in the war effort. Every week, school children brought nickels and dimes to school to buy stamps. When a book of stamps was filled, it could be traded in for a government bond that would help pay for the war. Civilians planted vegetable gardens, called victory gardens, took courses in first aid, and became air-raid wardens who made sure that people took cover during drills and that no light to guide enemy bombers escaped from heavily curtained windows.

The sixteen-year-old boys in *A Separate Peace* seem able to ignore the war much of the time. Their elite preparatory school and its emphasis on teaching the classics, as well as its heritage of competition both in the classroom and in sports, insulate the boys somewhat. In the back of their minds, however, they realize that in slightly over a year they will reach the age for military service. Along with the heightened feelings of patriotism comes the knowledge that they might very possibly be killed.

READING STRATEGIES   Gene, the narrator, is an adult relating events from his school days, and his insights are those of a person in his mid-thirties. As you read, be aware that you will find young people speaking and acting appropriately to their time and age, as well as the voice of a more mature person looking back on those actions. Notice that the point of view is first person. As a reader, you know only Gene's thoughts and impressions. When you read his "confessions," consider what the other characters might have felt. Finally, interact with the literature by using the active reading strategies: question, visualize, predict, correct, respond.

THEMES   You will encounter the following themes in *A Separate Peace:*

- Choices and consequences
- Self-realization
- The search for meaning
- Individuals in society
- Humans in conflict
- Values and beliefs
- Showing courage
- Reflecting on the past

The Wrestling Match

BACKGROUND   Buchi Emecheta, the author of *The Wrestling Match,* was born in 1944 in Lagos, Nigeria. Although she lives in London, she has not lost touch with her Nigerian culture. In fact, she is most recognized for her historical novels set in Nigeria. Her work is often autobiographical as she focuses on the situation of women in Nigerian society.

The Wrestling Match takes place in an Igbo village in Nigeria. In 1960 Nigeria won its independence from Great Britain. Ensuing ethnic rivalry caused one of the largest ethnic groups—the Igbo—to form a separate nation called Biafra. From 1967 to 1970 the Igbo people fought a civil war to gain their independence. Although they lost the fight, the Igbo have since become a strong part of Nigerian society. In many ways *The Wrestling Match* is a comment on the civil war. Emecheta suggests that the war was fought for the wrong reasons and that the resulting integration of the Igbo people into Nigerian society empowered the children of the war.

In every society there are special traditions and customs having to do with education, competition, family, hospitality, and other major aspects of life. In much of Africa, schools are not free, and many families cannot afford to give their children a formal education. Those who remain at home are educated in other ways, however, including traditional skills such as blacksmithing and medicine, and arts such as carving. Often, rivalry develops between those who are educated in the schools and those who are educated at home.

Unlike much athletic competition in the United States, Igbo athletic competition is community oriented. If rewards are not shared with the community, then the winner does not receive respect. The sport of wrestling illustrates this concept very well. The champion wrestler is a great hero in Igbo society, and the community helps the athlete in every way possible.

The Wrestling Match is a story about experiences that readers will find familiar: conflict between two rival groups; a romance between two young people; and tensions between young people and their parents. The young people in the novel learn how to function within the society, and come to respect the ways of the older generation. Along the way, they are encouraged to be independent and to think for themselves.

READING STRATEGIES As you read *The Wrestling Match,* keep in mind that time is an important part of a novel's setting. Emecheta frequently refers to the effects of the recent civil war. The Igbo people made a bid for independence and lost, only to find themselves stronger in the long run. Consider how the characters might have acted differently if they had not been affected by the civil war. Interact with the literature by using the active reading strategies: question, visualize, predict, connect, respond.

THEMES You will encounter the following themes in *The Wrestling Match:*

- Conflicts and challenges
- Values and beliefs
- Rites of passage
- Choices and consequences
- Showing courage

A Separate Peace

TREE TRUNKS, 1913
André Derain
Moscow, Pushkin Museum/Roos/Art Resource

GUIDE FOR READING

A Separate Peace, Chapters 1–4

Characters and Verisimilitude

Novels are about people, or **characters.** In fact, you probably could not have a novel without characters. It is the novelist's job to give these characters **verisimilitude.** This means that the novelist creates characters who, although fictional, seem like real-life human beings. In a modern novel, the hero, or protagonist, is usually presented as a fallable creature capable of making mistakes.

Focus

In a group of three or four people, discuss some of the difficulties and conflicts that can occur during the high-school years. Then prepare a chart with the headings *Personal Qualities, Motives, Feelings Toward Others, Attitudes,* and *Influences.* Explore each category as a group and complete the chart by listing the experiences you discuss. As you read *A Separate Peace,* complete this chart for Gene and Finny.

Vocabulary

Knowing the following words will help you as you read Chapters 1–4 of *A Separate Peace.*

tacit (tas′ it) *adj.*: Unspoken; not expressed or declared openly (p. 757)

vibrantly (vī′ brənt lē) *adv.*: Vigorously; energetically; throbbingly filled with life (p. 757)

capacious (kə pā′ shəs) *adj.*: Roomy; spacious (p. 757)

contentious (kən ten′ shəs) *adj.*: Quarrelsome (p. 758)

droll (drōl) *adj.*: Amusing in an odd or ironic way (p. 761)

prodigious (prə dij′ əs) *adj.*: Huge or powerful (p. 761)

rhetorically (ri tôr′ i klē) *adv.*: As if asking a question only for effect, without expecting an answer (p. 762)

anarchy (an′ ər kē) *n.*: Lawlessness; disorder (p. 772)

solace (säl′ is) *n.*: Something that comforts (p. 783)

vulnerable (vul′ nər ə bəl) *adj.*: Sensitive (p. 783)

John Knowles

(1926–   ) was born in Fairmont, West Virginia. At the age of fifteen, as World War II raged, he left home to attend Phillips Exeter Academy in New Hampshire. Later he served briefly in the armed services. After graduating from Yale University in 1949, Knowles worked at various writing and editing jobs. He modeled the setting for *A Separate Peace,* his first published novel, after Phillips Exeter. *A Separate Peace* has become one of the most widely read American postwar novels.

A Separate Peace

John Knowles

Chapter 1

I went back to the Devon School not long ago, and found it looking oddly newer than when I was a student there fifteen years before. It seemed more sedate than I remembered it, more perpendicular and strait-laced, with narrower windows and shinier woodwork, as though a coat of varnish had been put over everything for better preservation. But, of course, fifteen years before there had been a war going on. Perhaps the school wasn't as well kept up in those days; perhaps varnish, along with everything else, had gone to war.

I didn't entirely like this glossy new surface, because it made the school look like a museum, and that's exactly what it was to me, and what I did not want it to be. In the deep, tacit way in which feeling becomes stronger than thought, I had always felt that the Devon School came into existence the day I entered it, was vibrantly real while I was a student there, and then blinked out like a candle the day I left.

Now here it was after all, preserved by some considerate hand with varnish and wax. Preserved along with it, like stale air in an unopened room, was the well-known fear which had surrounded and filled those days, so much of it that I hadn't even known it was there. Because, unfamiliar with the absence of fear and what that was like, I had not been able to identify its presence.

Looking back now across fifteen years, I could see with great clarity the fear I had lived in, which must mean that in the interval I had succeeded in a very important undertaking: I must have made my escape from it.

I felt fear's echo, and along with that I felt the unhinged, uncontrollable joy which had been its accompaniment and opposite face, joy which had broken out sometimes in those days like Northern Lights[1] across black sky.

There were a couple of places now which I wanted to see. Both were fearful sites, and that was why I wanted to see them. So after lunch at the Devon Inn I walked back toward the school. It was a raw, nondescript time of year, toward the end of November, the kind of wet, self-pitying November day when every speck of dirt stands out clearly. Devon luckily had very little of such weather—the icy clamp of winter, or the radiant New Hampshire summers, were more characteristic of it—but this day it blew wet, moody gusts all around me.

I walked along Gilman Street, the best street in town. The houses were as handsome and as unusual as I remembered. Clever modernizations of old Colonial manses,[2] extensions in Victorian wood, capacious

---

1. Northern Lights: Irregular, luminous streamers of light that are visible at night in the north, including in the northern part of the United States; the aurora borealis (ô rôr′ ə bôr′ ē al′is).
2. manses (mans′ əz) *n.*: Large, imposing houses. Usually the manse was the parsonage or residence of the minister and as such was a stately and dignified structure.

Greek Revival temples[3] lined the street, as impressive and just as forbidding as ever. I had rarely seen anyone go into one of them, or anyone playing on a lawn, or even an open window. Today with their failing ivy and stripped, moaning trees the houses looked both more elegant and more lifeless than ever.

Like all old, good schools, Devon did not stand isolated behind walls and gates but emerged naturally from the town which had produced it. So there was no sudden moment of encounter as I approached it; the houses along Gilman Street began to look more defensive, which meant that I was near the school, and then more exhausted, which meant that I was in it.

It was early afternoon and the grounds and buildings were deserted, since everyone was at sports. There was nothing to distract me as I made my way across a wide yard, called the Far Common, and up to a building as red brick and balanced as the other major buildings, but with a large cupola and a bell and a clock and Latin over the doorway—the First Academy Building.

In through swinging doors I reached a marble foyer, and stopped at the foot of a long white marble flight of stairs. Although they were old stairs, the worn moons in the middle of each step were not very deep. The marble must be unusually hard. That seemed very likely, only too likely, although with all my thought about these stairs this exceptional hardness had not occurred to me. It was surprising that I had overlooked that, that crucial fact.

There was nothing else to notice; they of course were the same stairs I had walked up and down at least once every day of my Devon life. They were the same as ever. And I? Well, I naturally felt older—I began at that point the emotional examination to note how far my convalescence had gone—I was taller, bigger generally in relation to these stairs. I had more money and success and "security" than in the days when specters seemed to go up and down them with me.

I turned away and went back outside. The Far Common was still empty, and I walked alone down the wide gravel paths among those most Republican, bankerish of trees, New England elms,[4] toward the far side of the school.

Devon is sometimes considered the most beautiful school in New England, and even on this dismal afternoon its power was asserted. It is the beauty of small areas of order—a large yard, a group of trees, three similar dormitories, a circle of old houses—living together in contentious harmony. You felt that an argument might begin again any time; in fact it had: out of the Dean's Residence,[5] a pure and authentic Colonial house, there now sprouted an ell with a big bare picture window. Some day the Dean would probably live entirely encased in a house of glass and be happy as a sandpiper. Everything at Devon slowly changed and slowly harmonized with what had gone before. So it was logical to hope that since the buildings and the Deans and the curriculum could achieve this, I could achieve, perhaps unknowingly already had achieved, this growth and harmony myself.

I would know more about that when I

---

3. Greek Revival temples: Stately houses built in the style of ancient Greek temples with heavy columns.

4. New England elms: Once a common, ornamental, shade tree in New England, most of these tall, stately trees have been killed by Dutch elm disease.
5. Dean's Residence: The home of the head of the school administration.

had seen the second place I had come to see. So I roamed on past the balanced red brick dormitories with webs of leafless ivy clinging to them, through a ramshackle salient[6] of the town which invaded the school for a hundred yards, past the solid gymnasium, full of students at this hour but silent as a monument on the outside, past the Field House, called The Cage—I remembered now what a mystery references to "The Cage" had been during my first weeks at Devon, I had thought it must be a place of severe punishment—and I reached the huge open sweep of ground known as the Playing Fields.

Devon was both scholarly and very athletic, so the playing fields were vast and, except at such a time of year, constantly in use. Now they reached soggily and emptily away from me, forlorn tennis courts on the left, enormous football and soccer and lacrosse fields[7] in the center, woods on the right, and at the far end a small river detectable from this distance by the few bare trees along its banks. It was such a gray and misty day that I could not see the other side of the river, where there was a small stadium.

I started the long trudge across the fields and had gone some distance before I paid any attention to the soft and muddy ground, which was dooming my city shoes. I didn't stop. Near the center of the fields there were thin lakes of muddy water which I had to make my way around, my unrecognizable shoes making obscene noises as I lifted them out of the mire. With nothing to block

it the wind flung wet gusts at me; at any other time I would have felt like a fool slogging through mud and rain, only to look at a tree.

A little fog hung over the river so that as I neared it I felt myself becoming isolated from everything except the river and the few trees beside it. The wind was blowing more steadily here, and I was beginning to feel cold. I never wore a hat, and had forgotten gloves. There were several trees bleakly reaching into the fog. Any one of them might have been the one I was looking for. Unbelievable that there were other trees which looked like it here. It had loomed in my memory as a huge lone spike dominating the riverbank, forbidding as an artillery piece,[8] high as the beanstalk.[9] Yet here was a scattered grove of trees, none of them of any particular grandeur.

Moving through the soaked, coarse grass I began to examine each one closely, and finally identified the tree I was looking for by means of certain small scars rising along its trunk, and by a limb extending over the river, and another thinner limb growing near it. This was the tree, and it seemed to me standing there to resemble those men, the giants of your childhood, whom you encounter years later and find that they are not merely smaller in relation to your growth, but that they are absolutely smaller, shrunken by age. In this double demotion the old giants have become pigmies while you were looking the other way.

The tree was not only stripped by the cold season, it seemed weary from age, en-

---

6. salient (sāl′ yənt) *n*.: Projecting part or section.

7. lacrosse (lə krôs′) **fields:** Places where a game first played by Native Americans is played. Lacrosse is a game in which teams use long-handled pouched rackets to move a small rubber ball across the field into the opponents' goal.

8. artillery (är til′ ər ē) **piece**: A gun too heavy to carry that is mounted on wheels or on ships or planes.

9. beanstalk: An allusion to the beanstalk that reached up to the giant's kingdom in the sky in the fairy tale "Jack and the Beanstalk."

"It had loomed in my memory as a huge lone spike dominating the riverbank, forbidding as an artillery piece, high as the beanstalk."

feebled, dry. I was thankful, very thankful that I had seen it. So the more things remain the same, the more they change after all—*plus c'est la même chose, plus ça change.*[10] Nothing endures, not a tree, not love, not even a death by violence.

Changed, I headed back through the mud. I was drenched; anybody could see it was time to come in out of the rain.

The tree was tremendous, an irate, steely black steeple beside the river. I wasn't going to climb it. No one but Phineas[11] could think up such a crazy idea.

He of course saw nothing the slightest bit intimidating about it. He wouldn't, or wouldn't admit it if he did. Not Phineas.

"What I like best about this tree," he said in that voice of his, the equivalent in sound of a hypnotist's eyes, "what I like is that it's such a cinch!" He opened his green eyes wider and gave us his maniac look, and only the smirk on his wide mouth with its droll, slightly protruding upper lip reassured us that he wasn't completely goofy.

"Is that what you like best?" I said sarcastically. I said a lot of things sarcastically that summer; that was my sarcastic summer, 1942.

"Aey-uh," he said. This weird New England affirmative—maybe it is spelled "aie-huh"—always made me laugh, as Finny knew, so I had to laugh, which made me feel less sarcastic and less scared.

There were three others with us—Phineas in those days almost always moved in groups the size of a hockey team—and they stood with me looking with masked apprehension from him to the tree. Its soaring black trunk was set with rough wooden pegs leading up to a substantial limb which extended farther toward the water. Stand-ing on this limb, you could by a prodigious effort jump far enough out into the river for safety. So we had heard. At least the seventeen-year-old bunch could do it; but they had a crucial year's advantage over us. No Upper Middler,[12] which was the name for our class in the Devon School, had ever tried. Naturally Finny was going to be the first to try, and just as naturally he was going to inveigle[13] others, us, into trying it with him.

We were not even Upper Middler exactly. For this was the Summer Session, just established to keep up with the pace of the war. We were in shaky transit that summer from the groveling[14] status of Lower Middlers to the near-respectability of Upper Middlers. The class above, seniors, draft-bait,[15] practically soldiers, rushed ahead of us toward the war. They were caught up in accelerated courses and first-aid programs and a physical hardening regimen,[16] which included jumping from this tree. We were still calmly, numbly reading Virgil[17] and playing tag in the river farther downstream. Until Finny thought of the tree.

---

10. *plus c'est la même chose, plus ça change* (pluz se lǝ mem′ shōz pluz sa shanzh′)
11. Phineas (fin′ ē ǝs)

12. Upper Middler: A boy in the junior class at Devon School.
13. inveigle (in vē′ g'l) *v.*: Entice into doing something.
14. groveling (gruv′ liŋ) *adj.*: Crawling; humbling.
15. draft-bait *n.*: The age when young men would be drafted, or called up into the army. During World War II, all men between certain ages were subject to the draft. Although many young men and women enlisted, or volunteered to serve, most servicemen were drafted. Before the war started, the United States had an army of 1.6 million men. By the time the war was over, 15 million men and more than 200,000 women had served in the Armed Forces.
16. regimen (rej′ ǝ mǝn) *n.*: System. In this case, a system of exercises and other conditioning activities to prepare the students to fight in the war.
17. Virgil (vʉr′ jǝl): Name by which Publius Vergilius Maro (70–19 B.C.), Roman poet and author of the *Aeneid*, is known. The *Aeneid*, a story of Aeneas's wanderings and battles, is one of the great works that is often studied in a prep school like Devon. Such schools are noted for offering a classical education.

We stood looking up at it, four looks of consternation,[18] one of excitement. "Do you want to go first?" Finny asked us, rhetorically. We just looked quietly back at him, and so he began taking off his clothes, stripping down to his underpants. For such an extraordinary athlete—even as a Lower Middler Phineas had been the best athlete in the school—he was not spectacularly built. He was my height—five feet eight and a half inches (I had been claiming five feet nine inches before he became my roommate, but he had said in public with that simple, shocking self-acceptance of his, "No, you're the same height I am, five-eight and a half. We're on the short side"). He weighed a hundred and fifty pounds, a galling[19] ten pounds more than I did, which flowed from his legs to torso around shoulders to arms and full strong neck in an uninterrupted, unemphatic[20] unity of strength.

He began scrambling up the wooden pegs nailed to the side of the tree, his back muscles working like a panther's. The pegs didn't seem strong enough to hold his weight. At last he stepped onto the branch which reached a little farther toward the water. "Is this the one they jump from?" None of us knew. "If I do it, you're all going to do it, aren't you?" We didn't say anything very clearly. "Well," he cried out, "here's my contribution to the war effort!" and he sprang out, fell through the tops of some lower branches, and smashed into the water.

"Great!" he said, bobbing instantly to the surface again, his wet hair plastered in droll bangs on his forehead. "That's the most fun I've had this week. Who's next?"

I was. This tree flooded me with a sensation of alarm all the way to my tingling fingers. My head began to feel unnaturally light, and the vague rustling sounds from the nearby woods came to me as though muffled and filtered. I must have been entering a mild state of shock. Insulated by this, I took off my clothes and started to climb the pegs. I don't remember saying anything. The branch he had jumped from was slenderer than it looked from the ground and much higher. It was impossible to walk out on it far enough to be well over the river. I would have to spring far out or risk falling into the shallow water next to the bank. "Come on," drawled Finny from below, "stop standing there showing off." I recognized with automatic tenseness that the view was very impressive from here. "When they torpedo the troopship," he shouted, "you can't stand around admiring the view. Jump!"

What was I doing here anyway? Why did I let Finny talk me into stupid things like this? Was he getting some kind of hold over me?

"Jump!"

With the sensation that I was throwing my life away, I jumped into space. Some tips of branches snapped past me and then I crashed into the water. My legs hit the soft mud of the bottom, and immediately I was on the surface being congratulated. I felt fine.

"I think that was better than Finny's," said Elwin—better known as Leper[21]—Lepellier, who was bidding for an ally in the dispute he foresaw.

"All right, pal," Finny spoke in his cordial, penetrating voice, that reverberant[22]

18. consternation (kăn′ stər nā′ shən) n.: Fear or shock.
19. galling (gôl′ iŋ) adj.: Very annoying; irritating.
20. unemphatic (un em fat′ ik) adj.: Without emphasis; not forcible or definite.
21. Leper (lep′ ər): Nickname taken from Elwin Lepellier's last name that literally means someone suffering from the disease of leprosy. Throughout history, people have often shunned lepers because they fear catching the disease and because it disfigures its victims.
22. reverberant (ri vʉr′ bər ənt) adj.: Reechoing.

instrument in his chest, "don't start awarding prizes until you've passed the course. The tree is waiting."

Leper closed his mouth as though forever. He didn't argue or refuse. He didn't back away. He became inanimate.[23] But the other two, Chet Douglass and Bobby Zane, were vocal enough, complaining shrilly about school regulations, the danger of stomach cramps, physical disabilities they had never mentioned before.

"It's you, pal," Finny said to me at last, "just you and me." He and I started back across the fields, preceding the others like two seigneurs.[24]

We were the best of friends at that moment.

"You were very good," said Finny good-humoredly, "once I shamed you into it."

"You didn't shame anybody into anything."

"Oh yes I did. I'm good for you that way. You have a tendency to back away from things otherwise."

"I never backed away from anything in my life!" I cried, my indignation at this charge naturally stronger because it was so true. "You're goofy!"

Phineas just walked serenely on, or rather flowed on, rolling forward in his white sneakers with such unthinking unity of movement that "walk" didn't describe it.

I went along beside him across the enormous playing fields toward the gym. Underfoot the healthy green turf was brushed with dew, and ahead of us we could see a faint green haze hanging above the grass, shot through with the twilight sun. Phineas stopped talking for once, so that now I could hear cricket noises and bird cries of dusk, a gymnasium truck gunning along an empty athletic road a quarter of a mile away, a burst of faint, isolated laughter carried to us from the back door of the gym, and then over all, cool and matriarchal,[25] the six o'clock bell from the Academy Building cupola,[26] the calmest, most carrying bell toll in the world, civilized, calm, invincible, and final.

The toll sailed over the expansive tops of all the elms, the great slanting roofs and formidable chimneys of the dormitories, the narrow and brittle old housetops, across the open New Hampshire sky to us coming back from the river. "We'd better hurry or we'll be late for dinner," I said, breaking into what Finny called my "West Point[27] stride." Phineas didn't really dislike West Point in particular or authority in general, but just considered authority the necessary evil against which happiness was achieved by reaction, the backboard which returned all the insults he threw at it. My "West Point stride" was intolerable; his right foot flashed into the middle of my fast walk and I went pitching forward into the grass. "Get those hundred and fifty pounds off me!" I shouted, because he was sitting on my back. Finny got up, patted my head genially, and moved on across the field, not deigning to glance around for my counterattack, but relying on his extrasensory ears, his ability to feel in the air someone coming on him from behind. As I sprang at him he side-stepped easily, but I just managed to kick him as I shot past. He caught my leg and there was a brief wrestling match on the turf which he won. "Better hurry," he said, "or they'll put

<hr />

23. **inanimate** (in an′ ə mit) *adj.*: Dull; spiritless; not alive.
24. **seigneurs** (sen yɥrz′) *n.*: Men of rank; feudal lords.

25. **matriarchal** (mā′ trē är′ k′l) *adj.*: Motherly. In this case stately and dignified.
26. **cupola** (kyo͞o′ pə lə) *n.*: A small domelike structure on a roof.
27. **West Point:** The United States Military Academy, so-called because it is located on the west bank of the Hudson River in New York State.

you in the guardhouse.''[28] We were walking again, faster; Bobby and Leper and Chet were urging us from ahead to hurry up, and then Finny trapped me again in his strongest trap, that is, I suddenly became his collaborator. As we walked rapidly along I abruptly resented the bell and my West Point stride and hurrying and conforming. Finny was right. And there was only one way to show him this. I threw my hip against his, catching him by surprise, and he was instantly down, definitely pleased. This was why he liked me so much. When I jumped on top of him, my knees on his chest, he couldn't ask for anything better. We struggled in some equality for a while, and then when we were sure we were too late for dinner, we broke off.

He and I passed the gym and came on toward the first group of dormitories, which were dark and silent. There were only two hundred of us at Devon in the summer, not enough to fill most of the school. We passed the sprawling Headmaster's house[29]— empty, he was doing something for the government in Washington; past the Chapel —empty again, used only for a short time in the mornings; past the First Academy Building, where there were some dim lights shining from a few of its many windows, Masters[30] at work in their classrooms there; down a short slope into the broad and well-clipped Common, on which light fell from the big surrounding Georgian buildings.[31] A dozen boys were loafing there on the grass after dinner, and a kitchen rattle from the wing of one of the buildings accompanied their talk. The sky was darkening steadily, which brought up the lights in the dormitories and the old houses; a loud phonograph a long way off played "Don't Sit Under the Apple Tree," rejected that and played "They're Either Too Young or Too Old," grew more ambitious with *The Warsaw Concerto,* mellower with *The Nutcracker Suite,*[32] and then stopped.

Finny and I went to our room. Under the yellow study lights we read our Hardy assignments; I was halfway through *Tess of the D'Urbervilles,* he carried on his baffled struggle with *Far from the Madding Crowd,*[33] amused that there should be people named Gabriel Oak and Bathsheba Everdene. Our illegal radio, turned too low to be intelligible, was broadcasting the news. Outside there was a rustling early summer movement of the wind; the seniors, allowed out later than we were, came fairly quietly back as the bell sounded ten stately times. Boys ambled past our door toward the bathroom, and there was a period of steadily pouring shower water. Then lights began to snap out all over the school. We undressed, and I put on some pajamas, but Phineas, who had heard they were unmilitary, didn't; there was the silence in which it was understood we were saying some prayers, and then that summer school day came to an end.

---

28. guardhouse (gärd′ hous′) *n.*: A building where military prisoners are kept.
29. Headmaster's house: The home of the person who in a public school would be the principal.
30. Masters: Teachers.
31. Georgian (jôr′ jən) **buildings**: Those built in the style prevalent during the reign of King George V of England.

32. "Don't Sit . . . *Nutcracker Suite*: The first two songs were popular during World War II, because they were about being faithful to an absent serviceman and the shortage of eligible men at home. The last two are classical pieces by Addinsell and Tschaikowsky.
33. Hardy assignments . . . *Madding Crowd*: A reference to Thomas Hardy (1840–1928), English novelist and poet and to assignments to read two of the novels he wrote.

Chapter 2

Our absence from dinner had been noticed. The following morning—the clean-washed shine of summer mornings in the north country—Mr. Prud'homme[1] stopped at our door. He was broad-shouldered, grave, and he wore a gray business suit. He did not have the careless, almost British look of most of the Devon Masters, because he was a substitute for the summer. He enforced such rules as he knew; missing dinner was one of them.

We had been swimming in the river, Finny explained; then there had been a wrestling match, then there was that sunset that anybody would want to watch, then there'd been several friends we had to see on business—he rambled on, his voice soaring and plunging in its vibrant sound box, his eyes now and then widening to fire a flash of green across the room. Standing in the shadows, with the bright window behind him, he blazed with sunburned health. As Mr. Prud'homme looked at him and listened to the scatterbrained eloquence of his explanation, he could be seen rapidly losing his grip on sternness.

"If you hadn't already missed nine meals in the last two weeks . . ." he broke in.

But Finny pressed his advantage. Not because he wanted to be forgiven for missing the meal—that didn't interest him at all, he might have rather enjoyed the punishment if it was done in some novel[2] and unknown way. He pressed his advantage because he saw that Mr. Prud'homme was pleased, won over in spite of himself. The Master was slipping from his official position momentar-

ily, and it was just possible, if Phineas pressed hard enough, that there might be a flow of simple, unregulated friendliness between them, and such flows were one of Finny's reasons for living.

"The real reason, sir, was that we just had to jump out of that tree. You know that tree . . ." I knew, Mr. Prud'homme must have known, Finny knew, if he stopped to think, that jumping out of the tree was even more forbidden than missing a meal. "We had to do that, naturally," he went on, "because we're all getting ready for the war. What if they lower the draft age to seventeen? Gene and I are both going to be seventeen at the end of the summer, which is a very convenient time since it's the start of the academic year and there's never any doubt about which class you should be in. Leper Lepellier is already seventeen, and if I'm not mistaken he will be draftable before the end of this next academic year, and so conceivably he ought to have been in the class ahead, he ought to have been a senior now, if you see what I mean, so that he would have been graduated and been all set to be drafted. But we're all right, Gene and I are perfectly all right. There isn't any question that we are conforming in every possible way to everything that's happening and everything that's going to happen. It's all a question of birthdays, unless you want to be more specific and look at it from the sexual point of view, which I have never cared to do myself, since it's a question of my mother and my father, and I have never felt I wanted to think about their sexual lives too much." Everything he said was true and sincere; Finny always said what he happened to be thinking, and if this stunned people then he was surprised.

Mr. Prud'homme released his breath with a sort of amazed laugh, stared at Finny for a while, and that was all there was to it.

---

1. Prud'homme (prud ŏm′)
2. novel (năv′ 'l) *adj.*: New and unusual.

This was the way the Masters tended to treat us that summer. They seemed to be modifying their usual attitude of floating, chronic disapproval. During the winter most of them regarded anything unexpected in a student with suspicion, seeming to feel that anything we said or did was potentially illegal. Now on these clear June days in New Hampshire they appeared to uncoil, they seemed to believe that we were with them about half the time, and only spent the other half trying to make fools of them.

A streak of tolerance was detectable; Finny decided that they were beginning to show commendable signs of maturity.

It was partly his doing. The Devon faculty had never before experienced a student who combined a calm ignorance of the rules with a winning urge to be good, who seemed to love the school truly and deeply, and never more than when he was breaking the regulations, a model boy who was most comfortable in the truant's corner. The faculty threw up its

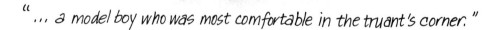

" ... a model boy who was most comfortable in the truant's corner. "

hands over Phineas, and so loosened its grip on all of us.

But there was another reason. I think we reminded them of what peace was like, we boys of sixteen. We were registered with no draft board,[3] we had taken no physical examinations. No one had ever tested us for hernia or color blindness. Trick knees and punctured eardrums were minor complaints and not yet disabilities which would separate a few from the fate of the rest.[4] We were careless and wild, and I suppose we could be thought of as a sign of the life the war was being fought to preserve. Anyway, they were more indulgent toward us than at any other time; they snapped at the heels of the seniors, driving and molding and arming them for the war. They noticed our games tolerantly. We reminded them of what peace was like, of lives which were not bound up with destruction.

Phineas was the essence of this careless peace. Not that he was unconcerned about the war. After Mr. Prud'homme left he began to dress, that is he began reaching for whatever clothes were nearest, some of them mine. Then he stopped to consider, and went over to the dresser. Out of one of the drawers he lifted a finely woven broadcloth shirt, carefully cut, and very pink.

"What's *that* thing?"

"This is a tablecloth," he said out of the side of his mouth.

"No, cut it out. What is it?"

"This," he then answered with some pride, "is going to be my emblem. Ma sent it up last week. Did you ever see stuff like this, and a color like this? It doesn't even button all the way down. You have to pull it over your head, like this."

"Over your head? Pink! It makes you look ridiculous!"

"Does it?" He used this preoccupied tone when he was thinking of something more interesting than what you had said. But his mind always recorded what was said and played it back to him when there was time, so as he was buttoning the high collar in front of the mirror he said mildly, "I wonder what would happen if I looked ridiculous to everyone."

"You're nuts."

"Well, in case suitors begin clamoring at the door, you can tell them I'm wearing this as an emblem." He turned around to let me admire it. "I was reading in the paper that we bombed Central Europe[5] for the first time the other day." Only someone who knew Phineas as well as I did could realize that he was not changing the subject. I waited quietly for him to make whatever fantastic connection there might be between this and his shirt. "Well, we've got to do something to *celebrate*. We haven't got a flag, we can't float Old Glory proudly out the window. So I'm going to wear this, as an emblem."

He did wear it. No one else in the school could have done so without some risk of having it torn from his back. When the sternest of the Summer Sessions Masters, old Mr. Patch-Withers, came up to him after history class and asked about it, I watched his drawn but pink face become pinker with amusement as Finny politely explained the meaning of the shirt.

It was hypnotism. I was beginning to see that Phineas could get away with anything. I couldn't help envying him that a little, which was perfectly normal. There was no harm in envying even your best friend a little.

---

3. draft board: An official board of civilians that selects qualified persons to serve in the U.S. armed forces.

4. No one . . . of the rest: Any of the disabilities mentioned was enough to disqualify a person from serving in the armed forces.

5. Central Europe: Germany and Austria.

In the afternoon Mr. Patch-Withers, who was substitute Headmaster for the summer, offered the traditional term tea to the Upper Middle class. It was held in the deserted Headmaster's house, and Mr. Patch-Withers' wife trembled at every cup tinkle. We were in a kind of sun porch and conservatory[6] combined, spacious and damp and without many plants. Those there were had large nonflowering stalks, with big barbaric[7] leaves. The chocolate brown wicker furniture shot out menacing twigs, and three dozen of us stood tensely teetering our cups amid the wicker and leaves, trying hard not to sound as inane[8] in our conversation with the four present Masters and their wives as they sounded to us.

Phineas had soaked and brushed his hair for the occasion. This gave his head a sleek look, which was contradicted by the surprised, honest expression which he wore on his face. His ears, I had never noticed before, were fairly small and set close to his head, and combined with his plastered hair they now gave his bold nose and cheekbones the sharp look of a prow.[9]

He alone talked easily. He discussed the bombing of Central Europe. No one else happened to have seen the story, and since Phineas could not recall exactly what target in which country had been hit, or whether it was the American, British, or even Russian air force which had hit it, or what day he read it in which newspaper, the discussion was one-sided.

That didn't matter. It was the event which counted. But after a while Finny felt he should carry the discussion to others. "I think we ought to bomb the daylights out of them, as long as we don't hit any women or children or old people, don't you?" he was saying to Mrs. Patch-Withers, perched nervously behind her urn.[10] "Or hospitals," he went on. "And naturally no schools. Or churches."

"We must also be careful about works of art," she put in, "if they are of permanent value."

"A lot of nonsense," Mr. Patch-Withers grumbled, with a flushed face. "How do you expect our boys to be as precise as that thousands of feet up with bombs weighing tons! Look at what the Germans did to Amsterdam! Look at what they did to Coventry!"[11]

"The Germans aren't the Central Europeans, dear," his wife said very gently.

He didn't like being brought up short. But he seemed to be just able to bear it, from his wife. After a temperamental pause he said gruffly, "There isn't any 'permanent art' in Central Europe anyway."

Finny was enjoying this. He unbuttoned his seersucker jacket, as though he needed greater body freedom for the discussion. Mrs. Patch-Withers' glance then happened to fall on his belt. In a tentative voice she said, "Isn't that the . . . our . . ." Her husband looked; I panicked. In his haste that morning Finny had not unexpectedly used a tie for a belt. But this morning the first tie at hand had been the Devon School tie.

This time he wasn't going to get away with it. I could feel myself becoming unexpectedly excited at that. Mr. Patch-Withers' face was reaching a brilliant shade, and his

---

6. conservatory (kən sur′ və tôr′ ē) *n*.: Greenhouse.
7. barbaric (bär ber′ ik) *adj*.: Uncivilized; wild.
8. inane (in ān′) *adj*.: Empty; foolish; silly.
9. prow (prou) *n*.: The forward part of a ship; the bow.

10. urn (urn) *n*.: Teapot.
11. Amsterdam (am′ stər dam′) and **Coventry** (kuv′ ən trē): Capital city of the Netherlands and city in central England that were devastated by German bombing raids.

wife's head fell as though before the guillotine.[12] Even Finny seemed to color a little, unless it was the reflection from his pink shirt. But his expression was composed, and he said in his resonant voice, "I wore this, you see, because it goes with the shirt and it all ties in together—I didn't mean that to be a pun,[13] I don't think they're very funny, especially in polite company, do you?—it all ties in together with what we've been talking about, this bombing in Central Europe, because when you come right down to it the school is involved in everything that happens in the war, it's all the same war and the same world, and I think Devon ought to be included. I don't know whether you think the way I do on that."

Mr. Patch-Withers' face had been shifting expressions and changing colors continuously, and now it settled into fixed surprise. "I never heard anything so illogical as that in my life!" He didn't sound very indignant, though. "That's probably the strangest tribute this school has had in a hundred and sixty years." He seemed pleased or amused in some unknown corner of his mind. Phineas was going to get away with even this.

His eyes gave their wider, magical gleam and his voice continued on a more compelling level, "Although I have to admit I didn't think of that when I put it on this morning." He smiled pleasantly after supplying this interesting additional information. Mr. Patch-Withers settled into a hearty silence at this, and so Finny added, "I'm glad I put on *something* for a belt! I certainly would hate the embarrassment of having my pants fall down at the Headmaster's tea. Of course he isn't here. But it would be just as embarrassing in front of you and Mrs. Patch-Withers," and he smiled politely down at her.

Mr. Patch-Withers' laughter surprised us all, including himself. His face, whose shades we had often labeled, now achieved a new one. Phineas was very happy; sour and stern Mr. Patch-Withers had been given a good laugh for once, and he had done it! He broke into the charmed, thoughtless grin of a man fulfilled.

He had gotten away with everything. I felt a sudden stab of disappointment. That was because I just wanted to see some more excitement; that must have been it.

We left the party, both of us feeling fine. I laughed along with Finny, my best friend, and also unique, able to get away with anything at all. And not because he was a conniver[14] either; I was sure of that. He got away with everything because of the extraordinary kind of person he was. It was quite a compliment to me, as a matter of fact, to have such a person choose me for his best friend.

Finny never left anything alone, not when it was well enough, not when it was perfect. "Let's go jump in the river," he said under his breath as we went out of the sun porch. He forced compliance by leaning against me as we walked along, changing my direction; like a police car squeezing me to the side of the road, he directed me unwillingly toward the gym and the river. "We need to clear our heads of that party," he said, "all that talk!"

"Yes. It sure was boring. Who did most of the talking anyway?"

---

12. guillotine (gĭl′ ə tēn) *n.*: An instrument used during the French Revolution for beheading people by a heavy blade dropped between two grooved uprights.
13. pun (pŭn) *n.*: The humorous use of a word, or of words, that sound alike but have different meanings; a play on words. In this case Finny uses the verb *ties* to explain why he is wearing the school tie as a belt.

14. conniver (kə nīv′ ər) *n.*: One who schemes in an underhanded way.

Finny concentrated. "Mr. Patch-Withers was pretty gassy, and his wife, and . . ."

"Yeah. And?"

Turning a look of mock shock on me, "You don't mean to infer that *I* talked too much!"

Returning, with interest, his gaping shock, "You? Talk too much? How can you accuse me of accusing you of that!" As I said, this was my sarcastic summer. It was only long after that I recognized sarcasm as the protest of people who are weak.

We walked along through the shining afternoon to the river. "I don't really believe we bombed Central Europe, do you?" said Finny thoughtfully. The dormitories we passed were massive and almost anonymous behind their thick layers of ivy, big, old-looking leaves you would have thought stayed there winter and summer, permanent hanging gardens[15] in New Hampshire. Between the buildings, elms curved so high that you ceased to remember their height until you looked above the familiar trunks and the lowest umbrellas of leaves and took in the lofty complex they held high above, branches and branches of branches, a world of branches with an infinity of leaves. They too seemed permanent and never-changing, an untouched, unreachable world high in space, like the ornamental towers and spires of a great church, too high to be enjoyed, too high for anything, great and remote and never useful. "No, I don't think I believe it either," I answered.

Far ahead of us four boys, looking like white flags on the endless green playing fields, crossed toward the tennis courts. To the right of them the gym meditated behind its gray walls, the high, wide, oval-topped windows shining back at the sun. Beyond the gym and the fields began the woods, our, the Devon School's woods, which in my imagination were the beginning of the great northern forests. I thought that, from the Devon Woods, trees reached in an unbroken, widening corridor so far to the north that no one had ever seen the other end, somewhere up in the far unorganized tips of Canada. We seemed to be playing on the tame fringe of the last and greatest wilderness. I never found out whether this is so and perhaps it is.

Bombs in Central Europe were completely unreal to us here, not because we couldn't imagine it—a thousand newspaper photographs and newsreels had given us a pretty accurate idea of such a sight—but because our place here was too fair for us to accept something like that. We spent that summer in complete selfishness, I'm happy to say. The people in the world who could be selfish in the summer of 1942 were a small band, and I'm glad we took advantage of it.

"The first person who says anything unpleasant will get a swift kick in the ass," said Finny reflectively as we came to the river.

"All right."

"Are you still afraid to jump out of the tree?"

"There's something unpleasant about that question, isn't there?"

"That question? No, of course not. It depends on how you answer it."

"Afraid to jump out of that tree? I expect it'll be a very pleasant jump."

After we had swum around in the water for a while Finny said, "Will you do me the pleasure of jumping out of the tree first?"

"My pleasure."

Rigid, I began climbing the rungs, slight-

---

15. hanging gardens: An allusion to the Hanging Gardens of Babylon, built by Nebuchadnezzar about 600 B.C. One of the Seven Wonders of the World, the gardens were built within the walls of the royal palace and were laid out on a series of terraces. Gene compares the ivy that looks as if it will continue to grow all over the walls of the dormitories with these Babylonian gardens, of which nothing remains.

ly reassured by having Finny right behind me. "We'll jump together to cement our partnership," he said. "We'll form a suicide society, and the membership requirement is one jump out of this tree."

"A suicide society," I said stiffly. "The Suicide Society of the Summer Session."

"Good! The *Super* Suicide Society of the Summer Session! How's that?"

"That's fine, that's okay."

We were standing on a limb, I a little farther out than Finny. I turned to say something else, some stalling remark, something to delay even a few seconds more, and then I realized that in turning I had begun to lose my balance. There was a moment of total, impersonal panic, and then Finny's hand shot out and grabbed my arm, and with my balance restored, the panic immediately disappeared. I turned back toward the river,

" *There was a moment of total, impersonal panic, and then Finny's hand shot out and grabbed my arm, ...* "

moved a few more steps along the limb, sprang far out and fell into the deep water. Finny also made a good jump, and the Super Suicide Society of the Summer Session was officially established.

It was only after dinner, when I was on my way alone to the library, that the full danger I had brushed on the limb shook me again. If Finny hadn't come up right behind me . . . if he hadn't been there . . . I could have fallen on the bank and broken my back! If I had fallen awkwardly enough I could have been killed. Finny had practically saved my life.

Chapter 3

Yes, he had practically saved my life. He had also practically lost it for me. I wouldn't have been on that limb except for him. I wouldn't have turned around, and so lost my balance, if he hadn't been there. I didn't need to feel any tremendous rush of gratitude toward Phineas.

The Super Suicide Society of the Summer Session was a success from the start. That night Finny began to talk abstractedly[1] about it, as though it were a venerable,[2] entrenched institution of the Devon School. The half-dozen friends who were there in our room listening began to bring up small questions on details without ever quite saying that they had never heard of such a club. Schools are supposed to be catacombed[3] with secret societies and underground brotherhoods, and as far as they knew here was one which had just come to the surface. They signed up as "trainees" on the spot.

We began to meet every night to initiate[4] them. The Charter Members, he and I, had to open every meeting by jumping ourselves. This was the first of the many rules which Finny created without notice during the summer. I hated it. I never got inured[5] to the jumping. At every meeting the limb seemed higher, thinner, the deeper water harder to reach. Every time, when I got myself into position to jump, I felt a flash of disbelief that I was doing anything so perilous. But I always jumped. Otherwise I would have lost face with Phineas, and that would have been unthinkable.

We met every night, because Finny's life was ruled by inspiration and anarchy, and so he prized a set of rules. His own, not those imposed on him by other people, such as the faculty of the Devon School. The Super Suicide Society of the Summer Session was a club; clubs by definition met regularly; we met every night. Nothing could be more regular than that. To meet once a week seemed to him much less regular, entirely too haphazard, bordering on carelessness.

I went along; I never missed a meeting. At that time it would never have occurred to me to say, "I don't feel like it tonight," which was the plain truth every night. I was subject to the dictates of my mind, which gave me the maneuverability of a straitjacket.[6] "We're off, pal," Finny would call out, and acting against every instinct of my nature, I went without a thought of protest.

As we drifted on through the summer,

1. abstractedly (ab strak′ tid lē) *adv.*: Absent-mindedly.
2. venerable (ven′ ər ə b'l) *adj.*: Long-established; impressive on account of age.
3. catacombed (kat′ ə kōm′ 'd) *adj.*: Full of; riddled with.

4. initiate (i nish′ ē āt′) *v.*: Admit as a member of a club.
5. inured (in yoor′d′) **to**: Accustomed to; used to.
6. maneauverability (mə noo′ vər ə bil′ ə tē) **of a straitjacket** (strāt′ jak′ it): Ability to move as if confined in a coatlike device used to restrain people who are in a violent state. In other words, Gene was not able to move at all.

with this one inflexible appointment every day—classes could be cut, meals missed, Chapel skipped—I noticed something about Finny's own mind, which was such an opposite from mine. It wasn't completely unleashed after all. I noticed that he did abide by certain rules, which he seemed to cast in the form of Commandments.[7] "Never say you are five feet nine when you are five feet eight and a half" was the first one I encountered. Another was, "Always say some prayers at night."

But the one which had the most urgent influence in his life was, "You always win at sports." This "you" was collective. Everyone always won at sports. When you played a game you won, in the same way as when you sat down to a meal you ate it. It inevitably and naturally followed. Finny never permitted himself to realize that when you won they lost. That would have destroyed the perfect beauty which was sport. Nothing bad ever happened in sports; they were the absolute good.

He was disgusted with that summer's athletic program—a little tennis, some swimming, clumsy softball games, badminton.[8] "Badminton!" he exploded the day it entered the schedule. He said nothing else, but the shocked, outraged, despairing note of anguish in the word said all the rest. *"Badminton!"*

"At least it's not as bad as the seniors," I said, handing him the fragile racquet and the fey shuttlecock. "They're doing calisthenics."[9]

"What are they trying to do?" He swatted the shuttlecock the length of the locker room. "Destroy us?" Humor infiltrated the outrage in his voice, which meant that he was thinking of a way out.

We went outside into the cordial afternoon sunshine. The playing fields were optimistically green and empty before us. The tennis courts were full. The softball diamond was busy. A pattern of badminton nets swayed sensually in the breeze. Finny eyed them with quiet astonishment. Far down the fields toward the river there was a wooden tower about ten feet high where the instructor had stood to direct the senior calisthenics. It was empty now. The seniors had been trotted off to the improvised obstacle course[10] in the woods, or to have their blood pressure taken again, or to undergo an insidious[11] exercise in The Cage which consisted in stepping up on a box and down again in rapid rhythm for five minutes. They were off somewhere, shaping up for the war. All of the fields were ours.

Finny began to walk slowly in the direction of the tower. Perhaps he was thinking that we might carry it the rest of the way to the river and throw it in; perhaps he was just interested in looking at it, as he was in everything. Whatever he thought, he forgot it when we reached the tower. Beside it someone had left a large and heavy leather-covered ball, a medicine ball.

He picked it up. "Now this, you see, is everything in the world you need for sports. When they discovered the circle they created sports. As for this thing," embracing the medicine ball in his left arm he held up the

---

7. Commandments (kə mand' mənts) *n.:* A reference to the Ten Commandments in the Bible (Exodus 20).
8. badminton (bad' min t'n) *n.:* A game in which a feathered shuttlecock is batted back and forth with light rackets across a net.
9. calisthenics (kal' əs then' iks) *n.:* Physical fitness exercises.

10. obstacle course: A pathway presenting obstructions such as walls to be climbed over, tunnels to be crawled through, and so on.
11. insidious (in sid' ē əs) *adj.:* Treacherous; more dangerous than apparent.

shuttlecock, contaminated, in his out-stretched right, "this idiot tickler, the only thing it's good for is eeny-meeny-miney-mo." He dropped the ball and proceeded to pick the feathers out of the shuttlecock, distastefully, as though removing ticks from a dog. The remaining rubber plug he then threw out of sight down the field, with a single lunge ending in a powerful downward thrust of his wrist. Badminton was gone.

He stood balancing the medicine ball, enjoying the feel of it. "All you really need is a round ball."

Although he was rarely conscious of it, Phineas was always being watched, like the weather. Up the field the others at badminton sensed a shift in the wind; their voices carried down to us, calling us. When we didn't come, they began gradually to come down to us.

"I think it's about time we started to get a little *exercise* around here, don't you?" he said, cocking his head at me. Then he slowly looked around at the others with the expression of dazed determination he used when the object was to carry people along with his latest idea. He blinked twice, and then said, "We can always start with this ball."

"Let's make it have something to do with the war," suggested Bobby Zane. "Like a blitzkrieg[12] or something."

"Blitzkrieg," repeated Finny doubtfully.

"We could figure out some kind of blitzkrieg baseball," I said.

"We'll call it blitzkrieg ball," said Bobby.

"Or just blitzball," reflected Finny. "Yes, blitzball." Then, with an expectant glance around, "Well, let's get started," he threw the big, heavy ball at me. I grasped it against my chest with both arms. "Well, run!" ordered Finny. "No, not *that* way!

Toward the river! Run!" I headed toward the river surrounded by the others in a hesitant herd; they sensed that in all probability they were my adversaries in blitzball. "Don't hog it!" Finny yelled. "Throw it to somebody else. Otherwise, naturally," he talked steadily as he ran along beside me, "now that we've got you surrounded, one of us will knock you down."

"Do what!" I veered away from him, hanging on to the clumsy ball. "What kind of a game is that?"

"Blitzball!" Chet Douglass shouted, throwing himself around my legs, knocking me down.

"That naturally was completely illegal," said Finny. "You don't use your *arms* when you knock the ball carrier down."

"You don't?" mumbled Chet from on top of me.

"No. You keep your arms crossed like this on your chest, and you just butt the ball carrier. No elbowing allowed either. All right, Gene, start again."

I began quickly. "Wouldn't somebody else have possession of the ball after—"

"Not when you've been knocked down illegally. The ball carrier retains possession in a case like that. So it's perfectly okay, you still have the ball. Go ahead."

There was nothing to do but start running again, with the others trampling with stronger will around me. "Throw it!" ordered Phineas. Bobby Zane was more or less in the clear and so I threw it at him; it was so heavy that he had to scoop my throw up from the ground. "Perfectly okay," commented Finny, running forward at top speed, "perfectly okay for the ball to touch the ground when it is being passed." Bobby doubled back closer to me for protection. "Knock him down," Finny yelled at me.

"Knock him down! Are you crazy? He's on my team!"

---

12. blitzkrieg (blits' krēg') *n.*: Sudden, overwhelming attack; a tactic used by the Germans during World War II.

"There aren't any teams in blitzball," he yelled somewhat irritably, "we're all enemies. Knock him down!"

I knocked him down. "All right," said Finny as he disentangled us. "Now you have possession again." He handed the leaden ball to me.

"I would have thought that possession passed—"

"Naturally you gained possession of the ball when you knocked him down. Run."

So I began running again. Leper Lepellier was loping along outside my perimeter, not noticing the game, taggling along without reason, like a porpoise escorting a passing ship. "Leper!" I threw the ball past a few heads at him.

Taken by surprise, Leper looked up in anguish, shrank away from the ball, and voiced his first thought, a typical one. "I don't want it!"

"Stop, stop!" cried Finny in a referee's tone. Everybody halted, and Finny retrieved the ball; he talked better holding it. "Now Leper has just brought out a really important fine point of the game. The receiver can *refuse* a pass if he happens to choose to. Since we're all enemies, we can and will turn on each other all the time. We call that the Lepellier Refusal." We all nodded without speaking. "Here, Gene, the ball is of course still yours."

"Still mine? Nobody else has had the ball but me, for God sakes!"

"They'll get their chance. Now if you are refused three times in the course of running from the tower to the river, you go all the way back to the tower and start over. Naturally."

Blitzball was the surprise of the summer. Everybody played it; I believe a form of it is still popular at Devon. But nobody can be playing it as it was played by Phineas. He had unconsciously invented a game which brought his own athletic gifts to their highest pitch. The odds were tremendously against the ball carrier, so that Phineas was driven to exceed himself practically every day when he carried the ball. To escape the wolf pack which all the other players became he created reverses and deceptions and acts of sheer mass hypnotism which were so extraordinary that they surprised even him; after some of these plays I would notice him chuckling quietly to himself, in a kind of happy disbelief. In such a nonstop game he also had the natural advantage of a flow of energy which I never saw interrupted. I never saw him tired, never really winded, never overcharged and never restless. At dawn, all day long, and at midnight, Phineas always had a steady and formidable flow of usable energy.

Right from the start, it was clear that no one had ever been better adapted to a sport than Finny was to blitzball. I saw that right away. Why not? He had made it up, hadn't he? It needn't be surprising that he was sensationally good at it, and that the rest of us were more or less bumblers in our different ways. I suppose it served us right for letting him do all the planning. I didn't really think about it myself. What difference did it make? It was just a game. It was good that Finny could shine at it. He could also shine at many other things, with people for instance, the others in our dormitory, the faculty; in fact, if you stopped to think about it, Finny could shine with everyone, he attracted everyone he met. I was glad of that too. Naturally. He was my roommate and my best friend.

Everyone has a moment in history which belongs particularly to him. It is the moment when his emotions achieve their most powerful sway over him, and afterward when you say to this person "the world today" or "life" or "reality" he will assume that you mean this moment, even if it is fifty years past. The world, through his unleashed emotions, imprinted itself upon him, and he carries the stamp of that passing moment forever.

For me, this moment—four years is a moment in history—was the war. The war was and is reality for me. I still instinctively live and think in its atmosphere. These are some of its characteristics: Franklin Delano Roosevelt is the President of the United States, and he always has been. The other two eternal world leaders are Winston Churchill[13] and Josef Stalin.[14] America is not, never has been, and never will be what the songs and poems call it, a land of plenty. Nylon, meat, gasoline, and steel are rare. There are too many jobs and not enough workers. Money is very easy to earn but rather hard to spend, because there isn't very much to buy. Trains are always late and always crowded with "servicemen." The war will always be fought very far from America and it will never end. Nothing in America stands still for very long, including the people, who are always either leaving or on leave.[15] People in America cry often. Sixteen is the key and crucial and natural age for a human being to be, and people of all other ages are ranged in an orderly manner ahead of and behind you as a harmonious setting for the sixteen-year-olds of this world. When you are sixteen, adults are slightly impressed and almost intimidated by you. This is a puzzle, finally solved by the realization that they foresee your military future, fighting for them. You do not foresee it. To waste anything in America is immoral. String and tinfoil are treasures. Newspapers are always crowded with strange maps and names of towns, and every few months the earth seems to lurch from its path when you see something in the newspapers, such as the time Mussolini, who had almost seemed one of the eternal leaders, is photographed hanging upside down on a meathook.[16] Everyone listens to news broadcasts five or six times every day. All pleasurable things, all travel and sports and entertainment and good food and fine clothes, are in the very shortest supply, always were and always will be. There are just tiny fragments of pleasure and luxury in the world, and there is something unpatriotic about enjoying them. All foreign lands are inaccessible except to servicemen; they are vague, distant, and sealed off as though behind a curtain of plastic. The prevailing color of life in America is a dull, dark green called olive drab.[17] That color is always respectable and always important. Most other colors risk being unpatriotic.

It is this special America, a very untypical one I guess, an unfamiliar transitional blur in the memories of most people, which is the real America for me. In that short-lived and special country we spent this summer at Devon when Finny achieved certain feats as an athlete. In such a period no one notices or rewards any achievements involving the body unless the result is to kill it or

---

13. Winston Churchill (1871–1947): Prime Minister of Great Britain during World War II.
14. Josef Stalin (1879–1953): Premier of the Soviet Union during World War II.
15. leaving or on leave: A reference to people leaving home to serve in the armed forces or coming home for a vacation from the armed forces.

16. Mussolini . . . meathook: Benito Mussolini (1882–1945), dictator of Italy during World War II, was killed by members of the Italian Resistance, and his body was hung with a meathook upside down in a gas station.
17. olive drab: The color of many uniforms of the armed forces.

save it on the battlefield, so that there were only a few of us to applaud and wonder at what he was able to do.

One day he broke the school swimming record. He and I were fooling around in the pool, near a big bronze plaque marked with events for which the school kept records —50 yards, 100 yards, 220 yards. Under each was a slot with a marker fitted into it, showing the name of the record-holder, his year, and his time. Under "100 Yards Free Style" there was "A. Hopkins Parker—1940—53.0 seconds."

"A. Hopkins Parker?" Finny squinted up at the name. "I don't remember any A. Hopkins Parker."

"He graduated before we got here."

"You mean that record has been up there the *whole time* we've been at Devon and nobody's busted it yet?" It was an insult to the class, and Finny had tremendous loyalty to the class, as he did to any group he belonged to, beginning with him and me and radiating outward past the limits of humanity toward spirits and clouds and stars.

No one else happened to be in the pool. Around us gleamed white tile and glass brick; the green, artificial-looking water rocked gently in its shining basin, releasing vague chemical smells and a sense of many pipes and filters; even Finny's voice, trapped in this closed, high-ceilinged room, lost its special resonance and blurred into a general well of noise gathered up toward the ceiling. He said blurringly, "I have a feeling *I* can swim faster than A. Hopkins Parker."

We found a stopwatch in the office. He mounted a starting box, leaned forward from the waist as he had seen racing swimmers do but never had occasion to do himself—I noticed a preparatory looseness coming into his shoulders and arms, a controlled ease about his stance which was unexpected in anyone trying to break a record. I said, "On your mark—Go!" There was a complex moment when his body uncoiled and shot forward with sudden metallic tension. He planed up the pool, his shoulders dominating the water while his legs and feet rode so low that I couldn't distinguish them; a wake rippled hurriedly by him and then at the end of the pool his position broke, he relaxed, dived, an instant's confusion and then his suddenly and metallically tense body shot back toward the other end of the pool. Another turn and up the pool again—I noticed no particular slackening of his pace—another turn, down the pool again, his hand touched the end, and he looked up at me with a composed, interested expression. "Well, how did I do?" I looked at the watch; he had broken A. Hopkins Parker's record by .7 second.

"So I really did it. You know what? I thought I was going to do it. It felt as though I had that stopwatch in my head and I could hear myself going just a little bit faster than A. Hopkins Parker."

"The worst thing is there weren't any witnesses. And I'm no official timekeeper. I don't think it will count."

"Well of course it won't *count*."

"You can try it again and break it again. Tomorrow. We'll get the coach in here, and all the official timekeepers and I'll call up *The Devonian* to send a reporter and a photographer—"

He climbed out of the pool. "I'm not going to do it again," he said quietly.

"Of course you are!"

"No, I just wanted to see if I could do it. Now I know. But I don't want to do it in public." Some other swimmers drifted in through the door. Finny glanced sharply at them. "By the way," he said in an even more subdued voice, "we aren't going to talk about this. It's just between you and me. Don't say anything about it, to . . . anyone.''

''Not say anything about it! When you broke the school record!''

''*Sh-h-h-h-h!*'' He shot a blazing, agitated glance at me.

I stopped and looked at him up and down. He didn't look directly back at me. ''You're too good to be true,'' I said after a while.

He glanced at me, and then said, ''Thanks a lot'' in a somewhat expressionless voice.

Was he trying to impress me or something? Not tell anybody? When he had broken a school record without a day of practice? I knew he was serious about it, so I didn't tell anybody. Perhaps for that reason his accomplishment took root in my mind and grew rapidly in the darkness where I was forced to hide it. The Devon School record books contained a mistake, a lie, and nobody knew it but Finny and me. A. Hopkins Parker was living in a fool's paradise, wherever he was. His defeated name remained in bronze on the school record plaque, while Finny deliberately evaded an athletic honor. It was true that he had many already—the Winslow Galbraith Memorial Football Trophy for having brought the most Christian sportsmanship to the game during the 1941–1942 season, the Margaret Duke Bonaventura ribbon and prize for the student who conducted himself at hockey most like the way her son had done, the Devon School Contact Sport Award, Presented Each Year to That Student Who in the Opinion of the Athletic Advisors Excels His Fellows in the Sportsmanlike Performance of Any Game Involving Bodily Contact. But these were in the past, and they were prizes, not school records. The sports Finny played officially—football, hockey, baseball, lacrosse—didn't have school records. To switch to a new sport suddenly, just for a day, and immediately break a record in it—that was about as neat a trick, as dazzling a reversal as I could, to be perfectly honest, possibly imagine. There was something inebriating[18] in the suppleness[19] of this feat. When I thought about it my head felt a little dizzy and my stomach began to tingle. It had, in one word, glamour, absolute schoolboy glamour. When I looked down at that stopwatch and realized a split second before I permitted my face to show it or my voice to announce it that Finny had broken a school record, I had experienced a feeling that also can be described in one word—shock.

To keep silent about this amazing happening deepened the shock for me. It made Finny seem too unusual for—not friendship, but too unusual for rivalry. And there were few relationships among us at Devon not based on rivalry.

''Swimming in pools is screwy anyway,'' he said after a long, unusual silence as we walked toward the dormitory. ''The only real swimming is in the ocean.'' Then in the everyday, mediocre tone he used when he was proposing something really outrageous, he added, ''Let's go to the beach.''

The beach was hours away by bicycle, forbidden, completely out of all bounds. Going there risked expulsion,[20] destroyed the studying I was going to do for an important test the next morning, blasted the rea-

---

18. inebriating (in ēb′ rē āt iŋ) *adj.*: Intoxicating; exciting.
19. suppleness (sup′ ′l nes) *n.*: Flexibility; resilience.
20. expulsion (ik spul′ sʜən) *n.*: A permanent removal from school.

sonable amount of order I wanted to maintain in my life, and it also involved the kind of long, labored bicycle ride I hated. "All right," I said.

We got our bikes and slipped away from Devon along a back road. Having invited me Finny now felt he had to keep me entertained. He told long, wild stories about his childhood; as I pumped panting up steep hills he glided along beside me, joking steadily. He analyzed my character, and he insisted on knowing what I disliked most about him ("You're too conventional,"[21] I said). He rode backward with no hands, he rode on his own handlebars, he jumped off and back on his moving bike as he had seen trick horseback riders do in the movies. He sang. Despite the steady musical undertone in his speaking voice Finny couldn't carry a tune, and he couldn't remember the melody or the words to any song. But he loved listening to music, any music, and he liked to sing.

We reached the beach late in the afternoon. The tide was high and the surf was heavy. I dived in and rode a couple of waves, but they had reached that stage of power in which you could feel the whole strength of the ocean in them. The second wave, as it tore toward the beach with me, spewed[22] me a little ahead of it, encroaching[23] rapidly; suddenly it was immeasurably bigger than I was, it rushed me from the control of gravity and took control of me itself; the wave threw me down in a primitive plunge without a bottom, then there was a bottom, grinding sand, and I skidded onto the shore. The wave hesitated, balanced there, and then hissed back toward the deep water, its tentacles not quite interested enough in me to drag me with it.

I made my way up on the beach and lay down. Finny came, ceremoniously took my pulse, and then went back into the ocean. He stayed in an hour, breaking off every few minutes to come back to me and talk. The sand was so hot from the all-day sunshine that I had to brush the top layer away in order to lie down on it, and Finny's progress across the beach became a series of high, startled leaps.

The ocean, throwing up foaming sunsprays across some nearby rocks, was winter cold. This kind of sunshine and ocean, with the accumulating roar of the surf and the salty, adventurous, flirting wind from the sea, always intoxicated Phineas. He was everywhere, he enjoyed himself hugely, he laughed out loud at passing sea gulls. And he did everything he could think of for me.

We had dinner at a hot dog stand, with our backs to the ocean and its now cooler wind, our faces toward the heat of the cooking range. Then we walked on toward the center of the beach, where there was a subdued New England strip of honky-tonks.[24] The Boardwalk[25] lights against the deepening blue sky gained an ideal, starry beauty and the lights from the belt of honky-tonks and shooting galleries[26] and beer gardens gleamed with a quiet purity in the clear twilight.

Finny and I went along the Boardwalk in

---

21. conventional (kən ven' shən 'l) *adj.*: Conforming to accepted standards.
22. spewed (spyo͞od) *v.*: Ejected; forced out.
23. encroaching (in krōch' iŋ) *adj.*: Intruding; advancing.

24. honky-tonks (hôŋ' kē tôŋks) *n.*: Cheap, disreputable taverns.
25. Boardwalk: A wooden sidewalk along the edge of a beach.
26. shooting galleries: Places at amusement parks where people shoot at targets to win prizes.

our sneakers and white slacks, Finny in a light blue polo shirt and I in a T-shirt. I noticed that people were looking fixedly at him, so I took a look myself to see why. His skin radiated a reddish copper glow of tan, his brown hair had been a little bleached by the sun, and I noticed that the tan made his eyes shine with a cool blue-green fire.

"Everybody's staring at you," he suddenly said to me. "It's because of that movie-star tan you picked up this afternoon . . . showing off again."

Enough broken rules were enough that night. Neither of us suggested going into any of the honky-tonks or beer gardens. We did have one glass of beer each at a fairly respectable-looking bar, convincing, or seeming to convince the bartender that we were old enough by a show of forged draft cards. Then we found a good spot among some sand dunes at the lonely end of the beach, and there we settled down to sleep for the night. The last words of Finny's usual nighttime monologue[27] were, "I hope you're having a pretty good time here. I know I kind of dragged you away at the point of a gun, but after all you can't come to the shore with just anybody and you can't come by yourself, and at this teen-age period in life the proper person is your best pal." He hesitated and then added, "which is what you are," and there was silence on his dune.

It was a courageous thing to say. Exposing a sincere emotion nakedly like that at the Devon School was the next thing to suicide. I should have told him then that he was my best friend also and rounded off what he had said. I started to; I nearly did. But something held me back. Perhaps I was stopped by that level of feeling, deeper than thought, which contains the truth.

Chapter 4

The next morning I saw dawn for the first time. It began not as the gorgeous fanfare over the ocean I had expected, but as a strange gray thing, like sunshine seen through burlap.[1] I looked over to see if Phineas was awake. He was still asleep, although in this drained light he looked more dead than asleep. The ocean looked dead too, dead gray waves hissing mordantly[2] along the beach, which was gray and dead-looking itself.

I turned over and tried to sleep again but couldn't, and so lay on my back looking at this gray burlap sky. Very gradually, like one instrument after another being tentatively rehearsed, beacons of color began to pierce the sky. The ocean perked up a little from the reflection of these colored slivers in the sky. Bright highlights shone on the tips of waves, and beneath its gray surface I could see lurking a deep midnight green. The beach shed its deadness and became a spectral[3] gray-white, then more white than gray, and finally it was totally white and stainless, as pure as the shores of Eden.[4] Phineas, still asleep on his dune, made me think of Lazarus,[5] brought back to life by the touch of God.

---

1. burlap (bʉr′ lap) *n.*: A coarse cloth of jute or hemp used for making sacks.

2. mordantly (môr′ dənt lē) *adv.*: Bitingly; sarcastically.

3. spectral (spek′ trəl) *adj.*: Ghostly.

4. Eden (ē′ d'n): In the Bible, the garden where Adam and Eve first lived until God expelled them for disobeying.

5. Lazarus (laz′ ə rəs): A young man raised from the dead by Jesus, in the New Testament book of John, Chapter 11.

---

27. monologue (män′ ə lôg′) *n.*: A long speech by one speaker.

"Perhaps I was stopped by that level of feeling, deeper than thought, which contains the truth."

I didn't contemplate this transformation for long. Inside my head, for as long as I could remember, there had always been a sense of time ticking steadily. I looked at the sky and the ocean and knew that it was around six-thirty. The ride back to Devon would take three hours at least. My important test, trigonometry, was going to be held at ten o'clock.

Phineas woke up talking. "That was one of the best night's sleep I ever had."

"When did you ever have a bad one?"

"The time I broke my ankle in football. I like the way this beach looks now. Shall we have a morning swim?"

"Are you crazy? It's too late for that."

"What time is it anyway?" Finny knew I was a walking clock.

"It's going on seven o'clock."

"There's time for just a short swim," and before I could say anything he was trotting down the beach, shedding clothes as he went, and into the ocean. I waited for him where I was. He came back after a while full of chilly glow and energy and talk. I didn't have much to say. "Do you have the money?" I asked once, suddenly suspecting that he had lost our joint seventy-five cents during the night. There was a search, a hopeless one, in the sand, and so we set off on the long ride back without any breakfast, and got to Devon just in time for my test. I flunked it; I knew I was going to as soon as I looked at the test problems. It was the first test I had ever flunked.

But Finny gave me little time to worry about that. Right after lunch there was a game of blitzball which took most of the afternoon, and right after dinner there was the meeting of the Super Suicide Society of the Summer Session.

That night in our room, even though I was worn out from all the exercise, I tried to catch up to what had been happening in trigonometry.

"You work too hard," Finny said, sitting opposite me at the table where we read. The study lamp cast a round yellow pool between us. "You know all about History and English and French and everything else. What good will Trigonometry do you?"

"I'll have to pass it to graduate, for one thing."

"Don't give me that line. Nobody at Devon has ever been surer of graduating than you are. You aren't working for *that.* You want to be head of the class, valedictorian, so you can make a speech on Graduation Day—in Latin or something boring like that probably—and be the boy wonder of the school. I know you."

"Don't be stupid. I wouldn't waste my time on anything like that."

"You never waste your time. That's why I have to do it for you."

"Anyway," I grudgingly added, "somebody's got to be the head of the class."

"You see, I knew that's what you were aiming at," he concluded quietly.

"Fooey."

What if I was. It was a pretty good goal to have, it seemed to me. After all, he should talk. He had won and been proud to win the Galbraith Football Trophy and the Contact Sport Award, and there were two or three other athletic prizes he was sure to get this year or next. If I was head of the class on Graduation Day and made a speech and won the Ne Plus Ultra Scholastic Achievement Citation, then we would both have come out on top, we would be even, that was all. We would be even. . . .

Was that it! My eyes snapped from the textbook toward him. Did he notice this sudden glance shot across the pool of light? He didn't seem to; he went on writing down his strange curlicue notes about Thomas Hardy in Phineas Shorthand. *Was that it!* With his head bent over in the lamplight I could discern a slight mound in his brow above the eyebrows, the faint bulge which is usually believed to indicate mental power. Phineas would be the first to disclaim any great mental power in himself. But what did go on in his mind? If I was the head of the class and won that prize, then we would be even. . . .

His head started to come up, and mine snapped down. I glared at the textbook. "Relax," he said. "Your brain'll explode if you keep this up."

"You don't need to worry about me, Finny."

"I'm not worried."

"You wouldn't—" I wasn't sure I had the control to put this question—"mind if I wound up head of the class, would you?"

"Mind?" Two clear green-blue eyes looked at me. "Fat chance you've got, anyway, with Chet Douglass around."

"But you wouldn't mind, would you?" I repeated in a lower and more distinct voice.

He gave me that half-smile of his, which had won him a thousand conflicts. "I'd kill myself out of jealous envy."

I believed him. The joking manner was a screen; I believed him. In front of my eyes the trigonometry textbook blurred into a jumble. I couldn't see. My brain exploded. He minded, despised the possibility that I might be the head of the school. There was a swift chain of explosions in my brain, one certainty after another blasted—up like a detonation went the idea of any best friend, up went affection and partnership and sticking by someone and relying on someone absolutely in the jungle of a boys' school, up went the hope that there was anyone in this school—in this world

—whom I could trust. "Chet Douglass," I said uncertainly, "is a sure thing for it."

My misery was too deep to speak any more. I scanned the page; I was having trouble breathing, as though the oxygen were leaving the room. Amid its devastation my mind flashed from thought to thought, despairingly in search of something left which it could rely on. Not rely on absolutely, that was obliterated as a possibility, just rely on a little, some solace, something surviving in the ruins.

I found it. I found a single sustaining thought. The thought was, You and Phineas are even already. You are even in enmity.[6] You are both coldly driving ahead for yourselves alone. You did hate him for breaking that school swimming record, but so what? He hated you for getting an A in every course but one last term. You would have had an A in that one except for him. Except for him.

Then a second realization broke as clearly and bleakly as dawn at the beach. Finny had deliberately set out to wreck my studies. That explained blitzball, that explained the nightly meetings of the Super Suicide Society, that explained his insistence that I share all his diversions. The way I believed that you're-my-best-friend blabber! The shadow falling across his face if I didn't want to do something with him! His instinct for sharing everything with me? Sure, he wanted to share everything with me, especially his procession of D's in every subject. That way he, the great athlete, would be way ahead of me. It was all cold trickery, it was all calculated, it was all enmity.

I felt better. Yes, I sensed it like the sweat of relief when nausea passes away; I felt

---

6. enmity (en' mə tē) *n.*: Bitter attitude or feelings of an enemy; hatred.

better. We were even after all, even in enmity. The deadly rivalry was on both sides after all.

I became quite a student after that. I had always been a good one, although I wasn't really interested and excited by learning itself, the way Chet Douglass was. Now I became not just good but exceptional, with Chet Douglass my only rival in sight. But I began to see that Chet was weakened by the very genuineness of his interest in learning. He got carried away by things; for example, he was so fascinated by the tilting planes of solid geometry that he did almost as badly in trigonometry as I did myself. When we read *Candide* it opened up a new way of looking at the world to Chet, and he continued hungrily reading Voltaire,[7] in French, while the class went on to other people. He was vulnerable there, because to me they were all pretty much alike—Voltaire and Molière and the laws of motion and the Magna Carta and the Pathetic Fallacy[8] and *Tess of the D'Urbervilles*—and I worked indiscriminately on all of them.

Finny had no way of knowing this, because it all happened so far ahead of him scholastically. In class he generally sat slouched in his chair, his alert face following the discussion with an expression of philosophical comprehension, and when he was forced to speak himself the hypnotic power of his voice combined with the singularity of his mind to produce answers which were often not right but could rarely be branded as wrong. Written tests were his downfall because he could not speak them, and as a result he got grades which were barely passing. It wasn't that he never worked, because he did work, in short, intense bouts now and then. As that crucial summer wore on and I tightened the discipline on myself Phineas increased his bouts of studying.

I could see through that. I was more and more certainly becoming the best student in the school; Phineas was without question the best athlete, so in that way we were even. But while he was a very poor student I was a pretty good athlete, and when everything was thrown into the scales they would in the end tilt definitely toward me. The new attacks of studying were his emergency measures to save himself. I redoubled my effort.

It was surprising how well we got along in these weeks. Sometimes I found it hard to remember his treachery, sometimes I discovered myself thoughtlessly slipping back into affection for him again. It was hard to remember when one summer day after another broke with a cool effulgence[9] over us, and there was a breath of widening life in the morning air—something hard to describe—an oxygen intoxicant, a shining northern paganism,[10] some odor, some feeling so hopelessly promising that I would fall back in my bed on guard against it. It was hard to remember in the heady and sensual

7. Candide . . . Voltaire: Written by French novelist Voltaire (1694–1778), *Candide* is a novel about a naive young man, Candide, whose teacher, Pangloss, insists that this is the best of all possible worlds despite the injustice and misery they continually encounter. The novel is a black comedy that pokes fun at the philosophy of optimism.

8. Molière . . . Pathetic Fallacy: Molière (mōl yer′) was a French dramatist (1622–1673); the laws of motion refer to principles of physics; the Magna Carta, a charter that King John of England was forced to grant in A.D. 1215, guaranteed certain civil and political liberties to English barons; in literature, the Pathetic Fallacy attributes human feelings and characteristics to inanimate things (the gym meditated).

9. effulgence (e ful′ jəns) *n.*: Radiance; brilliance.
10. paganism (pā′ gən is'm) *n.*: A belief in many gods that are found everywhere, including trees, rocks, and so on, so that people who are pagans feel a close communion with nature.

clarity of these mornings; I forgot whom I hated and who hated me. I wanted to break out crying from stabs of hopeless joy, or intolerable promise, or because these mornings were too full of beauty for me, because I knew of too much hate to be contained in a world like this.

Summer lazed on. No one paid any attention to us. One day I found myself describing to Mr. Prud'homme how Phineas and I had slept on the beach, and he seemed to be quite interested in it, in all the details, so much so that he missed the point: that we had flatly broken a basic rule.

No one cared, no one exercised any real discipline over us; we were on our own.

August arrived with a deepening of all the summertime splendors of New Hampshire. Early in the month we had two days of light, steady rain which aroused a final fullness everywhere. The branches of the old trees, which had been familiar to me either half-denuded or completely gaunt during the winter terms at Devon, now seemed about to break from their storms of leaves. Little disregarded patches of ground revealed that they had been gardens all along, and nondescript underbrush around the gymnasium and the river broke into color. There was a latent[11] freshness in the air, as though spring were returning in the middle of the summer.

But examinations were at hand. I wasn't as ready for them as I wanted to be. The Suicide Society continued to meet every evening, and I continued to attend, because I didn't want Finny to understand me as I understood him.

And also I didn't want to let him excel me in this, even though I knew that it didn't matter whether he showed me up at the tree or not. Because it was what you had in your heart that counted. And I had detected that Finny's was a den of lonely, selfish ambition. He was no better than I was, no matter who won all the contests.

A French examination was announced for one Friday late in August. Finny and I studied for it in the library Thursday afternoon; I went over vocabulary lists, and he wrote messages—je ne give a damn pas about le francais, les filles en France ne wear pas les pantelons—and passed them with great seriousness to me, as *aide-mémoire*.[12] Of course I didn't get any work done. After supper I went to our room to try again. Phineas came in a couple of minutes later.

"Arise," he began airily, "Senior Overseer Charter Member! Elwin 'Leper' Lepellier has announced his intention to make the leap this very night, to qualify, to save his face at last."

I didn't believe it for a second. Leper Lepellier would go down paralyzed with panic on any sinking troopship before making such a jump. Finny had put him up to it, to finish me for good on the exam. I turned around with elaborate resignation. "If he jumps out of that tree I'm Mahatma Gandhi."[13]

"All right," agreed Finny absently. He had a way of turning clichés[14] inside out like that. "Come on, let's go. We've got to be there. You never know, maybe he *will* do it this time."

---

11. latent (lāt′ 'nt) *adj.*: Hidden.

12. aide-mémoire (ed mā mwăr′) *n.*: French for "memory aid."
13. Mahatma Gandhi (mə hat′ mə gan′ dē) (1869–1948): Hindu leader of India during India's struggle for independence from British rule.
14. clichés (klē shāz′) *n.*: Trite, worn-out expressions.

" *Because it was what you had in your heart that counted.* "

I slammed closed the French book.

"What's the matter?"

What a performance! His face was completely questioning and candid.

"Studying!" I snarled. "Studying! You know, books. Work. Examinations."

"Yeah . . ." He waited for me to go on, as though he didn't see what I was getting at.

"Oh! You don't know what I'm talking about. No, of course not. Not you." I stood up and slammed the chair against the desk. "Okay, we go. We watch little lily-liver Lepellier not jump from the tree, and I ruin my grade."

He looked at me with an interested, surprised expression. "You want to study?"

I began to feel a little uneasy at this mildness of his, so I sighed heavily. "Never mind, forget it. I know, I joined the club, I'm going. What else can I do?"

"Don't go." He said it very simply and casually, as though he were saying, "Nice day." He shrugged, "Don't go. It's only a game."

I had stopped halfway across the room, and now I just looked at him. "What d'you mean?" I muttered. What he meant was clear enough, but I was groping for what lay behind his words, for what his thoughts could possibly be. I might have asked, "Who are you, then?" instead. I was facing a total stranger.

"I didn't know you needed to *study*," he said simply, "I didn't think you ever did. I thought it just came to you."

It seemed that he had made some kind of parallel between my studies and his sports. He probably thought anything you were good at came without effort. He didn't know yet that he was unique.

I couldn't quite achieve a normal speaking voice. "If I need to study, then so do you."

"Me?" He smiled faintly. "Listen, I could study forever and I'd never break C. But it's different for you, you're good. You really are. If I had a brain like that, I'd—I'd have my head cut open so people could look at it."

"Now wait a second . . ."

He put his hands on the back of a chair and leaned toward me. "I know. We kid around a lot and everything, but you have to be serious sometime, about something. If you're really good at something, I mean if there's nobody, or hardly anybody, who's as good as you are, then you've got to be serious about that. Don't mess around, for crying out loud." He frowned disapprovingly at me. "Why didn't you say you had to study before? Don't move from that desk. It's going to be all A's for you."

"Wait a minute," I said, without any reason.

"It's okay. I'll oversee old Leper. I know he's not going to do it." He was at the door.

"Wait a minute," I said more sharply. "Wait just a minute. I'm coming."

"No you aren't, pal, you're going to study."

"Never mind my studying."

"You think you've done enough already?"

"Yes." I let this drop curtly to bar him from telling me what to do about my work. He let it go at that, and went out the door ahead of me, whistling off key.

We followed our gigantic shadows across the campus, and Phineas began talking in wild French, to give me a little extra practice. I said nothing, my mind exploring the new dimensions of isolation around me. Any fear I had ever had of the tree was nothing beside this. It wasn't my neck, but my understanding which was menaced. He had never been jealous of me for a second. Now I knew that there never was and never could have been any rivalry between us. I was not of the same quality as he.

I couldn't stand this. We reached the others loitering around the base of the tree, and Phineas began exuberantly to throw off his clothes, delighted by the fading glow of the day, the challenge of the tree, the competitive tension of all of us. He lived and flourished in such moments. "Let's go, you and me," he called. A new idea struck him. "We'll go together, a double jump! Neat, eh?"

None of this mattered now; I would have listlessly agreed to anything. He started up the wooden rungs and I began climbing behind, up to the limb high over the bank. Phineas ventured a little way along it, holding a thin nearby branch for support. "Come out a little way," he said, "and then we'll jump side by side." The countryside was striking from here, a deep green sweep of playing fields and bordering shrubbery, with the school stadium white and minia-ture-looking across the river. From behind us the last long rays of light played across the campus, accenting every slight undulation[15] of the land, emphasizing the separateness of each bush.

Holding firmly to the trunk, I took a step toward him, and then my knees bent and I jounced the limb. Finny, his balance gone, swung his head around to look at me for an instant with extreme interest, and then he tumbled sideways, broke through the little branches below and hit the bank with a sickening, unnatural thud. It was the first clumsy physical action I had ever seen him make. With unthinking sureness I moved out on the limb and jumped into the river, every trace of my fear of this forgotten.

---

15. undulation (un' joo lā' shən) n.: Wavy, curving form.

RESPONDING TO THE SELECTION

Your Response

1. If you could ask Gene a question about the first accident, what would you ask? Why?
2. Imagine that you are fifteen years older, looking back on your high-school years. What aspects of your life do you think would seem different to you from that perspective? Explain.

Recalling

3. Give three examples of Finny's luring Gene into breaking the rules.
4. Explain the Super Suicide Society of the Summer Session.
5. Describe the events leading to Finny's accident at the tree.

Interpreting

6. Describe the relationship between Gene and Finny. Explain how the relationship would appear from the outside and the undercurrents at work in it that might not be apparent from the outside.
7. Explain how the setting of this novel—a private school, summer, the war—directly affects the events.

Applying

8. Do you accept that people can be friends but still harbor jealousy and resentment toward one another? Explain your answer.

ANALYZING LITERATURE

Understanding Characters

Novelists try to give their **characters** verisimilitude, or a lifelike quality. When you read a novel, ask questions about the characters, based on your experience with real people. For example, how did Gene's relationship with Finny develop? First, Gene followed Finny out of loyalty and rivalry; later, he became bitter from a sense of betrayal; finally, he acted cruelly from a sense of inferiority to Finny. Use examples from the novel to support your answers to these questions.

1. How does Finny view the world; that is, what seem to be his attitudes toward important issues of life?
2. Do you think the novelist achieved verisimilitude in creating the characters of Gene and Finny? Find evidence from the novel to support your answer.

CRITICAL THINKING AND READING

Contrasting Characters

Gene and Finny are different from each other in a number of ways. For example, Gene is a good, diligent student, while Finny is an indifferent one. Finny is the best athlete in the school, while Gene is only adequate in sports.

1. What are Gene's and Finny's attitudes toward school authority and rules?
2. What are Gene's and Finny's feelings about the jump from the tree?
3. What qualities does each boy have that explain why he is the leader or the follower?

THINKING AND WRITING

Presenting a Point of View

Choose one incident from Chapters 1 to 4, such as the first jump from the tree or the invention of blitzball. List the main events of the incident. Beside each event, note how Finny probably felt about it or would relate it to others. Then retell the incident from Finny's point of view. Revise your story, making sure you have maintained Finny's point of view throughout. Then proofread it and share it with your classmates.

LEARNING OPTIONS

1. **Writing.** Look through old school yearbooks, newspapers, and magazine articles to find photographs of young people during World War II. Try to find a group picture. Make a copy of the photo, and write a paragraph about what you imagine these particular people might have experienced while attending school during the war years. Use the photograph to create imaginary relationships and incidents that might have occurred.
2. **Cross-curricular Connection.** Read more about World War II in a history textbook or in other library resources. Explore the causes of the war, including the reasons for the United States' involvement. Then write a brief introduction to *A Separate Peace* in which you set the historical context for readers who are unfamiliar with World War II.

GUIDE FOR READING

A Separate Peace, Chapters 5–10

Conflict

The sequence of related events in a novel is called the **plot.** Often the plot centers on a struggle or problem, called the **conflict,** involving the main character. The conflict might be external, that is, a struggle with another person or a force of nature; or it may be internal, within the character. As the conflict develops, the plot reaches its **climax,** or turning point. Finally, there is a **resolution,** as the conflict is resolved or the struggle ends in some way.

An important external conflict in *A Separate Peace* is the competition between Gene and Finny. Gene also experiences internal conflict, as he tries to understand his feelings about himself.

Focus

In Chapters 5–10 of *A Separate Peace,* you will find many examples of conflict as the story builds toward a climax. Analyzing these conflicts can help you to understand what is happening in the plot. Imagine that you are Gene talking to Finny about his accident in the tree. How would you feel about what happened? What would you say to him? Write the conversation that might take place.

Vocabulary

Knowing the following words will help you as you read Chapters 5–10 of *A Separate Peace.*

detonate (det′ 'n āt) *v.:* Explode violently and noisily (p. 793)

delirious (di lir′ ē əs) *adj.:* In a state of mental confusion; hallucinating (p. 793)

ludicrous (lo͞o′ di krəs) *adj.:* Laughably absurd (p. 793)

erratic (er rat′ ik) *adj.:* Irregular; not following a normal pattern (p. 794)

contempt (kən tempt′) *n.:* Scorn (p. 801)

discern (di sʉrn′) *v.:* To recognize (p. 809)

vagaries (və ger′ ēz) *n.:* Odd or unexpected actions or ideas (p. 824)

culminate (kul′ mə nāt′) *v.:* To bring to its highest point of interest (p. 834)

aesthete (es′ thēt′) *n.:* Someone highly sensitive to art and beauty; someone who puts on such a sensitivity (p. 835)

querulous (kwer′ ə ləs) *adj.:* Inclined to find fault; complaining (p. 837)

Chapter 5

None of us was allowed near the infirmary during the next days, but I heard all the rumors that came out of it. Eventually a fact emerged; it was one of his legs, which had been "shattered." I couldn't figure out exactly what this word meant, whether it meant broken in one or several places, cleanly or badly, and I didn't ask. I learned no more, although the subject was discussed endlessly. Out of my hearing people must have talked of other things, but everyone talked about Phineas to me. I suppose this was only natural. I had been right beside him when it happened, I was his roommate.

The effect of his injury on the masters seemed deeper than after other disasters I remembered there. It was as though they felt it was especially unfair that it should strike one of the sixteen-year-olds, one of the few young men who could be free and happy in the summer of 1942.

I couldn't go on hearing about it much longer. If anyone had been suspicious of me, I might have developed some strength to defend myself. But there was nothing. No one suspected. Phineas must still be too sick, or too noble, to tell them.

I spent as much time as I could alone in our room, trying to empty my mind of every thought, to forget where I was, even who I was. One evening when I was dressing for dinner in this numbed frame of mind, an idea occurred to me, the first with any energy behind it since Finny fell from the tree. I decided to put on his clothes. We wore the same size, and although he always criticized mine he used to wear them frequently, quickly forgetting what belonged to him and what to me. I never forgot, and that evening I put on his cordovan[1] shoes, his pants, and I looked for and finally found his pink shirt, neatly laundered in a drawer. Its high, somewhat stiff collar against my neck, the wide cuffs touching my wrists, the rich material against my skin excited a sense of strangeness and distinction; I felt like some nobleman, some Spanish grandee.[2]

But when I looked in the mirror it was no remote aristocrat I had become, no character out of daydreams. I was Phineas, Phineas to the life. I even had his humorous expression in my face, his sharp, optimistic awareness. I had no idea why this gave me such intense relief, but it seemed, standing there in Finny's triumphant shirt, that I would never stumble through the confusions of my own character again.

I didn't go down to dinner. The sense of transformation stayed with me throughout the evening, and even when I undressed and went to bed. That night I slept easily, and it was only on waking up that this illusion was gone, and I was confronted with myself, and what I had done to Finny.

Sooner or later it had to happen, and that morning it did. "Finny's better!" Dr. Stanpole called to me on the chapel steps over the organ recessional[3] thundering behind us. I made my way haltingly past the members of the choir with their black robes flapping in the morning breeze, the doctor's words reverberating around me. He might denounce me there before the whole school. Instead he steered me amiably into the lane leading toward the infirmary. "He could stand a visitor or two now, after these very nasty few days."

"You don't think I'll upset him or anything?"

"You? No, why? I don't want any of these

---

1. cordovan (kôr′ də vən) *adj.*: Made of a fine-grained, colored leather.

2. grandee (gran dē′) *n.*: Important person; person of high rank.

3. recessional (ri sesh′ ən əl) *n.*: Music played while people are leaving a church service or ceremony.

teachers flapping around him. But a pal or two, it'll do him good.''

''I suppose he's still pretty sick.''

''It was a messy break.''

''But how does he—how is he feeling? I mean, is he cheerful at all, or—''

''Oh, you know Finny.'' I didn't, I was pretty sure I didn't know Finny at all. ''It was a messy break,'' he went on, ''but we'll have him out of it eventually. He'll be walking again.''

''*Walking* again!''

''Yes.'' The doctor didn't look at me, and barely changed his tone of voice. ''Sports are finished for him, after an accident like that. Of course.''

''But he must be able to,'' I burst out, ''if his leg's still there, if you aren't going to amputate it—you aren't, are you?—then if it isn't amputated and the bones are still there, then it must come back the way it was, why wouldn't it? Of course it will.''

Dr. Stanpole hesitated, and I think glanced at me for a moment. ''Sports are finished. As a friend you ought to help him face that and accept it. The sooner he does the better off he'll be. If I had the slightest hope that he could do more than walk I'd be all for trying for everything. There is no such hope. I'm sorry, as of course everyone is. It's a tragedy, but there it is.''

I grabbed my head, fingers digging into my skin, and the doctor, thinking to be kind, put his hand on my shoulder. At his touch I lost all hope of controlling myself. I burst out crying into my hands; I cried for Phineas and for myself and for this doctor who believed in facing things. Most of all I cried because of kindness, which I had not expected.

''Now that's no good. You've got to be cheerful and hopeful. He needs that from you. He wanted especially to see you. You were the one person he asked for.''

That stopped my tears. I brought my hands down and watched the red brick exterior of the infirmary, a cheerful building, coming closer. Of course I was the first person he wanted to see. Phineas would say nothing behind my back; he would accuse me, face to face.

We were walking up the steps of the infirmary, everything was very swift, and next I was in a corridor being nudged by Dr. Stanpole toward a door. ''He's in there. I'll be with you in a minute.''

The door was slightly ajar, and I pushed it back and stood transfixed on the threshold. Phineas lay among pillows and sheets, his left leg, enormous in its white bindings, suspended a little above the bed. A tube led from a glass bottle into his right arm. Some channel began to close inside me and I knew I was about to black out.

''Come on in,'' I heard him say. ''You look worse than I do.'' The fact that he could still make a light remark pulled me back a little, and I went to a chair beside his bed. He seemed to have diminished physically in the few days which had passed, and to have lost his tan. His eyes studied me as though I were the patient. They no longer had their sharp good humor, but had become clouded and visionary. After a while I realized he had been given a drug. ''What are *you* looking so sick about?'' he went on.

''Finny, I—'' there was no controlling what I said, the words were instinctive, like the reactions of someone cornered. ''What happened there at the tree? That tree, I'm going to cut down that tree. Who cares who can jump out of it. What happened, what happened? How did you fall, how could you fall off like that?''

''I just fell,'' his eyes were vaguely on my face, ''something jiggled and I fell over. I remember I turned around to look at you, it was like I had all the time in the world. I thought I could reach out and get hold of you."

I flinched violently away from him. "To drag me down too!"

He kept looking vaguely over my face. "To get hold of you, so I wouldn't fall off."

"Yes, naturally." I was fighting for air in this close room. "I tried, you remember? I reached out but you were gone, you went down through those little branches underneath, and when I reached out there was only air."

"I just remember looking at your face for a second. Awfully funny expression you had. Very shocked, like you have right now."

"Right now? Well, of course, I *am* shocked. Who wouldn't be shocked. It's terrible, everything's terrible."

"But I don't see why you should look so *personally* shocked. You look like it happened to you or something."

"It's almost like it did! I was right there, right on the limb beside you."

"Yes, I know. I remember it all."

There was a hard block of silence, and then I said quietly, as though my words might detonate the room, "Do you remember what made you fall?"

His eyes continued their roaming across my face. "I don't know, I must have just lost my balance. It must have been that. I did have this idea, this feeling that when you were standing there beside me, y— I don't know, I had a kind of feeling. But you can't say anything for sure from just feelings. And this feeling doesn't make any sense. It was a crazy idea, I must have been delirious. So I just have to forget it. I just fell," he turned away to grope for something among the pillows, "that's all." Then he glanced back at me, "I'm sorry about that feeling I had."

I couldn't say anything to this sincere, drugged apology for having suspected the truth. He was never going to accuse me. It was only a feeling he had, and at this moment he must have been formulating a new commandment in his personal decalogue:[4] Never accuse a friend of a crime if you only have a feeling he did it.

And I thought we were competitors! It was so ludicrous I wanted to cry.

If Phineas had been sitting here in this pool of guilt, how would he have felt, what would he have done?

He would have told me the truth.

I got up so suddenly that the chair overturned. I stared at him in amazement, and he stared back, his mouth breaking into a grin as the moments passed. "Well," he said at last in his friendly, knowing voice, "what are you going to do, hypnotize me?"

"Finny, I've got something to tell you. You're going to hate it, but there's something I've got to tell you."

"What energy," he said, falling back against the pillows. "You sound like General MacArthur."[5]

"I don't care who I sound like, and you won't think so when I tell you. This is the worst thing in the world, and I'm sorry and I hate to tell you but I've got to tell you."

But I didn't tell him. Dr. Stanpole came in before I was able to, and then a nurse came in, and I was sent away. The next day the doctor decided that Finny was not yet well enough to see visitors, even old pals like me. Soon after he was taken in an ambulance to his home outside Boston.

The Summer Session closed, officially came to an end. But to me it seemed irresolutely[6] suspended, halted strangely before its time. I went south for a month's vacation

---

4. decalogue (dek′ ə lōg′) *n.*: Ten Commandments.
5. General MacArthur: Douglas MacArthur (1880–1964), U.S. general and commander in chief of Allied forces in the Pacific during World War II.
6. irresolutely (ir rez′ ə lōot′ lē) *adv.*: Indecisively; waveringly.

"If Phineas had been sitting here in this pool of guilt, how would he have felt, what would he have done?"

in my home town and spent it in an atmosphere of reverie[7] and unreality, as though I had lived that month once already and had not been interested by it the first time either.

At the end of September I started back toward Devon on the jammed, erratic trains

of September, 1942. I reached Boston seventeen hours behind schedule; there would be prestige in that at Devon, where those of us from long distances with travel adventures to report or invent held the floor for several days after a vacation.

By luck I got a taxi at South Station, and instead of saying "North Station" to the driver, instead of just crossing Boston and catching the final train for the short last leg

---

7. reverie (rev′ ər ē) _n._: Dreamy thinking or imagining.

of the trip to Devon, instead of that I sat back in the seat and heard myself give the address of Finny's house on the outskirts.

We found it fairly easily, on a street with a nave[8] of ancient elms branching over it. The house itself was high, white, and oddly proper to be the home of Phineas. It presented a face of definite elegance to the street, although behind that wings and ells dwindled quickly in formality until the house ended in a big plain barn.

Nothing surprised Phineas. A cleaning woman answered the door, and when I came into the room where he was sitting, he looked very pleased and not at all surprised.

"So you *are* going to show up!" his voice took off in one of its flights, "and you brought me something to eat from down South, didn't you? Honeysuckle and molasses or something like that?" I tried to think of something funny. "Corn bread? You did bring something. You didn't go all the way to Dixie and then come back with nothing but your dismal face to show for it." His talk rolled on, ignoring and covering my look of shock and clumsiness. I was silenced by the sight of him propped by white hospital-looking pillows in a big armchair. Despite everything at the Devon Infirmary, he had seemed an athlete there, temporarily injured in a game; as though the trainer would come in any minute and tape him up. Propped now before a great New England fireplace, on this quiet old street, he looked to me like an invalid, house-bound.

"I brought . . . Well I never remember to bring anyone anything." I struggled to get my voice above this self-accusing murmur. "I'll send you something. Flowers or something."

"Flowers! What happened to you in Dixie anyway?"

"Well then," there was no light remark anywhere in my head, "I'll get you some books."

"Never mind about books. I'd rather have some talk. What happened down South?"

"As a matter of fact," I brought out all the cheerfulness I could find for this, "there was a fire. It was just a grass fire out behind our house. We . . . took some brooms and beat it. I guess what we really did was fan it because it just kept getting bigger until the Fire Department finally came. They could tell where it was because of all the flaming brooms we were waving around in the air, trying to put them out."

Finny liked that story. But it put us on the familiar friendly level, pals trading stories. How was I going to begin talking about it? It would not be just a thunderbolt. It wouldn't even seem real.

Not in this conversation, not in this room. I wished I had met him in a railroad station, or at some highway intersection. Not here. Here the small window panes shone from much polishing and the walls were hung with miniatures and old portraits. The chairs were either heavily upholstered and too comfortable to stay awake in or Early American and never used. There were several square, solid tables covered with family pictures and random books and magazines, and also three small, elegant tables not used for anything. It was a compromise of a room, with a few good "pieces" for guests to look at, and the rest of it for people to use.

But I had known Finny in an impersonal dormitory, a gym, a playing field. In the room we shared at Devon many strangers had lived before us, and many would afterward. It was there that I had done it, but it was here that I would have to tell it. I felt like a wild man who had stumbled in from the jungle to tear the place apart.

<hr>

8. nave (nāv) *n.*: Aisle.

I moved back in the Early American chair. Its rigid back and high armrests immediately forced me into a righteous[9] posture. My blood could start to pound if it wanted to; let it. I was going ahead. "I was thinking about you most of the trip up."

"Oh yeah?" He glanced briefly into my eyes.

"I was thinking about you . . . and the accident."

"There's loyalty for you. To think about me when you were on a vacation."

"I was thinking about it . . . about you because—I was thinking about you and the accident because I caused it."

Finny looked steadily at me, his face very handsome and expressionless. "What do you mean, you caused it?" his voice was as steady as his eyes.

My own voice sounded quiet and foreign. "I jounced the limb. I caused it." One more sentence. "I deliberately jounced the limb so you would fall off."

He looked older than I had ever seen him. "Of course you didn't."

"Yes I did. I did!"

"Of course you didn't do it. You fool. Sit down, you fool."

"Of course I did!"

"I'm going to hit you if you don't sit down."

"*Hit* me!" I looked at him. "*Hit* me! You can't even get up! You can't even come near me!"

"I'll kill you if you don't shut up."

"You see! Kill me! Now you know what it is! I did it because I felt like that! Now you know yourself!"

"I don't know anything. Go away. I'm tired and you make me sick. Go away." He held his forehead wearily, an unlikely way.

It struck me then that I was injuring him again. It occurred to me that this could be an even deeper injury than what I had done before. I would have to back out of it, I would have to disown it. Could it be that he might even be right? Had I really and definitely and knowingly done it to him after all? I couldn't remember, I couldn't think. However it was, it was worse for him to know it. I had to take it back.

But not here. "You'll be back at Devon in a few weeks, won't you?" I muttered after both of us had sat in silence for a while.

"Sure, I'll be there by Thanksgiving anyway."

At Devon, where every stick of furniture didn't assert that Finny was a part of it, I could make it up to him.

Now I had to get out of there. There was only one way to do it; I would have to make every move false. "I've had an awfully long trip," I said, "I never sleep much on trains. I guess I'm not making too much sense today."

"Don't worry about it."

"I think I'd better get to the station. I'm already a day late at Devon."

"You aren't going to start living by the rules, are you?"

I grinned at him. "Oh no, I wouldn't do that," and that was the most false thing, the biggest lie of all.

Chapter 6

Peace had deserted Devon. Although not in the look of the campus and village; they retained much of their dreaming summer calm. Fall had barely touched the full splendor of the trees, and during the height of the day the sun briefly regained its summertime power. In the air there was only an edge of coolness to imply the coming winter.

But all had been caught up, like the first fallen leaves, by a new and energetic wind. The Summer Session—a few dozen boys

---

9. righteous (rī′ chəs) *adj*.: Just; upright.

being force-fed education, a stopgap[1] while most of the masters were away and most of the traditions stored against sultriness[2]—the Summer Session was over. It had been the school's first, but this was its one hundred and sixty-third Winter Session, and the forces reassembled for it scattered the easygoing summer spirit like so many fallen leaves.

The masters were in their places for the first Chapel, seated in stalls in front of and at right angles to us, suggesting by their worn expressions and careless postures that they had never been away at all.

In an apse[3] of the church sat their wives and children, the objects during the tedious winter months of our ceaseless, ritual speculation (Why did he ever marry *her*? What in the world ever made her marry *him*? How could the two of them ever have produced *those* little monsters?). The masters favored seersucker on this mild first day, the wives broke out their hats. Five of the younger teachers were missing, gone into the war. Mr. Pike had come in his Naval ensign's uniform; some reflex must have survived Midshipman's School and brought him back to Devon for the day. His face was as mild and hopeless as ever; mooning above the snappy, rigid blouse, it gave him the air of an impostor.

Continuity was the keynote. The same hymns were played, the same sermon given, the same announcements made. There was one surprise; maids had disappeared "for the Duration,"[4] a new phase then. But continuity was stressed, not beginning again but continuing the education of young men according to the unbroken traditions of Devon.

I knew, perhaps I alone knew, that this was false. Devon had slipped through their fingers during the warm overlooked months. The traditions had been broken, the standards let down, all rules forgotten. In those bright days of truancy we had never thought of What We Owed Devon, as the sermon this opening day exhorted us to do. We had thought of ourselves, of what Devon owed us, and we had taken all of that and much more. Today's hymn was "Dear Lord and Father of Mankind Forgive Our Foolish Ways"; we had never heard that during the summer either. Ours had been a wayward gypsy music, leading us down all kinds of foolish gypsy ways, unforgiven. I was glad of it, I had almost caught the rhythm of it, the dancing, clicking jangle of it during the summer.

Still it had come to an end, in the last long rays of daylight at the tree, when Phineas fell. It was forced on me as I sat chilled through the Chapel service, that this probably vindicated[5] the rules of Devon after all, wintery Devon. If you broke the rules, then they broke you. That, I think, was the real point of the sermon on this first morning.

After the service ended we set out seven hundred strong, the regular winter throng of the Devon School, to hustle through our lists of appointments. All classrooms were crowded, swarms were on the crosswalks, the dormitories were as noisy as factories, every bulletin board was a forest of notices.

We had been an idiosyncratic,[6] leaderless band in the summer, undirected except by the eccentric notions of Phineas. Now the official class leaders and politicians could be seen taking charge, assuming as a matter of

---

1. stopgap (stăp′ gap′) *n.*: A temporary measure or substitute.
2. sultriness (sul′ trē nəs) *n.*: Oppressive heat.
3. apse (aps) *n.*: A semicircular projection at the east end of a church.
4. Duration (do͞o rā′ shən) *n.*: In this case, the time until the war is over.

5. vindicated (vin′ də kāt′ əd) *v.*: Upheld; defended.
6. idiosyncratic (id′ ē ō sin krat′ ik) *adj.*: Peculiar; individualistic.

course their control of these walks and fields which had belonged only to us. I had the same room which Finny and I had shared during the summer, but across the hall, in the large suite where Leper Lepellier had dreamed his way through July and August amid sunshine and dust motes[7] and windows through which the ivy had reached tentatively into the room, here Brinker Hadley had established his headquarters. Emissaries[8] were already dropping in to confer with him. Leper, luckless in his last year as all the others, had been moved to a room lost in an old building off somewhere in the trees toward the gym.

After morning classes and lunch I went across to see Brinker, started into the room and then stopped. Suddenly I did not want to see the trays of snails which Leper had passed the summer collecting replaced by Brinker's files. Not yet. Although it was something to have this year's dominant student across the way. Ordinarily he should have been a magnet for me, the center of all the excitement and influences in the class. Ordinarily this would have been so—if the summer, the gypsy days, had not intervened. Now Brinker, with his steady wit and ceaseless plans, Brinker had nothing to offer in place of Leper's dust motes and creeping ivy and snails.

I didn't go in. In any case I was late for my afternoon appointment. I never used to be late. But today I was, later even than I had to be. I was supposed to report to the Crew House,[9] down on the banks of the lower river. There are two rivers at Devon, divided by a small dam. On my way I stopped on the footbridge which crosses the top of the dam separating them and looked upstream, at the narrow little Devon River sliding toward me between its thick fringe of pine and birch.

As I had to do whenever I glimpsed this river, I thought of Phineas. Not of the tree and pain, but of one of his favorite tricks, Phineas in exaltation,[10] balancing on one foot on the prow of a canoe like a river god, his raised arms invoking the air to support him, face transfigured, body a complex set of balances and compensations, each muscle aligned in perfection with all the others to maintain this supreme fantasy of achievement, his skin glowing from immersions,[11] his whole body hanging between river and sky as though he had transcended gravity and might by gently pushing upward with his foot glide a little way higher and remain suspended in space, encompassing all the glory of the summer and offering it to the sky.

Then, an infinitesimal veering of the canoe, and the line of his body would break, the soaring arms collapse, up shoot an uncontrollable leg, and Phineas would tumble into the water, roaring with rage.

I stopped in the middle of this hurrying day to remember him like that, and then, feeling refreshed, I went on to the Crew House beside the tidewater river below the dam.

We had never used this lower river, the Naguamsett,[12] during the summer. It was ugly, saline, fringed with marsh, mud and seaweed. A few miles away it was joined to the ocean, so that its movements were governed by unimaginable factors like the Gulf Stream, the Polar Ice Cap, and the moon. It was nothing like the fresh-water Devon

---

7. dust motes: Tiny particles floating in the air.
8. Emissaries (em′ i ser′ ēz) *n.*: People on specific missions; secret agents.
9. Crew House: Headquarters for the rowing team.

10. exaltation (eg′ zôl tā′ sлən) *n.*: A feeling of great joy, pride, or power.
11. immersions (im mʉr′ sлənz) *n.*: Plunges into water.
12. Naguamsett (nə gwăm′ set)

above the dam where we'd had so much fun, all the summer. The Devon's course was determined by some familiar hills a little inland; it rose among highland farms and forests which we knew, passed at the end of its course through the school grounds, and then threw itself with little spectacle over a small waterfall beside the diving dam, and into the turbid[13] Naguamsett.

The Devon School was astride these two rivers.

At the Crew House, Quackenbush, in the midst of some milling oarsmen in the damp main room, spotted me the instant I came in, with his dark expressionless eyes. Quackenbush was the crew manager, and there was something wrong about him. I didn't know exactly what it was. In the throng of the winter terms at Devon we were at opposite extremities of the class, and to me there only came the disliked edge of Quackenbush's reputation. A clue to it was that his first name was never used—I didn't even know what it was —and he had no nickname, not even an unfriendly one.

"Late, Forrester," he said in his already-matured voice. He was a firmly masculine type; perhaps he was disliked only because he had matured before the rest of us.

"Yes, sorry, I got held up."

"The crew waits for no man." He didn't seem to think this was a funny thing to say. I did, and had to chuckle.

"Well, if you think it's all a joke . . ."

"I didn't say it was a joke."

"I've got to have some real help around here. This crew is going to win the New England scholastics, or my name isn't Cliff Quackenbush."

With that blank filled, I took up my duties as assistant senior crew manager. There is no such position officially, but it sometimes came into existence through necessity, and was the opposite of a sinecure.[14] It was all work and no advantages. The official assistant to the crew manager was a member of the class below, and the following year he could come into the senior managership with its rights and status. An assistant who was already a senior ranked nowhere. Since I had applied for such a nonentity[15] of a job, Quackenbush, who had known as little about me as I had about him, knew now.

"Get some towels," he said without looking at me, pointing at a door.

"How many?"

"Who knows? Get some. As many as you can carry. *That* won't be too many."

Jobs like mine were usually taken by boys with some physical disability, since everyone had to take part in sports and this was all disabled boys could do. As I walked toward the door I supposed that Quackenbush was studying me to see if he could detect a limp. But I knew that his flat black eyes would never detect my trouble.

Quackenbush felt mellower by the end of the afternoon as we stood on the float in front of the Crew House, gathering up towels.

"You never rowed did you." He opened the conversation like that, without pause or question mark. His voice sounded almost too mature, as though he were putting it on a little; he sounded as though he were speaking through a tube.

"No, I never did."

"I rowed on the lightweight crew for two years."

---

13. **turbid** (tur′ bid) *adj.*: Muddy; cloudy from having sediment stirred up.

14. **sinecure** (si′ nə kyoor′) *n.*: A position that brings advantage but involves little or no work.

15. **nonentity** (nän′ en′ tə tē) *n.*: A thing of little or no importance.

He had a tough bantam[16] body, easily detectable under the tight sweat shirt he wore. "I wrestle in the winter," he went on. "What are you doing in the winter?"

"I don't know, manage something else."

"You're a senior aren't you?"

He knew that I was a senior. "Yeah."

"Starting a little late to manage teams aren't you?"

"Am I?"

"Darn right you are!" He put indignant conviction into this, pouncing on the first sprig of assertiveness in me.

"Well, it doesn't matter."

"Yes it matters."

"I don't think it does."

"Who do you think you are anyway."

I turned with an inward groan to look at him. Quackenbush wasn't going to let me just do the work for him like the automaton[17] I wished to be. We were going to have to be pitted against each other. It was easy enough now to see why. For Quackenbush had been systematically disliked since he first set foot in Devon, with careless, disinterested insults coming at him from the beginning, voting for and applauding the class leaders through years of attaining nothing he wanted for himself. I didn't want to add to his humiliations; I even sympathized with his trembling, goaded egotism[18] he could no longer contain, the furious arrogance which sprang out now at the mere hint of opposition from someone he had at last found whom he could consider inferior to himself. I realized that all this explained him, and it wasn't the words he said which angered me. It was only that he was so ignorant, that he knew nothing of the gypsy summer, nothing of the loss I was fighting to endure, of skylarks and splashes and petal-bearing breezes, he had not seen Leper's snails or the Charter of the Super Suicide Society; he shared nothing, knew nothing, felt nothing as Phineas had done.

"You, Quackenbush, don't know anything about who I am." That launched me, and I had to go on and say, "or anything else."

"Listen you maimed . . ."

I hit him hard across the face. I didn't know why for an instant; it was almost as though I were maimed. Then the realization that there was someone who was flashed over me.

Quackenbush had clamped his arm in some kind of tight wrestling grip around my neck, and I was glad in this moment not to be a cripple. I reached over, grasped the back of his sweat shirt, wrenched, and it came away in my hand. I tried to throw him off, he lunged at the same time, and we catapulted into the water.

The dousing extinguished Quackenbush's rage, and he let go of me. I scrambled back onto the float, still seared by what he had said. "The next time you call anybody maimed," I bit off the words harshly so he would understand all of them, "you better make sure they are first."

"Get out of here, Forrester," he said bitterly from the water, "you're not wanted around here, Forrester. Get out of here."

I fought that battle, that first skirmish of a long campaign, for Finny. Until the back of my hand cracked against Quackenbush's face I had never pictured myself in the role of Finny's defender, and I didn't suppose that he would have thanked me for it now. He was too loyal to anything connected with himself—his roommate, his dormitory, his class, his school, outward in vastly expand-

---

16. bantam (ban' təm) *adj.:* Like a small and aggressive fowl.

17. automaton (ô täm' ə tän') *n.:* A person acting in an automatic or mechanical way.

18. goaded egotism (gōd' 'd ē' gō tiz' əm): Driven selfishness or conceit.

ed circles of loyalty until I couldn't imagine who would be excluded. But it didn't feel exactly as though I had done it for Phineas. It felt as though I had done it for myself.

If so I had little profit to show as I straggled back toward the dormitory dripping wet, with the job I had wanted gone, temper gone, mind circling over and over through the whole soured afternoon. I knew now that it was fall all right; I could feel it pressing clammily against my wet clothes, an unfriendly, discomforting breath in the air, an edge of wintery chill, air that shriveled, soon to put out the lights on the countryside. One of my legs wouldn't stop trembling, whether from cold or anger I couldn't tell. I wished I had hit him harder.

Someone was coming toward me along the bent, broken lane which led to the dormitory, a lane out of old London, ancient houses on either side leaning as though soon to tumble into it, cobblestones heaving underfoot like a bricked-over ocean squall —a figure of great height advanced down them toward me. It could only be Mr. Ludsbury; no one else could pass over these stones with such contempt for the idea of tripping.

The houses on either side were inhabited by I didn't know who; wispy, fragile old ladies seemed most likely. I couldn't duck into one of them. There were angles and bumps and bends everywhere, but none big enough to conceal me. Mr. Ludsbury loomed on like a high-masted clipper ship[19] in this rocking passage, and I tried to go stealthily by him on my watery, squeaking sneakers.

"Just one moment, Forrester, if you please." Mr. Ludsbury's voice was bass, British, and his Adam's apple seemed to move as much as his mouth when he spoke. "Has there been a cloudburst in your part of town?"

"No, sir. I'm sorry, sir, I fell into the river." I apologized by instinct to him for this mishap which discomforted only me.

"And could you tell me how and why you fell into the river?"

"I slipped."

"Yes." After a pause he went on. "I think you have slipped in any number of ways since last year. I understand for example that there was gaming in my dormitory this summer while you were living there." He was in charge of the dormitory; one of the dispensations[20] of those days of deliverance, I realized now, had been his absence.

"Gaming? What kind of gaming, sir?"

"Cards, dice," he shook his long hand dismissingly, "I didn't inquire. It didn't matter. There won't be any more of it."

"I don't know who that would have been." Nights of black-jack and poker and unpredictable games invented by Phineas rose up in my mind; the back room of Leper's suite, a lamp hung with a blanket so that only a small blazing circle of light fell sharply amid the surrounding darkness; Phineas losing even in those games he invented, betting always for what *should* win, for what would have been the most brilliant successes of all, if only the cards hadn't betrayed him. Finny finally betting his icebox and losing it, that contraption, to me.

I thought of it because Mr. Ludsbury was just then saying, "And while I'm putting the dormitory back together I'd better tell you to get rid of that leaking icebox. Nothing like that is ever permitted in the dormitory,

---

19. high-masted clipper ship: A sailing ship of the type that gave American merchants a considerable trading advantage during the early 1800's. The masts, sometimes 200 feet tall, carried huge canvas sails that caught every gust of wind and enabled these long, narrow ships to sail with great speed.

20. dispensations (dis' pən sā' shənz) n.: Releases; exemptions.

of course. I notice that everything went straight to seed during the summer and that none of you old boys who knew our standards so much as lifted a finger to help Mr. Prud'homme maintain order. As a substitute for the summer he couldn't have been expected to know everything there was to be known at once. You old boys simply took advantage of the situation."

I stood there shaking in my wet sneakers. If only I had truly taken advantage of the situation, seized and held and prized the multitudes of advantages the summer offered me; if only I had.

I said nothing, on my face I registered the bleak look of a defendant who knows the court will never be swayed by all the favorable evidence he has. It was a schoolboy look; Mr. Ludsbury knew it well.

"There's a long-distance call for you," he continued in the tone of the judge performing the disagreeable duty of telling the defendant his right. "I've written the operator's number on the pad beside the telephone in my study. You may go in and call."

"Thank you very much, sir."

He sailed on down the lane without further reference to me, and I wondered who was sick at home.

But when I reached his study—low-ceilinged, gloomy with books, black leather chairs, a pipe rack, frayed brown rug, a room which students rarely entered except for a reprimand—I saw on the pad not an operator's number from my home town, but one which seemed to interrupt the beating of my heart.

I called this operator, and listened in wonder while she went through her routine as though this were just any long-distance call, and then her voice left the line and it was pre-empted, and charged, by the voice of Phineas. "Happy first day of the new academic year!"

"Thanks, thanks a lot, it's a—you sound—I'm glad to hear your—"

"Stop stuttering, I'm paying for this. Who're you rooming with?"

"Nobody. They didn't put anyone else in the room."

"Saving my place for me! Good old Devon. But anyway, you wouldn't have let them put anyone else in there, would you?" Friendliness, simple outgoing affection, that was all I could hear in his voice.

"No, of course not."

"I didn't think you would. Roommates are roommates. Even if they do have an occasional fight. You were crazy when you were here."

"I guess I was. I guess I must have been."

"Completely over the falls. I wanted to be sure you'd recovered. That's why I called up. I knew that if you'd let them put anybody else in the room in my place, then you really *were* crazy. But you didn't, I knew you wouldn't. Well, I did have just a *trace* of doubt, that was because you talked so crazy here. I have to admit I had just a *second* when I wondered. I'm sorry about that, Gene. Naturally I was completely wrong. You didn't let them put anyone else in my spot."

"No, I didn't let them."

"I could shoot myself for thinking you might. I really knew you wouldn't."

"No, I wouldn't."

"And I spent my money on a long-distance call! All for nothing. Well, it's spent, on you too. So start talking, pal. And it better be good. Start with sports. What are you going out for?"

"Crew. Well, not exactly crew. Managing crew. Assistant crew manager."

"Assistant *crew* manager!"

"I don't think I've got the job—"

"Assistant crew *manager!*"

"I got in a fight this after—"

"*Assistant crew manager!*" No voice could course with dumfoundment like Finny's "You *are* crazy!"

"Listen, Finny, I don't care about being a big man on the campus or anything."

"Whaaat?" Much more clearly than anything in Mr. Ludsbury's study I could see his face now, grimacing in wide, obsessed stupefaction.[21] "Who said anything about whoever *they* are!"

"Well then what are you so worked up for?"

"What do you want to manage crew for? What do you want to *manage* for? What's that got to do with sports?"

The point was, the grace of it was, that it had nothing to do with sports. For I wanted no more of sports. They were barred from me, as though when Dr. Stanpole said, "Sports are finished" he had been speaking of me. I didn't trust myself in them, and I didn't trust anyone else. It was as though football players were really bent on crushing the life out of each other, as though boxers were in combat to the death, as though even a tennis ball might turn into a bullet. This didn't seem completely crazy imagination in 1942, when jumping out of trees stood for abandoning a torpedoed ship. Later, in the school swimming pool, we were given the second stage in that rehearsal: after you hit the water you made big splashes with your hands, to scatter the flaming oil which would be on the surface.

So to Phineas I said, "I'm too busy for sports," and he went into his incoherent groans and jumbles of words, and I thought the issue was settled until at the end he said, "Listen, pal, if *I* can't play sports, *you're* going to play them for me," and I lost part of myself to him then, and a soaring

" '*Listen, pal, if I can't play sports, you're going to play them for me,'...*"

21. **stupefaction** (stōō' pə fak' shən) *n.*: Stunned amazement; utter bewilderment.

sense of freedom revealed that this must have been my purpose from the first: to become a part of Phineas.

Chapter 7

Brinker Hadley came across to see me late that afternoon. I had taken a shower to wash off the sticky salt of the Naguamsett River—going into the Devon was like taking a refreshing shower itself, you never had to clean up after it, but the Naguamsett was something else entirely. I had never been in it before; it seemed appropriate that my baptism there had taken place on the first day of this winter session, and that I had been thrown into it, in the middle of a fight.

I washed the traces off me and then put on a pair of chocolate brown slacks, a pair which Phineas had been particularly critical of when he wasn't wearing them, and a blue flannel shirt. Then, with nothing to do until my French class at five o'clock, I began turning over in my mind this question of sports.

But Brinker came in. I think he made a point of visiting all the rooms near him the first day. "Well, Gene," his beaming face appeared around the door. Brinker looked the standard preparatory school article in his gray gabardine suit with square, hand-sewn-looking jacket pockets, a conservative necktie, and dark brown cordovan shoes. His face was all straight lines—eyebrows, mouth, nose, everything—and he carried his six feet of height straight as well. He looked but happened not to be athletic, being too busy with politics, arrangements, and offices. There was nothing idiosyncratic about Brinker unless you saw him from behind; I did as he turned to close the door after him. The flaps of his gabardine jacket

parted slightly over his healthy rump, and it is that, without any sense of derision at all, that I recall as Brinker's salient characteristic, those healthy, determined, not over-exaggerated but defined and substantial buttocks.

"Here you are in your solitary splendor," he went on genially. "I can see you have real influence around here. This big room all to yourself. I wish I knew how to manage things like you." He grinned confidingly and sank down on my cot, leaning on his elbow in a relaxed, at-home way.

It didn't seem fitting for Brinker Hadley, the hub of the class, to be congratulating me on influence. I was going to say that while he had a roommate it was frightened Brownie Perkins, who would never impinge[1] on Brinker's comfort in any way, and that they had two rooms, the front one with a fireplace. Not that I grudged him any of this. I liked Brinker in spite of his Winter Session efficiency; almost everyone liked Brinker.

But in the pause I took before replying he started talking in his lighthearted way again. He never let a dull spot appear in conversation if he could help it.

"I'll bet you knew all the time Finny wouldn't be back this fall. That's why you picked him for a roommate, right?"

"What?" I pulled quickly around in my chair, away from the desk, and faced him. "No, of course not. How could I know a thing like that in advance?"

Brinker glanced swiftly at me. "You fixed it," he smiled widely. "You knew all the time. I'll bet it was *all* your doing."

"Don't be nutty, Brinker," I turned back toward the desk and began moving books with rapid pointlessness, "what a crazy

---

1. **impinge** (im pinj′) *v.*: Intrude.

thing to say." My voice sounded too strained even to my own blood-pounded ears.

"Ah-h-h. The truth hurts, eh?"

I looked at him as sharply as eyes can look. He had struck an accusing pose.

"Sure," I gave a short laugh, "sure." Then these words came out of me by themselves, "But the truth will out."

His hand fell leadenly on my shoulder. "Rest assured of that, my son. In our free democracy, even fighting for its life, the truth will out."

I got up. "I feel like a smoke, don't you? Let's go down to the Butt Room."

"Yes, yes. To the dungeon with you."

The Butt Room was something like a dungeon. It was in the basement, or the bowels, of the dormitory. There were about ten smokers already there. Everyone at Devon had many public faces; in class we looked, if not exactly scholarly, at least respectably alert; on the playing fields we looked like innocent extroverts;[2] and in the Butt Room we looked, very strongly, like criminals. The school's policy, in order to discourage smoking, was to make these rooms as depressing as possible. The windows near the ceiling were small and dirty, the old leather furniture spilled its innards, the tables were mutilated, the walls ash-colored, the floor concrete. A radio with a faulty connection played loud and rasping for a while, then suddenly quiet and insinuating.

"Here's your prisoner, gentlemen," announced Brinker, seizing my neck and pushing me into the Butt Room ahead of him, "I'm turning him over to the proper authorities."

High spirits came hard in the haze of the Butt Room. A slumped figure near the radio, which happened to be playing loud at the moment, finally roused himself to say, "What's the charge?"

"Doing away with his roommate so he could have a whole room to himself. Rankest treachery." He paused impressively. "Practically fratricide."[3]

With a snap of the neck I shook his hand off me, my teeth set, "Brinker . . ."

He raised an arresting hand. "Not a word. Not a sound. You'll have your day in court."

"Shut up! I swear you ride a joke longer than anybody I know."

It was a mistake; the radio had suddenly gone quiet, and my voice ringing in the abrupt, releasing hush galvanized[4] them all.

"So, you killed him, did you?" A boy uncoiled tensely from the couch.

"Well," Brinker qualified judiciously, "not actually killed. Finny's hanging between life and death at home, in the arms of his grief-stricken old mother."

I had to take part in this, or risk losing control completely. "I didn't do hardly a thing," I began as easily as it was possible for me to do, "I—all I did was drop a little bit . . . a little pinch of arsenic in his morning coffee."

"Liar!" Brinker glowered at me. "Trying to weasel out of it with a false confession, eh?"

I laughed at that, laughed uncontrollably for a moment at that.

"We know the scene of the crime," Brinker went on, "high in that . . . that *funereal*

---

2. extroverts (eks′ trə vʉrts′) *n.*: People who are active, expressive, and directed toward things outside of themselves.

3. fratricide (frat′ rə sīd) *n.*: The killing of one's brother.
4. galvanized (gal′ və nīz′ 'd) *v.*: Stimulated as if by electric shock.

tree by the river. There wasn't any poison, nothing as subtle as that.''

"Oh, you know about the tree," I tried to let my face fall guiltily, but it felt instead as though it were being dragged downward. "Yes, huh, yes there was a small, a little *contretemps*[5] at the tree."

No one was diverted from the issue by this try at a funny French pronunciation.

"Tell us everything," a younger boy at the table said huskily. There was an unsettling current in his voice, a genuinely conspiratorial note, as though he believed literally everything that had been said. His attitude seemed to me almost obscene, the attitude of someone who discovers a sexual secret of yours and promises not to tell a soul if you will describe it in detail to him.

"Well," I replied in a stronger voice, "first I stole all his money. Then I found that he cheated on his entrance tests to Devon and I blackmailed his parents about that, then I made love to his sister in Mr. Ludsbury's study, then I . . .'' it was going well, faint grins were appearing around the room, even the younger boy seemed to suspect that he was being "sincere" about a joke, a bad mistake to make at Devon, "then I . . .'' I only had to add, "pushed him out of the tree" and the chain of implausibility[6] would be complete, "then I . . .'' just those few words and perhaps this dungeon nightmare would end.

But I could feel my throat closing on them; I could never say them, never.

I swung on the younger boy. "What did I do then?" I demanded. "I'll bet you've got a lot of theories. Come on, reconstruct the

crime. There we were at the tree. Then what happened, Sherlock Holmes?"[7]

His eyes swung guiltily back and forth. "Then you just pushed him off, I'll bet."

"Lousy bet," I said offhandedly, falling into a chair as though losing interest in the game. "You lose. I guess you're Dr. Watson,[8] after all."

They laughed at him a little, and he squirmed and looked guiltier than ever. He had a very weak foothold among the Butt Room crowd, and I had pretty well pushed him off it. His glance flickered out at me from his defeat, and I saw to my surprise that I had, by making a little fun of him, brought upon myself his unmixed hatred. For my escape this was a price I was willing to pay.

"French, French," I exclaimed. "Enough of this *contretemps*. I've got to study my French." And I went out.

Going up the stairs I heard a voice from the Butt Room say, "Funny, he came all the way down here and didn't even have a smoke."

But this was a clue they soon seemed to forget. I detected no Sherlock Holmes among them, nor even a Dr. Watson. No one showed any interest in tracking me, no one pried, no one insinuated.[9] The daily lists of appointments lengthened with the rays of the receding autumn sun until the summer, the opening day, even yesterday became by the middle of October something gotten out

---

5. contretemps (kôn tṛə tän′) *n.*: French for "an awkward mishap."

6. implausibility (im plô′ zə bil′ ə tē) *n.*: Something that does not seem reasonable; something that does not even have the appearance of being possible.

7. Sherlock Holmes (shŭr′ läk′ hōmz′): A fictional English detective.

8. Dr. Watson: Sherlock Holmes's friend and narrator of his fictional adventures. Watson lacked the powers of observation and the analytical skills of Holmes and so was incapable of solving the cases in which they were involved.

9. insinuated (in sin′ yōo wāt′ 'd) *v.*: Hinted; suggested indirectly.

of the way and forgotten, because tomorrow bristled with so much to do.

In addition to classes and sports and clubs, there was the war. Brinker Hadley could compose his Shortest War Poem Ever Written

The War
Is a bore

if he wanted to, but all of us had to take stronger action than that. First there was the local apple crop, threatening to rot because the harvesters had all gone into the army or war factories. We spent several shining days picking them and were paid in cash for it. Brinker was inspired to write his Apple Ode

Our chore
Is the core
of the war

and the novelty and money of these days excited us. Life at Devon was revealed as still very close to the ways of peace; the war was at worst only a bore, as Brinker said, no more taxing to us than a day spent at harvesting in an apple orchard.

Not long afterward, early even for New Hampshire, snow came. It came theatrically, late one afternoon; I looked up from my desk and saw that suddenly there were big flakes twirling down into the quadrangle, settling on the carefully pruned shrubbery bordering the crosswalks, the three elms still holding many of their leaves, the still-green lawns. They gathered there thicker by the minute, like noiseless invaders conquering because they took possession so gently. I watched them whirl past my window —don't take this seriously, the playful way they fell seemed to imply, this little show, this harmless trick.

It seemed to be true. The school was thinly blanketed that night, but the next morning, a bright, almost balmy day, every flake disappeared. The following weekend, however, it snowed again, then two days later much harder, and by the end of that week the ground had been clamped under snow for the winter.

In the same way the war, beginning almost humorously with announcements about maids and days spent at apple-picking, commenced its invasion of the school. The early snow was commandeered as its advance guard.[10]

Leper Lepellier didn't suspect this. It was not in fact evident to anyone at first. But Leper stands out for me as the person who was most often and most emphatically taken by surprise, by this and every other shift in our life at Devon.

The heavy snow paralyzed the railroad yards of one of the large towns south of us on the Boston and Maine line. At chapel the day following the heaviest snowfall, two hundred volunteers were solicited[11] to spend the day shoveling them out, as part of the Emergency Usefulness policy adopted by the faculty that fall. Again we would be paid. So we all volunteered, Brinker and I and Chet Douglass and even I noticed, Quackenbush.

But not Leper. He generally made little sketches of birds and trees in the back of his notebook during chapel, so that he had probably not heard the announcement. The train to take us south to the work did not arrive until after lunch, and on my way to the station, taking a short cut through a

---

10. commandeered (käm′ ən dir′d′) **as its advance guard:** Forced into service to be part of the small group of soldiers that investigate what lies ahead, protect the route, and lead the way for the rest of the troops.

11. solicited (sə lis′ it əd) v.: Asked.

meadow not far from the river, I met Leper. I had hardly seen him all fall, and I hardly recognized him now. He was standing motionless on the top of a small ridge, and he seemed from a distance to be a scarecrow left over from the growing season. As I plodded toward him through the snow I began to differentiate items of clothing—a dull green deer-stalker's cap, brown ear muffs, a thick gray woolen scarf—then at last I recognized the face in the midst of them, Leper's, pinched and pink, his eyes peering curiously toward some distant woods through steel-rimmed glasses. As I got nearer I noticed that below his long tan canvas coat with sagging pockets, below the red and black plaid woolen knickers and green puttees,[12] he was wearing skis. They were very long, wooden and battered, and had two decorative, old-fashioned knobs on their tips.

"You think there's a path through those woods?" he asked in his mild tentative voice when I got near. Leper did not switch easily from one train of thought to another, and even though I was an old friend whom he had not talked to in months I didn't mind his taking me for granted now, even at this improbable meeting in a wide, empty field of snow.

"I'm not sure, Leper, but I think there's one at the bottom of the slope."

"Oh yeah, I guess there is." We always called him Leper to his face; he wouldn't have remembered to respond to any other name.

I couldn't keep from staring at him, at the burlesque[13] explorer look of him. "What are you," I asked at last, "um, what are you doing, anyway?"

"I'm touring."

"Touring." I examined the long bamboo ski poles he held. "How do you mean, touring?"

"Touring. It's the way you get around the countryside in the winter. Touring skiing. It's how you go overland in the snow."

"Where are you going?"

"Well, I'm not *going* anywhere." He bent down to tighten the lacings on a puttee. "I'm just touring around."

"There's that place across the river where you could ski. The place where they have the rope tow on that steep hill across from the railroad station. You could go over there."

"No, I don't think so." He surveyed the woods again, although his breath had fogged his glasses. "That's not skiing."

"Why sure that's skiing. It's a good little run, you can get going pretty fast on that hill."

"Yeah but that's it, that's why it isn't skiing. Skiing isn't supposed to be fast. Skis are for useful locomotion." He turned his inquiring eyes on me. "You can break a leg with that downhill stuff."

"Not on that little hill."

"Well, it's the same thing. It's part of the whole wrong idea. They're ruining skiing in this country, rope tows and chair lifts and all that stuff. You get carted up, and then you whizz down. You never get to see the trees or anything. Oh you see a lot of trees shoot by, but you never get to really look at trees, at a tree. I just like to go along and see what I'm passing and enjoy myself." He had come to the end of his thought, and now he slowly took me in, noticing my layers of old clothes. "What are you doing, anyway?" he asked mildly and curiously.

"Going to work on the railroad." He kept gazing mildly and curiously at me. "Shovel out those tracks. That work they

---

12. puttees (pu tēz') *n*.: Coverings for the lower leg.
13. burlesque (bər lesk') *adj*.: Comically imitating.

talked about in chapel this morning. You remember."

"Have a nice day at it, anyway," he said.

"I will. You too."

"I will if I find what I'm looking for—a beaver dam. It used to be up the Devon a ways, in a little stream that flows into the Devon. It's interesting to see the way beavers adapt to the winter. Have you ever seen it?"

"No, I never have seen that."

"Well, you might want to come sometime, if I find the place."

"Tell me if you find it."

With Leper it was always a fight, a hard fight to win when you were seventeen years old and lived in a keyed-up, competing school, to avoid making fun of him. But as I had gotten to know him better this fight had been easier to win.

Shoving in his long bamboo poles he pushed deliberately forward and slid slowly away from me down the gradual slope, standing very upright, his skis far apart to guard against any threat to his balance, his poles sticking out on either side of him, as though to ward off any interference.

I turned and trudged off to help shovel out New England for the war.

We spent an odd day, toiling in that railroad yard. By the time we arrived there the snow had become drab and sooted, wet and heavy. We were divided into gangs, each under an old railroad man. Brinker, Chet and I managed to be in the same group, but the playful atmosphere of the apple orchard was gone. Of the town we could only see some dull red brick mills and warehouses surrounding the yards, and we labored away among what the old man directing us called "rolling stock"—grim freight cars from many parts of the country immobilized in the snow. Brinker asked him if it shouldn't

be called "unrolling stock" now, and the old man looked back at him with bleary dislike and didn't reply. Nothing was very funny that day, the work became hard and unvarying; I began to sweat under my layers of clothes. By the middle of the afternoon we had lost our fresh volunteer look, the grime of the railroad and the exhaustion of manual laborers were on us all; we seemed of a piece with the railroad yards and the mills and warehouses. The old man resented us, or we made him nervous, or maybe he was as sick as he looked. For whatever reason he grumbled and spat and alternated between growling orders and rubbing his big, unhealthy belly.

Around 4:30 there was a moment of cheer. The main line had been cleared and the first train rattled slowly through. We watched it advance toward us, the engine throwing up balls of steam to add to the heavy overcast.

All of us lined both sides of the track and got ready to cheer the engineer and passengers. The coach windows were open and the passengers surprisingly were hanging out; they were all men, I could discern, all young, all alike. It was a troop train.

Over the clatter and banging of the wheels and couplings we cheered and they yelled back, both sides taken by surprise. They were not much older than we were and although probably just recruits, they gave the impression of being an elite as they were carried past our drab ranks. They seemed to be having a wonderful time, their uniforms looked new and good; they were clean and energetic; they were going places.

After they had gone we laborers looked rather emptily across the newly cleared rails at each other, at ourselves, and not even Brinker thought of the timely remark. We turned away. The old man told us to go back

" ... we seemed to be nothing but children playing among heroic men."

to other parts of the yard, but there was no more real work done that afternoon. Stranded in this mill town railroad yard while the whole world was converging elsewhere, we seemed to be nothing but children playing among heroic men.

The day ended at last. Gray from the beginning, its end was announced by a deepening gray, of sky, snow, faces, spirits. We piled back into the old, dispiritedly lit coaches waiting for us, slumped into the uncomfortable green seats, and no one said much until we were miles away.

When we did speak it was about aviation training programs and brothers in the service and requirements for enlistment and the futility of Devon and how we would never have war stories to tell our grandchildren and how long the war might last and who ever heard of studying dead languages at a time like this.

Quackenbush took advantage of a break in this line of conversation to announce that he would certainly stay at Devon through the year, however half-cocked others might rush off. He elaborated without encouragement, citing the advantages of Devon's physical hardening program and of a high school diploma when he did in good time reach basic training. He for one would advance into the army step by step.

"You for one," echoed someone contemptuously.

"You *are* one," someone else said.

"Which army, Quackenbush? Mussolini's?"

"Naw, he's a Kraut."[14]

"He's a Kraut spy."

"How many rails did you sabotage today, Quackenbush?"

"I thought they interned all Quackenbushes the day after Pearl Harbor."[15]

To which Brinker added: "They didn't find him. He hid his light under a Quackenbush."

We were all tired at the end of that day.

Walking back to the school grounds from the railroad station in the descending darkness we overtook a lone figure sliding along the snow-covered edge of the street.

"Will you look at Lepellier," began Brinker irritably. "Who does he think he is, the Abominable Snowman?"[16]

"He's just been out skiing around," I said quickly. I didn't want to see today's strained tempers exploding on Leper. Then as we came up beside him, "Did you find the dam, Leper?"

He turned his head slowly, without breaking his forward movement of alternately planted poles and thrust skis, rhythmically but feebly continuous like a homemade piston engine's. "You know what? I did find it," his smile was wide and unfocused, as though not for me alone but for anyone and anything which wished to share this pleasure with him, "and it was really interesting to see. I took some pictures of it, and if they come out I'll bring them over and show you."

"What dam is that?" Brinker asked me.

"It's a . . . well a little dam up the river he knows about," I said.

"I don't know of any dam up the river."

"Well, it's not in the Devon itself, it's in one of the . . . tributaries."

"Tributaries! To the *Devon?*"

---

14. **Kraut:** Used during World War II as a derogatory term for a German.

15. **Pearl Harbor:** U.S. naval base in Hawaii attacked on December 7, 1941, by the Japanese, thus causing the United States to enter World War II. The name of the base is used to refer to the event.

16. **Abominable** (ə bäm′ ə nə bəl) **Snowman**: A legendary creature said to inhabit the slopes of the Himalayan Mountains.

"You know, a little creek or something."

He knit his brows in mystification. "What kind of a dam is this, anyway?"

"Well," he couldn't be put off with half a story, "it's a beaver dam."

Brinker's shoulders fell under the weight of this news. "That's the kind of a place I'm in with a world war going on. A school for photographers of beaver dams."

"The beaver never appeared himself," Leper offered.

Brinker turned elaborately toward him. "Didn't he really?"

"No. But I guess I was pretty clumsy getting close to it, so he might have heard me and been frightened."

"Well." Brinker's expansive, dazed tone suggested that here was one of life's giant ironies, "There you are!"

"Yes," agreed Leper after a thoughtful pause, "there you are."

"Here we are," I said, pulling Brinker around the corner we had reached which led to our dormitory. "So long, Leper. Glad you found it."

"Oh," he raised his voice after us, "how was your day? How did the work go?"

"Just like a stag at eve," Brinker roared back. "It was a winter wonderland, every minute." And out of the side of his mouth, to me, "Everybody in this place is either a draft-dodging Kraut or a . . . a . . ." the scornful force of his tone turned the word into a curse, "a *nat-u-ral-ist!*" He grabbed my arm agitatedly. "I'm giving it up, I'm going to enlist. Tomorrow."

I felt a thrill when he said it. This was the logical climax of the whole misbegotten[17] day, this whole out-of-joint term at Devon. I think I had been waiting for a long time for someone to say this so that I could entertain these decisive words myself.

To enlist. To slam the door impulsively on the past, to shed everything down to my last bit of clothing, to break the pattern of my life—that complex design I had been weaving since birth with all its dark threads, its unexplainable symbols set against a conventional background of domestic white and schoolboy blue, all those tangled strands which required the dexterity of a virtuoso[18] to keep flowing—I yearned to take giant military shears to it, snap! bitten off in an instant, and nothing left in my hands but spools of khaki which could weave only a plain, flat, khaki design, however twisted they might be.

Not that it would be a good life. The war would be deadly all right. But I was used to finding something deadly in things that attracted me; there was always something deadly lurking in anything I wanted, anything I loved. And if it wasn't there, as for example with Phineas, then I put it there myself.

But in the war, there was no question about it at all; it was there.

I separated from Brinker in the quadrangle, since one of his clubs was meeting and he could not go back to the dormitory yet —"I've got to preside at a meeting of the Golden Fleece Debating Society tonight," he said in a tone of amazed contempt, "the Golden Fleece Debating Society! We're mad here, all mad," and he went off raving to himself in the dark.

It was a night made for hard thoughts. Sharp stars pierced singly through the blackness, not sweeps of them or clusters or Milky Ways as there might have been in the South, but single, chilled points of light, as unromantic as knife blades. Devon, muffled under the gentle occupation of the snow, was dominated by them; the cold Yankee

---

17. misbegotten (mis' bi gät' 'n) *adj.*: Wrongly or unlawfully produced or thought out.

18. virtuoso (vʉr' cͪoo wō' sō) *n.*: Person displaying great technical skill in any field.

stars ruled this night. They did not invoke in me thoughts of God, or sailing before the mast, or some great love as crowded night skies at home had done; I thought instead, in the light of those cold points, of the decision facing me.

Why go through the motions of getting an education and watch the war slowly chip away at the one thing I had loved here, the peace, the measureless, careless peace of the Devon summer? Others, the Quackenbushes of this world, could calmly watch the war approach them and jump into it at the last and most advantageous instant, as though buying into the stock market. But I couldn't.

There was no one to stop me but myself. Putting aside soft reservations about What I Owed Devon and my duty to my parents and so on, I reckoned my responsibilities by the light of the unsentimental night sky and knew that I owed no one anything. I owed it to myself to meet this crisis in my life when I chose, and I chose now.

I bounced zestfully up the dormitory stairs. Perhaps because my mind still retained the image of the sharp night stars, those few fixed points of light in the darkness, perhaps because of that the warm yellow light streaming from under my own door came as such a shock. It was a simple case of a change of expectation. The light should have been off. Instead, as though alive itself, it poured in a thin yellow slab of brightness from under the door, illuminating the dust and splinters of the hall floor.

I grabbed the knob and swung open the door. He was seated in my chair at the desk, bending down to adjust the gross encumbrance[19] of his leg, so that only the familiar ears set close against his head were visible, and his short-cut brown hair. He looked up

with a provocative grin, "Hi pal, where's the brass band?"

Everything that had happened throughout the day faded like that first false snowfall of the winter. Phineas was back.

Chapter 8

"I can see I never should have left you alone," Phineas went on before I could recover from the impact of finding him there, "Where did you get *those* clothes!" His bright, indignant eyes swept from my battered gray cap, down the frayed sweater and paint-stained pants to a pair of clodhoppers.[1] "You don't have to advertise like that, we all know you're the worst dressed man in the class."

"I've been working, that's all. These are just work clothes."

"In the boiler room?"

"On the railroad. Shoveling snow."

He sat back in the chair. "Shoveling railroad snow. Well that makes sense, we always did that the first term."

I pulled off the sweater, under which I was wearing a rain slicker I used to go sailing in, a kind of canvas sack. Phineas just studied it in wordless absorption. "I like the cut of it," he finally murmured. I pulled that off revealing an Army fatigue shirt my brother had given me. "Very topical," said Phineas through his teeth. After that came off there was just my undershirt, stained with sweat. He smiled at it for a while and then said as he heaved himself out of the chair, "There. You should have worn that all day, just that. That has real taste. The rest of your outfit was just gilding that lily of a sweat shirt."

"Glad to hear you like it."

---

19. encumbrance (en kum′ brəns) *n*.: Burden.

1. clodhoppers (kläd′ häp′ ərz) *n*.: Coarse, heavy shoes such as those worn by farmers.

"Not at all," he replied ambiguously,[2] reaching for a pair of crutches which leaned against the desk.

I took the sight of this all right, I had seen him on crutches the year before when he broke his ankle playing football. At Devon crutches had almost as many athletic associations as shoulder pads. And I had never seen an invalid whose skin glowed with such health, accenting the sharp clarity of his eyes, or one who used his arms and shoulders on crutches as though on parallel bars, as though he would do a somersault on them if he felt like it. Phineas vaulted across the room to his cot, yanked back the spread and then groaned. "Oh, it's not made up. What is all this crap about no maids?"

"No maids," I said. "After all, there's a war on. It's not much of a sacrifice, when you think of people starving and being bombed and all the other things." My unselfishness was responding properly to the influences of 1942. In these past months Phineas and I had grown apart on this; I felt a certain disapproval of him for grumbling about a lost luxury, with a war on. "After all," I repeated, "there is a war on."

"Is there?" he murmured absently. I didn't pay any attention; he was always speaking when his thoughts were somewhere else, asking rhetorical questions[3] and echoing other people's words.

I found some sheets and made up his bed for him. He wasn't a bit sensitive about being helped, not a bit like an invalid striving to seem independent. I put this on the list of things to include when I said some prayers, the first in a long time, that night in bed. Now that Phineas was back it seemed time to start saying prayers again.

After the lights went out the special quality of my silence let him know that I was saying them, and he kept quiet for approximately three minutes. Then he began to talk; he never went to sleep without talking first and he seemed to feel that prayers lasting more than three minutes were showing off. God was always unoccupied in Finny's universe, ready to lend an ear any time at all. Anyone who failed to get his message through in three minutes, as I sometimes failed to do when trying to impress him, Phineas, with my sanctity,[4] wasn't trying.

He was still talking when I fell asleep, and the next morning, through the icy atmosphere which one window raised an inch had admitted to our room, he woke me with the overindignant shout, "What *is* all this crap about no maids!" He was sitting up in bed, as though ready to spring out of it, totally and energetically awake. I had to laugh at this indignant athlete, with the strength of five people, complaining about the service. He threw back his bedclothes and said, "Hand me my crutches, will you?"

Until now, in spite of everything, I had welcomed each new day as though it were a new life, where all past failures and problems were erased, and all future possibilities and joys open and available, to be achieved probably before night fell again. Now, in this winter of snow and crutches with Phineas, I began to know that each morning reasserted the problems of the night before, that sleep suspended all but changed nothing, that you couldn't make yourself over between dawn and dusk. Phineas however did not believe this. I'm sure that he looked down at his leg every morning first thing, as soon as he remembered it, to see if it had not

---

2. ambiguously (am big′ yo͞o əs lē) *adv.*: Vaguely; uncertainly.

3. rhetorical (ri tôr′ i kəl) **questions:** Questions asked only for effect, as to emphasize a point, not intended to be answered.

---

4. sanctity (saŋk′ tə tē) *n.*: Saintliness; holiness.

been totally restored while he slept. When he found on this first morning back at Devon that it happened still to be crippled and in a cast, he said in his usual self-contained way, "Hand me my crutches, will you?"

Brinker Hadley, next door, always awoke like an express train. There was a gathering rumble through the wall, as Brinker reared up in bed, coughed hoarsely, slammed his feet on the floor, pounded through the freezing air to the closet for something in the way of clothes, and thundered down the hall to the bathroom. Today, however, he veered and broke into our room instead.

"Ready to sign up?" he shouted before he was through the door. "You ready to en—Finny!"

"You ready to en—what?" pursued Finny from his bed. "Who's ready to sign and en what?"

"Finny, you're back!"

"Sure," confirmed Finny with a slight, pleased grin.

"So," Brinker curled his lip at me, "your little plot didn't work so well after all."

"What's he talking about?" said Finny as I thrust his crutches beneath his shoulders.

"Just talking," I said shortly. "What does Brinker ever talk about?"

"*You* know what I'm talking about well enough."

"No I don't."

"Oh yes you do."

"Are you telling me what I know?"

"I am."

"What's he *talking* about," said Finny.

The room was bitterly cold. I stood trembling in front of Phineas, still holding his crutches in place, unable to turn and face Brinker and this joke he had gotten into his head, this catastrophic joke.

"He wants to know if I'll sign up with him," I said, "enlist." It was the ultimate question for all seventeen-year-olds that year, and it drove Brinker's insinuations[5] from every mind but mine.

"Yeah," said Brinker.

"Enlist!" cried Finny at the same time. His large and clear eyes turned with an odd expression on me. I had never seen such a look in them before. After looking at me closely he said, "You're going to enlist?"

"Well I just thought—last night after the railroad work—"

"You thought you might sign up?" he went on, looking carefully away.

Brinker drew one of his deep senatorial breaths, but he found nothing to say. We three stood shivering in the thin New Hampshire morning light, Finny and I in pajamas, Brinker in a blue flannel bathrobe and ripped moccasins. "When will you?" Finny went on.

"Oh, I don't know," I said. "It was just something Brinker happened to say last night, that's all."

"I said," Brinker began in an unusually guarded voice, glancing quickly at Phineas, "I said something about enlisting today."

Finny hobbled over to the dresser and took up his soap dish. "I'm first in the shower," he said.

"You can't get that cast wet, can you?" asked Brinker.

"No, I'll keep it outside the curtain."

"I'll help," said Brinker.

"No," said Finny without looking at him, "I can manage all right."

"How can you manage all right?" Brinker persisted aggressively.

"I can *manage* all right," Finny repeated with a set face.

I could hardly believe it, but it was too plainly printed in the closed expression of

---

5. insinuations (in sin′ yo͞o ā′ shənz) *n.*: Sly hints or suggestions.

his face to mistake, too discernible[6] beneath the even tone of his voice: Phineas was shocked at the idea of my leaving. In some way he needed me. He needed me. I was the least trustworthy person he had ever met. I knew that; he knew or should know that too. I had even told him. I had told him. But there was no mistaking the shield of remoteness in his face and voice. He wanted me around. The war then passed away from me, and dreams of enlistment and escape and a clean start lost their meaning for me.

"Sure you can manage the shower all right," I said, "but what difference does it make? Come on. Brinker's always . . . Brinker's always getting there first. Enlist! What a nutty idea. It's just Brinker wanting to get there first again. I wouldn't enlist with you if you were General MacArthur's eldest son."

Brinker reared back arrogantly. "And who do you think I am!" But Finny hadn't heard that. His face had broken into a wide and dazzled smile at what I had said, lighting up his whole face. "Enlist!" I drove on, "I wouldn't enlist with you if you were Elliott Roosevelt."[7]

"First cousin," said Brinker over his chin, "once removed."

"He wouldn't enlist with you," Finny plunged in, "if you were Madame Chiang Kai-shek."[8]

"Well," I qualified in an undertone, "he really *is* Madame Chiang Kai-shek."

"Well fan my brow," cried Finny, giving us his stunned look of total appalled horrified amazement, "who would have thought that!"

But in a week I had forgotten that, and I have never since forgotten the dazed look on Finny's face when he thought that on the first day of his return to Devon I was going to desert him. I didn't know why he had chosen me, why it was only to me that he could show the most humbling sides of his handicap. I didn't care. For the war was no longer eroding the peaceful summertime stillness I had prized so much at Devon, and although the playing fields were crusted under a foot of congealed snow and the river was now a hard gray-white lane of ice between gaunt trees, peace had come back to Devon for me.

So the war swept over like a wave at the seashore, gathering power and size as it bore on us, overwhelming in its rush, seemingly inescapable, and then at the last moment eluded by a word from Phineas; I had simply ducked, that was all, and the wave's concentrated power had hurtled harmlessly overhead, no doubt throwing others roughly up on the beach, but leaving me peaceably treading water as before. I did not stop to think that one wave is inevitably followed by another even larger and more powerful, when the tide is coming in.

"I *like* the winter," Finny assured me for the fourth time, as we came back from chapel that morning.

"Well, it doesn't like you." Wooden plank walks had been placed on many of the school paths for better footing, but there were icy patches everywhere on them. A crutch misplaced and he could be thrown down upon the frozen wooden planking, or into the ice-encrusted snow.

Even indoors Devon was a nest of traps for him. The school had been largely rebuilt with a massive bequest from an oil family

---

6. discernible (di sʉrn′ ə b'l) *adj.*: Clearly recognizable.

7. Elliott Roosevelt: A son of President Franklin D. Roosevelt. Gene has made his refusal to enlist with Brinker even more emphatic by comparing him to the son of the President instead of to the son of a general.

8. Madame Chiang Kai-shek (chaŋ′ kī shek′): The wife of the head of the Chinese government during World War II.

" *So the war swept over like a wave at the seashore,* ... "

some years before in a peculiar style of Puritan grandeur, as though Versailles[9] had been modified for the needs of a Sunday school. This opulent sobriety[10] betrayed the divided nature of the school, just as in a different way the two rivers that it straddled did. From the outside the buildings were reticent,[11] severe straight lines of red brick or white clapboard, with shutters standing sentinel beside each window, and a few unassuming white cupolas placed here and there on the roofs because they were expected and not pretty, like Pilgrim bonnets.

But once you passed through the Colonial doorways, with only an occasional fan window or low relief pillar to suggest that a certain muted adornment was permissible, you entered an extravaganza of Pompadour[12] splendor. Pink marble walls and white marble floors were enclosed by arched and vaulted ceilings; an assembly room had been done in the manner of the High Italian Renaissance,[13] another was illuminated by chandeliers flashing with crystal teardrops; there was a wall of fragile French windows overlooking an Italian garden of marble bric-à-brac; the library was Provençal[14] on the first floor, rococo[15] on the second. And everywhere, except in the dormitories, the floors and stairs were of smooth, slick marble, more treacherous even than the icy walks.

"The winter loves me," he retorted, and then, disliking the whimsical[16] sound of that, added, "I mean as much as you can say a season can love. What I mean is, I love winter, and when you really love something, then it loves you back, in whatever way it has to love." I didn't think that this was true, my seventeen years of experience had shown this to be much more false than true, but it was like every other thought and belief of Finny's: it should have been true. So I didn't argue.

The board walk ended and he moved a little ahead of me as we descended a sloping path toward our first class. He picked his way with surprising care, surprising in anyone who before had used the ground mainly as a point of departure, as the given element in a suspended world of leaps in space. And now I remembered what I had never taken any special note of before: how Phineas used to walk. Around Devon we had gaits of every description; gangling shuffles from boys who had suddenly grown a foot taller, swinging cowboy lopes from those thinking of how wide their shoulders had become, ambles, waddles, light trippings, gigantic Bunyan[17] strides. But Phineas had moved in continuous flowing balance, so that he had seemed to drift along with no effort at all, relaxation on the move. He hobbled now

---

9. Versailles (vər sī′) *n.*: Magnificent French palace built in the seventeenth century by King Louis XIV and enlarged by King Louis XV. It housed over 5,000 members of the royal court and was the principal residence of the kings of France and the seat of government for over 100 years. It has become known as a symbol of royal extravagance.
10. opulent sobriety (äp′ yə lənt sə brī′ ə tē): Plush or extravagant seriousness.
11. reticent (ret′ ə s'nt) *adj.*: Having a restrained, quiet, or understated quality.
12. Pompadour (päm′ pə dôr′): Madame de Pompadour (1721–1764), an influential French patron of the arts who designed several palaces for King Louis XV.
13. High Italian Renaissance (ren′ ə säns′): The ornate style of Italian architecture of the fourteenth and fifteenth centuries.
14. Provençal (prō′ văn säl′) *adj.*: In the style of eighteenth-century France.

15. rococo (rə kō′ kō) *adj.*: A style of the early eighteenth century, characterized by much delicate ornamentation.
16. whimsical (hwim′ zi k'l) *adj.*: Playful; odd.
17. Bunyan (bun′ yən): A reference to Paul Bunyan, legendary, giant lumberjack of American folklore, who with his blue ox, Babe, performed various superhuman feats.

among the patches of ice. There was the one certainty that Dr. Stanpole had given —Phineas would walk again. But the thought was there before me that he would never walk like that again.

"Do you have a class?" he said as we reached the steps of the building.

"Yes."

"So do I. Let's not go."

"Not go? But what'll we use for an excuse?"

"We'll say I fainted from exertion on the way from chapel," he looked at me with a phantom's smile, "and you had to tend me."

"This is your first day back, Finny. You're no one to cut classes."

"I know, I know. I'm going to work. I really am going to work. You're going to pull me through mostly, but I *am* going to work as hard as I can. Only not today, not the first thing. *Not* now, not conjugating verbs when I haven't even looked at the school yet. I want to see this place, I haven't seen anything except the inside of our room, and the inside of chapel. I don't feel like seeing the inside of a classroom. Not now. Not yet."

"What do you want to see?"

He had started to turn around so that his back was to me. "Let's go to the gym," he said shortly.

The gym was at the other end of the school, a quarter of a mile away at least, separated from us by a field of ice. We set off without saying anything else.

By the time we had reached it sweat was running like oil from Finny's face, and when he paused involuntary tremors shook his hands and arms. The leg in its cast was like a sea anchor dragged behind. The illusion of strength I had seen in our room that morning must have been the same illusion he had used at home to deceive his doctor and his family into sending him back to Devon.

We stood on the ice-coated lawn in front of the gym while he got ready to enter it, resting himself so that he could go in with a show of energy. Later this became his habit; I often caught up with him standing in front of a building pretending to be thinking or examining the sky or taking off gloves, but it was never a convincing show. Phineas was a poor deceiver, having had no practice.

We went into the gym, along a marble hallway, and to my surprise we went on past the Trophy Room, where his name was already inscribed on one cup, one banner, and one embalmed football. I was sure that this was his goal, to mull over these lost glories. I had prepared myself for that, and even thought of several positive, uplifting aphorisms[18] to cheer him up. But he went by it without a thought, down a stairway, steep and marble, and into the locker room. I went along mystified beside him. There was a pile of dirty towels in a corner. Finny shoved them with a crutch. "What is all this crap," he muttered with a little smile, "about no maids?"

The locker room was empty at this hour, row after row of dull green lockers separated by wide wooden benches. The ceiling was hung with pipes. It was a drab room for Devon, dull green and brown and gray, but at the far end there was a big marble archway, glisteningly white, which led to the pool.

Finny sat down on a bench, struggled out of his sheep-lined winter coat, and took a deep breath of gymnasium air. No locker room could have more pungent air than Devon's; sweat predominated, but it was richly mingled with smells of paraffin and singed rubber, of soaked wool and liniment,

---

18. aphorisms (af′ ə riz′mz) *n.*: Short sayings expressing wise or clever observations about life.

and for those who could interpret it, of exhaustion, lost hope and triumph and bodies battling against each other. I thought it anything but a bad smell. It was preeminently the smell of the human body after it had been used to the limit, such a smell as has meaning and poignance[19] for any athlete, just as it has for any lover.

Phineas looked down here and there, at the exercise bar over a sand pit next to the wall, at a set of weights on the floor, at the rolled-up wrestling mat, at a pair of spiked shoes kicked under a locker.

"Same old place, isn't it?" he said, turning to me and nodding slightly.

After a moment I answered in a quiet voice, "Not exactly."

He made no pretense of not understanding me. After a pause he said, "You're going to be the big star now," in an optimistic tone, and then added with some embarrassment, "You can fill any gaps or anything." He slapped me on the back, "Get over there and chin yourself a few dozen times. What did you finally go out for anyway?"

"I finally didn't go out."

"You aren't," his eyes burned at me from his grimacing face, "still the assistant senior crew manager!"

"No, I quit that. I've just been going to gym classes. The ones they have for guys who aren't going out for anything."

He wrenched himself around on the bench. Joking was past; his mouth widened irritably. "What," his voice bounded on the word in a sudden rich descent, "did you do that for?"

"It was too late to sign up for anything else," and seeing the energy to blast this excuse rushing to his face and neck I stumbled on, "and anyway with the war on there won't be many trips for the teams. I don't

know, sports don't seem so important with the war on."

"Have you swallowed all that war stuff?"

"No, of course I—" I was so committed to refuting him that I had half-denied the charge before I understood it; now my eyes swung back to his face. "All what war stuff?"

"All that stuff about there being a war."

"I don't think I get what you mean."

"Do you really think that the United States of America is in a state of war with Nazi Germany and Imperial Japan?"

"Do I really think . . ." My voice trailed off.

He stood up, his weight on the good leg, the other resting lightly on the floor in front of him. "Don't be a sap," he gazed with cool self-possession at me, "there isn't any war."

"I know why you're talking like this," I said, struggling to keep up with him. "Now I understand. You're still under the influence of some medicinal drug."

"No, you are. Everybody is." He pivoted so that he was facing directly at me. "That's what this whole war story is. A medicinal drug. Listen, did you ever hear of the 'Roaring Twenties'?"[20] I nodded very slowly and cautiously. "When everybody who was young did just what they wanted?"

"Yes."

"Well what happened was that they didn't like that, all the stuffed shirts. So then they tried Prohibition[21] and arranged the Depression.[22] That kept the people who

---

19. poignance (poin′ yəns) n.: A feeling that is emotionally touching or moving.

20. "Roaring Twenties": The 1920's, a decade known for its exuberance and excesses.

21. Prohibition (prō′ i bish′ ən) n.: The period (1920–1933) when the manufacture, transportation, and sale of alcoholic beverages were forbidden by federal law.

22. Depression (dē presh′ ən) n.: The period of decrease in economic activity that began in 1929 and lasted through most of the 1930's; the Great Depression.

were young in the thirties in their places. But they couldn't use that trick forever, so for us in the forties they've cooked up this war fake."

"Who are 'they,' anyway?"

"The fat old men who don't want us crowding them out of their jobs. They've made it all up. There isn't any real food shortage, for instance. The men have all the best steaks delivered to their clubs now. You've noticed how they've been getting fatter lately, haven't you?"

His tone took it thoroughly for granted that I had. For a moment I was almost taken in by it. Then my eyes fell on the bound and cast white mass pointing at me, and as it was always to do, it brought me down out of Finny's world of invention, down again as I had fallen after awakening that morning, down to reality, to the facts.

"Phineas, this is all pretty amusing and everything, but I hope you don't play this game too much with yourself. You might start to believe it and then I'd have to make a reservation for you at the Funny Farm."

"In a way," deep in argument, his eyes never wavered from mine, "the whole world is on a Funny Farm now. But it's only the fat old men who get the joke."

"And you."

"Yes, and me."

"What makes you so special? Why should you get it and all the rest of us be in the dark?"

The momentum of the argument abruptly broke from his control. His face froze. "Because I've suffered," he burst out.

We drew back in amazement from this. In the silence all the flighty spirits of the morning ended between us. He sat down and turned his flushed face away from me. I sat next to him without moving for as long as my beating nerves would permit, and then I stood up and walked slowly toward anything which presented itself. It turned out to be the exercise bar. I sprang up, grabbed it, and then, in a fumbling and perhaps grotesque[23] offering to Phineas, I chinned myself. I couldn't think of anything else, not the right words, not the right gesture. I did what I could think of.

"Do thirty of them," he mumbled in a bored voice.

I had never done ten of them. At the twelfth I discovered that he had been counting to himself because he began to count aloud in a noncommittal, half-heard voice. At eighteen there was a certain enlargement in his tone, and at twenty-three the last edges of boredom left it; he stood up, and the urgency with which he brought out the next numbers was like an invisible boost lifting me the distance of my arms, until he sang out "thirty!" with a flare of pleasure.

The moment was past. Phineas I know had been even more startled than I to discover this bitterness in himself. Neither of us ever mentioned it again, and neither of us ever forgot that it was there.

He sat down and studied his clenched hands. "Did I ever tell you," he began in a husky tone, "that I used to be aiming for the Olympics?" He wouldn't have mentioned it except that after what he had said he had to say something very personal, something deeply held. To do otherwise, to begin joking, would have been a hypocritical denial of what had happened, and Phineas was not capable of that.

I was still hanging from the bar; my hands felt as though they had sunk into it. "No, you never told me that," I mumbled into my arm.

"Well I was. And now I'm not sure, not a hundred per cent sure I'll be completely, you know, in shape by 1944. So I'm going to coach you for them instead."

---

23. grotesque (grō tesk′) *adj.*: Ridiculous or distorted.

"But there isn't going to be any Olympics in '44. That's only a couple of years away. The war—"

"Leave your fantasy life out of this. We're grooming you for the Olympics, pal, in 1944."

And not believing him, not forgetting that troops were being shuttled toward battlefields all over the world, I went along, as I always did, with any new invention of Finny's. There was no harm in taking aim, even if the target was a dream.

But since we were so far out of the line of fire, the chief sustenance[24] for any sense of the war was mental. We saw nothing real of it; all our impressions of the war were in the false medium of two dimensions —photographs in the papers and magazines, newsreels, posters—or artificially conveyed to us by a voice on the radio, or headlines across the top of a newspaper. I found that only through a continuous use of the imagination could I hold out against Finny's driving offensive in favor of peace.

And now when we were served chicken livers for dinner I couldn't help conceiving a mental picture of President Roosevelt and my father and Finny's father and numbers of other large old men sitting down to porterhouse steak in some elaborate but secluded men's secret society room. When a letter from home told me that a trip to visit relatives had been canceled because of gas rationing it was easy to visualize my father smiling silently with knowing eyes—at least as easy as it was to imagine an American force crawling through the jungles of a place called Guadalcanal[25]—"Wherever that is," as Phineas said.

And when in chapel day after day we were exhorted to new levels of self-deprivation and hard work, with the war as their justification, it was impossible not to see that the faculty were using this excuse to drive us as they had always wanted to drive us, regardless of any war or peace.

What a joke if Finny was right after all!

But of course I didn't believe him. I was too well protected against the great fear of boys' school life, which is to be "taken in." Along with everyone else except a few professional gulls[26] such as Leper, I rejected anything which had the smallest possibility of doubt about it. So of course I didn't believe him. But one day after our chaplain, Mr. Carhart, had become very moved by his own sermon in chapel about God in the Foxholes,[27] I came away thinking that if Finny's opinion of the war was unreal, Mr. Carhart's was at least as unreal. But of course I didn't believe him.

And anyway I was too occupied to think about it all. In addition to my own work, I was dividing my time between tutoring Finny in studies and being tutored by him in sports. Since so much of learning anything depends on the atmosphere in which it is taught, Finny and I, to our joint double amazement, began to make flashing progress where we had been bumblers before.

Mornings we got up at six to run. I dressed in a gym sweat suit with a towel tucked around my throat, and Finny in pajamas, ski boots and his sheep-lined coat.

A morning shortly before Christmas vacation brought my reward. I was to run the course Finny had laid out, four times around an oval walk which circled the Headmas-

---

24. sustenance (sus′ ti nəns) n.: Maintenance; support.
25. Guadalcanal (gwä′ d'l kə nal′) n.: Largest island of the Solomon Islands in the southwest Pacific where the United States gained control in 1943 after a prolonged struggle.

26. gulls (gulz) n.: People who are easily cheated or tricked.
27. Foxholes (fäks′ hōlz′) n.: Holes dug in the ground as temporary protection for soldiers against enemy gunfire.

ter's home, a large rambling, doubtfully Colonial white mansion. Next to the house there was a patriarchal[28] elm tree, against the trunk of which Finny leaned and shouted at me as I ran a large circle around him.

This plain of snow shone a powdery white that morning; the sun blazed icily somewhere too low on the horizon to be seen directly, but its clean rays shed a blue-white glimmer all around us. The northern sunshine seemed to pick up faint particles of whiteness floating in the air and powdering the sleek blue sky. Nothing stirred. The bare arching branches of the elm seemed laid into this motionless sky. As I ran the sound of my footfalls was pitched off short in the vast immobile dawn, as though there was no room amid so many glittering sights for any sound to intrude. The figure of Phineas was set against the bulk of the tree; he shouted now and then, but these sounds too were quickly absorbed and dispelled.

And he needed to give no advice that morning. After making two circuits of the walk every trace of energy was as usual completely used up, and as I drove myself on all my scattered aches found their usual way to a profound seat of pain in my side. My lungs as usual were fed up with all this work, and from now on would only go rackingly through the motions. My knees were boneless again, ready any minute to let my lower legs telescope up into the thighs. My head felt as though different sections of the cranium were grinding into each other.

Then, for no reason at all, I felt magnificent. It was as though my body until that instant had simply been lazy, as though the aches and exhaustion were all imagined, created from nothing in order to keep me from truly exerting myself. Now my body seemed at last to say, "Well, if you must have

it, here!" and an accession of strength came flooding through me. Buoyed up, I forgot my usual feeling of routine self-pity when working out, I lost myself, oppressed mind along with aching body; all entanglements were shed, I broke into the clear.

After the fourth circuit, like sitting in a chair, I pulled up in front of Phineas.

"You're not even winded," he said.

"I know."

"You found your rhythm, didn't you, that third time around. Just as you came into that straight part there."

"Yes, right there."

"You've been pretty lazy all along, haven't you?"

"Yes, I guess I have been."

"You didn't even know anything about yourself."

"I don't guess I did, in a way."

"Well," he gathered the sheepskin collar around his throat, "now you know. And stop talking like that—'don't guess I did'!" Despite this gibe he was rather impersonal toward me. He seemed older that morning, and leaning quietly against that great tree wrapped in his heavy coat, he seemed smaller too. Or perhaps it was only that I, inside the same body, had felt myself all at once grown bigger.

We proceeded slowly back to the dormitory. On the steps going in we met Mr. Ludsbury coming out.

"I've been watching you from my window," he said in his hooting voice with a rare trace of personal interest. "What are you up to, Forrester, training for the Commandos?" There was no rule explicitly forbidding exercise at such an hour, but it was not expected; ordinarily therefore Mr. Ludsbury would have disapproved. But the war had modified even his standards; all forms of physical exercise had become conventional for the Duration.

---

28. patriarchal (pā′ trē ärk ′l) *adj.*: Fatherly.

I mumbled some abashed[29] answer, but it was Phineas who made the clear response.

"He's developing into a real athlete," he said matter-of-factly. "We're aiming for the '44 Olympics."

Mr. Ludsbury emitted a single chuckle from deep in his throat, then his face turned brick red momentarily and he assumed his customary sententiousness.[30] "Games are all right in their place," he said, "and I won't bore you with the Eton Playing Fields observation, but all exercise today is aimed of course at the approaching Waterloo.[31] Keep that in your sights at all times, won't you."

Finny's face set in determination, with the older look I had just detected in him. "No," he said.

I don't believe any student had ever said "No" flatly to Mr. Ludsbury before. It flustered him uncontrollably. His face turned brick red again, and for a moment I thought he was going to run away. Then he said something so rapid, throaty, and clipped that neither of us understood it, turned quickly and strode off across the quadrangle.

"He's really sincere, he thinks there's a war on," said Finny in simple wonder. "Now why wouldn't he know?" He pondered Mr. Ludsbury's exclusion from the plot of the fat old men as we watched his figure, reedy even in his winter wraps, move away from us. Then the light broke. "Oh, of course!" he cried. "Too thin. Of course."

I stood there pitying Mr. Ludsbury for his fatal thinness and reflecting that after all he had always had a gullible side.

Chapter 9

This was my first but not my last lapse into Finny's vision of peace. For hours, and sometimes for days, I fell without realizing it into the private explanation of the world. Not that I ever believed that the whole production of World War II was a trick of the eye manipulated by a bunch of calculating fat old men, appealing though this idea was. What deceived me was my own happiness; for peace is indivisible, and the surrounding world confusion found no reflection inside me. So I ceased to have any real sense of it.

This was not shaken even by the enlistment of Leper Lepellier. In fact that made the war seem more unreal than ever. No real war could draw Leper voluntarily away from his snails and beaver dams. His enlistment seemed just another of Leper's vagaries, such as the time he slept on top of Mount Katahdin in Maine where each morning the sun first strikes United States territory. On that morning, satisfying one of his urges to participate in nature, Leper Lepellier was the first thing the rising sun struck in the United States.

Early in January, when we had all just returned from the Christmas holidays, a recruiter from the United States ski troops showed a film to the senior class in the Renaissance Room. To Leper it revealed

---

29. abashed (ə bash′ 'd) *adj.*: Self-conscious; ashamed.

30. sententiousness (sen ten′ shəs nəs) *n.*: Manner of using pithy sayings in a moralizing way.

31. Eton Playing Fields observation . . . Waterloo: A quotation from Sir William Fraser's book *Words on Wellington* (1889): "The battle of Waterloo was won on the playing fields of Eton" was popular at the time. People believed that the skills, attitudes, and fortitude learned by taking part in athletic contests at school had made the English capable of finally defeating Napoleon at the battle of Waterloo in 1815 and would be responsible for the Allies finally defeating the Axis in World War II as well.

what all of us were seeking: a recognizable and friendly face to the war. Skiers in white shrouds[1] winged down virgin slopes, silent as angels, and then, realistically, herringboned[2] up again, but herringboned in cheerful, sunburned bands, with clear eyes and white teeth and chests full of vigor-laden mountain air. It was the cleanest image of war I had ever seen; even the Air Force, reputedly so high above the infantry's mud, was stained with axle grease by comparison, and the Navy was vulnerable to scurvy.[3] Nothing tainted these white warriors of winter as they swooped down their spotless mountainsides, and this cool, clean response to war glided straight into Leper's Vermont heart.

"How do you like that!" he whispered to me in a wondering voice during these scenes. "How do you like that!"

"You know, I think these are pictures of Finnish ski troops," Phineas whispered on the other side, "and I want to know when they start shooting our allies the Bolsheviks.[4] Unless that war between them was a fake too,[5] which I'm pretty sure it was."

---

1. shrouds (shroudz) *n.*: Clothes that conceal. Because the word also means a cloth used to wrap a corpse, its use here suggests death.
2. herringboned (her′ iŋ bōnd′) *v.*: Climbing a slope in skis with tips turned outward so the tracks form a pattern resembling the spine of a herring. This method prevents skiers from slipping back down the slope.
3. scurvy (skʉr′ vē) *n.*: A disease resulting from a lack of vitamin C (ascorbic acid) in the body.
4. Bolsheviks (bōl′ shə viks′): Bolsheviks were Russian Communists, our allies during World War II.
5. that war between them was a fake too: The war to which Finney refers is the Russo-Finnish War that occurred when the Soviet Union invaded Finland in 1939. Finland had refused to allow Russian military bases on its territory. The war, called the "winter war," continued until Finland surrendered in March 1940. The Soviet Union did not actually occupy Finland, but Finland did lose some of its territory.

After the movie ended and the lights came on to illuminate the murals of Tuscany and the painted classical galleries around us, Leper still sat amazed in his folding chair. Ordinarily he talked little, and the number of words which came from him now indicated that this was a turning point in his life.

"You know what? Now I see what racing skiing is all about. It's all right to miss seeing the trees and the countryside and all the other things when you've got to be in a hurry. And when you're in a War you've got to be in a hurry. Don't you? So I guess maybe racing skiers weren't ruining the sport after all. They were preparing it, if you see what I mean, for the future. Everything has to evolve or else it perishes." Finny and I had stood up, and Leper looked earnestly from one to the other of us from his chair. "Take the housefly. If it hadn't developed all those split-second reflexes it would have become extinct long ago."

"You mean it adapted itself to the fly swatter?" queried Phineas.

"That's right. And skiing had to learn to move just as fast or it would have been wiped out by this war. Yes, sir. You know what? I'm almost glad this war came along. It's like a test, isn't it, and only the things and the people who've been evolving the right way survive."

You usually listened to Leper's quiet talking with half a mind, but this theory of his brought me to close attention. How did it apply to me, and to Phineas? How, most of all, did it apply to Leper?

"I'm going to enlist in these ski troops," he went on mildly, so unemphatically that my mind went back to half-listening. Threats to enlist that winter were always declaimed like Brinker's, with a grinding of back teeth and a flashing of eyes; I had already heard plenty of them. But only Leper's was serious.

A week later he was gone. He had been within a few weeks of his eighteenth birthday, and with it all chance of enlistment, of choosing a service rather than being drafted into one, would have disappeared. The ski movie had decided him. "I always thought the war would come for me when it wanted me," he said when he came to say goodbye the last day. "I never thought I'd be going to it. I'm really glad I saw that movie in time, you bet I am." Then, as the Devon School's first recruit to World War II, he went out my doorway with his white stocking cap bobbing behind.

It probably would have been better for all of us if someone like Brinker had been the first to go. He could have been depended upon to take a loud dramatic departure, so that the school would have reverberated for weeks afterward with Brinker's Last Words, Brinker's Military Bearing, Brinker's Sense of Duty. And all of us, influenced by the vacuum of his absence, would have felt the touch of war as a daily fact.

But the disappearing tail of Leper's cap inspired none of this. For a few days the war was more unimaginable than ever. We didn't mention it and we didn't mention Leper, until at last Brinker found a workable point of view. One day in the Butt Room he read aloud a rumor in a newspaper about an attempt on Hitler's life. He lowered the paper, gazed in a visionary way in front of him, and then remarked, "That was Leper, of course."

This established our liaison[6] with World War II. The Tunisian campaign became "Leper's liberation"; the bombing of the Ruhr was greeted by Brinker with hurt surprise: "He didn't tell us he'd left the ski troops"; the torpedoing of the *Scharnhorst:*[7] "At it again." Leper sprang up all over the world at the core of every Allied success. We talked about Leper's stand at Stalingrad, Leper on the Burma Road, Leper's convoy to Archangel;[8] we surmised that the crisis over the leadership of the Free French[9] would be resolved by the appointment of neither de Gaulle[10] nor Giraud[11] but Lepellier; we knew, better than the newspapers, that it was not the Big Three[12] but the Big Four who were running the war.

---

7. Tunisian campaign (too nizh' ən kam pān') **. . . Scharnhorst** (sharn horst): From November 1942 until the Germans surrendered in Tunisia in May 1943, British and American forces had battled German forces for control of northern Africa. The bombing of the Ruhr refers to the bombing by the Allies of the Ruhr River region in central Germany, where many mining and industrial plants were located. In February 1942 the German battle cruiser *Scharnhorst* had made a daring raid up the English Channel and into the Straits of Dover in England. Although the ship was driven out by the British, it reached a German port safely, thus humiliating the British. In December 1943 the *Scharnhorst* was sunk by British ships off the coast of Norway.

8. Stalingrad (stä' lin grät') **. . . Archangel** (ärk' än' jəl): The Russian city of Stalingrad, which is now Volgograd, was besieged by the Germans during 1942, and in a valiant battle, the Russians forced the Germans to retreat in January 1943. The Burma Road had been the only land route by which the Allies could send desperately needed supplies to China. Despite the Allies' attempts to protect it, the Burma Road was closed in April 1942, when the Japanese captured the city at its southern end. In 1943 several attempts were made by British, American, and Chinese forces to regain control of the Burma Road, although the Allies were not successful until January 1945. Archangel was a Russian city near the Arctic Ocean. Convoys, groups of ships traveling together for protection, carrying supplies to Archangel suffered devastating attacks by German submarines in the North Atlantic.

9. Free French: French military forces that continued to fight the Germans after France's surrender.

10. de Gaulle (də gôl'): Charles de Gaulle (1890–1970), leader of the Free French, general, and president of France from 1959 to 1969.

11. Giraud (zhē rō'): Henri Giraud (1879–1949) competed with de Gaulle for leadership of the Free French. He retired in 1944 over differences with de Gaulle.

12. Big Three: United States, Britain, and the Soviet Union.

---

6. liaison (lē' ə zän') *n.:* A link or connection.

In the silences between jokes about Leper's glories we wondered whether we ourselves would measure up to the humblest minimum standard of the army. I did not know everything there was to know about myself, and I knew that I did not know it; I wondered in the silences between jokes about Leper whether the still hidden parts of myself might contain the Sad Sack, the outcast, or the coward. We were all at our funniest about Leper, and we all secretly hoped that Leper, that incompetent, was as heroic as we said.

Everyone contributed to this legend except Phineas. At the outset, with the attempt on Hitler's life, Finny had said, "If someone gave Leper a loaded gun and put it at Hitler's temple, he'd miss." There was a general shout of outrage, and then we recommended the building of Leper's triumphal arch around Brinker's keystone. Phineas

"The Tunisian campaign became 'Leper's liberation'; ..."

took no part in it, and since little else was talked about in the Butt Room he soon stopped going there and stopped me from going as well—"How do you expect to be an athlete if you smoke like a forest fire?" He drew me increasingly away from the Butt Room crowd, away from Brinker and Chet and all other friends, into a world inhabited by just himself and me, where there was no war at all, just Phineas and me alone among all the people of the world, training for the Olympics of 1944.

Saturday afternoons are terrible in a boys' school, especially in the winter. There is no football game; it is not possible, as it is in the spring, to take bicycle trips into the surrounding country. Not even the most grinding student can feel required to lose himself in his books, since there is Sunday ahead, long, lazy, quiet Sunday, to do any homework.

And these Saturdays are worst in the late winter when the snow has lost its novelty and its shine, and the school seems to have been reduced to only a network of drains. During the brief thaw in the early afternoon there is a dismal gurgling of dirty water seeping down pipes and along gutters, a gray seamy shifting beneath the crust of snow, which cracks to show patches of frozen mud beneath. Shrubbery loses its bright snow headgear and stands bare and frail, too undernourished to hide the drains it was intended to hide. These are the days when going into any building you cross a mat of dirt and cinders led in by others before you, thinning and finally trailing off in the corridors. The sky is an empty hopeless gray and gives the impression that this is its eternal shade. Winter's occupation seems to have conquered, overrun and destroyed everything, so that now there is no longer any resistance movement left in nature; all

the juices are dead, every sprig of vitality snapped, and now winter itself, an old, corrupt, tired conqueror, loosens its grip on the desolation, recedes a little, grows careless in its watch; sick of victory and enfeebled by the absence of challenge, it begins itself to withdraw from the ruined countryside. The drains alone are active, and on these Saturdays their noises sound a dull recessional to winter.

Only Phineas failed to see what was so depressing. Just as there was no war in his philosophy, there was also no dreary weather. As I have said, all weathers delighted Phineas. "You know what we'd better do next Saturday?" he began in one of his voices, the low-pitched and evenly melodic one which for some reason always reminded me of a Rolls-Royce moving along a highway. "We'd better organize the Winter Carnival."

We were sitting in our room, on either side of the single large window framing a square of featureless gray sky. Phineas was resting his cast, which was a considerably smaller one now, on the desk and thoughtfully pressing designs into it with a pocket knife. "What Winter Carnival?" I asked.

"*The* Winter Carnival. The Devon Winter Carnival."

"There isn't any Devon Winter Carnival and never has been."

"There is now. We'll have it in that park next to the Naguamsett. The main attraction will be sports, naturally, featuring I expect a ski jump—"

"A ski jump! That park's as flat as a pancake."

"—and some slalom races,[13] and I think a little track. But we've got to have some snow statues too, and a little music, and

---

13. slalom (slä′ ləm) **races:** Downhill ski races over a zigzag course marked by flag-topped poles, or gates.

something to eat. Now, which committee do you want to head?"

I gave him a wintry smile. "The snow statues committee."

"I knew you would. You always were secretly arty, weren't you? I'll organize the sports, Brinker can handle the music and food, and then we need somebody to kind of beautify the place, a few holly wreaths and things like that. Someone good with plants and shrubbery. I know. Leper."

From looking at the star he was imprinting in his cast I looked quickly up at his face. "Leper's gone."

"Oh yeah, so he is. Leper *would* be gone. Well, somebody else then."

And because it was Finny's idea, it happened as he said, although not as easily as some of his earlier inspirations. For our dormitory was less enthusiastic about almost everything with each succeeding week. Brinker for example had begun a long, decisive sequence of withdrawals from school activity ever since the morning I deserted his enlistment plan. He had not resented my change of heart, and in fact had immediately undergone one himself. If he could not enlist —and for all his self-sufficiency Brinker could not do much without company—he could at least cease to be so multifariously[14] civilian. So he resigned the presidency of the Golden Fleece Debating Society, stopped writing his school spirit column for the newspaper, dropped the chairmanship of the Underprivileged Local Children subcommittee of the Good Samaritan Confraternity, stilled his baritone in the chapel choir, and even, in his most impressive burst of irresponsibility, resigned from the Student Advisory Committee to the Headmaster's Discretionary Benevolent Fund. His well-bred clothes had disappeared; these days he wore khaki pants supported by a garrison belt,[15] and boots which rattled when he walked.

"Who wants a Winter Carnival?" he said in the disillusioned way he had lately developed when I brought it up. "What are we supposed to be celebrating?"

"Winter, I guess."

"Winter!" He gazed out of his window at the vacant sky and seeping ground. "Frankly, I just don't see anything to celebrate, winter or spring or anything else."

"This is the first time Finny's gotten going on anything since . . . he came back."

"He has been kind of nonfunctional, hasn't he? He isn't *brooding*, is he?"

"No, he wouldn't brood."

"No, I don't suppose he would. Well, if you think it's something Finny really wants. Still, there's never been a Winter Carnival here. I think there's probably a rule against it."

"I see," I said in a tone which made Brinker raise his eyes and lock them with mine. In that plotters' glance all his doubts vanished, for Brinker the Lawgiver had turned rebel for the Duration.

The Saturday was battleship gray. Throughout the morning equipment for the Winter Carnival had been spirited out of the dormitory and down to the small incomplete public park on the bank of the Naguamsett River. Brinker supervised the transfer, rattling up and down the stairwell and giving orders. He made me think of a pirate captain disposing of the booty. Several jugs of very hard cider which he had browbeaten away from some lowerclassmen were the most cautiously guarded treasure. They were buried in the snow near a clump of evergreens

---

14. multifariously (mul' tə far' ē əs lē) *adv.*: Diversely.

15. garrison belt: The type of belt worn by the armed forces with their best uniforms.

in the center of the park, and Brinker stationed his roommate, Brownie Perkins, to guard them with his life. He meant this literally, and Brownie knew it. So he trembled alone there in the middle of the park for hours, wondering what would happen if he had an attack of appendicitis, unnerved by the thoughts of a fainting spell, horrified by the realization that he might have to move his bowels, until at last we came. Then Brownie crept back to the dormitory, too exhausted to enjoy the carnival at all. On this day of high illegal competitiveness, no one noticed.

The buried cider was half-consciously plotted at the hub of the carnival. Around it sprang up large, sloppy statues, easily modeled because of the snow's dampness. Nearby, entirely out of place in this snowscape, like a dowager[16] in a saloon, there was a heavy circular classroom table, carried there by superhuman exertions the night before on Finny's insistence that he had to have *something* to display the prizes on. On it rested the prizes—Finny's icebox, hidden all these months in the dormitory basement, a set of York barbells, the *Iliad*[17] with the English translation of each sentence written above it, Brinker's file of Betty Grable[18] photographs, a lock of hair cut under duress from the head of Hazel Brewster, the professional town belle, a handwoven rope ladder with the proviso[19] that it should be awarded to someone occupying a room on the third floor or higher, a forged draft registration card, and $4.13 from the Headmaster's Discretionary Benevolent Fund. Brinker placed this last prize on the table with such

silent dignity that we all thought it was better not to ask any questions about it.

Phineas sat behind the table in a heavily carved black walnut chair; the arms ended in two lions' heads, and the legs ended in paws gripping wheels now sunk in the snow. He had made the purchase that morning. Phineas bought things only on impulse and only when he had the money, and since the two states rarely coincided his purchases were few and strange.

Chet Douglass stood next to him holding his trumpet. Finny had regretfully given up the plan of inviting the school band to supply music, since it would have spread news of our carnival to every corner of the campus. Chet in any case was an improvement over that cacophony.[20] He was a slim, fair-skinned boy with a ball of curly auburn hair curving over his forehead, and he devoted himself to playing two things, tennis and the trumpet. He did both with such easy, inborn skill that after observing him I had begun to think that I could master either one any weekend I tried. Much like the rest of us on the surface, he had an underlying obliging and considerate strain which barred him from being a really important member of the class. You had to be rude at least sometimes and edgy often to be credited with "personality," and without that accolade[21] no one at Devon could be anyone. No one, with the exception of course of Phineas.

To the left of the Prize Table Brinker straddled his cache[22] of cider; behind him was the clump of evergreens, and behind them there was after all a gentle rise, where the Ski Jump Committee was pounding snow into a little take-off ramp whose lip was perhaps a foot higher than the slope of

---

16. dowager (dou′ ə jər) *n.*: An elderly woman of wealth and dignity.
17. Iliad (il′ ē əd) *n.*: A Greek epic poem by Homer set in the tenth year of the Trojan War.
18. Betty Grable: Movie star popular during World War II.
19. proviso (prə vī′ zō) *n.*: Condition.

20. cacophony (kə käf′ ə nē) *n.*: Harsh sound.
21. accolade (ak′ ə lād′) *n.*: Approval.
22. cache (kash) *n.*: Anything stored or hidden in a secret or safe place.

the rise. From there our line of snow statues, unrecognizable artistic attacks on the Headmaster, Mr. Ludsbury, Mr. Patch-Withers, Dr. Stanpole, the new dietitian, and Hazel Brewster curved in an enclosing half-circle to the icy, muddy, lisping edge of the tidewater Naguamsett and back to the other side of the Prize Table.

When the ski jump was ready there was a certain amount of milling around; twenty boys, tightly reined in all winter, stood now as though with the bit firmly clamped between their teeth, ready to stampede. Phineas should have started the sports events but he was absorbed in cataloguing the prizes. All eyes swung next upon Brinker. He had been holding a pose above his cider of Gibraltar invulnerability;[23] he continued to gaze challengingly around him until he began to realize that wherever he looked, calculating eyes looked back.

"All right, all right," he said roughly, "let's get started."

The ragged circle around him moved perceptibly closer.

"Let's get going," he yelled. "Come on, Finny. What's first?"

Phineas had one of those minds which could record what is happening in the background and do nothing about it because something else was preoccupying him. He seemed to sink deeper into his list.

"Phineas!" Brinker pronounced his name with a maximum use of the teeth. "What is next?"

Still the sleek brown head bent mesmerized over the list.

"What's the big hurry, Brinker?" someone from the tightening circle asked with

dangerous gentleness. "What's the big rush?"

"We can't stand here all day," he blurted. "We've got to get started if we're going to have this thing. What's *next*? Phineas!"

At last the recording in Finny's mind reached its climax. He looked vaguely up, studied the straddling, at-bay figure of Brinker at the core of the poised perimeter of boys, hesitated, blinked, and then in his organ voice said good-naturedly, "Next? Well that's pretty clear. You are."

Chet released from his trumpet the opening, lifting, barbaric call of a bullfight, and the circle of boys broke wildly over Brinker. He flailed back against the evergreens, and the jugs appeared to spring out of the snow. "What," he kept yelling, off balance among the branches. *"What . . ."* By then his cider, which he had apparently expected to dole out according to his own governing whim, was disappearing. There was going to be no government, even by whim, even by Brinker's whim, on this Saturday at Devon.

From a scramble of contenders I got one of the jugs, elbowed off a counterattack, opened it, sampled it, choked, and then went through with my original plan by stopping Brinker's mouth with it. His eyes bulged, and blood vessels in his throat began to pulsate, until at length I lowered the jug.

He gave me a long, pondering look, his face closed and concentrating while behind it his mind plainly teetered between fury and hilarity; I think if I had batted an eye he would have hit me. The carnival's breaking apart into a riot hung like a bomb between us. I kept on looking expressionlessly back at him until beneath a blackening scowl his mouth opened enough to fire out the words, "I've been violated."

I jerked the jug to my mouth and took a huge gulp of cider in relief, and the violence

---

23. Gibraltar invulnerability (ji brôl′ tər in vul′ nər ə bil′ ə tē): A reference to the rocky peninsula at the southern tip of Spain that was a British crown colony. It guarded the entrance to the Mediterranean Sea and was considered to be an unassailable fortress.

latent in the day drifted away; perhaps the Naguamsett carried it out on the receding tide. Brinker strode through the swirl of boys to Phineas. "I formally declare," he bellowed, "that these Games are open."

"You can't do that," Finny said rebukingly. "Who ever heard of opening the Games without the sacred fire from Olympus?"

Sensing that I must act as the Chorus, I registered on my face the universally unheard-of quality of the Games without fire. "Fire, fire," I said across the damp snow.

"We'll sacrifice one of the prizes," said Phineas, seizing the *Iliad*. He sprinkled the pages with cider to make them more inflammable, touched a match to the pages, and a little jet of flame curled upward. The Games, alight with Homer and cider, were open.

Chet Douglass, leaning against the side of the Prize Table, continued to blow musical figures for his own enlightenment. Forgetful of us and the athletic programing Finny now put into motion, he strolled here and there, sometimes at the start of the ski jump competition, blowing an appropriate call, more often invoking the serene order of Haydn, or a high, remote, arrogant Spanish world, or the cheerful, lowdown carelessness of New Orleans.[24]

The hard cider began to take charge of us. Or I wonder now whether it wasn't our own exuberance which intoxicated us, sent restraint flying, causing Brinker to throw the football block on the statue of the Headmaster, giving me, as I put on the skis and slid down the small slope and off the miniature ski jump a sensation of soaring flight, of hurtling high and far through space; inspiring Phineas, during one of Chet's Spanish

inventions, to climb onto the Prize Table and with only one leg to create a droll dance among the prizes, springing and spinning from one bare space to another, cleanly missing Hazel Brewster's hair, never marring by a misstep the pictures of Betty Grable. Under the influence not I know of the hardest cider but of his own inner joy at life for a moment as it should be, as it was meant to be in his nature, Phineas recaptured that magic gift for existing primarily in space, one foot conceding briefly to gravity its rights before spinning him off again into the air. It was his wildest demonstration of himself, of himself in the kind of world he loved; it was his choreography of peace.

And when he stopped and sat down among the prizes and said, "Now we're going to have the Decathlon.[25] Quiet everybody, our Olympic candidate Gene Forrester, is now going to qualify," it wasn't cider which made me in this moment champion of everything he ordered, to run as though I were the abstraction of speed, to walk the half-circle of statues on my hands, to balance on my head on top of the icebox on top of the Prize Table, to jump if he had asked it across the Naguamsett and land crashing in the middle of Quackenbush's boathouse, to accept at the end of it amid a clatter of applause—for on this day even the schoolboy egotism of Devon was conjured away[26]—a wreath made from the evergreen trees which Phineas placed on my head. It wasn't the cider which made me surpass myself, it was this liberation we had torn from the gray encroachments of 1943, the escape we had concocted, this afternoon of momentary, illusory, special and separate peace.

---

24. Haydn . . . New Orleans: Chet plays classical music by Haydn, Spanish music, and New Orleans jazz.

---

25. Decathlon (di kath′ län′) *n.*: An athletic contest in which each contestant takes part in ten events.
26. conjured (kän′ jərd) **away:** Removed as if by magic.

" ... it was this liberation we had torn from the gray encroachments of 1943, ... "

And it was this which caused me not to notice Brownie Perkins rejoin us from the dormitory, and not to hear what he was saying until Finny cried hilariously, "A telegram for Gene? It's the Olympic Committee. They want you! Of course they want you! Give it to me, Brownie, I'll read it aloud to this assembled host." And it was this which drained away as I watched Finny's face pass through all the gradations between uproariousness and shock.

I took the telegram from Phineas, facing in advance whatever the destruction was. That was what I learned to do that winter.

I HAVE ESCAPED AND NEED HELP. I AM AT CHRIST-MAS LOCATION. YOU UNDERSTAND. NO NEED TO RISK ADDRESS HERE. MY SAFETY DEPENDS ON YOU COMING AT ONCE.

(signed) YOUR BEST FRIEND,
ELWIN LEPER LEPELLIER.

Chapter 10

That night I made for the first time the kind of journey which later became the monotonous routine of my life: traveling through an unknown countryside from one unknown settlement to another. The next year this became the dominant activity, or rather passivity, of my army career, not fighting, not marching, but this kind of nighttime ricochet;[1] for as it turned out I never got to the war.

I went into uniform at the time when our enemies began to recede so fast that there had to be a hurried telescoping of military training plans. Programs scheduled to culminate in two years became outmoded in six months, and crowds of men gathered for them in one place were dispersed to twenty others. A new weapon appeared and those of us who had traveled to three or four bases mastering the old one were sent on to a fifth, sixth, and seventh to master the new. The closer victory came the faster we were shuttled around America in pursuit of a role to play in a drama which suddenly, underpopulated from the first, now had too many actors. Or so it seemed. In reality there would have been, as always, too few, except that the last act, a mass assault against suicidally-defended Japan, never took place. I and my year—not "my generation" for destiny now cut too finely for that old phrase—I and those of my year were preeminently eligible for that. Most of us, so it was estimated, would be killed. But the men a little bit older closed in on the enemy faster than predicted, and then there was the final holocaust of the Bomb.[2] It seemed to have saved our lives.

So journeys through unknown parts of America became my chief war memory, and I think of the first of them as this nighttime trip to Leper's. There was no question of where to find him; "I am at Christmas location" meant that he was at home. He lived far up in Vermont, where at this season of the year even the paved main highways are bumpy and buckling from the freezing weather, and each house executes a lonely holding action against the cold. The natural state of things is coldness, and houses are fragile havens, holdouts in a death landscape, unforgettably comfortable, simple though they are, just because of their warmth.

Leper's was one of these hearths perched by itself on a frozen hillside. I reached it in the early morning after this night which presaged my war; a bleak, drafty train ride, a damp depot seemingly

---

1. ricochet (rik′ ə shā′) n.: Bouncing from one thing to another.

2. the Bomb: The atomic bomb.

near no town whatever, a bus station in which none of the people were fully awake, or seemed clean, or looked as though they had homes anywhere; a bus which passengers entered and left at desolate stopping places in the blackness; a chilled nighttime wandering in which I tried to decipher[3] between lapses into stale sleep, the meaning of Leper's telegram.

I reached the town at dawn, and encouraged by the returning light, and coffee in a thick white cup, I accepted a hopeful interpretation. Leper had "escaped." You didn't "escape" from the army, so he must have escaped from something else. The most logical thing a soldier escapes from is danger, death, the enemy. Since Leper hadn't been overseas the enemy must have been in this country. And the only enemies in this country would be spies. Leper had escaped from spies.

I seized this conclusion and didn't try to go beyond it. I suppose all our Butt Room stories about him intriguing around the world had made me half-ready to half-believe something like this. I felt a measureless relief when it occurred to me. There was some color, some hope, some life in this war after all. The first friend of mine who ever went into it tangled almost immediately with spies. I began to hope that after all this wasn't going to be such a bad war.

The Lepellier house was not far out of town, I was told. There was no taxi, I was also told, and there was no one, I did not need to be told, who would offer to drive me out there. This was Vermont. But if that meant austerity[4] toward strangers it also meant mornings of glory such as this one, in which the snow, white almost to blueness, lay like a soft comforter over the hills,

and birches and pines indestructibly held their ground, rigid lines against the snow and sky, very thin and very strong like Vermonters.

The sun was the blessing of the morning, the one celebrating element, an aesthete with no purpose except to shed radiance. Everything else was sharp and hard, but this Grecian sun evoked joy from every angularity and blurred with brightness the stiff face of the countryside. As I walked briskly out the road the wind knifed at my face, but this sun caressed the back of my neck.

The road led out along the side of a ridge, and after a mile or so I saw the house that must be Leper's, riding the top of the slope. It was another brittle-looking Vermont house, white of course, with long and narrow windows like New England faces. Behind one of them hung a star which announced that a son of the house was serving the country, and behind another stood Leper.

Although I was walking straight toward his front door he beckoned me on several times, and he never took his eyes from me, as though it was they which held me to my course. He was still at this ground-floor window when I reached the door and so I opened it myself and stepped into the hallway. Leper had come to the entrance of the room on the right, the dining room.

"Come in here," he said, "I spend most of my time in here."

As usual there were no preliminaries. "What do you do that for, Leper? It's not very comfortable, is it?"

"Well, it's a useful room."

"Yes, I guess it's useful, all right."

"You aren't lost for something to do in dining rooms. It's in the living room where people can't figure out what to do with themselves. People get problems in living rooms."

---

3. decipher (di sī′ fər) *v.*: Figure out the meaning of.
4. austerity (ô ster′ ə tē) *n.*: Severity.

"Bedrooms too." It was a try toward relieving the foreboding[5] in his manner; it only worked to deepen it.

He turned away, and I followed him into an under-furnished dining room of high-backed chairs, rugless floor, and cold fireplace. "If you want to be in a really functional room," I began with false heartiness, "you ought to spend your time in the bathroom then."

He looked at me, and I noticed the left side of his upper lip lift once or twice as though he was about to snarl or cry. Then I realized that this had nothing to do with his mood, that it was involuntary.

He sat down at the head of the table in the only chair with arms, his father's chair I supposed. I took off my coat and sat in a place at the middle of the table, with my back to the fireplace. There at least I could look at the sun rejoicing on the snow.

"In here you never wonder what's going to happen. You know the meals will come in three times a day for instance."

"I'll bet your mother isn't too pleased when she's trying to get one ready."

Force sprang into his expression for the first time. "What's she got to be pleased about!" He glared challengingly into my startled face. "I'm pleasing *myself!*" he cried fervently, and I saw tears trembling in his eyes.

"Well, she's probably pleased." Any words would serve, the more irrelevant and superficial the better, any words which would stop him; I didn't want to see this. "She's probably pleased to have you home again."

His face resumed its dull expression. The responsibility for continuing the conversation, since I had forced it to be superficial, was mine. "How long'll you be here?"

He shrugged, a look of disgust with my question crossing his face. The careful politeness he had always had was gone.

"Well, if you're on furlough you must know when you have to be back." I said this in what I thought of at the time as my older voice, a little businesslike and experienced. "The army doesn't give out passes and then say 'Come back when you've had enough, hear?'"

"I didn't get any pass," he groaned; with the sliding despair of his face and his clenched hands, that's what it was; a groan.

"I know you said," I spoke in short, expressionless syllables, "that you 'escaped.'" I no longer wanted this to be true, I no longer wanted it to be connected with spies or desertion or anything out of the ordinary. I knew it was going to be, and I no longer wanted it to be.

"I *escaped!*" the word surging out in a voice and intensity that was not Leper's. His face was furious, but his eyes denied the fury; instead they saw it before them. They were filled with terror.

"What do you mean, you escaped?" I said sharply. "You don't escape from the army."

"That's what you say. But that's because you're talking through your hat." His eyes were furious now too, glaring blindly at me. "What do you know about it, anyway?" None of this could have been said by the Leper of the beaver dam.

"Well I—how am I supposed to answer that? I know what's normal in the army, that's all."

"Normal," he repeated bitterly. "What a stupid word that is. I suppose that's what you're thinking about, isn't it? That's what you would be thinking about, somebody like you. You're thinking I'm not normal, aren't you? I can see what you're thinking—I see a lot I never saw before"—his voice fell to a querulous whisper—"you're thinking I'm psycho."

I gathered what the word meant. I hated the sound of it at once. It opened up a world I had not known existed—"mad" or "crazy" or "a screw loose," those were the familiar words. "Psycho" had a sudden mental-ward reality about it, a systematic, diagnostic sound. It was as though Leper had learned it while in captivity, far from Devon or Vermont or any experience we had in common, as though it were in Japanese.

Fear seized my stomach like a cramp. I didn't care what I said to him now; it was myself I was worried about. For if Leper was psycho it was the army which had done it to him, and I and all of us were on the brink of the army. "You make me sick, you and your army words."

"They were going to give me," he was almost laughing, everywhere but in his eyes which continued to oppose all he said, "they were going to give me a discharge, a Section Eight discharge."

As a last defense I had always taken refuge in a scornful superiority, based on nothing. I sank back in the chair, eyebrows up, shoulders shrugging. "I don't even know what you're talking about. You just don't make any sense at all. It's all Japanese to me."

"A Section Eight discharge is for the nuts in the service, the psychos, the Funny Farm candidates. Now do you know what I'm talking about? They give you a Section Eight discharge, like a dishonorable discharge only worse. You can't get a job after that. Everybody wants to see your discharge, and when they see a Section Eight they look at you kind of funny—the kind of expression you've got on your face, like you were looking at someone with their nose blown off but don't want them to know you're disgusted—they look at you that way and then they say, 'Well, there doesn't seem to be an opening here at present.' You're ruined for life, that's what a Section Eight discharge means."

"You don't have to yell at me, there's nothing wrong with my hearing."

"Then that's tough for you, Buster. Then they've got you."

"Nobody's *got* me."

"Oh they've got you all right."

"Don't tell me who's got me and who hasn't got me. Who do you think you're talking to? Stick to your snails, Lepellier."

He began to laugh again. "You always were a lord of the manor, weren't you? A swell guy, except when the chips were down. You always were a savage underneath. I always knew that only I never admitted it. But in the last few weeks," despair broke into his face again, "I admitted a lot to myself. Not about you. Don't flatter yourself. I wasn't thinking about you. Why should I think about you? Did you ever think about me? I thought about myself, and Ma, and the old man, and *pleasing* them all the time. Well, never mind about that now. It's you we happen to be talking about now. Like a savage underneath. Like," now there was the blind confusion in his eyes again, a wild slyness around his mouth, "like that time you knocked Finny out of the tree."

I sprang out of the chair. "You stupid crazy . . ."

Still laughing, "Like that time you crippled him for life."

I shoved my foot against the rung of his chair and kicked. Leper went over in his chair and collapsed against the floor. Laughing and crying he lay with his head on the floor and his knees up, ". . . always were a savage underneath."

Quick heels coming down the stairs, and his mother, large, soft, and gentle-looking, quivered at the entrance. "What on earth happened? Elwin!"

"I'm terribly—it was a mistake," I listened objectively to my own voice, "he said something crazy. I forgot myself—I forgot that he's, there's something the matter with his nerves, isn't there? He didn't know what he was saying."

"Well, good heaven, the boy is ill." We both moved swiftly to help up the chuckling Leper. "Did you come here to abuse him?"

"I'm terribly sorry," I muttered. "I'd better get going."

Mrs. Lepellier was helping Leper toward the stairs. "Don't go," he said between chuckles, "stay for lunch. You can count on it. Always three meals a day, war or peace, in this room."

And I did stay. Sometimes you are too ashamed to leave. That was true now. And sometimes you need too much to know the facts, and so humbly and stupidly you stay. That was true now too.

It was an abundant Vermont lunch, more like a dinner, and at first it had no more reality than a meal in the theater. Leper ate almost nothing, but my own appetite deepened my disgrace. I ate everything within reach, and then had to ask, face aflame with embarrassment, for more to be passed to me. But that led to this hard-to-believe transformation: Mrs. Lepellier began to be reconciled to me because I liked her cooking. Toward the end of the meal she became able to speak to me directly, in her high but gentle and modulated voice, and I was so clumsy and fumbling and embarrassed that my behavior throughout lunch amounted to one long and elaborate apology which, when she offered me a second dessert, I saw she had accepted. "He's a good boy underneath," she must have thought, "a terrible temper, no self-control, but he's sorry, and he is a good boy underneath." Leper was closer to the truth.

She suggested he and I take a walk after lunch. Leper now seemed all obedience, and except for the fact that he never looked at his mother, the ideal son. So he put on some odds and ends of clothing, some canvas and woolen and flannel pulled on to form a patchwork against the cutting wind, and we trailed out the back door into the splendor of the failing sunshine. I did not have New England in my bones; I was a guest in this country, even though by now a familiar one, and I could never see a totally extinguished winter field without thinking it unnatural. I would tramp along trying to decide whether corn had grown there in the summer, or whether it had been a pasture, or what it could ever have been, and in that deep layer of the mind where all is judged by the five senses and primitive expectation, I knew that nothing would ever grow there again. We roamed across one of these wastes, our feet breaking through at each step the thin surface crust of ice into a layer of soft snow underneath, and I waited for Leper, in this wintery outdoors he loved, to come to himself again. Just as I knew the field could never grow again, I knew that Leper could not be wild or bitter or psycho tramping across the hills of Vermont.

"Is there an army camp in Vermont?" I asked, so sure in my illusion that I risked making him talk, risked even making him talk about the army.

"I don't think there is."

"There ought to be. That's where they should have sent you. Then you wouldn't have gotten nervous."

"Yeah." A half chuckle. "I was what they call 'nervous in the service.'"

Exaggerated laughter from me. "Is that what they call it?"

Leper didn't bother to make a rejoinder.[6] Before there had always been his polite capping of remarks like this: "Yes, they do, that's what they call it"—but today he glanced speculatively at me and said nothing.

We walked on, the crust cracking uneasily under us. "Nervous in the service," I said. "That sounds like one of Brinker's poems."

"That Brinker!"

"You wouldn't know Brinker these days the way he's changed—"

"I'd know him if he'd changed into Snow White."[7]

"Well. He hasn't changed into Snow White."

"That's too bad," the strained laughter was back in his voice, "Snow White with Brinker's face on her. There's a picture," then he broke into sobs.

"Leper! What is it? What's the matter, Leper? Leper!"

Hoarse, cracking sobs broke from him; another ounce of grief and he would have begun tearing his country-store clothes. "Leper! Leper!" This exposure drew us violently together; I was the closest person in the world to him now, and he to me. "Leper, Leper." I was about to cry myself. "Stop that, now just stop. Don't do that. Stop doing that, Leper."

When he became quieter, not less despairing but too exhausted to keep on, I said, "I'm sorry I brought up Brinker. I didn't know you hated him so much." Leper didn't look capable of such hates. Especially now,

with his rapid plumes of breath puffing out as from a toiling steam engine, his nose and eyes gone red, and his cheeks red too, in large, irregular blotches—Leper had the kind of fragile fair skin given to high, unhealthy coloring. He was all color, painted at random, but none of it highlighted his grief. Instead of desperate and hate-filled, he looked, with his checkered outfit and blotchy face, like a half-prepared clown.

"I don't really hate Brinker, I don't really hate him, not any more than anybody else." His swimming eyes cautiously explored me. The wind lifted a sail of snow and billowed it past us. "It was only—" he drew in his breath so sharply that it made a whistling sound—"the idea of *his* face on a *woman's* body. That's what made me psycho. Ideas like that. I don't know. I guess they must be right. I guess I am psycho. I guess I must be. I must be. Did you ever have ideas like that?"

"No."

"Would they bother you if you did, if you happened to keep imagining a man's head on a woman's body, or if sometimes the arm of a chair turned into a human arm if you looked at it too long, things like that? Would they bother you?"

I didn't say anything.

"Maybe everybody imagines things like that when they're away from home, really far away, for the first time. Do you think so? The camp I went to first, they called it a 'Reception center,' got us up every morning when it was pitch black, and there was food like the kind we throw out here, and all my clothes were gone and I got this uniform that didn't even smell familiar. All day I wanted to sleep, after we got to Basic Training. I kept falling asleep, all day long, at the lectures we went to, and on the firing range, and everywhere else. But not at night. Next to me there was a man who had a cough that sounded like his stomach was going to come

---

6. rejoinder (ri join' dər) *n.*: A reply or answer.
7. Snow White: A reference to the heroine of the fairy tale "Snow White and the Seven Dwarfs."

up, one of these times, it sounded like it would come up through his mouth and land with a splatter on the floor. He always faced my way. We did sleep head to foot, but I knew it would land near me. I never slept at night. During the day I couldn't eat this food that should have been thrown away, so I was always hungry except in the Mess Hall. The Mess Hall. The army has the perfect word for everything, did you ever think of that?"

I imperceptibly nodded and shook my head, yes-and-no.

"And the perfect word for me," he added in a distorted voice, as though his tongue had swollen, "psycho. I guess I am. I must be. Am I, though, or is the army? Because they turned everything inside out. I couldn't sleep in bed, I had to sleep everywhere else. I couldn't eat in the Mess Hall, I had to eat everywhere else. Everything began to be inside out. And the man next to me at night, coughing himself inside out. That was when things began to change. One day I couldn't make out what was happening to the corporal's face. It kept changing into faces I knew from somewhere else, and then I began to think he looked like me, and then he . . ." Leper's voice had thickened unrecognizably, "he changed into a woman, I was looking at him as close as I'm looking at you and his face turned into a woman's face and I started to yell for everybody, I began to yell so that everyone would see it too, I didn't want to be the only one to see a thing like that, I yelled louder and louder to make sure every-one within reach of my voice would hear —you can see there wasn't anything crazy in the way I was thinking, can't you, I had a good reason for everything I did, didn't I—but I couldn't yell soon enough, or loud enough, and when somebody did finally come up to me, it was this man with the cough who slept in the next cot, and he was holding a broom because we had been sweeping out the barracks, but I saw right away that it wasn't a broom, it was a man's leg which had been cut off. I remember thinking that he must have been at the hospital helping with an amputation when he heard my yell. You can see there's logic in that." The crust beneath us continued to crack and as we reached the border of the field the frigid trees also were cracking with the cold. The two sharp groups of noises sounded to my ears like rifles being fired in the distance.

I said nothing, and Leper, having said so much, went on to say more, to speak above the wind and crackings as though his story would never be finished. "Then they grabbed me and there were arms and legs and heads everywhere and I couldn't tell when any minute—"

"*Shut up!*"

Softer, more timidly, "—when any min-ute—"

"Do you think I want to hear every gory detail! Shut up! I don't care! I don't care what happened to you, Leper. I don't care! Do you understand that? This has nothing to do with me! Nothing at all! I don't care!"

I turned around and began a clumsy run across the field in a line which avoided his house and aimed toward the road leading back into the town. I left Leper telling his story into the wind. He might tell it forever, I didn't care. I didn't want to hear any more of it. I had already heard too much. What did he mean by telling me a story like that! I didn't want to hear any more of it. Not now or ever. I didn't care because it had nothing to do with me. And I didn't want to hear any more of it. Ever.

RESPONDING TO THE SELECTION

Your Response

1. What feelings did you have in response to Leper's "escape" from the armed forces? Why do you think you responded this way?

Recalling

2. Why does Gene decide to tell Finny the truth and then feel sorry about doing so?
3. How does Finny's injury affect Gene's plans for participation in sports?
4. How does the war affect life at Devon?
5. Describe the Winter Carnival.

Interpreting

6. Explain what enlisting means to Gene. What does the army come to mean to Leper?
7. What is Finny's theory about the war and how is it typical of his way of thinking?
8. After Finny's accident, Gene's purpose was "to become a part of Phineas." What does he mean? Does he accomplish this?
9. Leper tells Gene, "You always were a savage underneath." How valid is that analysis of Gene? Give specific examples.

Applying

10. Gene tries to decide whether or not to enlist. How do you think a person should go about reaching such a major decision?

ANALYZING LITERATURE

Analyzing Conflict

A novel may have more than one conflict. To analyze conflicts ask yourself questions: What makes the conflict build? How will it be resolved? For example, Gene's internal conflict continues as he is torn between enlisting, thus entering the adult world, and his need to stay near Finny.

1. Describe the conflict between Gene and Brinker.
2. Explain how Gene's reaction to Leper when he goes to see him in his home is related to his internal conflict.

CRITICAL THINKING AND READING

Recognizing Symbols

A **symbol** is something that stands for something else. For example, the American flag is a symbol of the United States. In literature, authors use symbols to make a point or to present their ideas. Rain might symbolize a character's sadness, for example.

1. What do you think the tree symbolizes?
2. What might the Winter Carnival symbolize?
3. What do the Quackenbushes of the world symbolize?
4. John Ruskin has written, "At least be sure that you go to the author to get at *his* meaning, not to find yours." First, discuss the meaning of the quotation. Then explain why a reader must be careful when reading a novel with symbols.

THINKING AND WRITING

Analyzing a Symbol

Write an essay about the war as a symbol in this novel. Begin by listing different ideas about its symbolism. Then choose the idea best supported by evidence in the novel. Present this idea and the supporting evidence in your essay. When you revise, add one additional idea about the war as a symbol. Then write a final draft and proofread your essay.

LEARNING OPTION

Writing. In *A Separate Peace,* you know what Gene is thinking but you don't know much about what some of the other characters think or feel. Imagine that you are Finny, Leper, Brinker, or another character in the novel. Write diary entries about Finny's return to school after his accident. Tell how you feel about what happened, and how things might develop from here. Read your diary entries to your classmates.

GUIDE FOR READING

A Separate Peace, Chapters 11–13

Theme

The **theme** of a novel is the insight into life that it reveals. Sometimes, the theme is stated directly. More often, it is implied. The author may give hints about the theme while stepping away from the novel momentarily to address the reader. Such hints in key passages help a thoughtful reader identify the theme of the novel.

The theme will not always be easy for you to state. It may take a sentence, a paragraph, or even a whole essay. After identifying and stating the theme, it is important to test your understanding against actions of the characters and events of the plot. You will know if you have found the theme because events of the story will relate logically to it.

Focus

World War II is the backdrop to everything that takes place in *A Separate Peace.* An event outside your control—such as a war your country is fighting—can be terrifying. Survival can be a matter of luck, circumstance, or preparation. In a group of three or four, brainstorm about the effects of war on school-age students who are too young to fight but old enough to feel involved and threatened. With other members of the group, discuss what students could do to help in a war effort.

Vocabulary

Knowing the following words will help you as you read Chapters 11–13 of *A Separate Peace.*

surmise (sər mīz′) *v.*: To guess; to imagine or infer something without conclusive evidence (p. 851)

guileful (gīl′ fəl) *adj.*: Deceitful; tricky (p. 856)

incongruity (in′ kən grōō′ ə tē) *n.*: Lack of fitness or appropriateness (p. 858)

decrepit (di krep′ it) *adj.*: Broken down or worn out by old age or long use (p. 859)

impervious (im pʉr′ vē əs) *adj.*: Not affected by (p. 861)

parody (par′ ə dē) *n.*: Poor or weak imitation (p. 862)

assimilate (ə sim′ ə lāt′) *v.*: To absorb into one's thinking (p. 870)

Chapter 11

I wanted to see Phineas, and Phineas only. With him there was no conflict except between athletes, something Greek-inspired and Olympian in which victory would go to whoever was the strongest in body and heart. This was the only conflict he had ever believed in.

When I got back I found him in the middle of a snowball fight in a place called the Fields Beyond. At Devon the open ground among the buildings had been given carefully English names—the Center Common, the Far Common, the Fields, and the Fields Beyond. These last were past the gym, the tennis courts, the river and the stadium, on the edge of the woods which, however English in name, were in my mind primevally[1] American, reaching in unbroken forests far to the north, into the great northern wilderness. I found Finny beside the woods playing and fighting—the two were approximately the same thing to him—and I stood there wondering whether things weren't simpler and better at the northern terminus[2] of these woods, a thousand miles due north into the wilderness, somewhere deep in the Arctic, where the peninsula of trees which began at Devon would end at last in an untouched grove of pine, austere and beautiful.

There is no such grove, I know now, but the morning of my return to Devon I imagined that it might be just over the visible horizon, or the horizon after that.

A few of the fighters paused to yell a greeting at me, but no one broke off to ask about Leper. But I knew it was a mistake for me to stay there; at any moment someone might.

This gathering had obviously been Finny's work. Who else could have inveigled twenty people to the farthest extremity of the school to throw snowballs at each other? I could just picture him, at the end of his ten o'clock class, organizing it with the easy authority which always came into his manner when he had an idea which was particularly preposterous. There they all were now, the cream of the school, the lights and leaders of the senior class, with their high I.Q.'s and expensive shoes, as Brinker had said, pasting each other with snowballs.

I hesitated on the edge of the fight and the edge of the woods, too tangled in my mind to enter either one or the other. So I glanced at my wrist watch, brought my hand dramatically to my mouth as though remembering something urgent and important, repeated the pantomime in case anybody had missed it, and with this tacit explanation started briskly back toward the center of the school. A snowball caught me on the back of the head. Finny's voice followed it. "You're on our side, even if you do have a lousy aim. We need *somebody* else. Even you." He came toward me, without his cane at the moment, his new walking cast so much smaller and lighter that an ordinary person could have managed it with hardly a limp noticeable. Finny's coordination, however, was such that any slight flaw became obvious; there was an interruption, brief as a drum beat, in the continuous flow of his walk, as though with each step he forgot for a split-second where he was going.

"How's Leper?" he asked in an offhand way.

"Oh Leper's—how would he be? You know Leper—" The fight was moving toward us; I stalled a little more, a stray snowball caught Finny on the side of the face, he shot one back, I seized some ammunition from the ground and we were engulfed.

---

1. primevally (prī mē′ v'l lē) *adv.*: Belonging to earliest times.
2. terminus (tʉr′ mə nəs) *n.*: End; boundary.

"*Finny had scotch-taped newspaper pictures of the Roosevelt-Churchill meeting above his cot...,*"

would heighten the disorder. Loyalties became hopelessly entangled. No one was going to win or lose after all. Somewhere in the maze Brinker's sense of generalship disappeared, and he too became slippery. We ended the fight in the only way possible; all of us turned on Phineas. Slowly, with a steadily widening grin, he was driven down beneath a blizzard of snowballs.

When he had surrendered I bent cheerfully over to help him up, seizing his wrist to stop the final treacherous snowball he had ready, and he remarked, "Well I guess that takes care of the Hitler Youth[3] outing for one day." All of us laughed. On the way back to the gym he said, "That was a good fight. I thought it was pretty funny, didn't you?"

Someone knocked me down; I pushed Brinker over a small slope; someone was trying to tackle me from behind. Everywhere there was the smell of vitality in clothes, the vital something in wool and flannel and corduroy which spring releases. I had forgotten that this existed, this smell which instead of the first robin, or the first bud or leaf, means to me that spring has come. I had always welcomed vitality and energy and warmth radiating from thick and sturdy winter clothes. It made me happy, but I kept wondering about next spring, about whether khaki, or suntans or whatever the uniform of the season was, had this aura of promise in it. I felt fairly sure it didn't.

The fight veered. Finny had recruited me and others as allies, so that two sides fighting it out had been taking form. Suddenly he turned his fire against me, he betrayed several of his other friends; he went over to the other, to Brinker's side for a short time, enough to ensure that his betrayal of them

Hours later it occurred to me to ask him, "Do you think you ought to get into fights like that? After all, there's your leg—"

"Stanpole said something about not falling again, but I'm very careful."

"Oh, don't break it again!"

"No, of course I won't break it again. Isn't the bone supposed to be stronger when it grows together over a place where it's been broken once?"

"Yes, I think it is."

"I think so too. In fact I think I can feel it getting stronger."

"You think you can? Can you feel it?"

"Yes, I think so."

"Thank goodness."

"What?"

"I said that's good."

"Yes, I guess it is. I guess that's good, all right."

After dinner that night Brinker came to our room to pay us one of his formal calls. Our room had by this time of year the ex-

---

3. Hitler Youth: In Germany, an organization of boys and girls who supported Adolf Hitler, dictator from 1933 to 1945.

"*Over my cot I had long ago taped pictures which together amounted to a barefaced lie about my background....*"

hausted look of a place where two people had lived too long without taking any interest in their surround- ings. Our cots at either end of the room were sway- backed beneath their pink and brown cotton spreads. The walls, which were much farther off white than normal, expressed two forgotten inter- ests: Finny had scotch-taped newspaper pictures of the Roosevelt-Churchill meeting[4] above his cot ("They're the two most impor- tant of the old men," he had explained, "getting together to make up what to tell us next about the war"). Over my cot I had long ago taped pictures which together amounted to a barefaced lie about my background —weepingly romantic views of plantation mansions, moss-hung trees by moonlight, lazy roads winding dustily past cabins.

When asked about them I had acquired an accent appropriate to a town three states south of my own, and I had transmitted the impression, without actually stating it, that this was the old family place. But by now I no longer needed this vivid false identity; now I was acquiring, I felt, a sense of my own real authority and worth, I had had many new experiences and I was growing up.

"How's Leper?" said Brinker as he came in.

"Yeah," said Phineas, "I meant to ask you before."

"Leper? Why he's—he's on leave." But my resentment against having to mislead people seemed to be growing stronger every day. "As a matter of fact Leper is 'Absent Without Leave,' he just took off by himself."

"Leper?" both of them exclaimed to- gether.

---

4. Roosevelt-Churchill meeting: Roosevelt and Churchill met many times during World War II. This is probably a reference to their January 1943 meeting at Casablanca in Morocco to decide on future strategy for the Allies. It was at this conference that Roosevelt called for "unconditional surrender" of the Axis powers.

"Yes," I shrugged, "Leper. Leper's not the little rabbit we used to know any more."

"Nobody can change *that* much," said Brinker in his new tough-minded way.

Finny said, "He just didn't like the army, I bet. Why should he? What's the point of it anyway?"

"Phineas," Brinker said with dignity, "please don't give us your infantile[5] lecture on world affairs at this time." And to me, "He was too scared to stay, wasn't he?"

I narrowed my eyes as though thinking hard about that. Finally I said, "Yes, I think you could put it that way."

"He panicked."

I didn't say anything.

"He must be out of his mind," said Brinker energetically, "to do a thing like that. I'll bet he cracked up, didn't he? That's what happened. Leper found out that the army was just too much for him. I've heard about guys like that. Some morning they don't get out of bed with everybody else. They just lie there crying. I'll bet something like that happened to Leper." He looked at me. "Didn't it?"

"Yes. It did."

Brinker had closed with such energy, almost enthusiasm, on the truth that I gave it to him without many misgivings. The moment he had it he crumbled. "Well I'll be. I'll be. Old Leper. Quiet old Leper. Quiet old Leper from Vermont. He never could fight. You'd think somebody would have realized that when he tried to enlist. Poor old Leper. What's he act like?"

"He cries a lot of the time."

"Oh. What's the matter with our class anyway? It isn't even June yet and we've already got two men sidelined for the Duration."

"Two?"

Brinker hesitated briefly. "Well there's Finny here."

"Yes," agreed Phineas in his deepest and most musical tone, "there's me."

"Finny isn't out of it," I said.

"Of course he is."

"Yes, I'm out of it."

"Not that there's anything to be out of!" I wondered if my face matched the heartiness of my voice. "Just this dizzy war, this fake, this thing with the old men making . . ." I couldn't help watching Finny as I spoke, and so I ran out of momentum. I waited for him to take it up, to unravel once again his tale of plotting statesmen and deluded public, his great joke, his private toe hold on the world. He was sitting on his cot, elbows on knees, looking down. He brought his wideset eyes up, his grin flashed and faded, and then he murmured, "Sure. There isn't any war."

It was one of the few ironic remarks Phineas ever made, and with it he quietly brought to a close all his special inventions which had carried us through the winter. Now the facts were re-established, and gone were all the fantasies, such as the Olympic Games for A.D. 1944, closed before they had ever been opened.

There was little left at Devon any more which had not been recruited for the war. The few stray activities and dreamy people not caught up in it were being systematically corralled by Brinker. And every day in chapel there was some announcement about qualifying for "V-12," an officer-training program the Navy had set up in many colleges and universities. It sounded very safe, almost like peacetime, almost like

---

5. infantile (in′ fən tīl′) *adj.*: Characteristic of an infant; immature.

just going normally on to college. It was also very popular; groups the size of LST crews[6] joined it, almost everyone who could qualify, except for a few who "wanted to fly" and so chose the Army Air Force, or something called V-5 instead. There were also a special few with energetic fathers who were expecting appointments to Annapolis or West Point or the Coast Guard Academy or even —this alternative had been unexpectedly stumbled on—the Merchant Marine Academy. Devon was by tradition and choice the most civilian of schools, and there was a certain strained hospitality in the way both the faculty and students worked to get along with the leathery recruiting officers who kept appearing on the campus. There was no latent snobbery in us; we didn't find any in them. It was only that we could feel a deep and sincere difference between us and them, a difference which everyone struggled with awkward fortitude to bridge. It was as though Athens and Sparta[7] were trying to establish not just a truce but an alliance —although we were not as civilized as Athens and they were not as brave as Sparta.

Neither were we. There was no rush to get into the fighting; no one seemed to feel the need to get into the infantry, and only a few were talking about the Marines. The thing to be was careful and self-preserving. It was going to be a long war. Quackenbush, I heard, had two possible appointments to the Military Academy, with carefully prepared positions in V-12 and dentistry school to fall back on if necessary.

I myself took no action. I didn't feel free to, and I didn't know why this was so.

Brinker, in his accelerating change from absolute to relative virtue, came up with plan after plan, each more insulated from the fighting than the last. But I did nothing.

One morning, after a Naval officer had turned many heads in chapel with an address on convoy duty,[8] Brinker put his hand on the back of my neck in the vestibule outside and steered me into a room used for piano practice near the entrance. It was soundproofed, and he swung the vaultlike door closed behind us.

"You've been putting off enlisting in something for only one reason," he said at once. "You know that, don't you?"

"No, I don't know that."

"Well, I know, and I'll tell you what it is. It's Finny. You pity him."

"Pity him!"

"Yes, pity him. And if you don't watch out he's going to start pitying himself. Nobody ever mentions his leg to him except me. Keep that up and he'll be sloppy with self-pity any day now. What's everybody beating around the bush for? He's crippled and that's that. He's got to accept it and unless we start acting perfectly natural about it, even kid him about it once in a while, he never will."

"You're so wrong I can't even—I can't even *hear* you, you're so wrong."

"Well, I'm going to do it anyway."

"No. You're not."

"Yes I am. I don't have to have your approval, do I?"

"I'm his roommate, and I'm his best friend—"

6. LST crews: Sailors who manned landing craft during invasions.
7. Athens and Sparta: Ancient Greek city-states always at war with each other.

8. convoy duty: Convoy duty, in which navy ships escort merchant ships to protect them from attack, was one of the most dangerous assignments during World War II. In 1942 one convoy in the North Atlantic lost 24 of 35 ships.

"And you were there when it happened. I know. And I don't care. And don't forget," he looked at me sharply, "you've got a little personal stake in this. What I mean is it wouldn't do you any harm, you know, if everything about Finny's accident was cleared up and forgotten."

I felt my face grimacing in the way Finny's did when he was really irritated. "What do you mean by that?"

"I don't know," he shrugged and chuckled in his best manner, "nobody knows." Then the charm disappeared and he added, "unless you know," and his mouth closed in its straight expressionless line, and that was all that was said.

I had no idea what Brinker might say or do. Before he had always known and done whatever occurred to him because he was certain that whatever occurred to him was right. In the world of the Golden Fleece Debating Society and the Underprivileged Local Children subcommittee of the Good Samaritan Confraternity, this had created no problems. But I was afraid of that simple executive directness now.

I walked back from Chapel and found Finny in our dormitory, blocking the staircase until the others who wanted to go up sang "A Mighty Fortress Is Our God" under his direction. No one who was tone deaf ever loved music so much. I think his shortcoming increased his appreciation; he loved it all indiscriminately—Beethoven,[9] the latest love ditty, jazz, a hymn—it was all profoundly musical to Phineas.

". . . Our helper He a-mid the floods," wafted out across the Common in the tempo of a football march, "Of mortal ills prevailing!"

"Everything was all right," said Finny at the end, "phrasing, rhythm, all that. But I'm not sure about your pitch. Half a tone off, I would estimate offhand."

We went on to our room. I sat down at the translation of Caesar I was doing for him, since he had to pass Latin at last this year or fail to graduate. I thought I was doing a pretty good job of it.

"Is anything exciting happening now?"

"This part is pretty interesting," I said, "if I understand it right. About a surprise attack."

"Read me that."

"Well let's see. It begins, 'When Caesar noticed that the enemy was remaining for several days at the camp fortified by a swamp and by the nature of the terrain, he sent a letter to Trebonius instructing him' —'instructing him' isn't actually in the text but it's understood; you know about that."

"Sure. Go on."

"'Instructing him to come as quickly as possible by long forced marches to him' —this 'him' refers to Caesar of course."

Finny looked at me with glazed interest and said, "Of course."

"'Instructing him to come as quickly as possible by long forced marches to him with three legions; he himself'—Caesar, that is —'sent cavalry to withstand any sudden attacks of the enemy. Now when the Gauls[10] learned what was going on, they scattered a selected band of foot soldiers in ambushes; who, overtaking our horsemen after the leader Vertiscus had been killed, followed our disorderly men up to our camp.'"

"I have a feeling that's what Mr. Horn is going to call a 'muddy translation.' What's it mean?"

"Caesar isn't doing so well."

"But he won it in the end."

9. Beethoven (bā′ tō vən): Ludwig van Beethoven (1770–1827) was a famous German classical composer.

10. Gauls (gôlz) *n.*: People of Gaul, the region in western Europe that is today France and Belgium.

"Sure. If you mean the whole campaign —" I broke off. "He won it, if you really think there was a Gallic War[11] . . .." Caesar, from the first, had been the one historical figure Phineas refused absolutely to believe in. Lost two thousand years in the past, master of a dead language and a dead empire, the bane and bore of schoolboys, Caesar he believed to be more of a tyrant at Devon than he had ever been in Rome. Phineas felt a personal and sincere grudge against Caesar, and he was outraged most by his conviction that Caesar and Rome and Latin had never been alive at all . . . "If you really think there ever was a Caesar," I said.

Finny got up from the cot, picking up his cane as an afterthought. He looked oddly at me, his face set to burst out laughing I thought. "Naturally I don't believe books and I don't believe teachers," he came across a few paces, "but I do believe—it's important after all for me to believe *you*. I've got to believe you, at least. I know you better than anybody." I waited without saying anything. "And you told me about Leper, that he's gone crazy. That's the word, we might as well admit it. Leper's gone crazy. When I heard that about Leper, then I knew that the war was real, this war and all the wars. If a war can drive somebody crazy, then it's real all right. Oh I guess I always *knew*, but I didn't have to admit it." He perched his foot, small cast with metal bar across the bottom to walk on, next to where I was sitting on the cot. "To tell you the truth, I wasn't too completely sure about *you*, when you told me how Leper was. Of course I believed you," he added hurriedly, "but you're the nervous type, you know, and I thought maybe your imagination got a little inflamed up there in Vermont. I thought he might not

be quite as mixed up as you made out." Finny's face tried to prepare me for what came next. "Then I saw him myself."

I turned incredulously. "You saw Leper?"

"I saw him here this morning, after chapel. He was—well, there's nothing inflamed about my imagination and I saw Leper *hiding* in the shrubbery next to the chapel. I slipped out the side door the way I always do—to miss the rush—and I saw Leper and he must have seen me. He didn't say a word. He looked at me like I was a gorilla or something and then he ducked into Mr. Carhart's office."

"He must be crazy," I said automatically, and then my eyes involuntarily met Finny's. We both broke into sudden laughter.

"We can't do a thing about it," he said ruefully.

"I don't want to see him," I muttered. Then, trying to be more responsible, "Who else knows he's here."

"No one, I would think."

"There's nothing for us to do, maybe Carhart or Dr. Stanpole can do something. We won't tell anybody about it because . . . because they would just scare Leper, and he would scare them."

"Anyway," said Finny, "then I knew there was a real war on."

"Yes, I guess it's a real war all right. But I liked yours a lot better."

"So did I."

"I wish you hadn't found out. What did you have to find out for!" We started to laugh again, with a half-guilty exchange of glances, in the way that two people who had gone on a gigantic binge when they were last together would laugh when they met again at the parson's tea. "Well," he said, "you did a beautiful job in the Olympics."

"And you were the greatest news analyst who ever lived."

11. **Gallic** (gal' ik) **War:** War in which the Romans, under the leadership of Julius Caesar, conquered Gaul (58–49 B.C.).

"Do you realize you won every gold medal in every Olympic event? No one's ever done anything like that in history."

"And you scooped every newspaper in the world on every story." The sun was doing antics among the million specks of dust hanging between us and casting a brilliant, unstable pool of light on the floor. "No one's ever done anything like that before."

Brinker and three cohorts[12] came with much commotion into our room at 10:05 P.M. that night. "We're taking you out," he said flatly.

"It's after hours," I said. "Where?" said Finny with interest at the same time.

"You'll see. Get them." His friends half-lifted us half-roughly, and we were hustled down the stairs. I thought it must be some kind of culminating prank, the senior class leaving Devon with a flourish. Were we going to steal the clapper of the school bell, or would we tether a cow in chapel?

They steered us toward the First Building—burned down and rebuilt several times but still known as the First Building of the Devon School. It contained only classrooms and so at this hour was perfectly empty, which made us stealthier than ever. Brinker's many keys, surviving from his class-officer period, jingled softly as we reached the main door. Above us in Latin flowed the inscription, Here Boys Come to Be Made Men.

The lock turned; we went in, entering the doubtful reality of a hallway familiar only in daylight and bustle. Our footsteps fell guiltily on the marble floor. We continued across the foyer to a dreamlike bank of windows, turned left up a pale flight of marble steps, left again, through two doorways, and into the Assembly Room. From the high ceiling one of the celebrated Devon chandeliers, all glittering tears, scattered thin illumination. Row after row of black Early American benches spread emptily back through the shadows to long, vague windows. At the front of the room there was a raised platform with a balustrade[13] in front of it. About ten members of the senior class sat on the platform; all of them were wearing their black graduation robes. This is going to be some kind of schoolboy masquerade, I thought, some masquerade with masks and candles.

"You see how Phineas limps," said Brinker loudly as we walked in. It was too coarse and too loud; I wanted to hit him for shocking me like that. Phineas looked perplexed. "Sit down," he went on, "take a load off your feet." We sat in the front row of the benches where eight or ten others were sitting, smirking uneasily at the students on the platform.

Whatever Brinker had in his mind to do, I thought he had chosen a terrible place for it. There was nothing funny about the Assembly Room. I could remember staring torpidly[14] through these windows a hundred times out at the elms of the Center Common. The windows now had the closed blankness of night, a deadened look about them, a look of being blind or deaf. The great expanses of wall space were opaque with canvas, portraits in oil of deceased headmasters, a founder or two, forgotten leaders of the faculty, a beloved athletic coach none of us had ever heard of, a lady we could not identify —her fortune had largely rebuilt the school; a nameless poet who was thought when

---

12. cohorts (kō′ hôrts) *n*.: Companions; supporters.

13. balustrade (bal′ ə strād′) *n*.: A railing held up by small posts.

14. torpidly (tôr′ pid lē) *adv*.: Sluggishly; slowly.

under the school's protection to be destined primarily for future generations; a young hero now anonymous who looked theatrical in the First World War uniform in which he had died.

I thought any prank was bound to fall flat here.

The Assembly Hall was used for large lectures, debates, plays, and concerts; it had the worst acoustics in the school. I couldn't make out what Brinker was saying. He stood on the polished marble floor in front of us, but facing the platform, talking to the boys behind the balustrade. I heard him say the word "inquiry" to them, and something about "the country demands. . . ."

"What is all this hot air?" I said into the blur.

"I don't know," Phineas answered shortly.

As he turned toward us Brinker was saying ". . . blame on the responsible party. We will begin with a brief prayer." He paused, surveying us with the kind of wide-eyed surmise Mr. Carhart always used at this point, and then added in Mr. Carhart's urbane murmur, "Let us pray."

We all slumped immediately and unthinkingly into the awkward crouch in which God was addressed at Devon, leaning forward with elbows on knees. Brinker had caught us, and in a moment it was too late to escape, for he had moved swiftly into the Lord's Prayer. If when Brinker had said "Let us pray" I had said "No" everything might have been saved.

At the end there was an indecisive, semiserious silence and then Brinker said, "Phineas, if you please." Finny got up with a shrug and walked to the center of the floor, between us and the platform. Brinker got an armchair from behind the balustrade, and seated Finny on it with courtly politeness.

"Now just in your own words," he said.

"What own words?" said Phineas, grimacing up at him with his best you-are-an-idiot expression.

"I know you haven't got many of your own," said Brinker with a charitable smile. "Use some of Gene's then."

"What shall I talk about? You? I've got plenty of words of my own for that."

"*I'm* all right," Brinker glanced gravely around the room for confirmation, "you're the casualty."

"Brinker," began Finny in a constricted voice I did not recognize, "are you off your head or what?"

"No," said Brinker evenly, "that's Leper, our other casualty. Tonight we're investigating you."

"What are you talking about!" I cut in suddenly.

"Investigating Finny's accident!" He spoke as though this was the most natural and self-evident and inevitable thing we could be doing.

I felt the blood flooding into my head. "After all," Brinker continued, "there *is* a war on. Here's one soldier our side has already lost. We've got to find out what happened."

"Just for the record," said someone from the platform. "You agree, don't you, Gene?"

"I told Brinker this morning," I began in a voice treacherously shaking, "that I thought this was the worst—"

"And I said," Brinker's voice was full of authority and perfectly under control, "that for Finny's good," and with an additional timbre[15] of sincerity, "and for your own good too, by the way, Gene, that we should get all

---

15. timbre (tam′ bər) *n*.: The distinctive tone of a voice.

" 'Investigating Finny's accident!' "

this out into the open. We don't want any mysteries or any stray rumors and suspicions left in the air at the end of the year, do we?''

A collective assent to this rumbled through the blurring atmosphere of the Assembly Room.

"What are you talking about!" Finny's voice was full of contemptuous music. "What rumors and suspicions?"

"Never mind about that," said Brinker with his face responsibly grave. He's enjoying this, I thought bitterly, he's imagining himself Justice incarnate,[16] balancing the scales. He's forgotten that Justice incarnate is not only balancing the scales but also blindfolded. "Why don't you just tell us in your words what happened?" Brinker continued. "Just humor us, if you want to think of it that way. We aren't trying to make you feel bad. Just tell us. You know we wouldn't ask you if we didn't have a good reason . . . good reasons."

"There's nothing to tell."

"Nothing to tell?" Brinker looked pointedly at the small cast around Finny's lower leg and the cane he held between his knees.

"Well then, I fell out of a tree."

"Why?" said someone on the platform. The acoustics were so bad and the light so dim that I could rarely tell who was speaking, except for Finny and Brinker who were isolated on the wide strip of marble floor between us in the seats and the others on the platform.

"Why?" repeated Phineas. "Because I took a wrong step."

"Did you lose your balance?" continued the voice.

"Yes," echoed Finny grimly, "I lost my balance."

"You had better balance than anyone in the school."

"Thanks a lot."

"I didn't say it for a compliment."

"Well then, no thanks."

"Have you ever thought that you didn't just fall out of that tree?"

This touched an interesting point Phineas had been turning over in his mind for a long time. I could tell that because the obstinate, competitive look left his face as his mind became engaged for the first time. "It's very funny," he said, "but ever since then I've had a feeling that the tree did it by itself. It's an impression I've had. Almost as though the tree shook me out by itself."

The acoustics in the Assembly Room were so poor that silences there had a heavy hum of their own.

"Someone else was in the tree, isn't that so?"

"No," said Finny spontaneously, "I don't think so." He looked at the ceiling. "Or was there? Maybe there was somebody climbing up the rungs of the trunk. I kind of forget."

This time the hum of silence was prolonged to a point where I would be forced to fill it with some kind of sound if it didn't end. Then someone else on the platform spoke up. "I thought somebody told me that Gene Forrester was——"

"Finny was there," Brinker interrupted commandingly, "he knows better than anyone."

"You were there too, weren't you, Gene?" this new voice from the platform continued.

"Yes," I said with interest, "yes, I was there too."

"Were you——near the tree?"

Finny turned toward me. "You were down at the bottom, weren't you?" he asked, not in the official courtroom tone he had used before, but in a friend's voice.

---

16. incarnate (in kär′ nit) *adj.*: Endowed with a human body; in bodily form.

I had been studying very carefully the way my hands wrinkled when tightly clenched, but I was able to bring my head up and return his inquiring look. "Down at the bottom, yes."

Finny went on. "Did you see the tree shake or anything?" He flushed faintly at what seemed to him the absurdity of his own question. "I've always meant to ask you, just for the hell of it."

I took this under consideration. "I don't recall anything like that . . ."

"Nutty question," he muttered.

"I thought you were in the tree," the platform voice cut in.

"Well of course," Finny said with an exasperated chuckle, "of course I was in the tree—oh you mean Gene?—he wasn't in—is that what you mean, or—" Finny floundered with muddled honesty between me and my questioner.

"I meant Gene," the voice said.

"Of course Finny was in the tree," I said. But I couldn't make the confusion last, "and I was down at the bottom, or climbing the rungs I think . . ."

"How do you expect him to remember?" said Finny sharply. "There was a lot of confusion right then."

"A kid I used to play with was hit by a car once when I was about eleven years old," said Brinker seriously, "and I remember every single thing about it, exactly where I was standing, the color of the sky, the noise the brakes of the car made—I never will forget anything about it."

"You and I are two different people," I said.

"No one's accusing you of anything," Brinker responded in an odd tone.

"Well of course no one's *accusing* me—"

"Don't argue so much," his voice tried for a hard compromise, full of warning and yet striving to pass unnoticed by the others.

"No, we're not accusing you," a boy on the platform said evenly, and then I stood accused.

"I think I remember now!" Finny broke in, his eyes bright and relieved. "Yes, I remember seeing you standing on the bank. You were looking up and your hair was plastered down over your forehead so that you had that dumb look you always have when you've been in the water—what was it you said? 'Stop posing up there' or one of those best-pal cracks you're always making." He was very happy. "And I think I did start to pose just to make you madder, and I said, what did I say? something about the two of us . . . yes, I said 'Let's make a double jump,' because I thought if we went together it would be something that had never been done before, holding hands in a jump—" Then it was as though someone suddenly slapped him. "No, that was on the ground when I said that to you. I said that to you on the ground, and then the two of us started to climb . . ." he broke off.

"The two of you," the boy on the platform went on harshly for him, "started to climb up the tree together, was that it? And he's just said he was on the ground!"

"Or on the rungs!" I burst out. "I said I might have been on the rungs!"

"Who else was there?" said Brinker quietly. "Leper Lepellier was there, wasn't he?"

"Yes," someone said, "Leper was there."

"Leper always was the exact type when it came to details," continued Brinker. "He could have told us where everybody was standing, what everybody was wearing, the whole conversation that day, and what the temperature was. He could have cleared the whole thing up. Too bad."

No one said anything. Phineas had been sitting motionless, leaning slightly forward, not far from the position in which we prayed at Devon. After a long time he turned and reluctantly looked at me. I did not return his look or move or speak. Then at last Finny straightened from this prayerful position slowly, as though it was painful for him. "Leper's here," he said in a voice so quiet, and with such quiet unconscious dignity, that he was suddenly terrifyingly strange to me. "I saw him go into Dr. Carhart's office this morning."

"Here! Go get him," said Brinker immediately to the two boys who had come with us. "He must be in Carhart's rooms if he hasn't gone back home."

I kept quiet. To myself, however, I made a number of swift, automatic calculations: that Leper was no threat, no one would ever believe Leper; Leper was deranged, he was not of sound mind and if people couldn't make out their own wills when not in sound mind certainly they couldn't testify in something like this.

The two boys left and the atmosphere immediately cleared. Action had been taken, so the whole issue was dropped for now. Someone began making fun of "Captain Marvel,"[17] the head of the football team, saying how girlish he looked in his graduation gown. Captain Marvel minced for us in his size 12 shoes, the sides of his gown swaying drunkenly back and forth from his big hips. Someone wound himself in the folds of the red velvet curtain and peered out from it like an exotic spy. Someone made a long speech listing every infraction[18] of the rules we were committing that night. Someone else made a speech showing how by careful planning we could break all the others before dawn.

But although the acoustics in the Assembly Hall were poor, those outside the room were admirable. All the talk and horseplay ended within a few seconds of the instant when the first person, that is myself, heard the footsteps returning along the marble stairway and corridors toward us. I knew with absolute certainty moments before they came in that there were three sets of footsteps coming.

Leper entered ahead of the other two. He looked unusually well; his face was glowing, his eyes were bright, his manner was all energy. "Yes?" he said in a clear voice, resonant even in this room, "what can I do for you?" He made this confident remark almost but not quite to Phineas, who was still sitting alone in the middle of the room. Finny muttered something which was too indecisive for Leper, who turned with a cleanly energetic gesture toward Brinker. Brinker began talking to him in the elaborately casual manner of someone being watched. Gradually the noise in the room, which had revived when the three of them came in, subsided again.

Brinker managed it. He never raised his voice, but instead he let the noise surrounding it gradually sink so that his voice emerged in the ensuing silence without any emphasis on his part—"so that you were standing next to the river bank, watching Phineas climb the tree?" he was saying, and had waited, I knew, until this silence to say.

"Sure. Right there by the trunk of the tree. I was looking up. It was almost sunset, and I remember the way the sun was shining in my eyes."

"So you couldn't . . ." I began before I could stop myself.

There was a short pause during which every ear and no eyes were directed toward me, and then Brinker went on. "And what did you see? Could you see anything with the sun in your eyes?"

"Oh sure," said Leper in his new, confident, false voice. "I just shaded my eyes a

---

17. Captain Marvel: A comic book hero, after whom the football team's captain was nicknamed.
18. infraction (in frak' shən) n.: Violation.

little, like this," he demonstrated how a hand shades the eyes, "and then I could see. I could see both of them clearly enough because the sun was blazing all around them," a certain singsong sincerity was developing in his voice, as though he were trying to hold the interest of young children, "and the rays of the sun were shooting past them, millions of rays shooting past them like—like golden machine-gun fire." He paused to let us consider the profoundly revealing exactness of this phrase. "That's what it was like, if you want to know. The two of them looked as black as—as black as death standing up there with this fire burning all around them."

Everyone could hear, couldn't they? the derangement in his voice. Everyone must be able to see how false his confidence was. Any fool could see that. But whatever I said would be a self-indictment;[19] others would have to fight for me.

"Up there where?" said Brinker brusquely. "Where were the two of them standing up there?"

"On the limb!" Leper's annoyed, this-is-obvious tone would discount what he said in their minds; they would know that he had never been like this before, that he had changed and was not responsible.

"Who was where on the limb? Was one of them ahead of the other?"

"Well of course."

"Who was ahead?"

Leper smiled waggishly. "I couldn't see *that*. There were just two shapes, and with that fire shooting past them they looked as black as—"

"You've already told us that. You couldn't see who was ahead?"

"No, naturally I couldn't."

"But you could see how they were standing. Where were they exactly?"

"One of them was next to the trunk, holding the trunk of the tree. I'll never forget that because the tree was a huge black shape too, and his hand touching the black trunk anchored him, if you see what I mean, to something solid in all the bright fire they were standing in up there. And the other one was a little farther out on the limb."

"Then what happened?"

"Then they both moved."

"How did they move?"

"They moved," now Leper was smiling, a charming and slightly arch[20] smile, like a child who knows he is going to say something clever, "they moved like an engine."

In the baffled silence I began to uncoil slowly.

"Like an engine!" Brinker's expression was a struggle between surprise and disgust.

"I can't think of the name of the engine. But it has two pistons. What is that engine? Well anyway, in this engine first one piston sinks, and then the next one sinks. The one holding on to the trunk sank for a second, up and down like a piston, and then the other one sank and fell."

Someone on the platform exclaimed, "The one who moved first shook the other one's balance!"

"I suppose so." Leper seemed to be rapidly losing interest.

"Was the one who fell," Brinker said slowly, "was Phineas, in other words the one who moved first or second?"

Leper's face became guileful, his voice flat and impersonal. "I don't intend to implicate myself. I'm no fool, you know. I'm not going to tell you everything and then have it used against me later. You always did take me for a fool, didn't you? But I'm no fool any more. I know when I have information that might be dangerous." He was working him-

---

19. self-indictment (self in dīt′ mənt) *n.*: An accusation of himself.

20. arch (ärch) *adj.*: Mischievous.

self up to indignation. "Why should I tell you! Just because it happens to suit you!"

"Leper," Brinker pleaded, "Leper, this is very important—"

"So am I," he said thinly, "I'm important. You've never realized it, but I'm important too. You be the fool," he gazed shrewdly at Brinker, "you do whatever anyone wants whenever they want it. You be the fool now."

Phineas had gotten up unnoticed from his chair. "I don't care," he interrupted in an even voice, so full of richness that it overrode all the others. "I don't care."

I tore myself from the bench toward him. "Phineas—!"

He shook his head sharply, closing his eyes, and then he turned to regard me with a handsome mask of face. "I just don't care. Never mind," and he started across the marble floor toward the doors.

"Wait a minute!" cried Brinker. "We haven't heard everything yet. We haven't got all the facts!"

The words shocked Phineas into awareness. He whirled as though being attacked from behind. "You get the rest of the facts, Brinker!" he cried. "You get all your facts!" I had never seen Finny crying, "You collect every fact there is in the world!" He plunged out the doors.

The excellent exterior acoustics recorded his rushing steps and the quick rapping of his cane along the corridor and on the first steps of the marble stairway. Then these separate sounds collided into the general tumult of his body falling clumsily down the white marble stairs.

Chapter 12

Everyone behaved with complete presence of mind. Brinker shouted that Phineas must not be moved; someone else, realizing that only a night nurse would be at the Infirmary, did not waste time going there but rushed to bring Dr. Stanpole from his house. Others remembered that Phil Latham, the wrestling coach, lived just across the Common and that he was an expert in first aid. It was Phil who made Finny stretch out on one of the wide shallow steps of the staircase, and kept him still until Dr. Stanpole arrived.

The foyer and the staircase of the First Building were soon as crowded as at midday. Phil Latham found the main light switch, and all the marble blazed up under full illumination. But surrounding it was the stillness of near-midnight in a country town, so that the hurrying feet and the repressed voices had a hollow reverberance. The windows, blind and black, retained their look of dull emptiness.

Once Brinker turned to me and said, "Go back to the Assembly Room and see if there's any kind of blanket on the platform." I dashed back up the stairs, found a blanket and gave it to Phil Latham. He carefully wrapped it around Phineas.

I would have liked very much to have done that myself; it would have meant a lot to me. But Phineas might begin to curse me with every word he knew, he might lose his head completely, he would certainly be worse off for it. So I kept out of the way.

He was entirely conscious and from the glimpses I caught of his face seemed to be fairly calm. Everyone behaved with complete presence of mind, and that included Phineas.

When Dr. Stanpole arrived there was silence on the stairs. Wrapped tightly in his blanket, with light flooding down on him from the chandelier, Finny lay isolated at the center of a tight circle of faces. The rest of the crowd looked on from above or below on the stairs, and I stood on the lower edge. Behind me the foyer was now empty.

After a short, silent examination Dr. Stanpole had a chair brought from the

Assembly Room, and Finny was lifted cautiously into it. People aren't ordinarily carried in chairs in New Hampshire, and as they raised him up he looked very strange to me, like some tragic and exalted personage, a stricken pontiff.[1] Once again I had the desolating sense of having all along ignored what was finest in him. Perhaps it was just the incongruity of seeing him aloft and stricken, since he was by nature someone who carried others. I didn't think he knew how to act or even how to feel as the object of help. He went past with his eyes closed and his mouth tense. I knew that normally I would have been one of those carrying the chair, saying something into his ear as we went along. My aid alone had never seemed to him in the category of help. The reason for this occurred to me as the procession moved slowly across the brilliant foyer to the doors; Phineas had thought of me as an extension of himself.

Dr. Stanpole stopped near the doors, looking for the light switch. There was an interval of a few seconds when no one was near him. I came up to him and tried to phrase my question but nothing came out, I couldn't find the word to begin. I was being torn irreconcilably between "Is he" and "What is" when Dr. Stanpole, without appearing to notice my tangle, said conversationally, "It's the leg again. Broken again. But a much cleaner break I think, much cleaner. A simple fracture." He found the light switch and the foyer was plunged into darkness.

Outside, the doctor's car was surrounded by boys while Finny was being lifted inside it by Phil Latham. Phil and Dr. Stanpole then got into the car and drove slowly away, the headlights forming a bright paral-lel as they receded down the road, and then swinging into another parallel at right angles to the first as they turned into the Infirmary driveway. The crowd began to thin rapidly; the faculty had at last heard that something was amiss in the night, and several alarmed and alarming masters materialized in the darkness and ordered the students to their dormitories.

Mr. Ludsbury loomed abruptly out of a background of shrubbery. "Get along to the dormitory, Forrester," he said with a dry certainty in my obedience which suddenly struck me as funny, definitely funny. Since it was beneath his dignity to wait and see that I actually followed his order, I was able to budge free of him a moment later. I walked into the bank of shrubbery, circled past trees in the direction of the chapel, doubled back along a large building donated by the alumni which no one had ever been able to put to use, recrossed the street and walked noiselessly up the emerging grass next to the Infirmary driveway.

Dr. Stanpole's car was at the top of it, headlights on and motor running, empty. I idly considered stealing it, in the way that people idly consider many crimes it would be possible for them to commit. I took an academic interest in the thought of stealing the car, knowing all the time that it would be not so much criminal as meaningless, a lapse into nothing, an escape into nowhere. As I walked past it the motor was throbbing with wheezy reluctance—prep school doctors don't own very desirable getaway cars, I remember thinking to myself—and then I turned the corner of the building and began to creep along behind it. There was only one window lighted, at the far end, and opposite it I found some thin shrubbery which provided enough cover for me to study the window. It was too high for me to see directly into the room, but after I made sure that the

---

1. pontiff (pän' tif) *n.*: A high priest; a bishop.

ground had softened enough so that I could jump without making much noise, I sprang as high as I could. I had a flashing glimpse of a door at the other end of the room, opening on the corridor. I jumped again; someone's back. Again; nothing new. I jumped again and saw a head and shoulders partially turned away from me; Phil Latham's. This was the room.

The ground was too damp to sit on, so I crouched down and waited. I could hear their blurred voices droning monotonously through the window. If they do nothing worse, they're going to bore Finny to death, I said to myself. My head seemed to be full of bright remarks this evening. It was cold crouching motionless next to the ground. I stood up and jumped several times, not so much to see into the room as to warm up. The only sounds were occasional snorts from the engine of Dr. Stanpole's car when it turned over with special reluctance, and a thin, lonely whistling the wind sometimes made high in the still-bare trees. These formed the background for the dull hum of talk in Finny's room as Phil Latham, Dr. Stanpole and the night nurse worked over him.

What could they be talking about? The night nurse had always been the biggest windbag in the school. Miss Windbag, R.N. Phil Latham, on the other hand, hardly ever spoke. One of the few things he said was "Give it the old college try"—he thought of everything in terms of the old college try, and he had told students to attack their studies, their sports, religious waverings, sexual maladjustments, physical handicaps and a constellation of other problems with the old college try. I listened tensely for his voice. I listened so hard that I nearly differentiated it from the others, and it seemed to be saying, "Finny, give that bone the old college try."

I was quite a card tonight myself.

Phil Latham's college was Harvard, although I had heard that he only lasted there a year. Probably he had said to someone to give something the old college try, and that had finished him; that would probably be grounds for expulsion at Harvard. There couldn't possibly be such a thing as the old Harvard try. Could there be the old Devon try? The old Devon endeavor? The decrepit Devon endeavor? That was good, the decrepit Devon endeavor. I'd use that some time in the Butt Room. That was pretty funny. I'll bet I could get a rise out of Finny with—

Dr. Stanpole was fairly gabby too. What was he always saying. Nothing. Nothing? Well there must be something he was always saying. Everybody had something, some word, some phrase that they were always saying. The trouble with Dr. Stanpole was that his vocabulary was too large. He talked in a huge circle, he probably had a million words in his vocabulary and he had to use them all before he started over again.

That's probably the way they were talking in there now. Dr. Stanpole was working his way as fast as possible around his big circle, Miss Windbag was gasping out something or other all the time, and Phil Latham was saying, "Give 'er the old college try, Finny." Phineas of course was answering them only in Latin.

I nearly laughed out loud at that.

Gallia est omnis divisa in partes tres[2]—Finny probably answered that whenever Phil Latham spoke. Phil Latham would look rather blank at that.

Did Finny like Phil Latham? Yes, of course he did. But wouldn't it be funny if he suddenly turned to him and said, "Phil

---

2. *Gallia est omnis divisa in partes tres*: Latin for "All Gaul is divided into three parts," the first line of Julius Caesar's *Commentaries on the Gallic Wars*, a book often translated by Latin students.

Latham, you're a boob." That would be funny in a way. And what about if he said, "Dr. Stanpole, old pal, you're the most long-winded licensed medical man alive." And it would be even funnier if he interrupted that night nurse and said, "Miss Windbag, you're rotten, rotten to the core. I just thought I ought to tell you." It would never occur to Finny to say any of these things, but they struck me as so outrageous that I couldn't stop myself from laughing. I put my hand over my mouth; then I tried to stop my mouth with my fist; if I couldn't get control of this laughing they would hear me in the room. I was laughing so hard it hurt my stomach and I could feel my face getting more and more flushed; I dug my teeth into my fist to try to gain control and then I noticed that there were tears all over my hand.

The engine of Dr. Stanpole's car roared exhaustedly. The headlights turned in an erratic arc away from me, and then I heard the engine laboriously recede into the distance, and I continued to listen until not only had it ceased but my memory of how it sounded had also ceased. The light had gone out in the room and there was no sound coming from it. The only noise was the peculiarly bleak whistling of the wind through the upper branches.

There was a street light behind me somewhere through the trees and the windows of the Infirmary dimly reflected it. I came up close beneath the window of Finny's room, found a foothold on a grating beneath it, straightened up so that my shoulders were at a level with the window sill, reached up with both hands, and since I was convinced that the window would be stuck shut I pushed it hard. The window shot up and there was a startled rustling from the bed in the shadows. I whispered, "Finny!" sharply into the black room.

"Who is it!" he demanded, leaning out

from the bed so that the light fell waveringly on his face. Then he recognized me and I thought at first he was going to get out of bed and help me through the window. He struggled clumsily for such a length of time that even my mind, shocked and slowed as it had been, was able to formulate two realizations: that his leg was bound so that he could not move very well, and that he was struggling to unleash his hate against me.

"I came to——"

"You want to break something else in me! Is that why you're here!" He thrashed wildly in the darkness, the bed groaning under him and the sheets hissing as he fought against them. But he was not going to be able to get to me, because his matchless coordination was gone. He could not even get up from the bed.

"I want to fix your leg up," I said crazily but in a perfectly natural tone of voice which made my words sound even crazier, even to me.

"You'll fix my . . ." and he arched out, lunging hopelessly into the space between us. He arched out and then fell, his legs still on the bed, his hands falling with a loud slap against the floor. Then after a pause all the tension drained out of him, and he let his head come slowly down between his hands. He had not hurt himself. But he brought his head slowly down between his hands and rested it against the floor, not moving, not making any sound.

"I'm sorry," I said blindly, "I'm sorry, I'm sorry."

I had just control enough to stay out of his room, to let him struggle back into the bed by himself. I slid down from the window, and I remember lying on the ground staring up at the night sky, which was neither clear nor overcast. And I remember later walking alone down a rather aimless road which leads past the gym to an old water hole. I was trying to cope with something that might be called double vision. I saw the gym in the glow of a couple of outside lights near it and I knew of course that it was the Devon gym which I entered every day. It was and it wasn't. There was something innately[3] strange about it, as though there had always been an inner core to the gym which I had never perceived before, quite different from its generally accepted appearance. It seemed to alter moment by moment before my eyes, becoming for brief flashes a totally unknown building with a significance much deeper and far more real than any I had noticed before. The same was true of the water hole, where unauthorized games of hockey were played during the winter. The ice was breaking up on it now, with just a few glazed islands of ice remaining in the center and a fringe of hard surface glinting along the banks. The old trees surrounding it all were intensely meaningful, with a message that was very pressing and entirely indecipherable. Here the road turned to the left and became dirt. It proceeded along the lower end of the playing fields, and under the pale night glow the playing fields swept away from me in slight frosty undulations which bespoke meanings upon meanings, levels of reality I had never suspected before, a kind of thronging and epic grandeur which my superficial eyes and cluttered mind had been blind to before. They unrolled away impervious to me as though I were a roaming ghost, not only tonight but always, as though I had never played on them a hundred times, as though my feet had never touched them, as though my whole life at Devon had been a dream, or rather that everything at Devon, the playing fields, the gym, the water hole, and all the other buildings and all the people there were intensely real, wildly alive and totally meaningful,

and I alone was a dream, a figment[4] which had never really touched anything. I felt that I was not, never had been and never would be a living part of this overpoweringly solid and deeply meaningful world around me.

I reached the bridge which arches over the little Devon River and beyond it the dirt track which curves toward the stadium. The stadium itself, two white concrete banks of seats, was as powerful and alien to me as an Aztec ruin, filled with the traces of vanished people and vanished rites, of supreme emotions and supreme tragedies. The old phrase about "If these walls could only speak" occurred to me and I felt it more deeply than anyone has ever felt it, I felt that the stadium could not only speak but that its words could hold me spellbound. In fact the stadium did speak powerfully and at all times, including this moment. But I could not hear, and that was because I did not exist.

I awoke the next morning in a dry and fairly sheltered corner of the ramp underneath the stadium. My neck was stiff from sleeping in an awkward position. The sun was high and the air freshened.

I walked back to the center of the school and had breakfast and then went to my room to get a notebook, because this was Wednesday and I had a class at 9:10. But at the door of the room I found a note from Dr. Stanpole. "Please bring some of Finny's clothes and his toilet things to the Infirmary."

I took his suitcase from the corner where it had been accumulating dust and put what he would need into it. I didn't know what I was going to say at the Infirmary. I couldn't escape a confusing sense of having lived through all of this before—Phineas in the Infirmary, and myself responsible. I seemed to be less shocked by it now than I had the

---

3. innately (i nāt′ lē) *adv.*: Existing naturally rather than acquired.

4. figment (fig′ mənt) *n.*: Something merely imagined.

first time last August, when it had broken over our heads like a thunderclap in a flawless sky. There were hints of much worse things around us now like a faint odor in the air, evoked by words like "plasma" and "psycho" and "sulfa," strange words like that with endings like Latin nouns. The newsreels and magazines were choked with images of blazing artillery and bodies half sunk in the sand of a beach somewhere. We members of the Class of 1943 were moving very fast toward the war now, so fast that there were casualties even before we reached it, a mind was clouded and a leg was broken—maybe these should be thought of as minor and inevitable mishaps in the accelerating rush. The air around us was filled with much worse things.

In this way I tried to calm myself as I walked with Finny's suitcase toward the Infirmary. After all, I reflected to myself, people were shooting flames into caves and grilling other people alive, ships were being torpedoed and dropping thousands of men in the icy ocean, whole city blocks were exploding into flame in an instant. My brief burst of animosity, lasting only a second, a part of a second, something which came before I could recognize it and was gone before I knew it had possessed me, what was that in the midst of this holocaust?

I reached the Infirmary with Finny's suitcase and went inside. The air was laden with hospital smells, not unlike those of the gym except that the Infirmary lacked that sense of spent human vitality. This was becoming the new background of Finny's life, this purely medical element from which bodily health was absent.

The corridor happened to be empty, and I walked along it in the grip of a kind of fatal exhilaration. All doubt had been resolved at last. There was a wartime phrase coming into style just then—"this is it"—and although it later became a parody of itself, it had a final flat accuracy which was all that could be said at certain times. This was one of the times: this was it.

I knocked and went in. He was stripped to the waist, sitting up in bed leafing through a magazine. I carried my head low by instinct, and I had the courage for only a short glance at him before I said quietly, "I've brought your stuff."

"Put the suitcase on the bed here, will you?" The tone of his words fell dead center, without a trace of friendliness or unfriendliness, not interested and not bored, not energetic and not languid.[5]

I put it down beside him, and he opened it and began to look through the extra underwear and shirts and socks I had packed. I stood precariously[6] in the middle of the room, trying to find somewhere to look and something to say, wanting desperately to leave and powerless to do so. Phineas went carefully over his clothes, apparently very calm. But it wasn't like him to check with such care, not like him at all. He was taking a long time at it, and then I noticed that as he tried to slide a hairbrush out from under a flap holding it in the case his hands were shaking so badly that he couldn't get it out. Seeing that released me on the spot.

"Finny, I tried to tell you before, I tried to tell you when I came to Boston that time—"

"I know, I remember that." He couldn't, after all, always keep his voice under control. "What'd you come around here for last night?"

"I don't know." I went over to the window and placed my hands on the sill. I

_____

5. **languid** (laŋ′ gwid) *adj.*: Without vitality.
6. **precariously** (pri ker′ ē əs lē) *adv.*: Dependent upon the will or favor of another person.

looked down at them with a sense of detachment, as though they were hands somebody had sculptured and put on exhibition somewhere. "I had to." Then I added, with great difficulty, "I thought I belonged here."

I felt him turning to look at me, and so I looked up. He had a particular expression which his face assumed when he understood but didn't think he should show it, a settled, enlightened look; its appearance now was the first decent thing I had seen in a long time.

He suddenly slammed his fist against the suitcase. "I wish to God there wasn't any war."

I looked sharply at him. "What made you say that?"

"I don't know if I can take this with a war on. I don't know."

"If you can take—"

"What good are you in a war with a busted leg!"

"Well you—why there are lots—you can—"

He bent over the suitcase again. "I've been writing to the Army and the Navy and the Marines and the Canadians and everybody else all winter. Did you know that? No, you didn't know that. I used the Post Office in town for my return address. They all gave me the same answer after they saw the medical report on me. The answer was no soap. We can't use you. I also wrote the Coast Guard, the Merchant Marine, I wrote to General de Gaulle personally, I also wrote Chiang Kai-shek, and I was about ready to write somebody in Russia."

I made an attempt at a grin. "You wouldn't like it in Russia."

"I'll *hate* it *everywhere* if I'm not in this war! Why do you think I kept saying there wasn't any war all winter? I was going to keep on saying it until two seconds after I got a letter from Ottawa[7] or Chungking[8] or some place saying, 'Yes, you can enlist with us.'" A look of pleased achievement flickered over his face momentarily, as though he had really gotten such a letter. "Then there would have been a war."

"Finny," my voice broke but I went on, "Phineas, you wouldn't be any good in the war, even if nothing had happened to your leg."

A look of amazement fell over him. It scared me, but I knew what I said was important and right, and my voice found that full tone voices have when they are expressing something long-felt and long-understood and released at last. "They'd get you some place at the front and there'd be a lull in the fighting, and the next thing anyone knew you'd be over with the Germans or the Japs, asking if they'd like to field a baseball team against our side. You'd be sitting in one of their command posts, teaching them English. Yes, you'd get confused and borrow one of their uniforms, and you'd lend them one of yours. Sure, that's just what would happen. You'd get things so scrambled up nobody would know who to fight any more. You'd make a mess, a terrible mess, Finny, out of the war."

His face had been struggling to stay calm as he listened to me, but now he was crying but trying to control himself. "It was just some kind of blind impulse you had in the tree there, you didn't know what you were doing. Was that it?"

"Yes, yes, that was it. Oh that was it, but how can you believe that? How can you believe that? I can't even make myself pretend that you could believe that."

---

7. Ottawa (ăt′ ə wə) *n.*: Capital of Canada.
8. Chungking (chŏoŋ′ kiŋ′): Capital of China during World War II.

" 'Phineas, you wouldn't be any good in the war, ...' "

"I do, I think I can believe that. I've gotten awfully mad sometimes and almost forgotten what I was doing. I think I believe you, I think I can believe that. Then that was it. Something just seized you. It wasn't anything you really felt against me, it wasn't some kind of hate you've felt all along. It wasn't anything personal."

"No, I don't know how to show you, how can I show you, Finny? Tell me how to show you. It was just some ignorance inside me, some crazy thing inside me, something blind, that's all it was."

He was nodding his head, his jaw tightening and his eyes closed on the tears. "I believe you. It's okay because I understand and I believe you. You've already shown me and I believe you."

The rest of the day passed quickly. Dr. Stanpole had told me in the corridor that he was going to set the bone that afternoon. Come back around 5 o'clock, he had said, when Finny should be coming out of the anaesthesia.

I left the Infirmary and went to my 10:10 class, which was on American history. Mr. Patch-Withers gave us a five-minute written quiz on the "necessary and proper" clause of the Constitution. At 11 o'clock I left that building and crossed the Center Common where a few students were already lounging although it was still a little early in the season for that. I went into the First Building, walked up the stairs where Finny had fallen, and joined my 11:10 class, which was in mathematics. We were given a ten-minute trigonometry problem which appeared to solve itself on my paper.

At 12 I left the First Building, recrossed the Common and went into the Jared Potter Building for lunch. It was a breaded veal cutlet, spinach, mashed potatoes, and prune whip. At the table we discussed whether there was any saltpeter in the mashed potatoes. I defended the negative.

After lunch I walked back to the dormitory with Brinker. He alluded to last night only by asking how Phineas was; I said he seemed to be in good spirits. I went on to my room and read the assigned pages of *Le bourgeois gentilhomme.*[9] At 2:30 I left my room, and walking along one side of the oval Finny had used for my track workouts during the winter, I reached the Far Common and beyond it the gym. I went past the Trophy Room, downstairs into the pungent air of the locker room, changed into gym pants, and spent an hour wrestling. I pinned my opponent once and he pinned me once. Phil Latham showed me an involved method of escape in which you executed a modified somersault over your opponent's back. He started to talk about the accident but I concentrated on the escape method and the subject was dropped. Then I took a shower, dressed, and went back to the dormitory, reread part of *Le bourgeois gentilhomme,* and at 4:45, instead of going to a scheduled meeting of the Commencement Arrangements Committee, on which I had been persuaded to take Brinker's place, I went to the Infirmary.

Dr. Stanpole was not patrolling the corridor as he habitually did when he was not busy, so I sat down on a bench amid the medical smells and waited. After about ten minutes he came walking rapidly out of his office, his head down and his hands sunk in the pockets of his white smock. He didn't notice me until he was almost past me, and then he stopped short. His eyes met mine carefully, and I said, "Well, how is he, sir?"

---

9. *Le bourgeois gentilhomme* (lə boor zhwa′ jȧn tē yŏm′): *The Bourgeois Gentleman,* a play by the famous French playwright Molière.

in a calm voice which, the moment after I had spoken, alarmed me unreasonably.

Dr. Stanpole sat down next to me and put his capable-looking hand on my leg. "This is something I think boys of your generation are going to see a lot of," he said quietly, "and I will have to tell you about it now. Your friend is dead."

He was incomprehensible. I felt an extremely cold chill along my back and neck, that was all. Dr. Stanpole went on talking incomprehensibly. "It was such a simple, clean break. Anyone could have set it. Of course, I didn't send him to Boston. Why should I?"

He seemed to expect an answer from me, so I shook my head and repeated, "Why should you?"

"In the middle of it his heart simply stopped, without warning. I can't explain it. Yes, I can. There is only one explanation. As I was moving the bone some of the marrow must have escaped into his blood stream and gone directly to his heart and stopped it. That's the only possible explanation. The only one. There are risks, there are always risks. An operating room is a place where the risks are just more formal than in other places. An operating room and a war." And I noticed that his self-control was breaking up. "Why did it have to happen to you boys so soon, here at Devon?"

"The marrow of his bone . . ." I repeated aimlessly. This at last penetrated my mind. Phineas had died from the marrow of his bone flowing down his blood stream to his heart.

I did not cry then or ever about Finny. I did not cry even when I stood watching him being lowered into his family's strait-laced burial ground outside of Boston. I could not escape a feeling that this was my own funeral, and you do not cry in that case.

Chapter 13

The quadrangle surrounding the Far Common was never considered absolutely essential to the Devon School. The essence was elsewhere, in the older, uglier, more comfortable halls enclosing the Center Common. There the School's history had unrolled, the fabled riot scenes and Presidential visits and Civil War musterings, if not in these buildings then in their predecessors on the same site. The upperclassmen and the faculty met there, the budget was compiled there, and there students were expelled. When you said "Devon" to an alumnus ten years after graduation he visualized the Center Common.

The Far Common was different, a gift of the rich lady benefactress. It was Georgian like the rest of the school, and it combined scholasticism[1] with grace in the way which made Devon architecturally interesting. But the bricks had been laid a little too skillfully, and the woodwork was not as brittle and chipped as it should have been. It was not the essence of Devon, and so it was donated, without too serious a wrench, to the war.

The Far Common could be seen from the window of my room, and early in June I stood at the window and watched the war moving in to occupy it. The advance guard which came down the street from the railroad station consisted of a number of Jeeps, being driven with a certain restraint, their gyration-prone[2] wheels inactive on these old ways which offered nothing bumpier than a few cobblestones. I thought the Jeeps looked

---

1. scholasticism (skə las′ tə siz'm) *n.*: A philosophy based on ancient Greek, Roman, and Christian thought that suggests buildings designed in a traditional, rather Medieval style.

2. gyration-prone (jī rā′ shən prōn) *adj.*: Inclined to spin.

noticeably uncomfortable from all the power they were not being allowed to use. There is no stage you comprehend better than the one you have just left, and as I watched the Jeeps almost asserting a wish to bounce up the side of Mount Washington at eighty miles an hour instead of rolling along this dull street, they reminded me, in a comical and a poignant way, of adolescents.

Following them there were some heavy trucks painted olive drab, and behind them came the troops. They were not very bellicose-looking;[3] their columns were straggling, their suntan uniforms had gotten rumpled in the train, and they were singing "Roll Out the Barrel."

"What's that?" Brinker said from behind me, pointing across my shoulder at some open trucks bringing up the rear. "What's in those trucks?"

"They look like sewing machines."

"They *are* sewing machines!"

"I guess a Parachute Riggers' school has to have sewing machines."

"If only Leper had enlisted in the Army Air Force and been assigned to Parachute Riggers' school . . ."

"I don't think it would have made any difference," I said. "Let's not talk about Leper."

"Leper'll be all right. There's nothing like a discharge. Two years after the war's over people will think a Section Eight[4] means a berth on a Pullman car."[5]

"Right. Now do you mind? Why talk about something you can't do anything about?"

"Right."

I had to be right in never talking about what you could not change, and I had to make many people agree that I was right. None of them ever accused me of being responsible for what had happened to Phineas, either because they could not believe it or else because they could not understand it. I would have talked about that, but they would not, and I would not talk about Phineas in any other way.

The Jeeps, troops, and sewing machines were now drawn up next to the Far Common quadrangle. There was some kind of consultation or ceremony under way on the steps of one of the buildings, Veazy Hall. The Headmaster and a few of the senior members of the faculty stood in a group before the door, and a number of Army Air Force officers stood in another group within easy speaking distance of them. Then the Headmaster advanced several steps and enlarged his gestures; he was apparently addressing the troops. Then an officer took his place and spoke longer and louder; we could hear his voice fairly well but not make out the words.

Around them spread a beautiful New England day. Peace lay on Devon like a blessing, the summer's peace, the reprieve,[6] New Hampshire's response to all the cogitation[7] and deadness of winter. There could be no urgency in work during such summers; any parachutes rigged would be no more effective than napkins.

Or perhaps that was only true for me and a few others, our gypsy band of the summer before. Or was it rarer even than that; had Chet and Bobby sensed it then, for

---

3. bellicose-looking (bel′ ə kōs′ look′ iŋ) *adj.*: Appearing warlike; eager to fight.
4. Section Eight: The regulation under which people suffering from mental illness are released from the armed forces.
5. Pullman car (pool′ mən kär) *n.*: A railroad car with private compartments for sleeping.

6. reprieve (ri prēv′) *n.*: A temporary relief or escape.
7. cogitation (käj ə ta′ shən) *n.*: Meditation; seriousness.

instance? Had Leper, despite his trays of snails? I could be certain of only two people, Phineas and myself. So now it might be true only for me.

The company fell out and began scattering through the Far Common. Dormitory windows began to fly open and olive drab blankets were hung over the sills by the dozens to air. The sewing machines were carried with considerable exertion into Veazy Hall.

"Dad's here," said Brinker. "I told him to take his cigar down to the Butt Room. He wants to meet you."

We went downstairs and found Mr. Hadley sitting in one of the lumpy chairs, trying not to look offended by the surroundings. But he stood up and shook my hand with genuine cordiality when we came in. He was a distinguished-looking man, taller than Brinker so that his portliness[8] was not very noticeable. His hair was white, thick, and healthy-looking and his face was healthily pink.

"You boys look fine, fine," he said in his full and cordial voice, "better I would say than those doughboys[9]—G.I.'s—I saw marching in. And how about their artillery! Sewing machines!"

Brinker slid his fingers into the back pockets of his slacks. "This war's so technical they've got to use all kinds of machines, even sewing machines, don't you think so, Gene?"

"Well," Mr. Hadley went on emphatically, "I can't imagine any man in my time settling for duty on a sewing machine. I can't picture that at all." Then his temper switched tracks and he smiled cordially again. "But then times change, and wars change. But men don't change, do they? You boys are the image of me and my gang in the old days. It does me good to see you. What are you enlisting in, son," he said, meaning me, "the Marines, the Paratroops? There are doggone many exciting things to enlist in these days. There's that bunch they call the Frogmen, underwater demolition stuff. I'd give something to be a kid again with all that to choose from."

"I was going to wait and be drafted," I replied, trying to be polite and answer his question honestly, "but if I did that they might put me straight in the infantry, and that's not only the dirtiest but also the most dangerous branch of all, the worst branch of all. So I've joined the Navy and they're sending me to Pensacola.[10] I'll probably have a lot of training, and I'll never see a foxhole. I hope."

"Foxhole" was still a fairly new term and I wasn't sure Mr. Hadley knew what it meant. But I saw that he didn't care for the sound of what I said. "And then Brinker," I added, "is all set for the Coast Guard, which is good too." Mr. Hadley's scowl deepened, although his experienced face partially masked it.

"You know, Dad," Brinker broke in, "the Coast Guard does some very rough stuff, putting the men on the beaches, all that dangerous amphibious[11] stuff."

His father nodded slightly, looking at the floor, and then said, "You have to do what you think is the right thing, but just make sure it's the right thing in the long run, and not just for the moment. Your war memories will be with you forever, you'll be asked about them thousands of times after the war is over. People will get their respect for you from that—*partly* from that, don't get me wrong—but if you can say that you were up

---

8. portliness (pôrt' lē nis) *n.*: Stoutness; heaviness.
9. doughboys (dō' bois) *n.*: U.S. infantrymen. Used mainly during World War I, this term is used by Mr. Hadley because that was the war in which he fought.

10. Pensacola (pen' sə kō' lə) *n.*: Seaport and site of a naval base in northwest Florida, on an inlet of the Gulf of Mexico.
11. amphibious (am fib' ē əs) *adj.*: Operating on both land and water.

front where there was some real shooting going on, then that will mean a whole lot to you in years to come. I know you boys want to see plenty of action, but don't go around talking too much about being comfortable, and which branch of the service has too much dirt and stuff like that. Now I know you—I feel I know you, Gene, as well as I know Brink here—but other people might misunderstand you. You want to serve, that's all. It's your greatest moment, greatest privilege, to serve your country. We're all proud of you, and we're all—old guys like me—we're all darn jealous of you too."

I could see that Brinker was more embarrassed by this than I was, but I felt it was his responsibility to answer it. "Well, Dad," he mumbled, "we'll do what we have to."

"That's not a very good answer, Brink," he said in a tone struggling to remain reasonable.

"After all that's all we can do."

"You can do more! A lot more. If you want a military record you can be proud of, you'll do a heck of a lot more than just what you have to. Believe me."

Brinker sighed under his breath, his father stiffened, paused, then relaxed with an effort. "Your mother's out in the car. I'd better get back to her. You boys clean up—ah, those shoes," he added reluctantly, in spite of himself, having to, "those shoes, Brink, a little polish?—and we'll see you at the Inn at six."

"Okay, Dad."

His father, left, trailing the faint, unfamiliar, prosperous aroma of his cigar.

"Dad keeps making that speech about serving the country," Brinker said apologetically, "I wish he wouldn't."

"That's all right." I knew that part of friendship consisted in accepting a friend's shortcomings, which sometimes included his parents.

"I'm enlisting," he went on, "I'm going to 'serve' as he puts it, I may even get killed. But I won't have that Nathan Hale[12] attitude of his about it. It's all that World War I malarkey that gets me. They're all children about that war, did you never notice?" He flopped comfortably into the chair which had been disconcerting[13] his father. "It gives me a pain, personally. I'm not any kind of hero, and neither are you. And neither is the old man, and he never was, and I don't care what he says he almost did at Château-Thierry."[14]

"He's just trying to keep up with the times. He probably feels left out, being too old this time."

"Left out!" Brinker's eyes lighted up. "Left out! He and his crowd are responsible for it! And *we're* going to fight it!"

I had heard this generation-complaint from Brinker before, so often that I finally identified this as the source of his disillusionment during the winter, this generalized, faintly self-pitying resentment against millions of people he did not know. He did know his father, however, and so they were not getting along well now. In a way this was Finny's view, except that naturally he saw it comically, as a huge and intensely practical joke, played by fat and foolish old men bungling away behind the scenes.

I could never agree with either of them. It would have been comfortable, but I could not believe it. Because it seemed clear that wars were not made by generations and their special stupidities, but that wars were made instead by something ignorant in the human heart.

---

12. Nathan Hale (hāl): American soldier (1755–1776) in the Revolutionary War who just before being hanged by the British as a spy said, "I only regret that I have but one life to lose for my country."

13. disconcerting (dis′ kən sʉrt′ iŋ) v.: Upsetting the composure of; confusing.

14. Château-Thierry (shȧ tō tye rē′): Town in northern France that was the site of a famous battle in World War I.

Brinker went upstairs to continue his packing, and I walked over to the gym to clean out my locker. As I crossed the Far Common I saw that it was rapidly becoming unrecognizable, with huge green barrels placed at many strategic points, the ground punctuated by white markers identifying offices and areas, and also certain less tangible things: a kind of snap in the atmosphere, a professional optimism, a conscious maintenance of high morale. I myself had often been happy at Devon, but such times it seemed to me that afternoon were over now. Happiness had disappeared along with rubber, silk, and many other staples, to be replaced by the wartime synthetic, high morale, for the Duration.

At the gym a platoon was undressing in the locker room. The best that could be said for them physically was that they looked wiry in their startling sets of underwear, which were the color of moss.

I never talked about Phineas and neither did anyone else; he was, however, present in every moment of every day since Dr. Stanpole had told me. Finny had a vitality which could not be quenched so suddenly, even by the marrow of his bone. That was why I couldn't say anything or listen to anything about him, because he endured so forcefully that what I had to say would have seemed crazy to anyone else—I could not use the past tense, for instance—and what they had to say would be incomprehensible to me. During the time I was with him, Phineas created an atmosphere in which I continued now to live, a way of sizing up the world with erratic and entirely personal reservations, letting its rocklike facts sift through and be accepted only a little at a time, only as much as he could assimilate without a sense of chaos and loss.

No one else I have ever met could do this. All others at some point found something in themselves pitted violently against something in the world around them. With those of my year this point often came when they grasped the fact of the war. When they began to feel that there was this overwhelmingly hostile thing in the world with them, then the simplicity and unity of their characters broke and they were not the same again.

Phineas alone had escaped this. He possessed an extra vigor, a heightened confidence in himself, a serene capacity for affection which saved him. Nothing as he was growing up at home, nothing at Devon, nothing even about the war had broken his harmonious and natural unity. So at last I had.

The parachute riggers sprinted out of the hallway toward the playing fields. From my locker I collected my sneakers, jock strap, and gym pants and then turned away, leaving the door ajar for the first time, forlornly open and abandoned, the locker unlocked. This was more final than the moment when the Headmaster handed me my diploma. My schooling was over now.

I walked down the aisle past the rows of lockers, and instead of turning left toward the exit leading back to my dormitory, I turned right and followed the Army Air Force out onto the playing fields of Devon. A high wooden platform had been erected there and on it stood a barking instructor, giving the rows of men below him calisthenics by the numbers.

This kind of regimentation would fasten itself on me in a few weeks. I no longer had any qualms[15] about that, although I couldn't help being glad that it would not be at Devon, at anywhere like Devon, that I would have that. I had no qualms at all; in fact I

---

15. qualms (kwämz) *n.*: Feelings of doubt or uneasiness; misgivings.

" ... a way of sizing up the world ... "

could feel now the gathering, glowing sense of sureness in the face of it. I was ready for the war, now that I no longer had any hatred to contribute to it. My fury was gone, I felt it gone, dried up at the source, withered and lifeless. Phineas had absorbed it and taken it with him, and I was rid of it forever.

The P.T.[16] instructor's voice, like a frog's croak amplified a hundred times, blared out the Army's numerals, "Hut! Hew! Hee! Hore!" behind me as I started back toward the dormitory, and my feet of course could not help but begin to fall involuntarily into step with that coarse, compelling voice, which carried to me like an air-raid siren across the fields and commons.

They fell into step then, as they fell into step a few weeks later under the influence of an even louder voice and a stronger sun. Down there I fell into step as well as my nature, Phineas-filled, would allow.

I never killed anybody and I never developed an intense level of hatred for the enemy. Because my war ended before I ever put on a uniform; I was on active duty all my time at school; I killed my enemy there.

Only Phineas never was afraid, only Phineas never hated anyone. Other people experienced this fearful shock somewhere, this sighting of the enemy, and so began an obsessive labor of defense, began to parry[17] the menace they saw facing them by developing a particular frame of mind, "You see," their behavior toward everything and everyone proclaimed, "I am a humble ant, I am nothing, I am not worthy of this menace," or else, like Mr. Ludsbury, "How dare this threaten me, I am much too good for this sort of handling, I shall rise above this," or else, like Quackenbush, strike out at it always and everywhere, or else, like Brinker, develop a careless general resentment against it, or else, like Leper, emerge from a protective cloud of vagueness only to meet it, the horror, face to face, just as he had always feared, and so give up the struggle absolutely.

All of them, all except Phineas, constructed at infinite cost to themselves these Maginot Lines[18] against this enemy they thought they saw across the frontier, this enemy who never attacked that way—if he ever attacked at all; if he was indeed the enemy.

---

16. P.T.: Physical Training.

17. parry (par′ ē) *v*.: Ward off.
18. Maginot Lines (mazh′ ə nō′ līnz′): Fortifications built before World War II on the eastern frontier of France to prevent invasion that were by-passed by German armies and thus proved useless.

RESPONDING TO THE SELECTION

Your Response

1. What do you think about Finny's method of changing sides during a fight to ensure the ultimate confusion and disorder? What does this say about his desire to win? Explain.
2. What scene in the novel most lingers in your mind? Why?

Recalling

3. Why did Finny give up his theory about there being no war?
4. What is Brinker investigating, and who are the witnesses?
5. What happens to Finny after his fall down the staircase?
6. Explain the understanding Finny and Gene reach about the original accident.

Interpreting

7. How has Gene changed during the novel?
8. In what way was Finny a war casualty?
9. Interpret the last line of the novel.

Applying

10. Comment on Gene's view that "wars were not made by generations and their special stupidities, but . . . instead by something ignorant in the human heart."
11. Why do you think people set up "Maginot Lines"?

ANALYZING LITERATURE

Identifying a Theme

The **theme** of a novel is its insight into life. The main events in the plot usually reveal the theme. In addition, the novelist may include symbols that suggest thematic concerns.

1. State the theme of A Separate Peace.
2. Give a quotation that hints at the theme.
3. Name events in the story that relate to the theme and that support your idea about it.

CRITICAL THINKING AND READING

Evaluating the Novel

When **critics** evaluate the work of other writers, they consider many factors in their criticisms, including use of language and imagery, fullness of characterization, and logical consistency of plot.

1. How does Knowles use language to describe the setting or explain ideas?
2. Explain if and how the author makes you understand and care about the characters.
3. Is the plot logically consistent? Explain.

THINKING AND WRITING

Responding to Criticism

Read the excerpt from a critic's evaluation of A Separate Peace. Make notes about whether you agree or disagree with the critic's points. Then draft a response, adding your own evaluation of the novel. Proofread carefully.

> For style and imagery A Separate Peace ranks with the work of the very best young American novelists, such as William Styron. At the same time it has none of the false symbolism which so many Americans employ in an attempt to add depth to their work. But style and imagery are only the writer's tools; if a work of fiction has only these, it becomes mere decoration, with an immediate impact, but no depth. Here we may read messages which only become clear much later, after we have pondered long over the disturbing allegories. The interpretation of the messages must be highly subjective, which holds true of all major works of art. It is a fine first novel, one that should be read by every person who likes to think about a book after reading it.
>
> Douglas Aitken
> San Francisco Chronicle
> June 26, 1960

The Wrestling Match

MARKET SCENE
S. Kangau
LAMU, The Gallery of Contemporary African Art

THE WRESTLING MATCH

INTRODUCTION BY DR. ISIDORE OKPEWHO
Department of Afro-American and African Studies
State University of New York at Binghamton

Buchi Emecheta set her novel *The Wrestling Match* in Igbuno, an Igbo-speaking section of Nigeria. Igbuno is located in the tropical rain forest region of the Atlantic seaboard of West Africa, where the year is divided almost evenly into a rainy season and a dry one. Even in the rainy season, however, the sun can be very hot.

The Igbo-speaking communities have been seriously neglected by federal and state governments. As a result, they have received very few social benefits. They have remained basically rural in an era of change. Nevertheless, a certain amount of change has occurred in the community, causing tension between traditional conventions and modern aspirations. *The Wrestling Match* addresses this tension between the past and the present, the caution of the old and their ways as opposed to the vigor of the young.

The Organization of the Traditional Society. Traditionally, Igbo society is organized into a system of age-groups responsible for performing specific duties. The youngest group—ten- to twenty-five-year-olds—is in charge of making public announcements, keeping the environment clean, building meeting houses for the elders, digging graves for the dead, and providing cultural entertainment. The middle group—twenty-five- to fifty-year-olds—performs such tasks as waging war with other groups. The elders—people over age fifty—constitute the final authority on issues of law, culture, and religion. The highest traditional position in the community, the *obi* (ō bē'), or chieftain, is held by a male elder. For the most part, female members of the society have less influence than male members.

A Polygamous Society. Kinship in the community is based on the family, both nuclear and extended. The traditional nuclear family is inevitably polygamous, meaning a man may have more than one wife. In fact, the number of wives a man has is one sign of his material worth. The first wife married is considered the senior wife. In many cases the wives of one household peacefully coexist. However, jealousy, suspicion, and open hostility between wives are also common, since it is understood that the first son born to any of the wives in the family inherits most of the husband's property after his death.

Nevertheless, the potential for hostility is somewhat reduced by the design of the traditional household. The head of the family builds a compound in a circular pattern. His own house is located either at

the entrance to the compound or, more commonly, at the center. Surrounding his house is a series of huts, one for each wife and her children. In some cases a separate hut in the compound houses all the sons of the family, while each mother shares her hut with her daughter(s).

Family Traditions. Family traditions are very important in Igbo society. A young man and woman might fall deeply in love with each other, but their marriage is seen more as a joining of two families than as a linking of two individuals. There are various stages to the union, the first of which involves the groom's family offering the bride's family what is called a first round of drinks. After that first round of drinks is accepted, the girl is considered betrothed to her fiancé, and he and his relatives can refer to her as his wife. Eventually, both families negotiate a bride-price, a payment made by the groom's family to the bride's. After the bride-price is paid, a bridal train carries the girl and her belongings off to the groom's home.

Extended family relations are also very strong. Uncles and aunts have as much right to get involved in the lives of their nieces and nephews as the parents do. When a child loses her or his own parents, the uncle immediately becomes responsible for the child. In *The Wrestling Match*, for example, Okei (ō' kā ē) lives in the home of his uncle, Obi Agiliga (ä' gi li' gä), because Okei's parents have died.

An Agrarian Economy. The economy of these traditional, Igbo-speaking communities is basically agrarian, or a farm economy. Yam is the major crop, the basis of the economy, and the measure of both adulthood and wealth. The traditional week is made up of four market days devoted to the trading of yams and other foods.

A man's sons are expected to help ensure a good crop, and success in agriculture and trade allows a family to enhance its social

image. For example, a successful family can build brick or concrete houses rather than mud huts. In addition, clothes advertise economic success. Men with titles wear fine, hand-woven *otuogwu* (ō tŏŏ′ ō gwōō) cloth, and young people can indulge in fads like the "Appian Way" hairstyle mentioned in the novel. (This style calls for a large part in the middle, and several smaller parts). They can also wear *akwete* (ä kwā′ tā) cloth, or equally expensive *abada* (ä bä dä′) prints instead of mere rags. Such clothes are so expensive, however, that they are affordable only in installments or after much saving. For example, the girls in *The Wrestling Match* try to sell a "heavy load of plantain as expensively [as possible] . . . to buy the latest colorful outfits."

Cultural Education. At the end of a hard day on the farm or at the market, the family gathers after supper for various games designed to sharpen both physical and verbal skills. Storytelling and singing songs on moonlit nights are also common. In addition, the oral tradition of these communities includes praise poetry for celebrating achievements or positive qualities, and satirical poetry for denouncing negative social behavior.

The Yam Festival. At the end of the harvest season, mostly in September, there is a yam festival. The titled elders of the community lead a ceremony in which the newly harvested yam is cooked and eaten. This ceremony initiates many days of festivities, during which people perform satirical, joking poetry aimed at individuals within the community and at other communities. In addition, young men compete in wrestling matches like the one described in the novel. These wrestling matches are important because they allow adolescent males to prove that they are on the verge of adulthood and can be counted on to defend their community against attacks from outsiders.

Independence From Britain. *The Wrestling Match* also reflects the social change in Nigeria resulting from contact with the West. After nearly a century of British colonial rule, Nigeria gained full independence in 1960. Chief Awolowo (ä wō′ lô′ wō), the first prime minister of the Western Region, made education free at the elementary-school level. Widespread education and a shared colonial history encouraged a sense of a common Nigerian nationhood. At the same time, however, Western education alienated youths from traditions and encouraged generational conflicts, such as the one between Okei and Obi Agiliga in *The Wrestling Match*.

Civil War. In addition, strained relations between ethnic groups led to a series of internal conflicts in the Western Region. Eventually, this region seceded from Nigeria in 1967 and established itself as the nation of Biafra. The civil war that followed ended in 1970 with the surrender of the Biafran forces after numerous atrocities by soldiers on both sides and the loss of hundreds of thousands of lives. Fortunately, there was a swift reconciliation between opposing forces within the war-torn nation. Nigeria's head of state declared general amnesty and proclaimed that in a civil war there were "no victors, no vanquished." Emecheta echoes the general's memorable words in *The Wrestling Match*.

Characters and Terms in the Novel

compound: A family's premises, usually consisting of a house for the man and a house or houses for his wife or wives (p. 879)

Obi Agiliga (ō bē′ ä′ gi li′ gä): (p. 879)

Nne Ojo (n nā′ ō jō′): (p. 879)

Okei (ō′ kā ē): (p. 879)

otuogwu (ō tōō′ ō gwōō) cloth: Fine, hand-woven calico cloth with red patterns, worn by titled persons (p. 879)

Nduka (n′ dü kä): (p. 880)

Uche (ōō′ chä): (p. 880)

Mbekwu (m′ bä kwōō): Tortoise, the trickster in the folk tales of Igbo-speaking people (p. 880)

Umu aya Biafra (ü′ mü ä yä bē ä′ frä): (p. 880)

Eke (ā kā′), Olie (ō′ lē ä), Nkwo (n kwô′), Afo (ä fô′): (p. 882)

houseboys: Male, domestic servants (p. 883)

Kwutelu (kwōō te′ lü): (p. 884)

Onuoha (ô′ nü ô hä): (p. 887)

Awolowo (ä wō′ lô′ wō) free education: Chief Awolowo, the first prime minister of Nigeria's Western Region (1954–1962), made education free at the elementary-school level (p. 887)

Obi Uwechue (ō bē′ ōō wä′ chōō ē): (p. 887)

Obi Ogbeukwu (ō bē′ ōg′ bä ōō kwōō): (p. 893)

praise-names: Descriptive attributes used to glorify a person (p. 894)

Obi Uju (ō bē′ ōō jōō′):(p. 896)

wonkiness (wäŋ′ kē nis): Trendiness (p. 898)

praise-greetings: A string of praise-names offered when greeting someone (p. 909)

abada (ä bä dä′) cloth: Expensive, printed cotton cloth (p. 909)

Adaobi (ä dä′ ō bē): (p. 912)

Akwete (ä kwā′ tä) cloth: Expensive, hand-woven cloth of colorful patterns, named after a town in Eastern Nigeria (p. 917)

Kumbi (kōōm bē′): (p. 924)

lappas (lä päz′): Plural of lappa, a piece of cloth tied around the body from the waist down to the shin or ankle (p. 924)

GUIDE FOR READING

Buchi Emecheta

(1944–), who was born Florence Onye, has always considered storytelling important. As a child, she spent many hours in her Nigerian village listening to her aunt tell tales of her Igbo origins and ancestors. Emecheta was married at sixteen, but when her husband objected to her writing, the marriage ended. Then she began writing regularly, basing her work on personal experience. Considered Nigeria's best-known female writer, Emecheta has said, "Women are born storytellers. . . . It is what my aunt and my grandmother did, and their mothers before them."

The Wrestling Match, Chapters 1–7

Plot and Setting

Plot is the sequence of related events in a literary work. Since a novel is longer than a short story, novelists can develop plot more fully by engaging the characters in conflicts that are more complex. Plot is heavily influenced by **setting,** the time and place in which the events occur. For example, *The Wrestling Match* is set in an Igbo village in Nigeria after the Nigerian Civil War. (For more information about the war and Nigerian life, see the Introduction, pages 874–877.) Therefore, the characters and events in the novel reflect Igbo culture and show how the Nigerian Civil War affected the Igbo people.

Focus

In *The Wrestling Match,* a group of young people comes of age. As they mature, they find themselves struggling against the traditions and advice of the elder generation. Consider the ways in which your generation relates to your parents' generation. Then make a chart listing what you can learn from your elders and what they can learn from your generation.

Vocabulary

Knowing the following words will help you as you read *The Wrestling Match,* Chapters 1–7.

derision (di rizh' ən) *n.*: Contempt; ridicule (p. 879)

incredulous (in krej' ōō ləs) *adj.*: Showing disbelief (p. 882)

innuendoes (in' yōō en' dōz') *n.*: Indirect remarks that imply something derogatory (p. 883)

insinuations (in sin' yōō ā' shənz) *n.*: Hints or indirect suggestions (p. 884)

ambled (am' bəld) *v.*: Walked leisurely (p. 887)

airs (erz) *n.*: Superior manners (p. 887)

admonished (ad män' isht) *v.*: Strongly urged or cautioned (p. 894)

vulnerable (vul' nər ə bəl) *adj.*: Open to attack; easily hurt (p. 895)

insolence (in' sə ləns) *n.*: Bold disrespect (p. 903)

The Wrestling Match

Buchi Emecheta

Chapter 1

It was during that quiet part of the evening when all the buyers and sellers of the Eke market[1] had gone home. It was not yet time for the noises of children playing in the moonlight to be heard; they were all on the mud verandahs around their thatched huts, eating their evening meal. It was the time for the swishes of the fronds of the coconut palms to be heard; it was the time for the fire-insects of the night to hiss through the still air. It was the time for the frogs in the nearby ponds to croak to their mates, as if to say that they should now seek shelter because night was fast approaching.

But this quiet did not last long. In the compound of Obi Agiliga, his senior wife Nne Ojo was already murmuring. Soon the murmuring exploded into an outcry. "Look," she shouted, holding a piece of pounded yam she was about to swallow. "Look, if you are not satisfied with the best your family can do for you, go and live elsewhere. I don't care what anybody says. I am doing my best with you. If you are not satisfied. . . ."

"Now what is all that noise about? Not Okei again?" thundered Obi Agiliga, struggling into his outer otuogwu cloth and seething with anger. "What am I going to do about

you? I did not ask those federal soldiers to kill your parents. I have told you this so many times. Are you the only boy who had lost his parents during the civil war?"[2]

A young figure uncurled himself from the verandah where he had been sitting and eating with the others. He got up slowly, taking his time and almost stepping on the bowls of fish soup that stood on the mud floor. He extracted himself from the family, and was about to walk out of the compound when he changed his mind and said insultingly: "Oh, Uncle, we have heard that before. Why don't you think of something new to say?"

Obi Agiliga's wife could take no more. "You dare insult your father like that, you ungrateful boy? Every evening you have to eat badly, wading your dirty fingers in the soup-bowl as if you provided the food. If you don't stop this attitude, I will get boys of your age to beat you up."

"Boys of my age . . . ha, I'd like to see you do that!"

Nne Ojo was a quick-tempered woman. She threw the pounded yam she had been rolling in her hand on to Okei's shoulder. And he laughed again in derision.

"The way he behaves, one would have

---

1. **Eke market:** One of the four market days in the traditional Igbo week. The other three are called Olie, Nkwo, and Afo.

2. **civil war:** From 1967 to 1970 the Igbo people fought unsuccessfully to separate from Nigeria and form an independent nation called Biafra.

thought that I have never been young before," Obi Agiliga said, going back to his disrupted meal. "Go and find something to do. Go with us to the farm, or even try and catch those friends of yours who have been stealing things from old people, or go and fight a wrestling match. Do anything to prove that you're a man, Okei. Not sit here arguing over soup with my wives. Go and be a man, just as I was when I was your age."

"Yeah, when I was your age, when I was your age . . . I was not there to prove your claim, was I . . . when I was your age. . . ."

He strolled out of the compound with the angry voices of his uncle's wives still cutting the night air.

Immediately outside his uncle's compound, Okei was greeted with an easy laughter from two of his friends. They had been outside the compound waiting for him to finish his evening meal.

"The usual night song, I see," remarked Nduka. He was sixteen years old, the same age as Okei; but whilst Okei was thin and lanky, Nduka was stocky and short. He had a very sharp tongue as well. Okei was not given to much talking, but when he lost his temper he really lost it.

The third boy, Uche, was nicknamed Mbekwu—the easy-going tortoise. He had the irritating habit of laughing at everything and at everybody. He was a year younger than the other two, but they all belonged to the same age-group, Umu aya Biafra: babies born around the civil war.

The ripple of the great civil war started around 1964 and culminated in the creation of a new nation of Biafra in May 1967. But the children born at the very beginning of the political deadlock, and all those born during the war, and those born towards the end of the war were all called Umu aya Biafra, because it was the greatest happening that had ever occurred in Nigeria. It was a civil war, which started among the politicians; the army stepped in to keep the peace, then the military leaders started to quarrel among themselves, and one created a new state, taking his followers with him. That state was Biafra. It was a civil war that did cost Nigeria dear. Almost a million lives were lost, not just on the losing side; those who won the war lost thousands of people too—showing that in any war, however justified its cause, nobody wins.

But that was a long time ago. Now Uche was giggling at Okei's anger. The other two simply ignored him and went on talking as if he was not there.

"Did you hear what my uncle was saying—that some members of our age-group were stealing from old people? That cannot be true, can it?"

"Trouble with these old men is that they say things simply to hurt, without any proof," Nduka said, watching a group of children coming out of their huts into the open air to play.

"I don't know, but he has been saying this for the past few market days, and it's becoming boring. I hope they don't think I am one of the thieves!"

"Yes, that is the trouble. If a member of our age-group steals, the adults will say that we all steal. And what annoys me is that the thief gets all the attention and publicity and we get nothing."

"We get the nagging to go to the farm, to prove our manhood," laughed Uche.

"You won't prove your manhood like that when you laugh and eat all the time like a woman," snapped Okei. "This is not a laughing matter. I wish I knew what to do. I sometimes wish I hadn't gone out into the back yard when these soldiers came and killed my family. Sometimes I wish I had

NIGERIAN FAMILY COMPOUND
John Mainga
LAMU, The Gallery of Contemporary African Art

died with them. Listening to these women every evening . . . hm . . . I'm getting really fed up with life.''

"Oh come on!" said Nduka. "Life is only just beginning for us. It's not as bad as that. We've called on you to go to Akpei[3] with us, to meet Josephine and her friends. They are on their way from the market there.''

"You're really crazy about this girl, aren't you, Nduka?''

Nduka shrugged his shoulders. "Well, what else is there for me to do? Sit on our verandah and listen to my father telling me that I am hopeless, and that since my elder brother has been killed in the army there's no hope for our family line any more?''

"Does your father say that to you too?'' Okei asked, incredulous.

Uche started to laugh uncontrollably.

"What have I said to make you go mad like that? One of these days I'm going to show you that I don't like people who laugh when others are trying to be serious.''

"There is nothing to be serious about. You think you are the only one being nagged at? Well, you are wrong. The only good boys of our age-group are those who did not go to school at all—you know, who've been going to the farm with their parents all the four market days of the week—all through Eke, Olie, Nkwo, and Afo, and back again on another Eke day—since they took their first steps, and who will remain like that until their dying day. Those of us who went to school are no good.''

"Come on, let's go and meet the girls,'' said Nduka, finishing the argument. "At least they will be happy to see us.''

And they trotted into the darkening night on their way to Akpei.

---

3. Akpei (ăk pā′ ē): The nearest village to Igbuno.

Chapter 2

By the time Okei and his friends got to the little hill that bordered the Oboshi stream, the moon had risen full and clear. It illuminated the sands, highlighting their silvery color the more. The silver path through which the boys walked was thickly edged by dense evergreen bushes. Here they came to a clearing in which there was a cluster of cottages, most of them thatched but one or two roofed with corrugated iron sheets that glistened in the moonlight. There was an open clearing in which children and old people sat, telling stories and singing by the moonlight. The night was airy, and the young people on their way to Akpei enjoyed the feel of it all. There was no need for much conversation.

"We will have to run down the slope to the stream. I always enjoy doing that,'' Uche announced.

"Everybody enjoys that,'' Okei cut in. "I'll like to see you run up on your way back.''

"You can't run up, though,'' Nduka compromised, "because in most cases you're carrying something from the market or the stream.''

"Wait a minute. Why is it that Josephine and her friends had to go to Akpei to sell plantain[4] on an Eke day, when there is a big market here in Igbuno?'' asked Okei.

"You don't know our girls, you don't know them at all,'' Nduka said, looking wise. "They claim that in Akpei people are willing to pay more and that they are nicer.''

"So they walk all these miles for a few kobos?''[5]

---

4. plantain (plan′ tin) n.: A tropical banana plant eaten as a cooked vegetable; an important food in many tropical countries.

5. kobos (kō′ bōz′) n.: Units of Nigerian money.

"Well," Uche put in, "going to meet them at least gives us something to do. Isn't that what the adults have been accusing us of? That we are idle?" And he got ready to run down the slope.

"Hm . . . maybe you are right, Uche," said Okei. "But I am going to Akpei this night to accompany a friend and age-mate, not to meet any silly, giggling girl."

"So am I," laughed Uche.

"All right, all right, it is my own fault. But you cannot deny that it is a lovely evening, too lovely to stay indoors or sit by old women listening to their old-fashioned stories. Let us run down. I am sure we shall not reach Akpei, because the girls will have left the market a long time ago."

They tore down the slope, enjoying the wind whistling in their ears. At the bottom of the hill they all stopped short. They could hear voices. The voices of a group of girls.

"They are early. They must have left earlier than they normally do," remarked Nduka.

"I know what's happened," Okei said in a low voice. "I think they have had a good market and sold their plantain very quickly. You did say that they are eager for Igbuno plantain in Akpei. Lazy people, the people of Akpei. Can't they grow their own plantain?"

"They are singing again," laughed Uche.

"Sh . . . sh . . . we do not want them to know that we are here," Nduka said. "Otherwise they will not have their bath—and they won't thank us for that. So we just have to sit here quietly until they have finished washing, then we will surprise them with our presence."

Nobody contradicted him. They all flopped themselves down by the low bush near the stream. They lay on their backs, watching the slow movements of the moon whilst the voices of the chattering girls reached them distinctly.

The girls splashed and sang as they washed themselves. Then a voice said clear and loud: "You know, if I could afford it I would never go to Akpei again, not after today. Who do they think they are, that's what I'd like to know. They are playing the big people just because we take plantain to their villages. God, and their boys . . . aren't they annoying?"

"There is no smoke without fire, though. Maybe there is some truth in what they were saying."

"Well, if their accusations were true, should they not go to our young men and say it to them face to face? Why make all these innuendoes . . . and to us? We did not mug their old people, we did not break into the houses of our elders. If all those things had happened at all, only boys could have done them. Our elders make sure we girls are too busy to have time for such things."

"You know, the boys in our age-group are all capable of many things. Because they have been to school they do not wish to farm any more. And they are not educated enough to take up big jobs in the cities."

"They can be houseboys, though."

"Houseboys? These boys? Can you imagine a bighead like Okei being anybody's houseboy?"

There was a peal of laughter.

"Oh, I don't know. If there is any truth in all this, I won't be surprised if they were led by our Okei."

The girls laughed again, and went on splashing so much water that their voices were drowned by the sheer noises of their movements.

"If I lay my hands on that girl . . ." Okei growled from where he was sitting. He had sat bolt upright when he heard his name mentioned.

"Please, Okei, don't do anything rash," begged Nduka. "They are only girls, and don't forget that they were told this by those young people from Akpei.''

"But why me? Why me? I have nothing to do with it. My uncle was making such insinuations earlier on. Why me?''

"Because, Okei, you are taller than any of us. You are more polished. You know, you were born into a little wealth and you started life richer than any of us. All that has given you the makings of a leader. So you are the uncontested leader of our age-group. You get blamed for things like this. I must talk to Josephine, though. She should watch her tongue.''

"You better make sure you do. As for those Akpei weak-livered boys, we will deal with them. What do old people have that I'd like to take? Some of them are so poor.''

"We can do something, though. We can arrange a meeting of all our age-group, and take it in turns to police the areas where these thieves operate,'' Uche suggested, giggling at Okei's anger.

"But that's a good suggestion, Uche. Please don't spoil it by your stupid laughter. At least they will not accuse us of doing nothing. As for those people in Akpei . . .''

"No,'' Nduka said, "leave those people until we all meet, then we will decide how to deal with them.''

The girls, with their wares delicately balanced on their heads, walked out of the stream still talking of this and that, until they saw Okei and his friends. They stopped short, not at first knowing what to do.

Josephine stepped forward in a brave attempt to cover their confusion. "Have you been waiting here long?''

"No,'' said Nduka hurriedly, "we were just coming from the village. You must have left Akpei very early today, or we were late in leaving. You normally are not here by the time we meet you.''

"Yes, we sold our plantains very quickly today, didn't we?'' her friends agreed, but one small girl started to laugh.

"And why do you want to know if we have been waiting here long or not?'' growled Okei. "Have you been saying sly things about us?''

"Oh, Okei!'' shouted an elegant girl of seventeen, Kwutelu. She was the oldest of all the girls, the most sophisticated and the one that the others modeled their behavior by. "I didn't know you were here with the others! You are really beginning to care for us, coming to meet us on our way from Akpei. Thank you very much.''

"I did not come to meet you, Kwutelu. I only accompany my friend Nduka here,'' Okei snarled. "And am I so indistinct that you cannot see me in this clear moon?''

"Ahem, let us share your wares,'' Nduka said quickly. "Josephine, give me half of your things, I'll relieve you of the load.'' The others stood there and watched enviously as Nduka took all the heavy things from Josephine's basket and slung them across his thick shoulder.

Uche, not to be left out, took bits from each of the other five girls. But Okei was unmoved by all this show of affection. He was hurt and he was angry. He was dying to know more about the gossip from Akpei, but pride would not let him ask the girls. And the girls did not wish to pursue the conversation. Some of them had a suspicion that they had been overheard.

As they walked home the girls concentrated on being girls, being nice and being feminine. They brought out the roasted cashew nuts they had bought, and distributed them among themselves. They sang, made light conversation, and laughed just as Igbuno girls were expected to do.

Okei did not say a word, amidst all this show.

They parted at the market square. "You,

TEEN GIRLS RETURNING HOME AFTER MARKET
John Mainga
LAMU, The Gallery of Contemporary African Art

MULTICULTURAL CONNECTION

The Age-Group

In every culture, of course, young people grow up and become adults. In Nigeria, growing up and being responsible to one's peers as well as to the larger community are tied closely to the concept of the age-group. An age-group is an informal band of people who are linked by age and place of birth.

The traditional pattern. Traditionally, the age-group consisting of teenagers was assigned certain tasks. These included issuing public announcements as town-criers, making arrangements for sanitation, building meeting houses for the elders of the community, digging graves for the dead, and entertaining other community members. Through this work, teenagers played an important role in the life of the community and found an outlet for their energies. They also prepared themselves for assuming the even greater responsibilities of adult life.

Breaking the pattern. From 1967 to 1970, Nigeria was torn by civil war, and as a result, age-old traditions were affected. In *The Wrestling Match,* for instance, we see how the recently ended civil war has influenced the behavior of Okei and his friends. For example, Okei, apparently disturbed by the loss of his parents in the war, neither speaks respectfully to his uncle nor helps him in his work on the farm. In addition, he and his friends seem to be constantly getting into trouble, and the same situation prevails in other villages. After living through the horrors of war, young men find it difficult to assume their traditional role in society.

The Wrestling Match also shows how the spread of education has disrupted traditional patterns. Earlier, the members of an age-group may have shared a common background. In Okei's age-group, however, the young men have different educational backgrounds and different outlooks. Some members of the group work the land with their fathers, while others have attended secondary school and consider themselves too educated to work on a farm. Still others have gone to college. In addition, some of the young men speak only the native tongue, while others speak both the native language and English.

Growing up in other cultures. The concept of an age-group is not necessarily foreign to Western cultures, even though it may not entail the same duties and responsibilities as in Nigeria. In the United States, for instance, we speak of "the baby-boom generation," meaning all those born just after World War II, when many people were starting families. Not only were baby-boomers born at approximately the same time, but they also share certain cultural experiences. Most notably, they were children during the 1950's, when television was becoming an important medium of communication.

Sometimes key political developments can define a generation. In Poland, for instance, many people refer to "The Generation of '68," meaning those people who came of age during a time when the Communist regime was being challenged in 1968.

Discussing in Class

Do you and your classmates feel as if you belong to an age-group? What experiences and attitudes do you share that differentiate you from adults? Discuss these questions in small groups and then with the whole class.

Uche, go round and make the announcements. We must all meet tomorrow by the moonlight, in front of my uncle Obi Agiliga's compound," Okei said as he walked away very quickly, leaving the group to wonder about him.

"I don't like that young man very much," Kwutelu remarked.

"You don't have to like him. He does not go for girls like you," Uche said, sniggering.

"And what type of girls does he go for?" snapped Kwutelu.

"College girls, not gossip market girls from Akpei market. Here, take your stuff, I am going home. The moon is waning too," Uche said, half in joke and half in seriousness, confusing his listeners.

People never knew whether to take Uche seriously or not.

Chapter 3

The sun was very high in the sky and the heat was almost unbearably intense. All the leaves along the footpaths drooped from lack of moisture. All the bush animals had sought for shelter in the shades of trees and the giant grass. Even the ever-chattering wood-parrots were silent. So hot was the afternoon. Obi Agiliga knew that it was time for him and his farmhands to have a rest. It was time for him to go into the cool shed on his farm and lie on the beaten floor to smoke his pipe.

His paid helpers saw him and wordlessly followed his example. They all ambled into different parts of the bush in search of shelter.

"If only I could have more hands on this farm. Then I could be sure that all the yams would be harvested before the yam festival," Obi Agiliga moaned as he stretched his tall body on the cool floor. "Onuoha, go to the stream and get some water. We must have something to eat before we go on. This sun can burn life out of any man."

"I'll be back in no time at all, Father," said Onuoha, his twelve-year-old son. "Are you not happy about the progress of the harvesting?"

"Hmm, I am not too happy. When the sun is so hot it burns out all the moisture from the yams. So we will have to hurry."

"I wish you could make Okei come to the farm sometimes to help. He is very strong, yet he does not like coming to the farm at all."

"I know, but he is troubled about something, Onuoha. We don't know what it is. And he did not dream that he would ever be asked to come and work on the farm. That Awolowo free education has given him and his age-group airs. They will grow, never mind. They all will grow."

Father and son stopped talking as they listened carefully, knowing that a group of people were approaching their shed. Onuoha peeped into the bush-path, and the fear and curiosity in his young face were transformed and became a trusting and joyous glow.

"Father, you have visitors. It's Obi Uwechue from Akpei. I must run to the stream to get you all something to drink." So saying, he dashed into the bush-path, his young and determined feet crackling the dry fallen leaves as he went.

"It must be an important matter that brought you to my farm in this heat and at this time of year. Please sit down, sit down. The floor is cool at least."

"The matter is very urgent indeed, my friend," said Obi Uwechue. "And I do not want to come to your compound, because the women would interfere. How is your family?"

They all sat down and distributed kola nuts, and drank some cool palm-wine which Obi Uwechue had brought. Onuoha soon arrived from the stream and, with the help of his father's helpers, made a bush-meat soup which they all ate with pounded yam. Obi Agiliga studied his visitor all the time, wondering why he had come at such an odd time. But he was soon relieved of his suspense.

"My friend, you have a troublesome age-group in your village in Igbuno. We have the same in ours. I have never come across such stubborn young men. In Akpei it is now becoming difficult for women to walk down a footpath on moonless nights, a thing which we have never heard of before. Yesterday we had to send your girls away home early because they started picking quarrels with them. They say that your young men are equally bad. And of course a fight almost broke out. But during the argument, the name of your nephew was being mentioned all the time. . . ."

Obi Uwechue paused and looked around the farm hut, and laughed gently. "I was even hoping that I might find him on your farm today, since it is harvest-time."

"You are hoping for the moon, my friend," Obi Agiliga replied. "That boy is driving us all mad. And he is setting a very bad example for my younger sons. Onuoha here admires his strength. What shall we do, my friend? This must stop."

"Last Nkwo day, for example, some of your boys came into our stream to fish, when they know quite well that it is forbidden. They did not just fish, they muddled all the cassava pulp[6] which our women were soaking in the stream."

"Funny, I did not hear of all this, and my nephew did not say a word," Obi Agiliga remarked reflectively.

They were silent for a while, then as if on cue they both started to laugh. Obi Uwechue was the first one to speak.

"You remember what our fathers used to say, that when young men are idle the elders must give them something to worry about. I think we will have to create a big worry for our young men. By the time they have finished solving that problem they will be wiser."

"I was thinking of the same thing. The girls will be very useful. Women always have sharp tongues. Encourage your girls to start talking . . . you know, making pungent songs . . . and leave the rest to me," Obi Agiliga said with a knowing wink.

Chapter 4

Uche got up very early the following morning and rushed to the stream. This was very unusual, and his family thought that maybe he was having a change of heart. They hoped that he would probably be going to the farm with the rest of the men in the family.

He ran down the slope leading to the stream, as usual, and looked uncertainly at the clear water as it tumbled over tiny rocks and then formed a deep pool at the bottom of the stream. There were very few people about, one or two early risers. He did not say anything to them. He stood there scowling at the water. It was a chilly morning, and the thought of dipping into the stream took some courage. He was feeling the water with his feet when he heard his friend and age-mate whistling as he ran down the slope.

_____

6. cassava (kə sa′ və) **pulp:** Cheap and plentiful food prepared by cooking or soaking and pounding cassava, a very hard root.

TWO ELDERS
John Mainga
LAMU, The Gallery of Contemporary African Art

"Ah," sneered Nduka, "someone is feeling the water like an old woman."

"No I am not. I was only thinking," replied Uche, holding his breath and ready for a compulsory plunge. He knew that if he did not get into the water by himself his friend would push him in, and he would laugh at him as well. So before Nduka could reach him he threw his shorts on the nearby rocks and dashed into the water.

"You know I would have helped you to make up your mind," laughed Nduka.

"Well, I have cheated you of your fun. You are early. Going to Akpei with your Josephine?"

"She is not my Josephine. She is just a friend. And people don't go to Akpei on Olie day. They go on Eke days to sell. I want to have my bath early in order to start the announcements for our gathering this night."

"So do I," Uche said. "And look, I have a big gourd here to take home enough water to last my family the whole day. But they will not talk of that. They will only talk of the fact that I did not go to the farm."

"Hmm, I would have gone to the farm today myself, but this gathering is more important to me. I am taking home a lot of water too."

"Listen, Nduka, how are we going to make the announcements? Okei did not say . . . maybe he expects us to beat a drum. . . ." Uche started to laugh.

"Use whatever method you like, but make sure all our age-group in your area hear about it."

"All our age-group—what of those who did not go to school, those who are playing at being good boys and go to the farms with their fathers? Should we not leave them out?"

Both boys did not know how to deal with this situation. Before their time, an age-

group was an age-group. Now they had the educated ones and the uneducated ones. Should the uneducated ones be left out? Nduka was thinking of writing out the announcements for the meeting, instead of using a gong as people normally did. But if he wrote it out, would those of them who were illiterate get the message? He said reflectively: "I think we better include them. If they feel they cannot understand us, then they can absent themselves."

"Suppose we start speaking in English?" asked Uche, showing off.

"How many English words have you mastered? You are silly sometimes. Do you forget that we have many age-mates who are already in colleges? How would you feel if they excluded you in our age-gathering just because you stopped at Primary Six?"[7]

Uche gobbled his morning meal and waited for his people to leave for the farm, before he ransacked his mother's hut for a gong. He was not going to write the announcement. Nduka was right. He did not command enough English language for such a task. He started to beat the gong.

"All the males belonging to the Umu aya Biafra age-group are to meet in front of Obi Agiliga's compound when the moon is out this evening. All the males belonging. . . ."

A group of girls going to the stream saw him and wondered what the troublesome age-group had got to say to each other. "After all the trouble they have been causing. Go to your father's farm and help!" shouted one bold girl.

Uche ignored them and went on with his announcements. He would beat the gong three times to arrest attention, then deliver his message, and beat the gong three times

---

7. Primary Six: Sixth grade.

more to emphasize the end of his announcement.

Nduka took up the other side of Igbuno. But he copied out his message in shaky, large letters and distributed them by hand. He had to use plain sheets from his old school exercise book, because the age-group did not have much money. If we claim to be educated we must do things the way educated people do their things, he said to himself in justification for his action.

Okei enlisted the help of the young children in his uncle's compound and they swept the front of the compound leading to the footpath.

He was quiet and sullen, and the wives in the compound knew that something was on his mind. They teased him into anger, knowing that he would explode at the least provocation, but he seemed unaware of them. He was the more determined not to argue with anybody, when he noticed that his uncle Obi Agiliga was staying longer than usual on the farm.

"The Obi must be working so hard today. It is always like this during yam harvest time. Poor Obi. So much work," his senior wife Nne Ojo remarked pointedly.

The other, younger wives agreed, and all expressed the view that another pair of male hands would have been such a welcome gift to Obi Agiliga.

Okei knew that they were referring to his pair of idle hands. But he said nothing. If he picked up quarrel with any of them, the story would be repeated differently to his absent uncle.

By the time they had finished their evening meal many of the young people were already gathering. The meeting soon started.

Just as Okei had expected, he was elected as the leader of the age-group. Even though he himself doubted whether he had

been a good choice, yet the cheers with which the election was greeted showed him that his age-mates had confidence in him. They went through all the allegations that had been blamed on them, and nobody seemed to have done any of them. But towards the tail-end Uche, of all people, got up. He coughed and twiddled his ears for a time and then confessed:

"I got so fed up with all the lies told about us that last Nkwo day I went to Akpei to fish. Well, I must give them something to talk about. I did that on purpose with three of my younger half-brothers. It will not happen again."

"To think that you of all people should do a thing like that," Okei shouted. "Were you very hungry? Can't your father feed you? You disgrace us. Does the group think we have to punish him?"

"No," was the unanimous answer.

"He is silly and he has promised not to do so again. I will keep an eye on him," finished Nduka.

It was then decided that all the other insults heaped upon them from the young people of Akpei would be settled in a wrestling match. "It will be a friendly one, just like a play, but it will settle our superiority once and for all," Okei said.

This was greeted cheerfully too.

The match would be played strictly according to the wrestling rules. They would select their best wrestlers, and the Akpei young people would select theirs. They would not invite the elders from the two villages to decide the better of the two. The young men of Igbuno were quite sure of their winning, because they felt they had been wrongly accused.

"How come they started to accuse us in the first place?" asked Nduka.

"Because they hear our elders talking of our faults in the open, washing our dirty

TRADITIONAL YAM HARVEST
John Mainga
LAMU, The Gallery of Contemporary African Art

linen outside under the very noses of those chicken-livered Akpei boys," explained one farmer's boy from Obi Ogbeukwu's compound. "Never mind, we will teach them, we will teach them."

Well, he talked sense, thought Okei as he sat there on the silvery sand, watching his friends. To think that that farmer's boy never spent a day in school. Aloud he said: "But what are we going to do about this farming business?"

"How can we farm using the old, old method which our great-great-grandparents had used?" Nduka said. "Look at our fathers. They spend four days out of every five, from sunrise to sundown on the farm. What do they have to show for it? Only enough yams to feed each family, and during dry season we almost starve. And what do we get from yams? Only starch. They taught us this much at school. I am not going to throw my life away working on such a farm. I am still thinking of a way of avoiding it, if I am to stay in this village and be a farmer. I think we should let the elders know this." He heaved his hefty chest in anger.

And he too was cheered. But the boys who had never been to school did not know what their friends and age-mates were saying. They knew their limitations though, so they cheered with the rest.

It was amidst this cheering and comradeship that Obi Agiliga came from his farm, tired out after such a long day. "What is happening in front of my compound?" he roared. "Clear out, all of you lazy lot! Clear out, you lazy, good-for-nothing pilferers of fishes and muggers of the old. . . ."

"Come in, come in, come in!" begged his senior wife, Nne Ojo. "The Umu Biafra age-group are holding a meeting in front of your compound, that is all." Here she laughed a little. "Our future leaders and town planners. . . ."

Obi Agiliga allowed himself to be led in, and said in a low voice: "They should think of how to fill their bellies first. I must eat quickly. I have a word or two to say to the elders of Igbuno. This state of affairs must not go on."

The young people hurried over their deliberations and dispersed noisily. Okei and Nduka were to practice their wrestling skills, and the farmer's boy from Ogbeukwu was to go to Akpei the following day and throw the challenge to the loud mouths from Akpei.

"We will show them," Okei boasted in encouragement. "The wrestling match will decide who was in the wrong, and it will settle all the bickering and gossips once and for all."

Much later that evening Obi Agiliga went to see a few friends in their compound. He returned very late, when the moon was so clear and the footpaths so silent that the whole area looked like man-made glass. The air was so cool and light, the trees so clear in their thickness, that one was tempted to stay outside. But a mischievous smile played on the sealed lips of Obi Agiliga.

"These boys thought they were the only people who have ever been young. They will learn, sure they will learn," he murmured as he made his way to his own compound.

Chapter 5

Okei, at the age of sixteen, knew what was expected of him as a leader. He worried over it most of the night, but there was one thing he was determined on: The leadership was not going to be taken from him. He had been told stories of failed leaders when he was very little. Such ideas were woven into the native fables told to children by their grannies on moonlight nights. He was going to be a good leader, and would live up to the expectations of those who had elected him.

He got up early the next day. He ran up and down the incline that led to the stream, in order to toughen his feet. He knew that as a result of this kind of exercise his feet would not give way easily for his opponent to fell him in wrestling.

"Ah, you have started already?" greeted Nduka, who had come to the spot for his toughening-up and practicing with Okei.

"Yes, I have to do this part of it early to avoid the curious," Okei said as he panted.

"Oh, we can never prevent them from asking questions. Did you tell your uncle—I mean your little father, as you are expected to say—that you have been elected the leader of your age-group?"

"No. Whatever for? It won't interest him."

"I am sure it will. They say he was a great wrestler during his time."

"He never lets us forget it."

They ran up and down the slope many more times, until they were completely exhausted. Okei flopped on the nearby low bush, breathing hard. "I think all our age-group should toughen themselves up. You never know. I may lose the fight, and it could become an open one."

"There are rules to these wrestling matches, you know," Nduka said. "In any case, all our age-mates do wrestle for fun in their different compounds."

"That may be so, but I still would like it to become the accepted thing. They should all practice, not just the two of us."

"Ah, you are now talking as a leader," laughed Nduka.

"You all nominated me. . . . Come on, let us wrestle."

They moved to a sandier area and started to practice their wrestling. They both sweated profusely. People on their way to the stream soon started to pass them. Some gave them their praise-names in form of greetings, others just stared, encouraging this one against that one. It was all done in a lighthearted mood. The people of Igbuno loved such sports.

Soon a lighter, noisier group was approaching them. The wrestlers could tell that they were young people by the sounds their water-cans made against their carrier trays. They knew that they were girls. Then the approaching crowd saw them and stopped.

"Should we stop wrestling?" Nduka asked, uncertain.

"But why? They are going to the stream and we are wrestling. Just ignore them," Okei admonished his friend hoarsely.

But the two young men could see from the corners of their eyes that the girls were led by Kwutelu, and they both knew that she could be very provoking. They saw that she started to whisper something to the other girls, and this unnerved the wrestlers.

Then all of a sudden the girls burst out laughing. Kwutelu covered her mouth in amusement, and walked on her toes in an annoying manner towards Okei and Nduka.

"Oh, so you are wrestling?" she asked in suppressed laughter.

"What is bad in wrestling? Or are you frightened we might floor your friends from Akpei?" Nduka snapped.

"Why don't you keep quiet, for God's sake?" Okei shouted at his friend. But Nduka was not the one to be silenced. He cared for and respected Josephine, but not that arrogant Kwutelu. He did not hate her, only he did not so much as care for her.

"Why should we let her get away with her saucy remarks? Yes, we are practicing in order to challenge your friends from Akpei. Go and tell them. Come on, let's go, Okei. We've had enough for one morning anyway."

"Oh . . . so all this ballyhoo is for the Akpei boys," Kwutelu said. "Do you want to hear more of what they have been saying? They said you even pinch little sprats[8] from their streams, and steal from our old people." She looked in amusement towards the other girls, who were laughing at it all and encouraging her.

"Look, enough is enough, do you hear me?" Okei said menacingly. "Stop that nonsense. You know that there is no truth in all that. If you were a boy you wouldn't stand there saying all that to us. You are hiding behind the fact that you are a girl. But don't annoy me, because I can still beat girls up." He was showing his anger now. He was very tired from their early practice, and that made him rather vulnerable.

"So you have now come so low as to talk to ordinary girls like us? I thought you go for college girls. And how come you are wrestling? I thought you have become too civilized for that, Okei the son of Agiliga."

"There is no need in replying to you," Nduka said. "If you have retained anything you learnt at school you will remember that every nation on earth wrestles, even the white people."

"Well, that is nice to hear, but I hope you go and practice your prowess on the sneaking thieves that lurk in the bushes at night, and not on innocent boys from Akpei. After all, all they did was to complain about your stealing fish from their stream. . . ."

"I wish I knew who the thieves were. And if I did, I would encourage them to come and burgle your father's compound. And that, I think, would put your poisonous tongue in check."

"Oh, Okei, so you are threatening our compound now? You try it. My father will wait for you. And as for you and the boys from Akpei, you know what they say in our native fables, that the guilty person always loses in such an open fight. So you have to practice hard, to prove your innocence."

Okei made a move toward her, but Nduka held him back. "They will go and say that we are waylaying innocent girls. Don't do it, let us go."

Then the girls burst into a song:

"Umu aya Biafra.
Stealer of sprats from the streams,
Molester of innocent girls by the
    streams,
They will never go to the farms,
They will never help in the house.
Akpei boys will teach them a lesson,
    a lesson. . . ."

Okei was so angry that he did not bother to go to the stream to wash himself. He simply walked home with his friend, hoping to go back to the stream later on.

"Who is going to marry that chatterbox of a girl, Kwutelu?" he asked all of sudden.

"I don't know him personally. They say he is on government service in Ilorin,[9] one of the Yoruba[10] towns in the west."

"God help that man."

Nduka laughed. "I know what you mean. I wonder why she is going out of her way to annoy us, as if she had been set up into doing it. She was going to goad you into fighting her, and you know what that means. Her future parents-in-law and her real parents and their families would all go against us. That was why I was holding you."

---

8. sprats: Small, silvery herrings.

9. Ilorin (ē lōr′ in): Southwestern Nigerian city, far from the villages in the novel.
10. Yoruba (yō′ r$\overline{oo}$ bə): People of western Nigeria and neighboring regions.

"Thank you. But I will teach her a lesson one of these days if she continues this way. I don't think she was set up against us. I have never heard that girl utter a polite word to anybody."

"She is always cheeky, but not this far," Nduka maintained.

Chapter 6

As soon as Kwutelu got home from the stream, she felt it was her business to go and tell her friend Josephine all that had happened. Josephine did not go to the stream that early because she had to help in getting ready bits and pieces for the laborers who were going to help her father harvest the yams.

"This is the part of yam festivals that I hate most," she moaned to Kwutelu. "But how come you are not doing some work in your compound?"

"I am supposed to be claying the huts really, and my mother thought I was out in one of the groves getting the claying things. But I've just come to tell you this."

She went into a great detail of all that took place that morning. How she had successfully ruffled Okei's feathers; how he was so angry that he almost struck her. But thank goodness, Nduka was there to hold him back. She told Josephine how amused they were and how they had laughed. "Do you know, they really want to beat the Akpei boys in wrestling. What a big fun we are going to have watching them. Was it not a good thing that we started talking about it, eh?"

"I don't know, Kwutelu, if I like it all so much. I heard from my father this morning that they, the Umu Biafra, had a meeting last night. And the stupid boys had it in the open, and all the Agiliga household heard their deliberations."

"I did not hear that one. What have they decided to do? Kill us all on our sleeping-mats?"

"Oh, Kwutelu, you tend to dramatize everything. They are only going to wrestle with the boys from Akpei, and I heard my father saying that things were changing. He said that during his time young boys came of age with dancing and songs, but this group are coming of age with wrestling."

"Well, wrestling is a kind of sport, just like football the college boys play. At least Okei told me that much, this morning."

"Hm, if it is taken to be a friendly sport it will be nice. But this one is starting with a gossip. I wish we did not start it, Kwutelu. That boy Okei is very intense."

"Did your father tell you that we have done wrong?" Kwutelu asked.

"No, that's the funny part of it. I think the elders want us to goad them into anger. If you ask me, the elders from Akpei are doing the same," Josephine said reflectively.

They both laughed, and agreed that it could not be true. Though they would like some of those proud Igbuno boys, who thought they were going to be young for ever, taught a lesson.

"I am glad Okei did not beat you up. That would have been bad for you."

"And for him too."

When Kwutelu's father, Obi Uju, returned from the farm, his pet daughter Kwutelu told him of Okei's threats. Her father became angry and asked, "Can't our girls go to the stream without being molested? I must see his uncle Obi Agiliga. If he has to tie that nephew of his with a string to his door-post, I am going to make sure that I make him do so. If he wishes to practice

EVENING STORYTELLING
John Mainga
LAMU, The Gallery of Contemporary African Art

wrestling, why choose the pathway to the stream, just to be seen by everybody? If he threatens you again, just let me know. Since when have we stopped young girls from singing provoking songs? Is that not what women are made for, to provoke men? I don't understand these young people any more.''

Obi Uju did not feel like going out that evening. Few callers came to see him, and after they had all gone he felt he would retire early. He would have to get up early the following day to go and work on his farm with the few paid laborers he could afford. Laborers, especially paid ones, would look for any reason to dodge the work they were paid to do. The master had to be on the alert all the time. He must work hard himself, setting a good example. This was even more imperative with Obi Uju, because he could only get three workers and could only afford to pay them for four days. Four days, which he calculated would be just enough to finish the toughest part of his harvesting. He must make sure the workers worked for every kobo he paid them. He called his daughter to fill his evening pipe for him.

"You are retiring early," Kwutelu remarked indulgently. She was well loved by her father. She was always close to him, and he spoiled her. Many of Obi Uju's youngest wives resented this, but they all now took consolation in that she would be going away to her husband soon after the yam festival. Meanwhile Kwutelu knew that she was free to sleep in her father's sleeping-house or her mother's hut. Her father's house had spare inner rooms. She liked these better than her mother's thatched hut. When teased about it she used to say: "I like sleeping under corrugated iron sheets." Her listeners would smile indulgently, knowing full well that her future husband worked as a sales manager in one of the Nigerian companies in Ilorin.

She filled the pipe for her father, and with the youngest wife in the family swept and got ready his sleeping-place. Clean goatskins were spread on a wooden bed and a feather-filled pillow was placed on a wooden headrest.

"I think you have guests," the young wife told Kwutelu.

"Oh," she gasped as she listened to the noises that were coming into the inner room from the compound. "Yes, you are right. I can hear my future brothers-in-law whistling. I must go. I will entertain them in the compound. Father is too tired tonight to receive any more guests."

"Yes, he is dozing already. These harvests, they are men-killers."

"I know," Kwutelu said as she made her way out into the compound. She glanced at her father on her way and said casually: "I am in the compound, father, if you want anything."

"No, daughter, go and be nice to your future brothers. They are growing impatient, I can tell by the wonkiness of their whistle."

Kwutelu laughed lightly as she dashed out to welcome her fiancé's brothers. They were happy to see her. They had heard that Okei had waylaid her on her way to the stream, and had come to find out why. Kwutelu told them all that happened in a lighthearted way, because she did not wish to start trouble for her future in-laws. That, she knew, would give her a bad name. They were both farmers, very traditional, and would take no nonsense from anybody. By the time she had finished her story they were all laughing at the naïvety of the young people born around the civil war.

"They are so proud about being partly educated," Kwutelu emphasized. "They are like bats, neither birds nor animals. After all, people like your big brother were educated in this village. They did not burn our huts down."

She went into her mother's hut and brought them some nuts. They all ate, and they talked and kept her company till the moon had really gone pale. They wished her goodnight, and warned her to be a good girl because she was already their wife. Kwutelu knew all that on the day her bride-price[11] was paid. She promised to be good, and they saw her make her way to her father's house.

She did not like going to her mother's hut tonight, because she would wake up and tell her how late she was. Yes, all the young children playing outside had gone to sleep, but she was only chatting. She could hear her mother warning her against making herself cheap by over-exposure to her future in-laws, and these warnings had begun to get on her nerves. So she made her way to her father's sleeping-house. He would say nothing, nothing at all.

Obi Uju, Kwutelu's father, was deep in sleep, his tired body relaxed on the cool goatskins that had been lovingly laid out for him in his inner room by his daughter and youngest wife. He opened his eyes suddenly, not because the first bout of tiredness had ebbed away as a result of his retiring early but because he sensed that somebody was moving outside his outer door. He had got up earlier on, when it was very dark and when he guessed that his family were all asleep, and had hooked the heavy catch that held in the heavy wooden door. So he probably was dreaming.

Then he heard the sound again. This time he sat bolt upright. No, he was not dreaming. There was a determined rattling and pushing noise going on. The person was being careful not to wake the household. But for Obi Uju, whose well-trained ears were accustomed to hearing the slightest hiss of a snake, the noise at the door was loud enough. Then he remembered the threat Kwutelu told him that Okei had made to her earlier in the day.

"So, that stupid boy Okei thought he would carry out his threat? What is the world coming to? In the olden days one would have been justified in killing a thief like this one. But things have changed now. And I do not want to get involved in any unnecessary lawsuits over so silly a boy, and at this time of year too. But the boy must be taught a lesson, a lesson he will always remember for the rest of his life. He must learn never to defy and laugh at his elders. He must learn the fact that we, the older ones, have seen greater things happen than young people of his age."

He got up and soundlessly padded his way to the shelf by his head and took out a small cutlass which he used for cutting young corn. He crept quietly towards the door. "Sorry, son, that I have to teach you a lesson which you refused to learn from your uncle, and sorry that I have to teach you in this ghastly way. But you will live," Obi Uju thought. "This cutlass will scar you for life, but will not kill or break any bones of your body. To be threatened by such a tiny boy. What an insult!"

The pushing of the wooden door became stronger, and Obi Uju helped the thief outside by unhinging the door from the inside. The door gave way slightly with a whining noise.

The moon had waned, but the distinct shape of a young person's shoulder was visible in the dark. This fired the anger in

11. **bride-price:** In Igbo culture, the bride's family receives a contribution from the groom's family. The bride-price is a gesture of appreciation for the bride leaving her family to join the groom's.

Obi Uju's mind. "To think that I am even older than your father . . . you threatening me. . . ." With that he aimed the cutlass at the shoulder, making sure to control the force with which it would land on the silly thief. The person outside instinctively dodged it, and instead of scratching the shoulder-blade as Obi Uju had calculated, it landed on the side of the head, cutting a young ear neatly off.

Then a scream rang out, piercing and painful like that of a goat being killed. "Oh, Father . . . Father . . . why do you want to kill me? Father, it's only me, your daughter Kwutelu."

Obi Uju dropped the knife, looked at his own hands, and then stretched them both out to catch the sagging body of his beloved daughter before she hit the hard floor.

Then he took up the cry, but his was heavy with anguish and bitterness. "Wake up, wake up, everybody. Come and see the abomination, an abomination which has never happened in our village. I have killed my own daughter, with my own hands, all because of Umu aya Biafra. Wake up, wake up . . . an abomination . . . an abomination . . . ."

Chapter 7

The cry of "Umu aya Biafra, Umu aya Biafra" echoed from one end of Igbuno to the other. The cries cut through the otherwise still night like the sharp edges of so many shooting swords. The sounds seemed to give even the very still, dark leaves of trees bordering every footpath and open place a life of their own. They all seemed to quiver with the intensity of it all.

At first all the members of Obi Agiliga's compound were justly sleeping like everybody else. Obi Agiliga's house was in the innermost part of the compound. His wives' huts were built on both sides, and the whole set of buildings was surrounded with thatched walls made of very young, strong palm-fronds. A big gate sealed the whole compound from the rest of the village.

Nne Ojo's hut was the first one on the right. Because she was the nearest to the gate, she was always the first to hear shouts and gong announcements.

On this night, she could not believe her ears. "Umu aya Biafra—what have they been up to now?" she wondered. She sat up in the dark and would not wake her husband in the big house until she was quite sure what the trouble was. The noise grew louder and nearer. So she came out of the hut, and the words "Death, abomination, death, Umu aya Biafra" reached her. This was serious.

She wrapped her night waist-cloth around her and ran, shouting: "Obi Agiliga, wake up, they say that Umu aya Biafra have killed somebody, wake up." As she shouted and ran across the compound she went straight to the spare hut which the boys of the compound shared. She breathed a sigh of relief when she saw Okei, spread out in sleep next to his cousin Onuoha. "So whatever it is, we have nothing to do with it."

"What is it now, what are you shouting for?" Obi Agiliga shouted at his first wife.

"Just listen, listen to the whole Igbuno. They are saying that Umu aya Biafra have killed and burgled somebody—I don't know who."

"Oh my God, oh my God. These young boys. What of our son?" asked the Obi, now surrounded by most of the males in his compound.

"He is there, still sleeping."

"Then he has nothing to do with it. Wake him up. I must find out from him first."

Okei was still drowsy with sleep when he was led into Obi Agiliga's courtyard. "Now, I want to know everything. Don't leave anything behind. You know what our people say, that the day of blood relatives, friends would go? This night is the night of blood relatives. If we are going into a knife-fight to defend this compound, we must know the truth first. Who have you sent to go and kill somebody, Okei?"

Okei wanted to be sarcastic as usual, but he sensed the seriousness and urgency of the occasion. He shook his head violently, anger giving him strength. "I don't know anything about it. I did not send anybody to burgle or steal or kill. . . ."

"But they say that you are the leader. You did not feel us important enough to hear it from your own lips, but I know. So if you are the leader and an abomination has been committed in the name of your age-group, you should be the first to know. I believe you did not do it"—here Agiliga smiled a little—"and I believe you have nothing to do with it. No son of Agiliga would tell a lie to his own people."

"I am sorry, Father, I did not tell you about my nomination. I did not know that such a thing would interest you. I thought you would laugh at me."

"A leader is a leader, son, and this harvest-time is your coming-of-age time, and it is an important age in any man's life. But let all that be. Who could have done this, and for what reason?" Okei's mind went to giggling Uche, who had to muddle the Akpei stream just to annoy people—but killing a person? No, he did not think Uche could do such a thing. He did not have such a courage. Again Okei shrugged his shoulders and

shook his head. "I don't know, really I don't know."

"You had a gathering a few nights ago. You did not discuss anything like that?" Agiliga persisted.

"Discuss a thing like what?" Nne Ojo asked. "I was there in my hut, and I could hear all that they said. How I laughed about it all. They were just boys, groping their way to life. They discussed many things—wrestling, announcing this and that—but not killing or stealing. I can swear for my little husband Okei. But who would do a thing like this, to discredit a group of innocent boys, for God's sake?"

"All right, woman. Say no more until we know the full story. We know where we stand now."

So saying, he changed from his sleeping-loincloth and put on a pair of shorts which he covered with an outer otuogwu cloth. He frightened his family when he took out two curved knives and a cutlass and slung them around his waist. Nne Ojo started to cry when she saw them.

"But Okei did not do anything, Agiliga!"

"People do not know that now. They may know later, but meanwhile some stupid people may take it upon themselves to revenge on the leader of the age-group. You see, son, why it's no easy thing being a leader. I must go and find out."

"I am going with you," Okei said, standing out.

"That is good, son, but you can't and you won't. This time, you will obey me. I am your father's brother, born of the same parents. I am your father alive. You must do what I say. Nne Ojo, take the boy and hide him in your hut. No respectable man would search the wife of an Obi, to say nothing of the hut of his senior wife. You and the others just keep awake, and if anybody asks for me and Okei

AN ELDER WEARING OTUOGWU CLOTH
John Mainga
LAMU, The Gallery of Contemporary African Art

say we have gone to find out what is happening in Igbuno."

"Oh, father, suppose they attack you in anger, when you have nothing to do with it? I will go with you to prove our innocence," Okei begged, near tears.

"No son of Agiliga cries in the presence of the women in his compound. If you must do that, go and do it in private."

With that he left his family. And Nne Ojo's grip on Okei's wrist tightened as she led him into her hut.

Obi Agiliga had scarcely left when two angry young men burst into his compound, demanding to have a word with Okei. But Nne Ojo had hidden him in the darkest part of her hut, where he could hear nothing from the outside. She sat in her front room, peeping at the two men. "Only two people? Well, we can cope with those." She did not come out, but allowed the hired laborers who were still staying in the compound to deal with them. She could hear every word that was being uttered, and could see them all too clearly.

"They have gone to the center of Igbuno to see why everybody was shouting 'Murder, murder,'" said the laborers in their imperfect Igbo.

"They? Who are they?" asked one of the young men.

"Oh, the two people you are looking for. Obi Agiliga and his nephew Okei."

"Are all the members of this family dead, then? How come we can only have a word with hired laborers who can scarcely understand us?" one of the men asked in a loud voice of insolence.

Obi Agiliga's youngest wife was pregnant. She knew that they would not dare do any harm to her, and she could not stand there in the shadow and hear her compound insulted. Nne Ojo, she knew, was watching her and keeping an eye on Okei. So she came out from the corner of the compound, rubbing her eyes as if she had been woken from sleep. "What do we owe that you should come and visit us this time of night? Anyway, welcome. Our father has gone out, so we can't give you kola nut and palm-wine."

"Are you the only compound in Igbuno that has not heard all that has been going on for the past hours?"

"What has been going on?" the young wife demanded, stressing her innocence by opening her eyes wide.

"Have you not heard that Obi Uju has almost killed his beloved daughter Kwutelu, all because of a son of this compound?"

"Almost killed her? She is alive, then?"

"Do you want her dead? My brother in Ilorin has paid for her bride-price, and now she has only one ear. Her father has sliced the other one off."

"Oh dear, oh dear. And what has our Okei got to do with it?"

"What has he got to do with it? He threatened Kwutelu this morning by the stream that he would burgle her father's compound. So when she came in late her father thought it was your Okei, and cut her ear by mistake."

"I am sorry you are going to marry a young bride with only one ear, . . ." the young wife began, but she could not help laughing, and all the others who had been listening to the conversation started with a ripple of laughter and then laughed out loud.

Nne Ojo knew that it was time for her to take over. Thank goodness the girl is alive, she thought.

She welcomed the two angry men again and expressed her sorrow. It was a very nasty accident, and they should take it so. The Europeans could fix a new ear for their wife. They could use a piece of brown rubber; it would look like a brand new ear. "It's no use crying for revenge. Okei could have threatened to burgle Obi Uju's compound but he has not done it. And don't forget that Kwutelu is also of the same age-group. So you two come here to fight a small boy of sixteen? I am sure you are older than him by at least ten years. I am sorry for what has happened, though. But you all know how our people settle such things, by wrestling openly for the truth."

"Who will wrestle with that ninny? I'll break his bones in pieces."

"You see, we are saying the same thing. Okei is just a baby, and you two come here to revenge your wife-to-be's ear with knives. . . ."

"We haven't got any knives on us. We are not murderers."

"Then please go back to your compound and sleep off your anger. I am sorry about your wife's ear."

The two young men left shamefacedly. And Nne Ojo tried very hard to hush the laughter that would have overtaken all the members of Obi Agiliga's compound. She went back to her hut and said to Okei: "Go back to sleep. All is well."

When Obi Agiliga returned to his compound some time later, he and his senior wife stayed in the middle of their compound and went through the whole episode. They both agreed that Obi Uju had been a bit high-handed. "Suppose he had killed his daughter, all because she had an argument with Okei, and an argument which she started," Obi Agiliga wondered.

The Obi asked Nne Ojo whether she had told Okei anything. She said she had not, because she hid him in the darkest part of her hut. "But," she added, "the boy is sleeping now. I think he is beginning to trust us at last. He knew that you would take care of everything."

"Yes, let him sleep. I can see the faces of those mischievous boys in the morning. They say that Kwutelu has been a pain in the neck to them. Most of them did not like her very much. She is very cheeky."

"Oh, Obi Agiliga, the poor girl does not deserve to lose an ear just because she was cheeky," Nne Ojo said.

She made her way back to her hut, and slept soundly till morning.

■ RESPONDING TO THE SELECTION

Your Response

1. What advice would you give Okei when he says that he wishes he had died with the rest of his family?

2. For the Igbo, harvest time is coming-of-age time. What do you think it means to "come of age"?

Recalling

3. Who are the Umu aya Biafra?

4. What does Josephine unknowingly realize about the Igbuno and Akpei elders?

Interpreting

5. What are the sources of tension between the young people of Igbuno and the Akpei age-group?

6. Why do you think Okei and his companions are reluctant to work on farms?

7. The boys plan a wrestling match that will be "friendly," that will prove the Igbo superiority. Eventually, what else do the boys hope to accomplish by the match?

8. How does Okei's position in his age-group make him vulnerable to suspicion after Kwutelu's accident?

9. Does Okei show maturity when Obi Agiliga questions him about Kwutelu's accident? Explain.

Applying

10. The elders encourage Okei to "prove his manhood" by helping on the farm, catching the thieves, or wrestling. What do people in your culture do to prove their maturity?

ANALYZING LITERATURE

Analyzing Plot and Setting

In *The Wrestling Match,* plot and setting are closely related. The **plot,** or series of events in the novel, is influenced by the **setting** of the story, the time and place in which it occurs. The young people born in Nigeria around the civil war are coming of age as the story begins.

1. Why is Okei "fed up with life" at the end of the first chapter? What does the civil war have to do with his feelings?
2. What specific actions do the elders take in response to the frustrations of the Umu Biafra?
2. Do the elders' actions—as well as the actions of the young people—contribute to Kwutelu's accident at the end of Chapter 6? Explain.

CRITICAL THINKING AND READING

Comparing Cultural Backgrounds

Although *The Wrestling Match* is set in a traditional Nigerian community, the characters' experiences might compare to your own. For example, the young people expect to see their friends at the marketplace, much as you might meet your friends at a mall.

1. It is important to the elders that the young people work on the farm. What priorities do the older generation in your culture try to instill in young people?
2. Find two examples of comments from the elders that resemble comments you've heard from your parents' generation. Explain your choices.

THINKING AND WRITING

Writing From a Character's Point of View

As you read the first part of the novel, who intrigued you the most? With which character did you sympathize? Choose a character and write an account of key events in the novel from that character's point of view. You might identify with Okei, who struggles with the notion of working on the farm. On the other hand, you might understand Obi Agiliga's frustration with Okei. You might also wish to write from the point of view of Kwutelu before or immediately after her accident. Whichever character you choose, try to capture her or his innermost feelings.

LEARNING OPTIONS

1. **Cross-curricular Connection.** Knowing more about the Nigerian Civil War might give you greater insight into the characters in the novel. Find resources in your library and read more about the war. Why did the Igbo want their independence? Why did they lose their fight? How has the integration of the Igbo into Nigerian society been positive for them and for Nigeria? Share what you learn with your classmates in an informal class discussion.

2. **Performance.** At the end of Chapter 5, the girls sing a song taunting the boys. Get together with two or three classmates and write music for the song. Then perform it for the class, singing it as if you were the girls taunting the boys. Choose male members of your class to play the parts of the boys in the novel. As you perform, direct your singing toward them.

3. **Multicultural Activity.** The illustrations accompanying *The Wrestling Match* depict daily life as reflected in the novel. Choose one of the illustrations and compare it with a painting by a Western artist known for capturing daily life, such as Vermeer, Breughel, Mary Cassatt, or Norman Rockwell. How does each piece capture the everyday life of its culture? Write a brief comparison of the works you choose.

GUIDE FOR READING

The Wrestling Match, Chapters 8–14

Theme

Theme is the central idea or message the author conveys in a literary work. Usually, theme is implied, or stated indirectly, although it may be stated outright in the words of a character or narrator. Since a novel is more complex than shorter works of fiction, a novel may have more than one theme.

The themes of a novel may reflect a unique cultural experience or moment in history. At the same time, however, these themes may relate to other times and cultures as well. For example, the themes in *The Wrestling Match* relate specifically to the Igbo people in Nigeria, as well as to young and old people of many cultures.

Focus

In the second half of the novel, a wrestling match that was planned as a "friendly" challenge becomes much more serious to both the Akpei and Igbuno youth. Think of an athletic event you witnessed or heard about that became more than a simple test of ability. For example, perhaps it symbolized a rivalry between two schools. List some of the additional meanings that this event took on, and keep your list in mind as you read about the wrestling match in the novel.

Vocabulary

Knowing the following words will help you as you read *The Wrestling Match*, Chapters 8–14.

sensationalize (sen sā′ shə nə liz′) *v.:* To arouse excitement or interest by using startling or shocking descriptions (p. 908)
cynically (sin′ i kəl ē) *adv.:* Sarcastically (p. 909)
incensed (in senst′) *adv.:* Angry (p. 913)
conspiratorial (kən spir′ ə tôr′ ē əl) *adj.:* Suggesting a secret

plot planned by two or more people (p. 913)
agile (aj′ əl) *adj.:* Having the ability to move quickly and easily (p. 917)
wafted (wäft′ id) *v.:* Drifted through the air (p. 919)
resonant (rez′ ə nənt) *adj.:* Intense in sound and vibrations (p. 924)

Chapter 8

Okei woke up and for a time wondered where he was. Then the happenings of the night came flooding through his mind. He wondered at the whole set-up and would have liked to know exactly what had taken place. No one would tell him. In any case, it was too early for people to get up from their sleeping-places. He had now become used to getting up early, so he crept out of Nne Ojo's hut and jogged down to the stream's incline, hoping to have covered several rounds of his daily running exercises before Nduka arrived. Once or twice an eel of fear wriggled in his stomach, but he calmed himself by remembering what Nne Ojo had said to him before his going to sleep. Had she not said, "Go back to sleep, all is well" to him? He knew that Nne Ojo, being the senior wife, would never make a statement like that for fun. All must be well.

As he ran up and down the incline breathing heavily, feeling the strength building up in his young, thin but strong legs, a kind of confidence was gradually building inside him as well. In a wrestling match a contender was on the lose if he allowed his opponent to floor him. But if one had a pair of very strong legs that could stand the pushing and thumping and still be on one's feet, then that one was bound to win. He sometimes wondered who his opponent was going to be.

During his runs he disturbed many little animals who had been sleeping in peace before his arrival on the scene. Here he heard one angry bird singing croakily out of tune, as if in protest to his being there. There he saw a bush rabbit scurrying away into safety, no doubt wondering why such a person as Okei should take it upon himself to disturb them so. All the animals could not help hearing him, because the fallen, yellow-ing, dry leaves made loud crackling noises on his approach, like corn popping in an open fire. Never mind, little animals. The fight will be towards the end of the harvest, and then you will not see me again here to come and disturb your peace.

Then he stopped short. He heard a laughter that sounded more like that of a bush monkey than that of any human he had known. "Surely this part of the forest is too close to human habitation for monkeys to come this close," Okei thought as he looked around him, wondering whether he had imagined it. Then he heard the laughter again, this time closer to him, and with this second bout of uncontrollable, unnecessary laughter Uche, his friend and age-mate, emerged from that part of the forest that jutted itself into the pathway. He had been crouching there, watching him no doubt.

"I was not expecting to see you here this morning. Since when have you decided to come and exercise with me?" said Okei angrily.

"I know you were expecting Nduka, but I come early because I wish to congratulate you for what happened last night."

"What happened?"

"Have they not told you? They thought we cut Kwutelu's ear. It is so funny." Uche started to laugh again.

Okei was not amused, but was willing to wait for Uche to control himself before asking him for the full story. Uche was only too happy to comply. He told the story, dancing his demonstrations, making this funny sound and that silly one, just as if he had been there when Obi Uju was sharpening the knife with which he had accidentally sliced his daughter's ear. Okei had to laugh loud as Uche mimicked Obi Uju's cries of agony when he realized his mistake.

". . . And of course early this morning I

decided to go and see and show my sympathy to Kwutelu. But when I saw her, I could not laugh. Eh, you know something, that girl is really sick now. I saw her ear in a calabash bowl.[1] They had to tie her hair with bandages and a scarf. They are taking her to the big hospital in Benin.[2] Her father is still crying and cursing us all, especially you. I told them how sorry we are, and do you know, Kwutelu could not talk. . . .''

''Who could not talk?'' Nduka asked as he sprang on them from the part of the forest that jutted into the pathway.

''Kwutelu!'' Okei replied in astonishment. ''Have you ever heard of a thing like that before? That Kwutelu could not talk?''

''I can't believe it. I think her father did a nasty job. I think he ought to have cut her tongue or even her lips, instead of her innocent ear. Her future husband would not thank him for the loss of her ear, but he would thank him for the loss of her abusive tongue.''

''Oh, but we are awful,'' Okei said, becoming thoughtful as his mood changed. ''We should really be sorry for the poor soul, not making fun of her like this.''

''But that sharpened knife was meant for you, Okei,'' Uche pointed out.

''You did not believe for a moment that I was going there to steal anything? What I said was that if I had known those who did the burgling I would gladly tell them to come and burgle her father's compound. But of course she changed the story, to sensationalize it for her father. And now he has overreacted. . . . Pity. Come, let's go on with our wrestling practice.''

''You don't need to do that too seriously any more. This incident has shown that God is on our side,'' Uche said, wanting to back out from the rigorous exercise.

''Have you not heard that heavens help those who help themselves? God will not come down and wrestle with the Akpei boys for us. We will have to do it. He may help us if he wished, but the Akpei boys will be praying to him too,'' Okei said.

''That sounds like what one of my teachers used to say,'' Nduka replied. ''He claimed to have known somebody who had been a prisoner on both sides in the last war. He said that the person said that each side prayed to God to be on their side.''

''The man who had known another who had been in the great war said that somebody said—Gosh, you make me dizzy,'' laughed Uche. ''That may be so, but I am not going to kill myself running and wrestling. I am going to the market-place to watch Kwutelu go to the big hospital in Benin. The mammy lorry[3] will be there soon. And in particular I want to watch a crying Obi and a dumb Kwutelu. I wouldn't miss that scene for all the wrestling matches in the world.''

He left his two friends and faced the path towards home. Then he added for a good measure: ''I will tell you all about it when I see you later in the day.''

''Yes, and all garnished and spiced to your taste,'' Nduka said, and Okei laughed.

Uche went back into the village, and Okei asked Nduka if he had told the others to practice wrestling as he had advised them to do. Nduka had already done so and this pleased Okei. With that they went into the hard work of catching each other's legs and thumbing one another's arms and stomach to toughen all their young muscles.

---

1. calabash (kal′ ə bash) **bowl** n.: A bowl made from the dried, hollow shell of a gourd.
2. Benin (be nēn′): Nigerian city, named after an ethnic group famous for their bronze sculptures.

3. mammy lorry: Pick-up truck with a canvas cover.

At that moment, Obi Uwechue paid an early visit to Obi Agiliga on the farm. He had heard rumors of knifing, he said, and he wanted to know whether it was true that Umu aya Biafra had started it all.

"How news flies," marveled Obi Agiliga.

He soon told his friend from Akpei how it all happened, and they were both sorry, because they knew that indirectly they had encouraged the girls to goad the boys into anger. They agreed that the accident could have been worse. "Suppose Obi Uju had killed his daughter outright?" Obi Uwechu pondered aloud.

After a pause, he went on: "There is one good thing that is arising from all this—we do not have boys molesting anyone in the footpath any more. They are all busy practicing their wrestling and getting angry at the insults the other party is heaping on them."

"Have you noticed that in Akpei too? But for the last night's incident, the aya Biafra boys in Igbuno had been busy holding meetings and getting themselves toughened."

"Well, that is the whole point of the whole exercise, isn't it?" asked Obi Uwechue.

"You are right, my friend, after this incident they will learn to think a little like adults. Even my nephew is beginning to look at me as if I am somebody at last. Before, I was just an old man to be shouted at."

The two elders chuckled knowingly at their cleverness. They had successfully created problems for the "know-all" youngsters.

Chapter 9

It was another Eke market. There was much excitement in the air, and the girls of Igbuno were determined to make the best of the few Eke markets left. They would sell their heavy load of plantain as expensively as they possibly could; they would need the money to buy the latest colorful outfits. The relation between them and the boys was still uncertain, but a few boys had already made it up with some of their girlfriends. Even Kwutelu had started to exchange polite praise-greetings.

"Lord, your neck will sink into your chest with that big bunch of bananas," Josephine's mother observed. "It is too heavy. Why don't you sell them here? You will make some profit with such a big bunch."

"But I will make even more profit in Akpei. All my friends are going there this Eke market with as big a bunch as they can carry. I am not the only one."

"These modern girls and their love for money," Josephine's mother said, shaking her head.

Josephine balanced the bunch on the piece of old cloth she had coiled, and placed it all on her head. Yes, it was heavy, but the picture of the latest abada cloth she was going to wear on the day of the wrestling match was already imprinted in her mind. She had to work hard and save the money.

At the main crossing she saw some of her friends waiting for her. They all carried much heavier bunches than usual.

"I hope the Akpei people will buy all your plantain," said an old woman cynically, looking at them with contempt.

"I don't know why some people won't mind their business," said Josephine in a low voice.

"Well, if they all do mind their business, they won't be the people of Igbuno," Kwutelu said. She then looked around her enviously and continued: "My bunch is the

MARKET SCENE—BUYING AND SELLING
John Mainga
LAMU, The Gallery of Contemporary African Art

size of a small girl's. I don't know why that old woman did not make any remark about that."

"Don't talk like that, Kwutelu. When you were well we all know that you used to carry the biggest bunches of plantain of any of us. You must not carry anything big now, because it gives you headache," said Josephine consolingly.

Kwutelu sighed and was silent. This was the new attitude people noticed about her since the accident. Some thought that maybe she stopped being abusive because she was frightened in case people would call her "rubber ear." Because, as Nne Ojo had foretold on the night of the accident, an artificial ear had been glued to her head.

The spirit of the girls soon became light as they jogged their way to Akpei. They chattered about empty nothings as they climbed the steep hill that led to Akpei.

They arrived there very early as usual, hoping that by so doing they would sell their wares and leave for home early. After waiting for a while for the market to get full, they noticed that nobody from Akpei had come to ask them for their plantain. "Maybe they have stopped eating plantain," Josephine said with a nervous giggle.

"It's still early yet," Kwutelu said confidently.

The market became full and people started going home, yet all the Igbuno girls stood there staring at their unsold plantain.

"Do you think they are doing this on purpose?" a little girl of fourteen asked Kwutelu.

"But I don't know either. Maybe they too are going off food in order to save for their yam festival and the wrestling match," Kwutelu replied.

"It will be funny and humiliating if we have to go back home still carrying our bunches of plantain," Josephine remarked.

Kwutelu and the others were thinking of the same thing. They would be disappointed, to say nothing of the shame of it. Still, they all agreed to stay a little longer.

"I am so hungry," cried one girl in despair.

"You are not the only one," Josephine replied to her.

Normally by this time they would have almost finished selling and would have some food for themselves. But this afternoon they still had their plantain untouched by any customer, so there was no money to buy food.

Then came an old woman. She was in dark-patterned abada cloth and was walking with a stick, peering this way and that way critically as some old people do. She stopped in front of the girls and, having appraised them, advised them to give their plantain away to poor old people like herself. That way the bunches of plantain would be useful. "If you stand here all day and night, nobody will buy your plantain."

"But why, why?" Kwutelu cried.

"You ask me why?" she asked as she shook her stick in the air. "I shall tell you. Our Umu aya Biafra are planning a friendly wrestling match with your boys, and what do you think your boys are doing by turning the whole thing upside down?"

"Turning it upside down? What is she talking about?" the girls asked one another.

But the woman did not answer. Her mind went on to other things. "If you carry a bunch of your plantain to my hut, I will always bless you. If you take all your wares home, they will go rotten on you. If you think you are going to sell them here in Akpei, you will wait for ever." She went down the market square, still peering this way and that.

"What are we going to do?" cried Jose-phine. "If I have to carry that bunch back all the way to Igbuno I will never recover from the shame. Do you think we should ask them why they are boycotting our part of the market, Kwutelu?"

"And be insulted into the bargain? No, Josephine the daughter of Nwogbu, we won't stoop that low. We can dump some of the plantain in the bush on our way home if they are too heavy, but if not we must take them back to Igbuno with us. Can't you see what is happening, the way those people are looking at us slyly and laughing? All this was not accident. I know that we are hungry and tired, but we must go. And as far as I am concerned, I will always support my own people. I will always sell my plantain in our own Eke market, not come to a place like this and be insulted. You remove that woebe-gone look from your face, it is not the end of the world." Kwutelu finished addressing the latter part of her speech to the youngest girl, Adaobi, who had previously complained of hunger.

They packed their plantain again and helped each other into putting them on their heads, then went down the road leading to Igbuno, forcing themselves to make light jokes as if this type of thing happened to them every market day. They could hear people, one or two knots of gossip loungers, laughing out loudly. But the girls went on with determined steps.

When they knew that they were far from Akpei, they did away with their mask of pretense.

"Goodbye to my dream abada material," Josephine moaned.

"And welcome to our village pride. From now on we will have to boost the ego of our boys, not deflect it. The people of Akpei have turned a harmless joke into something seri-ous." Kwutelu was quiet for a while, realizing that all these rumors had almost cost her her life. So it must be serious.

Halfway between Akpei and Igbuno some of the girls threw away their plantain because they knew that they had a lot at home and it could not keep very long. They were all tired and could scarcely carry themselves, to say nothing of taking home heavy bundles of plantain which seemed to have become doubly weighty.

"It does not matter very much if we appear at the wrestling-square in our old abada cloth," said Kwutelu. "After all, the way the Akpei people are going about it, I don't think it is going to be all that friendly."

"Yes, that will be a good idea. Let us make it an old abada cloth day. Those silly Akpei girls will come in their very best, then we can pick up quarrel with them and mess their new outfits. Yes, that will teach them," said Josephine mischievously.

They all laughed, despite their failure to sell their plantain.

They were still laughing when they came to the hill bordering the Igbuno stream. They were met by a larger group of people, because many of their parents were anxious about them. It was a moonless night and very dark. But the friends and relatives met them with lamps and hand-torches.

The girls poured out their story and the young men became really incensed, determined to win the match.

But when the male elders heard it all later in the night, they all smiled with a conspiratorial wink.

Chapter 10

The next gathering of the Umu aya Biafra was held on a moonless night. The night was dark and forbidding. All the familiar trees and everyday shapes acquired greater solidity. Some trees even seemed to be moving when the night breeze fanned the landscape. The age-group carried hurricane lamps, and some modern and well-to-do boys brought powerful hand-torches.

This time they decided not to meet in the open, after their experience of the last meeting. They were moody almost to the last person. The insults, jibes, and abuses of the young men and women of Akpei had aroused the anger of the mildest member. Even Uche, who was always thought to be easy-going, had taken it almost as a personal insult that the Igbuno girls were shunned in Akpei market. So they met in an old abandoned hut at the corner of Akpuenu. This hut was large and used for occasional dance practices. The boys did not know who owned it, but they knew that they would not be chased away.

The matter of Kwutelu's ear was mentioned briefly. Some still found it funny, but many were beginning to feel sorry for Kwutelu, especially as she had now changed for the better.

Everybody was then allowed to display the tricks of wrestling they had mastered since their last gathering. They had fun with this, because there were those who were born to be non-wrestlers. Uche, for example, was always looking for a nice, soft place to fall instead of defending himself. "Oh, Uche, you wrestle like a pregnant woman," Okei shouted at the top of the laughter.

There was a big hush when Okei chose Nduka as a partner. The others were intrigued by the quickness of the two wrestlers, their lightness of touch, and the clever way with which they were polite to each other. It was a kind of wrestling, but a wrestling with an art. It was beautiful to watch. But the farmer boys among them started to grumble. The grumble became loud, and Okei had to stop the wrestling.

"And what is your problem, farmer's boy from Ogbeukwu?" he asked.

The so-addressed disregarded the insolent tone and answered sharply. "This is like a white man's wrestling, you two dancing about each other as if you are playing hide and seek. It is beautiful to watch, it is amusing. But it will not do for those Akpei people. Remember that I had to take message of the wrestle to them. I saw the spirit with which my news was received. They were determined. This type of dancing will win nothing for us."

"So how do you want us to wrestle?" asked Okei, panting with anger and breathless.

"The way real wrestlers wrestle."

Others applauded the statement from the farmer's boy. "After all, we elected you to be our leader. You should do your best to retain the post."

"I am not afraid of the leadership being taken away from me . . ." Okei began.

"Ahem, ahem," Uche butted in. "I like the dance, as you said, but where can we learn to improve it? Okei is very fast and strong, but if we can help him to be better it will be much more helpful than arguing about it." Then he started to laugh.

"You have made a good contribution," said the farmer's boy, "but I don't know why you are laughing. I saw the Akpei boys consulting with their elders even while I was still there. Okei can consult his uncle. They say that he was a good heavy wrestler in his time. Why can't we use his knowledge? I am sure he will be willing to teach us."

"No! No! This is our war, this is our problem. We don't want the elders to nose into our business. So keep him out of it. I won't like to consult with him for anything," Okei yelled, his voice echoing round the hushed gathering as if he were the only person there.

"But the Akpei young people are being helped by their elders," Nduka put in pointedly. "Why can't we use their knowledge too?"

"Because we are doing our thing our own way. We don't want their ways. They are old-fashioned, and as for my uncle . . . well, he is not bad for an uncle, but I don't like consulting him for anything."

"Then we are fighting a losing battle," the farmer's boy said, "because the young people of Akpei are bound to come out on top. And listen, Okei, are you going to do without the wrestling dance too? You know you will have to dance round the circle in a certain way. None of us here knows the wordings of the song, to say nothing of the way to dance it. Your uncle is a master at it. Are you going to do without that too?"

Okei looked at him in the dim light for a long time. Had they made a mistake in allowing those who had never sat behind desks at school to come and join them? Could they not do without the dance? A wrestling match without its dance was half a show, he knew. He must give in.

". . . We need our elders," the farmer's boy continued. "After all, they are our fathers, and they cannot direct us wrong. This is going to be a friendly match, and I hope it remains so. But suppose it should go out of hand?"

"All right, you have made your point. I'll see what help he can give us, to polish up our way of wrestling. I suppose one has to look up to one's elders."

"A village that has no elders has no future. I hope we will always have elders," Nduka said prayerfully.

Chapter 11

It was easy for Okei's age-mates to suggest that he should seek advice from his uncle, Obi Agiliga. He saw the point of his not making the mistakes which the elders had made before him. But until now it had never occurred to him that he and his age-mates could make mistakes at all. "Blast those Akpei boys! Why should they take it upon themselves to seek advice from their elders?" How was he going to start telling his troubles to his uncle? A man he had looked upon with tolerance, that type of tolerance that had to exist because there was no way out for him, because he had no other place to live. He feared that his uncle would feel proud and would hint, "I have always thought you would come to me to ask for advice."

"It is that humiliating part that I resent so much," he confessed to Nduka the second day. "I would have liked us to do without the likes of my uncle completely."

"Well, we can't, and we won't. We need the likes of him. What is wrong with his feeling proud about our seeking his advice? You never know, in a few years' time it will be your turn to advise his young sons. You will be the elder in your family then. Would it be wrong of you to feel proud then? I don't know what you are worrying about."

"I resented my parents' death and maybe his staying alive. Maybe if he had been my father and not my uncle, I would have been able to go to him naturally."

"Well, he cannot help staying alive, can he? It's not his fault your parents were killed. It was a war, and you and I know that in such wars, the innocent suffer. Don't lose the match for us because of your pride and stubbornness. I shall come with you, if you so desire."

"Thank you very much. I think that this is a family matter. I shall deal with it alone. Come on, let us run down the slope one more time."

Obi Agiliga was surprised to see Okei sitting in his courtyard in the evening. He was behaving in the normal traditional way, of sitting around in the evening after the day's work had been done and listening to the conversations of the adults and learning lessons from them. Agiliga glanced at him uneasily once or twice, and wondered what had come upon him. But he controlled himself from asking him any questions.

Okei helped in serving the adults the ever-present kola nuts and palm-wine, betraying no emotion but being extremely polite. One or two of Agiliga's friends who knew Okei's reputation arched their brows in a question, and Obi Agiliga simply shrugged his shoulders. He did not know the reason for this change of heart.

Okei started clearing and tidying up when the visitors had left. Agiliga watched him as he smoked his last pipe before retiring for the night. Then he asked: "What is it, Okei? What is worrying you?"

Okei looked up at his uncle and smiled. "It is the wrestling match," he replied promptly.

"You want to learn the songs and the style we used. Our style."

Okei would have liked to find out how his uncle knew exactly what he wanted, but he was so taken in by its suddenness that he nodded enthusiastically.

Then his uncle—who was also a tall man, but whose tallness was less pronounced because of his thickened body—got out from his sitting-place and took two simple but cunning steps towards Okei, and by the time he realized what he was doing Okei found himself lying on the floor.

AN ELDER WALKING ALONE
John Mainga
LAMU, The Gallery of Contemporary African Art

He got up and glared at his uncle. Obi Agiliga roared with laughter and said, "That is not a very fair way to treat your wrestling opponent. But if everything fails, it is a useful art to master. I will teach you that first."

Obi Agiliga did not stop with teaching him how to take his opponent unawares, especially if the person became violent; he taught him how to give his audience pleasure by luring his opponent round and round and then suddenly confronting him. "Most opponents are not prepared for this sudden halt, and you have to use their unpreparedness to floor them. You know that if an opponent's back reaches the ground, then you have won."

"I know that, uncle," Okei said with his mouth full of laughter at this Obi who in his enthusiasm had been transformed into an agile young man. He worked up his body into lumps and hooks, displaying many methods of trapping an opponent. It looked for a while as if the Obi was simply displaying his art only for himself. He became completely unaware of Okei's presence. Okei's respect for his uncle really soared high.

When it came to the words of the wrestling song, Obi Agiliga became supple and almost soft as a woman. He would jump into the air, and just as you thought he was going to land flatly on his back, you would see him touching the ground as lightly as a fallen dry leaf. Then like a cat he would tread softly on the balls of his feet, singing and moving to the rhythm of his own music.

He was thus preoccupied when his senior wife Nne Ojo came in. Okei made a sign for her to be quiet, and the two of them watched Obi Agiliga perform. It was only when he had danced to his heart's content that he said, "Now I have to teach you all that."

Nne Ojo laughed with tears in her eyes. "I used to see you in the wrestling circle performing like that. To think that you were that young once."

"Yes, that was a long time ago," the Obi said with some confusion. "I have to teach it all to this young man here. It is his turn now. My turn has come and gone."

"It was a lovely time, when we were always young," Nne Ojo said, and walked across the courtyard, making for the door leading into one of the rooms.

"Don't go, my senior wife. I was the leader of the wrestling group of my age, but not the leader of my age-group. But Okei here is the leader of his age-group and is required to defend their reputation. So it will be a big occasion for this family. Could you let him borrow one of your red Akwete cloths to use as a kind of cloak? I want him to come out in style to beat those crude Akpei boys. It is not always that a wrestling leader is also elected as the leader of his age-group. You will get the whole compound ready as well."

"We have done all the preparation in secret, hoping that one day our Okei will ask for your help. Now he has done it, we will all be behind him."

"Yes, that is right. The Akpei people and the whole of Igbuno will not forget the year in which Okei the son of Agiliga came of age," Obi Agiliga said proudly.

Nne Ojo soon left them and the two men, one middle-aged, the other a youth, practiced the art and songs of wrestling till late at night.

Chapter 12

The people of Igbuno, in their fever of excitement, started to count the days by saying that the day of the great wrestling match had only two market days to go. Then they started to count the days. It would be in four days' time, then three, then two, eventually the day after tomorrow.

Okei and his friend Nduka had become village heroes. As they practiced in the early morning they now had a large group of young enthusiasts who came to watch them. It was during the school holidays, and those boys who went to the farms were all free because the yams had been harvested. They cheered as the two boys punched each other mercilessly. They applauded as they danced in their art. They ran up and down the incline with them until they were out of breath. It was a time of great hope.

All the boys of that age went to a special barber, who had to cut their hair in a certain style called the Appian Way.[4] So they were easily recognizable. The old, the young men, and the women prayed for them to win the wrestling match.

"Our own age-group has got an original touch," boasted Uche as he trotted and puffed like a dog behind Okei and Nduka.

"What master touch?" Okei asked.

"All age-groups until now usually come out with some lousy dances. But we are wrestling our way into manhood."

"Maybe because we saw the gunning down and killing of many people in our babyhood."

"But that is true, though," Okei put in to enlighten his friend Nduka. "I keep wondering why it never occurred to us to dance our way out."

"It never occurred to us," said Nduka.

"But why since that would have been the normal thing?"

"I don't know. Don't ask me," Uche replied with a sickening giggle.

At home in Agiliga's compound, Okei was being treated to a place of honor. He was always being invited to eat with the Obi. He was no longer ordered to go and eat with the women, so Nne Ojo could not complain about his nasty eating manner. Once he started to eat with the elders, he began to behave himself.

Amidst the excitement and expectation, Okei asked Obi Agiliga one evening: "Suppose, father, I lose the contest?"

"In the first place, you will not lose. In the second place, even if you lost, it won't be a complete loss because you would have added a new art to the game of wrestling, and you would have taken part and done your best. Don't you think it is better to think on those lines, Okei the son of Agiliga?"

"You are right, father."

They had just finished their evening meal, the day before the official yam festival day, when they were suddenly forced to listen to a group of dancers coming towards the Agiliga's compound. As they drew nearer, the words of their songs became more distinct.

They were singing:

"Akpei people bumkum,[5]
The world bumkum, we don't care.
Why should we care?
When we have heroes like Okei . . .
Heroes like Okei the son of Agiliga
In our midst."

---

4. Appian (ā′ pē ən) **Way:** The main paved road through ancient Rome. The hairstyle has a big part or separation in the middle, and several smaller parts.

5. bumkum: A version of *bunkum*, which means "empty or insincere talk"; used here to ridicule the Akpei for not having a glorious wrestler like Okei.

They came to the front gate of the compound and made a circle. The dancers were the very girls who only a few months ago had been against the boys of Umu aya Biafra.

Kwutelu and another girl led the singing in turns. The rest of the group answered, shaking their beaded gourds in the air. They were so organized that the circle was never crowded. There were never more than two girls in the circle at the same time. Their male guide had a mock whip in his hands, ready to chase any unwanted dancer who was not invited to join in. So great was the happiness and excitement that everybody wished to display their own special dance. They kept on and on calling Okei to come out and dance for them. He would not. And people thought he was shy.

"I will dance for him," said the senior wife of the family, Nne Ojo. Her dance was a little comical, and it was clear that she was putting it on on purpose. She knew she could not crouch and jump as quickly and as gracefully as the young girls, so she overdid her stiff back. She placed one hand on her hip, and walked round the circle in imitation of the girls. She made faces at them, until the drummers and singers all collapsed in laughter.

"You must go and make a few dancing steps, Okei, at least to show your appreciation for all the girls' efforts," Obi Agiliga advised.

"I can't believe Kwutelu is singing my praises. She used to laugh at me."

"Everyone loves a winner," his uncle said wisely.

Okei eventually sprinted into the circle, dancing lightly as if he were a bird in flight. When he crouched slightly to the music, he looked like a bird pecking some food with its beak and then taking flight. He was so light. He was so agile, and they loved him.

The dancers were entertained, and they sang their way to other compounds. Everybody knew that the yam festival had started.

Chapter 13

The wrestling match day did arrive at last. The dawn was misty, but it was clear even from that early morning mist that it was going to be a sunny and dry day. No one expected it to rain at this time of year, but one could never tell for sure, especially as it was possible for some people who were not well disposed to the wrestling to intone to the skies and make it rain.

Okei was awakened by the drums of Igbuno. The special drummers knew how to make their drums talk and convey messages. This used to be a common thing a very, very long time ago. But now, these drums were used only on important occasions like this.

The doubt still lingered in Okei's mind. He had never been beaten in wrestling before, in Igbuno. But he did not know the style the opponents from Akpei would use. He did not let anybody know of his fear though, but he was determined to take his uncle's advice and do his best. And if he should lose, to accept it gallantly.

He was not left on his sleeping-mat long. Excited voices rang round the compound as young mothers called their children for the stream and their morning bath. The smell of roasted yams wafted all over the compound and the whole village. Smoke from wood fires rose from here and there and everywhere. On yam festival wrestling match

DRUMMERS OF IGBUNO
John Mainga
LAMU, The Gallery of Contemporary African Art

days, even the poorest widow could afford to dip a whole yam into the open fire. When roasted, they were dipped in palm oil and slightly salted and peppered. The crust of that roasted yam was a great treat for both children and adults. Okei knew that at least on this his great day, the crust of the yams would be left for him. At the thought of this, it looked to him as if the aroma of the food was strengthened especially for his nose. He got up and walked into the open compound.

"Oh, my strong little husband will come to my hut and eat my roasted yam?" Obi Agiliga's youngest wife asked hopefully.

Unfortunately for her, Nne Ojo was not too far away. She gave the young woman such a look that sent her scurrying like a squirrel into her own hut. "You must be careful of what you eat and where you eat today, Okei," she said.

Okei had to suppress the urge to show his eagerness. He was dying to have a taste, but he said manfully: "I must go to the stream to have a bath first."

"Well, don't stay too long and don't practice any more," Obi Agiliga shouted from the verandah of his house. He had heard all that Nne Ojo and his youngest wife had been saying. "When you return, your yam, specially prepared for you, will be here, hot and waiting."

At the stream many people wished Okei luck from afar. He acknowledged them all with a nod. Meeting Nduka at the men's area relaxed him a little.

"Did you see Kwutelu and the others last night?" Nduka asked.

"Yes, they came to our compound, and she was singing my praises," Okei said with a laugh.

"Did you not notice that all the girls were wearing their headscarves like a band, to cover their ears and display their hairdos?"

"I thought that was their latest fashion or something," Okei said naïvely.

"Well, it could become fashionable. But Kwutelu started it, to cover her damaged ear, and she willed the style so strongly on the other girls that it was accepted as part of their dancing outfit."

Both boys laughed conspiratorially.

"Poor Kwutelu," Okei said in sympathy.

"We have to hurry home, and good luck to you. The Akpei people are taking this very seriously, I heard," Nduka said.

"As far as we are concerned, it is a friendly match between the same age-groups. The adults can come and watch, but they must not interfere. We will choose our own judges and referees from both sides. They will be of the same age as all of us. Nothing to do with the adults and nothing at all that serious."

"Well, you'll have to warn the Igbuno girls. They see this wrestling match as a way of revenging the bad treatment they received over their plantain issue."

"That was their fault," said Okei. "We have an Eke market here in Igbuno. Why go all that way just to sell them? Yes, I know they make a few pennies extra. But if for any reason they have to go by a car or a bus of some kind, that money would be eroded."

"Anyway, few cars run that road. And they have stopped going to Akpei now. Yet they still want to use this match to get even with them."

Okei shrugged his shoulders. The two boys soon parted, each to his own compound to go and get ready for the wrestling.

By the afternoon there were drums being beaten in every big compound in Igbuno. People put on their best clothes, and went round to relatives' houses to eat yams and exchange gifts of yams. Everything and everybody was yammy. There would still be many dances for the rest of the season, but on wrestling match day the excitement was at its highest.

"Ah, I can hear a different kind of drum from ours," Obi Agiliga remarked. "And I think it is the Akpei people. They must be nearing our hill." He watched Nne Ojo, his senior wife, put the last touches on the Akwete cloak Okei was going to wear.

Okei, who had been lying on the mud couch in the courtyard, sat and listened carefully. Yes, he could hear a faint rhythm, different from the other, nearer ones. It was so faint that he had to strain his ears to hear it. Then he smiled at his uncle and said: "You have been expecting that sound, have you not?"

Obi Agiliga nodded, puffing confidently at his pipe. "Are you boys not having any elders there to see to the smooth running of things?"

"No, father, we are boys of a new breed. We want to do most of the whole things by ourselves. But since the Akpei boys consulted their elders to give them some tips, I had to come to you to teach me the tricky bits of wrestling and the dance to it. But you have helped us this far, I think we can now go on by ourselves. You all are invited to come and watch, though."

Obi Agiliga smiled into the smoke from his pipe. "You don't invite people to watch anything in Igbuno. We just go. And as far back as I can remember, the yam festival was always climaxed by boys on the verge of manhood entertaining everybody with a dance of some sort. But in your case, you want to celebrate yours with a fight."

"Not a fight, father. A sport."

"Well that may be so. But some people are not so good at losing. You must remember that. In any case, the whole village will be there."

The other people in the compound gave a shout of delight and cried, "We will show them, we will show them."

"They have heard the Akpei drums too. They are talking drums, and are saying that their wrestlers are the greatest and fastest wrestlers in the whole of Nigeria," explained Obi Agiliga.

"Is that what they are saying? I must get ready. We must go and meet them in style."

The men in the compound helped Okei to dress up. He only wore a plain pair of shorts and a pair of colorful plimsolls[6] to match. But on top of this, he had several charms slung round his neck. One of them was made with crocodile teeth, to prevent him from becoming breathless. Another was from nut kernels, to harden him like nuts which are hard to crack. His face had to be washed with waters mixed with many herbs, so that no evil eye would penetrate beyond his face to his heart. After all that, Okei was forced to drink a mixture which was supposed to get rid of any shyness he had.

The drink worked like a miracle. He started to sway to the drums of the Akpei people who were fast approaching the center of the village. He laughed loudly when he heard the thin voices of Igbuno girls going to meet the new arrivals. People told him that Kwutelu and the others were singing his praises to the Akpei people, and this was annoying the girls who came with them. Okei then shouted: "That is it. That is the spirit."

They soon finished dressing him up and getting him emotionally ready. Then the

---

6. plimsolls (plim′ səlz) *n.*: Rubber-soled, canvas shoes, like sneakers.

drums all stopped as if on cue. Their places were taken by the biggest drum of all, that of the age-group dancers. This drum was beaten only once a year, at every yam festival season. It boomed, and its sound seemed to shake the very earth. Okei leapt into the air, and all the members of Agiliga's compound and all the members of the nearby compounds ran out, some carrying their locally made guitars, some carrying beer bottles and teaspoons to make music with. Children got empty tins and their covers. These musical instruments were all kept in secret before, waiting for the time they thought the spirit of the yam harvest and the coming of age would descend upon Okei. He led the crowd on, leaping and whirling in the air, until he neared the open place called Kumbi, where he knew that the Akpei contestants would be waiting. Someone had to stop him, because it was said that if he saw his opponent first he would not live to be an old man.

Four young men got hold of him and held him, forcing him to lean against the mud wall of Obi Uju's compound. Even Obi Uju, Kwutelu's father, came out and said prayers for Okei that he should bring glory to Igbuno.

All the other young Umu aya Biafra came and went into the square with their own relatives and friends, singing their praise-names and dancing with them. The other people, young members of the age-group, were slightly more sober than Okei. They too had been given the mixture, but not as strong as Okei's. Nduka too came with a big crowd. He was to take the place of Okei if he had an accident or got beaten. He was to be kept in reserve.

The Umu aya Biafra drum boomed from Obi Uju's compound, where the drummers had been hidden. The wordings of the drums were very clear: "We will show you, we will show you."

The farmer's boy from Ogbeukwu went into the circle and welcomed the people of Akpei, reminding them that it was he who had come to them to ask them for this match, a friendly one. He welcomed them again and showed them the pile of food and drinks which the parents of those coming of age had prepared. He introduced them to the girls who would be ready to get them anything they wanted. He then told them to choose a judge, and someone to act as a referee: The Igbuno boys had already chosen theirs. Whatever decisions these four people made would be final.

The Akpei spokesman, a young man of the same age-group, thanked the Igbuno people and hoped that after this kind of friendly match a greater bond of friendship would exist between the two villages.

The elders, Obi Agiliga, Obi Uju, and Obi Uwechue, and many others watched the proceedings from afar. They listened to the glowing speeches. One or two of them coughed a little and winked at the other. They all smiled and shook their heads knowingly.

Chapter 14

The occasion started in a friendly way. The Igbuno dancers came and sang round the circle, they demonstrated their beautiful bodies and their agility. They were cheered and there was even great applause when girls performed acrobatic feats that took the breaths of the onlookers away. Josephine, Nduka's friend, was the leader of the acrobatic group. In acknowledging the cheers, they arranged themselves into such a pattern that they looked like the waters of

Igbuno streams tumbling down the rocks into the valley beyond. The fact that the girls were not dressed in the latest abada cloth did not bother them. They came in tunics which they had made themselves. After the acrobatics, they threw loose lappas round themselves and danced their way out of the circle, followed by the great cheers of so many people.

There was hardly any living person left in Igbuno who was not at Kumbi that late afternoon. The sun was going down and it was nearing the cool of the evening. The cool breezes fanned the people from the surrounding coconut and oil palms.

The Akpei dancers were so well dressed that they could not move so quickly. People admired their outfits and hairdos, but their dance was nothing compared to the determined performance of the Igbuno girls. They did not receive so loud a cheer as the other group, and one could see frowns beginning to form themselves on the faces of the young men. Even some of the older women who came with them were murmuring behind the back of their hands. They were not given much time to grumble, because the big drum that was in Obi Uju's compound had been quietly moved nearer to the square. Then it boomed, so loud and so resonant that those people nearest to the drummers jumped and almost ran away from the circle. They quickly came back though, because they knew that if they did not they would lose their places. The crowd was ten to twelve people thick, like an impenetrable wall surrounding this circle.

As the drum boomed faster and faster Nduka jumped into the circle, ran fast round it, and dropped his cloak in the center as a challenge to the Akpei people. The symbolic cloak was picked up by one of the referees. The drums beat even faster, and the circle was filled with all the boys of Igbuno born in and around the civil war. They had identical lappas, and their hair was cut in the same way. They were young, most of them slim and tall. They were proud and they showed it. Even the elders inched closer to admire the handsomeness of these young people who would take over the running of things when they were gone. They did a few light steps, and moved out of the circle.

Then the Akpei drummers took over, and their people were likewise shown. When the drums of the Igbuno people boomed again the four men holding Okei let him go. He danced into the square amidst the loudest cheer of that afternoon. He danced, and his young body pulsated in the cool of the evening. The Igbuno girls burst into song, praising him. His opponent watched him from his own side. Then at a sign from the referee, Okei threw his Akwete cloak on the ground and shouted: "Come out, whoever you are."

A young man, who was the same age as Okei but looked thicker and older somehow, leapt into the circle. And the wrestling started. The Akpei contestant kept looking for a way to pin down Okei, but he had been taught to wrestle like a dancer. He would leap here, run there, and dodge at the other place. They both sweated and panted, and Okei came closer only when he thought he had given his audience enough cheering and yelling for the afternoon. Okei was floored, almost at the very first close encounter. But he thanked his uncle in his heart. He used one of the surprise tactics he was taught, and his opponent was flat on the ground. He jumped on the boy from Akpei before he had time to recover from the shock, and held his arms in the air. Okei had won.

The excitement was terrific. The Igbuno people jumped and screamed in the air. But

MULTICULTURAL CONNECTION

The Universal Appeal of Wrestling

In "The Wrestling Match," Buchi Emecheta describes the importance of wrestling in the Nigerian culture. Although wrestling has been described as nothing more than two men trying to throw each other to the ground, few sports have exerted a more universal appeal. Practiced by peasants and kings alike, wrestling in its various forms has become popular in nearly every civilized country of the world.

The origins of wrestling. Exactly when wrestling began is not known. In the tombs of Beni Hasa found along the Nile River in Egypt, elaborately detailed images of wrestlers have been sculpted in stone, showing almost all the holds and techniques known today. These sculpted images date from three thousand years before the Christian era. In ancient Greece, the poet Homer wrote a memorable description of a wrestling match between two heroes. The sport also dates very far back in Japan, where wrestling has been practiced for over two thousand years.

In ancient Greece. The ancient Greeks had a high regard for wrestling, which was an important event in their athletic contests. In Greek wrestling, all holds were allowed, as were strangling, butting, kicking, and crushing an opponent's fingers. The match continued until one of the fighters admitted defeat. The most famous wrestler of ancient times was Milo of Crotona, who is reputed to have scored thirty-two victories in the Olympic games.

In Japan. In the ninth century, Emperor Shoumu made wrestling part of the annual harvest, or the "Festival of Five Grains." Even after Japanese emperors ceased to sponsor wrestling in the twelfth century, it remained a part of the soldier's or Samurai's training.

Japanese wrestling, or sumo, is the domain of very large men (some weigh as much as five hundred pounds) who have been specially trained since youth. The sumo match traditionally takes place in a ring twelve feet in diameter and is usually over in less than a minute. The first person to touch the mat with a part of his body other than his feet loses the bout. Three times each year, sumo wrestlers meet in Tokyo for fifteen days of championship matches, and the winners are accorded high status in Japanese society.

In Ireland, England, and Scotland. In parts of northern England and Scotland, an intricate style of wrestling known as "North Country" is common. Two men wrestle in stout, loosely cut linen jackets, with holds being restricted to those above the waist. A wrestler loses a match when two shoulders and a hip, or two hips and one shoulder, touch the mat at the same time.

In Turkey, Australia, and the United States. The wrestling we are most likely to see today comes from Lancashire, England, and is now practiced in Turkey, Australia, and the United States. Considered the legitimate descendant of the ancient Greek sport, this type of wrestling forbids kicking, striking, or strangling. A bout is won when both of the opponent's shoulders are made to touch the floor.

Discussing in Class

Together with your classmates, consider whether wrestling is a sport, a spectacle, an art form, or a combination of all three.

THE WRESTLERS
John Mainga
LAMU, The Gallery of Contemporary African Art

when the noise died down the Akpei people made it clear that an annual contest like that would not rest just on one wrestling match between two people only. They pushed in another boy, who floored Okei in no time at all. Arguments then started. The girls of Igbuno claimed that it was not fair for the Akpei people to have two contestants. So Nduka came in and the boy from Akpei floored him too. The Igbuno people became bitter and Okei could see that his people were becoming abusive, so he volunteered to wrestle with the same boy again. He did this, and he won.

Kwutelu was so excited that she jumped into the circle and started to wipe Okei's face with one of the handkerchiefs she was carrying. Then a shout came from one of the Akpei girls: "Why don't you use that handkerchief to wipe your rubber ear!"

Nobody knew who hit the other person first, but every Igbuno boy found himself wrestling and fighting a boy from Akpei. The confusion became so intense that younger people screamed, as the adults called on the fighters to stop. But fists were in the air, and all the bottled anger of the past months was let loose.

"I think they will need us now," said Obi Agiliga to the other Obis. They made their way into the confusion, and it took them a long time to disentangle the drumsticks from one of the drummers. They beat the drums as if they would bust, and shouted with their voices as well. Many of the fighters stopped unwillingly, as each was determined to get the better of the other.

Okei was grateful for the drums because two boys were really beating him without mercy. They asked him how he dared floor their best wrestlers. By the time the whole fight stopped blood was gushing down his nose, and both his feet felt like lead.

"This has been a very successful fight," said Obi Agiliga. "It has ended well . . . I mean the way we knew it would end. You have to stop punishing yourselves now. You all have to go home. We thank the girls for fanning the rumors and even taking part in fighting for their villages on this day. You can see for yourselves that you were all good wrestlers and fighters. And in all good fights, just like wars, nobody wins. You were all hurt and humiliated. I am sure you will always remember this day."

"What is he talking about?" asked Kwutelu of Josephine, as she tried to tie her headscarf properly.

"He said that we should be thanked for fanning the rumors. But did we fan the rumors, Kwutelu? Did the elders use us to organize this wrestling match?"

"But why?" asked Kwutelu.

"Just to keep the boys busy. They were getting on everybody's nerves a few months ago. I think we have been used. What actually started the quarrel between us and the Akpei Umu Biafra?" asked Josephine.

"That's the trouble, I can't even remember."

The two girls went back to their huts, very, very thoughtful.

Obi Agiliga and the other elders sat down to big kegs of palm-wine. "It has all gone well, has it not?" Obi Uwechue asked.

The others nodded and drank a toast to the elders of any land.

"My nephew told me this morning that we would not be needed. If we had not appeared there on time, those Akpei boys would have torn him into pieces. I am glad they have got the message—in a good war, nobody wins."

RESPONDING TO THE SELECTION

Your Response

1. Why do you think Kwutelu's personality changed after the accident?
2. If you were one of the young Igbuno people, how would you have felt when you discovered the elders' role in the wrestling match?

Recalling

3. In Chapter 9, what happens to the Igbuno girls when they go to the Eke Market in Akpei?
4. Why is Okei reluctant to consult his uncle before the wrestling match?

Interpreting

5. What do you learn about Okei's personality from the following comment? "But until now it had never occurred to [Okei] that he and his age-mates could make mistakes at all."
6. Do you think that if Obi Agiliga were Okei's natural father, Okei would have approached him more readily? Explain.

7. Okei and his age-mates refer to the wrestling match as a war. In what ways does the match resemble the war that he and his peers lived through?
8. Okei contradicts himself by calling the wrestling match "a war," on page 914, and "a friendly match," on page 921. How does Okei really view the match? Use passages from the novel to support your answer.
9. In what ways does Okei show that he is maturing in the second half of the novel? What causes him to "come of age"?
10. How does the wrestling match prove Obi Agiliga's claim that "in all good fights, just like wars, nobody wins"?

Applying

11. Describe a current event or an event from history that reflects the messages about war in the novel—"the innocent suffer" and "nobody wins."

ANALYZING LITERATURE

Analyzing Theme

Theme, the universal truth or message conveyed in a literary work, can be stated explicitly by the characters, or it can be implied. One of the main themes in *The Wrestling Match* is that "nobody wins" in a war. Obi Agiliga states this theme at the end of the novel. Another theme has to do with the conflicts that occur between generations.

1. How does Nduka touch on the theme of the relationship between generations when he urges Okei to approach Obi Agiliga? Do you think what Nduka says applies to other cultures as well? Explain.

2. Obi Agiliga claims that "nobody wins" in a fight or a war. In what sense, however, does everybody win as a result of the wrestling match?

CRITICAL THINKING AND READING

Exploring Dynamic Characters

In many works of literature there are **flat,** or static, **characters** who seem unaffected by the action in the plot. They change or grow very little by the time the novel comes to a close. By contrast, **dynamic characters** grow as a result of the conflicts and challenges that they face. In *The Wrestling Match,* we see two young people undergo dramatic changes as they come of age. Discuss the ways in which Kwutelu and Okei are dynamic characters. In your discussion, focus on the events that cause each character to grow, and describe how each changes.

THINKING AND WRITING

Responding to Themes

Imagine that Buchi Emecheta has asked to see your reactions to her novel *The Wrestling Match.* She is particularly interested in your responses to the themes in the novel. Write a thorough response to the novel and to the themes in the novel. Explain your responses in detail by drawing on specific information in the novel. In your response, you might also include any questions you might have about the novel. Once you have written a response you're comfortable with, share it with the class. In addition, explore possible answers to the questions each of you has about the novel.

LEARNING OPTIONS

1. **Performance.** In *The Wrestling Match,* the Igbuno villagers greet the wrestlers with praise-names. In a group of four or five people, think of praise-names for everyone in your group. The names should reflect something special about the individual. Then create a rap song, a poem, a piece of music, or even a dance that incorporates these praise-names. When your group is done, perform your work for the class.

2. **Community Connections.** What have you learned from *The Wrestling Match* that could apply to tensions between groups of people in your community? Write a letter to the editor of your local newspaper in which you draw on the themes in the novel to address community issues.

YOUR WRITING PROCESS

WRITING A BOOK INTRODUCTION

One of the novels in this unit provides a fascinating glimpse into the world of wrestling. Nonfiction books can also be useful sources of information about sports and games from around the world. Imagine that a publisher has asked you to write an introduction for such a book. How could you make your audience want to keep turning the pages, as with a good novel?

> **Focus**
>
> **Assignment:** Write an introduction to a book about a sport or game.
> **Purpose:** To describe the qualities needed to excel in the sport or game.
> **Audience:** Those interested in learning about the sport.

Prewriting

1. Choose and research your subject. To decide on a sport or game, look through the sports sections of newspapers and magazines, as well as in encyclopedias and histories of sports. Then use these resources to take notes about the rules of the sport, the abilities required, and the development of the game.

2. Observe the sport. If possible, watch the sport or game being played by attending an event or observing a game on television. Study pictures of players competing. Take notes on details you observe.

3. Explore your ideas. Using the notes you have gathered, explore the qualities a competitor needs to succeed in the sport you have selected. To help you generate and organize ideas, create a diagram.

Student Model

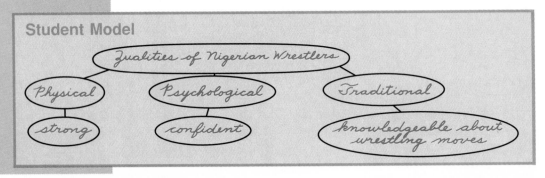

4. Consider your audience. Think about what your readers may already know about your subject. What new information would be most helpful for them to understand the sport you have chosen?

5. Find a focus. Study your notes. What generalization can you make about the qualities needed to excel in the sport you selected? If necessary, add details to your diagram to support the generalization you made.

Drafting

1. Write a strong beginning. How can you best capture your audience's interest from the start? One way is to use the generalization you made to announce your subject. This will help your readers to focus immediately on the most important aspects of your sport.

> ### Student Model
>
> In Nigeria wrestling is more than a sport—it is an art with a revered heritage. Wrestlers must not only be as psychologically perceptive as they are physically strong, but they must also never forget the traditions of their ancestors.

2. Use a consistent tone. Will you use a formal or informal tone in your introduction? Will you directly address your readers in a personal way? Decide whether you want to take a lively, humorous approach to your subject or a serious attitude; however, be consistent with your tone.

Revising and Editing

1. Consult with a peer editor. Read the draft of your introduction to a peer editor. Then see if you can improve your draft by asking your partner questions such as the following:
- Does my introduction arouse your interest in the sport enough so that you want to read the book?
- Does my introduction clearly describe the qualities needed to excel in the sport?
- Are there enough details about the rules and the history of the sport?
- Is my tone effective and consistent?

2. Connect ideas. Read over your work to see where you can make your writing flow more smoothly. Where might you link ideas by combining sentences or using transition words? Have you corrected sentence fragments?

Writer's Tip

Avoid sentence fragments. Except when used in a dialogue, sentence fragments tend to make writing choppy and difficult to follow because they break up the connections between ideas.

Options for Publishing

- Post your sports introduction on the bulletin board in the locker room or share it with your gym class.
- After you exchange introductions with classmates, comment on why you would or would not choose to read the entire book.
- Collect articles from newspapers and magazines about the sport you selected. Use your writing as an introduction to the collection of articles. Display your booklet in class.

Reviewing Your Writing Process

1. How did you gather information to help you write your introduction?

2. What revising strategy did you find worked best for this writing project? Explain.

YOUR WRITING PROCESS

WRITING A PERSUASIVE RECOMMENDATION

"I suppose I am a born novelist, for the things I imagine are more vital and vivid to me than the things I remember."

Ellen Glasgow

Were you able to picture in your mind each scene in the novels in this unit? What might the novels look like in movie versions? Imagine that you are a movie director who wants to persuade the head of a movie studio to make a film version of one of these novels. In a letter, how would you convince him or her that this novel will work as a film?

> **Focus**
>
> **Assignment:** Write a persuasive recommendation in the form of a letter.
> **Purpose:** To explain how a novel could be adapted as a film.
> **Audience:** The head of a film studio.

Prewriting

1. Review the novels. With a partner, discuss the novels you have read in terms of their visual potential as movies. Ask yourselves which novel has a conflict that would be most interesting to watch on the screen.

2. Outline the plot. The first question the head of a studio might ask is, "What is the novel about?" A summary of the plot can communicate key facts about the characters, settings, and theme of the story. Create a visual outline.

Student Model

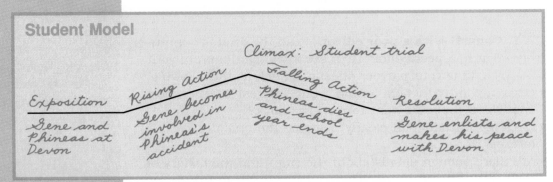

3. Write brief character sketches. Brainstorm with your partner to list characters' central personality traits.

4. Summarize the theme, setting, and point of view. Write brief summaries of the theme and settings for the story. From whose point of view will the story be told? Remember to note the reasons why you think the elements of the novel would contribute to making a good movie.

Drafting

1. Open with a persuasive note. Why do you and your partner feel this novel could be made into a successful film? Begin your letter with a persuasive comment that will hook the interest of the head of the film studio.

Student Model

Coming-of-age stories have frequently been made into compelling and successful films. *A Separate Peace* by John Knowles is a story about young men at a peaceful boarding school in the early 1940's who live with the threat of war. The conflicts that arise between characters in this dynamic novel would hold a film audience spellbound.

---

2. Use your diagram as a guide. Consider the limited time your reader may have to read your recommendation. To hold his or her attention, keep your letter short and to the point. Use your prewriting diagrams, lists, and notes selectively. Avoid mapping out every detail of your film.

3. Choose persuasive words. Use strong and precise language that you think will persuade your audience to accept your proposal. Choose adjectives and adverbs that vividly describe characters and events in the novel. Use exact nouns and active verbs to help the reader clearly visualize this story as a film.

Revising and Editing

1. Read your draft to a peer editor. After you have reviewed your draft, read it aloud to a partner and have him or her respond to the effectiveness of your letter. Does the beginning hook the interest of the reader? Are strong mental pictures created that help the reader visualize this story as a motion picture?

2. Check for organization and tone. Make a checklist to use as you revise your draft. Have you organized your material in the best way possible? Have you selected the strongest ideas from your prewriting notes? Is your language persuasive?

3. Hunt for errors. Proofread your letter carefully for errors in spelling, capitalization, and punctuation. Make sure that you have used the correct form for business letters.

Writer's Hint

Precise adjectives and adverbs as well as exact nouns and active verbs can help to create vivid mental pictures in your reader's mind. Use a thesaurus to help you find the most specific words to express your meaning.

Options for Publishing

• Read your letter aloud in class and have students vote on whether or not they would choose to adapt this novel for a film. Combine the letters into a booklet for each novel and make them available to all the students in your class.

• Use your letter to convince your teacher to let the class produce a video version of one of the scenes mentioned in your recommendation.

Review Your Writing Process

1. In your prewriting activities, how did you decide which novel could most effectively be adapted as a film?

2. What were the benefits and disadvantages of working with a partner?

HANDBOOK OF THE WRITING PROCESS
Lesson 1: Prewriting

The process of writing involves five major stages. In the *prewriting* stage, you plan the work to be done. In the *drafting* stage, you get your ideas down on paper. In the *revising* stage, you rework your written draft. In the *proofreading* stage, you check your final draft for errors in spelling and mechanics. Finally, in the *publishing* stage, you share your work with others. This lesson will explain the steps you should take during the prewriting stage.

STEP 1: ANALYZE THE SITUATION

Analysis is the process of dividing something into parts and then studying these parts to see what they are and how they are related. When you are given a writing assignment, begin by analyzing the following parts of the situation:

1. *Topic* (the subject you will be writing about): What, exactly, is this subject? Can you state it in a sentence? Is your subject too broad or too narrow?
2. *Purpose* (what you want the writing to accomplish): Is your purpose to tell a story? To describe? To explain? To persuade? To entertain?
3. *Audience* (the people for whom you are writing): What are the backgrounds of these people? Do they already know a great deal about your topic? Will you have to provide basic background information?
4. *Voice* (the way the writing will sound to the reader): What impressions do you want to make on your readers? What tone should your writing have? Should the writing be formal or informal? Should it be objective or subjective?
5. *Content* (the subject and all the information

provided about it): How much do you already know about your subject? What will you have to find out? Will you have to do some research? If so, what sources can you use? Can you use books? Magazines? Newspapers? Reference works? Interviews with other people? Your own memories and experiences?
6. *Form* (the shape that the writing will take, including its length and organization): What will the final piece of writing look like? How long will it be? Will it be written in one or more paragraphs? Will it have a distinct introduction, body, and conclusion? What method of organization will you use?

Asking questions such as these will help you to clarify the writing task. In the course of asking and answering these questions, you will have to make many decisions. These decisions will determine what your writing will be like and what steps you will have to take to produce it.

STEP 2: MAKE A PLAN

After analyzing the writing situation, you will probably find that some of your questions remain unanswered. For example, you might know what your topic, purpose, audience, voice, and form will be, but you might be unsure about your content. The next step in prewriting is to make a plan for answering your unanswered questions. For example, you might plan to do some research in your library to gather content information.

STEP 3: GATHER INFORMATION

There are many possible sources of information for use in writing. The following methods are useful for gathering the information you need:

1. *Freewriting:* Without stopping to punctuate or to think about spelling or form, write everything that comes to your mind as you think about your topic.
2. *Clustering:* Write your topic in the center of a sheet of blank paper. Then think about the topic and jot down other ideas that occur to you. Draw lines connecting these ideas to your topic. Then think about each of these ideas, write down new ideas, and connect them with lines. Continue until your paper is full.
3. *Questioning:* Make a list of *who, what, where, when, why,* and *how* questions related to your topic. Use your own knowledge or outside sources to answer these questions.
4. *Charting or listing:* Make lists of key ideas or concepts related to your topic. List the parts of your topic. If appropriate, make a chart of pros and cons, a timeline, a tree diagram, or some other type of chart of information related to your topic.
5. *Researching:* Check outside sources of information such as books, magazines, and reference works. Interview people who are knowledgeable about your topic.
6. *Analyzing:* Break your topic down into its parts, study these parts, and think about how they are related.

Each of these techniques can also be used to generate a topic idea.

STEP 4: ORGANIZE YOUR NOTES

After you have gathered the information you will use, organize this information in a logical way. Some common methods of organization include *chronological order, spatial order, degree order* (less to more or more to less), and *order of importance, value, utility,* or *familiarity.* Once you have organized your information, you may want to make a rough outline.

CASE STUDY: PREWRITING

Anthony's English teacher told the students to write descriptive paragraphs about their neighborhood or environment.

Anthony, a city-dweller, wanted to make the city his topic, but he wasn't sure about what to focus on. He tried clustering to come up with ideas.

As he worked, Anthony realized that by focusing on his own street, he was able to say something about the city as a whole. Then he was able to prepare the following plan:

- Topic: my street in the city
- Purpose: to describe and to inform
- Audience: the teacher and the class
- Voice: informal but positive; I want readers to like the street I describe
- Form: paragraph

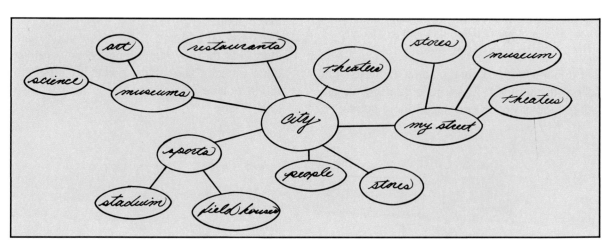

- Content: information on the things that are within walking distance of my apartment

Anthony decided to gather information in list form. He made his preliminary list in study hall. On his way home, he kept his eyes open and was able to add to his list as a result of his observations. Here is a portion of Anthony's list:

- Jade Pavilion Chinese restaurant

- small museum—1820 house

- all three- and four-story buildings

- people everywhere

- the Palace movie theater

- a college playhouse

- Yesteryear Antiques

- Sweaterville

- a video rental store

- Pop's Pop-In (convenience store)

- parking on just one side

- Gino's Pizza

- the park around the corner

When Anthony looked over his list, he realized that he had far too much information for a paragraph. He decided to focus on this main idea:

Living in the city is very convenient. Within a few blocks of my house, I can find almost anything I could ever need or want.

Anthony crossed out the items on his list that did not fit this idea. Then he organized his remaining ideas under three supporting points:

1. Shops for any need
2. Entertainment of every type
3. Food for any taste

Anthony grouped his details under these points and ended up with an outline that he could use as he began to write.

ACTIVITIES AND ASSIGNMENTS

A. Answer the following questions about the case study:
1. For what purpose did Anthony use clustering? For what purpose did he make a list?
2. Which items on Anthony's list did he probably cross out as he worked on step 3?
3. Which items on his list did he include under each of his planned supporting points?
    B. Do prewriting for a paragraph of your own. Follow these steps:
1. Choose one of the following topics or one of your own:

    your neighborhood   sports
    student concerns   music
2. Prepare a planning chart. Take notes about the topic, purpose, audience, voice, form, and content of your paragraph.
3. Use a prewriting technique—freewriting, clustering, questioning, making a list or chart, using outside sources, or outlining—to narrow your topic to a manageable size and to gather information.
4. Organize your notes. Decide on your main idea, find the key supporting points, and list details under supporting points to create a rough outline. Save your notes for use in a later lesson.

Lesson 2: Drafting and Revising

WRITING A DRAFT

Once you have found a topic, taken notes, and organized them, you are ready to write a preliminary version, or *draft,* of your paper. Keep the following points in mind as you draft a piece of writing:

1. Write the draft in a way that feels comfortable to you. Some writers like to dash off a draft as fast as possible, to keep their pens going as fast as their ideas flow. Others prefer to draft more slowly, considering how each idea should be presented and doing some revision as they go. Whichever way works best for you is the method you should use. You may find that the fast method works well in some writing situations, whereas the slow method works better in other situations.

2. Do not aim for perfection in the draft. If you work fast, you won't have time to worry; but even if you work slowly, do not get too caught up in any section. Move on; get something on paper. Some writers use codes: They underline words or sections they want to work on further, or put a small question mark above words they're not sure how to spell. These techniques are fine because they do not unduly interrupt the flow of writing.

3. Keep your notes beside you as you write, and keep your purpose and audience in mind. Doing so will guide you as you move from idea to idea.

4. As you draft, feel free to change your original plan. Remember that writing is a form of thinking. If you think of new ideas, add them. If you discover that some ideas in your rough outline don't seem to work after all, eliminate them.

5. If you discover a better approach as you are writing, feel free to start a new draft at any time. Some writers discard many drafts before they are happy with one. If the piece you are working on just doesn't seem right, start again.

REVISING YOUR DRAFT

Once you have completed your draft, you can begin revising it. This is the stage during which you work on your draft to make it as good as possible. If time permits, put your draft aside for a day before you revise; doing so will allow you to bring a fresh eye to your work.

Keep in mind that although some drafts may need very little revision, others may require major reworking.

Use the Checklist for Revision on page 938 as you revise your work.

The symbols in the following chart can be helpful when revising a piece of writing:

	EDITORIAL SYMBOLS	
Symbol	Meaning	Example
⟳	move text	˅screams suddenly
℘ℳ —	delete	the silent, quiet room
∧	insert	a lovely yellow dress
⌢ ⌣	close up; no space	sun shine
⊙	insert period	the end I knew
⋏	insert comma	left but they
˅	add apostrophe	Rons contribution
˅ ˅	add quotation marks	"Chee's Daughter"
∼	transpose	to quietly leave
¶	begin paragraph	trees. Next we
/	make lower case	the Main Street in the town
≡	capitalize	on main street

CHECKLIST FOR REVISION

Topic and Purpose
- ☐ Is my main idea clear?
- ☐ Does the writing achieve its purpose?

Content and Development
- ☐ Have I developed the main idea completely?
- ☐ Have I provided examples or details that support the statements I have made?
- ☐ Are my sources of information unbiased, up-to-date, and authoritative?
- ☐ Have I avoided including unnecessary or unrelated ideas?
- ☐ If I have used quotations, are these quotations verbatim, or word-for-word?

Form
- ☐ Have I following a logical method of organization?
- ☐ Have I used transitions to make the connections between ideas clear?
- ☐ Does the writing have a clear introduction, body, and conclusion?

Audience
- ☐ Will my audience understand what I have said?
- ☐ Will my audience find the writing interesting?
- ☐ Will my audience respond in the way I have intended?

Voice and Word Choice
- ☐ Does the writing convey the impression I have intended it to convey?
- ☐ Is my language appropriate?
- ☐ Have I avoided vague, undefined terms?
- ☐ Have I used vivid, specific nouns, verbs, and adjectives?
- ☐ Have I avoided jargon?
- ☐ Have I avoided clichés, slang, euphemisms, and gobbledygook except for humorous effect?

CASE STUDY: DRAFTING AND REVISING

Anthony kept his notes from the previous lesson next to him as he began drafting his paragraph. Then, as he worked on his draft, he used the Checklist for Revision shown on the left. Here is Anthony's revised draft:

> *Life at 1302 Lincoln Street*
> ~~Why where I live,~~ is very convenient.
> Whatever I need to buy is very close. Just
> next door is Pops Pop-In where I can get
> *paper and pens.* *a new sweater or a gift,*
> snacks and ~~supplies.~~ If I need ~~something,~~
> there's two shops within a block of my apartment. ~~I can get antiques at Yesteryear.~~ I can
> *find*
> ~~get~~ records and tapes just down the street at
> *whenever I want entertainment, that's close by, too.*
> Rockys music land. The Theater around the
> *prefer*
> corner has first-run movies, if I ~~want to get~~ a
> home movie there's a video store downstairs.
> Three or four times a year the local colledge
> puts on plays at there play house down the
> street. The minipark in the next block has a
> *As for food,*
> basketball court and a bocche court. I can
> walk to almost anything my heart desires ~~for as~~
> ~~food.~~ The Jade Pavilion chinese restaurant,
> Gino's Pizza, Hamburger Heaven, the Deli
> *All of this is within two blocks of*
> Delight. ~~I call that convenient.~~ *my apartment. Now that's what I call convenient*

ACTIVITIES AND ASSIGNMENTS

A. Answer the following questions about Anthony's draft:

1. Which sentence is Anthony's topic sentence? Why did he change the wording of this sentence?
2. What sentence did Anthony eliminate? Why did he do so?

3. What is the purpose of the sentence Anthony added between sentences 6 and 7?
4. Why did Anthony change the wording in the third-to-last sentence?
5. Why did Anthony change his last sentence?
6. In which sentences did Anthony replace general words with specific words?

B. Use the notes you prepared in the previous lesson to draft and revise a paragraph. Follow these steps:

1. If you have not already done so, prepare a rough outline. Indicate your main idea, group your notes into several subtopics, and list your details under each subtopic.
2. Write an introductory, or topic, sentence that states your main idea.
3. Keep your notes next to you as you draft the body of your paragraph.
4. Draft a conclusion that ties your ideas together.
5. Use the checklist in this lesson to revise your paragraph. Work until you can answer "yes" to each question. Use editorial symbols to indicate changes.

Lesson 3: Proofreading and Publishing

PROOFREADING

After you have revised your draft, you must proofread it to eliminate errors. Use the Checklist for Proofreading as you work:

CHECKLIST FOR PROOFREADING
Grammar and Usage ☐ Are all my sentences complete? That is, have I avoided sentence fragments? ☐ Do all my sentences express just one complete thought? That is, have I avoided run-on sentences? ☐ Do my verbs agree with their subjects? ☐ Have I used all the words in my paper correctly? Am I sure the meaning and connotation of each word fits the writing? ☐ Does each pronoun clearly refer to something? ☐ Have I used adjectives and adverbs correctly? *Spelling* ☐ Is every word correctly spelled? ☐ Have I double-checked the spelling of proper nouns? *Punctuation* ☐ Does each sentence end with a punctuation mark? ☐ Have I used commas, semicolons, colons, hyphens, dashes, parentheses, quotation marks, and apostrophes correctly? *Capitalization* ☐ Have I eliminated unnecessary capital letters? ☐ Have I correctly capitalized all words that need capital letters?

If your answer to any of these questions is "no," make the necessary corrections on your paper. Consult a dictionary, writing textbook, or handbook of style as necessary.

When you are satisfied with the grammar and mechanics of your paper, neatly recopy or type it. Use correct manuscript form:
1. Indent the first line(s) of the paragraph(s).
2. Write your name and the page number in the top right corner of each page.
3. If you type, double-space the manuscript.

Finally, proofread the final copy of your paper one more time, checking to make sure that it is free of errors.

PROOFREADING AND PUBLISHING

Some writing, such as diaries or journals, is intended to be kept private; other writing should be shared. You will, of course, submit most writing you do in school to your teachers. There are, however, other ways to publish it. Here are a few ideas:
1. Read your work to your family or give it to family members to read.
2. Make a second copy of your work and send it to a relative or friend.
3. Trade papers with a friend and read each other's writing.
4. Read your paper aloud in class.
5. Share your work with a small group of classmates.
6. Display your paper in your classroom.
7. Recast your ideas in the form of a letter, and send it to an appropriate recipient.
8. Submit your work to your school newspaper or to your school literary magazine.
9. Work with your classmates to put together a class magazine.
10. Submit your writing to a local newspaper or newsletter.
11. Enter your writing in a literary contest for student writers.
12. Submit your writing to a magazine that publishes work by young writers.

13. Save your writing in a folder and bind appropriate pieces together to create your own book.

CASE STUDY: PROOFREADING AND PUBLISHING

After Anthony revised his draft for content, form, and word choice, he used the Checklist for Proofreading in this lesson to find and correct errors in his paragraph. On the right is Anthony's paragraph with his corrections marked.

Anthony made two clean final copies of his paragraph and proofread them one last time. One copy he submitted in class; the other he sent to a cousin with whom he has a running argument: Anthony claims city life is best, whereas Ricky prefers suburban or country life.

ACTIVITIES AND ASSIGNMENTS

A. Answer the following questions about the case study in this lesson:
1. What run-on sentence did Anthony correct? How did he correct it?
2. What sentence fragment did Anthony find and correct? How did he correct it?
3. What errors in subject-verb agreement did Anthony correct?
4. What spelling errors did Anthony correct?
5. What punctuation errors did Anthony correct?
6. What errors in capitalization did Anthony correct?

B. Proofread and publish the paragraph you revised in the previous lesson. Follow these steps:
1. Use the Checklist for Proofreading as you work on your paragraph. Evaluate and correct your grammar and usage, spelling, punctuation, and capitalization. Consult reference books as necessary.

Life at 1302 Lincoln Street is very convenient. Whatever I need to buy is very close. Just next door is Pop's Pop-In where I can get snacks and soda, paper and pens. If I need a new sweater or a gift, there's *are* two shops within a block of my apartment. Records and tapes I can find just down the street at Rocky's music land. The *T*heater around the corner has first-run movies, *but* if I prefer a home movie there's a video store downstairs. Three or four times a year the local ~~colledge~~ *college* puts on plays at its play house down the street. The minipark in the next block has a basketball court and a ~~bocche~~ *bocce* court. As for food, I can walk to almost anything my heart desires. *T*he Jade Pavilion *c*hinese restaurant, Gino's Pizza, Hamburger Heaven, the Deli Delight. All of these are within two blocks of my apartment—now that's what I'd call a convenient neighborhood.

2. Write or type a clean final copy of your paragraph. Proofread this copy to be sure you have not introduced any new errors. Make any corrections very neatly.
3. Share your paragraph with a friend before you submit it in class.

HANDBOOK OF GRAMMAR AND REVISING STRATEGIES

Strategies for Revising Problems in Grammar and Usage 943

This section offers practical tips for revising your writing. Each topic includes an overall GUIDE FOR REVISING and one or more revising strategies. Strategies are illustrated by a first draft, a suggested revision, and sometimes a model sentence from a professional writer featured in *Prentice Hall Literature, Platinum.* The GUIDES FOR REVISING address the following issues:

Problems of Sentence Structure 943
■ **Run-on Sentences**
■ **Fragments**
■ **Illogical Combination of Subject and Predicate**

Problems of Clarity and Coherence 945
■ **Effective Transition**
■ **Vivid Modifiers**
■ **Incomplete and Illogical Comparisons**
■ **Pronoun-Antecedent Agreement**
■ **Dangling Modifiers**
■ **Misplaced Modifiers**

Problems of Consistency 950
■ **Subject-Verb Agreement**
■ **Confusion of Adjectives and Adverbs**
■ **Inconsistencies in Verb Tense**

Problems With Incorrect Words or Phrases 954
■ **Nonstandard Verb Forms**
■ **Nonstandard Pronoun Cases**
■ **Wrong Words or Phrases**
■ **Double Negatives**

Problems of Readability 956
■ **Sentence Variety**
■ **Stringy Sentences**
■ **Overuse of Common Words**

Problems of Conciseness 958
■ **Wordy Phrases**
■ **Redundancy**
■ **Unnecessary Intensifiers**

Problems of Appropriateness 959
■ **Inappropriate Diction**
■ **Clichés**

Summary of Grammar 961
Summary of Capitalization and Punctuation 964
Glossary of Common Usage 967

STRATEGIES FOR REVISING PROBLEMS IN GRAMMAR AND STANDARD USAGE
Problems of Sentence Structure

■ Run-on Sentences

GUIDE FOR REVISING: A run-on sentence results when no punctuation or coordinating conjunction separates two or more independent clauses. A run-on sentence also occurs when only a comma is used to join two or more independent clauses.

Strategy 1:	**Form two sentences by using a period to separate independent clauses.**
First Draft	Lorraine Hansberry was one of America's most gifted black writers her play *A Raisin in the Sun* is generally regarded as her finest work.
Revision	Lorraine Hansberry was one of America's most gifted black writers . Her play *A Raisin in the Sun* is generally regarded as her finest work.
Model From Literature	The pawnshop man let her take the violin at a reduced price. Marian never became very good on the violin. —*Langston Hughes, "Marian Anderson: Famous Concert Singer," p. 427*

Strategy 2:	**Use a semicolon to separate independent clauses.**
First Draft	Karen Blixen, who is also known as Isak Dinesen, published her reminiscences of life in Kenya in *Out of Africa* , this work was recently adapted into a very successful film with Meryl Streep and Robert Redford.
Revision	Karen Blixen, who is also known as Isak Dinesen, published her reminiscences of life in Kenya in *Out of Africa* ; this work was recently adapted into a very successful film with Meryl Streep and Robert Redford.
Model From Literature	Something was burning all right ; perhaps it was Mr. Prothero, who always slept there after midday dinner with a newspaper over his face. —*Dylan Thomas, "A Child's Christmas in Wales," p. 434*

Strategy 3:	**Join the sentences with a comma and a coordinating conjunction (*and, but, or, for, yet, so*).**
First Draft	At first Caesar yields to Calpurnia's pleas he orders Decius to inform the senators that he will not come to the Senate House that day.

Revision	At first Caesar yields to Calpurnia's pleas, and he orders Decius to inform the senators that he will not come to the Senate House that day.
Model From Literature	Probably no one man should have as many dogs in his life as I have had, but there was more pleasure than distress in them for me except in the case of an Airedale named Muggs. —*James Thurber, "The Dog That Bit People," p. 405*

Strategy 4: **Join the sentences with a semicolon and a conjunctive adverb.**

First Draft	In Jack Finney's story, Tom climbs out on the ledge to retrieve the sheet of paper with his notes the task proves to be more challenging than he had anticipated.
Revision	In Jack Finney's story, Tom climbs out on the ledge to retrieve the sheet of paper with his notes; however, the task proves to be more challenging than he had anticipated.
Model From Literature	Leiningen had been wrong when he supposed that the enemy would first have to fill the ditch with their bodies before they could cross; instead, they merely needed to act as stepping-stones, as they swam and sank, to the hordes ever pressing onwards from behind. —*Carl Stephenson, "Leiningen Versus the Ants," p. 47*

Strategy 5: **Make one clause subordinate by adding a subordinating conjunction.**

First Draft	Sergeant Major Morris mentions the monkey's paw Mr. White is curious to know more about it.
Revision	When Sergeant Major Morris mentions the monkey's paw, Mr. White is curious to know more about it.
Model From Literature	Even his wife's face seemed changed as he entered the room. —*W. W. Jacobs, "The Monkey's Paw," p. 38*

■ Fragments

GUIDE FOR REVISING: A sentence fragment is an incomplete sentence. Although a fragment begins with a capital letter and ends with a period, it lacks a subject or a verb and does not express a complete thought.

Strategy: **If possible, omit the subordinating conjunction, or connect the fragment to an independent clause.**

First Draft	Because Antigone respects the laws of the gods. She feels bound to bury her brother Polyneices. No matter how disloyal he has been to the city.

Revision	Because Antigone respects the laws of the gods, she feels bound to bury her brother Polyneices, no matter how disloyal he has been to the city.
Model From Literature	He could not kneel here hesitating indefinitely till he lost all courage to act, . . .
	—*Jack Finney, "Contents of the Dead Man's Pocket," p. 28*

■ Illogical Combination of Subject and Predicate

GUIDE FOR REVISING: The predicate of a sentence must be logically related to its subject.

Strategy 1:	**Rewrite the sentence so that the subject and predicate are logically related and compatible in meaning.**
First Draft	In Elizabeth Bishop's poem, the speaker has admiration of the fish that she lets it go.
Revision	In Elizabeth Bishop's poem, the speaker admires the fish so much that she lets it go.
Model From Literature	"The doctors agree in ordering me complete rest, an absence of mental excitement, and avoidance of anything in the nature of violent physical exercise," announced Framton, who labored under the tolerably widespread delusion that total strangers and chance acquaintances are hungry for the least detail of one's ailments and infirmities, their cause and cure.
	—*Saki, "The Open Window," p. 178*

Strategy 2:	**Change an awkward adverb clause to a noun or a noun phrase to make the subject and predicate compatible.**
First Draft	A myth is when a story tells about the actions of gods or heroes or the causes of natural phenomena.
Revision	A myth is a story about the actions of gods or heroes or the causes of natural phenomena.
Model From Literature	Weakness was what got him in the end.
	—*Anne Tyler, "With All Flags Flying," p. 229*

Problems of Clarity and Coherence

■ Effective Transitions

GUIDE FOR REVISING: Transitions are words or phrases that help the reader by signaling connections between words, sentences, and even paragraphs.

Strategy 1:	**Use transitions to show logical relationships. Transitions may be used to introduce another item in a series, an illustration or an example, a result or a cause, a restatement, a conclusion or a summary, or an opposing point.**
First Draft	Longfellow used traditional forms to handle universal themes; he became America's most popular poet during the nineteenth century.
Revision	Longfellow used traditional forms to handle universal themes; as a result, he became America's most popular poet during the nineteenth century.
Model From Literature	That is all of my story, for then I knew he was a man—I knew then that they had been men, neither gods nor demons. —*Stephen Vincent Benét, "By the Waters of Babylon," p. 144*

Strategy 2:	**Use transitions to indicate temporal relationships, such as sequence or progression in time. Transitions may be used to indicate frequency, duration, a particular time, the beginning, the middle, the end, and beyond.**
First Draft	Framton Nuttel describes his symptoms, and Mrs. Sappleton's attention wanders.
Revision	While Framton Nuttel describes his symptoms at some length, Mrs. Sappleton's attention wanders.
Model From Literature	Early in the month we had two days of light, steady rain which aroused a final fullness everywhere. —*John Knowles, A Separate Peace, p. 785*

Strategy 3:	**Use transitions to indicate spatial relationships. Transitions may be used to indicate closeness, distance, and direction.**
First Draft	The knight tells the questioner that "la belle dame sans merci" enchanted him.
Revision	Midway through Keats's poem, the knight tells the questioner that "la belle dame sans merci" enchanted him in her grotto.
Model From Literature	Next door, behind the hemlock hedge, another ample dwelling stood, suggesting in its style an Italian villa. —*Van Wyck Brooks, "Emily Dickinson," p. 415*

■ Vivid Modifiers

GUIDE FOR REVISING: Modifiers such as adjectives, adverbs, and prepositional phrases describe or limit subjects, verbs, objects, or other modifiers. Modifiers should be as vivid and specific as possible.

Strategy 1:	Make sure that you exchange vague and abstract modifiers for specific and concrete modifiers.
First Draft	Lewis Thomas has become well known for his easy-to-read, somewhat funny essays on science and medicine.
Revision	Lewis Thomas has become well known for his lucid, whimsically humorous essays on science and medicine.
Model From Literature	Chet released from his trumpet the opening, lifting, barbaric call of a bullfight, and the circle of boys broke wildly over Brinker. —*John Knowles*, A Separate Peace, *p. 831*

Strategy 2:	Try to use fresh, original modifiers instead of hackneyed, trite ones.
First Draft	Creon's ironclad edict confronts Antigone with a heart-rending choice.
Revision	Creon's stringent edict confronts Antigone with a lamentable choice.
Model From Literature	Would have to court Coquettish death, whose impudent and strange Possessive arms and beauty (of a sort) Can make a hard man hesitate—and change. —*Gwendolyn Brooks*, "The Sonnet-Ballad," *p. 582*

■ Incomplete and Illogical Comparisons

GUIDE FOR REVISING: When something is omitted from a comparison or only implied, the comparison may be incomplete and illogical.

Strategy 1:	Be sure that a comparison contains only items of a similar kind.
First Draft	Vickie thought that Bill's report on irony in *Julius Caesar* was more comprehensive than Mike.
Revision	Vickie thought that Bill's report on irony in *Julius Caesar* was more comprehensive than Mike's.
Model From Literature	"I think that was better than Finny's," said Elwin, . . . —*John Knowles*, A Separate Peace, *p. 762*

Strategy 2:	Be sure to include the words *other* or *else* in comparisons that compare one of a group with the rest of the group.
First Draft	After he had researched his massive biography of Lincoln, Carl Sandburg probably knew more about the sixteenth president than anyone in America did.

Revision	After he had researched his massive biography of Lincoln, Carl Sandburg probably knew more about the sixteenth president than anyone else in America did.
Model From Literature	Anyway, they were more indulgent toward us than at any other time; . . .—*John Knowles*, A Separate Peace, *p. 767*

Strategy 3:	Check to see if the words *better, less, more,* and *worse* and words formed with the suffix *-er* signal the need for a fully stated comparison; if so, use *than* and explain the comparison completely.
First Draft	By the end of the two orations in Act III, the people clearly feel that Antony has been more persuasive.
Revision	By the end of the two orations in Act III, the people clearly feel that Antony has been more persuasive than Brutus.
Models From Literature	On some days it will undoubtedly be better than on others ; . . . —*Aaron Copland*, "The Creative Process in Music," *pp. 515– 516*

"Nobody at Devon has ever been surer of graduating than you are. "   —*John Knowles*, A Separate Peace, *p. 752* |

■ Revising for Pronoun-Antecedent Agreement

GUIDE FOR REVISING: A personal pronoun must agree with its antecedent in number (singular or plural), person (first, second, or third), and gender (masculine, feminine, or neuter).

Strategy 1:	When you use a pronoun to stand for a noun that appears somewhere else in the sentence, check to see that it agrees in number (singular or plural) with that noun.
First Draft	From Mary Cassatt's beginnings as an art student, they were determined to follow the highest standards.
Revision	From Mary Cassatt's beginnings as an art student, she was determined to follow the highest standards.
Model From Literature	Black skimmers flew along the ocean's edge silhouetted against the dull, metallic gleam, or they went flitting above the sand like large, dimly seen moths. —*Rachel Carson*, "The Marginal World," *p. 529*

Strategy 2:	(a) When you use a pronoun to stand for two or more singular nouns joined by *or* or *nor,* make sure it is singular.
First Draft	Viswamithra reminds Rama that neither Vishnu nor Indra hesitated to use their power.

Revision	Viswamithra reminds Rama that neither Vishnu nor Indra hesitated to use his power.

(b) When you use a pronoun to stand for two or more nouns joined by *and*, make sure it is plural.

First Draft	In *A Separate Peace*, Gene and Finny sometimes cannot face up to the conflicts below the surface of his friendship.
Revision	In *A Separate Peace*, Gene and Finny sometimes cannot face up to the conflicts below the surface of their friendship.
Model From Literature	In *The Family*, the mother and child exist in positions of unease; the strong diagonals created by their postures of opposition give the pictures their tense strength, a strength that renders sentimental sweetness impossible.

—Mary Gordon, "Mary Cassatt," p. 500

Strategy 3:	**When you use a personal pronoun to stand for a singular indefinite pronoun, make sure it is also singular.**
First Draft	In the next scene, Cassius and Brutus meet in Brutus' tent; each has their reasons for angrily reproaching the other.
Revision	In the next scene, Cassius and Brutus meet in Brutus' tent; each has his reasons for angrily reproaching the other.
Model From Literature	And one by one dropped the revelers in the blood-bedewed halls of their revel, and died each in the despairing posture of his fall.

—Edgar Allan Poe, "The Masque of the Red Death," p. 172

Strategy 4:	**Do not use a pronoun to stand for a noun unless it is obvious which noun is its antecedent.**
First Draft	Both Brutus and Antony were eloquent, but I thought he was more so.
Revision	Both Brutus and Antony were eloquent, but I thought Antony was more so.
Model From Literature	Like all old, good schools, Devon did not stand isolated behind walls and gates but emerged naturally from the town which had produced it. —*John Knowles, A Separate Peace, p. 758*

■ Dangling Modifiers

GUIDE FOR REVISING: A prepositional phrase or a participial phrase should clearly modify some word in the sentence in which it appears. If there is no word in the sentence that the modifier can logically modify, it is called a dangling modifier or dangler.

Strategy 1:	**Reword the main part of the sentence to include a word that the dangler can modify.**
First Draft	Sitting opposite Uncle Hiram and Mae, the food at dinner was good.
Revision	Sitting opposite Uncle Hiram and Mae, Chig and his father thought that the food at dinner was good.
Model From Literature	Half squatting now, he dropped his left hand to the next indentation and then slowly reached with his right hand toward the paper between his feet. —*Jack Finney, "Contents of the Dead Man's Pocket," p. 21*

Strategy 2:	**Reword the dangling modifier as a subordinate clause. Choose a subordinator that reflects the relationship of the main idea in the modifier to the main idea of the sentence.**
First Draft	Letting go of the wheel, Leiningen's sense was of being coated from head to foot with a layer of ants.
Revision	After he had let go of the wheel, Leiningen realized that he was coated from head to foot with a layer of ants.
Model From Literature	At the age of three he still crawled along on all-fours while children of the same age were already walking. —*Sundiata, p. 725*

■ Misplaced Modifiers

GUIDE FOR REVISING: A misplaced modifier appears to modify the wrong word in a sentence.

Strategy:	**Move the modifying word, phrase, or clause closer to the word it should logically modify.**
First Draft	Chee decided that he must leave Little Canyon during the days that he herded sheep there.
Revision	During the days that he herded sheep there, Chee decided that he must leave Little Canyon.
Model From Literature	Unconscious of his wife's shriek, the old man smiled faintly, put out his hands like a sightless man, and dropped, a senseless heap, to the floor. —*W. W. Jacobs, "The Monkey's Paw," p. 37*

Problems of Consistency

■ Subject-Verb Agreement

GUIDE FOR REVISING: A verb must agree in number with its subject. A singular subject requires a singular verb, and a plural subject requires a plural verb.

Strategy 1:	**Check to see that if the subject is singular (it names only one thing), then the verb must also be singular. If the subject is plural (it names two or more things), then the verb must be plural.**
First Draft	Barry assure his father of his strength.
Revision	Barry assures his father of his strength.
Model From Literature	The second chamber was purple in its ornaments and tapestries, and here the panes were purple. —*Edgar Allan Poe, "The Masque of the Red Death," p. 168*

Strategy 2:	**Use a singular verb with a collective noun that represents a single group or collection of people or things.**
First Draft	The group plot to assassinate Julius Caesar on the Ides of March.
Revision	The group plots to assassinate Julius Caesar on the Ides of March.
Model From Literature	"The crew waits for no man. —*John Knowles,* A Separate Peace, *p. 799*

Strategy 3:	**Use a plural verb with two singular subjects joined by *and*.**
First Draft	Hyperbole and personification is figures of speech.
Revision	Hyperbole and personification are figures of speech.
Model From Literature	Both Chig's brother and sister, Peter and Connie, were packing for camp and besides were too young for such an affair.—*William Melvin Kelley, "A Visit to Grandmother," p. 69*

Strategy 4:	**Make sure that when a singular subject and a plural subject are joined by *or, either-or,* or *neither-nor,* the verb agrees in number with the subject closer to it.**
First Draft	Neither the myths about Rama nor the legend of King Arthur were familiar to me.
Revision	Neither the myths about Rama nor the legend of King Arthur was familiar to me.

Strategy 5:	**Be aware that in sentences in which the subject comes after the verb, the subject and verb must agree in number.**
First Draft	In *A Separate Peace*, there is several characters, objects, and events with symbolic meanings.

Revision	In *A Separate Peace,* there are several characters, objects, and events with symbolic meanings.
Model From Literature	There are also two other important ways in which the composer can add to his original material. —*Aaron Copland, "The Creative Process in Music," p. 520*

Strategy 6:	**Make sure that when a word group that includes one or more nouns comes between the subject and the verb, the verb agrees with its subject and not with a noun in the word group.**
First Draft	According to N. Scott Momaday, the houses on the plain is like sentinels.
Revision	According to N. Scott Momaday, the houses on the plain are like sentinels.
Model From Literature	One of the first things most people want to hear discussed in relation to composing is the question of inspiration. —*Aaron Copland, "The Creative Process in Music," p. 515*

■ Confusion of Adjectives and Adverbs

GUIDE FOR REVISING: Adjectives modify nouns and pronouns. Adverbs modify verbs, adjectives, or other adverbs; they may also modify phrases and clauses.

Strategy 1:	**Use an adjective to modify a noun or a pronoun.**
First Draft	At first the crowd reacts with naturally curiosity.
Revision	At first the crowd reacts with natural curiosity.
Model From Literature	The white mares of the moon rush along the sky Beating their golden hoofs upon the glass Heavens; . . . —*Amy Lowell, "Night Clouds," p. 612*

Strategy 2:	**Use an adverb to modify a verb, an adjective, or another adverb.**
First Draft	Mother thought that Muggs was sorry immediate.
Revision	Mother thought that Muggs was sorry immediately.
Model From Literature	Through planting time Chee worked zealously and tirelessly. —*Juanita Platero and Siyowin Miller, "Chee's Daughter," p. 84*

Strategy 3:	**Change an adverb to its adjective form when it is used as a subject complement after a sensory verb or the verb *to be*.**
First Draft	Annie Dillard says that after the hurricane the air smelled damply and acridly, like fuel oil.

Revision	Annie Dillard says that after the hurricane the air smelled damp and acrid, like fuel oil.
Model From Literature	The lions were sad and ugly and my panther was asleep. —*Julio Cortázar, "Axolotl," p. 107*

Strategy 4:	**Make sure that you make the correct use of troublesome adjective and adverb pairs such as *bad/badly* and *good/well*.**
First Draft	Lewis Thomas shows entertainingly in his essay that badly punctuation leads to confusion.
Revision	Lewis Thomas shows entertainingly in his essay that bad punctuation leads to confusion.
Models From Literature	"It is not as bad as it might be. It is not as though we are left with nothing." —*Juanita Platero and Siyowin Miller, "Chee's Daughter," p. 79* The visitor nodded in assent. "Badly hurt," he said quietly, "but he is not in any pain." —*W. W. Jacobs, "The Monkey's Paw," p. 36*
First Draft	Lorraine Hansberry must have felt well when she learned that the woman she had met in Maine lived to enjoy another summer.
Revision	Lorraine Hansberry must have felt good when she learned that the woman she had met in Maine lived to enjoy another summer.
Models From Literature	The hot coffee was good. It was not a fancy Colombian, aromatic blend, but it was so good! —*Darryl Babe Wilson, "Diamond Island: Alcatraz," p. 99* Perhaps the school wasn't as well kept up in those days; perhaps varnish, along with everything else, had gone to war. —*John Knowles,* A Separate Peace, *p. 757*

■ **Inconsistencies in Verb Tense**

GUIDE FOR REVISING: Verb tenses should not shift unnecessarily from sentence to sentence or within a single sentence.

Strategy 1:	**Make certain that the main verbs in a single sentence or in a group of sentences are in the same tense.**
First Draft	Doris Lessing left school at fifteen, worked at a variety of jobs in South Africa, and moved to England in 1949. The following year she publishes her first novel.

Revision	Doris Lessing left school at fifteen, worked at a variety of jobs in South Africa, and moved to England in 1949. The following year she published her first novel.
Model From Literature	He put on his goggles, fitted them tight, tested the vacuum. —Doris Lessing, "Through the Tunnel," p. 152

Strategy 2:	**In sentences describing two actions that occurred at different times in the past, the past perfect tense is used for the earlier action.**
First Draft	After his mother settled herself on the beach, Jerry descended the steep path to the bay.
Revision	After his mother had settled herself on the beach, Jerry descended the steep path to the bay.
Model From Literature	But Raghu soon moved away. There wasn't a sound once his footsteps had gone around the garage and disappeared. —Anita Desai, "Games at Twilight," p. 8

Problems With Incorrect Words or Phrases

■ Nonstandard Verb Forms

GUIDE FOR REVISING: A number of irregular verbs form their past tenses and past participles with changes in spelling or word form.

Strategy:	**Use the correct form when writing in the past tense.**
First Draft	I seen the movie *A Separate Peace* before I read the novel.
Revision	I saw the movie *A Separate Peace* before I read the novel.

■ Nonstandard Pronoun Cases

GUIDE FOR REVISING: When a pronoun is either the subject of a sentence or a predicate nominative, be sure to use the nominative case. Use the objective case when a pronoun is a direct object, an indirect object, or the object of a preposition.

Strategy 1:	**Take special care to identify the case of a pronoun correctly when the pronoun is part of a compound construction. You will often find it helpful to reword the sentence mentally.**
First Draft	The first students to submit entries in the essay contest were Brian and me.
Revision	The first students to submit entries in the essay contest were Brian and I. [Could be reworded: Brian and I were the first students to submit entries in the essay contest.]

Model From Literature	When his wife learnt of his death, she and her sons stormed in, roaring revenge on the saint. —*R. K. Narayan, the* Ramayana, *p. 721*

Strategy 2:	**Pronouns in the possessive case show possession before nouns. The possessive case is also regularly used when a pronoun precedes a gerund.**
First Draft	He jouncing the tree limb later caused Gene much guilt and anxiety.
Revision	His jouncing the tree limb later caused Gene much guilt and anxiety.
Model From Literature	"Out through that window, three years ago to a day, her husband and her two young brothers went off for their day's shooting." —*Saki, "The Open Window," p. 178*

■ Wrong Words or Phrases

GUIDE FOR REVISING: Words or phrases that are suitable in one context may be inappropriate in another.

Strategy 1:	**Check whether you have mistaken one word for another because they sound alike, are spelled similarly, or are easily confused.**
First Draft	From Chee's actions we can imply that the power of love is the theme of the story.
Revision	From Chee's actions we can infer that the power of love is the theme of the story.
Model From Literature	After the service ended we set out seven hundred strong, the regular winter throng of the Devon School, . . . —*John Knowles,* A Separate Peace, *p. 797*

Strategy 2:	**Make sure that your language is appropriately formal or informal, depending on your writing context.**
First Draft	Tom Benecke, the guy in the story, gets bent out of shape and can't get it together.
Revision	Tom Benecke, the main character in the story, panics and can't think clearly.
Model From Literature	Can the rough stuff . . . now a Mississippi steamboat pushes up the night river with a hoo-hoo-hoo-oo . . . and the green lanterns calling to the high soft stars . . . a red moon rides on the humps of the low river hills . . . go to it, O jazzmen. —*Carl Sandburg, "Jazz Fantasia," p. 644*

Handbook of Grammar and Revising Strategies   955

Strategy 3:	**Eliminate jargon if you are writing for a general audience.**
First Draft	Momaday writes informatively of culture-specific Kiowa traditions.
Revision	Momaday writes informatively of distinctive Kiowa traditions.
Model From Literature	The creative act with Palestrina is not the thematic conception so much as the personal treatment of a well-established pattern. —*Aaron Copland, "The Creative Process in Music," p. 518*

■ Double Negatives

GUIDE FOR REVISING: A double negative is the use of two or more negative words in one clause to express a negative meaning.

Strategy:	**Use only one negative word to give a sentence a negative meaning.**
First Draft	Chig was seventeen and didn't have nothing to do that summer.
Revision	Chig was seventeen and didn't have anything to do that summer.
Model From Literature	Upon reaching Antarctica they were unable to establish winter quarters on Cape Crozier as they had planned. —*Evan S. Connell, from* The White Lantern, *pp. 487–488*

■ Sentence Variety

GUIDE FOR REVISING: Varying the lengths and structures of your sentences will help you to hold your readers' attention.

Strategy 1:	**Expand short sentences by adding details.**
First Draft	Emily Dickinson joined in picnics with groups of other children.
Revision	When she was young, Emily Dickinson joined in picnics and walks over the hills of Amherst with groups of other children.
Model From Literature	He was evidently good, and sweet, and lovable, and guileless; and so it was exceedingly painful to see him stand there, as serene as a graven image, and deliver himself of answers which were veritably miraculous for stupidity and ignorance. —*Mark Twain, "Luck," p. 90*

Strategy 2:	**Break up lengthy, overly complicated sentences into simpler, shorter sentences.**
First Draft	Static characters do not change in the course of a story but remain the same, no matter what happens to them, in contrast to dynamic characters, who change and sometimes learn as a result of the events in a story.
Revision	Static characters do not change in the course of a story but remain the same, no matter what happens to them. Dynamic characters, in contrast, change and sometimes learn as a result of the events in a story.
Model From Literature	They thudded against chairs, whirling their mustached runners, kneading the rug nap, sucking gently at hidden dust. Then, like mysterious invaders, they popped into their burrows. Their pink electric eyes faded. The house was clean.
	—*Ray Bradbury, "There Will Come Soft Rains," p. 121*

Strategy 3:	**Use coordination to join simple sentences.**
First Draft	Ernesto needed to do some research on radio plays for his term paper. He wrote to the Museum of Broadcasting in New York City.
Revision	Ernesto needed to do some research on radio plays for his term paper, so he wrote to the Museum of Broadcasting in New York City.
Model From Literature	Someone called to Don Roméo that more guests were arriving, and with a final delighted pat on the stranger's shoulder, the little man scurried away.
	—*Josephina Niggli, "The Street of the Cañon," p. 128*

Strategy 4:	**Use subordination to join simple sentences.**
First Draft	Artificial intelligence refers to computer programs. These programs accomplish tasks. The tasks are usually associated with human agents.
Revision	Artificial intelligence refers to computer programs that accomplish tasks usually associated with human agents.
Model From Literature	At moments of failure, when he clowned to claim his mother's attention, it was with just this grave, embarrassed inspection that she rewarded him.
	—*Doris Lessing, "Through the Tunnel," p. 149*

■ Stringy Sentences

GUIDE FOR REVISING: Too many prepositional phrases can make writing wordy and monotonous.

Strategy:	Eliminate some prepositional phrases to reduce the number of words and make the meaning clearer.
First Draft	In *The Way to Rainy Mountain* by Momaday, there are many references to Kiowa legends from ancient times and to the traditions of culture in this tribe.
Revision	Momaday's *The Way to Rainy Mountain* refers to many ancient Kiowa legends and cultural traditions.

■ Overuse of Common Words

GUIDE FOR REVISING: Overuse of common or vague words makes your style monotonous and unoriginal.

Strategy:	Try not to overuse common words within a sentence.
First Draft	The story of King Arthur is unique among stories about knights for its appeal to the British.
Revision	The legend of King Arthur is unique among chivalric tales for its appeal to the imagination of British writers.
Model From Literature	And the rumor of this new presence having spread itself whisperingly around, there arose at length from the whole company a buzz, or murmur, expressive of disapprobation and surprise—then, finally, of terror, of horror, and of disgust. —*Edgar Allan Poe, "The Masque of the Red Death," p. 170*

Problems of Conciseness

■ Wordy Phrases

GUIDE FOR REVISING: Wordy phrases and clauses can weaken your writing by causing ideas to lose their sharpness and impact.

Strategy:	Shorten wordy phrases and clauses when you can do so without changing the meaning of a sentence.
First Draft	In "Two Tramps in Mud Time," Robert Frost uses a large number of clues to create the characterization of the speaker.
Revision	In "Two Tramps in Mud Time," Robert Frost uses numerous clues to characterize the speaker.
Model From Literature	A woman with shorn white hair is standing at the kitchen window. She is wearing tennis shoes and a shapeless gray sweater over a summery calico dress. —*Truman Capote, "A Christmas Memory," p. 443*

GUIDE FOR REVISING: Redundancy is the unnecessary repetition of an idea. Redundancy makes writing heavy and dull.

Strategy:	**Eliminate redundant modifiers in your sentences.**
First Draft	Jack Finney's "Contents of the Dead Man's Pocket" is a short story that contains a lot of suspense.
Revision	Jack Finney's "Contents of the Dead Man's Pocket" is a very suspenseful short story.
Model From Literature	He wrapped her warm in his seaman's coat Against the stinging blast; He cut a rope from a broken spar, And bound her to the mast. —*Henry Wadsworth Longfellow, "The Wreck of the Hesperus," p. 564*
First Draft	Gene was inclined to be envious and jealous of Finny's easy manners and naturalness.
Revision	Gene was inclined to be envious of Finny's easy manners.
Model From Literature	She frowned, conscientiously worrying over what amusements he might secretly be longing for, which she had been too busy or too careless to imagine. —*Doris Lessing, "Through the Tunnel," p. 147*

■ **Unnecessary Intensifiers**

GUIDE FOR REVISING: Intensifiers such as *really, very, truly,* and *of course* should be used to strengthen statements. Overuse of these words may, however, weaken a sentence.

Strategy:	**Eliminate unnecessary intensifiers from your writing.**
First Draft	I agree, of course, that Anne Tyler is a truly outstanding writer.
Revision	I agree that Anne Tyler is an outstanding writer.
Model From Literature	Leiningen, at the moment he made that leap through the flames, lost consciousness for the first time in his life. —*Carl Stephenson, "Leiningen Versus the Ants," p. 58*

Problems of Appropriateness

■ **Inappropriate Diction**

GUIDE FOR REVISING: Problems of inappropriate diction occur when words or phrases that are generally accepted in informal conversation or writing are inappropriately used in formal writing.

Strategy:	Choose the appropriate level of diction based on the audience for which you are writing, as well as the subject.
First Draft	Prince Prospero is an arrogant dude who thinks there's no way his bash is going to be spoiled by a gate-crasher.
Revision	Prince Prospero is an arrogant man who has no intention of letting his party be spoiled by an intruder.
Model From Literature	"Oh, you talking about that crazy horse GL brung home that time."
	—*William Melvin Kelley, "A Visit to Grandmother," p. 71*

■ Clichés

GUIDE FOR REVISING: Clichés are expressions that were once fresh and vivid but through overuse now lack force and appeal.

Strategy:	When you recognize a cliché, you should substitute a fresh expression of your own.
First Draft	When Creon confronts her, Antigone is bold as brass and hard as nails.
Revision	When Creon confronts her, Antigone is confident and stubborn.

SUMMARY OF GRAMMAR

Nouns   A **noun** is the name of a person, place or thing.

A **common noun** names any one of a class of people, places, or things. A **proper noun** names a specific person, place, or thing.

Common nouns	Proper nouns
author	Anne Tyler, W. W. Jacobs
country	Greece, New Zealand

Pronouns   **Pronouns** are words that stand for nouns or for words that take the place of nouns.

Personal pronouns refer to (1) the person speaking, (2) the person spoken to, or (3) the person, place, or thing spoken about.

	Singular	Plural
First Person	I, me, my, mine	we, us, our, ours
Second Person	you, your, yours	you, your, yours
Third Person	he, him, his she, her, hers it, its	they, them, their, theirs

A **reflexive pronoun** ends in *-self* or *-selves* and adds information to a sentence by pointing back to a noun or pronoun earlier in the sentence.

An **intensive pronoun** ends in *-self* or *-selves* and simply adds emphasis to a noun or pronoun in the same sentence.

> All these are different ways in which the musical idea may present *itself* to the composer. (reflexive)
> —Aaron Copland, *"The Creative Process in Music,"* p. 516
> After a time, I *myself* was allowed to go into the dead houses and search for metal. (intensive)
> —Stephen Vincent Benét, *"By the Waters of Babylon,"* p. 135

Demonstrative pronouns direct attention to specific people, places, or things.

this   that
these   those

A **relative pronoun** begins a subordinate clause and connects it to another idea in the sentence.

> Ribbons and immortality were mingled in her mind, *which* passed from one to the other with the speed of lightning, . . .
> —Van Wyck Brooks, *"Emily Dickinson,"* p. 423

Indefinite pronouns refer to people, places, or things, often without specifying which ones.

> And then, for a moment, *all* is still, . . .
> —Edgar Allan Poe, *"The Masque of the Red Death,"* p. 170

Verbs   A **verb** is a wrod that expresses time while showing an action, a condition, or the fact that something exists.

An **action verb** is a verb that tells what action someone or something is performing.

An action verb is transitive if it directs action toward someone or something named in the same sentence.

> He *was watering* the carnation plants in the greenhouse.
> —Toshio Mori, *"Abalone, Abalone, Abalone,"* p. 158

An action verb is intransitive if it does not direct action toward something or someone named in the same sentence.

> Jablonsky *smiled,* quite unexpectedly . . .
> —Isaac Asimov, *"The Machine That Won the War,"* p. 183

A **linking verb** is a verb that connects a word at or near the beginning of a sentence with a word at or near the end. All linking verbs are intransitive.

> Romance at short notice *was* her specialty.
> —Saki, *"The Open Window,"* p. 185

Helping verbs are verbs that can be added to another verb to make a single verb phrase.

> Nor *had* I ever *slept* in a dead place before—and yet, tonight, I *must sleep* there.
> —Stephen Vincent Benét, *"By the Waters of Babylon,"* p. 141

Adjectives   An **adjective** is a word used to describe a noun or pronoun or to give a noun or pronoun a more specific meaning. Adjectives answer these questions:

What kind?	*purple* shirt, *tall* ladder
Which one?	*this* ring, *those* spoons
How many?	*twelve* games, *both* cars
How much?	*enough* food, *sufficient* rain

The articles *the, a,* and *an* are adjectives. *An* is used before a word beginning with a vowel sound.

A noun may sometimes be used as an adjective.

   punctuation rule   *creation* myth

Adverbs   An **adverb** is a word that modifies a verb, an adjective, or another adverb. Adverbs answer the questions *Where? When? In what manner? To what extent?*

They lived *here.*	(modifies verb *lived*)
I run *daily.*	(modifies verb *run*)
Don't laugh *rudely.*	(modifies verb *laugh*)
Rita was *often* absent.	(modifies adjective *absent*)
He drove *too* fast.	(modifies adverb *fast*)

Prepositions   A **preposition** is a word that relates a noun or pronoun that appears with it to another word in the sentence. Prepositions are almost always followed by nouns or pronouns.

among us	*at* the end	*during* our trip
inside my desk	*with* you and me	*till* dark

Conjunctions   A **conjunction** is a word used to connect other words or groups of words.

Coordinating conjunctions connect similar kinds or groups of words.

peas *and* carrots   six *or* seven

Correlative conjunctions are used in pairs to connect similar words or groups of words.

both Val *and* Sid   *neither* they *nor* we

Subordinating conjunctions connect two complete ideas by placing one idea below the other in rank or importance.

He had been watching with mixed emotions *while* his father and his sister's husband cleared the fields beside the stream.
—*Juanita Platero and Siyowin Miller, "Chee's Daughter," p. 83*
Before he could answer, the chattering in the patio swelled to louder proportions.
—*Josephina Niggli, "The Street of the Cañon," p. 131*

Interjections   An **interjection** is a word that expresses feeling or emotion and that functions independently of a sentence.

"*Eh,* you're a stranger," she said.
—*Josephina Niggli, "The Street of the Cañon," p. 129*
"*Oh,* don't break it again!"
—*John Knowles, A Separate Peace, p. 844*

Sentences   A **sentence** is a group of words with two main parts: a complete subject and a complete predicate. Together these parts express a complete thought.

So Sir Launcelot went to Gaheris, and asked him to lend him his horse.
—*Sir Thomas Malory, "The Adventures of Sir Launcelot," p. 699*
Outside, the garage chimed and lifted its door to reveal the waiting car.
—*Ray Bradbury, "There Will Come Soft Rains," p. 121*

A **fragment** is a group of words that does not express a complete thought.
Yet not too much.
—*Robert Francis, "Pitcher," p. 632*

Subject-Verb Agreement   To make a subject and verb agree, make sure that both are *singular* or both are *plural.*

He is on vacation.
They swim well.
Soup or *salad is* a good first course.
Both the *chicken* and the *lamb were* delicious.
Either the *chairs* or the *table needs* dusting.
Neither *Sally* nor her *brothers want* to speak.
The *singer* as well as the *musicians were* excellent.
Candles on a Christmas tree *are* a serious hazard.

Phrases   A **phrase** is a group of words, without a subject and verb, that functions in a sentence as one part of speech.

A **prepositional phrase** is a group of words that includes a preposition and a noun or pronoun.

aboard ship	*behind* me
despite their success	*near* her window
through the night	*upon* entering

An **adjective phrase** is a prepositional phrase that modifies a noun or pronoun by telling what kind or which one.

When he had empty time he chose a chair *without rockers,* one that would not be a symbol *of age and weariness and lack of work.*
—*Anne Tyler, "With All Flags Flying," p. 235*

An **adverb phrase** is a prepositional phrase that modifies a verb, an adjective, or an adverb by pointing out where, when, in what manner, or to what extent.

On a sudden impulse, he got to his feet, walked to the front closet and took out an old tweed jacket; it would be cold outside.
—*Jack Finney, "Contents of the Dead Man's Pocket," p. 20*

An **appositive phrase** is a noun or pronoun with modifiers, placed next to a noun or pronoun to add information and details.

Adams, *the second President,* suspected the French Revolutionaries; . . .
—*Theodore H. White, "The American Idea," p. 512*

A **participial phrase** is a participle modified by an adjective or adverb phrase or accompanied by a complement. The entire phrase acts as an adjective.

Choosing such a tide, I hoped for a glimpse of the pool.
—*Rachel Carson, "The Marginal World," p. 528*
Having looked at his thematic material, the composer must now decide what sound medium will best fit it.
—*Aaron Copland, "The Creative Process in Music," p. 517*

A **gerund phrase** is a gerund with modifiers or a complement, all acting together as a noun.

. . . *moving along the ledge* was quite as easy as he had thought it would be.
—*Jack Finney, "Contents of the Dead Man's Pocket," p. 20*
The debate began with the *drafting of the Declaration of Independence.*
—*Theodore H. White, "The American Idea," p. 512*

An **infinitive phrase** is an infinitive with modifiers, complements, or a subject, all acting together as a single part of speech.

To juxtapose the great and the small, in unexpected ways, had been one of her prime amusements as the wit of her circle, . . .
—*Van Wyck Brooks, "Emily Dickinson," p. 424*

Ah no, it's always just my luck *to get / One perfect rose.*
—*Dorothy Parker, "One Perfect Rose," p. 584*

Clauses   A **clause** is a group of words with its own subject and verb.

An **independent clause** can stand by itself as a complete sentence. A **subordinate clause** cannot stand by itself as a complete sentence; it can only be part of a sentence. An **adjective clause** is a subordinate clause that modifies a noun or pronoun by telling what kind or which one.

For country people, *who only knew the dismantled tilting ground of Sir Ector's castle,* the scene which met their eyes was ravishing.
—*T. H. White, "Arthur Becomes King of Britain," p. 695*

Subordinate adverb clauses modify verbs, adjectives, adverbs, or verbals by telling where, when, in what manner, to what extent, under what condition, or why.

We step over the barbed wire into the pasture
Where they have been grazing all day, alone.
—*James Wright, "A Blessing," p. 598*

A **noun clause** is a subordinate clause that acts as a noun.

How they won their battles is *a story for the schoolbooks,* . . .
—*Theodore H. White, "The American Idea," p. 512*

SUMMARY OF CAPITALIZATION AND PUNCTUATION

CAPITALIZATION

Capitalize the first word in a sentence. Also capitalize the first word in a quotation if the quotation is a complete sentence.

He looked down, hesitated, then said, "Okay, sir. But take care of it."
—Thomas Boswell, "Gloves Labor Lost," p. 538

Capitalize all proper nouns and adjectives.

W. W. Jacobs	Saki	King Arthur
Flanders Fields	January	Colorado River
World War I	Peruvian	Rhodes Scholarship

Capitalize a person's title when it is followed by the person's name or when it is used in direct address.

Reverend   Dr. Stanpole   Captain Scott

Capitalize titles showing family relationships when they refer to a specific person unless they are preceded by a possessive noun or pronoun.

Grandmother   Aunt Rose   his father

Capitalize the first word and all other key words in the titles of books, periodicals, poems, stories, plays, paintings, and other works of art.

The Way to Rainy Mountain   Girl Looking at
Journal of the American   Landscape
  Medical Association   "A Letter From Home"
"A Visit to Grandmother"   Invasion From Mars

Capitalize the first word and all nouns in letter salutations and the first word in letter closings.

Dear Ms. Dillard,   Yours truly,

PUNCTUATION

End Marks Use a **period** to end a declarative sentence, an imperative sentence, an indirect question, and most abbreviations.

She broke off with a little shudder.
—Saki, "The Open Window," p. 178
Decius, go tell them Caesar will not come.
—William Shakespeare, The Tragedy of Julius Caesar, p. 314
Someone once asked me, in a public forum, whether I waited for inspiration.
—Aaron Copland, "The Creative Process in Music," p. 515

For reasons which will presently appear, I will withhold his real name and titles, and call him Lieutenant-General Lord Arthur Scoresby, V.C., K.C.B., etc., etc., etc.
—Mark Twain, "Luck," p. 89

Use a **question mark** to end a direct question, an incomplete question, or a statement that is intended as a question.

And what was Scoresby's blunder that time?
—Mark Twain, "Luck," p. 93
"Monkey's paw?" said Mrs. White curiously.
—W. W. Jacobs, "The Monkey's Paw," p. 32

Use an **exclamation mark** after a statement showing strong emotion, an urgent imperative sentence, or an interjection expressing strong emotion.

"Good!" he said. "Keep it up!"
—Toshio Mori, "Abalone, Abalone, Abalone," p. 158
Look! they say, look at what I just said!
—Lewis Thomas, "Notes on Punctuation," p. 508
"Good heavens!" cried Sir Kay.
—T. H. White, "Arthur Becomes King of England," p. 695

Commas Use a comma before the conjunction to separate two independent clauses in a compound sentence.

It was there that I had done it, but it was here that I would have to tell it.
—John Knowles, A Separate Peace, p. 795

Use commas to separate three or more words, phrases, or clauses in a series.

Animals took shape: yellow giraffes, blue lions, pink antelopes, lilac panthers cavorting in crystal substance.
—Ray Bradbury, "There Will Come Soft Rains," p. 122

Use commas to separate adjectives of equal rank. Do not use commas to separate adjectives that must stay in a specific order.

The driveway was a series of frozen, broken mudholes in a general direction across a field to his home.
—Daryl Babe Wilson, "Diamond Island: Alcatraz," p. 98
We had some deep spring sunshine about a month ago, in a drought; . . .
—Annie Dillard, "Flood," p. 473

Use a comma after an introductory word, phrase, or clause.

> *When Marian Anderson again returned to America,* she was a seasoned artist.
>
> —Langston Hughes, "Marian Anderson: Famous Concert Singer," p. 429

Use commas to set off parenthetical and nonessential expressions.

> It also seemed to me, *esthetically speaking,* that nature had got inexcusably carried away on the summer question . . .
>
> —Lorraine Hansberry, "On Summer," p. 493

Use commas with places, dates, and titles.

Alma, Georgia
August 4, 2026
Alfred, Lord Tennyson

Use commas after items in addresses, after the salutation in a personal letter, after the closing in all letters, and in numbers of more than three digits.

117 Maple Street, Columbus, Ohio
Dear Amy,   Affectionately,   10,773

Use a comma to indicate words left out of an elliptical sentence, to set off a direct quotation, and to prevent a sentence from being misunderstood.

> Lorraine Hansberry was born in Chicago; Toshio Mori, in Oakland.
>
> Then he was finished, and I must say, that horse looked mighty fine hitched to that buggy . . .
>
> —William Melvin Kelley, "A Visit to Grandmother," p. 73

Semicolons   Use a semicolon to join independent clauses that are not already joined by a conjunction.

> They could find no buffalo; *they had to hang an old hide from the sacred tree.*
>
> —N. Scott Momaday, *from* The Way to Rainy Mountain, p. 468

Use a semicolon to join independent clauses separated by either a conjunctive adverb or a transitional expression.

> For a moment he could not bring himself to lift his right foot from one ledge to the other; then he did it, and became aware of the harsh exhalation of air from his throat and realized that he was panting.
>
> —Jack Finney, "Contents of the Dead Man's Pocket," p. 22

Use semicolons to avoid confusion when independent clauses or items in a series already contain commas.

> There were the Useful Presents: engulfing mufflers of the old coach days, and mittens made for giant sloths; zebra scarfs of a substance like silky gum that could be tug-o'-warred down to the galoshes; blinding tam-o'-shanters like patchwork tea cozies . . .
>
> —Dylan Thomas, "A Child's Christmas in Wales," p. 436

Colons   Use a colon before a list of items following an independent clause.

> All together the five men grasped a Norwegian flag and thrust it into the snow: Amundsen, Sverre Hasel, Oskar Wisting, Helmer Hansen, Olav Bjaaland.
>
> —Evan S. Connell, *from* The White Lantern, p. 483

Use a colon to introduce a formal quotation.

> Now listen to Roald Amundsen on the same subject: "Success is a woman who has to be won, not courted."
>
> —Evan S. Connell, *from* The White Lantern, p. 487

Use a colon to introduce a sentence that summarizes or explains the sentence before it.

> Of the ingredients that go into our fruitcakes, whiskey is the most expensive, as well as the hardest to obtain: State laws forbid its sales.
>
> —Truman Capote, "A Christmas Memory," p. 446

Quotation Marks   A **direct quotation** represents a person's exact speech or thoughts and is enclosed in quotation marks.

> "Clara, my mind is made up."
>
> —Anne Tyler, "With All Flags Flying," p. 232

An **indirect quotation** reports only the general meaning of what a person said or thought and does not require quotation marks.

> She rattled on cheerfully about the shooting and the scarcity of birds, . . .
>
> —Saki, "The Open Window," p. 178

Always place a comma or a period inside the final quotation mark.

> "Well then," there was no light remark anywhere in my head, "I'll get you some books."
>
> —John Knowles, A Separate Peace, p. 795

Place a question mark or an exclamation mark inside the final quotation mark if the end mark is part of the quotation; if it is not part of the quotation, place it outside the final quotation mark.

> The letters themselves were brief and cryptic, usually only a line or two: "Do you look out tonight?" for example.
> —*Van Wyck Brooks, "Emily Dickinson," p. 416*

Use single quotation marks for a quotation within a quotation.

> "Well, let's see. It begins, 'When Caesar noticed that the enemy was remaining for several days at the camp fortified by a swamp and by the nature of the terrain, he sent a letter to Trebonius instructing him'—'instructing him' isn't actually in the text but it's understood; you know about that."
> —*John Knowles,* A Separate Peace, *p. 848*

Underline the titles of long written works, movies, television and radio shows, lengthy works of music, paintings, and sculptures. Also underline foreign words not yet accepted into English and words you wish to stress.

Julius Caesar	A Separate Peace
The Civil War	Appalachian Spring
Violinist at the Window	Hola
the essence of the plot	The Table
Wild Kingdom	au courant

Use quotation marks around the titles of short written works, episodes in a series, songs, and titles of works mentioned as parts of collections.

"The Monkey's Paw"	"Emily Dickinson"
"Jingle Bells"	"Making a Fist"
"Arthur Becomes King of Britain"	

Dashes   Use dashes to indicate an abrupt change of thought, a dramatic interrupting idea, or a summary statement.

> It made her so mad to see Muggs lying there, oblivious of the mice—they came running up to her—

that she slapped him and he slashed at her, but didn't make it.
> —*James Thurber, "The Dog That Bit People," p. 406*

Parentheses   Use parentheses to set off asides and explanations only when the material is not essential or when it consists of one or more sentences.

> We eat our supper (cold biscuits, bacon, blackberry jam) and discuss tomorrow.
> —*Truman Capote, "A Christmas Memory," p. 444*

Hyphens   Use a hyphen with certain numbers, after certain prefixes, with two or more words used as one word, and with a compound modifier coming before a noun.

fifty-two	self-satisfied
lady-in-waiting	greenish-blue water

Apostrophes   Add an apostrophe and *-s* to show the possessive case of most singular nouns.

> Leila's hat   a shopper's paradise

Add an apostrophe to show the possessive case of plural nouns ending in *-s* and *-es*.

> the cats' food   the Ortizes' apartment

Add an apostrophe and *-s* to show the possessive case of plural nouns that do not end in *-s* or *-es*.

> the people's wishes   the sheep's pasture

Use an apostrophe in a contraction to indicate the position of the missing letter or letters.

> "I *didn't* love any one of you more than any other."
> —*William Melvin Kelley, "A Visit to Grandmother," p. 74*
> "There *aren't* any teams in blitzball," he yelled somewhat irritably, "*we're* all enemies."
> —*John Knowles,* A Separate Peace, *p. 775*

GLOSSARY OF COMMON USAGE

a, an

The article *a* is used before consonant sounds; *an* is used before vowel sounds. Words beginning with *h, o,* or *y* sometimes have a consonant sound and sometimes a vowel sound.

> *A* history of modern African literature would have to include Chinua Achebe of Nigeria.
> The Nobel Prize is *an* honor that few writers would be likely to decline.

among, between

Among is usually used with three or more items. *Between* is generally used with only two items.

> *Among* the contents of Tom Benecke's pockets in Jack Finney's story are a dozen coins.
> Leslie Norris's story "Shaving" focuses on the relationship *between* Barry and his father.

amount, number

Amount refers to quantity or a unit, whereas *number* refers to individual items that can be counted. Therefore, *amount* generally appears with a singular noun, and *number* appears with a plural noun.

> Because Cassius feels that Brutus' membership in the conspiracy is vital, he spends a large *amount* of time trying to convince him to join the assassins.
> Cassius says that he will deliver a *number* of anonymous letters to Brutus.

anxious, eager

The adjective *anxious* implies uneasiness, worry, or fear. Do not use it as a substitute for *eager*.

> Portia's words show that she is *anxious* about Brutus' safety.
> Mr. White is *eager* to learn more about the monkey's paw from Sergeant Major Morris.

any, all

Any should not be used in place of *any other* or *all*.

> Thurber says that Muggs was more troublesome than *any other* dog he had ever owned.
> Of *all* Edgar Allan Poe's short stories, "The Masque of the Red Death" was Amy's favorite.

as, because, like, as to

The word *as* has several meanings and can function as several parts of speech. To avoid confusion use *because* rather than *as* when you want to indicate cause and effect.

> *Because* Jerry wanted to swim through the tunnel, he pestered his mother to buy him a pair of goggles.

Do not use the preposition *like* to introduce a clause that requires the conjunction *as*.

> Antigone does not behave *as* Creon believes *she* should: she disobeys the laws of the city.

The use of *as to* for *about* is awkward and should be avoided.

> Momaday combines personal reminiscences about his grandmother with informative comments about Kiowa history and traditions.

bad, badly

Use the predicate adjective *bad* after linking verbs such as *feel, look,* and *seem*. Use *badly* whenever an adverb is required.

> In line 2 of Keats's poem, the words "palely loitering" show that the knight looks *bad*.
> According to the speaker, Miss Rosie's appearance has *badly* deteriorated.

because of, due to

Use *due to* if it can logically replace the phrase *caused by*. In introductory phrases, however, *because of* is better usage than *due to*.

> Gene's internal conflicts are largely *due to* his guilt about jouncing the limb and causing Finny's accident.
> *Because of* his suspicion that the two tramps may want his job for pay, the speaker in Frost's poem regards them ambivalently.

being as, being that

Avoid these expressions. Use *because* or *since* instead.

> *Because* Mr. Carpenter does not want to be a burden to his family, he decides to move into a retirement home.
> *Since* the speaker in Elizabeth Bishop's poem admires the courage and beauty of the fish, she lets it go.

beside, besides

Beside is a preposition meaning "at the side of" or "close to." Do not confuse *beside* with *besides,* which means "in addition to." *Besides* can be a preposition or an adverb.

> As the three men cross the lawn and approach the open window, a brown spaniel trots *beside* them.
> There are many other Indian oral epics *besides* the Ramayana.
> Italo Calvino has written several distinguished novels; he has published fables and science fiction, *besides*.

can, may

The verb *can* generally refers to the ability to do something. The verb *may* generally refers to permission to do something.

> Dylan Thomas describes his childhood Christmases so vividly that most readers *can* visualize the scene.
>
> Creon's edict states that no one *may* bury Polyneices.

compare, contrast

The verb *compare* can involve both similarities and differences. The verb *contrast* always involves differences. Use *to* or *with* after *compare*. Use *with* after *contrast*.

> Jorge's report *compared* Dylan Thomas's "A Child's Christmas in Wales" *with* Truman Capote's "A Christmas Memory."
>
> In line 11 James Wright uses a simile to *compare* the two Indian ponies *to* wet swans.
>
> The characterization of Antigone in Sophocles' play *contrasts with* that of her sister Ismene.

different from, different than

The preferred usage is *different from*.

> The structure and rhyme scheme of a Shakespearean sonnet are *different from* the organization of a Petrarchan sonnet.

don't

Use *doesn't,* not *don't,* with third-person singular pronoun subjects and singular noun subjects.

> Framton Nuttel *doesn't* understand that Vera has mischievously tricked him.

emigrate, immigrate

Emigrate means "to move *out of* a country." *Immigrate* means "to move *into* a country."

> In 1949 Doris Lessing *emigrated* from South Africa and settled in London.
>
> Isaac Asimov's parents left Russia and *immigrated* to the United States when Asimov was three years old.

enthused, enthusiastic

Enthused is nonstandard. Replace it with *enthusiastic*.

> Tom Benecke is *enthusiastic* about his prospects for promotion at his company.

farther, further

Use *farther* when you refer to distance. Use *further* when you mean "to a greater degree" or "additional."

> The *farther* the ants travel, the more ominous and destructive they seem.

The last stanza of Updike's poem provides *further* hints that an athlete past his prime may tend to feel depressed.

fewer, less

Use *fewer* for things that can be counted. Use *less* for amounts or quantities that cannot be counted.

> According to Hindu myth, there are no *fewer* than 30 million gods.
>
> It takes *less* time to perform a Greek tragedy than to act a Shakespearean play.

former, latter

Former refers to the first of two previously mentioned items. *Latter* refers to the second.

> Octavio Paz and Jorge Luis Borges both wrote distinguished novels and poems; the *former* lived in Mexico, the *latter* in Argentina.

good, well

Use the predicate adjective *good* after linking verbs such as *feel, look, smell, taste,* and *seem.* Use *well* whenever you need an adverb.

> Caesar remarks that Cassius does not look *good;* on the contrary, his appearance is "lean" and "hungry."
>
> In "The Ring" Isak Dinesen describes the emotions of a young woman especially *well*.

hopefully

You should not loosely attach this adverb to a sentence, as in "Hopefully, the rain will stop by noon." Rewrite the sentence so that *hopefully* modifies a specific verb. Other possible ways of revising such sentences include using the adjective *hopeful* or a phrase like *everyone hopes that.*

> Theodore H. White writes *hopefully* about the American idea of equality and opportunity.
>
> Marie was *hopeful* that she could present her report on "Chee's Daughter" by the following Tuesday.
>
> *Most people hope that* we can solve the environmental problems that Rachel Carson identified and discussed so eloquently.

in, into

In refers to position and means "within" or "inside." *Into* implies motion from outside to inside.

> Chinua Achebe was born *in* Nigeria.
>
> When Jerry swims *into* the tunnel, the water pushes him up against the roof.

its, it's

Do not confuse the possessive pronoun *its* with the contraction *it's,* standing for "it is" or "it has."

In *its* very first lines, Burns's poem establishes a nostalgic mood.

In "The Street of the Cañon," Pepe knows that *it's* dangerous to attend Don Roméo's party.

just, only

When you use *just* as an adverb meaning "no more than," be sure that you place it directly before the word it modifies logically. Likewise, be sure that you place *only* before the word it logically modifies.

Many of the characters in *A Separate Peace* have *just* one event in the back of their minds: World War II.

A short story can usually develop *only* a few characters, whereas a novel can include many.

kind of, sort of

In formal writing you should not use these colloquial expressions. Instead, use a word such as *rather* or *somewhat*.

Poe portrays Prince Prospero as *rather* arrogant.

The end of Frost's poem is *somewhat* ambiguous: we never learn whether the speaker offers work to the tramps.

lay, lie

Do not confuse these verbs. *Lay* is a transitive verb meaning "to set or put something down." Its principal parts are *lay, laying, laid, laid. Lie* is an intransitive verb meaning "to recline." Its principal parts are *lie, lying, lay, lain.*

Brinker argues that a full investigation is necessary if the boys are to *lay* their doubts about Finny's accident to rest.

La belle dame sans merci enchants the knight as he *lies* in her "elfin grot."

learn, teach

Be careful not to use *learn,* meaning "to acquire knowledge," when your context requires *teach,* meaning "to give knowledge."

Jeanne *learned* a lot about Marian Anderson from Langston Hughes's essay.

Jorge Luis Borges *taught* English at the University of Buenos Aires.

leave, let

Be careful not to confuse these verbs. *Leave* means "to go away" or "to allow to remain." *Let* means "to permit."

Threatening Antigone not to disobey his orders, Creon angrily *leaves* the stage.

At first Mr. Carpenter's family does not want to *let* him enter the retirement home.

literally, figuratively

Literally means "word for word" or "in fact." The opposite of *literally* is *figuratively,* meaning "metaphorically." Be careful not to use *literally* as a synonym for *nearly,* as in informal expressions like "He was literally beside himself with rage."

A symbol must be interpreted both *literally* and *figuratively:* it stands for itself, and it also stands for something outside itself.

loose, lose

Loose can be either an adjective (meaning "unattached") or a verb (meaning "to untie"). *Lose* is always a verb (meaning "to fail to keep, have, or win").

Could there be a *loose* connection between some of the events in *A Separate Peace* and John Knowles's own experiences at Phillips Exeter Academy?

In A. R. Ammons's poem "Loss," the speaker says that when the daisies *lose* the sun they become half-wild.

many, much

Use *many* to refer to a specific quantity. Use *much* for an indefinite amount or for an abstract concept.

Many nineteenth-century French writers admired Edgar Allan Poe's use of atmosphere and symbolism.

Alan Paton spent *much* of his career battling the evils of apartheid in South Africa.

may be, maybe

Be careful not to confuse the verb phrase *may be* with the adverb *maybe* (meaning "perhaps").

Paradoxically, Brutus' idealism *may be* his tragic flaw.

Maybe Eldorado is a symbol for an unattainable ideal.

raise, rise

Raise is a transitive verb that usually takes a direct object. *Rise* is intransitive and never takes a direct object.

In his speech Antony unexpectedly *raises* the subject of Caesar's will.

When Framton Nuttel sees the men approaching, he *rises* from his seat in panic and dashes from the room.

set, sit

Do not confuse these verbs. *Set* is a transitive verb meaning "to put (something) in a certain place." Its principal parts are *set, setting, set, set. Sit* is an intransitive verb meaning "to be seated." Its principal parts are *sit, sitting, sat, sat.*

> Antigone's conduct *sets* high standards for all those who believe that conscience must be our ultimate guide.
>
> The uncles *sit* in the front parlor and smoke cigars.

so, so that
Be careful not to use the coordinating conjunction *so* when your context requires *so that. So* means "accordingly" or "therefore" and expresses a cause-and-effect relationship. *So that* expresses purpose.

> Robert Burns believed that poetry should appeal to the common reader, *so* he wrote much of his verse in Scots dialect.
>
> Antony uses eloquent rhetoric to stir up the people *so that* they will turn against the conspirators.

than, then
The conjunction *than* is used to connect the two parts of a comparison. Do not confuse *than* with the adverb *then,* which usually refers to time.

> Hazel enjoyed Lorraine Hansberry's essay "On Summer" more *than* Annie Dillard's "Flood."
>
> Marian Anderson gave a triumphant singing recital in New York that evening, and she *then* embarked on a coast-to-coast American tour.

that, which, who
Use the relative pronoun *that* to refer to things or people. Use *which* only for things and *who* only for people.

> The story *that* Ron liked most was "The Street of the Cañon."
>
> Haiku, *which* consists of only seventeen syllables, is often built around one or two vivid images.
>
> The assassin *who* strikes Caesar first is Casca.

them
Do not use *them* as a substitute for *those.*

> "Please handle *those* props carefully, Odell."

unique
Since *unique* means "one of a kind," you should not use it carelessly instead of the words "interesting" or "unusual." Avoid such illogical expressions as "most unique," "very unique," and "extremely unique."

> Emily Dickinson's unconventional themes and bold experiments with form make her *unique* in the history of nineteenth-century American poetry.

when, where
Do not directly follow a linking verb with *when* or *where.* Also be careful not to use *where* when your context requires *that.*

> Faulty: The exposition is *when* an author provides the reader with important background information.
>
> Revised: In the exposition an author provides the reader with important background information.
>
> Faulty: Madras, India, is *where* R. K. Narayan was born.
>
> Revised: R. K. Narayan was born in Madras, India.
>
> Faulty: Naomi read *where* Howard Koch won an Oscar for his screenplay for the movie *Casablanca.*
>
> Revised: Naomi read *that* Howard Koch won an Oscar for his screenplay for the movie *Casablanca.*

who, whom
In formal writing remember to use *who* only as a subject in clauses and sentences and *whom* only as an object.

> Aaron Copland, *who* wrote such classics of American music as *Appalachian Spring* and *El salon Mexico,* was born in Brooklyn, New York.
>
> The poet *whom* I most enjoyed reading this year was Gwendolyn Brooks.

HANDBOOK OF LITERARY TERMS AND TECHNIQUES

ACT   See *Drama*.

ALLEGORY   An *allegory* is a story with more than one level of meaning—a literal level and one or more symbolic levels. Allegory allows a writer both to tell a story about literal characters and to make a moral, religious, or political point. Besides having a literal surface meaning, the events, settings, or characters in an allegory also stand for ideas or qualities and have a second meaning on that level. Edgar Allan Poe's story "The Masque of the Red Death," on page 167, allegorically shows the inevitable arrival of death no matter how people try to avoid it.

ALLITERATION   *Alliteration* is the repetition of initial consonant sounds. Writers and poets use alliteration to create pleasing musical effects. Alma Villanueva uses alliteration in these lines from "I Was a Skinny Tomboy Kid":

> I grew like a thin, stubborn weed
> watering myself whatever way I could

See *Assonance, Consonance,* and *Rhyme*.

ALLUSION   An *allusion* is a reference to a well-known person, place, event, literary work, or work of art. Writers often make allusions to famous works such as the Bible or William Shakespeare's plays. They also make allusions to mythology, politics, current events, or other fields familiar to readers. For example, the title of Stephen Vincent Benét's story "By the Waters of Babylon" is an allusion to Psalm 137 in the Bible. A writer may use allusions as a sort of shorthand, briefly suggesting specific ideas or views.

ANACHRONISM   An *anachronism* is something presented out of its actual chronological time. For example, the events in *The Tragedy of Julius Caesar* take place in 44 B.C.. However, Shakespeare probably wrote the play in A.D. 1599. In the play William Shakespeare naturally includes many Roman customs, but he also mentions Elizabethan doublets, striking clocks, and chimney tops. These items from Shakespeare's time did not exist in Caesar's day and are therefore anachronisms.

ANALOGY   An *analogy* compares two different things to point out how they are similar. Mbuyiseni Oswald Mtshali uses an analogy to compare the sun to a "tossed coin" in the poem "Sunset" on page 613. The poet then compares a sunset to a parking meter that has "expired," illustrating a similarity between two very different objects.

ANAPEST   See *Meter*.

ANECDOTE   An *anecdote* is a brief story about an amusing or strange event. James Thurber, for example, fills "The Dog That Bit People," on page 405, with humorous anecdotes about his family and about the dog, Muggs. In the essay on page 415, Van Wyck Brooks presents anecdotes about Emily Dickinson's experiences and about her reactions to events.

ANTAGONIST   An *antagonist* is a character or force in conflict with the main character, or protagonist. In Alan Paton's "Sunlight in Trebizond Street," on page 207, the doctor is interrogated by his captor, Casper, who is his antagonist. In Carl Stephenson's short story on page 43, "Leiningen Versus the Ants," Leiningen battles nonhuman antagonists, the ants. A story does not have to have an antagonist, as Toshio Mori's "Abalone, Abalone, Abalone," on page 157, illus-

trates. Nevertheless, the conflict between the protagonist and an antagonist is often the basis for the plot.
See *Conflict* and *Protagonist*.

APHORISM   An *aphorism* is a general truth or observation about life, usually stated concisely and pointedly. Some writers have an aphoristic style, using many witty or wise statements to sum up their essays or to reinforce points or arguments. Benjamin Franklin is known for his aphorisms such as "Early to bed, early to rise, makes a [person] healthy, wealthy, and wise," from *Poor Richard's Almanack.*

APOSTROPHE   An *apostrophe* is a figure of speech in which a writer speaks directly to an idea, to a quality, to an object, or to a person who is not present. In the following lines, Emily Dickinson addresses a month of the year:

Dear March—come in—
How glad I am—
I hoped for you before—
Put down your Hat—
You must have walked—
How out of Breath you are—

Apostrophe is most often used in poetry and in speeches to add emotional intensity.
See *Figurative Language.*

ARGUMENTATION   *Argumentation* is the type of writing that presents and logically supports the writer's views about an issue. Argumentation is one of the forms of discourse, or formal discussion of a subject. It includes persuasive writing that not only presents the writer's opinion but also tries to move the reader to take some action or to adopt some way of thinking. Lorraine Hansberry's "On Summer," on page 493, is a *persuasive essay.*
See *Forms of Discourse* and *Persuasion.*

ASIDE   An *aside* is a short speech delivered to the audience by an actor in a play and spoken in an undertone to suggest that the rest of the characters on stage are unable to hear it. In William Shakespeare's *The Tragedy of Julius Caesar,* which begins on page 309, Caesar says, "and we (like friends) will straightway go together." Then Brutus says in an aside, "That every like is not the same, O Caesar,/The heart of Brutus earns to think upon." Brutus makes this comment in an aside so that Caesar will not hear it. The comment is heard, however, by the audience. An aside allows the writer to reveal a character's private thoughts, reactions, or motivations to the audience without making these known to the other characters.

ASSONANCE   *Assonance* is the close repetition of similar vowels in conjunction with dissimilar consonant sounds. Used particularly in poetry, assonance differs from rhyme because only the vowel sounds are repeated. For example, *at* and *bat* rhyme, but *at* and *ask* illustrate assonance. These lines from "Allí por la calle San Luís," by Carmen Tafolla, use assonance to describe the cooking of corn tortillas:

Cooked on the homeblack of a flat stove.
Flipped to slap the birth awake.
Wrapped by corn hands.

Here the repeated *a* sounds contribute to the poem's music and unity, enriching the description of the cooking process.
See *Consonance.*

ATMOSPHERE   See *Mood.*

AUTOBIOGRAPHY   An *autobiography* is a form of nonfiction in which a person tells his or her own life story. An autobiography may record personal thoughts as well as narrate events. Its focus is the individual, not the times or public incidents, though these of course play a part in anyone's life story. Unlike a journal, a collection of letters, or a diary, an autobiography is written and organized for a public audience. Notable examples of the genre include the autobiographies of

Benjamin Franklin and Frederick Douglass, as well as Dylan Thomas's "A Child's Christmas in Wales," which appears on page 433.
See *Biography*.

BALLAD   A *ballad* is a songlike poem that tells a story, often one dealing with adventure or romance. Ballads tell their stories with simple language, dramatic action, dialogue, and repetition, often in a refrain. Most ballads are about ordinary people and everyday life. Most deal with adventure, disaster, disappointment, love, tragedy, or other emotional themes.

This very old type of narrative poetry generally follows a traditional form called the *ballad stanza*. A ballad stanza may have four or six rhyming lines.

A *folk ballad* is passed along orally from generation to generation. Its writer is not known. Examples include the ballads of Robin Hood, Casey Jones, and John Henry. In contrast, a *literary ballad* is written by a specific person, following the model of the folk ballad. An example is Longfellow's "The Wreck of the Hesperus," on page 563.
See *Narrative Poem, Oral Tradition,* and *Refrain*.

BIOGRAPHY   A *biography* is a form of nonfiction in which a writer tells the life story of another person. A biographer uses the subject's letters or writings, interviews, personal knowledge, and other books or materials to find details about the main events of the subject's life. After gathering this information, the biographer generally selects a particular focus to concentrate on in the essay or book. For example, in "Marian Anderson: Famous Concert Singer," on page 427, Langston Hughes focuses on Marian Anderson's career as a singer.
See *Autobiography*.

BLANK VERSE   *Blank verse* is poetry written in unrhymed iambic pentameter lines. Each iambic foot has an unstressed syllable followed by a stressed syllable. A pentameter line has five of these feet. Robert Frost uses blank verse in "Birches":

> When I | see birch | es bend | to left | and right
> Across | the lines | of straight | er dark | er trees
> I like | to think | some boy's | been swing|ing them.

Because blank verse sounds like ordinary spoken English, it has been used in much famous poetry and drama, including William Shakespeare's *The Tragedy of Julius Caesar*.
See *Iambic Pentameter* and *Meter*.

CAESURA   A *caesura* is a pause or break in the middle of a line of poetry. Often, a caesura is indicated by punctuation. Double slash marks (//) have been used to indicate the caesuras in these lines from Paul Laurence Dunbar's "We Wear the Mask":

> We wear the mask//that grins and lies,
> It hides our cheeks//and shades our eyes,—
> This debt we pay//to human guile;
> With torn and bleeding//hearts we smile.

Poets use caesuras to reflect the ordinary sound patterns of English, to keep the rhythm from becoming monotonous, to emphasize certain words, and to create special effects.

CHARACTER   A *character* is a person or an animal who takes part in the action of a literary work. Characters are called round or flat, depending on how they are developed. *Round* characters are complicated and exhibit numerous qualities or traits. As a result, they seem like real people, as does Chee in "Chee's Daughter," on page 77. In contrast, *flat* characters have only one or two characteristics. For example, all that the reader learns about Chee's father-in-law, Old Man Fat, is that he is thriftless and greedy. Character types that readers easily recognize, such as the hard-boiled detective or the wicked stepmother, are called *stereotypes* or *stock characters*. Usually writers try to develop their main characters as lifelike, round characters. Other characters, however, may be flat because they are less important to the story and to readers.

Throughout the action of a story, a *static character* stays essentially the same. Scoresby in Mark Twain's "Luck," on page 89, is a static character. In contrast, a *dynamic* character is changed by events or by interactions with other characters, as is Tom Benecke in Jack Finney's "Contents of the Dead Man's Pocket," on page 17. Novels and plays often contain many dynamic characters. Short stories often have several static characters and only one or two dynamic characters.
See *Characterization* and *Motivation*.

CHARACTERIZATION   *Characterization* is the act of creating and developing a character. A writer uses *direct characterization* when stating or describing a character's traits. For example, in William Melvin Kelley's "A Visit to Grandmother," on page 69, GL is described as "part con man, part practical joker and part Don Juan." A writer uses *indirect characterization* when showing a character's personality through his or her actions, thoughts, feelings, words, and appearance, or through another character's observations and reactions. In the same story, Kelley presents Chig's observations and memories of his father. Kelley also shows the actions and words of Chig's father during the emotional scene with Chig's grandmother. Such indirect characterization relies on the reader to put together the clues in order to figure out the character's personality.
See *Character*.

CINQUAIN   See *Stanza*.

CLIMAX   The *climax* in a story or play is the high point of interest or suspense in a literary work. The climax generally occurs near the end of the work. In "Chee's Daughter," on page 77, the climax occurs when Chee takes the food to his in-laws at the trading post. At this point readers sympathize with Chee and feel great sus-

pense, wondering whether he will succeed in getting back his daughter.
See *Plot*.

COMEDY   A *comedy* is a work of literature, especially a play, that is less serious than a tragedy and that has a happy ending. Comedies often show ordinary people in conflict with their societies. Comedies may feature humorous physical action or witty dialogue.
See *Drama* and *Tragedy*.

CONCRETE POETRY   A *concrete poem* is one with a shape that suggests its subject. "A Christmas Tree," by William Burford, is one example:

Star,
If you are
A love compassionate,
You will walk with us this year.
We face a glacial distance, who are here
Huddled
At your feet.

CONFLICT   A *conflict* is a struggle between opposing forces. Sometimes this struggle is *internal,* or inside a character, as when a character strives to meet a self-imposed challenge. At other times the struggle is *external* and involves a force outside the character. This force may be another character, the antagonist; a force of nature; or a social convention or custom.

Many stories involve several types of conflict. In Italo Calvino's "Mushrooms in the City," on page 115, Marcovaldo faces both a conflict within himself and a conflict with nature.
See *Antagonist, Plot,* and *Protagonist*.

CONNOTATION   The *connotation* of a word is the set of associations that the word calls to mind. For example, most people would prefer a "vintage automobile" to an "old wreck." In fact some car dealers think a buyer would rather look at a "previously owned vehicle" than at a "used car." As these examples illustrate, words with similar

denotations, or literal, dictionary meanings, often have very different connotations. As a result, the words can create different emotional reactions and feelings. Careful writing involves choosing words with appropriate connotations as well as denotations.
See *Denotation*.

CONSONANCE *Consonance* is the repetition of consonant sounds in conjunction with dissimilar vowel sounds. The following word pairs illustrate consonance: *will–wall, flip–flop,* and *hid–head*. In "I Want to Write," Margaret Walker uses consonance within a line:

I want to catch their sunshine laughter in a bowl:
fling dark hands to a darker sky
and *fill* them *full* of stars.

Consonance is used to create musical effects, to link ideas, and to emphasize particular words.
See *Assonance*.

CONVENTION A *convention* is an artificial or unrealistic literary technique, form, or style that is nonetheless accepted by the audience or reader. For example, in a story or a play, a writer may jump backward in time by using the convention known as the *flashback*, even though such movement in time doesn't occur in real life. Similarly, a story or play may contain an all-knowing narrator, even though such a person could not actually exist. Common conventions in drama include asides, sound effects, and the use of a stage to represent a place other than a stage. Common conventions in poetry include rhyme, stanzas, and regular meters.

COUPLET A *couplet* is a pair of consecutive rhyming lines. These lines usually are of the same length and rhythmical pattern. Kathleen Raine's poem "In the Beck" describes "a fish, that quivers in [a] pool." The poem ends with this couplet:

It lives unmoved, equated with the stream,
as flowers are fit for air, man for his dream.

See *Stanza*.

CRISIS The *crisis* in the plot of a story or play is the turning point for the protagonist. At this point the protagonist changes his or her situation or reaches some new understanding. Often the crisis and the climax coincide. The crisis in Knowles's *A Separate Peace,* on page 757, occurs when Gene jounces the tree limb, causing Finny to fall.
See *Climax* and *Plot*.

DACTYL See *Meter*.

DEAD METAPHOR See *Metaphor*.

DENOTATION A *denotation* is the literal or exact meaning of a word. The denotation, or dictionary meaning, includes none of the feelings or suggestions that are part of a word's *connotations*.
See *Connotation*.

DENOUEMENT See *Plot*.

DESCRIPTION A *description* is a portrait, in words, of a person, a place, or an object. Its purpose is to provide the concrete details and lively images that make the appearance of people, places, and things easy for the reader to envision. For example, Bienvenido Santos uses description to set the scene in his essay "Scent of Apples":

In a backyard an old man burned leaves and twigs while a gray-haired woman sat on the porch, her red hands quiet on her lap, watching the smoke rising above the elms, both of them thinking the same thought, perhaps, about a tall, grinning boy with blue eyes and flying hair who went out to war; where could he be now this month when leaves were turning into gold and the fragrance of gathered apples was in the wind?

As this passage shows, vivid description uses details that appeal to the senses so that the reader can easily imagine how something looks, sounds, feels, tastes, or smells. Such details can also help to define the characters or to suggest the mood, or feeling, of the work.
See *Forms of Discourse.*

DEVELOPMENT   See *Plot.*

DIALECT   A *dialect* is the form of a language spoken by people in a particular region or group. Everyone speaks some dialect, usually that of the place where he or she grew up. Dialects differ in vocabulary, in grammar, and in pronunciation. Writers use dialect to make their characters sound realistic and to create local color. In Chinua Achebe's "Civil Peace," on page 215, the characters speak in a Nigerian dialect of English.
See *Local Color* and *Vernacular.*

DIALOGUE   A *dialogue* is a conversation between characters. Writers use dialogue to reveal character, to present events, to add variety to a narrative, and to interest readers.

DICTION   *Diction* is word choice. A writer chooses specific words to suit his or her audience, purpose, and subject. Diction is part of a writer's style and may be described in many ways—as formal or informal, as ordinary or technical, as abstract or concrete. In "Flood" on page 473, Annie Dillard's diction is both informal and exact. She chooses words that are fairly simple but that create a precise picture of the flood so that readers can share her experience.
See *Connotation, Denotation,* and *Style.*

DIMETER   See *Meter.*

DRAMA   A *drama* is a story written to be performed by actors. The playwright, or author of a drama, creates dialogue, or words for the actors to speak, and stage directions, or notes about elements of staging and performance. The audience accepts as believable the presentation on stage as well as whatever dramatic conventions are used, such as soliloquies, asides, poetic language, or the passage of time between acts or scenes. This textbook contains several dramas, including William Shakespeare's *The Tragedy of Julius Caesar,* on page 309. A drama is often divided into long sections called *acts* and into shorter sections called *scenes.* Types of drama include comedy, tragedy, melodrama, and farce.
See *Genre.*

DRAMATIC IRONY   See *Irony.*

DRAMATIC POEM   A *dramatic poem* is a verse that presents the speech of one or more characters. In a *dramatic monologue,* only one character speaks. In a *dramatic dialogue,* two or more characters speak. Dramatic poems are like little plays and usually involve many narrative elements such as setting, conflict, and plot. Such elements may be found in Rudyard Kipling's "Danny Deever," on page 569, and in W. H. Auden's "O What Is That Sound," on page 573.

DYNAMIC CHARACTER   See *Character.*

END-STOPPED LINE   An *end-stopped line* is a line, in a poem, that ends with a major pause. The pause is often punctuated by a comma, dash, colon, semicolon, or period. The following lines from "Beneath the Shadow of the Freeway," by Lorna Dee Cervantes, are end-stopped:

Before rain I notice seagulls.
They walk in flocks,
cautious across lawns:
splayed toes, indecisive beaks.
Grandma says seagulls mean a storm.

The pauses concluding end-stopped lines may vary in degree in order to vary the poem's emphasis and rhythm.
See *Run-on Line.*

EPIC An *epic* is a long narrative poem about the exploits of a hero or a god. Because of its length and its loftiness of theme, an epic usually presents a telling portrait of the culture in which it was produced. The ancient *folk epics* were recited aloud as entertainment at feasts and were not written down until long after they were composed.

The English poem *Beowulf* is a folk epic, as are the two classical Greek poems, the *Odyssey* and the *Iliad*. The *art epic* is modeled on the folk epic but has a known author and is written down as it is composed. Examples include the *Aeneid,* by the Roman poet Virgil, and *Paradise Lost,* by the English poet John Milton.
See *Narrative Poem*.

EPITHET An *epithet* is a brief descriptive phrase that is used like a name. Eve Merriam uses epithets such as "bright words" and "dark words" in "Metaphor," on page 608. *Homeric epithets,* such as "rosy-fingered Dawn," are common in epic poems, and *descriptive epithets* such as "land of liberty" are part of everyday speech and writing.

ESSAY An *essay* is a short, nonfiction work about a particular subject. Essays are of many types but may be grouped on the basis of tone, style, and structure as informal or formal.

The *informal essay* is generally brief, relaxed, and entertaining. It may be humorous, conversational, or unconventional. Whatever the subject or approach, an informal essay usually reveals the writer's character, as if the writer and the reader were sitting and talking together. James Thurber's "The Dog That Bit People," on page 405, shows how playful and entertaining informal essays can be.

By contrast, the *formal essay* is longer, more serious, and less personal. It is also organized more strictly according to some logical pattern. An example in this textbook of the formal essay is Theordore H. White's "The American Idea," on page 511.

An essay also may be categorized by its main purpose—to portray a person, place, or thing through description; to tell a story through narration; to explain and inform through exposition; or to support an opinion through persuasion or argumentation.
See *Argumentation, Description, Exposition, Forms of Discourse, Narration,* and *Persuasion.*

EXACT RHYME See *Rhyme.*

EXAGGERATION See *Hyperbole.*

EXPOSITION *Exposition* is writing or speech that explains, informs, or presents information. The main methods used in expository writing are illustration, classification, definition, comparison and contrast, and analysis. Examples of expository essays in this textbook are Annie Dillard's "Flood," on page 473; Lorraine Hansberrry's "On Summer," on page 493; and Rachel Carson's "The Marginal World," on page 527.

In the plot of a story or drama, the exposition is the part of the work that introduces the characters, the setting, and the basic situation. Such information is typically presented at the beginning of a work. The opening paragraphs of Isak Dinesen's "The Ring," on page 221, set the stage for the story because they immediately tell the reader who the two main characters are, where they are, and how they happen to be there.
See *Forms of Discourse.*

EXTENDED METAPHOR In an *extended metaphor,* as in regular metaphor, a subject is spoken or written of as though it were something else. However, extended metaphor differs from regular metaphor in that several comparisons are made. Eve Merriam uses extended metaphor in her poem "Metaphor," on page 608, to compare morning to "a new sheet of paper."

FABLE   A *fable* is a brief story, usually with animal characters, that teaches a lesson, or moral. The fable is an ancient literary form found in many cultures. The fables of Aesop, a Greek slave who lived in the sixth century B.C., are still popular with children. Other famous writers of fables include La Fontaine, a seventeenth-century Frenchman, and James Thurber, a twentieth-century American.

FANTASY   *Fantasy* is highly imaginative writing that contains elements not found in real life. A writer of fantasy presents improbable characters, places, and events, often ones involving magic or the supernatural. Many science-fiction stories, such as Ray Bradbury's "There Will Come Soft Rains," on page 121, contain elements of fantasy.

FARCE   *Farce* is a kind of comedy that features physical humor, stereotyped characters, and improbable plots. Writers of farces make considerable use of such literary devices as hyperbole, irony of situation, and surprising twists of the plot. Many farces involve mistaken identity and contain recognition scenes in which the true identities of characters are revealed. A farce may be a complete play or a scene within a play. William Shakespeare often used farce for contrast or for comic relief within his serious works. An example can be found in Act I, Scene i of *The Tragedy of Julius Caesar.*
See *Comedy* and *Drama.*

FICTION   *Fiction* is prose writing that tells about imaginary characters and events. The term is generally used to refer to narrative prose, to novels and short stories, rather than to poetry and drama. Fictional writing is sometimes based on real people, places, and events. However, the fiction writer reshapes these realistic elements, placing them in an imaginary or invented context. Doris Lessing's "Through the Tunnel," on page

147, and John Knowles's *A Separate Peace,* on page 757, are examples of fiction.
See *Genre, Novel,* and *Short Story.*

FIGURATIVE LANGUAGE   *Figurative language* is writing or speech not meant to be interpreted literally. Most writers, and especially poets, use figurative language to help readers to see things in new ways. For example, Naomi Long Madgett begins her poem "Black Woman" with these examples of figurative language:

My hair is springy like the forest grasses
That cushion the feet of squirrels—
Crinkled and blown in a south breeze
Like the small leaves of native bushes.

My black eyes are coals burning
Like a low, full jungle moon
Through the darkness of being.

Madgett does not mean, literally, that forest grasses grow from her head or that she has coals for eyes. Instead, she means her language to be interpreted figuratively. She is using types of figurative language known as simile and metaphor to describe herself imaginatively.

The many types of figurative language are called *figures of speech.* Poets and other writers use figurative language to create vivid word pictures, to make their writing emotionally intense and concentrated, and to state their ideas in new and unusual ways.
See *Figure of Speech.*

FIGURE OF SPEECH   A *figure of speech* is an expression or a word used imaginatively rather than literally. Types of figurative language include apostrophe, hyperbole, irony, metaphor, metonymy, oxymoron, paradox, personification, simile, synecdoche, and understatement.
See *Figurative Language.*

FIRST-PERSON POINT OF VIEW   See *Point of View.*

FLASHBACK A *flashback* is a section of a literary work that interrupts the sequence of events to relate an event from an earlier time. The events in a work are usually presented in chronological order, the order of their occurrence in time. However, a writer may present a flashback that describes an earlier event in order to shed light on the present situation. A flashback is often presented as a character's memory or recollection. For example, in William Melvin Kelley's "A Visit to Grandmother," on page 69, the grandmother tells about events that took place at least twenty-five years earlier. Writers often use flashbacks to show what motivates a character or to supply background information in a dramatic way.
See *Foreshadowing*.

FOIL A *foil* is a character who provides a contrast to another character. In William Shakespeare's *The Tragedy of Julius Caesar,* for example, both the ambitious Cassius and the shrewd Antony are foils for the idealistic Brutus.

FOLK BALLAD See *Ballad*.

FOLKLORE *Folklore* includes the stories, legends, myths, ballads, riddles, sayings, and other traditions handed down orally by ordinary people. Folklore reveals a great deal about the culture in which it originates. Folklore also influences written literature in many ways. John Keats's "La Belle Dame sans Merci," on page 553, draws on British fairy lore, whereas Edgar Allan Poe's "Eldorado," on page 577, draws on a folk legend of the Americas.
See *Oral Tradition*.

FOLK TALE A *folk tale* is a story composed orally and then passed from person to person by word of mouth. Folk tales originated among people who could not read and write. These people told the tales aloud. The tales were passed from generation to generation and then, in the modern era, were collected and written down by scholars. The well-known *Grimm's Fairy Tales* is a collection of European folk tales.
See *Oral Tradition*.

FOOT A *foot* is a group of two or three syllables with a particular pattern of stresses. Poets often create rhythmical patterns, or meters, by repeating specific types of feet. The most common feet in English poetry are iambs, trochees, anapests, and dactyls.
See *Meter* and *Scansion*.

FORESHADOWING *Foreshadowing* is the use, in a literary work, of clues that suggest events that have yet to occur. In W. W. Jacobs's "The Monkey's Paw," on page 31, many clues suggest what wishing on the monkey's paw will bring. For example, Mr. White's son says that he bets he never will see the money wished for by his father. This guess, of course, proves true and foreshadows the death of the son. Writers use foreshadowing to create suspense and to prepare readers for the outcome of the plot.
See *Flashback*.

FORM The *form* of a literary work is its structure, shape, pattern, organization, or style. A work's form is often distinguished from its content, or subject matter.

FORMS OF DISCOURSE The *forms of discourse* are the main types of writing, classified by purpose. Common forms of discourse include description, narration, exposition, persuasion, and argumentation. Sometimes a work is written entirely in one of these forms. More often, however, the forms of discourse are used together to support each other. For instance, a narrative story may include description, or an argument may begin with an expository section that explains key terms or that presents background information.
See *Argumentation, Description, Exposition, Narration,* and *Persuasion*.

FREE VERSE *Free verse* is poetry not written in a regular rhythmical pattern, or meter. Instead of having metrical feet and lines, free verse has a varying rhythm that suits its meaning and that uses the sounds of spoken language in lines of different lengths. Ana Castillo begins her free-verse poem "Napa, California" this way:

> We pick
>   the bittersweet grapes
>   at harvest
>   one
>   by
>   one
> with leather worn hands.

Free verse is one of the most common forms in twentieth-century poetry.
See *Meter* and *Rhythm*.

GENRE A *genre* is a division or type of literature. Literature is commonly divided into three major genres: poetry, prose, and drama. Each major genre is in turn divided into smaller genres, as follows:
1. *Poetry:* Lyric Poetry, Concrete Poetry, Dramatic Poetry, Narrative Poetry, and Epic Poetry
2. *Prose:* Fiction (Novels and Short Stories) and Nonfiction (Biography, Autobiography, Letters, Essays, and Reports)
3. *Drama:* Serious Drama and Tragedy, Comic Drama, Melodrama, and Farce
See *Drama, Poetry,* and *Prose.*

HAIKU *Haiku* is a three-line Japanese verse form. The first and third lines of a haiku have five syllables. The second line has seven syllables. See examples of haiku on pages 655 and 656.

HEPTAMETER See *Meter.*

HEPTASTICH See *Stanza.*

HERO/HEROINE A *hero* or *heroine* is a character whose actions are inspiring or noble. Often heroes struggle to overcome foes or to escape difficulties. The most obvious examples of heroes and heroines are the larger-than-life characters in myths and legends. However, more ordinary characters can, and often do, perform heroic deeds.

HEXAMETER See *Meter.*

HYPERBOLE *Hyperbole* is deliberate exaggeration or overstatement that is not meant to be taken literally. For example, as bad as Muggs is in James Thurber's "The Dog That Bit People," on page 405, a reader may suspect exaggeration when Thurber says, "He gave me more trouble than all the other fifty-four or -five [dogs] put together."
See *Figurative Language.*

IAMB See *Meter.*

IAMBIC PENTAMETER *Iambic pentameter* is a line of poetry with five iambic feet, each with one unstressed syllable followed by one stressed syllable (˘ ´). Iambic pentameter may be rhymed or unrhymed. Unrhymed iambic pentameter is called *blank verse.* These opening lines from Arna Bontemps's "A Note of Humility" are in iambic pentameter:

> When all | our hopes | are sown | on ston|y
>   ground
> and we | have yield|ed up | the thought | of
>   gain,
> long af|ter our | last songs | have lost|their
>   sound
> we may | come back, | we may | come back |
>   again.

Because iambic pentameter sounds like ordinary spoken language, it is one of the most commonly used rhythmical patterns.
See *Blank Verse* and *Meter.*

IMAGE An *image* is a word or phrase that appeals to one or more of the five senses—sight, hearing, touch, taste, or smell.
See *Imagery.*

IMAGERY *Imagery* is the descriptive language used in literature to re-create sensory experiences. The images in a work supply details of sight, sound, taste, touch, smell, or movement and help the reader to sense the experience being described. In her poem "Living Tenderly," May Swenson uses imagery of sight to describe a turtle:

> My body a rounded stone
> with a pattern of smooth seams.
> My head a short snake,
> retractive, protective.
> My legs come out of their sleeves
> or shrink within,
> and so does my chin.
> My eyelids are quick clamps.

INCITING INCIDENT See *Plot.*

INCONGRUITY *Incongruity* is the combination of incompatible or opposite elements. Sometimes a writer's wording may not match the subject. In Mark Twain's "Luck," on page 89, the speaker admires Scoresby as "that demigod," noting "the noble gravity of his countenance; the simple honesty that expressed itself all over him; the sweet unconsciousness of his greatness" only to hear from another guest that "Privately—he's an absolute fool." When a writer talks about something trivial in formal language, the surprise of the incongruity may create a comic or humorous effect.

INVERSION An *inversion* is a reversal of the regular word order in a sentence. For instance, Humbert Wolfe begins his poem "The Gray Squirrel" with "Like a small gray/coffeepot/sits the squirrel." These lines reverse the usual subject-predicate order, "The squirrel sits like a small gray coffeepot." Poets often use inversion to emphasize certain words and sometimes to fit them into the meter of a poem.

IRONY *Irony* is the general name given to literary techniques that involve surprising, interesting, or amusing contradictions. In *verbal irony* words are used to suggest the opposite of their usual meaning. In *dramatic irony* there is a contradiction between what a character thinks and what the reader or audience knows to be true. In *irony of situation,* an event occurs that directly contradicts the expectations of the reader or the audience.

During the funeral in William Shakespeare's *The Tragedy of Julius Caesar,* on page 309, Antony calls Brutus "an honorable man" when, in fact, he wants the people to think just the opposite. This is an example of verbal irony.

In the same play, dramatic irony occurs when the audience, knowing that Caesar will be assassinated, watches him set out on the ides of March.

In Italo Calvino's "Mushrooms in the City," on page 115, Marcovaldo expects the mushrooms to bring pleasure; instead, they turn out to be poisonous. This is an example of irony of situation.

IRONY OF SITUATION See *Irony.*

LEGEND A *legend* is a widely told story about the past, one that may or may not have a foundation in fact. One example, retold in many versions, is the legend of King Arthur. A legend often reflects a people's identity or cultural values. It generally has more historical truth and less emphasis on the supernatural than does a myth. See *Oral Tradition*

LIMITED POINT OF VIEW See *Point of View.*

LOCAL COLOR *Local color* is the use of characters and details from a specific geographic region. Local color suggests the special features of the area through the regional dialect, customs, clothing, manners, attitudes, scenery, and landscape. Josephina Niggli's "The Street of the Cañon," on page 127, uses local color to present Mexican village life, whereas Juanita Platero and Siyowin Miller's "Chee's Daughter," on page 77, uses local color to portray Navajo life.

LYRIC POEM   A *lyric poem* is a highly musical verse that expresses the observations and feelings of a single speaker. A lyric may follow a traditional pattern, as does a sonnet, or it may be in free verse. Unlike a narrative poem, a lyric presents an experience or creates a single effect, but it does not tell a full story. An example is Sara Teasdale's "There Will Come Soft Rains":

> There will come soft rains and the smell of the
>   ground,
> And swallows circling with their
>   shimmering sound;
> And frogs in the pools singing at night,
> And wild plum-trees in tremulous white.
>
> Robins will wear their feathery fire
> Whistling their whims on a low fence-wire;
> And not one will know of the war, not one
> Will care at last when it is done.
>
> Not one would mind, neither bird nor tree,
> If mankind perished utterly;
>
> And Spring herself, when she woke at dawn,
> Would scarcely know that we were gone.

This lyric poem concentrates on describing a particular moment, not on telling how it came about or why or what might happen next. In contrast, Ray Bradbury's story on page 121, which has the same title as the poem, shows how this theme can be treated in a short story. Among contemporary American poets, the lyric is the most common poetic form.

MAIN CHARACTER   See *Character*.

METAPHOR   A *metaphor* is a figure of speech in which one thing is spoken of as though it were something else. In a metaphor a comparison is suggested or implied through identification, as in "death *is* a long sleep" or "the sleeping dead." In contrast, "death is *like* a long sleep" is a *simile*. A simile uses *like, as, than,* or similar phrasing to make a comparison.

A metaphor may be brief, as in Simon J. Ortiz's "A Pretty Woman." He describes looking over the edge of a mesa and finding that "the land was a pretty woman/smiling at us." An *ex-tended metaphor,* however, is developed at length, as in the third section of "Four Glimpses of Night," by Frank Marshall Davis:

> Peddling
> From door to door
> Night sells
> Black bags of peppermint stars
> Heaping cones of vanilla moon
> Until
> His wares are gone
> Then shuffles homeward
> Jingling the gray coins
> Of Daybreak.

A *mixed metaphor* occurs when two metaphors are jumbled together. For example, thorns and rain are illogically mixed in "The thorns of life rained down on him." Because a mixed metaphor does not consistently stick to one idea, it is not clear and may even be funny. A *dead metaphor* is one that is not effective because it has been used too often. Many common expressions, such as "the foot of the stairs" or "toe the line" are dead metaphors because they have lost their freshness. They contrast with the metaphors used to make writing, especially poetry, more imaginative and more meaningful.
See *Figurative Language*.

METER   The *meter* of a poem is its rhythmical pattern. This pattern is determined by the number and types of stresses, or beats, in each line. To describe the meter of a poem, you must *scan* its lines. *Scanning* involves marking the stressed and unstressed syllables, as follows:

> Whĕn I | ăm áll | ălóne
> Énvў | mĕ thén,
> Fŏr I | hăve bétt|ĕr friénds
> Thăn wŏ|mĕn ănd mén.
>   —Sara Teasdale, "Thoughts"

Each strong stress is marked with a slanted line (´), and each weak stress is marked with a horseshoe symbol (˘). The weak and strong stresses are then divided by vertical lines (|) into groups called *feet*. The following types of feet are common in English poetry:

1. *Iamb:* a foot with one weak stress followed by one strong stress, as in the word "ărŏúnd"
2. *Trochee:* a foot with one strong stress followed by one weak stress, as in the word "flútter"
3. *Anapest:* a foot with two weak stresses followed by one strong stress, as in the phrase "ĭn ă cár"
4. *Dactyl:* a foot with one strong stress followed by two weak stresses, as in the word "glím-mĕrĭng"
5. *Spondee:* a foot with two strong stresses, as in the word "níghtfáll"
6. *Pyrrhic:* a foot with two weak stresses, as in the last foot of the word "ĕháust|ĭvĕly"
7. *Amphibrach:* a foot with a weak syllable, one strong syllable, and another weak syllable, as in "ă wónder|fŭl póĕm"
8. *Amphimacer:* a foot with a strong syllable, one weak syllable, and another strong syllable, as in "báck ănd fórth"

Depending on the type of foot that is most common in them, lines of poetry are described as *iambic, trochaic, anapestic,* or *dactylic.*

Lines are also described in terms of the number of feet that occur in them, as follows:

1. *Monometer:* verse written in one-foot lines

Ăll thíngs
Ăre ă
Bĕcómĭng
    —Heraclitus

2. *Dimeter:* verse written in two-foot lines

Yŏur gríef | ănd míne
Mŭst ĭn|tĕrtwíne
Lĭke séa | ănd rívĕr
    —Countee Cullen, "Any Human to Another"

3. *Trimeter:* verse written in three-foot lines

Tĕll me|ăno séc|rĕt, fríĕnd,
Mў héart | wĭll nót | sŭstáin
Ĭts lóad, | tŏo héav|ĭly
    —Francesca Yetunde Pereira, "The Burden"

4. *Tetrameter:* verse written in four-foot lines

Wŏod ŏf | pópplĕ | pále ăs | móonbeăm
Wŏod ŏf | oăk fŏr| yóke ănd | bárn-beăm
    —Edna St. Vincent Millay, "Counting-Out Rhyme"

5. *Pentameter:* verse written in five-foot lines

Ĭ scátt|ĕred séed | ĕnóugh | tŏ plánt | thĕ lánd
Ĭn róws | frŏm Cán|ădá | tŏ Méx|ĭcó
Bŭt fór | mў réap|ĭng ón|lў whát | thĕ hánd
Căn hóld | ăt ónce | ĭs áll | thăt Í | căn shów.
    —Arna Bontemps, "A Black Man Talks of Reaping"

A six-foot line is called a *hexameter.* A line with seven feet is a *heptameter.*

A complete description of the meter of a line tells how many feet there are in the line and what kind of foot is most common. Thus the lines from Bontemps's poem would be described as *iambic pentameter. Blank verse* is poetry written in unrhymed iambic pentameter. Poetry that does not have a regular meter is called *free verse.*

METONYMY *Metonymy* is a figure of speech that substitutes something closely related for the thing actually meant. In his poem "Spring," Richard Hovey says,

I said in my heart, "I am sick of four
    walls and a ceiling.
I have need of the sky. . . . "

Here "sky" stands for open air and space, expressing the speaker's need for outdoor activity and change, and "four walls and a ceiling" stand for both a room and a claustrophobic feeling. People use metonymy in everyday speech when they refer to the executive branch of government as "The White House."
See *Figurative Language* and *Synecdoche.*

MINOR CHARACTER   See *Character.*

MIXED METAPHOR   See *Metaphor.*

MONOLOGUE   A *monologue* is a speech made entirely by one person or character. A monologue may be addressed to another character or to the audience, or it may be a *soliloquy*—a speech that presents the character's thoughts as though the character were overheard when alone. In Howard Koch's *Invasion From Mars,* on page 251, Professor Richard Pierson's long monologue tells about his trip from Grovers Mill to Newark after the Martian attack.
See *Soliloquy.*

MONOMETER   See *Meter.*

MOOD   *Mood,* or atmosphere, is the feeling created in the reader by a literary work or passage. The mood may be suggested by the writer's choice of words, by events in the work, or by the physical setting. For example, the first paragraph in Juanita Platero and Siyowin Miller's "Chee's Daughter," on page 77, describes the angle of Chee's hat and his songless ride home, despite a fine horse and a sunny winter's day. The passage suggests Chee's unhappiness and grief as well as the power of the natural world to restore a person's spirit.
See *Setting* and *Tone.*

MORAL   A *moral* is a lesson taught by a literary work. Fables present morals that are directly stated. Poems, novels, short stories, and plays often present morals that are not directly stated but must be inferred by the reader.

MOTIVATION   A *motivation* is a reason that explains or partially explains a character's thoughts, feelings, actions, or speech. Convincing motivation usually combines outside forces with inside forces, linking events in the plot with the character's personality and needs. The more effectively and persuasively a writer presents a character's motivations, the more realistic and believable the character will seem.
See *Character.*

MYTH   A *myth* is a fictional tale that explains the actions of gods or heroes or the causes of natural phenomena. The *mythology* of a people or of a society is the group of myths created by them to explain where the world came from, why certain events occur, and what life means. Literary works often allude to or adapt stories from Greek, Roman, and Norse mythology.
See *Oral Tradition.*

NARRATION   *Narration* is writing that tells a story. The act of telling a story is also called narration. The *narrative,* or story, is told by a storyteller called the *narrator.* The story generally is told chronologically, in time order, but it may include flashbacks and foreshadowing. Narratives may be either fiction or nonfiction. Narration is one of the forms of discourse and is used in such works as novels, short stories, plays, narrative poems, essays, anecdotes, and newspaper reports.
See *Forms of Discourse, Narrative, Narrative Poem,* and *Narrator.*

NARRATIVE   A *narrative* is a story told in fiction, nonfiction, poetry, or drama.
See *Narration.*

NARRATIVE POEM   A *narrative poem* tells a story in verse. There are many types of narrative poems. Ballads use four- or six-line stanzas to tell of dramatic events involving ordinary people. *Epics* tell of the adventures of heroes or gods. *Metrical romances* tell tales of love and chivalry. Although ballads are still popular, especially when sung to music, narrative poetry now is less common than lyric poetry or narrative prose fiction. Examples of narrative poems in the textbook are John Keats's "La Belle Dame sans Merci," on page 553; Robert Frost's "Two Tramps in Mud Time," on page 557; and Henry Wadsworth Longfellow's "The Wreck of the Hesperus," on page 563.
See *Ballad, Epic, Lyric, Narrative,* and *Romance.*

NARRATOR   A *narrator* is a speaker or character who tells a story. A story or novel may be narrated by a main character, by a minor character, or by someone uninvolved in the story. The narrator may speak in the first person (using *I* or *we*), or in the third person (using *he, she, it,* or *they*). The third-person narrator may have an *omniscient* point of view, and know everything, or a *limited* point of view, and know only what one character knows. Because the writer's choice of narrator helps determine the point of view, this decision affects what version of a story is told and how readers will react to it.
See *Point of View*.

NONFICTION   *Nonfiction* is prose writing that presents and explains ideas or that tells about real people, places, objects, or events. The nonfiction writer tries to present what is true and accurate, without imaginary or invented additions. Nonfiction includes biography, autobiography, historical accounts, essays, and other writings about real people, places, events, or subjects.
See *Fiction*.

NOVEL   A *novel* is a long work of fiction. As a long narrative, a novel often has a complicated plot, many major and minor characters, several interrelated themes, and several settings. Novels can be grouped in many ways, based on the historical periods in which they were written, on the subjects and themes they treat, on the techniques the writers use, or on the literary movements that influenced them. Popular types of novels are historical novels, mysteries, science-fiction novels, and thrillers.
See *Fiction* and *Genre*.

OCTAVE   See *Stanza*.

OMNISCIENT POINT OF VIEW   See *Point of View*.

ONOMATOPOEIA   *Onomatopoeia* is the use of words that imitate sounds. Examples of such words include *hiss, hum, murmur,* and *rustle.* Robert Frost uses onomatopoeia in this line: "The *buzz* saw *snarled* and *rattled* in the yard." Onomatopoeia is used to create musical effects and to reinforce meaning, especially in poetry.

ORAL TRADITION   The *oral tradition* is the passing of songs, stories, and poems from generation to generation by word of mouth. The oral traditions of peoples around the globe have given us many myths, legends, spirituals, folk ballads, fairy tales, and other stories or songs.
See *Ballad, Folklore, Folk Tale, Legend,* and *Myth*.

OVERSTATEMENT   See *Hyperbole*.

OXYMORON   An *oxymoron* is a figure of speech that puts together two opposing or contradictory ideas. An oxymoron, such as "freezing fire," thus suggests a *paradox* in just a few words.
See *Figurative Language* and *Paradox*.

PARABLE   A *parable* is a brief story, usually with human characters, that is told to teach a moral lesson. The most famous parables are those told by Christ in the Bible. Many writers make allusions to these famous Biblical parables.

PARADOX   A *paradox* is a statement that seems to be contradictory but that actually presents a truth. Dorothy Donnelly uses paradox in "Glass World" when she says, "Ice/is setting the world on fire." Because a paradox is surprising or even shocking, it draws the reader's attention to what is being said.
See *Figurative Language* and *Oxymoron*.

PARALLELISM   *Parallelism* is the repetition of a sentence pattern, or grammatical structure. Elizabeth Barrett Browning uses parallelism in her "Sonnet 43," as the opening octave shows:

How do I love thee? Let me count the ways.
I love thee to the depth and breadth and height
My soul can reach, when feeling out of sight
For the ends of Being and ideal Grace.
I love thee to the level of everyday's
Most quiet need, by sun and candle light.
I love thee freely, as men strive for Right;
I love thee purely, as they turn from Praise.

Parallelism is used in poetry and in other writing to emphasize and to link related ideas.
See *Repetition.*

PARODY   A *parody* is an imitation of another work that exaggerates or distorts features of the work to make fun of it or simply to amuse readers. In *Don Quixote* on page 739, Miguel de Cervantes parodies the early romance literature.

PERSONIFICATION   *Personification* is a type of figurative language in which a nonhuman subject is given human qualities. In "Moonlight Night: Carmel," Langston Hughes personifies ocean waves:

Tonight the waves march
In long ranks
Cutting the darkness
With their silver shanks,

Cutting the darkness
And kissing the moon
And beating the land's
Edge into a swoon.

Effective personification of things or ideas makes them seem vital and alive, as if they were human.
See *Figurative Language.*

PERSUASION   *Persuasion* is writing or speech that attempts to convince the reader to adopt a particular opinion or course of action. Persuasion is used in advertising, editorials, sermons, political speeches, and in other writing and speech that urges people to think or act in certain ways. Lorraine Hansberry's essay "On Summer," on page 493, is a persuasive essay. Some critics

and scholars make a distinction between persuasion and argumentation, reserving the former for emotional appeals and the latter for appeals to reason.
See *Argumentation* and *Forms of Discourse.*

PETRARCHAN SONNET   The *Petrarchan,* or *Italian, sonnet* is a fourteen-line lyric poem. It is named for the Italian poet Francesco Petrarca, who wrote sonnets about his beloved Laura. The Petrarchan sonnet has no more than five rhymes, usually is written in iambic pentameter, and generally follows a traditional rhyme scheme. This type of sonnet has two parts. First is the eight-line *octave,* traditionally rhymed *abba abba.* This section asks a question, reveals a problem, or tells a brief story. Next comes the six-line *sestet,* generally rhymed *cde cde* or with some combination of *cd* rhymes. The sestet answers the question, solves the problem, or comments on the story in the octave. In this way the two parts of the Petrarchan sonnet work together to form a whole. "I Shall Go Back Again to the Bleak Shore," by Edna St. Vincent Millay, illustrates this sonnet pattern:

I shall go back again to the bleak shore	*a*
And build a little shanty on the sand,	*b*
In such a way that the extremest band	*b*
Of brittle seaweed will escape my door	*a*
But by a yard or two; and nevermore	*a*
Shall I return to take you by the hand;	*b*
I shall be gone to what I understand,	*b*
And happier than I ever was before.	*a*
The love that stood a moment in your eyes,	*c*
The words that lay a moment on your tongue,	*d*
Are one with all that in a moment dies,	*c*
A little under-said and over-sung.	*d*
But I shall find the sullen rocks and skies	*c*
Unchanged from what they were when I was young.	*d*

See *Lyric, Shakespearean Sonnet,* and *Sonnet.*

PLOT   *Plot* is the sequence of events in a literary work. In most novels, dramas, short stories and narrative poems, the plot involves both char-

acters and a central conflict. The plot usually begins with an *exposition,* which introduces the setting, the characters, and the basic situation. This is followed by the *inciting incident,* which introduces the central conflict. The conflict then increases during the *development* until it reaches a high point of interest or suspense, the *climax.* The climax is followed by the *resolution,* or end, of the central conflict. Any events that occur after the resolution make up the *denouement.* The *rising action* consists of all the events that precede the climax. The *falling action* consists of all the events that follow the climax.
See *Climax, Conflict,* and *Crisis.*

POETRY *Poetry* is one of the three major types of literature, the others being prose and drama. Defining poetry more precisely isn't easy, for there is no single, unique characteristic that all poems share. Poems are often divided into lines and stanzas and often employ regular rhythmical patterns, or meters. However, some poems are written out like prose, and some are written in free verse. Most poems make use of highly concise, musical, and emotionally charged language. Many also make use of imagery, figurative language, and special devices such as rhyme.
See *Genre.*

POINT OF VIEW The *point of view* is the perspective, or vantage point, from which a story is told. A story may be told by a narrator who supplies more information about all the characters and events than any one character could know. Such a narrator has an *omniscient,* or all-knowing, point of view. For example, the narrator in Anita Desai's "Games at Twilight," on page 3, provides Ravi's thoughts as well as information about the other children that only an omniscient narrator could provide.

Instead of knowing everything, the narrator may know only what one character knows. This character may or may not personally tell the story. If the character tells the story directly using *I, me,* and *we,* the writer has chosen a *first-person* point of view. For example, the narrator in Julio Cortázar's "Axolotl," on page 107, speaks in the first person, and the story is limited to his own words and knowledge.

If the narrator reveals only one character's inner thoughts and is not himself or herself a character in the story, then the story is told from a *limited third-person* point of view. Like an omniscient narrator, this narrator speaks in the third person, using *he, she, it,* and *they.* However, like a first-person narrator, this narrator reveals the inner life of only one character. Italo Calvino uses a limited third-person point of view in "Mushrooms in the City," on page 115.

Each point of view creates a different story with a different account of events. When the writer chooses a particular point of view and narrator, that choice affects both the nature of the story and the reader's understanding of the story.
See *Narrator* and *Speaker.*

PROSE *Prose* is the ordinary form of written language. Most writing that is not poetry, drama, or song is considered prose. Prose is one of the major genres of literature and occurs in two forms: fiction and nonfiction.
See *Fiction, Genre,* and *Nonfiction.*

PROTAGONIST The *protagonist* is the main character in a literary work. The protagonist is at the center of the action, often in conflict with an external antagonist or with internal forces. In Anne Tyler's "With All Flags Flying" on page 229, Mr. Carpenter is the protagonist. He struggles to keep his independence, against his family's good intentions and against his own physical weakness.
See *Antagonist* and *Conflict.*

PUN A *pun* is a play on words. Some puns involve a single word or phrase that has two different meanings. Others involve two different words or phrases with the same sound, such as the words *awl* and *all* in the scene from William Shakespeare's *The Tragedy of Julius Caesar* on page 309. Puns are often humorous but can have serious purposes.

PYRRHIC   See *Meter.*

QUATRAIN   A *quatrain* is a four-line poem or a stanza with four lines. If a quatrain is rhymed, it usually uses one of these rhyme schemes: *abab, aabb, abba,* or *abcb.* "For My Grandmother," by Countee Cullen, is a quatrain with the rhyme scheme *abcb:*

This lovely flower fell to see;	*a*
Work gently sun and rain;	*b*
She held it as her dying creed	*c*
That she would grow again.	*b*

See *Rhyme Scheme* and *Stanza.*

REFRAIN   A *refrain* is a regularly repeated line or group of lines in a poem or song. Most refrains come at the ends of stanzas, as does "An' they're hangin' Danny Deever in the mornin'" in Rudyard Kipling's "Danny Deever," on page 569.
See *Repetition.*

REPETITION   *Repetition* is the use, more than once, of any element of language—a sound, a word, a phrase, a clause, a sentence, or a rhythmical or grammatical pattern. In "The Marginal World," on page 527, Rachel Carson uses repetition to connect her points and to unify her writing. When she describes the pool within the cave, she repeats the key word *beauty* and the idea of "exquisite beauty" through related words like *magical, fragile, delicate,* and *enchanted.* Careless repetition bores a reader, but successful repetition links ideas, emphasizes main points, and makes the language forceful and musical.
See *Alliteration, Assonance, Consonance, Parallelism,* and *Rhyme.*

RESOLUTION   See *Plot.*

RHYME   *Rhyme* is the repetition of sounds at the ends of words. Rhymed words have the same vowel sounds in their accented syllables. The consonants before the vowels may be different, but the consonants after them are the same. Examples of rhyming words are *frog* and *bog,* and *willow* and *pillow.* The type of rhyme used most often is *end rhyme,* in which the rhyming words are repeated at the ends of lines. *Internal rhyme* occurs when the rhyming words fall within a line. In the first stanza of Edgar Allan Poe's "The Raven," rhymes link words at the ends of lines, within lines, and in different lines:

> Once upon a midnight *dreary,* while I pondered, weak and *weary,*
> Over many a quaint and curious volume of forgotten *lore—*
> While I nodded, nearly *napping,* suddenly there came a *tapping,*
> As of some one gently *rapping, rapping* at my chamber *door,*
> "'Tis some visitor," I muttered, *tapping* at my chamber *door—*
> Only this and nothing *more.*

Exact rhyme is present when the rhyming sounds are identical, as in *love* and *dove.* *Approximate,* or *slant, rhyme* is present when the sounds are similar, as in *prove* and *glove.* Both exact and approximate rhymes are illustrated in this stanza from "Mind," by Richard Wilbur:

> Mind in the purest play is like some *bat*
> That beats about in caverns all *alone,*
> Contriving by a kind of senseless *wit.*
> Not to conclude against a wall of *stone.*

Bat and *wit* illustrate approximate, or slant, rhyme, whereas *alone* and *stone* illustrate exact rhyme.
See *Rhyme Scheme.*

RHYME SCHEME   A *rhyme scheme* is a regular pattern of rhyming words in a poem. To describe a rhyme scheme, use different letters of the alphabet for the different sounds at the ends of the lines. For example, next to the lines of "Fire and Ice" by Robert Frost, *a* stands for the first sound, *b* for the next, and *c* for the third:

Some say the world will end in fire,	*a*
Some say in ice.	*b*
From what I've tasted of desire	*a*
I hold with those who favor fire.	*a*
But if it had to perish twice,	*b*
I think I know enough of hate	*c*
To say that for destruction ice	*b*
Is also great	*c*
And would suffice.	*b*

The rhyme scheme here is *abaabcbcb.* In this poem the rhyme scheme directly reinforces the meaning. Each *a* rhyme has to do with fire, each *b* with ice.

In many poems with more than one stanza, the pattern of the first stanza is repeated in each of the next two stanzas. As a result, each new stanza seems consistent with the others. Each also seems different because it uses its own rhyming sounds.
See *Rhyme* and *Stanza.*

RHYTHM *Rhythm* is the pattern of beats, or stresses, in spoken or written language. In prose this pattern is often irregular. In traditional poetry regular rhythmical pattern, or meter, is used. Poetry that is rhythmic but that does not have a regular pattern is called *free verse.* Instead of following a set metrical pattern, a poem in free verse has its own rhythm that suits its meaning.

In both poetry and prose, writers use rhythm to emphasize their ideas and feelings. In addition, the musical quality of rhythm is appealing because people enjoy expecting and finding a pattern.
See *Foot, Free Verse, Meter,* and *Scansion.*

RISING ACTION   See *Plot.*

ROMANCE   A *romance* is a story that presents fantastic events, especially ones involving love or chivalry. When written in verse, such a story is called a *metrical romance.* Traditional medieval romances, such as Sir Thomas Malory's tales of King Arthur, tell of the deeds and loves of noble knights and ladies. These stories are full of idealized characters, faraway settings, and mysterious or magical elements. In loosely structured, entertaining incidents, the heroic characters bravely battle their evil antagonists. During the nineteenth century, a revitalized romance tradition was opposed by the more realistic novel. This return to romance influenced many writers, including Alfred, Lord Tennyson, who retold the Arthurian legends in his long narrative poem *Idylls of the King.*
See *Narrative Poem.*

ROUND CHARACTER   See *Character.*

RUN-ON LINE   A *run-on line* is one that does not end with a pause. Instead, the idea is continued on the next line. Naoshi Koriyama's "Unfolding Bud" shows how one line can move to the next:

One is amazed
by a water-lily bud
Unfolding
With each passing day,
Taking on a richer color
And new dimensions.

Three run-on lines begin the poem, each leading the reader on to the next line. Thus the poem unfolds, line by line, just as a water-lily bud does. In contrast, lines four and six are end-stopped, as their punctuation shows. They stop the poem's movement after the unfolding and after the comment on its meaning. Besides reinforcing meaning, run-on lines can change a poem's rhythm, adding variety and helping the writer to avoid monotony.
See *Caesura, End-Stopped Line,* and *Rhythm.*

SATIRE   *Satire* is a type of writing that ridicules or criticizes the faults of individuals or groups. The satirist may use a tolerant, sympathetic tone or an angry, bitter tone. Some satire is written in poetry and some in prose.

Although a satire may be humorous, its purpose is not simply to make readers laugh but to correct, through laughter, the flaws and shortcomings it points out.

SCANSION   *Scansion* is the process of figuring out a poem's metrical pattern. When a poem is scanned, its stressed and unstressed syllables are marked. Their pattern shows what poetic foot is used and how many feet appear in each line.
See *Meter.*

SCENE   See *Drama.*

SCIENCE FICTION   *Science fiction* is writing that tells about imaginary events that involve science or technology. Many science-fiction stories are set in the future. Ray Bradbury's "There Will Come Soft Rains," on page 121, is an example of science fiction.

SCRIPT   A *script* is the written version of a play, a movie, a radio program, or a television show. The script provides the information needed to produce the work—the list of characters, the stage directions, the speaking parts for the characters, and any other directions the writer decides to include.

SENSORY LANGUAGE   *Sensory language* is writing or speech that appeals to one or more of the senses.
See *Image.*

SESTET   See *Stanza.*

SETTING   The *setting* of a literary work is the time and place of the action. A setting provides the location and background for the characters and plot and may help to create a particular atmosphere, or mood. Sometimes the central conflict of a story is a struggle against some element of the setting.

SHAKESPEAREAN SONNET   The *Shakespearean,* or *English, sonnet* is a fourteen-line lyric poem. It follows a traditional rhyme scheme and usually is written in iambic pentameter. It is named for William Shakespeare, who perfected the form in a series of sonnets that he wrote in his youth. This type of sonnet developed after English poets brought the Petrarchan sonnet home from Italy and changed its form.

The typical Shakespearean sonnet is made up of three quatrains and a couplet and follows the rhyme scheme *abab cdcd efef gg.* See William Shakespeare's sonnet "Shall I Compare Thee to a Summer's Day?" on page 650.
See *Lyric Poem, Petrarchan Sonnet,* and *Sonnet.*

SHORT STORY   A *short story* is brief work of fiction. The short story resembles the longer novel but generally has a simpler plot and setting. In addition, the short story tends to reveal character at a crucial moment rather than to develop it through many incidents. For example, Doris Lessing's "Through the Tunnel," on page 147, concentrates on what happens as Jerry learns to swim the tunnel.
See *Fiction, Genre,* and *Novel.*

SIMILE   A *simile* is a figure of speech that makes a direct comparison between two subjects using either *like* or *as.* In "Tiger Year" Laura Tokunaga uses this simile:

> planets circle in the gathering
> dark like pale insects
> around the opened throats of flowers.

By drawing together different things, effective similes make vivid and meaningful comparisons that enrich what the writer has to say.
See *Figurative Language.*

SLANT RHYME   See *Rhyme.*

SOLILOQUY   A *soliloquy* is a long speech made by a character who is alone. The character thus reveals his or her private thoughts and feelings to the audience. In William Shakespeare's

The Tragedy of Julius Caesar, on page 309, Brutus begins a soliloquy that is spoken while he is alone in his orchard. This soliloquy reveals Brutus' fears about how Caesar might change were he crowned as king.
See *Monologue.*

SONNET   The *sonnet* is a fourteen-line lyric poem focused on a single theme. Sonnets have many variations, but they are usually written in iambic pentameter, following either the Petrarchan or Shakespearean form.
See *Lyric Poem, Petrarchan Sonnet,* and *Shakespearean Sonnet.*

SPEAKER   The *speaker* is the imaginary voice assumed by the writer of a poem. In other words the speaker is the character who says the poem. This character often is not identified by name. The speaker in Gabriela Mistral's "I Am Not Lonely," page 591, is a woman describing her relationship with her child.

SPONDEE   See *Meter.*

STAGE DIRECTIONS   *Stage directions* are notes included in a drama to describe how the work is to be performed or staged. Stage directions are usually printed in italics and enclosed within brackets or parentheses. They may mention how the characters should speak or move, what the costumes or any scenery should look like, how the set should be arranged, how the lighting should work, and so on.

STANZA   A *stanza* is a group of lines in a poem, considered as a unit. Many poems are divided into stanzas that are separated by spaces. Stanzas often function just as paragraphs do in prose. Each stanza states and develops a single main idea.

Stanzas are commonly named according to the number of lines found in them, as follows:
1. *Couplet:* a two-line stanza
2. *Tercet:* a three-line stanza
3. *Quatrain:* a four-line stanza
4. *Cinquain:* a five-line stanza
5. *Sestet:* a six-line stanza
6. *Heptastich:* a seven-line stanza
7. *Octave:* an eight-line stanza

A *sonnet* is a fourteen-line poem that is composed either of an octave and a sestet or of three quatrains and a couplet.

STATIC CHARACTER   See *Character.*

STEREOTYPE   See *Character.*

STOCK CHARACTER   See *Character.*

STYLE   A writer's *style* is his or her typical way of writing. Style includes word choice, tone, degree of formality, figurative language, rhythm, grammatical structure, sentence length, organization—in short, every feature of a writer's use of language.

SUBPLOT   A *subplot* is a second, less important plot within a story. A subplot may add to, reflect, vary, or contrast with the main plot.
See *Plot.*

SURPRISE ENDING   A *surprise ending* is a conclusion that violates the expectations of the reader. Especially in a short story, the plot may take a sudden twist or turn when something crucial is revealed or concealed. An example in this textbook of a story with a surprise ending is Italo Calvino's "Mushrooms in the City," on page 115

SUSPENSE   *Suspense* is a feeling of growing curiosity or anxious uncertainty about the outcome of events in a literary work. Writers create suspense by raising questions in the minds of their readers.

SYMBOL   A *symbol* is anything that stands for or represents something else. A *conventional symbol* is one that is widely known and accepted, such as a voyage symbolizing life or a skull symbolizing death. A *personal symbol* is one created for a particular work by a particular author.

SYNECDOCHE *Synecdoche* is a figure of speech that uses a part of something to stand for the whole thing. In "February Evening in New York," Denise Levertov uses feet, heads, and bodies to refer to humans in the impersonal city crowds:

> As the buildings close, released autonomous
> feet pattern the streets
> in hurry and stroll; balloon heads
> drift and dive above them; the bodies
> aren't really there.

See *Figurative Language* and *Metonymy*.

TERCET   See *Stanza.*

TETRAMETER   See *Meter.*

THEME   A *theme* is a central idea, concern, or purpose in a literary work. An essay's theme might be its thesis, its point about the topic. The theme of a story, play, or poem might be its point about life—the insight that the writer wants to pass along to the reader. A light work, one meant strictly for entertainment, may not have a theme. In most serious poems, stories, and plays, the theme is expressed indirectly rather than directly. For example, in Juanita Platero and Siyowin Miller's "Chee's Daughter," on page 77, the authors do not directly say that Chee's actions show the power of love and the importance of one's values, but readers understand that this idea is the theme of the story.

THIRD-PERSON POINT OF VIEW   See *Point of View.*

TONE   The *tone* of a literary work is the writer's attitude toward the readers and toward the subject. A writer's tone may be formal or informal, friendly or distant, personal or impersonal. For example, although Lewis Thomas's advice is serious in "Notes on Punctuation," on page 507, his tone is lighthearted and amusing. Rachel Carson's awed and respectful tone in "The Marginal World," on page 527, expresses her intensity as she seeks the meaning behind the beauty of the natural world.
See *Mood.*

TRAGEDY   *Tragedy* is a type of drama or literature that shows the downfall or destruction of a noble or outstanding person. Traditionally this person has a character weakness called a *tragic flaw* that accounts for his or her fall. In William Shakespeare's *The Tragedy of Julius Caesar,* on page 309, Brutus is a brave and noble figure who is guilty of the tragic flaw of assuming that honorable ends justify dishonorable means. Such a tragic hero, through choice or circumstance, is caught up in a sequence of events that inevitably results in disaster. Because this hero is neither purely wicked nor purely innocent, the audience reacts with mixed emotions—both pity and fear. The outcome of a tragedy—the downfall of the tragic hero—contrasts with the happy ending found in a comedy. Thus tragedies tend to end with funerals and comedies with weddings.
See *Comedy* and *Drama.*

TRIMETER   See *Meter.*

TROCHEE   See *Meter.*

UNDERSTATEMENT   *Understatement* means saying less than is actually meant, generally in an ironic way. An example of understatement is the description of a flooded area as "slightly soggy" or of weather during a heat wave as "a bit warm."
See *Figurative Language* and *Hyperbole.*

VERBAL IRONY   See *Irony.*

VERNACULAR   The *vernacular* is the ordinary language used by the people in a particular place. Instead of using more formal literary language, writers may use the vernacular to create realistic characters or to approach readers informally.
See *Dialect.*

GLOSSARY

READING THE GLOSSARY ENTRIES

The words in this glossary are from selections appearing in your textbook. Each entry in the glossary contains the following parts:

1. Entry Word. This word appears at the beginning of the entry, in boldface type.

2. Pronunciation. The symbols in parentheses tell how the entry word is pronounced. If a word has more than one possible pronunciation, the most common of these pronunciations is given first.

3. Part of Speech. Appearing after the pronunciation, in italics, is an abbreviation that tells the part of speech of the entry word. The following abbreviations have been used:

n. noun   **p.** pronoun   **v.** verb
adj. adjective   **adv.** adverb   **conj.** conjunction

4. Definition. This part of the entry follows the parts-of-speech abbreviation and gives the meaning of the entry word as used in the selection in which it appears.

KEY TO PRONUNCIATION SYMBOLS USED IN THE GLOSSARY

The following symbols are used in the pronunciations that follow the entry words:

Symbol	Key Words	Symbol	Key Words
a	asp, fat, parrot	b	bed, fable, dub
ā	ape, date, play	d	dip, beadle, had
ä	ah, car, father	f	fall, after, off
		g	get, haggle, dog
e	elf, ten, berry	h	he, ahead, hotel
ē	even, meet, money	j	joy, agile, badge
		k	kill, tackle, bake
i	is, hit, mirror	l	let, yellow, ball
ī	ice, bite, high	m	met, camel, trim
		n	not, flannel, ton
ō	open, tone, go	p	put, apple, tap
ô	all, horn, law	r	red, port, dear
$\overline{oo}$	ooze, tool, crew	s	sell, castle, pass
oo	look, pull, moor	t	top, cattle, hat
y$\overline{oo}$	use, cute, few	v	vat, hovel, have
yoo	united, cure, globule	w	will, always, swear
oi	oil, point, toy	y	yet, onion, yard
ou	out, crowd, plow	z	zebra, dazzle, haze
u	up, cut, color	ch	chin, catcher, arch
ʉr	urn, fur, deter	sh	she, cushion, dash
		th	thin, nothing, truth
ə	a in ago	*th*	then, father, lathe
	e in agent	zh	azure, leisure
	i in sanity	ŋ	ring, anger, drink
	o in comply	′	[indicates that a
	u in focus		following **l** or **n** is a
ər	perhaps, murder		syllabic consonant, as in *able* (ā′ b'l)]

This pronunciation key is from *Webster's New World Dictionary,* Second College Edition. Copyright © 1986 by Simon & Schuster. Used by permission.

FOREIGN SOUNDS

à This symbol, representing the *a* in French *salle,* can best be described as intermediate between (a) and (ā).

ë This symbol represents the sound of the vowel cluster in french *coeur* and can be approximated by rounding the lips as for (ō) and pronouncing (e).

ö This symbol variously represents the sound of *eu* in French *feu* or of *ö* or *oe* in German *blöd* or *Goethe* and can be approximated by rounding lips as for (ō) and pronouncing (ā).

ô̂ This symbol represents a range of sounds between (ô) and (u); it occurs typically in the sound of the *o* in French *tonne* or German *korrekt;* in Italian *poco* and Spanish *torero,* it is almost like English (ô), as in *horn.*

ü This symbol variously represents the sound of *u* in French *duc* and in German *grun* and can be approximated by rounding the lips as for (ō) and pronouncing (ē).

kh This symbol represents the voiceless velar or uvular fricative as in the *ch* of German *doch* or Scots English *loch.* It can be approximated by placing the tongue as for (k) but allowing the breath to escape in a stream, as in pronouncing (h).

r This symbol represents any of various sounds used in languages other than English for the consonant *r.* It may represent the tongue-point trill or uvular trill of the *r* in French *reste* or *sur,* German *Reuter,* Italian *ricotta,* Russian *gorod,* etc.

ƀ This symbol represents the sound made by the letter *v* between vowels. It is pronounced like a *b* sound but without letting the lips come together.

A

abalone (ab′ ə lō′ nē) *n.* A shellfish with a flat shell and a pearly lining

abashed (ə basht′) *adj.* Self-conscious; ashamed

abate (ə bāt′) *v.* To lessen; to put an end to

absent (ab sent′) *v.* To keep away

abstract (ab strakt′) *adj.* Apart from any particular example; theoretical

accolade (ak′ ə lād′) *n.* Approval

accompaniment (ə kum′ pə nə mənt) *n.* A part, usually instrumental, performed together with the main part for richer effect

acquittal (ə kwit′ 'l) *n.* The judgment of a judge or jury that a person is not guilty of a crime as charged

ad-lib (ad′ lib′) *v.* To add words not in the script

admonish (ad män′ ish) *v.* To strongly advise; caution or warn

adobe (ə dō′ bē) *n.* Unburnt, sun-dried brick

adulation (a′ jōo lā′ shən) *n.* Excessive praise or admiration

aesthete   (es′ thēt′)   *n.* Someone highly sensitive to art and beauty; someone who puts on such a sensitivity

affable   (af′ ə bəl)   *adj.* Pleasant; friendly

affiliate   (ə fil′ ē āt′)   *v.* To associate

affront   (ə frunt′)   *n.* Intentional insult

agile   (aj′ əl)   *adj.* Quick and easy of movement

akin   (ə kin′)   *adj.* Having a similar quality or character

albatross   (al′ bə trôs′)   *n.* A large sea bird often used as a symbol of a burden or source of distress

albino   (al bī′ nō)   *n.* A person who because of a genetic factor has unusually pale skin and white hair

alchemy   (al′ kə mē)   *n.* An early form of chemistry in which the goal was to change baser metals into gold

alluvium   (ə lōō′ vē əm)   *n.* Material such as sand or gravel deposited by moving water

aloofness   (ə lōōf′ nəs)   *n.* The state of being distant, removed, or uninvolved

ambiguity   (am′ bə gyōō′ ə tē)   *n.* Uncertainty

amble   (am′ bəl)   *v.* To walk leisurely

amenable   (ə mē′ nə bəl)   *adj.* Responsive; open

amphibious   (am fib′ ē əs)   *adj.* That can operate or travel on both land and water

amulet   (am′ yōō lit)   *n.* Charm worn to protect against evil

anarchy   (an′ ər kē)   *n.* Lawlessness; disorder

Angelus   (an′ jə ləs)   *n.* Bell rung to announce the time for a prayer said at morning, noon, and evening

anthropomorphic   (an′ thrə pō′ môr′ fik)   *adj.* Having or suggesting human characteristics

antimacassar   (an′ ti mə kas′ ər)   *n.* A small cover on the arms or back of a chair or sofa to prevent soiling

anvil   (an′ vəl)   *n.* An iron or steel block

aphorism   (af′ ə riz′ əm)   *n.* Short sentence expressing wise or clever observation

apocryphal   (ə pä′ krə fəl)   *adj.* Fictitious; false

apoplexy   (ap′ ə plek′ sē)   *n.* A stroke

appertain   (ap′ ər tān′)   *v.* To belong

appurtenance   (ə pur′ t′n əns)   *n.* Accessory

apropos   (ap′ rə pō′)   *adv.* Aptly; fittingly for the occasion

arabesque   (ar′ ə besk′)   *adj.* Elaborately designed

arch   (ärch)   *adj.* Mischievous

ardent   (ärd′ ′nt)   *adv.* Intensely enthusiastic; devoted

arias   (ä′ rē əz)   *n.* Melodies in an opera, especially for solo voice with instrumental accompaniment

armada   (är mä′ də)   *n.* A fleet of warships

arnica   (är′ ni kə)   *n.* A preparation made from certain plants, once used for treating sprains, bruises, and so forth

arrant   (ar′ ənt)   *adj.* Extreme

arrogance   (ar′ ə gəns)   *n.* Pride; self-importance

arsenic   (är′ sən ik′)   *n.* A poison

assimilate   (ə sim′ ə lāt′)   *v.* To absorb into one's thinking

assumption   (ə sump′ shən)   *n.* Idea accepted as true without proof

astringency   (ə strin′ jən sē)   *n.* A harsh, biting quality

audaciously   (ô dā′ shəs lē)   *adv.* In a bold manner

augment   (ôg ment′)   *v.* To make greater

august   (ô′ gust)   *adj.* Imposing and magnificent

austerity   (ô ster′ ə tē)   *n.* Severity; self-denial

automaton   (ô täm′ ə tän′)   *n.* A person acting in an automatic or mechanical way

autonomous   (ô tän′ ə məs)   *adj.* Independent

avaricious   (av′ ə rish′ əs)   *adj.* Greedy for riches

avocation   (av ə kā′ shən)   *n.* Hobby

awl   (ôl)   *n.* A small, pointed tool for making holes in leather

awry   (ə rī′)   *adj.* Not straight; askew

azure   (azh′ ər)   *adj.* Clear blue

B

bailer   (bā′ lər)   *n.* A scoop for removing water from a boat

balustrade   (bal′ əs trād′)   *n.* A railing held up by small posts

banal   (bā′ nəl)   *adj.* Without originality or freshness; stale from overuse; commonplace

barbaric   (bär ber′ ik)   *adj.* Uncivilized; wild

bedight   (be dīt′)   *adj.* Adorned

bequeath   (bē kwēth′)   *v.* To pass on or hand down

bibulous   (bib′ yoo ləs)   *adj.* Given to drinking alcoholic beverages

bifocal   (bī fō′ kəl)   *n.* A pair of glasses with one part of each lens for close focus and the other part of each lens for distant focus

bigot   (big′ ət)   *n.* A person who holds blindly and intolerantly to a particular opinion

bilge   (bilj)   *n.* Dirty water in the bottom of a boat

billow   (bil′ ō)   *v.* To surge; swell

blasphemy   (blas′ fə mē′)   *n.* Disrespectful speech or action concerning God

blitzkreig   (blits′ krēg)   *n.* Sudden, overwhelming attack

boast   (bōst)   *v.* To show too much pride; brag

bounty   (boun′ tē)   *n.* Generosity

bouquet   (bōō kā′)   *n.* Fragrance

bowel   (bou′ əl)   *n.* Intestine; gut

brackish   (brak′ ish)   *adj.* Salty and marshy

brandish   (bran′ dish)   *v.* To wave or flourish menacingly

brazier   (brā′ zhər)   *n.* A metal pan or bowl to hold burning coals or charcoal

brittle   (brit′ ′l)   *adj.* Stiff and unbending; easily broken or shattered

bundling   (bun′ d′liŋ)   *v.* Moving quickly; bustling

burgh   (burg)   *n.* Small town

burlesque   (bər lesk′)   *n.* Comic imitation of

butte   (byōōt)   *n.* Flat-topped rock formation

C

cacaphony   (kə käf′ ə nē)   *n.* Harsh sound

cache   (kash)   *n.* Anything stored or hidden in a secret or safe place

cairn (kern) *n.* A cone-shaped heap of stones used as a marker or monument

caldron (kôl′ drən) *n.* Heat like that of a boiling kettle

calico (kal′ i kō′) *adj.* Made of cotton cloth, usually printed

cameo (kam′ ē ō′) *n.* A shell or stone carved with a head in profile and used as jewelry

candelabrum (kan′ də lä′ brəm) *n.* A large branched candlestick

cantor (kan′ tər) *n.* A singer of solos in a synagogue, who leads the congregation in prayer

capacious (kə pā′ shəs) *adj.* Roomy; spacious

capricious (kə prish′ əs) *adj.* Without apparent reason

caress (kə res′) *v.* To touch or stroke lightly or lovingly

carnage (kär′ nij) *n.* Slaughter; massacre

carrion (kar′ ē ən) *adj.* Flesh-eating

cavort (kə vôrt′) *v.* To leap or prance about

cerement (ser′ ə mənt) *n.* Wrapping or shroud

certitude (sʉrt′ ə tōōd′) *n.* Certainty; assurance

chafer (chāf′ ər) *n.* An insect that feeds on plants

chamiso (chə mē′ sō) *n.* Densely growing desert shrub

chastisement (chas tīz′ mənt) *n.* Punishment; severe criticism

check (chek) *n.* A move in chess that threatens to capture the king

chitinous (kī′ tin əs) *adj.* Of a material that forms the tough outer covering of insects, crustaceans, and so on

choleric (käl′ ər ik) *adj.* Quick-tempered

chorister (kôr′ is tər) *n.* A member of a chorus

circumvent (sʉr′ kəm vent′) *v.* To prevent from happening

citable (sīt′ ə b'l) *adj.* Able to be named

citron (si′ trən) *n.* A yellow, thick-skinned, lemonlike fruit

cliché (klē shā′) *n.* An overused phrase or expression

coaster (kōs′ tər) *n.* A ship that carries cargo or passengers from port to port along a coast

cogitation (käj′ ə tā′ shən) *n.* Meditation; seriousness

coherent (kō hir′ ənt) *adj.* Logically connected or ordered

cohort (kō′ hôrt′) *n.* Companion; supporter

collusion (kə loo′ zhən) *n.* A secret agreement for an illegal purpose

commandeer (käm′ ən dir′) *v.* To force into service

commiserate (kə miz′ ər āt′) *v.* To sympathize; share sufferings

complacence (kəm plās′ 'ns) *n.* Self-satisfaction

compulsory (kəm pul′ sə rē) *adj.* Mandatory

compunction (kəm puŋk′ shən) *n.* Sense of guilt or regret

conciliatory (kən sil′ ē ə tôr′ ē) *adj.* Soothing

confounded (kən found′ id) *adj.* Confused

conjecture (kən jek′ chər) *n.* An inference based on incomplete or inconclusive evidence

conjunction (kən juŋk′ shən) *n.* Union

conjure (kun′ jər) *v.* To remove as if by magic

consecrated (kän′ si krāt′ id) *adj.* Dedicated

conservatory (kən sʉr′ və tôr′ ē) *n.* Greenhouse

consort (kän′ sôrt′) *n.* Harmony of sounds

conspicuous (kən spik′ yoo əs) *adj.* Attracting attention by being unexpected

conspiracy (kən spir′ ə sē) *n.* 1. A group of people plotting an illegal or evil act 2. Such a plot itself

conspiratorial (kən spir′ ə tôr′ ē əl) *adj.* Planning and acting together secretly

constancy (kän′ stən sē) *n.* Firmness of mind or purpose; resoluteness

consternation (kän′ stər nā′ shən) *n.* Fear or shock

contemptuous (kən temp′ choo əs) *adj.* Full of contempt; scornful

contentious (kən ten′ shəs) *adj.* Quarrelsome

contretemps (kän′ trə tän′) *n.* French for "an awkward mishap"

contrition (kən trish′ ən) *n.* A feeling of remorse for having done something wrong

conventional (kən ven′ shən əl) *adj.* Of the usual kind; customary

convoluted (kän və loot′ id) *adj.* Intricate; twisted

convulsive (kən vul′ siv) *adj.* Marked by an involuntary, muscular contraction

coquettish (kō ket′ ish) *adj.* Flirtatious

coral (kôr′ əl) *n.* An animal with tentacles at the top of a tubelike body

cordon (kôr′ dən) *n.* A line or circle of police stationed around an area to guard it

coroner (kôr′ ə nər) *n.* A public official whose chief duty is to determine the cause of a death

cosmic (käz′ mik) *adj.* Relating to the universe

countenance (koun′ tə nəns) *n.* The expression of a person's face; facial feature

cowlish (koul′ ish) *adj.* Hood-shaped

cozen (kuz′ ən) *v.* To deceive

credence (krēd′ 'ns) *n.* Belief

credulity (krə doo′ lə tē) *n.* A tendency to believe too readily, especially without proof

criterion (krī tir′ ē ən) *n.* A standard or rule for making a judgment

crocheted (krō shād′) *adj.* Made with thread or yarn woven together with hooked needles

crofter (krôft′ ər) *n.* Tenant farmer

cryptic (krip′ tik) *adj.* Having a hidden or mysterious meaning

culminate (kul′ mə nāt′) *v.* To bring to its highest point of interest

cynically (sin′ i klē) *adv.* Sarcastically; sneering

czar (zär) *n.* The emperor of Russia

D

dacha (dä′ chä) *n.* In Russia, a country house or cottage

damson (dam′ zən) *n.* Small purple plum

davenport (dav′ ən pôrt′) *n.* A large couch or sofa

dean (dēn) *n.* Head of a school administration

decadent (dek′ ə dənt) *adj.* Decayed or declining, especially in morals

decalogue (dek′ ə lôg′) *n.* The Ten Commandments

decipher (dē sī′ fər) *n.* To figure out the meaning of

decora (di kor′ ə) *n.* Requirements of good taste

decrepitude (dē krep′ ə tood′) *n.* State of being worn out by old age or illness

deference (def′ ər əns) *n.* Respect and consideration

deftness (deft′ nis) *adj.* Skillfulness

dejectedly (dē jek′ tid lē) *adv.* As if depressed or disheartened

delineate (di lin′ ē āt′) *v.* To depict or describe

delirious (di lir′ ē əs) *adj.* Raving incoherently

delirium (di lir′ ē əm) *n.* State of extreme mental confusion

delusion (di loo′ zhən) *n.* A false belief held in spite of evidence to the contrary

dementia (di men′ shə) *n.* Insanity or madness

denouement (dā′ noo män′) *n.* Outcome or the end

density (den′ sə tē) *n.* Thickness

deploy (dē ploi′) *v.* To spread out

depravity (dē prav′ ə tē) *n.* Wickedness

deranged (dē rānjd′) *adj.* Disturbed out of the normal way of acting

derision (di rizh′ ən) *n.* Contempt; ridicule

desolation (des′ ə la′ shən) *n.* Wretchedness; loneliness

destitute (des′ tə toot′) *adj.* Poverty-stricken; in great need

desultory (des′ əl tôr′ ē) *adj.* Purposeless

diabolical (dī′ ə bäl′ ik əl) *adj.* Wicked; cruel

diffuse (di fyoos′) *adj.* Widely spread or scattered

dilapidated (di lap′ ə dāt′ id) *adj.* Fallen into a shabby and neglected state

dilettante (dil′ ə tant′) *n.* An amateur or dabbler in the arts

diminutive (də min′ yoo tiv) *adj.* Tiny; smaller than average

disapprobation (dis ap′ rə bā′ shən) *n.* Disapproval

discern (di zurn′) *v.* To recognize

discernible (di zurn′ ə b'l) *adj.* Clearly recognizable

disconcerted (dis′ kən surt′ id) *adj.* Embarrassed; confused

disconcerting (dis′ kən surt′ iŋ) *adj.* Upsetting the composure of; confusing

discourse (dis′ kôrs) *v.* To speak formally and at length

disdain (dis dān′) *n.* Scorn; lofty contempt

disillusionment (dis′ i loo′ zhən mənt) *n.* Disappointment

disown (dis ōn′) *v.* To deny ownership of or responsibility for

dispensation (dis′ pən sā′ shən) *n.* Release; exemption

disposition (dis′ pə zish′ ən) *n.* Inclination; tendency; choice

disreputable (dis rep′ yoo tə bəl) *adj.* Not respectable

dissect (di sekt′) *v.* To cut up into parts

dissipate (dis′ ə pāt′) *v.* To scatter

distemper (dis tem′ pər) *n.* An infectious virus disease of young dogs

divination (div′ ə nā′ shən) *n.* A correct guess

dominion (də min′ yən) *n.* Rule or power to rule

douche (doosh) *v.* To wash or flush away

doughty (dout′ ē) *adj.* Brave; valiant

dowager (dou′ ə jər) *n.* An elderly woman of wealth and dignity

drayman (drā′ mən) *n.* The driver of a horse-drawn cart with detachable sides for carrying heavy loads

droll (drōl) *adj.* Amusing in an odd or ironic way

drollery (drōl′ ər ē) *n.* Wry humor

drone (drōn) *v.* To make a continuous, dull humming sound

Dryad (drī′ ad′) *n.* A nature goddess who lives in a tree

E

ecstatic (ek stat′ ik) *adj.* Joyous

edifice (ed′ i fis) *n.* Building

effulgence (e ful′ jəns) *n.* Radiance; brillance

egress (ē′ gres′) *n.* The act of leaving

elocution (el′ ə kyoo′ shən) *n.* The art of clear and effective public speaking

elongated (e lôŋ′ gāt′ id) *adj.* Lengthened; stretched

emaciated (ē mā′ shē āt′ əd) *adj.* Abnormally thin because of starvation or illness

embryo (em′ brē ō′) *n.* Anything in an early stage of development

emulation (em′ yoo lā′ shən) *n.* Old word for envy, jealousy

encroaching (en krōch′ iŋ) *adj.* Intruding; advancing

engender (en jen′ der) *v.* To bring about; cause; produce

enigmatic (en′ ig mat′ ik) *adj.* Baffling

ensign (en′ sīn′) *n.* Old word for a standard bearer; one who carries a flag

enthrall (en thrôl′) *v.* To fascinate

entrail (en′ trāl) *n.* Intestine, gut

entreat (en trēt′) *v.* To beg; plead with

envy (en′ vē) *n.* Feeling of desire for another's possessions or qualities and jealousy at not having them

ephemeral (e fem′ ər əl) *adj.* Passing quickly

Epicurus (ep′ ə kyoor′ əs) A Greek philosopher who tried to find freedom from physical pain and emotional disturbance

epitome (ē pit′ ə mē′) *n.* A typical example

eradicate (ē rad′ i kāt′) *v.* To wipe out completely

ermine (ur′ min) *adj.* Of the soft, white, black-tipped fur of a weasel

errant (er′ ənt) *adj.* Straying outside the proper path or bounds

erratic (e rat′ ik) *adj.* Irregular; not following a normal pattern

esoteric (es′ ə ter′ ik) *adj.* Beyond the understanding of most people

essence (es′ əns) *n.* Real nature of something

esthetically (es thet′ ik lē) *adv.* Artistically

estranged (ə strānjd′) *adj.* Removed from; at a distance

estuary (es′ tyo͞o er′ ē) *n.* An inlet formed where a river enters the ocean

ethereal (ē thir′ ē əl) *adj.* Of the upper regions of space

eulogy (yo͞o′ lə jē) *n.* A formal speech in praise of someone who has recently died

evanescent (ev′ ə nes′ ənt) *adj.* Tending to fade from sight

evasion (ē vā′ zhən) *n.* The tendency to avoid or escape something

evocative (ē väk′ ə tiv) *adj.* Having the power to bring forth

exaltation (eg′ zôl tā′ shən) *n.* A feeling of great joy, pride, or power

exasperated (eg zas′ pər āt′ id) *adj.* Irritated; annoyed

excursion (eks kur′ zhən) *n.* A short trip

executive (eg zek′ yo͞o tiv) *adj.* Capable of carrying out duties

exhilarate (eg zil′ ə rāt′) *v.* To make cheerful, lively

exorcist (eks′ ôr sist) *n.* One who calls up spirits

expedient (ek spē′ dē ənt) *adj.* Useful; convenient

expend (ek spend′) *v.* To spend or use by consuming

exploit (eks′ ploit′) *n.* Act or deed, especially a heroic achievement

exquisite (eks′ kwi zit) *adj.* Delicately beautiful

extolled (eks tōld′) *v.* Praised

exuberance (eg zo͞o′ bər əns) *n.* Luxuriance

F

fagot (fag′ ət) *n.* A bundle of sticks used for fuel

fathom (fath′ əm) *v.* To understand thoroughly

fathomless (fath′ əm lis) *adj.* Too deep to be measured

feisty (fīst′ ē) *adj.* Spunky; touchy and quarrelsome

felicitations (fə lis′ i tā′ shənz) *n.pl.* Congratulations

fickle (fik′ əl) *adj.* Brief; to the point

fieldpiece (fēld′ pēs′) *n.* Mobile artillery

figment (fig′ mənt) *n.* Something merely imagined

fillet (fi lā′) *n.* Boned and sliced fish

flagrant (flā′ grənt) *adj.* Outrageous

flailing (flāl′ iŋ) *adj.* Beating or striking with a thrashing movement

flank (flaŋk) *n.* Side

flicker (flik′ ər) *n.* A species of woodpecker

flout (flout) *v.* To show contempt for

floweret (flou′ ər it) *n.* A small flower

flurriedly (flur′ əd lē) *adv.* In a flustered, agitated way

fomentation (fō′ mən tā′ shən) *n.* An application of warm, moist substances in the treatment of an injury; act of stirring up

foreboding (fôr bōd′ iŋ) *n.* Prediction of something bad or harmful

forfeiture (fôr′ fə chər) *n.* The act of giving up something as punishment for a crime

forlorn (fôr lôrn′) *adj.* Abandoned; deserted; hopeless, desperate

foxhole (fäks′ hōl′) *n.* A hole dug in the ground as temporary protection for soldiers against enemy gunfire

fragility (frə jil′ ə tē) *n.* State of being easily broken or damaged

franc (fraŋk) *n.* Unit of money in France

fratricide (fra′ trə sīd′) *n.* The killing of one's brother or sister

friction (frik′ shən) *n.* Resistance

frond (fränd) *n.* A leaflike shoot of seawood

furtive (fur′ tiv) *adj.* Sneaky; secretive

fusillade (fyo͞o′ sə läd′) *n.* Something that is like the rapid firing of many firearms

G

gait (gāt) *n.* Way of moving

gallantly (gal′ ənt lē) *adv.* Bravely; nobly

galleon (gal′ ē in) *n.* A large Spanish ship of the fifteenth and sixteenth centuries

gambol (gam′ bəl) *v.* To leap playfully

gargoyle (gär′ goil) *n.* A projecting ornament, usually a grostesquely carved animal or fantastic creature, on a building

gauche (gōsh) *adj.* Awkward

gendarme (zhän därm′) *n.* A French policeman

giddy (gid′ ē) *adj.* Mad or foolish

glen (glen) *n.* A secluded, narrow valley between mountains

gourd (gôrd) *n.* The dried, hollowed-out shell of a squash, used to hold the shape of the sock

gout (gout) *n.* A spurt, splash, or glob

grandee (gran dē′) *n.* Nobleman

grimace (gri mās′) *n.* A twisted facial expression

grisly (giz′ lē) *adj.* Horrifying; gruesome

grotesque (grō tesk′) *adj.* Ridiculous or distorted

groveling (gruv′ liŋ) *adj.* Crawling; humbling

guileful (gīl′ fəl) *adj.* Deceitful; tricky

guileless (gīl′ lis) *adj.* Without slyness or cunning; frank

gunnel (gun′ əl) *n.* The upper edges of the sides of a boat

H

habiliment (hə bil′ ə ment) *n.* Clothing

harmony (här′ mə nē) *n.* In music the study of chords (combinations of tones sounded together)

headstall (hed′ stôl′) *n.* The part of a bridle that fits over a horse's head

heirloom (er′ lo͞om′) *n.* A treasured possession handed down from generation to generation

hogan (hō′ gôn′) *n.* A traditional Navajo dwelling, built of wood and adobe

homage (häm′ ij) *n.* Public show of honor and allegiance

Homo sapiens (hō′ mō sā′ pē ənz′) *n.* A human being

hone (hōn) *n.* A stone used for sharpening cutting tools

horoscope (hôr′ ə skōp′) *n.* The position of the planets and stars with relation to one another at a given time, especially at the time of a person's birth

hue (hyōō) *n.* Color; shade of a given color

hulking (hulk′ iŋ) *adj.* Large; heavy; clumsy

hull (hul) *v.* To take the shells off nuts

hummock (hum′ ək) *n.* A low, rounded hill

hurdy-gurdy (hur′ dē gur′ dē) *n.* A musical instrument, like a barrel organ, played by turning a crank

husbandman (huz′ bənd mən) *n.* A farmer

I

ichthyologist (ik′ thē äl′ ə jist) *n.* One who studies fish

idiom (id′ ē əm) *n.* Meaning different from the literal; the style of artistic expression characteristic of an individual

idiosyncratic (id′ ē ō sin krat′ ik) *adj.* Peculiar

idyllic (ī dil′ ik) *adj.* Pleasing and simple

ignoble (ig nō′ bəl) *adj.* Common

Iliad (il′ ē əd) *n.* A Greek epic poem by Homer set in the tenth year of the Trojan War

immersion (i mur′ shən) *n.* A plunge into water

imminent (im′ ə nənt) *adj.* Likely to happen presently; threatening

impalpable (im pal′ pə bəl) *adj.* That which cannot be felt by touching

impassive (im pas′ iv) *adj.* Showing no emotion

imperative (im per′ ə tiv) *adj.* Absolutely necessary; urgent

imperatrix (im′ pə rā′ triks) *n.* A woman emperor

imperceptibly (im pər sep′ tə blē) *adv.* In such a slight way as to be almost unnoticeable

imperiously (im pir′ ē əs lē) *adv.* Arrogantly

imperturbable (im′ pər tur′ bə bəl) *adj.* Unable to be excited or disturbed

impervious (im pur′ vē əs) *adj.* Not affected by

impinge (im pinj′) *v.* To intrude

implacable (im plā′ kə bəl) *adj.* Unable to be appeased or pacified

implication (im′ plə kā′ shən) *n.* A suggestion

imploring (im plôr′ iŋ) *adj.* Quality of begging or asking earnestly

impudent (im′ pyōō dənt) *adj.* Shamelessly bold or disrespectful

inane (in ān′) *adj.* Empty; foolish; silly

inanimate (in an′ ə mit) *adj.* Dull; spiritless; not alive

inaugurate (in ô′ gyə rāt′) *v.* To make a formal beginning; celebrate the opening of

incapacited (in kə pas′ ə tāt′ əd) *adj.* Disabled

incensed (in senst′) *v.* Enraged

incongruity (in′ kən grōō′ ə tē) *n.* Something lacking harmony or agreement; inconsistency; lack of fitness or appropriateness

incongruous (in käŋ′ grōō əs) *adj.* Incompatible; inharmonious

incorporate (in kôr′ pər it) *adj.* United

incredulous (in krej′ oo ləs) *adj.* Unbelieving; doubtful

indolence (in′ də ləns) *n.* Idleness; a dislike for work

induce (in dōōs′) *v.* To cause

indulgence (in dul′ jəns) *n.* Leniency; forgiveness

inebriating (in ēb′ rē āt′ iŋ) *adj.* Intoxicating; exciting

inert (in urt′) *adj.* Unable to move or act

inestimable (in es′ tə mə bəl) *adj.* Priceless; beyond reckoning

inexplicability (in eks′ pli kə bil′ ə tē) *n.* A condition that cannot be explained

infantile (in′ fən tīl′) *adj.* Characteristic of an infant; immature

infectious (in fek′ shəs) *adj.* Tending to spread; catching

infirm (in furm′) *adj.* Weak; feeble

infirmity (in fur′ mə tē) *n.* A bodily weakness

infraction (in frak′ shən) *n.* A violation

ingrate (in′ grāt) *n.* Unappreciative person

ingress (in′ gres) *n.* Entering

inherent (in hir′ ənt) *adj.* Inborn

inherently (in hir′ ənt lē) *adv.* Basically; by its very nature

initiate (i nish′ ē āt′) *v.* To introduce or teach about

innately (i nāt′ lē) *adv.* Existing naturally rather than acquired

innuendo (in′ yōō en′ do) *n.* Insinuation; indirect remark or gesture that suggests wrongdoing

insidious (in sid′ ē əs) *adj.* Treacherous

insignificant (in′ sig nif′ i kənt) *adj.* Having little or no importance

insinuate (in sin′ yoo āt′) *v.* To hint; suggest indirectly

insinuation (in sin′ yōō ā′ shən) *n.* Sly hint or suggestion

insolence (in′ sə ləns) *n.* Boldly disrespectful speech or behavior

insurrection (in′ sə rek′ shən) *n.* A revolt

interminable (in tur′ mi nə bəl) *adj.* Seemingly endless

intimidate (in tim′ ə dāt′) *v.* To discourage or inhibit by making threats

inveigle (in vē′ g'l) *v.* To entice into doing something

irascible (i ras′ ə bəl) *adj.* Easily angered; quick-tempered

iridescent (ir′ i des′ ənt) *adj.* Showing changes in color

iris (ī′ ris) *n.* The round, colored part of an eye

isinglass (ī′ zin glas′) *n.* A semitransparent substance obtained from fish bladders and sometimes used for windows

J

jerked (jurkt) *adj.* Preserved by cutting into strips and drying in the sun

jostling (jäs′ liŋ) *adj.* Bumping; pushing

jurisdiction (joor′ is dik′ shən) *n.* Area of responsibility

juxtapose (juks′ tə pōz′) *v.* To put side by side to show contrast

K
keening (kēn′ iŋ) *adj.* Wailing for the dead
knave (nāv) *n.* A tricky rascal; a rogue

L
labyrinth (lab′ ə rinth′) *n.* Maze
laconic (lə kän′ ik) *adj.* Using few words; terse
lacquer (lak′ ər) *v.* To give a hard, highly polished finish
lament (lə ment′) *v.* To feel or express great sorrow
lamentation (lam′ ən ta′ shən) *n.* Mourning
languid (laŋ′ gwid) *adj.* Weak; listless; without vitality
languorous (laŋ′ gər əs) *adj.* Lacking vigor or vitality
latent (lāt′ 'nt) *adj.* Hidden
lather (la*th*′ ər) *n.* (Slang) An excited or disturbed state
layman (lā′ mən) *n.* A person not belonging to or skilled in a given profession
legacy (leg′ ə sē) *n.* Money, property, or position left in a will to someone
legerdemain (lej′ ər di mān′) *n.* Trickery; tricks with the hand
levity (lev′ i tē) *n.* Joking around
liaison (lē ā′ zän′) *n.* A link or connection
libation (lī bā′ shən) *n.* A liquid poured as an offering in a religious ritual
limpid (lim′ pid) *adj.* Clear
litany (lit′ 'n ē) *n.* Responsive religious readings
logistics (lō jis′ tiks) *n.* The providing and transporting of people and equipment
longevity (län jev′ ə tē) *n.* The length or duration of a life
lucent (lōō′ sənt) *adj.* Shining
lucidity (lōō sid′ ə tē) *n.* Clarity; ability to be understood
ludicrous (lōō′ di krəs) *adj.* Laughably absurd
luminous (lōō′ mə nəs) *adj.* Giving off light
luster (lus′ tər) *n.* Soft, reflected light; brilliance

M
machinations (mak′ ə nā′ shənz) *n.pl.* Secret schemes
mackintosh (mak′ in täsh′) *n.* A waterproof raincoat
maitre (māt′ ər) *n.* Mister, a term of address
malevolent (mə lev′ ə lənt) *adj.* Intended as evil or harmful
malice (mal′ is) *n.* A desire to harm or see harm done to others
malicious (mə lish′ əs) *adj.* Intentionally harmful
malign (mə līn′) *adj.* Evil; harmful
mandible (man′ də bəl) *n.* Biting jaw
mangrove (maŋ′ grōv) *n.* A tropical tree that grows in swampy ground with spreading branches that send down roots and thus form more trunks

manifestation (man′ ə fes tā′ shən) *n.* An appearance or evidence
manse (mans) *n.* A large, imposing house; minister's house
marginal (mär′ jə nəl) *adj.* Occupying the borderland of a stable area
martial law (mär′ shəl lô′) *n.* Temporary rule by the military authorities
marzipan (mär′ zi pan′) *n.* A candy made from almonds, sugar, and egg whites
masque (mask) *n.* A costume ball or masquerade theme
mate (māt) *n.* Checkmate, a chess move in which the king is captured and the game is over
matriarchal (mā′ trē är′ kəl) *adj.* Motherly
maul (môl) *v.* To handle roughly or clumsily
mead (mēd) *n.* A drink made of honey and water, often with spices or fruit added
mediocrity (mē′ dē äk′ rə tē) *n.* Inferior ability or value
melancholy (mel′ ən käl′ ē) *n.* Sadness; gloominess; depression
mellifluous (mə lif′ lōō əs) *adj.* Sweet and smooth
mesa (mā′ sə) *n.* A flattened hill with steep sides
metal (met′ 'l) *n.* Basic character; mettle
metamorphosis (met′ ə môr′ fə sis) *n.* A change in form, structure, or substance
meteorite (mēt′ ē ər īt′) *n.* Part of a heavenly body that passes through the atmosphere and falls to earth
mettle (met′ 'l) *n.* Basic character
militia (mə lish′ ə) *n.* An army of citizens rather than professional soldiers, called out in time of emergency
millinery (mil′ ə ner′ ē) *n.* Women's hats
mime (mīm) *n.* Pantomime
ministration (min′ is trā′ shən) *n.* The act of serving as a minister or clergyman
minute (mī nōōt′) *adj.* Tiny
misbegotten (mis′ bi gät′ 'n) *adj.* Wrongly or unlawfully produced
moidore (moi′ dor′) *n.* Gold coin of Portugal and Brazil
momentum (mō men′ təm) *n.* The ongoing force of a moving object
monotone (män′ ə tōn′) *n.* Uninterrupted repetition of the same tone
mordantly (môr′ dənt lē) *adv.* Bitingly; sarcastically
mortal (môr′ təl) *adj.* That eventually must die
mortgage (môr′ gij) *n.* The pledging of property for money
motive (mōt′ iv) *n.* The emotion or impulse that causes a person to act in a certain way
mottled (mät′ 'ld) *adj.* Marked with spots of different shades
multifariously (mul′ tə far′ ē əs lē) *adv.* Diversely
mummer (mum′ ər) *n.* A masked and costumed person who acts out pantomimes
muse (myōōz) *v.* To think deeply; meditate
mutable (myōōt′ ə bəl) *adj.* Capable of change

mute (my$\overline{oo}$t) *adj.* Silent; unspectacular

mutiny (my$\overline{oo}$t' 'n ē) *n.* Open rebellion against authority

N

nave (nāv) *n.* Aisle

negotiate (ni gō' shē āt') *v.* To master or successfully move through a situation

nonchalantly (nän' shə länt' lē) *adv.* Casually; indifferently

nonconductivity (nän kən' duk tiv' ə tē) *n.* The ability to contain and not transmit heat

nonentity (nän en' tə tē) *n.* A thing of little or no importance

novel (näv' əl) *adj.* New and unusual

nursery (nʉrs' ər ē) *n.* A place where young trees and plants are grown

O

obeisance (ō bā' səns) *n.* Gesture of respect

obligatory (əb lig' ə tôr' ē) *adj.* Required; necessary

obliquely (ə blēk' lē) *adv.* In a slanted, sloping way

obliterate (ə blit' ər āt') *v.* To destroy; erase without a trace

occult (ə kult') *adj.* Having to do with so-called mystic arts such as alchemy and astrology

officious (ə fish' əs) *adj.* Overly ready to serve; obliging

okapi (ō kä' pē) *n.* An African animal related to the giraffe but with a much shorter neck

ominous (äm' ə nəs) *adj.* Threatening; sinister

opacity (ō pas' ə tē) *n.* The quality of not letting light pass through

opaque (ō pāk') *adj.* Not letting light pass through

oracle (ôr' ə kəl) *n.* A source of knowledge or wise counsel

oration (ō rā' shən) *n.* A formal speech, especially one given at a state occasion, ceremony, or funeral

orthodox (ôr' thə däks') *adj.* Conforming to the usual beliefs

P

paddock (pad' ək) *n.* A small enclosed field

paganism (pā' gən iz əm) *n.* Lack of any religion

palfrey (pôl' frē) *n.* A saddle horse, especially one for a woman

palmetto (pal met' ō) *n.* A palm tree with fan-shaped leaves

palpable (pal' pə bəl) *adj.* Able to be perceived by the senses

pampas (päm' pəz) *n.* Treeless plains in South America

parabolic (par' ə bäl' ik) *adj.* Bowl-shaped

paradox (par' ə däks') *n.* Contradiction; inconsistent quality

paranoia (par' ə noi' ə) *n.* A mental disorder characterized by delusions of persecution

pariah (pə rī' ə) *n.* A social outcast

parody (par' ə dē) *n.* Poor or weak imitation

parry (par' ē) *v.* To ward off

parsimonious (pär' sə mō' nē əs) *adj.* Stingy

particularization (pər tik' yə lə rīz ā' shən) *n.* Presentation in minute detail

pathos (pā' thäs') *n.* Compassion; sympathy

patriarchal (pā' trē ärk' 'l) *adj.* Fatherly

pensively (pen' siv lē) *adv.* Sadly; reflectively

peon (pē' ən) *n.* A laborer in Spanish America

peony (pē' ə nē) *n.* A plant with large, showy flowers often red or pink in color

perplexing (pər pleks' iŋ) *adj.* Puzzling; difficult to understand

perspective (pər spek' tiv) *n.* Point of view

peso (pā' sō) *n.* Mexican unit of money

phantasm (fan' taz' əm) *n.* Something apparently seen but having to physical reality

philosophy (fə läs' ə fē) *n.* A system of values

phosphorescence (fäs' fə res' əns) *n.* Light

piety (pī' ə tē) *n.* Holiness; respect for the divine

pillage (pil' ij) *n.* The act of robbing and destroying, especially during wartime

piquancy (pē' kən sē) *n.* A pleasantly sharp quality

pique (pēk) *v.* To provoke

pith (pith) *n.* Force or strength

plague (plāg) *n.* A contagious epidemic disease

plaintive (plān' tiv) *adj.* Mournful; sad

plausibility (plô' zə bil' ə tē) *n.* Believability

poignancy (poin' yən sē) *n.* 1. A feeling that is emotionally touching or moving 2. The quality of being deeply affecting

poignant (poin' yənt) *adj.* Moving

poise (poiz) *n.* Self-assurance; ease of manner

pontiff (pänt' if) *n.* A high priest, bishop

portentous (pôr ten' təs) *adj.* Foreboding; full of unspecified meaning

portliness (pôrt' lē nes) *n.* Stoutness; heaviness

potent (pōt' 'nt) *adj.* Powerful

poultice (pōl' tis) *n.* An absorbent mass applied to a sore or inflamed part of the body

pragmatic (prag mat' ik) *adj.* Practical

precariously (prē ker' ē əs lē) *adv.* Dependent upon the will or favor of another person

predator (pred' ə tər) *n.* An animal that eats other animals

predestined (prē des' tin'd) *adj.* Decreed beforehand; foreordained

predilection (pred' 'l ek' shən) *n.* An inclination to like something; a special fondness

prelude (prel' y$\overline{oo}$d') *n.* Introduction

presuppose (prē' sə pōz') *v.* To assume beforehand

prey (prā) *n.* An animal hunted or killed for food

primeval (prī mē' vəl) *adj.* Ancient or primitive

primevally (prī mē' vəl lē) *adv.* Belonging to earliest times.

prodigious (prō dij' əs) *adj.* Impressively forceful; huge or powerful

promontory (präm′ ən tôr′ ē) *n.* A high place extending out over a body of water

propriety (prō prī′ ə tē) *n.* The quality of being proper, fitting, or suitable fitness

prosaic (prō zā′ ik) *adj.* Commonplace; dull; ordinary

prosecution (präs′ i kyōō′ shən) *n.* The conducting of criminal proceedings in court against a person

prosperous (präs′ pər əs) *adj.* Having continued success

provender (präv′ ən dər) *n.* Food

proviso (prə vī′ zō′) *n.* A condition

provocativeness (prō väk′ ə tiv nis) *n.* Stimulation; incitement

prowess (prou′ is) *n.* Skill; bravery

psychopathic (sī kō path′ ik) *adj.* With a mental disorder

punctilious (puŋk til′ ē əs) *adj.* Very careful about every detail of behavior

purify (pyoor′ ə fī′) *v.* To cleanse; rid of impurity

putrefactive (pyōō′ trə fak′ tiv) *adj.* Rotting; decomposing

Q

qualm (kwäm) *n.* Feelings of doubt or uneasiness; misgiving

querulous (kwer′ yōō ləs) *adj.* Inclined to find fault; complaining

queue (kyōō) *n.* A braid or pigtail worn down one's back

quickstep (kwik′ step′) *n.* The pace used in normal military marching, as contrasted with slower pace of the dead march

quince (kwins) *n.* Hard, green-yellow, apple-shaped fruit

quinquireme (kwin′ kwī rēm) *n.* An ancient ship propelled by sails and oars

R

raillery (rāl′ ər ē) *n.* Good-natured teasing; jest

recessional (ri sesh′ ən əl) *n.* Music played while people are leaving a church service or ceremony

redeem (ri dēm′) *v.* To rescue or save

redolence (red′ 'l əns) *n.* The quality of being fragrant or sweet-smelling

refuge (ref′ yōōj) *n.* Shelter or protection from danger

regimen (rej′ ə mən) *n.* System

rehabilitation (rē′ hə bil′ ə tā′ shən) *n.* Restoration of rank, privileges, and property

rejoinder (ri join′ dər) *n.* A reply or answer

relief (ri lēf′) *n.* The projection of shapes from a flat surface so that they stand out

repealing (ri pēl′ iŋ) *n.* Old word for "recalling," especially from exile

repertoire (rep′ ər twär′) *n.* The stock of songs that a singer is familiar with and is ready to perform

replication (rep′ lə kā′ shən) *n.* Echo or reverberation

repository (ri päz′ ə tôr′ ē) *n.* A place where things are stored and saved

repress (ri pres′) *v.* To hold back; restrain

repudiate (ri pyōō′ dē āt′) *v.* To deny

repulsive (ri pul′ siv) *adj.* Disgusting or offensive

requisite (rek′ wə zit) *adj.* Required by circumstance

residue (rez′ ə dōō′) *n.* Matter remaining after part has been taken away

resolution (rez′ ə lōō′ shən) *n.* Strong determination

resonant (rez′ ə nənt) *adj.* Increasing in intensity of sound

resplendent (ri splen′ dənt) *adj.* Splendid; dazzling

reticent (ret′ ə sənt) *adj.* Having a restrained, quiet, or understated quality

revel (rev′ əl) *v.* To take great pleasure in

reverberant (ri vʉr′ bər ənt) *adj.* Reechoing

reverie (rev′ ər ē) *n.* Dreamy thinking or imagining

rhetorical (ri tôr′ i kəl) *adj.* Elaborate in style

ribald (rib′ əld) *adj.* Characterized by coarse or vulgar joking

ricochet (rik′ ə shā′) *n.* Bouncing from one thing to another

righteous (rī′ chəs) *adj.* Just; upright

rigorous (rig′ ər əs) *adj.* Precisely accurate; strict

rile (rīl) *v.* To irritate; anger

rime (rīm) *n.* Another spelling for rhyme; poetry or verse in general

rime (rīm) *n.* Frost

rind (rīnd) *n.* The skin of oranges or lemons

roadster (rōd′ stər) *n.* An early sportscar with an open cab and a "rumble seat" in the rear

rosette (rō zet′) *n.* Pattern suggesting a rose

ruble (rōō′ bəl) *n.* The monetary unit of Russia

S

sacrilegious (sak′ rə lij′ əs) *adj.* Disrespectful or irreverent toward anything regarded as sacred

sadist (sad′ ist) *n.* One who gets pleasure from inflicting physical or psychological pain on others

sagacity (sə gas′ ə tē) *n.* Wisdom

salient (sāl′ yənt) *n.* A projecting part or angle

saline (sā′ līn) *adj.* Salty

sally (sal′ ē) *v.* To rush forth suddenly

sarcophagus (sär käf′ ə gəs) *n.* A stone coffin

sardonic (sär dän′ ik) *adj.* Sarcastic

sastrugus (sas′ troo gəs) *n.* A wavelike ridge of hard snow formed by the wind and common in polar regions

sate (sāt) *v.* To satisfy or please

satiated (sā′ shē at′ id) *adj.* Satisfied

saurian (sôr′ ē ən) *n.* A lizardlike animal

scholasticism (skə las′ tə siz′ əm) *n.* Tradition

schooner (skōō′ nər) *n.* A ship with two or more masts or supports for sails

scrupulously (skrōō′ pyə ləs lē) *adv.* Conscientiously; painstakingly

scrutinize (skrōōt′ 'n īz′) *v.* To examine closely

scythe (sīth) *n.* A tool with a long curving blade, used for mowing grass or grain

secular (sek′ yə lər) *adj.* Not sacred or religious

sedge (sej) *n.* A grassy plant that grows in wet areas

seigneur (sān yur′) *n.* A man of rank; feudal lord

seismograph (sīz′ mə graf′) *n.* An instrument that records the intensity and duration of earthquakes

selectmen (sə lekt′ mən) *n.* Board of officials who mange local affairs in many New England towns

self-indictment (self in dīt′ mənt) *n.* An accusation of oneself

sensationalize (sen sā′ shə nə līz) *v.* To use dramatic language or behavior to shock or excite

sensible (sen′ sə bəl) *adj.* Emotionally or intellectually aware

sententiousness (sen ten′ shəs nəs) *n.* Manner of using pithy sayings in a moralizing way

serene (sə rēn′) *adj.* Undisturbed

serenely (sə rēn′ lē) *adv.* In a calm, untroubled way

shackly (shak′ lē) *adj.* Dialect expression meaning "ramshackle," or falling apart

sheath (shēth) *n.* A case or covering

sheave (shēv) *n.* A bunch of cut stalks of grain bound up in a bundle

shilling (shil′ iŋ) *n.* A British silver coin

shimmy (shim′ ē) *n.* A jazz dance popular in the early 1920's involving shaking the body

shroud (shroud) *n.* Clothes that conceal

shrouds (shroudz) *n.* A set of ropes used to tie a mast to the side of a ship

sidereal (sī dir′ ē əl) *adj.* Of the star

silhouette (sil′ oo et′) *n.* An outline of something that appears dark against a light background

simian (sim′ ē ən) *adj.* Monkeylike

simulated (sim′ yoo lāt′ id) *adj.* Taking on the appearance of

sinecure (sī′ nə kyoor′) *n.* A position that brings advantage but involves little or no work

sinew (sin′ yoo) *n.* Tendon—the fibrous cord attaching muscle to bone

skinflint (skin′ flint′) *adj.* Miserly

slain (slān) *adj.* Killed

slanderous (slan′ dər əs) *adj.* Damaging to a person's reputation

sloth (slōth) *n.* A two-toed mammal that hangs from trees

smite (smīt) *v.* To strike strongly and suddenly

sojourn (sō′ jurn) *n.* A temporary stay

solace (säl′ is) *n.* Something that comforts

soldering (säd′ ər iŋ) *v.* Piecing together; uniting

solicited (sə lis′ it əd) *adj.* Asked

solicitor (sə lis′ it ər) *n.* British legal representative

solicitude (sə lis′ ə tood′) *n.* Caring or concern

sonorous (sə nôr′ əs) *adj.* Having a powerful, impressive sound

sovereign (säv′ rən) *n.* A British gold coin worth one pound

spar (spär) *n.* A pole that supports a sail

spare (sper) *adj.* Lean or thin

spectroscope (spek′ trə skōp) *n.* A scientific instrument used to identify substances

spew (spyoo) *v.* 1. To throw up from, or as from, the stomach 2. To eject; force out

spoor (spoor) *n.* The dropping of a wild animal

stalwart (stôl′ wərt) *adj.* Strong; with unwavering determination

stately (stāt′ lē) *adj.* Majestic

staunch (stônch) *adj.* Steadfast; loyal

stickler (stik′ lər) *n.* A person who insists uncompromisingly on the observance of something specified

stimulate (stim′ yoo lāt′) *v.* To rouse or excite to action

stipulate (stip′ yoo lāt′) *v.* To agree upon; guarantee

stratagem (strat′ ə jəm) *n.* Scheme or plan for deceiving an enemy in war

straightaway (strāt′ ə wā′) *n.* A straight course

stricken (strik′ ən) *adj.* Hit or wounded, as if by a missile

stripling (strip′ liŋ) *adj.* Young or youthful *n.* A young boy passing into manhood

stupefaction (stoo′ pə fak′ shən) *n.* Stunned amazement; utter bewilderment

sturgeon (stur′ jən) *n.* A large fish

suave (swäv) *adj.* Smoothly polite; polished

subjectively (səb jek′ tiv lē) *adv.* Personally

sublime (sə blīm′) *adj.* Noble; admirable

sublimity (sə blim′ ə tē) *n.* A noble or exalted state

subsequently (sub′ si kwənt lē) *adv.* After; following

subsidiary (səb sid′ ē er′ ē) *adj.* Secondary; supporting

subterfuge (sub′ tər fyooj′) *n.* A plan or action used to hide a true purpose

subtle (sut′ 'l) *adj.* Showing fine distinctions in meaning

subversion (səb vur′ zhən) *n.* A systematic attempt to overthrow a government from within

suit (soot) *n.* Old word for "petition"

sultriness (sul′ tri nəs) *n.* Oppressive heat

sumac (shoo′ mak′) *n.* Small tree or shrub with compound flowers and clusters of small greenish flowers followed by hair fruits. Some varieties cause an itching rash.

summit (sum′ it) *n.* The highest point of a mountain

sumptuous (sump′ choo əs) *adj.* Magnificent

superfluity (soo′ pər floo′ ə tē) *n.* An excess

suppleness (sup′ əl nes) *n.* Flexibility; resilience

supplication (sup′ lə kā′ shən) *n.* The act of asking humbly and earnestly

surcease (sur sēs′) *n.* An end

surly (sur′ lē) *adj.* Proud; commanding

surmise (sər mīz′) *v.* To guess; imagine or infer something

sustenance (sus′ tə nəns) *n.* Maintenance; support

svelte (svelt) *adj.* Slim; attractively slender

swarthy (swor′ the) *adj.* Having a dark complexion

sylvan (sil′ vən) *adj.* Wooded

syringa (sə riŋ′ gə) *n.* A hardy shrub with tiny fragrant flowers, also known as lilac

T

taciturn (tas′ ə turn′) *adj.* Not talkative

talisman (tal′ is mən) *n.* Anything believed to have magical power

taut (tôt) *adj.* Strained; tense

temperate (tem′ pər it) *adj.* Moderate in degree or quality

tempest (tem′ pist) *n.* A violent windstorm often with rain, snow, or hail

temporal (tem′ pə rəl) *adj.* Lasting only for a time, not eternal; wordly, not spiritual

tenuous (ten′ yōō əs) *adj.* Slight; flimsy; not substantial or strong

terminus (tur′ mə nəs) *n.* End, boundary

terse (turs) *adj.* Concise; polished

thrall (thrôl) *n.* Complete control; slavery

throe (thrō) *n.* A spasm or pang of pain

thwart (thwôrt) *n.* A rower's seat lying across a boat

timbre (tam′ bər) *n.* The distinctive tone of a voice

Titan (tīt′ 'n) *n.* Giant; any of a race of giant deities

titanic (tī tan′ ik) *adj.* Having great power

tithe (tith) *n.* One tenth of one's income; here, a small amount given to charity

torpidly (tôr′ pid lē) *adv.* Sluggishly; slowly

tortuous (tôr′ choo əs) *adj.* Full of twists and turns

tourniquet (tur′ ni kit) *n.* A bandage to stop bleeding by compressing a blood vessel

transcend (tran send′) *v.* To go above or beyond limits; exceed

transcendental (tran′ sen dent′ 'l) *adj.* Supernatural; not concrete

transient (tran′ shənt) *adj.* Not permanent; passing quickly

transmigration (trans′ mī grā′ shən) *n.* The act of passing from one state of existence to another

transverse (trans vurs′) *adj.* Crossing from side to side

travesty (trav′ is tē) *v.* To ridicule; represent in a crude, distorted, or ridiculous way

tremulous (trem′ yōō ləs) *adj.* Trembling; quivering

trifle (trī′ fəl) *v.* To deal lightly

tripod (trī′ päd′) *n.* A three-legged support

trod (träd) *v.* Walked

tureen (tōō rēn′) *n.* A deep dish with a cover

U

ubiquitous (yōō bik′ wə təs) *adj.* Present everywhere, at the same time

unethical (un eth′ ik əl) *adj.* Not moral; not conforming to certain rules

unfathomable (un fath′ əm ə bəl) *adj.* Incapable of being understood or measured

usurer (yōō′ zhər ər) *n.* A person who lends money at a high rate of interst

usurp (yōō zurp′) *v.* To take power over; hold by force

utilitarian (yōō til′ ə ter′ ē ən) *adj.* Meant to be useful

V

vagary (və ger′ ē) *n.* Odd or unexpected action or idea

vanguard (van′ gärd′) *n.* The part of an army that goes ahead of the main body in an advance

vanquish (vaŋ′ kwish) *v.* To conquer; force into submission

venerable (ven′ ər ə bəl) *adj.* Worthy of respect because of age and character; impressive on account of age

venison (ven′ i zən) *n.* The flesh of a game animal, now especially the deer, used as food

venture (ven′ chər) *n.* A chance

veracious (və rā′ shəs) *adj.* Truthful; accurate

veracity (və ras′ ə tē) *n.* Truthfulness; honesty

vermillion (vər mil′ yən) *adj.* Bright red or reddish orange in color

victrola (vic trōl′ ə) *n.* A record player

vigorous (vig′ ər əs) *adj.* Living or growing with full vital strength

vindicated (vin′ də kāt′) *v.* To uphold; defend

virtuoso (vur′ choo ō′ sō) *n.* Person displaying great technical skill in any field

vocation (vō kā′ shən) *n.* Occupation

vouchsafe (vouch sāf′) *v.* To grant a reply

vulnerable (vul′ nər ə bəl) *adj.* Sensitive; easily hurt

W

waft (wäft) *v.* To float through the air

wallow (wäl′ ō) *v.* To enjoy completely; take great pleasure

wariness (wer′ ē nis) *n.* Caution

warren (wôr′ ən) *n.* A crowded, mazelike passage

wattle (wät′ 'l) *n.* A small, flowering tree

weir (wir) *n.* A low dam

wheeling (hwēl′ iŋ) *adj.* Changing direction suddenly

whimper (hwim′ pər) *v.* To make a low, whining sound as in crying or in fear

whimsical (hwim′ zi kəl) *adj.* Playful; odd

willet (wil′ it) *n.* A large, gray and white, long-legged wading bird

withered (with′ ərd) *adj.* Weakened; dried up

writhe (rīth) *v.* To twist in pain and agony

Y

yew (yōō) *n.* An evergreen shrub and tree of the yew family

Z

zenith (zē′ nith) *n.* The highest point

INDEX OF FINE ART

Adam and Eve, Edvard Munch, 224

Adventures of Rama—Rama and Lakshman Battle the Demon Rakshasas, The, School of Akbar, 721

Adventures of Rama—Ceremony, The, School of Akbar, 719

Andrews, Michael, *Melanie and Me Swimming,* 609

Annie Old Crow, James Bama, 468

Anonymous Chinese Artist, Lintel and Pediment of a Tomb (detail), 735

Artist Unknown, *Crowning of Arthur,* 690

Artist Unknown, *Death of Arthur,* 706

Artist Unknown, *Gallahad's Sword in Stone,* 698

Asher, James, *Carmen,* 79

Bacon, Francis, *Portrait of Lucian Freud,* 209

Bama, James, *Annie Old Crow,* 468

Bama, James, *Rise With Force and Spirit,* 201

Bath, The, Mary Cassatt, 501

Battle of Bunker Hill, The, Howard Pyle, 569

Battle of Life (The Golden Knight), The, Gustav Klimt, 577

Beach Treat (detail), *The,* Suzanne Nagler, 148

Beardsley, Aubrey, *How Sir Bedivere Cast the Sword Excaliber Into the Water,* 711

Beckmann, Max, *Landschaft, Cannes (Landscape, Cannes),* Cover

Beethoven's Sterbezimmer Im Schwarzpanierhaus, Johann Nepomuk Hoechle, 519

Birthday, Marc Chagall, 595

Boy With Float, C. S. Mazarin, 607

Butler, Elizabeth, *Scotland Forever,* 92

Canyon, The, Jack Dudley, 77

Carmen, James Asher, 79

Carter, Clarence Holbrook, *Math Man #4,* 674

Cassatt, Mary, *The Bath,* 501

Cassatt, Mary, *The Family,* 502

Central Park, Maurice Prendergast, 551

Chagall, Marc, *Birthday,* 595

Chase, William Merritt, *Dorothy,* 177

Chase, William Merritt, *In the Studio,* 163

City Night, Georgia O'Keeffe, 143

Coast Scene, Isles of Shoals, Childe Hassam, 153

Coleman, Glenn O., *Street Scene in Lower New York,* 155

Couples, Kees Van Dongen, 579

Cover Illustration for *The Wandering Jew,* Ian Pollock, 615

Cover of *Sundiata,* Senegalese Glass Painting, 727

Crowning of Arthur, Artist Unknown, 690

da Silva, Maria Elena Vieira, *La Bibliothèque (The Library),* 461

Daumier, Honoré, *Don Quixote,* 741

Davis, Stuart, *Swing Landscape* (detail), 635

Dawei, Sun Jingbo, 198

Death of Arthur, Artist Unknown, 706

DeWitt, Johannes, *Swan Theatre, London,* 307

Degas, Edgar, *Diego Martelli,* 413

Derain, André, *Tree Trunks,* 755

Diebenkorn, Richard, *Girl Looking at Landscape,* 189

Diego Martelli, Edgar Degas, 413

Don Quixote, Honoré Daumier, 741

Don Quixote and the Windmill, Francisco J. Torrome, 743

Dorothy, William Merritt Chase, 177

Drummers of Igbuno in a Village, John Mainga, 920

Dudley, Jack, *The Canyon,* 77

Early Morning in Ro . . . , Paul Klee, 750

Egger-Lienz, Albin, *Entry of King Etzel (Attila) Into Vienna,* 684

Eichenberg, Fritz, *Etchings,* 438, 440

El Pez Luminoso (The Luminous Fish), Juan Soriano, 108

Elder Walking Alone, An, John Mainga, 916

Elder Wearing Otuogwu Cloth Talking to a Teen Boy, An, John Mainga, 902

Ensor, James, *Les Masques et la Mort,* 175

Entry of King Etzel (Attila) Into Vienna, Albin Egger-Lienz, 684

Etchings, Fritz Eichenberg, 438, 440

Evening, Monhegan Island, Samuel Reindorf, 67

Evening Storytelling, John Mainga, 897

Family, The, Mary Cassatt, 502

Fragonard, Jean-Honoré, *A Young Girl Reading,* 455

Frances Howard, Isaac Oliver, 650

Gallahad's Sword in Stone, Artist Unknown, 698

Gillray, James, *Hint to Modern Sculptors as an Ornament to a Future Square,* 90

Girl Looking at Landscape, Richard Diebenkorn, 189

Girl With Cat, Franz Marc, 663

Goya, Francisco, José de, *Señora Sabasa Garcia,* 131

Hassam, Childe, *Coast Scene, Isles of Shoals,* 153

Heade, Martin Johnson, *Newbury Hayfield,* 624

Heinze, Mitchell, *The Pitcher,* 632

Hide and Seek, Tony Wong, 11

Hint to Modern Sculptors as an Ornament to a Future Square, James Gillray, 90

Hios, Theo, *Sunrise in Crete,* 633

Hiroshige, Ando, *Snow-Laden Camellia and Sparrow,* 655

Hiroshige, Ando, *A Sudden Shower at Ohashi,* 656

Hockney, David, *Raised Stage With Masks, Narrator, and Auditorium,* 246

Hoechle, Johann Nepomuk, *Beethoven's Sterbezimmer Im Schwarzpanierhaus,* 519

Hopper, Edward, *Stairway,* 95

How Sir Bedivere Cast the Sword Excaliber Into the Water, Aubrey Beardsley, 711

Hoyos, Ana Mercedes, *Palenquera,* 647

Hunters, The, Gari Melchers, 179

Impressions of Hands, Antoni Tapies, 592

In the Studio, William Merritt Chase, 163

Jagger, David, *Portrait of Kitty Jagger, the Artist's Wife,* 567

Jingbo, Sun, *Dawei,* 198

Johnson, Lois, *Private Performance,* 85

Jonsson, Finnur, *Three Suns,* 613

Kangau, S., *Market Scene,* 873

Katz, Alex, *The Table,* 524

Klee, Paul, *Early Morning in Ro . . . ,* 750

Klimt, Gustav, *The Battle of Life (The Golden Knight),* 577

La Belle Dame sans Merci, John W. Waterhouse, 553

La Bibliothèque (The Library), Maria Elena Vieira da Silva, 461

Landschaft, Cannes (Landscape, Cannes), Max Beckmann, Cover

Les Masques et la Mort, James Ensor, 175

Lintel and Pediment of a Tomb (detail), Anonymous Chinese Artist, 735

Lonely Ones, The, Edvard Munch, 226

"Lots of People Reported Our Dog to the Police," James Thurber, 409

McGrew, R. Brownell, *Old Ones Talking,* 470

McMullan, James, *Untitled,* 194

Mainga, John, *Drummers of Igbuno in a Village,* 920

Mainga, John, *An Elder Walking Alone,* 916

Mainga, John, *An Elder Wearing Otuogwu Cloth Talking to a Teen Boy,* 902

Mainga, John, *Evening Storytelling,* 897

Mainga, John, *Market Scene—Buying and Selling,* 910

Mainga, John, *Nigerian Family Compound,* 881

Mainga, John, *Teen Girls Returning Home After Market,* 885

Mainga, John, *The Wrestlers,* 926

Mainga, John, *Traditional Yam Harvest,* 892

Mainga, John, *Two Elders Sitting in a Farm,* 889

Marc, Franz, *Girl With Cat,* 663

Market Scene—Buying and Selling, John Mainga, 910

Market Scene. S. Kangau, 873

Martin, Emily, Student, *View From a Car,* 402

Math Man #4, Clarence Holbrook Carter, 674

Matisse, Henri, *Violinist at the Window,* 587

Mazarin, C. S., *Boy With Float,* 607

Mediterranean Landscape, Pablo Picasso, 603

Melanie and Me Swimming, Michael Andrews, 609

Melchers, Gari, *The Hunters,* 179

Memory, Elihu Vedder, 619

Monet, Claude, *Regattas at Argenteuil,* 15

Munch, Edvard, *Adam and Eve,* 224

Munch, Edvard, *The Lonely Ones,* 226

Mushrooms, Sir William Nicholson, 117

Nagler, Suzanne, *The Beach Treat* (detail), 148

New Bear (Gros Ventre Tribe), *Untitled (Buffalo Hunt),* 642

Newbury Hayfield, Martin Johnson Heade, 624

Nicholson, Sir William, *Mushrooms,* 117

Nigerian Family Compound, John Mainga, 881

"Nobody Knew Exactly What Was the Matter With Him," James Thurber, 407

O'Keeffe, Georgia, *City Night,* 143

O'Keeffe, Georgia, *Red Hills and Bones,* 136

O'Keeffe, Georgia, *Red Poppies,* 544

Old Ones Talking, R. Brownell McGrew, 470

Oliver, Isaac, *Frances Howard,* 650

Orion, Martin Wong, 458

Palenquera, Ana Mercedes Hoyos, 647

Peirce, Joshua, *San Francisco,* 101

Picasso, Pablo, *Mediterranean Landscape,* 603

Pitcher, The, Mitchell Heinze, 632

Pollock, Ian, Cover Illustration for *The Wandering Jew,* 615

Portrait of Kitty Jagger, the Artist's Wife, David Jagger, 567

Portrait of Lucian Freud, Francis Bacon, 209

Prendergast, Maurice, *Central Park,* 551

Private Performance, Lois Johnson, 85

Prophet #1, The, Charles White, 671

Pyle, Howard, *The Battle of Bunker Hill,* 569

Rabell, Arnaldo Roche, *Toda la Sabiduria Viene del Cielo (All the Wisdom Comes From the Sky),* 111

Racing Game, Tony Wong, 6

Raised Stage With Masks, Narrator, and Auditorium, David Hockney, 246

Red Hills and Bones, Georgia O'Keeffe, 136

Red Poppies, Georgia O'Keeffe, 544

Regattas at Argenteuil, Claude Monet, 15

Reindorf, Samuel, *Evening, Monhegan Island,* 67

Rise With Force and Spirit, James Bama, 201

Road With Cypress and Star, Vincent van Gogh, 119

Ryder, Albert Pinkham, *Toilers of the Sea,* 612

San Francisco, Joshua Peirce, 101

School of Akbar, *The Adventures of Rama—Ceremony,* 719

School of Akbar, *The Adventures of Rama—Rama and Lakshman Battle the Demon Rakshasas,* 721

Scotland Forever, Elizabeth Butler, 92

Senegalese Glass Painting, Cover of *Sundiata,* 727

Señora Sabasa Garcia, Francisco José de Goya, 131

Shahn, Ben, *Song,* 505

Sisters, The, Stanley Spencer, 161

Snow-Laden Camellia and Sparrow, Ando Hiroshige, 655

Soriano, Juan, *El Pez Luminoso (The Luminous Fish),* 108

Song, Ben Shahn, 505

Spencer, Stanley, *The Sisters,* 161

Stairway, Edward Hopper, 95

Street Scene in Lower New York, Glenn O. Coleman, 155

Sudden Shower at Ohashi, A, Ando Hiroshige, 656

Sunrise in Crete, Theo Hios, 633

Swan Theatre, London, Johannes DeWitt, 307

Swing Landscape (detail), Stuart Davis, 635

Tapies, Antoni, *Impressions of Hands,* 592

Table, The, Alex Katz, 524
Teen Girls Returning Home After Market, John Mainga, 885
Three Suns, Finnur Jonsson, 613
Thurber, James, "Lots of People Reported Our Dog to the Police," 409
Thurber, James, "Nobody Knew Exactly What Was the Matter With Him," 407
Toda la Sabiduria Viene del Cielo (All the Wisdom Comes From the Sky), Arnaldo Roche Rabell, 111
Toilers of the Sea, Albert Pinkham Ryder, 612
Torrome, Francisco J., *Don Quixote and the Windmill,* 743
Traditional Yam Harvest, John Mainga, 892
Tree Trunks, André Derain, 755
Turner, J.M.W., *The Wreck of a Transport Ship,* 563
Two Elders Sitting in a Farm, John Mainga, 889

Untitled, James McMullan, 194
Untitled (Buffalo Hunt), New Bear (Gros Ventre Tribe), 642
Van Dongen, Kees, *Couples,* 579
van Gogh, Vincent, *Road With Cypress and Star,* 119
Vedder, Elihu, *Memory,* 619
View From a Car, Emily Martin, Student, 402
Violinist at the Window, Henri Matisse, 587
Waterhouse, John W., *La Belle Dame sans Merci,* 553
White, Charles, *The Prophet #1,* 671
Wong, Martin, *Orion,* 458
Wong, Tony, *Hide and Seek,* 11
Wong, Tony, *Racing Game,* 6
Wreck of a Transport Ship, The, J.M.W. Turner, 563
Wrestlers, The, John Mainga, 926
Young Girl Reading, A, Jean-Honoré Fragonard, 455

INDEX OF SKILLS

ANALYZING LITERATURE

Allegory, 166, 173
Alliteration, 637, 641
Appreciation, essay of, 498, 503
Arthurian legend, 689, 700
Aside, 346, 367
Assonance, 637
Atmosphere, 146, 154
Autobiography, 432, 441
Biography, 426, 431
    characterization in, 414, 425
Blank verse, 308, 327
Catharsis, 384
Characterization, 68
    in biography, 414, 425
    direct characterization, 68, 75
    indirect characterization, 68, 75
Characters, 756, 789
    dynamic characters, 88
    flat characters, 76, 87
    round characters, 76, 87
    static characters, 88, 94
    tragic characters, 290, 305
    verisimilitude, 756
Chivalry, 689, 703
Classification, 506, 509
Climax, 16, 29, 790
Complications, of plot, 16
Concrete poetry, 659, 660
Conflict, 42, 368, 383, 790, 841
    external conflict, 42, 59
    internal conflict, 42, 59
Couplet, 632
Crystallized moment, 220, 227
Definition, 510, 513
Descriptive essay, 472, 479
Dialogue, 576, 578
Direct characterization, 68, 75
Drama
    aside, 346, 367
    dramatic irony, 328, 345
    monologue, 346, 367
    plot structure, 274, 289
    radio play, 250, 271
    soliloquy, 346, 367
    tragedy, 384, 397
Dynamic characters, 88
Epic conflict, 724, 731
Epic hero, 716, 723
Epic poetry, 715

Essays
    of appreciation, 498, 503
    descriptive, 472, 479
    expository, 456, 463
    humorous, 412
    narrative, 480, 491
Exposition, 16, 29
Expository essay, 456, 463
External conflict, 42, 59
Fantasy, 60, 66
Feminine rhyme, 572, 574
Figurative language, 605, 611
Flat characters, 76, 87
Foreshadowing, 30, 41, 562, 566
Free verse, 597, 599, 679
Haiku, 654, 657
Historical context, 732, 737
Humorous essay, 412
Iamb, 574
Imagery, 621, 622, 624
    in essays, 464, 471
Images, and theme, 672
Indirect characterization, 68, 75
Interior monologue, 206, 213
Internal conflict, 42, 59
Internal rhyme, 641
Irony, 182, 188, 584
    dramatic irony, 328, 345
    irony of situation, 182, 188
    verbal irony, 182, 188
Key statements, 214, 219
Legends, 689, 700
    Arthurian legend, 689, 700
Local color, 126, 133
Lyric poem, 589, 591
Masculine rhyme, 572, 574
Metaphor, 605, 608
    extended metaphor, 611, 613
Meter, in poetry, 574, 637, 646
Metrical foot, 574
Monologue, 346, 367
Mood, 627, 628
Motivation, 14
Narrative essay, 480, 491
Narrative poem, 552, 555
Narrator, perspective of, 106, 113
Onomatopoeia, 637, 645
Parallelism, 639
Parody, 738, 745
Personal narrative, 539
Personification, 611, 618

Petrarchan sonnet, 652
Plot, 16, 29, 790, 878, 905
    climax, 16, 29, 790
    complications, 16
    exposition, 16, 29
    resolution, 16, 29, 790
Plot structure, in drama, 274, 289
Poetry
    blank verse, 308, 327
    concrete poetry, 659, 660
    couplet, 632
    dramatic poetry, 568, 571
    epic poetry, 715
    free verse, 597, 599, 679
    haiku, 654, 657
    lyric poem, 589, 591
    meter in, 574, 637, 646
    narrative poem, 552, 555
    rhyme in, 572, 574, 641
    rhythm in, 572, 574, 643
Point of view, 96, 103
    third-person limited, 114, 118
Radio play, 250, 271
Reminiscence, 442, 454
Repetition, 637, 639, 643
Resolution, 16, 29, 790
Rhyme in poetry, 572, 574, 641
    internal rhyme, 641
    masculine rhyme, 572, 574
Rhythm in poetry, 572, 574, 643
    meter, 574, 637, 646
Round characters, 76, 87
Sarcasm, 584
Setting, 120, 125, 876, 905
    time as aspect of, 134, 145
Shakespearean sonnet, 651
Simile, 605, 607
Soliloquy, 346, 367
Sonnet, 649, 651
    Petrarchan sonnet, 652
    Shakespearean sonnet, 651
Sound devices, 637
Speaker
    in poem, 556, 560
    tone of, 581, 583
Static characters, 88, 94
Suspense, 30, 41, 562
Symbols, 156, 159, 160, 165
    characters as, 241
Theme, 190, 203, 550, 665, 667, 842, 872, 906, 929
    and images, 672
    and key statements, 214, 219
Tone
    in dialogue, 176, 181
    and speaker, 581, 583
Tragedy, 384, 397
    tragic character, 290, 305

CRITICAL THINKING AND READING

Allusions, 550
Ambiguity, 213
Arguments, 383
Art
    conclusions about, 503
    making judgment about, 525
Author's purpose, 103
Biographer's purpose, 431
Cause and effect, 59, 533
Characters
    comparing and contrasting, 165, 789
    drawing conclusions about, 425
    dynamic characters, 929
    inference about, 75, 133, 181, 560
Chorus, role of, 289
Classifying, 679
Comparing and contrasting, 491
    characters, 165, 789
    cultural background, 905
    heroes, 723
Connotative meaning, 159, 173
Cultural background, comparing, 905
Cultural values, 737
Culture, inference about, 731
Details
    appreciation of, 227
    and mood, 600
    objective details, 441
    relevant details, 14
    subjective details, 441
    supporting details, 412, 521
Dynamic characters, 929
Emotive language, 454
Fact and opinion, 479
Figurative language, 203
Generalizations, 241
Humor, 94
Imagery, 327
Images, 625
    and mood, 634
Inference
    about author, 539
    about characters, 75, 133, 181, 560
    about culture, 731
    from evidence, 66
Inversion, 703
Main idea, 509
    and details, 412
Map, reading of, 471
Metaphorical language, 397
Mood
    and details, 600
    and images, 634
Novel, evaluation of, 872
Objective details, 441

Outcomes, prediction of, 41, 305, 345
Parody, tone in, 745
Perspective, shifts in, 113
Poetry
    form of, 675
    theme in, 593
Purpose, of essay, 463
Purpose of work, 643
Repetition, and theme, 672
Setting, effect of, 125
Stereotypes, 87
Subjective details, 441
Summarizing, a story, 219
Supporting details, 412, 521
Symbols, 841
Technique, evaluation of, 271
Theme
    in lyric poem, 593
    and repetition, 672
Tone, 367, 700
    in parody, 745

LEARNING OPTIONS

Art, 14, 59, 103, 113, 125, 133, 154, 159, 173, 289, 383,
    397, 425, 454, 471, 525, 533, 578, 631, 634, 639,
    641, 653, 669, 700
Community connections, 59, 241, 463, 561, 643, 669, 929
Cross-curricular connection, 41, 87, 118, 154, 159, 165,
    219, 271, 327, 383, 491, 503, 561, 578, 602, 631,
    639, 653, 672, 675, 731, 789, 905
Language, 602, 653, 679
Multicultural activity, 431, 441, 700, 737, 905
Performance, 29, 66, 227, 491, 905, 929
Speaking and listening, 118, 271, 571, 731
Writing, 41, 75, 113, 118, 145, 173, 181, 213, 367, 412,
    425, 441, 539, 561, 578, 602, 615, 631, 639, 641,
    653, 700, 703, 789, 841

READING IN THE ARTS AND SCIENCES

Critical writing, 522, 525
Definition, 510, 513
Inference, 526, 533
Observation, 526, 533
Process analysis, 514, 521

THINKING AND WRITING

Analyzing a symbol, 841
Assuming a character's identity, 289
Changing the point of view, 118
Comparing and contrasting characters, 87
Comparing and contrasting memories, 454
Comparing and contrasting sonnets, 653

Describing a pet, 412
Describing a place, 133
Exploring theme, 203
Interpreting character, 213
Patterning the style of the poem, 575
Preparing an argument, 397
Presenting a point of view, 789
Responding to criticism, 872
Responding to lyric poetry, 595
Responding to theme, 550, 672, 675, 929
Rewriting dialogue, 219
Rewriting in contemporary language, 383
Thinking about science, 533
Writing a biography, 431
Writing about a code of conduct, 703
Writing about a descriptive essay, 479
Writing about allegory, 173
Writing about a memorable place, 471
Writing about a narrative essay, 491
Writing about a person, 94
Writing about a place, 125
Writing about art, 154, 525
Writing about a symbol, 159
Writing about a title, 188
Writing about background music, 367
Writing about conflict, 59
Writing about cultural values, 737
Writing about Emily Dickinson's poetry, 425
Writing about epic poetry, 715
Writing about imagery, 625
Writing about initiation rites, 723
Writing about language arts, 509
Writing about lyric poetry, 594
Writing about meaning in free verse, 602
Writing about metaphors, 609
Writing about mood, 41, 631
Writing about motivation, 14
Writing about plot, 29
Writing about suspense, 566
Writing about the speaker, 561
Writing about tone, 181
Writing a character sketch, 75
Writing a different ending, 305
Writing a drama review, 271
Writing a fairy tale, 227
Writing a journal entry about history, 513
Writing a musical poem, 643
Writing a narrative poem, 555
Writing an autobiographical sketch, 441
Writing an essay about music, 521
Writing an essay of appreciation, 503
Writing a paraphrase of a poem, 662
Writing a parody of a fictional hero, 745
Writing a personal narrative, 539
Writing a sequel, 165
Writing a tribute, 463
Writing blank verse, 327

Writing concrete poetry, 660
Writing fantasy, 66
Writing from a character's point of view, 905
Writing from a different perspective, 113
Writing haiku, 657

Writing in contrast settings, 145
Writing in the first person, 103
Writing in the heroic tradition, 731
Writing with a symbol, 241
Writing with dramatic irony, 345

INDEX OF TITLES BY THEMES

APPRECIATING OTHERS

à pied, 614
Alex Katz's The Table, 523
Buffalo Dance Song, 642
Chee's Daughter, 77
Christmas Memory, A, 443
Constantly Risking Absurdity, 661
Diamond Island: Alcatraz, 97
Emily Dickinson, 415
Ex-Basketball Player, 677
First Lesson, 609
Fish, The, 629
Generations, 594
Homecoming Stranger, The, 191
I Am Not Lonely, 591
In Flanders Fields, 646
Jazz Fantasia, 644
K'ung-ming Borrows Some Arrows, 733
La Belle Dame sans Merci, 553
Leiningen Versus the Ants, 43
Making a Fist, 592
Marian Anderson: Famous Concert Singer, 427
Mary Cassatt, 499
Miss Rosie, 606
Morte d'Arthur, 704
Old People Speak of Death, The, 670
On Summer, 493
Pitcher, 632
Ramayana, from the, 717
Separate Peace, A, 757
Shall I Compare Thee to a Summer's Day?, 650
Size and Sheer Will, 607
Sonnet-Ballad, The, 582
Sundiata: An Epic of Old Mali, from, 725
To James, 666
Visit to Grandmother, A, 69
When Your Face Came Rising, 595
With All Flags Flying, 229
Wrestling Match, The, 879

CHOICES AND CONSEQUENCES

à pied, 614
Alabama Centennial, 547
Antigone, 275
Arthur Becomes King of Britain, 690
Chee's Daughter, 77
Civil Peace, 215
Contents of the Dead Man's Pocket, 17
Danny Deever, 569

Eldorado, 577
Ex-Basketball Player, 677
Games at Twilight, 3
Julius Caesar (See Tragedy of Julius Caesar, The)
Leiningen Versus the Ants, 43
Marian Anderson: Famous Concert Singer, 427
Marriage of King Arthur, The, 701
Mary Cassatt, 499
Monkey's Paw, The, 31
Morte d'Arthur, 704
Mushrooms in the City, 115
Notes on Punctuation, 507
O What Is That Sound, 573
Ring, The, 221
Separate Peace, A, 757
There Will Come Soft Rains, 121
Through the Tunnel, 147
Tragedy of Julius Caesar, The, 309
White Lantern, The, from, 481
With All Flags Flying, 229
Wreck of the Hesperus, The , 563
Wrestling Match, The, 879

CONFLICTS AND CHALLENGES

à pied, 614
Alabama Centennial, 457
Antigone, 275
Chee's Daughter, 77
Civil Peace, 215
Constantly Risking Absurdity, 661
Contents of the Dead Man's Pocket, 17
Creative Process in Music, The, 515
Diamond Island: Alcatraz, 97
Dog That Bit People, The, 405
Eldorado, 577
Ex-Basketball Player, 677
First Lesson, 609
Fish, The, 629
Flood, 473
Games at Twilight, 3
Homecoming Stranger, The, 191
Invasion From Mars, 251
Julius Caesar (See Tragedy of Julius Caesar, The)
K'ung-ming Borrows Some Arrows, 733
Letter Slot, 660
Making a Fist, 592
Marian Anderson: Famous Concert Singer, 427
Mary Cassatt, 499
Monkey's Paw, The, 31
Morte d'Arthur, 704

Mushrooms in the City, 115
Number Pi, The, 673
O What Is That Sound, 573
Ramayana, from the, 717
Reapers, 628
Ring, The, 221
Separate Peace, A, 757
Size and Sheer Will, 607
Sonnet-Ballad, The, 582
Sundiata: An Epic of Old Mali, from, 725
Sunlight in Trebizond Street, 207
Through the Tunnel, 147
To James, 666
To Satch, 585
Tragedy of Julius Caesar, The, 309
Visit to Grandmother, A, 69
White Lantern, The, from, 481
With All Flags Flying, 229
Wreck of the Hesperus, The, 563
Wrestling Match, The, 879

EXPLORING THE UNKNOWN

Axolotl, 107
By the Waters of Babylon, 135
Eldorado, 577
Invasion From Mars, 251
Marginal World, The, 527
Monkey's Paw, The, 31
Number Pi, The, 673
Old Man of the Temple, 61
Old People Speak of Death, The, 670
There Will Come Soft Rains, 121

HUMANS IN CONFLICT

à pied, 614
Alabama Centennial, 547
Antigone, 275
Chee's Daughter, 77
Diamond Island: Alcatraz, 97
Homecoming Stranger, The, 191
Julius Caesar (See Tragedy of Julius Caesar, The)
Morte d'Arthur, 704
O What Is That Sound, 573
Separate Peace, A, 757
Street of the Cañon, The, 127
Sunlight in Trebizond Street, 207
Tragedy of Julius Caesar, The, 309
Visit to Grandmother, A, 69
With All Flags Flying, 229
Wrestling Match, The, 879

ILLUSION AND REALITY

Axolotl, 107
Afterglow, 624

Don Quixote, from, 739
Invasion From Mars, 251
Julius Caesar (See Tragedy of Julius Caesar, The)
Luck, 89
Machine That Won the War, The, 183
Monkey's Paw, The, 31
Mushrooms in the City, 115
Old Man of the Temple, 61
Open Window, The, 177
Ring, The, 221
Tragedy of Julius Caesar, The, 309

INDIVIDUALS IN SOCIETY

American Idea, The, 511
Antigone, 275
Arthur Becomes King of Britain, 690
By the Waters of Babylon, 135
Civil Peace, 215
Danny Deever, 569
Emily Dickinson, 415
Ex-Basketball Player, 677
Flood, 473
I Am Not Lonely, 591
Julius Caesar (See Tragedy of Julius Caesar, The)
Luck, 89
Marian Anderson: Famous Concert Singer, 427
Marriage of King Arthur, The, 701
Mary Cassatt, 499
Masque of the Red Death, The, 167
Miss Rosie, 606
Mushrooms in the City, 115
O What Is That Sound, 573
Separate Peace, A, 757
Street of the Cañon, The, 127
Sunlight in Trebizond Street, 207
To James, 666
Tragedy of Julius Caesar, The, 309
Two Tramps in Mud Time, 557
White Lantern, The, from, 481
With All Flags Flying, 229
Wrestling Match, The, 879

OUR LIVING EARTH

Abalone, Abalone, Abalone, 157
Afterglow, 624
Autumn Song, 590
Big Wind, 622
Blessing, A, 598
Buffalo Dance Song, 642
By the Waters of Babylon, 135
Fish, The, 629
Flood, 473
Four Haiku, 655
Leiningen Versus the Ants, 43

Loss, 623
Marginal World, The, 527
My Heart's in the Highlands, 638
Night Clouds, 612
On Summer, 493
Reapers, 628
Sunset, 613
There Will Come Soft Rains, 121
Way to Rainy Mountain, The, from, 465
White Lantern, The, from, 481
Wind—tapped like a tired Man, The, 618
Wreck of the Hesperus, 563

REFLECTING ON THE PAST

Abalone, Abalone, Abalone, 157
Alabama Centennial, 547
By the Waters of Babylon, 135
Child's Christmas in Wales, A, 433
Christmas Memory, A, 443
Diamond Island: Alcatraz, 97
Ex-Basketball Player, 677
Glove's Labor Lost, 535
Homecoming Stranger, The, 191
In Commemoration: One Million Volumes, from, 457
Mary Cassatt, 499
Miss Rosie, 606
Old People Speak of Death, The, 670
On Summer, 493
Portrait, The, 161
Separate Peace, A, 757
Visit to Grandmother, A, 69
Way to Rainy Mountain, The, from, 465
Wrestling Match, The, 879

RITES OF PASSAGE

à pied, 614
Alabama Centennial, 547
Arthur Becomes King of Britain, 690
Autumn Song, 590
Axolotl, 107
Bees, The, 632
By the Waters of Babylon, 135
Child's Christmas in Wales, A, 433
Christmas Memory, A, 443
Civil Peace, 215
Diamond Island: Alcatraz, 97
Ex-Basketball Player, 677
First Lesson, 609
Games at Twilight, 3
Generations, 594
Glove's Labor Lost, 535
Homecoming Stranger, The, 191
In Commemoration: One Million Volumes, from, 457
In Flanders Fields, 646

Making a Fist, 592
Marriage of King Arthur, The, 701
Metaphor, 608
Miss Rosie, 606
Morte d'Arthur, 704
Old Man of the Temple, 61
Old People Speak of Death, The, 670
Portrait, The, 161
Separate Peace, A, 757
Size and Sheer Will, 607
Sunlight in Trebizond Street, 207
Through the Tunnel, 147
Visit to Grandmother, A, 69
Way to Rainy Mountain, The, from, 465
With All Flags Flying, 229
Wrestling Match, The, 879

THE SEARCH FOR MEANING

à pied, 614
Axolotl, 107
By the Waters of Babylon, 135
Diamond Island: Alcatraz, 97
Homecoming Stranger, The, 191
In Commemoration: One Million Volumes, from, 457
Letter from Home, A, 601
Marginal World, The, 527
Masque of the Red Death, The, 167
Street, The, 600
With All Flags Flying, 229

SELF-REALIZATION

Abalone, Abalone, Abalone, 157
Axolotl, 107
Child's Christmas in Wales, A, 433
Christmas Memory, A, 443
Contents of the Dead Man's Pocket, 17
Games at Twilight, 3
Homecoming Stranger, The, 191
Julius Caesar (See Tragedy of Julius Caesar, The)
My Heart's in The Highlands, 638
Portrait, The, 161
Ring, The, 221
Separate Peace, A, 757
Through the Tunnel, 147
Tragedy of Julius Caesar, The, 309
Visit to Grandmother, A, 69
With All Flags Flying, 229
Wrestling Match, The, 879

SHOWING COURAGE

à pied, 614
Alabama Centennial, 547
Antigone, 275
Arthur Becomes King of Britain, 690

Auto Wreck, 668
Chee's Daughter, 77
Contents of the Dead Man's Pocket, 17
Diamond Island: Alcatraz, 97
First Lesson, 609
Flood, 473
Homecoming Stranger, The 191
Julius Caesar (See Tragedy of Julius Caesar, The)
K'ung-ming Borrows Some Arrows, 733
Leiningen Versus the Ants, 43
Making a Fist, 592
Marian Anderson: Famous Concert Singer, 427
Marriage of King Arthur, The, 701
Mary Cassatt, 499
Miss Rosie, 606
Morte d'Arthur, 704
Old People Speak of Death, The, 670
On Summer, 493
Ramayana, from the, 717
Separate Peace, A, 757
Sonnet-Ballad, The, 582
Sundiata: An Epic of Old Mali, from, 725
Sunlight in Trebizond Street, 207
Through the Tunnel, 147
To James, 666
To Satch, 585
Tragedy of Julius Caesar, The, 309
White Lantern, The, from, 481
With All Flags Flying, 229
Wreck of the Hesperus, The, 563
Wrestling Match, The, 879

VALUES AND BELIEFS

à pied, 614
Abalone, Abalone, Abalone, 157
Alabama Centennial, 547
Alex Katz's The Table, 523
American Idea, The, 511
Antigone, 275
Buffalo Dance Song, 642

By the Waters of Babylon, 135
Chee's Daughter, 77
Child's Christmas in Wales, A, 433
Christmas Memory, A, 443
Civil Peace, 215
Contents of the Dead Man's Pocket, 17
Creative Process in Music, The, 515
Diamond Island: Alcatraz, 97
Eldorado, 577
Emily Dickinson, 415
Fish, The, 629
Flood, 473
Glove's Labor Lost, 535
Homecoming Stranger, The, 191
In Commemoration: One Million Volumes, from, 457
In Flanders Fields, 646
Julius Caesar (See Tragedy of Julius Caesar, The)
Machine That Won the War, The, 183
Marian Anderson: Famous Concert Singer, 427
Mary Cassatt, 499
Masque of the Red Death, The, 167
Monkey's Paw, The, 31
My Heart's in the Highlands, 638
O What Is That Sound, 573
Old Man of the Temple, 61
Old People Speak of Death, The, 670
On Summer, 493
One Perfect Rose, 584
Puritan Sonnet, 652
Reapers, 628
Shall I Compare Thee to a Summer's Day?, 650
Street of the Cañon, The, 127
Sunlight in Trebizond Street, 207
There Will Come Soft Rains, 121
Through the Tunnel, 147
Tragedy of Julius Caesar, The, 309
Two Tramps in Mud Time, 557
Visit to Grandmother, A, 69
Way to Rainy Mountain, The, from, 465
When Your Face Came Rising, 595
White Lantern, The, from, 481
With All Flags Flying, 229

INDEX OF AUTHORS AND TITLES

Page numbers in *italics* refer to biographical information.

A

à pied, 614
Abalone, Abalone, Abalone, 157
Achebe, Chinua, *214,* 215
Afterglow, 624
Alabama Centennial, 547
Alex Katz's The Table, 523
Allen, Samuel, *580,* 585
American Idea, The, 511
Ammons, A. R., *620,* 623
Anaya, Rudolfo A., *456,* 457
Antigone, 275
Arthur Becomes King of Britain, 690
Asimov, Isaac, *182,* 183
Auden, W. H., *572,* 573
Auto Wreck, 668
Autumn Song, 590
Axolotl, 107

B

Bashō, *654,* 655
Beattie, Ann, *522,* 523
Bees, The, 632
Benét, Stephen Vincent, *134,* 135
Big Wind, 622
Bishop, Elizabeth, *626,* 629
Blessing, A, 598
Blixen, Karen (*See* Dinesen, Isak)
Booth, Philip, *604,* 609
Borges, Jorge Luis, *620,* 624
Boswell, Thomas, 535, *538*
Bradbury, Ray, *120,* 121
Brooks, Gwendolyn, *580,* 582
Brooks, Van Wyck, *414,* 415
Buffalo Dance Song, 642
Burns, Robert, *636,* 638
By the Waters of Babylon, 135

C

Calvino, Italo, *114,* 115
Capote, Truman, *442,* 443
Carson, Rachel, *526,* 527
Cervantes, Miguel de, *738,* 739
Chee's Daughter, 77
Child's Christmas in Wales, A, 433
Chiyojo, *654,* 655
Christmas Memory, A, 443
Civil Peace, 215
Clemens, Samuel Langhorne (*See* Twain, Mark)

Clifton, Lucille, *604,* 606
Colette, *160,* 161
Connell, Evan S., *480,* 481
Constantly Risking Absurdity, 661
Contents of the Dead Man's Pocket, 17
Copland, Aaron, *514,* 515
Cortázar, Julio, *106,* 107
Creative Process in Music, The, 515

D

Danny Deever, 569
Dao, Bei, *190,* 191
Desai, Anita, 3, *13*
Diamond Island: Alcatraz, 97
Dickinson, Emily, *610,* 618
Dillard, Annie, *472,* 473
Dinesen, Isak, *220,* 221
Dog That Bit People, The, 405
Don Quixote, from, 739

E

Eldorado, 577
Emecheta, Buchi, *878,* 879
Emily Dickinson, 415
Ex-Basketball Player, 677

F

Ferlinghetti, Lawrence, *658,* 661
Finney, Jack, *16,* 17
First Lesson, 609
Fish, The, 629
Flood, 473
Four Haiku, 655
Francis, Robert, *626,* 632
Frost, Robert, *556,* 557

G

Games at Twilight, 3
Generations, 594
Glove's Labor Lost, 535
Gordon, Mary, *498,* 499, 504

H

Hansberry, Lorraine, *492,* 493
Hikmet, Nazim, *626,* 632
Homecoming Stranger, The, 191
Horne, Frank, *664,* 666
Hughes, Langston, *426,* 427
Hyakuchi, *654,* 655

I

I Am Not Lonely, 591
In Commemoration: One Million Volumes, from, 457
In Flanders Fields, 646
Invasion From Mars, 251
Issa, *654, 656*

J

Jacobs, W. W., *30,* 31
Jazz Fantasia, 644
Julius Caesar (See *Tragedy of Julius Caesar, The*)

K

Keats, John, *552, 553*
Kelley, William Melvin, *68, 69*
Kipling, Rudyard, *568, 569*
Knowles, John, *756, 757*
Koch, Howard, *250, 251*
K'ung-ming Borrows Some Arrows, 733

L

La Belle Dame sans Merci, 553
Leiningen Versus the Ants, 43
Lessing, Doris, *146, 147*
Letter from Home, A, 601
Letter Slot, 660
Lo Kuan-Chung, *732, 733*
Longfellow, Henry Wadsworth, *562, 563*
Loss, 623
Lowell, Amy, *588, 594, 610, 612*
Luck, 89

M

McCrae, John, *637, 646*
McElroy, Colleen J., *610,* 614, 616
Machine That Won the War, The, 183
Madgett, Naomi Long, 547, *550*
Making a Fist, 592
Malory, Sir Thomas, *688,* 701
Marginal World, The, 527
Marian Anderson: Famous Concert Singer, 427
Marriage of King Arthur, The, 701
Mary Cassatt, 499
Masque of the Red Death, The, 167
Merriam, Eve, *604,* 608
Metaphor, 608
Miller, Siyowin, *76,* 77
Miss Rosie, 606
Mistral, Gabriela, *588,* 591
Momaday, N. Scott, *464,* 465
Monkey's Paw, The, 31
Mori, Toshio, *156,* 157
Morte d'Arthur, 704
Mtshali, Mbuyiseni Oswald, *610,* 613
Munro, H. H. (*See* Saki)
Mushrooms in the City, 115
My Heart's in the Highlands, 638

N

Narayan, R. K., *60,* 61, *716,* 717
Niane, D. T., *724,* 725
Niggli, Josephina, *126,* 127
Night Clouds, 612
Notes on Punctuation, 507
Number Pi, The, 673
Nye, Naomi Shihab, *588,* 592

O

O What Is That Sound, 573
Old Man of the Temple, 61
Old People Speak of Death, The, 670
Olds, Sharon, *604,* 607
Oliver, Mary, *596,* 601
On Summer, 493
One Perfect Rose, 584
Open Window, The, 177

P

Parker, Dorothy, *580,* 584
Paton, Alan, *206,* 207
Pawnee, 636, 642
Paz, Octavio, *596,* 600
Pitcher, 632
Platero, Juanita, *76,* 77
Poe, Edgar Allan, *166,* 167, *576,* 577
Portrait, The, 161
Puritan Sonnet, 652

R

Ramayana, from the, 717
Reapers, 628
Ring, The, 221
Roethke, Theodore, *620,* 622

S

Saki, *176,* 177
Sandburg, Carl, *636,* 644
Separate Peace, A, 757
Shakespeare, William, *308,* 309, *648,* 650
Shall I Compare Thee to a Summer's Day?, 650
Shapiro, Karl, *664,* 668
Size and Sheer Will, 607
Sonnet-Ballad, The, 582
Sophocles, *274,* 275
Splendor Falls, The, 640
Stephenson, Carl, *42,* 43
Street, The, 600
Street of the Cañon, The, 127
Sundiata: An Epic of Old Mali, from, 725
Sunlight in Trebizond Street, 207
Sunset, 613
Szymborska, Wisława, *664,* 673

T

Tennyson, Alfred, Lord, *636,* 640, *688,* 704
There Will Come Soft Rains, 121

Thomas, Dylan, *432*, 433
Thomas, Lewis, *506*, 507
Through the Tunnel, 147
Thurber, James, 405, *411*
To James, 666
To Satch, 585
Toomer, Jean, *626*, 628
Tragedy of Julius Caesar, The, 309
Troupe, Quincy, *664*, 670
Twain, Mark, *88*, 89
Two Tramps in Mud Time, 557
Tyler, Anne, 229, *240*

U

Updike, John, *658*, 660, 677, *678*

V

Verlaine, Paul, *588*, 590

Vesey, Paul (*See* Allen, Samuel)
Visit to Grandmother, A, 69

W

Way to Rainy Mountain, The, from, 465
When Your Face Came Rising, 595
White Lantern, The, from, 481
White, T. H., *688*, 690
White, Theodore H., *510*, 511
Wilson, Darryl Babe, *96*, 97, 104
Wind—tapped like a tired Man, The, 618
With All Flags Flying, 229
Wreck of the Hesperus, The, 563
Wrestling Match, The, 879
Wright, James, *596*, 598
Wylie, Elinor, *648*, 652

Y

Yevtushenko, Yevgeny, *589*, 595

Acknowledgments

Rudolfo Anaya
"In Commemoration: One Million Volumes" by Rudolfo Anaya, from *A Million Stars: The Millionth Acquisition for the University of New Mexico General Library,* edited by Connie Capers Thorsen (Albuquerque: The University of New Mexico General Library, 1981). Reprinted by permission of the author.

Arte Público Press
Lines from "Napa, California" from *Women Are Not Roses* by Ana Castillo, 1987 (Second Edition), Arte Público Press, University of Houston. Reprinted by permission of Arte Público Press.

Asian American Studies Publications
"Abalone, Abalone, Abalone" from *The Chauvinist and Other Stories* by Toshio Mori. Copyright © 1979 by The Regents of the University of California. Reprinted by permission.

Elizabeth Barnett, Literary Executor of the Estate of Norma Millay Ellis
"I Shall Go Back Again to the Bleak Shore" and excerpt from "Counting-out Rhyme" by Edna St. Vincent Millay. Copyright © 1923, 1928, 1951, 1955 by Edna St. Vincent Millay and Norma Millay Ellis. Reprinted by permission.

Bilingual Press/Editorial Bilingüe
Lines from "Allí por la calle San Luis" by Carmen Tafolla from *Five Poets of Aztlán,* edited by Santiago Daydi-Tolson, © 1985 by Bilingual Press/Editorial Bilingüe, Arizona State University, Tempe, Arizona. Reprinted by permission.

BOA Editions, Ltd.
"miss rosie," copyright © 1987 by Lucille Clifton. Reprinted from *good woman: poems and a memoir 1969–1980* by Lucille Clifton with the permission of BOA Editions, Ltd., 92 Park Avenue, Brockport, NY 14420.

Estate of Jorge Luis Borges
"Afterglow" by Jorge Luis Borges, copyright © 1968 by Jorge Luis Borges and Norman Thomas di Giovanni. All rights reserved. Originally appeared in *The New Yorker* and subsequently reprinted in *The New Yorker Book of Poems.* Reprinted by permission of the Estate of Jorge Luis Borges.

Marion Boyars Publishers Ltd.
"When Your Face Came Rising" by Yevgeny Yevtushenko, from *Early Poems by Yevgeny Yevtushenko,* translated by G. Reavey. Reprinted by permission of Marion Boyars Publishers Ltd.

Brandt & Brandt Literary Agents, Inc.
"By the Waters of Babylon" from *The Selected Works of Stephen Vincent Benét,* Holt, Rinehart & Winston, Inc. Copyright 1937 by Stephen Vincent Benét, copyright renewed © 1964 by Thomas C. Benét, Stephanie B. Mahin, and Rachel Benét Lewis. Reprinted by permission of Brandt & Brandt Literary Agents, Inc.

George Braziller, Inc.
The Wrestling Match by Buchi Emecheta. Copyright © 1980 by Oxford University Press. Reprinted by permission of George Braziller, Inc.

Gwendolyn Brooks
"The Sonnet-Ballad" from *The World of Gwendolyn Brooks* by Gwendolyn Brooks, published by Harper & Row. Copyright © 1971 Gwendolyn Brooks, the David Company.

The Christian Science Monitor
Excerpt from "Unfolding Bud" by Naoshi Koriyama from *The Christian Science Monitor,* July 13, 1957. Copyright © 1957 by The Christian Science Publishing Society. Reprinted by permission from *The Christian Science Monitor.* All rights reserved.

Don Congdon Associates, Inc.
"There Will Come Soft Rains" by Ray Bradbury, published in *Collier's National Weekly Magazine,* 1950. Copyright 1950 by Ray Bradbury; renewed © 1977 by Ray Bradbury. "Contents of the Dead Man's Pocket" by Jack Finney, published in *Collier's,* 1956. Copyright © 1957 by Crowell-Collier Publishing Company; renewed 1984 by Jack Finney. Reprinted by permission of Don Congdon Associates, Inc.

Molly Malone Cook Literary Agency
"A Letter from Home" by Mary Oliver, published in *Mademoiselle, 1964,* Copyright © 1964 by Mary Oliver. Reprinted by permission of Molly Malone Cook Literary Agency.

The Estate of Aaron Copland
"The Creative Process in Music" from *What to Listen for in Music* by Aaron Copland. Copyright, Estate of Aaron Copland 1957, renewed 1985. Reprinted by permission of the Estate of Aaron Copland.

Curtis Brown Ltd.
A Separate Peace by John Knowles. Copyright © 1959 by John Knowles. Copyright renewed 1987 by John Knowles. Reprinted by permission of Curtis Brown Ltd.

Doubleday, a division of Bantam, Doubleday, Dell Publishing Group, Inc.
"The Machine That Won the War" by Isaac Asimov, copyright © 1961 by Mercury Press, Inc., from the book *Nightfall and Other Stories* by Isaac Asimov. "Glove's Labor Lost" from *How Life Imitates the World Series* by Thomas Boswell. Copyright © 1982 by Washington Post's Writers Group. "A Visit to Grandmother" by William Melvin Kelley, copyright © 1964 by William Melvin Kelley, from the book *Dancers on the Shore.* "Big Wind" by Theodore Roethke, copyright 1947 by

United Chapters of Phi Beta Kappa, from *The Collected Poems of Theodore Roethke.* Reprinted by permission of Doubleday, a division of Bantam, Doubleday, Dell Publishing Group, Inc.

Doubleday, a division of Bantam, Doubleday, Dell Publishing Group, Inc., and Harold Ober Associates, Inc.
"Civil Peace" from *Girls at War and Other Stories* by Chinua Achebe, copyright © 1972, 1973 by Chinua Achebe. Used by permission.

E.P. Dutton, an imprint of New American Library, a division of Penguin Books USA Inc
"Emily Dickinson" from *New England: Indian Summer, 1865– 1915* by Van Wyck Brooks. Copyright 1940, 1950 by Van Wyck Brooks, renewed 1968, 1978 by Gladys Brooks. Reprinted by permission of the publisher.

Ann Elmo Agency, Inc.
"Leiningen Versus the Ants" by Carl Stephenson. Reprinted by permission of Ann Elmo Agency, Inc., 60 East 42nd Street, New York, NY 10165.

Farrar, Straus & Giroux, Inc.
"The Portrait" by Colette, translated by Matthew Ward, from *The Collected Stories of Colette,* edited by Robert Phelps, translated by Matthew Ward. Translation copyright © 1983 by Farrar, Straus & Giroux, Inc. "The Fish" from *The Complete Poems 1927–1979* by Elizabeth Bishop. Copyright 1940 by Elizabeth Bishop. Copyright © 1979, 1983 by Alice Helen Methfessel. Reprinted by permission of Farrar, Straus & Giroux, Inc.

GRM Associates, Inc., Agents for the Estate of Ida M. Cullen
Lines from "Any Human to Another" from *The Medea and Some Other Poems* by Countee Cullen. Copyright © 1935 by Harper & Brothers; copyright renewed 1963 by Ida M. Cullen. Reprinted by permission of GRM Associates, Inc., Agents for the Estate of Ida M. Cullen.

Harcourt Brace Jovanovich, Inc.
"Spring: Mushrooms in the City" from *Marcovaldo or The Seasons in the City* by Italo Calvino, translated by William Weaver, copyright © 1963 by Giulo Enaudi editore S.P.A., Torino; English translation copyright © 1983 by Harcourt Brace Jovanovich, Inc. and Martin Secker and Warberg, Limited. "Antigone" from *The Antigone of Sophocles: An English Version* by Dudley Fitts and Robert Fitzgerald, copyright 1939 by Harcourt Brace Jovanovich, Inc. and renewed 1967 by Dudley Fitts and Robert Fitzgerald. "Jazz Fantasia" from *Smoke and Steel* by Carl Sandburg. Copyright 1920 by Harcourt Brace Jovanovich, Inc.; renewed 1948 by Carl Sandburg. Lines from "Mind" from *Things of This World,* copyright © 1956, renewed 1984 by Richard Wilbur. Reprinted by permission of Harcourt Brace Jovanovich, Inc.

HarperCollins Publishers Inc.
"Flood" from *Pilgrim at Tinker Creek* by Annie Dillard. Copyright © 1974 by Annie Dillard. Reprinted by permission of HarperCollins Publishers Inc.

HarperCollins Publishers Inc., and Jonathan Clowes Ltd., London, on behalf of Doris Lessing
"Through the Tunnel" from *The Habit of Loving* by Doris Lessing. Copyright © 1957 by Doris Lessing. Reprinted by permission.

Harvard University Press and the Trustees of Amherst College
Lines from "Dear March, come in" and "The Wind—tapped like a tired Man" reprinted by permission of the publishers and the Trustees of Amherst College from *The Poems of Emily Dickinson,* edited by Thomas H. Johnson, Cambridge, Massachusetts: The Belknap Press of Harvard University Press. Copyright 1951, © 1955, 1979, 1983 by The President and Fellows of Harvard College.

Henry Holt and Company, Inc.
"Two Tramps in Mud Time," "Fire and Ice," "Once by the Pacific," and lines from "Birches" from *The Poetry of Robert Frost,* edited by Edward Connery Lathem. Copyright © 1969 by Holt, Rinehart and Winston, Inc.; copyright © 1962 by Robert Frost; copyright © 1975 by Lesley Frost Ballantine. Reprinted by permission of Henry Holt and Company, Inc.

Houghton Mifflin Company
"The Marginal World" from *The Edge of the Sea* by Rachel Carson. Copyright © 1955 by Rachel L. Carson. Copyright © renewed 1983 by Roger Christie. "Generations" and "Night Clouds" from *The Complete Poetical Works of Amy Lowell.* Copyright © 1955 by Houghton Mifflin Company. Copyright © renewed 1983 by Houghton Mifflin Company, Brinton P. Roberts, Esquire, and G. D'Andelot Belin, Esquire. Reprinted by permission of Houghton Mifflin Company.

International Creative Management, Inc.
"Alex Katz's *The Table*" from *Alex Katz* by Ann Beattie. Text copyright © 1987 by Ann Beattie. "Invasion From Mars" from *The Panic Broadcast: Portrait of an Event* by Howard Koch. Copyright 1940 by Princeton University Press; © 1968 by Howard Koch. Reprinted by permission of International Creative Management, Inc.

Japan Publications, Inc.
"Falling upon earth" by Bashō, "Having viewed the moon" by Chiyojo, "With one who muses" by Hyakuchi, and "A gentle spring rain" by Issa, reprinted from *One Hundred Famous Haiku* translated by Daniel C. Buchanan, with permission from Japan Publications, Inc., © 1973.

Alfred A. Knopf, Inc.
"Size and Sheer Will" from *The Dead and the Living* by Sharon Olds. Copyright © 1983 by Sharon Olds. Marian Anderson: Famous Concert Singer" from *Famous American*

Negroes by Langston Hughes. Copyright 1954 by Langston Hughes; copyright renewed 1982 by George Houston Bass. "Moonlight Night: Carmel" copyright 1947 by Langston Hughes. Reprinted from *Selected Poems of Langston Hughes,* by Langston Hughes. "Ex-Basketball Player" from *The Carpentered Hen and Other Tame Creatures* by John Updike. Copyright © 1957, 1982 by John Updike. "Letter Slot" from *Verse* by John Updike. Copyright 1952 and renewed 1982 by John Updike. "Puritan Sonnet" from "Wild Peaches" from *Collected Poems* by Elinor Wylie. Copyright 1921 by Alfred A. Knopf, Inc. and renewed 1949 by William Rose Benét. Reprinted by permission of Alfred A. Knopf, Inc.

Latin American Review

Lines from "Beneath the Shadow of the Freeway" by Lorna Dee Cervantes, published in *Latin American Review* (Spring-Summer 1977). Copyright © 1977 by Lorna Dee Cervantes. Reprinted by permission of the editors of *Latin American Review.*

Liveright Publishing Corporation

"Reapers" is reprinted from *Cane* by Jean Toomer by permission of Liveright Publishing Corporation. Copyright 1923 by Boni & Liveright. Copyright renewed 1951 by Jean Toomer. Lines from "anyone lived in a pretty how town" from *Complete Poems 1904–1962* by E. E. Cummings, edited by George J. Firmage, by permission of Liveright Publishing Corporation. Copyright © 1940, 1968, 1991 by the Trustees for the E. E. Cummings Trust.

Macmillan Publishing Company

"There Will Come Soft Rains" and lines from "Thoughts" reprinted with permission of Macmillan Publishing Company from *Collected Poems* by Sara Teasdale, Copyright 1920 by Macmillan Publishing Company, Inc.; renewed 1948 by Mamie T. Wheless.

Naomi Long Madgett

"Alabama Centennial" from *Star by Star* by Naomi Long Madgett. Copyright 1965, 1970 by Naomi Long Madgett. Lines from "Black Woman" from *Pink Ladies in the Afternoon* by Naomi Long Madgett. Copyright © 1972 by Naomi Long Madgett. Reprinted by permission of the author.

Harold Matson Company, Inc.

Excerpt from *The White Lantern* by Evan S. Connell. Copyright © 1980 by Evan S. Connell. Reprinted by permission of Harold Matson Company, Inc.

NAL Penguin, a division of Penguin Books USA Inc.

"Eldorado" from *The Complete Poetry and Selected Criticism of Edgar Allan Poe,* edited by Allen Tate. From *The Tragedy of Julius Caesar* by William Shakespeare, edited by William and Barbara Rosen. Copyright © 1963 by William and Barbara Rosen. Reprinted by arrangement with NAL Penguin, New York, New York.

New Directions Publishing Corporation

"A Picture" from *Old Snow* by Bei Dao, translated by Bonnie S. McDougall and Chen Maiping. Translation copyright © 1991 by Bonnie S. McDougall and Chen Maiping. "The Homecoming Stranger" from *Waves* by Bei Dao. Copyright 1985, 1986 by Chinese University of Hong Kong. "Constantly Risking Absurdity" from Lawrence Ferlinghetti, *Endless Life.* Copyright © 1981 by Lawrence Ferlinghetti. Lines from "February Evening in New York" from Denise Levertov, *Collected Earlier Poems 1940–1960.* Copyright © 1959 by Denise Levertov Goodman. "The Street" from Octavio Paz, *Selected Poems.* Copyright © 1963 by Octavio Paz and Muriel Rukeyser. Reprinted by permission of New Directions Publishing Corporation.

New Directions Publishing Corporation, and David Higham Associates Ltd.

Dylan Thomas, *A Child's Christmas in Wales.* Copyright 1954 by New Directions Publishing Corporation. Published in Great Britain by J.M. Dent & Sons Ltd. Reprinted by permission.

The New Yorker

Lines from "Glass World" by Dorothy Donnelly. From the March 12, 1960 issue of *The New Yorker.* Copyright © 1960, 1988 by The New Yorker Magazine, Inc. Reprinted by permission of *The New Yorker.*

The New York Times

"The American Idea" by Theodore H. White from *The New York Times Magazine,* July 6, 1986. Copyright © 1986 by The New York Times Company. Reprinted by permission of The New York Times.

North Point Press

Excerpt from *The White Lantern,* copyright © 1980, 1988 by North Point Press, by Evan S. Connell. Published by North Point Press and reprinted by permission.

W.W. Norton & Company, Inc.

Reprinted from *Don Quixote,* Miguel de Cervantes, A Norton Critical Edition, The Ormsby Translation, Revised, Edited by Joseph R. Jones and Kenneth Douglas, by permission of W.W. Norton & Company, Inc. Copyright © 1981 by W.W. Norton & Company, Inc. "Loss" is reprinted from *Collected Poems,* 1951–1971 by A. R. Ammons, by permission of W. W. Norton & Company, Inc. Copyright © 1972 by A. R. Ammons.

Naomi Shihab Nye

"Making a Fist" from *Hugging the Jukebox* by Naomi Shihab Nye. Copyright © Naomi Shihab Nye, 1982. Reprinted by permission of the author.

Harold Ober Associates

"I Am Not Lonely" from *Selected Poems of Gabriela Mistral,* translated by Langston Hughes. Copyright © 1957 by the Estate of Gabriela Mistral as author and Langston Hughes as translator. Lines from "A Black Man Talks of Reaping" and lines from "A Note of Humility" from *Personals* by Arna Bontemps. Copyright © 1963 by Arna Bontemps. Reprinted by permission of Harold Ober Associates, Inc.

Oxford University Press, England

"Sunset" © Mbuyiseni Oswald Mtshali 1971. Reprinted with permission from *Sounds of a Cowhide Drum* by Mbuyiseni Oswald Mtshali (1971).

Pantheon Books, a division of Random House, Inc.
"K'ung-ming Borrows Some Arrows" from *Three Kingdoms* by Lo Kuan-Chung. Copyright © 1976 by Moss Roberts. "Axolotl" from *End of the Game and Other Stories* by Julio Cortázar, translated by Paul Blackburn. Copyright © 1967 by Random House, Inc. Reprinted by permission of Pantheon Books, a division of Random House, Inc.

Persea Books, Inc.
"The Bees" from *Selected Poems* by Nazim Hikmet, translated by Randy Blasing and Mutlu Konuk. Copyright © 1986 by Randy Blasing and Mutlu Konuk. Reprinted by permission of Persea Books, Inc.

Playbill Magazine
"On Summer" by Lorraine Hansberry, reprinted from *Playbill Magazine,* June 1960. Playbill® is a registered trademark of Playbill Incorporated, NYC. All rights reserved. Used by permission of *Playbill Magazine.*

Présence Africaine
"Childhood" and "The Lion's Awakening" from *Sundiata: An Epic of Old Mali* by D. T. Niane, translated by G. D. Pickett. © Présence Africaine 1960 (original French version: *Soundjata, ou l'Epopée Mandingue*). © Longman Group Ltd. (English Version) 1965. Reprinted by permission of Présence Africaine.

The Putnam Publishing Group
"In Flanders Fields" reprinted by permission of The Putnam Publishing Group from *In Flanders Fields* by John McCrae. Copyright © 1919 by G. P. Putnam's Sons. Renewed.

The Putnam Publishing Group, and Watkins/Loomis Agency, Inc.
Excerpt (titled, "Arthur Becomes King") reprinted by permission from *The Once and Future King* by T. H. White. Copyright © 1939, 1940, and 1958 by T. H. White. Renewed.

Quarterly Review of Literature Poetry Series
"The Number Pi" from *Quarterly Review of Literature Poetry Series,* Volume XXIII, edited by T. & R. Weiss. Reprinted by permission.

Random House, Inc.
"A Christmas Memory" copyright © 1956 by Truman Capote. Reprinted from *Breakfast at Tiffany's* by Truman Capote. Reprinted by permission of Random House, Inc.

Random House, Inc., and Faber and Faber Ltd.
"O What Is That Sound" copyright 1937 and renewed 1967 by W. H. Auden. Reprinted from *W. H. Auden: Collected Poems* by W. H. Auden, edited by Edward Mendelson. Reprinted by permission.

Random House, Inc., and Rungstedlund Foundation
"The Ring" from *Anecdotes of Destiny,* by Isak Dinesen. Copyright © 1958 by Isak Dinesen. Reprinted by permission.

Marian Reiner for Eve Merriam
"Metaphor" from *It Doesn't Always Have to Rhyme* by Eve Merriam. Copyright © 1964 by Eve Merriam. All Rights Reserved. Reprinted by permission of Marian Reiner for the author.

Rogers Coleridge and White Ltd.
"Games at Twilight" from *Games at Twilight and other stories* by Anita Desai. Copyright © Anita Desai, 1978. Published by Penguin Books. Reprinted by permission of Rogers Coleridge and White Ltd.

Scribner's Sons, an imprint of Macmillan Publishing Company
"Sunlight in Trebizond Street" reprinted with permission of Charles Scribner's Sons, an imprint of Macmillan Publishing Company from *Knocking on the Door* by Alan Paton. Copyright © 1975 Alan Paton.

Simon & Schuster, Inc.
Pronunciation key from *Webster's New World Dictionary,* Second College Edition. Copyright © 1984 by Simon & Schuster, Inc. Reprinted by permission of Simon & Schuster, Inc.

The Society of Authors as the literary representative of the Estate of W. W. Jacobs
"The Monkey's Paw" from *The Lady of the Barge* by W. W. Jacobs. Reprinted by permission.

Southern Methodist University Press
"A Christmas Tree" by William Burford from *Man Now* (Southern Methodist University Press, 1954). Reprinted by permission of the publisher and William S. Burford.

Sterling Lord Literistic, Inc.
"Mary Cassatt" from *Good Boys and Dead Girls and Other Essays* by Mary Gordon. Copyright © 1991 by Mary Gordon. Reprinted by permission of Sterling Lord Literistic, Inc.

May Swenson
Lines from "Living Tenderly" by May Swenson are reprinted by permission of the author, copyright © 1963 by May Swenson.

Rosemary A. Thurber
"The Dog That Bit People" copyright 1933, © 1961 by James Thurber. From *My Life and Hard Times,* published by Harper & Row. Reprinted by permission of Rosemary A. Thurber.

Quincy Troupe
"The Old People Speak of Death" by Quincy Troupe, reprinted from *Weather Reports: New and Selected Poems,* published December, 1991, by Harlem River Press. Copyright © 1991 by Qunicy Troupe. Used by permission of the author.

University of New Mexico Press
Reprinted from *The Way to Rainy Mountain* by N. Scott Momaday. First published in *The Reporter,* January 26, 1967, © 1969, The University of New Mexico Press and reprinted with their permission.

The University of North Carolina Press
"The Street of the Cañon" from *Mexican Village* by Josephina Niggli. Copyright 1945 The University of North Carolina Press. Reprinted by permission of the publisher.

Viking Penguin, a division of Penguin Books USA Inc.
"First Lesson" from *Relations: New and Selected Poems* by Philip Booth. Copyright 1957, renewed © 1985 by Philip Booth. "One Perfect Rose" from *The Portable Dorothy Parker* edited by Brendan Gill. Copyright 1926, renewed 1954 by Dorothy Parker. "The Open Window" from *The Complete Short Stories of Saki* by Saki (H. H. Munro). Copyright 1930, renewed 1958 by The Viking Press, Inc. "Notes on Punctuation" from *The Medusa and the Snail* by Lewis Thomas. Copyright © 1979 by Lewis Thomas. "Old Man of the Temple" from *Under the Banyan Tree and Other Stories* by R. K. Narayan. Copyright © 1985 by R. K. Narayan. Reprinted by permission of Viking Penguin, a division of Penguin Books USA Inc.

Alma Luz Villanueva
Lines from " I Was a Skinny Tomboy Kid" from *Bloodroot* by Alma Luz Villanueva. Copyright © 1977 by Alma Luz Villanueva. Reprinted by permission of the author.

Wallace Literary Agency for R. K. Narayan
"Rama's Initiation" from *The Ramayana: A Shortened Modern Prose Version of the Indian Epic* by R. K. Narayan. Published by Penguin Books. Copyright © 1972 by R. K. Narayan. Reprinted by permission of the author.

Wesleyan University Press
"A pied" from What *Madness Brought Me Here* by Colleen McElroy. Copyright 1990 by Colleen J. McElroy. "Pitcher" copyright 1953 by Robert Francis, reprinted from *The Orb Weaver* by permission of Wesleyan University Press. "A Blessing" copyright © 1961 by James Wright, reprinted from *Collected Poems* by permission of Wesleyan University Press. "A Blessing" first appeared in *Poetry*. Used by permission of Wesleyan University Press by permission of University Press of New England.

Wieser & Wieser, Inc.
"Auto Wreck" from *Collected Poems 1940–1978* by Karl Shapiro. Copyright 1942 and renewed 1970 by Karl Shapiro. Reprinted by permission of Wieser & Wieser, Inc.

Darryl Babe Wilson
"Diamond Island: Alcatraz" by Darryl Babe Wilson. © Darryl Babe Wilson, 1991. Reprinted by permission of the author.

Euphemia Ann Wolfe
Lines from "The Gray Squirrel" from *Kensington Gardens* by Humbert Wolfe. Reprinted by permission of Euphemia Ann Wolfe.

Note: Every effort has been made to locate the copyright owner of material reprinted in this book. Omissions brought to our attention will be corrected in subsequent editions.

ART CREDITS

Boldface numbers refer to the page on which the art is found.

Cover and Title Page: *Landschaft, Cannes* (*Landscape, Cannes*), 1934, Max Beckmann, Oil on canvas, $27\frac{5}{8} \times 38\frac{1}{2}''$, San Francisco Museum of Modern Art, Gift of Louise S. Ackerman, Photo by Don Myer; **v:** (top) *Private Performance* (detail), Lois Johnson, Courtesy of the artist; (bottom) *Toda la Sabiduria Viene del Cielo* (*All the Wisdom Comes From the Sky*) (detail), 1991, Arnaldo Roche Rabell, Galeria Alejandro Gallo; **vi:** (top) *Rise With Force and Spirit* (detail), 1988, James Bama, Oil, © The Greenwich Workshop, Inc., Trumbull, Connecticut; **vii:** *The Family,* c. 1892, Mary Cassatt (American, 1844–1926), Oil on canvas, $32\frac{1}{4} \times 26\frac{1}{8}''$, The Chrysler Museum, Norfolk, Virginia; **viii:** *Untitled (Buffalo Hunt)* (detail), New Bear (Gros Ventre tribe), Courtesy of Eastern Montana College Library; **ix:** (top) *Math Man #4,* 1967, Clarence Holbrook Carter, Acrylic on canvas, $54 \times 43''$, Courtesy of the artist; (bottom) *The Pitcher* (detail), Mitchell Heinze, Sal Barracca & Associates; **x:** (top) *Don Quixote* (detail), Honoré Daumier, Giraudon/Art Resource, New York; (bottom) *An Elder Walking Alone* (detail), John Mainga, LAMU, The Gallery of Contemporary African Art, Photo by John Lei/Omni-Photo Communications, Inc.; **xii:** *Midtown Sunset,* 1981, Romare Bearden, From the *Profile/Part II: The Thirties* series, Collage on board, Courtesy of the Estate of Romare Bearden, Photo by John Lei/Omni-Photo Communications, Inc.; **6:** *Racing Game,* 1982, Tony Wong, Oil pastel/paper, Courtesy of the artist; **11:** *Hide and Seek,* Tony Wong, Oil pastel/paper, Courtesy of the artist; **15:** *Régates à Argenteuil* (*Regattas at Argenteuil*), 1875, Claude Monet, Paris, Louvre, Giraudon/Art Resource, New York; **30:** *W. W. Jacobs,* 1910 (detail), Carlton Moore-Park, The Granger Collection, New York; **67:** *Evening, Monhegan Island,* 1963, Samuel Reindorf, Courtesy of the artist; **77:** *The Canyon,* Jack Dudley, Courtesy of the artist; **79:** *Carmen,* James Asher, Courtesy of the artist; **85:** *Private Performance,* Lois Johnson, Courtesy of the artist; **88:** *Samuel Langhorne Clemens* (detail), 1935, Frank Edwin Larson, The National Portrait Gallery, Smithsonian Institution; **90:** *Hint to Modern Sculptors as an Ornament to a Future Square,* James Gillray, Hand-colored etching, Victoria and Albert Museum Trustees; **92:** *Scotland Forever,* Elizabeth Butler, Leeds City Art Galleries; **95:** *Stairway,* c. 1925, Edward Hopper, Oil on wood, $16 \times 11\frac{7}{8}''$, Collection of Whitney Museum of American Art, Josephine N. Hopper

Bequest; **101:** *San Francisco,* 1849, Attributed to Joshua Peirce, Oil on canvas, Photo by John Lei/Omni-Photo Communications, Inc.; **108:** *El Pez Luminoso (The Luminous Fish),* 1956, Juan Soriano, Collection INBA–Museo de Arte Moderno, Mexico D.F., Reproduction authorized by the Instituto Nacional de Bellas Artes y Literatura; **111:** *Toda la Sabiduria Viene del Cielo (All the Wisdom Comes From the Sky),* 1991, Arnaldo Roche Rabell, Galeria Alejandro Gallo; **117:** *Mushrooms,* 1940, Sir William Nicholson, The Tate Gallery, London, Art Resource, New York; **119:** *Road With Cypress and Star,* Vincent van Gogh, Collection: State Museum, Kröller-Müller Otterlo, The Netherlands; **131:** *Señora Sabasa Garcia,* 1806–1807, Francisco José de Goya, © 1993 National Gallery of Art, Washington, Andrew W. Mellon Collection; **136:** *Red Hills and Bones,* 1941, Georgia O'Keeffe, Phildelphia Museum of Art, The Alfred Stieglitz Collection; **143:** *City Night,* 1926, Georgia O'Keeffe, Minneapolis Institute of Arts, Photo by Malcolm Varon, N.Y.C.; **148:** *The Beach Treat* (detail), Suzanne Nagler, Photograph © Stephen Tucker, Collection of Mr. and Mrs. X. Daniel Kafcas; **153:** *Coast Scene, Isles of Shoals,* 1901, Childe Hassam, The Metropolitan Museum of Art, Gift of George A. Hearn, 1909, Copyright © 1987 by The Metropolitan Museum of Art; **155:** *Street Scene in Lower New York,* c. 1926, Glenn O. Coleman, Oil on canvas, $30\frac{1}{4}$ × 25″, Collection of Whitney Museum of American Art, Gift of Mrs. Herbert B. Lazarus; **161:** *The Sisters,* 1940, Stanley Spencer, Leeds City Art Galleries; **163:** *In the Studio,* William Merritt Chase, Collection of Arthur G. Altschul, New York; **175:** *Les Masques et la Mort,* 1897, James Ensor, © Estate of James Ensor/VAGA, New York 1993, Art Resource, New York; **177:** *Dorothy,* William Merritt Chase, © 1989 Indianapolis Museum of Art, John Herron Fund; **179:** *The Hunters,* Gari Melchers, mid-1920s, Oil on canvas, $53\frac{3}{8}$ × $50\frac{1}{4}$″, Private Collection; **189:** *Girl Looking at Landscape,* 1957, Richard Diebenkorn, Oil on canvas, 59 × $60\frac{1}{4}$″, Collection of Whitney Museum of American Art, Gift of Mr. and Mrs. Alan H. Temple; **194:** *Untitled,* James McMullan, Courtesy of the artist; **198:** *Dawei* (detail), Sun Jingbo, 1982, Photography by Joan Lebold Cohen; **201:** *Rise With Force and Spirit,* 1988, James Bama, Oil, © The Greenwich Workshop, Inc., Trumbull, Connecticut; **209:** *Portrait of Lucian Freud,* 1951, Francis Bacon, Whitworth Art Gallery, University of Manchester; **220:** *Isak Dinesen,* Kay Christensen, The Granger Collection, New York; **224:** *Adam and Eve,* Edvard Munch, Munch Museum, Oslo, Scala/Art Resource, New York; **226:** *The Lonely Ones,* 1899, Edvard Munch, Munch-Museet, Oslo; **246:** *Raised Stage With Masks, Narrator, and Auditorium,* 1981, David Hockney, Drawing for Oedipus Rex, Gouache and Tempera on paper, 29 × 40″, © David Hockney, 1981; **274:** Sophocles, Vatican Museum, Scala/Art Resource, New York; **307:** *Swan Theatre, London,* c. 1596, Johannes DeWitt, The Granger Collection, New York; **308:** *William Shakespeare* (detail), Artist unknown, By courtesy of the National Portrait Gallery, London; **402:** *View From a Car,* Emily A. Martin, Student, Erie, Pennsylvania, Courtesy of the artist; **407:** "Nobody Knew Exactly What Was the Matter With Him," James Thurber,

From *My Life and Hard Times,* Copyright © 1933, 1961, Published by Harper & Row; **409:** "Lots of People Reported Our Dog to the Police," James Thurber, From *My Life and Hard Times,* Copyright © 1933, 1961, Published by Harper & Row; **413:** *Diego Martelli,* Edgar Degas, National Gallery of Scotland, Edinburgh, Bridgeman/Art Resource, New York; **414:** *Van Wyck Brooks* (detail), 1909, John Butler Yeats, The National Portrait Gallery, Smithsonian Institution; **426:** *Langston Hughes* (detail), c. 1925, Winold Reiss, The National Portrait Gallery, Smithsonian Institution, Gift of W. Tjark Reiss, In memory of his father, Winold Reiss, Art Resource, New York; **438, 440:** Fritz Eichenberg etching; **442:** *Truman Capote* (detail), 1974, Barnaby Conrad, The National Portrait Gallery, Smithsonian Institution, Washington D.C., Art Resource, New York; **455:** *A Young Girl Reading,* 1776, Jean-Honoré Fragonard, © 1993 National Gallery of Art, Washington, Gift of Mrs. Mellon Bruce in memory of her father, Andrew W. Mellon; **458:** *Orion,* 1984, Martin Wong, Acrylic on canvas, 36″ diameter, Courtesy of Exit Art Gallery, New York; **461:** La Bibliothèque (The Library), 1949, Maria Elena Vieira da Silva, Musée National d'Art Moderne, Centre National d'Art et de Culture Georges Pompidou, Photo by Philippe Migeat © Centre G. Pompidou; **468:** *Annie Old Crow,* James Bama, Courtesy of the artist; **470:** *Old Ones Talking,* R. Brownell McGrew, Courtesy of the artist; **501:** *The Bath,* 1891/1892, Mary Cassatt (American, 1844–1926), Oil on canvas, $39\frac{1}{2}$ × 26″, Robert A. Waller Fund, 1910.2 photograph © 1992, The Art Institute of Chicago, All rights reserved; **502:** *The Family,* c. 1892, Mary Cassatt (American, 1844–1926), Oil on canvas, $32\frac{1}{4}$ × $26\frac{1}{8}$″, The Chrysler Museum, Norfolk, Virginia; **505:** *Song,* 1950, Ben Shahn, Hirshhorn Museum and Sculpture Garden, Smithsonian Institution, Gift of Joseph H. Hirshhorn Foundation, 1966; **514:** *Aaron Copland* (detail), 1972, Marcos Blahove, The National Portrait Gallery, Smithsonian Institution; **519:** *Beethoven's Sterbezimmer Im Schwarzpanierhaus,* 1827, Johann Nepomuk Hoechle, Historisches Museum der Stadt Wien; **524:** *The Table,* 1984, Alex Katz, Courtesy of Marlborough Gallery; **544:** *Red Poppies,* Georgia O'Keeffe, Private Collection, Photo by Malcolm Varon; **551:** *Central Park,* 1901, Maurice Prendergast, Watercolor on paper, $14\frac{3}{8}$ × $21\frac{1}{2}$″, Collection of Whitney Museum of American Art, Purchase; **552:** *John Keats* (detail), 1818, Miniature by Joseph Severn, The Granger Collection, New York; **553:** *La Belle Dame sans Merci,* John W. Waterhouse, Hessisches Landes Museum, Darmstadt; **562:** *Henry Wadsworth Longfellow* (detail), Thomas B. Read, The National Portrait Gallery, Smithsonian Institution; **563:** *The Wreck of a Transport Ship,* 1810, J.M.W. Turner, Calouste Gulbenkian Foundation Museum; **567:** *Portrait of Kitty Jagger, the Artist's Wife,* David Jagger, Bridgeman/Art Resource, New York; **568:** *Rudyard Kipling* (detail), 1899, P. Burne-Jones, By courtesy of the National Portrait Gallery, London; **569:** *The Battle of Bunker Hill,* Howard Pyle, Delaware Art Museum, Howard Pyle Collection; **577:** *The Battle of Life (The Golden Knight),* Gustav Klimt, 1903, Courtesy Galerie St. Etienne, New York; **579:** *Couple,* Kees Van Dongen, Galleria d'Arte Moderna-Parigi, SEF Art

Resource, New York; **587:** *Violinist at the Window,* 1917/ 1918, Henri Matisse, Musée Nationale d'Art Moderne, Paris; **588:** *Paul Verlaine,* F. A. Cazals, Giraudon/Art Resource, New York; **592:** *Impressions of Hands,* 1969, Antoni Tapies, Soft-ground etching, Printed in black and aquatint, Printed in medium red-brown, Plate: 19⁹⁄₁₆ × 15½″, Collection, The Museum of Modern Art, New York, Donald Karshan Fund; **595:** *Birthday,* 1915, Marc Chagall, Oil on cardboard, 31¾ × 39¼″, Collection, The Museum of Modern Art, New York, Acquired through the Lillie P. Bliss Bequest, © 1993 ARS, New York/ ADAGP, Paris; **603:** *Mediterranean Landscape,* 1952, Pablo Picasso, Giraudon/Art Resource, New York, © 1993 ARS, New York/SPADEM, Paris; **607:** *Boy With Float,* C. S. Mazarin, Courtesy of the artist; **609:** *Melanie and Me Swimming,* 1978–1979, Michael Andrews, The Tate Gallery, London, Art Resource, New York; **610:** *Emily Dickinson,* Artist unknown, The Granger Collection, New York; **612:** Toilers of the Sea, Albert Pinkham Ryder, The Metropolitan Museum of Art, George A. Hearn Fund, 1915, Copyright © 1979 by The Metropolitan Museum of Art; **613:** *Three Suns,* 1966, © Finnur Jonsson/MYNDSTEF, owner: National Gallery of Iceland; **615:** Cover illustration for *The Wandering Jew* by Stefan Heym, Publisher Pan Books, Ian Pollock, Courtesy of the artist; **619:** *Memory,* 1870, Elihu Vedder, The Los Angeles County Museum of Art, Mr. and Mrs. William Preston Harrison Collection; **624:** *Newbury Hayfields,* 1862, Martin Johnson Heade, Memorial Art Gallery of the University of Rochester, Gift of Jacqueline Stemmler Adams, In memory of Mr. and Mrs. Frederick M. Stemmler; **626:** *Jean Toomer* (detail), c. 1925, Winold Reiss, The National Portrait Gallery, Smithsonian Institution; **632:** *The Pitcher,* Mitchell Heinze, Sal Barracca & Associates; **633:** *Sunrise in Crete, 1981,* Theo Hios, Watercolor, Courtesy of the artist; **635:** *Swing Landscape* (detail), 1938, Stuart Davis, Indiana University Art Museum; **636:** *Robert Burns* (detail), A. Nasmyth, The Granger Collection, New York; *Baron Alfred Tennyson* (detail), S. Laurence, By courtesy of the National Portrait Gallery, London; *Carl Sandburg* (detail), 1962, Miriam Svet, The National Portrait Gallery, Smithsonian Institution; **642:** *Untitled (Buffalo Hunt),* New Bear (Gros Ventre tribe), Courtesy of Eastern Montana College Library; **647:** *Palenquera,* 1988, Ana Mercedes Hoyos, Courtesy of the artist; **648:** *William Shakespeare* (detail), Artist unknown, By courtesy of the National Portrait Gallery, London; **650:** *Frances Howard,* Isaac Oliver, Victoria and Albert Museum Trustees; **655:** *Snow-Laden Camellia and Sparrow,* c. 1845, Ando Hiroshige, Metropolitan Museum of Art, Rogers Fund, 1936, Copyright © 1987 by The Metropolitan Museum of Art; **656:** *A Sudden Shower at Ohashi,* 1857, Ando Hiroshige, Metropolitan Museum of Art, Purchase, 1918, Joseph Pulitzer Bequest, Copyright © 1982 by The Metropolitan Museum of Art; **663:** *Girl With Cat,* Franz Marc, Superstock; **671:** *The Prophet #1,* 1975–1976, Color lithograph, Charles White, Courtesy of Heritage Gallery, Los Angeles; **674:** *Math Man #4,* 1967, Acrylic on canvas, 54 × 43″, Clarence Holbrook Carter, Courtesy of the artist; **684:** *Entry of King Etzel (Attila) Into Vienna—A Scene From the*

Epos of the Nibelungs (1909–1911), Albin Egger-Lienz, INv.3370, Erich Lessing/Art Resource, New York; **688:** *Baron Alfred Tennyson* (detail), 1840, S. Laurence, By courtesy of the National Portrait Gallery, London; **690:** *The Crowning of Arthur,* Royal MS, By permission of the British Library; **698:** *Gallahad's Sword in Stone,* Royal MS, By permission of the British Library; **706:** *Death of Arthur,* By permission of the British Library; **711:** *How Sir Bedivere Cast the Sword Excaliber Into the Water,* Aubrey Beardsley, By permission of the Houghton Library, Harvard University; **716:** Persian translation of the *Ramayana* of Valmiki (detail), Late 16th century, Mughal, School of Akbar, Indian manuscript, Miniatures in opaque colors and gold: average leaf, 27.5 × 15.2 cm., Courtesy of the Freer Gallery of Art, Smithsonian Institution, Washington, D.C., 07.271; **719, 721:** Persian translation of the *Ramayana* of Valmiki, Late 16th century, Mughal, School of Akbar, Indian manuscript, Miniatures in opaque colors and gold: average leaf, 27.5 × 15.2 cm., Courtesy of the Freer Gallery of Art, Smithsonian Institution, Washington, D.C., 07.271; **724:** Senegalese glass painting used on *Sundiata* (detail), From the collection of Professor Donal Cruise-O'Brien, Courtesy of Longman International Education; **727:** Senegalese glass painting used on *Sundiata,* from the collection of Professor Donal Cruise-O'Brien, Courtesy of Longman International Education; **732, 735:** Lintel and pediment of a tomb (detail) 1-left horizontal procession, 1st century B.C., China Westen Han dynasty, Denman Waldo Ross Collection, Courtesy, Museum of Fine Arts, Boston; **738:** *Miguel de Cervantes,* The Granger Collection, New York; **741:** *Don Quixote,* Honoré Daumier, Giraudon/Art Resource, New York; **743:** *Don Quixote and the Windmill,* c. 1900, Francisco J. Torrome, Bridgeman/Art Resource, New York; **750:** *Early Morning in Ro . . . [Früher Morgen in Ro . . .]* (detail), 1925, Paul Klee, Watercolor on paper, mounted on cardboard, 16⅝ × 21¼″, The Museum of Modern Art, New York, Gift of Mrs. Gertrud A. Mellon, Photograph © 1992, The Museum of Modern Art; **755:** *Tree Trunks,* André Derain, Moscow, Pushkin Museum, Roos, Art Resource, New York; **873:** *Market Scene,* S. Kangau, Kenyan wax batik on silk, LAMU, The Gallery of Contemporary African Art, Photo by John Lei/Omni-Photo Communications, Inc.; **881:** *Nigerian Family Compound,* John Mainga, LAMU, The Gallery of Contemporary African Art, Photo by John Lei/Omni-Photo Communications, Inc.; **885:** *Teen Girls Returning Home After Market,* John Mainga, LAMU, The Gallery of Contemporary African Art, Photo by John Lei/Omni-Photo Communications, Inc.; **889:** *Two Elders Sitting in a Farm,* John Mainga, LAMU, The Gallery of Contemporary African Art, Photo by John Lei/Omni-Photo Communications, Inc.; **892:** *Traditional Yam Harvest,* John Mainga, LAMU, The Gallery of Contemporary African Art, Photo by John Lei/Omni-Photo Communications, Inc.; **897:** *Evening Storytelling,* John Mainga, LAMU, The Gallery of Contemporary African Art, Photo by John Lei/Omni-Photo Communications, Inc.; **902:** *An Elder Wearing Otuogwu Cloth Talking to a Teen Boy,* John Mainga, LAMU, The Gallery of Contemporary African Art, Photo by John Lei/Omni-Photo Communications, Inc.; **910:**

Market Scene—Buying and Selling, John Mainga, LAMU, The Gallery of Contemporary African Art, Photo by John Lei/Omni-Photo Communications, Inc.; **916:** *An Elder Walking Alone,* John Mainga, LAMU, The Gallery of Contemporary African Art, Photo by John Lei/Omni-Photo Communications, Inc.; **920:** *Drummers of Igbuno in a Village,* John Mainga, LAMU, The Gallery of Contemporary African Art, Photo by John Lei/Omni-Photo Communications, Inc.; **926:** *The Wrestlers,* John Mainga, LAMU, The Gallery of Contemporary African Art, Photo by John Lei/Omni-Photo Communications, Inc.

PHOTOGRAPH CREDITS

vi: (bottom) Martha Swope; **2:** Courtesy of Marlene Sanchez; **13:** Thomas Victor; **17:** Joseph Nettis/Stock Boston, Inc.; **21:** Ken Karp; **25:** Hiroyuki Matsumoto/Black Star; **60:** AP/Wide World Photos; **64:** Charles Weckler/The Image Bank; **69:** David Hundley/The Stock Market; **72:** Alvis Upitis/The Image Bank; **96:** Darryl Babe Wilson; **97:** Photo of Native American Male (Wailaki tribe) by Edward S. Curtis, Courtesy of the Southwest Museum, Los Angeles, Photo #N.40042; **106:** Susan Meiselas/Magnum Photos, Inc.; **114:** Salgado, Jr./Magnum Photos, Inc.; **120:** Thomas Victor; **126:** Gary V. Fields; **134:** AP/Wide World Photos; **146:** Thomas Victor; **156:** Steven Y. Mori; **157:** Thomas Braise/The Stock Market; **158:** T. Fujihira/Monkmeyer Press; **160:** The Bettmann Archive; **166:** UPI/Bettmann Newsphotos; **176:** The Granger Collection, New York; **182:** Thomas Victor; **190:** Courtesy of Bei Dao; **206:** AP/Wide World Photos; **214:** Bill Cramer/AP/Wide World Photos; **216:** John Curtis/The Stock Market; **218:** Lawrence Manning/Black Star; **228:** Courtesy of Josh Lee; **233:** Michael Ventura/Folio, Inc.; **238:** Ken Karp; **240:** Thomas Victor; **250:** AP/Wide World Photos; **257, 262, 264:** Photofest; **272:** J. Alex Langley/DPI; **273:** Ray Shaw/The Stock Market; **277, 279, 282, 284, 291, 295, 299, 302:** Martha Swope; **313, 318:** Photofest; **333, 342:** Culver Pictures, Inc.; **350, 359, 362, 370, 376, 391:** Photofest; **404:** Courtesy of Beth Hasbrouck; **411:** UPI/Bettmann Newsphotos; **415, 418:** Dan McCoy/Rainbow; **423:** Coco McCoy Rainbow; **428:** UPI/Bettmann Newsphotos; **432:** The Bettmann Archive; **443:** Truman Capote and His Aunt, Photograph used with the permission of the Estate of Truman Capote, Alan U. Schwartz, Executor, Photograph by John Lei/Omni-Photo Communications, Inc.; **447, 449, 451, 453:** © 1993 Capital Cities/ABC, Inc.; **456:** Courtesy of Rudolfo Anaya; **464, 472:** Thomas Victor; **474:** Steve Proehl/The Image Bank; **480:** Nancy Crampton; **482:** Courtesy of the Library of Congress; **485:** National Archives, Washington, D.C.; **489:** Courtesy of the Library of Congress; **494:** Enrico Ferorelli; **496:** Robert Frerck/Woodfin Camp & Associates; **498:** Nancy Crampton; **506, 510:** Thomas Victor; **511:** Pete Turner/The Image Bank; **522:** Thomas Victor; **526:** UPI/Bettmann Newsphotos; **527:** Anne Wertheim/Animals Animals/Earth Scenes; **530:** Breck P. Kent; **532:** Stephen J. Krasemann/DRK Photo; **534:** Courtesy of Kristen Sweeney; **537:** Stephanie Maze/Woodfin Camp & Associates; **538:** Courtesy of *Playboy* Magazine, Copyright © 1983 by *Playboy;* **546:** Courtesy of Reginald Carnegie; **548:** James H. Karales/Peter Arnold Inc.; **550:** Courtesy of Naomi Long Madgett; **556:** Dmitri Kessel/*Life* Magazine, © Time Inc.; **558:** Philip Jon Bailey/Picture Cube; **572:** BBC Hulton/The Bettmann Archive; **576:** UPI/Bettmann Newsphotos; **580:** (top) Mark Leighton/UPI/Bettmann Newsphotos; (center) The Granger Collection, New York; **582:** Richard Nowitz/The Image Bank; **585:** AP/Wide World Photos; **588:** (center top) The Bettmann Archive; (center bottom) Marjorie Ramson; (bottom) The Bettmann Archive; **589:** TASS/Sovfoto; **590:** Joel Greenstein/Omni-Photo Communications, Inc.; **594:** Robert P. Carr/Bruce Coleman, Inc.; **596:** (top and center) Thomas Victor; (bottom) AP/Wide World Photos; **598:** Bill Weems/Woodfin Camp & Associates; **604:** (top) Rollie McKenna; (center top) Nancy Crampton; (center bottom) James Salzano; (bottom) Rollie McKenna; **610:** (top) The Bettmann Archive; (center bottom) Nihad Becirovic; **620:** (top) AP/Wide World Photos; (center) Thomas Victor; (bottom) Susan Meiselas/Magnum Photos, Inc.; **623:** Peter Mitter/The Image Bank; **626:** (center top) Thomas Victor; (center bottom and bottom) AP/Wide World Photos; **629:** William Johnson/The Stock Market; **640:** John Lewis Stage/The Image Bank; **645:** Enrico Ferorelli; **646:** Lorette Moureau; **648:** The Bettmann Archive; **658:** (top) Thomas Victor; (bottom) The Bettmann Archive; **664:** (top and center) AP/Wide World Photos; (bottom) Grace Davies/Omni-Photo Communications, Inc.; **666:** Co Rentmeester/The Image Bank; **676:** Courtesy of Sarah Hong; **677:** Adam J. Stoltman/Duomo Photography, Inc.; **678:** Thomas Victor; **688:** (top) AP/Wide World; **756:** New York Public Library Picture Collection; **874, 875, 876:** Herbert M. Cole; **878:** Melanie Friend.

ILLUSTRATION CREDITS

pp. 33, 39: The Art Source; **pp. 42, 43, 50–51, 57:** Gregory Manchess; **pp. 168–169, 171, 186–187, 467:** The Art Source; **pp. 760, 766, 771, 781, 786, 794, 803, 810, 817, 827, 833, 844, 845, 852, 864, 871:** Chris McAllister.